HOW TO USE THIS BOOK

List of Contents Page 5

TO SELECT A ROUTE

Consult the KEY MAP to the itineraries following page 40 or the ~~~
Maps which follow the key map.

The numbers on the key map are those of the itineraries. Those in black represent long-distance itineraries and through routes. Other routes are numbered in red.

Itinerary numbers also appear in the Gazetteer.

Roads in the itineraries are identified by Road Numbers, see page 30, and these road numbers are shown in the Atlas at the end of the book.

The article TOURING IN SCOTLAND, on page 29, with its accompanying map will assist in planning a general tour.

TO LOCATE A PLACE

Refer to the GAZETTEER which gives the page number of the Atlas on which it will be found, followed by the National Grid reference. This reference is fully explained on pages ii and iii of the Atlas. It gives the major square letter, and the numbers of the smaller square. The scale of the map does not allow every place name to be shown, but this system enables the approximate position of a place to be ascertained whether or not it is marked on the map.

All but the smallest places mentioned in the itineraries are included in the Gazetteer. Itinerary reference numbers are given in the Gazetteer entries for all places to which they apply, so that mileages to the other places on the same route can readily be found.

An asterisk before a place name in the itinerary, or its descriptive heading, indicates that it is a place of interest described in the Gazetteer.

ATLAS

The ATLAS at the end of the book has contour colouring. The roads are shown in three categories—Class A, including Trunk Roads; Class B; and other roads (unclassified) without road numbers. Some classified roads have a distinctive marking to indicate that special care is required. The road numbering system is explained on page 30.

TOWN PLANS

TOWN PLANS will be found throughout the Gazetteer and the names of towns for which there are plans are printed in heavy type in the itineraries.

PLACES OF INTEREST

PLACES OF INTEREST are fully described in the Gazetteer and short articles covering individual counties will be found on pages 8 to 26. These articles contain classified lists of places with special scenic, historical or architectural interest. A County map will be found on page i of the Atlas. On page 31 there is a short article dealing with Historic Buildings, The National Forest Parks, The Nature Reserves, and Scotland's Gardens, and on page 32 will be found information concerning The National Trust for Scotland. A comprehensive list of LITERARY ASSOCIATIONS with many of the places named in the Gazetteer is on page 27.

A combined GLOSSARY OF TECHNICAL TERMS AND GAELIC AND NORSE WORDS will be found at the end of the Gazetteer.

SPORTING FACILITIES IN SCOTLAND

Commencing on page 33 are articles dealing with Golf, Angling, Mountaineering and other sports.

HIGHLAND CLANS AND LOWLAND FAMILIES

The Clans are dealt with in an article commencing on page 267, and a location map is on page 36 of the Atlas.

FERRIES AND STEAMSHIP SERVICES

Details of FERRIES IN SCOTLAND AND SHIPPING SERVICES TO THE ISLANDS will be found on pages 271 and 274. A map showing the location of the Ferry Services is on page 270 while the Shipping Services are covered by a comprehensive map on pages 34 and 35 of the Atlas.

MILEAGE CHART

Inside the back cover will be found a quick reference Mileage Chart.

" Come forth, the sky is wide and it is a far cry to the world's end " . . . . " There is a road which leads to the Moon and the Great Waters . . . . . and it has no end; but it is a fine road, a braw road—who will follow it? . . . ."

JOHN BUCHAN
The Rime of True Thomas

The quotation above is taken from " The Moon Endureth " by John Buchan by kind permission of the Tweedsmuir Trustees, and Messrs. William Blackwood & Sons Ltd., the publishers.

From the lone shieling of the misty island
Mountains divide us, and the waste of seas,
Yet still the blood is strong, the heart is Highland,
And we in dreams behold the Hebrides.

Canadian Boat Song.

The Falls of Shin, in Sutherland, a mile to the north of Inveran Bridge and five miles south of Lairg.
They can be approached from B864, which follows the west bank of the river for some distance

ILLUSTRATED ROAD BOOK

OF SCOTLAND

WITH GAZETTEER, ITINERARIES, MAPS, & TOWN PLANS

First Impression 1960
Second Impression 1961

PRINTED AND BOUND IN ENGLAND BY
HAZELL WATSON AND VINEY LTD
AYLESBURY AND SLOUGH

THE AUTOMOBILE ASSOCIATION

FOUNDED 1905

HEAD OFFICE	Fanum House, Leicester Square, London WC2
TELEPHONE	WHItehall 1200
TELEGRAMS	INLAND Fanum London Telex
	OVERSEAS Fanum London WC2

PRESIDENT	His Grace The Duke of Norfolk KG, PC, GCVO
VICE-PRESIDENTS	The Rt. Hon. Viscount De L'Isle VC, PC, GCMG
	G. Shaw Scott MSC, FCIS
PAST PRESIDENT	HRH The Duke of Edinburgh KG, KT

COMMITTEE

CHAIRMAN	The Rt. Hon. Viscount Brentford
VICE-CHAIRMEN	Donald Stewart MD, FRCP
	Sir Denis H. Truscott GBE, TD
HON. TREASURER	Sir Hugh Fraser Bt, DL
COMMITTEE	Vernon Coles
	W. Michael Couper
	Patrick Gathorne-Hardy TD
	Sir William Graham Holford DCL, PRIBA, MTPI
	Andrew H. S. Lewis MBE, BSC, MRINA
	The Marquess of Linlithgow MC
	C. A. Miller TD, MA
	Sir Frank Newson-Smith Bt
	Lieutenant-General Sir Archibald Nye GCSI, GCMG, GCIE, KCB, KBE, MC
	G. Edward Payne
	Major R. A. B. Smith MC, AMICE, M Inst T
SECRETARY-GENERAL	K. L. Kelly
DEPUTY SECRETARY-GENERAL (Director of Administration)	H. A. Evans
DEPUTY SECRETARY-GENERAL (Director of Public Affairs)	H. Cecil Orr OBE
DIRECTOR OF SERVICES	G. J. Ryan

CONTENTS

A.A. OFFICES

Except where otherwise noted, the telegraphic address is 'Fanum', followed by the name of the town. Members may always obtain Emergency Service by telephoning Fanum House, London, or the office in any of the towns marked *

*LONDON, W.C.2
Fanum House, Leicester Square. T. WHItehall 1200.
Tel. Add. INLAND Fanum London Telex, OVERSEAS Fanum London WC2

LONDON, E.C.4
CITY OFFICE. Regis House, King William Street.
T. MANsion House 9993. Tel. Add. Fanumcity Cent London.

ABERDEEN
Fanum House, Golden Square. T. Aberdeen 51231.

BELFAST, 1
Fanum House, 5 Oxford Street. T. Belfast 26242.

*BIRMINGHAM, 16
Fanum House, 111 Hagley Road, Edgbaston. T. EDGbaston 6121.

*BOURNEMOUTH
Fanum House, 3 Wimborne Road. T. Bournemouth 25751.

*BRIGHTON, 7
Fanum House, 84 Marine Parade. T. Brighton 66161.

*BRISTOL, 8
Fanum House, Clifton Down (The Promenade). T. Bristol 38701.

*CAMBRIDGE
Fanum House, 35A Hills Road. T. Cambridge 51217.

*CARDIFF
Fanum House, Cathedral Road. T. Cardiff 30771.
Tel. Add. Carfanum Cardiff.

CARLISLE
Whitehall Chambers, Lowther Street. T. Carlisle 24274.

*CHELMSFORD
Fanum House, 198 New London Road. T. Chelmsford 3186.

COLWYN BAY
Fanum House, 77 Conway Road. T. Colwyn Bay 3384.

CORK
5 South Mall. T. Cork 21213.

DUBLIN, 2
23 Suffolk Street. T. Dublin 77677. Tel. Add. Dufanum Dublin.

DUNDEE (Sub-office)
Royal Exchange, Albert Square. T. Dundee 24161.
Tel. Add. Dunfanum Dundee.

*EDINBURGH, 3
Temporary Address: 11 Atholl Crescent. T. CALedonian 6591.

*EXETER
Fanum House, Bedford Street. T. Exeter 54281.

*GLASGOW, C.2
Fanum House, Blythswood Square. T. Glasgow CENtral 9191.
Tel. Add. Fanum Glasgow Telex.

*GUILDFORD
Fanum House, London Road. T. Guildford 2841.

JERSEY, Channel Islands
Esplanade Chambers, 5 Esplanade, St. Helier.
T. Jersey Central 23344. Tel. Add. Fanum Jersey.

*LEEDS
City Square, Leeds, 1. T. Leeds 57181. Tel. Add. Fanum Leeds 6.
Moorfield House, Alma Road, Leeds, 6. T. Leeds 57181.
Tel. Add. Fanum Leeds 6.

*LEICESTER
Fanum House, 142 Charles Street. T. Leicester 56075.

*LIVERPOOL, 2
Derby Square. T. Liverpool ROYal 6874.

*MAIDSTONE
Fanum House, London Road. T. Maidstone 55353.

*MANCHESTER, 2
Fanum House, York Street. T. DEAnsgate 8811.

*NEWCASTLE UPON TYNE, 2
Fanum House, 20 Great North Road. T. Newcastle upon Tyne 610111

*NORWICH
Fanum House, Thorpe Road, Norwich, Norfolk, NOR O8T.
T. Norwich 26231.

*NOTTINGHAM
Fanum House, 484 Derby Road. T. Nottingham 71181.
Tel. Add. Fanum Nottingham Telex.

PARIS, 16e
Fanum House, 39 Avenue d'Iéna. T. KLÉber 99.75.

*READING
Fanum House, 75 London Road. T. Reading 53481

*SHEFFIELD, 1
Mappin Buildings, Norfolk Street. T. Sheffield 27381.

*SOUTHAMPTON
Fanum House, 11 The Avenue. T. Southampton 27085.

*STANMORE, Middlesex
Fanum House, The Broadway. T. GRImsdyke 2345.

*STOKE-ON-TRENT
Normeir Buildings, St. Andrew's Square. T. Stoke-on-Trent 47541.

TRURO
Fanum House. Tregolls Road. T. Truro 2283.

A.A. PORT & AIRPORT OFFICES

In addition to those in the list below, the Association has Port Offices in Belfast, Dublin and Liverpool and also maintains full A.A. port service from its Area Offices in Cork, Glasgow, and Jersey. In these six cases, Members should use the addresses and telephone numbers given in the main list above. A.A. offices at ports and airports are open as required, for the assistance of Members arriving or leaving.

BOURNEMOUTH (HURN) AIRPORT
The A.A. Airport Office. T. Christchurch 2540.
Tel. Add. Fanumhurn, Christchurch.

DOUGLAS, I.O.M.
The A.A. Port Office, 12B Walpole Avenue.
T. Douglas 826. Tel. Add. as postal address.

DOVER
The A.A. Port Office, 1 Camden Crescent. T. Dover 1980.

FISHGUARD
The A.A. Port Office, Fishguard Harbour, Goodwick, Pembrokeshire.
T. Fishguard 3133.

FOLKESTONE
The A.A. Port Office, Folkestone Harbour. T. Folkestone 4290.

GUERNSEY
The A.A. Port Office, The White Rock, St. Peter Port.
T. Guernsey Central 2984. Tel. Add. as postal address.

HARWICH
The A.A. Port Office, Parkeston Quay.
T. Harwich 331. Tel. Add. Fanum Parkestonquay.

HEYSHAM
The A.A. Port Office, Heysham Harbour, Lancs.
T. Heysham 226.

HOLYHEAD
The A.A. Port Office, Holyhead Station, North Wales.
T. Holyhead 2740.

LARNE
The A.A. Port Office, Larne Harbour. T. Larne 2255.

LE TOUQUET
The A.A. Airport Officer, Aéroport du Touquet. T. Le Touquet 816
Tel. Add. as postal address.

LONDON, E.16
The A.A. Port Office, No. 8 Gate, Royal Victoria Dock.
T. ALBert Dock 3900. Tel. Add. Fanumdock London E.16.

LYDD (FERRYFIELD) AIRPORT
The A.A. Airport Office. T. Lydd 356. Tel. Add. Fanum Lydd.

NEWCASTLE UPON TYNE
The A.A. Port Office, Tyne Commission Quay, North Shields.
T. North Shields 2204 or Newcastle upon Tyne 610111.

NEWHAVEN
The A.A. Port Office, Newhaven Harbour. T. Newhaven 245.

ROSSLARE
The A.A. Port Officer, c/o British Railways, Rosslare Harbour.
T. Rosslare Harbour 15. Tel. Add. as postal address.

SOUTHAMPTON
The A.A. Port Office, No. 9 Berth (Entrance via No. 5 Gate, Canute Road), Southampton Docks. T. Southampton 28304.

SOUTHEND AIRPORT
The A.A. Airport Office.
T. Southend-on-Sea 544790. Tel. Add. Fanum Southend-on-Sea.

STRANRAER
The A.A. Port Office, Stranraer Harbour. T. Stranraer 570.

TILBURY
The A.A. Port Office, Tilbury Landing Stage. T. Tilbury 2796.

WEYMOUTH
The A.A. Port Office, Weymouth Quay. T. Weymouth 1057.

INTRODUCTION

THE FIRST post-war edition of the *A.A. Road Book of Scotland* appeared in 1953. Since that time there have been two reprints and recently a second revised edition was published. The A.A. touring library is now enriched by the addition of *The Illustrated Road Book of Scotland* to take its place beside *The Illustrated Road Book of England and Wales*. So far as is known, no such complete and authoritative touring guide covering the whole of Scotland has ever before appeared.

The book is so arranged that all illustrations refer to places described on the facing pages. Because of the limitations this plan has imposed, many items worthy of illustration have, unfortunately, had to be omitted. The drawings, of which there are more than 1,000, are all based on photographs, the majority of them taken by members of the A.A. staff in recent years.

The Association is indebted to H.M. Ministry of Works, the National Trust for Scotland, the Scottish Tourist Board and the British Travel and Holidays Association for permission to make use of photographs from their collections for the purpose of illustrating places and objects of special interest in the Hebrides, the islands of Orkney and Shetland, and elsewhere, and to the West Highland Museum, Fort William, for permission to make use of an official photograph to illustrate the interesting Secret Portrait of Prince Charles Edward on Plate 68. In addition, acknowledgment is made to the many sources from which information has been obtained. 'Scottish Country Life,' 'Country Life,' 'The Field,' 'The Autocar' and 'The Motor,' and the pages of 'The Times,' 'The Guardian' and 'The Scotsman' have all suggested subjects for illustration. Credit is also due to the ingenuity of the artists who have produced so many attractive illustrations, often under considerable technical difficulties. Mr. Angus Graham, F.S.A., F.S.A.(Scot.), who kindly checked the proofs of the illustrations, made many valuable suggestions which have been incorporated in the text and captions.

Throughout the book preference has been given to illustrations of things which can be seen by the public without intrusion on private property. In some cases a small fee is charged for admission, e.g. houses which are opened to the public by the owners, Scottish National Trust properties, and sites under the control of H.M. Ministry of Works.

With a book of this kind it is inevitable that some of the things illustrated are removed or destroyed after publication. So far as is known at the time of going to press, there is nothing illustrated which cannot be seen.

To those who may feel that something of particular interest in their locality has been omitted, and to those who may discover any inaccuracies in text or illustration which have escaped our careful checking, apologies are offered. It is hoped that this book will provide fresh interest and inspiration for those journeying in what is, in the opinion of many, the finest touring ground in Europe.

THE COUNTIES OF SCOTLAND

The following articles are designed to present a general picture of the topography and outstanding characteristics of the counties. Each is followed by classified lists showing the best of the various ecclesiastical buildings, ancient and historic castles, the most notable houses, attractive villages, and places with the greatest scenic interest. All places mentioned are listed separately in the Gazetteer, except certain Abbeys, Castles and Houses, which are described under the place-names given after them in brackets.

A striking feature of Scotland is its wealth of picturesque islands, large and small, said to number in all some 787, and situated mostly off the north and west coasts, the most important being Arran, Bute, the Inner and Outer Hebrides, and the Orkney and Shetland groups. Arran and Bute together constitute the county of Bute, while the Hebrides are divided between Argyll, Inverness and Ross and Cromarty. All these islands, together with the Orkneys and Shetland, both of which are counties in their own right, are fully described under their own headings in the Gazetteer, so that only a bare mention of them has been made in the county articles.

The mainland of Scotland is traditionally divided into the Highlands and the Lowlands, both of which districts are described in detail in the Gazetteer. The Lowlands belie their name, in that they are largely hilly, though only in the sparsely-populated Galloway area is a height of as much as 3,000 ft. approached. Included in the Lowlands are the Border Country, the Burns Country and the Scott Country, all of which are popular touring grounds, and for which there are a number of convenient centres.

The Highlands cover a much larger area, and in view of the mountainous nature of the country, narrower, and in general less well-surfaced roads will be encountered, but the magnificent scenery will more than compensate for this. Among the most notable examples of Highland grandeur are the wild peaks of historic Glencoe; the Lochaber district, with Ben Nevis, Britain's highest peak, facing the Mamores; the great Cairngorm range, incorporating a 40,000-acre National Nature Reserve; and, above all, the superb stretch of undeveloped hill country, ideal for one of the proposed Scottish National Parks, occupying almost the whole of the land to the north-west of the Great Glen, or Glen More, which virtually divides Scotland into two portions. These North-West Highlands contain the wildest mountain and loch scenery on the mainland, the greater part of it being concentrated near the deeply-indented coastline of Inverness, Wester Ross and Sutherland, with their superb sea lochs, though an outstanding exception is the grand inland scenery of Glen Affric and Glen Cannich, in northern Inverness-shire, where a great hydro-electric scheme, providing power for the Highlands, has opened up new vistas for the tourist by means of reconstructed roads.

Mountain scenery of an equally grand nature will be found also in the Hebridean islands of Mull, Rum, and particularly Skye, where the sensational knife-edge ridges of the Coolins are unique in Britain.

National Forest Parks have been established in certain districts and are mentioned under their respective counties, in addition to being marked on the atlas.

A county map will be found on the first page of the atlas at the end of the book.

ABERDEENSHIRE
(County Town: Aberdeen)

Scotland's most easterly county, and one of the largest in area, is divided into the five districts of Mar, Garioch, Formartine, Strathbogie and Buchan. Aberdeenshire is noted particularly for the breeding of prize pedigree cattle.

The Mar district includes the impressive granite-built Cathedral and University city of Aberdeen, the third largest in the country, and stretches westwards along the richly wooded valley of the Dee to take in Royal Deeside, beloved of Queen Victoria and all the Royal Family. Also within the confines of Mar rise the heights of the eastern Grampians, on the Angus and Banff borders. Garioch and Formartine are smaller districts, situated to the north of the fertile and winding Don valley, the former including the prominent hill of Bennachie, with the Mither Tap, to the west of Inverurie, and the latter taking in the flat coastal area around Newburgh and the Ythan river estuary. Strathbogie, near the Banff border, is mainly hilly, and watered by the Deveron, its chief centre being Huntly, with the ruined Palace, or Castle, of the

Gordons. Finally, Buchan is the name given to the rather bleak north-east corner of the county, which includes a lonely and undeveloped stretch of the North Sea coast between the herring fishing ports of Peterhead and Fraserburgh. A more attractive and rocky seaboard lies to the west of the last-named, in the direction of Troup Head, in Banffshire. The interior of Buchan is almost entirely flat, the monotony being relieved by the isolated Mormond Hill, near Strichen, with its carvings of a white horse and a stag.

Deeside is by far the best known and most beautiful part of the county, the scenery becoming gradually more mountainous towards the west, where the lofty Cairngorm plateau and ridges, the source of the River Dee, and now partly a large National Nature Reserve, are situated. Here, Ben Macdhui, the second highest of Scotland's peaks, rises on the Banff border; Braeriach, overlooking the famous Lairig Ghru pass, is shared with the county of Inverness; while Cairn Toul is wholly within Aberdeenshire. Away to the north-east of the Cairngorms is Cock Bridge, on the upper Don, from where the desolate and lonely Lecht road climbs steeply to 2,090 ft., near the Banff border, on its way to Tomintoul.

The county is also famous for its splendid series of baronial castles, many being still inhabited, and foremost among which must be placed the modern Royal Castle of Balmoral. This stands in a beautiful forest setting on the Dee, to the east of the well-known Highland resort of Braemar, and has for its southern background the outline of the famous peak of Lochnagar. Among the more ancient castles, those of Fyvie, Craigievar, Midmar and Castle Fraser are the finest, and together form a group that is without equal of its kind in Scotland. Of numerous still earlier, but ruined structures, the picturesque castles of Kildrummy, Huntly, and Tolquhon, near Tarves, are perhaps the most notable examples.

Places of Scenic Interest. Aboyne, Ballater, Braemar, Cock Bridge, Collieston, Cruden Bay, Inverey, Lochnagar, Old Deer, Oyne, Pennan, Rosehearty.

Places of Architectural or Historic Interest. Aberdeen, Balmoral Castle, Braemar, Castle Fraser (Kemnay), Craig Castle (Lumsden), Craigievar Castle, Crathie Church, Delgatie Castle (Turriff), Drum Castle (Drumoak), Fyvie, Huntly, Inveramsay, Kildrummy, Kintore, Midmar Castle, Old Meldrum, Pitsligo, Tolquhon Castle (Tarves).

ANGUS
(County Town: Forfar)

The name of this county, which extends from the North Sea to the heights of the Grampians, was formerly Forfarshire. The title Forfar is, however, now generally confined to the county town.

The most picturesque part of Angus is known as the " Braes of Angus ", and lies to the north-west and north, where the lofty outliers of the eastern Grampian, or Benchinnan mountains penetrate into the county, which is here broken up into a series of deep and lonely glens of great beauty. The best known are Glen Isla, Glen Prosen, Glen Clova, and the delightful valley of the North Esk river, terminating with Loch Lee, backed by the lonely peak of Mount Keen, on the Aberdeen border. These glens, although traversed by roads, are comparatively little visited, due perhaps to the fact that none of them, except Lower Glen Isla, provides a through route to the west for motorists. For long-distance walkers, however, a wide field of exploration is opened up by means of the various lofty tracks leading towards the Dee valley and the White Mounth and Lochnagar mountains from a number of points at the remote heads of the glens.

In the highly cultivated south-west corner of Angus, which is famous also for its prize cattle, the Sidlaw Hills extend towards Forfar. In the vicinity of this town are two of the most interesting places in the county: Kirriemuir, with its memories of Sir James Barrie; and Glamis, famous for the great Castle, so intimately associated with the present Royal family, and overlooking part of the fertile Vale of Strathmore, here known as the Howe of Angus.

The finest part of the coast lies between Arbroath and the port and resort of Montrose, where much wild rock scenery and sandstone cliffs will be found around Red Head, and also near the quaint fishing village of Auchmithie, lying to the south. Dundee is by far the largest centre in Angus, and ranks fourth in population among Scottish cities, being famous for jute, and noted also for the fine Old Steeple of the City Churches. Linking it to the Fife coast across the Firth of Tay is the celebrated two-mile-long Tay Bridge, carrying the main railway line to the south.

Among ecclesiastical buildings, Brechin Cathedral, where one of Scotland's three round towers, reminiscent of those found in Ireland, can be seen, is of interest, while the ruined Abbey at Arbroath is also notable. The Parish Church at Fowlis Easter contains an elaborately carved Sacrament House, one of the finest to have survived. Claypots Castle, near Broughty Ferry, is a curious old stronghold, and at Edzell is a ruined castle preserving an early 17th cent. walled garden, which is unique in the country.

Places of Scenic Interest. Auchmithie, Braedownie, Clova Church, Dykehead, Edzell, Gannochy Bridge, Kirkton of Glenisla, Kirriemuir, Lochlee Church, Tarfside, Usan.

Places of Architectural or Historic Interest. Affleck Castle (Monikie), Arbroath, Brechin, Claypotts Castle (Broughty Ferry), Cortachy Castle, Dundee, Edzell, Fowlis Easter, Glamis, Guthrie, Hospitalfield (Arbroath), Inverquharity Castle (Kirriemuir), Kirriemuir, Pitcur, Restenneth Priory (Forfar), St. Vigean's.

ARGYLLSHIRE
(County Town: Inveraray)

Second in size among the Scottish counties, and at one time known as the kingdom of Dalriada, Argyllshire incorporates in addition many of the Inner Hebridean islands, one of the largest of which is the rugged and picturesque Isle of Mull, in which Ben More rises to more than 3,000 ft. Jura and Islay are also of considerable size, but more famous are the small islands of Iona and Staffa, off the coast of Mull, the former celebrated for its Cathedral and associations with St. Columba, and the latter renowned for some remarkable basaltic rock scenery and the well-known Fingal's Cave.

The mainland of Argyll is cut up into peninsulas, and deeply indented by magnificent sea lochs. Outstanding among these are Loch Sunart, dividing the districts of Ardnamurchan and Morven; Outer Loch Linnhe, which separates Morven and Ardgour from Appin; the narrow trough of Loch Etive, situated in the land of Benderloch and

Lorne; and the long and narrow Loch Fyne, which divides Knapdale from the hilly land of Cowal, the shores of which are washed by the well-known Kyles of Bute. South and east of Cowal, in which the large resort of Dunoon faces Cloch Point on the Renfrew coast, are the waters of the Firth of Clyde, beloved of yachtsmen, and of which the Holy Loch and Loch Long are picturesque inlets. The head of the latter is dominated by Ben Arthur, popularly known as The Cobbler, overlooking the extensive Argyll National Forest Park in the vicinity of Glen Croe, with its well-known hill of Rest and be Thankful. Farther south, the long and narrow Kintyre peninsula stretches away from Knapdale towards the distant Northern Irish coast, and terminates in the wild headland of the Mull of Kintyre, with its lighthouse.

Inland, far to the north, on the Inverness border, the beautiful southern, but roadless shores of Loch Shiel, with its memories of Prince Charles Edward, belong to Argyll, and here mountain and loch combine to portray an exceptionally rich and varied picture. Eastwards of Ballachulish and its well-known car ferry, finely situated on Loch Leven, lies the entrance to the grim and forbidding Pass of Glencoe, scenically and historically probably the most famous in Scotland, and hemmed in by 3,000-ft. high rock peaks culminating in Bidean nam Bian, the monarch of Argyll. Near the eastern entrance to the glen, where the finely-engineered new road is at a lower level than the disused old road, stands the " Kingshouse " Inn. Above it rises the spectacular rock bastion of Buchaille Etive Mor, the " Shepherd of Etive," famous among climbers, and towering above the lonely wastes of Rannoch Moor, one of the country's principal watersheds, dominated to the east by the lofty Drum Alban ridge of the Grampian range. Much of all this grand mountain district is the property of the National Trust for Scotland, notably the Dalness Forest area, which borders Glen Etive, leading towards the lonely shores of Loch Etive, at the head of which rises Ben Starav.

Beyond Loch Linnhe stretch the remote, but picturesque districts of Ardgour and Morven, threaded by Loch Sunart, to the north of which rise the fine peaks of Garbh Bheinn and Ben Resipol, the former being a prominent feature of the view across Loch Linnhe from the ferry at Ballachulish. Farther west still is Ardnamurchan, where the lonely Ardnamurchan Point marks the most westerly point on the Scottish mainland. The roads in these districts are narrow and at times poorly surfaced, but frequent passing-places have been constructed on certain stretches.

Loch Awe, dominated at its head by the twin-peaked Ben Cruachan, is the largest inland loch, with roads traversing the whole length of both its southern and northern shores. To the west lies Oban, perhaps the best known resort in the county, and an excellent centre for visiting the various

Inner Hebridean islands by steamer. Near Ardrishaig, on Loch Fyne, is the eastern end of the Crinan Canal, built originally to provide an easier passage for ships making for the Sound of Jura and the Atlantic, thus avoiding the often stormy voyage round the Mull of Kintyre.

The Royal Burgh of Inveraray, on Loch Fyne, where the 18th cent. Castle is the ancestral home of the Duke of Argyll, the head of Clan Campbell, forms one of the pleasantest of small Scottish towns. The county also possesses a number of romantically situated old castles, now mostly in ruins, notably Kilchurn Castle on Loch Awe, Castle Stalker near Portnacroish in Appin, Castle Tioram near Acharacle, and Dunstaffnage Castle to the north of Oban.

In addition, a number of prehistoric antiquities, notably Chambered Cairns and Cup and Ring marked rocks from the Bronze Age, as well as several finely sculptured churchyard Crosses, are a feature of the county, particularly in the neighbourhood of Kilmartin.

Places of Scenic Interest. Acharacle, Ardgour, Ballachulish, Benmore Estate, Bridge of Orchy, Clachan Bridge, Falls of Cruachan, Glencoe, Inversanda, Kilchoan, Kilmelford, Kingshouse, Loch Awe, Loch Fyne, Lochgoilhead, Loch Shiel, Mull of Kintyre, Oban, Rest-and-be-Thankful, Southend, Strontian, Tarbert.

Places of Architectural or Historic Interest. Ardtornish Castle (Lochaline), Barcaldine Castle, Carnasserie Castle (Kilmartin), Carrick Castle (Lochgoilhead), Castle Stalker (Portnacroish), Castle Sween (Kilmory Knap), Castle Tioram (Acharacle), Dundarave Castle (Inveraray), Dunstaffnage Castle, Glencoe, Gylen Castle (Oban), Inveraray, Kilchurn Castle, Kilmartin, Kilmichael, Mingary Castle (Kilchoan), Saddell.

Places of interest in the Inner Hebridean islands of Colonsay, Iona, Jura and Staffa will be found by referring to the gazetteer articles for those islands. Islay and Mull have separate entries for all individual places of interest, these being cross-indexed in the parent articles.

AYRSHIRE
(County Town: Ayr)

The name of Robert Burns is inseparably bound up with Ayrshire, and of the various places with which his name is associated, Ayr itself and its neighbour Alloway, with the famous Auld Brig spanning the River Doon, are perhaps the most visited. Nevertheless, Catrine, Kilmarnock, Kirkoswald, Mauchline and Tarbolton all have their own special claims.

The county is divided from north to south into the three districts of Cunningham, Kyle and Carrick, the last-named having once formed part of Galloway. A long coastline on the shores of the Firth of Clyde gives splendid views from many places towards the island of Bute, the twin

Cumbraes, and the lofty mountains of Arran. Facing the resort of Girvan, and situated some ten miles out to sea, is the prominent, lonely islet of Ailsa Craig, with its lighthouse and ruined castle. Between the Renfrew border in the north and the town of Ayr on its bay are situated a number of well-known coastal resorts, including historic Largs, and Ardrossan, the port for Arran. Among numerous golfing centres, Troon, Turnberry and Prestwick are perhaps most renowned, the last-named now doubly famous due to the proximity of the great airport. Away to the south, between Girvan and the mouth of Loch Ryan, which bites deep into Wigtownshire, lies perhaps the finest coastal stretch in southern Scotland. This is traversed by the picturesque road through Kennedy's Pass and round Bennane Head to Ballantrae and the finely wooded Glen App, this glen lying a little inland.

Parts of the Cunningham district have been industrialised, the most important town being Kilmarnock, but the remainder of the county is devoted mainly to agriculture and dairy farming, the Ayrshire breed of cattle being world famous. There are lonely hills and moors bordering Dumfries and Kirkcudbright, to the south-east, rising in places to more than 2,500 ft. in height, and to the south of Dalmellington, in the foothills of Galloway, lies Loch Doon, which forms the Kirkcudbright boundary for most of its length. In the heart of the Carrick country are the pleasant villages of Straiton and Barr, the latter situated in the delightful Stinchar valley, while in the neighbourhood are the Carrick and Changue Forests, forming part of the Glen Trool National Forest Park. To the east of Barr, a narrow hill road leads southwards over the Nick o' the Balloch pass, with views of the Galloway hills, and giving access to Glen Trool, in Kirkcudbrightshire.

Ayr itself, apart from its links with Burns, is a town and resort of varied interest, having associations with William Wallace, and being also the birthplace of John Macadam, of road-making fame. To the south of Ayr stands the small town of Maybole, once the capital of Carrick, preserving in the High Street the former town house of the Earls of Cassillis, and in the vicinity of which is the ruined Crossraguel Abbey, neighboured by the old tower of Baltersan.

Among numerous ancient castles, the finest are Culzean, where the former Kennedy stronghold is incorporated in Robert Adam's fine mansion of 1777, now the property of the Scottish National Trust; Killochan, near Girvan; and Rowallan, to the north-east of Kilmaurs. The remaining fragment at Turnberry is of interest as having perhaps been the birthplace of Robert Bruce. A feature of the county which is perhaps unique is the so-called "Electric Brae" at Croy, near Dunure, where, as the result of a curious optical illusion, a car will roll backwards along what would appear

to be a descending gradient, this being nevertheless an ascent.

Places of Scenic Interest. Ballantrae, Barr, Colmonell, Dunure, Kirkoswald, Lendalfoot, Pinwherry, Sorn, Straiton.

Places of Architectural or Historic Interest. Alloway, Ardstinchar Castle (Ballantrae), Auchinleck, Ayr, Crossraguel Abbey, Culzean Castle, Dumfries House (Cumnock), Kelburne Castle (Fairlie), Kilbirnie, Killochan Castle (Girvan), Largs, Loch Doon Castle, Loudoun Castle (Galston), Mauchline, Maybole, Penkill Castle (Dailly), Rowallan Castle (Kilmaurs), Tarbolton, Turnberry.

BANFFSHIRE
(County Town: Banff)

A long and narrow county of considerable physical contrasts, Banffshire extends from the lofty fastnesses of the Cairngorms and eastern Grampians in the south-western extremity, through a predominantly agricultural countryside around Keith to the characteristic fishing villages and towns along the rocky, cliffbound coast.

Ben Macdhui, Scotland's second highest mountain, and Cairn Gorm, almost as lofty, two famous Cairngorm peaks, are situated on the Aberdeen and Inverness borders respectively, while the remote Loch Avon, with its well-known Shelter Stone, lies under Beinn Mheadoin between the two first-mentioned mountains. An extensive National Nature Reserve is now included within the Cairngorms. The boundary with Aberdeen traverses the summits of Beinn a'Bhuird and Ben Avon, and away to the north-east, the remarkable Lecht road, reaching an altitude of 2,090 ft., crosses from the Aberdeenshire village of Cock Bridge to enter Banffshire on its way towards Tomintoul. This is the loftiest village in the Highlands, though not in the whole of Scotland.

The River Avon flows northwards through the county from its source in the Cairngorms, and beyond Tomintoul is overlooked by the Cromdale Hills on the Inverness and Moray borders. Later it unites with the rapid-flowing Spey beyond Dalnashaugh Inn and the Bridge of Avon in a picturesque wooded setting. Northwards from here, the Spey forms the Moray boundary for some distance, with a particularly lovely stretch around Craigellachie, where it is joined by the Fiddich. To the south stands Dufftown, at the head of the long and pleasant Glen Rinnes, with Ben Rinnes rising in the background, while farther to the south-west is Glen Livet, where the famous distillery is perhaps the best known of the many which are to be found in the county. Through the flatter north-eastern sector of Banff flows the Deveron, on the Aberdeen border, reaching the sea between the twin ports of Banff and Macduff, with their important fisheries.

The coastline is flat in the west, but often rocky

and cliffbound in the east, with a number of prominent headlands between Logie Head, near Cullen, and Troup Head, far to the east on the Aberdeen border. Among various picturesque, though often lonely fishing villages are Findochty and Portknockie, to the west of Cullen, and also Crovie and Gardenstown, lying under the cliffs to the east of Macduff. In the pleasant village of Fordyce, between Cullen and Portsoy, stands a delightful little 16th cent. castle, while Balvenie Castle, outside Dufftown, is a picturesque ruin. At Deskford, the Church preserves what is perhaps the finest of the interesting Sacrament Houses which are almost confined to this area of Scotland, and another can be seen in the church at Cullen, which stands almost adjacent to Cullen House, where the old town was formerly situated.

Places of Scenic Interest. Craigellachie, Crovie, Dalnashaugh, Findochty, Gardenstown, Glenlivet, Portknockie, Tomintoul.

Places of Architectural or Historic Interest. Auchindown, Balvenie Castle (Dufftown), Boyne Castle (Portsoy), Cullen, Deskford, Duff House (Banff), Findlater Castle (Cullen), Fordyce, Kinnairdy Castle (Aberchirder).

BERWICKSHIRE
(County Town: Duns)

The name of the county is taken from the town of Berwick-upon-Tweed, though this latter is now regarded as belonging to Northumberland. At one time Berwickshire was known as The Merse, and this title is still applied to the wide plain which lies to the north of the River Tweed, and contains some of the richest agricultural land in Scotland.

The Tweed, a famous salmon stream, forms the southern border with England for some miles. Farther to the south-west, parts of Roxburgh extend northwards across the river, and at the seaward end the Tweed flows through a small portion of Northumberland and is joined by the Whiteadder Water. In the northern half of Berwickshire, the long range of the Lammermuirs, is tenanted largely by sheep. Its rather bleak moorlands slope gradually towards the Merse, extending from the viewpoint of Soutra Hill, on the borders of East Lothian and Midlothian, to the coast in the neighbourhood of Cockburnspath, and traversed by several narrow and hilly roads. To the south-west of the main Lammermuir ridge is the district of Lauderdale, watered by the Leader Water, and containing the small, but historic town of Lauder, the sole Royal Burgh in the county. In the vicinity of the town stand the old and new castles of Thirlestane.

The coast is largely rocky, with lofty, red cliffs in many places, the most notable headland being that of St. Abb's Head, to the west and south of which the maritime scenery is at its most impressive. Both Eyemouth and picturesque Burnmouth are noted for their fisheries, and to the north-west of the former is Coldingham, where the interesting Priory has been restored, and is now in use as the Parish Church.

The most famous building in the county is Dryburgh Abbey, which, apart from its beautiful situation near the Tweed, and also its architectural interest, is visited yearly by thousands who come to pay homage to Sir Walter Scott and to Field-Marshal Earl Haig, both of whom lie buried within its walls. Bemersyde House, the old home of the Haigs, is situated a little to the north of the Abbey, and the view from Bemersyde Hill, ranging over the windings of the Tweed backed by the Eildon Hills, was particularly loved by Scott.

At Coldstream, with its fine bridge spanning the Tweed, the famous Coldstream Guards were first raised in 1650 by General Monk, and away to the north-east, facing the river, is the beautiful old church of Ladykirk, built originally by James IV.

Places of Scenic Interest. Burnmouth, Cockburnspath, Cranshaws, Duns, Earlston, Eyemouth, St. Abb's, Soutra Hill.

Places of Architectural or Historic Interest. Abbey St. Bathans, Bemersyde, Chirnside, Coldingham, Cranshaws, Dryburgh Abbey, Greenknowe Castle (Gordon), Hume Castle (Greenlaw), Ladykirk, Mellerstain, Nisbet House (Duns), Thirlestane Castle (Lauder).

BUTESHIRE
(County Town: Rothesay)

This county consists of the large islands of Arran and Bute, together with the smaller Cumbraes, all of which are situated in the Firth of Clyde. The two first-named are fully described under their own headings in the gazetteer, while individual places of interest on both islands have their own separate entries, which are cross-indexed in the parent articles. A description of the twin Cumbraes will be found under the heading of Millport, their chief centre.

CAITHNESS-SHIRE
(County Town: Wick)

Situated in the distant and somewhat bleak far north-eastern corner of Scotland, and largely unknown to the majority of tourists, Caithness is in some respects more akin to a Lowland county. It contains nevertheless an irresistible magnet for the curious traveller in the magic name of John o' Groats, the fame of which rests largely on its very remoteness. This is the terminal point of the great trunk road from Edinburgh through the central Highlands to the lonely outpost facing the little island of Stroma. Although John o' Groats is scenically of minor interest, only a few miles to the east is the magnificent headland of Duncansby Head, with its lighthouse, and a trio of prominent detached sandstone stacks to the south, which should certainly be seen by all visitors to this "Ultima Thule."

The northern shores of Caithness are washed by the turbulent waters of the Pentland Firth, beyond which lie the Orkneys, of which the great cliffs and isolated Old Man of Hoy are often visible from a number of points on the mainland. The fishing port of Thurso is noted also for its quarries, from which emanate the characteristic Caithness flagstones lining so many of the local roads and fields. Across Thurso Bay, to the west, is the little harbour of Scrabster, the port for the Orkney mail steamer, and beyond it are the riven cliffs of Holborn Head, looking across the expanse of the bay towards Dunnet Head, the most northerly point on the mainland. Farther west along the coast is Dounreay, where Scotland's first nuclear power station has been built.

Wick, on the east coast, is an important fishing port and Royal Burgh, with splendid cliff scenery, both to the south and north of the town, while the hilly coast road leading south-westwards gives an excellent picture of the southern Caithness landscape. Beyond Dunbeath this is composed mainly of an elevated tableland, broken up in various places by streams, the scenery being particularly impressive and picturesque around Berriedale, and near the Ord of Caithness on the Sutherland border.

Inland from Berriedale rise the lonely hills of Scaraben and Morven, the latter being the best known height in the county, and forming a landmark for many miles. Much of the interior of Caithness is boggy and undeveloped, and the early Norse invaders are recalled by many of the place-name terminations, while numerous prehistoric antiquities, such as hut circles and Pictish remains, have survived, notably in the Latheron valley between Dunbeath and Lybster.

Places of Scenic Interest. Berriedale, Bridge of Forss, John o' Groats, Latheron, Wick.

Places of Architectural or Historic Interest.
Ackergill Tower (Reiss), Brawl Castle (Halkirk), Canisbay Church, Castle Girnigo (Wick), Castle of Mey (East Mey), Dunbeath, Dunnet, Keiss, Mid Clyth.

CLACKMANNANSHIRE
(County Town: Alloa)

Scotland's smallest county is situated between the widening Forth estuary and the highest parts of the Ochil Hills, with the fertile, low-lying country below the range traversed by the serpentine windings of the River Devon, which flows into the estuary near Tullibody.

The grass-covered Ochils extend along the whole northern border of the county, facing Perthshire, the highest point in the range, Ben Cleuch, attaining well over 2,000 ft. It rises above the little weaving towns of Alva and Tillicoultry, both of which stand at the foot of delightful glens, the meeting-point of tiny burns flowing down from the hills. In the foothills of the Ochils, below King's Seat Hill, and looking down towards the town of Dollar, noted for its Academy, stands the ancient, ruined Castle Campbell, in one of the most picturesque settings in Scotland, giving a view across the Fife levels to the Forth estuary and the distant Pentland Hills.

Both Alloa and Clackmannan have preserved ancient towers, the former, which has associations with Mary, Queen of Scots, standing in close proximity to a modern mansion.

Places of Scenic Interest. Alva, Dollar, Tillicoultry.

Places of Architectural or Historic Interest.
Alloa, Castle Campbell (Dollar), Clackmannan.

DUMFRIESSHIRE
(County Town: Dumfries)

Extending from the low, sandy shores of the Solway Firth into the heart of the Lowlands, this county displays a wealth of hills and dales, outstanding among which are the three parallel dales of Nithsdale, Annandale and Eskdale. In the first-named is some of the loveliest scenery in Dumfries, notably between Thornhill and Sanquhar, where the Nith flows between ranges of shapely, green hills. A trio of picturesque passes, those of Dalveen, Mennock and Enterkin, link the Nith valley with Clydesdale, in Lanarkshire, the two first-named being traversed by good motoring roads. The last-named is a mere track, and joins the Mennock near the mining village of Wanlockhead, the highest situated in Scotland, overlooked by the bulky hill of Green Lowther.

Annandale stretches northwards from the Solway Firth, the river flowing between Lockerbie and Lochmaben, and the dale becoming lonelier and at its wildest to the north of the little spa of Moffat. Here, it is noted for the winding pass overlooking the Devil's Beef Tub, a hollow set deep below steep green hills near the borders of Dumfries, Lanark and Peebles, close to the important watershed where the Rivers Clyde, Tweed and Annan rise. Beyond Moffat, the Selkirk road to the north-east follows the Moffat Water under the slopes of Hart Fell and White Coomb, and passes near the well-known waterfall of the Grey Mare's Tail, at the summit of the Birkhill Pass, looking into Selkirkshire. The burn at this point comes down from the high-lying Loch Skene, in the vicinity of which Dumfries, Peebles and Selkirk meet.

Eskdale, the most easterly of the three dales, commences near the English border, here guarded by the Scots Dyke, on the borders of the former "Debatable Land." It continues through Canonbie and Langholm, amid characteristic Border scenery, to lose itself away to the north in the wild and lonely Ettrick hills beyond Eskdalemuir.

The town of Dumfries, situated on the Nith near its estuary, has important Burns associations, and near Auldgirth, also on the river, is the well-known farmhouse of Ellisland, where the poet composed " Tam o' Shanter " among other works. Another famous literary association is claimed by Ecclefechan, where Thomas Carlyle was born, and near Dunscore is the farm of Craigenputtock, where his great work "Sartor Resartus" was written.

Among other places of interest in the county are Lochmaben, said to have been the birthplace of Robert Bruce, and Gretna, which was long notorious for its runaway marriage ceremonies. Sanquhar, in Nithsdale, together with the Lowther Hills to the east, has many associations with the persecuted Covenanters. In the little Church at Ruthwell is preserved the celebrated 8th cent. Ruthwell Cross, the most notable of the county's ecclesiastical remains, and at Durisdeer the Church contains a remarkable range of monuments. Drumlanrig Castle is a magnificent Renaissance house in a lovely setting, and Maxwelton House, near Moniaive, is famous as the one-time home of Annie Laurie. Among numerous castles and towers, Caerlaverock Castle, with its remarkable façade; Comlongon Castle near Clarencefield; and the exceptionally well-preserved Amisfield Tower, are perhaps the most notable examples.

Places of Scenic Interest. Auldgirth, Birkhill, Canonbie, Carronbridge, Enterkinfoot, Eskdalemuir, Langholm, Mennock, Moffat, Wanlockhead.

Places of Architectural or Historic Interest. Amisfield, Caerlaverock, Closeburn, Comlongon Castle (Clarencefield), Craigenputtock (Dunscore), Drumlanrig Castle, Dumfries, Durisdeer, Ecclefechan, Ellisland (Auldgirth), Gretna, Hollows Tower (Canonbie), Isle Tower (Auldgirth), Lochmaben, Maxwelton House (Moniaive), Moniaive, Ruthwell, Spedlins Tower (Lockerbie).

DUNBARTONSHIRE
(County Town: Dumbarton)

This county was at one time known as Lennox, and formed part of an ancient district comprising also portions of Stirling, Perth and Renfrew, the name being now preserved in the general title of the Lennox Hills, which is applied to the Kilpatricks, the Campsie Fells and the neighbouring hill ranges. Dunbarton is unique among Scottish counties in that it possesses also a small detached portion on the mainland, lying to the east, bordered by Lanark and Stirling. This includes the town of Kirkintilloch, where a fort on the Antonine, or Roman Wall, was formerly situated.

The bulk of the county stretches north-westwards from the environs of Glasgow, its boundaries being the Clyde estuary, Loch Long and Loch Lomond, while at the northern extremity it meets Perthshire beyond Ardlui at the head of the last-named loch. The great mass of Ben Vorlich dominates the scene at this point, and to the south-west of the mountain lies Loch Sloy, whose waters have been harnessed

to one of Scotland's large hydro-electric schemes. Some of the loveliest scenery in the country is to be found on the road which traverses the whole length of Loch Lomond's western shores, passing the attractive village of Luss. Another scenic road is that which follows the Gare Loch to its head, and then continues along the eastern shores of the lengthy and narrow Loch Long to Arrochar, situated on the narrow neck of land separating Loch Long from Loch Lomond. Several of the well-known Clyde coast resorts lie on the shore of the Gare Loch, and also in the narrow Rosneath peninsula separating its waters from those of Loch Long, the best known being perhaps Helensburgh.

The Royal Burgh of Dumbarton, an important shipbuilding town, is noted for its castle, which dominates the Clyde estuary from the heights of Dumbarton Rock. To the north of the town, along the shores of the River Leven, which issues from Loch Lomond at the railhead of Balloch, is a district specialising in bleaching, and in which the town of Alexandria has associations with Tobias Smollett. Nearer to Glasgow the Clyde becomes highly industrialised, and Clydebank, which was severely damaged during the second World War, is famous for its shipbuilding yards, where, among many historic ships, the great liners *Queen Mary* and *Queen Elizabeth* were built. At Bowling, below the Kilpatrick Hills, between Dumbarton and Clydebank, the Forth and Clyde canal enters the estuary, and here was the western terminus of the Roman Wall, which stretched across the narrow waist of the country to the Forth estuary. Some portions are still to be seen in Dunbartonshire near the town of Bearsden.

Places of Scenic Interest. Ardlui, Arrochar, Garelochhead, Loch Lomond, Luss, Rosneath, Tarbet.

Places of Architectural or Historic Interest. Bearsden, Bowling, Dumbarton, Knockderry Castle (Kilcreggan), Ross Priory (Gartocharn).

EAST LOTHIAN
(County Town: Haddington)

One of the most fertile of the Scottish counties, notably near Dunbar, where, in the red soil, are grown the celebrated " Red Dunbar " potatoes. The long and lonely range of the Lammermuirs, given over largely to sheep, forms the southern background to East Lothian, while the land to the north of the hills slopes gradually towards the coastal plain overlooking the Firth of Forth. Lammer Law, rising to the south of Gifford, is the highest point in the Lammermuirs, and to the west, near the Midlothian and Berwick borders, is Soutra Hill, a well-known viewpoint on the main Edinburgh to Jedburgh road.

East Lothian has a coastline which is mainly flat, and the neighbourhood of the famous resorts of Gullane and North Berwick is largely devoted to golf. Out to sea beyond North Berwick, and a prominent object in the view from the picturesque, ruined castle of Tantallon, is the notable landmark of the Bass Rock, now a haunt of sea birds.

Both Dunbar and Prestonpans are renowned in Scottish history for the battles with which they are associated and near the latter is the little fishing village of Cockenzie. The Royal Burgh of Haddington, which formerly gave its name to the county, is supposed to be the birthplace of John Knox, and its fine, though mutilated Church has been called the "Lamp of Lothian." Dirleton, East Linton and Gifford are attractive villages, the first-named having an old castle, while near the last-named is the Adam mansion of Yester House, beyond which lies the curious underground "Goblin Ha'" from the former castle. At White-kirk and Seton there are interesting churches, the latter, which is unfinished, being collegiate, and noted for its vaulted chancel and apse. A number of other fine old houses grace the county, among which may be mentioned Gosford House, Pilmuir near Bolton, and both Winton House and Penkaet in the vicinity of Pencaitland.

Places of Scenic Interest. Dirleton, East Linton, Garvald, Gifford, Pencaitland, Soutra Hill.

Places of Architectural or Historic Interest.
Biel (Stenton), Dirleton, Dunbar, Dunglass, Elphinstone Tower (Tranent), Falside Castle (Tranent), Gosford House, Haddington, Hailes Castle (East Linton), Lennoxlove (Bolton), Northfield (Prestonpans), Pencaitland, Penkaet (Pencaitland), Pilmuir (Bolton), Prestonpans, Saltcoats Castle (Gullane), Seton, Spott, Tantallon Castle (North Berwick), Tynninghame, Whitekirk, Whittinghame, Winton (Pencaitland), Yester (Gifford).

FIFE
(County Town: Cupar)

Situated between the Firths of Forth and Tay, and sometimes still known as the "Kingdom of Fife," this pleasant county included, until 1426, also Kinross within its boundaries. Although lacking the more spectacular physical features associated with some other Scottish counties, Fife has nevertheless achieved a niche of its own by virtue of the world-wide fame of St. Andrews, and the delightful old-world maritime burghs gracing the shores of the Firth of Forth, the most picturesque surviving of their kind. On the extreme north-west border rise the Ochil Hills, separated by the fertile Howe of Fife from the Lomonds, which lie farther south, and are shared with Kinross. Away to the south-west, Benarty Hill and the Cleish Hills, with their high point of Dumglow, are also situated on the Kinross border.

The remainder of Fife is mostly fertile and undulating, with flat country along the eastern shores from Tents Moor, beyond Leuchars, to Fife Ness, the most easterly point, facing the North Sea from the promontory known as the East Neuk of Fife. The two most famous railway bridges in Scotland link the county with West Lothian and Angus respectively, the Forth Bridge, spanning the Firth of Forth from Queensferry North, and the less impressive, but longer Tay Bridge crossing the Firth of Tay a little to the south-west of Newport. A road bridge across the Firth of Forth is being built. An important coalfield lies in the south-western sector of the county around Cowdenbeath.

St. Andrews is by far the most renowned Royal Burgh in Fife, and is today best known as the Mecca of golf, its Royal and Ancient Club ranking as the ruling authority on the game. The Cathedral, now reduced to ruin, and neighboured by the tall tower of St. Rule's Church, was once the largest in Scotland, while the University, with its fine chapel of St. Salvator, is the oldest in the country. The picturesque remains of the castle are impregnated with memories of Cardinal Beaton and John Knox. To the north of the town, beyond the Eden estuary, is Leuchars, with its famous Norman church and the fine old mansion of Earlshall, while westwards lies the exceptionally attractive little village of Ceres.

Among the small coastal towns, Crail, Pittenweem and St. Monance are all delightful, with their fishing harbours and numerous old houses, while near Pittenweem is the fine 16th cent. Kellie Castle. Farther west are situated Largo, associated with "Robinson Crusoe," and Dysart, another attractive old burgh, now linked to the larger town of Kirkcaldy. Dunfermline, a Royal Burgh with a long history, retains a striking Norman nave in its restored Abbey Church, in which Robert Bruce lies buried, and the town was the birthplace of the great philanthropist, Andrew Carnegie. Falkland, another pleasant little Royal Burgh, situated below the Lomonds, is celebrated for the delightful 16th cent. Palace, with its memories of Scottish Kings.

Lastly, and the loveliest of its kind in Scotland, is Culross, now largely cared for by the Scottish National Trust, and situated on the Forth estuary west of Dunfermline, being easily reached from the south by means of the fine bridge over the estuary at Kincardine-on-Forth. At Culross, the numerous old houses of the tiny Royal Burgh, with their crow-stepped gables and red pantiled roofs, the picturesque Tolbooth, and the beautiful little Palace, with its painted rooms and quaint walled gardens, are overlooked by the Abbey Church on the hillside above. They combine to produce a picture that is without a peer, and are deserving of even greater fame than they have already achieved.

Places of Scenic Interest. Auchtermuchty, Ceres, Crail, Culross, Dairsie, Falkland, Kilconquhar, Pitscottie, Pittenweem, St. Monance, Tayport.

Places of Architectural or Historic Interest.
Balmerino Abbey, Crail, Culross, Dunfermline, Dysart, Earlshall (Leuchars), Falkland Palace,

Inchcolm Island, Kellie Castle (Pittenweem), Kincardine-on-Forth, Leslie, Leuchars, Lindores Abbey, Melville House (Monimail), St. Andrews, St. Monance, Scotstarvit (Cupar).

INVERNESS-SHIRE
(County Town: Inverness)

The largest county in Scotland, extending from the Atlantic to the North Sea, and scenically perhaps the finest, including within its boundaries examples of almost every type of Highland scenery. Its deeply indented western shores are notable for the magnificent sea lochs of Hourn and Nevis, the first-named of which exhibits scenery comparable with the fjords of Norway. These lochs are, however, difficult of access by road, though the inner and outer reaches of Loch Hourn can be visited by means of rough and narrow roads from Tomdoun and Glenelg respectively. The road leading to Glenelg from the shores of Loch Duich, in Ross and Cromarty, climbs over the lofty Mam Rattachan pass, one of the finest viewpoints in the Highlands. Several other sea lochs farther to the south are only little less remarkable for their wild beauty, and have, in addition, romantic associations with Prince Charles Edward and the '45. These Jacobite memories extend to the whole of the Moidart district, bordered by the highly picturesque, but roadless Loch Shiel, on the Argyll border, at the head of which stands Glenfinnan, with the well-known monument to the Prince in its superb mountain setting.

To Inverness-shire belongs also a large part of the Inner and Outer Hebrides, including the beautiful Island of Skye, in which the spectacular, jagged rock peaks of the Coolins overlook the wild and desolate Loch Coruisk. In the extreme north of the island, near Staffin, is situated the strange, rocky amphitheatre known as the Quiraing. Both Rum and Eigg, whose outlines figure so prominently in views from the mainland, in addition to the whole chain of the Outer Hebrides, with the exception of Lewis, but including the lonely and distant islands of St. Kilda, are all also Inverness territory.

On the mainland, the Great Glen of Alban, or Glen More, with its chain of lochs, linked by the Caledonian Canal, is overlooked in the Lochaber district by Ben Nevis (4,406 ft.), the highest mountain in the British Isles. This glen virtually divides Scotland into two portions, and is one of its most remarkable physical features. The largest of the lochs in the Great Glen is Loch Ness, which has achieved fame as the domicile of the fabulous "Loch Ness Monster," first seen in 1932. Northwest of the Great Glen lies a wild and lonely area of mountain and loch, including the remote Knoydart and "Rough Bounds" district beyond picturesque Loch Quoich, where a hydro-electric scheme now operates. This district is as yet comparatively poorly developed for touring, but exhibits a rugged landscape which ranks among the loveliest in the country. Much of the varied beauty of this part of Scotland can be appreciated from two roads; first, the far-famed Road to the Isles, " By Ailort and by Morar to the sea," linking Fort William with Morar, famous for its white sands and deep inland loch, and terminating at Mallaig, on Outer Loch Nevis; and secondly the roads through Glen Garry and Glen Moriston, which meet near Loch Cluanie, in Ross and Cromarty, to form an alternative Road to the Isles and lead by way of Glen Shiel to Kyle of Lochalsh, the well-known " Gateway to Skye." The views from the improved Mallaig road, in particular, will come as a revelation to those without previous experience of West Highland scenery, and the exceptionally lovely colourings are at times more akin to Mediterranean surroundings, while the picturesque, island-studded Loch Eilt, near Lochailort, is one of the gems of the Scottish mainland.

Some of the roads in the wilder parts of the county, and also in the Island of Skye and the Outer Hebrides are narrow and at times poorly surfaced, but frequent passing-places have been constructed on a number of stretches.

In the north of the county, the delightful valley of Strath Glass gives access from Cannich to the superbly-wooded mountain scenery of Glen Affric and Glen Cannich, with their lochs, which are, however, not through routes to the west. Their erstwhile peace has been somewhat shattered by the introduction of a large hydro-electric scheme, though the re-aligned and well-surfaced roads which have now been provided along these two glens are of considerable benefit to motorists.

To the east of Loch Ness and the Great Glen rise the Monadhliath mountains, and below them lies Badenoch, and also Speyside, or Strath Spey, richly wooded in parts, and overlooked by the great range of the Cairngorms, now including an extensive National Nature Reserve. Their remote, flat-topped 4,000-ft. high summits, partly shared by the counties of Aberdeen and Banff, at whose meeting-point is situated Ben Macdhui (4,275 ft.), the loftiest Cairngorm peak, are surpassed in altitude only by Ben Nevis.

On Speyside are situated a number of pleasant summer and winter resorts, among the best known of which are Aviemore and Kingussie, the former being convenient for the Glenmore National Forest Park, with Loch Morlich, and also for Rothiemurchus Forest, at the entrance to the famous Lairig Ghru pass in the Cairngorms. Inverness and Fort William, the most important touring centres in the county, guard the eastern and western extremities of the Great Glen respectively, and are linked by a splendid modern highway, which traverses the entire length of the glen. Easy of access from Fort William, and reached by way of Spean Bridge and Roy Bridge, are the remarkable " Parallel Roads " of Glen Roy. The town of

Inverness preserves memories of Prince Charles Edward, while the battlefield of Culloden, where the tragic finale of the '45 was played out, lies a little to the east.

Places of Scenic Interest. Arnisdale, Aviemore, Ben Nevis, Cannich, Fort William, Foyers, Glenelg, Glenfinnan, Kingussie, Kinloch Hourn, Kinlochmoidart, Lairig Ghru, Lochailort, Loch Arkaig, Loch Hourn, Loch Lochy, Loch nan Uamh, Loch Ness, Loch Nevis, Loch Quoich, Loch Shiel, Mallaig, Morar, Rothiemurchus, Roy Bridge, Spean Bridge, Struy Bridge, Tomdoun.

Places of Architectural or Historic Interest. Beaufort Castle (Kilmorack), Beauly, Castle Stewart (Inverness), Culloden, Dalcross Castle (Croy), Fort Augustus, Glenelg, Invergarry, Inverlochy Castle (Fort William), Inverness, Kilravock Castle (Croy), Urquhart Castle (Drumnadrochit).

A description of the Inner Hebridean island of Skye will be found by referring to its gazetteer article, while separate entries are made for all individual places of interest, most of which are also cross-indexed in the parent article. For the Outer Hebrides, see under Hebrides, Outer.

KINCARDINESHIRE
(County Town: Stonehaven)

Known also by the alternative name of The Mearns, this county has a long North Sea coastline, with rock scenery at various points, notably in the stretch between Bervie, or Inverbervie and Johnshaven, and also in the neighbourhood of Muchalls. Inland, between the River North Esk and the Bervie Water, is a fertile, level tract of country called the "Howe of the Mearns," an extension of the Howe of Angus and Strathmore valley lying away to the south-west.

Beyond the flat country, the level of the land rises gradually to the foothills of the eastern Grampians, much of them given over to grouse and deer, with Mount Battock rising to more than 2,500 ft. near the meeting point of Kincardine, Angus and Aberdeen. The only road to traverse this mountain district is the famous Cairn o' Mounth pass, attaining nearly 1,500 ft., and linking the attractive village of Fettercairn, known for its Macbeth associations, with Banchory, situated on wooded Deeside. This small Kincardineshire stretch of the Dee valley, overlooked to the north by the Hill of Fare, on the Aberdeen border, includes the picturesque 16th cent. Crathes Castle, a valuable acquisition of the Scottish National Trust and perhaps the finest building in the county.

Another hill road, known in part as the Slug Road, goes south-eastwards from Banchory to link Deeside with the coast. The river divides the county from Aberdeenshire from a point east of Banchory to Girdle Ness, on the coast, overlooking Aberdeen Bay. Away to the south of the Ness, beyond Muchalls, is the fishing port and resort of Stonehaven, near which, in a picturesque setting of cliffs, are considerable remains of the historic Dunnottar Castle.

Places of Scenic Interest. Banchory, Cairn o' Mounth, Cove, Fettercairn, Inverbervie, Johnshaven, Muchalls, St. Cyrus.

Places of Architectural or Historic Interest. Allardyce Castle (Inverbervie), Arbuthnott, Crathes Castle, Dunnottar Castle, Fiddes Castle (Drumlithie), Kincardine Castle (Fettercairn), Muchalls.

KINROSS-SHIRE
(County Town: Kinross)

One of the smallest in area among the Scottish counties, at one time forming part of Fife, from which it was separated in 1426.

Kinross is bordered to the north by the Ochil Hills, and to the east by the lesser range of the Lomonds, the county boundary in each case traversing some of the highest of the ridges. Between the hills lies Loch Leven, well known to fishermen, and perhaps the most notable physical feature of the county, being also historically famous for the celebrated escape of Mary, Queen of Scots from its romantically-situated island castle. Part of Benarty Hill, and much of the Cleish Hills, are included within the southern half of Kinross. In the extreme south-west, the picturesque gorges and waterfalls of the winding River Devon provide the country's finest scenery, notably in the vicinity of Rumbling Bridge and Crook of Devon, where the river forms the boundary with Perthshire.

The manufacture of woollens and linens is of some importance, and one of the chief centres of the industry is the small town of Milnathort, situated to the north-west of Loch Leven. Kinross House, in its splended setting, is one of the finest houses of its period in Scotland, and the mansion of Blairadam is associated with William Adam, the architect, one of whose sons was the even more famous architect, Robert Adam.

Places of Scenic Interest. Crook of Devon, Kinnesswood, Loch Leven, Rumbling Bridge.

Places of Architectural or Historic Interest. Blairadam, Burleigh Castle (Milnathort), Kinross, Loch Leven Castle, Portmoak, Tullibole Castle (Crook of Devon).

KIRKCUDBRIGHTSHIRE
(County Town: Kirkcudbright)

Sometimes also referred to as the Stewartry, recalling its former jurisdiction by a Royal Steward, this county, together with its western neighbour, Wigtown, constitutes the Galloway district, and includes within its borders the wild and beautiful scenery of the "Galloway Highlands." This mountain landscape, which has been graphically described in the novels of S. R. Crockett, is concentrated in the north-western corner, on the

Ayrshire border, where the lonely Merrick rises above the surrounding heights to take its place as the highest mainland hill south of the Highlands proper. Below the Merrick, to the west and south, lie, among others, the remote lochs of Enoch and Neldricken, and beyond the former rise Corserine and Carlins Cairn, the monarchs of the Rhinns of Kells range. These are only a little inferior in height to the Merrick itself, and look northwards across the valley of the Gala Lane to the shores of Loch Doon, which forms the boundary with Ayrshire.

To the south-west of the hills lies Glen Trool, the loveliest in Galloway, with the Bruce Memorial overlooking Loch Trool in a delightful and picturesque setting. The extensive Glen Trool National Forest Park includes much of this fine country, while two of its outlying sub-divisions, Cairn Edward Forest, west of New Galloway, and Kirroughtree Forest, north-east of the little Wigtownshire town of Newton Stewart, and overlooked by the lofty Cairnsmore of Fleet, also lie within the county boundaries.

The remaining parts of Kirkcudbright are largely undulating, and given over to cattle and sheep rearing, the dark Galloway cattle and the local breed of horses both being well known. The county extends eastwards as far as the Nith estuary, over which towers the bulky hill of Criffell, while Maxwelltown, which is divided from the town of Dumfries by the river, was united to the latter in 1929. Much of the long coastline overlooks the Solway Firth and the distant Cumbrian mountains, and, while mainly flat in the east, becomes increasingly bolder and more scenic to the west, with a number of " Smugglers' " caves, and also associations with Scott's " Guy Mannering." There are several large inlets, notably Rough Firth and Auchencairn Bay south of Dalbeattie; Kirkcudbright Bay, below the county town; and Fleet Bay, to the south-west of Gatehouse of Fleet. The coast road from the last-mentioned town along the shores of Wigtown Bay to Creetown, on the Cree estuary, is one of the loveliest in Scotland, passing several ruined castles, and also Dirk Hatteraick's Cave, west of Ravenshall Point.

The extensive Galloway Power Scheme utilises much of the local water power, notably in the Ken basin around New Galloway in the Glenkens district, and a number of reservoirs and power stations have been brought into operation, of which the Clatteringshaws reservoir and dam are outstanding.

The chief architectural interest lies in the Abbeys of Dundrennan, Lincluden, and New, or Sweetheart Abbey. Among the ruined castles, Cardoness and Rusco near Gatehouse of Fleet, Threave, to the west of Castle Douglas, and Maclellan's Castle at Kirkcudbright are all of note.

Places of Scenic Interest. Auchencairn, Bargrennan, Carsphairn, Clatteringshaws, Creetown, Douglas Hall, Gatehouse of Fleet, Irongray, Kippford, Loch Trool, Southerness.

Places of Architectural or Historic Interest.
Anwoth Church, Cardoness Castle (Gatehouse of Fleet), Dundrennan Abbey, Hills Castle (Lochfoot), Lincluden Abbey, Maclellan's Castle (Kirkcudbright), New (or Sweetheart) Abbey, Orchardton Tower (Palnackie), Rusco Castle (Gatehouse of Fleet), Shawhead, Threave Castle (Castle Douglas).

LANARKSHIRE
(County Town: Hamilton)

The county of Lanark is sub-divided into three districts, known as the Upper, Middle and Lower Wards. The first-named is pastoral, and includes the range of the Lowther Hills; the second is largely composed of the orchard country of Lower Clydesdale, between Lanark and Hamilton, to the north-west of which stands the imposing ruin of Bothwell Castle; and the last-named contains the industrial area in the neighbourhood of Glasgow, where, in the city, stands one of Scotland's finest Cathedrals. The Upper Ward is the home of the well-known Clydesdale draught-horse, and the mining of lead and other minerals has long been associated with the district around Leadhills.

Due to the inclusion within its boundaries of the great city and seaport of Glasgow, and also the extensive coal and iron basin to the south-east, Lanarkshire has the largest population of all the Scottish counties. Although often thought of primarily as given over to industry, there is nevertheless much attractive scenery, commencing with the long valley of the River Clyde. Above its junction with the Avon near Motherwell, the Clyde traverses a landscape becoming increasingly pastoral, notably around Crossford, in a rich setting of orchards, near which stands Craignethan Castle, supposed to be the Tillietudlem of Scott's " Old Mortality." In the vicinity of the town of Lanark are the picturesque Falls of the Clyde, of which Cora Linn is perhaps the finest.

Away to the south-east, near Symington, is the isolated Tinto Hill, a prominent landmark and viewpoint, from which the even higher Culter Fell, on the Peebles border, can be seen. In the extreme south of the county, overlooking the heart of Upper Clydesdale, are the green hills of Lowther, rising to more than 2,000 ft. in places, and famous as the haunt of persecuted Covenanters in the latter half of the 17th century. Facing the hills is the bleak and loftily situated village of Leadhills, exceeded in altitude only by its Dumfriesshire neighbour Wanlockhead. From Elvanfoot, two roads link Clydesdale with the Nith valley across the Dumfries border, the former going through Leadhills and the Mennock Pass, and the latter keeping farther south and traversing the Dalveen Pass.

Places of Scenic Interest. Crawford, Douglas, Elvanfoot, Kirkfieldbank, Leadhills.

Places of Architectural or Historic Interest.
Barncluith (Hamilton), Biggar, Bothwell, Cadzow Castle (Hamilton), Craignethan Castle (Crossford), Crookston Castle (Paisley), Dalzell House (Motherwell), Douglas, Glasgow, Hallbar Tower (Crossford), Pollok House (Pollokshaws).

MIDLOTHIAN
(County Town: Edinburgh)

The fame of the city of Edinburgh has very largely overshadowed the county in which it is situated. Nevertheless, Midlothian, or Edinburghshire, contains architectural features of considerable interest, some of the best farming land in the whole of Scotland, and scenery of a pleasantly diversified nature, from the Pentland Hills in the west to the Moorfoots in the east.

The Pentlands, which are some 16 miles in length, and attain nearly 2,000 ft. at Scald Law near Penicuik, were much beloved of Robert Louis Stevenson, and form an admirable outlet for the energies of Edinburgh's citizens. A number of reservoirs are situated on their slopes, and the range is crossed by numerous footpaths, and also various old drove roads, of which the Cauld Stane Slap, between the East and West Cairn Hills, is one of the best known. The Moorfoots are lonelier hills, exceeding the 2,000-ft. level at Blackhope Scar, while a narrow, but picturesque road threads their southern slopes, commencing at Heriot, and reaching a height of more than 1,000 ft. before descending into Tweeddale.

Soutra Hill, a well-known viewpoint on the main Edinburgh to Jedburgh road, and situated at the junction of Midlothian, East Lothian and Berwickshire, links the Moorfoot outliers with the Lammermuir Hills farther to the east. Away to the south lies the delightful winding valley of the Gala Water, in which lies the pleasant village of Stow in its setting of hills.

Among the notable buildings of Midlothian are the churches of Crichton, Duddingston, Temple, and above all Roslin; the castles of Borthwick, Craigmillar, Crichton and Roslin; and the fine old houses of Dalkeith, Pinkie, Hawthornden, to the south-west of Lasswade, and Auchendinny near Penicuik. Edinburgh, with its wealth of historic and architectural interest in the city, and also a number of interesting old mansions in the outer suburbs of Colinton, Corstorphine, Duddingston and Liberton, is, of course, a chapter in itself, and is very fully described in the gazetteer section of the book.

Places of Scenic Interest. Cramond Bridge, Duddingston, Glencorse, Lasswade, Roslin, Soutra Hill, Stow, Swanston, Temple.

Places of Architectural or Historic Interest.
Arniston (Gorebridge), Auchendinny (Penicuik), Borthwick, Cakemuir Castle (Blackshiels),

Carrington, Colinton, Corstorphine, Craigmillar Castle, Crichton, Dalhousie (Cockpen), Dalkeith, Drum (Gilmerton), Duddingston, Edinburgh, Glencorse, Hawthornden (Lasswade), Holyroodhouse (Edinburgh), Lauriston Castle (Barnton), Liberton, Mid Calder, Newbattle, Pinkie House, Prestonfield (Duddingston), Roslin, Temple.

MORAY
(County Town: Elgin)

This maritime county, once part of a province extending over a much larger area, has low, sandy shores facing the Moray Firth. Farther inland lies the broad and fertile Laigh of Moray, in the centre of which stands Elgin, famous for the ruins of its once-magnificent Cathedral, desecrated in 1390 by the notorious Wolf of Badenoch.

The fast-flowing River Findhorn traverses part of north-west Moray, exhibiting picturesque, wooded scenery at Randolph's Leap by its junction with the Divie, near Logie, to the north-east of Ferness, which lies just inside the county of Nairn. Later, the Findhorn flows between Darnaway Forest and Altyre Woods in the vicinity of Forres, before entering Findhorn Bay, an inlet of the Moray Firth. This is bordered to the west by the famous Culbin Sands, now largely afforested, but which, in the great sandstorm of 1694, completely engulfed a formerly fertile and prosperous district.

The southern half of the county is hilly, an altitude of more than 2,300 ft. being reached in the Cromdale Hills, on the Inverness and Banff border. To the north-west of the hills flows the turbulent River Spey, the second longest in Scotland, and famous for its salmon, forming the county boundary with Banff for some miles, and reaching the end of its long journey from Badenoch at Spey Bay beyond Fochabers. There are beautiful stretches near the point where it is joined by the Avon below the Hill of Delnapot, near Dalnashaugh Inn, in Banffshire, and again in the neighbourhood of Craigellachie, also just over the Banff border. Here, the Fiddich enters the main stream, before the latter turns northwards towards Rothes, beyond which lies the pleasant Glen of Rothes.

Two well-known resorts in the county are Lossiemouth, on the coast, and the delightful Highland resort and touring centre of Grantownon-Spey, with the massed summits of the Cairngorms rising away to the south. Among the old buildings of Moray, Elgin Cathedral, Pluscarden Priory and Spynie Palace, together with the sinister island castle of Lochindorb, and Coxton Tower near Lhanbryde, are perhaps of the greatest interest. Darnaway Castle, in its forest setting near Forres, although considerably later in date, preserves portions of an earlier structure.

Places of Scenic Interest. Culbin Sands, Findhorn, Forres, Grantown-on-Spey, Lochindorb, Logie, Mosstodloch, Rothes.

Places of Architectural or Historic Interest.
Birnie, Castle Grant (Grantown-on-Spey), Coxton Tower (Lhanbryde), Darnaway Castle (Forres), Duffus, Elgin, Forres, Innes House (Elgin), Lochindorb, Pluscarden Priory, Spynie Palace.

NAIRNSHIRE
(County Town: Nairn)

One of the smaller Scottish counties, with an expanse of flat coastline on the shores of the Moray Firth, which is overlooked by the well-known resort and golfing centre of Nairn, noted for its dry and sunny climate. A little to the east is the pleasant village of Auldearn, where Montrose, in 1645, won a battle against the Covenanters. To the south-west of the town, beyond the River Nairn, stands the fine old castle of Cawdor, one of the most interesting and picturesque in the whole country, and associated with Shakespeare's "Macbeth." In the vicinity is Kilravock Castle, which has links with Prince Charles Edward, and to the south of Nairn stands the ruined Rait Castle.

The southern half of Nairn is hilly and sparsely populated, an altitude of more than 2,000 ft. being reached on the Inverness border in Strath Dearn. Here, the lonely Streens district is traversed by the River Findhorn, a rapid-flowing stream, on the banks of which the finest scenery in the county is to be found. At Dulsie Bridge, the river flows through a narrow, rocky gorge, overlooked by woodlands, and the view from the single-span 18th century bridge is exceptionally picturesque. Beyond the bridge, to the north-east, in the grounds of Glenferness House, is the romantic Princess Stone, and from this point the Findhorn flows in a series of curves to reach Ferness. Still farther north-east is Daltulich Bridge, where the river again threads its way through delightful wooded scenery to enter Morayshire, near the beauty spot of Randolph's Leap, where the Divie joins the main stream.

Places of Scenic Interest. Auldearn, Dulsie Bridge, Ferness.

Places of Architectural or Historic Interest.
Ardclach Church, Brodie, Cawdor Castle, Inshoch Tower (Auldearn), Kilravock Castle (Croy), Rait Castle (Nairn).

ORKNEY
(County Town: Kirkwall)

The islands forming this group are fully described, both generally and individually, including all places of interest, under their own heading in the gazetteer.

PEEBLESSHIRE
(County Town: Peebles)

This pleasant Border county exhibits the characteristic valleys and rounded green hills of the Lowlands, and much of its scenery and past history has been used for local colour in the works of Sir Walter Scott and John Buchan. Peeblesshire is devoted mainly to agriculture and sheep farming, but the wool industry is of importance in several of the towns in the Tweed valley, notably Peebles and Innerleithen.

The River Tweed, famous for its salmon, flows through the centre of the county, which is known sometimes by the alternative name of Tweeddale. Some of the loveliest scenery associated with the river will be found around Peebles itself, and in particular farther to the west, where the hills become higher and lonelier. Here, the infant river has its source at Tweed's Well, near the watershed on the borders of Dumfries and Lanark in the shadow of Hart Fell, one of the loftiest of the Lowland hills. To the north of Hart Fell is situated the large Talla reservoir, overlooked by the flat-topped Broad Law, and reached from Tweedsmuir, which lies on the fine road linking Peebles with Moffat. Among the numerous tributaries of the Tweed, one of the best known is the Leithen Water. This joins the parent stream at Innerleithen, after flowing through picturesque Glentress, surrounded by hills, of which Windlestraw Law, rising near the meeting-point of Peebles, Midlothian and Selkirk, is the highest.

In the vicinity of the Royal Burgh and inland resort of Peebles are several delightful valleys, notably that of the Manor Water, which extends southwards into the hills from Manor Church. There is also the much less known and roadless Glensax, which lies to the south-east of the town. The Pentland Hills lie in the extreme north of the county, the boundary line with Midlothian traversing the lofty East and West Cairn Hills, between which goes the old drove road known as the Cauld Stane Slap, commencing beyond the village of West Linton. Outliers of the slightly higher Moorfoot Hills extend into the north-eastern corner of Peebleshire beyond the valleys of the Eddleston and Leithen Waters, and on the slopes of the hills lies the little Portmore Loch, near Eddleston.

There are interesting small churches at Stobo and Lyne, the former of which is backed by the celebrated Dawyck Woods. Facing the Tweed, outside Peebles, stands the very picturesque, ruined tower of Neidpath, once battered by Cromwell's guns, and associated later with the Dukes of Queensberry. The finest old house in the county is the mansion of Traquair, with its romantic associations and delightful setting in the valley of the Quair Water. Beyond Traquair village rises the hill road known as the "Paddy Slacks," forming the boundary with Selkirk, and crossing into Ettrick Forest and the Vale of Yarrow.

Places of Scenic Interest. Carlops, Crook Inn, Manor, Peebles, Skirling, Stobo, Traquair, Tweedsmuir, West Linton.

Places of Architectural or Historic Interest.
Barns Tower (Lyne), Drochil Castle (Romanno Bridge), Lyne, Neidpath Castle (Peebles), Stobo, Traquair House, Whim (Leadburn).

PERTHSHIRE
(County Town: Perth)

Situated almost in the centre of the country, with the grassy, or heather-clad Grampian mountains and their subsidiary spurs occupying the greater part of the northern half, Perthshire is one of the loveliest of Scottish counties, and exhibits Highland scenery in its most characteristic settings while its historical associations are no less outstanding.

In the south-eastern corner rise the Ochil and Sidlaw Hills, the latter separated from the Firth of Tay by the low-lying and fertile Carse of Gowrie. Away to the west, beyond the windings of the Forth, on the Stirling border, lies the romantic and beautifully wooded Trossachs district, overlooked by Ben Venue, with Lochs Katrine and Vennachar, made famous by the genius of Sir Walter Scott, and visited annually by thousands of tourists. Some of Perthshire's best known mountains lie to the north of this area, notably Ben Ledi near Callander; Ben More and its neighbour Stobinian dominating Crianlarich; Ben Vorlich, forming the background to Loch Earn; and Ben Lui, on the Argyll border, south-west of Tyndrum.

The fracture known as the Highland Line, or "fault," which divides the Highlands from the Lowlands, as shown by the changes in the rock structure of the hills, passes across Perthshire in a line going from Aberfoyle to the River Tay south-east of Dunkeld, and in the vicinity of Comrie slight earth tremors are felt from time to time.

Loch Tay and Loch Rannoch are the largest of the lochs, both being traversed by roads on either bank, this applying also to the smaller, but very delightful Loch Earn. Above the northern shores of Loch Tay towers Ben Lawers (3,984 ft.), a botanist's paradise, and the highest mountain in the county. Beyond the Ben, and parallel to the loch, stretches Glen Lyon, one of the longest in Scotland, being particularly lovely immediately to the west of Fortingall. The lonely head of the glen is closed in by the lofty Drum Alban ridge of the Grampians, and hydro-electric developments are taking place in the vicinity. Much of General Wade's great military road from Dunkeld to Inverness, now part of the splendid modern highway, passes through the county, crossing the Grampians by means of the bleak Drumochter Pass. On his link road, commencing at Crieff, and joining the main highway at Dalnacardoch, lies Aberfeldy, where what is perhaps Wade's finest bridge still spans the Tay. To the north of Aberfeldy is the delightful Tummel valley, with the famous Queen's View, looking towards the prominent cone of Schiehallion and the Rannoch country. Extensive hydro-electric developments which have taken place between Loch Tummel and Pitlochry are creating new interests for the tourist.

The picturesque, wooded gorge of Killiecrankie, near the meeting-place of Tummel and Garry, was the scene, in 1689, of a memorable battle; at Sheriffmuir, near Dunblane, in 1715, the Old Pretender's forces fought an indecisive action; and the legendary battle of Mons Graupius, c. A.D. 84, was responsible for the erroneous naming of the Grampian mountains. South of the fertile vale of Strathmore, and situated on the Tay, which has the largest volume of water in Scotland, stands the "Fair City" of Perth, boasting a long and interesting history. It is today an important touring centre, being within easy reach of the very lovely Sma' Glen, leading to Glen Almond; the gorges and waterfalls of the Devon near Rumbling Bridge, on the Kinross border; and the pleasant valley of Strath Earn, linking Crieff with St. Fillan's.

Aberfoyle, on the threshold of the Queen Elizabeth National Forest Park; Callander, in a district beloved by Scott; the famous golfing centre at Gleneagles Hotel; and both Killin and Pitlochry, are all well-known Perthshire resorts. Far to the north-east of the last-named, beyond Glen Shee, is the Cairnwell Pass, in the Grampians, near the Aberdeen border, where the summit, at 2,199 ft., is the highest main road altitude reached in Great Britain. Among the notable buildings of the county are the Cathedrals of Dunblane and Dunkeld, the round tower of the church at Abernethy, the interesting group of domestic buildings at Stobhall, and the fine castles of Blair, at Blair Atholl, Castle Huntly near Longforgan, Doune and Huntingtower.

Places of Scenic Interest. Bridge of Balgie, Callander, Crianlarich, Fortingall, Glenshee, Killiecrankie, Killin, Kinloch Rannoch, Lochearnhead, Loch Tay, Meikleour, Moulin, Pitcairngreen, Pitlochry, Queen's View, Rumbling Bridge, St. Fillan's, Sma' Glen, Struan, Trossachs, Tummel Bridge, Tyndrum.

Places of Architectural or Historic Interest. Aberfoyle, Abernethy, Ardoch (Braco), Blair Castle (Blair Atholl), Bridge of Earn, Castle Huntly (Longforgan), Doune, Drummond Castle (Crieff), Dunblane, Dunkeld, Elcho Castle (Perth), Finlarig Castle (Killin), Fowlis Wester, Grandtully, Huntingtower, Inchmahome Priory (Port of Menteith), Innerpeffray (Crieff), Killiecrankie, Kinnaird, Meggernie Castle (Bridge of Balgie), Menzies Castle (Weem), Perth, Scone, Sheriffmuir (Dunblane), Stobhall, Tullibardine.

RENFREWSHIRE
(County Town: Renfrew)

A small county, bounded to the north by the widening estuary of the Clyde, which is backed by the distant hills of Cowal. In population Renfrewshire ranks high, including within its boundaries the important industrial towns of Paisley, Greenock and Renfrew, in addition to a part of Glasgow itself. Paisley is the world's largest thread-producing centre, and both Renfrew and Greenock are noted for shipbuilding. The roadstead in the Clyde off the shores of the latter is famous as the "Tail of the Bank."

To the north-west of Paisley, the well-known Erskine Ferry across the Clyde gives access to the Highlands, and is much used by travellers from the south wishing to by-pass Glasgow. On the fringe of the industrial area are considerable stretches of moorland, notably to the south, where the high-lying Eaglesham Moor lies beyond the 18th cent. village of that name. Again near the Ayrshire border, west of Lochwinnoch, there are lonely moors attaining a height of over 1,700 ft.

Along the shores of the Clyde coast are situated the well-known resorts of Wemyss Bay and Gourock, linked by a road which passes the white Cloch lighthouse, and giving fine views over the estuary towards Dunoon. To the south-east of Greenock lies the fertile valley of Strath Gryfe, with its reservoirs, and in the centre of which is situated the pleasant inland resort of Kilmacolm.

The fine, restored Abbey Church at Paisley is the most important building in the county. The ruined castle of Newark, outside Port Glasgow, on the Clyde, and the old mansion of Dargavel, near Bishopton, are also of some interest.

Places of Scenic Interest. Eaglesham, Gourock, Inverkip, Kilmalcolm.

Places of Architectural or Historic Interest.
Cathcart Castle (Clarkston), Dargavel (Bishopton), Eaglesham, Houston, Kilbarchan, Newark Castle (Port Glasgow), Paisley, Renfrew.

ROSS AND CROMARTY
(County Town: Dingwall)

A large and mountainous northern county, only a small proportion of which is arable, stretching across Scotland from coast to coast and exhibiting some notable physical contrasts, from the North-West Highland grandeur of Wester Ross to the comparatively level country of Easter Ross.

The finest scenery is concentrated in the hill country, mainly deer forest, adjacent to its western shores. Here, the beautiful seaboard is deeply indented by picturesque lochs along the entire distance from the Coigach district near Ullapool, on Loch Broom, in the north, to Loch Alsh and lovely Loch Duich, with its perfect background of shapely hills, in the south. The grand defile of Glen Shiel, which gives access to the last-named loch, is thought by many competent judges to be even more impressive than the better-known Glencoe. It owes much of its fame to the finely-grouped, quintet of peaks known as the Five Sisters of Kintail, which face the knife-edge ridges of the Saddle across the glen, to form the centrepiece of the superb view from the lofty Mam Rattachan Pass leading over to Glenelg, in Inverness-shire. The

Five Sisters are part of the magnificent National Trust estate of Kintail, contiguous to which is another estate, also Trust property, with the spectacular but remote Falls of Glomach, some of the highest in Britain, and accessible, partly on foot, from Ardelve on Loch Alsh. A picturesque road from Kyle of Lochalsh, the terminal point of one of the Roads to the Isles, and the "Gateway to Skye," traverses the shores of Loch Alsh and beautiful Loch Duich, on which stands the romantic Eilean Donan Castle near Dornie bridge. The road then climbs through Glen Shiel to Cluanie, with its loch, and crosses some low hills to reach Loch Garry, now harnessed to a hydro-electric scheme, to the east of Tomdoun, before descending to Invergarry, in Inverness-shire. The scenery along the whole of this route is among the grandest in Britain.

Gairloch, on its beautiful sandy bay, is one of the most delightful of small Wester Ross resorts, and away to the south, beyond Outer Loch Torridon, is the almost isolated Applecross peninsula, which can only be approached by sea, or by the notorious Bealach nam Bo, or Pass of the Cattle. This climbs very steeply over wild hills, reaching a height of 2,054 ft., with a series of acute hairpin bends, affording magnificent views from the summit, and provides the nearest approach in these islands to the conditions of an Alpine pass. Among the mountains dominating Inner Loch Torridon, the most noteworthy lie in the Kinlochewe district, where the striking peaks of red Torridon sandstone, topped in places by gleaming white quartzite, and dominated by the great mass of Liathach, are of particular interest to geologists.

To the north-east of the trough of Glen Torridon are the picturesque, wooded shores of Loch Maree, where Britain's first National Nature Reserve is situated on the slopes of Ben Eighe in Kinlochewe deer forest. Beyond the eastern shores of the loch, which is dominated by the fine peak of Slioch, lies a wilderness of trackless, rocky hills culminating in An Teallach, near Dundonnell, often described as the wildest peak on the mainland. Westwards are the inlets of Little Loch Broom and Gruinard Bay, the latter one of the loveliest in the Highlands, in a setting of low, rocky hills, well seen from the steep Gruinard Hill.

To the north of Ullapool, in the extreme north-western corner of Ross and Cromarty, is the fascinating, but little visited Loch Lurgain. Its shores are traversed by a narrow, winding road, overlooked by the fantastic, rock-crowned hill known as Stack Polly, with the isolated peaks of Cul Mor and Cul Beag rising in the background. The coast beyond Loch Lurgain, on the northern fringe of the wild Coigach district, is traversed by an exceptionally lovely, but winding and hilly road overlooking Enard Bay which leads towards the Sutherland border at Inverkirkaig.

Many of the roads in the hilly western half of the

county are narrow and at times poorly-surfaced, but frequent passing-places have been constructed on certain stretches.

In the eastern half of the county, the bulky mass of Ben Wyvis towers over a comparatively low-lying district and faces the well-known inland resort of Strathpeffer. The land of Easter Ross is composed mainly of the former county of Cromarty, which was annexed to Ross in 1889. The inlets of the Dornoch and Moray Firths, with their low, sandy shores, form the boundaries of this area, which is almost cut in half by the narrow Cromarty Firth lying to the north of the fertile Black Isle. In addition to its territory on the mainland, the Outer Hebridean island of Lewis, with the exception of the Harris peninsula, and famous for the Standing Stones of Callanish, belongs to Ross and Cromarty, as do also several of the outlying islands, among them the Flannan group.

Places of Scenic Interest. Achiltibuie, Applecross, Ardelve, Baddagyle, Braemore Lodge, Cluanie, Dornie, Dundonnell, Falls of Glomach, Gairloch, Glen Shiel, Gruinard Bay, Kinlochewe, Loch Broom, Loch Duich, Loch Lurgain, Loch Maree, Mam Rattachan, Plockton, Shiel Bridge, Strathpeffer, Tornapress, Torridon, Ullapool.

Places of Architectural or Historic Interest.
Balnagown Castle (Logie Easter), Castle Leod (Strathpeffer), Dingwall, Edderton, Eilean Donan Castle (Dornie), Fortrose, Foulis Castle (Evanton), Kilcoy Castle (Muir of Ord), Tain.

Places of interest in the Outer Hebridean island of Lewis will be found by referring to its gazetteer entry under Hebrides, Outer.

ROXBURGHSHIRE
(County Town: Jedburgh)

In this Lowland county will be found the quintessence of Border scenery in its most characteristic vein, a land of rounded green hills, rushing streams and delightful valleys, of which Liddesdale and Teviotdale, both traversed by picturesque roads, are the best known. Part of the Border National Forest Park, which extends also into England, lies in Liddesdale.

Many places in Roxburghshire are impregnated with memories of Border legends and warfare, and the presence of Abbotsford House makes the county of the very greatest interest to lovers of Sir Walter Scott. Other places having links with the great writer are Branxholm Tower near Hawick, Darnick Tower near Melrose, and the lonely Smailholm Tower, in its wild setting, neighboured by Sandyknowe farm, where part of Scott's youth was spent. Abbotsford, beautifully situated on the Tweed, and accessible to the public, was the writer's last and favourite home, remaining today almost untouched since the Waverley novels were written.

The three great ruined Abbeys of Melrose,

Kelso and Jedburgh are among the finest in Scotland, the very notable architectural features and beautiful setting of the first-named, situated between the Tweed and the triple-peaked Eildon Hills, being quite outstanding. Of Kelso Abbey, perhaps once the greatest of the trio, the existing remains are less extensive, but the town, with its wide square, and Rennie's five-arched bridge spanning the Tweed looking towards the splendid pile of Floors Castle, is most attractive. The red sandstone Abbey at Jedburgh is still most impressive in its roofless state, while in the town stands the fine old Queen Mary's House, associated with that ill-fated monarch.

Liddesdale stretches northwards from the English border, where the Cheviot foothills near Newcastleton are being thickly afforested by the State, and in a branch valley which forks northwestwards is situated the ruined, but immensely strong Hermitage Castle, where Mary, Queen of Scots nearly died from fever in 1566. The longer valley of Teviotdale is threaded by the Teviot Water, which flows across the northern half of the county from the lonely hills on the Dumfries border, and unites finally with the Tweed outside Kelso. In the heart of the dale lies the important woollen manufacturing town of Hawick, and to the north-west, near Denholm, is the lofty height of "dark" Ruberslaw, an ancient haunt of the persecuted Covenanters.

To the south of Jedburgh stands the picturesque old Ferniehirst Castle, now a Youth Hostel, beyond which a fine road follows the Jed Water towards England. This ascends gradually on to the Cheviot ridge, the 1,371-ft. high summit being reached at the splendid viewpoint of Carter Bar, from which the panorama across the Lowlands extends from the Cheviot itself to the Eildons far away to the north-west. Another road descends back into Scotland from this ridge towards Bonchester Bridge, on the Rule Water, where it is joined by the road from Liddesdale, which has climbed previously to well over 1,000 ft. at Note o' the Gate. Eastwards of Carter Bar, the line of the Roman "Dere Street" of Agricola crosses the Cheviots near the remarkable Chew Green earthworks, just inside the Northumbrian border. It then descends towards Oxnam, beyond which stands the ruined Cessford Castle, preserving walls 14 ft. in thickness. In the vicinity is Morebattle, at the foot of the lonely Kale Water valley, once a Covenanters' refuge, and away to the north-east, at the foot of the Cheviots, are the adjacent villages of Kirk and Town Yetholm. These lie on either side of the Bowmont Water, and were formerly the headquarters of the Scottish gipsies.

Places of Scenic Interest. Ancrum Bridge, Bonchester Bridge, Carter Bar, Denholm, Melrose, Morebattle, Newcastleton, Oxnam, Riccarton, Teviothead, Yetholm.

Places of Architectural or Historic Interest.
Abbotsford House, Bowden, Branxholm Tower (Hawick), Cessford Castle (Morebattle), Darnick Tower, Fatlips Castle (Denholm), Ferniehirst Castle, Floors Castle, Hermitage Castle, Jedburgh Abbey, Kelso Abbey, Melrose Abbey, Newstead, Sandyknowe, Smailholm, Southdean.

SELKIRKSHIRE
(County Town: Selkirk)

At one time known as Ettrick Forest, which consisted largely of a vast Royal hunting ground, Selkirkshire is a Border county of much scenic beauty, showing characteristic Lowland hills, particularly in the west, near the boundaries of Peebles and Dumfries. Here, Broad Law and the lonely Ettrick Pen are two of the most prominent heights, and Lochcraig Head rises at the meeting-point of all the three counties. To the east of the higher hills, in what is still described as Ettrick Forest, lie St. Mary's Loch and its neighbour the tiny Loch of the Lowes, beyond which stretches the celebrated Yarrow Vale, threaded by the Yarrow Water, and in parts richly wooded. The praises of this delectable region have been sung by many well-known writers, among them being Sir Walter Scott and William Wordsworth. St. Mary's Loch is the most picturesque sheet of water in the Borders, and its romantic associations with James Hogg, the "Ettrick Shepherd," give it an added interest. The well-known "Tibbie Shiel's" Inn, at its southern extremity, has been visited by many famous personages. The Megget Water flows into the loch from the west, and near the northern shore, beyond the churchyard of St. Mary's Kirk, stands the ruined Dryhope Tower, which has associations with Scott's ancestors.

To the south of Yarrow Vale is the valley of the Ettrick Water, where, at Tushielaw, in 1528, James V hanged a notorious Border raider in his own stronghold. Two picturesque roads diverge from here into the hills, the easterly branch leading towards Hawick, and the more southerly climbing to nearly 1,100 ft., on its way into Upper Eskdale.

Galashiels and Selkirk are both noted for their tweed mills, and the first-named is situated on the pleasant Gala Water, which joins the Tweed beyond the town. On the south bank of the Tweed, near Clovenfords, stands the mansion of Ashiestiel, where Scott lived for 8 years as sheriff of the county, and where several of the best known of his earlier works were written. To the north-west of Galashiels, a small portion of Selkirkshire projects into a district of lonely hills in which the Caddon Water rises, and near the meeting-point with Peebles and Midlothian is the high point of Windlestraw Law.

Selkirk itself, a Royal Burgh, noted for a picturesque annual Border Riding ceremony, stands in a delightful setting, and to the west of the town the Yarrow and the Ettrick Water unite, the combined streams flowing north-eastwards to join the Tweed within a short distance. The little church at Ettrick was the burial-place of both Hogg and Tibbie Shiel. Among the numerous ruined castles, or towers in the county, those of Newark near Broadmeadows, Oakwood near Ettrick Bridge End, and Elibank, facing the Tweed east of Walkerburn, are perhaps of most interest.

Places of Scenic Interest. Broadmeadows, Ettrick Bridge End, Fairnilee, Gordon Arms, St. Mary's Loch, Selkirk, Tushielaw, Yarrow.

Places of Architectural or Historic Interest. Ashiestiel, Bowhill (Selkirk), Elibank Tower (Walkerburn), Ettrick, Newark Castle (Broadmeadows), Oakwood Tower (Ettrick Bridge End), "Tibbie Shiel's" Inn.

SHETLAND
(County Town: Lerwick)

The islands forming this group are fully described, both generally and individually, including all places of interest, under their own heading in the gazetteer.

STIRLINGSHIRE
(County Town: Stirling)

Occupying a strategic position across the narrow waist of Scotland, at the meeting of the Lowlands and the Highlands, Stirlingshire has played a leading part in the history of the country. No place was of greater importance in the Middle Ages than the old bridge over the River Forth at Stirling, which is still in use for foot passengers, and stands near a newer bridge. Farther down the estuary, beyond Airth, the more recent Kincardine Bridge spans the widening course of the river, giving access to the Fife coast.

The county can be divided into three sectors. The first lies to the east, and includes the industrial area around Falkirk, with its coal and iron industry, and also the oil refineries and docks of Grangemouth on the Forth estuary. The second sector takes in the winding and fertile valley of the Forth to the east and west of Stirling, mainly on the Perthshire border. Lastly, and occupying the central area of the county, are the hills, comprising the Fintry, Gargunnock and Kilsyth ranges and also the Campsie Fells, in what is known as the land of Lennox. The heart of the hills is threaded by a road leading westwards from Denny, which follows the course of the River Carron and the Endrick Water towards the village of Fintry before debouching into the flat country to the east of Loch Lomond. Another road leads southwards over the Campsies to reach the well-known Campsie Glen.

A narrow tongue of Stirlingshire extends north-westwards along the picturesque shores of Loch

Lomond towards its head, with Loch Arklet and Loch Katrine farther to the east, and Glen Gyle, preserving memories of Rob Roy, forming the boundary with Perthshire beyond Stronachlachar. Above Rowardennan, on Loch Lomond, where the road along the eastern shore terminates, rises Ben Lomond, a noted viewpoint and the monarch of the surrounding district.

Stretching from east to west across the county, and often in close proximity, are the Forth and Clyde canal and the line of the Antonine, or Roman Wall, the remains of which, though slight compared with the more famous Hadrian's Wall in Northumberland, are nevertheless of interest. Some of the best preserved portions are situated in the vicinity of Falkirk, notably in the grounds of Callendar House.

The historic town of Stirling, known as the "Gateway to the Highlands," is the most important in the county, and is renowned for its great Castle and Palace, which has been associated with several Scottish Kings, and also with Mary, Queen of Scots. The fine old houses of Argyll's Lodging and Mar's Wark give an added interest to the town, while the Church of the Holy Rude is one of the finest in Scotland. In the immediate neighbourhood of Stirling are the loftily situated Wallace Monument at Causewayhead; the remains of Cambuskenneth Abbey, situated in the fertile Links of the Forth; and the famous battlefield of Bannockburn, which lies beyond the village of St. Ninian's.

Places of Scenic Interest. Bridge of Allan, Campsie Glen, Fintry, Inversnaid, Killearn, Kippen, Loch Lomond, Rowardennan, St. Ninian's, Stockiemuir, Strathblane.

Places of Architectural or Historic Interest. Airth, Bannockburn, Callendar House (Falkirk), Cambuskenneth Abbey (Stirling), Culcreuch Tower (Fintry), Kilsyth, Kippen, Stirling, Wallace Monument (Stirling).

SUTHERLAND
(County Town: Dornoch)

This maritime and sparsely populated county has a rugged Atlantic seaboard occupying the far north-west corner of Scotland. Its less spectacular eastern shores are washed by the waters of the North Sea. The western coast, stretching from lonely Cape Wrath to the borders of Ross and Cromarty at Enard Bay, is wild and beautiful, and indented by the sea lochs of Inchard, Laxford, and Cairnbawn, the last-named being an inlet of the lovely island-studded Eddrachillis Bay. This lies to the south of Scourie, a small fishing resort, well known for the nearby island of Handa, now a sanctuary for sea-fowl.

The scenery in the south-western part of the county is bare and mountainous, and of exceptional geological interest in the Assynt district. Here, the strangely-shaped peaks of Suilven, Canisp and Quinag, in particular the first-named, described sometimes as the "Matterhorn" of Scotland, are built up of red Torridon sandstone and rise individually in isolated majesty from a bed of Archæan pinky-grey gneiss, some of the oldest rocks in the world. The highest mountain in the county, Ben More Assynt (3,273 ft.), near Inchnadamph, is composed almost entirely of this gneiss, while other peaks farther to the north in the remote Reay Forest, notably Foinaven and Arcuil, which dominate the neighbourhood of Rhiconich, are composed mainly of quartzite. Almost the whole of this wild Northern Highland district is given over to deer forest. From the small Assynt resorts of Lochinver and Inchnadamph, and, in particular from the steep and narrow coastal road linking the first-named with the ferry at Kylesku, in its exceptionally wild and beautiful setting at the meeting-point of three lochs, a good idea can be obtained of the memorable, though rather austere scenery of this fascinating landscape. Due to the innumerable small lochans, this is a fisherman's paradise, and, when viewed from the summit of any of the mountain tops in the district, the impression is given that there is almost more water than land. The roads in this part of the county are narrow and at times rough, but frequent passing places have been constructed on a number of stretches.

On the bleak northern coast is Loch Eriboll, a good anchorage, and a long and beautiful inlet, with roads on both the eastern and western shores. Westwards, beyond the celebrated Smoo Cave, is Durness, overlooking the Kyle of Durness and the lonely moors leading to Cape Wrath and its lighthouse. The mountains in this area include Ben Hope, the most northerly 3,000-ft. peak in Scotland. Farther to the east rises the many-peaked Ben Loyal, well seen from the Kyle of Tongue and forming a notable landmark. Much of this part of the country suffered severely as a result of the penal enactments of 1747, and also from the "Sutherland Clearances" in the early 19th century, when some 15,000 of the inhabitants were forced to move elsewhere. In more recent years efforts have, however, been made to improve conditions for the crofting population.

Near the Caithness border, on the east coast, the landscape resembles a lofty plateau, which has been carved out by its rivers, the shores being rocky, with some cliff scenery. Farther south, near the Dornoch Firth, the seaboard is for the most part low and sandy, and to the north-east of Golspie, overlooking the sea, stands the great pile of Dunrobin Castle in its park.

Places of Scenic Interest. Altnaharra, Cape Wrath, Drumbeg, Durness, Eriboll, Inchnadamph, Inverkirkaig, Kinlochbervie, Kylesku, Laxford Bridge, Loch Assynt, Lochinver, Rhiconich, Rispond, Scourie, Smoo Cave, Stoer, Tongue.

Places of Architectural or Historic Interest.
Altnaharra, Ardvreck Castle (Inchnadamph), Dornoch, Dunrobin Castle, Golspie, Helmsdale, Skibo Castle.

WEST LOTHIAN
(County Town: Linlithgow)

This small county has for its northern boundary the flat shores of the Forth estuary, and is composed mainly of good farming land, though visible signs of the oil-shale industry in the vicinity of Winchburgh somewhat mar the landscape. West Lothian is less remarkable for its scenic beauty than for its architectural interest, which is dominated by the famous Palace and Church at Linlithgow, the name of which was formerly applied to the county as a whole.

The short coastline, from the mouth of the River Avon in the west to that of the Almond in the east, is mainly flat, with a harbour at Bo'ness. This town marks the terminal point of the Antonine, or Roman Wall, which extends across the waist of Scotland to the Clyde estuary. From Queensferry South, the spectacular Forth Bridge, an outstanding achievement of the late 19th cent., spans the widening estuary and carries the main railway line to the Fife coast and the north. This is being supplemented in due course by a new road bridge, thus obviating the need for the car ferry.

Linlithgow Palace, though largely in ruins, is of considerable interest, and here was born the ill-fated Mary, Queen of Scots, who played such a vital part in Scottish history, and is associated also with another West Lothian stronghold, that of Niddry near Kirkliston. The splendid church at Linlithgow is one of the finest in the country, and exhibits unusual French characteristics. To the south are the low Bathgate Hills, and on their western fringe lies Torphichen, where the church is also of much interest. Dalmeny church is perhaps the finest of Scottish Norman churches, and the little church at Abercorn is remarkable for its furnishings. Among the old mansions of West Lothian, that of Hopetoun House, the work of Sir William Bruce and William and Robert Adam, is outstanding. The Binns, now National Trust property, situated near Abercorn, and also Houston near Uphall, are other fine old buildings.

Places of Scenic Interest. Cramond Bridge, Linlithgow, Torphichen.

Places of Architectural or Historic Interest.
Abercorn, Binns (Abercorn), Blackness, Bridge Castle (Torphichen), Dalmeny, Hopetoun House, Houston (Uphall), Kinneil (Bo'ness), Kirkliston, Linlithgow, Niddry Castle (Kirkliston), Queensferry South, Torphichen.

WIGTOWNSHIRE
(County Town: Wigtown)

The extreme south-western county of Scotland, forming, together with its eastern neighbour Kirkcudbright, the attractive district known as Galloway. Wigtown is divided into three distinct regions: the double peninsula of the Rhinns of Galloway, washed by the waters of Loch Ryan and Luce Bay; the Machers peninsula, separating Luce Bay from Wigtown Bay; and the inland country around New Luce, known as The Moors.

The whole county, with the exception of some low hills and moorlands on the Ayrshire border, is flat, or undulating, and devoted mainly to agriculture and grazing. There is a long coastline, often characterised by rock scenery, with "Smugglers" caves in places, while three prominent headlands stand out, those of Corsewall Point on Loch Ryan; the Mull of Galloway, Scotland's most southerly point; and Burrow Head, at the bleak extremity of the Machers district. A coastal road makes the almost complete circuit of Luce Bay, from the Mull of Galloway in the west to Whithorn in the east, providing some notable seascapes. Stranraer, at the head of Loch Ryan, is of importance as a port for Northern Ireland, and has superseded Portpatrick, where the harbour was too exposed to gales.

Newton Stewart, on the River Cree, one of the most delightful of small Scottish towns, stands on the threshold of much lovely country, including part of the National Forest Park of Glen Trool, and the river forms the boundary with Kirkcudbright for some miles to the north. Monreith House in the Machers peninsula, and Logan House near Port Logan, in the southern horn of the Rhinns of Galloway, are both famous for their very beautiful woodland gardens, and at Port Logan is a remarkable tidal fish-pond, where the fish are tame and fed by hand. The ruins of the ancient Castle Kennedy are neighboured by the modern Lochinch Castle, also well known for its splendid grounds, the two buildings being situated on a narrow neck of land separating the Black and White Lochs. Other interesting old buildings in the county are Craigcaffie Tower at Innermessan, the Old Place of Mochrum near Kirkcowan, and Carscreuch Castle, in the vicinity of Glenluce.

Both Whithorn and the nearby Isle of Whithorn, on the coast, claim to be the site of the early Chapel of St. Ninian, who first introduced Christianity into Scotland, and his shrine at the former place became later an important place of pilgrimage, being visited regularly by James IV.

Places of Scenic Interest. Bargrennan, Cairn Ryan, Glenluce, Lochnaw Castle, Mull of Galloway, Newton Stewart, Port Logan, Portpatrick, Port William.

Places of Architectural or Historic Interest.
Castle Kennedy, Castle of Park (Glenluce), Craigcaffie Castle (Innermessan), Cruggleton, Isle of Whithorn, Lochinch Castle (Castle Kennedy), Lochnaw Castle, Logan House (Port Logan), Luce Abbey (Glenluce), Monreith, Old Place of Mochrum (Kirkcowan), Whithorn.

LITERARY ASSOCIATIONS OF PLACES NAMED IN GAZETTEER

Many places in Scotland have interesting associations with famous or lesser-known men and women of letters In the case of certain authors, entire districts have come to be associated with their works, such as the Scott Country, covering much of the Border Country in the Lowlands, and the Burns Country, which covers a different part of the Lowlands, centred on Ayrshire. Certain parts of Argyllshire have many links with the works of Robert Louis Stevenson.

Of the individual towns and villages, some are of interest for one or more literary works, others as the birthplace or place of rest of a particular writer. The following list, though not exhaustive, does give a comprehensive picture of the literary haunts of Scotland and all the places mentioned will be found in the gazetteer section of the book.

Sir James Barrie	Outer Hebrides (Harris), Kirriemuir.
James Boswell	Auchinleck, Broadford, Glenelg, Mam Rattachan Pass, Skye.
George Douglas Brown	Ochiltree.
Dr. John Brown	Biggar.
Michael Bruce	Kinnesswood, Portmoak.
John Buchan	Broughton, Creetown, Galloway, Loch Coruisk, Peebles, Tweedsmuir.
Robert Burns	Alloway, Auldgirth, Ayr, Dumfries, Gatehouse of Fleet, Kilmarnock. Kirkoswald, Lincluden Abbey, Mauchline, Moffat, Tarbolton.
Lord Byron	Banff, Bridge of Ess, Cambus o'May.
Thomas Campbell	Calgary, Salen (Isle of Mull), Ulva.
Thomas Carlyle	Annan, Ecclefechan, Kirkcaldy.
S. R. Crockett	Auchencairn, Galloway, Laurieston, Lendalfoot, Loch Trool, Peebles.
R. B. Cunninghame-Graham	Cardross, Dumbarton.
Daniel Defoe	Largo.
Sir Arthur Conan Doyle	Edinburgh.
William Drummond	Hawthornden, Lasswade.
John Galt	Irvine.
James Hogg	Ettrick, St. Mary's Loch, Selkirk, "Tibbie Shiel's" Inn, Yarrow.
Dr. Johnson	Banff, Broadford, Dundonald, Glenelg, Glen Shiel, Renton, Skye.
Ben Jonson	Lasswade.
Margaret Kennedy-Fraser	Iona.
John Knox	Edinburgh, Perth, St. Andrews.
Andrew Lang	Selkirk.
J. G. Lockhart	Darnick, Dryburgh.
H. F. Lyte	Ednam.
Alexander Macdonald	Arisaig, Dalilea.
Duncan Ban MacIntyre	Dalmally.
Dr. Kenneth MacLeod	Gigha.
James Macpherson	Kingussie, Moffat.
Thomas Macaulay	Killiecrankie.
Sir Thomas Maxwell	Monreith.
Hugh Miller	Cromarty.
Neil Munro	Corrieyairack Pass, Inveraray, Kingshouse.
Alexander Peden	Denholm, Sorn.
Thomas de Quincey	Lasswade.
Allan Ramsay	Carlops, Leadhills, Penicuik.
Dante Gabriel Rossetti	Dailly.
John Ruskin	Perth
Sir Walter Scott	Abbotsford, Aberfoyle, Ashiestiel, Blairgowrie, Caddonfoot, Callander, Clovenfords, Crossford, Darnick, Dryburgh, Dunfermline, Edinburgh, Gordon Arms, Innerleithen, Irongray, Lasswade, Loch Leven, Melrose, Orkney, Peebles, St. Mary's Loch, Selkirk, Smailholm, Trossachs.
William Shakespeare	Birnam, Cawdor, Inverness.
Adam Smith	Kirkcaldy.
Alexander Smith	Isle Ornsay.
Tobias Smollett	Alexandria, Renton.
Robert Southey	Banff.
Robert Louis Stevenson	Appin, Ballachulish, Ballantrae, Borgue, Bridge of Allan, Bunessan, Dalwhinnie, Dirleton, Edinburgh, Fairmilehead, Glencoe, Glencorse, Kingshouse, Lanark, Moulin, Peebles, Swanston, Torryburn.
Robert Tannahill	Paisley.
James Thompson	Ednam.
Dorothy Wordsworth	Inversnaid.
William Wordsworth	Broadmeadows, Lanark, St. Mary's Loch, Sma' Glen, Yarrow.

TOURING
IN
SCOTLAND

Scale
0   10   20   30   40 M.

LEWIS

Durness
Tongue
Thurso
John O'
Groats
WICK

Scourie
FERRY No.59
225
225
230
229
224
230
200
Helmsdale

West

Ullapool
Laing
Bonar
Bridge
200

Gairloch
222

ELGIN
199
Fraserburgh
BANFF
182
Buchan
Peterhead

DINGWALL
Black Isle
199 NAIRN
INVERNESS
195
Huntly
195

SKYE
RAASAY
FERRY No.57
Strome
FERRY No.56
222
210
210
Glen Affric
Caledonian Canal
140,150
Grantown-
on-Spey

ABERDEEN
175
182
155

Kyle of
Lochalsh
Kintail
220
Aviemore
140,150
Cairngorms
Deeside
168
STONEHAVEN

CANNA
RUM
Knoydart
FERRY No.54
Braemar
BALMORAL
CASTLE
155
Montrose

MUCK
EIGG
209
Moidart
Fort
William
Ardgour
Ardnamurchan
210
125
Lochaber
Badenoch
Devil's Elbow
168
Strathmore
155

COLL
Morven
GlenCoe
140,150
Pitlochry
Aberfeldy
139

TIREE
MULL
125
Oban
139
Dunkeld
150
DUNDEE
155
Arbroath
FERRY No.60
154
St.Andrews
Crail

INVERARAY
88
Trossachs
Lomond
Callander
PERTH
140
135
131
94
94
Elie

118
118
139
STIRLING
133
Dunfermline
94
Kirkcaldy

Lochgilphead
Greenock
88
FERRY No.44
101 99
96
FERRY No.61
2
North Berwick
Dunbar

Cowal
BUTE
Largs
59
88
GLASGOW
15 *Lothians*
EDINBURGH
2
BERWICK-
UPON-TWEED

ISLAY
JURA
ARRAN
Troon
88
14
11
13
MELROSE
Border Country
30
KELSO

Kintyre
Knapdale
AYR
Burns Country
27
PEEBLES
*Scott
Country*
14
DRYBURGH ABBEY
46 43
JEDBURGH

Girvan
80
Carrick
SELKIRK
13
11 Hawick
Moffat

80
Galloway
DUMFRIES
The Stewartry
27
13
Cheviots

Stranraer
Newton
Stewart
33
73
CARLISLE
11

KIRKCUDBRIGHT

1148/ RB.60
DRAWN AND PUBLISHED BY THE AUTOMOBILE ASSOCIATION

The numbers are those of the itineraries.

TOURING IN SCOTLAND

Scotland makes a double appeal to the motorist. There is the wild mountain and loch scenery of the Highlands, and the less spectacular, but none the less beautiful Lowland country, with its strong romantic and literary flavour, which forms for many people an equal or an even greater attraction. Apart from the industrial area, concentrated in the narrow waist of Scotland between the Clyde and the Forth, the land is but sparsely populated, and nowhere in Great Britain can a feeling of solitude be so easily obtained as by wandering off the beaten track in the remote Highlands.

The map opposite shows the itinerary numbers for a suggested tour through the more popular touring districts. A few of the many possible alternatives are also indicated, including an extended tour to the North-West Highlands. The main tour totals approximately one thousand miles, and tourists with time at their disposal will find it convenient to choose suitable centres from which to explore the surrounding countryside. With the aid of the Itinerary Key Map and the Road Atlas, tours covering most of the less-frequented districts can be planned. These should appeal to those already familiar with the better known touring areas. Any comprehensive tour of Scotland should include a visit to some of the many islands situated off the West Coast. Details of tours in these islands are given in the itinerary section of the book, commencing with number 241. More detailed descriptions will be found under individual headings in the Gazetteer. A map showing the line of the various steamship communications will be found on pages 34 and 35 of the Atlas, though in some cases the cost does not justify transportation of the car.

Whilst much fine scenery can be enjoyed without leaving main roads, the motorist will miss a great deal if he is not prepared to venture occasionally on to the lesser-used roads, and he should not be deterred by fear of rough or dangerous stretches.

Main roads to the south and east of the line Fort William–Inverness are generally good, and severe gradients are few. Owing to the indented nature of the coastline there are a number of ferry crossings, full details of which are given later in the book. Delays may sometimes be experienced due to tide and weather conditions and also to the traffic demands during the touring season. Certain ferries, particularly those for Skye and at Strome, do not operate on Sunday. Although most of the crossings can be avoided, the detours may be lengthy.

In the wilder parts of the north and west the roads generally are of a lower standard, some being very narrow, and occasionally rough. See article on " Driving on Highland Roads " on following page. Since hotel accommodation in the north-west is limited, it is important to make due allowance when estimating the daily average mileage. When on tour and advance bookings have not been made, hotels at intended stopping places should be telephoned as early as possible, but during the touring season, it is always advisable to arrange hotel accommodation in advance. It should also be remembered that in the north-west long distances can be covered without encountering garages or filling stations.

The early visitor to Scotland has the advantage of the long hours of daylight. The grandeur of the Highlands is probably seen at its best in September, when the heather-clad hills enhance the scene. July and August are preferable for seeing traditional events such as the Highland Gatherings, Festivals and other summer events. Access to some of the hills is restricted during the August shooting season.

SCOTTISH ROADS—ROAD NUMBERS AND CLASSIFICATIONS

The official Ministry of Transport Road Numbers are shown throughout the itineraries and on the Maps in the Atlas.

Although originally introduced for administrative reasons, road numbers, as well as place names, now appear on all Ministry of Transport signs for classified roads. Besides helping the traveller to find his way, there is the assurance that a numbered road will eventually lead somewhere and will, except perhaps in the more remote Highlands, have at least a reasonable surface.

In 1919 the Ministry was given power to classify roads by the Ministry of Transport Act, Section 17 (2), and subsequently roads have been numbered " A " or " B." The plan for numbering is a simple one though some anomalies have arisen during the years.

Scotland is split up into three main zones centred on Edinburgh, with key highways forming the boundaries of, and giving their numbers to, zones 7, 8 and 9. Zones 1–6 are centred on London and are the basis of the numbering system of England and Wales.

The three key highways of Scotland are: —

The Edinburgh-Carlisle Road	A7
The Edinburgh-Glasgow Road	A8
The Edinburgh-Inverness-John O'Groats Road	A9

The area of each zone is that from the road concerned to the next road numbered in sequence in a clockwise direction; e.g. zone 7 is from the Edinburgh-Carlisle road A7, to the Edinburgh-Glasgow road A8, and zone 8 is from the Edinburgh-Glasgow road A8 to the Edinburgh-Inverness-John O'Groats road A9. Zone 9 lies east of A9 in roughly the area covered by the triangle Edinburgh, Nairn, Peterhead. The area Edinburgh, Berwick-upon-Tweed, Carlisle, includes the Scottish portion of zone 6 with small portions of zone 1 east of the Great North Road A1 between Edinburgh and Berwick-upon-Tweed.

The numbers of the roads originating in any zone begin with the zone number, no matter how many figures the individual road number may have. For example A70 Edinburgh-Ayr, and A76 Dumfries-Kilmarnock are in zone 7, and all the class B roads originating in this zone begin with 7 both for 3 and 4 figure numbers, similarly for zones 8 and 9. Occasionally a road number is carried beyond the zone boundary by an important highway, an example being A73 which crosses A8 from zone 7 into zone 8 at Newhouse and continues through Airdrie to Cumbernauld on the Glasgow-Stirling road A80.

Road numbers have a further important use, for with the aid of a map showing them, the motorist can locate his position exactly at any signpost showing two or more. For example B8074 joins A85 between Dalmally and Tyndrum at the south end of Glen Orchy, and farther north A832 joins A835 between Ullapool and Garve at the Braemore A.A. Box. A black and white chequer along the top of an advance direction sign indicates the way to a road of major importance. As an example the sketches show the position at Barnton Hotel on A90—4½m. west of Edinburgh. Here the chequer indicates the road leading to both A8 and A9. The number of this road is A902 but it does not appear on the sign.

DRIVING ON HIGHLAND ROADS

In general, Scottish roads are of quite a high standard, but in the extreme north-west the fact that a road is labelled and numbered as class A or class B does not necessarily mean that its surface, width, or condition is going to be anything like similarly classified roads farther south. This is also true of many of the roads in other wild and mountainous parts of the country.

In the Highlands many garages are closed on Sundays and petrol pumps are relatively scarce, so it is a good plan to keep the tank full.

In the north-west corner substantial improvements have been made in recent years in connection with road surfaces, but there are still rough stretches especially on the western seaboard and on unclassified roads. There is, however, nothing that cannot be dealt with by reduced speeds and judicious use of the gearbox. Estimates of journey times should be adjusted to allow for those slower speeds, and also for possible delays at ferries. Most roads are narrow—little more than single width, but passing bays are provided and if care is taken no difficulty should be experienced. In view of the narrow roads motorists with trailer caravans may find it more convenient to select a centre and tour the surrounding area by car only.

There are a few simple rules to remember when using these narrow Highland roads.

1. Please be courteous and considerate in the use of passing bays on single-track roads. The bays are usually well marked by white, diamond-shaped signs, thus: ◇ If due care is exercised, it should not be necessary for vehicles to be reversed. It should be remembered that it is more difficult for buses, transport vehicles, or cars towing caravans to reverse on a single-lane road, than it is for a car to do so.

2. Always adjust the speed of the vehicle to the prevailing conditions, and keep in mind the lack of visibility on bends.

3. A driver nearest a passing bay should give way to an approaching vehicle.

4. If a passing bay is on the driver's right, or off-side, it is not necessary to draw across the road and enter it. Stop opposite the bay and allow any approaching vehicle the maximum carriageway to deviate into the bay in passing.

5. Passing bays are provided for vehicles to pass in safety, and except in an emergency, should not be used as lay-bys for parking purposes.

6. Drivers of vehicles such as caravans, etc., whose speed is restricted, should draw into or stop opposite a passing bay to allow a faster-moving vehicle to overtake.

HISTORIC BUILDINGS, THE NATIONAL FOREST PARKS, NATURE RESERVES AND SCOTLAND'S GARDENS

For so small a country Scotland is unusually rich in "beauty spots" and historic buildings. Scotland's natural scenery is, of course, world famous, and her turbulent and romantic history has also left a large number of relics in the way of buildings and monuments.

HISTORIC BUILDINGS. The monuments of Scotland can be divided into two classes. Firstly there are the prehistoric remains from those dim times before Scotland was a kingdom proper, when wolves were nearly as common as foxes today, when the land was covered by the great "Caledonian Forest" and when that mysterious race, the Picts, occupied most of the land. Secondly there are those Castles, Abbeys, Churches, palaces and historical houses which are a product of the last thousand years of Scotland's life and are a part of her recorded history.

Some 230 of the best of these monuments are under the guardianship of the Ministry of Works. They vary from the prehistoric village of Jarlshof and the celebrated broch at Mousa, both in Shetland, to the exquisite beauty of the partially destroyed Melrose Abbey in the Border Country. Apart from these there are many relics of early Christian times, and secular buildings such as the Palace of Holyroodhouse and Edinburgh Castle—to take two of the most obvious examples.

All guardianship monuments are accessible to the public. Admission is sometimes free, but is usually 6d. or 1s. according to the importance and size of the monument or building. Except in places of military importance, visitors are allowed to take photographs. Nearly all the important places of historical interest are easily accessible by road. An illustrated guide, *Ancient Monuments of Scotland*, is published by H.M. Stationery Office, Castle Street, Edinburgh, at 7s. 6d. Individual guides of many of the monuments are also published.

NATIONAL FOREST PARKS. The large amount of public forestry work which began after World War I, and which has increased since World War II, has resulted in the establishment of National Forest Parks for public recreation. State afforestation has thrown open to all who love the countryside of Scotland and who like to roam and camp in it at leisure, several large tracts of the wilder parts of Scotland: The Argyll National Forest Park embraces 58,000 acres and extends from Arrochar near Loch Long to Loch Goil and the Holy Loch near Dunoon. There are camping and caravan sites near Arrochar.

On the east side of Loch Lomond there is the Queen Elizabeth Forest Park which stretches for about twelve miles to the north and east of Rowardennan, and includes Ben Lomond (3,192 ft.). The approach is from Drymen in Stirlingshire. A camping ground and caravan park are situated close together in Rowardennan Forest.

Glenmore National Forest Park is conveniently reached from Aviemore, Inverness-shire. It extends for 12,500 acres and embraces several of the highest peaks in Britain, including Cairn Gorm (4,084 ft.). In addition to mountain climbing, the area is now an important centre for winter sports, and there is a public camping ground near Glen More Lodge.

In the south-west of Scotland lies the Glen Trool National Forest Park, reached from Bargrennan. Though perhaps less rugged than the others this area contains 116,000 acres of beautiful Galloway hill country and includes a chain of lovely lochs. There is a site for caravans and camping close to Loch Trool. Also in the south is the Border Forest Park which contains the largest planted forest in Great Britain, and again bears witness, as in other cases, to the very important work of the Forestry Commission. The main area lies over the Border in England, but two of the main parks, namely Wauchope and Newcastleton are in Scotland. Road access is not too easy. The approach points from the Scottish side are Hawick for Wauchope, or Langholm and Newcastleton for the Newcastleton Forest. The approach from the south is via Bellingham. A camping and caravan park is provided.

NATURE RESERVES. Scotland led the way with the first nationally owned nature reserve in Great Britain. This is near Kinlochewe in Ross and Cromarty, and is known as the Beinn Eighe National Nature Reserve, which was opened in 1951 and contains some 10,450 acres. Since then the work of the Nature Conservancy has expanded in area and in interest, and there are now 22 reserves in Scotland, the largest being the 40,000 acres in the Cairngorms.

The majority of the Nature Reserves are still privately owned, but have been set up under special agreements with the Nature Conservancy, who will supply details of any of the Reserves on application to The Nature Conservancy, 12 Hope Terrace, Edinburgh 9.

SCOTLAND'S GARDENS SCHEME. Throughout the spring, summer and autumn seasons there are a number of private gardens attached to houses and country mansions which are open to the public by courtesy of the owners. Those interested in

31

flowers and in the beauty of gardens will find much of interest in these "Open Gardens" which are located in every county of Scotland. Admission charges vary, but are generally about 1s. per person, and parking charges for cars 2s. The fees are for the benefit of the Scottish branch of the Queen's Institute of District Nursing, for the bene-fit of the Benevolent Fund, the Education Fund, and other similar schemes, as well as for the benefit of local Nursing Associations. Handbooks giving details are issued free from the secretary of the "Scotland's Gardens Scheme," 26 Castle Terrace, Edinburgh 1, or from the A.A. Offices in Edinburgh, Glasgow or Aberdeen.

THE NATIONAL TRUST FOR SCOTLAND

The National Trust for Scotland is an independent body and is recognised by Act of Parliament as a charity. Relying entirely on donations, legacies and the subscriptions of its members, the Trust exists to preserve for public enjoyment, places and buildings of historical and architectural interest and also areas of natural beauty in the Scottish countryside. More than sixty castles and country houses, cottages and gardens are now included in Trust properties.

The Trust owns and guards large stretches of Scotland's superb mountain scenery which are now made accessible to all. Among these is the wild beauty of Glencoe, the Pass of Killiecrankie, Ben Lawers, renowned for its alpine flowers, Goat Fell, the highest peak on Arran, and, perhaps finest of all, Kintail in Wester Ross.

A number of the great houses and castles of Scotland are now in the Trust's care, such as Crathes Castle on Deeside, the Royal Palace of Falkland in Fife, Culzean Castle in Ayrshire, the Scottish home of President Eisenhower, and most recently, Brodick Castle on the Isle of Arran. These properties, with the gardens which surround many of them, are living symbols of the nation's heritage. Among the other outstanding gardens which the Trust maintains or has re-created are the famous Highland garden of Inverewe in Wester Ross and the 17th-century garden of Pitmedden in Aberdeenshire.

Not only the great houses attract the attention of the Trust, but many of the "little houses," built in the vernacular style of the past have now been restored and preserved. At Culross in Fife and Dunkeld in Perthshire, imaginative group restoration schemes have been undertaken. Often of equal delight to the eye are the cottages and humble houses which were associated with famous Scots. Hugh Miller, J. M. Barrie, Thomas Carlyle and Robert Burns are honoured by the Trust in this way, whilst what is often called Prince Charles's Monument at lonely Glenfinnan is now preserved as a memorial to the Highlanders who followed the Prince in the '45 Rising. It is fitting, therefore, that Culloden, the scene of the last battle on British soil, is also now a property of the nation through the Trust.

At properties where a charge is made, N.T.S. members have free admission, and members of the National Trust too have this privilege. Minimum annual subscription is 10s. for N.T.S. membership. Guide-books and leaflets giving information about its work, its properties and details of membership are readily available from the Trust Offices at 5 Charlotte Square, Edinburgh 2.

LIST OF COUNTIES WITH 1951 CENSUS POPULATION FIGURES

County			Population	County			Population	County			Population
Aberdeen	...	...	308,055	East Lothian	...	...	52,240	Peebles	...	...	15,226
Angus	...	...	274,870	Fife	...	...	306,855	Perth	...	...	128,072
Argyll	...	...	63,270	Inverness	...	...	84,924	Renfrew	...	...	324,652
Ayr	...	...	321,184	Kincardine	...	...	47,341	Ross and Cromarty			60,503
Banff	...	...	50,135	Kinross	...	...	7,418	Roxburgh	...	...	45,562
Berwick	...	...	25,060	Kirkcudbright	...	...	30,742	Selkirk	...	...	21,724
Bute	...	...	19,285	Lanark	...	...	1,614,125	Shetland	...	...	19,343
Caithness	...	...	22,705	Midlothian	...	...	565,746	Stirling	...	...	187,432
Clackmannan	...	...	37,528	Moray	...	...	48,211	Sutherland	...	...	13,664
Dumfries	...	...	85,656	Nairn	...	...	8,719	West Lothian	...	...	88,576
Dunbarton	...	...	164,263	Orkney	...	...	21,258	Wigtown	...	...	31,625

SPORTING FACILITIES IN SCOTLAND

GOLF. In this particular volume mention of golf is of course a "must"; Scotland and the royal and ancient game have always been and remain inseparables and the motorist, visitor or resident, will, except perhaps in the North-West Highlands, almost always find a course within easy distance.

Amid the many changes the years have brought in many things, Scotland's place in golf remains unique as the very fount and home of the game, its traditional and still operative seat of government whose writ runs to the end of the earth and whose repute for courses of characteristic quality is world-wide.

Whatever your starting point, or whichever way you head your car in this country of so many spots obviously intended by Providence for golf, you will find your journey rewarding. You may play in the northern isolation of Sutherland's Brora, or after your rounds at glorious Argyllshire's Machrihanish, be lulled to slumber by the Atlantic, and between these distant points experience the pleasures and variety, seaside and inland alike, of the game at many places.

You can still play, for instance, on links of apparent popularity in 1457, when King James II's Parliament, concerned at the neglect of archery, "decreed and ordained that wapinschawingis [weapon show] be halden be the Lordis and Barinis

spirituale and temporale foure times in the zeir [year], and that the Fute-ball and Golf be utterly cryit doune and nocht usit."

At St. Andrews, for example, the centuries meet, for its classic green is at once an honoured shrine and a supreme test for modern champions; while guests of members may still view in the treasure case of the Royal and Ancient Club priceless relics of the past, including the first Silver Club and the original Championship Belt.

For the rich attractions, however, awaiting the golfing motorist north of the Border, and which are too numerous for mention or description here, the appended list will supply some finger-posts.

You will find them in Fife, where beside storied St. Andrews are other delights; East Lothian, the fabled "Holy Land of Golf" including much-picturised North Berwick; the shores of the Firth of Clyde where, with your score good, bad or indifferent, you will have scenery and sunsets that will linger in your memory for long; and finally the famous Gleneagles Hotel courses carved out of the moorland in and adjacent to Strath Earn.

But see for yourself, and you will agree that Robert Louis Stevenson needs in this case some amendment, for while you will travel hopefully you will not necessarily find that better than to arrive.

The following list of golf-courses has been arranged in County order. The name of the club or course is followed, in brackets, by the number of holes. The letter S denotes Sunday play, but information should be obtained locally as to the hours of play. The list includes courses owned by local authorities and many clubs where visitors are admitted without introduction. A few clubs at which it is necessary for an intending player to be introduced by a member have been omitted from the list, although the Gazetteer entry may include the word GOLF.

ABERDEENSHIRE

Aberdeen
  Balnagask (18. S.)
  Bieldside (18. S.)
  King's Links (18 and 9. S.)
  Hazelhead (18 and 9. S.)
  Murcar G.C. (18 and 9. S.)
Ballater G.C. (18. S.)
Braemar G.C. (18. S.)
Cruden Bay G.C. (18. S.)
Ellon G.C. (9. S.)
Fraserburgh G.C. (18 S.)
Huntly G.C. (9)
Inverurie G.C. (9. S.)
Kemnay G.C. (9. S.)
Kintore G.C. (9. S.)
Lumphanan G.C. (9. S.)
Newburgh G.C. (9)
Peterhead G.C. (18 and 9. S.)
Rosehearty G.C. (9)
Tarland G.C. (9. S.)
Turriff G.C. (9. S.)

ANGUS

Arbroath G.C. (18. S.)
  Elliot Course (18. S.)
Barry
  Panmure C.C. (18. S.)
Brechin G.C. (18. S.)
Carnoustie
  Championship Course (18. S.)
  Burnside Course (18. S.)
Dundee
  Caird Park Public G.C. (18 and 9. S.)
  Downfield G.C. (18. S.)
  Camperdown G.C. (18. S.)
Edzell G.C. (18. S.)
Forfar G.C. (18. S.)
Kirriemuir G.C. (18. S.)
Monifieth G.C. (18. S.) 2 courses

Montrose
  Medal Course (18. S.)
  Auxiliary Course (18. S.)

ARGYLLSHIRE

Blairmore and Strone G.C. (9. S.)
Carradale G.C. (9)
Dunoon. Cowal G.C. (18)
Innellan G.C. (9. S.)
Islay, Isle of, G.C., Port Ellen (18. S.)
Machrihanish G.C. (18. S.)
Mull, Isle of
  Western Isles G.C. Tobermory (9)
Oban
  Glen Cruitten (18. S.)
Southend
  Dunaverty G.C. (18)
Tarbert G.C. (9)

AYRSHIRE

Ayr. Belleisle G.C. (18) 2 courses
    Seafield (18)
Barassie G.C. (18. S.)
Beith G.C. (9. S.)
Dalry G.C. (9)
Gailes
    Western G.C. (18. S.)
Galston
    Loudoun G.C. (18. S.)
Girvan Burgh G.C. (18. S.)
Irvine Municipal Course (18. S.)
    Bogside (18. S.)
Kilbirnie
    Place G.C. (9. S.)
Kilmarnock Caprington Course (18)
    Annanhill (18. S.)
Largs G.C. (18)
    Routenburn G.C. (18. S.)
Mauchline. Ballochmyle G.C. (18. S.)
Maybole G.C. (9)
New Cumnock G.C. (9. S.)
Prestwick
    St. Cuthbert G.C. (18. S.)
    St. Nicholas G.C. (18. S.)
    Prestwick G.C. (18. S.) Introduction
Saltcoats
    Ardrosssan and Saltcoats G.C. (9)
Skelmorlie G.C. (13. S.)
Stevenston
    Ardeer G.C. (18. S.)
Troon Municipal G.C. (18) 2 courses
Turnberry G.C. (18. S.) 2 courses
West Kilbride G.C. (18)

BANFFSHIRE

Banff
    Duff House Royal G.C. (18. S.)
Buckie
    Strathlene G.C. (18. S.)
Cullen Municipal G.C. (18)
Macduff
    Royal Tarlair G.C. (18. S.)

BERWICKSHIRE

Coldstream
    Lennel G.C. (9)
Duns G.C. (9. S.)
Eyemouth G.C. (9)

BUTESHIRE

Arran, Isle of
    Brodick G.C. (18. S.)
    Corrie G.C. (9)
    Kildonan G.C. (9)
    Lamlash G.C. (18. S.)
    Lochranza G.C. (9)
    Machrie Bay G.C. (9)
    Shiskine G.C., Nr. Blackwaterfoot
        (12)
    Whiting Bay G.C. (18. S.)
Bute, Isle of
    Port Bannatyne G.C. (13)
    Rothesay G.C. (18. S.)
Cumbrae, Isle of
    Millport G.C. (18. S.)

CAITHNESS-SHIRE

Lybster G.C. (9)
Thurso G.C. (9)
Wick G.C. (18)

CLACKMANNANSHIRE

Alloa G.C. (18. S.)
    Braehead G.C. (9. S.)
Alva G.C. (9. S.)
Dollar G.C. (18. S.)
Tillicoultry G.C. (9. S.)

DUMFRIESSHIRE

Annan
    Powfoot G.C. (18. S.)
Dumfries
    Dumfries and Galloway G.C. (18. S.)
    Dumfries and County G.C. (18. S.)
Lochmaben G.C. (9)
Lockerbie G.C. (9. S.)
Moffat G.C. (18. S.)
Sanquhar G.C. (9)
Thornhill G.C. (9. S.)

DUNBARTONSHIRE

Alexandria
    Vale of Leven G.C. (18. S.)
Bearsden
    Douglas Park G.C. (18. S.)
Cardross G.C. (18. S.)
Clydebank and District G.C. (18. S.)
    Dalmuir Municipal G.C. (18. S.)
Dullatur G.C. Nr. Cumbernauld
    (18. S.)
Dumbarton G.C. (18. S.)
Helensburgh G.C. (18. S.)
Kirkintilloch G.C. (18. S.)
    Lenzie G.C. (18. S.)
Milngavie G.C. (18. S.)
    Hilton Park (18. S.)
    Allander (18. S.)
    Milngavie (18. S.)
Shandon G.C. (9. S.)

EAST LOTHIAN

Aberlady
    Kilspindie G.C. (18. S.)
    Luffness New G.C. (18. S.)
Dunbar G.C. (18. S.)
    Winterfield G.C. (18. S.)
Gifford G.C. (19. S.)
Gullane Nos. 1, 2 and 3 courses (18. S.) (see also Muirfield.)
Haddington G.C. (18. S.)
Longniddry G.C. (18. S.)
Muirfield. Honourable Company of
    Edinburgh Golfers (18. S.)
North Berwick G.C. (18. S.)
    New Club G.C. (18 and 9)

FIFE

Aberdour G.C. (18. S.)
Anstruther G.C. (9)
Burntisland G.C. (18. S.)
Cardenden-Auchterderran G.C. (9. S.)
Crail. Balcomie (18. S.)
Cupar G.C. (9. S.)
Dunfermline G.C. Nr. Newmills
    (18. S.)
    Canmore G.C. (18. S.)
    Pitreavie G.C. (18. S.)

Elie (18. S.)
Kincardine-on-Forth
    Tulliallan G.C. (18. S.)
Kinghorn Municipal G.C. (18. S.)
Kirkcaldy G.C. (18. S.)
Ladybank G.C. (9. S.)
Leslie G.C. (9. S.)
Leuchars
    St. Michael's G.C. (9. S.)
Leven G.C. (18)
Lundin Links G.C. (18)
St. Andrews G.C. (18. S.) 4 courses
Saline G.C. (9. S.)
Tayport
    Scotscraig G.C. (18. S.)
Wemyss G.C. (9. S.)

INVERNESS-SHIRE

Arisaig
    Traigh G.C. (9)
Boat of Garten G.C. (18. S.)
Fort William (9)
Inverness G.C. (18. S.)
Kingussie G.C. (18. S.)
Nethybridge
    Abernethy G.C. (9. S.)
Newtonmore G.C. (18)
Skye, Isle of
    Portree (9)
South Uist
    Askernish G.C. (Lochboisdale)
        (9. S.)
Spean Bridge (9)

KINCARDINESHIRE

Auchenblae G.C. Nr. Fordoun (9)
Banchory G.C. (18. S.)
Muchalls (9)
Stonehaven G.C. (18. S.)

KINROSS-SHIRE

Kinross G.C. (9. S.)
Milnathort G.C. (9. S.)

KIRKCUDBRIGHTSHIRE

Colvend G.C. (9. S.)
Dalbeattie G.C. (9. S.)
Gatehouse of Fleet G.C. (9. S.)
Kirkcudbright G.C. (9. S.)
New Galloway G.C. (9. S.)
Southerness-on-Solway G.C. (18. S.)

LANARKSHIRE

Airdrie G.C. (18)
    Easter Moffat G.C. (18. S.)
Bellshill G.C. (18. S.)
Biggar G.C. (18)
Bothwell Castle G.C. (18. S.)
Cambuslang G.C. (9)
    Kirkhill G.C. (18. S.)
Carluke G.C. (18. S.)
Carnwath G.C. (18. S.)
Coalburn, Hollandbush G.C. Nr.
    Lesmahagow (9)
Coatbridge. Drumpelier G.C. (18. S.)
Douglas G.C. (9)
East Kilbride G.C. (18. S.)

Glasgow
Public courses 8 (18 and 9. S.)
Glasgow G.C. (18. S.)
Balmore G.C. (18. S.)
Bishopbriggs G.C. (18. S.)
Cawder G.C. (18. S.) 2 courses
Cathcart Castle G.C. (18. S.)
Cathkin Braes G.C. (18. S.)
Cowglen G.C. (18. S.)
Crow Wood G.C. (18)
Deaconsbank G.C. (18. S.)
East Renfrewshire G.C. (18. S.)
Eastwood G.C. (18. S.)
Gartcosh, Mount Ellen (18. S.)
Haggs Castle G.C. (18. S.)
Killermont (18. S.)
Lethamhill (18. S.)
Linn Park (18. S.)
Littlehill (18. S.)
Mount Ellen G.C. (18. S.)
Pollock G.C. (18. S.)
Sandyhills (18. S.)
Williamwood G.C. (18. S.)
Windyhill (18. S.)
Hamilton Municipal G.C. (18. S.)
Lanark G.C. (18 and 9)
Leadhills G.C. (9)
Lenzie G.C. Nr. Kirkintilloch (18. S.)
Motherwell
Colville Park G.C. (18)
Shotts G.C. (18. S.)
Strathaven G.C. (9. S.)
Uddingston
Calderbraes G.C. (9. S.)
Wishaw G.C. (18)

MIDLOTHIAN

Broomieknowe. Bonnyrigg G.C.
Nr. Bonnyrigg (18. S.)
Dalkeith
Newbattle G.C. (18. S.)
Edinburgh
Public courses 6 (18 and 9)
Royal Burgess Golfing Society (18. S.)
Baberton G.C. (18. S.)
Bruntsfield Links Golfing Society (18. S.)
Craigmillar Park G.C. (18. S.)
Dalmahoy G.C. (18. S.) 2 courses
Duddingston G.C. (18. S.)
Ingliston G.C. (18. S.)
Kingsknowe G.C. (18. S.)
Liberton G.C. (18. S.)
Lothianburn G.C. (18. S.)
Merchants of Edinburgh (18. S.)
Mortonhall G.C. (18. S.)
Murrayfield G.C. (18. S.)
Prestonfield G.C. (18. S.)
Ratho Park G.C. (18. S.)
Ravelston G.C. (9. S.)
Swanston G.C. (18. S.)
Torphin Hill G.C. (18. S.)
Turnhouse G.C. (18. S.)
Glencorse G.C. (18. S.)
Harburn G.C. Nr. West Calder (18. S.)
Musselburgh G.C. (18. S.)
Royal Musselburgh G.C. (18. S.)
Pumpherston G.C. Nr. Uphall (9. S.)

MORAYSHIRE

Elgin G.C. (18. S.)
Forres G.C. (18. S.)
Garmouth (9)
Grantown-on-Spey G.C. (18. S.)
Hopeman G.C. (9)
Lossiemouth
Moray G.C. (18 and 9)
Spey Bay G.C. (18. S.)

NAIRNSHIRE

Nairn G.C. (18 and 9. S.)
Dunbar G.C. (18)

ORKNEY

Kirkwall
Orkney G.C. (18. S.)
Stromness G.C. (18)
Westray G.C. (9)

PEEBLESSHIRE

Innerleithen G.C. (9)
Peebles Municipal G.C. (18. S.)
West Linton G.C. (9. S.)

PERTHSHIRE

Aberfeldy G.C. (9)
Aberfoyle G.C. (9. S.)
Alyth G.C. (18. S.)
Auchterarder G.C. (9. S.)
Blairgowrie G.C. (18 and 9. S.)
Callander G.C. (18. S.)
Comrie G.C. (9. S.)
Crieff G.C. (18. S.)
Dunblane New G.C. (18. S.)
Dunkeld and Birnam G.C. (9. S.)
Gleneagles Hotel G.C. (18 and 9. S.)
Kenmore
Taymouth Castle (18. S.)
Killin G.C. (9. S.)
Muckhart G.C. Nr. Yetts of Muckhart (9. S.)
Muthill G.C. (9. S.)
Perth Municipal G.C. (18)
King James VI G.C. (18. S.)
Craigie Hill G.C. (18. S.)
Pitlochry G.C. (18. S.)
St. Fillans G.C. (9. S.)
Strathtay G.C. Nr. Grandtully (9)

RENFREWSHIRE

Barrhead
Fereneze G.C. (18. S.)
Bishopton
Erskine G.C. (18)
Bridge of Weir
Ranfurly Old Course G.C. (18. S.)
Ranfurly Castle G.C. Ltd. (18. S.)
Elderslie G.C. (18. S.)
Giffnock
Eastwood G.C. (18. S.)
Gourock G.C. (18. S.)
Greenock G.C. (18 and 9)
Whinhill G.C. (18. S.)
Johnstone
Cochrane Castle G.C. (18)
Kilmacolm G.C. (18. S.)
Lochwinnoch G.C. (9. S.)
Paisley G.C. (18. S.)
Renfrew G.C. (18. S.)
Whitecraigs G.C. Nr. Busby (18. S.)

ROSS AND CROMARTY

Alness G.C. (9)
Fortrose and Rosemarkie G.C. (18)
Invergordon G.C. (9)
Muir of Ord G.C. (18)
Portmahomack
Tarbat G.C. (9)
Stornoway G.C. (18)
Strathpeffer G.C. (18)
Tain G.C. (18. S.)

ROXBURGHSHIRE

Hawick G.C. (18)
Jedburgh G.C. (9. S.)
Kelso G.C. (9. S.)
Melrose G.C. (9. S.)

SELKIRKSHIRE

Galashiels G.C. (18. S.)
Torwoodlee G.C. (9. S.)
Selkirk G.C. (9. S.)

SHETLAND

Lerwick
Shetland G.C. Nr. Bressay (9)

STIRLINGSHIRE

Bonnybridge G.C. (9. S.)
Bridge of Allan G.C. (9. S.)
Drymen
Buchanan Castle G.C. (18. S.)
Falkirk
Falkirk G.C. (18. S.)
Kilsyth
Burgh of Kilsyth G.C. (9. S.)
Larbert
Falkirk Tryst G.C. (18. S.)
Glenbervie G.C. (18. S.)
Lennoxtown
Campsie G.C. (9. S.)
Polmont G.C. (9. S.)
Stirling G.C. (18)

SUTHERLAND

Brora G.C. (18)
Dornoch
Royal Dornoch G.C. (18 and 9)
Golspie G.C. (18)

WEST LOTHIAN

Bathgate G.C. (18. S.)
Bo'ness
West Lothian G.C. (18. S.)
Fauldhouse G.C. Nr. Whitburn (12)
Linlithgow G.C. (9. S.)
Uphall G.C. (9. S.)

WIGTOWNSHIRE

Glenluce
Wigtownshire County G.C. (9. S.)
Newton Stewart G.C. (9. S.)
Portpatrick
Dunskey G.C. (18 and 9. S.)
Port William
St. Medan G.C. (9. S.)
Stranraer G.C. (18. S.)

ANGLING in Scotland is, in the best sense of that much misused word, a "democratic" sport. That is to say it is enjoyed by all members of society and by those from all income groups. Moreover, the fish that these anglers pursue are for the most part game fish—salmon, sea trout, trout and occasionally char. This may surprise visitors who have looked upon angling for game fish as the recreation of the rich or the comparatively well-off. This is not so in Scotland, where to be seen carrying a trout or salmon rod is the surest way of getting into conversation in a railway carriage, bus, or village street, as well as in more luxurious surroundings.

While it is true that there are in Scotland waters where game fish are highly preserved, and waters which are expensive to fish, it is also true that the majority of trouting water in this country can be fished for the cost of reasonably priced and often cheap tickets, or is attached free of charge to hotels. In many instances trouting water is altogether open and free. To a lesser extent this also applies to salmon and sea trout. You may fish for salmon on a ticket for five shillings or even less. For the motorist, then, Scotland offers a larger variety of angling for game fish suited to any purse than does anywhere else in Britain.

Roughly speaking, the mainland of Scotland is for the angler divided into two halves. These two halves are not the north and south of the country, but are marked by a diagonal line from the North-East to the South-West, again very roughly speaking, coinciding with the line that separates the Highlands from the Lowlands. (The Highland line is fully described in the article on the Highlands in the Gazetteer section of the book.) North and west of this line loch fishing predominates; south and east of it the rivers and streams hold pride of place.

For the motoring angler who wishes to "get about" as well as enjoy his sport this generalisation is capable of further sub-divisions: —

(1) In the extreme south-west, in Galloway (that little Highlands beyond the Lowlands) there is both loch and river fishing. The lochs provide fair sport in brown trout. Some are attached to hotels in Gatehouse of Fleet, Castle Douglas and Newton Stewart. Others are free, or are fishable on cheap tickets. There is good salmon and sea-trout fishing to be had in the rivers of the Nith, the Fleet, the Border Esk, the Cree, and the Annan.

(2) In the south-east (the Borders proper) that noble river the Tweed is king of the waters; therein it are born, and to it return each year, some of the finest salmon in Western Europe. Parts are carefully preserved, others can be fished on a very reasonably priced ticket. There are also free stretches. The Tweed contains sea trout and some excellent brown trout, though naturally in so popular a water they tend to be highly educated. This also applies to the trout in the upper stretches of the Clyde and other smaller rivers amongst the Border hills. There is not much loch fishing in south-east Scotland; but if one stretches one's definition to include Fife and Kinross, there is, of course, the celebrated Loch Leven, with its own special trout, of recent years averaging over a pound. There are some who find fishing on Loch Leven "too commercial." But it is worthy of note that there are few who would refuse a day on that world-famous water.

(3) In central Scotland, which is largely occupied by Perthshire and parts of Inverness-shire, the Highland line is crossed and loch fishing predominates. It is easy to get permits through hotels or associations to fish most lochs, though some (notably Loch Lubnaig, south of Strathyre, which contains salmon as well as trout) are free. Loch Lomond, though so near to Glasgow, may be included in this area. It is famous for its salmon and sea trout and the price of tickets on it is reasonable.

(4) The Western Central Highlands, so noted for their beauty, give the angler a continuation of the loch fishing of the more central parts. Though most of the rivers running into the Atlantic on this coast are preserved, there is salmon and sea-trout fishing to be had here on enquiry.

(5) In Aberdeenshire and the Buchan bulge to the north-east, there is practically no loch fishing, but there is some of the best river fishing in Scotland. The Dee, the Don (by some held to be "the best trouting river in Scotland"), the Ythan, the Deveron and other streams flow easily and at length through country that is not nearly so precipitous as in the west. The waters are therefore not subject to sudden rises and falls. Fish can linger in and return to them sure of comfort and feeding. From these facts the river angler profits in the "near North-East." Naturally such waters, particularly the Dee, are preserved. But by means of hotels and with tickets it is possible for the visiting angler to have a large variety of excellent river fishing—salmon, sea trout and trout.

(6) Away and across the Moray Firth in the far north-east the river fishing is largely preserved. In Caithness, however, the most northerly county on the mainland of Britain, there are a number of lochs which yield a good average of brown trout nearly up to the present Loch Leven size, and more numerous. The rights of fishing these lochs are nearly all held by hotels, and

most lochs are easily accessible by road and from the hotels. The charges are not high.

(7) The extreme North-West of Scotland, which is occupied by the counties of Sutherland and Ross, is the goal of angling motorists who love remote scenery, loch fishing, and large numbers of brown trout, without being consistently ambitious about size. This is not to say that there are not lochs in these parts containing large trout. At Durness, for instance, near to Cape Wrath, there are four lochs in which some of the record brown trout of Scotland have been taken. The average weight too is remarkably high; but for the most part in Sutherland the myriad little hill lochs do not yield trout of much over half a pound in weight, sometimes three to the pound or even less. But if you like plenty of fish with plenty of fight in their small bodies this is the place to find them. The hill lochs are so numerous that some of them are free, but most are attached to the hotels in this district.

Apart from these seven divisions of the mainland of Scotland there are, of course, the islands (the Hebrides, and Orkney and Shetland), in which in certain places some of the best angling in Scotland is to be found.

The average visiting motorist may find them difficult and expensive of access, but this article would not be complete without mention of fishing in the islands.

To fish for game fish in Scotland in any comfort one is confined to the months of mid-April to the end of September. There is of course a spring run of salmon beginning earlier, and an autumn run in places going on till November, but the average motorist who wishes to fish will probably be mostly concerned with brown trout, the fishing grounds for which are so easy of access and which can, even in the most unpromising weather, be guaranteed to provide *some* sport.

As brown trout are so plentiful in Scotland, especially in the lochs of the West and North-West, the visiting angler must not expect in these places anything very large. He will, especially if he fishes the rivers on the east side, get trout of between one and two pounds, sometimes over, but in the majority of open or easily accessible lochs and streams and burns he must recognise that a trout of three-quarters of a pound is a reasonable size and that the average is more like half a pound.

Moderate tackle then is all that is needed for the motorist who wishes to try for trout in various districts of Scotland. A rod of nine and a half or ten feet will do excellently for all brown-trout fishing. A smooth-running reel, to give plenty of play and light gut or nylon of 3X or 3X equivalent, gives the best fun on nearly all trout waters of the country. Flies naturally vary according to district and season, but as far as wet fly fishing is concerned, the ordinary well-tried favourites, Peter

Ross, Greenwell's Glory, Woodcock and Yellow, March brown, the butcher, grouse and claret, teal and green, soldier palmer and Zulu (the last named being more effective the farther north you go) as well as others of stock pattern will provide the basis of, if not all, the collection of flies you need. Others can be bought locally.

Wet fly fishing is most extensively used upon the lochs, though it also has its uses in fast-flowing rivers and streams. On the whole, however, dry fly fishing is becoming more extensively used upon Scottish rivers, and there are days when only the dry fly will do upon lochs. There is nothing like the regular pattern amongst dry flies as there is amongst wet. Visiting anglers should not only study the local conditions for the right dry flies but take the advice of local tackle-dealers.

Salmon and sea trout naturally require heavier tackle. But in these days of high prices it is quite possible to use a ten-and-a-half or eleven-foot rod which will give you pleasure when into sea trout, but which is quite capable of dealing with the ordinary salmon.

Fishing with fly (wet or dry) is the traditional method of angling for all game fish in Scotland; and, despite a certain amount of perennial discussion on the subject, most Scottish anglers get the greatest pleasure from catching their fish on the fly. Nevertheless, whether he be a fly purist or not, the visitor to Scotland must reconcile himself to the prospect (and the pleasure of variety) of using bait and other lures than fly. This is particularly true of the months of July and August, which are not the best fly months, and yet are the usual holiday months for motoring visitors.

It may surprise trout anglers accustomed to the waters of Southern England to learn that the humble worm is by no means despised by all in Scotland. Indeed there are days when the worm is almost the only lure for trout. A heavy spate (or flood) makes the use of fly impracticable. Worm fishing in such conditions is the only resource the angler has. Nor should he despise its use. While it is true that nothing like the same delicacy that goes with fly fishing is needed, there is a certain amount of skill in using your worm in swollen waters and studying the bed of the river to make its passage in the water natural. Moreover this is the kind of time when the large trout who have resisted the fly over many summers can be tempted from their lairs.

At the opposite extreme, and when the summer streams are very low, clear water worm angling with small red worms on the finest gut imaginable not only offers good sport, but calls for a high degree of skill. That is to say skill in negotiating the shallow clear pools, working one's worm in them in a lifelike way and, above all, keeping out of sight.

It may be added (though with a distinct reserve) that even the lordly salmon has been known to take a large lob worm or a bunch of worms on a hook. Anyone who intends to try this last extremity of salmon angling should make careful enquiries as to whether such methods are permissible on the water he intends to fish.

Finally, as an alternative to fly, both for trout and salmon, there is that method which has sprung into such prominence of recent years—spinning with a thread-line from a fixed spool reel. This art or craft in angling has made great strides owing to the scientific advances which the makers of rods, and particularly the new reels, have achieved. As with the worm on clear water days, spinning can prove deadly. Most keen resident anglers in Scotland carry at least one fly rod and a bait-casting rod with a bait-casting reel as well. It is, however, possible to buy a rod which will cope with the fly and with bait-casting, but in the long run this is an economy that is not recommended. The two styles of fishing are different, and a compromise is inclined to reduce the pleasure of each.

At the risk of repetition it must be stressed that the visitor will be surprised at the amount of angling for game fish that is available in Scotland. Indeed it is so obvious that many an angling motorist, especially in the wilder, remoter, more loch and burn filled districts, will be tempted to stop his car by the roadside and "have a go" at a lochan or running water that clearly "smells of trout." While it is true that in these remote districts such waters are sometimes free, or so nearly free that no one will object, the conscientious angler should make enquiries (usually in advance of his day's journey) as to whether there is any objection to him fishing the roadside waters. If he is lucky enough in Sutherland or the more remote west to strike such a patch of free, or near-free waters, he will find great pleasure in wandering on in his car from lochan to lochan, from burn to burn, trying his luck as he goes. But he *should make sure in advance* that he is entitled to do so. There is no licence for game fishing in Scotland, and if a water is free it is completely free to any legitimate method of angling; at the same time it should be stressed that even the remotest hill lochs are often preserved by hotels, angling associations, as well as by private individuals.

Salmon fishing, occurring as it does in spring and late autumn, is largely outside the scope of this article, which is primarily addressed to touring motorists. It is possible, however, to secure permission on the East Coast rivers and in some of the Highland lochs for late spring or early summer salmon. But luck plays a large part in such fishing. No one should count on salmon during the holiday months.

Luck, but to a lesser degree, arises in the angling for that lively and sporting fish, the sea trout. In most parts of the mainland of Scotland sea trout start coming up the rivers and streams and into the lochs in July. Dry weather, however, may hold them back, or, if they have got into fresh water the same dry weather may drive them down to the depths to sulk. Therefore, while sea trout during the holiday months are not nearly so chancy as salmon, they are not nearly so reliable as those delightful and usually smaller fish (whom some would call their humbler cousins) the brown trout. But, if a visiting angler is fortunate enough to strike a time when the sea trout are running, he will have an unforgettable experience. Pound for pound there is no game fish that in sport can surpass the sea trout. He fights like a demon to the last, and has an exciting trick of spending almost as much time in the air as in the water after he is hooked. He is the world's high jump expert amongst fish.

Sea trout waters are not *usually* free. They are generally attached to hotels (when not privately owned) and these hotels are mostly on the West Coast. The usual sea trout flies are all that the angler needs, but when fishing in estuary waters such as the Ythan, a famous sea trout spot, those long feathered contraptions known as demons, or sand eels, or even strips from a mackerel belly, are used with great effect. In certain parts of Scotland, notably in Shetland, anglers go after sea trout outside the actual estuaries and in the purely salt-water sea lochs, known in Shetland as "voes."

The preponderance of game fish in Scotland does not mean that there is not some excellent coarse fishing to be had. There is not the variety of coarse fish that there are in England, and as the season for most of them is in the winter they will not usually interest the tourist. There are grayling, particularly in the Perthshire streams, which can be fished for in the summer months. There are perch in many lochs; and the pike of the south-west lochs in Galloway and in the Lake of Menteith (the only lake as distinct from loch in Scotland) are not to be despised.

Finally there is sea fishing. In Scotland, where some really large pollock as well as cod are to be had in the north-west waters, the sport has been not so much neglected as not mapped out. The angler who finds himself near the coast during a dry holiday spell when the game fish are sulking at the bottom or off the take can have something of the pleasures of an explorer as well as of a sportsman if he can persuade a fisherman to take him out in his boat off the rock-bound and fish-teeming coast.

The angler coming to Scotland is indeed a fortunate man—or should be with such a wide variety of fishing at his disposal and at very moderate outlay. All over the country angling clubs, hotels and other proprietors of fishing rights expend a great deal of care and money in restocking or improving their waters. In recent years too the Hydro Electric Board has spent many thousands of pounds in re-stocking their reservoirs.

To sum up: the motoring angler on a holiday, even if he carries only one trout rod and a moderate amount of tackle, can be sure of having some sport with brown trout. If he comes prepared with a spinning rod he will be sure of more. If he comes armed with heavier tackle, if he plans his route and the weather is kind to him, he should be able to enjoy himself, even in the holiday months, with the most sporting fish, the sea trout. If he has pertinacity and luck he may well get a few salmon.

He will have some sport even if he merely wanders in his car along the roads of Scotland, but he would be well advised to plan his route and book his rooms in advance in angling hotels. He should come protected against wet weather, but should he strike a dry spell he should realise that with modern tackle trout can be caught to a certain extent in all weathers.

The intending angler in Scotland would be well advised to obtain a copy of " Scotland for Fishing," which is published annually by the Scottish Tourist Board, 2 Rutland Place, West End, Edinburgh 1. This book is revised annually and usually costs 3s. (plus 6d. postage). It gives most comprehensive information on all aspects of fishing in Scotland, including maps, lists of Angling Clubs from whom permits can be obtained, fishing hotels, and summaries of the various rivers and lochs in which fishing is available.

SHOOTING. Although August 12, " the glorious twelfth," is a notable date in the Sportsman's Calendar, the majority of shooting estates are let privately and there are very few facilities for the passing tourist. Some hotels may be able to offer occasional rough shooting, but due to the frequently changing conditions, it is not practicable to give any reliable list. Members interested are recommended to consult gunsmiths at such places as Edinburgh, Glasgow, Perth, Aberdeen or Inverness. The Scottish Tourist Board, 2 Rutland Place, West End, Edinburgh 1, may also be able to offer suggestions.

SKI-ING. Although Scotland cannot claim snow conditions as good as the high altitude continental resorts, ski-ing is generally possible for three to four months, starting from the end of January. It is over 50 years since the sport was first introduced into Scotland but until recently only a few enthusiasts practised it. During recent years however ski-ing has become immensely popular. New clubs have sprung up and hotels in the best snow areas are making great efforts to provide facilities for this rapidly developing sport. Ski-roads, chair-lifts and Alpine huts are planned for all the best snow areas.

The main centres are Aviemore in Inverness-shire for the Cairngorms; Killin, Perthshire for Ben Lawers; and Kingshouse for the slopes of the Glen-coe Mountains.

Ski-ing in Scotland may at times mean hard work, but it is none the less enjoyable and the accident rate is negligible. A number of the hotels now

have Swiss or Norwegian instructors who cater for novices as well as for advanced ski-ers who wish to improve their technique. Some hotels also provide ski-ing equipment on hire.

The Scottish Ski Club, the Scottish Council of Physical Recreation and local ski clubs are among the bodies which in the past year or two have backed the growth of ski-ing in Scotland. Their efforts include a new ski-road to the Cairngorms, which will allow ski-ers to be transported to Coire Cas, saving many miles of hard walking when the snow is high on the mountains.

MOUNTAINEERING AND HILL-WALKING. Scotland's highest mountain, Ben Nevis, is only 4,406 ft. high—small compared with continental peaks. But the ruggedness and infinite variety of Scottish mountains—there are 543 of them over 3,000 ft. in height—has meant that rock-climbing and fell-walking have long been established as a major attraction in Scotland.

Some of the finest pitches in the world for rock-climbers are found in the Coolins of Skye. The Coolins have the best of all rocks for climbers—gabbro, and the climbs range from the simple to the virtually impossible.

On the mainland, the most popular centre is Glencoe, and there is good climbing also to be found on Arran and in parts of the Cairngorms. For snow climbing in winter Ben Nevis is the centre, though there is good sport to be found in other parts of the Highlands.

Ben Nevis, ascended by an easy afternoon's walk from one side in summer, yet has the longest and most difficult snow climbs in Britain on the other side in winter, and should not be tackled by the inexpert or the under-equipped climber.

For the moorland and fell-walker, there is a wide variety of terrain. There is fine ridge-walking to be had on Arran, in the Mamore Forest, in Kintail and in Wester Ross, all with superb views over long lochs and steep hills. The Perthshire uplands, western Inverness-shire, the Cairngorms and Argyll are the best areas.

May, June and September are the best months of the year for the mountaineers and rock-climbers, and for walking generally spring and early autumn are likely to be finer and drier than the height of summer.

PONY TREKKING. Scotland claims to have been the pioneer of pony trekking holidays, which have captured the imaginations of thousands of young people from Britain and overseas since their introduction at Newtonmore in 1952.

Pony trekking in its simplest form offers the chance to explore wide countryside at a steady pace in congenial company. The ponies used are steady, sure-footed and know their job, as they carry people long distances over moorland, mountains, and burns and rivers.

The main centres for pony trekking are Inverness-shire, Morayshire and Perthshire, although the sport is extending rapidly to other and lower hill areas of Scotland. Many hotels in these districts are making a speciality of pony trekking holidays, and tuition is provided not only in the necessary elementary form of simple trekking, but for those who want it in more advanced forms of horsemanship.

SAILING. Scotland, with its long and largely unspoilt coastline and many fishing harbours, its great firths and innumerable lochs, is obviously well-placed to develop the attractions of sailing and yachting, sports which are steadily increasing in popularity.

The Scottish Council for Physical Recreation alone in one year recently sponsored no less than eight sailing schools providing instruction for over a thousand beginners and novices, and the number of such courses, both from the S.C.P.R. and other organisations, is growing annually. One of the leading centres is the S.C.P.R.'s base at Inverclyde, near Largs, on the Firth of Clyde, and they also run a centre at Glenmore National Forest Park, near Aviemore, in the Cairngorms.

The main centre, however, remains the Clyde coast, where also two other water sports have developed rapidly of recent years. One is the sailing of catamarans—this has been taken up enthusiastically by some sailing clubs on the Clyde coast, who now run special events for this odd-looking craft. The other development is in water ski-ing; while it is not usually possible for the casual visitor to hire a catamaran for a short period, water-ski-ing tuition is available in several places.

CRUISING. Cruising has also grown of late years. Formerly restricted to the few who could afford their own crafts, this sport has been extended by the Scottish Council of Physical Recreation, who now run cruising courses in the West of Scotland, where the pattern of islands and inlets is most suitable: safe havens abound and yet there are open passages where all the adventures of the ocean-racing yachtsman can be experienced.

On these cruising courses members become one of the crew of a big yacht, helping to sail and work it from day to day, and making new landfalls every night. The cruises normally last a week or a fortnight.

The season is from Easter to October, and the yachts work out of the Firth of Clyde and Oban.

KEY MAP TO THE ITINERARIES
SCALE: TWELFTH-INCH TO MILE

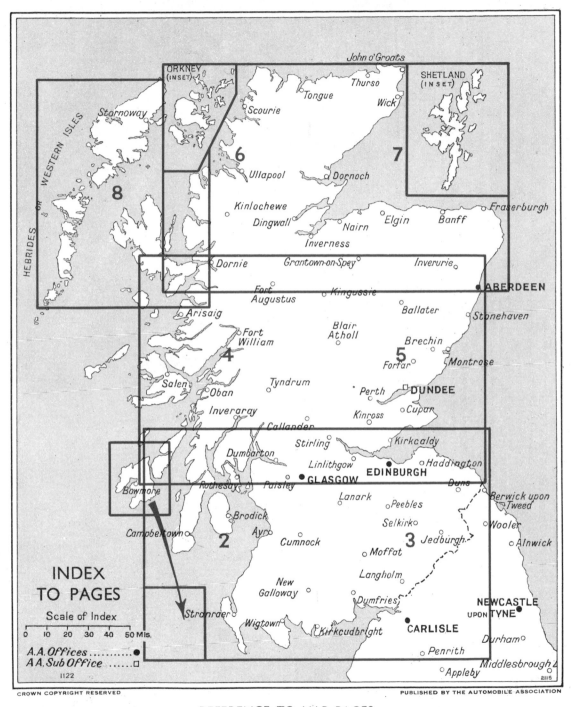

John o'Groats
Thurso
Tongue
Scourie
Wick

ORKNEY (INSET)

SHETLAND (INSET)

7

6

Ullapool
Dornoch
Stornoway

Kinlochewe
Dingwall
Nairn
Elgin
Banff
Fraserburgh

8

Inverness

Dornie
Grantown-on-Spey
Inverurie
ABERDEEN

Fort Augustus
Kingussie

Arisaig
Ballater
Stonehaven

Fort William
Blair Atholl
Brechin

4
Forfar
5
Montrose

Salen
Oban
Tyndrum
Perth
DUNDEE

Inveraray
Kinross
Cupar

Callander
Stirling
Kirkcaldy

Dumbarton
Linlithgow
Haddington
Rothesay
Paisley
GLASGOW
EDINBURGH
Duns

Bowmore
Berwick upon Tweed

Lanark
Peebles
Wooler

Brodick
Selkirk
Alnwick

Campbeltown
Ayr
Jedburgh

2
Cumnock
Moffat
3

Langholm

New Galloway
Dumfries

INDEX TO PAGES

Scale of Index

0 10 20 30 40 50 Mis.

A.A. Offices .... ●
A.A. Sub Office ...... □

1122

Stranraer
Wigtown
Kirkcudbright
CARLISLE

NEWCASTLE UPON TYNE ●

Durham
Penrith
Middlesbrough
Appleby

2115

PUBLISHED BY THE AUTOMOBILE ASSOCIATION

REFERENCE TO MAP PAGES

Through-route Itineraries	**100**	Other Itineraries ___74___
Alternative Routes ___(80)___	Roads under construction _____	Car Ferries [F25]
Dotted roads refer to itinerary descriptive notes	Adjoining Map Page Numbers [7]	

SCALE OF MAP PAGES

0   5   10   15   20   25   30   35 English Miles
0 5 10 15 20 25 30 35 40 45 50 55 Kilometres

See special Through Ro

following Key Map

6

4

See special Through Ro...

Printed by John Bartholomew & Son Ltd., Edinburgh

Butt of Lewis
Port of Ness
258
258
Barvas
Tolsta
260
258
(258)
S
Tiumpan Hd.
260
Callernish
260
Uig
260
257
257
Garynahine
257
259
Ardroil Sands
257
Stornoway
W
256
260
E
257
NORTH
L
Balallan
256
Husinish
MINCH
(256)
256
Tarbert
256
HARRIS
256
Aultbea
256
Ewe
(256)
Leverburgh
L. Gairloch
Poolewe
Rodel
Gairloch
Kilmaluig
Duntulm
208,222
205,222
261
254
Tighary
Lochmaddy
Staffin
L. Torridon
Diabaig
261
Loch Snizort
254
NORTH
262
(254)
L. Torridon
(223)
Clachan
261
UIST
Trumpan
Uig
Shieldaig
219,223
228
Carinish
262
LITTLE
(255)
255
254
219
223
L. Dunvegan
Applecross
(219)
Gramisdale
MINCH
Bernisdale
255
262
Benbecula
Skeabost
254
Kishorn
219
Creagorry
Dunvegan
255
S
Portree
F57
Carnan
Bracadale
K
Strome
Plockton
255,253
Port-na-long
251,253
(222)
SOUTH
Carbost
255
Y
255
Kyle of Lochalsh
220,219
207
UIST
Talisker Bay
(252)
Sligachan
251,253
Kyleakin
207
262
252
E
Auchter
(220)
222
262
Daliburgh
Lochboisdale
262
Broadford
F56
F55
262
Torrin
252
253
Kylerhea
Steamer only
(262)
252
(207)
Glenelg
Pollachar
Glenbrittle
Isle Ornsay
253
Armadale
Eriskay
Elgol
L. Eishort
L. Hourn
Nevis
Armadale
253
Canna
F54
Previous booking necessary
Mallaig
209
Barra
Rum

North Minch

Sound of Raasay
Inner Sound
Raasay

Sound of Sleat

Copyright by the Automobile Association

Printed by John Bartholomew & Son Ltd., Edinburgh

THROUGH ROUTES
FROM
EDINBURGH

The numbers are those of the Itineraries.

*For ferry and steamship details
see end of book.*

SCALE OF MILES

0   10   20   30   40

1131 (A)/R.B.60

COPYRIGHT BY THE AUTOMOBILE ASSOCIATION

THROUGH ROUTES
FROM
GLASGOW

The numbers are those of the Itineraries.

*For ferry and steamship details
see end of book.*

THROUGH ROUTES
FROM
ABERDEEN AND
DUNDEE

The numbers are those of the Itineraries.

*For ferry and steamship details
see end of book.*

COPYRIGHT BY THE AUTOMOBILE ASSOCIATION

THROUGH ROUTES
FROM
CARLISLE AND
NEWCASTLE-UPON-TYNE

The numbers are those of the Itineraries.
For ferry and steamship details
see end of book.

ITINERARIES

<u>TO SELECT A ROUTE.</u> Consult the Key Map following page 40 or one of the special maps which indicate THROUGH ROUTES to be found immediately following the Key Map.

The numbers are those of ITINERARIES—not book pages—or road numbers.

<u>GENERAL.</u> The descriptions given at the top of all itineraries will assist in the selection of routes. These notes include the gradients of significant hills, especially those steeper than 1 in 10.

On page 29 will be found an article dealing with Touring in Scotland, and opposite a map giving the itinerary numbers for a suggested general tour.

Edinburgh - Town plans will be found in the Gazetteer section for all place names shown in heavy type. Reference to these plans will assist in deciding the best route through or round the town.

* - - An asterisk printed before the place name means that it is mentioned under its own heading in the Gazetteer.

A.7 - - To provide an easy method for identification of roads, and to indicate changes in direction, the Ministry of Transport Road Numbers are given in the *left-hand column*. Changes are shown against the place at which they occur, except where this is between two places, when it is shown thus: Junc. A.7/A.6106.

"uncl." - This abbreviation denotes that the road is not classified and therefore un-numbered.

(By-pass) - These words after a place name, show that there is a choice of routes, through or avoiding the town, but the mileage given is that to the town centre.

Ferry to - Particulars of ferry services, with map, will be found at the end of the book.

The *first mileage column* gives the progressive mileage from the starting point of the route, while the *column immediately before* the place names shows the distance between each place. The distance to the end of the route is given *after the place names*.

The itineraries have been designed for use in either direction and the following examples will serve to demonstrate the points mentioned above. Reverse mileages are not given on alternative routes.

ITINERARY No. 24. EDINBURGH TO DUMFRIES VIA PEEBLES.
USED IN THE DIRECTION GIVEN.

From Edinburgh to Peebles is 23 miles. **Edinburgh** and **Peebles** being printed in heavy type indicate that Town Plans for both places will be found in the Gazetteer. From Leadburn to Eddleston is 5¼ miles. From Eddleston to Peebles is 4½ miles. From Peebles to Dumfries is 54 miles as shown in the last column.

2¼ miles from Edinburgh the road number changes from A.7 to A.701 and at Leadburn it again changes to A.703. From Peebles A.72 is taken for 3 miles, followed by an unclassified road for one mile when B.712 is joined. From Rachan Mill to Dumfries A.701 is followed, but near Beattock the Glasgow-Carlisle Trunk road is taken for ½ mile, the lower number A.74 taking precedence, as is usual.

Peebles, Tweedsmuir, Moffat, etc., all marked with an asterisk, have descriptive entries in the Gazetteer.

ITINERARY No. 24. USED IN THE REVERSE DIRECTION FOR THE ROUTE FROM DUMFRIES TO EDINBURGH.

The A.701 road is followed from Dumfries to the junction with A.74 near Beattock, rejoining A.70 beyond Beattock. Taking the first mileage column, 29¾ miles at Stobo represents the distance still to b covered to reach Edinburgh.

The right-hand column now indicates the progressive mileage reading from Dumfries, *i.e.* 47¼ at Stob shows that this distance has been covered from Dumfries.

The following abbreviations are used in the Itinerary section:

Br.	= Bridge.	P.O.	= Post Office.
Ch.	= Church.	Sta.	= Station.
Iter.	= Itinerary.	Uncl.	= Road not classified by the Ministry of Transport
Junc. A.7/A.6106	= Junction of two roads.	W.M.	= War Memorial.
P.H.	= Public House.	X-rds.	= Cross-roads.

1. EDINBURGH to BERWICK-UPON-TWEED for NEWCASTLE-UPON-TYNE. A pleasant, easy route following the Great North Road, with coast scenery between Broxburn and Cockburnspath and again between Ayton and Berwick. A stone near Broxburn commemorates the battle of Dunbar. During the winter months this route to Newcastle should be used in preference to the shorter way given in Iter. 4. The quickest route to Scotch Corner is by Carlisle, see Iter. 10.

A.1				
			*Edinburgh ..	56¾
..	5¾	5¾	*Musselburgh ..	51
..	7	1¼	Levenhall ..	49¾
..	7¼	¼	Wallyford Toll X-rds. ..	49
..	10	2¼	*Tranent ..	46¾
..	11¼	1¼	Macmerry ..	45
..	13¼	1½	Gladsmuir ..	43½
..	16½	3¼	*Haddington (By-pass) ..	40¼
..	22	5½	*East Linton (By-pass) ..	34¾
..	28½	6½	*Broxburn ..	28¼
..	35½	7	*Cockburnspath	21¼
..	40¼	4¾	*Grant's House	16½
..	48¾	8½	*Ayton ..	8
..	53¾	5	*Lamberton Toll (The Border)	3
..	56¾	3	***Berwick-upon-Tweed**	

Thence by Gt. North Rd. (A.1.):—

..	119½	62¾	Newcastle-upon-Tyne
..	161½	42	Scotch Corner
..	397½	236	London

2. EDINBURGH to BERWICK-UPON-TWEED via the Coast. A coastal route for the greater part, and passes through the golfing district and seaside resorts of East Lothian. *Prestonpans, *Cockenzie and Port Seton can be visited by following B.1348 between Musselburgh and Aberlady, whilst *Portobello may be included by leaving

Edinburgh by A.1140, thence by A.199 to Musselburgh. On leaving the Great North Road this route skirts the battlefield of Prestonpans, and passes *Seton Castle to reach the coast by *Gosford Bay. After North Berwick there is a fine view of the *Bass Rock from Canty Bay, while just beyond are the ruins of *Tantallon Castle. After Dunbar, a stone is passed near Broxburn commemorating the battle of Dunbar, and beyond Cockburnspath, a detour is made to visit the fine cliff scenery in the vicinity of St. Abb's. See Iter. 1 for the main road route.

A.1				
			*Edinburgh	69¾
..	5¾	5¾	*Musselburgh ..	64
..	7	1¼	Levenhall ..	62¾
A.198	7¼	¼	Wallyford Toll X-rds.	62
..	9¼	1½	Prestonpans Sta.	60½
..	12¾	3½	*Longniddry ..	57
..	16	3¼	*Aberlady ..	53¾
..	18¼	2¼	*Gullane ..	51
..	19¼	½	*Muirfield ..	50½
..	21	1¼	*Dirleton ..	48¾
..	23¼	2¼	***North Berwick**	46¼
..	29	5¾	*Whitekirk ..	40¾
..	30¾	1¾	*Tynninghame	39
A.1	31¾	1	Junc. A.198/A.1	38
A.1087	33¼	1½	Junc. A.1/A.1087	36¼
..	34½	¾	West Barns	35½
..	35	¾	Belhaven	34¾
..	36	1	***Dunbar**	33¾
A.1	37½	1½	*Broxburn	32¼
..	44½	7	*Cockburnspath	25¼
A.1107	45¾	1¼	Junc. A.1/A.1107	24
B.6438	54¼	8½	*Coldingham ..	15¼
..	56¼	1¾	*St. Abb's	13½

Return to:—

A.1107	58		1¾	*Coldingham ..	11¾
..	61	3	*Eyemouth ..	8¾
..	63½	2½	*Burnmouth (Sta.)	6¼
A.1	63¾	¼	Junc. A.1107/A.1	6
..	66¾	3	*Lamberton Toll (The Border)	3
..	69¾	3	***Berwick-upon-Tweed**	

3. EDINBURGH to BERWICK-UPON-TWEED via the Lammermui Hills. An attractive by-road crossin the Lammermuir Hills beyond Gifford Between Gifford and Cranshaw the road is hilly and narrow i parts, with gradients up to 1 in 6, an includes the crossing of two easy ford between which the road is known a the Hungry Snout. The direct roa via Preston (B.6355) avoids Duns, bu involves the crossing of a more difficul ford. 5 miles from Gifford anothe narrow and hilly road, with a goo surface, branches off by way of *Long formacus to Duns. The easiest rout between Edinburgh and Duns is b Greenlaw, Iter. 5 and 33, and th quickest to Berwick is by Iter. 1.

A.1				
			*Edinburgh	57
..	5¾	5¾	*Musselburgh ..	51
..	7	1¼	Levenhall ..	50
..	7¼	¼	Wallyford Toll X-rds.	49
B.6371	10	2¼	*Tranent ..	47
B.6355	10½	½	Junc. B.6371/B.6355	46
..	11¼	1¼	*Winton ..	45
..	13¼	2	*Pencaitland ..	43
..	16	2¼	*East Salton ..	41
..	19¼	3¼	*Gifford ..	37
..	32	12¼	*Cranshaws ..	25
..	37¼	5¼	*Burnhouses ..	19
B.6365	38	¾	Junc. B.6355/B.6365	19
A.6112	40¼	2¼	Junc. B.6365/A.6112	16
A.6105	41¼	1¼	***Duns** ..	15
..	52	10½	*Foulden ..	5
A.699	56	4	Junc. A.6105/A.699	
..	57	1	***Berwick-upon-Tweed**	

4. EDINBURGH to CARTER BAF for NEWCASTLE-UPON-TYNE. A pleasant, easy run through agricultura and moorland country, with fine ope views to the north from the summit o

Soutra Hill (1,131 feet), followed by a gradual descent through Lauderdale to cross the River Tweed at Leaderfoot Bridge, with the Eildon Hills to the west. After Jedburgh, *Ferniehirst Castle is passed, and there are extensive views to the north on the ascent approaching the summit at Carter Bar (1,371 feet) on the Cheviot ridge, where the Border is crossed into England. Owing to the high altitudes and undulating open roads it is advisable to use the Great North Road to Newcastle (Iter. 1) during the winter months. The recommended route from Edinburgh to Scotch Corner and the south is via Carlisle, see Iter. 10.

Road			Place	
A.7			*Edinburgh	58½
..	4¼	4¼	*Gilmerton	54¼
A.6106	6	1¾	Junc. A.7/A.6106	52½
A.68	6¼	¼	Junc. A.6106/A.68	52¼
..	7	¾	*Dalkeith	51½
..	12¼	5¼	*Pathhead	46¼
..	15½	3¼	*Blackshiels	43
..	18½	3	*Soutra Hill	40
..	22¾	4¼	*Carfraemill	35¾
..	26¾	4	*Lauder	31¾
..	33¾	7	*Earlston	24¾
..	36¼	2½	Leaderfoot Bridge	22¼
..	38½	2¼	*Newtown St. Boswells	20
..	39½	1	*St. Boswells Green	19
..	44¾	5¼	*Ancrum Bridge	13¾
..	46	1¼	Bonjedward	12½
..	48	2	*Jedburgh	10½
..	58½	10½	*Carter Bar (The Border)	

Thence by roads A.68 and A. 696 to:—

..	105¾	47¼	Newcastle-upon-Tyne	

OR

Roads A.68 and B.6275 to:—

..	139½	81	Scotch Corner Great North Rd. (A.1)	
..	375½	236	London	

5. EDINBURGH to WOOLER for NEWCASTLE-UPON-TYNE.

Pleasant moorland scenery, with open views to the north from the summit of Soutra Hill (1,131 feet), afterwards descending along the east side of Lauderdale to Greenlaw. The River Tweed is reached at Coldstream, where the Border is crossed into England. A stone to the south of the road between Cornhill and Milfield commemorates the battle of Flodden, and there are views of the Cheviots hereabouts. This is a good alternative to Newcastle, other routes being given in Iters. 1 and 4. The best way to Scotch Corner is by Carlisle, Iter. 10.

Road			Place	
A.7			*Edinburgh	62¾
..	4¼	4¼	*Gilmerton	58½
A.6106	6	1¾	Junc. A.7/A.6106	56¾
A.68	6¼	¼	Junc. A.6106/A.68	56½
..	7	¾	*Dalkeith	55¾
..	12¼	5¼	*Pathhead	50½
..	15½	3¼	*Blackshiels	47¼
..	18½	3	*Soutra Hill	44¼
A.697	22¾	4¼	*Carfraemill	40
..	38	15¼	*Greenlaw	24¾
A.698	46¼	8½	Junc. A.697/A.698	16
..	48¼	1½	*Coldstream	14½
..	49¼	1¼	Cornhill	13¾
A.697	49¼	¼	Coldstream Sta.	13
..	56¼	7	Milfield	6
..	59¾	3	Akeld	3
..	62¾	3	Wooler	

Thence by roads A.697 and A.1 (Great North Road) to:—

..	108¾	45¾	Newcastle-upon-Tyne	
..	150¾	42	Scotch Corner	
..	386¾	236	London	

6. EDINBURGH to WOOLER via Kelso.

After Carfraemill, the road gradually descends along the east side of Lauderdale, with moorland and agricultural scenery, and passes close to *Mellerstain House before reaching the Tweed valley at Kelso. A pleasant, hilly by-road is then followed skirting the *Cheviot Hills, and the Border is crossed into England before reaching Mindrum Mill. The main road via Greenlaw is given in Iter. 5, whilst a better route between Kelso and Wooler is via Coldstream, see Iter. 32.

Road			Place	
			*Edinburgh	64¼
			By Iter. 4 to:—	
A.697	22¾	22¾	*Carfraemill	41½
A.6089	30¼	7½	Junc. A.697/A.6089	34
..	35	4½	*Gordon	29¼
..	39½	4½	*Nenthorn	24¾
A.698	43¼	3¾	*Kelso	21
B.6352	44	¾	Junc. A.698/B.6352	20¼
..	44¼	¼	Maxwellheugh	20
B.6396	45½	1¼	Junc. B.6352/B.6396	18¾
B.6352	53	7½	Mindrum Mill	11¼
B.6351	55½	2½	Junc. B.6352/B.6351	8¾
..	58½	3	Kirknewton	5¼
A.697	61¼	2¾	Akeld	3
..	64¼	3	Wooler	

7. EDINBURGH to WOOLER via Smailholm and Yetholm.

This forms a pleasant winding, but less hilly alternative to Iter. 6 between Carfraemill and Kelso, passing near *Mellerstain House before Smailholm. After Kelso, a detour through Yetholm passes along the foothills of the *Cheviots, the Border being crossed into England between Yetholm and Mindrum Mill. The quickest way from Kelso to Wooler is by Coldstream (Iter. 32), whilst the best road from Edinburgh to Wooler is by Iter 5.

Road			Place	
			*Edinburgh	69¼
			By Iter. 4 to:—	
A.6105	33¼	33¼	*Earlston	35¾
B.6397	35	1¼	Junc. A.6105/B.6397	34¼
..	39¼	4¼	*Smailholm	29½
A.6089	44¼	4½	Junc. B.6397/A.6089	25
A.698	46	1¾	*Kelso	23¼
B.6352	46¾	¾	Junc. A.698/B.6352	22½
..	47	¼	Maxwellheugh	22¼
..	53¾	6¾	*Yetholm	15½
..	58	4¼	Mindrum Mill	11¼
B.6351	60½	2½	Junc. B.6352/B.6351	8¾
..	63½	3	Kirknewton	5¼
A.697	66¼	2¾	Akeld	3
..	69¼	3	Wooler	

8. EDINBURGH to BERWICK-UPON-TWEED via Greenlaw.

An alternative to the main road given in Iter. 1. Beyond Carfraemill traverses the east side of Lauderdale through pleasant moorland country to Greenlaw, thence undulating agricultural districts.

Road			Place	
			*Edinburgh	58¼
			By Iter. 4 to:—	
A.697	22¾	22¾	*Carfraemill	35½
	38	15¼	*Greenlaw	20¼
B.6460	39½	1½	Junc. A.697/B.6460	18¾
..	42¾	3¼	Fogorig	15½
..	44¾	2	Mount Pleasant X-rds.	13½
..	53¾	8½	*Paxton	4¾
A.699	53¾	¼	Junc. B.6460/A.699	4¾
..	58¼	4½	*Berwick-upon-Tweed	

9. EDINBURGH to BERWICK-UPON-TWEED via Stow.

A pleasant touring route utilising by-roads on the middle part. At Eskbank, a short detour can be made past *Newbattle Abbey, afterwards rejoining the winding road across the moors to Stow, where there is an ascent of 1 in 8 from the main road. Hilly, cross country moorland roads are then followed to Duns, after which the country is flat and rural. The quickest way from A.697 to Duns is by Greenlaw (Iters. 8 and 33).

Road			Place	
A.7			*Edinburgh	64½
..	4¼	4¼	*Gilmerton	60¼
..	6½	2¼	*Eskbank	58
..	11¼	4¾	*Fushiebridge	53¼
..	12¼	1	*Middleton	52¼
..	17	4¾	*Heriot (Sta.)	47½
B.6362	25¼	8¼	*Stow	39¼
A.68	30¼	5¼	Junc. B.6362/A.68	34
..	30¾	¼	*Lauder	33¾
A.697	31¼	½	Junc. A.68/A.697	33¼
B.6456	36	4¾	Junc. A.697/B.6456	28¼
..	38¼	2½	*Westruther	26
A.6105	46	7½	Junc. B.6456/A.6105	18¼
..	49	3	*Duns	15½
..	59½	10½	*Foulden	5
A.699	63¼	4	Junc. A.6105/A.699	1
..	64½	1	*Berwick-upon-Tweed	

10. EDINBURGH to CARLISLE.

This is the easiest and shortest road to Carlisle and also the quickest way into England (except to places in Northumberland and Durham). At first through agricultural districts, with views of the Pentland Hills, until beyond Broughton, where lonely moorland country is traversed. Near the summit, between Tweedsmuir and Moffat, is the source of the River Tweed, and shortly afterwards the famous *Devil's Beef Tub is passed on the descent into Annandale.

A pleasant, undulating road through picturesque scenery then leads to the Border, which is crossed into England at Sark Bridge. Several alternative routes to Carlisle are available, including those shown in Iter. 11 and 12 and that via Abington (Iter. 25 and 51).

A.7			*Edinburgh	93
A.701	2¼	2¼	Junc. A.7/A.701	90¾
..	3	¾	*Liberton	90
..	5	2	Straiton	88
..	6½	1½	*Bilston	86½
..	8	1½	*Milton Bridge	85
..	8½	½	*Glencorse	84½
..	10	1½	*Penicuik	83
..	13¼	3¼	*Leadburn	79¾
..	15½	2¼	*Lamancha	77½
..	20	4½	*Romanno Bridge	73
A.72	22½	2½	*Blyth Bridge	70½
A.701	25¼	3¼	Junc. A.72/A.701	67¾
..	28¼	3	*Broughton	64¾
..	30½	1½	Rachan Mill	62½
..	35½	5½	*"Crook" Inn	57½
..	37	1½	*Tweedsmuir	56
..	52¼	15¼	*Moffat	40¾
A.74	54	1¾	Junc. A.701/A.74	39
..	54½	½	*Beattock (Sta.)	38½
..	61	6¾	*Johnstone Bridge	32
..	68¼	7¼	*Lockerbie	24¾
..	74	5¾	*Ecclefechan	19
..	77½	3½	*Kirtlebridge	15½
..	80¼	3	*Kirkpatrick Fleming	12¾
..	83½	3¼	*Gretna Green	9½
..	84	½	*Gretna	9
..	84½	½	*Sark Bridge (The Border)	8½
A.7	90½	6¼	Kingstown	2½
..	93	2½	†Carlisle	

Thence by road A.6 to:—

..	111¼	18¼	Penrith
..	212	100¾	Manchester

† OR

Carlisle

Thence by A.6 to:—

..	111¼	18¼	Penrith

Then by A.66 to:—

..	161	49¾	Scotch Corner Great North Road (A.1)
..	397	236	London

11. EDINBURGH to CARLISLE via Selkirk. At Eskbank, a short detour can be made past *Newbattle Abbey, afterwards rejoining the winding main road across the moorlands to Galashiels. Becoming rather hilly between Selkirk and Hawick, followed by a fine scenic run through Teviotdale to Langholm in Eskdale. This is a pleasant, but slower alternative to the recommended route given in Iter. 10. A detour to include the many places of interest adjacent to the road is shown in Iter. 13.

A.7			*Edinburgh	94
..	4¼	4¼	*Gilmerton	89¾
..	6½	2¼	*Eskbank	87½
..	11¼	4¾	*Fushiebridge	82¾
..	12¼	1	*Middleton	81¾
..	17	4¾	*Heriot (Sta.)	77
..	25¼	8¼	*Stow	68¾
..	29	3¾	*Bowland	65
..	33¼	4¼	*Galashiels	60¾
..	39	5¾	*Selkirk	55
..	44½	5½	Ashkirk	49½
..	50¾	6¼	*Hawick	43¾
..	55½	4½	Newmill	38¼
..	59½	4¼	*Teviothead	34¼
..	63¼	3¾	"Mosspaul" Hotel	30¾
..	69¼	6	*Ewes P.O.	24¾
..	73¼	4	*Langholm	20¼
..	79¼	6¼	*Canonbie	14¼
..	82	2¾	The Border	12
..	85¼	3¼	Longtown	8¾
..	91½	6¼	Kingstown	2½
..	94	2½	Carlisle	

12. EDINBURGH to CARLISLE via the Moorfoot Hills and Ettrick Forest. An attractive by-road to Langholm through moorland country, narrow in places, but with a good surface. At Eskbank, a short detour can be made past *Newbattle Abbey, afterwards rejoining the main road. Beyond Middleton, a secondary road is followed over the Moorfoot Hills to Innerleithen. There is an alternative valley road (B.709) leaving A.7 farther south at Heriot Station. Between Traquair and Gordon Arms this is known as the Paddy Slacks road. The descent through Ettrick Forest to Yarrow Water is followed by another climb to reach the Ettrick valley, and the road then descends the Tima valley to cross the ridge into Eskdale, where the Thomas Telford memorial is passed before reaching Westerkirk. A pleasant run through wooded country then follows until the Border is crossed into England between Canonbie and Longtown. In general this is a hilly route without any serious gradients. See Iter. 10, 11, 13 and 14 for alternatives.

A.7			*Edinburgh	93¼
..	4¼	4¼	*Gilmerton	89
..	6½	2¼	*Eskbank	86¾
..	11¼	4¾	*Fushiebridge	82
..	12¼	1	*Middleton	81
B.7007	13¼	1	Junc. A.7/B.7007	80
B.709	19¼	6	Junc. B.7007/B.709	74
..	25	5¾	Whitehope	68¼
..	29	4	*Innerleithen	64¼
..	30½	1½	*Traquair	62¾
..	37½	7	*"Gordon Arms" Inn	55¾
..	44	6½	*"Tushielaw" Inn	49¼
..	46½	2¾	*Ettrick	46½
..	59¼	12¾	*Eskdalemuir Ch.	34
..	67	7¾	*Westerkirk	26¼
A.7	72¾	5¾	*Langholm	20½
..	79	6¼	*Canonbie	14¼
..	81¼	2¾	The Border	12
..	84¼	2¾	Longtown	8¾
..	90½	6¼	Kingstown	2½
..	93¼	2½	Carlisle	

13. EDINBURGH to CARLISLE via the Scott County and Yarrow Vale. A touring route in the Lowlands through mainly agricultural and moorland districts and including places of interest in the *Scott Country. From the summit of Soutra Hill (1,131 feet) there are fine open views to the north, and after a gradual descent through Lauderdale to Earlston, the main road is left to visit Bemersyde and Dryburgh Abbey. On returning to the main road at St. Boswells, the Eildon Hills are encircled by way of Melrose and Abbotsford House. A short detour can be made to include the old-world village of *Newstead between St. Boswells and Melrose, and on leaving the town another detour would include *Darnick Tower. Beyond Selkirk, the road ascends the picturesque Yarrow Vale, which is well wooded on the earlier part. Crosses the moorlands of Ettrick Forest and then passes the delightful *St. Mary's Loch, to reach the summit at Birkhill (1,105 feet). Descends past the Grey Mare's Tail waterfall (on rt.) to Moffat, then by a pleasant, undulating road in Annandale to cross the Border into England at Sark Bridge.

A.7			*Edinburgh	129¼
..	4¼	4¼	*Gilmerton	125
A.6106	6	1¾	Junc. A.7/A.6106	123¼
A.68	6¼	¼	Junc. A.6106/A.68	123
..	7	¾	*Dalkeith	122¼
..	12¼	5¼	*Pathhead	117
..	15½	3¼	*Blackshiels	113¾
..	18½	3	*Soutra Hill	110¾
..	22¾	4¼	*Carfraemill	106¼
..	26¾	4	*Lauder	102½
A.6105	33¾	7	*Earlston	95½
B.6356	34	¼	Junc. A.6105/B.6356	95¼
..	37¼	3¼	*Bemersyde Hill	92
..	38	¾	*Bemersyde House	91¼
..	39½	1½	*Dryburgh Abbey	89¾
B.6404	41½	2	Junc. B.6356/B.6404	87¾
..	43	1½	*St. Boswells	86¼
A.68	43¼	¼	Junc. B.6404/A.68	86
..	44¼	1	*Newtown St. Boswells	85
A.6091	44¾	½	Junc. A.68/A.6091	84¼
..	47	2¼	*Melrose	82¼
B.6360	48½	1½	Junc. A.6091/B.6360	80¾
..	50	1½	*Abbotsford House	79¼
A.7	52¼	2¼	Junc. B.6360/A.7	77
A.707	54¼	2¼	*Selkirk	74¾
A.708	55	½	Junc. A.707/A.708	74¼
..	59	4	*Broadmeadows	70¼
..	63	4	*Yarrow Ch.	66¼
..	67	4	*"Gordon Arms" Inn	62¼
..	71¼	4¼	Copplecleuch	58
..	72¼	1	*"Rodono" Hotel	57
..	73¼	1	*"Tibbie Shiel's" Inn	56
..	77¼	4	*Birkhill	52
..	78½	1¼	*Grey Mare's Tail	50¾
..	84	5¼	Shortwoodend	45¼
A.701	88¼	4¼	*Moffat	40¾
A.74	90¼	1¾	Junc. A.701/A.74	39
..	90½	¼	*Beattock (Sta.)	38¾
..	97¼	6¾	*Johnstone Bridge	32
..	104¼	7¼	*Lockerbie	24¾
..	110¼	5¾	*Ecclefechan	19
..	113½	3¼	*Kirtlebridge	15½
..	116½	3	*Kirkpatrick Fleming	12¾
..	119½	3¼	*Gretna Green	9½
..	120¼	½	*Gretna	9
..	120½	¼	*Sark Bridge (The Border)	8½
A.7	126¾	6¼	Kingstown	2½
..	129¼	2½	Carlisle	

14. EDINBURGH to SELKIRK via Peebles.

From Edinburgh to Leadburn shows alternative roads to the main route given in Iter. 10. Agricultural at first, with views of the Pentland Hills, followed by moor and woodlands to Lyne, whence there is a pretty, undulating road along the Tweed valley. The direct route to Peebles is by Iter. 24 and to Selkirk by Iter. 11.

A.702			*Edinburgh	51
	4¼	4¼	*Fairmilehead ..	46¾
A.703	5¼	1	*Hillend ..	45¾
A.701	7¼	2	Junc. A.703/A.701	43¾
B.7026	8	¾	Junc. A.701/B.7026	43
..	8½	½	*Auchendinny ..	42½
A.6094	11	2½	*Howgate ..	40
A.701	12½	1¾	*Leadburn ..	38¼
..	15	2¼	*Lamancha ..	36
B.7059	19½	4½	*Romanno Bridge	31½
A.72	23	3½	Junc. B.7059/A.72	28
..	25¾	2¾	*Lyne Ch. ..	25¼
..	30	4¼	*Peebles ..	21
..	36½	6½	*Innerleithen ..	14½
..	38½	2	*Walkerburn ..	12½
A.707	43½	5	Junc. A.72/A.707	7½
..	44½	1	*Caddonfoot ..	6½
..	46½	1¾	*Fairnilee ..	4½
..	51	4½	*Selkirk	

15. EDINBURGH to GLASGOW.

A fast, industrial road linking the two cities, with no scenic interest. The mast of the B.B.C. Kirk O'Shotts television transmitter is beside the road about half-way between Harthill and Newhouse.

A.8			*Edinburgh ..	43¾
..	4¼	4¼	*Corstorphine ..	39¼
..	6	1¾	*Gogar ..	37¾
..	9	3	*Newbridge ..	34¾
..	14½	17½	*Harthill ..	20¼
..	30½	7	Newhouse ..	13¼
..	43¾	13¼	*Glasgow	

16. EDINBURGH to GLASGOW via Airdrie.

An industrial road with no special features of interest. See Iter. 15 for the main road avoiding the towns.

A.8			*Edinburgh ..	45
..	4¼	4¼	*Corstorphine ..	40¾
..	6	1¾	*Gogar ..	39
..	9	3	*Newbridge ..	36
A.899	2	5	Junc. A.8/A.899	34
..	11¾	¾	*Broxburn ..	33¼
..	13	1¼	*Uphall ..	32
..	14¾	1¾	Dechmont ..	30¼
A.8	15	¼	Junc. A.899/A.8	30
A.89	17¾	2¾	Junc. A.8/A.89	27¼
..	19½	1¾	*Bathgate ..	25½
..	21¾	2¼	*Armadale ..	23¼
..	29½	7¾	*Caldercruix ..	15½
..	33½	4	*Airdrie ..	11½
..	35½	2	*Coatbridge ..	9½
..	38¼	3½	*Baillieston ..	6¼
..	41½	2½	*Shettleston ..	3½
..	45	3½	*Glasgow	

17. EDINBURGH to GLASGOW via Bo'ness and Falkirk.

At first a pleasant, easy road passing beneath the Forth Bridge, with views across the estuary to Fife. Becomes industrial beyond Grangemouth, the latter part being mainly a commercial route through agricultural and mining districts. For the direct road to Falkirk see Iter. 95 and for Glasgow Iter. 15. Some places of interest near the south bank of the River Forth are visited in Iter. 96.

A.90			*Edinburgh ..	49
..	2½	2½	Blackball ..	46½
..	4½	2	*Barnton ..	44½
..	5	½	*Cramond Bridge	44
A.904	8½	3½	*S. Queensferry (Forth Bridge)	40¾
..	8¾	½	*Queensferry ..	40¼
..	10¾	2	Newton ..	38¼
..	18	7¼	*Bo'ness ..	31
..	23	5	*Grangemouth ..	26
A.9	26¾	3¾	*Falkirk ..	22¼
A.803	27½	1	*Camelon ..	21½
..	30½	3	*Bonnybridge ..	18½
A.80	31½	1	Junc. A.803/A.80	17½
..	31¾	¼	*Dennyloanhead ..	17¼
..	33¼	1½	*Castlecary ..	15¾
..	35	1¾	*Cumbernauld ..	14
..	38	3	Condorrat ..	11
..	39½	1½	Mollinburn ..	9½
..	42	2½	*Muirhead ..	7
..	43¾	1¾	*Stepps ..	5¼
..	44½	¾	Millerston ..	4½
..	49	4½	*Glasgow	

18. EDINBURGH to PAISLEY via Mid Calder.

Mainly industrial, until joining the main Edinburgh-Glasgow road near Whitburn. The mast of the B.B.C. Kirk O'Shotts television transmitter is beside the road between Harthill and Newhouse. Avoids Glasgow, but there are built-up areas beyond Newhouse and the route is complicated. The quickest way from Edinburgh to Harthill is by Iter. 15.

A.71			*Edinburgh ..	54
..	5½	5½	*Hermiston ..	48½
..	11½	6¼	East Calder ..	42¼
A.705	12½	¾	*Mid Calder ..	41¼
..	15	2½	Livingston ..	39
..	18½	3½	Blackburn ..	35½
..	21	2½	*Whitburn ..	33
A.8	22	1	Junc. A.705/A.8	32
..	23½	1½	*Harthill ..	30½
..	30½	7	Newhouse ..	23½
A.775	30¾	¼	Junc. A.8/A.775	23¼
..	32½	1¾	*Holytown ..	21½
..	33¾	1¼	Mossend ..	20¼
A.725	34¼	¾	*Bellshill ..	19¾
B.7012	36½	2	*Bothwell Bridge	17½
A.776	38¼	1¾	Junc. B.7012/A.776	15¾
..	38½	¼	*High Blantyre ..	15½
A.749	41¼	2¾	Junc. A.776/A.749	12¾
A.726	42	¾	*East Kilbride ..	12
..	45½	3½	Busby ..	8½
..	46½	1	*Clarkston ..	7½
..	47½	1¼	*Giffnock ..	6¼
..	50½	2¾	Nitshill ..	3¾
..	54	3½	*Paisley	

19. EDINBURGH to TROON via Motherwell.

Agricultural on the earlier part, with mining districts on the moors to Newmains, and becoming industrial approaching the Clyde valley. After East Kilbride, Eaglesham Moor is crossed, and beyond Kilmarnock passes through flat agricultural country. Through traffic can avoid the centre of Motherwell by following road B.754. The fastest road from Edinburgh to Motherwell, Hamilton and East Kilbride is by Iter. 15 to Newhouse, then Iter. 87 for Motherwell and Hamilton, or Iter. 18 for East Kilbride. The recommended route between Edinburgh and Kilmarnock is by Strathaven, see Iter. 20 and 69.

A.71			*Edinburgh ..	72½
..	5½	5½	*Hermiston ..	66¾
..	11½	6¼	East Calder ..	60¾
..	12½	¾	*Mid Calder ..	59¾
..	15	2½	Bellsquarry ..	57½
..	17½	2¼	*West Calder ..	55
A.722	30½	13½	*Newmains ..	41½
A.721	32½	2	*Wishaw ..	39½
A.723	36½	3½	*Motherwell ..	36
A.724	38½	2¼	*Hamilton ..	33¾
A.776	40	1½	Burnbank ..	32¼
..	40½	¾	*High Blantyre ..	31¾
A.749	43½	2½	Junc. A.776/A.749	28¾
A.726	44½	1	*East Kilbride ..	28
B.764	45½	1	Junc. A.726/B.764	27
..	48¾	3½	*Eaglesham ..	23¾
A.77	54¼	6	Junc. B.764/A.77	17¼
A.77	57¼	3	*Fenwick (By-pass) ..	14¼
A.759	62	4¼	*Kilmarnock ..	10¼
A.78	68¼	6¼	Junc. A759/A.78	3¼
A.759	70¼	1½	*Loans ..	2
..	72¼	2	*Troon	

20. EDINBURGH to AYR.

Agricultural then mining districts to Strathaven, afterwards becoming mainly agricultural. See Iter. 21 for an alternative summer route with greater scenic interest.

A.71			*Edinburgh ..	73½
..	5½	5½	*Hermiston ..	67¾
..	11½	6¼	East Calder ..	61¾
..	12½	¾	*Mid Calder ..	60¾
..	15	2½	Bellsquarry ..	58½
..	17½	2¼	*West Calder ..	56
A.73	30½	13½	*Newmains ..	42½
A.71	31½	1	Junc. A.73/A.71	42
..	32½	1½	Waterloo ..	40½
..	33½	¾	Overtown ..	40
..	39	5½	Stonehouse ..	34½
..	43	4	*Strathaven ..	30½
..	48¾	5½	*Drumclog ..	24¾
..	52	3½	*Loudounhill ..	21½
..	54	2	*Darvel ..	19½
..	55½	1½	*Newmilns ..	17½
A.719	58½	2½	*Galston ..	15
..	71½	13	Whitletts ..	2
..	73½	2	*Ayr	

21. EDINBURGH to AYR via Cumnock.

A fine, open moorland road to Carnwath, skirting the Pentland Hills on the line of the old drove road known as the Lang Whang. Traverses rural country to Cumnock, where there is some mining. Mainly agricultural on the latter part. With fewer restricted areas than in the previous route, this makes a pleasant summer run, but during winter months the Strathaven route (Iter. 20) is to be preferred.

A.70			*Edinburgh ..	77½
..	3	3	Slateford ..	74½
..	5½	2½	*Juniper Green ..	71½
..	6½	1	*Currie ..	70½
..	14	7½	*Causewayend ..	63½
..	26	12	*Carnwath ..	51½
..	28¾	2¾	*Carstairs ..	48½
..	29½	1	Ravenstruther ..	47½
..	32½	2½	*Hyndford Bridge	45
..	37½	5½	Rigside ..	39½

..	41½	4	*Douglas	.. 35½
..	51½	10½	*Muirkirk	.. 25½
..	59½	7¾	*Lugar	.. 17½
..	61½	2	*Cumnock	.. 15½
..	65½	4½	*Ochiltree	.. 11½
..	71½	6	*Coylton	.. 5½
..	77½	5½	*Ayr	

22. EDINBURGH to LANARK.

Mainly agricultural to West Calder, thence a fine moorland road. During the summer months the more scenic route via Carnwath (Iter. 23) may be preferred, but otherwise there is little to choose.

A.71			*Edinburgh	.. 33¼
..	5½	5½	*Hermiston	.. 28
..	11¾	6¼	East Calder	.. 21¾
..	12½	¾	*Mid Calder	.. 21
..	15	2½	Bellsquarry	.. 18½
..	17½	2¼	*West Calder	.. 16¼
A.704	18¼	1	Junc. A.71/A.704	15¼
A.706	22½	4	Junc. A.704/A.706	11¼
..	24½	2¼	*Wilsontown	.. 9
..	25¼	¾	Forth	.. 8¼
..	33½	8¼	*Lanark	

23. EDINBURGH to LANARK via Carnwath.

A fine, open moorland run to Carnwath, skirting the Pentland Hills along the line of the old drove road known as the Lang Whang. The alternative given in Iter. 22 is a slightly easier road.

A.70			*Edinburgh	.. 32¼
..	3	3	Slateford	.. 29¼
..	5½	2½	*Juniper Green	.. 27¼
..	6½	1	*Currie	.. 26¼
..	14	7½	*Causewayend	.. 18¼
..	26	12	*Carnwath	.. 6¼
..	28½	2½	*Carstairs	.. 4
A.743	29¼	1	Ravenstruther	.. 3
..	32¼	3	*Lanark	

24. EDINBURGH to DUMFRIES via Peebles.

Pleasant agricultural country, with views of the Pentland Hills to Leadburn, followed by moorland scenery and becoming wooded in the Tweed valley after Peebles. Near the summit between Tweedsmuir and Moffat is the source of the Tweed, and shortly afterwards the famous *Devil's Beef Tub is passed on the descent to Annandale, where the country becomes wooded and agricultural. See Iter. 10 for the direct road to Moffat.

A.7			*Edinburgh	.. 77
A.701	2¼	2¼	Junc. A.7/A.701	74¾
..	3	¾	*Liberton	.. 74
..	5	2	Straiton	.. 72
..	6½	1½	*Bilston	.. 70½
..	8	1½	*Milton Bridge	.. 69
..	8½	½	*Glencorse	.. 68½
..	10	1½	*Penicuik	.. 67
A.703	13½	3½	*Leadburn	.. 63½
..	18½	5¼	*Eddleston	.. 58½
A.72	23	4½	*Peebles	.. 54
Uncl.	26	3	Junc. A.72/Uncl.	51
B.712	27	1	Junc. Uncl./B.712	50
..	29½	2½	*Stobo	.. 47½
..	32½	2½	*Drumelzier	.. 44½
A.701	34	1½	Rachan Mill	.. 43
..	39½	5½	*" Crook " Inn	.. 37½
..	40¾	1¼	*Tweedsmuir	.. 36¼
..	56	15¼	*Moffat	.. 21

A.74	57½	1½	Junc. A.701/A.74	19¼
..	58	½	*Beattock (Sta.)	19
A.701	58½	½	Junc. A.74/A.701	18½
..	63½	5½	*St. Ann's	.. 13½
..	68½	5	Parkgate	.. 8½
..	69½	1	*Ae Bridge	.. 7½
..	72½	3	*Amisfield	.. 4½
..	73¾	1½	Locharbriggs	.. 3¼
..	77	3¼	*Dumfries	

25. EDINBURGH to STRANRAER.

An easy, undulating road to Dolphinton, with views of the Pentland Hills, thence through fine, open country. Follows the Clyde valley from Biggar to Elvanfoot, after which there are extensive views of the Lowther Hills, and reaching an altitude of 1,140 feet before descending through the winding Dalveen Pass. *Durisdeer Church lies to the east of the road before reaching Carronbridge in Nithsdale. Moor and hill scenery in the Galloway district, becoming agricultural beyond Newton Stewart.

A.702			*Edinburgh	.. 129¼
..	4¼	4¼	*Fairmilehead	.. 125
..	5¼	1	*Hillend	.. 124
..	10½	5¼	*Silverburn	.. 118¾
..	12¾	2¼	Nine Mile Burn	.. 116½
..	14¼	1½	*Carlops	.. 115
..	17	2¾	*West Linton	.. 112¼
..	20¾	3¾	*Dolphinton	.. 108½
A.72	27½	6¾	Junc. A.702/A.72	101¾
..	28½	1	*Biggar	.. 100¾
A.702	29½	1	Junc. A.72/A.702	99¾
..	31¼	1¾	*Culter	.. 98
..	34½	3¼	*Lamington	.. 94¾
A.73	39	4½	Junc. A.702/A.73	90¼
A.74	40¾	1¾	*Abington	
			(By-pass)	.. 88½
..	44	3¼	*Crawford	.. 85¼
A.702	45¼	1¼	Junc. A.74/A.702	83¾
..	46½	1¼	*Elvanfoot	.. 82¾
A.76	61¾	15¼	*Carronbridge	.. 67¼
B.732	62½	1	Junc. A.76/B.732	66½
A.702	63¼	¾	Junc. B.732/A.702	65¾
..	64¼	1	Burnhead	.. 65
..	65½	1¼	*Penpont	.. 63¾
..	69¾	4¼	*Kirkland	.. 59½
..	71¾	2	*Moniaive	.. 57½
A.769	82½	11	Bogue Toll	.. 46½
A.712	84½	1½	Junc. A.769/A.712	44¾
..	85	½	Ken Br.	.. 44½
..	85¾	¾	*New Galloway	.. 43½
..	92¼	6½	*Clatteringshaws Dam	37
A.75	103	10½	Junc. A.712/A.715	26¼
..	104¼	1¼	*Newton Stewart	25
..	119½	15¼	*Glenluce	.. 9¼
..	123	3½	Dunragit	.. 6¼
..	126	3	*Castle Kennedy	3¼
..	129¼	3¼	*Stranraer	

26. CARLISLE to STRANRAER.

The main road to Galloway, crossing the Border at Sark Bridge. Pleasant agricultural and moorland country is traversed, with coastal scenery between Gatehouse of Fleet and Creetown.

A.7			Carlisle	.. 108¾
A.74	2½	2½	Kingstown	.. 106¼
..	8¾	6¼	*Sark Bridge (The Border)	100
A.75	9	¼	*Gretna	.. 99¾
..	11	2	Rigg	.. 97½
..	14	3	Eastriggs	.. 94½

..	14½	¾	*Dornock	.. 94
..	17½	2½	*Annan	.. 91½
..	23¼	6¼	Carrutherstown	85
..	29¼	5½	Collin	.. 79½
..	32½	3¼	*Dumfries	.. 76
..	42½	9½	*Crocketford	.. 66½
..	44½	2½	Springholm	.. 64¼
..	50¾	6¼	*Castle Douglas	58
..	56½	5½	*Ringford	.. 52¼
..	59¼	2¾	*Twynholm	.. 49½
..	65¼	6	*Gatehouse of Fleet	.. 43¼
..	77½	12	*Creetown	.. 31½
..	80½	3¼	*Palnure	.. 28¼
..	83¾	3¼	*Newton Stewart	25
..	99	15¼	*Glenluce	.. 9¼
..	102½	3¼	Dunragit	.. 6¼
..	105½	3	*Castle Kennedy	3¼
..	108¾	3¼	*Stranraer	

27. CARLISLE to AYR.

After crossing the Border at Sark Bridge, passes through pleasant agricultural country to Dumfries, where a short detour can be made to visit *Lincluden Abbey. Traverses the pretty Nith valley to Sanquhar, with mining in places towards Cumnock, but becoming mainly agricultural again on the latter part. Dumfries, Auldgirth and Ayr have associations with the poet Burns.

A.7			Carlisle	.. 92
A.74	2½	2½	Kingstown	.. 89½
..	8¾	6¼	*Sark Bridge (The Border)	83¼
A.75	9	¼	*Gretna	.. 83
..	11	2	Rigg	.. 81
..	14	3	Eastriggs	.. 78
..	14½	¾	*Dornock	.. 77¼
..	17½	2½	*Annan	.. 74½
..	23¾	6¼	Carrutherstown	68¼
..	29¼	5½	Collin	.. 62½
A.76	32½	3¼	*Dumfries	.. 59½
..	35½	2½	*New Bridge	.. 56½
..	36½	1	Holywood	.. 55½
..	40½	4	*Auldgirth	.. 51½
..	45	4½	*Closeburn	.. 47
..	47½	2½	*Thornhill	.. 44½
..	49	1½	*Carronbridge	.. 43
..	53	4	*Enterkinfoot	.. 39
..	57½	4½	*Mennock	.. 34½
..	59½	2¼	*Sanquhar	.. 32½
..	63	3½	*Kirkconnel	.. 29
..	70½	7½	*New Cumnock	.. 21½
A.70	76½	5½	*Cumnock	.. 15½
..	80½	4½	*Ochiltree	.. 11½
..	86½	6	*Coylton	.. 5½
..	92	5½	*Ayr	

28. CARLISLE to DUMFRIES via the Coast.

After crossing the Border at Sark Bridge, this forms an interesting alternative to the main road (Iter. 26) and is mainly through flat country close to the Solway Firth. Between Cummertrees and Bankend, a short detour can be made to visit *Ruthwell Church, which lies north-east of the junction of roads B.724 and B.725, from which point the direct road to Dumfries is given in Iter. 47. There is also a direct unclassified road from Bankend to Dumfries.

A.7			Carlisle	.. 39¼
A.74	2½	2½	Kingstown	.. 36¼
..	8¾	6¼	*Sark Br. (Border)	.. 30½

A.75	9	¼	*Gretna	.. 30¼
..	11	2	Rigg	.. 28¼
..	14	3	Eastriggs	.. 25¼
..	14¼	¼	*Dornock	.. 24½
..	17¼	2½	*Annan	22
B.724	17¾	½	Junc. A.75/B.724	21½
..	20¾	3	*Cummertrees	.. 18½
B.725	24	3¼	Junc. B.724/B.725	15¼
..	28¾	4¾	*Bankend (for *Caerlaverock Church)	.. 10½
..	30½	1¾	*Caerlaverock (Castle)	.. 8¾
..	34	3½	*Glencaple	.. 5¼
..	39¼	5¼	*Dumfries	

29. CARLISLE to PAISLEY.

After crossing the Border into Scotland at Sark Bridge, there is a fine open run through agricultural country in Annandale, changing to moorland on the gradual ascent over Beattock summit (1,025 feet). Beyond Lesmahagow a mining and industrial district is entered.

A.7			Carlisle	.. 103¼
A.74	2½	2½	Kingstown	.. 100¾
..	8¾	6¼	*Sark Bridge (The Border)	94¾
..	9	¼	*Gretna	94½
..	9½	½	*Gretna Green	.. 93¾
..	12¼	3¼	*Kirkpatrick Fleming	90½
..	15¼	3	*Kirtlebridge	.. 87½
..	19	3¼	*Ecclefechan	.. 84¼
..	24¼	5¼	*Lockerbie	.. 78¾
..	32	7¼	*Johnstone Bridge	71¼
..	38¼	6¼	*Beattock (Sta.)	64¾
..	49¼	10¼	*Beattock Summit	54
..	54¼	5	*Crawford	.. 49
..	57½	3¼	*Abington (By-pass)	.. 45¾
..	72	14½	*Lesmahagow	.. 31¼
A.71	77½	5½	Junc. A.74/A.71	25¾
..	79	1½	Stonehouse	.. 24¼
A.726	83	4	*Strathaven	.. 20¼
..	85½	2½	Chapelton	.. 17½
..	91¼	5¼	*East Kilbride	.. 12
..	95	3¾	Busby	.. 8¼
..	95½	½	*Clarkston	.. 7½
..	97	1½	*Giffnock	.. 6¼
..	99½	2½	Nitshill	.. 3¾
..	103¼	3½	*Paisley	

30. CARLISLE to BERWICK-UPON-TWEED.

A fine scenic run by the main road through the *Border Country. This route crosses the Border twice, entering Scotland between Longtown and Canonbie, and re-entering England at Cornhill. Open country at first in the Esk valley, then crosses the moors into Teviotdale for Hawick, where the country becomes agricultural. Flat in the Tweed valley beyond Kelso, with views of the *Cheviot Hills.

A.7			Carlisle	.. 88
..	2½	2½	Kingstown	.. 85½
..	8¾	6¼	Longtown	.. 79¼
..	12	3¼	The Border	.. 76
..	14¼	2¼	*Canonbie	.. 73¾
..	20¼	6¼	*Langholm	.. 67¾
..	24½	4¼	*Ewes P.O.	.. 63¾
..	30¼	6	" Mosspaul " Hotel	57¾
..	34¼	3¾	*Teviothead	.. 53¾
..	38¼	4¾	Newmill	.. 49¾
A.698	43¼	4½	*Hawick	.. 44¾
..	48¼	5	*Denholm	.. 39¾

..	55	6¼	Bonjedward	.. 33
..	57½	2½	Crailing	.. 30¼
..	59¼	2	*Eckford Church	28¾
..	64¼	5	*Kelso	.. 23¾
..	69¼	5¼	*Birgham	.. 18½
..	73½	4	*Coldstream	.. 14½
..	74¼	1½	Cornhill	.. 13¾
..	88	13½	*Berwick-upon-Tweed	

31. CARLISLE to HAWICK via Newcastleton.

Crosses the Border into Scotland between Longtown and Canonbie, with pleasant scenery in *Liddesdale on the earlier part. Traverses moorlands after Newcastleton, 5 miles beyond which *Hermitage Castle lies to the west of the road. This is an alternative to the main road given in Iter. 30.

A.7			Carlisle	45
..	2½	2½	Kingstown	.. 42½
..	8¾	6¼	Longtown	.. 36¼
..	12	3¼	The Border	33
..	14¼	2¼	*Canonbie	.. 30¾
B.6357	14¾	¼	Junc. A.7/B.6357	30¼
..	15½	1	Rowanburn	.. 29½
..	24½	9	*Newcastleton	.. 20½
B.6399	26	1½	Junc. B.6357/B.6399	19
..	37¾	11¾	*Shankend (Sta.)	7¼
..	40¾	3	Stobs Camp (entrance)	4¼
..	45	4¼	*Hawick	

32. PEEBLES to WOOLER.

A scenic road mainly following the Tweed valley. After passing near the Eildon Hills at Melrose, the country is agricultural and becomes less hilly. Approaching Kelso the scanty remains of *Roxburgh Castle are passed, and there is a fine view of *Floors Castle on the north bank of the River Tweed, while at Cornhill the Border is crossed into England. A stone to the south of the road between Cornhill and Milfield, commemorates the battle of Flodden. Views of the *Cheviot Hills to the south, on the latter part.

A.72			*Peebles	.. 60¼
..	6¼	6¼	*Innerleithen	.. 53¾
..	8½	2	*Walkerburn	.. 51¾
..	15	6½	*Clovenfords	.. 45¼
A.6091	18½	3½	*Galashiels	.. 41¾
..	22½	4	*Melrose	.. 37¾
A.68	24¼	2¼	Junc. A.6091/A.68	35½
..	25¼	½	*Newtown St. Boswells	35
A.699	26¼	1	*St. Boswells Green	34
..	28	1¾	*Maxton	.. 32¼
A.698	36¼	8¼	*Kelso	.. 23¾
..	41½	5¼	*Birgham	.. 18½
..	45¼	4	*Coldstream	.. 14½
..	47	1¾	Cornhill	.. 13¾
A.697	47¼	¼	Coldstream Sta.	13
..	54¼	7	Milfield	.. 6
..	57¼	3	Akeld	.. 3
..	60¼	3	Wooler	

33. PEEBLES to BERWICK-UPON-TWEED via Duns.

A cross-country route at first along the pleasant Tweed valley to Galashiels, then avoiding Melrose, using narrow, undulating roads in places, to reach Greenlaw. Flat rural country between Duns and Berwick. The recommended route to Berwick is by Coldstream Iter. 32 and 30, and the shortest way from Greenlaw to Berwick is by Iter. 8.

A.72			*Peebles	.. 59¼
..	6¼	6¼	*Innerleithen	.. 53¼
..	8½	2	*Walkerburn	.. 51¼
..	15	6½	*Clovenfords	.. 44¾
A.6091	18½	3½	*Galashiels	.. 41¼
B.6360	21¼	2¾	Junc. A.6091/B.6360	38¼
..	22	¾	Gattonside	.. 37¼
A.68	24	2	Leaderfoot Bridge (near side)	.. 35¼
A.6105	26¼	2¼	*Earlston	.. 33¼
..	32¾	6½	*Gordon	27
..	37¼	4½	*Greenlaw	.. 22½
..	40¼	3	*Polwarth	.. 19¼
..	44¼	3¾	*Duns	.. 15¼
..	54¼	10¼	*Foulden	5
A.699	58¼	4	Junc. A.6105/A.699	1
..	59¼	1	*Berwick-upon-Tweed	

34. PEEBLES to HAWICK via Ettrick Forest.

A cross-country moorland route utilising narrow and hilly roads in places, but with no serious gradients. If preferred, an alternative road (B.7062) along the south bank of the wooded River Tweed can be used to Traquair instead of the main road via Innerleithen. Between Traquair and Gordon Arms the route crosses from the Tweed valley to Yarrow Vale in Ettrick Forest and is known as the Paddy Slacks road. The climb over the next ridge to reach the Ettrick valley is followed by a winding moorland road leading to Hawick, in Teviotdale. The main road route is by Selkirk, Inter. 14 and 11.

A.72			*Peebles	.. 37¼
B.709	6¼	6¼	*Innerleithen	.. 30¾
..	8	1¾	*Traquair	.. 29¼
..	15	7	*" Gordon Arms " Inn	22¼
B.711	21½	6½	*" Tushielaw " Inn	15¾
..	24¼	2¾	*Buccleuch	13
..	32¼	8	*Roberton	5
A.7	35½	3¼	Junc. B711/A.7	1½
..	37¼	1¾	*Hawick	

35. PEEBLES to AYR via Mauchline.

Pleasant moorlands beyond the Lyne valley, and later through agricultural country, with mining developments in places. A better way between Muirkirk and Ayr is by Cumnock, see Iter. 21.

A.72			*Peebles	.. 72
..	4¼	4¼	*Lyne Ch.	.. 67¾
..	9½	5¼	*Blyth Bridge	.. 62½
..	15¼	5¼	*Skirling	.. 56¾
..	17¾	2½	*Biggar	.. 54¼
..	21¼	3½	*Symington	.. 50¾
A.73	22	¾	Junc. A.72/A.73	50
A.70	27¼	5¼	*Hyndford Bridge	44¾
..	33	5¼	Rigside	39
..	37	4	*Douglas	35
..	47¼	10¼	*Muirkirk	.. 24¾
B.743	49¼	2	Junc. A.70/B.743	22¾
..	56¾	7½	*Sorn	.. 15¼
A.758	60¼	4	*Mauchline	.. 11½
..	63¼	2¼	*Failford	.. 8¼
..	68¼	5½	*Auchincruive	.. 3¼
A.719	70	1	Whitletts	2
..	72	2	*Ayr	

36. NORTH BERWICK to HAWICK.

A cross-country route to Humbie through the golfing district of East Lothian, with coastal scenery at first. Fine, open views from the summit of Soutra Hill (1,131 feet), then through moorland and agricultural country in Lauderdale. The Eildon Hills are seen to the west after crossing the Tweed at Leaderfoot Bridge, after which an easy road beyond Ancrum Bridge leads through Teviotdale.

A.198			*North Berwick	63½
..	2½	2½	*Dirleton	61
..	4½	1½	*Muirfield	59¼
..	4¾	½	*Gullane	58¾
A.6137	7½	2¾	*Aberlady	56
..	13	5½	*Haddington	50½
..	16	3	*Bolton	47½
..	22	6	*Humbie (P.O.)	41½
A.68	24½	2½	Junc. A.6137/A.68	39
..	30½	6	*Carfraemill	33
..	34½	4	*Lauder	29
..	41½	7	*Earlston	22
..	44	2½	Leaderfoot Bridge	19½
..	46¼	2¼	*Newtown St. Boswells	17¼
..	47¼	1	*St. Boswells Green	16¼
..	52¼	5¼	*Ancrum Bridge	11
A.698	52¾	½	Junc. A.68/A.698	10¾
..	58¼	5¼	*Denholm	5
..	63½	5	*Hawick	

37. NORTH BERWICK to LANARK via Dalkeith.

A cross-country link, at first through the golfing district of East Lothian. Coastal scenery at *Gosford Bay, near Aberlady, then passing *Seton Castle beyond Longniddry and skirting the battlefield of *Prestonpans. After Leadburn, mainly agricultural to Lanark. The quickest way is by Edinburgh, Iter. 2 and 22.

A.198			*North Berwick	57½
..	2½	2½	*Dirleton	54½
..	4½	1½	*Muirfield	53
..	4¾	½	*Gullane	52¾
..	7½	2¾	*Aberlady	49¾
..	10½	3½	*Longniddry	46½
..	14½	3½	Prestonpans Sta.	43
A.6094	15¾	1½	Wallyford Toll X-rds.	41½
..	16½	½	*Wallyford	41
..	20½	4	*Dalkeith	37
..	20¾	¼	*Eskbank	36¾
..	22	1¼	*Bonnyrigg	35¾
..	24½	2½	Rosewell	33
..	28½	4	*Howgate	28½
A.701	30¼	1½	*Leadburn	27
..	32½	2¼	*Lamancha	24¾
..	37	4½	*Romanno Bridge	20¼
..	39½	2½	*Blyth Bridge	17¾
A.721	40½	1	Junc. A.701/A.721	17
..	44½	4	Elsrickle	13
..	48½	4	*Newbigging	9
A.70	50½	2½	*Carnwath	6¾
..	53¼	2½	*Carstairs	4
A.743	54½	1	Ravenstruther	3
..	57½	3	*Lanark	

38. NORTH BERWICK to COLD-STREAM.

A pleasant road touching the coast in places to Cockburnspath, after which the road is rather winding through mainly agricultural country. Two miles from North Berwick there is a fine view of the *Bass Rock from Canty Bay, and the ruins of *Tantallon Castle lie just beyond. At Broxburn a stone commemorates the battle of Dunbar.

A.198			*North Berwick	46½
..	5½	5½	*Whitekirk	41
..	7¼	1¾	*Tynninghame	39¼
A.1	8½	1	Junc. A.198/A.1	38¼
..	13½	5	*Broxburn	33¼
..	20½	7	*Cockburnspath	26¼
A.6112	25	4½	*Grant's House	21½
..	31½	6½	*Preston	15¼
..	34	2½	*Duns	12½
..	37	3	Mount Pleasant X-rds.	9½
..	40	3	*Swinton	6½
..	45½	5½	Lennel	1
..	46½	1	*Coldstream	

39. DUNBAR to KELSO.

Pleasant coast scenery to Cockburnspath, then a rather winding road through a mainly agricultural district. At Broxburn a stone commemorates the battle of Dunbar.

A.1087			*Dunbar	38
A.1	1½	1½	*Broxburn	36½
..	8½	7	*Cockburnspath	29½
A.6112	13½	4½	*Grant's House	24½
..	19½	6¼	*Preston	18½
..	22¼	2¼	*Duns	15¾
B.6460	25¼	3	Mount Pleasant X-rds.	12¾
Uncl.	25½	¼	Junc. B.6460/Uncl.	12½
A.699	28¼	2¾	Swinton Mill X-rds.	9¾
..	30	1½	Leitholm	8
..	32½	2½	*Eccles	5½
..	35¾	3¼	*Ednam	2¼
..	38	2¼	*Kelso	

40. DUNBAR to PEEBLES via TEMPLE.

A fast and easy road to Haddington, then a cross-country route, with rural scenery changing to moorland approaching the Moorfoot Hills, beyond Temple.

A.1087			*Dunbar	42¾
..	1	1	Belhaven	41¾
..	1¾	¾	West Barns	41
A.1	2¼	½	Junc. A.1087/A.1	40¼
..	5¾	3¼	*East Linton (By-pass)	37
A.6093	10½	4¾	Junc. A.1/A.6093	32¼
..	11¼	¾	*Haddington	31½
..	16¾	5½	*Pencaitland	26
A.68	21¼	4½	Junc. A.6093/A.68	21½
B.6372	21¾	½	Junc. A.68/B.6372	21
..	25¼	3½	*Gorebridge	17½
..	28¼	3	*Temple	14½
Uncl.	31	2¾	Junc. B.6372/Uncl.	11¾
A.703	35¾	4¾	Junc. Uncl./A.703	7
..	38¼	2½	*Eddleston	4½
..	42¾	4½	*Peebles	

41. SELKIRK to EYEMOUTH.

A cross-country link, with pleasant scenery in the *Scott Country and Tweed valley at first. Narrow, undulating roads between Earlston and Greenlaw, moorland in places, becoming mainly agricultural on the latter part. The fastest way to Duns is by Kelso, see Iter. 46 and 39.

A.7			*Selkirk	44
B.6360	2½	2½	Junc. A.7/B.6360	41¾
..	4½	2¼	*Abbotsford House	39½
A.6091	6	1½	Junc. B.6360/A.6091	38
B.6361	7½	1½	*Melrose	36½
..	8¾	1¼	*Newstead	35¼
A.68	9¾	1	Leaderfoot Bridge	34¼
A.6105	12¼	2½	*Earlston	31¾
..	18½	6¼	*Gordon	25½
..	23	4½	*Greenlaw	21
..	26¼	3¼	*Polwarth	17¾
..	30	3¾	*Duns	14
B.6355	36	6	Junc. A.6105/B.6355	8
..	36½	½	*Chirnside	7½
A.1	41¼	4¾	Junc. B.6355/A.1	2¾
B.6355	41¾	½	*Ayton	2¼
..	44	2¼	*Eyemouth	

42. SELKIRK to CARLISLE via Ettrick Forest and Annan.

A touring route, through fine open moorlands following the Ettrick and Tima valleys over the ridge into Eskdale. Narrow between Eskdalemuir and Lockerbie. Flat agricultural scenery in Annandale. See Iter. 11, 12 and 13 for alternative routes.

B.7009			*Selkirk	72¼
..	7¼	7¼	*Ettrick Bridge End	65
B.709	14½	7¼	Junc. B.7009/B.709	57¾
..	15	½	*"Tushielaw" Inn	57¼
..	17¾	2¾	*Ettrick	54½
B.723	30¼	12½	*Eskdalemuir Ch.	42
..	37½	7¼	Boreland	34¾
A.74	44	6½	Junc. B.723/A.74	28¼
..	44½	½	*Lockerbie	27¾
B.723	45	½	Junc. A.74/B.723	27¼
..	50½	5½	*Hoddom Bridge	21¾
A.75	54½	3¾	Junc. B.723/A.75	18
..	55	½	*Annan	17¼
..	57½	2½	*Dornock	14¾
..	58¼	¾	Eastriggs	14
..	61¼	3	Rigg	11
A.74	63¼	2	*Gretna	9
..	63½	¼	*Sark Bridge (The Border)	8¼
A.7	69¾	6¼	Kingstown	2½
..	72¼	2½	Carlisle	

43. SELKIRK to CARTER BAR via the Scott Country.

A touring route visiting places of interest in the *Scott Country. Between Abbotsford House and Melrose the Eildon Hills are seen to the south-east, and a detour can be made to *Darnick Tower. The tour then proceeds via Earlston to reach Bemersyde and Dryburgh Abbey, returning to the main road at St. Boswells. *Ferniehirst Castle is passed just beyond Jedburgh, and there are extensive views northwards on the ascent approaching the summit at Carter Bar (1,371 feet) on the Cheviot ridge, where the Border is crossed into England. See Iter. 4 for alternative destinations in England and Iter. 46 for the direct road between Selkirk and St. Boswells Green.

A.7			*Selkirk	41
B.6360	2½	2½	Junc. A.7/B.6360	38½
..	4½	2¼	*Abbotsford House	36½

A.6091	6	1½	Junc.	
			B.6360/A.6091	35
B.6361	7½	1½	*Melrose ..	33½
..	8½	1¼	*Newstead ..	32¼
A.68	9¼	1	Leaderfoot Bridge	31¼
A.6105	12¼	2½	*Earlston ..	28¼
B.6356	12½	¼	Junc.	
			A.6105/B.6356	28¼
..	15¾	3¼	*Bemersyde Hill	25¼
..	16¼	½	*Bemersyde House	24½
..	18	1½	*Dryburgh Abbey	23
B.6404	20	2	Junc.	
			B.6356/B.6404	21
..	21½	1½	*St. Boswells ..	19½
A.68	21¾	¼	Junc. B.6404/A.68	19¼
..	22	¼	*St. Boswells	
			Green ..	19
..	27¼	5¼	*Ancrum Bridge	13¾
..	28½	1¼	Bonjedward ..	12½
..	30½	2	*Jedburgh ..	10½
..	41	10½	*Carter Bar	

44. HAWICK to CARTER BAR.

An undulating road, with fine moorland scenery, gradually ascending to Carter Bar (1,371 feet) on the Cheviot ridge.

A.698			*Hawick ..	16
A.6088	1½	1½	Junc.	
			A.698/A.6088	14½
..	3¾	2	Kirkton ..	12¼
..	7½	3¾	*Bonchester Bridge	8½
..	10½	3	*Southdean ..	5½
A.68	15¾	5¼	Junc. A.6088/A.68	¼
..	16	¼	*Carter Bar	

45. DUMFRIES to HAWICK.

Agricultural to Lockerbie, then a scenic cross-country moorland road to Langholm. An easy climb to Mosspaul is followed by a pleasant run through Teviotdale.

A.709			*Dumfries ..	53¼
..	4¼	4¼	*Torthorwald ..	49
..	8½	4¼	*Lochmaben ..	44¾
..	12½	4	*Lockerbie ..	40¾
..	15½	3	Tundergarth ..	37¾
..	16¾	1¼	Bankshill ..	36½
A.7	30¼	13½	*Langholm ..	22¾
..	34¾	4½	*Ewes P.O. ..	18½
..	40¾	6	"Mosspaul" Hotel	12½
..	44½	3¾	*Teviothead ..	8¾
..	48¾	4¼	Newmill ..	4½
.	53¼	4½	*Hawick	

46. DUMFRIES to BERWICK-UPON-TWEED via Selkirk.

Pleasant, wooded agricultural country to Moffat. After passing the Grey Mare's Tail waterfall (on left), the road climbs to the moorlands of Ettrick Forest. Picturesque scenery on the descent past *St. Mary's Loch to Yarrow Vale, and well wooded in places approaching Selkirk. Hilly to St. Boswells, passing close to the village of *Bowden at the foot of the Eildon Hills, then an easy road in the Tweed valley, passing the scanty remains of *Roxburgh Castle. *Floors Castle is well seen entering Kelso. The quickest way from Dumfries to Kelso is by Hawick, Iter. 45 and 30, while places of interest in the *Scott Country can be visited by following Iter. 43 from Selkirk to St. Boswells. Between Kelso and Berwick agricultural districts are traversed, but the main road (Iter. 30) continues with the Tweed valley via Coldstream, although there is little to choose between these two roads. At Swinton a diversion can be made to include *Ladykirk and Norham Castle, by following B.6470 across the Tweed (The Border) and thence by A.698 to Berwick.

A.701			*Dumfries ..	97¼
..	3½	3½	Locharbriggs ..	94
..	4½	1¼	*Amisfield ..	92¾
..	7½	3	*Ae Bridge ..	89¾
..	8½	¾	Parkgate ..	89
..	13½	5	*St. Ann's ..	84
A.74	18½	5½	Junc. A.701/A.74	78¾
..	19	½	*Beattock (Sta.)	78½
A.701	19¼	¼	Junc. A.74/A.701	78
A.708	21	1¾	*Moffat ..	76¼
..	25½	4½	Shortwoodend ..	71¾
..	31	5½	*Grey Mare's Tail	66¼
..	32½	1½	*Birkhill ..	65
..	36¼	4	*"Tibbie Shiel's"	
			Inn ..	61
..	37½	1	*"Rodono" Hotel	60
..	38¼	1	Coppercleuch ..	59
..	42½	4¼	*"Gordon Arms"	
			Inn ..	54¾
..	46½	4	*Yarrow Ch. ..	50¾
..	50½	4	*Broadmeadows	46¾
A.707	54¼	4	Junc. A.708/A.707	42¾
A.7	55	½	*Selkirk ..	42¼
A.699	55¾	¾	Junc. A.7/A.699	41½
..	63¾	8	*St. Boswells	
			Green ..	33½
..	65½	1¾	*Maxton ..	31¾
..	74	8½	*Kelso ..	23¾
..	76¼	2¼	*Ednam ..	21
..	79½	3¼	*Eccles ..	17¾
..	82	2½	Leitholm ..	15½
..	83¾	1¾	Swinton Mill	
			X-rds. ..	13¾
..	85½	1¾	*Swinton ..	11¾
..	97¼	11¾	*Berwick-upon-Tweed	

47. DUMFRIES to BERWICK-UPON-TWEED via the Border Country.

A touring route, utilising by-roads in the *Border Country for the greater part. A pleasant alternative to the main road as far as Annan, passing near *Ruthwell Church, which lies to the north of the road just beyond Clarencefield, then an undulating by-road to Canonbie. The quickest way to Canonbie is by Iter. 67 to Gretna Green thence by roads A.6071 and A.7 (32½ miles). Pretty scenery in Liddesdale to Riccarton, after which the road ascends across lonely moorlands to the summit (1,250 feet) near Note o' the Gate, 5 miles beyond Riccarton. There are extensive views hereabouts before descending to Bonchester Bridge. A hilly by-road is then followed to Jedburgh, and after a short stretch of main road a detour is made past the foothills of the *Cheviots to Yetholm. The Border is then crossed into England, close to the scene of the battle of Flodden, which lies to the north of the road. Traverses pleasant undulating agricultural country on the latter part. The quickest way from Crailing to Berwick is by Kelso and Coldstream, Iter. 30.

A.75			*Dumfries ..	107½
B.724	3½	3½	Collin ..	103½
..	9½	6½	*Clarencefield ..	97¼
..	13½	3½	*Cummertrees ..	94
A.75	16½	3	Junc. B.724/A.75	91
..	16¾	¼	*Annan ..	90¼
B.6357	17½	½	Junc. A.75/B.6357	90
..	23	5¼	*Kirkpatrick	
			Fleming ..	84¾
..	26	3	Chapelknowe ..	81¾
A.7	32	6	*Canonbie ..	75¼
B.6357	32½	½	Junc. A.7/B.6357	75
..	33½	1	Rowanburn ..	74
..	42½	9	*Newcastleton ..	65
..	49	6½	*Riccarton ..	58¼
A.6088	60	11	Junc.	
			B.6357/A.6088	47¼
B.6357	61	1	*Bonchester	
			Bridge ..	46¼
A.68	67	6	Junc. B.6357/A.68	40¼
..	68½	1½	*Jedburgh ..	38½
A.698	70½	2	Bonjedward ..	36½
..	73	2½	Crailing ..	34½
..	75	2	*Eckford Ch. ..	32¼
B.6401	75½	½	Junc.	
			A.698/B.6401	32
..	79¾	4¼	*Morebattle ..	27½
B.6352	84	4¼	*Yetholm ..	23½
..	88¼	4¼	Mindrum Mill ..	19
A.697	94	5¾	Junc.	
			B.6352/A.697	13¾
B.6354	94½	½	Junc.	
			A.697/B.6354	12¾
..	97	2½	Etal ..	10¼
..	107¼	10¼	*Berwick-upon-Tweed	

48. DUMFRIES to LANARK via Mennock Pass or via Sanquhar.

On leaving Dumfries, a short detour can be made to visit *Lincluden Abbey before joining the main road along the pretty Nith valley, afterwards ascending the winding Mennock Pass to Wanlockhead, the highest village in Scotland (1,380 feet). The summit is reached between Wanlockhead and Leadhills where the road attains a height of 1,531 feet, with extensive views of the Lowther Hills. A long descent leads to Abington through moorland country, afterwards becoming agricultural. The alternative by Sanquhar follows the narrow, winding valleys of the Crawick and Duneaton Waters to A.74. The recommended route to Abington is by Beattock (Iter. 46 and 50) and between Abington and Lanark by Iter. 50. A further alternative is via the Dalveen Pass, see Iter. 56.

A.76			*Dumfries ..	57
..	2¼	2¼	*New Bridge ..	54¾
..	3½	1	Holywood ..	53¼
..	7½	4	*Auldgirth ..	49¼
..	12¼	4¾	*Closeburn ..	44¾
..	14½	2¼	*Thornhill ..	42½
..	16¼	1¾	*Carronbridge ..	40¾
..	20¼	4	†*Enterkinfoot ..	36¾
B.797	24¼	4	Junc. A.76/B.797	32¾
..	30½	6¼	*Wanlockhead ..	26½
..	32¼	1¾	*Leadhills ..	24¾
A.74	38½	6¼	*Abington	
			(By-pass) ..	18¼
A.70	47½	8½	Junc. A.74/A.70	9½
..	49¼	1¾	Rigside ..	7¾
A.73	54½	5¼	*Hyndford Bridge	2½
..	57	2½	*Lanark	
			†	
			OR	
			via Sanquhar	
			*Enterkinfoot	
A.76	20¼		*Mennock	
..	24¼	4¼	*Mennock	
..	26¼	2¼	*Sanquhar	

B.740	27½	¾	Junc. A.76/B.740	
..	39¾	12¼	*Crawfordjohn	
A.74	41½	1½	Junc. B740/A.74	
A.70	46¾	5¼	Junc. A.74/A.70	
..	48¼	1½	Rigside	
A.73	53½	5¼	*Hyndford Bridge	
..	56¼	2½	*Lanark	

49. MOFFAT to AYR via the Mennock Pass.

A touring route through the Lowlands, reaching an altitude of 1,025 feet at Beattock summit, and again ascending from Elvanfoot, with views of the Lowther Hills, to another summit (1,531 feet) between Leadhills and Wanlockhead, the latter being the highest village in Scotland (1,380 feet). Descends by the Mennock Pass, over 1,400 feet high, to the main road in upper Nithsdale, until, beyond Kirkconnel, a hilly cross-country moorland road is followed to Straiton. Afterwards continues through undulating country, and, nearing the coast between Maybole and Dunure, the *Croy (electric) Brae is traversed. A short diversion is made to visit Dunure, whence there is a fine coastal run into Ayr.

A.701			*Moffat ..	77½
B.719	2½	2½	Junc. A.701/B.719	75
A.74	5½	3	Junc. B.719/A.74	72
..	9¼	3¾	*Beattock Summit	68¼
A.702	12¾	3½	Junc. A.74/A.702	64¾
B.7040	13¾	1	*Elvanfoot ..	63¾
B.797	18¼	4¼	*Leadhills ..	59
..	20¼	1½	*Wanlockhead ..	57¼
A.76	26¼	6¼	Junc. B.797/A.76	51
..	26¾	¼	*Mennock ..	50¾
..	29	2¼	*Sanquhar ..	48½
..	32¼	3¼	*Kirkconnel	45
B.741	39¼	7¼	Junc. A.76/B.741	37¼
A.713	50	10¼	*Dalmellington	27¼
B.741	50½	½	Junc. A.713/B.741	27
..	57	6½	*Straiton	20¼
Uncl.	60	3	Junc. B.741/Uncl.	17½
B.7023	60¾	¾	Crosshill	16¾
..	63¼	2½	*Maybole ..	14
A.719	65¾	2¼	Junc. B.7023/A.719	11¾
Uncl.	69¼	3½	*Dunure Mains ..	8¼
..	70¼	1	*Dunure	7¼
A.719	71	¾	Junc. Uncl./A.719	6¼
..	75¾	4½	Doonfoot	1½
..	77¼	1½	*Ayr	

50. CARLISLE to STIRLING.

After crossing the Border at Sark Bridge, this main road into central Scotland is a fine, easy run through picturesque open country in Annandale. Traverses moorland scenery after Beattock, and reaches an altitude of 1,025 feet at the summit, followed by a pleasant stretch along the Clyde valley. Mining and agricultural districts, with several level crossings, between Lanark and Stirling.

A.7			Carlisle ..	111¼
A.74	2½	2½	Kingstown ..	109
..	8¾	6¼	*Sark Bridge	
			(The Border)	102½
..	9	¼	*Gretna ..	102½
..	9½	½	*Gretna Green	102
..	12¼	3¼	*Kirkpatrick	
			Fleming ..	98¾
..	15¼	3	*Kirtlebride ..	95¾
..	19	3¼	*Ecclefechan ..	92¼
..	24½	5½	*Lockerbie ..	86¾
..	32	7½	*Johnstone Bridge	79¼
..	38¾	6¾	*Beattock (Sta.)	72½

..	49¼	10½	*Beattock Summit	62¼
..	54¼	5	*Crawford ..	57¼
A.73	57½	3¼	*Abington	
			(By-pass) ..	54
..	60½	3¼	Roberton ..	50¾
..	72½	11¾	*Hyndford Bridge	39
..	75	2½	*Lanark ..	36¼
..	79¼	4¼	*Braidwood ..	32¼
..	80½	1¼	*Carluke ..	30¾
..	84¼	3¾	*Newmains ..	27
..	88¼	4	Newhouse	23
..	89¾	1½	Chapelhall	21½
..	91¼	1½	*Airdrie ..	19½
A.80	98¼	7	*Cumbernauld	12¼
..	100¼	1½	*Castlecary	11
..	102	1½	*Dennyloanhead	9¼
..	104¼	2½	*Denny ..	7
A.9	110¼	5¼	*St. Ninian's ..	1¼
..	111½	1¼	*Stirling	

51. GLASGOW to CARLISLE or LONGTOWN (for Newcastle upon Tyne).

An easy road through industrial and mining districts on the earlier part, later crossing open moorlands. Beyond Crawford, the road reaches an altitude of 1,025 feet at Beattock summit, and then descends through picturesque open country in Annandale. Crosses the Border into England at Sark Bridge. Near Gretna Green, an alternative road branches across the Border to Longtown and provides the recommended route to Newcastle during the winter months, See Iter. 52 for the route via Carter Bar.

A.721			*Glasgow ..	94¼
A.74	4¾	4¾	Mount Vernon	89¼
..	5½	¾	Broomhouse	88¾
..	7½	2	*Uddingston	86¾
..	8¼	1¼	*Bothwell	85¼
..	9½	1¼	*Bothwell Bridge	84¾
..	11	1½	*Hamilton	83¼
..	14½	3½	*Larkhall	79¾
..	22¼	7¾	*Lesmahagow ..	72
..	36¼	14¼	*Abington	
			(By-pass)	57¾
..	40	3¾	*Crawford	54¼
..	45	5	*Beattock Summit	49¼
..	55½	10½	*Beattock (Sta.)	38½
..	61¼	6¼	*Johnstone Bridge	32
..	69¼	7½	*Lockerbie	24¾
..	75¼	5½	*Ecclefechan ..	19
..	78½	3¼	*Kirtlebride	15¾
..	81½	3	†*Kirkpatrick	
			Fleming	12¾
..	84¼	3¼	*Gretna Green ..	9¼
..	85¼	½	*Gretna	9
..	85¼	¼	*Sark Br. (Border)	8¾
A.7	91¼	6¼	*Kingstown ..	2½
..	94¼	2½	Carlisle	
			Thence by road A.6 to:—	
..	112¼	18¼	Penrith.	
..	213¼	100¼	Manchester	
			OR	
..	112¼	18¼	Penrith. By A.66 to	
..	162¼	49¼	Scotch Corner	
			Great North Road. (A.1)	
..	398¼	236	London	
†			OR	
			*Kirkpatrick Fleming	
A.6071	84	2¼	Junc. A.74/A.6071	
..	84¼	¼	*Springfield	
..	85	½	The Border	
A.7	87¾	2½	Junc. A.6071/A.7	
..	88¼	½	Longtown	
			Thence by roads A.6071 and A.69 to :—	
..	149¼	61	Newcastle upon Tyne	

52. GLASGOW to CARTER BAR (for Newcastle upon Tyne).

A fast road, at first through industrial and mining districts, with several level crossings between Newhouse and Carluke. Afterwards, a moorland road is succeeded by a fine scenic run, mainly along the Tweed valley to Melrose, where the Eildon Hills are seen to the south. After Jedburgh, *Ferniehirst Castle is passed, and there are extensive views to the north on the ascent approaching the summit at Carter Bar (1,371 feet) on the Cheviot ridge, where the Border is crossed into England. Owing to the high altitudes and undulating open roads it is advisable to use the route via Longtown (Iter. 51) during the winter months. A detour to include the places of interest in the *Scott Country can be made via Selkirk, see Iter. 14 and 43.

A.8			*Glasgow ..	96
A.73	13½	13½	Newhouse ..	82¼
..	17½	4	*Newmains ..	78¾
A.721	21	3½	*Carluke	75
A.70	27½	6½	Junc. A.721/A.70	68½
A.721	30	2½	*Carnwath	66
..	32¼	2¼	*Newbigging ..	63¾
..	36¼	4	Elsrickle	59¾
A.72	40¼	4	Junc. A.721/A.72	55¾
..	41	¾	*Blyth Bridge	55
..	46½	5½	*Lyne Church ..	49½
..	50½	4¼	*Peebles ..	45¼
..	57¼	6½	*Innerleithen	38¼
..	59¼	2	*Walkerburn ..	36¼
..	65¾	6½	*Clovenfords ..	30¼
A.6091	69¼	3½	*Galashiels ..	26¾
..	73¼	4	*Melrose ..	22¾
A.68	75¼	2¼	Junc. A.6091/A.68	20¼
..	76	½	*Newtown St.	
			Boswells	20
..	77	1	*St. Boswells	
			Green	19
..	82¼	5¼	*Ancrum Bridge	13¼
..	83¼	1½	Bonjedward ..	12¼
..	85½	2	*Jedburgh ..	10½
..	96	10¼	*Carter Bar (The	
			Border)	
			Thence by roads A.68 and A.696 to :—	
..	143¼	47¼	Newcastle-upon-Tyne	

53. GLASGOW to PEEBLES via the Clyde Valley.

Heavy traffic through an industrial district to Hamilton, then pleasant orchard scenery in the Clyde valley to Lanark. Crosses moorland country before joining the Tweed valley near Lyne. The fastest route to Lanark and Peebles is by Newhouse and Carluke (Iter. 52 and 54), while a better way to Hamilton is by Uddingston (Iter. 51).

A.724			*Glasgow ..	55¾
..	4¾	4¾	*Cambuslang	51
..	9¾	5	Burnbank	46
A.74	11¼	1½	*Hamilton ..	44½
A.72	14	2¾	Junc. A.74/A.72	41½
..	18¼	4¼	Rosebank	37¼
..	20¼	2½	*Crossford	35
..	22	1¾	Hazelbank	33¾
..	24½	2½	*Kirkfieldbank ..	31¼
A.73	25¼	1	*Lanark	30¼
..	28	2¾	*Hyndford Bridge	27¼
A.72	33½	5½	Junc. A.73/A.72	22
..	34¼	¾	*Symington ..	21¼

..	38	3½	*Biggar	17¾
..	40½	2½	*Skirling	15¼
..	46	5½	*Blyth Bridge	9¾
..	51½	5½	*Lyne Ch.	4¼
..	55¾	4¼	*Peebles	

54. GLASGOW to LANARK via Motherwell.
Mainly industrial in character with heavy traffic to Wishaw. For fast travel the route via Newhouse is recommended, see Iter. 52.

A.721			*Glasgow	26
A.74	4½	4½	*Mount Vernon	21¼
..	5½	½	Broomhouse	20½
A.721	6½	1¼	Junc. A.74/A.721	19½
..	9½	2¾	*Bellshill	16½
..	12	2½	**Motherwell**	14
..	15½	3½	*Wishaw	10½
..	16½	1¼	Waterloo	9¼
A.73	18	1½	Junc. A.721/A.73	8
..	20½	2½	*Carluke	5¾
..	21½	1½	*Braidwood	4¼
..	26	4¼	**Lanark**	

55. GLASGOW to STRANRAER.
Heavy traffic to Giffnock, then a fast arterial road, with open moorland in places, to Kilmarnock and then becoming agricultural until reaching the coast at Prestwick, where the Airport is passed. After Ayr, the road is undulating with pleasant valley scenery, returning to the coast at Girvan, afterwards following the shore through Kennedy's Pass to Ballantrae, beyond which there is a climb inland before descending through Glen App to the shores of Loch Ryan. If proceeding to Glenluce, Stranraer may be avoided by following A.751 from Innermessan to join A.75 east of Stranraer.

A.77			*Glasgow	84¼
..	5	5	*Giffnock	79¾
..	7½	2½	*Newton Mearns	77¼
..	16¾	9½	*Fenwick (By-pass)	68
..	21	4¼	**Kilmarnock**	63¾
..	22½		Riccarton	62½
..	30¼		*Prestwick (By-pass)	54½
..	33	2¾	*Ayr	51¼
..	38½	5½	Minishant	46¼
..	42½	3½	*Maybole	42¼
..	44½	2¼	*Crossraguel Abbey	40¼
..	46½	2½	*Kirkoswald	38
..	54½	7¾	*Girvan	30¼
..	61	6½	*Lendalfoot	23¾
..	67½	6½	*Ballantrae	17½
..	78¾	11¼	*Cairn Ryan	6
..	82¼	3½	*Innermessan	2½
..	84¾	2½	*Stranraer	

56. GLASGOW to DUMFRIES via Strathaven and the Dalveen Pass.
A good alternative exit from Glasgow, with heavy traffic at first, then climbing to the moorlands, with pleasant views in places. Follows the Clyde valley for several miles beyond Abington, after which there are extensive views towards the Lowther Hills, and reaches an altitude of 1,140 feet at the head of the Dalveen Pass, before descending towards the Nith. *Durisdeer Church lies to the east of the road in Nithsdale, and after New Bridge a short detour can be made to visit *Lincluden Abbey. The main road is by Beattock, Iter. 51 and 24.

A.749			*Glasgow	77
..	3½	3½	*Rutherglen	73½
A.726	8½	5½	*East Kilbride	68½
..	14	5½	Chapelton	63
..	16¾	2¼	*Strathaven	60¼
Uncl.	22½	6	Boghead	54¼
A.74	25	2½	Junc. Uncl./A.74	52
..	25¼	¼	*Lesmahagow	51¾
..	39¾	14¼	*Abington (By-pass)	37¼
..	43	3¼	*Crawford	34
A.702	44½	1½	Junc. A.74/A.702	32¼
..	45½	1	*Elvanfoot	31½
A.76	60½	15¼	*Carronbridge	16¼
..	62½	1½	*Thornhill	14½
..	64¾	2¼	*Closeburn	12¼
..	69½	4¾	*Auldgirth	7¾
..	73½	4	Holywood	3¾
..	74½	1	*New Bridge	2¾
..	77	2½	**Dumfries**	

57. GLASGOW to ARDROSSAN.
An easy road through agricultural country beyond the suburbs of Glasgow. Becomes industrial near Kilwinning.

A.736			*Glasgow	29¼
..	3½	3½	*Pollokshaws	25¾
..	8	4½	**Barrhead**	21¼
..	14¾	6¾	Lugton	14½
..	17¼	2½	Burnhouse	12
B.778	19½	2¼	Junc. A.736/B.778	9¾
A.78	24¼	4¾	*Kilwinning	5
..	26¾	2½	*Stevenston (By-pass)	2½
A.738	28½	2	Junc. A.78/A.738	½
..	29¼	½	*Ardrossan	

58. GLASGOW to LARGS.
Industrial to Paisley, then through agricultural country. Ascends to the moors beyond Kilbirnie; care required on the descent of Hailey Brae (1 in 10) with two hairpin bends half a mile before joining the main coast road into Largs.

A.737			*Glasgow	30
..	7	7	*Paisley	23
..	9½	2½	*Elderslie	20½
..	13¼	3¾	*Howwood	16¾
A.760	16	2¾	Junc. A.737/A.760	14
..	16¾	¾	*Lochwinnoch	13¼
..	20¼	4	*Kilbirnie	9½
A.78	29	8¾	Junc. A.760/A.78	1
..	30	1	*Largs	

59. GLASGOW to GOUROCK or WEMYSS BAY.
Busy industrial route at first running along the shores of the Clyde. Govan can be avoided—see Glasgow town plan. The alternative shows the direct road from Greenock to Inverkip and Wemyss Bay, but the coast road via Gourock (Iter. 65) is easier and more scenic.

A.8			*Glasgow	25½
..	4	4	*Govan	21½
..	6½	2½	*Renfrew	19¼
..	12	5½	*Bishopton	13½
..	15½	3½	Langbank	10
..	19¼	3¾	*Port Glasgow	6¼
..	22½	3¼	†*Greenock	3
..	25½	3	*Gourock	
			†	
			OR	
A.742	22½		*Greenock	
A.78	27	4½	Junc. A.742/A.78	
..	27¾	¾	*Inverkip	
..	30½	2¾	*Wemyss Bay	

60. PAISLEY to AYR.
An easy road through agricultural districts, becoming flat beyond Irvine. Passes Prestwick Airport between Monkton and Prestwick.

A.726			*Paisley	33½
B.771	1½	1½	Junc. A.726/B.771	31¾
A.736	4	2½	*Barrhead	29¼
..	10½	6½	Lugton	22½
..	13½	2½	Burnhouse	20½
A.78	22	8½	*Irvine	11½
..	27	5	*Loans	6½
A.77	30¼	3¾	*Prestwick (By-pass)	2¾
..	33½	2¼	*Ayr	

61. PAISLEY to KILMARNOCK.
Industrial at first, then mainly agricultural districts, but crossing moorlands between Newton Mearns and Fenwick.

A.726			*Paisley	22¼
..	3½	3½	Nitshill	18½
A.77	6½	2¾	*Giffnock	16
..	8½	2½	*Newton Mearns	13½
..	18	9½	*Fenwick (By-pass)	4¼
..	22¼	4¼	**Kilmarnock**	

62. PAISLEY to KILMARNOCK via Kilmaurs.
A slower alternative to Iter. 61. Mainly agricultural, with industrial development in places.

A.726			*Paisley	21¼
B.771	1½	1½	Junc. A.726/B.771	19¾
A.736	4	2½	*Barrhead	17½
A.735	10½	6½	*Lugton	10½
..	13½	2½	*Dunlop	8¼
..	15¾	2½	*Stewarton	5¾
..	19	3¼	*Kilmaurs	2¼
..	21¼	2½	**Kilmarnock**	

63. PAISLEY to ARDROSSAN.
Agricultural scenery for the greater part, with industrial districts at each end.

A.737			*Paisley	25½
..	2½	2½	*Elderslie	23
..	6¼	3¾	*Howwood	19¼
..	11½	5½	*Beith (By-pass)	13¾
..	16½	4¾	*Dalry	9
A.78	20½	4	*Kilwinning	5
..	23	2½	*Stevenston (By-pass)	2½
A.738	25	2	Junc. A.78/A.738	½
..	25½	½	*Ardrossan	

64. PAISLEY to WEMYSS BAY via Kilmacolm.
Industrial at first, but avoids *Johnstone, afterwards traversing pleasant, open countryside through Strath Gryfe to Port Glasgow. Industrial along the Clyde estuary to Greenock. Views across the Firth of Clyde beyond Inverkip. See Iter. 65 for alternative routes.

A.737			*Paisley	26
A.761	1½	1½	Junc. A.737/A.761	24½
..	2¼	¾	Linwood	23¾
..	7	4¾	*Bridge of Weir	19
..	10½	3½	*Kilmacolm	15½
A.8	14½	4	Junc. A.761/A.8	11½
..	14½		*Port Glasgow	11½
A.742	18	3½	*Greenock	8
A.78	22½	4½	Junc. A.742/A.78	3½
..	23½	¾	*Inverkip	2½
..	26	2½	*Wemyss Bay	

65. PAISLEY to GOUROCK and WEMYSS BAY. Mainly industrial districts. Follows the Clyde estuary from Langbank, with pleasant views across the Firth of Clyde. See Iter. 64 for alternative route.

A.726			*Paisley ..	27¾
A.8	3¼	3¼	Junc. A.726/A.8	24½
..	6	2¾	*Bishopton ..	21¾
..	9½	3½	Langbank ..	18¼
..	13¼	3¾	*Port Glasgow ..	14½
..	16¼	3	*Greenock ..	11¼
A.78	19¼	3	*Gourock ..	8¼
..	22¼	2¾	*Cloch Lighthouse	5½
..	25	2¾	*Inverkip ..	2¾
..	27¾	2¾	*Wemyss Bay	

66. GOUROCK to AYR or KILMARNOCK. A fine coastal route, close to the shore for several miles with views of the islands of Bute, the *Cumbraes and Arran in the Firth of Clyde and across to the hills of Cowal. *West Kilbride lies to the east of the main road beyond Fairlie, and the other coastal resorts including Ardrossan and Troon can also be included by reference to Iter. 88. Partly industrial near Stevenston and flat beyond Irvine, and passes Prestwick Airport between Monkton and Prestwick. There are some mining developments on the alternative to Kilmarnock.

A.78			*Gourock ..	45
..	2¾	2¾	*Cloch Lighthouse	42¼
..	5½	2¾	*Inverkip ..	39½
..	8¼	2¾	*Wemyss Bay ..	36¾
..	8¼	¼	*Skelmorlie ..	36¾
..	14½	5¼	*Largs ..	30½
..	17	2½	*Fairlie ..	28
..	22	5	*Sea Mill ..	23
..	27¾	5¼	*Stevenston (By-pass) ..	17¼
..	30¼	2¾	*Kilwinning ..	14¾
..	32¼	2¼	Rd. to Bogside Racecourse ..	12½
..	33¼	1	†*Irvine ..	11¾
..	38¼	5	*Loans ..	6½
A.77	42¼	3¾	*Prestwick (By-pass) ..	2¾
..	45	2¾	*Ayr	
		†	OR	
A.71	33¼		*Irvine	
..	35¼	2¼	*Dreghorn	
..	38¼	2¾	Crosshouse	
..	41	2¾	*Kilmarnock	

67. KILMARNOCK to LONGTOWN. Through agricultural country, with mining developments and moorland in a few places to Sanquhar. Pretty in Nithsdale to New Bridge, after which a short detour can be made to visit *Lincluden Abbey. Beyond Dumfries, flat agricultural districts are traversed to Gretna Green, later crossing the Border into England.

A.71			*Kilmarnock ..	86¾
A.76	1¾	1¾	*Hurlford ..	85
..	8¾	7	*Mauchline ..	78
..	13¼	4½	*Auchinleck ..	73¼
..	15¼	1½	*Cumnock ..	71½
..	20¾	5¼	*New Cumnock	66
..	28¼	7½	*Kirkconnel ..	58¼
..	32	3½	*Sanquhar ..	54¾
..	34¼	2¼	*Mennock ..	52½
..	38¼	4¼	*Enterkinfoot ..	48¼

..	42½	4	*Carronbridge ..	44¼
..	44¼	1½	*Thornhill ..	42½
..	46½	2¼	*Closeburn ..	40¼
..	51	4½	*Auldgirth ..	35¾
..	55	4	Holywood ..	31¾
..	56	1	*New Bridge ..	30¾
A.75	58½	2½	*Dumfries ..	28
..	62¼	3¾	Collin ..	24¼
..	67½	5½	Carrutherstown	19
..	74¼	6¾	*Annan ..	12½
..	76¾	2½	*Dornock ..	10
..	77½	¾	Eastriggs ..	9¼
..	80½	3	Rigg ..	6¼
B.721	81½	1	Junc. A.75/B.721	5¼
..	82½	1	*Gretna Green ..	4¼
A.6071	82½	¼	Junc. B.721/A.6071	4
..	83	½	*Springfield ..	3¾
..	83¼	¼	The Border ..	3¼
A.7	86¼	2¾	Junc. A.6071/A.7	½
..	86¼	½	Longtown	

68. STRATHAVEN to GIRVAN via Cumnock. An undulating cross-country road with open moorland scenery to Cumnock, then through rural countryside to reach the coast 5 miles before Girvan. A faster route is via Ayr, see Iter. 20 and 55.

A.723			*Strathaven ..	55¾
A.70	13¼	13¼	*Muirkirk ..	42½
..	21	7¾	*Lugar ..	34¾
..	23	2	*Cumnock ..	32¾
..	27¼	4¼	*Ochiltree ..	28¼
B.742	33¼	6	*Coylton ..	22¼
..	38¼	5¼	Dalrymple ..	17¼
A.77	42	3¾	Junc. B.742/A.77	13¾
..	43¼	1¾	*Maybole ..	12¼
..	45¼	2¼	*Crossraguel Abbey	10
..	48	2¾	*Kirkoswald ..	7¾
..	55¾	7¾	*Girvan	

69. LANARK to ARDROSSAN. Pleasant in the Clyde valley at first, then undulating across moorlands. Later passes through an agricultural district, with mining developments in places, and industrial towards the end.

A.72			*Lanark ..	52¾
..	1	1	*Kirkfieldbank ..	51¾
..	4¼	3¼	*Crossford ..	47¾
..	7¼	2¾	Rosebank ..	45¼
A.71	8¼	1¼	Junc. A.72/A.71	44
..	12¼	4¼	Stonehouse ..	39¾
..	16¼	4	*Strathaven ..	35¾
..	22¼	5¾	*Drumclog ..	30
..	25¼	3¼	*Loudounhill ..	26¾
..	27¼	2	*Darvel ..	24¾
..	29¼	1½	*Newmilns ..	23
..	32	2½	*Galston ..	20¼
..	35	3	*Hurlford ..	17¼
..	36¼	1½	*Kilmarnock ..	15¾
..	39¼	2½	Crosshouse ..	13¼
..	42	2½	*Dreghorn ..	10½
A.78	44¼	2¼	*Irvine ..	8¼
..	45¼	¾	Rd. to Bogside Racecourse ..	7¼
..	47½	2¼	*Kilwinning ..	5
..	50	2½	*Stevenston (By-pass) ..	2¼
A.738	52	2	Junc. A.78/A.738	½
..	52½	½	*Ardrossan	

70. DUMFRIES to KIRKCUDBRIGHT. Pleasant agricultural scenery.

A.75			*Dumfries ..	27½
..	9½	9½	*Crocketford ..	18
..	11¾	2¼	Springholm ..	15¾

..	18	6¼	*Castle Douglas	9½
A.711	22	4	Junc. A.75/A.711	5½
..	25½	3½	*Tongland ..	2
..	27½	2	*Kirkcudbright	

71. DUMFRIES to GIRVAN via New Galloway. At first a lonely road through the hills of Galloway with fine moorland scenery, followed by attractive wooded country in the Cree valley as far as Bargrennan. Thence a fine moorland run, after which a pleasant valley road leads to the coast at Girvan. A short but interesting detour can be made from Bargrennan to visit the picturesque *Loch Trool, for the Glen Trool National Forest Park. Between Challoch and Barrhill there is a less-frequented route (B.7027). The normal route to Newton Stewart is via Castle Douglas (Iter. 26).

A.75			*Dumfries ..	73¾
A.712	9½	9½	*Crocketford ..	64¼
..	15½	6	Corsock ..	58¼
..	23	7½	*Balmaclellan ..	50¾
..	24¼	1¼	Ken Bridge ..	49½
..	25	¾	*New Galloway ..	48¾
..	31½	6½	*Clatteringshaws Dam ..	42¼
A.75	42½	10¼	Junc. A.712/A.75	31¼
A.714	43½	1¼	*Newton Stewart	30¼
..	45½	2¼	Challoch ..	28
..	52¼	6½	*Bargrennan ..	21¼
..	61¼	9	*Barrhill ..	12¼
..	65½	4¼	*Pinwherry (Sta.) ..	8¼
..	69	3¼	Pinmore (Sta.) ..	4¾
A.77	72½	3¾	Junc. A.714/A.77	1
..	73¼	¾	*Girvan	

72. DUMFRIES to NEWTON STEWART via Dalbeattie and Kirkcudbright. A touring route traversing pleasant agricultural districts, passing New (or Sweetheart) Abbey before circling Criffell Hill to Dalbeattie and touching the coast at several places. Rather narrow between Dalbeattie and Kirkcudbright. The shores of Wigtown Bay are followed between Gatehouse of Fleet and Creetown, with views of the Galloway Hills. See Iter. 26, 71, 73 and 76 for alternatives.

A.710			*Dumfries ..	64
..	7½	7½	*New Abbey ..	56½
..	12	4½	*Kirkbean ..	52
..	14½	2½	*Mainsriddle ..	49½
A.745	16¼	1¾	*Southwick ..	47¾
A.711	23½	7¼	*Dalbeattie ..	40¼
A.745	24¼	¾	Junc. A.711/A.745	39¾
B.727	26¼	1¾	Junc. A.745/B.727	37¾
..	29	2¾	Gelston ..	35
A.755	37½	8¼	*Kirkcudbright ..	26¾
A.75	42	4½	Junc. A.755/A.75	22
..	45½	3½	*Gatehouse of Fleet ..	18½
..	57½	12	*Creetown ..	6½
..	60½	3¼	*Palnure ..	3¼
..	64	3¼	*Newton Stewart	

73. DUMFRIES to NEWTON STEWART via the Coast. An interesting touring route following the coast as far as possible and passing New (or Sweetheart) Abbey and Dundrennan Abbey. At Mainsriddle a side road leads to *Southerness lighthouse, and between Colvend and Dalbeattie short detours can be made to visit the small resorts of *Rockcliffe and *Kippford. Views of the Galloway hills on the latter part. For alternative routes see Iter. 26, 71, 72 and 76.

A.710			*Dumfries	74¼
..	7¼	7¼	*New Abbey	67
..	12	4¼	*Kirkbean	62¼
..	14½	2½	*Mainsriddle	60¼
..	16¼	1¾	*Southwick	58¼
..	19	2¾	*Douglas Hall	55¼
..	20¾	1¾	*Colvend	54
..	22¾	2	Barnbarroch	52
A.711	25¾	3	*Dalbeattie	49
..	29¼	3½	*Palnackie	45¼
..	33¼	4	*Auchencairn	41¼
..	38	4¾	*Dundrennan	36¼
A.755	44½	6½	*Kirkcudbright	30¼
B.727	45½	1	Junc. A.755/B.727	29¼
..	50	4½	*Borgue	24¼
A.75	53½	3½	Junc. B.727/A.75	21¼
..	56¼	2¾	*Gatehouse of Fleet	18¼
..	68¼	12	*Creetown	6¼
..	71½	3¼	*Palnure	3¼
..	74¾	3¼	*Newton Stewart	

74. DUMFRIES to GIRVAN via Moniaive. On leaving Dumfries, short detours can be made to visit *Lincluden Abbey and *Irongray. A quiet cross-country route, hilly and winding to Moniaive, then across moorland, passing Kendoon Loch nearing Carsphairn. The northern extremity of *Loch Doon is passed on the way to Dalmellington, where there are some mining developments. Pleasant valley scenery beyond Straiton. The quickest way to Carsphairn is by Dalry, see Iter. 75.

A.76			*Dumfries	64¼
B.729	2¼	2¼	*New Bridge	62
..	9¼	6½	*Dunscore	55½
A.702	14¾	5½	*Kirkland	50
B.729	16¾	2	*Moniaive	48
A.713	31¾	15	Junc. B.729/A.713	33
..	32¼	½	*Carsphairn	32½
..	42¼	10¼	*Dalmellington	22¼
B.741	43	¾	Junc. A.713/B.741	21¼
..	49¼	6¼	*Straiton	15¼
..	57½	8¼	*New Dailly	7
A.77	64	6¼	Junc. B.741/A.77	¾
..	64¼	¼	*Girvan	

75. DUMFRIES to AYR via Dalmellington. Pleasant moorland scenery in the Galloway Hills for the greater part. Mining in the vicinity of Dalmellington, which stands near the northern extremity of *Loch Doon. Agricultural on the latter part. The quickest way is by Cumnock (Iter. 27). Another road (B.7000) from Dalry to Carsphairn follows the eastern side of Glen Ken and passes the shores of Kendoon Loch.

A.75			*Dumfries	61¼
A.712	9¼	9¼	*Crocketford	51¼
..	15¼	6	Corsock	45¼
..	23	7¾	*Balmaclellan	38¼
A.713	24¼	1¼	Ken Bridge	37
..	26¾	2½	*Dalry	34½
..	36	9¼	*Carsphairn	25¼
..	46¼	10¼	*Dalmellington	15
..	51¼	5	*Patna	10
..	61¼	10	*Ayr	

76. DUMFRIES to AYR via Dalbeattie. Pleasant agricultural district at first, and then follows the shores of Loch Ken between Castle Douglas and Ken Bridge. Crosses moorland and passes near the northern extremity of *Loch Doon, before Dalmellington, where there are some mining developments. Agricultural on the latter part. Another road (B.7000) from Dalry to Carsphairn follows the eastern side of Glen Ken and passes the shores of Kendoon Loch. For the recommended routes from Dumfries to Ayr, see Iter. 27; to Ken Bridge, see Iter. 75; and to Castle Douglas, see Iter. 70.

A.711			*Dumfries	70½
..	6½	6½	Beeswing	64
..	9	2½	*Kirkgunzeon	61½
..	13½	4½	*Dalbeattie	57
A.745	14¼	¾	Junc. A.711/A.745	56¼
A.75	19½	5¼	Junc. A.745/A.75	51
A.713	20	½	*Castle Douglas	50½
..	23½	3½	*Crossmichael	46¾
..	27	3½	Parton	43½
..	33½	6½	Ken Br.	37
..	36	2½	*Dalry	34½
..	45½	9½	*Carsphairn	25¼
..	55½	10¼	*Dalmellington	15
..	60½	5	*Patna	10
..	70½	10	*Ayr	

77. KIRKCUDBRIGHT to AYR. Pretty scenic road, agricultural at first, then past lochs, hills, moors and close to the northern extremity of *Loch Doon, near Dalmellington, where is some mining. Developments in connection with hydro-electric power schemes north of New Galloway. Agricultural on the latter part.

A.711			*Kirkcudbright	56
A.762	1½	1½	Junc. A.711/A.762	54½
A.75	3½	2	Junc. A.762/A.75	52½
A.762	4¼	1	*Ringford	51¼
..	9¼	5	*Laurieston	46¼
..	13¼	4	New Galloway Sta.	42½
..	18¼	5	*New Galloway	37½
A.713	22½	3½	Junc. A.762/A.713	33½
..	30¼	8½	*Carsphairn	25¼
..	41	10¼	*Dalmellington	15
..	46	5	*Patna	10
..	56	10	*Ayr	

78. NEWTON STEWART to GIRVAN via Luce Bay and New Luce. Pleasant rural scenery to the coast at Port William, then follows the sandy shores of Luce Bay to Auchenmalg, later passing Luce Abbey between Glenluce and New Luce. Beyond this point, narrow and hilly moorland by-roads are traversed between New Luce and Barrhill, with numerous gates. After Pinwherry, a detour is made to include part of the Stinchar valley to Barr, whence the road over the hills is narrow and winding. The quickest way from Glenluce to Girvan is by A.75 and A.751 to Innermessan, thence by the coast road, A.77. The direct road from Newton Stewart to Pinwherry and Girvan is shown in Iter. 80.

A.714			*Newton Stewart	68¼
B.7005	6	6	Junc. A.714/B.7005	62¼
A.714	7¼	1¼	*Bladnoch	60¾
..	11	3¼	Whaup Hill	57½
A.747	17¼	6¼	*Port William	51¼
..	26¼	9¼	Auchenmalg	42
A.75	30¼	4	Junc. A.747/A.75	38
..	31¼	¾	*Glenluce	37¼
Uncl.	31¼	¾	Junc. A.75/Uncl.	36¼
..	36¼	4¼	*New Luce	32
..	41½	5	*Glenwhilly	27
..	42½	1¼	Miltonish	25¼
..	45¼	2½	Chirmorie	23¼
A.714	49¼	4	*Barrhill	19¼
..	53¼	4¼	*Pinwherry (Sta.)	15
B.734	55¼	1¼	Junc. A.714/B.734	13¼
..	60¼	5½	*Barr	7¼
..	65¼	5	*Old Dailly	2¼
A.77	68	2¼	Junc. B.734/A.77	½
..	68½	½	*Girvan	

79. NEWTON STEWART to AYR via the Galloway and Carrick Hills. A touring route across the Galloway Hills, following the wooded Cree valley to Bargrennan, where a short detour can be made to visit the picturesque *Loch Trool for the Glen Trool National Forest Park. Care required on the section from Bargrennan to Straiton, which is a narrow, hilly and winding moorland road, rising to 1,421 feet, with a descent of 1 in 10, 3 miles before Straiton. A winding, valley road is then followed until joining the main road near Minishant. From Rowantree, an alternative road leads over the hills by the Nick o' the Balloch Pass (1,280 feet) to the Stinchar valley at North Balloch, thence by Iter. 84 to Ayr (42 miles). The main road is by Girvan and Maybole, Iter. 80 and 55.

A.714			*Newton Stewart	44½
..	2¼	2¼	Challoch	42¼
Uncl.	8¼	6¼	*Bargrennan	35¾
..	18¼	9¼	*Rowantree	26¼
B.741	30	11¼	*Straiton	14½
B.7045	30¼	¼	Junc. B.741/B.7045	14¼
..	34¼	4	Kirkmichael	10¼
A.77	38¼	4	Junc. B.7045/A.77	6¼
..	39	¾	Minishant	5¼
..	44½	5½	*Ayr	

80. NEWTON STEWART to AYR, touring route. At first the road passes through pleasant agricultural and moorland country, thence along the east side of Loch Ryan. It then turns inland along Glen App and later descends to the coast at Ballantrae. Thereafter it is a fine coast road, and passes Turnberry golf course. There are views of Culzean Castle and Dunure Castle (ruins), between which the famous *Croy (Electric) Brae is traversed.

A.75			*Newton Stewart	74¼
..	15¼	15¼	*Glenluce	59½
..	18¼	3½	Dunragit	56
..	21¼	3	*Castle Kennedy	53
A.751	23	1¼	Junc. A.75/A.751	51¼
A.77	24¼	1¼	*Innermessan	50
..	28¼	3½	*Cairn Ryan	46¼
..	39¼	11¼	*Ballantrae	35
..	46	6¼	*Lendalfoot	28¼
..	52½	6½	*Girvan	22¼
A.719	57½	5	Junc. A.77/A.719	17¼
..	57½		*Turnberry	17
..	59¼	1½	*Maidens	15¼
..	61½	2¼	*Culzean Castle	13¼

..	67	5½	*Dunure Mains	7¾
..	73	6	Doonfoot ..	1¼
..	74¼	1¼	*Ayr	

81. NEWTON STEWART to PORTPATRICK via Wigtown.

Agricultural and moorland country. The direct road to Glenluce is given in Iter. 25.

A.714			*Newton Stewart	38½
B.733	7	7	*Wigtown ..	31½
..	15½	8½	*Kirkcowan ..	23¼
A.75	16½	1½	Junc. B.733/A.75	21¾
..	24¼	7½	*Glenluce ..	14¼
A.715	26½	2½	Junc. A.75/A.715	11¾
A.757	29	2½	Junc. A.715/A.757	9¼
A.716	32½	3½	Kildrochet ..	6
A.757	33	½	Junc. A.716/A.757	5½
A.77	33½	½	*Lochans ..	5
..	38½	5	*Portpatrick	

82. NEWTON STEWART to STRANRAER via Luce Bay and the Mull of Galloway.

Pleasant rural scenery along the coast of Wigtownshire to the Mull of Galloway, touching the shores of Luce Bay between Monreith and Auchenmalg, and again between Sandhead and Drummore. A short detour can be made from Kirkinner via B.7004 to *Garliestown and on to Whithorn, or by B.7004 and B.7063 passing *Cruggleton Church and direct to Isle of Whithorn. From Drummore to the Mull of Galloway, the most southerly point in Scotland, can be omitted by proceeding direct from Damnaglaur to Kirkmaiden. The direct road to Port William is given in Iter. 78 and to Glenluce in Iter. 25.

A.714			*Newton Stewart	92½
..	7	7	*Wigtown ..	85½
..	8½	1½	*Bladnoch ..	84¼
A.746	9½	1¼	Junc. A.714/A.746	83¼
..	10½	½	*Kirkinner ..	82¼
..	13½	3¼	*Sorbie ..	79¼
A.750	18	4½	*Whithorn ..	74½
..	21½	3½	*Isle of Whithorn	71¼
			Return to:—	
A.747	23½	1½	Junc. A.750/A.747	69¼
..	25½	2½	*Glasserton ..	67
..	30	4½	*Monreith ..	62½
..	32½	2½	*Port William ..	60¼
..	41½	9½	Auchenmalg ..	51
A.75	45¼	4	Junc. A.747/A.75	47
..	46½	¾	*Glenluce ..	46¼
A.715	49	2½	Junc. A.75/A.715	43¾
A.716	54½	5½	Junc. A.715/A.716	38
..	55½	1	*Sandhead ..	37
..	58½	3	*Ardwell (P.O.)	34
B.7041	65½	6½	*Drummore ..	27½
..	66½	1	Damnaglaur ..	26½
Uncl.	67½	1¼	Junc. B.7041/Uncl.	25¼
..	70½	2½	*Mull of Galloway	22½
			Return to:—	
B.7065	74½	4	Damnaglaur ..	18½
..	75½	1	*Kirkmaiden ..	17½
..	78½	3½	*Port Logan ..	14
A.716	80½	2	Junc. B.7065/A.716	12
..	82½	1½	*Ardwell (P.O.)	10½
..	85½	3	*Sandhead ..	7½
..	87½	2	Stoneykirk ..	5½
..	89½	2	Kildrochet ..	3½
A.77	90½	1	Junc. A.716/A.77	2½
..	92¾	2½	*Stranraer	

83. A Tour from STRANRAER via Aldouran Glen and Loch Ryan.

A picturesque tour in the quiet by-ways of the northern half of the Rhinns of Galloway, with distant glimpses of Ireland after Portpatrick. After passing Lochnaw Castle, the road follows the wooded Aldouran Glen, and a short detour is then made before approaching the shores of Loch Ryan.

A.77			*Stranraer ..	30¼
..	2¾	2¾	*Lochans ..	27½
..	7¾	5	*Portpatrick ..	22½
			Return to:—	
A.764	8½	¾	Junc. A.77/A.764	21¾
B.738	11½	3½	Junc. A.764/B.738	18½
..	13	1½	Larbrax School	17½
B.7043	14½	1½	Junc. B.738/B.7043	15¾
..	15	½	*Lochnaw Castle	15¼
B.798	17	2	Leswalt ..	13¼
..	19½	2½	Ervie (P.O.) ..	10¾
B.738	19¾	¼	Junc. B.798/B.738	10½
A.718	22¾	3	Junc. B.738/A.718	7½
..	24	1¼	*Kirkcolm ..	6¼
..	30¼	6¼	*Stranraer	

84. STRANRAER to AYR via the Stinchar Valley.

A touring route following the main road by the shores of Loch Ryan for some miles before ascending Glen App, then descending to the coast at Ballantrae. Thence by a pretty, undulating road along the wooded valley of the River Stinchar to North Balloch, followed by a narrow, moorland run over the hills to Crosshill. Care required when passing on this section. An easy run through agricultural districts on the latter part. See Iter. 55 for the direct route.

A.77			*Stranraer ..	57
..	2½	2½	*Innermessan ..	54½
..	6	3½	*Cairn Ryan ..	51
B.7044	17½	11½	*Ballantrae ..	39½
A.765	20¾	3¼	Junc. B.7044/A.765	36¼
..	22½	1¾	*Colmonell ..	34½
A.714	25¾	3¼	*Pinwherry (Sta.)	31¼
B.734	27½	1¾	Junc. A.714/B.734	29½
Uncl.	33	5½	*Barr ..	24
..	37½	4½	*North Balloch	19¾
B.7023	45¾	8½	Crosshill ..	11¼
A.77	48½	2¾	*Maybole ..	8½
B.7024	48¾	¼	Junc. A.77/B.7024	8¼
..	54½	5½	*Brig o' Doon ..	2¾
..	54¾	¼	*Alloway ..	2½
..	57	2¼	*Ayr	

85. A tour from GIRVAN to GOUROCK.

A by-road route through Ayrshire, following the Girvan valley to Kirkmichael, then a cross-country road to Irvine through mainly agricultural districts and visiting Tarbolton, in the Burns country. Beyond Lochwinnoch, crosses moorland to Kilmacolm and becomes industrial on the estuary of the Clyde. The main road is by Ayr and Largs, see Iter. 55 and 66.

A.77			*Girvan ..	78
B.741	¾	¾	Junc. A.77/B.741	77¼
..	7	6¼	*New Dailly ..	71
B.7023	10¾	3¾	Junc. B.741/B.7023	67¼
Uncl.	12¾	2	Crosshill ..	65¼
B.7045	14¼	1½	Junc. Uncl./B.7045	63¾
Uncl.	15	½	Kirkmichael ..	63
A.713	20¼	5¼	*Patna ..	57¾
B.730	21¼	1	Junc. A.713/B.730	56¾
..	26½	5½	*Drongan ..	51¼
A.70	27½	½	Junc. B.730/A.70	50½
B.730	27¾	¼	Junc. A.70/B.730	50¼
..	29	1¼	Trabboch ..	49
..	30	1	*Stair ..	48
..	32½	2½	*Tarbolton ..	45½
A.719	33¾	1½	Junc. B.730/A.719	44¼
B.730	34¼	½	Junc. A.719/B.730	43¾
..	39½	5¼	*Dundonald ..	38¼
A.71	42	2½	*Dreghorn ..	36
A.78	44½	2½	*Irvine ..	33¼
..	45¼	1	Rd. to Bogside Racecourse ..	32¾
A.737	47½	2¼	*Kilwinning ..	30¼
B.780	51½	4	*Dalry ..	26¼
A.760	55½	3¾	*Kilbirnie ..	22½
B.786	59¼	4	*Lochwinnoch ..	18¾
A.761	67¼	8¼	*Kilmacolm ..	10½
A.8	71½	4	Junc. A.761/A.8	6½
..	71¾	¼	*Port Glasgow ..	6¼
..	75	3¼	*Greenock ..	3
..	78	3	*Gourock	

86. LANARK to PERTH via Kincardine Bridge and the Ochil Hills.

Open moorland to Longridge, then agricultural and mining districts, whilst the interesting village of *Torphichen lies to the east of the road between Armadale and Linlithgow. Crosses the River Forth at Kincardine Bridge, and beyond Rumbling Bridge traverses the Ochil Hills by a pleasant scenic route with fine views. This forms an alternative to the main roads across the Ochils by Glenfarg (Iter. 91) and Glen Devon (Iter. 89). Attractive at Forteviot in Strath Earn. The direct road (A.801) avoiding Linlithgow via Maddiston is narrow and difficult to follow. From Lanark, the recommended route is by Stirling to Perth (Iter. 50 and 135) and Iter. 50 and 136 to Yetts of Muckhart. From Kincardine Bridge the best route to Perth is by Kinross (Iter. 91).

A.706			*Lanark ..	69¼
..	8¼	8¼	Forth ..	61
..	9	¾	*Wilsontown ..	60¼
..	13¾	4¾	Longridge ..	55½
..	15¼	1½	*Whitburn ..	53¾
..	18	2¾	*Armadale ..	51¼
A.9	25¼	7¼	*Linlithgow ..	43¾
..	30	4¾	*Polmont ..	39¼
A.905	30½	½	Junc. A.9/A.905	38¾
..	34	3½	Bothkennar ..	35¼
A.876	34½	½	Junc. A.905/A.876	34¾
..	37	2½	*Kincardine Bridge	32½
A.977	37½	½	*Kincardine-on-Forth	31¾
..	42¼	4¾	Forest Mill ..	27
..	45½	3¼	Blairingone ..	23¾
..	48	2½	Powmill ..	21¼
A.823	49	1	*Rumbling Bridge	20¼
..	50½	1½	*Yetts of Muckhart	18¾
B.934	50¾	¼	Junc. A.823/B.934	18½
..	59¾	9	*Dunning ..	9½
..	62½	2¾	*Forteviot (Sta.)	6¾
B.9112	63	½	Junc. B.934/B.9112	6¼
..	65½	2½	Aberdalgie ..	3¾
A.9	67¾	2¼	Cherrybank ..	1½
..	69¼	1½	*Perth	

87. STRATHAVEN to STIRLING via Motherwell.

Traverses mining and agricultural districts. The quickest way is by Newmains. Iter. 20 and 50.

Road			Place	
A.723			*Strathaven	37½
..	7½	7½	*Hamilton	29¾
..	9¾	2¼	*Motherwell	27½
..	11¾	2	*Carfin	25½
..	12½	¾	*Newarthill	24¾
A.73	14¼	1¾	Newhouse	23
..	15½	1¼	Chapelhall	21¾
..	17½	2	*Airdrie	19¾
A.80	24½	7	*Cumbernauld	12¾
..	26¼	1¾	*Castlecary	11
..	27¾	1½	*Dennyloanhead	9½
..	30¼	2½	*Denny	7
A.9	36	5¾	*St. Ninian's	1¼
..	37¼	1¼	*Stirling	

88. AYR to INVERARAY, touring route.

Fine scenery along the Ayrshire coast, the Firth of Clyde, Loch Lomond, and in the hills and by the sea lochs of Argyll. Prestwick Airport is passed before leaving the main road to visit the golfing centre of Troon. After a brief stretch of industrial development near Stevenston, a short detour leads to Saltcoats and Ardrossan, while after rejoining the main road another can be made from Sea Mill to *West Kilbride. The road then keeps close to the shore for several miles through the Clyde resorts, with views of the islands of Arran, the Cumbraes and Bute, in the Firth of Clyde, and across to the hills of Cowal. It is mainly industrial along both sides of the river for some miles and Glasgow is avoided by utilising the Erskine ferry. Attractive scenery along the shores of *Loch Lomond from Arden to Tarbet, with views of Ben Lomond. Turning westward through the hills of Argyll, there are views of Ben Arthur (The Cobbler) approaching Arrochar, at the head of Loch Long. A gradual ascent is made by the reconstructed road in Glen Croe to the summit at Rest and be Thankful, with an undulating descent to the shores of *Loch Fyne.

Road			Place	
A.77			*Ayr	113½
..	2¼	2¼	*Prestwick	110½
A.78	4	1¾	*Monkton	109½
B.749	4½	½	Junc. A.78/B.749	109
A.759	7¼	3½	*Troon	105¾
B.746	8	¾	Junc. A.759/B.746	105¼
..	9	1	*Barassie	104½
A.78	10	1	Junc. B.746/A.78	103½
..	14	4	*Irvine	99½
..	15	1	Rd. to Bogside Racecourse	98½
..	17½	2½	*Kilwinning	96¼
A.738	19½	2	Junc. A.78/A.738	94¼
..	19¾	½	*Stevenston	93¾
..	21¼	1½	*Saltcoats	92¼
..	22¼	1½	*Ardrossan	90¾
A.78	23¼	½	Junc. A.738/A.78	90¼
..	27	3¾	*Sea Mill	86½
..	32	5	*Fairlie	81½
..	34½	2½	*Largs	78½
..	40¼	5¾	*Skelmorlie	73¼
..	40¼	½	*Wemyss Bay	77¾
..	43½	2¾	*Inverkip	70
..	46¼	2¾	*Cloch Lighthouse	67¾
A.8	49	2¼	*Gourock	64½
..	52	3	*Greenock	61½
..	55½	3½	*Port Glasgow	58¼
..	59	3½	Langbank	54½
B.815	62½	3½	Junc. A.8/B.815	51½
A.726	64¼	2	Junc. B.815/A.726	49¼
..	64¾	¼	*Erskine Ferry to	
A.814			*Old Kilpatrick	49
..	66½	1¾	*Bowling	47¼
A.82	66¾	¼	Junc. A.814/A.82	46¾
..	67½	¾	Milton	46
..	71½	4¼	*Bonhill	41½
..	72½	¾	*Alexandria	41
..	76	3½	Arden	37½
..	81½	5½	*Luss	32
A.83	90	8½	*Tarbet	23½
..	91½	1½	*Arrochar	21½
..	98½	6¾	*Rest and be Thankful	15
..	103½	5¼	*Cairndow	9¼
..	113½	9¾	*Inveraray	

89. EDINBURGH to KINLOCH RANNOCH via Dunfermline.

A scenic, but hilly road throughout, winding in places, and utilising the ferry crossing near the Forth Bridge. Fine mountain views near Rumbling Bridge, approaching the Ochil Hills, which are crossed by a winding road in Glen Devon followed by the long descent to Gleneagles. Pleasant in Strath Earn to Crieff, after which there is fine Highland scenery as the road traverses the *Sma' Glen to Amulree. At Milton, a long climb over the hills by Glen Cochill is followed by a lengthy descent to Aberfeldy. Fine views of the Perthshire Hills hereabouts. Beyond Coshieville, ascends across moorland country skirting the peak of Schiehallion. Care on the winding descent three miles before Kinloch Rannoch. The recommended route for fast travel to Crieff is by Stirling (Iter. 95 and 140) and other alternatives are by Perth (Iter. 90, 91 or 92) thence by Iter. 149 to Aberfeldy or via Pitlochry to Kinloch Rannoch (Iter. 150 and 148).

Road			Place	
A.90			*Edinburgh	86¼
..	2¼	2¼	Blackhall	83¾
..	4½	2	*Barnton	81¾
..	5	½	*Cramond Bridge	81¼
..	8¼	3¼	*South Queensferry	
			(Forth Rd. Br. under construction)	
			Ferry to *North Queensferry	78
A.823	9¾	1½	Junc. A.90/A.823	76½
..	11¼	1½	*Rosyth	75
..	13¾	2½	*Dunfermline	72½
..	23½	9¾	Powmill	62¾
..	24½	1	*Rumbling Bridge	61¾
..	26	1½	*Yetts of Muckhart	60¼
..	28½	2½	*Glendevon	58
..	34½	6¼	Loaninghead X-rds.	51¾
..	35½	¾	*Gleneagles (Hotel)	51
A.822	39¾	4¼	Junc. A.823/A.822	46½
..	41¼	2	*Muthill	44½
A.85	45¼	3½	*Crieff	41
A.822	47¼	2	*Gilmerton	39
..	53¾	6½	*Newton Bridge	32½
..	57½	3½	*Amulree	28½
A.826	59¼	1½	*Milton	27
B.846	68¼	9¼	*Aberfeldy	17¼
..	69¼	1	*Weem	16¼
..	73½	4¼	*Coshieville	12¼
..	77	3½	*White Bridge	9¼
Uncl.	77½	½	Junc. B.846/Uncl.	8¼
..	86¼	8¾	*Kinloch Rannoch	

90. EDINBURGH to PERTH via Queensferry.

Utilises the ferry crossing near the Forth Bridge which is well seen from the ferry boat. Pretty scenery, except for a small mining area near Cowdenbeath. Views of *Loch Leven approaching Kinross and picturesque in Glenfarg. For another crossing over the River Forth see Iter. 91, or by Stirling, Iter. 95 and 135.

Road			Place	
A.90			*Edinburgh	41¼
..	2¼	2¼	Blackhall	39¼
..	4½	2	*Barnton	37¼
..	5	½	*Cramond Bridge	36¾
..	8¼	3¼	*South Queensferry	
			(Forth Rd. Br. under construction)	
			Ferry to *North Queensferry	33½
..	10¼	2	*Inverkeithing	31¼
..	14¼	4	*Crossgates	27¼
..	16¼	2¼	*Cowdenbeath	25¼
..	22½	5½	*Gairneybridge	19¼
..	24½	2¼	*Kinross	17¼
..	26¼	1½	*Milnathort	15¼
..	31	4½	*Glenfarg	10¼
..	33½	2½	"Bein" Inn	8¼
..	35½	2	Aberargie	6¼
..	37¼	2¼	*Bridge of Earn	4
..	41¼	4	*Perth	

91. EDINBURGH to PERTH via Kincardine Bridge.

Utilises the bridge crossing over the Forth nearest to Edinburgh until completion of the Forth Road Bridge. A pleasant, easy road to Kincardine Bridge, then mainly rural scenery, particularly attractive in Glenfarg. This route provides an alternative to the ferry crossings from Edinburgh. The route via Stirling (Iter. 95 and 135), is 5½ miles farther.

Road			Place	
A.8			*Edinburgh	65
..	4¼	4¼	*Corstorphine	60¾
A.9	5¼	1	Junc. A.8/A.9	59¾
..	7¼	2	*Turnhouse Airport	57¾
..	9	1¾	*Kirkliston	56
..	11¼	2¼	*Winchburgh	53¾
..	17¼	6	*Linlithgow	47¾
..	21¼	4¼	*Polmont	43¾
A.905	22½	¼	Junc. A.9/A.905	42¼
..	25¼	3½	Bothkennar	39¼
A.876	26¼	1	Junc. A.905/A.876	38¼
..	28¼	2¼	*Kincardine Bridge	36¾
A.977	29¼	½	*Kincardine-on-Forth	35¾
..	34	4¾	Forest Mill	31
..	37¼	3½	Blairingone	27¾
..	39¾	2½	Powmill	25¼
..	41¼	2	*Crook of Devon	23¾
A.90	47½	6	*Kinross	17¼
..	49¼	1¾	*Milnathort	15¼
..	54¼	4½	*Glenfarg	10¼
..	56¾	2½	"Bein" Inn	8¼
..	58½	2	Aberargie	6¼
..	61	2¼	*Bridge of Earn	4
..	65	4	*Perth	

92. EDINBURGH to PERTH via Dunfermline.

Uses the ferry crossing near the Forth Bridge which is well seen from the ferry boat. Thence a pleasant scenic run except for a small mining area around Kelty. Views of *Loch Leven on the approach to Kinross and picturesque through Glenfarg.

A.90			*Edinburgh ..	43¾
..	2½	2½	Blackhall ..	41¼
..	4½	2	*Barnton ..	39¾
..	5	½	*Cramond Bridge	38¾
..	8¼	3¼	*South Queensferry	
(Forth Rd. Br. under construction) Ferry to				
			*North Queensferry ..	35½
A.823	9½	1½	Junc. A.90/A.234	34
..	11¼	1½	*Rosyth ..	32½
..	13¾	2½	*Dunfermline ..	30
B.915	16¼	2½	Junc. A.823/B.915	27¾
B.914	18	1¾	Junc. B.915/B.914	25¾
..	20½	2½	*Kelty ..	23¼
A.90	21	½	Junc. B.914/A.90	22¾
..	24¼	3¼	*Gairneybridge	19¾
..	26¼	2½	*Kinross ..	17½
..	28¼	1¾	*Milnathort ..	15½
..	33	4¾	*Glenfarg ..	10¾
..	35½	2½	"Bein" Inn ..	8¼
..	37½	2	Aberargie ..	6¼
..	39¼	2¼	*Bridge of Earn	4
..	43¾	4	*Perth	

93. EDINBURGH to ST. ANDREWS via Queensferry.

Utilises the ferry crossing near the Forth Bridge. A pleasant, easy road through rural scenery, except for a small industrial area near Kirkcaldy.

A.90			*Edinburgh ..	50
..	2½	2½	Blackhall ..	47½
..	4½	2	*Barnton ..	45½
..	5	½	*Cramond Bridge	45
..	8¼	3¼	*South Queensferry	
(Forth Rd. Br. under construction) Ferry to				
			*North Queensferry ..	41½
A.92	10½	2½	*Inverkeithing	39½
..	12	1½	Hillend ..	38
B.924	14	2	Junc. A.92/B.924	36
A.907	16¼	2½	Junc. B.924/A.907	33½
A.92	22½	6¼	*Kirkcaldy ..	27½
..	24¼	1½	Sinclairtown ..	25½
..	24¾	½	Gallatown ..	25¼
..	27¼	2½	*Thornton ..	22¾
..	29	1¾	*Glenrothes ..	21
..	30	1	Cadham ..	20
..	34	4	Kettlebridge ..	16
..	36¼	2¼	*Pitlessie ..	13¾
..	40½	4¼	*Cupar ..	9½
..	43½	3	*Dairsie ..	6½
..	46	2½	*Guardbridge ..	2½
..	50	4	*St. Andrews	

94. EDINBURGH to DUNDEE via Queensferry and the Fife Coast.

A tour along the coast of Fife, utilising ferries across the Rivers Forth and Tay. The famous Forth Bridge is well seen from the ferry boat at Queensferry, after which there is a pleasant run before reaching the small industrial area near Kirkcaldy. This route avoids the industrial district on the coast road through Leven (see Iter. 128), and later follows a winding, scenic road through some of the Fife coast Royal Burghs to St. Andrews. Beyond Guardbridge, a short detour is made to Tayport, where there are views across the Firth of Tay, before crossing the ferry from Newport to Dundee, in sight of the well-known Tay Bridge. Pretty scenery throughout, although the road only occasionally approaches the sea-shore. For alternative routes see Iter. 93, 126, 127, 128 and 129. A direct road (A.921) from Upper Largo to Crail through *Colinsburgh passes Kellie Castle; there is also a direct road (A.959) from Anstruther to St. Andrews (9½ miles).

A.90			*Edinburgh ..	75
..	2½	2½	Blackhall ..	72½
..	4½	2	*Barnton ..	70½
..	5	½	*Cramond Bridge	70
..	8¼	3¼	*South Queensferry	
(Forth Rd. Br. under construction) Ferry to				
			*North Queensferry ..	66½
A.92	10½	2½	*Inverkeithing	64½
..	12	1½	Hillend ..	63
B.924	14	2	Junc. A.92/B.924	61
A.907	16¼	2½	Junc. B.924/A.907	58½
A.92	22½	6¼	*Kirkcaldy ..	52½
..	24¼	1½	Sinclairtown ..	50¾
..	24¾	½	Gallatown ..	50¼
A.915	25¼	½	Junc. A.92/A.915	49¾
..	30½	5¼	*Windygates ..	44½
..	33	2½	*Scoonie ..	42
..	35	2	*Lundin Links ..	40
A.921	36	1	*Upper Largo ..	39
A.917	38¼	2¼	Junc. A.921/A.917	36¼
..	41¼	2½	*Elie ..	33¾
..	43¼	2¼	*St. Monance ..	31¾
..	45¼	2	*Pittenweem ..	29¾
..	46¼	1	*Anstruther ..	28¾
..	47¼	1	*Kilrenny ..	27¾
A.918	51	3½	*Crail ..	24
..	54	3	*Kingsbarns ..	21
A.91	60½	6½	*St. Andrews ..	14½
A.919	64½	4	*Guardbridge ..	10½
..	66½	1½	*Leuchars ..	8½
B.945	67¾	1¼	"St. Michaels" Hotel ..	7¼
B.946	72	4¼	*Tayport ..	3
A.914	74¼	2¼	Junc. B.946/A.914	¼
..	75	½	*Newport	
			Ferry to	
			*Dundee	

95. EDINBURGH to STIRLING.

A pleasant, easy road for the greater part, with narrow streets in Falkirk and Camelon. Later passes near to the battlefield at Bannockburn. See Iter. 96 for alternative from Polmont to Stirling.

A.8			*Edinburgh ..	36
..	4¼	4¼	*Corstorphine ..	31¾
A.9	8¼	1¼	Junc. A.8/A.9 ..	30¼
..	7¼	2	*Turnhouse Airport	28¾
..	9	1¾	*Kirkliston ..	27
..	11¼	2¼	*Winchburgh ..	24¾
..	17¼	6	*Linlithgow ..	18¾
..	21¼	4¼	*Polmont ..	14¾
..	23½	1½	Laurieston ..	12½
..	25	1½	*Falkirk ..	11
..	26	1	*Camelon ..	10
..	27½	1½	*Larbert ..	8½
..	28¾	1¼	N. Broomage ..	7½
..	31¼	3	Plean ..	4¾
..	33½	2¼	*Bannockburn ..	2½
..	34½	1¼	*St. Ninian's ..	1½
..	36	1½	*Stirling	

96. EDINBURGH to STIRLING, touring route.

A pleasant, easy touring route, visiting places of interest near the south bank of the River Forth. 3 miles from Barnton, a short detour can be made to visit the famous Norman church at *Dalmeny before passing beneath the impressive Forth Bridge, where there are views across the river. Very shortly, between Queensferry and Abercorn, *Hopetoun House is passed, after which another detour is made past the mansion of The *Binns to include Blackness Castle. At Linlithgow, the main road is followed for a short distance before branching off along a pleasant, level road avoiding the manufacturing district around Falkirk. The main road is shown in Iter. 95 and a further alternative route to Falkirk is given in Iter. 17.

A.90			*Edinburgh ..	42
..	2½	2½	Blackhall ..	39½
..	4½	2	*Barnton ..	37½
..	5	½	*Cramond Bridge	37
A.904	8¼	3¼	*South Queensferry ..	33¾
..	8¾	½	Queensferry ..	33¾
Uncl.	10½	2	Junc. A.904/Uncl.	31½
..	12½	1¾	*Abercorn ..	29½
A.904	13¼	1¼	Junc. Uncl./A.904	28¾
B.9109	15½	1½	Junc. A.904 B.9109	26½
B.903	17½	2	Junc. B.9109/B.903	24½
..	19	1½	*Blackness ..	23
A.9	22½	3½	*Linlithgow ..	19½
..	27¼	4½	*Polmont ..	14¾
A.905	28	½	Junc. A.9/A.905	14
..	31¼	3½	Bothkennar ..	10½
..	34	2¼	*Airth ..	8
..	39¼	5¼	Fallin ..	2¾
..	42	2¼	*Stirling	

97. GLASGOW to KIRKCALDY via Kincardine Bridge.

A commercial route at first, through industrial, mining and agricultural districts. Later, utilises the Kincardine Bridge to cross the River Forth, after which pleasant rural countryside is traversed. See Iter. 134 for an alternative road from Kincardine passing through the very interesting little Royal Burgh of *Culross (N.T. Scot.).

A.80			*Glasgow ..	52½
..	4½	4½	Millerston ..	48
..	5¼	¾	*Stepps ..	47¼
..	7	1¾	*Muirhead ..	45¼
..	9½	2½	Mollinburn ..	43
..	11	1½	Condorrat ..	41½
..	14	3	*Cumbernauld ..	38½
..	15¼	1¼	*Castlecary ..	37¼
..	17¼	1½	*Dennyloanhead	35¼
A.803	17½	½	Junc. A.80/A.803	34¾
A.876	18¼	½	Junc. A.803/A.876	34¼
A.9	21¼	3	*Larbert ..	31¼
A.876	22	¾	N. Broomage ..	30¼
..	27¼	5¼	*Kincardine Bridge	24¾
A.985	28¼	½	*Kincardine-on-Forth	24¼
..	33¼	5¼	*Newmills ..	18¼
..	34¼	¾	*Torryburn ..	18
A.994	35¼	¾	Junc. A.985/A.994	17¼
..	36	¾	Cairneyhill ..	16¼
..	37¼	1¼	Crossford ..	15¼
A.907	39	1¾	*Dunfermline ..	13½
..	41¼	2¼	Halbeath ..	11¼
..	42½	1¼	*Crossgates ..	10
..	44	1½	Donibristle ..	8½
..	52½	8½	*Kirkcaldy	

98. GLASGOW to CRAIL via Kincardine Bridge. Commercial at first, then through an agricultural district, with mining developments, the best way to Dennyloanhead being by Cumbernauld (Iter. 97). Pleasant rural scenery after crossing the River Forth by Kincardine Bridge, with views of the Ochil Hills nearing Kinross. Pleasant by *Loch Leven, shortly after Milnathort, and later reaches the coast near Lundin Links, afterwards traversing a winding road, with pretty scenery, through the Fife coast Royal Burghs. The quickest way to Windygates is by Cumbernauld, Dunfermline and Kirkcaldy (Iter. 97 and 94), whilst there is a direct road (A.921) from Upper Largo to Crail, through *Colinsburgh, which passes Kellie Castle.

A.803			*Glasgow	..	86¼
..	2¼	2¼	Springburn	..	83¾
..	4¼	1½	*Bishopbriggs	..	82¼
..	8¼	4	*Kirkintilloch		
			(By-pass)	..	78¼
..	13¼	5	*Kilsyth	..	73¼
A.80	18¼	5	Junc. A.803/A.80	68¼
..	18¾	½	*Dennyloanhead	67¾
A.803	19¼	½	Junc. A.80/A.803	67¼
A.876	19¾	½	Junc. A.803/A.876	66¼
A.9	22¾	3	*Larbert	..	63¾
A.876	23½	¾	N. Broomage ..	63
			*Kincardine Bridge	
A.977	29¾	6¼	*Kincardine-on-	
			Forth	..	56¾
..	34¼	4½	Forest Mill	..	52
..	37¾	3½	Blairingone	..	48½
..	40¼	2½	Powmill	..	46¼
..	42¼	2	*Crook of Devon	44¼
A.90	48¼	6	*Kinross	..	38¼
A.911	50	1¾	*Milnathort	..	36¼
..	54	4	*Kinnesswood	..	32¼
..	54¾	¾	*Portmoak	..	31½
..	55	1	*Scotlandwell	..	31¼
..	59¼	4¼	*Leslie	..	27¼
..	61¼	2	Cadham	..	25¼
..	62½	1½	*Markinch	..	24
..	64¼	1½	*Milton of	
			Balgonie	..	22¼
A.915	66	1¾	*Windygates	..	20¼
..	68½	2½	*Scoonie	..	18
..	70½	2	*Lundin Links	16
A.921	71½	1	*Upper Largo	15
A.917	74	2½	Junc. A.921/A.917	12¼
..	76¾	2¾	*Elie	..	9¼
..	79¼	2½	*St. Monance	..	7¼
..	81¼	2	*Pittenweem	..	5¼
..	82¼	1	*Anstruther	..	4¼
..	83¼	1	*Kilrenny	..	3¼
..	86¼	3¼	*Crail		

99. GLASGOW to STIRLING. A commercial route through industrial mining and agricultural districts.

A.80			*Glasgow	..	26¼
..	4¼	4¼	Millerston	..	22¼
..	5¼	1	*Stepps	..	21¼
..	7	1¾	*Muirhead	..	19¼
..	9½	2½	Mollinburn	..	17¼
..	11	1½	Condorrat	..	15¼
..	14	3	*Cumbernauld	..	12¼
..	15¼	1¼	*Castlecary	..	11
..	17¼	1¾	*Dennyloanhead	9¼
..	19½	2¼	*Denny	..	7
A.9	25¼	5¾	*St. Ninian's	..	1¼
..	26¼	1¼	*Stirling		

100. GLASGOW to FORT WILLIAM. This main road to the Western Highlands is one of the finest highways in Scotland. There is a variety of loch, woodland and mountain scenery on the journey from the industrial banks of the Clyde, by *Loch Lomond and historic *Glencoe to Fort William, which lies at the foot of *Ben Nevis, the highest mountain in Great Britain. After Alexandria, the road, winding in places, follows the west shore of Loch Lomond for more than twenty miles into the Highlands through woodland scenery, with views of Ben Lomond, which rises from the far side of the Loch. Beyond Inveruglas, where the Loch Sloy hydro-electric power station is passed, the road ascends through Glen Falloch to Crianlarich. For 30 miles commencing at Tyndrum, the re-constructed Glencoe road is carefully graded and has an excellent surface. Beyond Bridge of Orchy, Loch Tulla is attractive and contrasts with the bleaker aspect as the Black Mount is skirted to reach a height of 1,143 feet on the open Moor of Rannoch, where part of the old road is seen leading past the *Kingshouse Hotel, on the right. There are magnificent views of the Three Sisters of Glencoe as the road enters the rugged and historic pass of Glencoe and descends past Loch Triochatan to sea level at Carnach (see Iter. 142 for an alternative route from this point, avoiding Kinlochleven and the circuit of the Loch by means of the Ballachulish Ferry, saving 12½ miles). The main road then circles Loch Leven, passing some industrial developments at Kinlochleven, afterwards continuing along the shore of *Loch Linnhe, with extensive views towards the *Ardgour Hills.

A.82			*Glasgow	..	115
..	3	3	Anniesland	..	112
..	7¼	4¼	*Duntocher	..	107¾
..	11¼	4	Milton	..	103¾
..	16	4¼	*Bonhill	..	99
..	16¼	¾	*Alexandria	..	98¼
..	20¼	3¼	Arden	..	94¾
..	25¼	5¼	*Luss	..	89¼
..	34¼	8¼	*Tarbet	..	80½
..	37¼	3¼	*Inveruglas	..	77¼
..	42¼	4¼	*Ardlui	..	72½
..	51	8¼	*Crianlarich	..	64
..	56¼	5¼	*Tyndrum	..	58¼
..	63	6¼	*Bridge of Orchy	52
..	86¼	23¼	*Carnach	..	28¼
..	93¼	6¼	*Kinlochleven	..	21¼
..	102¼	9½	*N. Ballachulish	12¼
..	104¼	2	*Onich	..	10¼
..	106¼	1½	Rd. to *Corran	
			Ferry	..	8¼
..	115	8¼	*Fort William		

101. GLASGOW to INVERARAY. Industrial along Clydeside, but beyond Alexandria a scenic road, at first along the shores of *Loch Lomond to Tarbet, with views of Ben Lomond. Beyond Arrochar, at the head of Loch Long, is the Argyll National Forest Park with a fine view of Ben Arthur (The Cobbler). Then the gradual ascent of the recon-

structed road in Glen Croe to the summit at Rest and be Thankful is made, followed by an undulating descent to the shores of *Loch Fyne.

A.82			*Glasgow	..	57½
..	3	3	Anniesland	..	54¾
..	7½	4½	*Duntocher	..	50
..	11½	4	Milton	..	46
..	16	4½	*Bonhill	..	41¾
..	16½	¾	*Alexandria	..	41
..	20¼	3½	Arden	..	37½
..	25¼	5¼	*Luss	..	32
A.83	34½	8¼	*Tarbet	..	23½
..	36	1¼	*Arrochar	..	21½
..	42¼	6¼	*Rest and be	
			Thankful		15
..	48	5¼	*Cairndow	..	9¼
..	57¼	9¼	*Inveraray		

102. A tour from GLASGOW to INVERARAY through Cowal. Industrial along Clydeside to Dumbarton, then fine mountain and loch scenery by the shores of the Gare Loch and Loch Long, with an ascent of 1 in 7 between Garelochhead and Whistlefield, followed by a similar descent. Views of Ben Arthur (The Cobbler) approaching Arrochar. See Iter. 101 for an alternative route by Loch Lomond to Arrochar. Passes through the *Cowal district with the lochs and mountains of the Argyll National Forest Park, partly by narrow roads with steep gradients, portions of which can be omitted as desired. Leaving Loch Long, there is a gradual ascent by the reconstructed road in Glen Croe to the summit at Rest and be Thankful, where a detour is made to picturesque Lochgoilhead. This narrow road has passing places and a gradient of 1 in 7. The tour then traverses Hell's Glen (1 in 5) to *Loch Fyne, and after a short stretch along the shore goes inland through the hills overlooking Loch Eck, to turn off by a narrow, hilly road (1 in 4) to Glen Finart and the shores of Loch Long at Ardentinny. Thereafter a level coast road gives views of the Rosneath peninsula, before circling the Holy Loch by Hunter's Quay to Dunoon. See Iter. 137 for the direct route. On the detour along the coast past Toward Point to the road end at Inverchaolin, there are views of the islands of Bute and the *Cumbraes in the Firth of Clyde. Leaving Dunoon, the tour turns inland again by a scenic, narrow and winding road through hills, near the head of pretty Loch Striven, where there is a descent of 1 in 8 and an ascent of 1 in 5 to reach Colintraive on the well-known *Kyles of Bute. Returning from Colintraive, the lovely Glendaruel is traversed before crossing the hills with a 1 in 7 ascent and descent to the main road. A left turn at this point towards Strathlachlan (¾ m.) permits an optional extension to Tighnabruaich (see Iter. 103), an additional 47 miles.

A.82			*Glasgow	..	182¼
..	3	3	Anniesland	..	179¼
..	7¼	4¼	*Duntocher	..	174½
..	11¼	4	Milton	..	170¼

A.814	12	¼	Junc. A.82/A.814	170¼
..	14	2	*Dumbarton	168¼
..	17½	3½	*Cardross	164¾
..	21¼	3¾	Rd. to *Craigendoran Pier	161
..	22	¾	*Helensburgh	160¼
..	24¼	2¼	*Rhu	158
..	27	2¾	*Shandon	155¼
..	28½	1½	*Faslane	153¾
..	29½	1	*Garelochhead	152¾
..	31	1½	*Whistlefield (Sta.)	151¼
..	32½	1½	*Finnart	149¾
..	39½	7	*Arrochar	142¾
B.828	46¼	6¾	*Rest and be Thankful	136
B.839	49½	3¼	Junc. B.828/B.839	132¾
..	52¼	2¾	*Lochgoilhead	130
			Return	
A.815	58½	6¼	Junc. B.839/A.815	123¾
..	61¼	2¾	*St. Catherine's	121
..	65¼	4	*Strachur Pier	117
..	66¼	1	*Strachur	116
Uncl.	72½	6¼	Junc. A.815/Uncl.	109¾
A.880	77¾	5¼	*Ardentinny	104¼
..	81½	3¾	*Blairmore	100¾
..	82¼	¾	*Strone	100
..	83¾	1½	*Kilmun	98½
A.815	85¼	1½	Cothouse Bridge	97
..	87½	2¼	*Sandbank	94¾
..	88	½	*Ardnadam	94¼
..	89½	1½	*Hunter's Quay	92¾
..	90¼	¾	*Kirn	92
..	91½	1¼	*Dunoon	90¾
..	95¾	4¼	*Innellan	86¾
Uncl.	102	6¼	Junc. A.815/Uncl.	80¼
..	105½	3½	*Inverchaolin Ch.	76¾
			Return to:—	
A.885	119½	14	*Dunoon	62¾
A.815	122¼	2¾	*Sandbank	60
B.836	123¾	1¼	Junc. A.885/B.836	58¾
..	125½	2	Clachaig	56¾
B.8000	134	8½	Junc. B.836/B.8000	48¼
..	139¼	5¼	*Colintraive	42¾
			Return to:—	
B.836	145	5½	Junc. B.8000/B.836	37¼
..	147½	2½	*Glendaruel	34¾
A.886	158¼	10¾	Junc. B.836/A.886	24
A.815	162¼	4	Junc. A.886/A.815	20
..	162¾	½	*Strachur Pier	19½
..	166¾	4	*St. Catherine's	15½
A.83	171¾	5	Junc. A.815/A.83	10¾
..	172½	¾	*Cairndow	9¾
..	182¼	9¾	*Inveraray	

103. GLASGOW to TIGHNABRUAICH or COLINTRAIVE (for the Kyles of Bute). Fine mountain and loch scenery in the *Cowal district of Argyll, with views of Ben Arthur (The Cobbler) across Loch Long approaching Arrochar. See Iter. 102 for an alternative route to Arrochar, by Loch Long. A gradual ascent from Loch Long by the reconstructed road in Glen Croe to the summit at Rest and be Thankful is followed by an undulating descent to *Loch Fyne, the shores of which are followed for over 25 miles. Narrow and hilly from Otter Ferry, with fine views of the *Kyles of Bute from the shore road between Kames and Tighnabruaich. The alternative to Colintraive turns off by a 1 in 7 ascent, followed by a gradual descent along a narrow road through pretty Glendaruel, thence by a scenic shore road along Loch Riddon to the *Kyles of Bute.

			*Glasgow	84½
			By Iter. 100 to:—	
A.83	34½	34½	*Tarbet	50
..	36	1½	*Arrochar	48½
..	42¾	6¾	*Rest and be Thankful	41½
A.815	47½	4½	Junc. A.83/A.815	37
..	52½	5	*St. Catherine's	32
..	56½	4	†*Strachur Pier	28
A.886	56¾	¼	Junc. A.815/A.886	27¾
..	61¼	4½	*Strathlachlan	22¾
..	72½	10¾	*Otter Ferry	12
..	76¼	4	*Kilfinan	8
..	82	5¾	Millhouse	2¾
..	83¼	1¼	*Kames	1
..	83½	¼	*Auchenlochan	½
..	84¼	½	*Tighnabruaich	
		†	OR	
A.815	56½		*Strachur Pier	
A.886	56¾	½	Junc. A.815/A.886	
B.836	60¾	4	Junc. A.886/B.836	
..	71½	10¾	*Glendaruel	
B.8000	74	2½	Junc. B.836/B.8000	
..	79½	5½	*Colintraive	

104. GLASGOW to ROWARDENNAN. After leaving the suburbs of Glasgow, there is a pleasant run across *Stockiemuir to Drymen. Between Balmaha and Rowardennan, at the foot of Ben Lomond, a narrow, wooded road (with several short hills up to 1 in 6), follows the shores of *Loch Lomond, with views of the prettily wooded islands on the loch.

A.82			*Glasgow	28¼
A.806	3	3	Anniesland	25¼
A.809	4¼	1¼	Junc. A.806/A.809	23¾
..	5¼	1	*Bearsden	22¾
A.811	17	11¾	Junc. A.809/A.811	11¼
B.837	17¾	¾	*Drymen	10½
Uncl.	21¼	4	*Balmaha	6½
..	28¼	6¾	*Rowardennan	

105. GLASGOW to INVERSNAID. Pleasant in Strathblane, after leaving the suburbs of Glasgow, with views of the Campsie Fells. Open country to Aberfoyle, after which the narrow road passes between the hills and by several lochs, including Loch Arklet. There is a steep descent (1 in 10) to Inversnaid on *Loch Lomond. The steamer pier on Loch Katrine, at *Stronachlachar, lies ¾ m. to the east from the end of B.829.

A.82			*Glasgow	42¼
A.806	3	3	Anniesland	39¼
A.81	4¼	1¼	Junc. A.806/A.81	37¾
..	5¼	¾	Hillfoot (Sta.)	37
..	6¾	1½	*Milngavie	35½
..	11	4¼	*Strathblane	31¼
..	11½	¾	Blanefield	30¾
..	19¾	8	Ballat X-rds.	22½
A.821	26¼	6½	Junc. A.81/A.821	16
B.829	27¼	1	*Aberfoyle	15
Uncl.	38¼	11	Junc. B.829/Uncl.	4
..	42¼	4	*Inversnaid	

106. GLASGOW to CALLANDER via the Trossachs. A touring route, with splendid loch and woodland scenery on the latter part. After leaving the suburbs of Glasgow, there is a pleasant run across *Stockiemuir to Drymen, followed by open country to Aberfoyle. A picturesque, winding road then climbs over the hills, with magnificent views towards Loch Vennachar and the Trossachs. Returning from Loch Katrine, the prettily wooded shores of Loch Achray are followed at first, then on to the larger Loch Vennachar to Callander. The quickest way to Ballat X-rds. is by Iter. 105 and from that point to Callander by Iter. 109.

A.82			*Glasgow	45¼
A.806	3	3	Anniesland	42¼
A.809	4¼	1¼	Junc. A.806/A.809	40¼
..	5½	1	*Bearsden	39¼
A.811	17	11½	Junc. A.809/A.811	28¼
..	17½	¾	*Drymen	27¾
A.81	21½	3¾	Ballat X-rds.	23¾
A.821	28	6½	Junc. A.81/A.821	17¼
..	29	1	*Aberfoyle	16¼
..	35½	6½	*Loch Katrine Pier	9¼
..	36¾	1¼	*" Trossachs " Hotel	8½
..	38¼	1½	*Brig o' Turk	6¾
A.84	44	5½	Kilmahog	1¼
..	45¼	1¼	*Callander	

107. GLASGOW to ABERFELDY via the Campsie Fells and Glen Lyon. A touring route throughout, using narrow and hilly by-roads in places, although these can easily be omitted as desired. Leaves the main road before Torrance, crosses flat country to Lennoxtown, then a long climb by *Campsie Glen to the summit (1,154 feet) on the Campsie Fells, from which there are extensive views. A long descent leads through Fintry and skirts the Fintry Hills to Kippen, followed by a flat stretch to Thornhill, whence it is rather hilly to Callander. The main road to Callander is by Milngavie and Ballat X-rds. (Iter. 105 and 109). Alternatively the touring route via The Trossachs (Iter. 106) can be used. Onwards to Killin is by the main road, with an attractive stretch between Callander and Strathyre, by the Falls of Leny, where road and river wind through the pass to the shores of Loch Lubnaig. Views of Loch Earn approaching Lochearnhead, after which there is a gradual ascent through Glen Ogle over the ridge to descend into Glen Dochart and Killin. After a short run along *Loch Tay, the route turns off by the slopes of Ben Lawers along a narrow track, towards a gap in the hills. This is a rough and rutted mountain road, giving magnificent views on the gradual 4 mile ascent (max. gradient 1 in 6). The lonely Lochan na Lairige is passed before reaching the summit at 1,805 feet, after which there is a similar 4 mile descent to Bridge of Balgie in Glen Lyon. This road is easier to traverse from north to south, but can be omitted if desired, by proceeding direct along the north shore of Loch

Tay to Fortingall (Iter. 138) or to Lawers and Aberfeldy (Iter. 120). Glen Lyon is one of the longest in the country, and for those not venturing by the direct road over to Bridge of Balgie, a delightful and easy return journey can be made from Fortingall through the pretty Pass of Lyon. From Bridge of Balgie, a motoring road continues, past Meggernie Castle, with a gradually deteriorating surface, towards the wild head of the glen. Between Fortingall and Aberfeldy it is an easy valley road.

A.803			*Glasgow	..	90
..	2¾	2¾	Springburn	..	87¼
..	4¼	1½	*Bishopbriggs	..	85¾
A.807	6¼	2	Junc. A.803/A.807	83¾
B.822	7	¾	Junc. A.807/B.822	83
..	7¼	¼	Torrance	..	82¾
A.891	10	2¾	Junc. B.822/A.891	80
B.822	10¾	¾	*Lennoxtown	..	79¼
B.818	18	7¼	Junc. B.822/B.818	72
..	18½	½	*Fintry	..	71½
B.822	19¼	¾	Junc. B.818/B.822	70¾
..	25¾	6½	*Kippen	..	64¼
..	30	4¼	Thornhill	..	60
A.81	33¾	3¾	Junc. B.822/A.81	56¼
A.84	35½	2	*Callander	..	54¼
..	37	1½	Kilmahog	..	53
..	44½	7½	*Strathyre	..	45½
..	47¼	2¾	*Balquhidder Sta.	42¾
A.85	49¼	2	*Lochearnhead ..	40¾
A.827	54¼	5	Lix Toll	..	35¾
..	56¾	2½	*Killin	..	33¼
Uncl.	61¼	4½	Junc. A.827/Uncl.	28¾
..	70½	9	*Bridge of Balgie	19¼
..	71¼	1	*Innerwick Ch.	18¾
..	73¼	2	Camusvrachan	16¾
..	76¼	3	Invervar	..	13¾
..	81¾	5½	*Fortingall	..	8¼
B.846	84½	2¾	*Coshieville	..	5½
..	89	4½	*Weem	..	1
..	90	1	*Aberfeldy		

108 GLASGOW to STIRLING via Killearn. Pleasant in Strathblane, after leaving the suburbs of Glasgow, with views of the Campsie Fells, later through open country and following a level road for the last ten miles. Passes close to the villages of *Kippen and *Gargunnock. For through journeys it is quicker to avoid Killearn via Ballat X-rds. (Iter. 105 and 112), while the direct route is given in Iter. 99.

A.82			*Glasgow	..	38½
A.806	3	3	Anniesland	..	35½
A.81	4½	1½	Junc. A.806/A.81	34
..	5¼	¾	Hillfoot (Sta.)	..	33¼
..	6¾	1½	*Milngavie	..	31¾
..	11	4¼	*Strathblane	..	27½
..	11¾	¾	Blanefield	..	26¾
A.875	14½	2¾	Junc. A.81/A.875	24
..	16¾	2¼	*Killearn	..	21¾
..	19½	2¾	*Balfron	..	19
A.811	21½	2	Junc. A.875/A.811	17
..	23¾	2¼	*Buchlyvie	..	14¾
..	26¼	2½	Arnprior	..	12¼
..	38½	12¼	*Stirling		

109. PAISLEY to CALLANDER via Erskine Ferry. A useful link route avoiding Glasgow by means of the Erskine Ferry. Featureless country to Bonhill, then fine open scenery, later passing the Lake of Menteith before reaching Port of Menteith. About half-

way between this point and Callander the road is hilly, with an ascent and descent of 1 in 9.

A.726			*Paisley	..	42¾
..	5¼	5¼	*Erskine Ferry	
A.814			*Old Kilpatrick	37
..	7½	1½	*Bowling	..	35¼
A.82	8	½	Junc. A.814/A.82	34¾
..	8¾	¾	Milton	..	34
A.811	13	4¼	*Bonhill	..	29¾
..	14	1	Jamestown	..	28¾
..	18	4	*Gartocharn	..	24¾
..	22½	4½	*Drymen	..	20¼
A.81	26	3½	Ballat X-rds.	..	16¾
..	36	10	*Port of Menteith	6¾
..	42¾	6¾	*Callander		

110. PAISLEY to OBAN via Erskine Ferry. Except for the crossing of the Clyde estuary, where the Erskine Ferry is utilised to avoid Glasgow, this is an excellent road through beautiful loch and mountain scenery. After Alexandria, the road winds along the shores of *Loch Lomond into the Highlands, with views of Ben Lomond. At Inveruglas is the Loch Sloy hydro-electric power station, and the road then goes by way of Glen Falloch to Crianlarich and Tyndrum, near which Ben Lui is well seen. There is a fine view of Ben Cruachan approaching Dalmally, before crossing Loch Awe by the new bridge near *Kilchurn Castle, and there are more extensive views as the road follows the lochside towards the narrowing Pass of Brander. Pleasant along the shore road of Loch Etive before passing beneath Connel Bridge, after which *Dunstaffnage Castle lies just north of the road.

A.726			*Paisley	..	90¼
..	5¼	5¼	*Erskine Ferry	
A.814			*Old Kilpatrick	84½
..	7½	1½	*Bowling	..	82¾
A.82	8	½	Junc. A.814/A.82	82¼
..	8¾	¾	Milton	..	81½
..	13	4¼	*Bonhill	..	77¼
..	13¾	¾	*Alexandria	..	76½
..	17¼	3½	Arden	..	73
..	22¾	5½	*Luss	..	67½
..	31¼	8½	*Tarbet	..	59
..	34¾	3½	*Inveruglas	..	55½
..	39¼	4½	*Ardlui	..	50¾
..	48	8½	*Crianlarich	..	42¼
A.85	53½	5½	*Tyndrum	..	36¾
..	65½	12	*Dalmally	..	24¾
..	68½	3	*Loch Awe	
			(Hotel)	..	21¾
..	72	3½	*Falls of Cruachan	18¼
..	75½	3½	Bridge of Awe	..	14¾
..	78	2½	*Taynuilt	..	12¼
..	85	7	*Connel	..	5¼
..	90½	5¼	*Oban		

111. A tour from PAISLEY to STIRLING via Loch Long and the Trossachs. A tour embracing the sea lochs of Dunbartonshire, together with some of the lochs and mountains of the Perthshire Highlands, and including the Trossachs district. Avoiding Glasgow by the Erskine Ferry, the tour traverses flat country on the industrial north bank of the Clyde to Dumbarton. Beyond Helensburgh, there is fine mountain and loch scenery on the

shores of the Gare Loch and Loch Long. Between Garelochhead and Whistlefield there is an ascent of 1 in 7 followed by a similar descent. Views of Ben Arthur (The Cobbler) approaching Arrochar, before crossing to the shore of *Loch Lomond, where there is a fine view of Ben Lomond. If preferred, the direct road along Loch Lomondside can be followed from the ferry, see Iter. 110. Continuing into the Highlands, by the shores of Loch Lomond, the Loch Sloy hydro-electric power station is passed at Inveruglas, the tour then ascending through Glen Falloch to Crianlarich, and traversing in turn Glen Dochart and Glen Ogle, with Ben More overlooking the former. Lochearnhead is situated above Loch Earn, and an attractive stretch beyond Strathyre leads by the winding shores of pretty Loch Lubnaig, and afterwards by way of the Pass and Falls of Leny to Kilmahog, where a short detour can be made to visit Callander, before taking the road to the Trossachs along the edge of Loch Vennachar and the wooded Loch Achray. Returning from Loch Katrine, a picturesque, winding road crosses over the hills, giving extensive views, before descending to Aberfoyle and past the Lake of Menteith to the open country.

A.726			*Paisley	..	118
..	5¼	5¼	*Erskine Ferry	
A.814			*Old Kilpatrick	112½
..	7½	1½	*Bowling	..	110½
A.82	8	½	Junc. A.814/A.82	110
..	8¾	¾	Milton	..	109¼
A.814	9	¼	Junc. A.82/A.814	109
..	11	2	*Dumbarton	..	107
..	14½	3½	*Cardross	..	103½
..	18½	3½	Rd. to *Craigen-	
			doran Pier	..	99¾
..	19	½	*Helensburgh	..	99
..	21½	2½	*Rhu	..	96½
..	24	2½	*Shandon	..	94
..	25½	1½	*Faslane	..	92½
..	26½	1	*Garelochhead ..	91½
..	28	1½	*Whistlefield	
			(Sta.)	..	90
..	38	1½	*Finnart	..	88½
A.83	36½	7	*Arrochar	..	81½
A.82	38½	1½	*Tarbet	..	79¾
..	41¾	3½	*Inveruglas	..	76¼
..	46½	4½	*Ardlui	..	71½
A.85	55	8½	*Crianlarich	..	63
..	66½	11½	Lix Toll	..	51½
A.84	71½	5	*Lochearnhead	..	46½
..	73½	2	*Balquhidder Sta. ..	44½
..	76	2½	*Strathyre	..	42
A.821	83½	7½	Kilmahog	..	34½
..	89	5½	*Brig o' Turk	..	29
..	90¼	1¼	*" Trossachs "	
			Hotel	..	27½
..	92	1¼	*Loch Katrine	
			Pier	..	26
..	98½	6½	*Aberfoyle	..	19½
A.81	99½	1	Junc. A.821/A.81	18½
..	103	3½	*Port of Menteith	15
A.873	104½	1½	Junc. A.81/A.873	13½
..	108½	4	Thornhill	..	9½
A.84	112	3½	Junc. A.873/A.84	6
..	118	6	*Stirling		

112. GOUROCK to STIRLING via Erskine Ferry. Industrial on the south bank of the River Clyde, then utilises the Erskine Ferry to avoid Glasgow. Traverses pleasant, open agricultural country beyond Bonhill, with views of the Campsie Fells, to the south-east, and following a level road for the last ten miles, passing close to the villages of *Kippen and *Gargunnock.

A.8			*Gourock	..	54¼
..	3	3	*Greenock	..	51¼
..	6¼	3¼	*Port Glasgow	..	48
..	10	3¾	Langbank	..	44¼
B.815	13¼	3¼	Junc. A.8/B.815		41
A.726	15¼	2	Junc. B.815/A.726		39
..	15½	¼	*Erskine Ferry		
A.814			*Old Kilpatrick		38¼
..	17¼	1½	*Bowling	..	37
A.82	17¼	½	Junc. A.814/A.82		36¼
..	18¼	¼	Milton	..	35¼
A.811	22¾	4¼	*Bonhill	..	31¼
..	23¼	1	Jamestown	..	30¼
..	27¼	4	*Gartocharn	..	26¼
..	32¼	4½	*Drymen	..	22
..	36	3¼	Ballat X-rds.	..	18¼
..	39¼	3½	*Buchlyvie	..	14¼
..	42	2½	Arnprior	..	12¼
..	54¼	12¼	*Stirling		

113. FALKIRK to GOUROCK via Erskine Ferry. At first through agricultural districts, with mining developments in places. From Kirkintilloch an intricate cross-country route is followed, avoiding Glasgow to the north and crossing the River Clyde by the Erskine Ferry. Industrial on the banks of the Clyde.

A.9			*Falkirk	..	46¼
A.803	1	1	*Camelon	..	45¼
..	4	3	*Bonnybridge	..	42¼
A.80	5	1	Junc. A.803/A.80		41¼
..	5½	½	*Dennyloanhead		40¾
A.803	6	½	Junc. A.80/A.803		40¼
..	11	5	*Kilsyth	..	35¼
..	16	5	*Kirkintilloch (By-pass)		30¼
A.807	18¼	2¼	Junc. A.803/A.807		28
..	19	¾	Torrance	..	27¼
..	20¼	1¼	Balmore	..	26
A.81	23¼	3¼	Junc. A.807/A.81		22¼
A.808	24¼	1¼	Hillfoot (Sta.)	..	21¼
A.809	25¼	½	*Bearsden	..	21
A.810	25¼		Junc. A.809/A.810		20¼
..	28¼	2½	Hardgate	..	18
A.82	29	¾	*Duntocher	..	17¼
A.814	30¼	1¼	Junc. A.82/A.814		16
..	30¼	½	*Old Kilpatrick		
A.726			*Erskine Ferry	..	15¼
B.815	31	½	Junc. A.726/B.815		15¼
A.8	33	2	Junc. B.815/A.8		13¼
..	36¼	3¼	Langbank	..	10
..	40	3¾	*Port Glasgow	..	6¼
..	43¼	3¼	*Greenock	..	3
..	46¼	3	*Gourock		

114. FALKIRK to HELENSBURGH via Fintry. Industrial to Denny, then a tourist route by a narrow and hilly moorland road to Fintry, which lies between the Fintry Hills and Campsie Fells. Undulating on the latter part, and touches the shore of Loch Lomond for a short distance. The quickest way to Gartocharn is by Stirling (Iter. 95 and 137).

A.9			*Falkirk	..	45¼
A.803	1	1	*Camelon	..	44¼
A.883	2¼	1¼	Junc. A.803/A.883		43
B.818	5¼	3¼	*Denny	..	39¼

..	18¼	13	*Fintry	..	26¼
A.875	24¼	6¼	Junc. B.818/A.875		20¼
B.834	25¼	1	*Killearn	..	19¼
A.809	28	2¼	Junc. B.834/A.809		17¼
A.811	30¼	2¼	Junc. A.809/A.811		15
..	33¼	3½	*Gartocharn	..	11¼
A.813	37	3¼	Junc. A.811/A.813		8¼
..	37½	½	*Balloch	..	7¼
A.82	37¾	¼	Junc. A.813/A.82		7¼
B.831	40¼	2½	Arden	..	5
B.832	41¼	1½	Junc. B.831/B.832		3½
..	45¼	3½	*Helensburgh		

115. FALKIRK to ROWARDENNAN via Kilsyth. A cross-country link, with mining developments in places to Kilsyth, then pleasant agricultural scenery with views of the Campsie Fells to the north. Between Balmaha and Rowardennan, at the foot of Ben Lomond, a narrow, wooded road (with several short hills up to 1 in 6) follows the shores of *Loch Lomond, with views of the prettily wooded islands on the loch. Iter. 114 shows an alternative route through Fintry, but the quickest route is via Stirling (Iter. 95 and 137) to Drymen.

A.9			*Falkirk	..	42
A.803	1	1	*Camelon	..	41
..	4	3	*Bonnybridge	..	38
A.80	5	1	Junc. A.803/A.80		37
..	5½	½	*Dennyloanhead		36½
A.803	6	½	Junc. A.80/A.803		36
..	11	5	*Kilsyth	..	31
A.891	14	3	Junc. A.803/A.891		28
..	15¼	1¼	Milton	..	26¼
..	17¼	1¼	*Lennoxtown	..	24¼
..	18¼	1¼	*Campsie Glen	..	23¼
A.81	22¼	3½	*Strathblane	..	19¼
..	23	¾	Blanefield	..	19
B.834	27¼	4¼	Junc. A.81/B.834		14¼
A.809	28¼	1	Junc. B.834/A.809		13¼
A.811	30¼	2¼	Junc. A.809/A.811		11¼
B.837	31¼	¾	*Drymen	..	10¼
Uncl.	35¼	4	*Balmaha	..	6¼
..	42	6¼	*Rowardennan		

116. HELENSBURGH to COULPORT (Rosneath peninsula). Except between Rosneath and Kilcreggan, where there is a short ascent and descent, this is a practically level road circling the shores of the Gare Loch to the Rosneath peninsula, and finally along the shores of Loch Long.

A.814			*Helensburgh	..	21¼
..	2¼	2¼	*Rhu	..	19¼
..	5	2¼	*Shandon	..	16¼
..	6½	1½	*Faslane	..	15¼
..	7½	1	*Garelochhead	..	14¼
B.833	7¾	¼	Junc. A.82/B.833		14
..	12¼	4½	Clynder	..	9¼
..	13¼	¾	*Rosneath	..	8¼
..	15¼	2½	*Kilcreggan	..	6
..	17¼	2	*Cove	..	4
..	21¼	4	*Coulport		

117. INVERARAY to OBAN. Splendid views of Loch Awe and Ben Cruachan from the crest of the hill between Inveraray and Cladich, where there is a short 1 in 8 gradient. Crosses the new bridge near *Kilchurn Castle and follows the banks of Loch Awe towards the narrowing Pass of Brander. Pleasant along the shore road by Loch

Etive before passing under Connel Bridge, after which *Dunstaffnage Castle lies just to the north of the road. For alternative routes see Iter. 118 and 119. Just before Taynuilt a side road (B.845) leads to *Kilchrenan, beyond which the narrow road along the west shore of Loch Awe is rough and not advised. The ferry across Loch Awe to Portsonachan is unsuitable for vehicles.

A.819			*Inveraray	..	38¼
..	9¼	9¼	*Cladich	..	29¼
A.85	15	5¼	Junc. A.819/A.85		23¾
..	17	2	*" Loch Awe " Hotel		21¼
..	20¼	3¼	*Falls of Cruachan		18¼
..	24	3¼	Bridge of Awe	..	14¼
..	26¼	2¼	*Taynuilt	..	12¼
..	33¼	7	*Connel	..	5¼
..	38¼	5¼	*Oban		

118. INVERARAY to OBAN via Lochgilphead. A very fine scenic route, with a variety of loch and mountain scenery, becoming hilly on the latter part. Follows the shore of *Loch Fyne to Lochgilphead, and is level to Kilmartin. Approaching Kintraw the road becomes hilly (max. gradient 1 in 8). Later follows the edge of Loch Melfort, through the wooded Pass of Melfort to Kilninver, after which there is a pleasant stretch along Loch Feochan. See Iter. 117 and 119 for alternative routes.

A.83			*Inveraray	..	61¼
..	8	8	*Furnace	..	53¼
..	10	2	*Crarae	..	51¼
..	11½	1½	*Minard	..	50¼
..	17	5½	*Lochgair	..	44¼
A.816	24¼	7¼	*Lochgilphead	..	37¼
..	28¼	3¾	*Kilmichael	..	33¼
..	32¼	4½	*Kilmartin	..	29
..	38¼	5¾	*Kintraw	..	23¼
..	46¼	8¼	*Kilmelford	..	15¼
..	53¼	7	*Kilninver	..	8¼
..	61¼	8¼	*Oban		

119. INVERARAY to OBAN or ARDRISHAIG via Loch Awe. Splendid views of Ben Cruachan and *Loch Awe from the crest of the hill between Inveraray and Cladich, afterwards following a secondary road with fair surface alongside Loch Awe for many miles. Hilly after joining the main road beyond Ford Hotel, with a maximum gradient of 1 in 8. Later follows the edge of Loch Melfort and through the wooded Pass of Melfort to Kilninver, after which there is a pleasant stretch along Loch Feochan. The alternative follows a level road back to Loch Fyne at Ardrishaig.

A.819			*Inveraray	..	60¼
B.840	9¼	9¼	*Cladich	..	51¼
..	12¼	3¼	*Portsonachan	..	48
..	21¼	8¼	*Portinnisherrich		39½
..	30¼	9¼	†*Ford (Hotel)	..	30¼
A.816	33¼	4	Junc. B.840/A.816		23½
..	37¼	4	*Kintraw	..	23¼
..	45¼	8¼	*Kilmelford	..	15¼
..	52¼	7	*Kilninver	..	8¼
..	60¼	8¼	*Oban		
†			OR		
B.840	30¼		*Ford (Hotel)		

A.816	33¾	2½	Junc. B.840/A.816	
..	34½	1½	*Kilmartin	
..	39	4½	*Kilmichael	
A.817	42½	3	Junc. A.816/A.817	
A.83	42¾	½	Junc. A.817/A.83	
..	44¼	1½	**Ardrishaig**	

120. INVERARAY to PITLOCHRY.

Splendid views of Ben Cruachan and Loch Awe from the crest of the hill between Inveraray and Cladich, then an easy, undulating road through the hills to Killin, where there is a grand view of Ben Lawers. The whole length of *Loch Tay is then traversed to Kenmore, after which it is pleasant in the Tay and Tummel valleys.

A.819			*Inveraray	..	84¼
..	9¼	9¼	*Cladich	..	75
A.85	15	5¾	Junc. A.819/A.85		69¼
..	16	1	*Dalmally	..	68¼
A.82	28	12	*Tyndrum	..	56¼
..	33½	5½	*Crianlarich	..	50¾
A.827	44¾	11¼	Lix Toll	..	39½
..	47¼	2½	*Killin	..	37
..	55¾	8½	*Lawers	..	28½
..	60	4¼	*Fearnan	..	24¼
..	63¾	3¾	*Kenmore	..	20½
..	69¾	6¼	**Aberfeldy**	..	14½
..	74¾	5	*Grandtully	..	9½
..	79	4¼	*Logierait	..	5¼
A.9	79¾	¾	Ballinluig	..	4½
..	84¼	4½	**Pitlochry**		

121. INVERARAY to CAMPBELTOWN.

A fine scenic run at first along the shores of *Loch Fyne to Tarbert, then crossing a narrow isthmus to the shores of West Loch Tarbert, and following the Atlantic coast road on the west side of the *Kintyre peninsula. Hilly between Whitehouse and Clachan, with a maximum gradient of 1 in 7.

A.83			*Inveraray	..	76¼
..	8	8	*Furnace	..	68¼
..	10	2	*Crarae	..	66¼
..	11½	1½	*Minard	..	64¾
..	17	5½	*Lochgair	..	59¼
..	24½	7½	*Lochgilphead	..	51¾
..	26½	2	**Ardrishaig**	..	49¾
..	38¼	11¾	*Tarbert	..	38
..	39¾	1½	*W. Loch Tarbert		
			Pier	..	36¾
..	44¼	4½	Whitehouse	..	32
..	49¼	5	Clachan	..	27
..	57¼	8	*Tayinloan	..	19
..	58¼	1	Killean	..	18
..	63¾	5½	*Glenbarr	..	12½
..	66¾	3	Bellochantuy	..	9½
..	72	5¼	Kilkenzie	..	4¼
..	76¼	4¼	*Campbeltown		

122. CAMPBELTOWN to OBAN via the East Coast of Kintyre.

A fine scenic tour along the east coast of *Kintyre, later touching the west coast of Argyll with its numerous islands off-shore. A narrow, winding and hilly road to West Loch Tarbert, particularly hilly between Saddell and Carradale, where there are gradients of 1 in 7, with hairpin bends. Fine views of the Isle of Arran across Kilbrennan Sound. A short detour can be made from Claonaig to visit *Skipness (2½ miles). The main road to Tarbert is by the west coast of Kintyre, see

Iter. 121 Beyond Tarbert a level road along the shore of *Loch Fyne is followed to Ardrishaig, then inland to Kilmartin. In *Knapdale a hilly road (B.8024) provides a loop from Tarbert to Ardrishaig, passing by West Loch Tarbert and Loch Killisport. Approaching Kintraw the road becomes hilly (maximum gradient 1 in 8). Later the road follows the edge of Loch Melfort and then through the wooded Pass of Melfort to Kilninver, after which there is a pleasant stretch along Loch Feochan. Between Ardrishaig and Kilmichael, a detour can be made along the Crinan Canal via *Cairnbaan to visit *Crinan, with possible extensions by Loch Sween to *Kilmory Knap and *Tayvallich. Another detour can be made at Kilninver for *Clachan Bridge leading to the slate-quarrying island of Seil.

B.842			*Campbeltown		89¼
..	10	10	*Saddell	..	79½
..	15	5	*Carradale (P.O.)		74½
..	19½	4½	*Grogport	..	70
B.8001	29	9½	*Claonaig	..	60¼
A.83	33½	4½	Junc. B.8001/A.83	55¾
..	37¾	4	*W. Loch Tarbert		
			Pier	..	51¾
..	39¼	1½	*Tarbert	..	50¼
..	51	11¾	**Ardrishaig**	..	38½
A.817	52½	1½	Junc. A.83/A.817	37
A.816	53	½	Junc. A.817/A.816	36½
..	56	3	*Kilmichael	..	33½
..	60½	4½	*Kilmartin	..	29
..	66	5½	*Kintraw	..	23½
..	74¾	8¾	*Kilmelford	..	15¼
..	81¾	7	*Kilninver	..	8¼
..	89½	8¼	**Oban**		

123. CAMPBELTOWN to MACHRIHANISH and MULL OF KINTYRE.

Two independent routes covering the southern extremity of the *Kintyre peninsula. A level road is followed to Machrihanish on the Atlantic coast. The road to Southend is hilly, then follows the coast to Carskey, after which it is only a rough private track (gradient 1 in 7).

A.83			*Campbeltown	..	5¾
B.843	1¾	1¾	Stewarton	..	4
..	4	2¼	Drumlemble	..	1¾
..	5¾	1¾	*Machrihanish		
			OR		
A.83			*Campbeltown	..	18½
B.842	1¾	1¾	Stewarton	..	16¾
Uncl.	9¼	7½	*Southend	..	9
..	13	3¾	Carskey	..	5½
..	18½	5½	*Mull Lighthouse		
			(Mull of Kintyre)		

124. OBAN to FORT WILLIAM via Connel Bridge.

A coast route, with fine mountain and loch scenery, and utilising the road-rail toll bridge across Loch Etive at Connel. *Dunstaffnage Castle lies just north of the road before reaching Connel, and *Barcaldine Castle is to the west beyond Benderloch. A side road to *Port Appin is passed before reaching the coast at Portnacroish, with a view of Castle Stalker, on its island, and there are extensive prospects across *Loch Linnhe towards the *Ardgour Hills. At Ballachulish, the

road turns inland to encircle *Loch Leven, with some fine views of the Glencoe Hills. There is some industrial development at Kinlochleven, and if preferred the journey around Loch Leven can be avoided by crossing the ferry at Ballachulish, saving 19¼ miles. The latter part of the route is by a shore road alongside Loch Linnhe to Fort William, at the foot of *Ben Nevis, the highest mountain in Great Britain. A detour can be made from Connel North along the north shore of Loch Etive passing the ruined priory of *Ardchattan, and thence by B.845 over the hill and by Glen Salach to rejoin the main road around Loch Creran. There is a ferry across Loch Etive linking B.845 to Bonawe. For an alternative touring route through Glencoe and avoiding Connel Bridge, see Iter. 125.

A.85			*Oban	..	68
Uncl.	4¾	4¾	Junc. A.85/Uncl.	63¼
..			*Connel Br. (Toll)	
A.828	5¼	½	Connel North	..	62¾
..	7½	2¼	Ledaig	..	60½
..	8	½	*Benderloch	..	60
..	20½	12½	*Creagan	..	47½
..	23½	3	*Appin (P.O.)	..	44½
..	24	½	*Portnacroish	..	44
..	29½	5½	*Duror (Sta.)	..	38½
..	33½	3½	*Kentallen (Sta.)	34½
..	36¼	2¾	†*" Ballachulish "		
			Hotel	..	31¾
..	37½	1¼	*Ballachulish Sta.	30¼
A.82	39¾	2¼	*Carnach	..	28¼
..	46¼	6½	*Kinlochleven	..	21¾
..	55¾	9½	*N. Ballachulish	12¼
..	57½	2	*Onich	..	10¼
..	59¼	1½	Rd. to *Corran		
			Ferry	..	8¾
..	68	8¾	**Fort William**		
		†	OR		
A.828	36¼		*" Ballachulish " Hotel	
			Ferry to		
			" Loch Leven " Hotel	
82	36½	¼	*N. Ballachulish	
..	38½	2	*Onich	
..	40	1½	Rd. to *Corran Ferry	
..	48¾	8¾	**Fort William**	

125. OBAN to FORT WILLIAM via the Pass of Glencoe.

Magnificent mountain and loch scenery throughout. *Dunstaffnage Castle lies just north of the road before passing under Connel Bridge, after which a pleasant road is followed along the shore of Loch Etive, on which *Bonawe is situated, just off the road from Taynuilt. Views of Ben Cruachan before reaching the Pass of Brander, then a shore road alongside Loch Awe, later passing *Kilchurn Castle. Easy to Tyndrum, then for 30 miles follows the reconstructed *Glencoe road, carefully graded and with an excellent surface. The direct road (B.8074) from Dalmally by Glen Orchy to Bridge of Orchy is an attractive valley road, with fine views, but has a rough surface in places and is rather narrow, with numerous passing bays. Beyond Bridge of Orchy, Loch Tulla is attractive, and contrasts with the bleaker aspect of the Black Mount, which is skirted to reach a height of 1,143 feet on the open Moor of Rannoch. Part of the old road is seen leading past the *Kingshouse Hotel on the right, while another road to the left through Glen Etive ends at Loch Etive head. There are magnificent views of the Three Sisters of Glencoe as the road enters the rugged and historic Pass of Glencoe and descends, past Loch Triochatan to sea level at *Loch Leven. See Iter. 142 for an alternative from this point using the Ballachulish ferry to avoid Kinlochleven and the circuit of the loch thus saving 12¼ miles. The main road then circles Loch Leven, passing some industrial development at Kinlochleven, afterwards continuing along the shores of *Loch Linnhe, with extensive views towards the *Ardgour hills, to reach Fort William, at the foot of *Ben Nevis, the highest mountain in Great Britain. The direct road from Oban is given in Iter. 124.

Road			Place		
A.85			*Oban	..	95¼
..	5¼	5¼	*Connel		90
..	12¼	7	*Taynuilt		83
..	14¾	2½	Bridge of Awe		80¼
..	18¼	3½	*Falls of Cruachan		77
..	21¾	3½	*Loch Awe (Hotel)		73½
..	24¾	3	*Dalmally		70½
A.82	36¾	12	*Tyndrum		58¼
..	43¼	6½	*Bridge of Orchy		52
..	67	23¾	*Carnach		28¼
..	73½	6½	*Kinlochleven		21¼
..	83	9½	*N. Ballachulish		12¼
..	85	2	*Onich		10¼
..	86½	1½	Rd. to *Corran Ferry		8¾
..	95¼	8¾	*Fort William		

126. KIRKCALDY to DUNDEE.
Open agricultural country, utilising the ferry between Newport and Dundee, from which there is a fine view of the Tay Bridge. Before reaching Kilmany a detour can be made to the ruined *Balmerino Abbey.

Road			Place		
A.92			*Kirkcaldy	..	28¼
..	1½	1½	Sinclairtown		26¾
..	2	½	Gallatown		26¼
..	4½	2½	*Thornton		23¾
..	6¼	1¾	*Glenrothes		22
..	7¼	1	Cadham		21
A.914	9¼	2	Junc. A.92/A.914		19
..	22¾	13½	*Kilmany		5½
..	26½	3¾	*Wormit		1¾
..	28¼	1¾	*Newport Ferry to *Dundee		

127. KIRKCALDY to DUNDEE via Cupar.
Pleasant, open agricultural country for the greater part. Hilly between Windygates and Cupar, with an ascent of 1 in 9 at Kennoway. Utilises the ferry across the Tay between Newport and Dundee, from which there is a view of the Tay Bridge. The normal route is given in Iter. 126 and a better way to Cupar is by Iter. 93.

Road			Place		
A.92			*Kirkcaldy	..	29¼
..	1½	1½	Sinclairtown		27¾
..	2	½	Gallatown		27¼
A.915	2½	½	Junc. A.92/A.915		26¾
A.916	7¾	5¼	*Windygates		21½
..	9¼	1½	Kennoway		20
..	15¼	6	*Craigrothie		14
A.92	17½	2¼	Junc. A.916/A.92		11¾
A.91	18¼	¾	*Cupar		11
A.92	21¼	3	*Dairsie		8
A.92	21½	¼	Junc. A.91/A.92		7¾
..	25½	3¾	" St. Michaels " Hotel		4
..	29¼	4	*Newport Ferry to *Dundee		

128. KIRKCALDY to ST. ANDREWS via Leven.
Colliery developments on the coast road to Lundin Links. Between Dysart and Coaltown there is a side road leading to *West Wemyss. Hilly, agricultural country on the latter part. The quickest way to Lundin Links is by Windygates, Iter. 94, and to St. Andrews the quickest is by Cupar, see Iter. 93. Another alternative is given in Iter. 129.

Road			Place	
A.92			*Kirkcaldy	24
A.955	1¼	1¼	Junc. A.92/A.955	22¾
..	2	¾	*Dysart	22
..	4½	2½	Coaltown of Wemyss	19½
..	5¾	1¼	*East Wemyss	18¼
..	7¼	1½	*Buckhaven	16¾
..	8¼	1	*Methil	15¾
..	9¼	1	*Leven	14¾
A.915	10	¾	*Scoonie	14
..	12	2	*Lundin Links	12
..	13	1	*Upper Largo	11
..	17¼	4¼	Largoward	6¾
..	18¼	1	Lathones	5¾
..	24	5¾	*St. Andrews	

129. KIRKCALDY to ST. ANDREWS via Ceres.
Pleasant agricultural country. Hilly between Windygates and Ceres, with an ascent of 1 in 9 at Kennoway. Utilises secondary roads from Craigrothie. For other alternatives see Iter. 93, 94, 127 and 128.

A.92			*Kirkcaldy	..	24¼
..	1½	1½	Sinclairtown		23¾
..	2	½	Gallatown		22¾
A.915	2½	½	Junc. A.92/A.915		22¼
A.916	7¾	5¼	*Windygates		17
..	9¼	1½	Kennoway		15½
B.939	15¼	6	*Craigrothie		9½
..	16½	1¼	*Ceres		8
..	18¼	1½	*Pitscottie		6½
..	24¼	6¼	*St. Andrews		

130. KIRKCALDY to PERTH.
An easy road, with varied scenery, mainly through agricultural country, with views of the Lomond and Ochil Hills. Pretty in Glenfarg near the Bein Inn.

Road			Place		
A.92			*Kirkcaldy	..	28¼
..	1½	1½	Sinclairtown		26¾
..	2	½	Gallatown		26¼
..	4½	2½	*Thornton		23¾
..	6¼	1¾	*Glenrothes		22
..	7¼	1	Cadham		21
A.912	9¼	2	Junc. A.92/A.912		19
..	11½	2¼	*Falkland		16¾
..	15	3½	*Strathmiglo		13¼
A.91	15¼	¼	Junc. A.912/A.91		13
A.912	17	1¾	Gateside		11¼
A.90	20	3	" Bein " Inn		8¼
..	22	2	Aberargie		6¼
..	24¼	2¼	*Bridge of Earn		4
..	28¼	4	*Perth		

131. ST. ANDREWS to PERTH.
Pretty scenery, with fine views of the River Tay on the latter part.

Road			Place		
A.91			*St. Andrews	..	31¼
..	4	4	*Guardbridge		27¼
..	6½	2½	*Dairsie		24¾
A.913	9½	3	*Cupar		21¾
..	17½	8¼	*Lindores		13¾
..	20	2½	*Newburgh		11¼
..	23¼	3¼	*Abernethy		8
A.90	25	1¾	Aberargie		6¼
..	27¼	2¼	*Bridge of Earn		4
..	31¼	4	*Perth		

132. PERTH to CRAIL or ELIE.
Pretty scenery, with views of the River Tay on the first part. Hilly from Cupar to Crail and also from Cupar to Elie.

Road			Place		
A.90			*Perth	..	39¼
..	4	4	*Bridge of Earn		35¼
A.913	6¼	2¼	Aberargie		33
..	8	1¾	*Abernethy		31¼
..	11¼	3¼	*Newburgh		28
..	13½	2¼	*Lindores		25¾
B.940	21½	8¼	*Cupar		17½
..	24½	3	*Pitscottie		14½
..	28½	3½	†" Peat " Inn		11
A.918	38½	10½	Junc. B.940/A.918		¼
..	39½	½	*Crail		
		†	OR		
B.941	28½		" Peat " Inn		
..	30	1½	Largoward		
..	34½	4½	*Kinconquhar		
A.917	35¼	¾	Junc. B.941/A.917		
..	36¼	1	*Elie		

133. STIRLING to KIRKCALDY via Dunfermline.
A pleasant, easy road with views of the Ochil Hills on the first part.

A.9			*Stirling	..	35
A.91	1¼	1¼	*Causewayhead		33¾
A.907	2¼	1	Junc. A.91/A.907		32¾
..	5¼	2½	Cambus		29¾
..	7½	2¼	*Alloa		27½
..	9¼	1¾	*Clackmannan		25¼
..	16¾	7½	*Oakley		18¼
..	18	1¼	Carnock		17
..	21½	3½	*Dunfermline		13½
..	23¾	2¼	Halbeath		11¼
..	25	1¼	*Crossgates		10
..	26½	1½	Donibristle		8½
..	35	8½	*Kirkcaldy		

134. STIRLING to KIRKCALDY via Culross.
Views of the Ochil Hills at first, and beyond Kincardine some fine scenery along the shores of the River Forth, including a detour to visit Culross (N.T. Scot.) and views of the Forth Bridge. Hilly beyond Aberdour, where there is an ascent of 1 in 6½. A shorter route (by 1½ miles) to Kincardine is by the south side of the River Forth, then across Kincardine Bridge. The direct road from Kincardine to Newmills is shown in Iter. 97. and the coast road through Burntisland and Kinghorn can be avoided by proceeding via B.923 from Kirkton. The quickest route from Stirling to Kirkcaldy is by Dunfermline (Iter. 133) and from Inverkeithing by Iter. 94.

Road			Place		
A.9			*Stirling	..	39¼
A.91	1¼	1¼	*Causewayhead		38

A.907	2¾	1	Junc. A.91/A.907	37
..	5¼	2½	Cambus ..	34½
..	7½	2¼	*Alloa ..	32¼
..	9¼	1¾	*Clackmannan ..	30½
A.985	10½	1¼	Junc.A.907/A.985	29¼
A.977	11	½	Junc.A.985/A.977	28¾
Uncl.	12¼	1¼	Junc. A.977/Uncl.	27½
..	12¾	½	*Kincardine-on-Forth ..	27
..	16¾	4	*Culross ..	23
A.985	17¾	1	Junc. Uncl./A.985	22
..	18½	¾	*Newmills ..	21¼
..	19¼	¾	*Torryburn ..	20½
..	21	1¾	Crombie ..	18¾
..	25½	4½	*Rosyth ..	14
A.90	26¼	¾	Junc. A.985/A.90	13¾
A.92	26¾	¼	*Inverkeithing ..	13
..	28¼	1½	Hillend ..	11¼
..	31	2¾	*Aberdour ..	8½
..	33¾	2¾	Kirkton ..	6
..	34¼	½	**Burntisland** (W.M.) ..	5½
..	36¼	2½	*Kinghorn ..	3
..	39¼	3	**Kirkcaldy**	

135. STIRLING to PERTH. An easy main road through fine country, with views of the Ochil Hills at first. Carsebreck Pond lies to the north of the road between Greenloaning and Blackford. Extensive views of the Perthshire hills on the latter part.

A.9			*Stirling ..	34½
..	1¾	1¾	*Causewayhead	32¾
..	3¾	1¾	*Bridge of Allan	31¼
..	6	2¼	*Dunblane ..	28½
..	11½	5½	*Greenloaning ..	23
..	16	4½	*Blackford ..	18½
..	18	2	Loaninghead X-rds.	16½
..	18¾	¾	Gleneagles (Sta.)	15¾
..	20¼	1½	*Auchterarder	14¼
..	23	2¾	*Aberuthven ..	11½
..	33	10	Cherrybank ..	1½
..	34½	1½	*Perth	

136. STIRLING to ST. ANDREWS. Fine scenery along the foot of the Ochil Hills to Milnathort, with views of Castle Campbell at Dollar. Later, a pleasant, easy road with pretty scenery, through agricultural country.

A.9			*Stirling ..	51½
A.91	1¾	1¾	*Causewayhead	49¾
..	4¼	2½	*Blairlogie ..	47¼
..	5¾	1½	Menstrie ..	45¾
..	7¾	2	*Alva ..	43¾
..	10	2¼	*Tillicoultry ..	41½
..	13	3	*Dollar ..	38½
..	16½	3½	*Yetts of Muckhart ..	35
..	20	3½	Carnbo ..	31½
..	24¼	4¼	*Milnathort ..	27¼
..	29	4¾	Gateside ..	22½
..	31	2	*Strathmiglo ..	20½
..	33	2	*Auchtermuchty	18½
..	38½	5½	Bow of Fife ..	13¼
..	42	3½	**Cupar** ..	9½
..	45	3	*Dairsie ..	6½
..	47½	2½	*Guardbridge ..	4
..	51½	4	**St. Andrews**	

137. STIRLING to DUNOON. Traverses a variety of agricultural, loch, woodland and mountain scenery. A broad level road for the first ten miles, with views of the Campsie Fells to the south, and passing close to the villages of *Gargunnock and *Kippen. Through pleasant, open agricultural districts to Balloch, after which the road follows the shore of *Loch Lomond to Tarbet, with views of Ben Lomond. Pleasant at Arrochar, on Loch Long, where there is a fine view of Ben Arthur (The Cobbler), before the gradual ascent by the reconstructed road in Glen Croe to the summit at Rest and be Thankful. An undulating descent leads to the shore of *Loch Fyne, which is followed for several miles before turning inland through the *Cowal district of Argyll. Very pretty along the shore road beside *Loch Eck, and shortly passes the well-wooded Benmore Estate of the Argyll National Forest Park, later touching the shore of the Holy Loch near Sandbank.

A.811			*Stirling ..	88½
..	12¼	12¼	*Arnprior ..	76¼
..	14¾	2½	*Buchlyvie ..	73¾
..	18¼	3½	Ballat X-rds. ..	70¼
..	22	3¾	*Drymen ..	66½
..	26½	4½	*Gartocharn ..	62
A.813	29¾	3¼	Junc. A.811/A.813	58¾
..	30¼	½	*Balloch ..	58¼
A.82	30½	¼	Junc. A.813/A.82	58
..	33	2½	Arden ..	55½
..	38½	5½	*Luss ..	50
A.83	47	8½	**Tarbet** ..	41½
..	48¾	1¾	*Arrochar ..	39¾
..	55½	6¾	*Rest and be Thankful ..	33
A.815	60	4½	Junc. A.83/A.815	28½
..	65	5	*St. Catherine's	23½
..	69	4	*Strachur Pier ..	19½
..	70	1	*Strachur ..	18½
..	81¼	11¼	*Benmore Estate	7
..	83½	2	Cothouse Bridge	5
A.885	85¾	2¼	*Sandbank ..	2¾
..	88½	2¾	**Dunoon**	

138. A tour from STIRLING to AVIEMORE via Loch Earn, the Tummel Valley and Speyside. A tour through the lochs and mountains of the Perthshire Highlands, later crossing the Grampian mountains to skirt *Rothiemurchus Forest. Views of the Ochil hills at first, and passing the great Roman Station of Ardoch near Braco, then a pleasant road over the hills to Comrie, afterwards following the north shore of Loch Earn. There is also a narrow and hilly road along the south shore of the loch leading past Ardvorlich House and the Edinample Falls, while other routes to Lochearnhead are given in Iter. 141 and 142. A gradual ascent through Glen Ogle leads over the ridge to Killin. Views of Ben Lawers from the road along the north shore of *Loch Tay, while after Fearnan a pleasantly wooded valley leads to Coshieville. A long climb over moorlands, reaching an altitude of 1,263 feet just beyond White Bridge, affords a view of Schiehallion, before a similar descent to the hydro-electric power station at Tummel Bridge. Picturesque by the wooded Loch Tummel to Queen's View, after which there is some development in connection with the hydro-electric power scheme. The road becomes hilly and winding to Bridge of Garry, where the main road is joined close by the historic Pass of Killiecrankie. Beyond Blair Atholl, desolate moorland country in the Grampians is traversed as the road climbs gradually to the summit of Drumochter Pass (1,506 feet). After the long descent, a narrow by-road is followed on the south side of well-timbered Strath Sprey and finally skirts Rothiemurchus Forest. The best way from Dalwhinnie is by the main road through Kingussie (Iter. 140).

A.9			*Stirling ..	136¼
..	1¾	1¾	*Causewayhead	134¼
..	3¼	1½	*Bridge of Allan	133
..	6	2¾	*Dunblane ..	130¼
A.822	11½	5½	*Greenloaning ..	124¾
..	13¼	1¾	*Braco ..	123
B.827	13¾	½	Junc. A.822/B.827 ..	122½
A.85	24¼	10½	*Comrie ..	112
..	29¾	5½	*St. Fillans ..	106¼
..	36¾	7	*Lochearnhead ..	99¼
A.827	41¼	5	Lix Toll ..	94½
..	44½	2¼	*Killin ..	92
..	52¾	8½	*Lawers ..	83¼
Uncl.	57	4¼	*Fearnan ..	79¼
..	59¼	2¼	*Fortingall ..	77
B.846	62¼	3	*Coshieville ..	74
..	65½	3¼	*White Bridge ..	70½
B.8019	70½	5	*Tummel Bridge	65½
..	77	6½	*Queen's View ..	59¼
..	78¾	1¾	*Fincastle P.O. ...	57¼
..	81	2¼	*Bridge of Garry	55¼
A.9	81¼	¼	Junc. B.8019/A.9	55
..	82¼	1	*Killiecrankie ..	54
..	85½	3¼	**Blair Atholl** ..	50¼
..	89¾	4¼	*Calvine ..	46½
..	95¼	5½	*Dalnacardoch	40½
..	101¾	5½	*Dalnaspidal ..	35
..	103	1¼	*Drumochter Pass (summit) ..	33¼
..	109	6	*Dalwhinnie ..	27¼
B.970	118½	9½	Junc. A.9/B.970	17¾
..	122¼	3¾	*Ruthven ..	14
..	124	1¾	*Tromie Bridge	12¼
..	126	2	*Insh ..	10¼
..	129¼	3¼	*Feshie Bridge ..	6¼
..	135½	5½	Inverdruie ..	1
..	136¼	1	*Aviemore	

139. A tour from STIRLING to PITLOCHRY via the Trossachs and the Tay Valley. A tour embracing the Trossachs and the loch, mountain and woodland scenery of the Perthshire Highlands. Open country, passing the Lake of Menteith to Aberfoyle, then climbs over the hills by a picturesque, winding road, with magnificent views of the Trossachs and Loch Vennachar. Returning from Loch Katrine, the tour passes the edge of Lochs Achray and Vennachar before reaching Callander. For alternative routes to Callander see Iter. 141 and 142. An attractive stretch between Kilmahog and Strathyre by the Falls of Leny, where the road winds through the Pass of Leny to the shores of pretty Loch Lubnaig. Views of Loch Earn approaching Lochearnhead, after which there is a gradual ascent through Glen Ogle over the ridge to descend to Glen Dochart and Loch Tay. The wooded road along the south side of the loch is narrow and hilly, but there are splendid views of Ben Lawers. The main road by Killin and the north side of the loch (Iter. 120) has a better surface, but is less scenic. Pleasant along Strath Tay through Aberfeldy to the delightful, well-timbered district around Dunkeld, where the river is crossed, and the tour doubles back to follow the opposite side of the valley to Ballinluig, and afterwards by the banks of the Tummel to Pitlochry.

A.84			*Stirling	.. 107¾
A.873	6	6	Junc. A.84/A.873	101¾
..	9¼	3¼	Thornhill	98
A.81	13¾	4	Junc. A.873/A.81	94
..	15	1¼	*Port of Menteith	92¾
A.821	18½	3½	Junc. A.81/A.821	89¼
..	19½	1	*Aberfoyle	88¼
..	26	6½	*Loch Katrine Pier	.. 81¾
..	27½	1½	*" Trossachs " Hotel	80¼
..	29	1½	*Brig o' Turk	.. 78¾
A.892	33½	4½	Junc. A.821/A.892	74¼
A.81	35	1½	Junc. A.892/A.81	72¾
A.84	35¼	¼	*Callander	72½
..	36¼	1¼	Kilmahog	71¾
..	44	7¾	*Strathyre	63¾
..	46½	2½	*Balquhidder Sta.	61
..	48¾	2	*Lochearnhead	.. 59
A.827	53¾	5	Lix Toll	54
Uncl.	55¾	2	Junc. A.827/Uncl.	52
..	62½	6½	Ardeonaig	45½
..	65½	3½	Ardtalnaig	42
..	70½	4½	Acharn	37¼
A.827	72	1½	Junc. Uncl./A.827	35½
..	78	6	*Aberfeldy	29¾
B.898	83	5	*Grandtully	.. 24¾
A.9	95	12	Junc. B.898/A.822/A.9	12½
..	95½	½	*Dunkeld	.. 12¼
..	103½	8	Ballinluig	.. 4½
..	107¾	4½	*Pitlochry	

140. STIRLING to INVERNESS via the Sma' Glen. During the summer months this is recommended as a through route across the Grampian mountains to the north, since this picturesque way to Dunkeld is also the shortest. For the winter months, and in periods of bad weather, the best way is by Perth (Iter. 135 and 150). Views of the Ochil hills at first, and passing the great Roman Station of Ardoch near Braco, then pleasant, though rather winding in Strath Earn to Crieff, after which there is fine Highland scenery as the road ascends the *Sma' Glen to Amulree. Later descends by Strath Bran to the well-wooded district around Dunkeld, afterwards following parts of the valleys of the Tay, Tummel and Garry, then through the wooded Pass of Killiecrankie. Beyond Blair Atholl, desolate moorland country is entered as the road climbs gradually to the summit of Drumochter Pass (1,506 feet), then descends, later by the well-timbered Strath Spey, to about 700 feet at Aviemore, after which another gradual climb over the open moorlands leads to Slochd Summit (1,333 feet). Rather winding as Strath Dearn and Strath Nairn are crossed on the long gradual descent to sea level at Inverness.

A.9			*Stirling	.. 144¾
..	1½	1½	*Causewayhead	142¾
..	3¼	1½	*Bridge of Allan	141½
..	6	2¾	*Dunblane	.. 138½
A.822	11½	5½	*Greenloaning	.. 133
..	13½	1½	*Braco	131¼
..	19½	6½	*Muthill	.. 125
A.85	23	3½	*Crieff	.. 121½
A.822	25	2	*Gilmerton	.. 119½
..	31½	6½	*Newton Bridge	113
..	35½	3½	*Amulree	.. 109¼
..	37	1½	*Milton	.. 107¼
..	41	4	Trochry	.. 103¼
A.9	44½	3½	Junc. A.822/A.9	100
..	44¾	¼	*Dunkeld	.. 99¾
..	52¾	8	Ballinluig	.. 91¾
..	57¼	4½	*Pitlochry	.. 87½
..	61	3¾	*Killiecrankie	.. 83¾
..	64¼	3½	*Blair Atholl	.. 80¼
..	68½	4¼	*Calvine	.. 76
..	74½	6	*Dalnacardoch	.. 70
..	80	5½	*Dalnaspidal	.. 64¾
..	81¾	1¾	*Drumochter Pass (summit)	.. 62¾
..	87¾	6	*Dalwhinnie	.. 56¾
..	98½	10½	*Newtonmore	.. 46
..	101¼	2¾	*Kingussie	.. 43½
..	107	5¾	*Kincraig	.. 37½
..	110¾	3¾	*Lynwilg	.. 33¾
..	113¼	2½	Aviemore	.. 31¼
..	120½	7	*Carrbridge	.. 24¼
..	126	5½	*Slochd Summit	.. 18½
..	128½	2½	*Tomatin	.. 16
..	133¼	4½	*Moy (Sta.)	.. 11¼
..	138¾	5½	*Daviot	.. 5¾
..	144½	5½	*Inverness	

141. A tour from STIRLING to GRANTOWN-ON-SPEY via Lochearnhead, Dunkeld and Balmoral. A scenic tour of the lochs, valleys and hills of Perthshire, afterwards crossing the Grampian mountains to Braemar in the Dee Valley, then skirting the Cairngorm mountains by way of Strathdon and the Lecht Road. Very high altitudes are attained and the road is liable to be blocked by snow during the winter months particularly at the Devil's Elbow beyond Spittal of Glenshee and also between Cock Bridge and Tomintoul. At first traverses pleasant agricultural country with views of the hills approaching Callander, the main road to which is shown in Iter. 142. An attractive stretch between Kilmahog and Strathyre by the Falls of Leny, where the road winds through the Pass of Leny to the shores of pretty Loch Lubnaig. Follows the north shore of Loch Earn, although just before reaching Lochearnhead a narrow and hilly road, leading along the south shore, could be followed past Edinample Falls and Ardvorlich House. Fine scenery ascending the *Sma' Glen to Amulree, afterwards descending by Strath Bran to the wooded district around Dunkeld, the direct route to which is given in Iter. 140. Pretty along the foot of the hills, where several lochs and the village of *Clunie lie adjacent to the road, then at Blairgowrie turns northwards into the hills by a long gradual ascent of Glen Shee. Between Spittal of Glenshee and Cairnwell summit the road becomes steeper until at Devil's Elbow the general gradient is 1 in 9, with a maximum of

1 in 5 on the awkward S bends. This summit (2,199 feet) is the highest altitude reached by any classified motoring road in Great Britain. After a gradual descent to wooded *Deeside, the Royal residence of *Balmoral Castle is passed. Leaving the Dee Valley at Cambus O'May the road passes close to Lochs Kinord and Davan, then by the Don Valley to Cock Bridge beyond which the road is narrow with a 1 in 5 ascent leading to the summit of the Lecht Road (2,090 feet), followed by a long descent to Tomintoul. After several ascents and descents (maximum gradient 1 in 7) between Bridge of Avon and the summit beyond Bridge of Brown, a gradual descent leads to the wooded Strath Spey. For the direct road between Braemar and Cock Bridge see Iter. 160.

A.9			*Stirling	.. 186
..	1½	1½	*Causewayhead	184½
..	3¼	1½	*Bridge of Allan	182¾
A.820	6	2¾	*Dunblane	.. 180
A.84	10¼	4¼	*Doune	.. 175¾
..	17½	7½	*Callander	.. 168½
..	19	1½	Kilmahog	.. 167
..	26½	7½	*Strathyre	.. 159½
..	29¼	2¾	*Balquhidder Sta.	156½
A.85	31½	2	*Lochearnhead	154½
..	38½	7	*St. Fillans	.. 147½
..	43¾	5½	*Comrie	.. 142¼
..	50½	6¾	*Crieff	.. 135½
A.822	52½	2	*Gilmerton	.. 133½
..	59	6½	*Newton Bridge	127
..	62½	3½	*Amulree	.. 123½
..	64½	1½	*Milton	.. 121½
..	68½	4	Trochry	.. 117½
A.9	72	3½	Junc. A.822/A.9	114
..	72½	½	*Dunkeld	.. 113½
A.923	72¾	¼	Junc. A.9/A.923	113¼
..	76½	3½	*Butterstone	.. 109¾
A.93	83½	7½	*Blairgowrie	.. 102½
..	84½	¾	*Rattray	.. 101¾
..	89¾	5½	*Bridge of Cally	96¼
..	97¾	8	*Lair	.. 88¼
..	102¾	5	*Spittal of Glenshee	.. 83¼
..	108¼	5½	*Cairnwell Pass (summit)	.. 77¾
..	117¾	9½	*Braemar	.. 68¼
..	127	9¼	*Crathie Ch.	.. 59
..	133	6	Bridge of Gairn	53
..	134½	1½	*Ballater	.. 51½
..	138	3½	*Cambus o' May	48
A.97	139	1	Junc. A.93/A.97	47
Uncl.	141½	2½	Junc. A.97/Uncl.	44½
A.97	143	1½	Junc. Uncl./A.97	43
..	143¾	¾	Logie Coldstone	42¼
B.973	151½	7½	Junc. A.97/B.973	34½
..	153½	2½	*Strathdon	.. 32¼
A.939	159½	6	Colnabaichin	.. 26¼
..	161½	1½	*Corgarff	.. 24½
..	165½	1½	*Cock Bridge	.. 23½
..	172½	9½	*Tomintoul	.. 13½
..	174½	2	*Bridge of Avon	11½
..	176½	2½	*Bridge of Brown	9½
A.95	184½	8	Junc. A.939/A.95	1½
..	186		*Grantown-on-Spey	

142. STIRLING to FORT WILLIAM via Ballachulish Ferry. Pleasant agricultural country at first, with views of the hills approaching Callander, whence the road passes through the heart of the Highlands, traversing splendid mountain loch and moorland scenery. An attractive stretch between Kilmahog and Strathyre, by the Falls of Leny, where the road winds through the Pass of Leny to the shores of pretty Loch Lubnaig. Views of Loch Earn approaching Lochearnhead, after which the road ascends to the ridge through Glen Ogle and then descends to Glen Dochart, which is traversed under the slopes of Ben More to Crianlarich. For 30 miles from Tyndrum follows the reconstructed *Glencoe road, which is carefully graded and has an excellent surface. Beyond Bridge of Orchy, Loch Tulla is attractive, and contrasts with the bleaker aspect as the Black Mount is skirted to cross the open Moor of Rannoch at a height of 1,143 feet, where part of the old road is seen leading past the *Kingshouse Hotel on the right. There are magnificent views of the Three Sisters of Glencoe as the road enters the Pass of Glencoe and descends past Loch Triochatan to sea level, then by the shores of *Loch Leven to the Ballachulish Ferry. (If desired the ferry can be avoided by following the main road encircling Loch Leven by Kinlochleven, 12¼ miles farther, see Iter. 100). Afterwards the shore of *Loch Linnhe is followed, with extensive views towards the *Ardgour hills, to reach Fort William, at the foot of *Ben Nevis, the highest mountain in Great Britain.

Road			Place	
A.84			*Stirling	97¼
..	6¼	6¼	*Kincardine Ch.	91
..	8¼	2	*Doune	89
..	15¾	7½	*Callander	81½
..	17	1¼	Kilmahog	80¼
..	24½	7½	*Strathyre	72¾
..	27¼	2¾	*Balquhidder (Sta.)	70
A.85	29¼	2	*Lochearnhead	68
..	34¼	5	Lix Toll	63
A.82	45¼	11¼	*Crianlarich	51¼
..	51	5¾	*Tyndrum	46¼
..	57¼	6¼	*Bridge of Orchy	39¾
A.828	81¼	23¾	*Carnach	16
..	83½	2¼	*Ballachulish (Sta.)	13¾
..	84¼	1¼	*" Ballachulish " Hotel Ferry to " Loch Leven " Hotel	12¼
A.82	85	¼	*N. Ballachulish	12¼
..	87	2	*Onich	10¼
..	88½	1½	Rd. to *Corran Ferry	8¾
..	97¼	8¾	*Fort William	

143. PITLOCHRY to FORT WILLIAM. Fine mountain and moorland scenery, at first through the wooded Pass of Killiecrankie to Blair Atholl, then across the desolate Grampian mountains by a gradual ascent, reaching the summit at Drumochter Pass (1,506 feet). Leaves the main road near Dalwhinnie, and reaches the Upper Spey valley at Drumgask, then follows the shores of Loch Laggan and through pretty Glen Spean to Roy Bridge and Spean Bridge. Open country on the latter part, with views of *Ben Nevis.

Road			Place	
A.9			*Pitlochry	76
..	3¾	3¾	*Killiecrankie	72¼
..	7	3¼	*Blair Atholl	69
..	11¼	4¼	*Calvine	64¾
..	17¼	6	*Dalnacardoch	58¾
..	22¾	5½	*Dalnaspidal	53¼
..	24½	1¾	*Drumochter Pass (summit)	51½
..	30½	6	*Dalwhinnie	45½
A.889	31¼	¾	Junc. A.9/A.889	44¾
A.86	37¾	6½	*Drumgask	38¼
..	44½	6¾	*Loch Laggan (Hotel)	31½
..	57¾	13¼	Rd. to *Tulloch Sta.	18¼
..	63¼	5½	*Roy Bridge	12¾
A.82	66½	3¼	*Spean Bridge	9½
..	73¾	7¼	Lochy Bridge (near side)	2¼
..	76	2¼	*Fort William	

144. STIRLING to OBAN. Pleasant agricultural country at first, with views of the hills approaching Callander, whence the road passes through the heart of the Highlands traversing splendid mountain, loch and moorland scenery. An attractive stretch between Kilmahog and Strathyre by the Falls of Leny, where the road winds through the Pass of Leny to the shores of pretty Loch Lubnaig. Views of Loch Earn approaching Lochearnhead, after which there is a gradual ascent through Glen Ogle over the ridge to descend into Glen Dochart, which is then followed under the slopes of Ben More to Crianlarich and on to Tyndrum. There is a fine view of Ben Cruachan approaching Dalmally, before crossing Loch Awe by the new bridge near *Kilchurn Castle, and there are more extensive views as the road follows the lochside towards the narrowing Pass of Brander. Pleasant along the shore of Loch Etive before passing beneath Connel Bridge, after which *Dunstaffnage Castle lies just north of the road.

Road			Place	
A.84			*Stirling	87¾
..	6¼	6¼	*Kincardine Ch.	81½
..	8¼	2	*Doune	79¾
..	15¾	7½	*Callander	72
..	17	1¼	Kilmahog	70¾
..	24½	7½	*Strathyre	63¼
..	27¼	2¾	*Balquhidder Sta.	60½
A.85	29¼	2	*Lochearnhead	58½
..	34¼	5	Lix Toll	53½
A.82	45¼	11¼	*Crianlarich	42¼
A.85	51	5¾	*Tyndrum	36¾
..	63	12	*Dalmally	24¾
..	66	3	*Loch Awe (Hotel)	21¾
..	69½	3½	*Falls of Cruachan	18¼
..	73	3½	Bridge of Awe	14¾
..	75½	2½	*Taynuilt	12¼
..	82½	7	*Connel	5¼
..	87¾	5¼	*Oban	

145. PERTH to OBAN. Beautiful scenery, by way of Strath Earn and the shores of Loch Earn to the Highlands, with views of the Perthshire hills. An alternative narrow and hilly road along the south shore of Loch Earn leads past Ardvorlich House and the Edinample Falls. After Lochearnhead, there is a gradual ascent through Glen Ogle over the ridge to descend into Glen Dochart, which is then followed under the slopes of Ben More to Crianlarich and on to Tyndrum. There is a fine view of Ben Cruachan approaching Dalmally, before crossing Loch Awe by the new bridge near *Kilchurn Castle, and there are more extensive views as the road follows the lochside towards the narrowing Pass of Brander. Pleasant along the shore of Loch Etive before passing beneath Connel Bridge, after which *Dunstaffnage Castle lies just north of the road.

Road			Place	
A.85			*Perth	95¼
..	2¼	2¼	*Huntingtower	92¼
..	6¼	3¾	*Methven	88¾
..	12¾	6¼	*New Fowlis	82¾
..	15½	2¾	*Gilmerton	79¾
..	17½	2	*Crieff	77¾
..	24¼	6¾	*Comrie	71
..	29¾	5½	*St. Fillans	65½
..	36¾	7	*Lochearnhead	58½
..	41¼	5	Lix Toll	53½
A.82	53	11¾	*Crianlarich	42¼
A.85	58½	5½	*Tyndrum	36¾
..	70½	12	*Dalmally	24¾
..	73½	3	*Loch Awe (Hotel)	21¾
..	77	3½	*Falls of Cruachan	18¼
..	80½	3½	Bridge of Awe	14¾
..	83	2½	*Taynuilt	12¼
..	90	7	*Connel	5¼
..	95¼	5¼	*Oban	

146. PERTH to CALLANDER. A pleasant, undulating road in Strath Earn, with views of the Ochil hills on the middle part. Carsebreck Pond lies to the north of the road between Blackford and Greenloaning. There is a descent of 1 in 9 at Dunblane, after which it is pleasant open country giving views of the hills approaching Callander.

Road			Place	
A.9			*Perth	40¼
..	1½	1½	Cherrybank	38¾
..	11¼	10	Aberuthven	28¾
..	14¼	2¾	*Auchterarder	26
..	15¾	1½	*Gleneagles (Sta.)	24¼
..	16½	¾	Loaninghead X-rds.	23¾
..	18½	2	*Blackford	21¾
..	23	4½	*Greenloaning	17¼
A.820	28½	5½	*Dunblane	11¼
A.84	32¼	4¼	*Doune	7½
..	40¼	7¾	*Callander	

147. A tour from PERTH to AVIEMORE via the Sma' Glen and Loch Rannoch. A tour through the Perthshire Highlands to Loch Rannoch, afterwards crossing the Grampian mountains to Strath Spey. After passing Huntingtower, a pretty by-road is followed along the valley of the River Almond passing Trinity College, Glenalmond, before reaching the *Sma' Glen. At Milton, a long climb over the hills by Glen Cochill is succeeded by a similar descent to Aberfeldy, where there are extensive views. Beyond Coshieville, ascends across moorland country, skirting the mountain of Schiehallion. Care on the winding descent three miles before Kinloch Rannoch. If desired, the circuit of Loch Rannoch can be omitted, but there are some very fine views from the lochside. Leaving Kinloch Rannoch, a moorland road is followed by Trinafour in Glen Erochy, passing near the village of *Struan just before joining the main road at Calvine. (The direct way from Trinafour to the main road at Dalnacardoch has a rough surface, with awkward hairpin bends and a steep ascent of 1 in 5.) Traverses desolate moorland country on the long, gradual ascent to the summit of Drumochter Pass (1,506 feet), and also on the descent, until reaching the wooded Strath Spey, near Newtonmore. The best way from Perth to Aberfeldy is by Birnam (Iter. 149) and from Aberfeldy to Dalwhinnie by Pitlochry (Iter. 120 and 150).

A.85			*Perth	130
..	2¾	2¾	*Huntingtower	127¼
Uncl.	6	3¼	Junc. A.85/Uncl.	124
B.8063	13½	7½	Buchanty	116½
A.822	15¼	1¾	Junc. B.8063/A.822	114¾
..	18	2¾	*Newton Bridge	112
..	21¼	3¼	*Amulree	108¾
A.826	23½	1¾	*Milton	106½
B.846	32¼	9¼	*Aberfeldy	97¾
..	33¼	1	*Weem	96¾
..	38	4½	*Coshieville	92
..	41¼	3¼	*White Bridge ..	88¾
Uncl.	41¾	½	Junc. B.846/Uncl.	88¼
B.846	50¼	8½	*Kinloch Rannoch	79¾
..	58¼	7¾	Killichonan	71¾
Uncl.	61¼	3	Junc. B.846/Uncl.	68¾
..	61½	¼	Bridge of Gaur ..	68½
B.846	72¼	11¼	*Kinloch Rannoch	57¾
B.847	75¼	2½	Junc. B.846/B.847	54¾
..	79¼	4	*Trinafour	50¾
A.9	85¼	6	*Calvine	44¾
..	91¼	6	*Dalnacardoch ..	38¾
..	96¾	5½	*Dalnaspidal	33¼
..	98½	1¾	*Drumochter Pass (summit)	31½
..	104½	6	*Dalwhinnie ..	25½
..	115¼	10¾	*Newtonmore ..	14¾
..	118	2¾	*Kingussie	12
..	123½	5½	*Kincraig ..	6½
..	127½	3¾	*Lynwilg ..	2½
..	130	2½	*Aviemore	

148. PERTH to RANNOCH STATION via Stanley.

Follows the Tay and Tummel valleys throughout, with extensive views in places. As far as Dunkeld this forms a pleasant alternative to the main road (Iter. 150) through mainly agricultural country, becoming well-wooded around Dunkeld. Leaves the main road near Bridge of Garry to follow a hilly, winding road to Queen's View, after which an easier, undulating road follows the shores of Loch Tummel and Loch Rannoch, with views of Schiehallion. Open moorland on the latter part. There are a number of developments in connection with hydro-electric power schemes on the second half of this route.

A.9			*Perth	66
..	4½	4½	*Luncarty	61½
B.9099	5¼	¾	Junc. A.9/B.9099	60¾
..	7½	2¼	*Stanley	58¾
..	10¾	3¼	*Murthly	55¼
A.984	12¼	1½	*Caputh	53¾
A.9	17	4¾	*Dunkeld	49
..	25	8	Ballinluig	41
..	29¼	4¼	*Pitlochry	36¾
B.8019	32¼	2¾	Junc. A.9/B.8019	33¾

..	32½	¼	*Bridge of Garry	33½
..	34¾	2¼	*Fincastle (P.O.)	31¼
..	36½	1¾	*Queen's View ..	29½
B.846	43	6½	*Tummel Bridge	23
..	50	7	*Kinloch Rannoch	16
..	57¼	7¼	Killichonan ..	8¾
..	66	8¾	*Rannoch Sta.	

149. PERTH to GRANTOWN-ON-SPEY via Aberfeldy and the Rothiemurchus Forest.

Well wooded at first and utilising secondary roads beyond Aberfeldy, crossing moorland country in the Grampian mountains before reaching Strath Spey and the *Rothiemurchus Forest. Leaving the main road at Birnam, the wooded Strath Tay is followed to Coshieville, after which there is a long climb over moorlands, reaching an altitude of 1,263 feet just beyond White Bridge, affording a view of Schiehallion, before a similar descent to the hydro-electric power station at Tummel Bridge. Ascends again to over 1,000 feet near Trinafour. Continuing by Glen Erochy, the road passes close to *Struan, just before rejoining the main road at Calvine. (The direct way from Trinafour to the main road at Dalnacardoch has a rough surface, with awkward hairpin bends and a steep ascent of 1 in 5.) Desolate moorland country is traversed as the road climbs gradually over the Grampians to the summit of Drumochter Pass (1,506 feet). After the descent to the wooded Strath Spey, a rough, narrow by-road is followed on the south side of the valley, and one mile before Inverdruie a short detour can be made to Loch-an-Eilean, in Rothiemurchus Forest, after which the road improves.

A.9			*Perth	117¼
..	4½	4½	*Luncarty	112¾
..	8¼	4¼	*Bankfoot ..	108½
B.898	14½	5¾	Junc. A.9/A.822/B.898	102¾
A.827	26½	12	*Grandtully	90¾
B.846	31½	5	*Aberfeldy	85¾
..	32½	1	*Weem	84¾
..	36¾	4¼	*Coshieville	80½
..	40	3¼	*White Bridge	77¼
..	45	5	*Tummel Bridge	72¼
Uncl.	45¾	¾	Junc. B.846/Uncl.	71½
B.847	49¼	3½	Junc. Uncl./B.847	68
..	49¾	½	*Trinafour	67½
A.9	55¾	6	*Calvine	61½
..	61¾	6	*Dalnacardoch ..	55½
..	67½	5¾	*Dalnaspidal	50
..	69	1¾	*Drumochter Pass (summit) ..	48¼
..	75	6	*Dalwhinnie ..	42¼
B.970	84¾	9¾	Junc. A.9/B.970	32¾
..	88¼	3¾	*Ruthven	29
..	90	1¾	*Tromie Bridge	27¼
..	92	2	*Insh	25¼
..	95¾	3¾	*Feshie Bridge ..	21¾
..	101¾	5¾	Inverdruie	16
..	102¾	1	*Coylumbridge ..	15
..	112	9¼	*Nethybridge ..	5¾
A.95	116¾	4¼	Junc. B.970/A.95	1
..	117¾	1	*Grantown-on-Spey	

150. PERTH to INVERNESS.

This main route to the north is a valley road on the early part, afterwards crossing the desolate Grampian mountains, partly relieved by a well-wooded stretch in Strath Spey. At first follows the valleys of the Tay, Tummel and Garry through agricultural scenery, with well-wooded districts around Dunkeld and in the famous Pass of Killiecrankie. Beyond Blair Atholl, desolate moorland country is entered as the road climbs gradually to the summit at Drumochter Pass (1,506 feet), then descends through the well-timbered Strath Spey to about 700 feet at Aviemore, after which another gradual climb over the open moorlands leads to Slochd Summit (1,333 feet). Rather winding as Strath Dearn and Strath Nairn are crossed on the long gradual descent to sea level.

A.9			*Perth	114¼
..	4½	4½	*Luncarty	110
..	8¼	4¼	*Bankfoot	105¾
..	14	5¾	*Birnam	100¼
..	14¾	¾	*Dunkeld	99½
..	22¾	8	Ballinluig	91½
..	27¼	4½	*Pitlochry	87¼
..	31	3¾	*Killiecrankie	83¼
..	34¼	3¼	*Blair Atholl	80¼
..	38½	4¼	*Calvine	76
..	44½	6	*Dalnacardoch ..	70
..	50	5½	*Dalnaspidal	64¼
..	51¼	1¼	*Drumochter Pass (summit)	62¾
..	57¼	6	*Dalwhinnie	56¾
..	68¼	10¾	*Newtonmore	46
..	71¼	2¾	*Kingussie	43¼
..	77	5¾	*Kincraig	37¼
..	80¼	3¾	*Lynwilg	33¾
..	83¼	2½	*Aviemore	31¼
..	90¼	7	*Carrbridge	24¼
..	96	5¾	*Slochd Summit	18¼
..	98¾	2½	*Tomatin	16
..	103¼	4¾	*Moy (Sta.) ..	11¼
..	108¼	5¾	*Daviot	5¾
..	114¼	5¾	*Inverness	

151. PERTH to ABERDEEN.

An easy main road through pleasant, open agricultural country, with views of the Sidlaw hills and passing Glamis Castle before Forfar. Fine views on the coast road beyond Stonehaven, after which the village of *Muchalls lies just off the main road. The old road (B.9134) from Forfar to Brechin via *Aberlemno is 1½ miles shorter, but is narrow in places and not suitable for fast travel.

A.94			*Perth	82¼
..	2	2	*New Scone ..	80¼
..	5¼	3¼	*Balbeggie ..	77
..	10¼	5	Burrelton ..	72
..	12½	2¼	*Coupar Angus	69¾
..	17¾	2¼	*Meigle ..	64½
..	22	4¼	*Eassie ..	60¼
..	24½	2½	*Glamis ..	57¾
..	29¼	5¼	*Forfar ..	52¾
..	35¼	6	*Finhaven ..	46¾
..	42¾	6¼	*Brechin ..	39¾
..	53¼	11	*Laurencekirk ..	28¾
..	57	3½	*Fordoun (Sta.)	25¼
..	60¼	3¼	Mondynes Bridge	22
A.92	67¼	7¼	*Stonehaven ..	14¼
..	76¼	8¾	Hillside ..	6
..	80¼	4	*Bridge of Dee ..	2
..	82¼	2	*Aberdeen (See town plan for By-pass)	

152. PERTH to ABERDEEN via Braemar and Deeside. A splendid touring route, contrasting the crossing of the bare Grampian mountains with the delightful, wooded *Deeside. Pleasant, open country in the Tay Valley at first, passing the famous *Meikleour beech hedge a little beyond Bridge of Isla, then gradually ascends, by Glen Shee into the hills. Between Spittal of Glenshee and Cairnwell summit, the road becomes steeper, until, at the Devil's Elbow, the general gradient is 1 in 9, with a maximum of 1 in 5 on the awkward S bends. The summit at Cairnwell (2,199 feet) is the highest altitude reached by any classified motoring road in Great Britain and is liable to become blocked by snow during winter months. Glen Clunie is traversed to reach Braemar, after which the picturesque Dee Valley is followed to Aberdeen. Ballater can be avoided by a short cut (B.972) through the pretty Pass of Ballater, and the road on the south side of the river can be reached by several connecting bridges. The Royal residence of *Balmoral Castle is seen between Braemar and Crathie Church, and Loch Kinord lies just off the road near Cambus o' May. Crathes Castle, near Banchory, is interesting.

A.93			*Perth	.. 108
..	2¼	2¼	*Old Scone	.. 105½
..	5½	3½	*Guildtown	.. 102½
..	10¾	5	*Bridge of Isla	.. 97¼
..	15¼	4½	*Blairgowrie	.. 92¾
..	15¾	½	*Rattray	92¼
..	21¼	5½	*Bridge of Cally	86¾
..	29¼	8	*Lair	78¾
..	34¼	5	*Spittal of Glenshee	73¾
..	39¼	5½	*Cairnwell Pass (summit)	.. 68¾
..	49¼	9½	*Braemar	.. 58¾
..	58½	9¼	*Crathie Church	49½
..	64½	6	Bridge of Gairn	43½
..	66	1½	*Ballater	42
..	69½	3½	*Cambus o' May	38½
..	73	3½	*Dinnet	35
..	77½	4½	*Aboyne	30½
..	82¼	4¾	*Kincardine o' Neil	.. 25¾
..	90	7¾	*Banchory	.. 18
..	93½	3½	*Crathes	.. 14½
..	96¾	3¼	*Drumoak	.. 11¼
..	100½	3¾	*Peterculter	.. 7½
..	108	7½	*Aberdeen	
			(See town plan for By-pass)	

153. PERTH to MONTROSE. Pleasant, open agricultural country, with views of the Sidlaw hills to Forfar, and passing Glamis Castle. The direct road (B.9113) from Forfar past the ruins of *Restenneth Priory is 1¼ miles shorter, but is somewhat narrow.

A.94			*Perth	.. 49
..	2	2	*New Scone	47
..	3½	1½	*Balbeggie	.. 43½
..	10¼	5	Burrelton	38¾
..	12½	2¼	*Coupar Angus	36½
..	17¾	5¼	*Meigle	.. 31¼
..	22	4¼	*Eassie	.. 27
..	24½	2½	*Glamis	.. 24½
A.932	29¾	5½	*Forfar	.. 19½
..	37	7¼	*Guthrie (Sta.)	.. 12
A.933	38½	1½	*Friockheim	.. 10½
A.934	40½	2½	Junc. A.933/A.934	8½
A.92	48	7¼	Junc. A.934/A.92	1
..	49	1	*Montrose	

154. PERTH to DUNDEE. A fast, level road across the open *Carse of Gowrie, with the village of *Kinnaird to the north of the road at the foot of the Sidlaw hills. There is an alternative by-road through *Errol (B.958) branching off before Glencarse and rejoining near Dundee.

A.85			*Perth	.. 21¼
..	6	6	*Glencarse	.. 15¼
..	12¼	6¼	*Inchture	9
..	15¼	2½	*Longforgan (By-pass)	6½
..	17½	2¼	Invergowrie	.. 4¼
..	21¼	4¼	*Dundee	
			(See town plan for By-pass)	

155. DUNDEE to ABERDEEN. An easy main road through open country along the coast, with fine views in places, although not touching the shore. The alternative includes the coast resorts and golfing district between Dundee and Carnoustie. *Auchmithie and *Johnshaven lie east of the road, the former just beyond Arbroath, and the latter between St. Cyrus and Inverbervie. *Dunnottar Castle is passed before reaching Stonehaven, beyond which *Muchalls is adjacent to the main road. Approaching Aberdeen, a detour can be made to include the rocky coastline from *Cove to Girdle Ness.

A.92			*Dundee	.. 67
..	11	11	Muirdrum	.. 56
..	16¼	5¼	*Arbroath	.. 50¼
..	19	2¾	Marywell	.. 48
..	22½	3½	*Inverkeilor	.. 44½
..	29¾	7¼	*Montrose	.. 37¼
..	35	5¼	*St. Cyrus	.. 32
..	42½	7½	*Inverbervie	.. 24½
..	52¼	9¾	*Stonehaven	.. 14¾
..	61	8¾	Hillside	.. 6
..	65	4	*Bridge of Dee	.. 2
..	67	2	*Aberdeen	
			(See town plan for By-pass)	

Alternative via Carnoustie

A.930			*Dundee	
..	3½	3½	*Broughty Ferry	
..	6¼	2¾	*Monifieth	
..	9	2¾	*Barry	
..	10½	1½	*Carnoustie	
A.92	13	2¼	Muirdrum	
..	18¾	5¾	*Arbroath	

156. DUNDEE to ABERDEEN via Edzell. Undulating at first, on the edge of the Sidlaw hills to Forfar, then flat open country. The direct road (B.9134) from Forfar to Brechin via *Aberlemno is not so fast, but is 1½ miles shorter. Leaves the main road beyond Brechin to follow by-roads along the foot of the hills, later rejoining the main road to Stonehaven. Fine coast scenery on the latter part, and passes the edge of *Muchalls, 4 miles beyond Stonehaven. Approaching Aberdeen a detour can be made to include the rocky coastline from *Cove to Girdle Ness.

A.929			*Dundee	.. 69½
..	6	6	Todhills	.. 63½
A.94	14	8	*Forfar	.. 55½
..	20	6	Finhaven	.. 49½
..	26¼	6¼	*Brechin	.. 42½
B.966	29	2¼	Junc. A.94/B.966	40¼
..	30¼	1¼	Inchbare	.. 38½
..	32½	2¼	*Edzell	.. 36¼
..	34	1¼	*Gannochy Bridge	35¼
..	37½	3½	*Fettercairn	.. 31¾
A.94	45½	7½	Junc. B.966/A.94	24
..	47¼	2	Mondynes Bridge	22
A.92	54½	7¼	*Stonehaven	.. 14¾
..	63¼	8¾	Hillside	6
..	67¼	4	*Bridge of Dee	.. 2
..	69¼	2	*Aberdeen	
			(See town plan for By-pass)	

157. DUNDEE to ABERFELDY via Dunkeld. Rather winding on the crossing of the Sidlaw hills, with an easy descent of Tullybaccart Hill. Joins the Tay Valley at Meikleour, becoming wooded at Dunkeld, where the river is crossed. See Iter. 158 for an alternative.

A.923			*Dundee	.. 47
..	5¼	5¼	*Muirhead	.. 41¾
..	12	6¾	*Pitcur	.. 35
..	14¼	2¼	*Coupar Angus	32¼
A.984	16¼	1½	Junc. A.923/A.984	30¾
..	19¾	3½	*Meikleour	.. 27¼
..	25	5¼	*Caputh	22
A.9	29¼	4¼	*Dunkeld	.. 17¼
B.898	30	¾	Junc. A.9/A.822/B.898	17
A.827	42	12	*Grandtully	.. 5
..	47	5	*Aberfeldy	

158. DUNDEE to PITLOCHRY or ABERFELDY. Rather winding on the crossing of the Sidlaw hills, with an easy descent of Tullybaccart Hill, afterwards a rather undulating road. Passes several lochs between Blairgowrie and Butterstone, and *Clunie village is adjacent to the road. Joins the well-wooded Tay Valley just north of Dunkeld, and shows divergent routes to either Pitlochry or Aberfeldy. See Iter. 157 and 159 for alternatives.

A.923			*Dundee	.. 42¼
..	5¼	5¼	*Muirhead	.. 37¼
..	12	6¾	*Pitcur	.. 30¼
..	14¼	2¼	*Coupar Angus	27¼
..	18	3½	Rosemount (Sta.)	24¼
..	19½	1½	*Blairgowrie	.. 23
..	27	7½	*Butterstone	.. 15½
A.9	30½	3½	Junc. A.923/A.9	12
..	38	7½	†Ballinluig	.. 4½
..	42	4½	*Pitlochry	
			† OR	
A.827	38		Ballinluig	
..	38¾	¾	*Logierait	
..	43	4¼	*Grandtully	
..	48	5	*Aberfeldy	

159. DUNDEE to PITLOCHRY via Kirkmichael. Rather winding on the crossing of the Sidlaw hills, with an easy descent of Tullybaccart Hill. Ascends gradually into the hills from Blairgowrie, with pleasant scenery in Glen Brerachan, and views from the summit (1,260 feet) before the long descent to Pitlochry and the Tummel Valley. The quickest way is by Ballinluig, Iter. 158.

A.923			*Dundee	..	45
..	5¼	5¼	*Muirhead	..	39¾
..	12	6¾	*Pitcur	..	33
..	14¼	2¼	*Coupar Angus	..	30¾
..	18	3½	Rosemount (Sta.)		27
A.93	19½	1½	**Blairgowrie**	..	25½
..	20	½	*Rattray		25
A.924	25½	5½	*Bridge of Cally		19½
..	32½	7	*Kirkmichael	..	12½
..	34½	2	Enochdhu		10½
..	44¼	9¾	*Moulin		¾
..	45	¾	**Pitlochry**		

160. DUNDEE to GRANTOWN-ON-SPEY via Glen Isla and Tomintoul.

A very hilly, scenic route, utilizing narrow roads in Glen Isla and on the Lecht Road crossing of the north-eastern Grampians. Very high altitudes are attained and the road is liable to be blocked by snow during the winter, particularly in the Grampians, at the Devil's Elbow beyond Spittal of Glenshee and again between Braemar and Tomintoul. An easy road is first followed from Dundee through a gap in the Sidlaw hills to Newtyle. 3 miles beyond Meigle, a detour can be made to *Alyth before joining the hilly road leading to Glen Isla. There are several gradients of 1 in 7 along the picturesque valley, and the road is narrow over the hill to the main road at Lair in Glen Shee. The easiest and quickest way to Glen Shee is by Blairgowrie, Iter. 158 and 152. Between Spittal of Glenshee and Cairnwell summit the road becomes steeper, until, at the Devil's Elbow, the general gradient is 1 in 9, with a maximum of 1 in 5 on the awkward S bends. The summit at Cairnwell (2,199 feet) is the highest altitude reached by any classified motoring road in Great Britain. Glen Clunie is traversed to reach Braemar, thence along wooded *Deeside, passing the Royal residence of *Balmoral Castle before turning off by a narrow, hilly road across the mountains. After the climb from the Dee Valley, there is a 1 in 5 descent before Gairnshiel Lodge. Afterwards, a climb to 1,800 feet (max. grad. 1 in 5) is followed by a long descent to Strath Don (see Iter. 141 for an alternative route via Ballater and Strathdon to Cock Bridge). There is a 1 in 5 ascent from Cock Bridge leading to the summit of the Lecht Road (2,090 feet), and another long descent follows to Tomintoul. After several ascents and descents (maximum gradient 1 in 7) between Bridge of Avon and the summit beyond Bridge of Brown, a gradual descent leads to the wooded Strath Spey.

A.923			*Dundee	..	100
A.927	5¼	5¼	*Muirhead	..	94¾
..	11½	6	*Newtyle	..	88½
..	13½	2¼	*Meigle	..	86¼
B.954	16½	3	Junc. A.927/B.954		83½
..	21	4½	*Bridge of Craig		79
B.951	23½	2½	*Dykend		76½
..	26¼	3	*Kirkton of Glenisla		73¼

A.93	33½	6¼	*Lair	..	66½
..	38½	5	*Spittal of Glenshee		61½
..	44	5½	*Cairnwell Pass (summit)		56
..	53½	9½	**Braemar**	..	46½
A.939	62½	8½	Junc. A.93/A.939		37½
..	67½	5¼	*Gairnshiel Lodge		32½
..	73½	6¼	Colnabaichin	..	26¼
..	75¼	1½	*Corgarff		24¾
..	76½	1¼	*Cock Bridge	..	23½
..	86¼	9¾	*Tomintoul		13¾
..	88¼	2	*Bridge of Avon		11¾
..	90½	2¼	*Bridge of Brown		9½
A.95	98½	8	Junc. A.939/A.95		1½
..	100	1½	**Grantown-on-Spey**		

161. DUNDEE to GLEN CLOVA.

Crosses the Sidlaw hills and passes Glamis Castle before Kirriemuir, then a hilly, but delightful by-road in picturesque Glen Clova. At Dykehead, a branch road diverges westwards to traverse Glen Prosen, while 3 miles up Glen Clova the road divides, and either side of the valley can be followed, but these roads are not through ways.

A.929			**Dundee**	..	35¼
A.928	6	6	Todhills	..	29¼
..	12	6	*Glamis	..	23¼
A.926	17	5	**Kirriemuir**	..	18¼
B.955	17½	½	Junc. A.826/B.955		17¾
..	22¼	4¾	*Dykehead	..	13
Uncl.	32¼	10	*Clova Church	..	3
..	35¼	3	*Braedownie		

162. CARNOUSTIE to PITLOCHRY via Glen Isla.

Pleasant, wooded, agricultural districts to Kirriemuir, then following a hilly, secondary road passing Loch Lintrathen before reaching Dykend. There are several gradients of 1 in 7 along the picturesque Glen Isla, and the road is narrow over the hill to the main road at Lair in Glen Shee. Traverses moorland country on the latter part, with views from the summit (1,260 feet) beyond Glen Brerachan, before the long descent through Moulin to Pitlochry in the Tummel Valley. A faster route is via Dundee, Iter. 155 and 158.

A.930			*Carnoustie	..	60¼
A.958	2¼	2¼	Muirdrum	..	58
..	10	7¾	Craichie	..	50¼
..	12	2	Kingsmuir	..	48¼
A.94	14	2	*Forfar	..	46¼
A.926	14½	½	Junc. A.94/A.926		45¾
..	20	5¼	**Kirriemuir**	..	40¼
B.951	20½	¼	Junc. A.926/B.951		39½
..	23¾		Kirkton of Kingoldrum	..	36½
..	30½	6¾	*Dykend	..	29¾
..	33½	3	*Kirkton of Glenisla		26¾
A.93	40¼	6¾	*Lair	..	20
B.950	43½	3¼	Junc. A.93/B.950		16¾
A.924	47½	3¾	Junc. B.950/A.924		12¾
..	47¾	¼	*Kirkmichael	..	12½
..	49¼	2	Enochdhu	..	10½
..	59¼	9¾	*Moulin	..	¾
..	60¼		**Pitlochry**		

163. ARBROATH to BANCHORY via Cairn o' Mounth.

Pleasant, open country to Fettercairn, then a difficult cross-country road, with fine panoramic views, crossing Cairn o' Mounth to the Dee Valley. From Clattering Bridge, the road is narrow, with frequent passing bays, and there are several steep gradients, especially the long ascent to Cairn o' Mounth (maximum gradient 1 in 5½) and at Bridge of Dye (maximum gradient 1 in 6). The summit of the Cairn o' Mounth road is at 1,475 feet, and the road between Fettercairn and Strachan is frequently blocked by snow during the winter months, the easiest way being via Stonehaven and the Slug Road (Iter. 190).

A.933			**Arbroath**	..	42½
..	3½	3½	Gowanbank	..	39
..	6½	3	*Friockheim	..	36
A.94	14¼	7¾	**Brechin**	..	28¼
B.966	16½	2¼	Junc. A.94/B.966		26
..	18½	1½	Inchbare	..	24¼
..	20½	2	*Edzell	..	22¼
..	21½	1½	*Gannochy Bridge		21
B.974	25	3½	*Fettercairn	..	17½
..	28½	3½	*Clattering Bridge		14
..	30½	2	*Cairn o' Mounth (summit)		12
..	34½	4	*Bridge of Dye ..		8
..	39¼	4¾	*Strachan	..	3¼
A.943	41¼	2¼	*Bridge of Feugh (near side)	..	¾
..	42½	¾	*Banchory		

164. MONTROSE to LOCHLEE CHURCH (GLEN ESK).

A flat main road to Brechin, then a by-road ascending into the hills. After Gannochy Bridge, becomes winding, as the beautiful valley of the North Esk is followed to the road end at Lochlee Church, finely situated amongst the eastern Grampian mountains.

A.92			**Montrose**	..	30½
A.935	½	½	Junc. A.92/A.935		30
A.94	8½	8	**Brechin**	..	22
B.966	10½	2¼	Junc. A.94/B.966		19½
..	12½	1½	Inchbare	..	18
..	14½	2	*Edzell	..	16
..	15¾	1¼	*Gannochy Bridge		14¾
Uncl.	16	¼	Junc. B.966/Uncl.		14¼
..	26¼	10¼	*Tarfside	..	4¼
..	30½	4¼	*Lochlee Church		

165. MONTROSE to HUNTLY via Cairn o' Mounth.

Pleasant open country to Fettercairn, then a difficult cross-country road, with fine panoramic views crossing the Cairn o' Mounth to the Dee Valley at Potarch Bridge, thereafter an easy, but twisting road through moorland and agricultural districts passing *Craigievar Castle about 4 miles from Lumphanan. The summit at Cairn o' Mounth is at 1,475 feet, and the road between Fettercairn and Feughside Inn is frequently blocked by snow during the winter months. From Clattering Bridge the road is narrow, with frequent passing bays, and there are several steep gradients, especially the long ascent to Cairn o' Mounth (maximum gradient 1 in 5½) and at Bridge of Dye (maximum gradient 1 in 6). There are two small fords on the unclassified road between Bridge of Dye and Feughside. A faster route is via Aberdeen (Iter. 155 and 175). The direct road from Bridge of Alford to Huntly via *Tullynessle and *Kennethmont is hilly, narrow and winding.

A.92			*Montrose	68¼
A.937	1	1	Junc. A.92/A.937	67¼
B.974	6	5	*Marykirk	62¼
..	11¼	5¼	*Fettercairn	56¾
..	15¼	3½	*Clattering Bridge	53
..	17¼	2	*Cairn o' Mounth (summit)	51
..	21¼	4	*Bridge of Dye	47
Uncl.	23¼	2	Junc. B.974/Uncl.	45
..	25¼	2¼	*" Feughside " Inn	42½
A.93	29¼	4	*Potarch Bridge	38½
B.993	31	1¼	Junc. A.93/B.993	37¼
A.980	33¼	2¼	*Torphins	34½
..	37¼	3½	*Lumphanan	31
A.944	47¼	10¼	Junc. A.980/A.944	20¼
..	48	¼	*Bridge of Alford	20¼
A.97	54	6	Junc. A.944/A.97	14¼
..	55¼	1½	*Lumsden	12¼
..	59¼	4	*Rhynie	8¼
..	68¼	8¾	*Huntly	

166. DUNKELD to MONTROSE. An undulating cross-country route through open agricultural districts, along the edge of the hills at first. Passes several lochs between Dunkeld and Blairgowrie, and *Clunie village is adjacent to the road. Rather narrow between Blairgowrie and Finhaven. *Alyth lies to the north of the road near New Alyth.

A.9			*Dunkeld	50
A.923	½	½	Junc. A.9/A.923	49½
..	4	3½	*Butterstone	46
A.93	11½	7½	*Blairgowrie	38½
A.926	12	½	*Rattray	38
..	16¼	4¼	*New Alyth	33¾
..	19	2¾	Ruthven	31
..	22	3	Craigton	28
B.957	26¼	4¼	*Kirriemuir	23¼
..	32	5¼	Justinhaugh Bridge	18
..	33¼	1¼	*Tannadice	16¼
A.94	34½	1½	*Finhaven	15¼
A.935	41½	6½	*Brechin	8½
A.92	49½	8	Junc. A.935/A.92	½
..	50	½	*Montrose	

167. PITLOCHRY to HUNTLY. A tour across the bare Grampian mountains to the delightful, wooded *Deeside, and later a part of the upper Don valley. A long climb from Pitlochry across moorland country, reaching the summit at 1,260 feet, then a gradual descent through Glen Brerachan to Kirkmichael, afterwards ascending by way of Glen Shee. Beyond Spittal of Glenshee the road becomes steeper until, at the Devil's Elbow, the general gradient is 1 in 9, with a maximum of 1 in 5 on the awkward S bends. The summit at Cairnwell (2,199 feet) is the highest altitude reached by any classified motoring road in Great Britain, and during winter months this road is liable to become blocked by snow. Moorland scenery through Glen Clunie to Braemar, then a picturesque road along the Dee valley, passing the Royal residence of *Balmoral Castle. Ballater can be avoided by the short cut (B.972) through the pretty Pass of Ballater. Leaving the Dee valley at Cambus o' May, the road passes close to Lochs Kinord and Davan, then traverses moor land and agricultural country, including several miles along the Don valley to Kildrummy.

A.924			*Pitlochry	97½
..	¼	¼	*Moulin	96¾
..	10¼	9¾	Enochdhu	87
..	12½	2	*Kirkmichael	85
B.950	12¾	¼	Junc. A.924/B.950	84¼
A.93	16¼	3¼	Junc. B.950/A.93	81
..	20	3½	*Lair	77½
..	25	5	*Spittal of Glenshee	72½
..	30½	5½	*Cairnwell Pass (summit)	67
..	40	9½	*Braemar	57½
..	49¼	9¼	*Crathie Church	48¼
..	55¼	6	Bridge of Gairn	42¼
..	56¼	1½	*Ballater	40¾
..	60¼	3½	*Cambus o' May	37¼
A.97	61¼	1	Junc. A.93/A.97	36¼
Uncl.	63¼	2¼	Junc. A.97/Uncl.	33¼
A.97	65¼	1½	Junc. Uncl./A.97	32¼
..	66	¾	Logie Coldstone	31¼
..	78	12	*Glenkindie	19¼
..	81½	3½	*Kildrummy	16
..	84½	3½	*Lumsden	12¼
..	88½	4	*Rhynie	8¾
..	97¼	8¼	*Huntly	

168. PITLOCHRY to ABERDEEN via Deeside. A tour across the bare Grampian mountains to the delightful, wooded Royal *Deeside. A long climb from Pitlochry across moorland country reaching the summit at 1,260 feet, then a gradual descent through Glen Brerachan to Kirkmichael, afterwards ascending by way of Glen Shee. Beyond Spittal of Glenshee the road becomes steeper, until, at the Devil's Elbow, the general gradient is 1 in 9, with a maximum gradient of 1 in 5 on the awkward S bends. The summit at Cairnwell (2,199 feet) is the highest altitude reached by any classified motoring road in Great Britain and during winter months this road is liable to become blocked by snow. Moorland scenery through Glen Clunie to Braemar, where the route crosses to the south side of the picturesque Dee valley as far as Potarch Bridge, where the river is re-crossed. Beyond Banchory, the tour reverts to the south bank, shortly crossing the pretty, but narrow Bridge of Feugh, and continues by the open valley to Aberdeen. Between Braemar and Aberdeen there are several connecting bridges between the parallel roads on opposite banks of the river, the main road being given in Iter. 152.

A.924			*Pitlochry	98¼
..	¼	¼	*Moulin	97½
..	10¼	9¾	Enochdhu	87¾
..	12½	2	*Kirkmichael	85¾
B.950	12¾	¼	Junc. A.924/B.950	85¼
A.93	16¼	3¼	Junc. B.950/A.93	81¾
..	20	3½	*Lair	78¼
..	25	5	*Spittal of Glenshee	73¼
..	30½	5½	*Cairnwell Pass (summit)	67½
..	40	9½	*Braemar	58¼
A.973	49	9	Junc. A.93/A.973	49¼
..	49¼	¼	*Balmoral Castle (gates)	49
..	57¼	8	*Ballater Bridge (near side)	41
..	59¼	2	*Pannanich Wells	39
..	64	4¼	*Dinnet Bridge (near side)	34¼
..	67	3	*Bridge of Ess	31¼
..	68½	1½	Birsemore	29¼
A.93	74	5½	*Potarch Bridge	24¼
A.943	80	6	*Banchory	18¼
..	80¼	¼	*Bridge of Feugh	17¼
..	85	4¼	Durris	13¼
..	91¼	6¼	*Maryculter	7
..	92¼	1¼	*Blairs	5¼
..	95	2¼	Banchory Devenick	3¼
A.92	96¼	1¼	*Bridge of Dee	2
..	98¼	2	*Aberdeen (See town plan for By-pass)	

169. AVIEMORE to CULLEN via Tomintoul. Undulating and well-wooded in Strath Spey for the first 15 miles, then a narrow, hilly, moorland road, with views of the Cairngorm mountains. There are several ascents and descents from near Bridge of Brown to Tomintoul, with a maximum gradient of 1 in 7. Later passes near the famous *Glenlivet distillery, near Tomnavoulin. Then follows an attractive run through Glen Rinnes to Dufftown (to which the easiest way is by the Spey Valley, Iter. 170 and 195). Pretty at Drummuir, in Strath Isla, and afterwards traverses agricultural country. The direct road from Aviemore to Keith is given in Iter. 170.

A.9			*Aviemore	70½
A.95	4¼	4¼	Junc. A.9/A.95	66¼
Uncl.	5	¾	Junc. A.95/Uncl.	65½
..	6¼	1¼	*Boat of Garten	64¼
B.970	7	¾	Junc. Uncl./B.970	63½
..	10½	3½	*Nethybridge	60
A.95	14¾	4¼	Junc. B.970/A.95	55¾
A.939	15¼	½	Junc. A.95/A.939	55¼
..	23¼	8	*Bridge of Brown	47¼
..	25¼	2¼	*Bridge of Avon	45
..	27½	2	*Tomintoul	43
B.9008	27¾	¼	Junc. A.939/B.9008	42¾
..	32¼	4¼	Knockandhu	38¼
..	34	1¾	*Tomnavoulin	36½
B.9009	35½	1½	Achbreck (Church)	34¾
..	41¼	5½	*Glenrinnes	29¼
A.941	46¼	5	*Dufftown	24¼
A.920	46¾	½	Junc. A.941/A.920	23¾
..	51¼	4½	*Drummuir	19¼
..	54¼	3	Auchindachy	16¼
A.96	56¼	2¼	*Fife Keith	13¼
A.95	57¼	½	*Keith	13¼
B.9018	59¼	2	Junc. A.95/B.9018	11¼
..	66¼	7	*Deskford	4¼
..	69	2¾	Lintmill	1½
A.98	69¾	¾	Junc. B.9018/A.98	¾
..	70½	¾	*Cullen	

170. AVIEMORE to BANFF. Attractive in Strath Spey to Craigellachie, well-wooded on the earlier part. An undulating agricultural district beyond Keith.

A.9			*Aviemore	69¼
A.95	4¼	4¼	Junc. A.9/A.95	65¼
Uncl.	5	¾	Junc. A.95/Uncl.	64¼
..	6¼	1¼	*Boat of Garten	63¼
B.970	7	¾	Junc. Uncl./B.970	62¼
..	10½	3½	*Nethybridge	59¼

A.95	14¼	4¼	Junc. B.970/A.95	55
..	17¼	3	*Cromdale	52
..	27¼	10	*"Dalnashaugh" Inn	42
..	35½	7¼	*Aberlour	34¼
..	37½	2	*Craigellachie	32¼
..	40	2½	*Maggieknockater	29¾
..	44¼	4¼	Mulben (W.M.)	25¼
A.96	48¼	4	Junc. A.95/A.96	21¼
..	49	¾	*Fife Keith	20¾
A.95	49¼	¼	*Keith	20½
..	58½	9	Glenbarry	11¼
..	61½	3	*Cornhill	8¼
A.98	65	3½	Junc. A.95/A.98	4¾
..	69¼	4¼	*Banff	

171. AVIEMORE to SPEY BAY via Strath Spey.

Secondary roads following the Spey Valley, well-wooded on the earlier part, then open agricultural country beyond Rothes. The main road to Grantown is given in Iter. 172 whilst a quicker route to Rothes is via Craigellachie (Iter. 170 and 192).

B.970			*Aviemore	56½
..	1	1	Inverdruie	55½
..	2	1	*Coylumbridge	54½
..	11¾	9¾	*Nethybridge	44¾
A.95	16	4¼	Junc. B.970/A.95	40½
A.939	17	1	*Grantown-on-Spey	39½
B.9102	17½	½	Junc. A.939/B.9102	39
..	33½	16	*Knockando Church	23
..	36½	3	Archiestown	20
A.941	40¼	4¼	Junc. B.9102/A.941	15¾
..	42¾	2	*Rothes	13¾
B.9015	43¼	½	Junc. A.941/B.9015	13¼
..	46½	3¼	*Orton (Sta.)	10
A.96	51¼	4¾	*Mosstodloch	5¼
B.9104	52¼	1	Junc. A.96/B.9104	4¼
..	56½	4¼	*Spey Bay	

172. AVIEMORE to FORRES.

Well-wooded in Strath Spey to Grantown, then crosses Dava Moor and joins the Findhorn Valley at Logie.

A.9			*Aviemore	36¼
A.95	4¼	4¼	Junc. A.9/A.95	32
..	11¾	7½	*Dulnain Bridge	24½
A.939	14¾	3	*Grantown-on-Spey	21½
A.940	22¼	7½	*Dava	14
..	29	6¾	Dunphail (Sta.)	7¼
..	30¾	1¾	*Logie	5½
..	36¼	5½	*Forres	

173. AVIEMORE to FORRES via Ferness.

Beyond Carrbridge, a narrow moorland road, passing a little to the west of the lonely *Lochindorb. Before Ferness, a short detour can be made to the picturesque valley of the River Findhorn, threading a rocky gorge at *Dulsie Bridge. Between Ferness and Logie the River Divie is crossed near the beauty spot of Randolph's Leap and the grounds of Relugas House. Beyond Logie, the Findhorn flows through another fine gorge, both road and river later passing between Darnaway Forest and the Altyre woods. The easiest way is via Grantown, Iter. 172.

A.9			*Aviemore	33¾
A.938	7	7	*Carrbridge	26¾

B.9007	8¾	1¾	Junc. A.938/B.9007	25
..	22¼	13¼	*Ferness	11½
A.940	28	5¾	Junc. B.9007/A.940	5¾
..	28¼	¼	*Logie	5½
..	33¾	5½	*Forres	

174. ABERDEEN to TOMINTOUL via Deeside.

Mainly follows the south bank of the wooded Dee Valley to Ballater, afterwards continuing to Tomintoul by a narrow, hilly road which is liable to be blocked by snow during the winter months. Pretty at the narrow Bridge of Feugh, where a diversion is made beside the Feugh Water to rejoin Deeside near Birsemore. From Gairnshiel Lodge there is a long ascent and descent to Colnabaichin in the Don Valley. At Cock Bridge, a 1 in 5 ascent leads to the summit of the Lecht Road (2,090 feet), from which there is a long descent to Tomintoul. The main road to Ballater is given in Iter. 152, while other routes to the Don Valley are given in Iter. 176 and 191; also to Tomintoul in Iter. 176 and 177, the quickest way being by Huntly, Iter. 175, 195 and 177.

A.92			*Aberdeen	67¼
A.943	2	2	*Bridge of Dee	65¼
..	3¼	1¼	Banchory Devenick	64¼
..	5½	2¼	*Blairs	62¼
..	7	1½	*Maryculter	60¾
..	13¼	6¼	Durris	54¼
B.974	17¼	4¼	*Bridge of Feugh	50
B.976	20¼	2½	*Strachan	47½
..	22¼	2	*"Feughside" Inn	45½
..	25	2¾	Finzean (P.O.)	42¾
..	27¼	2¼	Marywell	40¼
A.973	27¾	½	Junc. B.976/A.973	40
..	30¾	3	Birsemore	37
..	32¼	1½	*Bridge of Ess	35½
..	35¼	3	*Dinnet Bridge (near side)	32¼
..	40	4¾	*Pannanich Wells	27¾
B.971	42	2	Ballater Bridge	25¾
A.93	42¼	¼	*Ballater	25¼
..	43¾	1½	Bridge of Gairn	24
B.972	44	¼	Junc. A.93/B.972	23¾
A.939	49	5	*Gairnshiel Lodge	18¾
..	55½	6½	Colnabaichin	12½
..	56½	1½	*Corgarff	11
..	58	1½	*Cock Bridge	9¾
..	67¾	9¾	*Tomintoul	

175. ABERDEEN to INVERNESS.

A pleasant, easy main road through agricultural country.

A.96			*Aberdeen	104
..	3¾	3¾	Bucksburn	100¼
..	8¾	5	Blackburn	95¼
..	12¼	3½	*Kintore	91¾
..	14½	2¼	Port Elphinstone	89½
..	15¾	1¼	*Inverurie	88¼
..	19½	3¾	*Inveramsay	84½
..	21	1½	*Pitcaple	83
..	28½	7½	*Colpy	75½
..	38¾	10¼	*Huntly	65¼
..	49¼	10½	*Keith	54¾
..	50	½	*Fife Keith	54
..	57¼	7¼	*Fochabers	46¾
..	58¼	1½	*Mosstodloch	45¼
..	62¼	3½	*Lhanbryde	41¾
..	66¼	3¾	*Elgin	37¾
..	71½	5¼	*Alves	32½
..	78	6½	*Forres	26

..	82	4	*Brodie (Sta.)	22
..	86	4	*Auldearn	18
..	88¼	2¼	*Nairn	15¾
A.9	103	14¾	Junc. A.96/A.9	1
..	104	1	*Inverness	

176. A tour from ABERDEEN to INVERNESS via the Lecht Road and Grantown-on-Spey.

Agricultural districts at first, passing near Dunecht House and *Castle Fraser, which lie on opposite sides of the road near Waterton Dunecht. Follows the Don Valley from Alford to Cock Bridge, whence the narrow road to Tomintoul is liable to be blocked by snow during the winter months. At Cock Bridge an ascent of 1 in 5 leads to the summit of the Lecht Road (2,090 feet), followed by a long descent to Tomintoul. After several ascents and descents (maximum gradient 1 in 7) between Bridge of Avon and the summit beyond Bridge of Brown, there is a gradual descent to the wooded Strath Spey. Beyond Grantown, Dava Moor is crossed to Ferness, in the pretty Findhorn Valley, to reach Nairn, on the Moray Firth. Flat agricultural country on the latter part. See Iter. 175, 177 and 195 for alternative routes. The quickest way to Inverness is by Elgin (Iter. 175), and to Grantown or Tomintoul is via Huntly and Dufftown, Iter. 175, 195 and 177. From Grantown to Inverness the quickest way is by Carrbridge, Iter. 195.

A.944			*Aberdeen	116
..	8	8	*Skene	108
..	12¼	4¼	*Waterton-Dunecht	103¾
..	20	7¾	*Tillyfourie	96
..	25¼	5¼	*Alford	90¾
..	26¾	1½	*Bridge of Alford	89¼
A.97	32½	6	Junc. A.944/A.97	83¼
..	34¼	1¾	*Kildrummy	81¾
..	38	3¾	*Glenkindie	78
B.973	42½	4½	Junc. A.97/B.973	73¼
..	45	2½	*Strathdon	71
A.939	51	6	Colnabaichin	65
..	52½	1½	*Corgarff	63¼
..	53¾	1¼	*Cock Bridge	62¼
..	63½	9¾	*Tomintoul	52½
..	65½	2	*Bridge of Avon	50½
..	67¼	2¼	*Bridge of Brown	48¼
A.95	75¼	8	*Junc. A.939/A.95	40¼
A.939	77¼	1½	*Grantown-on-Spey	38½
..	84¼	7½	*Dava	31¼
..	90	5¼	*Ferness	26
A.96	99¼	9¼	Junc. A.939/A.96	16¼
..	100¼	½	*Nairn	15¾
A.9	115	14¾	Junc. A.96/A.9	1
..	116	1	*Inverness	

177. A tour from ABERDEEN to INVERNESS via Grantown-on-Spey and the Findhorn Valley.

An alternative to the direct road as far as Tillyfourie, mostly following the River Don, through agricultural country. *Castle Fraser lies to the south of the road beyond Kemnay. Winding and hilly across moorlands, ascending from Rhynie to Cabrach, then by the Glacks of Balloch Pass (1,197 feet) to Dufftown. The direct road (B.9002) from north of Lumsden to Cabrach is narrow and more difficult.

Pretty in Glen Rinnes, leading to Tomnavoulin, near the famous *Glenlivet distillery, then becomes hilly beyond Tomintoul, with several ascents and descents (maximum gradient 1 in 7) between Bridge of Avon and the summit beyond Bridge of Brown, after which there is a gradual descent to the wooded Spey Valley. Beyond Grantown, crosses Dava Moor, then leaves the main road to visit the delightful Findhorn valley at Dulsie Bridge, thence by Cawdor Castle to Culloden Moor. Between Dava and Inverness, a narrow, winding and hilly road is followed, and there is a ford before reaching Dulsie Bridge. See Iter. 176 for the main road via Nairn. A short detour can be made along the banks of *Lochindorb, by turning off just before reaching Dava, and proceeding uphill by a narrow moorland road, rejoining the main route before Dulsie Bridge. For alternative routes see Iter. 175, 176 and 195. The quickest way to Dufftown, Grantown or Tomintoul is by Huntly, Iter. 175, 195 and 177. From Grantown to Inverness the quickest way is by Carrbridge, Iter. 195.

A.96			*Aberdeen	127¾
..	3¾	3¾	Bucksburn	124
..	8¾	5	Blackburn	119
B.994	11½	2¾	Junc. A.96/B.994	116¼
B.993	14¼	3¼	Junc. B.994/B.993	113
..	15¾	1	*Kemnay	112
..	18¼	3	*Monymusk	109
A.944	22	3¾	*Tillyfourie	105¾
..	27¼	5¼	*Alford	100¾
..	28¾	1½	*Bridge of Alford	99
A.97	34¾	6	Junc. A.944/A.97	93
..	36¼	1½	*Lumsden	91½
A.941	40¼	4	*Rhynie	87½
..	48¼	8	*Cabrach	79½
B.9009	58¾	10¼	*Dufftown	69
..	63¾	5	*Glenrinnes	64
B.9008	69¼	5½	Achbreck (Church)	58½
..	71	1¾	*Tomnavoulin	56¾
..	72¾	1¾	Knockandhu	55
A.939	77¼	4½	Junc. B.9008/A.939	50½
..	77½	¼	*Tomintoul	50¼
..	79½	2	*Bridge of Avon	48¼
..	81¾	2¼	*Bridge of Brown	46
A.95	89¾	8	Junc. A.939/A.95	38
A.939	91¼	1½	*Grantown-on-Spey	36¼
..	98¾	7½	*Dava	29
Uncl.	101¼	2½	Junc. A.939/Uncl.	26¼
..	104¾	3½	*Dulsie Bridge	23
B.9090	113½	8¾	Junc. Uncl./B.9090	14¼
..	113¾	¼	*Cawdor	14
B.9091	115¾	2	Junc. B.9090/B.9091	12
B.9006	117¼	1½	*Croy	10½
..	122¼	5	*Culloden Cairn	5½
A.9	125	2¾	Junc. B.9006/A.9	2¾
..	127¼	2¼	*Inverness	

178. ABERDEEN to BUCKIE via Insch. Through pleasant agricultural districts and following an alternative to the main road (Iter. 175) between Pitcaple and Huntly.

A.96			*Aberdeen	65
..	3¾	3¾	Bucksburn	61¼
..	8¾	5	Blackburn	56¼
..	12¼	3½	*Kintore	52¾
..	14½	2¼	Port Elphinstone	50½
..	15¾	1¼	*Inverurie	49¼
..	19¾	3¾	*Inveramsay	45¼
..	21	1¼	*Pitcaple	44
A.979	23	2	Junc. A.96/A.979	42
..	24¼	1¼	*Oyne	40¾
..	27¼	3	*Insch (Sta.)	37¾
..	33¼	6	*Kennethmont	31¾
A.97	36	2¾	Junc. A.979/A.97	29
A.96	41¼	5¼	*Huntly	23¾
..	52¼	10¾	*Keith	12¼
..	52¾	½	*Fife Keith	12¼
B.9016	54¾	2	Junc. A.96/B.9016	10¼
..	55½	¾	Aultmore	9½
..	61	5½	*Tynet	4
A.98	61½	½	Junc. B.9016/A.98	3½
A.942	64	2½	Junc. A.98/A.942	1
..	65	1	*Buckie	

179. ABERDEEN to BRAEMAR and LINN OF DEE via Tarland. Pleasant, rural country at first, passing *Midmar Castle 2 miles beyond Echt, while Lochs Davan and Kinord are adjacent to the road between Tarland and Cambus o' May. Ballater can be avoided by the short cut (B.972) through the pretty Pass of Ballater. Delightful in wooded *Deeside, with a view of the Royal residence of *Balmoral Castle after Crathie Church. Narrow and winding along the secluded valley to Linn of Dee, where the motoring road doubles back along the opposite bank of the river to Linn of Quoich, but there is no through way. The main road from Aberdeen to Braemar is given in Iter. 152 and a further alternative appears in Iter. 168.

A.944			*Aberdeen	65¼
A.974	5¾	5¾	Junc. A.944/A.974	59¾
..	9¾	4	Garlogie	55½
..	12½	2¾	*Echt	52¾
..	31	18½	*Tarland	34¼
A.97	34	3	Junc. A.974/A.97	31¼
A.93	37½	3½	Junc. A.97/A.93	27¾
..	38½	1	*Cambus o' May	26¾
..	42	3½	*Ballater	23¼
..	43½	1½	Bridge of Gairn	21¾
..	49¼	5¾	*Crathie Church	15¾
Uncl.	58¾	9¼	*Braemar	6½
..	63¾	5	*Inverey	1½
..	65¼	1½	*Linn of Dee	

180. ABERDEEN to BANFF or MACDUFF. An undulating road through flat agricultural country.

A.96			*Aberdeen	45¾
A.947	3¾	3¾	Bucksburn	42
..	6	2¼	*Dyce	39¾
..	10¼	4¼	Newmachar	35½
..	13¼	3¼	Whiterashes	32¼
..	17¼	4	*Old Meldrum	28¼
..	25¼	7¾	*Fyvie	20¼
..	30	4¾	*Auchterless	15¾
..	34¼	4¼	*Turriff	11¼
..	40¼	6	*King Edward (P.O.)	5½
A.98	45¼	5	†Banff Bridge	½
..	45¾	½	*Banff	
			OR	
			†	
A.98	45¼		Banff Bridge (near side)	
..	46¼	1	*Macduff	

181. ABERDEEN to BANFF via Peterhead and Fraserburgh. An undulating main road connecting Aberdeen, Peterhead, Fraserburgh and Banff through mainly agricultural country, with glimpses of the North Sea. See Iter. 180, 182 and 183 for alternative routes.

A.92			*Aberdeen	77½
..	2½	2½	*Bridge of Don	75
..	8	5½	Balmedie	69½
..	16½	8½	*Ellon	60¼
A.952	21¼	4½	Birness	56¼
..	24¾	3½	Hatton	52¾
..	28¼	4	Longhaven	48¾
..	31	2¾	*Boddam	46¼
..	32¾	1¾	*Burnhaven	44¾
..	34¼	1½	*Peterhead	43¼
..	39¼	5	St. Fergus	38¼
..	43¼	4¼	*Crimond	34
..	46¼	3	*Lonmay	31
A.92	47¼	¾	Junc. A.952/A.92	30¼
A.98	52¼	5	*Fraserburgh	25¼
..	57¼	5¼	Tyrie	19¼
..	73¼	15¾	Longmanhill	4¼
..	76	2¾	*Macduff	1½
..	77	1	Banff Bridge	½
..	77½	½	*Banff	

182. ABERDEEN to BANFF via the Coast. A touring route, mainly through agricultural country, with fine coast views in places, especially between Fraserburgh and Banff, where the road is hilly and winding, with a steep descent and ascent near Pennan (maximum gradient 1 in 6). *Collieston lies on an alternative narrow road nearer the coast between Newburgh and Cruden Bay, whilst *Old Rattray and *St. Combs lie to the east of the road between Peterhead and Fraserburgh. Approaching Rosehearty, the road passes near *Pitsligo Castle and beyond Protstonhill detours can be made to visit the picturesque fishing villages of *Crovie and *Gardenstown. For the main roads between the towns, see Iter. 180 and 181.

A.92			*Aberdeen	78
..	2½	2½	*Bridge of Don	75½
..	8	5½	Balmedie	70
A.975	11	3	Junc. A.92/A.975	67
..	13½	2½	*Newburgh	64½
..	23¼	9½	*Cruden Bay	54¾
A.952	26¼	3¼	Junc. A.975/A.952	51¾
..	26¾	½	Longhaven	51¼
..	29	2¼	*Boddam	49
..	30¼	1¼	*Burnhaven	47¾
..	32¼	1½	*Peterhead	45¾
..	37¼	5	St. Fergus	40¾
..	41¼	4¼	Crimond	36¾
..	44¼	3	*Lonmay	33½
B.9033	46	1¾	Junc. A.952/B.9033	32
..	47¼	1¼	Crofts of Savoch	30¾
..	51¼	4¼	*Bridge of Philorth	26¼
A.92	53	1¾	Junc. B.9033/A.92	25
A.98	54	1	*Fraserburgh	24
B.9031	54¾	¾	Junc. A.98/B.9031	23¼
..	56½	1¾	*Sandhaven	21½
..	58½	2	*Rosehearty	19½
..	63¼	4¾	*New Aberdour	14¾
..	66½	3¼	*Pennan	11½
..	68½	2	Protstonhill	9½
A.98	75¼	6¾	Junc. B.9031/A.98	2¾
..	76¼	1	*Macduff	1½
..	77¾	1	Banff Bridge	¾
..	78	½	*Banff	

183. ABERDEEN to BANFF via Ellon.

A cross-country alternative to the main road by Turriff (Iter. 180). Through rural districts, hilly between New Deer and New Byth, with a descent of 1 in 8.

Road			Place	
A.92			*Aberdeen	50
..	2½	2½	*Bridge of Don	47½
..	8	5½	Balmedie	42
A.948	16½	8½	*Ellon	33½
..	24½	7¾	Auchnagatt	25½
..	29	4½	*New Deer	21
Uncl.	34½	5½	Junc. A.948/Uncl.	15½
B.9027	35	¼	Junc. Uncl./B.9027	15
..	37½	2½	*New Byth	12½
Uncl.	38½	1	Junc. B.9027/Uncl.	11½
A.98	39½	¾	Junc. Uncl./A.98	10¾
..	45¾	6½	Longmanhill	4½
..	48½	2¾	*Macduff	1½
..	49½	1	Banff Bridge	½
..	50	½	*Banff	

184. ABERDEEN to CULLEN.

A rural cross-country route, utilizing undulating secondary roads between Inverurie and Portsoy. The recommended route is by Banff (Iter. 180 and 198).

Road			Place	
A.96			*Aberdeen	57½
..	3½	3½	Bucksburn	54
..	8¾	5	Blackburn	49
..	12½	3½	*Kintore	45½
..	14½	2½	Port Elphinstone	43½
..	15¾	1¼	*Inverurie	42
B.9001	17	1½	Junc. A.96/B.9001	40½
..	26¼	9¼	*Rothie Norman	31½
..	36½	10¼	*Forgue	21¼
A.97	37½	1	Junc. B.9001/A.97	20½
..	40	2½	Bridge of Marnoch	17¾
..	43	3	*Aberchirder	14¾
B.9025	45½	2½	Blacklaw (P.O.)	12¼
A.98	49¾	4¼	Junc. B.9025/A.98	8
..	52¼	2½	*Portsoy	5½
..	57¾	5½	*Cullen	

185. ABERDEEN to FRASERBURGH.

An easy main road through open agricultural country.

Road			Place	
A.92			*Aberdeen	42¾
..	2½	2½	*Bridge of Don	40¼
..	8	5½	Balmedie	34¾
..	16½	8½	*Ellon	26
..	21½	4½	Birness	21½
..	28	6½	Clola	14½
..	30½	2½	*Mintlaw	12¼
..	34½	4	New Leeds	8¼
..	42¾	8¼	*Fraserburgh	

186. ABERDEEN to FRASERBURGH via Tarves.

Utilizes secondary roads through rural countryside for the greater part. See Iter. 185 for the main road.

A.92			*Aberdeen	46¼
..	2½	2½	*Bridge of Don	43¾
B.999	4½	1½	Junc. A.92/B.999	42
..	8¾	4¼	Whitecairns	37¾
..	15	6¼	*Pitmedden	31¼
..	18½	3½	*Tarves	28
A.981	20½	2¼	Junc. B.999/A.981	25¾
..	23½	2½	*Methlick	23
..	25¾	2½	Cairnorrie	20½
..	30	4½	*New Deer	16¼
..	37½	7½	*Strichen	8¾
..	42¾	5½	Memsie	3½
..	46¼	3½	*Fraserburgh	

187. PETERHEAD to LOSSIEMOUTH via Cruden Bay.

A secondary route through agricultural country. The quickest way from Peterhead to Huntly is by Turriff (Iter. 189 and 196), while the direct road from Peterhead to Ellon is given in Iter. 181.

Road			Place	
A.952			*Peterhead	84½
..	1½	1½	*Burnhaven	83
..	3¼	1¾	*Boddam	81¼
..	5½	2½	Longhaven	79
A.975	5¾	¼	Junc. A.952/A.975	78¾
..	9	3½	*Cruden Bay	75½
Uncl.	9¼	¼	Junc. A.975/Uncl.	75¼
A.952	11¼	2	Junc. Uncl./A.952	73¼
..	12¼	1	Hatton	72¼
A.92	15½	3¼	Birness	68¾
B.9004	20¼	4½	*Ellon	64¼
B.999	25¼	5	Junc. B.9004/B.999	59¼
B.9000	26	¾	*Pitmedden	58¼
A.947	30¾	4¾	Junc. B.9000/A.947	53¾
A.981	31½	¾	*Old Meldrum	53
B.9000	31¾	¼	Junc. A.981/B.9000	52¾
..	42½	10¾	*Culsalmond	42
A.96	43	½	Junc. B.9000/A.96	41½
..	53	10	*Huntly	31½
..	63¾	10¾	*Keith	20¾
..	64¼	½	*Fife Keith	20¼
..	71½	7¼	*Fochabers	13
..	73	1½	*Mosstodloch	11½
..	76¾	3¾	*Lhanbryde	7¾
B.9103	77¾	1	Junc. A.96/B.9103	6¾
..	79¾	1½	Calcots (Sta.)	5¼
A.941	83½	4¼	Junc. B9103/A.941	1
..	84½	1	*Lossiemouth	

188. PETERHEAD to BANFF.

An easy road through agricultural country, flat at first, later becoming undulating.

Road			Place	
A.950			*Peterhead	35¼
..	6½	6½	Longside	28¾
..	9	2½	*Mintlaw	26¼
..	19	10	*New Pitsligo	16¼
A.98	20¼	1¼	Junc. A.950/A.98	15
..	31	10¾	Longmanhill	4½
..	33¾	2¾	*Macduff	1½
..	34½	1	Banff Bridge	½
..	35¼	½	*Banff	

189. PETERHEAD to ELGIN via Turriff.

A cross-country route mainly utilizing secondary roads through agricultural districts. *Old Deer can be included by following B.9029 from beyond Mintlaw to Maud, but the route shown is easier to follow. Pretty scenery in places, especially in the Deveron Valley between Aberchirder and Keith, where *Rothiemay lies just off the road, and again in the Spey Valley near Orton. The quickest way from Peterhead to Elgin is by Banff (Iter. 188 and 198) and from Keith to Elgin is by Fochabers (Iter. 175).

Road			Place	
A.950			*Peterhead	71¾
..	6½	6½	Longside	65¼
..	9	2½	*Mintlaw	62¾
B.9106	13	4	Junc. A.950/B.9106	58¾
B.9029	14½	1½	Maud	57¼
A.981	16¼	1¾	Junc. B.9029/A.981	55½
A.948	17½	1	*New Deer	54¼

190. STONEHAVEN to ELGIN.

A useful cross-country link, forming a pleasant alternative to the main road by Aberdeen and Huntly (Iter. 155 and 175). Although winding and hilly in places, the roads are good and there is little traffic. At first a steady climb across the moors by the Slug Road and over the pretty Bridge of Feugh to Banchory in the Dee Valley. *Craigievar Castle is passed 4 miles from Lumphanan, and later the Don Valley is traversed for several miles. Winding and hilly across moorland, ascending from Rhynie to Cabrach, then by the Glacks of Balloch Pass (1,197 feet) to Dufftown. The direct road (B.9002) from north of Lumsden to Cabrach is narrow and more difficult. Moorland and agricultural on the latter part, with pretty scenery around Craigellachie in the Spey Valley.

Road			Place	
A.957			*Stonehaven	85
..	4½	4½	Rickarton	80½
A.943	14	9½	Junc. A.957/A.943	71
..	15½	1½	*Bridge of Feugh	69½
A.93	16¼	¾	*Banchory	68¾
A.980	16¼	½	Junc. A.93/A.980	68¼
..	23½	7	*Torphins	61½
..	27½	3½	*Lumphanan	57½
A.944	37½	10½	Junc. A.980/A.944	47½
..	38	½	*Bridge of Alford	47
A.97	44	6	Junc. A.944/A.97	41
..	45½	1½	*Lumsden	39½
A.941	49½	4	*Rhynie	35½
..	57½	8	*Cabrach	27½
..	68	10½	*Dufftown	17
..	72½	4½	*Craigellachie	12½
..	75	2½	*Rothes	10
..	84½	9½	New Elgin	½
..	85	½	*Elgin	

191. STONEHAVEN to TOMINTOUL.

At first a steady climb across the moors by the Slug Road and over the pretty Bridge of Feugh to the River Dee at Banchory. Continuing with *Deeside to Dinnet, moorland and agricultural country is traversed to the Don Valley, which is followed to Cock Bridge, beyond which the road is narrow with a 1 in 5 ascent leading to the summit of the Lecht Road (2,090 feet) followed by a long descent to Tomintoul. This road from Cock Bridge is liable to be blocked by snow during the winter months.

A.957			*Stonehaven	66
..	4½	4½	Rickarton	61½

(Continuation of Iter. 189, from first column data)

Road			Place	
..	23½	6¼	Cuminestown	48¼
A.947	28	4½	Junc. A.948/A.947	43¾
B.9025	30	2	*Turriff	41¾
A.97	37	7	Junc. B.9025/A.97	34¾
..	37½	½	*Aberchirder	34¼
B.9117	40	2½	Junc. A.97/B.9117	31¾
..	40¾	¾	Marnoch	31
A.95	48	7¼	Junc. B.9117/A.95	23¾
A.96	53½	5½	*Keith	18¼
..	53¾	¼	*Fife Keith	18
A.95	54½	¾	Junc. A.96/A.95	17¼
B.9103	58½	4	Mulben (W.M.)	13¼
B.9015	61½	3	Junc. B.9103/B.9015	10¼
..	62	½	*Orton (Sta.)	9¾
B.9103	63½	1½	Junc. B.9015/B.9103	8¼
A.96	69	5½	Junc. B.9103/A.96	2¾
..	71¼	2¼	*Elgin	

A.943	14	9¾	Junc. A.957/A.943	52
..	15½	1½	*Bridge of Feugh	50½
A.93	16½	¾	*Banchory ..	49¾
..	24	7½	*Kincardine o' Neil ..	42
..	28¼	4¼	*Aboyne ..	37¾
B.9119	33½	4¼	*Dinnet ..	32¼
..	35½	2	Ordie ..	30½
A.97	35½	¼	Junc. B.9119/A.97	30½
..	37½	2	Logie Coldstone ..	28½
B.973	45	7½	Junc. A.97/B.973	21
..	47½	2½	*Strathdon ..	18½
A.939	53½	6	Colnabaichin ..	12½
..	55	1½	*Corgarff ..	11
..	56¼	1¼	*Cock Bridge ..	9¾
..	66	9¾	*Tomintoul	

192. TOMINTOUL to LOSSIEMOUTH. Moorland to Tomnavoulin, passing near the famous *Glenlivet distillery. If preferred, the alternative road (B.9136) through Strath Avon to Downan can be used, although there is little to choose. Follows the wooded Strath Spey from Dalnashaugh to Rothes, and traverses a flat agricultural district on the latter part. The ruined *Spynie Palace is adjacent to the road between Elgin and Lossiemouth.

A.939			*Tomintoul ..	42¼
B.9008	¼	¼	Junc. A.939/B.9008	42
..	4½	4¼	Knockandhu ..	37¾
..	6¼	1¾	*Tomnavoulin ..	35¾
..	8¼	1½	Achbreck (Church)	34
..	10½	2¼	*Downan ..	31¾
A.95	14	3½	*" Dalnashaugh " Inn ..	28¼
..	21½	7½	*Aberlour ..	20½
A.941	23½	2	*Craigellachie ..	18½
..	26¼	2¼	*Rothes ..	15¾
..	35¾	9½	New Elgin ..	6½
..	36¼	½	*Elgin ..	5¾
..	37¼	¾	Bishopmill ..	5
..	42¼	5	*Lossiemouth	

193. HUNTLY to CULLEN. Pleasant open agricultural land, with coastal views between Portsoy and Cullen. *Rothiemay lies to the east of the road half way between Huntly and Glenbarry.

A.96			*Huntly ..	23¾
B.9022	1	1	Junc. A.96/B.9022	22¾
A.95	10¾	9¾	Glenbarry ..	13
B.9022	12	1¼	Junc. A.95/B.9022	11¾
A.98	17½	5½	Junc. B.9022/A.98	6
..	18¼	¾	*Portsoy ..	5½
..	23¾	5½	*Cullen	

194. HUNTLY to BANFF. A pleasant undulating road through agricultural country.

A.96			*Huntly ..	20¾
A.97	1	1	Junc. A.96/A.97	19¾
..	6½	5½	Bogniebrae ..	14½
..	8¾	2¼	Bridge of Marnoch	12
..	11¾	3	*Aberchirder ..	9
..	14¼	2½	Blacklaw (P.O.)	6½
..	20¾	6½	*Banff	

195. HUNTLY to INVERNESS via Grantown-on-Spey. A picturesque alternative to the main road by Elgin Iter. 175. Pretty in the Deveron Valley at first, then hilly across the moors to Dufftown. Attractive in Strath Spey between Craigellachie and Grantown, changing to moorland after Carrbridge, where the road gradually ascends to Slochd summit (1,333 feet), later becoming rather winding as Strath Dearn and Strath Nairn are crossed on the long, gradual descent to sea level.

A.96			*Huntly ..	75¾
B.9014	½	½	Junc. A.96/B.9014	75¼
..	11½	11	*Auchindown ..	64¼
A.941	12¾	1¼	Junc. B.9014/A.941	63
..	13½	1	*Dufftown ..	62
A.95	18	4½	*Craigellachie ..	57¾
..	20	2	*Aberlour ..	55¾
..	27¾	7¾	*" Dalnashaugh " Inn ..	48
..	37¾	10	*Cromdale ..	38
..	42	4¼	*Grantown-on-Spey ..	33¾
A.938	45	3	*Dulnain Bridge	30¾
..	49½	4½	Duthil ..	26¼
A.9	51½	2	*Carrbridge ..	24¼
..	57½	5¾	*Slochd Summit	18¼
..	59½	2½	*Tomatin ..	16
..	64½	4½	*Moy (Sta.) ..	11¼
..	70	5½	*Daviot ..	5¾
..	75¾	5¾	*Inverness	

196. HUNTLY to FRASERBURGH. A pleasant cross-country route through agricultural districts, rather winding in places to Aberchirder.

A.96			*Huntly ..	41½
A.97	1	1	Junc. A.96/A.97	40½
..	6½	5½	Bogniebrae ..	35¼
..	8¾	2¼	Bridge of Marnoch	32¾
..	11¾	3	*Aberchirder ..	29¾
B.9025	12¼	½	Junc. A.97/B.9025	29¼
A.947	19¼	7	*Turriff ..	22¼
B.9105	21¼	2	Junc. A.947/B.9105	20¼
A.98	27	5¾	Junc. B.9105/A.98	14¼
..	36	9	Tyrie ..	5½
..	41½	5½	*Fraserburgh	

197. BANCHORY to FRASERBURGH via Inverurie. A cross-country route utilizing secondary roads through pleasant rural scenery.

A.93			*Banchory ..	56¼
A.980	½	½	Junc. A.93/A.980	56
B.977	2¾	2¼	Junc. A.980/B.977	53¾
..	8¾	6	*Echt ..	47¾
..	11¼	2½	*Waterton-Dunecht ..	45¼
..	12½	1¼	Lyne of Skene ..	44
..	14½	2	Leylodge ..	42
A.96	16½	2	Junc. B.977/A.96	40
..	17	½	*Kintore ..	39¼
..	19¼	2¼	Port Elphinstone	37¼
A.981	20¼	1¼	*Inverurie ..	36
A.947	25¼	5¼	*Old Meldrum ..	30¾
A.981	26¼	¾	Junc. A.947/A.981	30
..	33½	7	*Methlick ..	23
..	36	2½	Cairnorrie ..	20¼
..	40¼	4¼	*New Deer ..	16¼
..	47½	7½	*Strichen ..	8¾
..	53	5½	Memsie ..	3½
..	56½	3½	*Fraserburgh	

198. BANFF to INVERNESS via Culloden. Follows an inland route parallel to the coast through pleasant countryside. See Iter. 199 for alternatives including the seaside resorts. *Fordyce lies to the south of the road between Portsoy and Cullen. Between Elgin and Forres there are quiet alternatives (uncl.) to the south of the main road, passing *Pluscarden Priory and *Dallas (B.9010) respectively. From Forres to Inverness a diversion is made to pass Cawdor Castle and the historic battlefield at Culloden, the main road being given in Iter. 175.

A.98			*Banff ..	74½
..	8	8	*Portsoy ..	66½
..	13½	5½	*Cullen ..	61
..	22½	9	*Tynet Bridge ..	52
A.96	25½	3	Junc. A.98/A.96	49
..	25¾	¼	*Fochabers ..	48¼
..	27¼	1½	*Mosstodloch ..	47¼
..	31	3¾	*Lhanbryde ..	43¼
..	34½	3½	*Elgin ..	39¾
..	40	5½	*Alves ..	34¼
..	46½	6½	*Forres ..	28
..	50½	4	*Brodie (Sta.) ..	24
B.9101	54½	4	*Auldearn ..	20
B.9090	57¾	3½	Junc. B.9101/B.9090	16¾
..	60½	2¾	*Cawdor ..	14
B.9091	62½	2	Junc. B.9090/B.9091	12
B.9006	64	1½	*Croy ..	10½
..	69	5	*Culloden Cairn	5½
A.9	71½	2½	Junc. B.9006/A.9	2¾
..	74½	2¾	*Inverness	

199. BANFF to INVERNESS via the Coast. This touring route embraces most of the sandy seaside resorts in the counties of Banff, Moray and Nairn, the main road to Elgin being given in Iter. 198 and Elgin to Inverness in Iter. 175. Some other places of interest to the south of the main road are also mentioned in Iter. 198. Just off the coast road there are a number of places which can be visited, if desired, including *Whitehills, between Banff and Portsoy, *Spey Bay beyond Portgordon, and also *Garmouth and *Kingston from Mosstodloch. A detour can be made (Iter. 187) through *Lossiemouth on the coast north of Elgin, but at present the direct road from Lossiemouth to Duffus is closed. Other excursions which can be made, are from Kinloss to *Findhorn and from Forres to the *Culbin Sands.

A.98			*Banff ..	85¾
B.9139	1¼	1¼	Junc. A.98/B.9139	84½
..	1½	¼	*Boyndie Bay ..	84¼
A.98	6½	5	*Portsoy ..	79¼
..	12	5½	*Cullen ..	73¾
A.942	13½	1½	Junc. A.98/A.942	72¼
..	14¼	1	*Portknockie ..	71¼
..	16¾	2¼	*Findochty ..	69
..	18½	1¾	*Portessie ..	67¼
A.990	19½	1	*Buckie ..	66¼
Uncl.	22	2½	*Portgordon ..	63¾
B.9104	24¼	2¼	Junc. Uncl./B.9104	61
A.96	26¼	2	Junc. B.9104/A.96	59
..	27¼	1	*Mosstodloch ..	58
..	31¼	3¾	*Lhanbryde ..	54¼
A.941	35¼	3¾	*Elgin ..	50½
B.9012	36	¾	Bishopmill ..	49¾
..	40½	4½	*Duffus ..	45¼
..	42½	2	*Hopeman ..	43¼
..	43½	1	Cummingstown ..	42¼
..	45	1½	*Burghead ..	40¾
B.9089	45½	½	Junc. B.9012/B.9089	40

..	52¼	6¼	*Kinloss ..	33½
A.96	54½	2	Junc. B.9011/A.96	31½
..	55	¼	*Forres ..	30¾
..	59	4	*Brodie (Sta.) ..	26¾
..	63	4	*Auldearn ..	22¾
..	65½	2½	*Nairn ..	20¼
B.9092	67½	2	Junc. A.96/B.9092	18½
B.9006	71½	4¼	Junc. B.9092/B.9006	14¼
..	72	½	*Ardersier ..	13¾
..	73½	1½	*Fort George ..	12½
			Return to:—	
B.9039	75	1½	*Ardersier ..	10½
A.96	80¼	5¼	Junc. B.9039/A.96	5¼
A.9	84¼	4¼	Junc. A.96/A.9 ..	1
..	85¼	1	*Inverness	

200. INVERNESS to JOHN O' GROATS. The main road to the far north of Scotland. Follows an inland route parallel to the coast through agricultural country, with moorland in places, and is level for the greater part. At first skirts Beauly Firth and then alongside Cromarty Firth beyond Dingwall. During the winter months, when the direct road over the hills by Aultnamain is affected by bad weather conditions, the longer, but level coast road by Tain (Iter. 201) is recommended. After circling Dornoch Firth by Bonar Bridge, *Skibo Castle is passed between Spinningdale and Clashmore and the coast is regained at Golspie, shortly afterwards passing *Dunrobin Castle. Hilly and winding between Helmsdale and Latheron, with a steep descent and ascent (maximum gradient 1 in 9) at Berriedale, thereafter becoming level again. Undulating on the latter part, keeping a little inland but with some fine seascapes in places, especially to the east of John o' Groats.

A.9	..		*Inverness ..	140¼
..	2¼	2¼	*Clachnaharry ..	138
..	11½	9¼	*Lovat Bridge ..	128½
..	12¾	1¼	*Beauly ..	127¼
..	15¼	2½	*Muir of Ord ..	125
..	19	3¾	*Conon Bridge ..	121¼
..	20	1	*Dingwall ..	120¼
..	21½	1½	Maryburgh ..	118¾
..	28	6¼	*Evanton ..	112¼
A.836	30	2	Junc. A.9/A.836	110¼
..	39¼	9¼	*"Aultnamain" Inn ..	100¼
A.9	44¾	5	June. A.836½A.9	95½
..	47¾	3	*Ardgay ..	92½
..	48¾	1	*Bonar Bridge ..	91½
..	51¼	2½	*Creich ..	89
..	53¾	2½	*Spinningdale ..	86½
..	58¼	4½	*Clashmore ..	82
..	59¼	1½	*Evelix ..	80¾
..	65¼	6	*Mound Sta. ..	74½
..	70	4¼	*Golspie ..	70¼
..	75	5	*Brora ..	65¼
..	82	7	*Loth ..	58¼
..	84¼	2¼	*Portgower ..	55½
..	86½	2	**Helmsdale** ..	53½
..	96½	10	*Berriedale ..	43¾
..	102	5½	*Dunbeath ..	38¼
..	106¼	4¼	*Latheron ..	33¾
..	110	3¾	*Lybster ..	30¼
..	111¼	1¼	Occumster ..	29
..	114	2¾	*Mid Clyth ..	26¼
..	119¼	5¼	*Thrumster ..	20¼
..	123¼	4	**Wick** ..	16¼
..	126¼	3¼	*Reiss ..	13¼
..	131¼	4½	*Keiss ..	9
..	133½	2¼	Auckingill ..	6¼
..	135½	2	*Freswick ..	4½
..	140¼	4½	**John o' Groats**	

201. INVERNESS to BONAR BRIDGE via Strathpeffer and Tain. Mainly through agricultural country, at first skirting Beauly Firth, then making a diversion from the main road to include Strathpeffer. A level coast road is followed from Dingwall, alongside Cromarty Firth to Barbaraville, and by the edge of Dornoch Firth beyond Tain. During the winter months this route from Dingwall to Bonar Bridge is recommended in preference to the direct road via Aultnamain (Iter. 200) which is 13¼ miles shorter, but liable to be affected by bad weather.

A.9	..		*Inverness ..	68¾
..	2¼	2¼	*Clachnaharry ..	66½
..	11½	9¼	*Lovat Bridge ..	57¼
..	12¾	1¼	*Beauly ..	56
A.832	15¼	2½	*Muir of Ord ..	53¼
..	19¼	4¼	*Marybank ..	49¼
Uncl.	21¼	1¾	Junc. A.832/Uncl.	47¼
A.834	21¾	½	Junc. Uncl./A.834	47
..	23½	1¾	**Strathpeffer** ..	45¼
A.9	28¼	4¾	**Dingwall** ..	40¼
..	34½	6¼	*Evanton ..	34
..	38¼	3¾	*Alness ..	30¼
..	42	3¾	*Invergordon ..	26¾
..	43¼	1¼	*Saltburn ..	25¼
..	45½	2¼	Barbaraville ..	23¼
..	48½	3	*Logie Easter ..	20¼
..	53½	5	*Tain ..	15¼
..	59	5½	*Edderton ..	9¾
..	67¾	8¾	*Ardgay ..	1
..	68¾	1	**Bonar Bridge**	

202. INVERNESS to DINGWALL via Kessock Ferry. A direct route, utilizing the Kessock Ferry, and thence by a secondary road through an agricultural district. The recommended route is by Beauly, Iter. 200.

B.9161	..		*Inverness	13½
..	1¼	1¼	*South Kessock Ferry to *North Kessock	11¼
B.9162	3¼	2	Junc. B.9161/B.9162	9¼
..	6¼	2½	Tore ..	7¼
A.9	11	4¾	*Conon Bridge ..	2½
..	12	1	Maryburgh ..	1½
..	13½	1½	**Dingwall**	

203. INVERNESS to DINGWALL via Cromarty. A tour through the *Black Isle, with an alternative utilizing the Kessock Ferry to avoid the long detour around Beauly Firth. Pleasant, wooded agricultural country, with attractive coastal views and following the shore in several places.

A.9	..		*Inverness ..	60¼
..	2¼	2¼	*Clachnaharry ..	58¼
..	11½	9¼	*Lovat Bridge ..	49¼
..	12¾	1¼	*Beauly ..	48
B.9169	14¼	1½	Junc. A.9/B.9169	46¼
A.832	15¼	1	Junc. B.9169/A.832	45¼
..	18¼	3¼	*Redcastle (Church)	42¼
..	20¼	1¾	Tore ..	40¼
..	26¼	6¼	*Avoch ..	34
..	28¼	1¾	*Fortrose ..	32¼
..	29¼	1	*Rosemarkie ..	31¼
B.9163	38¼	8¾	*Cromarty ..	22¼
..	45¼	7	Balbair ..	15¼
..	49¼	4	*Cullicudden ..	11¼
..	56¼	7	Alcaig ..	4¼
B.9162	58	1½	Junc. B.9163/B.9162	2¾
A.9	58¼	¼	*Conon Bridge ..	2¼
..	59¼	1	Maryburgh ..	1½
..	60¾	1½	*Dingwall	
			Alternative via Kessock Ferry	
B.9161			*Inverness	
..	1¼	1¼	*South Kessock Ferry to *North Kessock	
..	6¼	5	Munlochy	
A.832	7	¼	Junc. B.9161/A.832	
..	10½	3½	*Avoch	

204. INVERNESS to ULLAPOOL. Skirts Beauly Firth at first, then follows a valley road to Loch Garve, passing the *Falls of Rogie near the Achilty Inn. Beyond Garve, the road is narrow, with frequent passing bays, and crosses the open moorlands of the Dirrie More to reach the Falls of Measach at Braemore Lodge. Beautiful mountain and loch scenery on the latter part, the last few miles being through Strath More and then along the shores of Loch Broom.

A.9	..		*Inverness ..	60¼
..	2¼	2¼	*Clachnaharry ..	58¼
..	11½	9¼	*Lovat Bridge ..	49¼
..	12¾	1¼	*Beauly ..	48
A.832	15¼	2½	*Muir of Ord ..	45¼
..	19½	4¼	*Marybank ..	41¼
..	22	2½	*Contin ..	38¾
..	22¼	¼	*" Achilty " Inn	38
..	28¼	5½	*Garve ..	32¼
A.835	29	¾	Junc. A.832/A.835	31¼
..	38¼	9¼	*" Altguish " Inn	22¼
..	48¼	10¼	*Braemore Lodge	12¼
..	60¾	12¼	*Ullapool	

205. INVERNESS to GAIRLOCH. Skirts Beauly Firth at first, then follows a valley road to Loch Garve, passing the *Falls of Rogie near the Achilty Inn. Crosses moorland country beyond Garve, with beautiful loch and mountain scenery, particularly after descending Glen Docherty to Kinlochewe, where the Ben Eighe Nature Reserve is situated. Thence an attractive, winding road follows the banks of Loch Maree for several miles, with the peak of Slioch dominating the farther shore. Later descends by the wooded Kerrysdale to Gairloch.

A.9	..		*Inverness ..	73¾
..	2¼	2¼	*Clachnaharry ..	71½
..	11½	9¼	*Lovat Bridge ..	62¼
..	12¾	1¼	*Beauly ..	61
A.832	15¼	2½	*Muir of Ord ..	58¾
..	19½	4¼	*Marybank ..	54¼
..	22	2½	*Contin ..	51¼
..	22¼	¼	*" Achilty " Inn	51
..	28¼	5½	*Garve ..	45¼
..	38¼	10	Achanalt ..	35¼
..	44¼	6¼	**Achnasheen** ..	29
..	54¼	9¼	*Kinlochewe ..	19¼
..	64	9¼	*Loch Maree (Hotel) ..	9¾
..	73¼	9¼	*Gairloch	

206. A tour from INVERNESS to GAIRLOCH via Cannich (for Glen Affric) and Gruinard Bay. A touring route, embracing some of the finest north-west Highland scenery, but utilizing narrow and hilly roads in places. At first along the shore of *Loch Ness, then by Glen Urquhart to Cannich, where picturesque detours can be made along the richly-wooded Glen Affric and Glen Cannich. Here there are some hydro-electric power scheme developments. Strath Glass is followed to the main road at Beauly, turning off at Dingwall through Strathpeffer, and passing the *Falls of Rogie near Achilty Inn. Beyond Garve the road becomes narrow, with frequent passing places, and crosses open moorland to the Falls of Measach near Braemore Lodge. Beautiful coast and mountain scenery, with excellent views on the remainder of the tour, but the road is narrow and hilly, including the 1 in 6 ascent of Gruinard Hill. Fine views of the An Teallach peaks on the descent from the so-called Destitution Road to Dundonnell, then follows Little Loch Broom to Gruinard Bay and the ascent of Gruinard Hill. *Aultbea, on Loch Ewe, lies just off the road between Laide and Poolewe. Fine views of Loch Maree and the Gair Loch on the latter part. For the direct routes to Beauly, Garve or Gairloch see Iter. 205; for Dingwall see Iter. 200 and for Strathpeffer, Iter. 201.

A.82			**Inverness**	131½
A.831	14¼	14¼	*Drumnadrochit	116¾
..	15¼	1	Milton	115¾
..	27¼	11½	*Cannich	104¼
..	34½	7	*Struy Bridge	97¼
..	39¼	5	*Crask of Aigas	92¼
..	41¼	2¼	*Kilmorack	89¾
A.9	43¼	1½	Junc. A.831/A.9	88¼
..	44¼	1¼	*Beauly	87
..	47	2¼	*Muir of Ord	84½
..	50¼	3¼	*Conon Bridge	80¾
..	51¼	1	Maryburgh	79½
A.834	53¼	1½	**Dingwall**	78¼
..	58	4¼	**Strathpeffer**	73½
A.832	60½	2½	*Contin	71
..	61¼	¾	*" Achilty " Inn	70¼
..	66¾	5½	*Garve	64¾
A.835	67½	¾	Junc. A.832/A.835	64
..	76¾	9¼	*" Altguish " Inn	54¾
A.832	87	10¼	*Braemore Lodge	44½
..	100¼	13¼	*Dundonnell	31
..	112¼	11¼	*Gruinard Bay	19¼
..	116¼	4¼	Laide	15
..	125½	9	*Poolewe	6
..	131½	6	*Gairloch	

207. INVERNESS to KYLE OF LOCHALSH (for the Isle of Skye) or GLENELG and ARNISDALE. At first along the *Caledonian Canal through the Great Glen or *Glen More, later passing the ruined Urquhart Castle beyond Drumnadrochit, on the shore of *Loch Ness, which is followed to Invermoriston. A gradual ascent is then made through the wooded Glen Moriston to Cluanie, afterwards descending (maximum gradient 1 in 8) by the lonely Glen Shiel along the route of one of the " Roads to the Isles," with magnificent mountain scenery. Fine views of the Kintail hills, including the Five Sisters, as the road follows the shore of *Loch Duich, past Eilean Donan Castle, before crossing Loch Long by the fine modern bridge at Dornie. Hilly between Inverinate and Dornie as the road climbs high above the loch, with an ascent and descent of 1 in 6, while beyond Balmacara, on the shore of Loch Alsh, there is another ascent of 1 in 10, after which the hills of Skye come into view. On the alternative to Arnisdale there are fine panoramic views from the winding ascent of Mam Rattachan (maximum gradient 1 in 6, hairpin bends), where an altitude of 1,116 feet is reached, followed by an easier descent. The road then divides. One branch leads through Glenelg to reach Glen Beag, where a visit can be made to the remarkable Pictish Brochs; thereafter a narrow and hilly road is followed high above the Sound of Sleat and along the shore of picturesque *Loch Hourn to the road end at Arnisdale. The other branch road diverges before Glenelg village and leads to a ferry which operates during the summer months to Kylerhea (Isle of Skye). From Kylerhea there is a long climb (maximum gradient 1 in 5) by a narrow road through Glen Arroch, followed by a long descent to the main road halfway between Kyleakin and Broadford (Shiel Bridge to Broadford is 20¾ miles).

A.82			**Inverness**	83½
..	14¼	14¼	*Drumnadrochit	68¾
..	15½	¾	*Lewiston	68
A.887	27¼	11¾	*Invermoriston	56¼
..	35½	8¼	*Torgyle Bridge	47¾
A.87	51¼	16	*Cluanie	31¼
..	63½	11¾	†*Shiel Bridge	20
..	66	2½	*Croe Bridge	17½
..	69¼	3¼	*Inverinate	14¼
..	73	3¾	*Dornie	10½
..	73¾	¾	*Ardelve	9¾
..	76	2¼	*Auchtertyre	7½
..	77½	1½	*Balmacara	6
..	83½	6	*Kyle of Lochalsh	
			OR	
Uncl.	63½		†Shiel Bridge	
..	66¾	3¼	*Mam Rattachan (summit)	
..	72	5¼	*Glenelg	
..	82	10	*Arnisdale	

208. FORT WILLIAM to AVIEMORE. Passes through a variety of mountain, moorland, loch and woodland scenery, with views of *Ben Nevis from the open country on the earlier part. Beyond Spean Bridge, the pretty Glen Spean is traversed, afterwards passing along the shores of Loch Laggan. Attractive woodland scenery in the Upper Spey Valley from Drumgask.

A.82			**Fort William**	61¼
..	2¼	2¼	Lochy Bridge (near side)	59
A.86	9½	7¼	**Spean Bridge**	51¾
..	12¾	3¼	*Roy Bridge	48½
..	18¼	5½	Rd. to *Tulloch Sta.	43
..	31½	13¼	*Loch Laggan (Hotel)	29¾
..	38¼	6¾	*Drumgask	23
..	38¾	½	*Laggan Bridge	22½
A.9	46½	7¾	*Newtonmore	14¾
..	49½	2¾	*Kingussie	12
..	55	5½	*Kincraig	6½
..	58¼	3¼	*Lynwilg	2¾
..	61¼	2¾	*Aviemore	

209. FORT WILLIAM to MALLAIG. Although narrow and winding on the second half, this " Road to the Isles " is scenically one of the very finest in the Highlands. A variety of loch, mountain and woodland scenery is traversed at first along the shores of Loch Eil, then passing the Prince Charles Edward Monument on the edge of *Loch Shiel near Glenfinnan. Later along the shores of picturesque Loch Eilt, and afterwards passing the heads of Loch Ailort and *Loch Nan Uamh, before reaching the silver sands and Falls of Morar. There is only a passenger ferry service between Mallaig and Skye, although vehicles may be carried by previous arrangement on the steamer services (see details at end of book).

A.82			**Fort William**	47¾
A.830	2¼	2¼	*Lochy Bridge	45½
..	3½	1¼	*Banavie	44¼
..	4½	1	*Corpach	43¼
..	12¼	8	*Kinlocheil	35¼
..	18½	6¼	*Glenfinnan	29
..	28¼	9¾	*Lochailort	19¼
..	38¼	10¼	*Arisaig	9¼
..	45	6½	*Morar	2¾
..	47¾	2¾	**Mallaig**	

210. FORT WILLIAM to INVERNESS. A delightful main road following the line of the Great Glen, or *Glen More, threaded by the *Caledonian Canal, which joins a series of lochs to form a continuous waterway between the Atlantic Ocean and the North Sea. There are fine views of *Loch Lochy, *Loch Oich and *Loch Ness as the road keeps near to the waterside for most of the way, and passes the ruined Urquhart Castle before Lewiston. The alternative detour by Glen Urquhart and Strath Glass can be extended by excursions from Cannich along the beautiful Glen Affric and Glen Cannich, where there are some hydro-electric power scheme developments.

A.82			**Fort William**	65¼
..	2¼	2¼	Lochy Bridge (near side)	63¼
..	9½	7¼	**Spean Bridge**	56¼
..	21	11½	*Laggan Locks	44¼
..	24¾	3¾	**Invergarry**	41
..	27¼	2¼	*Oich Bridge	38¾
..	32	4¾	*Fort Augustus	33¼
..	38¼	6¼	**Invermoriston**	27¼
..	50¼	11¾	*Lewiston	15½
..	51	¾	†*Drumnadrochit	14¾
..	65¼	14¼	**Inverness**	
†			OR	
			via Cannich	
A.831	51		*Drumnadrochit	
..	52	1	Milton	
..	63½	11½	*Cannich	
..	70¼	7	*Struy Bridge	
..	75½	5	*Crask of Aigas	
..	78	2½	*Kilmorack	
A.9	79¼	1¼	Junc. A.831/A.9	
..	79¾	½	*Lovat Bridge	
..	89	9¼	*Clachnaharry	
..	91¼	2¼	**Inverness**	

211. FORT WILLIAM to INVERNESS via Errogie or Foyers.

There are several routes between Fort Augustus and Inverness, the main road by Invermoriston being shown in Iter. 210, but there are fine views from the more winding, hilly and less frequented roads on the east side of *Loch Ness, which are indicated below. Leaving Fort Augustus, there is a steep ascent (maximum gradient 1 in 9) to Glen Doe, afterwards gradually rising to reach the summit at 1,275 feet, followed by a long descent to Whitebridge. There is a choice of routes from here, the best road, by Errogie, having a steep descent to Loch Ness at Dores, although there is a narrow secondary road which branches off 3 miles from Torness and follows a more gradual descent. The alternative, but narrow and hilly, road from Whitebridge goes by way of the Falls of Foyers before reaching the shores of Loch Ness which is then followed to Dores. Thereafter it is an easy level road to Inverness.

			*Fort William ..	65½
		By Iter. 210 to:—		
A.862	32	32	*Fort Augustus	33½
..	41½	9½	*Whitebridge ..	24¼
..	45¼	4	Gorthleck ..	20¼
..	47½	2¼	*Errogie ..	18
..	51½	4	*Torness ..	14
..	57½	6	*Dores ..	8
..	65½	8	**Inverness**	

OR

via Foyers

			*Fort William	64¼
		By Iter. 210 to:—		
A.862	32	32	*Fort Augustus	32¼
..	41½	9½	*Whitebridge ..	23
B.852	42½	1	Junc. A.862/B.852	22
..	45¼	3	*Foyers ..	19
..	47½	2¼	*Inverfarigaig ..	16¾
A.862	56¼	8½	*Dores ..	8
..	64¼	8	**Inverness**	

212. FORT WILLIAM to NAIRN via Cawdor Castle.

From Fort Augustus this is a cross-country route utilizing secondary roads, with a steep ascent (maximum gradient 1 in 9) leading to Glen Doe, afterwards rising to the summit at 1,275 feet, followed by a long descent to Whitebridge, and then follows the south side of Strath Nairn. On reaching the main Aviemore-Inverness road a detour can be made to *Culloden through *Daviot and thence by road B.851 along the north side of Strath Nairn. The fastest route is by Inverness, Iter. 210 and 175.

			*Fort William ..	81¼
		By Iter. 210 to:—		
A.862	32	32	*Fort Augustus	49¼
..	41½	9½	*Whitebridge ..	40
..	45¼	4	Gorthleck ..	36
..	47½	2¼	*Errogie ..	33¾
B.851	49½	2	Junc. A.862/B.851	31½
..	55	5½	Aberarder ..	26¼
..	59½	4½	Farr ..	21¾
..	60½	1	*Dalvourn ..	21
A.9	63½	3½	Junc. B.851/A.9	17½
Uncl.	64½	½	Junc. A.9/Uncl.	17
..	64½	½	Rd. to Daviot Sta.	16½
B.9090	73½	9	Junc.	
			Uncl./B.9090	7½
..	75	1½	*Cawdor ..	6¼
..	81¼	6¼	**Nairn**	

213. FORT WILLIAM to DINGWALL.

Beyond Fort Augustus, follows the shore of *Loch Ness through the Great Glen, or *Glen More, threaded by the *Caledonian Canal, and passing the ruined Urquhart Castle before Lewiston, near Drumnadrochit. It then utilizes a cross-country link, with a 1 in 6 ascent from Milton, giving extensive views from the summit before descending wooded Glen Convinth. Agricultural on the latter part.

			*Fort William	74
		By Iter. 210 to:—		
..	32	32	*Fort Augustus	42
..	38½	6½	**Invermoriston** ..	35½
..	50½	11½	*Lewiston ..	23¾
A.831	51	½	*Drumnadrochit	23
A.833	52	1	Milton ..	22
..	59	7	Glackbea ..	15
A.9	62	3	Junc. A.833/A.9	12
..	64	2	*Lovat Bridge ..	10
..	65¼	1¼	*Beauly ..	8¾
..	67¼	2½	*Muir of Ord ..	6¼
..	71½	3¾	*Conon Bridge ..	2½
..	72½	1	Maryburgh ..	1½
..	74	1½	**Dingwall**	

214. FORT WILLIAM to KINLOCH HOURN via Loch Arkaig.

A touring route at first through the Great Glen, or *Glen More, and following the banks of the *Caledonian Canal to *Loch Lochy, and then by the " Dark Mile " to Loch Arkaig. Returning by Loch Lochy, the Falls of Mucomer are passed before joining the main road to Invergarry. Pretty in Glen Garry past Loch Garry to Tomdoun, whence the road is very rough. Grand mountain and loch scenery by *Loch Quoich, with the fine peak of Gairich rising to the south, and onwards to *Loch Hourn, but there is a steep descent (maximum gradient 1 in 6) for the last 2½ miles. There is no through road along either Loch Arkaig or Loch Hourn. The direct road to Invergarry is shown in Iter. 210.

A.82			*Fort William ..	66½
A.830	2¼	2¼	Lochy Bridge ..	64¼
B.8004	3½	1¼	*Banavie ..	63
B.8005	9½	6	Junc.	
			B.8004/B.8005	57
..	15	5½	*Loch Arkaig ..	51½
			Return to:—	
B.8004	20½	5½	Junc.	
			B.8005/B.8004	46
..	20½	¼	*Gairlochy ..	45¾
A.82	23½	2½	Junc. B.8004/A.82	43¼
..	36½	13	*Laggan Locks ..	30¼
A.87	40	3¾	**Invergarry** ..	26½
Uncl.	50½	10½	*Tomdoun	
			(Hotel) ..	16
..	60½	10	*Quoich Bridge ..	6
..	66½	6	*Kinloch Hourn	

215. FORT WILLIAM to ARDGOUR.

Fine mountain and loch scenery, with views of *Ben Nevis as the route circles round Loch Eil to reach the west shore of *Loch Linnhe. The road is level, but beyond Kinlocheil becomes narrow and winding. The long detour can be avoided by following the A.82 southwards from Fort William and utilizing the *Corran Ferry to Ardgour.

A.82			*Fort William ..	35½
A.830	2¼	2¼	Lochy Br. ..	33¼
..	3½	1¼	*Banavie ..	32
..	4½	1	*Corpach ..	31
..	12½	8	*Kinlocheil ..	23
A.861	13¾	1¼	Junc. A.830/A.861	21¾
..	24	10¼	*Camusnagaul ..	11½
..	35½	11½	*Ardgour (Hotel)	

216. ARDGOUR to KILCHOAN (for Ardnamurchan Point).

Fine mountain and loch scenery, although the road is narrow and winding, particularly beyond Salen, where the surface deteriorates and passing places are infrequent. At first along the edge of *Loch Linnhe, then from Strontian to Glenborrodale follows the wooded shore of *Loch Sunart, dominated to the north by Ben Resipol. After a short deviation inland, the ruins of Mingary Castle are passed before reaching Kilchoan. A road continues for 6 miles beyond Kilchoan to *Ardnamurchan Point, the most westerly extremity of the Scottish mainland. There is a passenger ferry from Mingary Pier, near Kilchoan, to Tobermory, Isle of Mull.

A.861			*Ardgour (Hotel)	44½
..	6½	6½	*Inversanda ..	38
..	14½	8	*Strontian ..	30
B.8007	24½	10	Junc.	
			A.861/B.8007	20
..	24½	¼	*Salen ..	19¾
..	32¼	7½	Glenborrodale	
			Castle ..	12¼
..	44½	12¼	*Kilchoan	

217. ARDGOUR to KINLOCHMOIDART.

Fine mountain and loch scenery, although the road is narrow and hilly, particularly on the last ten miles, where the surface is rough and passing places are infrequent. At first along the edge of *Loch Linnhe, then for 10 miles from Strontian follows the wooded shore of *Loch Sunart, dominated to the north by Ben Resipol. Touches the shores of *Loch Shiel and Loch Moidart on the latter part, while about half-way between Acharacle and Kinlochmoidart, a short by-road (B.8006) to the east leads to *Dalilea, on Loch Shiel, associated with Prince Charles Edward.

A.861			*Ardgour (Hotel)	34
..	6½	6½	*Inversanda ..	27½
..	14½	8	*Strontian ..	19½
B.850	24½	10	Junc. A.861/B.850	9½
..	26½	2	*Acharacle ..	7½
..	34	7½	*Kinlochmoidart	

218. ARDGOUR to LOCHALINE or DRIMNIN.

Fine mountain and loch scenery in the lonely *Morven district of Argyll, the road being narrow and hilly. Follows the shore of *Loch Linnhe to Inversanda, and by Glen Tarbert to the south shore of *Loch Sunart, thence a long climb over the hills. A narrow alternative road B.8043 from Inversanda continues by Loch Linnhe to *Camasnacroise, joining the road from Loch Sunart (A.884). Just before Lochaline, a branch road leads off along the Sound of Mull to Drimnin. The passenger steamer between Oban and Tobermory, Isle of Mull, calls at Lochaline and Drimnin.

A.861			*Ardgour (Hotel)	32½
..	6½	6½	*Inversanda	26
A.884	13	6½	Junc. A.861/A.884	19½
..	29½	16½	†*Larachbeg	3½
..	32½	3¼	*Lochaline	
		† OR		
A.884	29½		*Larachbeg	
B.849	31½	2	Junc. A.884/B.849	
..	42½	11¼	*Drimnin	

219. STROME FERRY to SHIELDAIG or APPLECROSS. Utilizes the ferry across Loch Carron (no Sunday service), then follows the shore for 3 miles, whence narrow and hilly roads are used. There is a 1 in 6 ascent from the main road, followed by a gradual descent, with views across Loch Kishorn. After Tornapress, the road surface deteriorates, but is fairly easy to Shieldaig. The alternative to Applecross climbs the well-known Pass of the Cattle, which is one of the most difficult roads in the country. It is narrow, without passing bays, and has several hairpin bends. On the 6 mile ascent the gradient steepens to a maximum of 1 in 4, with magnificent views from the summit at 2,054 feet. On the long descent to the sea at Applecross the road and gradients are similar but easier. This road is liable to be blocked by snow during the winter months.

A.890			*Strome Ferry (Sta.)	18
			Ferry to Strome North	
B.857	3½	3½	Junc. A.890/B.857	14½
..	7¾	4¼	*Kishorn	10¼
..	9½	1¾	†*Tornapress	8½
..	18	8½	*Shieldaig	
		† OR		
Uncl.	9½		*Tornapress	
..	15½	6	*Pass of the Cattle (summit)	
..	21	5½	*Applecross	

220. FORT WILLIAM to KYLE OF LOCHALSH (for Isle of Skye) or STROME FERRY. At first through open country to the wooded shores of *Loch Lochy and *Loch Oich to Invergarry, after which it is a winding and hilly Highland road, forming an alternative " Road to the Isles." Beautiful loch and mountain scenery by Loch Garry and Glen Garry then a long gradual ascent and descent to Loch Cluanie. There are important hydro-electric developments in this area. After Cluanie there is a long descent through the lonely Glen Shiel, a magnificent mountain defile. Fine views of the Kintail hills, including the Five Sisters, as the road follows the shore of *Loch Duich past Eilean Donan Castle, before crossing Loch Long by the fine modern bridge at Dornie. Hilly between Inverinate and Dornie as the road climbs above the loch, with an ascent and descent of 1 in 6. Beyond Balmacara, on the shore of Loch Alsh, there is another ascent of 1 in 10, after which the hills of Skye come into view. The alternative to Strome Ferry is hilly with ascents and descents up to 1 in 6, but affords more fine views of Loch Duich and the Five Sisters of Kintail from Auchtertyre Hill.

A.82			*Fort William	78½
..	2¼	2¼	Lochy Bridge (near side)	76¼
..	9½	7¼	*Spean Bridge	69
..	21	11½	*Laggan Lochs	57¼
A.87	24¾	3¾	*Invergarry	53¼
..	46¾	22	*Cluanie	31¾
..	58½	11½	*Shiel Bridge	29
..	61	2½	*Croe Bridge	17½
..	64¼	3¼	*Inverinate	14¼
..	68	3¾	*Dornie	10½
..	68¾	¾	*Ardelve	9¾
..	71	2¼	†*Auchtertyre	7½
..	72½	1½	*Balmacara	6
..	78½	6	*Kyle of Lochalsh	
		† OR		
A.890	71		*Auchtertyre	
..	76½	5½	*Achmore	
..	77¾	1¼	*Strome Ferry (Sta.)	

221. KYLE OF LOCHALSH to INVERNESS via Strome Ferry. Hilly to Strome, with a 1 in 10 descent approaching Balmacara on Loch Alsh, and an ascent and descent of 1 in 6 before Strome Ferry, with fine views of Loch Duich and the Five Sisters of Kintail from Auchtertyre Hill. There is a hairpin bend approaching the ferry which is utilized to cross Loch Carron. In addition to the ferry, there is an alternative service by rail between Kyle or Strome and Strathcarron stations (see ferry details), but neither operates on Sundays. Mountain and loch scenery and across moorlands to Garve, becoming agricultural on the latter part, following Beauly Firth for the last few miles. The *Falls of Rogie are passed near Achilty Inn. A quicker route to Inverness is via Invermoriston (Iter. 207).

A.87			*Kyle of Lochalsh	84½
..	6	6	*Balmacara	78¾
A.890	7½	1½	*Auchtertyre	77¼
..	13	5½	*Achmore	71¾
..	14¼	1¼	*Strome Ferry (Sta.)	
			Ferry to *Strome (North)	70¼
..	18½	4¼	*Lochcarron	66¼
..	21¼	2¾	Rd. to *Strathcarron (Sta.)	63¼
..	25¼	4	Balnacra	59¼
..	27	1¾	*Achnashellach	57¼
A.832	39¼	12¼	Junc. A.890/A.832	45
..	40	¾	*Achnasheen	44¼
..	46½	6½	Achanalt	38¼
..	56½	10	*Garves	28¼
..	62	5½	*" Achilty " Inn	22¾
..	62½	¾	*Contin	22
..	65¼	2¾	*Marybank	19¼
A.9	69½	4¼	*Muir of Ord	15¼
..	72	2½	*Beauly	12¼
..	73½	1½	*Lovat Bridge	11¼
..	82½	9¼	*Clachnaharry	2¼
..	84¾	2¼	*Inverness	

222. A tour from KYLE OF LOCHALSH to ULLAPOOL via Loch Maree and Gairloch. A picturesque tourist route through beautiful mountain, loch and coast scenery, with magnificent views, but utilizing some hilly and narrow roads provided with passing places. Hilly to Strome, with a 1 in 10 descent approaching Balmacara on Loch Alsh, and descent of 1 in 8 before Strome Ferry, with fine views of Loch Duich and the Five Sisters of Kintail from Auchtertyre Hill. 2 miles from Kyle, a secondary road (with gradients up to 1 in 5) branches off through Drumbuie and Duirinish to reach the coast at the picturesquely situated village of *Plockton. The road from Duirinish by Duncraig Castle to Strome is hilly, and becomes narrow and rough on the latter part, which is unsuitable for motors. There is a hairpin bend approaching the ferry which is utilized to cross Loch Carron. In addition to the ferry, there is an alternative service by rail between Kyle or Strome and Strathcarron stations (see ferry details), but neither operates on Sundays. After the long descent through Glen Docherty (maximum gradient 1 in 9) to Kinlochewe, where the Ben Eighe Nature Reserve is situated, an attractive road follows the winding shore of Loch Maree, with views of Slioch rising from the opposite bank. Later descends through wooded Kerrysdale to Gairloch on the coast, after which a climb inland leads to Poolewe on Loch Ewe. *Aultbea lies just off the road between Poolewe and Laide. The road onwards to Braemore Lodge is narrower and has gradients of 1 in 8, in addition to the 1 in 7 descent of Gruinard Hill (care required), but there are some magnificent coast and mountain views at Gruinard Bay and along Little Loch Broom, where the Ardessie Falls are passed before Dundonnell. Views of An Teallach on the long ascent over the so-called Destitution Road to the Falls of Measach near Braemore Lodge, and finally after descending through Strath More, follows the shores of Loch Broom to Ullapool.

A.87			*Kyle of Lochalsh	125¼
..	6	6	*Balmacara	119¼
A.890	7½	1½	*Auchtertyre	117¼
..	13	5½	*Achmore	112¼
..	14¼	1¼	*Strome Ferry (Sta.)	
			Ferry to *Strome (North)	111
..	18½	4¼	*Lochcarron	106¾
..	21¼	2¾	Rd. to *Strathcarron (Sta.)	104
..	25¼	4	Balnacra	100
..	27	1¾	*Achnashellach	98¼
A.832	39¼	12¼	Junc. A.890/A.832	85¼
..	49	9¾	*Kinlochewe	76¼
..	58¾	9¾	*Loch Maree (Hotel)	66¼
..	68¼	9¼	*Gairloch	56¾
..	74¼	6	*Poolewe	50¾
..	83½	9	Laide	41¼
..	87½	4¼	*Gruinard Bay	37½
..	99¾	11¾	*Dundonnell	25¾
A.835	113	13¼	*Braemore Lodge	12¼
..	125¼	12¼	*Ullapool	

223. SHIELDAIG to TORRIDON. A narrow road to Tornapress, with views across Loch Kishorn, before the long ascent and descent (maximum gradient 1 in 6) to Loch Carron. A pleasant, easy road through Glen Carron, later descending Glen Docherty to Kinlochewe, where the Ben Eighe Nature Reserve is situated. Afterwards follows a by-road through Glen Torridon, with splendid views of the Torridon peaks of Ben Eighe and Liathach. This is the shortest way for motors between Shieldaig and Torridon until the construction of the seven-mile road on the south side of Loch Torridon is completed in 1962. The hilly track by the Coulin Pass from Achnashellach to the Torridon road at Loch Clair is a narrow, private road only available by permission. Beyond Torridon the road continues for 8 miles, partly alongside the hilly shores of Inner Loch Torridon, but later there is a severe ascent and descent (maximum gradient 1 in 3½) over to Diabaig, on the Outer Loch.

B.857			*Shieldaig	..	56¼
..	8½	8½	*Tornapress	..	48
..	10¼	1¾	*Kishorn	..	46¼
A.890	14¼	4	Junc. B.857/A.890		42
..	15¼	¾	*Lochcarron	..	41¼
..	18	2¾	Rd. to *Strath-		
			carron (Sta.)	..	38¼
..	22	4	Balnacra	..	34¼
..	23¾	1¾	*Achnashellach		32¾
A.832	36½	12¾	Junc. A.890/A.832		20
B.858	45¾	9¼	*Kinlochewe	..	10¾
..	56¼	10¼	*Torridon		

224. ULLAPOOL to LAIRG. Hilly and narrow to Ledmore, with frequent passing bays, thereafter a good Highland road. Fine views of the mountains of Wester Ross and the Assynt peaks of Sutherland on the first part, including Ben More Coigach, Cul Mor and Cul Beag. The peaks of Stack Polly and Canisp are prominent, while the sharp eastern cone of Suilven comes into view near Elphin. Crosses open moorland country from Ledmore, following Strath Oykell by way of Rosehall.

A.835			*Ullapool	..	45½
..	3¼	3¼	*Ardmair Bay	..	42¼
..	7¾	4½	*Strathkanaird	..	37¾
..	16	8¼	*Elphin	..	29½
A.837	18¼	2¼	Ledmore Fork	..	27¼
..	19¾	1½	*Altnacealgach		
			(Hotel)	..	25¾
..	30¼	10½	*Oykell Bridge	..	15¼
A.839	37	6¾	*Rosehall (W.M.)		8½
A.836	45¼	8¼	Junc. A.839/A.836		¼
..	45½	¼	*Lairg		

225. A tour from ULLAPOOL to TONGUE via Kylesku Ferry. A tour through the Northern Highlands, touching the coast at several places. Hilly and narrow roads (max. grad. 1 in 7) throughout with frequent passing places. There are certain restrictions on the use of the ferry at Kylesku (see ferry details), which can be avoided by proceeding via Lairg, Iter. 224 and 229 or 230. Fine views of the mountains of Wester Ross and Sutherland on the first part, including Ben More Coigach, Cul Mor and Cul Beag. The peaks of Stack Polly and Canisp are prominent, while Suilven comes into view near Elphin. Passes the ruins of Ardvreck Castle on the shore of *Loch Assynt beyond Inchnadamph (with views of Ben More Assynt and Quinag), where a detour can be made to *Lochinver on the coast, 11 miles away. A hilly, narrow and winding road is followed over the hills from Skaig Bridge

to the ferry at Kylesku, afterwards continuing through a wild landscape of bare gneiss dotted with innumerable lochans. Touches the coast in several places to Rhiconich, with fine views of the peaks of the Reay Forest to the south-west, and later passing close to the Cape Wrath Hotel, the nearest motoring point to Cape Wrath. From Durness, the indented north coastline is first followed past Smoo Cave, after which *Rispond lies just off the road before encircling Loch Eriboll. After passing the northern end of Loch Hope, there are views of Ben Hope and Ben Loyal as the road rounds the head of the Kyle of Tongue. A by-road along the western shore of the Kyle of Tongue leads to *Melness and *Port Vasco.

A.835			*Ullapool	..	107¾
..	3¼	3¼	*Ardmair Bay	..	104½
..	7¾	4½	*Strathkanaird	..	100
..	16	8¼	*Elphin	..	91¾
A.837	18¼	2¼	Ledmore Fork	..	89½
..	24¼	6	*Inchnadamph	..	83½
A.894	26¼	2¼	Skaig Bridge	..	81¼
..	32¼	6	*Unapool	..	75¼
..	34	1½	*Kylesku	..	73¾
			Ferry to		
..	34¾	¾	*Kylestrome	..	73
..	42¼	7¼	*Eddrachillis		
			Church	..	65¼
..	45	2½	*Scourie	..	62¾
A.838	51¾	6¾	*Laxford Bridge		56
..	56¾	5	*Rhiconich	..	51
..	69¼	12½	Rd. to *Cape		
			Wrath Hotel	..	38¾
..	71	1¾	*Durness	..	36¾
..	72¾	1¾	*Smoo Cave	..	35
..	87¼	14½	*Eriboll	..	20½
..	90¼	3	*Heilim	..	17½
..	92	1¾	*Hope Lodge	..	15¾
..	98¾	6¾	Achuvoldrach		9
..	107¾	9	*Tongue		

226. ULLAPOOL to LOCHINVER or ACHILTIBUIE. Wild loch and mountain scenery, with views of Ben More Coigach and Cul Beag before turning off by a narrow road along the lonely shores of *Loch Lurgain, close by the splintered peak of Stack Polly. Beyond Baddagyle, very narrow, winding and hilly, with gradients up to 1 in 7, but giving splendid views of Enard Bay and the fantastic peaks of Stack Polly and Suilven. The main road from Ullapool to Lochinver is by Inchnadamph, Iter. 225 and 228. The alternative from Baddagyle reaches the coast near Achiltibuie, where there are fine views of the Summer Isles.

A.835			*Ullapool	..	30
..	3¼	3¼	*Ardmair Bay	..	26¾
..	7¾	4½	*Strathkanaird	..	22¼
Uncl.	10	2¼	Junc. A.835/Uncl.		20
..	18¼	8¼	†*Baddagyle		
			(Rd. junc.)	..	11¾
..	27	8¾	*Inverkirkaig	..	3
..	28¾	1¾	Strathan	..	1¼
..	30	1¼	*Lochinver		
		†	OR		
Uncl.	18¼		*Baddagyle (Rd. junc.)		
..	24¾	6½	*Achiltibuie		

227. LOCHINVER to KYLESKU FERRY or INCHNADAMPH via Drumbeg. A hilly and winding by-road

following the coastline through wild desolate country, with fine views of the Assynt mountains of Sutherland, especially of Suilven and the Quinag. Magnificent mountain and loch scenery on the latter part, with a maximum descent and ascent of 1 in 5 between Drumbeg and A.894. The alternative to Inchnadamph is hilly and winding by Skaig Bridge, where the shores of *Loch Assynt are followed past the ruins of Ardvreck Castle, with views of Ben More Assynt. The easiest way from Lochinver to Kylesku and Inchnadamph is by the direct road (A.837) to Skaig Bridge.

A.837			*Lochinver	..	25
B.869	¾	¾	Junc. A.837/B.869		24¼
..	6½	5¾	*Stoer		18½
..	8½	2	Clashnessie		16½
..	14	5½	*Drumbeg		11
..	15¼	1¼	Nedd		9¾
A.894	22½	7¼	†Junc. B.869/A.894		2½
..	23½	¾	*Unapool		1¼
..	25	1½	*Kylesku Ferry		
		†	OR		
A.894	22½		Junc. B.869/A.894		
..	28	5½	Skaig Bridge		
..	30¼	2¼	*Inchnadamph		

228. BONAR BRIDGE to LOCHINVER. Open moorland country, following Strath Oykell to Altnacealgach, where there are extensive views of the mountains of Wester Ross and the Assynt peaks, including Cul Beag, Cul Mor, Suilven and Canisp. Narrow beyond Inchnadamph, following the shore of *Loch Assynt, and passing the ruins of Ardvreck Castle, with views of Quinag, and afterwards following the River Inver to the coast at Lochinver.

A.836			*Bonar Bridge	..	49¾
..	3¼	3¼	*Invershin (Sta.)		46¼
A.837	4	¾	Junc. A.836/A.837		45¾
..	4¾	¾	*Inveran Bridge		45
..	11¾	7	*Rosehall (W.M.)		38
..	18¼	6¾	*Oykell Bridge	..	31¼
..	29	10½	*"Altnacealgach"		
			Hotel	..	20¾
..	30¼	1½	Ledmore Fork	..	19¼
..	36¼	6	*Inchnadamph	..	13¼
..	38¾	2¼	Skaig Bridge	..	11
..	49¾	11	*Lochinver		

229. BONAR BRIDGE to DURNESS or KINLOCHBERVIE. Follows the main road to Lairg, an alternative by the River Shin and the Shin Falls being given in Iter. 232. Beyond Lairg, crosses open moorland country, passing Lochs Shin, Merkland, More and Stack. Ben Stack and the Reay Forest mountains are well seen before reaching Laxford Bridge, beyond which the road is hilly. Crosses open moorland after Rhiconich, later passing close to the Cape Wrath Hotel, the nearest motoring point to Cape Wrath. The alternative traverses a narrow road (with a descent of 1 in 8) along the shore of Loch Inchard to Kinlochbervie. This road continues for another 4 miles to Sheigra, near the open sea, from which the remote, but beautiful Sandwood Bay can be reached on foot.

A.836			*Bonar Bridge	..	66¾
..	3¼	3¼	*Invershin (Sta.)		63¼
..	10¾	7½	*Lairg	..	56

A.838	12¼	2	Junc. A.836/A.838	54
..	26¼	13¾	*Overscaig	40¼
..	30¼	4¼	*Merkland Lodge	36
..	41	10¼	*Achfary	25¼
..	47¼	6¼	*Laxford Bridge	19¼
..	52¼	5	†*Rhiconich	14¼
..	65	12¼	Rd. to *Cape Wrath Hotel ..	1½
..	66¼	1¼	*Durness	
†			OR	
B.801	52¼		*Rhiconich	
..	56¼	4¼	*Kinlochbervie	

230. BONAR BRIDGE to TONGUE.
Follows the main road to Lairg, an alternative by the River Shin and Shin Falls being given in Iter. 232. Beyond Lairg, crosses open moorland country by the Pass of Crask and Strath Bagastie, with distant views of the Sutherland mountains to the west, to reach Altnaharra. Later follows the shore of Loch Loyal, with views of Ben Loyal. From Altnaharra a narrow, rough and hilly by-road leads along the shore of Loch Hope to Hope Lodge on A.838.

A.836			*Bonar Bridge ..	48
..	3¼	3¼	*Invershin (Sta.)	44¼
..	10¼	7¼	*Lairg	37¼
..	23¼	13	*Crask	24¼
..	31½	7¼	*Altnaharra	16¼
..	48	16½	*Tongue	

231. BONAR BRIDGE to HELMSDALE via Dornoch. A fine coast run along the Dornoch Firth passing *Skibo Castle between Spinningdale and Clashmore, afterwards diverging from the main road to visit Dornoch. The coast is regained at Golspie, where shortly afterwards *Dunrobin Castle is passed. The direct road is given in Iter. 200.

A.9			*Bonar Bridge ..	40¼
..	2½	2½	*Creich	37¾
..	5	2½	*Spinningdale ..	35¼
..	9¼	4¼	*Clashmore ..	30¼
B.9167	11	1½	Evelix	29¼
B.9168	13	2	*Dornoch ..	27¼
A.9	15¼	2¼	*Junc. B.9168/A.9	25
..	19½	4¼	*Mound Sta. ..	20¼
..	23¾	4¼	*Golspie	16¼
..	28¼	5	*Brora	11¼
..	35¼	7	*Loth	4¼
..	38¼	2½	*Portgower	2
..	40¼	2	*Helmsdale	

232. BONAR BRIDGE to THURSO via Strath Naver. A touring route, at first following the Rover Shin past the Shin Falls to Lairg, the main road being given in Iter. 230. Afterwards crosses open moorland country by the Pass of Crask and Strath Bagastie, with distant views of the Sutherland mountains to the west, to reach Altnaharra, then follows a narrow, undulating road along the shores of Loch Naver and by Strath Naver to the coast at Bettyhill. Fine coast scenery on the latter part, but the road is narrow, winding and hilly to Melvich. A number of crofting villages, including *Farr *Armadale and *Portskerra lie just off the road. See Iter. 200 and 236 for the recommended route, via Helmsdale.

A.836			*Bonar Bridge	86½
..	3¼	3¼	*Invershin (Sta.)	83¼
A.837	4	¾	Junc. A.836/A.837	82½
B.864	4¼	¼	*Inveran Bridge	81¼
..	8¼	4	Gruids Mill	77¼
A.839	9¼	1	Junc. B.864/A.839	76½
A.836	10½	¾	Junc. A.839/A.836	76
..	10¾	¼	*Lairg	75¾
..	23¾	13	*Crask	62¾
..	31½	7¾	*Altnaharra	55
B.873	32	½	Junc. A.836/B.873	54½
B.871	43½	11½	*Syre Church ..	43
..	46	2½	*Strath Naver (P.O.)	40½
A.836	52¼	6¼	Junc. B.871/A.836	33¾
..	55¾	3	*Bettyhill	30¾
..	66	10¼	*Strathy	20½
..	68¼	2¼	*Melvich	17¼
..	75¼	7	*Reay	10¼
..	77½	1¼	Rd. to *Dounreay	9
..	81	3½	*Bridge of Forss	5½
..	86½	5½	*Thurso	

233. LAIRG to HELMSDALE. Moorland country at first, the coast being reached at Golspie, where shortly afterwards *Dunrobin Castle is passed.

A.839			*Lairg	35¼
..	10¼	10¼	*Rogart (W.M.)	24¾
A.9	14¼	4	*Mound Sta. ..	20¼
..	18¾	4¼	*Golspie	16½
..	23¾	5	*Brora	11½
..	30¾	7	*Loth	4½
..	33¼	2½	*Portgower	2
..	35¼	2	*Helmsdale	

234. HELMSDALE to TONGUE or THURSO via Strath Halladale. A desolate, narrow moorland road by Strath Ullie and Strath Halladale to the coast at Melvich. Fine coast views on the latter part, but the road is hilly and winding, with a maximum gradient of 1 in 7 at Borgie Bridge. *Portskerra, *Armadale and *Farr lie just off the road between Strathy and Bettyhill. This route to Thurso avoids the hills of the main coast road by Berriedale (Iter. 236), but is longer and narrower.

A.897			*Helmsdale ..	66¼
..	9	9	*Kildonan Church	57¼
..	17¼	8¼	*Kinbrace	49
..	24¼	7¼	*Forsinard (Sta.)	41¼
..	32¼	8¼	*Dalhalvaig (P.O.)	33¼
A.836	38	5¼	†Junc. A.897/A.836 ..	28¼
..	40	2	*Melvich	26¼
..	42¼	2¼	*Strathy	23½
..	53	10¼	*Bettyhill	13¼
..	59	6	*Borgie Bridge ..	7¼
..	63¼	4¼	Coldbackie	3
..	66¼	3	*Tongue	
†			OR	
A.836	38		Junc. A.897/A.836	
..	43	5	*Reay	
..	44¾	1¾	Rd. to *Dounreay	
..	48¼	3½	*Bridge of Forss	
..	53¾	5½	*Thurso	

235. HELMSDALE to TONGUE via Strath Naver. A narrow, undulating cross-country route through loch and moorland scenery to Strath Naver. Hilly on the latter part, with a maximum gradient of 1 in 7 at Borgie Bridge.

A.897			*Helmsdale ..	52¼
..	9	9	*Kildonan Church	43¼
B.871	17¼	8¼	*Kinbrace	35¼
..	21¼	4¼	Baddanloch ..	30¾
..	32¾	11	*Syre Church ..	19¼
..	35¼	2½	*Strath Naver (P.O.) ..	17¼
A.836	42	6¾	Junc. B.871/A.836	10¼
..	45¼	3¼	*Borgie Bridge ..	7¼
..	49¼	4¼	Coldbackie ..	3
..	52¼	3	*Tongue	

236. HELMSDALE to THURSO and SCRABSTER (for Orkney). A pleasant, hilly and winding coast road to Thurso, with a steep descent at Berriedale (maximum gradient 1 in 9). Open moorland on the latter part, reaching the coast again at Thurso. For alternative see Iter. 234.

A.9			*Helmsdale	45¼
..	10	10	*Berriedale ..	35¼
..	15¼	5¼	*Dunbeath ..	30
A.895	20	4¼	*Latheron ..	25¼
..	26¼	6¼	Achavanich ..	19¼
..	32¾	6¼	Mybster ..	12¼
..	37	4¼	*Georgemas Junction	8¼
A.882	37½	½	Junc. A.895/A.882	8
..	38¼	¾	*Halkirk Roadside P.O. ..	7¼
A.836	43¼	5¼	*Thurso	2
..	44¼	¼	Junc. A.836/A.882	1¼
..	45¼	1¼	*Scrabster	

237. WICK to THURSO. An easy road through flat country.

A.882			*Wick ..	20¼
..	8¼	8¼	*Watten ..	12¼
..	15½	7¼	*Halkirk Roadside P.O. ..	5¼
..	20¼	5¼	*Thurso	

238. WICK to THURSO via CASTLETOWN. Through flat, open country. An alternative to the main road given in Iter. 237 with little to choose.

A.9			*Wick ..	20¼
B.876	3¼	3¼	*Reiss ..	17¼
..	7	3¼	Kirk ..	13¼
..	11¼	4¼	Bower (P.O.) ..	9¼
A.836	15¼	4	Junc. B.876/A.836	5¼
..	15¾	¼	*Castletown ..	5
..	20¼	5	*Thurso	

239. WICK to THURSO via Halkirk. A secondary route through flat country, and going parallel to the main road given in Iter. 237, but includes a diversion to Halkirk.

A.9			*Wick ..	23¼
B.874	1¼	1¼	Junc. A.9/B.874	22¼
..	11¾	10½	Gillock ..	12
..	15¼	4	*Halkirk Roadside P.O. ..	8
..	16¼	½	Hoy (Sta.) ..	7¼
..	17¼	1¼	*Halkirk ..	6¼
..	23¼	6¼	*Thurso	

240. TONGUE to JOHN O' GROATS.

An undulating coast road, with fine seascapes in places, especially near Dunnet, where a short detour (B.855) can be made to the most northerly point of the mainland at Dunnet Head, a bold promontory affording fine views of the Orkneys. *Farr and *Armadale lie just off the road between Bettyhill and Strathy.

A.836			*Tongue	..	64		38½	3½	*Bridge of Forss	25½
..	3	3	Coldbackie		61		44	5½	*Thurso	..	20
..	7¼	4¼	*Borgie Bridge	..	56¾		49	5	*Castletown	..	15
..	13¼	6	*Bettyhill		50¾		52½	3½	*Dunnet	..	11½
..	23¾	10½	*Strathy		40½		56¾	4¼	*Mey	..	7¼
..	26¼	2½	*Melvich		37¾		58	1¼	*East Mey	..	6
..	33¼	7	*Reay		30¾		62	4	*Huna		2
..	35	1¾	Rd. to *Dounreay	29	A.9	63½	1½	Junc. A.836/A.9	½
							64	½	*John o' Groats	

THE ISLANDS OF SCOTLAND

The itineraries tabulated below indicate the extent and nature of the main roads on the more important islands; the road mileage on the other islands is insufficient to warrant taking a vehicle for a short period.

Road conditions are extremely variable, and, in general, main roads on the islands are narrow with fair surface, although they are often winding and hilly. Side roads are usually inferior. Conditions vary from time to time and members are invited to apply to any A.A. Office for the latest information.

Particulars of the ferry and shipping services are given in the two separate articles entitled: 'Ferries in Scotland' and 'Shipping Services to the Islands,' which will be found at the end of the book.

Except on the smaller islands, bus services are usually provided to connect with the steamer sailings and cars are normally available for hire. Regular air services are also operated to many of the islands and particulars will be supplied by any office of British European Airways or by most travel agencies.

BUTE

The island is only 15 miles long and 5 miles broad, so that the road mileage is limited, but in its small compass the island offers a variety of attractive scenery, including moorland and lochs, while there are many delightful coastal views and sandy bays. The route given below utilizes the ferry from the mainland across the *Kyles of Bute, but alternative services are available between Rothesay and other Clyde ports.

241. COLINTRAIVE to ROTHESAY and KILCHATTAN BAY.

The road follows the east coast of the island with views of the Kyles of Bute, the Firth of Clyde and the twin Cumbraes. A number of excursions from the route can be made to places on the west coast, including Kilmichael, Ettrick Bay, St. Ninians Bay, Scalpsie Bay and St. Blane's Chapel.

			*Colintraive Ferry to	
B.8000			*Rhubodach	..	17½
A.844	5¼	5¼	Junc. B.8000/A.844	11¼
..	6¼	1	*Port Bannatyne	10¼
..	8¼	2	*Rothesay	..	8¼
..	9¼	1	*Craigmore	..	7¼
..	11½	1¼	*Ascog	..	6
B.881	16	4½	Kingarth	1½
..	17½	1½	*Kilchattan Bay	

ARRAN

This delightful island has a wide variety of scenery, including rugged mountains, wild glens, rolling hills and farmlands. The coastline offers attractive views of the Firth of Clyde to the east and Kilbrennan Sound to the west. In addition to the circular tour described below, there is a link from Brodick to the west coast by way of the String Road, which later divides, one branch going past the Standing Stones of Tormore to Machrie, and the other to Blackwaterfoot. The only other motoring road is that leading south-west from Lamlash through the Monamore Glen and Glen Scorrodale to the coast road at Bennecarrigan Church, near Lagg. Passenger steamship services are available on weekdays from certain Clyde ports to Brodick, Whiting Bay and Lochranza; vehicles are conveyed between Brodick and Fairlie and also to Ardrossan during the season.

242. A TOUR OF THE ISLE OF ARRAN.

The winding coast road passes through a variety of scenery, with extensive views at first north-east across the Clyde to the islands of Bute and the Cumbraes, and then north to the Cowal hills. Later, on the west side, the views extend to the Kintyre peninsula. Between Lagg and Dippin, on the south side, a short detour can be made to the ruined *Kildonan Castle. There are fine views of Holy Island and the granite peak of Goat Fell on the latter part.

A.841			*Brodick	..	55½
..	6½	6½	*Corrie	..	49
..	7½	1½	*Sannox	..	47½
..	14½	6¾	*Lochranza	..	40½
..	16½	2	*Catacol	..	38½
..	21	4½	*Pirnmill	..	34½
..	23½	2½	Imachar	..	31½
..	26	2½	Dougrie Lodge	29½
..	27½	1½	*Machrie	..	27½
..	32	4½	*Blackwaterfoot	23½
..	36½	4½	Corriecravie	19
..	37	¾	Sliddery	..	18½
..	38	1	Bennecarrigan Ch.	17½
..	39	1	*Lagg (Kilmory P.O.)	..	16¼
..	45	6	Dippin (*Kildonan P.O.)	..	10¼
..	47½	2½	*Whiting Bay	..	7½
..	51½	4	*Lamlash	..	3½
..	55½	3½	*Brodick	

ISLAY

There is no road right round the island, but there are a number of roads linking the main villages, which are all situated on the coast. Although not very hilly, some of these roads afford extensive views and also give access to the many fine sandy beaches of the island. The steamer service operates on alternate week-days from Port Ellen on the south and Port Askaig on the east, calling at West Loch Tarbert on the mainland. Connections are provided to the islands of Gigha, Jura and Colonsay. A passenger ferry also operates from Port Askaig across the Sound of Islay to Feolin Ferry in Jura. Air services are operated from Glasgow to Glenegedale Airport.

243. PORT ELLEN to PORT ASKAIG via Bowmore.

This route follows a straight, level road to Bowmore, known as the "Low Road," the shortest way to Bridgend and Port Askaig being described in Iter. 246. Not far from Port Ellen, a side road leads to the extensive Machrie Sands, another approach being indicated in Iter. 244. Wooded around Bridgend, otherwise mainly moorland country is traversed. Near Port Askaig, a short detour, affording splendid views of Jura and Mull, can be made northwards along a narrow, hilly road beside the Sound of Islay to Bonahaven Bay.

A.846			*Port Ellen	..	21½
..	3¼	3¼	Rd. to *Machrie	18¼
..	5	1¾	*Glenegedale Airport	16¼
..	10½	5½	*Bowmore	..	11
..	13½	3	*Bridgend	..	8
..	18¼	4½	Ballygrant	3¼
..	21¼	3¼	*Port Askaig	

244. PORT ELLEN to MULL OF OA. This short route provides some extensive views beyond Cragabus, but becomes narrow and winding as it crosses the high moorlands. There are some fine sands and an American memorial at Kilnaughton Bay, about 1¼ miles from Port Ellen. Here a side road leads off to the extensive Machrie Sands on the west coast. The magnificent cliff scenery at the Mull of Oa well repays the twenty-minute walk to reach the American soldiers' monument erected at this point.

A.846			*Port Ellen	..	7
Uncl.	¼	¼	Junc. A.846/Uncl.		6¾
..	1½	1¼	Rd. to *Machrie		5½
..	3	1½	Cragabus	..	4
..	4¼	1¼	Oa Church	..	2¾
..	7	2¾	Killeyan		
			(for *Mull of Oa)		

245. PORT ELLEN to CLAGGAIN BAY. Traverses a variety of scenery, with fine stretches of rocky coast, later passing through the Kildalton estate, where the road becomes narrow. Fine views of Kintyre to the east, and of Jura to the north, and also of Beinn Bheigeir (1,609 feet), the highest point of the island.

A.846			*Port Ellen	..	9¼
..	1½	1½	Laphroaig	..	7¾
..	2¾	1¼	*Lagavulin	..	6½
Uncl.	3½	¾	Ardbeg	..	5¾
..	5	1½	*Kildalton (Castle Lodge)	..	4¼
..	9¼	4¼	*Claggain Bay		

246. PORT ELLEN to SANAIGMORE or KILCHOMAN (for Machir Bay). This direct road from Port Ellen to Bridgend is known as the "High Road," the alternative by Bowmore being shown in Iter. 243. About 7 miles from Port Ellen, the narrow "Glen Road" strikes north-east and forms the most direct way between Port Ellen and Port Askaig, although the best way is by Bridgend. After following the shore of Loch Indaal beyond Bridgend, the road turns inland across agricultural and moorland country and shortly divides, one branch leading to the rocky coast at Sanaigmore, and the other leading to Kilchoman and the sandy Machir Bay. An alternative loop road (B.8017) to Sanaigmore turns off 2¼ miles from Bridgend and crosses Gruinart Flats, where an excursion can be made along Loch Gruinart to Loch Ardnave. Beyond Sanaigmore there is a narrow road linking it with Kilchoman by way of Saligo Bay.

A.846			*Port Ellen	..	22
B.8016	1½	1½	Junc. A.846/B.8016		20½
A.846	10½	9¼	Junc. B.8016/A.846		11½
A.847	11¼	¾	*Bridgend	..	10¼
B.8018	15½	4¼	†Junc. A.847/B.8018		6½
..	22	6½	*Sanaigmore		
			OR		
D.0018		15½	Junc. A.847/B.8018		
Uncl.	17½	2	Junc. B.8018/Uncl.		
..	20¼	2¾	*Kilchoman (Coastguard Sta.)		

247. PORT ASKAIG to PORTNAHAVEN. Moorland country, wooded around Bridgend, after which the shore of Loch Indaal is followed. At Port Charlotte there is a narrow side road which crosses the Rhinns of Islay to the rocky coast at Kilchiaran Bay, whence a rough, narrow road ascends over moorlands to Portnahaven.

A.846			*Port Askaig	..	23¼
..	3¼	3¼	Ballygrant	..	20
A.847	8	4¼	*Bridgend	..	15¼
..	14	6	*Bruichladdich	..	9¼
..	16	2	*Port Charlotte		7¼
..	23¼	7¼	*Portnahaven		

MULL

The island is well known for its picturesque scenery, but there are few roads apart from those detailed in the following itineraries. With the exception of the Tobermory-Salen road, all are narrow and winding and follow the coast for the greater part, affording fine mountain and loch views. The main access to the island is by the week-day steamer which operates from Oban to Salen and Tobermory. There are other passenger boat connections with the mainland, as well as to several other islands, including historic Iona, the basalt rock island of Staffa, and the distant Outer Hebrides.

248. A TOUR OF THE ISLAND OF MULL (Northern). This tour covers the northern half of the island, following narrow roads for the greater part. Crosses moorlands at first and passes the Mishnish Lochs, then descends by hairpin bends to Dervaig, beyond which woodland country is traversed to Calgary, where there is an excellent sandy bay. There are more hairpin bends on the descent before reaching Kilninian, and the Laggan Falls are passed some distance before the short side road leading to the passenger ferry to the island of Ulva. The road then winds high above the rocks along Loch na Keal, with views of Ben More, the highest mountain on Mull. From Gruline, a narrow neck of land is crossed to Salen, where the main road along the Sound of Mull is followed.

A.848			*Tobermory	..	43¾
..	7¼	7¼	*Dervaig	..	36
B.8073	12¼	4½	*Calgary	..	31¼
..	18¾	6½	*Kilninian	..	25
..	24¼	5½	*Ulva Ferry	..	19¼
A.849	31¼	6¾	Gruline Church	..	12½
A.848	33¾	2½	*Salen	..	10
..	43¾	10	*Tobermory		

249. A TOUR OF THE ISLE OF MULL (Southern). This tour covers the southern part of the island, at first following the most direct road to the *Iona passenger ferry at Fionphort, beyond Bunessan. Between Tobermory and Salen there are delightful views of the Sound of Mull and the mainland hills of Morven. From Salen to Gruline is the narrowest part of Mull, and is a pretty run through woodland and then moorland country. The road winds along the shores of Loch na Keal, with many lovely views of the western isles, Ulva, Gometra and Staffa being prominent. There are fine panoramic views as the road follows the shore to the head of Loch Scridain, with the peak of Ben More to the north. The tour can be shortened by following the alternative return from this point, and omitting the excursion to Iona, which follows the southern shore of Loch Scridain to Fionphort and returns by the same road. At Pennyghael, a side road leads to *Carsaig Bay on the south coast. From Loch Scridain, a long gradual ascent and descent through the wild Glen More leads past Loch Spelve and Loch Don, with extensive views of the Appin hills and the Isle of Lismore. Near Craignure, the Morven hills lie to the north of Loch Linnhe, beyond the distant head of which can be glimpsed Ben Nevis, and the road then keeps close by the Sound of Mull to Salen and Tobermory. To permit more time in Iona, the outward route should be used for the return journey.

A.848			*Tobermory	..	107
A.849	10	10	*Salen	..	97
..	12½	2½	Gruline Church	..	94½
..	21¼	8¼	*Gribun	..	85¾
..	26¼	5	*Kilfinichen Church	..	80¾
..	33	6¾	*Pennyghael	..	74
..	43	10	*Bunessan	..	64
..	49	6	*Fionphort	..	58
			(Passenger ferry to Iona)		
			Return to:—		
..	55	6	*Bunessan	..	52
..	65	10	*Pennyghael	..	42
B.8035	68	3	Junc. A.849/B.8035		39
..	83¼	15¼	*Lochdonhead	..	23¾
..	85¾	2½	*Craignure	..	21¼
A.848	97	11½	*Salen	..	10
..	107	10	*Tobermory		

250. TOBERMORY to LOCHBUIE. This alternative way to Salen follows a hilly, winding road, past the Mishnish Lochs, with hairpin bends on the descent to Dervaig, then by Glen Aros to Salen. Extensive views from the coast road along the Sound of Mull, including the mainland hills of Morven, the Isle of Lismore and the Appin hills. Near Craignure there is a distant view of Ben Nevis at the head of Loch Linnhe. After Lochdonhead, the main road is left near Loch Spelve, and winds over Ardura Hill (gradient 1 in 8) to follow the attractive shore road beside Lochs Spelve and Uisg, with the peaks of Ben Buie and Creach Bheinn to the north.

A.848			*Tobermory	..	44¼
Uncl.	7¼	7¼	*Dervaig	..	36¾
A.848	18	10¼	Junc. Uncl./A.848		26¼
B.8035	19½	1½	*Salen		25
..	31	11½	*Craignure	..	13½
..	33½	2½	*Lochdonhead		11¼
Uncl.	37	3½	Junc. B.8035/Uncl.		7¼
..	44¼	7¼	*Lochbuie		

SKYE

The island of Skye is some 50 miles long, and provides a striking variety of scenery, with open moorlands, charming lochs, a rocky coastline affording lovely seascapes, the whole being dominated from most points by the serrated peaks of the Black Coolins, while there is also considerable historic interest, notably in the island's associations with Prince Charles Edward and Flora Macdonald. There are few roads other than those detailed in the following itineraries, which keep mainly to the indented coastline.

Most of the roads included are narrow and winding, with variable surfaces, and become hilly in places, although there are no serious gradients. The island is easily reached on weekdays, by the ferry from Kyle of Lochalsh to Kyleakin. There is also a steamship service on weekdays between Mallaig and Armadale on which previous booking is necessary. During the summer an additional ferry service is operated between Glenelg and Kylerhea. **There are no Sunday services.**

251. KYLE OF LOCHALSH to PORTREE. Utilizes the ferry service across Kyle Akin, and then follows the main coast road to Sligachan, passing the Red Hills beyond Broadford, and with a fine view of Blaven before rounding Loch Ainort. Striking views of the Black Coolin peak of Sgurr nan Gillean at Sligachan, after which the road keeps inland across the moors through Glen Varragill.

			*Kyle of Lochalsh	36¼
			Ferry to	
A.850			*Kyleakin	
..	5½	5½	Breakish	.. 30¾
..	7½	2	Harrabol	.. 28¾
..	8¼	¾	*Broadford	.. 28
..	13	4¾	*Dunan	.. 23¼
..	23¾	10¾	Sconser	.. 12½
..	26¾	3	*Sligachan	.. 9½
A.855	36	9¼	Junc. A.850/A.855	.. ¼
..	36¼	¼	*Portree	

252. ELGOL to GLENBRITTLE. At Elgol there is an impressive view of the Coolins across *Loch Scavaig. The wild and picturesque *Loch Coruisk in the secluded heart of the Coolins can be reached by motor boat or on foot from Elgol. The narrow and hilly road between Elgol and Torrin passes the head of Loch Slapin and there are fine views of the Red Hills and the Coolin peak of Blaven. Thereafter an easier road is followed around the Red Hills and passes through Broadford and along the main coast road to Loch Ainort, where the Island of Scalpay is seen across the narrow channel. There is a striking view of Sgurr nan Gillean from Sligachan, after which the road passes over moorland country and winds through Glen Drynoch. A narrow, rough by-road is then followed to the climbing centre of Glenbrittle. Another branch road continues westwards along the west side of

Loch Harport to the *Talisker distillery at *Carbost, from which two by-roads diverge. One leads to the splendid cliffs of Talisker Bay and the other to *Port na Long, well known for its weaving industry.

A.881			*Elgol	.. 47½
	9	9	*Torrin	.. 38¼
A.850	14¼	5½	*Broadford	.. 32¾
..	19¼	4¾	*Dunan	.. 28
..	30	10¾	Sconser	.. 17¼
A.863	33	3	*Sligachan	.. 14¼
B.8009	38¼	5¼	Junc.	
			A.863/B.8009	9
Uncl.	39¾	1½	Junc. B.8009/Uncl.	7½
..	47¼	7½	*Glenbrittle	

253. PORTREE to ARMADALE. Follows the main road southwards across the moorlands of Glen Varragill, with fine views of the peak of Sgurr nan Gillean in the Black Coolins approaching Sligachan. Afterwards follows the coast, with a view of the peak of Blaven after Loch Ainort is circled, and later passes the Red Hills nearing Broadford, beyond which the route turns inland, rejoining the coast near Isle Ornsay on the Sound of Sleat. There is only a passenger ferry between Armadale and Mallaig, although vehicles will be carried on the steamer services by previous arrangement.

A.855			*Portree	.. 44¾
A.850	¼	¼	Junc. A.855/A.850	44¼
..	9½	9¼	*Sligachan	.. 35¼
..	12½	3	Sconser	.. 32¼
..	23¼	10¾	*Dunan	.. 21¼
..	28	4¾	*Broadford	.. 16¾
..	28¾	¾	Harribol	.. 16
A.851	29¾	1	Junc. A.850/A.851	15
..	37¼	7½	*Isle Ornsay	.. 7½
..	40¼	3¼	*Teangue	.. 4¼
..	44¼	4¼	*Armadale (Pier)	

254. A tour from PORTREE via DUNTULM CASTLE and THE QUIRAING. A tour through the Trotternish district in the north-west corner of Skye, crossing moorlands to Loch Snizort and Uig Bay, on the north side of which there is a sharp turn up Idrigil Hill, near the summit of which a road branches off direct to Staffin. It is narrow and hilly, with a sharp 1 in 9 descent and hairpin bends, giving a panoramic view of Staffin Bay, but goes closer to the jagged mass of the Quiraing than the main tour, which continues by the easier road round the north coast by Kilmuir, passing the ruined Duntulm Castle and Flodigarry. The fantastic rock pinnacles of the Quiraing lie to the right near Staffin, while beyond are the Mealt Falls. After Culnaknock, the Lealt Falls are passed, as the precipitous Storr, the culminating point of the long Trotternish ridge, and noted for the detached pinnacle known as the Old Man of Storr, comes into view. The road then passes the Storr Lochs, now harnessed to the new hydro-electric power scheme inaugurated in 1952.

A.855			*Portree	.. 50
A.850	¼	¼	Junc. A.855/A.850	49¾

A.856	4	3¼	Junc. A.850/A.856	46
..	8¼	4¼	*Snizort Church	41¾
..	13¾	5½	Earlish	36¼
..	15¾	2	*Uig	34¼
A.855	16¾	1	Junc. A.856/A.855	33¼
..	20¾	4	*Kilmuir	29¼
..	24¾	4	*Duntulm	25¼
..	25¾	1	*Kilmaluag	24¼
..	28¾	3	*Flodigarry	21¼
..			*Quiraing (to rt.)	
..	32½	3¾	*Staffin	17¼
..	36	3½	*Culnaknock	14
..			*Storr (to rt.)	
..	50	14	*Portree	

255. A tour from PORTREE via DUNVEGAN CASTLE. Follows the main road southwards across the moorlands of Glen Varragill, with fine views of the peak of Sgurr nan Gillean in the Black Coolins approaching Sligachan, where the tour turns westwards through Glen Drynoch. Continues along the east side of Loch Harport and round the head of little Loch Beag to Bracadale, where there is a rough, narrow road (B.885) to Portree (11 miles). The tour then proceeds close by Loch Bracadale, branching off to visit the famous Dunvegan Castle, on the loch of that name, with views of the twin flat-topped Macleod's Tables to the southwest. The return is then made by way of Edinbain and the heads of Loch Greshornish and Loch Snizort Beag. 3¾ miles beyond Dunvegan a branch road (B. 886) leads to *Trumpan.

A.855			*Portree	.. 55¾
A.850	¼	¼	Junc. A.855/A.850	55¼
A.863	9¼	9¼	*Sligachan	46
..	15	5½	*Drynoch Br.	.. 40½
..	23¾	8¾	*Bracadale	
			(Struan P.O.)	31¾
..	26¾	3	*Ose (P.O.)	.. 28¾
..	30¾	4	Roskhill (P.O.)	.. 24¾
A.850	33¾	3	*Dunvegan	.. 21¾
..	42	8¼	*Edinbain	.. 13¾
..	43¾	1¾	Arnisort	.. 11½
..	48¼	4½	Bernisdale	.. 7¼
..	50¼	2	*Skeabost Bridge	.. 5¼
A.855	55¼	5	Junc. A.850/A.855	¼
..	55½	¼	*Portree	

OUTER HEBRIDES

The Outer Hebrides group comprises the chain of islands stretching from the Butt of Lewis to Barra Head, but for the motorist the main interest lies in the largest island of Lewis and Harris, since the islands of North Uist, Benbecula, South Uist and Barra, which lie to the south have a much smaller road mileage. Benbecula and North and South Uist are connected by bridges and causeways. The roads are gradually being improved, and, in general, main roads are fair, but great care must be exercised, as they are often narrow and tortuous, while side roads are inferior. One of the features of the islands is the variety of pre-historic cairns, duns, brochs and forts, which include the famous group of Standing Stones at Callernish. A comprehensive article dealing with the islands as a whole, and at the same time describing the various places of interest, will be found in the gazetteer under the heading of **Hebrides, Outer.**

There are steamship connections every weekday from Stornoway to Kyle of Lochalsh and Mallaig, and a regular circular service links Harris, North Uist and South Uist with Mallaig and Kyle of Lochalsh. In addition, there is a service from South Uist and Barra to Tobermory (Mull) and Oban.

The airports situated at Stornoway and also on Benbecula and Barra are served from Glasgow, and in addition there is a direct service from Inverness to Stornoway.

256. STORNOWAY to RODEL.

This is the longest, but also one of the finest drives in the island, and gives an excellent comparison between the moorlands of Lewis and the hills of Harris. After crossing moorlands the country becomes hilly beyond Laxay, the road winding round the many lochs. There are delightful scenes of mountain, moor and loch as the road continues by Loch Seaforth, and shortly after crossing the boundary of Lewis and Harris at Aline, there is a long, gradual ascent round a shoulder of Clisham, the highest peak in the Outer Hebrides. Fine panoramic views approaching West Loch Tarbert near Ardhasig Bridge, where a side road (B.887) leads off to Husinish Bay, passing Amhuinnsuidhe Castle. Beyond Tarbert, which is prettily situated on the narrow neck of land separating East and West Loch Tarbert, the main road follows Glen Laxdale to the west coast, and then traverses more pastoral country, passing several sandy bays on the shores of the Sound of Harris on the way to Leverburgh and Rodel, with its famous church. 4½ miles from Tarbert there is a narrow, winding and hilly road along the east coast through Finsbay to Rodel. Great care is required on this road as there are many blind corners and acute bends. *For * places see Hebrides, Outer, in Gazetteer.*

A.857			*Stornoway	..	60½
A.858	1	1	Junc. A.857/A.858		59½
A.859	1¼	¾	Junc. A.858/A.859		58¾
..	2¾	1	Creed Lodge	..	57¾
..	11¾	9	Laxay	..	48¾
..	14½	2¾	Balallan (P.O.)	..	46
..	24	9½	*Aline (Lewis-Harris boundary)		36½
..	33½	9½	Ardhasig Bridge		27¼
..	36½	3¼	*Tarbert	..	24
..	50	13½	Borve Lodge	..	10½
..	57	7	*Obbe	..	3½
..	57¾	¾	*Leverburgh	..	2¾
..	60½	2¾	*Rodel		

257. STORNOWAY to UIG or ARDROIL SANDS.

As far as Garynahine pleasant moorland country is traversed, with some pretty loch scenery near Achmore. A narrow road is then followed between the hills and round the

lochs, with many lovely views. Beyond Meavig, Glen Valtos is followed to the fork roads where one branch leads to Uig and the other to the fine sandy bay at Ardroil. *For * places see Hebrides, Outer, in Gazetteer.*

A.857			*Stornoway	..	35
A.858	1	1	Junc. A.857/A.858		34
..	9½	8½	Achmore	..	25½
B.8011	14¼	4¾	*Garynahine	..	20¾
..	27	12¾	Eneclate	..	8
..	30½	3½	Carashader	..	4½
..	32	1½	Meavig	..	3
Uncl.	34	2	†Junc. B.8011/Uncl.		1
..	35	1	*Uig		
		†	OR		
Uncl.	34		Junc. B.8011/Uncl.		
..	36½	2½	*Ardroil Sands		

258. STORNOWAY to PORT of NESS (for Butt of Lewis).

To Barvas there are long straight stretches over open moors dotted with tiny lochans, and afterwards the road keeps parallel to the west coast, passing close by the Clach an Trushal monolith, near Shader. At Port of Ness, a secondary road (B.8014) leads to the Butt of Lewis, the most northerly point of the island. From Laxdale, there is a secondary road (B.895) along the east coast of the island past several sandy bays to Gress (noted for its caves), and Tolsta (12 miles), with fine coast scenery. *For * places see Hebrides, Outer, in Gazetteer.*

A.857			*Stornoway	..	27¾
..	1¼	1¼	Laxdale	..	26½
..	12	10¾	*Barvas	..	15½
..	16	4	*Shader	..	11¾
..	25¾	9¾	Swainbost	..	2
..	27¾	2	*Port of Ness		

259. STORNOWAY to THE EYE PENINSULA (for Tiumpan Head).

The road crosses the narrow isthmus linking the main part of the island to the Eye peninsula, with the sandy shores of Broad Bay to the north, and the open seas of the North Minch to the south. Beyond the isthmus stands the old church of Eye, noted for the Macleod tombs. From Tiumpan Head there are extensive views north towards Tolsta Head and north-east towards Cape Wrath on the mainland. *For * places see Hebrides, Outer, in Gazetteer.*

A.866			*Stornoway	..	11½
..	1½	1½	Sandwick	..	10
..	6¼	4¾	Garrabost	..	5¼
..	6¾	½	*Eye Church	..	4¾
..	8	1¼	Shulishader	..	3½
..	10	2	Portnaguran	..	1½
..	11½	1½	Tiumpan Head (Lighthouse)		

260. A tour from STORNOWAY via CALLERNISH.

Crosses open moorland country dotted with sparkling lochs, and with extensive views of the Harris hills to the south-west. A short

detour may be made to visit the famous Standing Stones of Callanish (second only in interest to the better known Stonehenge), after which the road continues within sight of the west coast, at first by East Loch Roag, and later by the Atlantic Ocean, passing near Carloway Broch, whence there is a direct road to Stornoway. The main road continues close by a number of crofting villages to Barvas, after which there are long straight stretches across moorland. *For * places see Hebrides, Outer, in Gazetteer.*

A.857			*Stornoway	..	46¾
A.858	1	1	Junc. A.857/A.858		45¾
..	9½	8½	Achmore	..	37¼
..	14¼	4¾	*Garynahine	..	32½
..	16¼	2	*Callanish	..	30½
..	17	¾	Breasclete	..	29¾
..	23	6	*Carloway	..	23¾
..	28½	5½	Shawbost	..	18¼
..	30½	2	Bragair	..	16¼
..	31¾	1¼	Arnol	..	15
A.857	34¾	3	*Barvas	..	12
..	45½	10¾	Laxdale	..	1¼
..	46¾	1¼	*Stornoway		

261. A TOUR IN NORTH UIST.

North Uist seems to consist more of water than of land, so numerous are the lochs and arms of the sea running in to it. *For * places see Hebrides, Outer, in the Gazetteer.*

A.865			*Lochmaddy	..	34¼
..	8¾	8¾	Grenetote	..	25½
..	10	1¼	Sollas	..	24¼
..	18	8	Tighary	..	16¼
..	20¾	2¾	Bayhead	..	13½
A.867	25¾	5	Clachan	..	8½
..	33¼	7½	Junc. A.867/A.865		1
..	34¼	1	*Lochmaddy		

262. LOCHMADDY (North Uist) to LOCHBOISDALE (South Uist).

This route traverses the islands of North Uist, Benbecula and South Uist which are linked by the North and South Ford Causeways.

The Balivanich Airport is situated on road B.892 2 miles west of Gramisdale, Benbecula.

From Daliburgh in South Uist there is a branch road (B.888) leading south to *Pollachar, the nearest point to the islands of Eriskay and Barra.

3¼ miles north of Daliburgh, Flora MacDonald's birthplace at Milton, lies just off the road. *For * places see Hebrides, Outer, in Gazetteer.*

A.865			Lochmaddy		42¼
A.867	1	1	Junc. A.865/A.867		41¼
A.865	8½	7½	Clachan	..	33¾
..	11¾	2¾	*Carnish	..	31
			North Ford Causeway		
..	15¾	4	*Gramisdale	..	27
..	21	5¼	*Creagorry	..	21¼
			South Ford Causeway		
..	22	1	*Carnan	..	20¼
..	27¾	5¾	Stilligarry	..	14½
..	29¼	1½	Howmore	..	13
..	39¼	10	*Daliburgh Church		3
..	42¼	3	*Lochboisdale		

ORKNEY

The Orkney group consists of numerous islands some 20 miles north from the mainland port of Scrabster (Thurso). The motorist is chiefly interested in the island called Mainland, or Pomona, on which there are about 150 miles of motoring roads, about half of them being of good surface, and the remainder mainly fair, although subsidiary roads are poor. There are no gradients of any consequence and road widths are sufficient to permit passing without difficulty. The second largest island, called Hoy, is notable for its cliff scenery, and is reached by steamer from Stromness, but there are few motoring roads.

During the last war the Churchill Barriers, linking Mainland to the islands of Lamb Holm, Glimps Holm, Burray and South Ronaldsay were completed. Steamer and motor boat services are available to many of the other islands. The Orkneys are noted for fine seascapes and magnificent cliff scenery, although the latter is best viewed from the water. There is also much of antiquarian interest, notably the famous Standing Stones of Stenness and the prehistoric village of Skara Brae. A comprehensive article dealing with the islands as a whole and describing the various places of interest will be found in the gazetteer under the heading of **Orkney.**

In addition to the weekday steamer between Scrabster (Thurso) and Stromness, there are also services from Aberdeen and Leith (Edinburgh) to Kirkwall and Stromness with regular connections to the Shetlands.

Air services are available from Glasgow, Aberdeen and Inverness to Grimsetter Airport near Kirkwall and also to Sumburgh Airport, Shetland.

263. A tour from KIRKWALL via STROMNESS and BIRSAY. Follows the direct road to Stromness across moorland and agricultural country, passing near the gallery grave of Rennibister, on the shores of the Bay of Firth, while beyond Finstown is the notable Maeshowe cairn. The south shores of the Loch of Stenness are followed to Stromness, and returning from there the tour keeps to the west sides of the Lochs of Stenness and of Harray. Later there is a distant view of the Kitchener Memorial on Marwick Head. The tour continues round the north-east coast past Evie, where a side road leads to the large, ruined broch of Aikerness, to reach Finstown. Between Finstown and Kirkwall there is an alternative secondary road skirting the viewpoint of Wideford Hill. *For * places see Orkney, in Gazetteer.*

A.965			*Kirkwall	..	52
..	6¾	6¾	*Finstown	..	45¼
..	9½	2¾	*Maeshowe	..	42½
..	10½	1	*Stenness (P.O.)	..	41½
..	15	4½	*Stromness	..	37
			Return to:—		
A.967	16	1	Junc. A.965/A.967	36	
..	25½	9½	Twatt Church	..	26½

A.966	28	2½	Junc. A.967/A.966	24	
..	28½	½	*Birsay (Earl's Palace)	..	23½
..	37½	9	*Evie Church	..	14½
..	42	4½	Rendall (P.O.)	..	10
A.965	45¼	3¼	*Finstown	..	6¾
..	52	6¾	*Kirkwall		

264. A tour from KIRKWALL via SKARA BRAE. Follows the coast road to the Loch of Stenness, with views of Scapa Flow, and later crosses the Bridge of Brogar, which separates Stenness Loch from Harray Loch, to reach the Standing Stones of Stenness and Ring of Brogar. A detour is then made to the pre-historic Skara Brae, near Aith, on the west coast, and later the Kitchener Memorial on Marwick Head comes into view. On the return route, a diversion can be made by B.9057 from Dounby to Klick Mill, afterwards continuing either by Evie and Iter. 263, or by returning to Dounby. There are alternative roads between Finstown and Kirkwall, a secondary road skirting the viewpoint of Wideford Hill. *For * places see Orkney, in Gazetteer.*

A.963			*Kirkwall		47
A.964	½	½	Junc. A.963/A.964	46½	
..	8	7½	*Orphir (P.O.)		39
A.965	14½	6½	Junc. A.964/A.965	32¾	
..	15¾	1½	*Stenness (P.O.)		31¼
B.9055	16	¼	Junc. A.965/B.9055	31	
..	16½	½	Bridge of Brogar		30½
..	21½	5	*Aith	..	25½
B.9056	22¾	1¼	*Skara Brae	..	24¼
..	23	¼	Bay of Skaill	..	24
..	24¼	1¼	Scarwell	..	22¾
..	26¼	2	*Marwick	..	20¾
A.967	28½	2¼	Junc. B.9056/A.967	18¼	
..	30¼	1¾	Twatt Church	..	16¾
A.986	30½	¼	Junc. A.967/A.986	16½	
..	33¼	2¾	*Dounby	..	13¾
..	36	2¾	Harray (P.O.)	..	11
A.965	38¼	2¼	Junc. A.986/A.965	8¼	
..	40¼	1½	*Finstown	..	6¾
..	47	6¾	*Kirkwall		

265. A tour from KIRKWALL via DEERNESS. This short drive covers the area known as the East Mainland, and is mainly through pleasant country, with occasional moorland. Just beyond Toab, a narrow neck of land is crossed, with Deer Sound on the one side and the North Sea on the other. On the north of the Deerness peninsula is a Covenanters' monument at Scarva Taing, accessible on foot. Returning to Toab, moorland country is crossed before reaching the coast at Holm Sound, with views of the islands to the south, while the latter part to Kirkwall is mainly through agricultural districts. *For * places see Orkney, in Gazetteer.*

A.960			*Kirkwall	..	28½
..	7	7	Toab (P.O.)	..	21½
B.9050	9¼	2¼	Junc. A.960/B.9050	18¼	
..	10	¼	Deerness (P.O.) ..	18¼	

..	12	2	*Deerness Church (Sandside Bay)	16½	
			Return to:—		
A.960	17	5	Toab (P.O.)	..	11½
B.9052	17¼	¼	Junc. A.960/B.9052	11¼	
A.961	21	3¾	Junc. B.9052/A.961	7½	
..	21¾	¾	*St. Mary's Holm	6¾	
A.960	27¾	6	Junc. A.961/A.960	¾	
..	28½	¾	*Kirkwall		

266. KIRKWALL to BURWICK (South Ronaldsay) via Churchill Barriers. Crosses agricultural country to St. Mary's Holm, then utilizes the Churchill Barriers, which link Mainland with the islands of Lamb Holm, Glimps Holm, Burray and South Ronaldsay, to terminate at Burwick, on the Pentland Firth. The Barriers are liable to be closed from time to time for maintenance work. *For * places see Orkney, in Gazetteer.*

A.960			*Kirkwall	..	22½
A.961	¾	¾	Junc. A.960/A.961	22	
..	6¾	6	*St. Mary's Holm	16	
..	8¼	1½	Lamb Holm	..	14½
..	9¼	1	Glimps Holm	..	13½
..	12¾	3½	Burray	..	10
B.9040	16¼	3½	*St. Margaret's Hope (South Ronaldsay)	6¼	
..	22¾	6½	*Burwick		

SHETLAND

The 100 or so Islands in the Shetland group lie 185 miles north of Aberdeen. For the motorist the largest island called Mainland claims chief attention. The road mileage on the other islands, with the exception of Unst and Yell, is limited and the road conditions rather poor. The coastline is broken by innumerable sea lochs, or "Voes" as they are called in Shetland, so that no part of the Islands is more than three miles from the sea. Along the coast there is some magnificent scenery, most of it within easy reach of roads.

A comprehensive article dealing with the Islands as a whole and describing the various places of interest will be found in the Gazetteer under the heading of **Shetland.**

The roads on the Mainland are generally in good condition and the main roads from the airport at Sumburgh to Lerwick and from Lerwick to Walls and Hillswick are excellent. The roads are generally undulating with no severe gradients, but care must be taken on narrow stretches and blind corners. The other large Islands, Yell and Unst, possess quite serviceable roads, but in each of these there are waterbound stretches, although these are gradually being tar sprayed.

Communication with Shetland (Mainland) is by steamer from Aberdeen direct to Lerwick, or from Leith via Aberdeen and Kirkwall. There are air services from Aberdeen, Edinburgh,

Glasgow, Inverness and Wick to Sumburgh.

A steamer connects Lerwick with the North Isles of Shetland three times a week. A bus and ferry route is also in operation leaving Lerwick every morning, but passengers cannot return the same day. In the summer season a tour is operated every Tuesday returning the same day. This covers a considerable portion of the Mainland and also large stretches of Yell and Unst.

267. LERWICK to HILLSWICK, ESHANESS or ISBISTER. Most of this route to the northern part of the Mainland lies through moorland country with low-lying hills, and the road is seldom out of sight of either an inland loch, a sea loch or the open sea. Mavis Grind, which is situated at the head of Sullom Voe, is a narrow neck of land separating the Atlantic Ocean from the North Sea by something like fifty yards or so. About six miles to the north of this, the road divides, the left-hand branch leading to the sandy bay and rocky coast at Hillswick, an excellent centre for trout fishing. Just before reaching Hillswick, a narrow secondary road leads to Eshaness, and while here an opportunity should be taken to visit the Grind of the Navir, a huge breach in the cliff face made by the force of the stormy sea. Another sight worth seeing is the Holes of Scraada, so called because there were at one time two of these holes, but the connecting bridge fell down about half a century ago and one hole now remains.

The other branch of the main road continues northward to Isbister.

A number of detours from the direct road are indicated in Iter. 270.

For places of interest marked * see Shetland, in Gazetteer.

A.970			*Lerwick	..	35¼
..	3¾	3¾	Bridge of Fitch	..	31½
..	6	2¼	Gott (P.O.)	..	29¼
..	9½	3½	Girlsta	..	25¾
..	18½	9	*Voe (P.O.)	..	16¾
..	23½	5	Brae	..	11½
..	25¼	1½	‡*Mavis Grind	..	10
..	33½	8	†Urafirth	..	2
..	35½	2	*Hillswick		
	†		OR		
A.970	33½		Urafirth		
B.9078	34¾	1¼	Junc. A.970/B.9078		
Uncl.	40	5¼	Junc. B.9078/Uncl.		
..	40¼	¼	*Esha Ness (Light-house)		
	‡		OR		
A.970	25¼		*Mavis Grind		
..	35½	10	Collafirth		
..	39¾	4¼	North Roe (P.O.)		
..	41¼	1½	*Isbister		

268. LERWICK to WALLS or SANDNESS. This route to the western part of the Mainland crosses the usual Shetland moorland country through the fertile valley of Weisdale to the head of Weisdale Voe, then up the incline to the top of the road which now slopes down to Tresta. From the top of this hill one of the finest views in the Islands can be had looking towards the south. After the head of Bixter Voe is passed at Parkhall, a secondary road leads in a southerly direction to Reawick with its nice sandy bay (6 miles). Two roads diverge at the Bridge of Walls, the left-hand one leading to Walls and the right-hand one to Sandness, with views of Papa Stour and St. Magnus Bay. The other divergent road on this itinerary is just after Bixter is passed, and runs in a somewhat north-easterly direction to the township of Aith, continuing round the head of Aith Voe via Gonfirth to Voe.

For places of interest marked * see Shetland, in Gazetteer.

A.970			*Lerwick	..	24¼
..	3½	3½	Bridge of Fitch		21
A.971	5	1½	Junc. A.970/A.971		19½
..	8½	3¾	Whiteness	..	16
..	12½	4	Weisdale	..	12
..	15½	3	Tresta	..	9
..	17½	2	Bixter	..	7
..	19	1½	Twatt	..	5½
..	23	4	†Bridge of Walls	1½
..	24¾	1¾	*Walls		
	†		OR		
A.971	23		Bridge of Walls		
..	29½	6½	*Sandness		

269. LERWICK to SUMBURGH. This route follows the east coast to the southern part of the Mainland, passing through Quarff with the Cunningsburgh hills to the west and fine views of the coastline. After passing the head of the Voe of Quarff, a loop road leads through the old-fashioned village of Fladdabister, which, in recent years, has been greatly modernized. The loop road continues through the fertile valley of Cunningsburgh and rejoins the main road at Mail. A mile or so farther on another detour can be made through Leebitton, where a boat can be hired to convey passengers to Mousa, where the best preserved specimen of a so-called Pictish broch can be examined. Continuing through Sandwick, the road splits just before Levenwick; the right-hand branch going in a westerly direction through Scousburgh and down to the Voe of Spiggie. It continues round the west side of Spiggie Loch, a very good trout loch, permission to fish in which must be obtained from the proprietor. The road rejoins the main road close to Boddam and continues down to Sumburgh. While there the opportunity should not be missed to visit the remarkable archaeological sites at Jarlshof, comprising the remains of three prehistoric and protohistoric village settlements dating from the Stone Age, the Iron Age and also a Viking House.

For places of interest marked * see Shetland, in Gazetteer.

A.970			*Lerwick	..	25¼
..	6½	6½	Quarff (P.O.)	..	18¾
..	10½	4	Cunningsburgh	..	14¾
..	13	2½	Rd. to *Sandwick	12¼
..	17½	4½	Levenwick (P.O.)	7¾
..	21½	4	*Dunrossness	..	3¾
..	25¼	3¾	*Sumburgh Airport (for Sumburgh Head)	

270. A TOUR FROM LERWICK. This tour covers the central part of the Mainland, making several detours from the main roads. Going first towards Scalloway, it then branches to the right through the very fertile valley of Tingwall before circling round Weisdale Voe, with very fine views at the top of the hill between Weisdale and Bixter. Here a branch road, running in a northerly direction, crosses the moors to reach the sea at Aith. Passing Gonfirth, the road connects with the north main road at Voe, where, still continuing northwards, a detour is made to Toft's Voe, near Mossbank, where there is a ferry service to the Island of Yell. A return to the main road at Voe is made by a high road overlooking Dales Voe, and then a narrow, winding coast road is followed through the parish of Nesting, with views of the Island of Whalsay, rejoining the main road to Lerwick before Girlsta.

For places of interest marked * see Shetland, in Gazetteer.

A.970			*Lerwick	..	83¾
..	3¾	3¾	Bridge of Fitch	..	80
..	7¼	3½	*Scalloway	..	76¾
			Return to:—		
B.9074	8¼	1	Junc. A.970/B.9074	75½
..	10¾	2½	*Tingwall Church	73
A.971	11½	¾	Junc. B.9074/A.971	72¼
..	14¾	3½	Whiteness	..	69
..	18¾	4	Weisdale	..	65
..	21¾	3	Tresta	..	62
..	23¾	2	Bixter	..	60
B.9071	24	¼	Junc. A.971/B.9071	59¾
..	26¾	2¾	Aith	..	57
..	31¾	5	Gonfirth Church	52
..	34½	2¾	*Voe	..	49¼
A.970	35	½	Junc. B.9071/A.970	48¾
..	35½	½	Voe (P.O.)	..	48¼
..	40½	5	Brae	..	43¼
B.9076	40¾	¼	Junc. A.970/B.9076	43
..	42¼	1½	Voxter	..	41½
A.968	47¾	5½	Junc. B.9076/A.968	36
..	49¼	1½	*Mossbank	..	34½
			Return to:—		
A.970	59¼	9½	Voe (P.O.)	..	24½
B.9071	60	¾	Junc. A.970/B.9071	23¾
B.9075	62¼	2¼	*Laxo	..	21½
..	67¼	5	South Nesting Bay	16½
..	69¼	2	Skellister (P.O.)	14½
..	70¼	1	Catfirth	13½
A.970	71¼	1½	Junc. B.9075/A.970	12
..	74	2¼	Girlsta	..	9¾
..	77¾	3¾	Gott (P.O.)	..	6
..	80	2¼	Bridge of Fitch	..	3¾
..	83¾	3¾	*Lerwick		

GAZETTEER

The county is given after each place name. This is followed by the population figures, taken mainly from the 1951 census and later sources. The following abbreviations are used: LB for Large Burgh; SB for Small Burgh.

The map square reference number appears on the right-hand side at the top of each entry, e.g. Map 10, **NT 27.** This reference is fully explained on pages ii and iii of the Atlas. It gives the major square letter, and the numbers of the smaller square. The scale of the map does not allow every place name to be shown, but this system enables the approximate position of a place to be ascertained whether or not it is marked on the map.

Early Closing and Market Days are indicated by the abbreviations E.C. and M.D. Where there is a golf course in the vicinity, this is shown by the word GOLF.

The times of opening for places of interest are included. These are correct up to the time of going to press, but members are strongly advised to verify the times, either locally or through the nearest A.A. Office. An annual publication " Houses, Castles and Gardens open to the public " is issued, giving up-to-date opening times and is available to members free on application.

In view of the fact that Gaelic spelling is not standardized, there is considerable variation in the spelling of place names. No authority is therefore claimed in this difficult question, and it may also be found that the spelling of certain places in the Gazetteer differs from that shown on the map.

The numbers of the Itineraries in which the places are mentioned are printed in the text in italics and should not be confused with page numbers.

Features of interest referred to in the text are printed in italics.

The abbreviations used in the Gazetteer are as follows:

A.M. .. Ancient Monument (*such as building, earthwork, etc., generally under Government care, usually accessible to the public*)

c. .. circa

cent. .. century

Iter. .. Itinerary

LB. .. Large Burgh

N.T. Scot. Property or land in the care of The National Trust for Scotland (see article on page 32)

SB. .. Small Burgh

A combined glossary of technical terms and Gaelic and Norse words will be found at the end of the Gazetteer.

Town Plans appear in or near their appropriate places throughout the Gazetteer. Mileages shown on town plan exits are calculated from town centres.

Below are the markings used on the larger type of town plans, those on the " thumb-nail " type being self-explanatory.

Recommended Routes ...

Congested Routes ...

One Way Streets ...

Traffic Roundabouts ...

Car Parks ...

Public Conveniences ...

Golf Courses ...

An exit name printed in brackets indicates that there is a better route by another exit.

ILLUSTRATED ROAD BOOK

OF SCOTLAND

GAZETTEER

Abbey St. Bathans, Berwick. An unusual warning sign, situated on an unclassified road to the south of the village

Abbotsford House, Roxburgh. Sir Walter Scott's 19th century home, most of which he himself designed, having changed the name to Abbotsford from Clarty Hole, when he purchased the estate in 1811. It stands near the River Tweed, off B6360

Aberdeen, Aberdeen. The 14th century Auld Brig O'Don, or Bridge of Balgownie, the work of Bishop Cheyne. The bridge is mentioned in Byron's '*Don Juan*'

Abercorn, West Lothian. One of the many quaintly carved tombstones in the churchyard. Bishop Trumuini established an Anglian bishopric here in the 7th century

Aberchirder, Banff. Kinnairdy Castle, once a Crichton stronghold. It stands 3 miles to the south-west, on an unclassified road

Aberdeen, Aberdeen. Provost Ross's House, dating from 1593, the oldest in the city. It has been restored by the National Trust for Scotland

PLATE 1 (facing page 91)   [For ABERDEEN see also following plate

ABBEY ST. BATHANS, Berwick. 169.
Map 11, **NT 7** 6.
Situated on the Whiteadder Water in the region of the *Lammermuir* hills. In the Parish Church is preserved the tomb of a prioress, portraying her pet dog, from the former 12th cent. Abbey Church. The Holy Well of *St. Bathans* is in the nearby grounds of the manor house. To the south, on the slopes of *Cockburn Law*, 1,065 ft., is the ancient Pictish tower, or broch, known as *Edinshall* (A.M.), one of the very few examples known outside the Northern Highlands. (See **Glenelg.**) North-westwards of Abbey St. Bathans rises the long ridge of *Monynut Edge*, with *Heart Law* attaining 1,283 ft.

ABBOTSFORD HOUSE, Roxburgh.
Map 10, **NT 5** 3.
This last and most famous of Sir Walter Scott's homes, where he died in 1832, stands in a delightful, wooded setting near the banks of his beloved River Tweed, and was designed largely by Scott himself, while many of the trees on the estate were planted by his hand. The house dates from 1817 to 1824, and contains a collection of personal memorials and also historical Scottish relics. In the library is a bust of Scott by Chantrey, and the drawing-room contains interesting portraits. The armoury has a notable collection of weapons of all ages, and the study remains much as the author left it. Abbotsford is shown weekdays, 10 to 5, April to late Oct. Also on Sun., 2 to 5, from June to late Sept. (See page 90.) To the south-east rise the triple-peaked *Eildon* hills, a prominent landmark in the Scott country, with a view-indicator. See **Ashiestiel, Darnick, Dryburgh Abbey, Galashiels** and **Smailholm.** *Iter. 13, 41, 43.*

ABERARGIE, Perth. Map 17, **NO 1** 1.
Iter. 90, 91, 92, 130, 131, 132.

ABERCHIRDER, Banff. 785. SB. Map 27, **NJ 6** 5.
The village was founded in 1746. About **3 m. S.W.,** where the River Deveron is joined by the Auchintoul Burn, stands the fine old *Kinnairdy Castle*, a former Crichton stronghold. *Iter. 184, 189, 194, 196.*

ABERCORN, West Lothian. Map 16, **NT 0** 7.
A little village by the Firth of Forth, on the opposite shore of which stands the naval base of *Rosyth* (q.v.). The restored Church contains retiring rooms and an elaborate laird's pew, designed by Sir William Bruce, the builder of the nearby *Hopetoun House* (q.v.). The curious *Binns* aisle is of note. Some ancient carved stones are preserved. There is also a pre-Reformation pulpit, and the Celtic cross-shafts are notable. **½ m. S.W.** is *Midhope Tower*, dating from the 16th cent. **3 m. W.S.W.** is the mansion of *The Binns* (N.T. Scot.), dating from 1478 and later, with 17th cent. plaster ceilings. Open daily, 2 to 5, mid-June to mid-Sept. (See page 90.) Here, General Tam Dalyell, who defeated the Covenanters at Rullion Green in 1666, raised the Royal Scots Greys in 1681. *Iter. 96.*

ABERDALGIE, Perth. Map 16, **NO 0** 2.
Iter. 86.

ABERDEEN, Aberdeen. 186,190. Map 21, **NJ 9** 0.
E.C. Wed., Sat. **M.D.** Fri. **GOLF.** An important Royal Burgh, Cathedral, University and maritime city, in the district of Mar, on the estuaries of the Rivers Dee and Don, the former flowing into the harbour, and the latter entering the sea to the north of Aberdeen Bay, beyond *Old Aberdeen*. The city, which is the third largest in Scotland, is built almost entirely of the granite for which it is perhaps best known, and presents a remarkably clean and

CENTRAL ABERDEEN.
A.A. OFFICE: FANUM HOUSE, GOLDEN SQUARE. Telephone Aberdeen 51231.

Art Gallery, War Memorial and Cowdray Hall	3.	Grammar School and Byron Statue	8.	Provost Ross's House (N.T. Scot.) 1593	14.
County and Municipal Buildings	4.	Harbour Offices	13.	Provost Skene's House, 17th cent. (Museum)	9.
East and West Churches	5.	Information Bureau	15.	St. Mary's Cathedral	
Fishmarket	5.	Marischal College	1.	(R.C.)	7.
Gordon's College	2.	Mercat Cross (1686)	12.	Union Bridge	11.
		New Markets	6.		

solid picture to the eye. Its watchword is the phrase " Bon Accord." From the harbour are shipped granite, fish and cattle, and as a resort Aberdeen is noted for its fine, sandy bathing beach in the bay. The charters of the city date back to c. 1179, but the former Castle has entirely vanished. In 1296, Edward I came here, and Bruce was a refugee after the battle of *Methven* (q.v.) in 1306. Edward III burned Aberdeen in 1337, and Montrose thrice occupied it, the last time in 1644. After the burning of 1337, the city was rebuilt, and consisted of Aberdeen and Old Aberdeen, the latter including the Cathedral precincts, and being made a Burgh of Barony in 1498, but in 1891 the two were united.

Union St. is a splendid modern thoroughfare, off which stands the Church of *St. Nicholas*, divided at the Reformation into the *East* and *West* Churches. They were later reconstructed, the former being a rebuilding of the 19th cent., and the latter, a design of James Gibbs, dating from 1763, and forming the best example of Scottish ecclesiastical architecture of that period. Of the original structure remain the 12th to 13th cent. transepts, and the 15th cent. crypt below the apse, in which much woodwork of the period has been preserved. A rare Scottish brass is to be seen in the south transept, or " Drum's " aisle. West of the Union Bridge, in Huntly St., is the R.C. Cathedral. Near *Robert Gordon's Colleges*, founded in 1739, is the interesting Art Gallery and Museum. A statue of Byron stands in front of the Grammar School. The 17th cent. *Provost Skene's House* has been restored as a museum. The Duke of Cumberland stayed here in 1746. *Provost Ross's House*, built in 1593, the oldest in Aberdeen, has been restored by the Scottish National Trust. It is open Mon. and Fri., 2.30 to 4.30 (See note page 90). In Castle St. is the Mercat Cross, dating from 1686, built for the sum of £100, paid out of the guild wine funds, and not on its original site. A statue of the 5th Duke of Gordon, Scott's

ABERDEEN

Scale

0   ¼   ½   1 MI.

Times of High Tide can be found by referring to the Tide Table in the Members Handbook

R.B.60

DRAWN AND PUBLISHED BY THE AUTOMOBILE ASSOCIATION

[For Central Aberdeen Plan see page 91.

92

Auld Brig O'Don (Bridge of Balgownie) 3.   Bridge of Dee 4.   Information Bureau (May–Sept.) 5.   King's College 2.   St. Machar's Cathedral 1.

The 17th century Provost Skene's House, now a
museum. The Duke of Cumberland occupied this house
in 1746

The seven-arched Bridge of Dee, built 1520–27 by
Bishop Gavin Dunbar, and decorated with coats of arms

The Chapel (c.1500) and tower of the old University building. The
'crown' at the top of the tower was rebuilt after a storm in 1633

The Mercat Cross of 1686. It cost
£100 to build, which was paid out of
the Guild wine funds

St. Machar's Cathedral in Old Aberdeen,
mainly the work of Bishop Lichtoun
in the mid-15th century and Bishop Gavin
Dunbar between 1519 and 1532

The 19th century buildings of Marischal College. It was founded
in 1593 by George Keith, the Earl Marischal

PLATE 2 (facing page 92)   [For ABERDEEN see also preceding plate

Abergeldie Castle, Aberdeen. Abergeldie Castle, on Royal Deeside, where King Edward VII stayed at times when Prince of Wales. The Castle was garrisoned by Mackay in 1689. It stands off A973, on the south bank of the river

Aberdour, Fife. The ruined 17th century and earlier Castle, the latest additions having been the work of the eighth Earl of Morton

Aberfoyle, Perth. 'Bailie Nicol Jarvie's poker,' the plough coulter hanging from a tree, which recalls a scene from Sir Walter Scott's '*Rob Roy*'

Aberlady, East Lothian. The old mounting stone, or 'loupin-on-stane' outside the Church

Aberfeldy, Perth. General Wade's bridge, spanning the River Tay, erected in 1733 at a cost of £4,095 5s. 10d.

Aberfeldy, Perth. The Memorial, erected in Queen Victoria's Jubilee Year (1887) to commemorate the enrolling of the Black Watch Regiment in October, 1739

PLATE 3 (facing page 93)

" Cock o' the North," is in Golden Square. The Municipal Buildings, in the same street, incorporate the tower and spire of the 14th cent. Tolbooth, and preserve the so-called " Aberdeen Maiden," the ancient executioner's weapon, on which was modelled the famous French guillotine. In the near vicinity stands the modern *St. Andrew's* Cathedral. The *Marischal College*, part of the University, and an imposing granite structure of the 19th cent., was founded originally in 1593, being housed in the former buildings of the old *Greyfriars* Monastery. From the 233-ft. high *Mitchell* tower of the College, a splendid view can be obtained.

Smeaton and Telford both shared in the construction of the harbour, and the Fish Market is a scene of much interest in the early morning. James Gibbs, the eminent 18th cent. architect, was born in Aberdeen in 1682. Near Hazlehead Park are the Rubislaw granite quarries. In *Old Aberdeen* stands the Cathedral of *St. Machar*, built of granite, and founded c.1136, though the earliest part of the present building goes back only to the mid-14th cent. (A.M.). The main part of the structure is a century later in date, and, apart from the spires, all the nave stonework is of granite. The choir has completely vanished. Of particular note are the West front, with its twin towers; the painted wooden nave ceiling of 1540; the 17th cent. monument to Bishop Scougal, and also the one to Bishop Dunbar; and the " Nuns " library. There is a very fine series of heraldic, wooden nave bosses, dating from the early 16th cent. In the High St. is *King's College*, also part of the University, founded in 1494, preserving the 16th cent. Chapel and the notable " crown " tower of the 17th cent. from the old buildings, the remainder being mostly 19th cent. reconstruction. The Chapel is famous for its rich woodwork, the screen having a wide rood-loft, and the carved stalls being canopied. The " crown " tower resembles those of *St. Giles'* at *Edinburgh* (q.v.) and the Tolbooth at *Glasgow* (q.v.), but is surmounted by a fine Renaissance crown, added in 1634. The Library, containing some fine MSS., and also the Senators' Room are of much interest.

Beyond the Cathedral is the picturesque " Auld Brig o' Don," or Bridge of Balgownie, a single span of early 14th cent. date, in a wooded setting. **2 m. S.S.W.** of the city centre is the even finer, widened Bridge of Dee, built 1520–1527, and showing seven fine arches decorated with coats of arms. **6 m. N.N.W.**, on the Turriff road, is *Dyce* (q.v.), where the airport for the city is situated. See **Blairs, Cove** and **Culter** (Aberdeen). For " Through Routes," see page 43. *Iter. 151, 152, 155, 168, 174, 175, 176, 177, 178, 179, 180, 181, 182, 183, 184, 185, 186.*

ABERDOUR, Fife. 1,502.   Map 17, **NT 1** 8.
E.C. Wed. GOLF. A small Firth of Forth resort, with sands and bathing. The restored Church is Norman and 16th cent., and has a leper window blocked by what is known as the Pilgrim's Stone. There is a ruined 14th to 17th cent. Castle, neighboured by an old doocot (A.M.). In Dalgetty Bay, to the west, is the mansion of *Donibristle House*, the surviving portion dating from c. 1720. It has fine wrought-iron entrance gates. In the vicinity, to the north-east, is the ruined Church (A.M.) of *St. Bridget*, at *Dalgetty*, dating from the 12th cent., the burial place of the early Bishops of *Dunkeld* (q.v.). Near Donibristle took place, in 1592, the murder of the Earl of Moray by the Earl of Huntly, which is commemorated in an old ballad. East of the Bay is Braefoot Point, looking out towards *Inchcolm Island* (q.v.). *Iter. 134.*

ABERFELDY, Perth. 1,486. SB.   Map 19, **NN 8** 4.
E.C. Wed. **M.D.** Alt. Thurs. GOLF. A touring centre in Strath Tay, on the south bank of the river, which is spanned, to the north-west, by one of General Wade's finest bridges, dating from 1733. The cost of building the bridge is said to have amounted to £4,095 5s. 10d. Near the bridge is the Black Watch Monument, the regiment having been enrolled in 1739. The poem by Burns entitled " The Birks of Aberfeldy " is thought to refer probably to a place by the name of Abergeldie, in Aberdeenshire. (See **Crathie Church.**) Away to the north of Aberfeldy, beyond

the lochs of Glassie and Derculich, rises *Farragon Hill*, 2,559 ft., a fine viewpoint. **1 m. S.**, reached by footpath from Bank St., and situated on the Moness Burn, are the

1. Wade Bridge.   2. Black Watch Monument.   3. Information Bureau.

three Falls of Moness. The Amulree road goes south through Glen Cochill, and climbs to a height of over 1,400 ft., among lonely moors, with *Meall Dearg*, 2,258 ft., rising to the south. See **Amulree, Dull, Grandtully, Wade Roads** and **Weem.** *Iter. 89, 107, 120, 139, 147, 149, 157, 158.*

ABERFOYLE, Perth. 1,134.   Map 15, **NN 5** 0.
E.C. Wed. GOLF. This small holiday resort, situated to the east of Loch Ard, is known as the " Gateway to the Trossachs." The former clachan of Aberfoyle, associated with Scott's " Rob Roy," lay **1 m. E.** of the present village. The well-known " *Bailie Nicol Jarvie* " Hotel is the successor to the inn made famous by Scott in " Rob Roy," and a plough coulter hanging from a tree opposite recalls a scene from the book. Two mortsafes in the churchyard recall the horrible exploits of the early 19th cent. body-snatchers, Burke and Hare, who were finally brought to trial at Edinburgh. The well-known *Duke's Road* to the *Trossachs* (q.v.) goes due north over high ground, giving fine views, notably towards Loch Drunkie and the larger Loch Vennachar, backed by *Ben Ledi*, 2,875 ft. To the west is the road through the Pass of Aberfoyle to Loch Ard, in its picturesque setting, and near the west end of the loch are two waterfalls on the Ledard Burn, described in Scott's " Waverley." Eastwards and westwards stretches Loch Ard Forest, part of the extensive Queen Elizabeth National Forest Park. The road continues to Loch Chon, and terminates at *Stronachlachar* (q.v.), on the shores of Loch Katrine, another branch going westwards to *Inversnaid* (q.v.) on *Loch Lomond* (q.v.). To the east of the village rise the grassy *Menteith* hills, attaining 1,289 ft. See **Port of Menteith.** *Iter. 105, 106, 111, 139.*

ABERGELDIE CASTLE, Aberdeen.   Map 20, **NO 2** 9.
See **Crathie Church.**

ABERLADY, East Lothian. 1,172.   Map 10, **NT 4** 7.
GOLF. A quiet holiday resort on the Firth of Forth, with a sandy beach and bathing, once the port of *Haddington* (q.v.). The Church has a 15th cent. tower and the 1762 monument to Lady Elibank by Canova is notable. Aberlady Bay, a local Nature Reserve, is a haunt of sea-birds. On its shores stands *Luffness House*, late 16th cent., with modern additions, ornate chimneys, and preserving a fine 16th cent. circular dovecote. See **Gosford House** and **Gullane.** *Iter. 2, 36, 37.*

ABERLEMNO, Angus. 664. Map 21, **NO 5** 5.
In the churchyard stands a notable cross-slab with Pictish symbols (A.M.), and at *Flemington* farm, in the vicinity, two Celtic stones, with reliefs of fights, are preserved (A.M.). Westwards rises the *Hill of Finhaven*, a good viewpoint, with a vitrified fort on the eastern summit. Away to the east lies the wooded expanse of Montreathmont Moor. See **Finhaven.** *Iter. 151, 156.*

ABERLOUR, Banff. 1,159. SB. Map 26, **NJ 2** 4.
E.C. Wed. A Spey valley village, the full name of which is *Charlestown of Aberlour,* named after its 19th cent. founder, Charles Grant. There are distilleries in the neighbourhood, and from the high ground in the vicinity fine views of the valley are obtainable. **6 m. S.S.W.** rises *Ben Rinnes,* 2,755 ft., and on the Aberlour Burn, flowing northwards from the mountains, is the cascade known as the *Linn of Ruthie. Iter. 170, 192, 195.*

ABERNETHY, Perth, 651. SB. Map 17, **NO 1** 1.
E.C. Wed. To the north of the village, the River Earn flows into the Firth of Tay, and to the south rise the *Ochil* hills. Once a Pictish capital, *Abernethy* is notable for the 12th cent. round church tower (A.M.), 74 ft. high, reminiscent of the numerous Irish examples, and one of the only two to be found on the Scottish mainland. At *Carpow,* **1 m. N.E.,** once a Roman port, Roman baths have been uncovered. See **Brechin.** *Iter. 131, 132.*

ABERUTHVEN, Perth. Map 16, **NN 9** 1.
Lies in Strath Earn, to the north of the *Ochil* hills. Near the ruined old Parish Church of *St. Kattan* stands the mausoleum of the Dukes of Montrose. About **4 m. N.N.E.,** beyond Dalreoch Bridge, across the River Earn, and to the north of the modern *Gask House,* is a five-mile stretch of Roman road, where excavation has taken place at various points from time to time, notably in 1770 by Pennant, and again in 1890. In the grounds of the mansion, which preserves relics of Prince Charles Edward, is a fragment of the 17th cent. house in which the Prince spent several hours on his way to Edinburgh, in 1745. See **Braco** and **Forteviot.** *Iter. 135, 146.*

ABINGTON, Lanark. 250. Map 9, **NS 9** 2.
E.C. Thurs. Attractively situated in Clydesdale in a ring of Lowland hills. To the former coaching inn came Prince

By-pass now available.

Louis Napoleon, in 1839, on his way to the tournament at *Eglinton Castle* near *Kilwinning* (q.v.). There is a memorial on A.73 to a local postmaster and fisherman, Matthew McKendrick (1848–1926). In the valley of the *Glengonnar Water,* to the south - west, where gold has been found, the road through the valley climbs gradually to over 1,400 ft., the summit being reached near the mining village of *Leadhills* (q.v.). See **Crawford, Crawfordjohn** and **Elvanfoot.** *Iter. 25, 29, 48, 50, 51, 56.*

ABOYNE, Aberdeen. 1,009. Map 21, **NO 5** 9.
E.C. Thurs. **M.D.** Alt. Mon. A well-known *Deeside* (q.v.) resort, bordered to the south by the extensive Forest of Birse, in the eastern Grampians, and backed by the *Hill of Cat,* 2,435 ft. The important annual Highland Gathering takes place in the first week of September. *Aboyne Castle,* a Gordon stronghold, to the north of the village, is mainly modern, but the west side is a rebuilding of 1671. In the private grounds is a megalithic circle.

South-west of the village, the long, wooded valley of Glen Tanner (See **Bridge of Ess**), stretches into the hills to Glen Tanner Forest and the lofty peak of *Mount Keen,* 3,077 ft. Two well-known walkers' tracks leave Glen Tanner at different points. The Fir Mounth road leads from the Church in the glen and crosses the hills east of the *Hill of Cat* to reach Glen Esk near *Tarfside* (q.v.), while the Mounth road diverges much higher up the glen, and after crossing a shoulder of *Mount Keen,* reaches Glen Mark near *Lochlee* (q.v.). A third track, known as the Fungle Road, proceeds southwards from Aboyne, and penetrates deep into the Forest of Birse. *Iter. 152, 191.*

ABRIACHAN, Inverness Map 25, **NH 5** 3.
The village is situated near the western shores of *Loch Ness* (q.v.), and a steep and winding descent leads down to the pier. A poor and narrow road goes north-westwards from Abriachan into the hills, passing the tiny Loch Laide, and descending later into Glen Convinth. See **Lovat Bridge.**

ACHANALT, Ross and Cromarty. Map 24, **NH 2** 6.
Iter. 205, 221.

ACHARACLE, Argyll. 500. Map 12, **NM 6** 6.
A little anglers' resort, situated at the western extremity of the 18-mile long *Loch Shiel* (q.v.), and the terminal point for the steamer from *Glenfinnan* (q.v.) which plies on the loch. The neighbouring countryside and hills are associated with Prince Charles Edward. To the east rises *Ben Resipol,* 2,774 ft., a notable landmark in the Sunart district, from the summit of which the view is remarkable. Northwards from Acharacle, a road parallels the Shiel River, past Shiel Bridge, to its outlet in Loch Moidart near *Dorlin,* in a richly-wooded setting, opposite which is the large island of Eilean Shona. Offshore, but linked to the mainland, except at high spring tides, stands the picturesque, ruined 14th cent. *Castle Tioram* of the MacDonalds of Clanranald, which was burnt in 1715. To the west of Acharacle, a by-road leads across Kentra Moss to *Ardtoe,* in Kentra Bay, in the Ardnamurchan district, from which the islands of Eigg and Rum are well seen. See **Dalilea, Kinlochmoidart, Loch Sunart** and **Salen** (Argyll). *Iter. 217.*

ACHARN, Perth. Map 16, **NN 7** 4.
Iter. 139.

ACHAVANICH, Caithness. Map 30, **ND 1** 4.
Iter. 236.

ACHBRECK, Banff. Map 26, **NJ 2** 2.
Iter. 169, 177, 192.

ACHFARY, Sutherland. Map 28, **NC 2** 3.
Situated between Loch Stack and Loch More, two of the chain of lochs which give character to the road leading from Lairg to Loch Laxford, on the wild coast of Sutherland. See **Laxford Bridge.** *Iter. 229.*

ACHILTIBUIE, Ross and Cromarty. Map 29, **NC 0** 0.
A remote little *Wester Ross* resort, providing fine maritime scenery, and most beautifully situated on the North-West Highland coast, on Baden Bay, in which lie the delightful Summer Islands. The largest of these is Tanera More, and to the south-east is Horse Island. On the mainland, farther to the south-east, rises *Ben More Coigach,* 2,438 ft., a splendid viewpoint in the Coigach district, overlooking the whole length of *Loch Broom* (q.v.). Northwards extends the Rhu More peninsula, with Rhu Coigach at its northern tip, looking over Enard Bay and the Minch, with the lonely Sutherland peaks of *Suilven,* 2,399 ft., and *Canisp,* 2,779 ft., dominating the country to the north-east. See **Baddagyle** and **Loch Lurgain.** *Iter. 226.*

ACHILTY INN, Ross and Cromarty. Map 25, **NH 4** 5.
An old coaching inn, situated in a wooded setting on the Blackwater River. To the west is the little Loch Achilty, beyond which are the Conon Falls, on the river of that name, reached by paths which lead to the south-eastern extremity of Loch Luichart. See **Contin, Falls of Rogie** and **Marybank.** *Iter. 204, 206, 221.*

Aberlemno, Angus. A churchyard cross-slab, probably 8th-century, inscribed with Pictish symbols on the reverse face

Abernethy, Perth. One of the only two examples of an Irish-type round Church tower on the Scottish mainland. It is probably early 12th century. See Brechin (Plate 22)

Acharacle, Argyll. The wooded shores of Loch Moidart, with a distant view of the 14th century Castle Tioram, on its island. The loch lies on an unclassified road to the north-west

Achfary, Sutherland. A 'stag and hind' weather-vane by the entrance to Loch More Lodge, near the shores of Loch More, off A838, in a deer-stalking district

Abington, Lanark. The Memorial on A73, overlooking the River Clyde, to Matthew McKendrick, a local postmaster and angler (1848–1926)

Achiltibuie, Ross and Cromarty. The peak of Ben More Coigach, seen from an unclassified road on Outer Loch Broom, a little to the south-east

PLATE 4 (facing page 94)

Achmore, Ross and Cromarty. A view towards Loch Carron as seen from A890 to the south of Strome Ferry

Achnashellach, Ross and Cromarty. The mountain of Fuar Tholl, nearly 3,000 feet, which overlooks the whole length of Glen Carron

Achnacarry, Inverness. The 'Dark Mile' of trees, near which Bonnie Prince Charlie hid in 1746. It lies to the north of the Achnacarry estate, on B8005, leading to Loch Arkaig. Commandos were trained here during the Second World War

Affric, Inverness. A view of Loch Benevean, in the richly wooded Glen Affric, to the south-west of Inverness, on an unclassified road off A831. A large hydro-electric scheme is in operation here

Airth, Stirling. The Mercat Cross, which displays the Elphinstone arms and is dated 1697

Alexandria, Dunbarton. The old house of Dalquharn, the birthplace in 1721 of Tobias Smollett the novelist

[For AFFRIC see also under GLEN AFFRIC (Plate 74)

PLATE 5 (facing page 95)

ACHMORE, Isle of Lewis, Ross and Cromarty.
Iter. 257, 260.   Map 32, **NB 3** 2.

ACHMORE, Ross and Cromarty.   Map 23, **NG 8** 3.
Lies in the level valley of Strath Ascaig, on the picturesque road leading from *Strome* (*q.v.*) to the shores of Loch Alsh by way of the fine viewpoint of *Auchtertyre* (*q.v.*) hill. See **Plockton** (for *Duncraig Castle*). *Iter. 220, 221, 222.*

ACHNACARRY, Inverness.   Map 18, **NN 1** 8.
See **Loch Arkaig.**

ACHNASHEEN, Ross and Cromarty.   Map 24, **NH 1** 5.
E.C. Wed. Situated between Strath Bran and Glen Carron, dominated to the north by the peak of *Fionn Bheinn,* 3,060 ft., beyond which lies the lonely Loch Fannich, with the *Fannich* peaks in the background. A large hydro-electric scheme in the Fannich district is now in operation. To the west, on the road to *Loch Maree* (*q.v.*), is Loch a' Chroisg, or Rosque, beyond which a climb is made to the head of

Glen Docherty, from which a magnificent distant view of Loch Maree is obtained. The road to *Kyle of Lochalsh* (*q.v.*) crosses the Drum Alban watershed west of Loch Gowan, to the south-west of which rises *Moruisg,* 3,033 ft., in Glencarron Forest. To the south-east of Achnasheen is *Sgurr Vuillin,* 2,845 ft., overlooking the lonely Glen Conon, with the remote Loch Beannachan. See **Kinlochewe.** *Iter. 205, 221.*

ACHNASHELLACH, Ross and Cromarty.
              Map 24, **NH 0** 4.
In Glen Carron and Achnashellach Forest, by Loch Doule, dominated by the peaks of *Fuar Tholl,* 2,968 ft., and *Sgurr Ruadh,* 3,142 ft., to the north-west, while away to the east rises *Moruisg,* 3,033 ft., in Glencarron Forest. A most beautiful private road goes from here over the Coulin Pass in a north-easterly direction, past Lochs Coulin and Clair, to Glen Torridon and *Kinlochewe* (*q.v.*), but the public motoring road is by way of *Achnasheen* (*q.v.*). *Iter. 221, 222, 223.*

ACHUVOLDRACH, Sutherland.
Iter. 225.   Map 28, **NC 5** 5.

AE BRIDGE, Dumfries.   Map 4, **NY 0** 8.
This bridge spans the Water of Ae, flowing eastwards to join the Annan in the vicinity of *Lochmaben* (*q.v.*). The Ae rises on the 2,285-foot high *Queensberry Hill,* away to the north, near the Lanark border. 2½ m. N.W., in a newly-planted forest, is the village of *Ae,* created by the Forestry Commission in 1947. *Iter. 24, 46.*

AFFLECK CASTLE, Angus.
See **Monikie.**   Map 17, **NO 5** 3.

AFFRIC, Inverness.   Map 24, **NH 1** 2.
See **Cannich.**   and **NH 2** 2.

AILSA CRAIG, Ayr.   Map 2, **NX 0** 9
See **Girvan.**   and **NS 0** 0.

AIRDRIE, Lanark. 32,494. LB.   Map 9, **NS 7** 6.
E.C. Wed. **GOLF.** A large town with coal mines and ironworks in the vicinity. *Iter. 16, 50, 87.*

AIRTH, Stirling. 691.   Map 16, **NS 8** 8.
Lies near the southern extremity of the Kincardine road bridge spanning the Forth. In the 15th cent. a Royal dockyard was situated here. There is an old Mercat Cross, dated 1697, with two sundials, and displaying the Elphinstone arms, with their motto : " Doe well let them say." *Airth Castle,* modernized, incorporates Wallace's tower, of 14th cent. origin. *Iter. 96.*

AITH, Orkney.   Map 33, **HY 2** 1.
See **Orkney Islands** (Mainland). *Iter. 264.*

AITH, Shetland.   Map 33, **HU 3** 5.
Iter. 270.

ALCAIG, Ross and Cromarty.   Map 25, **NH 5** 5.
Iter. 203.

ALEXANDRIA, Dunbarton. 9,715.   Map 15, **NS 3** 8.
E.C. Wed. **GOLF.** One of a group of three neighbouring bleaching and manufacturing towns, the others being *Renton* and *Bonhill,* lying along the River Leven, which flows from the south end of *Loch Lomond* (*q.v.*) into the Clyde. Tobias Smollett, the novelist, was born at the old house of *Dalquharn,* in 1721, and is commemorated by a monument at *Renton* (*q.v.*). See **Balloch.** *Iter. 88, 100, 101, 110.*

ALFORD, Aberdeen. 100.   Map 27, **NJ 5** 1.
E.C. Wed. **M.D.** Tues. The River Don flows to the north of the village through the fertile Howe of Alford, with the *Correen* hills to the north-west and *Bennachie,* 1,733 ft., rising to the north-east. A Civil War battle was fought here in 1645, when the Marquis of Montrose defeated General Baillie, and relics of the fight have been dug up from time to time. The scene of the battle was near the Church, **2 m. W.,** and in the vicinity is the ruined *Asloun Castle.* To the north-east of the church is Bridge of Alford, where the Huntly road crosses the Don. **1 m. S.E.** of Alford is the decayed *Balfluig Castle,* dating from 1556. See **Craigievar Castle** and **Kildrummy.** *Iter. 176, 177.*

Town Hall. Information Bureau.

ALINE, Isle of Lewis (Harris) Inverness; Ross and Cromarty. Map 32, **NB 1** 1.
Here, facing Seaforth Island, in Loch Seaforth, the road from Lewis enters the district of Harris. See **Hebrides, Outer** (Lewis). *Iter. 256.*

ALLARDYCE CASTLE, Kincardine. Map 21, **NO 8** 7.
See **Inverbervie.**

ALLOA, Clackmannan. 13,884. SB. Map 16, **NS 8** 9.
E.C. Tues. GOLF. The largest town in Scotland's smallest county, standing just north of the River Forth,

1. Alloa Tower. 2. Alloa House. 3. St. Mungo's Church. 4. House with sundial, 1695.

with the long range of the *Ochil* hills in the background. Double tides are a feature of the river in the vicinity. The town is noted for the spinning of worsted yarns. Near the 19th cent. *Alloa House* stands the 13th cent. *Alloa Tower*, associated on more than one occasion with Mary, Queen of Scots. In the Kirkgate stands a house dating from 1695 and preserving a magnificent sundial of the same date. The modern Church of *St. Mungo* retains an older tower. *Iter. 133, 134.*

ALLOWAY, Ayr. 2,497. Map 8, **NS 3** 1.
Situated a little to the south of *Ayr (q.v.)*, and famous as the birthplace, on January 25th, 1759, of Robert Burns, the great Scots poet. The cottage in which he was born has been preserved, and adjoining it is the Burns museum, housing various personal relics. The poet's father is buried in front of the roofless " haunted " Kirk, and across the street stands the Burns Monument, containing, among other objects, Bibles belonging to Burns and his " Highland Mary." Spanning the River Doon, in a delightful setting, is the well-known " Auld Brig,' associated with Tam o' Shanter, and dating back perhaps to the 13th cent. See **Kirkoswald.** *Iter. 84.*

ALNESS, Ross and Cromarty. 320. Map 25, **NH 6** 6.
GOLF. A Cromarty Firth village, on the Alness River, where it flows into the Firth after its journey down Strath Rusdale. On *Fyrish Hill*, 1,483 ft., to the west, is a curious monument, said to be a copy of the Indian gate of Negapatam. *Iter. 201.*

ALTGUISH INN, Ross and Cromarty. Map 24, **NH 3** 7.
This lonely coaching inn stands on the moorland road leading from *Garve (q.v.)* to *Ullapool (q.v.)*. By the road flows the Glascarroch River, to be joined by other streams before flowing into Loch Garve to the south-east. In the

vicinity, on A.835, is a new reservoir in connection with the Fannich hydro-electric scheme. Away to the east rises *Ben Wyvis*, 3,429 ft., and westwards are the *Fannichs*, a group of lofty peaks, the highest of which is *Sgurr Mor*, 3,637 ft. **5 m. W.N.W.** is Loch Droma, at a height of 915 ft., on the desolate stretch known as the Dirrie More. *Iter. 204, 206.*

ALTNACEALGACH, Sutherland. Map 29, **NC 2** 1.
To the east, a thin wedge of Ross and Cromarty projects into Sutherland, and is said to have been claimed for the first-named county by men who walked the ground with Ross soil in their boots. A lonely inn stands here, on the shores of Loch Borralan, and the mountain views are impressive, with *Cul Beag*, 2,523 ft., and *Cul Mor*, 2,786 ft., to the west, and the sharp cone of *Suilven*, 2,399 ft., seen in the distance. *Breabag*, 2,670 ft., which rises to the north, is part of a line of hills extending to *Ben More Assynt*, 3,273 ft., Sutherland's highest peak. Caves on the spurs of Breabag have yielded evidence of the Stone Age, and near the tiny Loch Awe, on the road to *Inchnadamph (q.v.)*, there are Burial Cairns dating from the Bronze Age. **4 m. N.W.** of the inn is the Cam Loch and its western neighbour Loch Veyatie, lying in the heart of the strange, isolated Sutherland mountains of Torridon sandstone. See **Loch Lurgain.** *Iter. 224, 228.*

ALTNAHARRA, Sutherland. Map 28, **NC 5** 3.
E.C. Fri. An angling resort, situated at the western extremity of Loch Naver, in *Strath Naver (q.v.)*, and dominated by the schist peak of *Ben Klibreck*, 3,154 ft., which rises to the south. On the farther side of the mountain lies the lonely Loch Choire. Near *Klibreck* farm, at the southwestern extremity of Loch Naver, there are hut circles and a Celtic Cross, and farther along the loch-side is a Pictish broch known as *Dun Creagach*. Almost facing it, across Loch Naver, is another broch, situated on the road traversing Strath Naver. A very rough and narrow road leads north-westwards from Altnaharra, passing Loch na Meadie, and reaching Strath More near its junction with Glen Golly. In Strath More, and **10 m. N.W.** of Altnaharra, stands *Dun Dornadilla*, one of the best known brochs on the mainland. To the north rises *Ben Hope*, 3,040 ft., a splendid viewpoint, the most northerly Scottish peak of over 3,000 ft., overlooking the narrow Loch Hope. A little farther to the north beyond Dun Dornadilla is the Allt-na-Caillich waterfall, east of the road in Strath More. *Iter. 230, 232.*

ALVA, Clackmannan. 3,988. SB. Map 16, **NS 8** 9.
E.C. Wed. GOLF. A weaving town at the base of the *Ochil* hills, whose principal summit, *Ben Cleuch*, 2,363 ft., rises to the north-east of the town, and is a notable viewpoint. The River Devon flows to the south of Alva. At the head of Alva Glen is the Craighall waterfall, and in the Silver Glen a silver mine was worked from 1712 until it became exhausted. Two Communion Cups in Alva Church are made of the local silver. Records of the woollen industry in this district go back to 1550. *Iter. 136.*

ALVES, Moray. Map 26, **NJ 1** 6.
This small village lies in the fertile Laigh of Moray, and is neighboured by the hamlet of *Crook of Alves*. To the south-west, beyond Alves Wood, stands the ruined *Asliesk Castle*, and to the north-east is the modern *York Tower*, on the summit of the *Knock*, the traditional meeting-place of Macbeth with the " Weird Sisters." *Iter. 175, 198.*

ALYTH, Perth, 2,013. SB. Map 20, **NO 2** 4.
E.C. Wed. M.D. Sat. GOLF. A small linen-manufactur-

Alloway, Ayr. The Burns Monument, built in 1820, which contains many relics of the poet, including the Bible which he gave to his ' Highland Mary '

Alloa, Clackmannan. The ornate sundial of 1695 on a house in Kirkgate. It was built by Thomas Beauchop, the master mason of Kirross House and the Mid Steeple of Dumfries

Alloway, Ayr. The cottage in which Robert Burns was born in 1759. It was re-built by the poet's father

Alves, Moray. The modern York Tower, on the Knock, off A96. On this hill Macbeth is said to have met the ' Weird Sisters '

Altguish Inn, Ross and Cromarty. The reservoir on the Garve to Ullapool road (A835) in connection with the Fannich hydro-electric scheme

Alness, Ross and Cromarty. The curious Negapatam Monument on Fyrish Hill, as seen from A9. It was set up by Sir Hector Munro of Novar (1726–1805), who helped to capture the Indian town of that name

PLATE 6 (facing page 96)

Amisfield, Dumfries. The 16th century Amisfield Tower, one of the finest of its period in Scotland. It has been associated with the Charteris family since the 12th century

Appin, Argyll. The car ferry across Loch Leven at Ballachulish, at the northern extremity of the Appin country

Ancrum Bridge, Roxburgh. The Waterloo Monument, a well-known Border Country landmark, which stands on Peniel Heugh, 2 miles north-east. It was set up by the Marquis of Lothian and his tenants in 1815

Applecross, Ross and Cromarty. Cottages facing Applecross Bay, in a remote village accessible by road only over the famous 2,054-foot high Pass of the Cattle. An illustration of this appears under Tornapress (Plate 163)

Anstruther, Fife. The old manse, or minister's house, of Anstruther Easter, which carries the date 1590, and is said to be the oldest inhabited manse in Scotland

Annan, Dumfries. The old Grammar School at which Thomas Carlyle was educated

PLATE 7 (facing page 97)   For ARBROATH see following plate ing town in *Strathmore* (*q.v.*), overlooked by the *Hill of Alyth*, to the east of which is *Barry Hill*, preserving a British fort. The town lies a little to the north of the Blairgowrie to Kirriemuir road. **4 m. N.E.**, beyond the River Isla, is *Airlie Castle*, of which only a small portion of the old building, burnt in 1640, has survived. Nearby is a rare Pict's house with a rudely sculptured roof. See **Bridge of Craig, Kirkton of Glenisla** and **Meigle**. *Iter. 160, 166.*

AMISFIELD, Dumfries. Map 4, **NX 9** 8.
Another name for this village is *Amisfield Town*. **1 m. N.W.** is *Amisfield Tower*, an ancient seat of the Charteris family. It is one of the best preserved and most picturesque of the ancient towers still remaining in Scotland, and was built largely in the latter half of the 16th cent., the date 1600 being inscribed on some heraldic panels. An oak door, with carvings, formerly in the tower, is now preserved in the National Museum of Antiquities at Edinburgh. **3 m. S.W.,** beyond the small village of *Kirkmahoe*, is *Carnsalloch House*, dating from 1759, with its walled gardens. *Iter. 24, 46.*

AMULREE, Perth. Map 16, **NN 9** 3.
Situated at the western extremity of Strath Bran, and a good centre for exploring Glen Quaich, with Loch Freuchie, and also for Glen Cochill and Glen Almond. (See **Newton Bridge.**) The road through Glen Cochill, leading to *Aberfeldy* (*q.v.*) is partly on the line of one of General Wade's old roads, and southwards from Amulree the Wade road goes through the delightful *Sma' Glen* (*q.v.*). Another road goes north-westwards through Glen Quaich, and climbs to a height of 1,672 ft., before descending very steeply (1 in 4) with a poor surface and sharp bends, to *Kenmore* (*q.v.*), on *Loch Tay* (*q.v.*). To the south-west, beyond beautiful Glen Almond, rises *Ben Chonzie*, 3,048 ft. In 1715, the Clans met at Amulree, and were armed for the Jacobite rising. *Iter. 89, 140, 141, 147.*

ANCRUM BRIDGE, Roxburgh. Map 10, **NT 6** 2.
The bridge spans the Teviot, and a little to the north-west is the village of *Ancrum*, on the Ale Water, which flows southwards to join the larger river. Part of a 13th cent. Cross stands on the village green. *Ancrum House* lies in a fine wooded setting, and nearby, on the banks of the Ale, are a number of old caves, used perhaps in ancient Border warfare. *Chesters House* dates from 1790. Away to the north of the village is Ancrum Moor, or Lilliard's Edge, the scene of one of the last major Border conflicts, fought in 1545, a Roman road threading the site. **2 m. N.E.** of Ancrum, on *Peniel Heugh*, 774 ft., is the Waterloo Monument, erected in 1815. *Iter. 4, 36, 43, 52.*

ANNAN, Dumfries. 5,033. SB. Map 4, **NY 1** 6.
E.C. Wed. **M.D.** Fri. **GOLF.** A small Solway Firth town, on the River Annan, looking across to Bowness in Cumberland and the distant peak of Skiddaw in the Lake District. The river is tidal and noted for its fish. Thomas Carlyle was educated at the old Grammar School, described later by the author as "Hinterschlag Gymnasium" in his "Sartor Resartus." The inscribed *Brus Stone* in the Town Hall may possibly be associated with Robert the Bruce. A nuclear power station has been built on the outskirts of the town at *Chapelcross*. Annandale extends northwards from the Firth, and the scenery in the dale becomes gradually hillier, the finest parts being reached beyond *Moffat* (*q.v.*). **3 m. N.E.** of the town is *Stapleton Tower*, dating from the 16th cent., and modernized. See **Dunscore, Kirtlebridge, Powfoot** and **Ruthwell**. *Iter. 26, 27, 28, 42, 47, 67.*

ANNIESLAND (GLASGOW), Lanark. Map 8, **NS 5** 6.
Iter. 100, 101, 102, 104, 105, 106, 108.

ANSTRUTHER, Fife. 3,302, SB with Kilrenny.
Map 17, **NO 5** 0.
E.C. Wed. **M.D.** Fri. **GOLF.** The ancient Royal Burghs of *Anstruther Easter* and *Anstruther Wester* lie on either side of the harbour, which has become an important herring fishing port. The manse of Anstruther Easter dates from 1590. Both burghs have Churches with unbuttressed

16th cent. towers, showing picturesque outlines, while the Church at *Kilrenny*, a little inland, has a similar tower. *St. Ayles House* is associated with the monks who once occupied *Balmerino Abbey* (*q.v.*). Adjacent to Anstruther Easter, on the north-east side, is *Cellardyke*, another Royal Burgh, these being now united under Kilrenny. Out to sea is the tiny Isle of May, with its bird-watching station and lighthouse, one of the earliest sites for a lighthouse off the coast of Scotland. It is now a National Nature Reserve, where more than 200 species of birds have been recorded. *Iter. 94, 98.*

ANTONINE WALL, Dunbarton; Lanark; Stirling; West Lothian. Map 8, **NS 4** 7 etc., and 16 **NT 0** 8 etc.
See **Roman Wall.**

ANWOTH CHURCH, Kirkcudbright. Map 3, **NX 6** 5.
This ruined Church, built in 1627, retains a mediæval bell and a remarkable 8-ft. high inscribed 17th cent. *Gordon* tomb. Samuel Rutherford was minister here in the 17th cent. and is commemorated by an obelisk on a hill in the parish.

APPIN, Argyll. Map 14, **NM 9** 4.
Situated on the fine Oban to Ballachulish road, and near the point of divergence of the by-road leading westwards to the village of *Port Appin* (*q.v.*), which faces the island of *Lismore* (*q.v.*). The name *Appin* is applied generally to the stretch of picturesque country lying between Loch Creran and the confluence of Loch Leven and *Loch Linnhe* (*q.v.*), and is really part of the land of *Lorne* (*q.v.*). Included in the district is the massif of *Ben Vair*, with its two peaks of over 3,000 ft., stretching in a semi-circle from Glen Duror to *Ballachulish* (*q.v.*), and forming a magnificent viewpoint. R. L. Stevenson described the country in his novel "Kidnapped," which treats also of the celebrated Appin murder in 1752, when Colin Campbell, known as the Red Fox, was shot. Later, James Stewart (James of the Glen) was brought to trial at *Inveraray* (*q.v.*) as the alleged murderer, and, after a trial considered to have been unfair, was hanged at Ballachulish. See **Duror** and **Portnacroish** (for *Castle Stalker*). *Iter. 124.*

APPLECROSS, Ross and Cromarty. Map 22, **NG 7** 4.
A remote West Highland village at the foot of wild hills, situated on Applecross Bay, facing the island of Raasay in the Inner Sound, beyond which lies Skye. The patron saint, named Maelrubha, or Maree, founded a monastery here in A.D. 673, being later buried in the little Church north of the village. Motor boats from Kyle of Lochalsh serve *Toscaig*, which lies some 4 miles to the south, at the head of the small inlet of Loch Toscaig. By road, the only approach is over the famous 2,054-ft. high Pass of "Bealach nam Bo," the Pass of the Cattle, a most difficult route, described under *Tornapress*, and liable to be blocked by snow in winter. The descent from the summit of the pass to Applecross Bay is without serious difficulty. Beyond Loch Toscaig lie the three small Crowlin Islands. A walkers' track goes northwards from Applecross to the mouth of Outer Loch Torridon, giving splendid views, and continuing in a easterly direction to *Shieldaig* (*q.v.*), on the loch of that name, looking towards the splendid *Torridon* (*q.v.*) mountains. *Iter. 219.*

ARBIGLAND, Kirkcudbright. Map 4, **NX 9** 5.
See **Kirkbean.**

ARBIRLOT, Angus. 667. Map 21, **NO 6** 4.
On the Elliot Water. A little to the south-east is *Kelly Castle*, an ancient tower.

ARBROATH, Angus. 19,785. LB. Map 17, **NO 6** 4.
E.C. Wed. **M.D.** Thurs. **GOLF.** A fishing port, Royal Burgh, industrial town and resort, the name being a contraction of *Aberbrothock*. The town is associated with Scott's novel "The Antiquary," under the name of "Fairport." There are sands and a bathing pool, and the coastal stretch away to the north-east is noted for its cliffs and caves, among the latter being Dickmont's Den, Mason's and the Forbidden Cave. A

curious rock stack is known as the Pint Stoup. The Brothock Water flows through the town to enter the North Sea. The notable, ruined Abbey Church of Arbroath (A.M.) is in the style of the early 13th cent., the most impressive portions being the South transept gable and the West front, with its tower and portal. In the South transept is the circular window known as the "O" of Arbroath, formerly lit up and used as a beacon for mariners. In 1951, the Stone of *Scone* (*q.v.*), after having been removed from Westminster Abbey, found a temporary resting place in the Abbey before being returned

1. Abbey.

to England. The Sacristy contains the tomb of William the Lion, who founded the Abbey in 1176, and the Abbot's House, with its 12th cent. vaulted kitchen, has a Folk Museum, and is associated with Robert Bruce. In 1320, the Declaration of Independence was signed in the Abbey. The Arbroath Abbey Pageant has been held in most years during the summer since 1947, and takes place in the Abbey precincts. The fine old restored mansion of *Hospitalfield*, situated a little to the west of the town, is associated with Jonathan Oldbuck in Scott's "The Antiquary," and now contains a collection of Scottish pictures. The house is open from 2 to 5 on Fri. in July and Aug. (see note page 90). Out to sea, some 11 miles south-east, is the *Bell Rock*, or Inchcape Rock lighthouse, marking a dangerous reef. The lighthouse is considered the outstanding achievement of Robert Stevenson, an ancestor of Robert Louis Stevenson. A well-known Scottish ballad tells how the Bell Rock received its name. See **Arbirlot, Auchmithie, Carnoustie** and **St. Vigeans.** *Iter.* 155, 163.

ARBUTHNOTT, Kincardine.   Map 21, **NO 8** 7.
This remotely situated place in the valley of the Bervie Water possesses a very interesting Church, where the Arbuthnott Missal was written in 1491. The Church was Collegiate, and shows 13th and 15th cent. work, being especially notable for the Arbuthnott Aisle, heavily buttressed outside and vaulted inside. *Arbuthnott House* is an old mansion, dating back to the 16th cent. and contains fine 17th cent. plaster ceilings.

ARCHIESTOWN, Moray.   Map 26, **NJ 2** 4.
Iter. 171.

ARDBEG, Isle of Islay, Argyll.   Map 6, **NR 4** 4.
Iter. 245.

ARDCHATTAN, Argyll.   Map 14, **NM 9** 3.
Iter. 124. See **Connel**.

ARDCLACH CHURCH, Nairn.   Map 25, **NH 9** 4.
Near this Church is an unusual detached bell tower (A.M.), perhaps of 17th cent. date and situated high above the River Findhorn.

ARDELVE, Ross and Cromarty.   Map 23, **NG 8** 2.
E.C. Wed. Picturesquely situated at the junction of *Loch Alsh* (*q.v.*) with *Loch Duich* (*q.v.*), in a setting of North-West Highland mountains. From the west side of the road bridge at *Dornie* (*q.v.*), lying a little to the south-east, a passenger ferry connects with *Totaig*, across Loch Duich, from which are fine views up the loch towards the *Five Sisters of Kintail*. A by-road goes north-eastwards from Ardelve, at first following the shores of Loch Long, and passing Killilan. *Ben Killilan*, 2,466 ft., and *Sguman Coinntich*, 2,881 ft., both very fine viewpoints, dominate this part of the valley, which leads into Glen Elchaig. From the western end of the little Loch na Leitreach access is then gained by means of a stiff climb on foot to the lofty *Falls of Glomach* (*q.v.*), which can also be approached from quite a different direction, for which see under *Croe Bridge*. By means of long-distance walkers' paths from the head of Glen Elchaig, it is possible to reach Glen Cannich, farther to the east, described under *Cannich*. *Iter.* 207, 220.

ARDEN, Dunbarton.   Map 15, **NS 3** 8.
Iter. 88, 100, 101, 110, 114, 137.

ARDENTINNY, Argyll.   Map 14, **NS 1** 8.
The terminal point of a fine road from *Dunoon* (*q.v.*) in the land of *Cowal* (*q.v.*). Traversing the shores of Loch Long, the road looks towards the Rosneath peninsula, on which stands, facing Ardentinny, the village of *Coulport* (*q.v.*). There is also a hilly and narrow road continuing up Glen Finart to the shores of *Lock Eck* (*q.v.*), dominated to the west by *Beinn Mhor*, 2,433 ft. This connects with a better road towards *Strachur* (*q.v.*) near the shores of *Loch Fyne* (*q.v.*). *Iter.* 102.

ARDEONAIG, Perth.   Map 16, **NN 6** 3.
Iter. 139.

ARDERSIER, Inverness.   Map 25, **NH 7** 5.
An Inner Moray Firth fishing village, known also as *Campbelltown*. *Iter.* 199.

ARDGARTAN (Argyll National Forest Park), Argyll.
See **Arrochar**.   Map 14, **NN 2** 0.

ARDGAY, Ross and Cromarty.   Map 29, **NH 6** 9.
E.C. Wed. Lies on the Inner Dornoch Firth. In the market square is the White Stone of Kincardine, marking the annual winter market, and formerly built into the walling of what was once an inn. To the west extends Strath Carron, with its river, and roads along both banks, which terminate on the outskirts of Amat Forest, in a setting of lonely hills farther to the west, with the extensive Diebidale and Freevater Forests in the background. *Iter.* 200, 201.

ARDGOUR, Argyll. 371.   Map 18, **NN 0** 6.
The village is situated where the Corran Narrows almost divide *Loch Linnhe* (*q.v.*) into two parts, and *Corran* (*q.v.*) car ferry connects with the opposite shore for *Fort William* (*q.v.*) and the south. This avoids the detour around Loch Eil to the north, which adds some 25 miles to the journey along a narrow and winding road. The Corran lighthouse guards the narrows at this point and dominating the scene in the background rises *Sgurr na h'Eanchainne*, 2,397 ft. The name Ardgour is generally applied to the whole district lying between Loch Linnhe and *Loch Shiel* (*q.v.*), and its finest mountain, though not the highest, is *Garbh Bheinn*, 2,903 ft., which is described under *Inversanda*. About **3 m. S.W.** of Ardgour, on Loch Linnhe, is the entrance to Glen Gour, which has no road.

Arbroath, Angus. The ruined 13th century Abbey, the circular south transept window of which is known as the ' O ' of Arbroath. It was formerly lit up as an aid to shipping off the coast

Arbroath, Angus. The entrance to the old mansion of Hospitalfield, which houses a collection of Scottish pictures

Ardelve, Ross and Cromarty. An old heather-thatched crofter's house, of a type now almost vanished. It stands by Loch Alsh, and was used in the filming of R. L. Stevenson's '*Master of Ballantrae*'

Ardgour, Argyll. A view of the Ardgour hills across Loch Linnhe, at the Corran narrows, which are crossed by a car ferry

Arbuthnott, Kincardine. The 13th to 15th century Church, which is noted for the heavily buttressed Arbuthnott Aisle

Ardclach, Nairn. The detached bell tower of the Church, which is considered to be of 17th century date

PLATE 8 (facing page 98)

Ardmair Bay, Ross and Cromarty. A view across Loch Kanaird towards the Coigach mountains

Ardnamurchan Point, Argyll. The lonely lighthouse at Ardnamurchan Point, the most westerly place on the mainland of Scotland, its name meaning 'Cape of the Great Seas'

Arisaig, Inverness. The Church, with its memorial clock commemorating the Gaelic poet, Alexander Macdonald

Ardrossan, Ayr. The modern Roman Catholic Church of St. Peter-in-Chains, built in Swedish style

Armadale, Isle of Skye, Inverness. The modern Castle (c. 1815), which replaces a former house where Dr. Johnson and Boswell were entertained during their tour of the Hebrides in 1773

Ardoch Roman Camp, Perth. Part of the well-preserved defences of the extensive Roman fort, one of the largest in Great Britain. It is situated near Braco, off A822

PLATE 9 (facing page 99)

and is overlooked at its far end by *Sgurr Dhomhail*, 2,915 ft., the highest peak in Ardgour. **4 m. N.W.** of Ardgour, on the same loch, is *Inverscaddle Bay*, where Glen Scaddle and Cona Glen, both roadless, converge. From here, the views into *Lochaber* (*q.v.*) over Loch Linnhe, looking towards *Ben Nevis* (*q.v.*), are very fine. See **Camusnagaul.** *Iter. 215, 216, 217, 218.*

ARDHASIG BRIDGE (Isle of Lewis), Harris, Inverness. *Iter. 256.* Map 32, **NB 1** 0.

ARDLUI, Dunbarton. Map 15, **NN 3** 1.
Picturesquely situated in a mountain setting, dominated by *Ben Vorlich*, 3,092 ft., to the south-west, and at the northern extremity of *Loch Lomond* (*q.v.*), being the terminal place of call for the loch steamers. In the vicinity is a curious pulpit, hewn out of the solid rock-face, from which sermons have been delivered. The road which has traversed the western shores of Loch Lomond continues northwards from here through lovely Glen Falloch, in Perthshire, towards *Crianlarich* (*q.v.*), with *Beinn Oss*, 3,374 ft., rising away to the west, and *Cruach Ardran*, 3,428 ft., to the east. See **Inveruglas.** *Iter. 100, 110, 111.*

ARDLUSSA, Isle of Jura, Argyll. Map 13, **NR 6** 8.
See **Jura.**

ARDMAIR BAY, Ross and Cromarty. Map 29, **NH 1** 9.
Faces Loch Kanaird, an offshoot of Loch Broom and looks out across Isle Martin towards the *Coigach* mountains. *Iter. 224, 225, 226.*

ARDNADAM, Argyll. Map 14, **NS 1** 8.
On the south shore of the Holy Loch and noted for yachting. *Iter. 102.*

ARDNAMURCHAN POINT, Argyll. Map 12, **NM 4** 6.
The most westerly point on the Scottish mainland, on which stands a lonely lighthouse, from where the views extend northwards out to sea towards the islands of Muck, Eigg and *Rum* (*q.v.*), and westwards to the islands of Coll and *Tiree* (*q.v.*). A rough, gated road connects the lighthouse with *Kilchoan* (*q.v.*). To the north-east of the Point is Sanna Bay, with its white sands, overlooked by Sanna Point. The name Ardnamurchan is also given to the whole of the peninsula which stretches westwards to the Point, and is bounded to the east by the sea lochs of Moidart and *Sunart* (*q.v.*). The last-named is traversed on its northern shores by the road which links Ardnamurchan with the head of the loch. See **Acharacle.** *Iter. 216.*

ARDOCH ROMAN CAMP, Perth. Map 16, **NN 8** 0.
See **Braco.** *Iter. 138, 140.*

ARDRISHAIG, Argyll. 1,058. Map 14, **NR 8** 8.
E.C. Wed. Lies on Loch Gilp, an inlet of *Loch Fyne* (*q.v.*). Here is the eastern end of the 9-mile long *Crinan Canal*, linking Loch Fyne with the Sound of Jura, and terminating at *Crinan* (*q.v.*). The road leading southwards from Ardrishaig forks within 2¼ miles, the rather hilly western branch leading through the *Knapdale* (*q.v.*) hills towards

Loch Killisport, and the main road continuing along the shores of Loch Fyne to *Tarbert* (*q.v.*) See **Cairnbaan** and **Lochgilphead.** *Iter. 119, 121, 122.*

ARDROIL SANDS, Isle of Lewis, Ross and Cromarty. *Iter. 257.* See **Hebrides, Outer** (Lewis). Map 32, **NB 0** 3.

ARDROSSAN, Ayr. 9,532. SB. Map 8, **NS 2** 4.
E.C. Wed. **GOLF.** A holiday resort with sands and bathing, and also a port of departure for steamers to the island of *Arran* (*q.v.*). The modern Church of St. Peter-

1. Castle ruins, 12th cent. 2. St. Peter-in-Chains Church (R.C.).

in-Chains (R.C.) is a striking building in the Swedish style. There are slight remains of a 12th cent. Castle of the Montgomerys. The town stands between the North and South Bays, and beyond the last-named lies *Saltcoats* (*q.v.*), a well-known resort. Horse Island lies off-shore in the North Bay. There are magnificent views to be obtained of the granite peaks of Arran, 15 miles distant across the Firth of Clyde. *Iter. 57, 63, 69, 88.*

ARDTALNAIG, Perth. Map 16, **NN 7** 3.
Iter. 139.

ARDWELL, Wigtown. Map 2, **NX 1** 4.
On the western shores of Luce Bay, in the narrow Rhinns of Galloway peninsula, which extends southwards to the *Mull of Galloway* (*q.v.*). *Ardwell* is a restored late 17th cent. house, with fine gardens. See **Port Logan.** *Iter. 82.*

ARGYLL NATIONAL FOREST PARK, Argyll.
Map 14, **NS 1** 9 etc.
See **Arrochar** (for *Ardgartan*) and **Benmore Estate.**

ARISAIG, Inverness. 500. Map 12, **NM 6** 8.
E.C. Tues. **GOLF.** Situated in the green landscape of South Morar, beyond the hills, with a wonderful outlook from the romantic " Road to the Isles " across Loch nan Cilltean to the islands of Eigg and Rum, and also northwards towards the distant Coolins of Skye. The tower of the Catholic Church is a local landmark, and near a ruined 16th cent. Chapel, in the burial ground, are some old sculptured slabs. In the Church is a memorial clock to Alexander Macdonald, or Alasdair MacMhaigstir Alasdair, the famous Gaelic poet. *Arisaig House* is noted for its rhododendron and shrub gardens, and in the vicinity is a cave in which Prince Charles Edward hid before escaping to France in 1746. Southwards lies the Sound of Arisaig, with the inlet of *Loch nan Uamh* (*q.v.*), noted for its wealth of associations with the Prince. Across the water rise the hills of *Moidart* (*q.v.*), culminating in *Fros Beinn*, 2,876 ft. See **Dalilea, Lochailort** and **Morar.** *Iter. 209.*

ARMADALE, Isle of Skye, Inverness. Map 23, **NG 6** 0.
Lies in the fertile peninsula of Sleat, in the far south of

the island, its shores washed by the Sound of Sleat and the waters of Loch Eishort. There is a steamer service, carrying cars, to *Mallaig* (q.v.) on the mainland. Sleat has been called the " Garden of Skye," and has numerous trees, which were admired by Dr. Johnson and Boswell during their visit in 1773. The house in which they were entertained has been replaced by the modern *Armadale Castle*. A road leads south-westwards along the coast past *Ardvasar*, and terminates by the Aird of Sleat. The views across to the mainland mountains at the head of *Loch Nevis* (q.v.) are very fine. A path continues to the Point of Sleat, with a sandy bay, the most southerly point in Skye. **2 m. N.E.**, off the coast road to Broadford, a narrow by-road climbs north-westwards over a water-shed, giving magnificent views of the *Coolins* (q.v.) before descending to Tarskavaig Bay on Loch Eishort, facing Straithaird Point. See **Isle Ornsay** and **Teangue**. *Iter. 253.*

ARMADALE, Sutherland. Map 30, **NC 7** 6.
A small crofting and fishing township, noted for its sheep. It lies on the stormy northern coast of Scotland, just off the Bettyhill to Thurso road. There is a pleasant bay, with rocky shores. **4 m. W.** is the remote Kirtomy Bay, to the north of which is Kirtomy Point, where boats may pass under the rocks by means of a curious tunnel, as described originally by Thomas Pennant. *Iter. 232, 234, 240.*

ARMADALE, West Lothian. 6,174. SB. Map 9, **NS 9** 6.
A mining town, situated at a height of over 500 ft. *Iter. 16, 86.*

ARNISDALE, Inverness. Map 23, **NG 8** 1.
This remote and tiny village is reached by a hilly, narrow and rough road from *Glenelg* (q.v.), which affords magnificent views, from high ground, across the Sound of Sleat to the islands of Skye and Rum. *Arnisdale* is situated on Outer *Loch Hourn* (q.v.), in a picturesque setting of mountain and loch. West of the village are the Rassaidh islands in the loch. Behind the village rises the steep, twin-peaked *Ben Sgriol*, 3,196 ft., and across the loch is *Ladhar Bheinn*, 3,343 ft., the most westerly of the 3,000-ft. peaks on the mainland, both being exceptionally fine viewpoints. A poorly-defined path leads south-eastwards from Arnisdale, passing the clachan of *Corran*, where the Arnisdale River flows into Loch Hourn from Glen Arnisdale and Glen Dubh, under the slopes of *Druim Fada*, 2,401 ft. This path gives access to the magnificent scenery of Inner Loch Hourn, facing Barrisdale Bay on the south side of the loch. See **Kinloch Hourn**. *Iter. 207.*

ARNISORT, Isle of Skye, Inverness. Map 22, **NG 3** 5.
Iter. 255.

ARNPRIOR, Stirling. Map 16, **NS 6** 9.
Iter. 108, 112, 137.

ARRAN, ISLE OF, Bute. Map 7, **NR 9** 3 etc.
The picturesque island of *Arran* lies in the Firth of Clyde, some 14 miles from the mainland coast. Its attractive western shores are washed by the Kilbrennan Sound, less than 4 miles in width at its narrowest point, and separating it from the narrow *Kintyre* (q.v.) peninsula. Arran is some 20 miles long and 10 miles wide, the finest scenery being concentrated in the northern half. Here, the fine Highland ridges of granite, interesting geologically, are dominated by *Goat Fell*, 2,866 ft. (N.T. Scot.), the highest, though not the wildest peak, and are bitten into from west to east by Glen Iorsa, Glen Rosa and Glen Sannox. Robert Bruce is said to have crossed from the island, in 1307, to *Turnberry* (q.v.), where he commenced his struggle to achieve Scotland's independence. A good road, 56 miles in length, encircles the island, and two others cross it from east to west, the best known being the so-called " String " road, linking Brodick with the south-west coast. There are a number of resorts and villages, with bathing, fishing and other amenities, all of which are described under separate headings. One of the most important approaches from the mainland is by steamer from *Ardrossan* (q.v.) to *Brodick*. The view from the summit of *Goat Fell* is one of the most extensive in Scotland. In addition, fine panoramic views of Arran are obtained from a number of

points on the mainland, notably the Kintyre peninsula, the Ayrshire coast, and also from the island of *Bute* (q.v.). See **Blackwaterfoot, Brodick, Corrie, Kildonan, Lagg, Lamlash, Lochranza, Machrie, Pirnmill, Sannox** and **Whiting Bay.** *Iter. 242.*

ARROCHAR, Dunbarton. 1,367. Map 15, **NN 2** 0.
E.C. Wed. (Winter). Situated at the northern end of the long and narrow *Loch Long* (q.v.), with a steamer pier, and only 2 miles distant from the western shores of *Loch Lomond* (q.v.). To the north-west of the village are some of Argyll's finest peaks, notably *Ben Arthur*, familiarly known as *The Cobbler*, 2,891 ft., *Ben Narnain*, 3,036 ft., and *Ben Ime*, 3,318 ft., the two first-named being famous for rock-climbing, and all being notable *Cowal* (q.v.) viewpoints. **2 m. S.W.** is *Ardgartan*, in the extensive Argyll National Forest Park, covering some 37,000 acres, developed largely by the Forestry Commission, and overlooked to the west by the rocky peak of *The Brack*, 2,580 ft. The park includes also *The Cobbler* and the neighbouring peaks. From here the road climbing westwards through Glen Croe passes *Rest and Be Thankful* (q.v.) before descending to *Loch Fyne* (q.v.). To the south-west of Glen Croe is the Ardgoil Estate of the National Forest Park, in which rises *Ben Donich*, 2,774 ft. There are camping grounds belonging to the Park both at Arrochar and Ardgartan. See **Benmore Estate** and **Tarbet**. *Iter. 88, 101, 102, 103, 117, 137.*

ASCOG, Bute. Map 7, **NS 1** 6.
On the eastern shore of the island, with Loch Ascog to the west. *Iter. 241.*

ASHIESTIEL, Selkirk. Map 10, **NT 4** 3.
Ashiestiel (or *Ashiesteel*) *House* lies on the south bank of the Tweed, and here Scott lived, as sheriff of the county, from 1804 to 1812, while during this period were written " The Lay of the Last Minstrel," " The Lady of the Lake " and " Marmion." Mungo Park, the explorer, visited Scott at Ashiestiel. See **Abbotsford House**.

ASHKIRK, Selkirk. Map 10, **NT 4** 2.
Iter. 11.

ASSYNT, Sutherland. Map 29, **NC 1** 2
and **2** 2.
See **Inchnadamph, Loch Assynt** and **Lochinver**.

ATHELSTANEFORD, East Lothian. Map 17, **NT 5** 7.
The rebuilt Church dates originally from c. 1100. Nearby is a very fine example of a stone-built and crow-stepped gabled doocot. John Home, the writer of " Douglas," produced at Covent Garden, London, in 1757, was at one time minister here. Athelstaneford is associated with a 10th cent. battle fought by the Saxon King Athelstan against the Picts and Scots, which is said to have originated the St. Andrew's Cross as the Scottish flag.

ATHOLL, Perth. Map 19, **NN 6** 7 etc.
This district includes most of northern Perthshire, a mountainous region, bounded to the west by the great trunk road linking Perth with Inverness. It includes within its boundaries the extensive Forest of Atholl, neighboured by the Gaick Forest to the north, all lying in the *Grampians* (q.v.). At *Blair Atholl* (q.v.) is *Blair Castle*, the seat of the Duke of Atholl, and to the north of the village extends the long and narrow Glen Tilt, hemmed in by lofty hills, and extending to the Aberdeen border.

AUCHENCAIRN, Kirkcudbright. 200. Map 3, **NX 7** 5.
E.C. Thurs. An attractive little seaside village, facing Auchencairn Bay, in which lies Hestan Island, with its lighthouse, described in S. R. Crockett's " Raiders " as " Isle Rathan." Near the school is an ancient circular burial cairn, and to the south-east is *Balcary House*, built originally by smugglers. Beyond the house is Balcary Point, overlooking the Solway Firth. *Iter. 73.*

AUCHENCROW, Berwick. Map 11, **NT 8** 6.
This small village, below the 860-ft. high *Horseley Hill*, is associated with gruesome stories of the 18th cent. practices of dealing with witches.

Arrochar, Dunbarton. A bridge on A83, in the heart of the Macfarlane country, in which, at one time, the new moon is said to have been known as ' Macfarlane's Lantern '

Arran, Isle of, Bute. The peak of Goat Fell, 2,866 feet (N.T. Scot.), the highest point in the island. It rises above Brodick Bay, and the first recorded ascent was in 1628

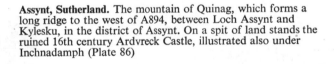

Assynt, Sutherland. The mountain of Quinag, which forms a long ridge to the west of A894, between Loch Assynt and Kylesku, in the district of Assynt. On a spit of land stands the ruined 16th century Ardvreck Castle, illustrated also under Inchnadamph (Plate 86)

Athelstaneford, East Lothian. A notable example of an old stone-built dovecote, showing a crow-stepped gable. It stands behind the church

Atholl, Perth. A toll cottage on A9, at Edendon Bridge to the north-west of Dalnacardoch, on the edge of the vast Forest of Atholl in the Grampian mountains

PLATE 10 (facing page 100)

Auchmithie, Angus. Sandstone cliff scenery at a village which is associated with Sir Walter Scott's novel, ' *The Antiquary,*' under the name of ' Musselcrag '

Auchindown, Banff. The remains of the Castle, built partly by Thomas Cochrane, the favourite of James III. It stands on an unclassified road beyond Parkhead Farm, some 2 miles south-east of Dufftown, off A941

Auchtermuchty, Fife. The ' Thirlestane,' a stone block used formerly for the beam holding the wool-scales. It stands some 3 miles north-west of the village, on the Mournipea road (unclassified) leading westwards off A983

Auldearn, Nairn. The 17th century Boath dovecote (N. T. Scot.). Here, the Royal Standard was raised by Montrose in 1645, when he defeated the Covenanters

Auldgirth, Dumfries. The late 18th century bridge across the River Nith, which Thomas Carlyle's father helped to build

Aultnamain Inn, Ross and Cromarty. A tree, planted in July 1937, to commemorate the march of the London Scottish through the Highlands. It is situated 3 miles north, on A9

[For AVIEMORE see following plate
[For AUCHTERMUCHTY see also Plate 175
[For AUCHTERTYRE see under KINTAIL (Plate 100)

PLATE 11 (facing page 101)

AUCHENDINNY HOUSE, Midlothian. Map 9, **NT 2** 6.
See **Penicuik.** *Iter. 14.*

AUCHENLOCHAN, Argyll. Map 7, **NR 9** 7.
See **Tighnabruaich.** *Iter. 103.*

AUCHENMALG, Wigtown. Map 2, **NX 2** 5.
Iter. 78, 82.

AUCHINBLAE, Kincardine. Map 21, **NO 7** 7.
GOLF. See **Fordoun.** *Iter. 151.*

AUCHINCRUIVE, Ayr. Map 8, **NS 3** 2.
Auchincruive House and its extensive grounds lying in a
wooded setting on the River Ayr, with its sandstone cliffs,
now houses a West of Scotland Agricultural College, and
was presented to the nation in 1930. There are associations with both Burns and Wallace, the latter having reputedly hid in woods in the vicinity. *Iter. 35.*

AUCHINDACHY, Banff. Map 26, **NJ 4** 4.
Iter. 169.

AUCHINDOIR CHURCH, Aberdeen. Map 26, **NJ 4** 2.
See **Lumsden.**

AUCHINDOWN, Banff. Map 26, **NJ 3** 3.
The Castle (A.M.) stands **2 m. S.,** on an eminence surrounded by prehistoric earthworks overlooking the Fiddich
River. It is said to have been founded in the 11th cent.,
and includes a 15th cent. tower, much of the structure
having been destroyed c. 1600. *Iter. 195.*

AUCHINLECK, Ayr. 4,837. Map 8, **NS 5** 2.
Auchinleck House, known locally as *Place Affleck,* lies
3 m. W., near the banks of the River Lugar, and was built
by the father of the famous James Boswell, the biographer
of Dr. Johnson. The house is partly the work of the
brothers Adam, dating from c. 1780, and nearer the river
are the remains of the former Castle. Boswell was buried
in Auchinleck Church in 1795. *Iter. 67.*

AUCHMITHIE, Angus. Map 21, **NO 6** 4.
A quaint little village, situated high up on a rocky part of
the Angus coast, with its sandstone cliffs, which extend
north-eastwards towards the impressive Red Head and
Lang Craig, overlooking Lunan Bay. Both Auchmithie
and Red Head are associated with Scott's "The Antiquary." A picturesque stretch of foreshore also lies to the
south, with the caves of Dickmont's Den, Mason's and
the Forbidden Cave, and also the detached stack of the
Pint Stoup. *Iter. 155.*

AUCHNAGATT, Aberdeen. Map 27, **NJ 9** 4.
Iter. 183.

AUCHTERARDER, Perth. 2,404. SB. Map 16, **NN 9** 1.
E.C. Wed. GOLF. Consists mainly of a single street over
a mile in length, situated to the north of the *Ochil* hills.
In 1716, the old town was burnt by the Earl of Mar. **1 m.
S.,** near the Ruthven Water, is the ancient *Kincardine
Castle,* dismantled in 1645, while in the vicinity stands the
modern Castle. **2½ m. N.W.,** near the Machany Water, is
Strathallan Castle. See **Blackford, Gleneagles Hotel** and
Tullibardine. *Iter. 135, 146.*

AUCHTERDERRAN, Fife. Map 17, **NT 2** 9.
A village on the winding River Ore, with an 18th cent.
Church which preserves a doorway dated 1676. The large
Bowhill colliery is in the vicinity. **2½ m. N.E.,** at *Dogton*
farm, is the inscribed Celtic *Dogton Stone* (A.M.).

AUCHTERLESS, Aberdeen. Map 27, **NJ 7** 4.
A little to the south-west, and just off the Fyvie to Turriff
road, stands *Towie-Barclay* farm, incorporating the remains of *Tolly Castle,* an erstwhile Barclay residence, and
of which the 14th cent. hall is of note. See **Kirktown of
Auchterless.** *Iter. 180.*

AUCHTERMUCHTY, Fife. 1,334. SB. Map 17, **NO 2** 1.
Once a Royal Burgh, this little town stands on the edge of
the fertile Howe of Fife, looking north-westwards to the
Ochil hills. On the Perth road is the *Thirlestane,* a stone
block once used for the beam holding the wool-scales.
An old Tolbooth still remains, dating from 1728, and in

the town are houses with thatched roofs, a comparatively
rare sight in Scotland. *Myres Castle* is 16th cent. and
later. *Iter. 136.*

AUCHTERTOOL, Fife. Map 17, **NT 2** 9.
The ruined *Knockdavie Castle* stands some **2½ m. S.,** on
the farther side of A.907.

AUCHTERTYRE, Ross and Cromarty. Map 23, **NG 8** 2.
From Auchtertyre Hill, to the north-east, on the hilly road
leading towards *Strome* (*q.v.*), there is a magnificent view
towards the lofty mountains at the head of *Loch Duich*
(*q.v.*), notably the picturesque *Five Sisters of Kintail,*
dominated by *Scour Ouran,* 3,505 ft. Below the hill, in
Glen Udalain, a small hydro-electric scheme is in operation. *Iter. 207, 220, 221, 222.*

AUCKINGILL, Caithness. Map 30, **ND 3** 6.
Iter. 200.

AULDEARN, Nairn. 331. Map 25, **NH 9** 5.
A pleasant village, situated a little inland from the Moray
Firth. The circular 17th cent. *Boath* dovecote (N.T. Scot)
stands on the spot where *Montrose* raised the Royal
Standard before the battle in 1645, in which he decisively
routed a force of Covenanters. **½ m. E.** is the ruined
Parish Church. Cairns and cists from the Bronze Age
are to be found in the neighbourhood. **2 m. N.E.** is
Inshoch Tower, now in ruins. **3 m. E.,** off the Forres road,
is the *Hardmuir,* a wooded stretch, supposedly the scene
of the encounter of Macbeth and Banquo with the witches.
Iter. 175, 198, 199.

AULDGIRTH, Dumfries. Map 4, **NX 9** 8.
The River Nith flows through a picturesque gorge below
the bridge, dating from c. 1780, which Carlyle's father
helped to build. **2 m. S.E.,** near the river, is *Ellisland*
farm, where Burns composed Tam o' Shanter among other
works. **2 m. W.** is the ruined 16th cent. tower of *Lag.*
3 m. S.E. is *Isle Tower,* dated 1587, in a good state of
preservation, situated on the west bank of the Nith. See
Dunscore. *Iter. 27, 48, 56, 67.*

AULTBEA, Ross and Cromarty. 500. Map 22, **NG 8** 8.
E.C. Wed. **M.D.** Tues./Fri. This crofting village is
situated in a remote part of *Wester Ross,* on Loch Ewe,
facing the Isle of Ewe, and lies just off the Poolewe to
Ullapool road. In both the World Wars Loch Ewe was
of considerable naval importance. Northwards extends
the peninsula of Rudha Mor, terminated by Greenstone
Point. The road continuing northwards towards *Gruinard
Bay* (*q.v.*) passes the curiously-named clachans of *First
Coast* and *Second Coast.* See **Poolewe.** *Iter. 206, 222.*

AULTMORE, Banff. Map 26, **NJ 4** 5.
Iter. 178.

AULTNAHARRIE, Ross and Cromarty.
  Map 29, **NH 1** 9.
Lies on the south side of Loch Broom, facing *Ullapool*
(*q.v.*), to which it is connected by passenger ferry. *Ben
Goleach,* 2,052 ft., a good viewpoint, is the prominent hill
rising to the west, overlooking Loch Broom and Little
Loch Broom. A track leads southwards, climbing steeply
over the hills, with fine views of the great *Teallach* moun-
tains, before descending to *Dundonnell* (*q.v.*). Near
Aultnaharrie are two examples of ruined brochs.

AULTNAMAIN INN, Ross and Cromarty.
  Map 31, **NH 6** 8.
Stands on the fine moorland road linking *Evanton* (*q.v.*)
and *Bonar Bridge* (*q.v.*), an alternative to the longer route
by way of *Tain* (*q.v.*). The inn was formerly a resting-place
for drovers on their southward journey. Away to the
south-west rises *Beinn Tharsuinn,* 2,270 ft. On the descent
of Struie Hill (A.A. viewpoint), **3 m. N.,** a fine view is obtained over Dornoch Firth. *Iter. 200.*

AVIEMORE, Inverness. 650. Map 25, **NH 8** 1.
E.C. Wed. A well-known Highland resort in a richly-
wooded stretch of Strath Spey, the broad valley dividing
the *Monadhliath* and *Cairngorm* (*q.v.*) mountains, and on
the western fringe of the great forests of *Rothiemurchus*

(q.v.) and Glenmore, between the Spey and the lofty Cairngorm summits. The last-named forest is reached by way of *Coylumbridge* (q.v.), on the road to *Nethybridge* (q.v.), which keeps to the east of the Spey. Climbing, walking, and winter sports are all a feature of Aviemore. To the south-west of the village rises the *Rock of Craigellachie*, which gave its name to the well-known slogan of the Grants: "Stand fast—Craigellachie." In the Queen's Forest of Glenmore is one of the newly-created National Forest Parks, extending to 12,500 acres, in which *Glen-*

Academy, founded 13th cent.	12.	Carnegie Library County Buildings	10. 9.	"Tam o'Shanter" Inn Town Hall, Town	7.
Auld Brig	2.	Loudoun Hall	11.	Buildings and	
Auld Kirk (1655)	5.	New Brig	1.	Information Bureau	3.
Burns' Statue	8.	St. John's Tower	4.	Wallace Tower	6.

more Lodge, at the eastern end of lovely *Loch Morlich* (q.v.), backed by *Cairn Gorm*, 4,084 ft., and *Cairn Lochan*, 3,983 ft., is now a training centre for mountaineering. Nearby is a public camping ground. Winter ski-ing takes place in this district. A path from here climbs over the Ryvoan Pass, with the picturesque Green Loch, and leads eventually to Nethybridge through the Forest of Abernethy, another way being by means of the Sluggan Pass, farther to the west. The views of the Cairngorms are particularly fine as seen from Aviemore, and the cleft of the well-known *Lairig Ghru* (q.v.) Pass can be clearly discerned in the distance. See **Kincraig** and **Lynwilg.** *Iter. 138, 140, 147, 150, 169, 170, 171, 172, 173, 208.*

AVOCH, Ross and Cromarty. 1,270. Map 25, **NH 7** 5. **E.C.** Thurs. A fishing village, situated in the *Black Isle* (q.v.), on the shores of the Inner Moray Firth. To the

south, on Ormond Hill, are traces of the former *Avoch Castle. Iter. 203.*

AYR, Ayr. 43,685. LB. Map 8, **NS 3** 2. **E.C.** Wed. **M.D.** Tues. GOLF. An attractive resort, seaport and industrial Royal Burgh, in the Kyle division of the county, on Ayr Bay in the Firth of Clyde, with a sandy beach and forming a convenient centre for the *Burns Country* (q.v.). The neighbouring resorts of *Prestwick* (q.v.), with its important airport, and *Troon* (q.v.), are both well-known golfing centres. Ayr is famous for its Burns associations, notably the old thatched "*Tam o' Shanter*" Inn, and the "*Twa Brigs,*" of which the "*Auld Brig*" dates back possibly to the 13th cent. (See **Alloway.**) The Town Buildings are surmounted by a slender spire, and the Academy is a 13th cent. foundation. *Wallace's* tower, built in 1832, has a statue of Wallace, and near the station is the Burns statue. The *Auld Kirk* dates from 1655, with Cromwellian associations, and in it Burns was baptized. The *Fort Castle* is the tower of the old Greyfriars Church of *St John*, in which Bruce's Parliament met in 1315, and forms a splendid viewpoint, including within its orbit the island of Arran. The 16th cent. *Loudoun Hall*, of much architectural interest, has been restored. The Hall is the oldest building in the town, the original owner having been James Tait, a burgess of Ayr, while later owners, the Campbells, enlarged the house. In the late 18th cent. the fortunes of Loudoun declined rapidly, until the commencement of its restoration in 1938. John Macadam, the well-known maker of roads, was born at Ayr, in 1756. There is a racecourse, situated to the east of the town. 2½ m. S., on the coast, stands the ruined *Greenan Castle*, and beyond it is the cape known as the *Heads of Ayr.* See **Auchincruive, Culzean Castle, Dunure, Kirkoswald, Maybole** and **Tarbolton.** *Iter. 20, 21, 27, 35, 49, 55, 60, 66, 75, 76, 77, 79, 80, 84, 88.*

AYTON, Berwick. 572. Map 11, **NT 9** 6. **E.C.** Thurs. Stands on the north bank of the Eye Water, whose wooded reaches are here spanned by a single-arched bridge. There is a modern Castle. The church lodge was once a toll-house. The old Church, now in ruins, has been replaced by a modern structure. See **Eyemouth.** *Iter. 1, 41.*

BADDAGYLE, Ross and Cromarty. Map 29, **NC 0** 1. Situated at the western extremity of Loch Baddagyle, in the district known as the Aird of Coigach. Here, the road from Ullapool forks, the left branch going westwards past Loch Owskeich to *Achiltibuie* (q.v.), dominated by *Ben More Coigach*, 2,438 ft., and the right fork climbing by means of a reverse turn on to moorland, to continue its tortuous way towards *Inverkirkaig* (q.v.) and *Lochinver* (q.v.). From the summit, a magnificent panoramic view of the distant, isolated Sutherland peaks to the north, dominated by the long ridge of *Suilven*, 2,399 ft., is gained. To the south-east of Loch Baddagyle is the beautiful mountain-encircled *Loch Lurgain* (q.v.) on the road to *Ullapool* (q.v.). 2½ m. N. of Baddagyle, after crossing the River Polly, the strangely-shaped Loch Sionascaig is seen to the right. *Iter. 226.*

BADDANLOCH, Sutherland. Map 30, **NC 7** 3. *Iter. 235.*

Aviemore, Inverness. A view from Strath Spey across Rothiemurchus Forest towards Carn Eilrig, in the foothills of the Cairngorm mountains. To the east of this hill goes the long-distance walkers' path through the rugged Lairig Ghru pass, leading through a cleft of the Cairngorms towards the upper reaches of the River Dee in Glen Dee

Ayton, Berwick. The church lodge, which was at one time used as a toll house on the Berwick to Edinburgh road until tolls were abolished

Ayr, Ayr. The Auld Kirk of 1655, in which Robert Burns was baptized. The building was restored in 1952, and the interior contains three lofts, known as the Merchants', Sailors' and Traders' Lofts

Ayr, Ayr. The 'Tam O'Shanter' Inn, associated with Robert Burns. It was bought for the town in 1943

Ayr, Ayr. The late mediaeval Auld Brig, now used for foot passengers only. It is one of the famous 'Twa Brigs' of the town, the other being a modern replacement of a bridge first erected in 1788

PLATE 12 (facing page 102)

Badenoch, Inverness. Ruthven Barracks, to the east of the River Spey, at Kingussie, off B970. They were built in 1716 and enlarged by General Wade in 1734. The Highlanders destroyed them after the '45 Rising

Balfron, Stirling. A signpost near the station, which gives distances in miles and yards

Ballachulish, Argyll. The Monument to James of the Glens, who was hanged for allegedly shooting Colin Roy Campbell of Glenure, known as the 'Red Fox,' on 14th May, 1752, a crime he never committed. The white stone at the top of the monument is visible from the ferry when in mid-stream

Ballantrae, Ayr. The ruined stronghold of Ardstinchar, once held by the Bargany Kennedys. Robert Louis Stevenson came here in 1876, but the scene of his '*Master of Ballantrae*' is not laid here

Balmacara, Ross and Cromarty. The Monument facing Loch Alsh, erected in 1863 to Colonel Donald Murchison, factor to the Earl of Seaforth during the '45 Rising. He sent the Seaforth rents for seven years to the exiled Earl, and is said to have been ignored after his return

Balmaclellan, Kirkcudbright. The churchyard monument to Robert Paterson, famous as Sir Walter Scott's 'Old Mortality.' His wife kept a school here for 20 years, while he repaired Covenanters' tombstones all over Scotland

PLATE 13 (facing page 103)

[For BALLATER see Plate 172

BADENOCH, Inverness. Map 19, **NN 5** 8 etc.
This mountainous district in the *Grampians* (*q.v.*) stretches roughly from the neighbourhood of *Loch Laggan* (*q.v.*) and the lonely head-waters of the Upper Spey valley to the lofty *Cairngorms* (*q.v.*). A good centre for its exploration is *Kingussie* (*q.v.*), where the ruins of *Ruthven Barracks* are associated with the notorious Wolf of Badenoch, whose former stronghold stood on the site. Prior to that, Badenoch was Comyn country, passing, after their annihilation, to the Earls of Moray. At the western extremity of Loch Laggan is Glen Spean, where Badenoch meets the district of *Lochaber* (*q.v.*). See **Lochindorb.**

BAILLIESTON, Lanark. 6,070. Map 8, **NS 6** 6.
A town engaged in the coal and iron industry. *Iter. 16.*

BALALLAN, Isle of Lewis, Ross and Cromarty.
Iter. 256. Map 32, **NB 2** 2.

BALBEGGIE, Perth. Map 17, **NO 1** 2.
To the north-east rise the *Sidlaw* hills, with the prominent *Dunsinane Hill*, 1,012 ft., on the summit of which is an ancient fort, said to have been Macbeth's castle. *Iter. 151, 153.*

BALBLAIR, Ross and Cromarty. Map 25, **NH 7** 6.
Iter. 203.

BALERNO, Midlothian. Map 9, **NT 1** 6.
See **Currie.**

BALFRON, Stirling. 1,107. Map 15, **NS 5** 8.
An attractively situated village near the Endrick Water, with the *Campsies* and the *Fintry* hills rising away to the south and east. See **Killearn.** *Iter. 108.*

BALINTORE, Ross and Cromarty. 349. Map 31, **NH 8** 7.
A fishing village on the Moray Firth, once known as *Abbotshaven*. A little to the north is *Hilton of Cadboll*, where a sculptured 7th cent. stone was found, and is now in the Edinburgh Museum of National Antiquities. See **Shandwick.**

BALLACHULISH, Argyll. 727. Map 18, **NN 0** 5.
E.C. Wed. A straggling village, situated about a mile east of the busy car ferry over Loch Leven to *North Ballachulish* (*q.v.*). Roofing slates are quarried in the neighbourhood. Behind the village rises *Ben Vair*, with its two 3,000-ft. peaks, and away to the north, beyond the loch, are the mountains of *Mamore Forest* (*q.v.*). Near the ferry is the monument marking the spot where James of the Glen was hanged, in 1752, after the famous *Appin* (*q.v.*) murder trial at *Inveraray* (*q.v.*). The identity of the real murderer has never been solved, and R. L. Stevenson has graphically portrayed the events in his novel "Kidnapped." The views from here across Loch Linnhe towards the Ardgour Hills, dominated by *Garbh Bheinn*, 2,903 ft. (See **Inversanda**) are exceptionally fine, and gorgeous sunsets are a feature at times. Equally fine are the views looking up Loch Leven towards the entrance to the famous pass of *Glencoe* (*q.v.*), dominated from this end by the conical *Pap of Glencoe*, 2,430 ft. The ferry avoids the long detour around Loch Leven for motorists proceeding from Glencoe towards *Fort William* (*q.v.*). South-westwards from Ballachulish, the road to *Oban* (*q.v.*) through the *Appin* (*q.v.*) country traverses the shores of Outer Loch Linnhe amid delightful scenery below the massif of *Ben Vair*, with its peaks of *Sgurr Dhearg*, 3,362 ft., and *Sgurr Dhonuill*, 3,284 ft., both fine viewpoints. See **Ardgour, Duror** and **Kentallen.** *Iter. 124, 142.*

BALLANTRAE, Ayr. 887. Map 2, **NX 0** 8.
A pleasant little holiday resort in the *Carrick* (*q.v.*) district, on Ballantrae Bay, north of the estuary of the River Stinchar, with a sand and shingle beach. The view out to sea is dominated by the 1,114-ft. high rock of *Ailsa Craig*. Near the bridge over the Stinchar is the ruined *Ardstinchar Castle*, an ancient Kennedy stronghold, and up the delightful river valley are two further Kennedy castles, those of *Knockdolian* and *Kirkhill*. South of Ballantrae, on the road to *Stranraer* (*q.v.*), is the beautifully wooded Glen App, in which stands a small mid-19th cent.

Church, restored in the present century in memory of the Hon. Elsie Mackay, lost when flying the Atlantic in 1928. To the north, on the *Girvan* (*q.v.*) road, is *Kennedy's Pass*, the highlight of one of the finest coastal drives in southern Scotland. R. L. Stevenson used the name of Ballantrae for his well-known novel "The Master of Ballantrae." See **Colmonell.** *Iter. 55, 80, 84.*

BALLATER, Aberdeen. 1,155. SB. Map 20, **NO 3** 9.
E.C. Thurs. GOLF. A well-known holiday resort on Royal *Deeside* (*q.v.*), at a height of nearly 700 ft., surrounded by wooded hills, and dominated by *Lochnagar*, 3,786 ft. (*q.v.*), rising far to the south-west. North of the town is *Craig-an-Darroch*, 1,250 ft., a good viewpoint, below which the pretty pass of Ballater is threaded by the old Deeside road, on which stands the ruined Kirk of *St. Nathalan of Tullich*, preserving some sculptured Celtic stones. South-west of the town is the long valley of Glen Muick, with picturesque Loch Muick, dominated by the *Broad Cairn*, 3,268 ft., and beloved of Queen Victoria. It gives access for long-distance walkers to the *White Mounth* plateau and *Lochnagar*, and by the long Capel Mounth track to *Braedownie* (*q.v.*), at the head of Glen Clova. In Glen Muick is *Birkhall*, dating from 1715, a Royal home, bought by King Edward VII when Prince of Wales. A motoring road extends for some 9 miles down the glen, but the loch is accessible only on foot. Eastwards of Glen Muick lies the Forest of Glen Tanner, with *Mount Keen*, 3,077 ft. The narrow road linking the Dee valley with the upper valley of the Don, to the north, goes through the hills by way of *Gairnshiel Lodge* (*q.v.*), the lofty section beyond this point being liable to become snow-bound in winter. 1½ m. N.E. of Ballater, on the main Aboyne road, is Bridge of Tullich, a noted viewpoint, from which Lochnagar is prominent. See **Balmoral, Cambus o' May, Crathie Church** and **Pannanich Wells.** *Iter. 141, 152, 167, 168, 174, 179.*

BALLINDALLOCH CASTLE, Banff. Map 26, **NJ 1** 3.
See **Dalnashaugh Inn.**

BALLINLUIG, Perth. Map 20, **NN 9** 5.
Iter. 120, 139, 140, 148, 150, 158.

BALLOCH, Dunbarton. 1,719. Map 15, **NS 3** 8.
E.C. Wed. Here is the pier from which steamers start on their journey up picturesque *Loch Lomond* (*q.v.*). The town stands actually on the River Leven, which flows southwards from the loch into the Clyde. In the park is the mound of the vanished Castle associated with both Wallace and Bruce. To the north of Balloch, on the eastern shores of Loch Lomond, are the modern houses of *Balloch Castle* and, farther north, *Boturich Castle*. *Iter. 114, 137.*

BALLYGRANT, Isle of Islay, Argyll. Map 6, **NR 3** 6.
Iter. 243, 247.

BALMACARA, Ross and Cromarty. 50. Map 23, **NG 8** 2.
E.C. Thurs. The 8,000-acre *Balmacara* estate, extending over most of the peninsula which includes *Kyle of Lochalsh* (*q.v.*) and *Plockton* (*q.v.*), incorporates *Balmacara House*, now a school, and belongs to the N.T. Scot. There are fine views over Loch Alsh and Kyle Rhea, beyond which lies the island of Skye, in which *Beinn na Caillich*, 2,396 ft., faces Balmacara across the waters of *Loch Alsh* (*q.v.*). See **Auchtertyre.** *Iter. 207, 220, 221, 222.*

BALMACLELLAN, Kirkcudbright. Map 3, **NX 6** 7.
A delightful hillside village in *Galloway* (*q.v.*), in the churchyard of which is a monument to Robert Paterson, Scott's "Old Mortality." There is also a Covenanter's tombstone with an inscription. Another tombstone shows weapons used in the Crimean War. Celtic relics have been excavated in the vicinity and are preserved in one of the Edinburgh museums. See **Caerlaverock.** *Iter. 71, 75.*

BALMAGHIE, Kirkcudbright. Map 3, **NX 7** 6.
See **Laurieston.**

BALMAHA, Stirling. Map 15, **NS 4** 9.
A calling-place for the *Loch Lomond* (*q.v.*) steamers. A

picturesque group of wooded islands lies in the loch at this point. The road along the loch-side continues north-westwards through the Pass of Balmaha towards *Rowar-dennan* (*q.v.*). *Iter. 104, 115.*

BALMANNO, Perth.   Map 17, **NO 1** 1.
See **Bridge of Earn.**

BALMEDIE, Aberdeen.   Map 27, **NJ 9** 1.
Iter. 181, 182, 183, 185.

BALMERINO ABBEY, Fife. 533.   Map 17, **NO 3** 2.
This ruined Cistercian Abbey (N.T. Scot.), founded in 1229, stands in a delightful setting on the south shore of the Firth of Tay. The beautiful Chapter House dates from the 15th cent. Monks from Melrose built the Abbey, which was burnt in 1547 and sacked in 1559. (Not open.) *Naughton House* has a fine old doocot. Each one of a block of modern houses facing the Firth carries an inscription giving the last words addressed to his troops by Lt.-Col. David Scrymgeour-Wedderburn before the Anzio battle in the Second World War. *Iter. 126.*

BALMORAL CASTLE, Aberdeen.   Map 20, **NO 2** 9.
The Highland residence of Her Majesty, the Queen, situated on a curve of the river in Royal *Deeside* (*q.v.*), in the district of Mar, and faced by the wooded *Craig Gowan*, 1,319 ft., a viewpoint crowned by a cairn. Balmoral Castle was first mentioned in 1484, and was at that time known as *Bouchmorale*. In 1848 it was first visited by Queen Victoria, and in 1852 the estate was purchased by the Prince Consort, who had it rebuilt in the present " Scottish Baronial " style, the new structure being first occupied by the Royal Family in 1855. Later, Queen Victoria added the Ballochbuie Forest to the property, and it has ever since remained a Royal residence. The grounds are generally open to the public from 10 to 5, on Tues., Wed. and Thurs. during the summer in the absence of the Royal Family (see note page 90). This is Clan Farquharson country, and a mile west of Balmoral is a mound known as Carn na Cuimhne, associated with the clan. To the south of the Castle is Glen Gelder, leading to Balmoral Forest and the lofty *White Mounth* (*q.v.*) group, and it was by this route that Queen Victoria and the Prince Consort climbed *Lochnagar* (*q.v.*) on ponies, in 1848. Away to the north-west of Balmoral, beyond Invercauld Forest, rises *Ben Avon*, 3,843 ft., one of the loftiest of the *Cairngorm* (*q.v.*) peaks. See **Ballater, Braemar** and **Crathie Church.** *Iter. 152, 160, 167, 168, 179.*

BALMORE, Stirling.   Map 8, **NS 6** 7.
Iter. 113.

BALNACRA, Ross and Cromarty.   Map 24, **NG 9** 4.
Iter. 221, 222, 223.

BALNAGOWN CASTLE, Ross and Cromarty.
See **Logie Easter.**   Map 31, **NH 7** 7.

BALQUHIDDER, Perth. 671.   Map 15, **NN 5** 2.
E.C. Wed. Beautifully situated to the east of Loch Voil, about **2 m. W.** of Balquhidder station on the Callander to Lochearnhead road, in the country of the MacGregors, and upon which looks down the lofty ridge known as the *Braes of Balquhidder*. In the churchyard of the roofless old Kirk is buried Rob Roy, the famous freebooter and hero of Scott's well-known novel of that name. Three sculptured stones are said to mark the grave of Rob Roy and some of his family, and one stone is carved with the MacGregor arms. Another stone commemorates members of the Clan Laurin, murdered in 1588 by incendiarists from Glen Dochart. South of Balquhidder, the short Glen Buckie penetrates into the green hills. **7 m. W.,** beyond Loch Voil and its continuation Loch Doine, reached by a rough and narrow by-way, is *Inverlochlaraig*, where Rob Roy died in 1734. *Stobinian*, 3,821 ft., and *Beinn Tulachan*, 3,099 ft., overlook this lonely place. *Iter. 107, 111, 139, 141, 142, 144.*

BALVENIE CASTLE, Banff.   Map 26, **NJ 3** 3.
See **Dufftown.**

BANAVIE, Inverness.   Map 18, **NN 7** 7.
Stands on the road from *Corpach* (*q.v.*) to *Gairlochy* (*q.v.*), and provides a splendid view of *Ben Nevis*, 4,406 ft. (*q.v.*). **2 m. N.E.,** on the west bank of the River Lochy, is *Tor Castle*, near which stands a ruined tower of the Clan Chattan. Two miles farther, in the same direction, to the west of the road, is the entrance to the roadless Glen Loy, down which Prince Charles Edward marched in 1745. *Iter. 209, 214, 215.*

BANCHORY, Kincardine. 1,877. SB.   Map 21, **NO 6** 9.
E.C. Thurs. **M.D.** Alt. Wed. GOLF. A pleasant holiday resort on Royal *Deeside* (*q.v.*), near the point where the Water of Feugh, here spanned by the narrow Bridge of Feugh, carrying the date 1799, but probably of earlier construction, and lying in a picturesque, wooded setting, joins the Dee. Away to the north rises the *Hill of Fare*, 1,545 ft., on the slopes of which a battle was fought, in 1562. From Banchory a road leads southwards, following the Water of Feugh through Glen Dye towards the *Cairn o' Mounth Pass* (*q.v.*). The road leading south-eastwards to Stonehaven, which rises to nearly 800 ft., with fine views, is known, when crossing the hills, as the *Slug Road*. To the south of this road, and about **4 m.** from Banchory, lies the 16th cent. *Tilquhillie Castle*, now a farmhouse. See **Crathes Castle.** *Iter. 152, 163, 168, 190, 191, 197.*

BANCHORY DEVENICK, Kincardine.   Map 21, **NJ 9** 0.
Iter. 168, 174.

BANFF, Banff. 3,347. SB.   Map 27, **NJ 6** 6.
E.C. Wed. GOLF. An ancient seaport, Royal Burgh and resort, with sands and bathing, on Banff Bay at the mouth of the River Deveron. On the opposite shore of the river stands *Macduff* (*q.v.*). Banff has fragmentary remains of the former Castle. *Duff House* (A.M.),

Castle remains	1.	Library and Museum	4.
Church remains and old churchyard	2.	Town House (1796), Biggar Fountain and the Old	
Duff House, c. 1735	3.	Cross	5.

William Adam's masterpiece, dating from c. 1735, has fine grounds, which are now a public park belonging to the town. It is open weekdays, 10 to 4 or 7; Sun., 2 to 4 or 7 (see note page 90). The shaft of an old Cross stands at the Planestanes. The Town House dates from 1796. There are some remains of the old Church, and a few 17th cent. houses have survived. On the site of the former gallows is the *Biggar* fountain. Southey, Byron and Doctor Johnson all have associations with the town.

Balmerino Abbey, Fife. The inscribed portico in a block of houses built by Mr. Henry J. Scrymgeour-Wedderburn, Hereditary Standard Bearer of Scotland. They are in memory of his brother, a colonel of the Scots Guards, who died of wounds at Anzio, in Italy, in 1944

Balquhidder, Perth. The grave of Rob Roy, the famous freebooter, who died on December 28th, 1734

Banchory, Kincardine. A memorial fountain, dated 1870, on A93

Balvenie Castle, Banff. The ruined 15th century Atholl castle of Balvenie, which retains its original 'yett,' or iron gate. Earlier owners were the Comyns, followed by the Douglases. It stands near Dufftown station, off A941

Banff, Banff. The Biggar Fountain, on the site of the former gallows, where, in 1701, James Macpherson, the outlaw and fiddler, offered his instrument to the crowd before going to his death

Banff, Banff. Duff House, built c. 1735, and considered to be William Adam's masterpiece. It was donated to the town by the Duke of Fife

PLATE 14 (facing page 104)

Barcaldine Castle, Argyll. Barcaldine Castle, a 16th century home of the Campbells of Barcaldine, which was restored by the 10th Laird in 1896

Bannockburn, Stirling. The flagpole, set up in 1870, marking the reputed site of Robert Bruce's headquarters in the battle of June 24th, 1314. The traditional site of the battlefield is now partly the property of the National Trust for Scotland

Bargrennan, Kirkcudbright; Wigtown. The Martyrs' Stone, at the south-west extremity of Loch Trool, in the Glen Trool National Forest Park. It lies about 4 miles north-east of Bargrennan, off an unclassified road

Barnton (Edinburgh), Midlothian. Lauriston Castle, mainly modern, but incorporating 16th century work by Sir Archibald Napier, father of the inventor of logarithms. It was once the home of Sir John Law, who sponsored the disastrous ' Mississippi Scheme ' of 1720

Bass Rock, East Lothian. The Bass Rock, which stands out to sea some 3 miles north-east of North Berwick. It was used as a Covenanters' prison after 1671

PLATE 15 (facing page 105)

2½ m. W.N.W., on a rocky piece of coast, is the village of *Whitehills* (*q.v.*), sheltered by Knock Head. **3 m. S.**, off the Huntly road, is *Kirktown of Alvah* (*q.v.*). See **Boyndie Bay**. *Iter. 170, 180, 181, 182, 183, 188, 194, 198, 199.*

BANKEND, Dumfries. Map 4, **NY 0** 6.
See **Caerlaverock**. *Iter. 28.*

BANKFOOT, Perth. 726. Map 16, **NO 0** 3.
E.C. Thurs. A *Strathmore* (*q.v.*) village, on the Garry Burn, with the level Cornleith Moss and beyond it the Muir of Thorn, both lying to the north-east. *Iter. 149, 150.*

BANKSHILL, Dumfries. Map 4, **NY 1** 8.
Iter. 45.

BANNOCKBURN, Stirling. 4,759. Map 16, **NS 8** 9.
E.C. Wed. A coal-mining village, on the Bannock Burn, a mile to the north of which, and nearer to *St. Ninian's* (*q.v.*), is the famous battlefield where Bruce defeated the English under Edward II in 1314. The *Borestone* (N.T. Scot.), nearby, is, by tradition, where Bruce displayed the Scottish Royal Standard. As an immediate result of the battle, Stirling surrendered, Edward II fled to Dunbar, and Scotland achieved her independence. Scott's "Lord of the Isles" describes the conflict between Bruce and De Bohun. In the vicinity was fought also the battle of Sauchieburn, in 1488, when James III was defeated and afterwards fatally stabbed. Prince Charles Edward made *Bannockburn House* his headquarters in January, 1746. *Iter. 95.*

BARASSIE, Ayr. Map 8, **NS 3** 3.
GOLF. See **Troon**. *Iter. 88.*

BARBARAVILLE, Ross and Cromarty. Map 25, **NH 7** 7.
Iter. 201.

BARCALDINE CASTLE, Argyll. Map 14, **NM 9** 4.
This old castle is situated on a level piece of land which juts out from the main *Benderloch* (*q.v.*) district, and is bounded on three sides by Ardmucknish Bay, the Lynn of Lorne and Loch Creran. The castle is a typical example of the 16th cent. Scottish baronial style (1579) and has been restored. A by-road leads to the castle, diverging from the main Oban to Ballachulish road at Benderloch station, and terminating on the shores of Loch Creran opposite the small island of Eriska.

BARGRENNAN, Kirkcudbright; Wigtown. 280.
  Map 2, **NX 3** 7.
From *Bargrennan* Church, near the River Cree, a road turns north-eastwards, leading shortly to *Loch Trool* (*q.v.*) in Glen Trool with the extensive National Forest Park, one of the most beautiful pieces of country in *Galloway* (*q.v.*). Beyond rises the *Merrick*, 2,764 ft., the loftiest mountain in the Lowlands, and farther east is *Corserine*, 2,668 ft., the monarch of the *Rhinns of Kells*. Westwards from Bargrennan are three small lochs, those of Ochiltree, Dornal and Maberry. **10½ m. N.**, on the narrow and winding moorland road leading towards Maybole, is the lonely Nick o' the Balloch Pass, 1,280 ft., in a fine, hilly setting, looking eastwards to *Shalloch on Minnoch*, 2,520 ft., beyond which lies the remote Loch Macaterick. Before the pass is reached, the road crosses into Ayrshire, with Loch Moan to the west, and *Kirriereoch Hill*, 2,562 ft., away to the east, facing *Mullwharchar*, 2,270 ft. See **Rowantree**. *Iter. 71, 79.*

BARNBARROCH, Kirkcudbright. Map 3, **NX 8** 5.
Iter. 73.

BARNTON (Edinburgh), Midlothian. Map 9, **NT 1** 7.
A little to the north-east stands *Lauriston Castle*, late 16th cent., attached to a modern house, now public property, and once the home of John Law, author of the disastrous early 18th cent. Mississippi scheme. Open in summer, daily, except Fri., 2 to 5; winter, Sat. and Sun. only, 2 to 4 (see note page 90). The grounds of the neighbouring *Barnton House* are also public. See **Cramond Bridge**. *Iter. 17, 89, 90, 92, 93, 94, 96.*

BARR, Ayr. Map 2, **NX 2** 9.
A little anglers' resort of the *Carrick* (*q.v.*) district, in the valley of the Upper Stinchar River looking south-eastwards to *Polmadie Hill*, 1,852 ft. **6 m. E.S.E.**, on a narrow, winding moorland road leading from Maybole in a southerly direction towards *Bargrennan* (*q.v.*), is the Nick o' the Balloch Pass, at a height of 1,280 ft., with views towards *Shalloch on Minnoch*, 2,520 ft., and the *Merrick*, 2,764 ft., the monarch of the *Galloway* (*q.v.*) Highlands. South of Barr is Changue Forest, and farther to the east is Carrick Forest, both being part of the fine Glen Trool National Forest Park. See **Loch Trool**. *Iter. 78, 84.*

BARRA, ISLE OF, Inverness. Map 32, **NF 6** 0 etc.
See **Hebrides, Outer** (Barra).

BARRHEAD, Renfrew. 13,752. SB. Map 8, **NS 4** 5.
E.C. Tues. GOLF. A manufacturing town, standing on

the Levern Water, with an extensive and lofty moorland area lying to the south, in which a number of reservoirs are situated. See **Clarkston** and **Neilston**. *Iter. 57, 60, 62.*

BARRHILL, Ayr. 277. Map 2, **NX 2** 8.
E.C. Tues. Situated in the Duisk valley, with moorland country to the west and east. The road leading southwards towards *New Luce* (*q.v.*), in Wigtownshire, traverses lonely moorlands which are threaded by the Cross Water of Luce, the way being gated, narrow and hilly. See **Bargrennan**. *Iter. 71, 78.*

BARROGILL CASTLE, Caithness. Map 30, **ND 2** 7.
See **East Mey**.

BARRY, Angus. Map 17, **NO 5** 3.
GOLF. See **Carnoustie**. *Iter. 155.*

BARVAS, Isle of Lewis, Ross and Cromarty.
Iter. 258, 260. Map 32, **NB 3** 4.

BASS ROCK, East Lothian. Map 10, **NT 6** 8.
See **North Berwick**. *Iter. 2, 38.*

BATHGATE, West Lothian. 11,968. SB. Map 9, **NS 9** 6.
E.C. Wed. GOLF. There are iron and steel foundries. The town is also engaged in the shale oil industry. A silver mine was formerly worked in the neighbourhood. Sir James Simpson, who introduced chloroform into midwifery, was born at Bathgate in 1811. To the north are situated the *Bathgate* hills, with *The Knock* attaining 1,017 ft. See **Torphichen**. *Iter. 16.*

BEARSDEN, Dunbarton. 10,143. Map 8, **NS 5** 7.
GOLF. On the line of the Antonine, or *Roman Wall* (*q.v.*), some of the best preserved portions of which are to be found to the north-west and north-east of the town, which is also known as *New Kilpatrick*. *Iter. 104, 106, 113.*

BEATTOCK, Dumfries. Map 9, **NT 0** 0.
On the Evan Water, in Upper Annandale, in a hilly setting. Above the station there are four prehistoric forts, notably

one on Beattock Hill. **1 m. N.N.W.** is *Auchen Castle*, late 13th cent., and farther north, in the Evan valley, leading to Beattock summit, 1,025 ft., which is situated some 10 miles from the village, are the ruined towers of *Blacklaw, Mellingshaw* and *Raecleuch*. **4 m. S.** of Beattock is *Lochwood Tower*, 15th cent., in a wooded setting, once a Johnstone seat. See **Beattock Summit** and **Moffat**. *Iter. 10, 13, 24, 29, 46, 50, 51.*

BEATTOCK SUMMIT, Lanark.   Map 9, **NS 9** 1.
The highest point (1,029 ft.) on the road from Beattock to the Clyde valley at Elvanfoot. It is situated some 10 miles north-west of Beattock. See **Beattock**. *Iter. 29, 49, 50, 51.*

BEAUFORT CASTLE, Inverness.   Map 25, **NH 5** 4.
See **Kilmorack.**

BEAULY, Inverness. 1,112.   Map 25, **NH 5** 4.
E.C. Thurs. Situated on the River Beauly, a river noted for its salmon, and where it begins to widen into the Beauly Firth. The name is a corruption of Beaulieu, meaning " beautiful place " in French. There is a ruined Priory (A.M.), founded in 1230, with monuments and graves to the Chisholms, Frasers, and the Mackenzies of Kintail. In the market place a monument commemorates the raising of the Lovat Scouts. To the south, in the direction of *Lovat Bridge* (*q.v.*), is the fertile district known as *The Aird*. *Iter. 200, 201, 203, 204, 205, 206, 213, 221.*

BEESWING, Kirkcudbright.   Map 4, **NX 8** 6.
South of Loch Arthur rises *Lotus Hill*. *Iter. 76.*

BEITH, Ayr. 4,347.   Map 8, **NS 3** 5.
E.C. Wed. GOLF. A town manufacturing linen thread and furniture. To the north-east rises *Cuff Hill*, crowned by a long barrow, and looking down on to the Threepwood reservoir. *Iter. 63.*

BELHAVEN, East Lothian.   Map 10, **NT 6** 7.
Iter. 2, 40.

BELLOCHANTUY, Argyll.   Map 6, **NR 6** 3.
Iter. 121.

BELLSHILL, Lanark. 15,561.   Map 9, **NS 7** 6.
E.C. Wed. GOLF. A mining town, situated to the north-east of the Clyde valley. *Iter. 18, 54.*

BELLSQUARRY, Midlothian.   Map 9, **NT 0** 6.
Iter. 19, 20, 22.

BEMERSYDE, Berwick.   Map 10, **NT 5** 3.
Bemersyde House is famous as the hereditary home of the Haigs, and was presented by the nation in 1921 to Field-Marshal Earl Haig, who lies buried in *Dryburgh Abbey* (*q.v.*). The house is shown Wed., Sat. and Sun., 10 to 6, May to end of Sept. (see note page 90). It incorporates an ancient but restored tower which was burnt in a raid in 1545, and there is a museum containing personal relics of Earl Haig. Sir Walter Scott was a frequent visitor to the house, and delighted in the splendid viewpoint of *Bemersyde Hill* (A.A. viewpoint), with its panorama of the winding Tweed, backed by the triple-peaked *Eildon* hills to the west. See **Scott's View** and **Smailholm**. *Iter. 13, 43.*

BENBECULA, ISLE OF, Inverness.   Map 32, **NF 7** 5.
See **Hebrides, Outer** (Benbecula). *Iter. 262.*

BENDERLOCH, Argyll.   Map 14, **NM 9** 3 etc.
Near *Benderloch* station, on the shores of Ardmucknish Bay, rises a low twin-peaked hill, crowned by a vitrified fort, and forming a good viewpoint. The name *Beregonium*, by which it is sometimes known, would appear to have been given to it in error. The hilly district lying between Loch Etive and Loch Creran, dominated by *Beinn Sguliaird*, 3,059 ft., is generally known as Benderloch, which is really a part of the much larger district of *Lorne* (*q.v.*). A by-road leads north-westwards from Benderloch station to *Barcaldine Castle* (*q.v.*). *Iter. 124.*

BEN EIGHE NATIONAL NATURE RESERVE, Ross and Cromarty. See **Kinlochewe**.   Map 24, **NG 9** 6.

BEN MACDHUI, Aberdeen; Banff.   Map 20, **NN 9** 9.
See **Cairngorms.**

BENMORE ESTATE, Argyll.   Map 14, **NS 1** 8.
This estate forms part of the extensive Argyll National Forest Park, and *Benmore House* is now the Forester Training School. The sector of the Park to the north includes the forests of *Glenbranter* and *Glenfinart*. There is magnificent mountain and loch scenery in this *Cowal* (*q.v.*) district, notably around *Loch Eck* (*q.v.*) and Loch Long. Glen Masson, to the north-west of the Holy Loch, and the picturesque little *Puck's Glen*, just beyond the head of the loch, are of special note, the latter incorporating a fine viewpoint. See **Arrochar**. *Iter. 137.*

BENNECARRIGAN, Isle of Arran, Bute. Map 7, **NR 9** 2. *Iter. 242.*

BEN NEVIS, Inverness.   Map 18, **NN 1** 7.
The highest mountain in Great Britain, a conglomerate of granite, schists and lavas, rising to a height of 4,406 ft., and dominating *Fort William* (*q.v.*) and the district of *Lochaber* (*q.v.*), at the south-western extremity of the Great Glen, or *Glen More* (*q.v.*). Around its western and southern flanks extends *Glen Nevis*, one of the loveliest of Scottish glens, with the finely-wooded gorge of the River Nevis near its farther end. A narrow, switchback road traverses the glen for much of its length, keeping to the west side of the river, and passing near *Glen Nevis House*, the headquarters of Lochiel when besieging Fort William in 1746. *Dun Dearduil*, a hill on the west side of the road, has remains of a vitrified fort, and within a few miles the road reaches the Polldubh waterfall. After this point the road turns east and deteriorates considerably, while at the end of the glen, reached on foot only, is seen the lofty Steall waterfall, in its wild setting among the peaks of the *Mamores*, at the commencement of the long and lonely track leading towards Loch Treig.

Although the Ben is often considered to be unshapely as seen from most angles, the stupendous range of cliffs, about two miles in length, which fall away on its northern flanks, can only be seen properly from the remote Mhuilinn Glen at its foot, or from the upper slopes of *Carn Mor Dearg*, 4,012 ft., which is linked to the Ben by a spectacular, narrow arête overlooking upper Glen Nevis. Snow lingers generally until late in the summer, or even all the year round, in the remote corries of these great cliffs. On the summit of Ben Nevis, an exposed wilderness of massive boulders, stood formerly an observatory, first erected in 1883, but this is now in ruins, having been closed down in 1904, while a hotel, or hostel, which also once stood here was shut in 1915. A mountain indicator gives particulars of the wide view which can be enjoyed in clear weather, ranging over the whole country from the Cairngorms to the Hebrides, as well as occasionally taking in the far distant Irish coast. The fine *Mamore Forest* (*q.v.*) group, seen almost in its entirety, forms a prominent feature in the aspect across Glen Nevis to the south, with the white quartzite peak of *Sgurr a' Mhaim*, 3,601 ft., dominating the lesser heights. The upper reaches of the glen are dominated by *Aonach Beag*, 4,060 ft., and *Aonach Mor*, 3,999 ft., which form a ridge over 3 miles in length.

The ascent of Ben Nevis is usually made along a well-defined, but rough and stony path commencing at *Achintee* farm in Glen Nevis, this being reached by road from Fort William by crossing the River Nevis a little to the north-east of the town, and then keeping to the east bank of the river. Halfway up the mountain is the little Lochan Meall-an-t-Suidhe, near which a descent can be made over moorland into the Mhuilinn Glen, in order to see the precipices on the north side. When the observatory was in operation, supplies were taken up the path, at that time a track, up which, at a later date a car was actually driven to the mountain top, but with the course of time the track has gradually degenerated into the present narrow foot-track. A 15-mile long pipeline for the Lochaber Power Scheme has been driven through the Ben from Loch Treig, near *Tulloch* (*q.v.*), in order to feed the power house on the outskirts of Fort William. Away to the east of the Ben, beyond *Carn Mor Dearg* and the *Aonach* peaks are the seldom visited *Grey Corries*, 3,858 ft.,

Beauly, Inverness. The remains of the Priory, founded by Sir John Bisset of Lovat in 1230. Abbot Reid erected the façade after 1530. The restored north transept is the burial place of the Mackenzies of Kintail

Bemersyde, Berwick. Bemersyde House, the home of the Haigs, presented to Field-Marshal Earl Haig by the nation in 1921. An old prophecy by Thomas the Rhymer says:

'Tide, 'tide, what'er betide,
There'll aye be Haigs of Bemersyde.

Ben Eighe National Nature Reserve, Ross and Cromarty. The northern spurs of Ben Eighe, seen from Grudie Bridge, on A832, near Loch Maree. On its slopes is situated Britain's first National Nature Reserve

Benmore Estate, Argyll. Newly-afforested hill slopes overlooking Loch Eck, between Loch Fyne and Loch Long, in the Argyll National Forest Park. A road follows the eastern shores of the loch for the whole of its length

Ben Nevis, Inverness. The highest mountain in Great Britain, 4,406 feet, as seen from Corpach across the head of Loch Linnhe. In the great northern corries of the Ben, snow lies sometimes all the year round

PLATE 16 (facing page 106)   [For BENDERLOCH see Plate 175

Berriedale, Caithness. The smithy, decorated with stags' antlers, at the foot of Berriedale Hill

Birkhill, Dumfries. The 200-foot high waterfall known as the 'Grey Mare's Tail', which is situated a mile to the south-west, off A708

Berriedale, Caithness. Stones near the bridge over the Berriedale Water, marking the height of flood waters in 1896 and 1912

Bettyhill, Sutherland. A view of the estuary of the River Naver, where it flows into Torrisdale Bay, to the north-west of Bettyhill

Biggar, Lanark. The 'Cadger's Brig' in the main street

Binns, West Lothian. The 15th to 17th century house of The Binns (N.T. Scot.), where General Tam Dalyell raised the Royal Scots Greys in 1681. It stands off A904 between Blackness and Abercorn.

PLATE 17 (facing page 107)

overlooking Glen Spean and *Roy Bridge* (q.v.). Iter. 100, 124, 125, 142, 143, 208, 215.

BERNERAY, ISLE OF, Inverness.   Map 32, NL 5 7.
See **Hebrides, Outer** (Barra).   and **5** 8.

BERNISDALE, Isle of Skye, Inverness.   Map 22, NG 4 5.
Iter. 255.

BERRIEDALE, Caithness. 570.   Map 31, ND 1 2.
The Berriedale Water flows here into the sea from its long valley, the last part of which is richly wooded, and the stream is joined near its mouth by the Langwell Water, which rises on the distant slopes of the conical peak of *Morven*, 2,313 ft. Nearer to the village is the long ridge of *Scaraben*, 2,054 ft., overlooking the bare expanse of Langwell Forest. There are scanty remains of the 14th cent. *Berriedale Castle.* The Post Office is decorated with stags' antlers, as is also the old smithy. The main road to the south is steep and winding, skirting a number of deep ravines on its way to the Ord of Caithness. To the north, the coast is wild and rocky, and has been described in the novels of Neil Gunn. Iter. 200, 236.

BERVIE, Kincardine.   Map 21, NO 8 7.
See **Inverbervie.**

BERWICK-UPON-TWEED, Northumberland (England). 12,570.   Map 11, NT 9 5.
E.C. Thurs. **M.D.** Sat. GOLF. The ancient border town of *Berwick-upon-Tweed* has a long history, and changed hands

A.6105 DUNS 15½
A.1 NORTH TERRACE
EYEMOUTH 8¾ EDINBURGH 56¾
BERWICK-upon-TWEED
Scale.
0   ¼ ml.
CASTLE TERRACE
SWINTON 11¾ A.699
Municipal Golf Course
Hosp.
CASTLE GATE
Royal border Br.
RIVER
QUAY
ROYAL TWEED BR.
BERWICK BR.
MARY GATE
GOLDN SQ.
G.P.O.
Cricket Ground
COLDSTREAM 14½
A.698
FORD DRIVE
PRINCE EDWARD RD.
TWEED
Pier
TWEED MOUTH
HIGHGATE
DOCK ROAD
SPITTAL
Association Football Ground
B.6435
←To A.698
B.6354
Eral 10
BELFORD ROAD
To Berwick G.C.(Goswick)
NEWCASTLE 62¾ MORPETH 48¾
A.1
R.B.60
SPITTAL ROAD
Times of High Tide can be found by referring to the Tide Table in the Members Hand-book
CROWN COPYRIGHT RESERVED   PUBLISHED BY THE AUTOMOBILE ASSOCIATION

Barracks, designed by Vanbrugh	7.
Castle Walls	1.
Church, 17th cent.	3.
Museum	4.

Scotch Gate, rebuilt 1815	6.
Town Hall, 18th cent.	5.
Town Walls, 13th and 16th cent.	2.

on numerous occasions in medieval times, reverting finally to England in 1482, when it became a bastion against the Scots, with a government of its own. At one period it was an important Scottish port, and was frequently visited by the early kings of the country, who were given hospitality by the

town's merchants. Berwick is today a fishing port and resort, with good sands, while both sea and river fishing are available, the Tweed being especially famous for its salmon. The river is one of the most important in Scotland, being nearly 100 miles long, and forming the boundary between the two countries for some 16 miles of its course. Three bridges span its waters at Berwick : the early 17th cent. fifteen-arched Old Bridge ; the Royal Tweed Bridge of 1928 carrying the Great North Road ; and the Royal Border Bridge of the railway. Of the town walls, there remain slight traces of those built in the 13th cent., together with larger stretches of those constructed in Elizabethan times, which are of much interest. Near the station are situated scanty remains of the former Norman Castle. The Parish Church is of the 17th cent., and the Town Hall carries the date 1754. The fine ranges of barracks are the work of the great architect Vanbrugh, and date from 1717 to 1721. There are a number of late Georgian houses in the town, some of the finest being situated along the Quay Walls. **2 m.** N.W. of the town is *Halidon Hill*, the scene of a Scottish defeat by the English in 1333. See **Burnmouth, Ladykirk, Lamberton** and **Paxton.** Iter. 1, 2, 3, 8, 9, 30, 33, 46, 47.

BETTYHILL, Sutherland. 600.   Map 30, NC 7 6.
E.C. Wed. Once known as *Bettyhill of Farr*, and founded originally as a fishing and agricultural centre. It is now a touring and fishing resort on Torrisdale Bay, with bathing from good, though exposed sands, and is noted for sea birds and alpine plants. Beyond the bay, to the north-west, are the islands of Eilean Co'omb and the precipitous Roan Island. The River Naver flows here into the sea from the long valley of *Strath Naver* (q.v.), in which many prehistoric remains, tumuli, hut circles and cairns are to be found. **4 m.** S., on a by-road to the east of the River Naver, are some horned burial cairns near *Skelpick Lodge.* See **Farr** and **Syre.** Iter. 232, 234, 240.

BIGGAR, Lanark. 1,444 SB.   Map 9, NT 0 3.
E.C. Wed. **M.D.** Thurs. GOLF. Lies in the broad vale of the Biggar Water, a tributary of the Tweed, but whose waters reach the Clyde, to the west, in times of flood. There are slight traces of the former *Boghall Castle*, south of the town. At the end of the wide main street is the restored bridge, or " Cadger's brig." The restored, cruciform Church was commenced in 1545, and has in its churchyard a tomb in which lie the ancestors of Gladstone. A bust in the School recalls the fact that Dr. John Brown, author of " Rab and his Friends," was born in the nearby manse. *Culter House*, 17th cent. has a mile-long avenue of trees. See **Symington** (Lanark). Iter. 25, 35, 53.

BILSTON, Midlothian.   Map 10, NT 2 6.
See **Roslin.** Iter. 10, 24.

BINNS, THE, West Lothian   Map 9, NT 0 7.
See **Abercorn.** Iter. 96.

BIRGHAM, Berwick.   Map 11, NT 7 3.
A Tweed-side village on the edge of the fertile plain of the *Merse* (q.v.). The Treaty of Birgham, signed in 1290, established the details of Scotland's independence. The fine gardens of *Springhill House* are sometimes open to view (see note page 90). Iter. 30, 32.

BIRKHALL, Aberdeen.   Map 20, NO 3 9.
See **Ballater.**

BIRKHILL, Dumfries.   Map 9, NT 1 1.
Surrounded by green Lowlands hills, *Birkhill*, which stands at the 1,105-ft. high summit of the Birkhill Pass, is overshadowed by *White Coomb*, 2,695 ft., and lies almost on the Selkirk border. In the near vicinity is Dob's Linn, formerly a refuge for the persecuted Covenanters. **1 m.** S.W. is the well-known waterfall, some 200 ft. high, known as the *Grey Mare's Tail*, where the Tail Burn joins the Moffat Water, while beyond the junction, to the north, is the wild Loch Skene, in its lonely setting under *Lochcraig Head*, 2,625 ft. See **Moffat** and **St. Mary's Loch.** Iter. 13, 46.

BIRNAM, Perth. 629.   Map 16, NO 0 4.
E.C. Thurs. The village lies in a delightful wooded setting be-

tween *Birnam Hill*, 1,324 ft., and the River Tay, the narrow Birnam Pass being the traditional " Mouth of the Highlands," having been traversed by both Montrose and Prince Charles Edward. " Duncan's Castle," a hill fort on Birnam Hill, is associated with Shakespeare's King Duncan, and the " Birnam Oaks," actually an oak and a sycamore, standing on the south bank of the Tay behind Birnam Hotel, are thought to be the survivors of Shakespeare's " Great Birnam Wood." **4 m. S.E.** is *Murthly Castle*, standing in fine wooded grounds in a bend of the Tay, and beyond it is Caputh Bridge across the river. **See Dunkeld.** *Iter. 149, 150.*

BIRNESS, Aberdeen. Map 27, NJ 9 3.
Iter. 181, 185, 187.

BIRNIE, Moray. Map 26, NJ 2 5.
The little Kirk, dating from the 12th cent., has chancel windows and a font of Norman date, and preserves a Celtic bell, known as the " Ronnel Bell." Other points of interest are an 18th cent. sundial and a Druid stone in the kirkyard. To the west flows the little River Lossie.

BIRSAY, Orkney. Map 33, HY 2 2.
See Orkney Islands (Mainland). *Iter. 263.*

BIRSEMORE, Aberdeen. Map 21, NO 5 9.
Iter. 168, 174.

BISHOPBRIGGS, Lanark. 5,272. Map 8, NS 6 7.
GOLF. Lies on the northern outskirts of Glasgow, in the vicinity of the Forth and Clyde canal and the line of the *Roman Wall* (*q.v.*). *Iter. 98, 107.*

BISHOPMILL, Moray. Map 26, NJ 2 6·
Iter. 192, 199.

BISHOPTON, Renfrew. 1,586. Map 8, NS 4 7.
E.C. Wed. GOLF. On the Glasgow to Gourock road and to the north-west of which a view is opened up of *Dumbarton* (*q.v.*) Castle, backed by the distant peak of *Ben Lomond*, 3,192 ft., on the farther side of the Clyde estuary. **1½ m. S.** is the 16th cent. and modernized *Dargavel House*, an old Maxwell possession, a gable carrying their arms, with the date 1584. **2 m. S.W.** is the modern mansion of *Formakin*, built by Sir Robert Lorimer. See **Erskine Ferry.** *Iter. 59, 65.*

BLACKBURN, Aberdeen. Map 27, NJ 8 1.
Iter. 175, 177, 178, 184.

BLACKBURN, West Lothian. Map 9, NS 9 6.
Iter. 18.

BLACKFORD, Perth. 522. Map 16, NN 8 0.
Situated on the Allan Water. In the vicinity, about **4 m. W.N.W.**, is the Carsebreck Curling pond, where the annual match between North and South Scotland formerly took place. **1 m. S.E.** of Blackford stand the remains of *Ogilvie Castle*, backed by the ridges of the *Ochil* hills. **See Gleneagles Hotel.** *Iter. 135, 146.*

BLACKHALL (Edinburgh), Midlothian. Map 9, NT 2 7.
Iter. 17, 89, 90, 92, 93, 94, 96.

BLACK ISLE, Ross and Cromarty. Map 25, NH 6 5 etc.
The name given to the broad and fertile strip of land which lies between the Firth of Cromarty and the Beauly and Inner Moray Firths, terminating in the South Sutor headland beyond the town of Cromarty (*q.v.*). In the centre of the Black Isle is a wooded ridge, known as *Millbuie*, or Ardmeanach, the lordship of which was granted originally to Darnley by Mary, Queen of Scots. See **Fortrose** and **Rosemarkie.** *Iter. 203.*

BLACKLAW, Banff. Map 27, NJ 6 5.
Iter. 184, 194.

BLACK MOUNT, Argyll. Map 18, NN 2 4.
The name given to the bleak and hilly moors lying between Loch Tulla and Rannoch Moor. The present Glencoe road traverses its eastern border, the old road having taken a higher course farther to the west. On this western side rise the fine peaks of *Stob Ghabhar*, 3,565 ft., *Clachlet*, 3,602 ft. and *Meall a Bhuiridh*, 3,636 ft. See **Inveroran** and **Kingshouse.**

BLACKNESS, West Lothian. Map 16, NT 0 7.
Once the third port of Scotland, and now but a small village. The Castle (A.M.), dates from the 15th cent. and later. After having been used as a prison in Covenanting times, became at a later date a powder magazine. There are views across the Firth of Forth, and eastwards to the Forth Bridge. *Iter. 96.*

BLACKSHIELS, Midlothian. 100. Map 10, NT 4 6.
E.C. Wed. *Blackshiels* and *Fala* lie below *Soutra Hill* (*q.v.*), an outlier of the extensive *Lammermuirs*, a sparsely populated area devoted to sheep. **2½ m. S.W.**, by the Cakemuir Burn, is *Cakemuir Castle*, 16th to 18th cent., associated with Mary, Queen of Scots and Bothwell. The chamber in which the Queen is said to have changed her page's clothes after escaping from *Borthwick Castle* (*q.v.*), in 1567, is on the first floor. *Iter. 4, 5, 13.*

BLACKWATERFOOT, Isle of Arran, Bute. Map 7, NR 8 2.
GOLF. A small village on Drumadoon Bay, with some cliff scenery and views over Kilbrennan Sound to the *Kintyre* (*q.v.*) peninsula. Here, the String Road from *Brodick* (*q.v.*) links up with the coast road following the western shores of the island. **2 m. N.E.**, off the Brodick road, is *Shiskine* Church, in which a carved tombstone is preserved. See **Lagg** and **Machrie.** *Iter. 242.*

BLADNOCH, Wigtown. Map 2, NX 4 5.
This little village stands on the Bladnoch Water, here spanned by a bridge, the river flowing eastwards past an old quay to enter Wigtown Bay north of the Baldoon Sands. About a mile to the south-east of the village lie the remains of *Baldoon Castle*, associated with Scott's " Bride of Lammermoor," and once the home of David Dunbar, the original of the bridegroom in the novel. *Iter. 78, 82.*

BLAIRADAM, Kinross. Map 17, NT 1 9.
Once known as *Maryburgh*, and the birthplace of William Adam, the father of the four distinguished architects who bear the name. The most famous was Robert Adam, 1728-1792, who worked in Edinburgh and also in England. The house of *Blairadam* was visited by Sir Walter Scott, and the neighbourhood is described in his novel " The Abbot." To the west are the *Cleish* hills, with *Dumglow* attaining 1,241 ft., and north-eastwards rises *Benarty Hill*, 1,167 ft.

BLAIR ATHOLL, Perth. 300. Map 19, NN 8 6.
E.C. Wed. This pleasant *Atholl* (*q.v.*) village stands on the River Garry, in a setting of woods, hills and moors. Many glens meet in the vicinity, which accounts for its former importance as the key to the Central Highlands. The fine *Blair Castle*, in its extensive park, noted for the larch plantations, is an old seat of the Clan Murray, the head of which is the Duke of Atholl, and dates back to 1269. It was Georgianised in the mid-18th cent. and given a castellated appearance by David Bryce in 1869. The interior is noted for its period furniture, weapons and other relics.

BLAIR ATHOLL

1. Blair Castle. 3. Kilmaveonaig
2. St. Bride's Church. Church.

There are associations with James V, Mary, Queen of Scots, Montrose and Prince Charles Edward, and the Castle at one period held a Cromwellian garrison. It is said to be the last castle in Britain to have withstood a siege. The oldest part of the castle is the Cumming's Tower. It is

Birnie, Moray. The 'Druid Stone' in the churchyard

Black Isle, Ross and Cromarty. The 16th century Castle Craig, a former Black Isle residence of the Bishops of Ross. It faces Cromarty Firth, beyond B9163, from which it is hidden from view, and can be seen from A9, on the farther shores of the Firth

Blackness, West Lothian. The Castle, of the 15th century and later. It was once used as a prison for Covenanters, and in more recent times as an ordnance depot

Blackshiels, Midlothian. Cakemuir Castle, some 2½ miles south-west, on a by-road off B6458. Here Mary, Queen of Scots, is said to have changed from her page's clothes after her escape from Borthwick Castle in 1567

Bladnoch, Wigtown. Baldoon Castle, off an unclassified road to the south-east, which has associations with Sir Walter Scott's '*Bride of Lammermoor*'

Blair Atholl, Perth. Blair Castle, the ancient seat of the Clan Murray. It was Georgianised in the mid-18th century and given its present castellated appearance in 1869

PLATE 18 (facing page 100)

Blantyre, Lanark. Shuttle Row, where David Livingstone was born in 1813. It is now a Livingstone Memorial

Boddam, Aberdeen. The lighthouse at Buchan Ness Scotland's most easterly point

Blyth Bridge, Peebles. An example of a whalebone archway in the village

TRAVELLER.
STOP and *Read* with *GRATITUDE*
The names of the *PARLIAMENTARY COMMISSIONERS*
appointed in the Year 1803 to direct the making
of above Five Hundred miles of Roads through
the Highlands of Scotland and of numerous
Bridges particularly those at BEAULY
SCUDDEL, BONAR, FLEET, and HELMSDALE
connecting those Roads viz,

RIGHT HONOURABLE CHARLES ABBOT
RIGHT HONOURABLE NICHOLAS VANSITTART
RIGHT HONOURABLE WILLIAM DUNDAS
Sir WILLIAM PULTENEY BAR.T
ISAAC HAWKINS BROWN ESQ.R
CHARLES GRANT ESQ.R
WILLIAM SMITH ESQ.R
    to whom were afterwards added
ARCHIBALD COLQUHOUNE ESQ.R LORD ADVOCATE
CHARLES DUNDAS ESQ.R
RIGHT HONOURABLE NATHANIEL BOND

This *BUILDING* was begun Sept.R 1811.
and finished Nov.R 1812.
THOMAS TELFORD Architect, SIMPSON & CARGILL Builders
    This *STONE* was placed here by
    GEORGE DEMPSTER of Dunnichen
    In the Year 1815.

Bolton, East Lothian. The well near the Gifford Water, where Robert Burns's mother drew water. The well is inscribed: 'Drink of the pure crystals and not only be ye succoured but also refreshed in mind. Agnes Broun, 1732–1820'

Bonar Bridge, Sutherland. A tablet on the bridge recording the building of the original structure by Telford (1811–12)

PLATE 19 (facing page 109

shown weekdays, 10 to 6 (Sun., after 2), early May to end of Sept. Also on Sun. and Mon. in April. (See note page 90). The 16th cent. Parish Church of *Kilmaveonaig* was rebuilt in 1794. In *St. Bride's* Churchyard at *Old Blair* is buried Claverhouse of Dundee, slain in 1689, at the battle of *Killiecrankie* (*q.v.*). To the north of the village is Glen Tilt, extending far into the mountains of the Forest of Atholl, with *Ben-y-Gloe*, 3,671 ft., to the east. At the commencement of the glen, near the Old Bridge of Tilt, are the Falls of Fender. Farther north, the glen is hemmed in by steep hills, and extends for some six miles in an almost dead straight line, the river meanwhile flowing through a granite dyke. Later the Tarf Water, with its numerous falls, joins the Tilt amid a wilderness of lonely hills. Beyond the meeting of the rivers lie the remote Aberdeenshire deer forests of Glen Ey and Mar, with *Beinn Bhrotain*, 3,797 ft., in the *Cairngorm* range, dominating the latter. See **Struan** (for *Falls of Bruar*). *Iter.* 138, 140, 143, 150.

BLAIRGOWRIE, Perth. 5,250 SB. with Rattray.
Map 20, **NO 1 4**.
E.C. Thurs. M.D. Tues. GOLF. On the River Ericht, and linked by the 19th cent. Brig o'Blair to *Rattray*, on the edge of *Strathmore* (*q.v.*). By the bridge is a fish pass, built in 1958. It is noted as the centre of a raspberry and strawberry growing district. The main road leading north-

wards from the town crosses the river twice within a few miles, and then enters the fine Ericht gorge, where the river flows between cliffs 200 ft. high. Nearby, on high ground to the right, stands the mansion of *Craighall Rattray*, which has claims to be the original of Scott's " Tully-Veolan " in his novel " Waverley." The road continues by way of *Bridge of Cally* (*q.v.*) and climbs steadily through Glen Shee on its way to the lofty *Cairnwell* (*q.v.*) Pass and Braemar. Off the Dunkeld road, to the west of the town, are Lochs Ardblair and Marlee, with the 16th cent. mansion of *Ardblair Castle* near the first-named. See **Clunie, Meikleour, Stobhall** and **Traquair.** *Iter.* 141, 152, 158, 159, 166.

BLAIRINGONE, Kinross; Clackmannan. Map 16, **NS 9 9**.
Iter. 86, 91, 98.

BLAIRLOGIE, Stirling. Map 16, **NS 8 9**.
A village under the *Ochil* hills, with *Dumyat*, 1,375 ft., a viewpoint, rising in the background. Sir William Alexander, founder of Nova Scotia, once worshipped in the former old church. *Iter.* 136.

BLAIRMORE, Argyll. Map 14, **NS 1 8**.
GOLF. See **Strone.** *Iter.* 102.

BLAIRS, Kincardine. Map 21, **NJ 8 0**.
Here is *Blairs House*, now a R.C. College, in which is

preserved a splendid portrait of Mary, Queen of Scots, one of the very few considered to be authentic. It was originally found concealed at Douai after the French Revolution. *Iter.* 168, 174.

BLANEFIELD, Stirling. Map 15, **NS 5 7**.
Iter. 105, 108, 115.

BLANTYRE, Lanark. 16,854. Map 8, **NS 6 5**.
The Clyde flows a little to the north, in a wooded setting. Nearby is the building known as *Shuttle Row*, where Livingstone was born in 1813, and which has been restored as a National Memorial, housing relics. On the tower of the *Livingstone* memorial church is the explorer's statue. There are slight remains of *Blantyre Priory*, **2 m. N.**, near the river. The district is largely devoted to coal-mining. A little to the west of Blantyre, near the Rotten Calder Water, stands *Crossbasket Castle*, 16th cent., with large modern additions. See **Bothwell.** *Iter.* 18, 19.

BLYTH BRIDGE, Peebles. Map 9, **NT 1 4**.
On the Tarth Water, in a setting of Lowland hills. See **Romanno Bridge.** *Iter.* 10, 35, 37, 52, 53.

BOAT OF GARTEN, Inverness. 247. Map 25, **NH 9 1**.
E.C. Thurs. A Strath Spey resort, on the fringe of the extensive Forest of Abernethy, which lies to the east with its many paths and shelters the tiny Loch Garten. The name Boat of Garten refers to the former ferry, by means of which the river was crossed prior to the construction of the bridge in 1898. Away to the south rise the peaks of the *Cairngorms* (*q.v.*), which can be reached by a track over the Sluggan Pass, at the foot of *Craiggowrie*, 2,237 ft., to the east of the road from Nethybridge to Aviemore. See **Aviemore, Carrbridge** and **Nethybridge.** *Iter.* 169, 170.

BODDAM, Aberdeen. Map 27, **NK 1 4**.
Buchan Ness, with its lighthouse, the most easterly point in Scotland, shelters this little pink granite fishing village, lying just off the Peterhead road, and to the south of which stands the ruined 14th cent. Castle. To the south-west are the large Peterhead granite quarries. See **Cruden Bay.** *Iter.* 181, 182, 187.

BOGHEAD, Lanark. Map 9, **NS 7 4**.
Iter. 56.

BOGNIEBRAE, Aberdeen. Map 27, **NJ 5 4**.
Iter. 194, 196.

BOGSIDE, Ayr. Map 8, **NS 3 3**.
Noted for its race-course. See **Irvine.** *Iter.* 66, 69, 85, 88.

BOGUE TOLL, Kirkcudbright. Map 3, **NX 6 8**.
Iter. 25.

BOLTON, East Lothian. Map 10, **NT 5 7**.
In the Churchyard lie buried Burns's mother, sister and brother. A well near the Gifford Water, which Burns's mother used, was restored in 1932. **2 m. S.W.** is *Pilmuir House*, a delightful gabled and crow-stepped mansion, built in 1624 by the Cairns family, and retaining a contemporary dovecote. **2 m. N.** is *Lennoxlove*, a mansion of several dates, the nucleus of which is a fine 15th cent. tower. The great hall, and also two sundials, dated 1644 and 1679 respectively, are of interest, while above the entrance door, which still preserves its iron yett, is an inscription with the date 1626. The house was formerly known as *Lethington Tower*, and was associated with William Maitland, the "Mr. Secretary Lethington" to Mary, Queen of Scots. It is shown daily, 2 to 5, July 1 to Sept. 30, also Easter and Whitsun weekend and each weekend in June. (See note page 90). *Iter.* 36.

BONAR BRIDGE, Sutherland. 288. Map 29, **NH 6 9**.
E.C. Wed. The bridge, which spans the channel connecting the Inner Dornoch Firth with the Kyle of Sutherland, replaces one built originally by Telford. Before its construction occurred the Meikle Ferry disaster, in 1809, when 99 lives were lost. Hut circles and stone-age burial cairns are to be found in the vicinity, and on *Duncreich*, **4 m. S.E.**, is a vitrified fort. Strath Carron to the west, and Strath Oykell to the north-west, are two picturesque glens, the latter traversed by the road leading to *Oykell Bridge* (*q.v.*) and the mountains of the west coast. A little to the east of

BONAR BRIDGE

LAIRG, LOCHINVER
A.836

Ch.   Golf Course

R. Carron

STRATH CARRON

DORNOCH, JOHN O'GROATS

Ardgay   Bonar Br. Sta

Dornoch Firth

A.9

A.9
TAIN, DINGWALL, INVERNESS

R.B.60   CROWN COPYRIGHT RESERVED

Bonar Bridge lies the small Loch Migdale, in a wooded setting. *Iter. 200, 201, 228, 229, 230, 231, 232.*

BONAWE, Argyll.
Map 14, NN 0 3.
Lies on Airds Bay, near the point where the River Awe flows into *Loch Etive* (*q.v.*), dividing it into the lower and upper lochs, the latter domi-nated by *Ben Starav*, 3,541 ft. *Inverawe House*, partly 16th cent., and associated with a curious ghost story, stands on the east bank of the river. Beyond the north side of the loch, and reached by ferry, are the Bonawe granite quarries. *Ben Cruachan*, 3,689 ft., with its twin peaks, rises to the south-east of the village, and below the northern flanks of the mountain lies the lonely Glen Noe, hemmed in by lofty hills. See **Falls of Cruachan.** *Iter. 125.*

BONCHESTER BRIDGE, Roxburgh.   Map 5, NT 5 1.
The bridge is over the Rule Water, flowing in a northerly direction to join the Teviot, and is overlooked by *Bonchester Hill*, 1,059 ft. *Greenriver House*, late Georgian, was re-named after a place in Jamaica. Roads fork here for Jedburgh and Hawick, and to the south is another fork, where the road climbing south-eastwards towards *Carter Bar* (*q.v.*) leaves the fine Liddesdale road. This goes south-westwards into the hills, and reaches a height of 1,250 ft. at Note o' the Gate, below the main *Cheviot* (*q.v.*) range dominated here by *Peel Fell*, 1,975 ft. and *Carter Fell*, 1,815 ft. This is the Wauchope Forest area, which, together with *Newcastleton* (*q.v.*) Forest, forms part of the Border National Forest Park, extending across the English border. See **Southdean.** *Iter. 44, 47.*

BO'NESS, West Lothian. 10,280. SB.   Map 16, NS 9 8.
GOLF. The name is a contraction of *Borrowstounness*. An industrial town and port on the Forth estuary, Bo'ness is associated with Henry Bell, who launched an early steam-boat, the " Comet ", on the Clyde in 1812, and also with James Watt, who experimented, in 1764, with his steam engine on the nearby *Kinneil* estate, now a public park. Mid-16th cent. wall paintings, perhaps Flemish or French work, and illustrating the story of the Good Samaritan, have been discovered on one of the walls of a room in *Kinneil House* (A.M.), which is open weekdays, 10 to 7 or 12 to 4; Sunday, after 2 (see note page 90). Bo'ness Hill climb for cars takes place in the grounds. The *Antonine* or *Roman Wall* (*q.v.*) terminated just to the east of Bo'ness, and in 1868, a Distance Slab, now in the National Museum of Antiquities at Edinburgh was unearthed. A copy of this has been erected, set in a framework of Roman stones, and situated near *Bridgeness Tower*, at the east end of the town. 1½ m. E. is the modernised *Carriden House*, the old portion of which is dated 1602. See **Bowling** and **Falkirk.** *Iter. 17.*

BONHILL, Dunbarton. 3,984.   Map 15, NS 3 7.
On the River Leven, between the Clyde estuary and the southern extremity of *Loch Lomond* (*q.v.*) and engaged in bleaching. See **Alexandria.** *Iter. 88, 100, 101, 109, 110, 112.*

BONJEDWARD, Roxburgh.   Map 10, NT 6 2.
Iter. 4, 30, 43, 47, 52.

BONNYBRIDGE, Stirling. 6,065.   Map 16, NS 8 8.
GOLF. An industrial town on the Forth and Clyde canal and also on the line of the *Roman Wall* (*q.v.*). *Iter. 17, 113, 115.*

BONNYRIGG, Midlothian. 5,674. SB. with Lasswade.
Map 10, NT 3 6.
GOLF. A colliery town. See **Lasswade.** *Iter. 37.*

BORDER COUNTRY, THE.   Maps 4, 5, 9, 10, and 11.
The term Border Country is generally applied to the Lowland counties of Roxburgh, Peebles, Selkirk and also parts of Berwick and Dumfries, though the essence of true Border scenery is confined mainly to the first three counties. This land of rounded green hills, delightful glens and dales, together with numerous ruined castles and peel towers, is separated from England by the long line of the *Cheviot* (*q.v.*) hills, and is impregnated with legends and stories of Border warfare and raids in medieval times. Above all, the district is associated with the life and works of Sir Walter Scott, whose last and most famous home of *Abbotsford* (*q.v.*) is situated in the very heart of the Border Country, in which are also to be found the four great ruined Abbeys of *Melrose*, *Jedburgh*, *Dryburgh* and *Kelso* (all *q.v.*). See **Lowlands** and **Scott Country.** *Iter. 30, 47.*

BORDER NATIONAL FOREST PARK, Roxburgh.
Map 5, NY 4 8 and NT 5 1 etc.
See **Bonchester Bridge** and **Newcastleton.**

BORELAND, Dumfries.   Map 4, NY 1 9.
Iter. 42.

BORGIE BRIDGE, Sutherland.   Map 28, NC 6 5.
The bridge spans the River Borgie, which flows northwards from here into Torrisdale Bay. A by-road follows the river towards the coast before veering north-westwards for the crofting township of *Skerray* (*q.v.*). *Iter. 234, 235, 240.*

BORGUE, Kirkcudbright.   Map 3, NX 6 4.
A quiet village, to the west of Kirkcudbright Bay, and noted for its flowers. Its setting was used by R. L. Stevenson for part of his novel " The Master of Ballantrae." *Plunton Castle* is a 16th cent. ruin. *Iter. 73.*

BORRODALE, Inverness.   Map 12, NM 6 8.
See **Loch Nan Uamh.**

BORTHWICK, Midlothian.   Map 10, NT 3 5.
The splendid, massive, double-towered *Borthwick Castle*, with its machicolated parapet, dating from 1430, and now restored, was the home of Mary, Queen of Scots and Bothwell after their marriage in 1566. The Queen escaped from the Castle later, disguised as a man, and rejoined her husband on his way to *Dunbar* (*q.v.*). In 1650 the Castle surrendered to Cromwell. The great hall retains a splendid hooded fireplace and has a massive barrel vault. The modern Church retains the 15th cent. aisle from the former structure, burnt in 1775, and contains well-preserved effigies of the first Lord and Lady Borthwick. See **Blackshiels** and **Crichton.**

BOTHKENNAR, Stirling.   Map 16, NS 9 8.
Iter. 86, 91, 96.

BOTHWELL, Lanark. 3,180.   Map 8, NS 7 5.
E.C. Wed. GOLF. In 1679 was fought near here the battle of Bothwell Brig, ending in the defeat of the Covenanters. The prisoners, to a number of 1,200, were confined for 5 months in the Greyfriars churchyard at *Edinburgh* (*q.v.*). The bridge over the Clyde, built originally c. 1400, was modernized in 1826. *Bothwell Castle* (A.M.), belonging to the Douglas family, is one of the most impressive ruined strongholds in Scotland, dating from the 13th and 15th cents., and situated in a picturesque setting above the Clyde Valley to the north-west of the town. The great hall was formerly one of the finest in the country, but the whole structure has suffered many vicissitudes. The great tower resembles its prototype at Coucy, in France. Sir Walter Scott wrote " Young Lochinvar " at Bothwell. The Castle is open weekdays, 10 to 4 or 7; Sun., after 2 (see note page 90). The Collegiate Church of Bothwell dates partly from 1398, and contains 18th cent. monuments to the Douglas family, being noted architecturally for its pointed barrel vault. *Iter. 51.*

BOTHWELL BRIDGE, Lanark.   Map 8, NS 7 5.
See **Bothwell.** *Iter. 18, 51.*

BOWDEN, Roxburgh.   Map 10, NT 5 3.
The restored Church dates mainly from the 17th cent. and contains a laird's loft. A church was founded here in the 12th cent. The 16th cent. Market Cross has been restored as a

Border Country, The. The 'Capon Tree' at Jedburgh, Roxburghshire, a survivor of the ancient Jed, or Jethart Forest, which formerly covered the region. It stands south of the town, to the right of A68

Bo'ness, West Lothian. A copy of a distance slab, set up in 1868, marking the terminal point of the Antonine, or Roman Wall. The original, which was excavated here, is now in the National Museum of Antiquities at Edinburgh

Bothwell, Lanark. The Monument commemorating the defeat of the Covenanters at Bothwell Brig in 1679

Bothwell, Lanark. The ruined 13th to 15th century Castle, incorporating the Douglas tower, which took 36 years to complete, and was probably built by French craftsmen

Borthwick, Midlothian. Borthwick Castle, 15th century and restored, once the home of Mary, Queen of Scots and Bothwell

Border Country, The. The iron 'yett', or gate, of the 15th century Comlongon Castle, which stands on an unclassified road west of Clarencefield, in Dumfriesshire, not far from the English border

PLATE 20 (facing page 110)   [For BOWDEN see following plate

Braemar, Aberdeen. Invercauld Bridge, carrying A93 across the River Dee to the east of Braemar

Bowden, Roxburgh. The mainly 17th century Church, which contains an example of a laird's loft. A church was founded here originally in the 12th century

Bowden, Roxburgh. The restored 16th century village Cross, now a War Memorial

Braemar, Aberdeen. Braemar Castle, built in 1628 and partly re-built c.1748

Braemar, Aberdeen. The Old Bridge of Dee, some 3 miles east of the resort

Bracadale, Isle of Skye, Inverness. The flat-topped twin hills known as Macleod's Tables, seen from A863, near the shores of Loch Bracadale, on the way to Dunvegan

PLATE 21 (facing page 111)

War Memorial. Bowden's market dates from 1571, the first non-burghal Scottish one to be licensed. To the north rise the prominent triple-peaked *Eildon* hills, and from the high ground in the vicinity the view extends southwards towards the distant *Cheviots* (q.v.). *Iter. 46.*

BOWER, Caithness.   Map 30, **ND 2** 6.
Iter. 238.

BOWHILL, Selkirk.   Map 10, **NT 4** 2.
See **Selkirk.**

BOWLAND, Midlothian; Selkirk.   Map 10, **NT 4** 4.
On the Gala Water. To the south is the road to the Tweed valley, between Knowes Hill and the Torwoodlee Woods, among which stands the old Castle of *Torwoodlee*, near the Georgian house, dating from c. 1783. Nearby is *Crosslee Hill*, where, within a British Camp, are the foundations of a broch known as " The Rings." *Iter. 11.*

BOWLING, Dunbarton. 1,245.   Map 8, **NS 4** 7.
E.C. Wed. The point where the Forth and Clyde Canal, 38 miles long, crossing the narrow waist of Scotland, and built by Smeaton in 1790, enters the Clyde. The first practical steamboat, Symington's " Charlotte Dundas," was tried out here in 1802, and in 1812, Bell launched here the famous " Comet," the first Clyde passenger steamer. The western terminus of the Antonine, or *Roman Wall* (q.v.) was near Bowling. Farther to the west, by the Clyde, at Dunglass Point, is a ruined Castle, near which stands an obelisk to Henry Bell. In the background rise the *Kilpatrick* hills, attaining 1,313 ft., with their numerous small reservoirs. See **Bo'ness, Helensburgh, Leadhills, Neilston** and **Torphichen.** *Iter. 88, 109, 110, 111, 112.*

BOWMORE, Isle of Islay, Argyll.   Map 6, **NR 3** 5.
A large fishing village on Loch Indaal, noted for the curious circular Parish Church of *Kilmarrow*, on the tower of which an inscribed panel records its construction in 1767 by Daniel Campbell, " Lord of this island." From 1718 to 1843 the Islay Parliament met at Bowmore. There are alternative roads leading southwards towards *Port Ellen* (q.v.), the " low " road keeping near the shores of Laggan Bay, and the " high " road following an inland course. *Iter. 243.*

BOW OF FIFE, Fife.   Map 17, **NO 3** 1.
Fernie Castle, to the north, is a 16th cent. and later house. *Iter. 136.*

BOYNDIE BAY, Banff.   Map 27, **NJ 6** 6.
A bungalow resort, with fine sands and bathing and a bridge spanning the Burn of Boyndie. To the west is Knock Head, while inland, a little to the west, is the ruined church of *St. Brandan*, preserving some Jacobean tomb-stones in the churchyard. See **Whitehills.** *Iter. 199.*

BRACADALE, Isle of Skye, Inverness.   Map 23, **NG 3** 3.
    (Struan P.O.)
On Loch Beag, an inlet of Loch Harport, and the junction of a very rough hill road from *Portree* with a better road linking *Sligachan* (q.v.) to the Vaternish peninsula away to the north-west. A little to the west of the village is the ruined *Dun Beag*, one of the best preserved brochs in the island, and farther to the west is Loch Bracadale, with its islands, beyond which lies the Duirinish peninsula, dominated by the flat-topped, twin *Macleod's Tables*. See **Dunvegan.** *Iter. 255.*

BRACO, Perth. 273.   Map 16, **NN 8** 0.
To the east of the old bridge over the Knaik Water is the great Roman station of *Ardoch*, in the grounds of *Ardoch House*. The earthworks are of great strength, and are among the most striking of their kind in Great Britain. Coins excavated here date from the period of Hadrian. A little farther to the north-west is another Roman Camp, known as the Great Camp, adjacent to which is another and smaller example, the two camps together being considered to have had space for nearly 40,000 troops at a time. See **Forteviot.** *Iter. 138, 140.*

BRAE, Shetland.   Map 33, **HU 3** 6.
Iter. 267, 270.

BRAEDOWNIE, Angus.   Map 20, **NO 2** 7.
Beautifully situated in the Braes of Angus mountains at the head of the long valley of Glen Clova, where the road ends, and two roadless valleys fork north-westwards into the high hills, the more easterly of which gives access to the lofty *White Mounth* (q.v.) plateau, and *Lochnagar* (q.v.), lying to the north. A branch track, known as the Capel Mounth, diverges to the north, and leads to Loch Muick, in Glen Muick, giving access to *Ballater* (q.v.). The westerly valley, known as Glen Doll, is traversed by a track leading to the curiously named Jock's Road, a path which climbs high above the White Water into the hills below *Broad Cairn* 3,268 ft. The hills of *Driesh*, 3,105 ft., to the south, and *Craig Mellon*, 2,815 ft., to the north, overshadow this lonely glen, which, near its head, is overlooked by the crags of *Craig Rennet*, 2,442 ft. See **Clova Church.** *Iter. 161.*

BRAEMAR, Aberdeen. 440.   Map 20, **NO 1** 9.
E.C. Thurs. GOLF. This famous Royal *Deeside* (q.v.) summer and winter resort in the Highlands, at an altitude of 1,100 ft., consists actually of *Castleton of Braemar* and *Auchindryne*, situated on either side of the Clunie Water, which flows into the Dee a little to the north of the village. The scenery is some of the most notable in Scotland, with heather-clad hills rising all round, dominated by the *Cairngorm* (q.v.) massif of *Cairn Toul*, 4,241 ft., away to the west, and to the south-east by the peak of *Lochnagar*, 3,786 ft. (q.v.), in the lofty *White Mounth* (q.v.) group, reached by way of Glen Callater. The neighbourhood was popularized originally by Queen Victoria, who spent many holidays at the Royal Castle of *Balmoral* (q.v.). On a mound, on which stands now the " *Invercauld Arms* " Hotel, the Earl of Mar raised the Jacobite Standard in 1715. *Braemar Castle*, dating from 1628, was largely rebuilt c. 1748, and is situated to the north of the resort, near the Dee, looking towards Invercauld Forest and the distant Cairngorm peak of *Ben Avon*, 3,843 ft. R. L. Stevenson wrote part of " Treasure Island " in a cottage at the south end of Castleton Terrace. The an-

BRAEMAR

1. Stevenson Cottage.
2. Castle.
3. Princess Roya Park.

nual Braemar Gathering, held in September, is an important social event, and takes place in the Princess Royal Park.

Below Invercauld Bridge, **3 m. E.**, is the old Bridge of Dee, and access is sometimes possible from the lodge here to the Garbh-Allt Falls in the Royal Forest of Ballochbuie. *Invercauld House*, north of the river, is partly 15th cent., and the view of Lochnagar from Invercauld Bridge over the Dee is extremely fine. *Morrone Hill*, 2,819 ft., to the south-west of Braemar, is a splendid viewpoint, looking north-westwards towards the Cairngorms. The main road leading southwards from Braemar climbs through Glen Clunie, and over the *Cairnwell* (q.v.) Pass, prior to descending over the famous *Devil's Elbow* (frequently blocked by snow in winter) to reach Spittal of *Glenshee* (q.v.). The continuation along Glen Shee leads to lower-lying country watered by the River Ericht, and gives access to Blairgowrie. Private roads leave the main Deeside road (A.93) to the east of Braemar, from points near Invercauld Bridge and Inver; these roads later unite and lead northwards to the remote *Loch Builg*, on the eastern fringe of *Ben Avon*, in the Cairngorms. At one point this road reaches a height of 2,391 ft., making it almost the highest in Great Britain, but in addition to being private it is at the present time completely unserviceable for motor vehicles. A steep and narrow road inking the Dee valley with the upper valley of the Don, leaves Deeside near Balmoral Castle, climbing into the hills by way of *Gairnshiel Lodge* (*q.v.*), in Glen Gairn. The lofty section beyond this point attains 1,805 ft., and is liable to become snow-bound in winter. From a point approaching Gairnshiel Lodge, a by-road diverges to the west, following the River Gairn, but becoming private beyond Daldownie. The continuation of this road gives access to Loch Builg by an easier route. See **Crathie Church** and **Inverey** (for *Linn of Dee*). *Iter. 141, 152, 160, 167, 168, 179.*

BRAEMORE LODGE, Ross and Cromarty.
Map 29, **NH 2** 7.
Here, the roads from *Dundonnell* (*q.v.*) and *Ullapool* (*q.v.*) converge on their way eastwards to Inverness. On the former, just before the junction, is the very impressive *Corrieshalloch Gorge* (N.T. Scot), well seen from a fragile bridge spanning the deep and narrow chasm, below which lie the spectacular *Falls of Measach*, some of the finest in Scotland. The road descending to Ullapool, on Loch Broom, goes through the beautiful fertile valley of Strath More, and in the background, to the east, are the lofty peaks of *Beinn Dearg*, 3,547 ft., and *Cona Mheall*, 3,200 ft., the latter sheltering the wild little Loch Choire Ghranda, in its precipitous setting. The remote, vertical cliffs of *Seana Bhraigh*, 3,041 ft., rise away to the north between the Inverlael and Freevater Forests. To the south of Braemore Lodge is the extensive *Fannich* group, in which *Sgurr Mor*, 3,637 ft., overlooks the lonely Loch Fannich. The road leading south-eastwards towards Inverness traverses the bleak moorland known as the Dirrie More, on which lies the little Loch Droma. The Dundonnell road, which rises to over 1,100 ft., was made during the 1851 famine, and is called the " Destitution Road." Magnificent views of the wild *Teallach* mountains nearly 3,500 ft. in height, which form the background to the lonely Dundonnell Forest, can be obtained from it. *Iter. 204, 206, 222.*

BRAGAIR, Isle of Lewis, Ross and Cromarty.
Iter. 260.   Map 32, **NB 2** 4.

BRAIDWOOD, Lanark.   Map 9, **NS 8** 4.
Known for its limestone quarries. **2 m. S.S.E.**, in a park, is *The Lee*, a mansion associated with a famous amulet known as the " Lee Penny," which suggested Scott's novel " The Talisman." *Iter. 50, 54.*

BRANDERBURGH,, Moray. 5,161 SB. with Lossiemouth. See **Lossiemouth**.   Map 26, **NJ 2** 7.

BRANXHOLM TOWER, Roxburgh.   Map 5, **NT 4** 1. See **Hawick**.

BREADALBANE, Perth.   Maps 15, **NN 33** etc.
The name given to a large part of north-west Perthshire, extending from the Inverness border to the basin of the rivers Earn and Forth, lying to the south towards the Stirling border. The *Grampian* (*q.v.*) mountains cover most of the area, which includes also Loch Rannoch and Glen Lyon, one of the longest and finest of Scottish glens. The view from the summit of *Ben Lawers*, 3,984 ft., gives a far-reaching panorama over the tangled ranges of the Breadalbane hills, which include the lofty *Forest of Mamlorn* group. See **Bridge of Balgie**, **Fortingall**, **Kinloch Rannoch** and **Lawers**.

BREAKISH, Isle of Skye, Inverness.   Map 23, **NG 6** 2. *Iter. 251.*

BREASCLETE, Isle of Lewis, Ross and Cromarty.
Iter. 260.   Map 32, **NB 2** 3.

BRECHIN, Angus. 7,393. SB.   Map 21, **NO 6** 6.
E.C. Wed. M.D. Tues. GOLF. Stands on the South Esk River, facing the valley of *Strathmore* (*q.v.*), with a background of hills rising gradually to the eastern Grampians. The old town, with its steep streets, is well seen from the river bridge on the Arbroath road. Parts of the Cathedral, now the Parish Church, are of 12th cent. date. After partial demolition in 1807, the building was restored in 1902. The spired tower dates from c. 1360, and the prominent Round Tower (A.M.), 87 ft. high, one of the two examples on the Scottish mainland, is held to be 10th or

BRECHIN

Scale
0   ¼M

CROWN COPYRIGHT RESERVED   RB.60   PUBLISHED BY THE AUTOMOBILE ASSOCIATION

1. Castle.
2. Cathedral, with Round Tower.
3. Municipal Buildings.
   Information Bureau.

11th cent. work, and recalls similar examples in Ireland. In the town stands a fragment of the 13th cent. Maison Dieu Chapel (A.M.). The Castle, separated from the Cathedral by a burn, withstood a siege in 1303, but has been completely modernized, and has a fine park. **5 m. W.** is *Careston Castle*, a 15th cent. and later structure. **6 m. N.W.** are two prehistoric hill forts (A.M.), known as the Black Caterthun and the White Caterthun, situated on a ridge commanding extensive views over the Howe of the Mearns and towards the eastern Grampians. **5 m. S.E.**, in a deer-park of 1,300 acres, is *Kinnaird Castle*, a 19th cent. structure, retaining a portion dating from 1405. See **Aberlemno**, **Abernethy** and **Edzell**. *Iter. 151, 156, 163, 164, 166.*

BRESSAY, Shetland.   Map 33, **HU 4** 3 etc.
See **Shetland Islands** (Mainland).

BRIDGEND, Isle of Islay, Argyll.   Map 6, **NR 3** 6.
At the head of Loch Indaal, in a wooded setting, and a junction of roads proceeding westwards and south-westwards along its shores. *Islay House* stands in wooded grounds. **2½ m. W.**, on the coast at *Blackrock*, is a sandy bathing beach. A road leads northwards from here across Gruinart Flats to the head of Loch Gruinart, where a clan battle took place in 1598. A branch road follows the west shores of the loch as far as Ardnave, beyond which is Ardnave Point and Nave Island, on a rocky stretch of coast. See **Bowmore**. *Iter. 243, 246, 247.*

BRIDGE OF ALFORD, Aberdeen.   Map 26, **NJ 5** 1.
See **Alford**. *Iter. 165, 176, 177, 190.*

BRIDGE OF ALLAN, Stirling. 3,261 SB. Map 16, **NS 7** 9.
E.C. Wed. GOLF. This pleasant watering-place and touring centre, on the Allan Water, which unites with the Forth to the south of the town, stands in a wooded setting at the foot of the *Ochil* hills, with *Dumyat*, 1,375 ft., a good viewpoint, rising to the east. There is a modern Pump Room and baths. R. L. Stevenson was formerly a frequent visitor to the resort. **2 m. N.W.** is *Keir House*, where Chopin was a guest in 1848. *Iter. 135, 138, 140, 141.*

BRIDGE OF AVON, Banff.   Map 26, **NJ 1** 2.
Here, the road leading northwards from *Tomintoul* (*q.v.*) forks, the left branch going over the hills by way of *Bridge*

Brechin, Angus. The 10th or 11th century round tower, which stands apart from the Cathedral. It is one of the only two examples of a structure native to Ireland to be found on the mainland of Scotland. See Abernethy (Plate 4)

Braemore Lodge, Ross and Cromarty. The deep Corrieshalloch ravine, belonging to the National Trust for Scotland, in which lie the impressive Falls of Measach

Bridge of Allan, Stirling. The Spa buildings. Robert Louis Stevenson was a frequent visitor to Bridge of Allan

Bridge of Avon, Banff. Here, the Tomintoul to Grantown-on-Spey road (A939) crosses the River Avon

Breadalbane, Perth. A bridge over the River Lyon at Fortingall, north of Loch Tay, at the entrance to Glen Lyon, among the Breadalbane hills of north-west Perthshire

PLATE 22 (facing page 112)

Brig O'Doon, Ayr. The Auld Brig at Alloway, immediately to the south of Ayr, on B7024. It is of late mediaeval date, and is associated with Robert Burns's '*Tam O'Shanter*'

Bridge of Ess, Aberdeen. The tomb of Byron's 'Mary,' who died at Aberdeen in 1887. It is situated in the churchyard of Glentanner, on an unclassified road some 2 miles west

Bridge of Forss, Caithness. The remains of the 16th century Brims Castle, now part of a farm, on Crosskirk Bay, to the north

Bridge of Orchy, Argyll. A curious forestry workers' 'bucket bridge' over the River Orchy, operated by a hand rope. It is situated 3 miles south-west, in Glen Orchy, on B8074

Bridge of Orchy, Argyll. This old bridge on A82 stands at the entrance to Glen Orchy, where the new Glencoe road leaves the line of the old road

Bridge of Brown, Banff; Moray. A moorland bridge carrying A939 across a stream in Glen Brown, on the Banff–Moray border

[For **BRIDGE OF FEUGH** see under DEESIDE (Plate 44)

PLATE 23 (facing page 113)

of Brown (*q.v.*) to Strath Spey, and the right branch following the River Avon northwards, with the *Cromdale* hills to the west. *Iter. 141, 160, 169, 176, 177.*

BRIDGE OF AWE, Argyll. Map 14, **NN 0** 2.
Iter. 110, 117, 125, 144, 145.

BRIDGE OF BALGIE, Perth. Map 15, **NN 5** 4.
Situated in beautiful Glen Lyon, and the point of divergence of the steep (1 in 6), narrow and poorly surfaced mountain road leading southwards to *Loch Tay* (*q.v.*) over a 1,805-ft. high shoulder of *Ben Lawers*, 3,984 ft., and passing the little Lochan na Lairige. To the south-east of the lochan rise the peaks of the *Tarmachan* group, 3,421 ft. There are hydro-electric developments in this district. The narrow road continuing westwards from Bridge of Balgie into Upper Glen Lyon soon passes near the picturesque *Meggernie Castle*, by the River Lyon, and dating partly from c. 1582. The road eventually reaches Loch Lyon, near which a large new dam has been constructed. The head of the glen is surrounded by lofty, green hills, dominated by *Ben Achallader*, 3,404 ft., to the north-west, and *Ben Heasgarnich*, 3,530 ft., to the south. The latter is the highest peak of the Forest of Mamlorn group in the *Breadalbane* (*q.v.*) country. See **Fortingall, Innerwick Church** and **Lawers.** *Iter. 107.*

BRIDGE OF BROWN, Banff ; Moray.
 Map 26, **NJ 1** 2.
The bridge stands at the county boundary, on the lofty moorland road from *Tomintoul* (*q.v.*) to *Grantown-on-Spey* (*q.v.*). To the south lies Glen Brown. The Grantown road climbs to more than 1,400 ft., before commencing the descent towards the wooded Strath Spey, and there are views of the lofty *Cairngorm* (*q.v.*) mountains away to the south-west, in which *Ben Avon*, 3,843 ft., is prominent. To the north rise the nearer, but lower *Cromdale* hills. *Iter. 141, 160, 169, 176, 177.*

BRIDGE OF CALLY, Perth. 300.
 Map 20, **NO 1** 5.
This bridge spans the River Ardle, flowing through Strath Ardle, the stream being joined a short distance away by the Black Water, coming down from Glen Shee, the two forming the River Ericht. Westwards lies the moorland area of Clunie Forest, and to the east is the Forest of Alyth. The main road from Blairgowrie divides at Bridge of Cally, the left fork leading to Pitlochry, and the right fork climbing through Glen Shee to the lofty *Cairnwell* (*q.v.*) Pass on its way to Braemar. *Iter. 141, 152, 159.*

BRIDGE OF CRAIG, Angus. Map 20, **NO 2** 5.
The bridge spans the River Isla, and a little to the east are the fine falls known as the Reekie Linn. Still farther east is the waterfall of the Slug of Auchrannie. To the north is Loch Lintrathen, a reservoir for Dundee's water supply. See **Dykend.** *Iter. 160.*

BRIDGE OF DEE, Aberdeen. Map 27, **NJ 9** 0.
See **Aberdeen.** *Iter. 151, 155, 156, 168, 174.*

BRIDGE OF DON, Aberdeen. Map 27, **NJ 9** 0.
See **Aberdeen.** *Iter. 181, 182, 183, 185, 186.*

BRIDGE OF DYE, Kincardine. Map 21, **NO 6** 8.
See **Cairn o' Mounth.** *Iter. 163, 165.*

BRIDGE OF EARN, Perth. 400. Map 17, **NO 1** 1.
E.C. Thurs. M.D. Fri. Part of the medieval bridge may still be seen. **1 m.** W. are *Pitkeathly Wells*, once well known. **1 m.** N.E. is *Moncreiffe House*, dating from c. 1679 and ascribed to Sir William Bruce. It was badly damaged by fire in 1957. **2½ m.** S.E. is the fine old mansion of *Balmanno*, well restored by Sir Robert Lorimer. See **Abernethy.** *Iter. 90, 91, 92, 130, 131, 132.*

BRIDGE OF ESS, Aberdeen. Map 21, **NO 5** 9.
At the entrance to the wooded valley of Glen Tanner, in which stands *Glentanar House*, in a delightful setting. In the churchyard of *Glentanner*, some **2 m.** W., on the south bank of the Dee, is buried Byron's " Mary." (See **Cambus o' May).** The various hill-paths which lead out of the valley into the eastern Grampian mountains are described under *Aboyne. Iter. 168, 174.*

BRIDGE OF FEUGH, Kincardine. Map 21, **NO 7** 9.
See **Banchory.** *Iter. 163, 168, 174, 190, 191.*

BRIDGE OF FITCH, Shetland. Map 33, **HU 4** 4.
Iter. 267, 268, 270.

BRIDGE OF FORSS, Caithness. Map 30, **ND 0** 6.
An old tree-surrounded mill stands here near the rapids of the Forss Water, flowing towards Crosskirk Bay, on the eastern arm of which is Brims Ness, sheltering the ruined 16th cent. *Brims Castle*, now incorporated in a farm. To the north-west is the little chapel of *St. Mary*, perhaps of 12th cent. date. *Iter. 232, 234, 240.*

BRIDGE OF GAIRN, Aberdeen. Map 20, **NO 3** 9.
Iter. 141, 152, 167, 174, 179.

BRIDGE OF GARRY, Perth. Map 20, **NN 9** 6.
A little to the south, the River Garry flows into the Tummel, a path leading to the junction of the rivers, near which are the Falls of Tummel (N.T. Scot.). Bridge of Garry is sometimes considered to stand almost in the exact centre of Scotland. The hydro-electric developments in the vicinity are part of the Tummel-Garry scheme, and are described under *Pitlochry*. The falls are accessible by road from that resort by means of the new Aldour Bridge and road built in connection with the scheme, and leading past the newly-created Loch Faskally, near the west bank of the Tummel. The road continues westwards from Bridge of Garry towards Loch Tummel and passes the famous *Queen's View* (*q.v.*), at the eastern end of the loch. See **Killiecrankie.** *Iter. 138, 148.*

BRIDGE OF GAUR, Perth. Map 19, **NN 5** 5.
Iter. 147.

BRIDGE OF ISLA, Perth. Map 17, **NO 1** 3.
See **Meikleour** and **Stobhall.** *Iter. 152.*

BRIDGE OF MARNOCH, Banff. Map 27, **NJ 6** 4.
Iter. 184, 194, 196.

BRIDGE OF ORCHY, Argyll. 50. Map 15, **NN 2** 3.
E.C. Wed. The old and the new roads to *Glencoe* (*q.v.*) diverge here, the new road, completed in 1935, continuing northwards round the eastern side of Loch Tulla, where old pine trees, relics of the former extensive Caledonian Forest, are still standing. This road avoids the exposed climb over the *Black Mount* which the old road was forced to take, the new alignment merely skirting the *Mount*, attaining a height of 1,143 ft. on Rannoch Moor, and passing near Loch Ba. *Ben Dorain*, 3,524 ft., dominates the surrounding country, its steep, furrowed slopes rising in a continuous sweep to the summit. Farther to the north, on the east side of Loch Tulla, in the Drum Alban ridge, and near the country's main watershed, is *Ben Achallader*, 3,404 ft. Below stands the ruined *Achallader Castle*, on a rough by-road in Glen Tulla, in which are the ancient pine trees of Crannach. Glen Orchy extends south-westwards from Bridge of Orchy, and is traversed by a narrow and rather rough road, which is later joined by the main Oban road through Glen Lochy, the two roads converging on *Dalmally* (*q.v.*). See **Inveroran** and **Kingshouse.** *Iter. 100, 125, 142.*

BRIDGE OF PHILORTH, Aberdeen. Map 27, **NK 0** 6.
See **Inverallochy.** *Iter. 182.*

BRIDGE OF WALLS, Shetland. Map 33, **HU 2** 5.
Iter. 268.

BRIDGE OF WEIR, Renfrew. 3,148. Map 8, **NS 3** 6.
E.C. Wed. GOLF. A residential and golfing district on the Gryfe Water. Tanning is an important local industry. *Ranfurly Castle* was formerly the home of John Knox's ancestors. To the north-west lie the well-known *Quarrier's Orphan Homes*. See **Houston.** *Iter. 64.*

BRIG O' DOON, Ayr. Map 8, **NS 3** 1.
See **Alloway.** *Iter. 84.*

BRIG O' TURK, Perth. Map 15, **NN 5** 0.
See **Trossachs.** *Iter. 106, 111, 139.*

BROADFORD, Isle of Skye, Inverness. 900.
 Map 23, **NG 6** 2.
E.C. Wed. A small tourist resort on Broadford Bay,

looking to the little island of Pabay, known for its fossils, and beyond it to the Applecross mountains on the mainland. *Beinn na Caillich*, 2,403 ft., and *Beinn Dearg Mhor*, 2,323 ft., in the Broadford group of *Red* hills, dominate the village to the west. At the foot of the hills is the ruined *Coire Chatachan*, a former Mackinnon home, where Dr. Johnson and Boswell were entertained in 1773. The coast road leading north-westwards towards *Sligachan* (*q.v.*) provides superb views of mountain and sea, and makes the complete circuit of the sea loch of *Loch Ainort*, at the mouth of which is the island of Scalpay. The finest excursion from Broadford is a visit to the magnificent scenery of *Lochs Scavaig* and *Coruisk* (both described under their own headings), the hilly and narrow road proceeding by way of Loch Slapin, dominated by the great peak of *Blaven*, 3,042 ft., an outlier of the *Coolins* (*q.v.*). It then crosses the low Strathaird peninsula to reach the village of *Elgol* (*q.v.*), the remainder of the journey having to be made by motor boat on Loch Scavaig. See **Dunan, Kyleakin, Kylerhea** and **Torrin**. *Iter. 251, 252, 253.*

BROADMEADOWS, Selkirk.　　　　Map 10, **NT 4** 3.
Beautifully situated in the pastoral Vale of Yarrow, threaded by the Yarrow Water. An old drovers' track, the *Minch* road, goes over the hills in a north-easterly direction from here towards *Traquair* (*q.v.*). **1 m. S.E.** is *Newark Castle*, an impressive 15th cent. ruin, the retreat of the widowed Anne, Duchess of Buccleuch, to whom Scott made the " Last Minstrel" address his "Lay," and visited by Scott and Wordsworth together. On the opposite side of the river is Mungo Park's birthplace, a small cottage at *Foulshiels*, where the explorer was born in 1771. The Yarrow flows here through a most picturesque wooded reach. **1 m. W.** of Broadmeadows is *Hangingshaw*, on the Yarrow, here joined by the Hangingshaw Burn. There are remains of an old Castle of the outlaw Murray. See **Ettrick Bridge End** and **Yarrow Church.** *Iter. 13, 46.*

BRODICK, Isle of Arran, Bute. 1,033.　　Map 7, **NS 0** 3.
E.C. Wed. GOLF. Finely placed on the sandy Brodick Bay, with a pier served by the Clyde steamers, one of the most important approaches being from *Ardrossan* (*q.v.*), on the mainland across the Firth of Clyde. The real name of the village is *Invercloy*. *Brodick Castle* (N.T. Scot.), once the home of the Dukes of Hamilton, is open, with its fine gardens, daily in summer except Sun., 1 to 5 p.m. (See note page 90). Parts of the Castle date from the 14th century and it was enlarged by Cromwell's garrison. The western end and the tower were built in 1844. The National Trust for Scotland also now owns *Goat Fell*, 2866 ft., the highest of Arran's mountains, and some 7,000 acres, above the 750-ft. level. This includes Glen Rosa and *Cir Mhor*, 2618 ft., whose south-west ridge and the Rosa pinnacle, together with the nearby *a'Chir* ridge, provide some of Scotland's finest rock climbing and ridge walking. There are, however, a number of easy routes to the summits, which provide magnificent viewpoints. *Caisteal Abhail* (Peak of the Castles), 2,817 ft., *Beinn Tarsuinn* (N.T. Scot.) and *Beinn Nuis* (N.T. Scot.) also offer splendid climbing. A road, known as the String Road, proceeds south-westwards from Brodick through Glen Shurig, affording fine views from the high ground which it traverses, and reaching the west coast at *Blackwaterfoot* (*q.v.*). A branch from this road leads to *Machrie* (*q.v.*). higher up the coast, and passes within sight of the Standing Stones of Tormore, with remains of some 10 circles, situated to the south of the Machrie Water, nearing the shores of Kilbrennan Sound. The Glen Rosa valley, north-west of Brodick, offers some of the finest scenery in the neighbourhood, and from its head, a climb over a col gives access for walkers to Glen Sannox and *Sannox* (*q.v.*). South of Brodick, the *Lamlash* (*q.v.*) road goes inland, but a path circles the low *Clauchland* hills, keeping near the coast, with fine views. See **Corrie**. *Iter. 242.*

BRODIE, Moray.　　　　　　Map 25, **NH 9** 5.
The imposing *Brodie Castle* stands a little to the north, with the Muckle Water flowing to the east on its way to Findhorn Bay. *Iter. 175, 198, 199.*

BROOMHALL, Fife.　　　　　Map 16, **NT 0** 8.
See **Charlestown.**

BROOMHOUSE, Lanark.　　　　Map 8, **NS 6** 6.
Iter. 51, 54.

BRORA, Sutherland. 1,074.　　　Map 31, **NC 9** 0.
E.C. Wed. GOLF. A small resort, with a harbour, sands and bathing, on the River Brora, noted for salmon. Here the river enters the sea after flowing through Loch Brora, over which, a few miles inland, hangs the *Carrol Rock*, nearly 700 ft. high. To the west of the loch is Strath Brora. Brora Bridge was the only one in the county prior to Telford's 19th cent. road-making. A coal mine, first opened at Brora in 1598, is said to be the sole example in the north of Scotland. There are a number of Pictish brochs in the vicinity, including *Cole Castle*, near the head of Loch Brora, and *Kintradwell*, the latter, a particularly notable example, being situated **3 m. N.E.** of Brora, off the Helmsdale road. **3 m. S.W.** is *Uppat House*, dating from the 18th cent. See **Loth**. *Iter. 200, 231, 233.*

BROUGHTON, Peebles. 355.　　　Map 9, **NT 1** 3.
Here, Biggar Water and the Broughton Burn unite to flow together into the Tweed to the south-east of the village. Beside the ruined old church, in the cemetery, is a restored vault, thought to be the remains of a cell, founded in the 7th cent. by St. Llolan, a Pictish saint. There are numerous hill-forts on the surrounding hills. The village is associated with John Buchan (Lord Tweedsmuir) who spent many holidays here. The modern mansion of *Broughton Place* has fine gardens, which are shown at times in the summer (see note page 90). The former house was the home of Murray of Broughton, who was secretary to Prince Charles Edward in 1745, and was later captured, subsequently turning King's Evidence and eventually dying in England. See **Drumelzier** and **Lyne**. *Iter. 10.*

BROUGHTY FERRY, Angus. 11,380.　　Map 17, **NO 4** 3.
E.C. Wed. GOLF. A pleasant resort and suburb of Dundee, with sands and bathing. Opposite, across the Firth of Tay, stands Tayport. *Broughty Castle*, 15th cent. (A.M.), was restored in 1860, and is used for military training. *Claypotts Castle* (A.M.), built between 1569 and 1588, is a quaint example of its period, notably the angle towers, with their crew-stepped gables. Claverhouse of Dundee once owned the castle. It is open weekdays, 10 to 4 or 7 ; Sun., after 2 (See note page 90). See **Monifieth**. *Iter. 155.*

BROW, Dumfries.　　　　　　Map 3, **NY 0** 6.
On an inlet of the Solway Firth, and once a small watering-place, visited in 1796 by Robert Burns, a week prior to his death. The Brow Well recalls the visit.

BROXBURN, East Lothian.　　　Map 10, **NT 6** 7.
Just off the Great North Road, to the south-east, is the site of the battle of *Dunbar* (*q.v.*), fought in 1650, in which Cromwell defeated Leslie and the Covenanters. A stone was erected in 1950 to commemorate the fight. To the east. on the coast, are white sands and the Barn's Ness lighthouse. *Iter. 1, 2, 38, 39.*

BROXBURN, West Lothian. 7,555.　　Map 9, **NT 0** 7.
A mining village. At *Kirkhill* farm, to the north-west, is a curious, inscribed "solar" stone, erected by the 11th Earl of Buchan in the 18th cent. See **Uphall**. *Iter. 16.*

BRUAR FALLS, Perth.　　　　　Map 19, **NN 8** 6.
See **Struan.**

BRUICHLADDICH, Isle of Islay, Argyll.　Map 6, **NR 2** 6.
A small port on the western shores of Loch Indaal. There are distilleries in the neighbourhood. *Iter. 247.*

BUCCLEUCH, Selkirk.　　　　　Map 10, **NT 3** 1.
Near *Buccleuch* farm stood formerly a tower, which gave its name to the title of the Dukes of Buccleuch. *Iter. 34.*

BUCHAN, Aberdeen.　　　　　Map 27, **NJ 8** 5 etc.
The name given to the north-eastern and rather bleak sector of the county, which includes the fishing ports of Fraserburgh and Peterhead, and a long, mainly undeveloped stretch of coastline north and south of Rattray Head. The land is almost entirely flat, a notable land-

Brora, Sutherland. The broch of Kintradwell, situated some 3 miles to the north-east, off A9

Broughton, Peebles. An inscribed gate on the Rachan estate

Broughty Ferry, Angus. The 16th century Claypotts Castle. It was allegedly once the home of a mistress of Cardinal Beaton, and Claverhouse of Dundee lived there for a time

Brow, Dumfries. The Brow Well, visited by Robert Burns a week before his death in 1796. It stands on B725, a mile south-west of Ruthwell Church

Broxburn, West Lothian. The curious inscribed 'Solar Stone' at Kirkhill Farm. It was set up in the 18th century by the 11th Earl of Buchan, who founded the Society of Antiquaries of Scotland

Broxburn, East Lothian. A stone, placed just off the Great North Road (A1), commemorating the Battle of Dunbar, fought in 1650. The inscription quotes words written by Thomas Carlyle

[For BUCHAN see following plate
For BRODICK see under ARRAN (Plate 10)

PLATE 24 (facing page 114)

Buchan, Aberdeen. The Town House of 1788 at Peterhead, a fishing port in the Buchan, or north-east corner of the county

Bullers of Buchan, Aberdeen. The strange, rocky amphitheatre, which lies a mile to the north-east of Cruden Bay. Dr. Johnson, in his tour of 1773, visited it by boat, and pronounced it a 'rock perpendicularly tubulated'

Bunkle, Berwick. In this re-built Church is preserved what may be one of the earliest Norman arches in Scotland. The original Norman Church was taken down in 1820

Burns Country, Ayr; Dumfries. The late 19th century Burns Memorial Tower, which stands to the north of Mauchline, an Ayrshire town, on A76. In the vicinity is Mossgiel Farm, where his early poems were written

Burntisland, Fife. The Church, built in 1592, probably to a Dutch design. The tower was added in 1759

PLATE 25 (facing page 115)

[For BUTE see following plate

mark being the low *Mormond Hill*, with its two carved animals, a white horse and a stag, situated near *Strichen* (*q.v.*). The River Deveron forms the western boundary of Buchan for a short distance, and along the southern boundary flows the less-important Ythan, on the banks of which is situated the splendid castle of *Fyvie* (*q.v.*). On the Buchan coast is Buchan Ness, the most easterly point in Scotland, situated to the south of Peterhead.

BUCHANTY, Perth. Map 16, **NN 9** 2.
Iter. 147.

BUCHLYVIE, Stirling. 349. Map 15, **NS 5** 9.
E.C. Wed. A hand-weaving industry is established here. **2 m. W.** is *Auchentoig*, a house dating from 1702, which is associated with Rob Roy. *Iter. 108, 112, 137.*

BUCKHAVEN, Fife. 21,488. SB. with Methil.
Map 17, **NT 3** 9.
E.C. Thurs. Once a ferry-port and fishing centre, this quaint little place has "streets" of steps and also old-world corners, common to many Fife villages. It is now united with *Methil* (*q.v.*). *Iter. 128.*

BUCKIE, Banff. 8,067. SB. Map 26, **NJ 4** 6.
E.C. Wed. GOLF. An important fishing town, with a good harbour and sands, situated on Spey Bay. Along the coast, to the east, are a number of small fishing villages nestling in the cliffside, among which, beyond Craig Head, *Findochty* (*q.v.*) and *Portnockie* (*q.v.*) are the most attractive. See **Portessie.** *Iter. 178, 199.*

BUCKSBURN, Aberdeen. 3,751. Map 27, **NJ 8** 0.
Iter. 175, 177, 178, 180, 184.

BULLERS OF BUCHAN, Aberdeen. Map 27, **NK 1** 3.
See Cruden Bay.

BUNESSAN, Isle of Mull, Argyll. Map 13, **NM 3** 2.
Lies in the peninsula of the Ross of Mull, noted for granite quarries, and on the road which links the eastern part of the island with *Fionphort*, some five miles to the west, from where a passenger ferry connects with *Iona* (*q.v.*). Away to the south is the small island of *Erraid*, associated with R. L. Stevenson's "Kidnapped," and out to sea are the Torran Rocks. North of Bunessan is the sea loch of Na Lathaich, and to the south-east is Loch Assapol. *Iter. 249.*

BUNKLE CHURCH, Berwick. Map 11, **NT 8** 5.
See Preston.

BURGHEAD, Moray. 1,384. SB. Map 26, **NJ 1** 6.
A fishing village, with a harbour and lighthouse, on the eastern horn of Burghead Bay overlooking the Moray Firth. There are extensive sands in the bay. The past is recalled by a rampart known as the "Broch Bailies," and also by a rock-cistern (A.M.) called the "Roman Bath." Ptolemy's "Alata Castra" may be identified with the village. The 505-ft. high mast of the B.B.C. radio transmitter, erected in 1936, is a notable local landmark. A curious old custom, still kept up on Old Yule Night, January 11th, is "Burning the Clavie," a tar-filled barrel being set alight and rolled down Dorrie Hill in order to ward off evil spirits. See **Duffus** and **Hopeman.** *Iter. 199.*

BURNBANK, Lanark. Map 8, **NS 7** 5.
Iter. 19, 53.

BURNHAVEN, Aberdeen. Map 27, **NK 1** 4.
Dates from the 19th cent. and lies adjacent to *Peterhead* (*q.v.*) prison. The village is situated between Peterhead and Sandford Bays and looks south-eastwards to Buchan Ness. *Iter. 181, 182, 187.*

BURNHEAD, Dumfries. Map 3, **NX 8** 9.
Iter. 25.

BURNHOUSE, Ayr. Map 8, **NS 3** 5.
Iter. 57, 60.

BURNHOUSES, Berwick. Map 11, **NT 7** 5.
Above the hamlet, to the north, rises *Cockburn Law*, 1,065 ft., and to the east are the curves of the Whiteadder Water. See **Abbey St. Bathans.** *Iter. 3.*

BURNMOUTH, Berwick. Map 11, **NT 9** 6.
A delightful little fishing village, at the foot of sandstone cliffs, sheltered by Ross Point, to the south. Northwards, beyond Ross Bay, is a rocky stretch of coast leading to Nestends, facing Hare Point across the Eye estuary. Two treaties between Scotland and England, in 1384, and again in 1497, were signed at Burnmouth. See **Eyemouth** and **Lamberton.** *Iter. 2.*

BURNS COUNTRY, THE, Ayr ; Dumfries.
Map 3, **NX 9** 7 etc. and 8, **NS 3** 2 etc.
Ayrshire is the county most intimately connected with the works of the great poet Robert Burns, and the town of *Ayr* itself, together with its neighbour *Alloway*, the birthplace of Burns, makes an admirable centre for visits to those places which are most associated with his life and works. Outside the county, the town of *Dumfries* is very closely connected with Burns, he having lived and worked there for five years, and being buried, together with members of his family, in the churchyard of *St. Michael's* Church. In the vicinity of Dumfries, near Auldgirth, is *Ellisland*, a farm, where Burns composed " Tam o'Shanter." Outside Mauchline, an Ayrshire town, is the farmhouse of *Mossgiel*, where some of his earliest works were written. See **Alloway, Auldgirth, Ayr, Catrine, Dumfries, Kilmarnock, Kirkoswald, Mauchline, Moffat** and **Tarbolton.**

BURNTISLAND, Fife. 6,016, SB. Map 17, **NT 2** 8.
E.C. Wed. GOLF. This Royal Burgh and coaling port on the Firth of Forth is overlooked by the hill known as *The Binn*,
632 ft. Bathing is from sands. The Church, modelled perhaps on the North Church at Amsterdam, dates from 1592, the tower having been built in 1749. It has a magistrate's pew, constructed in 1606, and there are seats especially marked for the various town guilds. Some characteristic 17th cent. houses line Somerville Street. In the

1. Church (1592).

Civil War, Burntisland was occupied by Cromwell. The town faces *Granton* (*q.v.*), some five miles across the Firth of Forth. See **Aberdour, Inchcolm** and **Inchkeith.** *Iter. 134.*

BURRAY, Orkney. Map 33, **ND 4** 9.
Iter. 266.

BURRELTON, Perth. Map 17, **NO 2** 3.
Iter. 151, 153.

BURWICK, Orkney. Map 33, **ND 4** 8.
See **Orkney Islands** (South Ronaldsay). *Iter. 266.*

BUSBY, Lanark ; Renfrew. Map 8, **NS 5** 5.
GOLF. *Iter. 18, 29.*

BUTE, ISLE OF, Bute. Map 7, **NS 0** 6 etc.
The island is situated off the *Cowal* (*q.v.*) coast, from which it is separated by the picturesque *Kyles of Bute* (*q.v.*). To the south, the Sound of Bute, in which lies the tiny island of *Inch Marnock*, divides it from the larger island of *Arran* (*q.v.*), well seen from various points. These islands, together with the smaller *Cumbraes* (see **Millport**), in the Firth of Clyde to the east, constitute the county of Bute. The island of Bute itself is about 15 miles long, averaging 3 to 5 miles in width, and, except in the northern sector, it is well provided with roads. The only high ground is in the north, beyond *Port Bannatyne*. The resort of *Rothesay* is one of the best known in Scotland, and in the south-eastern extremity of the island is *Kilchattan Bay*, the nearest point to the Cumbraes. Access to the island, which has a number of

sandy bays for bathing, is gained by steamer services connecting Rothesay with various Clyde ports, and also by means of the car ferry linking *Rhubodach* with *Colintraive* (*q.v.*), on the Kyles of Bute. See **Kilchattan Bay, Port Bannatyne, Rothesay** and **Rhubodach.** *Iter. 241.*

BUTTERSTONE, Perth.   Map 20, NO 0 4.
To the south is the little Loch Butterstone, and almost adjoining it is the Loch of the Lows, with the tiny Loch Craignish to the north. Away to the north lie the lofty moorlands of the Forest of Clunie, with the lonely lochs of Ordie and Benachally. See **Clunie.** *Iter. 141, 158, 166.*

CABRACH, Banff.   Map 26, NJ 3 2.
Stands about 1,000-ft. high, on a fine road leading north-westwards over the hills towards *Dufftown* (*q.v.*), crossing first the Deveron valley and then the 1,197-ft. high Glacks of Balloch pass. East of the village, the road to Rhynie attains 1,350 ft. on the Aberdeenshire border. To the south-east of Cabrach, on the Aberdeen border, rises the *Buck of Cabrach*, 2,368 ft., away to the west of which the Deveron has its lonely source among the hills. *Iter. 177, 190.*

CADDONFOOT, Selkirk. 946.   Map 10, NT 4 3.
Situated in the wooded Tweed valley, between *Craig Hill*, 1,252 ft., to the south, and *Meigle*, 1,387 ft., and its neighbours, to the north-east. The Caddon Water flows into the river a little to the west. See **Ashiestiel.** *Iter. 14.*

CADHAM, Fife.   Map 17, NO 2 0.
Iter. 93, 98, 126, 130.

CAERLAVEROCK, Dumfries.   Map 4, NY 0 6.
In the churchyard, which lies about a mile to the north-west of *Bankend*, off a by-road, and near the Lochar Water, lies Robert Paterson (1715-1801), the "Old Mortality" made famous by Sir Walter Scott. **4 m. S.,** off the *Glencaple* (*q.v.*) road, is *Caerlaverock Castle* (A.M.), a Maxwell stronghold, first mentioned in 1220, but dating mainly from the 15th cent., and the enclosure of which is triangular in plan. The building has had a stormy history, notably the attack on it by Edward I in 1300. Its final siege, by the Covenanters, which lasted three months, took place in 1640, after which it fell gradually into ruins. The impressive remains include a notable Renaissance façade, dating from 1638, and the Maxwell crest appears over the gateway between two formidable circular towers. The castle is open weekdays, 10 to 4 or 7 ; Sun., 2 to 4 or 7. (See note page 90.) Caerlaverock is held to be the "Ellangowan" of Scott's "Guy Mannering." The 6,200 acre Caerlaverock Estate is now a Nature Reserve. To the north is *Wardlaw Hill*, crowned by a prehistoric fort, with views over the Solway Firth and across the estuary of the Nith to *Criffell*, 1,866 ft., overlooking the Solway Firth. See **Balmaclellan** and **Dunnottar Castle.** *Iter. 28.*

CAIRNBAAN, Argyll.   Map 14, NR 8 9.
Situated midway along the Crinan Canal, on which the summit level is a little to the west. At Cairnbaan is a series of nine locks on the canal. Some 200 yards north of the hotel are two Cup and Ring-marked rocks (A.M.), relics of the prehistoric age. See **Crinan** and **Kilmichael.** *Iter. 122.*

CAIRNDOW, Argyll.   Map 14, NN 1 1.
Stands at the western end of Glen Kinglas, a little below the re-aligned main road and on the shores of upper *Loch Fyne* (*q.v.*), overlooked by *Binnein an Fhidhleir*, 2,658 ft. To the north, the River Fyne flows into the loch from Glen Fyne, to the east of which, at a height of 1,278 ft., are the impressive, but not so well-known Eagle's Falls. **1 m. S.W.** is *Ardkinglas House*, a modern mansion, built by Sir Robert Lorimer. See **Rest and be Thankful.** *Iter. 88, 101, 102.*

CAIRNEYHILL, Fife.   Map 16, NT 0 8.
Iter. 97.

CAIRNGORMS, Aberdeen ; Banff ; Inverness.
                                            Map 20, NH 9 0 etc.
The *Cairngorms* form an extensive group of lofty flat-topped mountains, broken by lonely corries, and stretching from *Deeside* (*q.v.*) to Speyside, to the north-east of the main *Grampian* (*q.v.*) range. Their outlook across the Dee Valley is towards the famous peak of *Lochnagar* (*q.v.*),

the monarch of the *Mounth* group. In the Cairngorms lies the largest area of ground in Scotland over the 4,000-ft. level, including four well-defined peaks. These are *Ben Macdhui*, 4,296 ft., the second highest of Scottish mountains, with an indicator on the summit, from which an extensive view is obtainable ; *Braeriach*, 4,248 ft., on whose upper slopes is the source of the River Dee, and which overlooks the well-known pass of the *Lairig Ghru* (*q.v.*), used by long-distance walkers ; *Cairn Toul*, 4,241 ft., prominent in the westerly view from *Braemar* (*q.v.*) ; and lastly *Cairn Gorm*, 4,084 ft., the most northerly of the quartet, which has given its name to the entire range. Near *Cairn Gorm* is *Cairn Lochan*, 3,983 ft., on the edge of the wild Coire an t-Sneachda, overlooked by the spectacular Fiacaill Ridge. Below *Cairn Gorm* lies the remote and gloomy Loch Avon, in its wild mountain setting, with the Shelter Stone at the western extremity. *Beinn Mheadoin*, 3,883 ft., also overlooks the loch, and to the south-west lies the tiny Loch Etchachan, at a height of more than 3,000 ft. This loch is said to remain frozen over for more than half the year. Another wild loch, that of Einich, deep below the great cliffs of *Sgoran Dubh*, 3,658 ft., on the western fringe of the range, is overlooked by the bare and lofty plateau known as the Great Moss, or Am Moine Mhor, sheltering the tiny Lochan nan Cnapan. In 1859, Queen Victoria climbed to the summit of *Ben Macdhui*, once considered to be Britain's highest peak.

Among the lesser peaks are *Ben Avon*, 3,843 ft., in the extreme east, overlooking the great Slochd Mor rift, and the waters of the Upper Avon ; *Bheinn a'Bhuird*, 3,924 ft., and 3,860 ft., rising above Glen Quoich ; *Derry Cairngorm*, 3,788 ft., between Glen Derry and Glen Lui Beg ; and *Beinn Bhrotain*, 3,797 ft., to the west of Glen Dee, and on the edge of Mar Forest. Owing to their great bulk, the Cairngorms can be seen at a distance from many parts of Scotland, while some of the best of the nearer views are those obtainable from parts of the Spey valley, in particular near *Aviemore* (*q.v.*). The two main passes through the hills linking Deeside and Speyside, the *Lairig Ghru*, and the less well-known *Lairig an Laoigh*, are ancient rights-of-way, and were formerly much used by cattle drovers. They are, however, only suitable for very strong walkers, as the distances are long and the going very difficult in places, while bad weather can turn the crossings into hazardous expeditions.

The Cairngorms are composed mainly of granite, and in some places quartz crystals, known as "Cairngorms," are to be found, and are often mounted in articles of jewellery. On the lower slopes of the hills large expanses of heather give a vivid colouring to the scene. The old name for the Cairngorms is the *Monadruadh*, or Red Mountains, as opposed to the much lower *Monadliath*, or Grey Mountains, which lie west of the Spey valley. Snow lies to a great depth for many months on certain of the peaks and also in the remote corries, notably on *Braeriach*. Winter sports can be enjoyed from some of the well-known resorts on the fringe of the high hills, such as Aviemore, Kingussie, Braemar and Tomintoul. All of these are described under their own headings, and the first-named is convenient for visiting the fine Glen More National Forest Park. This lies to the east of the great forest of *Rothiemurchus* (*q.v.*), in which remain scanty portions of the former Caledonian Forest once covering much of the Highlands. The Cairngorm district forms one of the proposed Scottish National Parks, which is expected to cover some 180 square miles. The Cairngorm National Nature Reserve is 40,000 acres in extent and is rich in local fauna and flora, notably of arctic-alpine type. Bird life includes the greenshank, dotterel and snow bunting. See **Inverey, Loch Morlich** and **Nethybridge.**

CAIRN O' MOUNTH, Kincardine.   Map 21, NO 6 8.
One of the best known of the passes traversing the lower, or eastern *Grampians* (*q.v.*), linking *Banchory* (*q.v.*) with *Fettercairn* (*q.v.*), and liable to be blocked by snow in winter. The summit of the pass, at a height of 1,475 ft., a fine viewpoint, is **5 m. N.** of Fettercairn, gradients on the ascent reaching 1 in 5½, and on the subsequent descent 1 in 6¼. Far to the west is *Mount Battock*, 2,555 ft., and to the north is *Clachnaben*, 1,944 ft. Eastwards, the view

Bute, Isle of, Bute. The remains of the mainly 13th century Castle at Rothesay, the most important resort on the island.

Caerlaverock, Dumfries. The impressive, ruined Maxwell stronghold, invested by Edward I in 1300, and attacked by the Covenanters in 1640. It stands 3 miles to the south, off B725

Cairnbaan, Argyll. Examples of prehistoric cup and ring marked rocks

Cairngorms, Aberdeen; Banff; Inverness. Alvie Church, on Loch Alvie, near Lynwilg, as seen from A9. To the north-west rises Geal Charn Mor, 2,702 feet, from which the view of the Cairngorms is perhaps the finest in Strath Spey

Cairngorms, Aberdeen; Banff; Inverness. The Cairngorm mountains, seen from the unclassified road from Aviemore to Loch Morlich, in the Glen More National Forest Park

Cairn O'Mounth, Kincardine. A footbridge and ford near the A.A. box at Glen Dye (B974), on the descent from the pass towards Deeside

[For CAIRNBAAN see also under KNAPDALE (Plate 103)

PLATE 26 (facing page 116

Cairn Ryan, Wigtown. White-harled houses on Loch Ryan. Part of the 'Mulberry' harbour used for the invasion of Normandy during the Second World War was constructed here

Cairnwell Pass, Aberdeen; Perth. Near the summit of the pass in the Grampian mountains, where A93 attains 2,199 feet, the highest altitude of any main road in Great Britain

Caledonian Canal, Inverness. The series of eight locks at Corpach, near Fort William, off A830, which are known as 'Neptune's Staircase'

California, Stirling. The surprising village sign

Callander, Perth. The sundial of 1753, which stands in South Church Street, near the River Teith. The inscription reads:

"I mark not the hours
   unless they bring light,
I mark not the hours of
   darkness and night,
My promise is solely to
   follow the sun,
And point out the course
   his chariot doth run"

Cambuskenneth Abbey, Stirling. The late 13th-century tower of the Abbey, founded in 1147, and now in ruins. It was the scene of Robert Bruce's Parliament in 1326, and stands near the River Forth, north-east of Stirling, on an unclassified road

PLATE 27 (facing page 117)

ranges over the fertile Howe of the Mearns and the distant Kincardine coast. The names of Macbeth, Edward I, Montrose and Claverhouse, are all associated with the Pass, the first-named having fled northwards to *Lumphanan* (*q.v.*) across the Dee. The bridge over the Dye Water, **4 m.** N. of the summit in the heart of the delightfully wooded Glen Dye, dates from 1680, and was one of the earliest bridges in the district. *Iter. 163, 165.*

CAIRNORRIE, Aberdeen. Map 27, **NJ 8** 4.
Iter. 186, 197.

CAIRN RYAN, Wigtown. Map 2, **NX 0** 6.
Once known as *Macherie*, this little village of whitewashed houses is situated on the western shores of Loch Ryan, sheltered by Cairn Point. *Lochryan*, a house of 1701, has fine gardens. To the north, on Leight Moor, is the so-called " Taxing Stone," said to mark the tomb of a Scottish King, murdered in 741. Beyond the Moor is lovely Glen App, traversed by the Water of App, flowing into Loch Ryan at Finnart Bay. See **Ballantrae.** *Iter. 55, 80, 84.*

CAIRNWELL PASS, Aberdeen; Perth. Map 20, **NO 1** 7.
The summit of the pass, at 2,199 ft., is the highest main road altitude reached in Great Britain, and forms part of the original military road linking Coupar Angus with Braemar, first constructed in the mid-18th cent. by General Caulfeild, one of Wade's successors. The *Devil's Elbow* section was not, however, on the line of the original road, and probably dates from the early 19th cent. The road over the pass is liable to be blocked by snow in winter. The *Cairnwell*, 3,059 ft., to the west, and *Glas Maol*, 3,502 ft., to the east, the latter across the Angus border, dominate the Cairnwell Pass, and below the summit, on the road leading southwards to *Blairgowrie* (*q.v.*), is the well-known *Devil's Elbow*, described under *Glenshee*. Excellent ski-ing can be enjoyed in the vicinity when conditions are suitable. The northerly descent from the summit of the pass gives access through Glen Clunie to *Braemar* (*q.v.*). A path, essentially for long-distance walkers, crosses the eastern shoulder of *Glas Maol*, and is known as the *Monega Pass*. It attains 3,318 ft., the highest right-of-way in the country, and gives access to the head of Glen Isla and *Kirkton of Glenisla* (*q.v.*). An unbroken chain of lofty hills stretches north-eastwards from *Glas Maol* by way of *Cairn na Glasha*, 3,484 ft., to *Lochnagar* (*q.v.*) in the *Whit Mounth* (*q.v.*) group. *Iter. 141, 152, 160, 167, 168.*

CALCOTS, Moray. Map 26, **NJ 2** 6.
Iter. 187.

CALDERCRUIX, Lanark. 2,917. Map 9, **NS 8** 6.
To the east is the large Hillend reservoir. *Iter. 16.*

CALEDONIAN CANAL, Inverness.
Map 18, **NN 1** 7 etc. and 25, **NH 6** 4 etc.
Thomas Telford began, in 1803, the construction of this artificial waterway through the Great Glen of Alban, or *Glen More* (*q.v.*), which virtually splits Scotland into two portions. The work was completed after 44 years, at the end of which sailing vessels were enabled to pass from the North Sea to the Atlantic and the West Coast of Scotland, avoiding the stormy journey around Cape Wrath. The advent of steam has since made the canal largely unnecessary, and its use is now mainly for fishing vessels. By means of the canal, the towns of *Inverness* (*q.v.*), on the Inner Moray Firth, and *Fort William* (*q.v.*), on Loch Linnhe, were brought into touch, utilizing the waters of Loch Ness, Loch Oich, and Loch Lochy, which are links in the canal proper. The latter extends in length to some 22 miles out of a total length of 60½ miles along the glen, and no fewer than 29 locks had to be constructed, the most notable being the series known as " Neptune's Staircase " near *Corpach* (*q.v.*). See **Loch Lochy, Loch Ness, Loch Oich** and **Westerkirk.** *Iter. 207, 210, 213, 214.*

CALGARY, Isle of Mull, Argyll. Map 12, **NM 3** 5.
Lies in the north-western extremity of the island, on Calgary Bay, with fine sands for bathing. Emigrants from here founded a Calgary in Canada. Away to the north, near the lonely Callach Point, the poet Campbell once lived as a tutor, and here some of his works were composed. From Calgary there are views of the scattered Treshnish Islands away to the south-west, while almost due westwards lie the larger islands of Coll and *Tiree* (*q.v.*). *Iter. 248.*

CALIFORNIA, Stirling. Map 16, **NS 9** 7.
A village on high ground in a mining district.

CALLANDER, Perth. 1,627. SB. Map 15, **NN 6** 0.
E.C. Wed. GOLF. A well-known touring centre and " Gateway of the Highlands," especially convenient for the *Trossachs* (*q.v.*). Sir Walter Scott was a frequent visitor to the district, which he has depicted in the " Lady of the Lake." The " *Roman Camp* " Hotel has associations with J. M. Barrie. In South Church Street is an inscribed sundial dated 1753. The town stands on the River Teith, which is joined to the west by the Leny, flowing through the beautiful Pass of Leny from Loch Lubnaig. In the Pass are the picturesque Falls of Leny. *St. Bride's Chapel*, partly restored as a memorial to Sir Walter Scott, stands beyond the Pass, on the way to Loch Lubnaig.

1. Sundial (1753).

North-west of Callander is *Ben Ledi*, 2,875 ft., the monarch of the district, a noted viewpoint, and on its northern slopes lies the tiny Lochan nan Corp, with which is associated the tragedy of a burial party due to breaking ice. To the north-east of the town are the Falls of Bracklinn, on the Keltie Water, from which a path continues through the hills to lonely Glen Artney, by means of which the town of *Comrie* (*q.v.*) can be reached. The road leading westwards from Callander traverses the northern shores of Loch Vennachar, described in Scott's " Lady of the Lake," and later reaches the *Brig o' Turk*, for which see under *Trossachs*. See **Balquhidder, Doune and Strathyre.** *Iter. 106, 107, 109, 139, 141, 142, 144, 146.*

CALLANISH, Isle of Lewis, Ross and Cromarty.
Map 32, **NB 2** 3.
See **Hebrides, Outer (Lewis).** *Iter. 260.*

CALVINE, Perth. Map 19, **NN 8** 6.
See **Struan.** *Iter. 138, 140, 143, 147, 149, 150.*

CAMASNACROISE, Argyll. Map 18, **NM 8** 5.
Situated on a small inlet of *Loch Linnhe* (*q.v.*), with the smaller Loch a' Choire lying a little to the west. In the background rises *Creach Bheinn*, 2,800 ft., at the head of Glenalmadale. The views across Loch Linnhe from Camasnacroise are very fine, and extend from the island of *Lismore* (*q.v.*) along the picturesque *Appin* (*q.v.*) coast towards the distant *Lochaber* (*q.v.*) mountains. The road leading north-eastwards into the hills forks after about six miles, the northern branch giving access to the shores of *Loch Sunart* (*q.v.*), and the south-western branch continuing through Gleann Geal towards the *Morven* (*q.v.*) country and the shores of the Sound of Mull at *Lochaline* (*q.v.*). *Iter. 218.*

CAMBUS, Clackmannan. Map 16, **NS 8** 9.
Iter. 133, 134.

CAMBUSKENNETH ABBEY, Stirling. Map 16, **NS 8** 9.
See **Stirling.**

CAMBUSLANG, Lanark. 26,861. Map 8, **NS 6** 6.
E.C. Wed. GOLF. On the outskirts of Glasgow, with extensive iron and steel works. To the south-west lies the attractive, wooded public park of Cathkin Braes. See **Rutherglen.** *Iter. 53.*

CAMBUS O' MAY, Aberdeen. 40.   Map 20, **NO 4 9.**
E.C. Thurs. Nearby flows the Dee in a richly wooded stretch, and to the north-east are the two small lochs of Kinord and Davan. On the latter is an ancient " crannog," or lake-dwelling. Across the Dee, to the south, is the farm-house of *Ballaterach*, where Byron spent part of his youth (see **Bridge of Ess**). On *Culblean Hill*, 1,567 ft., to the north of Cambus o' May, where a battle was fought in 1335, is a curious rock-chamber called the " Vat," and beyond rises *Morven*, 2,862 ft., the highest mountain in the district. *Iter. 141, 152, 167, 179.*

CAMELON, Stirling. 9,398.   Map 16, **NS 8 8.**
E.C. Wed. Situated on the site of a former Roman town, and now possessing iron foundries. The Antonine, or Roman (*q.v.*) Wall ran to the south of the town, and a little to the north, overlooking the River Carron, is the site of a double camp. *Iter. 17, 95, 113, 114, 115.*

CAMPBELTOWN, Argyll. 7,022. SB.   Map 7, **NR 7 2.**
E.C. Wed. M.D. Mon. A Royal Burgh, fishing port and resort, once known as *Kilkerran*, in the *Kintyre* (*q.v.*) penin-sula, with a shingle beach, and situated on Campbeltown Loch, forming a good anchorage. There is a steamer pier. At the entrance to the loch is Davaar Island, with its light-house. A cave on the island has a painting of the crucifixion by Archibald Mackinnon. It is accessible by boat. Flora MacDonald and her family sailed from this port to America in 1774. In the town is a notable, ornamented Celtic Cross, dating from c. 1500. There are distilleries and also a coal-mine at Campbeltown. **1** m. S.E. is the ruined Castle of *Kilkerran*, near the shores of the bay, and **1** m. farther, near Achinhoan Head to the east of the coast road, is *St. Kieran's Cave*, 25 ft. above high water, which may be the earliest Christian Chapel in Scotland. To the west of the town is the *Machrihanish* (*q.v.*) airport, with services to Glasgow (Renfrew airport), and still farther west is Machrihanish itself, famous for golf. See **Mull of Kintyre, Saddell** and **Southend;** *Iter. 121, 122, 123.*

CAMPSIE GLEN, Stirling.   Map 15, **NS 6 7.**
Stands at the foot of the well-known glen in the *Campsie Fells*, through which climbs the Crow Road, leading from *Lennoxtown* (*q.v.*) to *Fintry* (*q.v.*), reaching a height of 1,154 ft., with good views. *Earl's Seat*, 1,896 ft., away to the west, is the highest point in the hills, and forms a notable view-point. *Iter. 107, 115.*

CAMUSNAGAUL, Argyll.   Map 18, **NN 0 7.**
At the head of *Loch Linnhe* (*q.v.*) on its western shore, and near the meeting with Loch Eil. *Camusnagaul* stands on the narrow, winding road linking *Kinlocheil* (*q.v.*) with *Ardgour* (*q.v.*), and gives a view across Loch Linnhe to Fort William, backed by the great bulk of *Ben Nevis*, 4,406 ft., which from this point dominates the town and the surrounding *Lochaber* (*q.v.*) country. The hill-ridge rising west of Camus-nagaul attains 2,527 ft. with *Stob Choire a' Chearcail*, a fine viewpoint, overlooking the junction of the Cona Glen with Glen Scaddle. *Iter. 215.*

CANISBAY CHURCH, Caithness.   Map 30, **ND 3 7.**
This is the most northerly church on the mainland and over-looks Gills Bay. Much of the structure is early 18th cent. work and a slab on the south wall is the actual gravestone of the original John de Groot, whose famous house stood formerly at *John O'Groats* (*q.v.*).

CANNA, ISLE OF, Inverness.   Map 23, **NG 2 0.**
See **Rum.**

CANNICH, Inverness. 243.   Map 24, **NH 3 3.**
E.C. Wed. Situated in a beautiful, wooded setting, at the south-western extremity of the picturesque and long valley of Strath Glass (see **Struy Bridge**), and in the immediate vicinity of the confluence of the Rivers Cannich and Glass. Two of Scotland's loveliest and most famous glens, those of Affric and Cannich, noted especially for their richly-wooded scenery, extend westwards from Cannich into the bare and lonely mountain country on the borders of Ross and Cromarty, but neither glen provides a throughway for motor traffic. The proposed Affric National Park will eventually cover the area contiguous to the two glens. A large hydro-electric scheme, inaugurated by the Duke of Edinburgh, in October 1952, now operates in the Cannich district, and has changed touring conditions to some extent. The power station for the whole scheme is situated at Fasnakyle, some 2½ m. S.W. of Cannich, on the Glass. The new road to Glen Affric leads south-westwards from Cannich, passing near Fasnakyle, in the woods around which Prince Charles Edward wandered as a fugitive in 1746. It then traverses the picturesque Chisholm's Pass, with the Dog Fall, to emerge later by the shores of Loch Benevean, in a rich setting of birch and pine trees. The level of this loch has been raised, resulting in the formation of many tiny wooded islets, and a dam has been constructed at the eastern end, beyond which, to the south, lies the extensive Guisachan Forest. The road follows the northern shores of the loch, amid scenery of increasing grandeur,. and later reaches Loch Affric, above which rises the peak of *Sgurr na Lapaich*, 3,401 ft. In the background are the still higher summits of *Mam Sodhail*, 3,862 ft. and *Carn Eige*, 3,877 ft., the highest, though by no means the wildest mountains north of the Great Glen of Scotland, and forming notable viewpoints. Lonely tracks continue westwards beyond Loch Affric, passing under the slopes of the remote peak of *Sgurr nan Ceathreamhnan*, 3,771 ft., and giving access for long-distance walkers to *Croe Bridge* (*q.v.*) on Loch Duich.

Glen Cannich is reached by a re-made road leading first north-westwards from Cannich under *Beinn Acharain*, 2,119 ft., and then penetrating westwards through rugged, densely-wooded hills, later passing the tiny Loch Car, and then following the River Cannich to Loch Mullardoch. At the eastern end of this loch the main dam for the hydro-electric scheme has been built. The waters of the loch have been taken by tunnel to Loch Benevean. Lofty, bare hills rise to the north-west of the loch, *Sgurr na Lapaich*, 3,773 ft. (Ross-shire), and *An Riabhachan*, 3,730 ft., being the princi-pal summits. Long distance walkers' tracks continue west-wards beyond Loch Mullardoch, passing Loch Lungard, and eventually reaching Glen Elchaig and Loch Long, in Wester Ross (See **Ardelve**). The peaks of *Mam Sodhail* and *Sgurr na Lapaich* (Ross-shire) were chosen as key-points in the principal triangulation of the Ordnance Survey of Great Britain in the years 1846 and 1848.

The road which links Cannich through Glen Urquhart to *Drumnadrochit* (*q.v.*), on Loch Ness, was constructed by Telford. Although the coming of the hydro-electric scheme to the Cannich district has brought in its train undoubted advantages, there are nevertheless many who will regret the need to have tampered with the magnificent scenery with which the area was endowed by nature, while the feeling of peace and solitude formerly associated with these two exceptionally lovely glens may never again be recaptured in its entirety. *Iter. 206, 210.*

CANONBIE, Dumfries. 1,455.   Map 4, **NY 3 7.**
E.C. Wed. The pleasant village of *Canonbie*, with its old coaching inn, stands on the river Esk, at the southern extremity of Eskdale. The river is joined, a little to the south, near the Liddel Moat, by the Liddel Water, traversing the long valley of *Liddesdale* (*q.v.*), which is associated with Dandie Dinmont in Scott's " Guy Mannering." The Esk, flowing towards the Solway Firth, was formerly the boundary between England and Scotland, and the tract between the Esk and the Sark became the so-called " debatable land," which deteriorated gradually into an area of lawlessness, until, in 1552, the *Scots Dyke* was constructed across the district to form a new territorial boundary. The former Priory of Canonbie was destroyed by the English in 1542. **2** m. N., to the east of the Esk, is a Roman Camp, situated to the north of Gilnockie station. **2** m. N.N.W., beyond Gilnockie Bridge, on the main Langholm road, stands *Hollows Tower*, dating from the 16th cent. and preserving walls 6 ft. thick. It was once the home of the 16th cent. Border reiver, Johnny Armstrong, whose other home of *Gilnockie* stood formerly near Gilnockie Bridge. See **Langholm** and **Teviothead.** *Iter. 11, 12, 30, 31, 47.*

CAPE WRATH, Sutherland.   Map 28, **NC 2 7.**
This wild, cliff-bound headland, the most northerly point of Scotland's north-west seaboard, cannot be reached by car

Canonbie, Dumfries. The 16th century Hollows Tower, where Johnny Armstrong, the celebrated Border ' reiver,' or freebooter, once lived. It stands 2 miles north-west of Canonbie, off A7

Canisbay, Caithness. The gravestone in the Church of the original John de Groot, whose house gave the name of John O' Groat's to the lonely outpost a little to the east

Canisbay, Caithness. The most northerly Church on the Scottish mainland. It was built in the 18th century

Campbeltown, Argyll. The richly-decorated Celtic Cross

Cannich, Inverness. The dam on Loch Benevean, erected in connection with a large hydro-electric scheme operating in Glen Affric and Glen Cannich

PLATE 28 (facing page 118)

Carfin, Lanark. The famous Grotto, to which thousands of pilgrims come each year

Carluke, Lanark. The plaque at the site of Miltonhead, the birthplace of Major-General William Roy, 1726–90, known as the 'father' of the Ordnance Survey. Out of his military map of Scotland, drawn between 1747 and 1755, grew the Ordnance Survey of Great Britain. It is situated on an unclassified road 2 miles west, near Milton Lockhart farm

Carnwath, Lanark. The shaft of the Market Cross of 1516, giving road distances, including that to Ayr, misspelt AIR

Carrbridge, Inverness. The arch of the old bridge across the River Dulnain, seen from the modern bridge. It was built in 1715 by the Earl of Seafield for the use of funeral parties to Duthil

Carrbridge, Inverness. The remains of Inverlaidnan House, where Bonnie Prince Charlie slept on the way to Culloden in 1746. It stands on an unclassified road near the River Dulnain, some 3½ miles west

Carrick, Ayr. The 17th century Castle at Maybole, the former capital of Carrick. It was once the town house of the Kennedys, Earls of Cassillis, of whom an old rhyme says:

"Twixt Wigtown and the town of Ayr, Portpatrick and the Cruives of Cree,
No man may think for to bide there unless he court St. Kennedie"

PLATE 29 (facing page 119)

For CARRBRIDGE see also under WADE ROADS (Plate 167)

as only a passenger ferry is available for crossing the narrow Kyle of Durness. At times a hire car, belonging to the " *Cape Wrath* " Hotel (See **Durness**), was kept on the west side of the Kyle, but this is at present not available. The lighthouse is 11 miles distant, over a stretch of lonely moorland known as The Parph, which is overlooked to the north by *Scrishven*, 1,216 ft., and to the south by *Fashven*, 1,498 ft. This lighthouse was constructed in 1828, and provides distant views across the Minch to the island of Lewis in the Outer Hebrides. There are fine cliffs of gneiss in the vicinity. The remote Atlantic islands of *North Rona* and *Sula Sgeir*, some 50 miles to the north-west, are now National Nature Reserves. They are the home of the rare Atlantic grey seal, and the equally rare Leach's fork-tailed petrel breeds there. See **Kinlochbervie**. *Iter. 225, 229.*

CAPUTH, Perth. 1,012.   Map 16, NO 0 3.
Lies just to the north of the River Tay, here spanned by a bridge. **3 m. E.** is the Roman Camp of *Inchtuthil*, situated in the private grounds of *Delvine House*. Across the river, to the west, is *Murthly Castle*, in a fine, wooded setting. A Sitka spruce tree in the park is some 160 feet tall. *Iter. 148, 157.*

CARBERRY HILL, Midlothian.   Map 10, NT 3 6.
Famous for the skirmish, fought in 1567, when Mary, Queen of Scots, after Bothwell had fled, surrendered to the Lords of the Congregation, and was taken thence to *Loch Leven Castle* (*q.v.*). A little to the west is *Carberry Tower*, rebuilt in 1830, but incorporating an old tower. See **Pinkie House.**

CARBISDALE CASTLE, Ross and Cromarty.
     Map 29, NH 5 9.
See **Invershin.**

CARBOST, Isle of Skye, Inverness.   Map 23, NG 3 3.
To the south, a road leads through Glen Eynort to the loch of that name, where recent afforestation is changing the face of the landscape. See **Talisker.** *Iter. 252.*

CARDROSS, Dunbarton. 1,199.   Map 8, NS 3 7.
E.C. Thurs. GOLF. Here, in a castle now vanished, Robert Bruce died in 1329. The Parish Church was destroyed in the Second World War. The grandfather of Macaulay, the historian, was at one period minister at Cardross. In *Ardoch House*, an 18th cent. mansion facing the Clyde, lived R. B. Cunninghame-Graham, the author and explorer. To the north of Cardross is the ruined *Kilmahew Castle.* The 15th cent. *Kilmahew* Chapel was restored in 1955. See **Dumbarton.** *Iter. 102, 111.*

CARFIN, Lanark. 1,795.   Map 9, NS 7 5.
A mining village, with a population largely of Irish extraction. A grotto, dedicated to Our Lady of Lourdes in 1922, is the yearly venue of thousands of pilgrims. Two fragments of rock from Lourdes are inset in a marble block from Iona above the pool of holy water. There are several shrines in a well-designed garden setting. *Iter. 87.*

CARFRAEMILL, Berwick.   Map 10, NT 5 5.
Situated in Lauderdale, with the *Lammermuir* hills rising away to the north-east. From here the Leader Water flows southwards between the main roads leading to Lauder and Greenlaw. To the north-west of Carfraemill, the Edinburgh road climbs steadily towards the viewpoint of *Soutra Hill* (*q.v.*). See **Oxton.** *Iter. 4, 5, 6, 8, 13, 36.*

CARINISH, North Uist, Inverness.   Map 32, NF 8 6.
See **Hebrides, Outer** (North Uist). *Iter. 261.*

CARLISLE, Cumberland (England). 68,500.
For " Through Routes " see page 44.   Map 5, NY 4 5.
E.C. Thurs. M.D. Wed./Sat. GOLF. *Iter. 10, 11, 12, 13, 26, 27, 28, 29, 30, 31, 42, 50, 51.*
(For description see Road Book of **England and Wales**).

CARLOPS, Peebles.   Map 9, NT 1 5.
A *Pentland* hills village, on the North Esk river, well known as a small inland holiday resort. A curious rock outcrop overshadows the northern extremity of the village. There are associations with Allan Ramsay, author of the pastoral play " The Gentle Shepherd." A path follows the river into the hills past the North Esk reservoir to the Bore

Stone, from which *East Cairn Hill*, 1,839 ft., a notable viewpoint, can be reached. See **Penicuik** and **Polwarth.** *Iter. 25.*

CARLOWAY, Isle of Lewis, Ross and Cromarty.
     Map 32, NB 2 4.
See **Hebrides, Outer** (Lewis). *Iter. 260.*

CARLUKE, Lanark. 7,126.   Map 9, NS 8 5.
E.C. Wed. GOLF. Stands at an altitude of over 600 ft., above the fertile Clyde valley, and with moors to the east. The tower of the former 18th cent. Church still stands. The growing of fruit in the valley dates back as far as the 12th cent. See **Braidwood.** *Iter. 50, 52, 54.*

CARNACH, Argyll.   Map 18, NN 0 5.
At the western end of *Glencoe* (*q.v.*) on Loch Leven, and the point of divergence of the picturesque road circling Loch Leven to North Ballachulish from the direct road to *Ballachulish* (*q.v.*). The latter route, by utilising the ferry over Loch Leven, shortens the distance to Fort William considerably. Across the glen rises the *Pap of Glencoe*, 2,430 ft., a conical peak, being an outlier of the long ridge of *Aonach Eagach*, with its 3,000-ft. high summits, facing *Bidean nam Bian*, 3,766 ft., across the deep rift of Glencoe. See **Kinlochleven.** *Iter. 100, 124, 125, 142.*

CARNAN, South Uist, Inverness.   Map 32, NF 7 4.
See **Hebrides, Outer** (South Uist). *Iter. 262.*

CARNBO, Kinross.   Map 16, NO 0 0.
Iter. 136.

CARNOCK, Fife.   Map 16, NT 0 8.
Iter. 133.

CARNOUSTIE, Angus. 5,220. SB.   Map 17, NO 5 3.
E.C. Tues. GOLF. A well-known golfing resort on the North Sea coast, with a fine, sandy beach and bathing. To the south-west are the Barry links, extending to Buddon Ness, a military training area. See **Arbroath** and **Monikie.** *Iter. 155, 162.*

CARNWATH, Lanark. 787.   Map 9, NS 9 4.
E.C. Wed. GOLF. Only the aisle remains from the old Church, built c. 1424. The Market Cross dates from 1516 and gives road distances. The road leading north-eastwards towards Edinburgh traverses the lower slopes of the *Pentland* hills, and is known as the " Lang Whang," once much used as a drove road. **2 m. N.W.** of Carnwath are slight remains of *Cowthally Castle*, a Somerville stronghold, which consisted at one time of three separate towers. James IV, V and VI were entertained here at different periods. *Iter. 21, 23, 37, 52.*

CARRADALE, Argyll.   Map 7, NR 8 3.
GOLF. A small *Kintyre* (*q.v.*) resort, with a fishing harbour, situated on Kilbrennan Sound facing the Isle of Arran, and about 1½ m. E. of the Campbeltown road. Near the pier is the ruined *Aird Castle*, and on the west side of the bay is a vitrified fort. Carradale Bay, sheltered by Carradale Point, lies a little to the south. Farther inland rises *Beinn an Tuirc*, 1,491 ft., the highest point in Kintyre. See **Saddell.** *Iter. 122.*

CARRBRIDGE, Inverness. 233.   Map 25, NH 9 2.
E.C. Thurs. A pleasant Highland resort, on the River Dulnain, here spanned by a modern bridge, beside which the arch of a much older one is still in position. 2½ m. W., on the river, is Wade's old *Sluggan Bridge*, on one of his military roads. In the vicinity is the ruined *Inverlaidnan House*, where Prince Charles Edward spent the night on the way to Culloden. 1½ m. N.E., a narrow moorland road diverges northwards from the Grantown-on-Spey road towards Forres, and a right fork, after another seven miles, gives access to the lonely *Lochindorb* (*q.v.*), with its romantic island castle. See **Boat of Garten** and **Slochd Summit.** *Iter. 140, 150, 173, 195.*

CARRICK, Ayr.   Map 2, NX 2 9 etc.
The name given to the southernmost division of the county, lying to the south of the River Doon, and formerly part of the district of *Galloway* (*q.v.*), which was, until 1747, administered by hereditary stewards. The scenery is at its

best in the south-east, where the foothills of the " Galloway Highlands " of Kirkcudbright extend over the border, and of which *Kirriereoch Hill*, 2,562 ft., and *Shalloch on Minnoch*, 2,520 ft., are perhaps the best known Carrick hills. The two narrow and hilly moorland roads which lead northwards from *Rowantree* (*q.v.*) towards *Maybole* (*q.v.*) wind through the heart of the hills of Carrick, the more westerly road climbing over the Nick o' the Balloch Pass, which attains nearly 1,300 ft. Between *Ballantrae* (*q.v.*) and *Girvan* (*q.v.*) is a particularly fine stretch of coastline, which includes the picturesque Kennedy's Pass. See **Barr**.

CARRINGTON, Midlothian.   Map 10, NT 3 6.
The little cruciform Church, with its ogee-capped tower, dates from 1710.

CARRONBRIDGE, Dumfries.   Map 3, NX 8 9.
A Nithsdale village, where the Carron Water joins the River Nith a little to the south-west. From here, a fine road forks north-eastwards leading to the picturesque, winding Dalveen Pass, the summit of which is at a height of 1,140 ft., near the Lanark border, above which rises *Comb Head*, 1,998 ft., an outlier of the *Lowther* hills. West of the village, across the Nith, are scanty remains of *Tibbers Castle*. 2½ m. N.E. is the ruined *Morton Castle*, perhaps 15th cent., in a glen overlooking Morton Loch. See **Drumlanrig Castle, Durisdeer** and **Enterkinfoot**. *Iter. 25, 27, 48, 56, 67.*

CARRUTHERSTOWN, Dumfries.   Map 4, NY 1 7.
Iter. 26, 27, 67.

CARSAIG BAY, Isle of Mull, Argyll.   Map 13, NM 5 2.
On the wild, rocky southern shores of the island, with cliffs rising to nearly 1,000 ft. in places. *Carsaig Bay* is reached by a narrow road leading southwards through Glen Leidle from the road which traverses the southern shores of Loch Scridain. The film " I Know Where I'm Going " was shot in the vicinity. Away to the south-west, on the coast, not accessible by road, are the remarkable Carsaig Arches, basalt tunnels in the rock, and farther to the east is the Nun's Cave, with carvings supposed to be the original designs of a Cross on Iona. To the east of Carsaig Bay is the seaward end of Loch Buie, dominated at its head by *Ben Buie*, 2,354 ft. See **Pennyghael**. *Iter. 249.*

CARSE OF GOWRIE, Perth.   Map 17, NO 2 2
                                                      and 3 2.
The name given to the strip of fertile, level country which lies between the *Sidlaw* hills and the Firth of Tay, and is especially noted for the cultivation of strawberries. See **Errol, Kinnaird** and **Longforgan**. *Iter. 154.*

CARSETHORN, Kirkcudbright.   Map 3, NX 9 5.
A small harbour on Carse Bay.

CARSKEY, Argyll.   Map 6, NR 6 0.
Iter. 123.

CARSPHAIRN, Kirkcudbright. 240.   Map 3, NX 5 9.
E.C. Wed. A small *Galloway* (*q.v.*) village situated on the Water of Deugh, between two ranges of lofty hills, *Cairnsmore of Carsphairn*, 2,612 ft., to the north-east, and *Corserine*, 2,688 ft., and *Carlins Cairn*, 2,650 ft., to the southwest. North-west of the village is *Lagwine*, a ruined tower, belonging formerly to the Macadams. *Cairn Avel*, south of the village, is a pre-historic chambered cairn. East of the village is *Knockgray Park*, where a cairn indicates the place where the last wild deer in the Lowlands is said to have been slain. A track goes westwards from Carsphairn past the Woodhead lead mines to the shores of *Loch Doon* (*q.v.*), and its former island-castle, to the south of *Dalmellington* (*q.v.*). Away to the west of Carsphairn is Carrick Forest, part of the extensive Glen Trool National Forest Park, included in which are the lonely Lochs Recar and Macaterick, situated in the heart of the Galloway hills. 3 m. S.E. of the village, in the Glenkens district, on the more easterly of the two roads leading towards New Galloway, is the newly-created Kendoon Loch, connected with the Galloway Power Scheme. In this loch, the gorge known as the Tinkler's Loup has been engulfed. Beyond the loch, the High Bridge of Ken spans the Water of Ken. Farther to the south is the large Carsfad dam. See **Loch Trool**. *Iter. 74, 75, 76, 77.*

CARSTAIRS, Lanark. 1,488.   Map 9, NS 9 4.
E.C. Thurs. To the south are the many windings of the Clyde, flowing through a broad and fertile valley, and to the north is the Mouse Water, which joins the Clyde above *Lanark* (*q.v.*). In the Parish Church is preserved a rare 15th cent. Crucifixion stone. To the east lies the White Loch noted for curling. *Iter. 21 23, 37.*

CARTER BAR, Roxburgh.   Map 5, NT 6 0.
Situated on the summit ridge of the *Cheviots* (*q.v.*), where the main road from Newcastle enters Scotland and divides into two, the right fork descending to *Jedburgh* (*q.v.*) and the left fork to *Bonchester Bridge* (*q.v.*) and *Hawick* (*q.v.*). The view from the 1,371-ft. high Carter Bar is famous, and extends towards the Cheviot itself and well into the Lowlands, with the triple-peaked *Eildon* hills appearing in the distance to the north-west. The last Border battle, the Redeswire Raid, took place here, in 1575. Away to the east, on the crest of the hills, near the source of the River Coquet, are the notable camp and earthworks of *Chew Green*, situated just inside Northumberland, across the English border. Here, the earliest of the Roman roads into Scotland, the Dere Street of Agricola, crosses the border at a height of some 1,500 ft., and later descends towards *Oxnam* (*q.v.*). *Iter. 4, 43, 44, 52.*

CASTLEBAY, Isle of Barra, Inverness.   Map 32, NL 6 9.
See **Hebrides, Outer** (Barra).

CASTLE CAMPBELL, Clackmannan.   Map 16, NS 9 9.
See **Dollar**. *Iter. 136.*

CASTLECARY, Stirling.   Map 16, NS 7 7.
One of the forts of the *Roman Wall* (*q.v.*) is situated in the vicinity. Castlecary takes its name from a former square tower, which was largely destroyed in 1715. The Forth and Clyde Canal reaches its highest elevation at this point. *Iter. 17, 50, 87, 97, 99.*

CASTLE DOUGLAS, Kirkcudbright. 3,346. SB.
                                                      Map 3, NX 7 6.
E.C. Thurs. M.D. Mon. A market town and commercial capital of the *Stewartry* (*q.v.*) of Kirkcudbright, the name of the town having at one time been *Carlingwark*, which is the title of the loch situated immediately to the south. Castle Douglas has associations with S. R. Crockett, the novelist, and is noted for fishing. 1½ m. S.W. is the *Threave* Estate. with a 19th cent. mansion (N.T. Scot.). The gardens are noted for their wealth of daffodils and rhododendrons, and are shown generally on Thurs. and Sun., 2.15 to 6.15, from April to early June. 3 m. farther to the north-west, and reached after having first crossed the River Dee, stands the ancient *Threave Castle* (N.T. Scot.), situated on an island in the river. This Douglas stronghold dates from the 14th cent., with a 15th cent. courtyard, and is open weekdays (except Thurs.), 10 to 7; Sun., 2 to 7, April to end of Sept. (see note page 90). In 1640, the interior of the castle was wrecked by the Covenanters. The main road leading northwestwards from the town to *New Galloway* (*q.v.*) passes by the shores of Loch Ken for some miles, the loch having been extended considerably to the south-east in connection with the Galloway Power Scheme (See Crossmichael). Away to the south of Castle Douglas rises *Bengairn*, which attains 1,250 ft. See **Galloway, Laurieston** and **Palnackie**. *Iter. 26, 70, 76.*

CASTLE FRASER, Aberdeen.   Map 27, NJ 7 1.
See **Kemnay**. *Iter. 176, 177.*

CASTLE GRANT, Moray.   Map 26, NJ 0 3.
See **Grantown-on-Spey**.

CASTLE KENNEDY, Wigtown.   Map 2, NX 1 6.
Between the Black and White Lochs, to the north, stands the modern *Lochinch Castle*, famous for its magnificent grounds, laid out on landscape lines. Facing it, to the east, is the ivy-clad ruin of *Castle Kennedy*, dating from the early 17th cent., and burnt in 1715. *Lochinch* gardens are shown Wed. and Sun., 2 to 5, mid-April to end of July (see note page 90). *Iter. 25, 26, 80.*

Carsphairn, Kirkcudbright. The remains of Lagwine Tower, of the Macadams, which was burnt down before the birth of John Loudon Macadam, famous in the history of road-making. It stands to the north-west of the village, off A713

Castle Kennedy, Wigtown. The ruined Kennedy stronghold, built by the 5th Earl of Cassillis in 1607 and burnt in 1715. It stands in the famous Lochinch gardens, laid out originally by the second Earl of Stair, Commander-in-Chief to George II. They have since been re-created. The present mansion of Lochinch dates from 1867

Carter Bar, Roxburgh. The Border between Scotland and England, at the summit ridge of the Cheviot Hills, on A68

Castle Campbell, Clackmannan. A ruined 14th to 16th century stronghold, built by the first Earl of Argyll, and once known as Castle Gloume. Montrose burnt it in 1645. It stands below the Ochil Hills, in the Dollar Glen, on an unclassified road off A91

Carrington, Midlothian. The Church, which dates from 1710

PLATE 30 (facing page 120)

Castle Stalker, Argyll. The 16th century former home of the Stewarts of Appin, which stands on an island off-shore from Portnacroish. It was built originally as a hunting lodge in order to entertain James IV

Ceres, Fife. A carving of the last Provost of Ceres (1578) on a wall in the village

Ceres, Fife. The carving of a bale being weighed on the old iron scales, above the door of the former 17th century weigh-house. The inscription reads: 'God bless the just'

Chapel of Garioch, Aberdeen. The 'Maiden Stone,' carved with Pictish symbols, including a comb and mirror. It is situated near Drumdurno Farm, on an unclassified road to the north-west

Castle Semple, Renfrew. The remains of the Collegiate Church, founded by the first Lord Sempill, who was killed at Flodden Field in 1513

Castletown, Caithness. An example of fencing utilising the local flagstones

PLATE 31 (facing page 121)

CASTLE OF MEY, Caithness.　　　　Map 30, ND 2 7.
See **East Mey.**

CASTLE SEMPLE, Renfrew.　　　　Map 8, NS 3 6.
Near Castle Semple Loch is the Collegiate Church (A.M.), which has a three-sided apse, and a monument dated 1513 in memory of John, Lord Semple, killed at Flodden.

CASTLE STALKER, Argyll.　　　　Map 14, NM 9 4.
See **Portnacroish.** *Iter. 124.*

CASTLE STEWART, Inverness.　　　Map 25, NH 7 4.
See **Inverness.**

CASTLETOWN, Caithness. 600.　　　Map 30, ND 1 6.
E.C. Thurs. Noted formerly for the production of flagstones, an industry founded in 1837. These are also used locally for fencing. A brooch, found in a burial cist here in 1786, is now in the National Museum of Antiquities in Edinburgh. The wide expanse of Dunnet Bay lies to the north of the village. *Iter. 238, 240.*

CASTLE SWEEN, Argyll.　　　　Map 6, NR 7 7.
See **Kilmory Knap.**

CATACOL, Isle of Arran, Bute.　　　Map 7, NR 9 4.
See **Lochranza.** *Iter. 242.*

CATRAIL, Roxburgh ;　Selkirk.　　Map 5, NT 5 0.
　　　　　　　　　　　　　　　　and 10, NT 4 3.

See **Galashiels** and **Shankend.**

CATRINE, Ayr. 2,672.　　　　　　Map 8, NS 5 2.
A village on the River Ayr, with a mill once noted for its huge water-wheel. *Ballochmyle House,* a little to the north-west, forms the setting for two well-known songs of Burns, while at *Catrine House,* to the south-west of Catrine, Burns dined with Professor Dugald Stewart before visiting Edinburgh in 1786. See **Mauchline** and **Sorn.**

CAUSEWAYEND, Midlothian.　　　Map 9, NT 0 6.
A little to the east is the Harper Rig reservoir, with slight remains of *Cairns Castle,* and near the shores of which goes the old drove road known as the Cauld Stane Slap, with *East Cairn Hill,* 1,839 ft., one of the loftiest *Pentland* hills rising beyond. About **6 m. S.W.** of Causewayend, to the west of the Lanark road, is the larger Cobbinshaw reservoir. *Iter. 21, 23.*

CAUSEWAYHEAD, Stirling. 1,000.　　Map 16, NS 8 9.
See **Stirling.** *Iter. 133, 134, 135, 136, 138, 140, 141.*

CAWDOR, Nairn.　　　　　　　　Map 25, NH 8 4.
A pleasant village, the Church having an unusual tower and a Norman doorway. To the south is Cawdor Wood, threaded by the Hermitage Burn. *Cawdor Castle,* one of the finest and most picturesque of Scotland's medieval buildings, retains a central tower dating from 1454, a drawbridge with its gateway and iron yett, and preserves some 16th cent. portions, which have been altered at a slightly later period. There are also notable gardens surrounding the castle. Shakespeare's Macbeth was Thane of Cawdor, and the castle is traditionally the scene of the murder of Duncan. To the south-west of Cawdor there are roads on both sides of the River Nairn leading towards *Daviot* (*q.v.*), that on the north bank going by way of *Culloden* (*q.v.*). **3 m. W.** of Cawdor, across the Nairn, stands *Kilravock Castle,* described under *Croy.* **8 m. S.E.,** in the valley of the Findhorn, is some very attractive scenery around *Dulsie Bridge* (*q.v.*), reached by means of a road traversing the line of one of the former military roads. *Iter. 177, 198, 212.*

CELLARDYKE, Fife.　　　　　　Map 17, NO 5 0.
See **Anstruther.**

CERES, Fife.　　　　　　　　　Map 17, NO 3 1.
A most attractive little village, with an old bridge, known as the Bishop's Bridge. Adjoining the Parish Church is the medieval mausoleum of the Crawfords. On a wall in the village is a carving of the last Provost of Ceres, who received this office in 1578. Annual games take place on the last Saturday in June, in commemoration of the return of the villagers in 1314, after fighting in Robert Bruce's army. An obelisk in the Bow Butts has an inscription recording the association with Bannockburn. Above the doorway of the 17th cent. weigh-house is an interesting carving of a bale being weighed, surmounted by an inscription, while nearby hang the medieval jougs. **1 m. S.E.** is the ruined 17th cent. *Craighall Castle.* *Iter. 129.*

CHALLOCH, Wigtown.　　　　　Map 2, NX 3 6.
Iter. 71, 79.

CHANNELKIRK CHURCH, Berwick.　Map 10, NT 4 5.
See **Oxton.**

CHAPELCROSS, Dumfries.　　　　Map 4, NY 1 6.
See **Annan.**

CHAPELHALL, Lanark. 2,497.　　　Map 9, NS 7 6.
Iter. 50, 87.

CHAPELKNOWE, Dumfries.　　　Map 4, NY 3 7.
Iter. 47.

CHAPEL OF GARIOCH, Aberdeen.　Map 27, NJ 7 2.
A little to the north-west, by *Drumdurno* farm, is the *Maiden Stone,* a remarkable 10-ft. high carved slab, carrying Pictish characters, and depicting a comb and mirror. **1 m. S.E.** of Chapel of Garioch is the ruined *Balquhain Tower,* dating from 1530.

CHAPELTON, Lanark.　　　　　Map 8, NS 6 4.
Iter. 29, 56.

CHARLESTOWN, Fife.　　　　　Map 16, NT 0 8.
A small Forth estuary coal port. A little to the east is *Limekilns,* associated with R. L. Stevenson's " Kidnapped." In the vicinity stands the fine mansion of *Broomhall.*

CHARLESTOWN OF ABERLOUR, Banff. 1,153.
　　　　　　　　　　　　　　　　Map 26, NJ 2 4
E.C. Wed. See **Aberlour.** *Iter. 170, 192, 195.*

CHARTERHALL, Berwick.　　　　Map 11, NT 7 4.
Here is a motor racing track.

CHERRYBANK, Perth.　　　　　Map 16, NO 1 2.
Iter. 86, 135, 146.

CHEVIOT HILLS, Roxburgh.　　　Map 5, NY 5 9 etc.
　　　　　　　　　　　　　　　　and 11, NT 8 1 etc.
This range of lonely, grassy hills forms the boundary with England for much of its length, its highest point, *The Cheviot,* 2,676 ft., being over the Northumberland border, part of the range being included within the Northumberland National Park. Other prominent heights are *Peel Fall,* 1,964 ft., and *Carter Fell,* 1,815 ft., both rising to the south-west of the viewpoint of *Carter Bar* (*q.v.*), 1,371 ft. high, where the road from Hawick and Jedburgh to Newcastle crosses the border to the west of the line followed by the Roman Dere Street. Away to the south-west of *Peel Fell,* the road from *Riccarton* (*q.v.*) cuts through the hills at a comparatively low altitude, and gives access to the lonely North Tyne valley across the Northumberland border. Many of the hill slopes are grazed by the characteristic Cheviot and black-faced sheep. *Iter. 6, 7, 47.*

CHIRMORIE, Ayr.　　　　　　Map 2, NX 2 7.
Iter. 78.

CHIRNSIDE, Berwick.　　　　　Map 11, NT 8 5.
The Parish Church retains a Norman south door with tympanum. The junction of the Whiteadder Water with that of the Blackadder takes place a little to the south of the village. See **Edrom Church.** *Iter. 41.*

CHURCHILL BARRIERS, Orkney.　Map 33, ND 4 9.
See **Orkney Islands** (Mainland and South Ronaldsay).
Iter. 266.)

CLACHAIG, Argyll.　　　　　　Map 14, NS 1 8.
Iter. 102.

CLACHAIG INN, Argyll.　　　　Map 18, NN 1 5.
See **Glencoe.**

CLACHAN, Argyll.　　　　　　Map 7, NR 7 5.
Iter. 121.

CLACHAN, North Uist, Inverness.　Map 32, NF 8 6.
Iter. 261.

CLACHAN BRIDGE, Argyll.   Map 14, NM 7 1.
This picturesque single-arched bridge, designed by Telford in 1792, which links the mainland with the island of *Seil*, has achieved fame as being probably the only bridge to " span the Atlantic." The waters are actually those of the narrow Seil Sound, which joins the Firth of Lorne to Outer Loch Melfort, but they can, nevertheless, with some justification, claim to be an arm of the Atlantic. On Seil there are slate quarries at *Balvicar*, while off the west coast lies the smaller island of *Easdale*, also noted for its slates. The Cuan Sound, crossed by the *Cuan* ferry, separates Seil from *Luing*, yet another slate-quarrying island, on the coast of which is the little port of *Cullipool*. The Luing Sound separates this island from Lunga, hilly Scarba, and the smaller Garvellach group, among which is Eileach an Naoimh, which retains a ruined chapel, associated with *St. Brendan* and *St. Columba*. Nearby are the remains of a double beehive house. To the south of Scarba is the Gulf of Corryvreckan, with its treacherous tide-race, the noise of which can be heard from a great distance. The island of *Scarba* attains almost 1,500 ft. at one point and is noted for its deer. **3 m. S.** of Clachan Bridge on the mainland, and situated close to Seil Sound, is the ancient seat of *Ardmaddy Castle*, overlooking the bay of that name. See **Kilninver**. *Iter. 122.*

CLACHNAHARRY, Inverness.   Map 25, NH 6 4.
Situated on the south side of the Beauly Firth, at the point where the *Caledonian Canal* (*q.v.*), after its journey across the Highlands by way of the Great Glen, or *Glen More* (*q.v.*), enters the Firth with the aid of six locks. On *Craig Phadraig*, 550 ft., a little to the south, there is a notable vitrified fort. *Iter. 200, 201, 203, 204, 205, 210, 221.*

CLACKMANNAN, Clackmannan. 2,356.
                                      Map 16, NS 9 9.
E.C. Tues. This name town of the smallest Scottish county lies on the Black Devon River, which flows southwards into the estuary of the Forth, to the south, at *Clackmannan Pow*. In the town is an old Tolbooth, neighboured by the ancient Stone of Manau. *Clackmannan Tower* (A.M.), 79 ft. high, on a hill to the west, is 14th or 15th cent. work, with 17th cent. additions, and is finely machicolated. Tradition has it that Robert Bruce built the tower. See **Culross**. *Iter. 133, 134.*

CLADICH, Argyll.   Map 14, NN 0 2.
Here the road from Dalmally along the shores of *Loch Awe* (*q.v.*) divides into two, the westerly fork continuing along the loch-side, and the southerly fork climbing over the hills, with fine views of *Ben Cruachan*, 3,689 ft., away to the north. The subsequent descent through the delightful, wooded Glen Aray leads towards *Inveraray* (*q.v.*). See **Kilchurn Castle** and **Portsonachan**. *Iter. 117, 119, 120.*

CLAGGAIN BAY, Isle of Islay, Argyll.   Map 6, NR 4 5.
This rocky and sandy bay is overlooked from the west by *Beinn Bheigeir*, 1,609 ft., the highest point on the island. The road from *Port Ellen* (*q.v.*) along the south-east coast of the island terminates here. There are views of the island of Jura and of the *Kintyre* (*q.v.*) peninsula. *Iter. 245.*

CLAONAIG, Argyll.   Map 7, NR 8 5.
See **Skipness**. *Iter. 122.*

CLARENCEFIELD, Dumfries.   Map 4, NY 0 6.
A little to the west is *Comlongon Castle*, a well preserved 15th cent. tower, with walls 10 to 13ft. in thickness, and retaining an iron yett. A modern building is now joined to the tower. See **Caerlaverock** and **Ruthwell**. *Iter. 47.*

CLARKSTON, Renfrew. 7,303.   Map 8, NS 5 5.
About **2 m. N.**, on the White Cart River, are the remains of *Cathcart Castle*, partly demolished in the 15th cent., and later replaced by the nearby *Cathcart House*. The ruined castle is associated with Mary, Queen of Scots, who is said to have watched the battle of Langside, in 1568, from the so-called " Queen Mary's Window." The result of the battle was fatal to the Queen's cause, and from here she fled to *Dundrennan* (*q.v.*), before finally departing from Scottish shores. *Iter. 18, 29.*

CLASHMORE, Sutherland.   Map 31, NH 7 8.
See **Skibo Castle**. *Iter. 200, 231.*

CLASHNESSIE, Sutherland.   Map 28, NC 0 3.
Iter. 227.

CLATTERING BRIDGE, Kincardine.   Map 21, NO 6 7.
At the foot of the fine moorland road over the *Cairn o' Mounth* (*q.v.*) leading to the Dee valley at *Banchory* (*q.v.*). A little to the north is the Slack Burn, in its deep gorge, overlooked by *Finella Hill*, 1,358 ft., which is encircled by the road leading towards *Fordoun* (*q.v.*) by way of *Drumtochty Castle*, now a school. *Iter. 163, 165.*

CLATTERINGSHAWS DAM, Kirkcudbright.
                                      Map 3, NX 5 7.
This large dam was erected across the Black Water of Dee, thus creating a new inland reservoir, the water being then taken through a tunnel to a hydro-electric station of the *Galloway* (*q.v.*) power scheme. The district has associations with Robert Bruce, and is now part of the Cairn Edward Forest, belonging to the Glen Trool National Forest Park. A boulder on Moss Raploch (N.T. Scot.) marks the site of one of Bruce's early fights. **4½ m. S.W.**, off the Newton Stewart road, is the prominent *Murray Monument*, commemorating a late 18th cent. professor. Away to the south-west, beyond the remote Loch Grennoch, rises *Cairnsmore of Fleet*, 2,331 ft., in the Galloway hills, associated with John Buchan's " The Thirty-nine Steps." To the north is *Meikle Millyea*, 2,446 ft., the most southerly peak in the fine *Rhinns of Kells* range, and beyond it lies the lonely Loch Dungeon. South-west of Meikle Millyea is Loch Dee, in the vicinity of which is the lonely area of bog known as the Silverflowe Nature Reserve. See **Dalry** (Kirkcudbright) and **Loch Trool**. *Iter. 25, 71.*

CLEISH, Kinross.   Map 16, NT 0 9.
A rare burial boundary stone is set into the churchyard wall. *Cleish Castle* is a restored 16th cent. house. **4 m. W.** is the restored *Aldie Castle*.

CLOCH LIGHTHOUSE, Renfrew.   Map 8, NS 2 7.
This notable landmark stands at Cloch Point, and overlooks the outer Clyde estuary, opposite which lies the famous resort of *Dunoon* (*q.v.*) on the *Cowal* (*q.v.*) coast. The white-painted lighthouse was constructed in 1797. *Iter. 65, 66, 88.*

CLOLA, Aberdeen.   Map 27, NK 0 4.
Iter. 185.

CLOSEBURN, Dumfries.   Map 3, NX 8 9.
The massive 14th cent. *Closeburn Tower*, visited by Burns, still preserves its iron yett. **2½ m. N.**, in a ravine, is *Crichope Linn*, described in Scott's " Old Mortality." To the east rise lonely moors and hills, culminating in *Queensberry*, 2,285 ft., a good viewpoint. *Iter. 27, 48, 56, 67.*

CLOVA CHURCH, Angus.   Map 20, NO 3 7.
Situated in the lonely and picturesque Glen Clova, threaded by the South Esk River, and forming one of the fine Braes of Angus glens, which lead into the heart of the eastern Grampian, or *Benchinnan* mountains. The tiny village is known as *Milton of Clova*, and to the north-west are scanty remains of the former castle. A walkers' track leads northwards from a point near the church, and penetrates into the hills to reach the mountain-encircled Loch Brandy, at a height of 2,098 ft., overlooked by a sharp ridge known as the " Snub of Clova," with *Boustie Ley*, 2,868 ft., rising to the west. The road continuing towards the lonely head of the glen, near *Braedownie* (*q.v.*), traverses scenery of increasing wilderness as the hills close in on either side. To the south-east of Clova Church, the road through the glen divides into two branches, one on each bank of the river, these roads reuniting after some six miles and leading to *Dykehead* (*q.v.*). *Iter. 161.*

CLOVENFORDS, Selkirk. 150.   Map 10, NT 4 3.
E.C. Thurs. On the Caddon Water, flowing southwards from lonely hill country to its junction with the Tweed. Scott once lodged at an inn here, as sheriff of Selkirk, before moving to *Ashiestiel* (*q.v.*). In 1803, Dorothy and William Wordsworth came to Clovenfords. There is a monument

Clackmannan, Clackmannan. The old Tolbooth, neighboured by the ancient Stone of Manau and the stepped Town Cross

Cleish, Kinross. A rare example of a burial boundary stone, set in the churchyard wall

Clashmore, Sutherland. A standing stone, traditionally believed to commemorate the killing of a Danish chief of the name of Ospis. It stands some 2 miles west, by the side of A9

Cloch Lighthouse, Renfrew. The white-painted lighthouse at Cloch Point, a notable Clyde estuary landmark

Clarkston, Renfrew. The stone near Cathcart Castle, from which Mary, Queen of Scots, is said to have watched the battle of Langside in 1568. It stands near Cathcart House, some 2 miles north, off an unclassified road

Clachan Bridge, Argyll. This is often described as the only bridge to 'span the Atlantic.' It crosses the narrow Seil Sound, which is, in fact, an arm of the Atlantic Ocean

[For CLOVENFORDS see following plate
[For CLARENCEFIELD see under BORDER COUNTRY (Plate 20)
[For CLATTERINGSHAWS DAM see under GALLOWAY (Plate 70)

PLATE 32 (facing page 122)

Clovenfords, Selkirk. The inscribed tablet to John Leyden, the poet and orientalist, who was a schoolmaster here in 1792

Cock Bridge, Aberdeen. The Well of the Lecht, some 4 miles north-west, which records the construction of the well known Lecht road (A939) by the 33rd regiment under Lord Charles Hay, in 1754

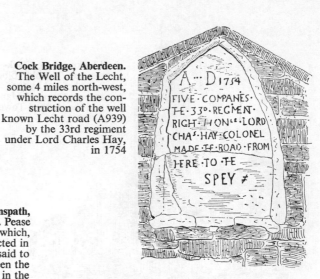

Cockburnspath, Berwick. Pease Bridge, which, when erected in 1837, is said to have been the highest in the world (124 feet)

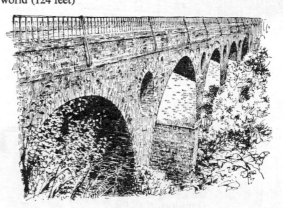

Coatbridge, Lanark. A fountain on the site of the track of the Monkland and Kirkintilloch railway (1824–72), on which an experimental form of traction by wind power using umbrellas was first used. For travel to windward, the services of a Clydesdale horse were utilised

Coldingham, Berwick. The Parish Church, which incorporates the remains of the former 12th century Priory, colonised originally by Benedictine monks from Durham

Coigach, Ross and Cromarty. The peaks of Stack Polly, Cu Beag and Ben More Coigach, seen from an unclassified road along Loch Baddagyle, in the Coigach district, near Achiltibuie

PLATE 33 (facing page 123)

to John Leyden, who taught here in 1792. The Tweed Vineries are situated here. *Iter. 32, 33, 52.*

CLUANIE, Ross and Cromarty.　　Map 24, NH 0 1.
Here, in a grand setting of lonely hills overlooking Glen Cluanie, the road to *Kyle of Lochalsh* (q.v.), for the island of Skye, commences the long traverse through picturesque *Glen Shiel* (q.v.). The road to the south, which formerly went over the hills to *Tomdoun* (q.v.), is to be submerged where it crosses Loch Loyne, a new hydro-electric scheme having necessitated the construction of a large reservoir here. A new road has been built, turning southwards to the east of Loch Cluanie (also now forming a reservoir), and crossing some low hills to reach the shores of Loch Garry, from which Tomdoun can be reached by following the enlarged loch towards the west. The hills around Cluanie, both to the north and south, are well known to climbers. The highest point is *A'Chralaig*, 3,673 ft., which rises to the north, on the Inverness border, and gives a fine view of the remote peak of *Sgurr nan Ceathreamhnan*, 3,771 ft. *Iter. 207, 220.*

CLUNIE, Perth.　　Map 20, NO 1 4.
Lies a little to the south of the Blairgowrie to Dunkeld road, and immediately west of the Loch of Clunie, on an island of which stands the ruined 16th cent. *Clunie Castle*, which was perhaps the early home of the "Admirable Crichton," born in 1560. 2½ m. E. of Clunie, on the Blairgowrie road, is the Loch of Marlee. See **Mennock**. *Iter. 141, 158, 166.*

CLYDEBANK, Dunbarton. 49,761. LB.　　Map 8, NS 5 6.
E.C. Wed. GOLF. An important Clyde shipbuilding centre, with docks and factories. Among many great ships built here are the liners "Queen Mary" and "Queen Elizabeth." Bomb damage in the Second World War was severe. A little to the south-east is *Yoker* (q.v.), with a car ferry over the river giving access to *Renfrew* (q.v.) and the south.

CLYDE FALLS, Lanark.　　Map 9, NS 8 4.
See **Lanark**.

CLYNDER, Dunbarton.　　Map 14, NS 2 8.
Iter. 116.

COALTOWN OF WEMYSS, Fife. 1,065. Map 17, NT 3 9.
Iter. 128.

COATBRIDGE, Lanark. 51,951. LB.　　Map 8, NS 7 6.

E.C. Wed. GOLF. An industrial town, noted especially for its large ironworks. *Iter. 16.*

COCK BRIDGE, Aberdeen.　　Map 26, NJ 2 0.
Situated at a height of more than 1,300 ft., on the River Don, and the starting-point of the well-known *Lecht* road, crossing the north-eastern *Grampians* (q.v.), known here as the *Ladder Hills*, in which *Carn Mor* attains 2,636 ft. This road forms part of a military road of 1754, the date being carved on the Well of the Lecht, some 4 m. N.N.W. of Cock Bridge. The road continues together with the Conglass Water in a gradual descent to *Tomintoul* (q.v.), and later descends still farther to reach the valley of the Spey. The Lecht road, once the terror of motorists, with its steep gradients and sharp bends, has been reconstructed, but remains one of the loftiest roads in the kingdom, the summit, 2½ m. N. of Cock Bridge, being at a height of 2,090 ft., with hills on either side rising to more than 2,600 ft. The steepest section, gradient 1 in 5, is on the ascent out of Cock Bridge over the Hill of Allargue, and the whole road is liable to become snow-bound in severe weather. Away to the west stretches the long valley of Glen Avon, dominated by *Ben Avon*, 3,843 ft., at the eastern extremity of the great *Cairngorm* (q.v.) range. 2½ m. E. of Cock Bridge, a road turns southwards off the *Strathdon* (q.v.) road and climbs into the hills, reaching a height of over 1,800 ft. in the steep and narrow Glas Choille section, sometimes blocked by snow. This road leads to *Gairnshiel Lodge* (q.v.), in the lonely Glen Gairn, thence giving access to the various resorts on *Deeside* (q.v.). See **Corgarff**. *Iter. 141, 160, 174, 176, 191.*

COCKBURNSPATH, Berwick. 761.　　Map 11, NT 7 7.
E.C. Thurs. Near the point where the long range of the *Lammermuir* hills slopes down to the rocky North Sea coast stands this village. To the south-east is a deep, wooded valley, traversed both by the Great North Road and the Edinburgh to London main railway line. The ruined *Cockburnspath Tower* stands near the junction of the road through the valley with the road to *Coldingham* (q.v.), the latter crossed by Pease Bridge, said to have been the highest in the world when erected in 1837. In the village is an old thistle-crowned Mercat Cross, which is early 17th cent. The Church is partly 14th cent., with a curious round tower. 2 m. E., near the sandy shores of Pease Bay, is the ruined Norman Church of *St. Helen*. 6½ m. E., reached by a farm road leading eastwards off the Great North Road, is the ruined *Fast Castle*, situated on the cliffs, and associated with Scott's "Bride of Lammermoor." See **Abbey St. Bathans** and **Dunglass**. *Iter. 1, 2, 38, 39.*

COCKENZIE, East Lothian. 3,335. SB. with Port Seton.
　　Map 10, NT 4 7.
A little Firth of Forth fishing village, where, in the autumn, the picturesque custom of the "Fishermen's Walks" is still kept up. See **Prestonpans** and **Seton**. *Iter. 2.*

COCKPEN, Midlothian. Map 10, NT 3 6.
The small Church, set on rising ground, is the resting place of the Marquis of Dalhousie, who was Viceroy of India at the time of the mutiny. *Dalhousie Castle*, near the west bank of the South Esk River, and dating originally from the 12th cent., has been much modernized, but retains its original drawbridge grooves in the old entrance.

COIGACH, Ross and Cromarty.
　　Map 29, NC 1 0.
See **Achiltibuie, Loch Lurgain, Strathkanaird** and **Ullapool**.

COLDBACKIE, Sutherland.
　　Map 28, NC 6 5.
Iter. 234, 235, 240.

COLDINGHAM, Berwick. 375.
　　Map 11, NT 9 6.
E.C. Wed. This pleasant village is situated a little inland from the sandy shores of Coldingham Bay. Here, a Priory was founded c. 1147, which was burnt and plundered on many later occasions, being

COATBRIDGE

Municipal Buildings. Information Bureau.

finally partially blown up by Cromwell in 1648. In 1854, the remains were restored and added to, and now form the Parish Church, much 12th and 13th cent. work having been preserved. The discovery, in the 19th cent., of a female skeleton embedded upright in the South transept, was turned to account by Scott in "Marmion." See St. Abb's. *Iter.* 2.

COLDSTREAM, Berwick. 1,287. SB.   Map 11, NT 8 3.
E.C. Thurs. GOLF. The River Tweed flows between the village and Cornhill, on the English side of the water. The ford here, used by Edward I entering Scotland in 1296, was used also for many later invasions. Smeaton designed the bridge, first opened in 1766, and up to 1856 marriages were frequently performed at the former toll-house at the Scottish end of the bridge. A tablet placed on the bridge in 1926, records the fact that on May, 7th, 1787, Robert Burns first visited England by this route. A tall, fluted column commemorates Charles Marjoribanks, a former M.P. for Berwick. General Monk originally raised the famous Coldstream Guards here in 1650. A house in the Market Square has a plaque recalling the regimental headquarters. **2 m. N.W.** is the mansion of *The Hirsel*, in its splendid grounds, with a small loch. See **Ladykirk.** *Iter.* 5, 30, 32, 38.

COLINSBURGH, Fife.   Map 17, NO 4 0.
A village dating mainly from 1718, and noted for its cattle shows. A little to the north-west is the fine mansion of *Balcarres House*, which dates partly from 1595, and is a seat of the Lindsays. A "folly" tower stands on Balcarres Crag. *Iter.* 94, 98.

COLINTON (Edinburgh), Midlothian.   Map 9, NT 2 6.
GOLF. On the Water of Leith. The imposing modern Church preserves an old mortsafe in the churchyard. R. L. Stevenson, in his youth, was a frequent visitor at the Manse. The new buildings of *Merchiston* School are situated at Colinton, and here are also the *Redford Barracks*. The old Castle of *Merchiston*, dating from the 16th cent., where John Napier, the inventor of logarithms, was born in 1550, lies to the north-east on the road leading back into the city. Nearby stands *George Watson's* College, a well-known school. Away to the south, in the foothills of the *Pentlands*, is *Bonaly Tower*, formerly the home of the well-known judge, Lord Cockburn. Nearby stands *Dreghorn Castle*, where lived the 18th cent. author of the ballad "William and Margaret." Westwards, beyond *Juniper Green*, lies *Baberton House*, 1622–23, in which Charles X of France once lived. See **Swanston.**

COLINTRAIVE, Argyll. 173.   Map 7, NS 0 7.
A small *Kyles of Bute* (q.v.) and *Cowal* (q.v.) resort, with a shingle beach. Cattle were formerly made to swim across the strait near this point to reach the island of Bute. To the north-west is the inlet of Loch Riddon, and to the south-east, beyond Strone Point, linked by a coast road from Colintraive, is the larger inlet of Loch Striven. A car ferry connects with *Rhubodach* (q.v.) in Bute, giving access to the well-known resort of *Rothesay* (q.v.). See **Glendaruel.** *Iter.* 102, 103, 241.

COLL, ISLE OF, Argyll.
See **Tiree.**

COLLAFIRTH, Shetland.   Map 33, HU 3 8.
Iter. 267.

COLLIESTON, Aberdeen. 147.   Map 27, NK 0 2.
An attractive little fishing village, in a cove, noted for "speldings," or small haddock, and situated some **5 m.** east of the Aberdeen to Peterhead road. In the vicinity are smugglers' caves in the cliffs. In St. Catherine's Dub, a deep creek to the north, a Spanish Armada ship sank in 1588. **2 m. N.E.** are slight remains of *Old Slains Castle*, demolished in 1594. Away to the south-west, near the Ythan estuary, facing *Newburgh* (q.v.), are the Sands of Forvie, beyond Forvie Ness, covering a buried village. See **Cruden Bay.** *Iter.* 182.

COLLIN, Dumfries.   Map 4, NY 0 7.
Iter. 26, 27, 47, 67.

COLMONELL, Ayr. 1,611.   Map 2, NX 1 8.
E.C. Tues. Lies inland from Ballantrae Bay, in the attrac-

tive valley of the River Stinchar. In the churchyard is a Covenanter's memorial. *Kirkhill Castle* dates from 1589, and has received modern additions. Across the stream is the ruined 13th cent. *Craigneil Castle*, and farther west, on the opposite side, stands the 17th. cent. *Knockdolian Tower*, under the hill of that name. *Iter.* 84.

COLNABAICHIN, Aberdeen.   Map 26, NJ 2 0.
Iter. 141, 160, 174, 176, 191.

COLONSAY, ISLE OF, Argyll.   Map 13, NR 3 9.
The two small Inner Hebridean islands of *Colonsay* and *Oronsay* lie to the west of *Jura* (q.v.), and Colonsay is linked by steamer to *Tarbert* (q.v.), on the mainland, by way of *Islay* (q.v.). The islands are separated from each other by a narrow strait, which is dry at low tide for a period of three hours. Colonsay has a pier at *Scalasaig*, and on the island is good pasture land. *Colonsay House*, near Kiloran, inland to the north, has sub-tropical gardens. Oronsay possesses the interesting remains of a 14th. cent. Priory, in the churchyard of which is a notable sculptured Cross, and other sculptured stones have also been preserved. Out to sea, to the north-west of Colonsay, stands the lonely *Dubh Heartach* lighthouse, on an isolated reef. It was the work of David and Thomas Stevenson.

COLPY, Aberdeen.   Map 27, NJ 6 3.
See **Culsalmond** and **Wells of Ythan.** *Iter.* 175.

COLVEND, Kirkcudbright.   Map 3, NX 8 5.
GOLF. The little White Loch lies immediately to the north, and farther to the north-west are the smaller Clonyard and Barean Lochs. A short by-road leads south-westwards from Colvend to the quiet resort of *Rockcliffe* (q.v.), on Rough Firth. *Iter.* 73.

COMRIE, Perth. 1,196.   Map 16, NN 7 2.
E.C. Wed. GOLF. A small summer resort, on the River Earn, in Strath Earn, within easy reach of the attractive Loch Earn, at the eastern end of which lies *St. Fillan's* (q.v.). At Hogmanay, a midnight torch procession takes place, featuring mummers with quaint costumes. *Dunmore Hill*, 837 ft., crowned by the Melville monument, is a good viewpoint. Comrie Church dates from 1805, the steeple being by John Stewart. To the north of Comrie is Glen Lednock, with its falls, and to the south is Glen Artney, these two glens facing each other across the Highland "fault," which has given rise at various times to minor earthquake shocks in this district. Scott used Glen Artney as the setting for parts of the "Lady of the Lake" and "Legend of Montrose." From the former glen, long-distance paths lead through to Loch Tay, and from the latter, a path eventually reaches *Callander* (q.v.), after following the course of the Keltie Water. **2 m. W.S.W.** of Comrie is *Aberuchill Castle*, mainly of 17th cent. date. See **Crieff.** *Iter.* 138, 141, 145.

CONDORRAT, Dunbarton. 1,023.   Map 9, NS 7 7.
Iter. 17, 97, 99.

CONNEL, or CONNEL FERRY, Argyll. 180.
      Map 14, NM 9 3.
E.C. Wed. Situated on the south side of *Loch Etive* (q.v.), where, beyond the narrows, its waters mingle with those of the Firth of *Lorne* (q.v.). The Falls of Lora, a sea cataract, seen at their best during low spring tides, lie immediately to the east of the cantilever rail bridge, the largest in Europe after the Forth Bridge, incorporating a toll-track for vehicles. The bridge spans the loch, giving access to *Benderloch* (q.v.) and the picturesque *Appin* (q.v.) country. From the north side, a by-road leads north-eastwards, skirting the Moss of Achnacree, and passing *Ardchattan* Church to reach the ruined Priory of *Ardchattan*, which adjoins the mansion, on the shores of Loch Etive. The Priory, a 13th cent. foundation, preserves slight remains, including some carved stones, an 11th cent. cross slab, and a carved coffin-cover. These are associations with Robert Bruce's Parliament of 1308, and also with the famous Appin murder (See **Ballachulish**). Beyond here the road forks, one branch continuing to the *Bonawe* (q.v.) granite quarries, and the other turning north and climbing through Glen Salach to reach the shores of Loch Creran, on the road leading to the Appin district. *Iter.* 110, 117, 125, 144, 145.

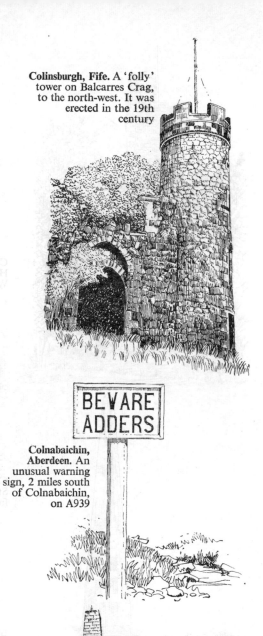

Colinsburgh, Fife. A 'folly' tower on Balcarres Crag, to the north-west. It was erected in the 19th century

Coldstream, Berwick. The plaque on a house recording the former head-quarters of the Coldstream Guards in 1659 which General Monk raised here

Colmonell, Ayr. Kirkhill Castle, built originally in 1589 as a Kennedy stronghold

Colnabaichin, Aberdeen. An unusual warning sign, 2 miles south of Colnabaichin, on A939

Comrie, Perth. The Melville Monument, on the summit of Dunmore Hill. It was set up in 1812 in memory of Viscount Melville, who died the previous year

Connel, Argyll. The road and rail bridge spanning the mouth of Loch Etive, with the Falls of Lora below. It is the largest cantilever bridge in Europe after the Forth Bridge

PLATE 34 (facing page 124)

For COLDSTREAM see also under MERSE (Plate 121)

Corgarff, Aberdeen. The 16th century tower of Corgarff, which underwent a siege in 1571, and has associations with the Jacobite Risings of 1715 and 1745

Corstorphine, Midlothian. Clermiston Tower, on Corstorphine Hill, erected in 1872 to commemorate the centenary of Sir Walter Scott

Corrieyairack Pass, Inverness. General Wade's 18th century Garva, or St. George's Bridge, which spans the Upper Spey on the way to his famous road over the Pass, now unusable

Corpach, Inverness. The obelisk at Kilmallie Church to Colonel John Cameron, who fell at the battle of Quatre Bras during the Waterloo campaign of 1815. It stands to the west, off A830

Conon Bridge, Ross and Cromarty. The former toll house on the bridge over the River Conon

PLATE 35 (facing page 125)

CONNEL, NORTH, Argyll.   Map 14, NM 9 3.
See **Connel.** *Iter. 124.*

CONON BRIDGE, Ross and Cromarty. 339.
                             Map 25, NH 5 5.
E.C. Thurs. An attractive village, at the eastern extremity
of the wooded Strath Conon and lying on the River Conon,
which flows almost immediately into the Firth of Cromarty
to the north-east. On the bridge over the river stands the
former toll-house. A hydro-electric scheme is to operate in
the Conon valley. North-eastwards of Conon Bridge, a
road traverses the shores of Cromarty Firth, with the *Black
Isle* (*q.v.*) lying to the east, and later reaches Udale and
Cromarty Bays, beyond which stands the town of *Cromarty*
(*q.v.*). **2 m. S.** of Conon Bridge, near the river, is *Conon
House*, in the grounds of which is a beech tree 25 ft. in girth.
Iter. 200, 202, 203, 206, 213.

CONTIN, Ross and Cromarty. 1,260.   Map 25, NH 4 5.
A meeting-place of two roads from *Dingwall* (*q.v.*). The
River Blackwater here forms two channels, the Church
standing in the island formed by the branches of the river.
In the vicinity stood *Kilchrist* Church, which, in 1603, while
the Mackenzies were worshipping, is said to have been set
on fire by the Macdonalds, whose piper then marched round
the burning building. See **Achilty Inn** and **Marybank.** *Iter.
204, 205, 206, 221.*

COOLINS, Isle of Skye, Inverness.   Map 23, NG 4 2.
This grand range of mountains, the most precipitous and
striking in Great Britain, is known also as the *Cuillin,* or
the *Cuchullins,* the last-named referring to its possible
association with an Ossianic hero. The main Coolin ridges,
sometimes known as the Black Coolins in order to distinguish
them from the much less impressive Red Coolins, extend in
an irregular semi-circle, some 6 miles in length, overlooking
the spectacular Loch Coruisk in the south-western sector of
the island, and are composed of black gabbro, a rock
particularly suitable for climbing. The highest peak is *Sgurr
Alasdair,* 3,251 ft., but the finest is perhaps *Sgurr nan
Gillean,* 3,167 ft., which rises dramatically above the village
of Sligachan. The Coolins are of much interest to geologists,
and are noted for the misty conditions with which they are
often affected, a danger to inexperienced climbers. The
views from the summit ridges are superb, and quite unequalled elsewhere in Scotland. The Red Coolins, or Red
Hills, face the main ridge from the opposite side of Glen
Sligachan, and their chief peaks, *Glamaig,* 2,537 ft., and
Marsco, 2,414 ft., are rounded and smooth, being composed
of a crumbly pink granite. Beyond them, to the south, rises
Blaven, 3,042 ft., a magnificent outlier of the Black Coolins,
noted for the rock traverse of *Clach Glas,* and overlooking
Loch na Creitheach and Loch Slapin, both in the Strathaird
peninsula. The main Coolin ridge is essentially for expert
climbers, but it is possible to reach the peak of *Bruach na
Frithe,* 3,143 ft., from the famous climbing centre of Sligachan, without serious difficulty, and the view of the fantastic-
ally curved summit ridge and wild corries from this belvedere
is most impressive. From the mainland, the serrated Coolin
ridge can be seen from the summits of some of the loftiest
of the Ross-shire and Inverness-shire peaks, while nearer
views of their splendour can be obtained from a boat on
Loch Scavaig, above which rises *Gars Bheinn,* 2,934 ft., the
most southerly of the Coolins. See **Broadford, Dunan,
Elgol, Glenbrittle, Loch Coruisk, Loch Scavaig** and **Sligachan.**

COPPERCLEUCH, Selkirk.   Map 10, NT 2 2.
Iter. 13, 46.

CORGARFF, Aberdeen.   Map 26, NJ 2 0.
The old tower of *Corgarff* was besieged in 1571, and played a
part in the Jacobite risings of 1715 and 1745. Later it
became a barracks, and was used as a military depot against
smugglers until c. 1830. See **Cock Bridge.** *Iter. 141, 160,
174, 176, 191.*

CORNHILL, Banff.   Map 27, NJ 5 5.
Park House, 16th cent., has fine gardens. *Iter. 170.*

CORNHILL, Northumberland (England). Map 11, NT 8 3.
E.C. Thurs. *Iter. 5, 30, 32.*

CORPACH, Inverness. 209.   Map 18, NN 0 7.
E.C. Wed. Here, near the shores of Loch Linnhe, where the
narrows lead into Loch Eil, looking across to *Fort William*
(*q.v.*), are the eight locks on the Caledonian Canal which
are known as " Neptune's Staircase." A little to the west
is *Kilmallie* Church, where an obelisk to the memory of Col.
John Cameron, with whom Prince Charles Edward once
stayed, has an inscription thought to be by Sir Walter Scott.
The " Road to the Isles " leads westwards from here by the
shores of Loch Eil towards *Glenfinnan* (*q.v.*). See **Banavie**
and **Kinlocheil.** *Iter. 209, 215.*

CORRAN FERRY (NETHER LOCHABER), Inverness.
                            Map 18, NN 0 6.
On the east side of the Corran Narrows, which almost divide
Loch Linnhe (*q.v.*) into two parts, and situated just off the
main Ballachulish to Fort William road. This car ferry
connects with *Ardgour* (*q.v.*), on the opposite shore, and
gives access to the beautiful Ardgour district, which can also
be visited by continuing along the eastern shore of Loch
Linnhe as far as *Fort William* (*q.v.*), and then making the
complete circuit of Loch Eil before reaching Ardgour village
across the narrows. By this means the ferry crossing is
avoided, but an addition of some 25 miles will have to be
reckoned with on the journey, along a narrow and winding
road. Nether Lochaber is the name given to this whole
district, which is Cameron country, stretching from Loch
Leven to Fort William and *Ben Nevis* (*q.v.*), as opposed to
Brae Lochaber, which lies beyond the Ben in the direction
of Glen Spean. See **Lochaber** and **North Ballachulish.** *Iter.
100, 124, 125, 142.*

CORRIE, Isle of Arran, Bute.   Map 7, NS 0 4.
GOLF. A delightful little coastal village, at the foot of
Goat Fell, 2,866 ft., Arran's loftiest mountain. White posts
on the nearby hillside as far north as Sannox Bay indicate the
well-known " Measured Mile " for large vessels on speed
trials. Farther north, on the coast, a path leads to the
picturesque Fallen Rocks. See **Sannox** and **Skelmorlie.**
Iter. 242.

CORRIECRAVIE, Isle of Arran, Bute.   Map 7, NR 9 2.
Iter. 242.

CORRIESHALLOCH GORGE, Ross and Cromarty.
(Falls of Measach).   Map 29, NH 2 7.
See **Braemore Lodge.**

CORRIEYAIRACK PASS, Inverness.   Map 19, NN 4 9.
This famous Pass, which carried the road built by General
Wade in 1735 in order to link *Kingussie* (*q.v.*) with *Fort
Augustus* (*q.v.*), has deteriorated to such an extent that it is
now quite impassable for vehicles, but long-distance walkers
can still make the crossing. Prince Charles Edward crossed
in 1745 from west to east, and droves of sheep made the
journey regularly over the pass until 1899. The summit,
approached from the east by a series of 13 zig-zags, is at a
height of 2,507 ft., the *Corrieyairack* itself attaining 2,922 ft.
immediately to the north. The view is very extensive, and
ranges from the Moray Firth to the distant Coolins of Skye.
The east side of the pass from *Drumgask* (*q.v.*) is paralleled
by the River Spey, while the descent on the north-west side
goes through GlenTarff. Neil Munro, in his " New Road,"
has described the construction of the road. Although little
remains today of the road over the pass, it ranks as one of
the greatest achievements of Wade. See **Wade Roads.**

CORSOCK, Kirkcudbright.   Map 3, NX 7 7.
Iter. 71, 75.

CORSTORPHINE (Edinburgh), Midlothian.
                            Map 9, NT 1 7.
Here is the Edinburgh Zoological Park, situated on the slopes
of *Corstorphine Hill,* 530 ft., on which is the viewpoint of
Rest and be Thankful, associated with R. L. Stevenson's
" Kidnapped." On the summit of the hill stands the *Clermiston Tower,* commemorating Sir Walter Scott. Corstorphine Church, of 15th cent. date, became collegiate in
1429, and is noted for the Forrest memorials, the separate
gabled roofs, and the coats of arms on the exterior. To the
east of the hill is the early 17th cent. *Craigcrook Castle,* with
later alterations and additions. Nearby is *Ravelston*

House, with its lovely gardens, associated with Tully-Veolan in Scott's "Waverley." **2 m. E.** is the famous Rugby Football ground of *Murrayfield*, the home of Scotland's international matches, and near it stands *Roseburn House*, 1562 and later, in which Cromwell is said to have passed the night in 1650. See **Gogar**. *Iter. 15, 16, 91, 95.*

CORTACHY, Angus.　　　　　Map 20, **NO 3** 5.
The Church retains a 15th cent. window. *Cortachy Castle*, a seat of the Earl of Airlie, the head of Clan Ogilvie, has a well known herd of cattle.

COSHIEVILLE, Perth.　　　　Map 19, **NN 7** 4.
A road junction in the Strath of Appin, where the road to *Fortingall* (*q.v.*) and beautiful Glen Lyon diverges from that linking *Aberfeldy* (*q.v.*) with Lochs Rannoch and Tummel. A little to the north is the ruined 14th cent. *Garth Castle*. Farther north still, off the road which mounts steadily over moorlands towards *White Bridge* (*q.v.*), a walkers' track diverges westwards, by which the graceful peak of *Schiehallion*, 3,547 ft., may be climbed. *Iter. 89, 107, 138, 147, 149.*

COTHOUSE BRIDGE, Argyll.　　Map 14, **NS 1** 8.
Iter. 102, 137.

COULPORT, Dunbarton.　　　Map 14, **NS 2** 8.
On the east shores of *Loch Long* (*q.v.*), facing *Ardentinny* (*q.v.*) across its waters. At Coulport terminates the road which almost encircles the narrow Rosneath peninsula. *Iter. 116.*

COUPAR ANGUS, Perth.　2,133. SB.　Map 17, **NO 2** 3.
E.C. Wed. The centre of a fruit-growing district, situated in the valley of *Strathmore* (*q.v.*), immediately to the south of the winding Tay. There are slight remains of a Cistercian Abbey, founded in 1164, standing in a corner of the churchyard. Away to the south are the *Sidlaw* hills, with *King's Seat*, 1,235 ft., and *Dunsinane Hill*, 1,012 ft. (See **Balbeggie**). At *Lintrose*, 2 m. S., are the outlines of an extensive Roman Camp. Off the Blairgowrie road, to the north-west of the town, lies the Stormont Loch. See **Meikleour, Pitcur** and **Stobhall**. *Iter. 151, 153, 157, 158, 159.*

COVE, Dunbarton.　　　　　Map 14, **NS 2** 8.
See **Kilcreggan**. *Iter. 116.*

COVE, Kincardine.　　　　　Map 21, **NJ 9** 0.
A small village, off the Aberdeen to Stonehaven road, and on an interesting stretch of coastline, with the rocky shores of Nigg Bay lying 2½ m. N.N.E., sheltered by Girdle Ness, with its lighthouse. A road traverses the shores as far as the Ness, and continues towards Aberdeen Bay. See **Findon**. *Iter. 155, 156.*

COVESEA, Moray.　　　　　Map 26, **NJ 1** 7.
See **Lossiemouth**.

COWAL, Argyll.　　　　　Map 14, **NS 0** 8 etc.
The name given to the extensive tract of hilly country, forming a peninsula, which lies between *Loch Fyne* (*q.v.*) and the Clyde estuary, and which is indented by a number of picturesque sea lochs, notably Loch Striven and Loch Goil. To the east of the last-named is Loch Long, at the head of which stands *Arrochar* (*q.v.*), in a setting of lofty hills, most of which form part of the Argyll National Forest Park. To the south of Cowal, and separated from it by the *Kyles of Bute* (*q.v.*), is situated the island of Bute, access to which is gained by car ferry from *Colintraive* (*q.v.*). See **Ardentinny, Benmore Estate, Dunoon** (*for Cowal Highland Gathering*), **Kilmun, Lochgoilhead, Rest and be Thankful, Strachur** and **Tighnabruaich**. *Iter. 102, 103, 137.*

COWDENBEATH, Fife. 13,572. SB.　Map 17, **NT 1** 9.
E.C. Wed. The principal town on the Fife coalfield. To the east of the town lies Loch Gelly, and away to the west is Loch Fitty, backed by the low *Roscobie* hills. See **Blairadam**. *Iter. 90.*

COWIE, Kincardine.　　　　　Map 21, **NO 8** 8.
A small fishing village, on a rocky bay, with a ruined chapel.

COXTON TOWER, Moray.　　　Map 26, **NJ 2** 6.
See **Lhanbryde**.

COYLTON, Ayr.　　　　　Map 8, **NS 4** 1.
Lies in a coal-mining area. A little to the east are the many windings of the Water of Coyle. 2½ m. S.W. is Martnaham Loch. See **Drongan**. *Iter. 21, 27, 68.*

COYLUMBRIDGE, Inverness.　　Map 25, **NH 9** 1.
On the outskirts of *Rothiemurchus* (*q.v.*) Forest, and situated on the road leading to the Glenmore National Forest Park, described under *Aviemore*. Coylumbridge is also on the walkers' track leading to the well-known *Lairig Ghru* (*q.v.*) pass in the *Cairngorms* (*q.v.*). A little to the west, beyond *Inverdruie*, a short by-road gives access to Loch an Eilean, described under Rothiemurchus. A road leads northwards from Coylumbridge by way of the attractive little Loch Pityoulish, and later passes *Kincardine* Church on the way to the Forest of Abernethy and *Nethybridge* (*q.v.*). *Iter. 149, 171.*

CRAGABUS, Isle of Islay, Argyll.　Map 6, **NR 3** 4.
Iter. 244.

CRAICHIE, Angus.　　　　　Map 25, **NO 5** 4.
Iter. 162.

CRAIGELLACHIE, Banff. 400.　　Map 26, **NJ 2** 4.
E.C. Thurs. A village beautifully situated in the wooded Strath Spey, near the point where the Fiddich joins the larger river. The bridge over the Spey leading into Morayshire was designed by Telford. This district is well known for its distilleries. The village is sometimes known as *Lower Craigellachie*, to avoid confusion with the well-known *Rock of Craigel-*

Coshieville, Perth. The statue to Major-General David Stewart (1788–1829), erected by the Stewart Society in 1925

Coupar Angus, Perth. Remains of the Cistercian Abbey, founded by Malcolm IV in 1164 and destroyed in 1559

Cowal, Argyll. Hunter's Quay, a Clyde yachting rendezvous, at the mouth of the Holy Loch

Cowal, Argyll. The obelisk to J. Duncan, at Kilmun, on the north shore of the Holy Loch. His chemical research in the 19th century is said to have revolutionised the British sugar refining industry

Coxton Tower, Moray. The white-harled tower of 1641, the work of the Innes family of Invermarkie. It stands on an unclassified road off A96, south of Lhanbryde

Craigellachie, Banff. The old Spey Bridge, constructed by Thomas Telford

PLATE 36 (facing page 126)

Cramond Bridge, Midlothian; West Lothian. The 'Cramond' Inn, where Robert Louis Stevenson once cut his initials on a table. It stands at Cramond village, 2 miles north, on the Firth of Forth

Crail, Fife. The Mercat Cross, topped by a unicorn

Cramond Bridge, Midlothian; West Lothian. A pillar in the churchyard of Cramond village, near the Firth of Forth

Craigievar Castle, Aberdeen. The early 17th century Castle, one of the finest in Scotland. The great hall displays a notable Renaissance ceiling. It stands to the west of A980, between Lumphanan and Alford

Craigmillar Castle, Midlothian. The 14th century Castle of the Prestons, where, in 1566, Mary, Queen of Scots, in company with Bothwell, plotted the murder of Darnley

PLATE 37 (facing page 127) [For CRAIL see also under EAST NEUK (Plate 56) and also Plates 172 and 175
[For CRANSHAWS see under LAMMERMUIRS (Plate 105)

lachie at *Aviemore* (*q.v.*). 3½ m. E.S.E., above Glen Fiddich, is the old mansion of *Kininvie*. 2½ m. N.E. is *Ben Aigan*, 1,544 ft., from which a remarkable view of the Spey Valley can be obtained. See **Aberlour**. *Iter. 170, 190, 192, 195.*

CRAIGENDORAN, Dunbarton. Map 15, NS 3 8.
One of the most important railhead centres for steamers on the Clyde coast, situated on the south-east outskirts of the resort of *Helensburgh* (*q.v.*). *Iter. 102, 111.*

CRAIGENPUTTOCK, Dumfries. Map 3, NX 7 8.
See Dunscore.

CRAIGHOUSE, Isle of Jura, Argyll. Map 6, NR 5 6.
See Jura.

CRAIGIEVAR CASTLE, Aberdeen. Map 27, NJ 5 0.
One of the loveliest of Scottish Castles, built to an L-plan in the baronial style, and situated to the north of the Aberdeen to Tarland road, on high ground above the Leochel Burn, with views across the Don valley. The structure dates from 1610 to 1624, with a fine show of turrets and high-pitched roofs, while the interior is noted for its splendid Renaissance ceiling in the Hall. Over the fireplace is the inscription " Doe not vaiken sleeping dogs." *Iter. 165, 190.*

CRAIGMILLAR CASTLE (Edinburgh), Midlothian.
Map 10, NT 2 7.
This fine, ruined Castle (A.M.), with its massive 14th cent. keep, a noted viewpoint, has been added to at later periods, and was a favourite residence of Mary, Queen of Scots, who, within its walls, in 1566, plotted with Bothwell to murder Darnley. Earlier, in 1477, the Castle was the prison of the Earl of Mar, who is said to have been bled to death here. It is open weekdays, 10 to 4 or 7; Sun., 2 to 4 or 7. (See note page 90). In the vicinity, on the road to Dalkeith, are some old houses known as *Little France*, where some of the Queen's French attendants once lived. 1½ m. N.E. of the Castle is *Niddrie Marischal*, the ancient home of the Wauchope family, dating partly from 1600, 1636 and 1661, with later alterations by the brothers Adam.

CRAIGMORE, Bute. Map 7, NS 1 6.
Iter. 241.

CRAIGNURE, Isle of Mull, Argyll. Map 12, NM 7 3.
Stands at the meeting of the waters of the Sound of Mull and *Loch Linnhe* (*q.v.*), with a small pier. *Craignure* faces the flat island of *Lismore* (*q.v.*), and looks to the mainland mountains of Appin and also the distant peak of Ben Nevis. 3½ m. S.E., at Duart Point, is the famous, restored *Duart Castle*, the ancestral home of the chiefs of the Macleans, the 26th of whom died in 1937 at the age of 101. The road leading southwards from Craignure, by way of the head of Loch Don, traverses later the shores of the almost landlocked Loch Spelve, in the midst of fine mountain and cliff scenery, dominated by *Creach Bheinn*, 2,289 ft. A branch from this road penetrates the lonely Glen More, backed by wild hills, with *Ben Buie* attaining 2,354 ft., and later reaches the shores of Loch Scridain. Another range of hills, exceeding 2,500 ft. in height, dominates the road which leads north-westwards from Craignure along the shores of the Sound of Mull past Scallastle Bay in the direction of *Salen* (*q.v.*). See **Lochbuie**. *Iter. 249, 250.*

CRAIGROTHIE, Fife. Map 17, NO 3 1.
To the south are scanty remains of the one-time palatial *Struthers Castle*, which, in 1547 was known by the name of *Auchtervthyrstruthyr*. It was occupied by Cromwell in 1653. See Ceres. *Iter. 127, 129.*

CRAIGTON, Angus. Map 20, NO 3 5.
Iter. 166.

CRAIL, Fife. 1,168. SB. Map 17, NO 6 0.
E.C. Wed. GOLF. A most picturesque fishing town and ancient Royal Burgh, the oldest in the East Neuk, with a number of old crow-stepped and red-tiled houses, notably near the harbour. The Tolbooth dates from the early 16th cent., displaying a fish weather-vane, and a coat of arms with the date 1602. There have been 18th and early 19th cent. additions. The Collegiate Church is a 13th cent structure, with later alterations, and retains a plain short-spired tower. There is some 17th cent. woodwork, an ancient carved cross, and in the chancel is a picture of a sailor taking a bearing with a sextant. The churchyard is rich in carved memorials. Near the shore stands an ancient doocot and in the Victoria Gardens is the ancient *Sauchope Stone*. The Town Cross displays a unicorn. On the Isle of May, out to sea to the south-east, and once a place of pilgrimage, is a powerful lighthouse. 2 m. N.E., on the coast, is the tower of *Balcomie Castle*, where Mary of Guise, the mother of Mary, Queen of Scots, was entertained in 1538. Beyond the Castle is Fife Ness, in the " East Neuk of Fife," facing the North Carr lighthouse, marking the perilous Carr Rocks. Away to the north-east, visible in clear weather, is the lonely Bell Rock lighthouse. 2 m. S.W. of the town are the caves of *Caiplie*, the largest being 40 ft. long. *Iter. 94, 98, 132.*

CRAILING, Roxburgh. Map 10, NT 6 2.
Crailing House, dating from 1803, is a fine Regency mansion. *Iter. 30, 47.*

CRAMOND BRIDGE, Midlothian; West Lothian. 500.
Map 17, NT 1 7.
The modern bridge spanning the Almond, built by Rennie, stands in sight of the old bridge, in its wooded setting, and dated 1619, which lies a little way to the north. Beyond here, the river flows into the Firth of Forth at the village of *Cramond*, with Cramond Island lying on the edge of the Drum Sands. A predecessor of the old bridge figures in Rossetti's " The King's Tragedy," which describes the warning of impending tragedy given by a prophetess to James 1, in 1436, when journeying from Edinburgh to Perth, where he was murdered. Another legend of the bridge tells of the rescue of James V from footpads in the 16th cent. (See **Fenwick**), while some years later the bridge figured in an incident with which Mary, Queen of Scots was associated. Cramond Church stands on the site of a Roman fort, and the village was described in R. L. Stevenson's " St. Ives." *Cramond House* dates from the 17th and 18th cents. See **Barnton** (Edinburgh) and **Dalmeny**. *Iter. 17, 89, 90, 92, 93, 94, 96.*

CRANSHAWS, Berwick. 119. Map 10, NT 6 6.
A tiny village in a picturesque, lonely setting on the White-adder Water in the *Lammermuir* hills. Near the remains of the old Church stands *Cranshaws Tower*, a fine Border peel, still inhabited, and once a Douglas stronghold. The arms of James VI, once in the old Church, have been transferred to the inner north door of the present Church. The narrow and hilly road leading north-westwards into the hills towards *Gifford* (*q.v.*) crosses the " Hungry Snout," and reaches an altitude of well over 1,000 ft., with *Spartleton Edge* rising away to the east. A right fork from this road gives access, under the slopes of *Clints Dod*, 1,307 ft., a good viewpoint, to the village of *Garvald* (*q.v.*). See **Abbey St. Bathans**. *Iter. 3.*

CRARAE, Argyll. Map 14, NR 9 9.
A pleasant village on *Loch Fyne* (*q.v.*). *Crarae Lodge* has notable gardens, shown 9 to dusk, April to end of Oct. (See note page 90). *Iter. 118, 121.*

CRASK, Sutherland. Map 28, NC 5 2.
A little to the north is the low road pass of *The Crask*, 828 ft., a watershed, from which the view extends to *Ben Klibreck*, 3,154 ft., to the east, and *Ben More Assynt*, 3,273 ft., the highest mountain in the county, to the west. Below the first-named mountain, to the east of Crask, lies the remote Loch Choire. *Iter. 230, 232.*

CRASK OF AIGAS, Inverness. Map 25, NH 4 4.
The Beauly River, in a very beautiful wooded setting, flows here, dividing at one point into two arms, which encircle *Eilean Aigas* house, a refuge of Lord Lovat, in 1697, and once the home of Sir Robert Peel. The house is also associated with the two brothers known as the Sobiéski Stuarts, who claimed to be descendants of Prince Charles Edward, and were well known as sportsmen and naturalists. The gardens are of especial note. Farther to the north-east is the low Druim Pass, with richly wooded cliffs, and a little way beyond are the Falls of *Kilmorack* (*q.v.*). *Iter. 206, 210.*

CRATHES CASTLE, Kincardine.　　Map 21, **NO 7** 9.
To-the north of the River Dee stands this fine Castle, or double square tower, presented in 1952 to the Scottish National Trust, and open Wed. and Thurs., 11 to 8 (Sun. from 2.30), May to end of Sept.; Wed. and Sat., 11 to 4.30, Oct. to end of April. (See note page 90). The structure was commenced in 1553 and completed between 1596 and 1600, forming a notable example of the Scottish baronial style, rich in turrets and gables. It is famous for its wood-work, and several painted ceilings, which date from 1599, considered to be the finest in Scotland. There are also beautiful walled gardens, including some massive yew hedges. Among the rare antiquities preserved in the Castle is the jewelled " Horn of Leys," of 1324, possibly connected with Robert Bruce. Crathes has belonged to the Burnetts of Leys since 1323. *Iter. 152.*

CRATHIE CHURCH, Aberdeen.　　Map 20, **NO 2** 9.
This small Royal *Deeside* (q.v.) Church is attended by the Royal Family when they are in residence at *Balmoral Castle* (q.v.). The Church is built of granite, and dates from 1895. Queen Victoria laid the foundation stone, and in the grave-yard of the ruined Old Church is buried John Brown, her personal attendant for many years. **1 m. E.**, on the south side of the Dee, is *Abergeldie Castle*, an old tower, with modern additions, where King Edward VII lived when Prince of Wales. See **Aberfeldy**. *Iter. 141, 152, 167, 179.*

CRAWFORD, Lanark. 354.　　Map 9, **NS 9** 2.
E.C. Thurs. A Clydesdale resort, surrounded by green Lowland hills, and well suited for walking. There is an old stone pillar, associated with the owners of the local hotel who ran the last mail coach. *Tower Lindsay* is a fragment of an old castle, visited by both James IV and James V. The Camps Water, issuing from the Camps reservoir, in its amphitheatre of hills to the east, flows into the Clyde at Crawford. See **Elvanfoot**. *Iter. 25, 29, 50, 51, 56, 125.*

CRAWFORDJOHN, Lanark.　　Map 9, **NS 8** 2.
The village stands at the foot of *Mountherrick Hill*, 1,400 ft., and on a narrow road linking Clydesdale with Nithsdale, in Dumfries-shire, the latter part of the road following the winding valley of the Crawick Water, in a setting of Lowland hills. **2 m. E.**, under the slopes of *Drake Law*, 1,584 ft., is the old mansion of *Gilkerscleuch*, 17th cent., with modern additions. *Iter. 48.*

CREAGAN, Argyll.　　Map 14, **NM 9** 4.
On the shores of Loch Creran, around the head of which winds the picturesque road linking Benderloch with Appin. Beyond the head extend Glens Creran and Ure, dominated by *Beinn Sguliaird*, 3,059 ft., and *Beinn Fhionnlaidh*, 3,139 ft. *Iter. 124.*

CREAGORRY, Isle of Benbecula, Inverness.
　　　　　　　　　　　　　　Map 32, **NF 7** 4.
See **Hebrides, Outer** (Benbecula). *Iter. 262.*

CREETOWN, Kirkcudbright. 887.　　Map 2, **NX 4** 5.
E.C. Wed. Stands on Wigtown Bay, near the widening estuary of the Cree, and was formerly named *Ferrytown*. From the local granite quarries came the stone for part of Liverpool's docks. The clock tower commemorates Queen Victoria's Diamond Jubilee. The neighbourhood is associa-ted with Scott's " Guy Mannering," notably the mansion of *Cassencary*, to the south of the town. The old road to *Gatehouse of Fleet* (q.v.) went inland, but the present road follows the curve of Wigtown Bay, and is one of the most beautiful coast roads in southern Scotland. The ruined castles of *Carsluith* and *Barholm*, the latter once a hiding place of John Knox, lie off the road between Creetown and Ravenshall Point, to the west of which is *Dirk Hatteraick's Cave*. Near Barholm, up the valley of the Kirkdale Burn, are the long cairns at *Cairnholy*, relics of the New Stone Age. Away to the north of Creetown rises the lonely mass of *Cairnsmore of Fleet*, 2,331 ft., a prominent landmark, which is associated with John Buchan's " The Thirty-nine Steps." See **Newton Stewart** and **Palnure**. *Iter. 26, 72, 73.*

CREICH, Sutherland.　　Map 31, **NH 6** 8.
Near the Church stands the 7-ft. high *St. Demhan's Cross. Dun Creich*, to the south-east, is a vitrified fort on the

Dornoch Firth. In the vicinity are chambered cairns. *Iter. 200, 231.*

CRIANLARICH, Perth. 400.　　Map 15, **NN 3** 2.
E.C. Wed. A centre for climbing, walking and winter sports, in the *Breadalbane* (q.v.) country, situated at the meeting-place of Strath Fillan, Glen Dochart and Glen Falloch, and in the midst of some of the finest mountain scenery in the Highlands. The road leading south-eastwards by way of Glen Falloch to *Ardlui* (q.v.), at the head of *Loch Lomond* (q.v.), is very picturesque. In Glen Dochart, the Dochart River flows through Loch Dochart and Loch Iubhair, backed by the well-known twin peaks of *Ben More*, 3,843 ft., and *Stobinian*, 3,821 ft., while a little to the west rises *Cruach Ardran*, 3,428 ft. On a small wooded island in Loch Dochart are scanty remains of an old castle. **3 m. N.W.**, in Strath Fillan, east of the Fillan Water, are slight remains of *St. Fillan's* Chapel, dating from 1314, and dedicated by Bruce as a thanks-offering for the victory of Bannockburn. St. Fillan's bell is now preserved in the National Museum of Antiquities at Edinburgh. To the west of Crianlarich rises *Beinn Oss*, 3,374 ft., almost on the Argyll border. See **Tyndrum**. *Iter. 100, 110, 111, 120, 142, 144, 145.*

CRICHTON, Midlothian.　　Map 10, **NT 3** 6.
Above the steep, wooded banks of the Tyne Water stands the little Collegiate Church, dating from 1449, notable for its tower and barrel vaulting, and a quaint bell-cote. To the south is the fine Castle (A.M.), 14th to 16th cent., showing a curious Italianate north wing, with numerous projecting bosses in the courtyard walls. The building was originally composed of a single tower, but developed into a three-sided enclosure, and finally received the unique north wing. The dungeon is known as the " Massie More." The Castle was visited by Mary, Queen of Scots in 1562, and is associated with Scott's " Marmion." Open weekdays (except Fri.): summer 10 to 7, winter 10 to 4; Sun., 2 to 7 or 4. (See note page 90). See **Borthwick**.

CRIEFF, Perth. 5.384. SB.　　Map 16, **NN 8** 2.
E.C. Wed. M.D. Tues. GOLF. A good touring centre in Strath Earn. To the north of Crieff, the Earn is joined by the Turret Water flowing from the picturesque Loch Turret in the remote glen of that name, with its falls, lying at the base of *Ben Chonzie*, 3.048 ft. Outside the Town Hall are the

1. Town Hall with Drummond 　2. Market Cross. 　Cross and stocks. 　3. Information Bureau.

Crathes Castle, Kincardine. The late 16th century Castle of the Burnetts of Leys (N.T. Scot.). It stands to the north of A93, east of the Deeside resort of Banchory

Crawford, Lanark. A stone pillar, set up in the late 19th century, which was once the tombstone of the Cranston family, former owners of the 'Crawford' Hotel, who ran the last mail coach in this district. It was to have been set up in the churchyard, but owing to a family quarrel this was never carried out

Crathie Church, Aberdeen. The Church, built in 1895, of which Queen Victoria laid the foundation stone. The Royal Family worship here when in residence at Balmoral Castle

Creich, Sutherland. The 7-foot high St. Demhan's Cross

Creetown, Kirkcudbright. The ruined Barholm Castle, situated about half-way to Gatehouse of Fleet, on A75. It was once a hiding-place of John Knox

Crichton, Midlothian. The 14th to 16th century Castle, associated with Sir Walter Scott's '*Marmion*.' The north wing, the work of the Earl of Bothwell, was probably copied from a Veronese palace

[For CRIEFF see following plate

[For CRICHTON see also Plate 173

PLATE 38 (facing page 128)

Crieff, Perth. A cross slab, re-used as a Market Cross, probably 10th century

Cromarty, Ross and Cromarty. The 17th century cottage (N.T. Scot.), which was the birthplace of Hugh Miller, the geologist, in 1802

Crieff, Perth. The Drummond Cross of 1688. The iron stocks below were in use until 1816

Crook Inn, Peebles. A well known posting inn of coaching days, now rebuilt and enlarged. A former Jacobite landlord, captured at Culloden, in 1746, saved his life by dashing down the steep slopes of the Devil's Beef Tub (see Plate 45), near Moffat, when on his way to be tried at Carlisle

Crossford, Lanark. The 16th century Craignethan Castle, which may be the 'Tillietudlem' of Sir Walter Scott's '*Old Mortality*'

Crossmichael, Kirkcudbright. The tombstone to William Graham, a Covenanter martyr of 1682

PLATE 39 (facing page 129)

old stocks, and nearby is the octagonal *Drummond Cross*, dated 1688. The old Market Cross, ornamented with runic knots, is perhaps 10th cent. work. Crieff was burnt in 1716, being further damaged in 1745. Prince Charles Edward held a council of war in the " *Drummond Arms* " Hotel in 1746. To the north of the town is the *Knock of Crieff*, 911 ft., surmounted by an indicator, and forming a fine viewpoint. It overlooks the mansion of *Ochtertyre*, with its small loch, visited by Burns in 1787. **3 m. W.** is *Tomachastle Hill*, crowned by a monument to Sir David Baird, the hero of Seringapatam. **3½ m. S.S.W.** is *Drummond Castle*, once bombarded by Cromwell, and partially dismantled in 1745. An old tower, now an armoury, still remains, but the rest of the structure is mostly rebuilt. The multiple sundial is dated 1630, and there are notable gardens. **4 m. S.E.** is the ruined *Innerpeffray Castle*, dated 1610. Nearby is the oldest library in Scotland, founded in 1691, and housed in a late 18th cent. building. The library is open to the public on week-days. The adjoining burial-chapel of the Drummonds was once a Collegiate Church, dating from 1508, and has quaint tombs. See **Fowlis Wester, Gilmerton** (Perth), **Sma' Glen** and **Muthill.** *Iter. 89, 140, 141, 145.*

CRIMOND, Aberdeen.   Map 27, NK 0 5.
See **Old Rattray.** *Iter. 181, 182.*

CRINAN, Argyll. 40.   Map 14, NR 7 9.
A small village, situated at the foot of a remarkable rock garden on Crinan Loch. Here, the Crinan Canal terminates its journey from *Ardrishaig* (*q.v.*) and flows into the Sound of Jura. This 9-mile long waterway dates from 1793 to 1801, but it is now comparatively little used. The purpose of its construction was to enable ships to reach the Atlantic from Loch Fyne, without having to make the long and often stormy circuit of the Kintyre peninsula away to the south. Queen Victoria traversed the canal by barge in 1847. **3 m. S.W.,** to the north of the canal, is the Moss of Crinan, or Moine Mhor. Away to the south, in the *Knapdale* (*q.v.*) district, is the well-wooded Loch Sween, with roads along both east and west shores, which terminate with views over the Sound of Jura to the island of Jura, with its prominent *Paps.* See **Cairnbaan, Kilmartin, Kilmory Knap** and **Tayvallich.** *Iter. 122.*

CROCKETFORD, Kirkcudbright. 115.   Map 3, NX 8 7.
E.C. Thurs. About halfway between the little lochs of Auchenreoch and Milton, and slightly to the north, stands the village, which was founded by a religious sect, known as the Buchanites. On the hills to the north-west are a tombstone and monument to four Covenanting martyrs, shot in 1685. See **Irvine and Shawhead.** *Iter. 26, 70, 71, 75.*

CROE BRIDGE, Ross and Cromarty.   Map 24, NG 9 2.
Situated near the head of picturesque *Loch Duich* (*q.v.*), on the lovely road leading towards *Kyle of Lochalsh* (*q.v.*). A long-distance walkers' path goes 7 miles through the hills from here, by way of Dorusduain, and over the rough and steep 2,000-ft. high Bealach na Sroine towards the magnificent *Falls of Glomach* (*q.v.*). These can also be approached from quite a different direction, for which see under *Ardelve.* Another path goes south-eastwards, through Glen Lichd, under the slopes of *Ben Attow*, or *Beinn Fhada*, 3,383 ft., and follows the River Croe and the Allt Granda over the Inverness border to the headwaters of the Affric River, giving access for hardy walkers to Glen Affric. (See **Cannich.**) West of Croe Bridge, on the way to *Inverinate* (*q.v.*), is the little Church and manse of *Kintail* (*q.v.*). See **Shiel Bridge.** *Iter. 207, 220.*

CROFTS OF SAVOCH, Aberdeen.   Map 27, NK 0 5.
Iter. 182.

CROMARTY, Ross and Cromarty. 678. SB.
     Map 25, NH 7 6.
E.C. Wed. A small *Black Isle* (*q.v.*) seaport of Easter Ross, guarding the narrows of Cromarty Firth, with the North Sutor headland over the water, and the South Sutor headland to the east of the town, looking out towards the Moray Firth. The two are known together as the Sutors of Cromarty. Cromarty was the birthplace of Hugh Miller, the geologist, and his cottage, dating from c. 1650 (N.T. Scot.), contains a

1. Hugh Miller's birthplace   2. Parish Church.
    (N.T. Scot.).

geological collection. Open week-days only, 10 to 12 and 2 to 5. (See note page 90). A statue to him stands on a hill above the town. Among the characteristic 17th to 18th cent. houses in the town is *Albion House*, in Church Street. The Parish Church is of interest for its interior furnishings. On the site of the former

Castle, to the south-east of the town, stands *Cromarty House*. A passenger ferry crosses the Firth to *Dunskeath* (*q.v.*) on the opposite shore. *Iter. 203.*

CROMBIE, Fife.   Map 16, NT 0 8.
Iter. 134.

CROMDALE, Moray.   Map 26, NJ 0 2.
To the south-east rise the *Cromdale* hills, several of whose summits top the 2,000-ft. mark, the highest being *Carn Eachie*, 2.136 ft., and along the crest of which goes the Banffshire county boundary. The winding course of the River Spey is a little to the north of the village. **2 m. E.,** in the Haughs of Moray, is the site of a battle fought and lost by the Jacobites in 1690. *Iter. 170, 195.*

CROOK INN, Peebles.   Map 9, NT 1 2.
At a height of nearly 750 ft., in a setting of hills, this inn was once a famous posting house on the Edinburgh to Dumfries road. By following the Hearthstane Burn it is possible to climb south-eastwards and reach the flat summit of *Broad Law*, 2,754 ft., rising to the east of the lonely Talla Reservoir. Farther to the north is *Dollar Law*, 2,680 ft. See **Tweedsmuir.** *Iter. 10, 24.*

CROOK OF ALVES, Moray.   Map 26, NJ 1 6.
See **Alves.** *Iter. 175, 198.*

CROOK OF DEVON, Kinross.   Map 16, NO 0 0.
The River Devon, flowing southwards through a picturesque defile, makes a sharp bend, or " crook " here on its way to *Rumbling Bridge* (*q.v.*). It would appear that the flow of the river from here was formerly in an easterly direction, along the course of the present Gairney Water. Away to the south-east rise the *Cleish* hills, with *Dumglow* attaining 1,241 ft. **1 m. E.N.E.** is *Tullibole Castle*, an old tower, dated 1608. *Iter. 91, 98.*

CROSSFORD, Fife.   Map 16, NT 0 8.
Iter. 97.

CROSSFORD, Lanark. 618.   Map 9, NS 8 4.
A Clydesdale village, in a district of orchards, near which the River Nethan flows into the main stream. **1 m. W.S.W.,** overlooking the Nethan, is *Craignethan Castle*, now a ruin, preserving two towers and portions of the walls, and dating from the 16th cent. (A.M.). It is supposed to be the "Tillietudlem Castle " of Scott's " Old Mortality." **1 m. N.E.,** situated in a ravine of the Fiddler's Burn, is the 16th cent. *Hallbar Tower*. See **Kirkfieldbank.** *Iter. 53, 69.*

CROSSGATES, Fife. 1,771.   Map 17, NT 1 8.
A little to the south-east are the low, wooded *Cullalo* hills, overlooking the Burntisland reservoir. *Iter. 90, 97, 133.*

CROSSHILL, Ayr.   Map 8, NS 3 0.
Iter. 49, 84, 85.

CROSSHOUSE, Ayr. 2,009.   Map 8, NS 3 3.
Iter. 66, 69.

CROSSMICHAEL, Kirkcudbright. 1,731. Map 3, NX 7 6.
E.C. Wed. Situated on the River Dee, where it broadens

out into a reservoir which has been constructed by means of the Glenlochar barrage, and the waters of which are united with those of Loch Ken, to the north-west. In the Kirkyard is a Covenanter's gravestone of 1682. **2 m. N.E.** of Cross-michael, and on high ground, is the tiny Loch Roan. See **Laurieston.** *Iter. 76.*

CROSSRAGUEL ABBEY, Ayr. Map 8, NS 2 0.
This Cluniac Abbey (A.M.), founded in the 12th cent., is now an interesting ruin, most of the present structure dating from the 15th cent. Of special interest are the gate-house, the dove-cote and the Abbot's tower. A little to the north-east is the tower of *Baltersan,* a one-time Kennedy stronghold, dating from 1584, from which an extensive view can be obtained. *Iter. 55, 68.*

CROVIE, Banff. Map 27, NJ 8 6.
A secluded little fishing village, lying at the base of lofty red cliffs in Gamrie Bay, sheltered by Crovie Head. A little farther to the north-east is the larger headland of Troup Head. See **Gardenstown.** *Iter. 182.*

CROWN OF SCOTLAND, Peebles. Map 4, NT 0 1.
See **Tweeddale.**

CROY, Inverness. Map 25, NH 7 4.
To the north lies the little Flemington Loch. A short distance to the east, near the River Nairn, is *Kilravock Castle,* dating from 1460, in which Prince Charles Edward was entertained in 1746. **2 m. S.W.** of Croy is *Dalcross Castle,* built in 1621, and later modernized. See **Cawdor.** *Iter. 177, 198.*

CROY BRAE, Ayr. Map 8, NS 2 1.
See **Dunure.** *Iter. 49, 80.*

CRUACHAN, Argyll. Map 14, NN 0 2.
See **Falls of Cruachan.**

CRUDEN BAY, Aberdeen. 600. Map 27, NK 0 3.
E.C. Thurs. GOLF. A well-known resort, with fine sands, and noted for golf. The Bishop's Bridge, spanning the Cruden Water, dates from 1697. A little to the east is the ruined *Slains Castle,* built in 1664 to replace the old Castle near *Collieston (q.v.),* and visited in 1773 by Dr. Johnson. To the south of the castle, on a headland, is the fishing village of *Port Erroll,* overlooking the waters of Cruden Bay. Some **2 m.** N.E. of the resort are the well known *Bullers of*

1. Bishop's Bridge (1697).

Buchan, a great rock amphitheatre, 200 ft. deep and 50 ft. wide, particularly impressive in rough weather, and once described by Dr. Johnson. To the south-east of the Bullers is the Dun Buy, or Yellow Rock, associated with Scott's "The Antiquary." *Iter. 182, 187.*

CRUGGLETON, Wigtown. Map 2, NX 4 4.
Here is a little Norman Church, the chancel arch, doors and windows dating from the 12th cent. Near the shore are the remains of *Cruggleton Castle,* and farther to the north, beyond Sliddery Point, is Cruggleton, or Rigg Bay. *Iter. 82.*

CUAN FERRY, Argyll. Map 14, NM 7 1.
See **Clachan Bridge.**

CUILLIN, Isle of Skye, Inverness. Map 23, NG 4 2.
See **Coolins.**

CULBIN SANDS, Moray. Map 25, NH 9 6. and NJ 0 6.
These famous sands lie to the west of Findhorn Bay, facing the Moray Firth. They extend to over 3,600 acres and are 100 ft. high, being now to a large extent afforested with Scots and Corsican pine. In 1694, a disastrous sandstorm over-whelmed what was at that time an exceptionally fertile district, and even to this day the shifting sands from time to time expose some relic of the past. The Barony of Culbin had already previously been affected by sandstorms, and in the final storm the mansion of *Culbin,* a former home of the Kinnairds, was completely engulfed. *Iter. 199.*

CULLEN, Banff. 1,526. SB. Map 26, NJ 5 6.
E.C. Wed. GOLF. A resort and fishing town, formerly known as *Invercullen,* with a sandy beach and bathing, situated on Cullen Bay, between Scar Nose to the west, and Logie Head to the east. On the shore are three rocks known as the "Three Kings of Cullen." In the square is a Mercat

1. St. Mary's Church, 16th cent.
2. Cullen House, 16th cent.

Cross. Behind the town is the fine mansion of *Cullen House,* partly 16th cent., and shown Wed., Thurs. and 2nd Sun. in month, 2 to 6, from June to Sept. (see note page 90). The house enjoys fine views out to sea, and is situated where the Old Town formerly stood, before being demolished in 1822. Near the house is the cruciform *St. Mary's* Church, 16th cent., but much altered. It was founded by Bruce, and became Collegiate in 1543. In the Chancel are a Sacrament House, the prominent Ogilvie monument and the 17th cent. laird's pew of the Seafield family of Clan Grant, with its 17th cent. woodwork. The churchyard is noted for its numerous fine table tombs. Some **2 m. E.,** on the coast, is the picturesque, ruined *Findlater Castle.* **3 m. S.W.** is the *Bin of Cullen,* 1,050 ft., a good viewpoint. See **Deskford, Fordyce** and **Portknockie.** *Iter. 169, 184, 193, 198, 199.*

CULLICUDDEN, Ross and Cromarty. Map 25, NH 6 6.
About **2 m. W.,** on the shores of Cromarty Firth, are the remains of the 16th cent. *Castle Craig,* at one time a residence of the Bishops of Ross. *Iter. 203.*

CULLODEN, Inverness. Map 25, NH 7 4.
A great cairn (N.T. Scot.) marks the site of the famous battle, fought in 1746 on Culloden, or Drummossie Muir, where Prince Charles Edward lost for ever all hope of restoring the fortunes of the Stuarts, when his army of some 5,000 Highlanders was crushed by the Duke of Cumberland's forces. *Old Leanach* Farmhouse (N.T. Scot.) survived the battle which was fought around it. "Cumberland's Stone" was used by the general to survey the ground. Near the Graves of the Clans is the Well of the Dead. (All N.T. Scot.), *Culloden House,* late 18th cent., **2 m. N.W.,** stands on the site of the former mansion where the Prince spent some hours before the fight. **1 m. S.E.,** across the River Nairn, are the *Stones of Clava* (N.T. Scot.), cairns and standing stones from the Bronze Age, some of the most extensive in the country. *Iter. 177, 198, 212.*

CULNAKNOCK, Isle of Skye, Inverness. Map 22, NG 5 6.
On the east coast of the Trotternish peninsula, and a little to the south of which are the Lealt Falls, the river Lealt having issued from the wild and lonely range of hills in the back-ground which culminate farther south in The Storr (q.v.).

Crossraguel Abbey, Ayr. The old dovecote of the Abbey, which has 240 nesting boxes. The monks of Crossraguel formerly minted their own pennies and farthings

Cruggleton, Wigtown. The little Norman Church, which dates back to the 12th century

Cruden Bay, Aberdeen. The remains of Slains Castle (1664), which Dr. Johnson and Boswell visited in 1773

Culbin Sands, Moray. Afforestation on the wastes of the Culbin Sands. A great sandstorm took place here in 1694 and devastated the area

Cullen, Banff. Rocks on the foreshore known as the ' Three Kings of Cullen '

Culloden, Inverness. The ' Cumberland Stone,' from which the Duke of Cumberland watched the battle of 1746 which marked the end of the Jacobite Rising

[For CROSSRAGUEL ABBEY see also Plate 172
[For CULLODEN see also Plate 173
[For CRUDEN BAY see also under BULLERS OF BUCHAN (Plate 25)

PLATE 40 (facing page 130)

Culross, Fife. The Tolbooth, dating from 1626, with a tower added after some 57 years

Cupar, Fife. The Mercat Cross, brought back to the town from Wemysshall Hill in 1897. It is surmounted by a unicorn

Culter, Aberdeen. The statue of Rob Roy, the famous freebooter, which stands above the Leuchar Burn, at Peterculter, on A93

Culross, Fife. The old Palace, dated 1597 and 1611, once the home of Sir George Bruce of Carnock. In the vicinity is the 'snuffmaker's' house, of 1673, inscribed 'Who would have thocht it, noses would have bocht it'

Culross, Fife. The paved road known as the 'Crown o' the Causey', the raised crown of which was for the use of the 'upper classes' only

Culzean, Ayr. Robert Adam's late 18th century mansion (N.T. Scot.), built for the 10th Earl of Cassillis. The top flat has been given to General Eisenhower as his Scottish residence

[For CURRIE see following plate
[For CULROSS see also Plate 173

PLATE 41 (facing page 131)

Out to sea is the island of South Rona, with the larger island of Raasay to the south. *Iter. 254.*

CULROSS, Fife. 600. SB.   Map 16, NS 9 8.
This picturesque little Royal Burgh, associated with both St. Serf and St. Kentigern, stands in Torry Bay, on the estuary of the River Forth, and well justifies its reputation as the loveliest of the old Fife Burghs. It has the supreme benefit of being largely under the control of the Scottish National Trust, who have admirably preserved many of the old buildings, among which are some typical 16th and 17th cent. houses with crow-stepped gables and red pantiled roofs. The famous " Palace," dated 1597 and 1611, the work of George Bruce (Lord Carnock), and once visited by James VI, is notable for the panelled and painted rooms, and also the curious terraced and walled gardens (A.M.). It is open weekdays, 10 to 7 in summer, 10 to 4 in winter; Sundays, from 2. (See note page 90). The delightful Tolbooth, facing the estuary, dates from 1626, and the ' snuffmaker's ' house, dated 1673, carries the inscription, " Who would have thocht it, noses would have bocht it." In the village are an attractive 17th cent. house known as " The Study "; *Parleyhill House*; the Manse; and the Hospital, founded in 1637. The modern Mercat Cross, on the original steps, is approached by the ' Crown o' the Causey,' the raised crown of which was for the use of the " upper classes." The Abbey (A.M.), on the hillside to the north, was founded in 1217, and the 13th cent. Church preserves the choir and central tower, the latter built over the rood-screen and pulpitum, but the nave of the Church is ruined. There are interesting 17th cent. alabaster effigies to the Bruce family. The Abbey House, 17th and 19th cent., and latterly reduced in size, stands in close proximity to the Church, and was built partly from stones belonging to the former monastic buildings. The town was formerly noted for " girdles," and James VI visited its salt-pans. A little to the west of Culross is *Dunimarle Castle. Iter. 134.*

CULSALMOND, Aberdeen.   Map 27, NJ 6 3.
The full name of the village is *Kirkton of Culsalmond*. To the north-west, threaded by the main road from Aberdeen to Huntly, is Glen Foudland, above which rises the *Hill of Foudland*, 1,529 ft. A little to the south of Culsalmond is *Williamston House*, the fine gardens of which are sometimes shown in the summer (see note page 90). *Iter. 187*

CULTER, Aberdeen.   Map 21, NJ 8 0.
GOLF. A village on the River Dee, known more generally as *Peterculter*. The paperworks on the Leuchar Burn, which flows here into the Dee, date from 1751. Above the burn is a statue of Rob Roy. To the south-west of the village are the *Normandykes* earthworks. Near the modern *Maryculter* Church, across the Dee in Kincardine, is the Corbie Linn, a wild ravine. See **Blairs** and **Drumoak**. For Iter. see *Maryculter* and *Peterculter*.

CULTER, Lanark.   Map 9, NT 0 3.
An attractive village on the Culter Water, near its junction with the Clyde. *Culter House* is a white-harled building of the 17th cent., with a mile-long avenue of trees. Away to the west is *Tinto Hill*, 2,335 ft., and to the south-east is *Culter Fell*, 2,454 ft., over the summit of which goes the Lanark and Peebles county boundary. *Iter. 25.*

CULZEAN CASTLE, Ayr.   Map 8, NS 2 1.
This splendid pile (N.T. Scot.), situated in a commanding position facing Culzean Bay, and about a mile to the west of the Ayr to Girvan road, is one of Robert Adam's most notable creations, and dates mainly from 1777, though an earlier tower is incorporated in the structure. The Castle has long been a Kennedy stronghold, they having succeeded the Earls of Carrick, and becoming later Earls of Cassillis. Interesting Kennedy relics are preserved, and the top flat in the Castle has been presented to General Eisenhower as a Scottish residence. The splendid grounds and Castle are shown 10 to dusk, March to end of Nov. (See note page 90). Below the Castle are rock caves known as the Coves of Culzean. See **Dunure** and **Maybole**. *Iter. 80.*

CUMBERNAULD, Dunbarton. 3,000.   Map 16, NS 7 7.
GOLF. Lies in a detached portion of the county. A new

town is in process of development. To the south-east is Fannyside Muir and the small loch, once part of the extensive former Caledonian Forest. *Iter. 17, 50, 87, 97, 99.*

CUMBRAE ISLANDS, GREAT AND LITTLE, Bute.
See **Millport**.   Map 7, NS 1 5.

CUMINESTOWN, Aberdeen.   Map 27, NJ 8 5.
Iter. 189.

CUMMERTREES, Dumfries. 914.   Map 4, NY 1 6.
E.C. Tues. A Solway Firth village from which the notorious spring tides of the Firth can be observed. The Church is said to have been founded by Robert Bruce. The district is described in Scott's " Redgauntlet." Some 3 m. N. is *Kinmount*, replacing a Queensberry mansion burnt in the 18th cent., and said, until recently, to have contained no wood of any description. See **Powfoot** and **Ruthwell**. *Iter. 28, 47.*

CUMMINGSTOWN, Moray.   Map 26, NJ 1 6.
Iter. 199.

CUMNOCK, Ayr. 5,168. SB.   Map 8, NS 5 1.
E.C. Wed. M.D. Thurs. Stands on the Lugar Water, and is the centre of a mining district. There is a restored Mercat Cross. Snuffboxes were once manufactured here. 2 m. N.E. is *Lugar* (*q.v.*), where the great ironworks were built in 1845. Between Cumnock and Lugar, the river is spanned by a viaduct 150 ft. high, overlooking a deep gorge. 2 m. W. is *Dumfries*

House, an exceptionally fine and unspoilt Adam mansion, and within its grounds is the ruined *Terrenzean Castle*. See **New Cumnock**. *Iter. 21, 27, 67, 68.*

CUPAR, Fife. 5,663. SB.   Map 17, NO 3 1.
E.C. Thurs. M.D. Tues. GOLF. This Royal Burgh has a charter dating back to 1363. Outside the town, to the south, flows the Eden, coming from the Howe of Fife, and entering the sea in St. Andrew's Bay, to the north-east. The Parish Church tower dates from 1415, but the spire is two centuries later. A 17th cent. gravestone carved with two heads and a hand records the murder of martyrs of the period. The Mercat Cross is topped by a unicorn, which stood once on Wemysshall Hill; the hill is associated with a treaty of 1559 between the Queen Regent and the Lords of the Congregation, as a result of which French troops were to leave Fife. 2 m. S. is the fine *Scotstarvit Tower*, dating partly from 1627, and standing on the *Hill of Tarvit* estate (N.T. Scot.), in which the mansion, open Wed. and Sun., 2.30-6, from May to the end of Oct. (see page 90), was restored in 1906 by Sir Robert Lorimer. It contains art treasures and overlooks the Howe of Fife. 3 m. N.W., off the Newburgh road, an obelisk to the 4th Earl of Hopetoun stands on *Mount Hill*. Farther to the north-west stands the ruined 16th cent. *Collairnie Castle*. See **Ceres**, **Dairsie** and **Monimail**. *Iter. 93, 127, 131, 132, 136.*
(See page 132 for Town Plan of **CUPAR**.)

CURRIE, Midlothian. 1,101.   Map 9, NT 1 6.
GOLF. Through the village flows the Water of Leith, in its deep valley, and southwards is the long range of the *Pentland* hills. Both here and at *Balerno*, the neighbouring village to the south-west, paper-mills are an important industry. An ancient bridge crosses the river near the little 18th cent. Church, and about half-way to Balerno is the ruined *Lennox Tower*. The road leading south-westwards towards Carnwath traverses the lower slopes of the Pent-

CROWN COPYRIGHT RESERVED

PUBLISHED BY THE AUTOMOBILE ASSOCIATION

RB.60

1. Parish Church.   2. Mercat Cross.

lands, and is known as the "Lang Whang," once well known as a drove road. 2½ m. S. of Balerno, on the slopes of the Pentlands, is the old hunting seat of *Bavelaw Castle*, probably 17th cent. or earlier, with modern additions, and situated beyond the Threipmuir reservoir, beyond which rises the main ridge of the Pentlands, dominated by *Scald Law*, 1,898 ft. *Iter.* 21, 23.

DAILLY, Ayr. 472.   Map 2, NS 2 0 and NX 2 9.
E.C. Wed. The villages of *New* and *Old Dailly* stand some three miles apart in the wooded valley of the Water of Girvan. A little to the north of the former is the ruined *Dalquharran Castle*, and to the west stands the 16th cent. *Brunston Castle*. New Dailly Church is 18th cent. and contains the former lairds' lofts. To the south of Old Dailly, in the Penwhapple Glen, is *Penkill Castle*, one of the oldest inhabited houses in the county, dating back to the 16th and 17th cents., and associated with Dante Gabriel Rossetti. In the vicinity of Old Dailly, near the river, is the 17th cent. house of *Bargany*, with its very notable gardens. See **Straiton**. For *Iter.* see *New Dailly and Old Dailly*.

DAIRSIE, Fife. 492.   Map 17, NO 4 1.
E.C. Thurs. The village is situated three miles east of Cupar, on the main Cupar–St. Andrews road. A mile south, on the Pitscottie road, the River Eden is spanned by a bridge dating from 1522. On a height is the ruined *Dairsie Castle*. The little Church dates from 1621. Southwards from the bridge, the road traverses the charmingly wooded *Dura Glen*, where fossilized fishes have been discovered. To the north is the 16th cent. *Pitcullo Castle*. *Iter.* 93, 127, 131, 136.

DALAVICH, Argyll.   Map 14, NM 9 1.
See **Kilchrenan**.

DALBEATTIE, Kirkcudbright. 3,387. SB.   Map 3, NX 8 6.
E.C. Thurs. M.D. Sat. GOLF. This small town in the wooded valley of the Urr Water, flowing southwards into Rough Firth, is noted chiefly for its important granite quarries, which are situated at *Craignair*, a little to the west. 1½ m. N.W. is the tower of *Buittle Place*, where formerly a castle stood. 2½ m. N.W., off a road to New Galloway, is the *Mote of Urr*, an impressive Saxon, or early Norman fortification. See **Auchencairn** and **Palnackie**. *Iter.* 72, 73, 76.

DALHALVAIG, Sutherland.   Map 30, NC 8 5.
A Strath Halladale hamlet, in the vicinity of which are remains of brochs and also several hut circles. *Iter.* 234.

DALHOUSIE CASTLE, Midlothian
                                    Map 10, NT 3 6.
See **Cockpen**.

DALIBURGH CHURCH, South Uist, Inverness.
                                    Map 32, NF 7 2.
See **Hebrides, Outer** (South Uist). *Iter.* 262.

DALILEA, Inverness.   Map 12, NM 7 6.
A stopping-place for the little *Loch Shiel* (*q.v.*) steamer, and a resort of anglers, in the historic *Moidart* (*q.v.*) district, reached by way of *Acharacle* (*q.v.*), to the south-west. *Dalilea* has two associations of note. Alexander Macdonald, the earliest, and perhaps the best-known of Gaelic Jacobite bards, once lived here, and in 1745, Prince Charles Edward and his Clanranald followers sailed up the loch from here in three boats to Glenaladale, a lonely, road-less glen, leading northwards into the hills farther up the loch, where they received hospitality. Across the loch, to the south-east, is *Ben Resipol*, 2,774 ft., a notable landmark and viewpoint in the district of Sunart. See **Arisaig**. *Iter.* 217.

DALKEITH, Midlothian, 9,150. SB.
                                    Map 10, NT 3 6.
E.C. Tues. GOLF. This market town is situated on high ground between the North and South Esk rivers, which unite beyond the park of *Dalkeith Palace*, to the north-east. The original stronghold dates from the 12th cent., but the present Palace was built c. 1700 by Vanbrugh for Anne, Duchess of Buccleuch, who married the unfortunate Duke of Monmouth, executed in London in 1685, and is associated with Scott's "Lay of the Last Minstrel." Among the famous visitors to the Palace have been James IV, James VI and Prince Charles Edward. *St. Nicholas'* Church, restored in 1852, contains, in the roofless eastern apse, the tomb of Monmouth's widow, who lived for some years at

CROWN COPYRIGHT RESERVED

DRAWN AND PUBLISHED BY THE AUTOMOBILE ASSOCIATION

1. St. Nicholas' Church.   2. Dalkeith Palace.
3. Newbattle Abbey.

Newark Castle near *Broadmeadows* (*q.v.*) in the Vale of Yarrow. See **Cockpen, Dundee, Hawick, Lasswade** and **Newbattle**. *Iter.* 4, 5, 13, 37.

DALLAS, Moray.   Map 26, NJ 1 5.
Dallas Lodge, built in 1680 and circular in style, has fine gardens.

Currie, Midlothian. The road to Carnwath, across the Pentland foothills, which follows the line of an old drove road, known as the 'Lang Whang'

Dailly, Ayr. The 16th to 17th century Penkill Castle, associated with Dante Gabriel Rossetti, who composed poetry here in 1869. It is situated near Old Dailly

Dailly, Ayr. A roadside stone, a mile to the east of New Dailly, recording the death at this spot of a local road man

Dailly, Ayr. The shell of the 17th century Dalquharran Castle, which stands near New Dailly. In the vicinity stands the newer castle of 1790, designed by Robert Adam

Dairsie, Fife. The old bridge over the River Eden, a mile south of the village, dates from 1522

Dalkeith, Midlothian. St. Nicholas' Church, with its roofless eastern apse, in which is the grave of Anne, Duchess of Buccleuch, who had married the Duke of Monmouth, beheaded in 1685

PLATE 42 (facing page 132)

Dalmally, Argyll. The Monument to the bard, Duncan Ban MacIntyre, some 2 miles south-west, on the old unclassified road to Inverarary. He has been described as the 'Burns of the Highlands'

Dalmeny, West Lothian. One of the finest Norman churches in Scotland. The tower is modern, its predecessor having collapsed in the 15th century

Dalnacardoch, Perth. The 8-foot high Wade Stone, dated 1729, situated off A9, some 2 miles north-west. General Wade is said to have placed a coin on the top and found it still in position a year later

Dalnashaugh Inn, Banff. The entrance lodge and gate of the 16th century and later Ballindalloch Castle, which carries the arms of the Macpherson-Grants

Dalry, Kirkcudbright. The ancient St. John's Stone, recalling the dedication name of John the Baptist, given originally to the Church by the Knights Templars

Daltulich Bridge, Moray; Nairn. Randolph's Leap, named after Randolph, first Earl of Moray, whose opponent jumped the river during a combat. It is situated on the River Findhorn, off B9007, some 7 miles south of Forres

[For DALNACARDOCH see also under ATHOLL (Plate 10) and WADE ROADS (Plate 167)
For DALWHINNIE see under GRAMPIANS (Plate 78)

PLATE 43 (facing page 133)

DALMALLY, Argyll. 1,000.   Map 14, NN 1 2.
E.C. Wed. The River Orchy flows here through Strath
Orchy into *Loch Awe* (*q.v.*), to the west, the road to the loch-
side and Taynuilt now utilizing a new bridge over an inner
reach of the loch, and passing near *Kilchurn Castle* (*q.v.*),
with views of *Ben Cruachan*, 3,689 ft. Nearly **2 m.** S.W.
of Dalmally, off the old road to Inveraray, and on high
ground, forming a good viewpoint, stands a monument to
the famous bard, Duncan Ban MacIntyre. (See **Inveroran**).
Beyond Glen Strae, to the north, rises *Ben Eunaich*, 3,242 ft.
6 m. E. of Dalmally, overlooking Glen Orchy and Glen
Lochy, rises *Ben Lui*, 3,708 ft., one of Argyll's highest
mountains. Eastwards from Dalmally, a rather rough and
narrow road leaves the *Tyndrum* (*q.v.*) road and traverses
Glen Orchy, surrounded by lofty hills. *Iter. 110, 120,
125, 144, 145.*

DALMELLINGTON, Ayr. 4,702.   Map 8, NS 4 0.
E.C. Wed. A small iron-working town at a height of 800 ft.,
to the west of which is Bogton Loch, with the waterfall of
Dalcairnie Linn, and threaded by the River Doon, which
has its source in the long and narrow *Loch Doon* (*q.v.*), to
the south. This loch lies in the shadow of the *Rhinns of
Kells*, dominated by *Corserine*, 2,668 ft., and *Carlins Cairn*,
2,650 ft. At its northern end is the picturesque Ness Glen.
Benbeoch, 1,521 ft., a hill to the north of Dalmellington, is a
good viewpoint. See **Barr, Loch Trool** and **Straiton**.
Iter. 49, 74, 75, 76, 77.

DALMENY, West Lothian. 274.   Map 10, NT 1 7.
The little 12th cent. Parish Church is perhaps the finest
example of the Norman style in the whole of Scotland. Of
special interest are the richly carved south doorway. and
also the chancel and semi-circular vaulted apse, with their
fine arches. Some of the carvings represent curious
mythological wild beasts. The Church has been restored,
and the tower is of recent date. East of the village is the park
of *Dalmeny House*, modern, with the restored *Barnbougle
Castle*, looking towards the Drum Sands on the Firth of
Forth. The Royal Elizabeth naval victualling yard dates from
1948. See **Queensferry, South.** *Iter. 96.*

DALNACARDOCH, Perth.   Map 19, NN 7 7.
Here, the Wade road, now a rough track, dating from 1730,
and striding across the hills from *Trinafour* (*q.v.*), joins the
present main highway through Glen Garry leading to Inverness, itself also largely one of Wade's roads. General Wade
had a hut at Dalnacardoch, which later became an inn, and
here Prince Charles Edward spent a night in 1745. Beyond
the junction, about **2 m.** N.W., in a lonely setting of hills, is
the *Wade Stone*, an 8-foot high pillar, carrying the date 1729,
marking the completion of that particular sector of the road.
Wade, a man of great stature, is said to have placed a coin
on the pillar, and to have found it still there when re-visiting
the site in a year's time. To the north is the vast hill and
moorland area known as the Forest of Atholl. See **Tromie
Bridge** and, **Wade Roads.** *Iter. 138, 140, 143, 147, 149, 150.*

DALNASHAUGH INN, Banff.   Map 26, NJ 1 3·
To the north, on the Grantown-on-Spey road, the fine old
Bridge of Avon, in a picturesque, wooded setting, spans the
river which flows northwards to join the Spey beyond the
lovely grounds of *Ballindalloch Castle*. This 16th cent.
tower is linked to a modern building, and approached from
the Craigellachie road. Beyond the junction of the two
rivers rises the *Hill of Delnapot*, 1,001 ft., in Moray. Southwards from Dalnashaugh Inn, a road follows the Avon to
its junction with the Livet Water near *Downan* (*q.v.*), in
the vicinity of the famous *Glenlivet* (*q.v.*) distillery. *Iter. 170,
192, 195.*

DALNASPIDAL, Perth.   Map 19, NN 6 7.
At this lonely spot in the *Grampian* (*q.v.*) moorlands, the
main road and railway from Perth to Inverness leave Glen
Garry to traverse the bleak and lofty Pass of *Drumochter*
(*q.v.*), the road reaching a height of 1,507 ft. A little to
the south is Loch Garry, which is now joined by a tunnel
to Loch Ericht, a larger loch to the west, in connection with a
big hydro-electric scheme. *Ben Alder*, 3,757 ft., dominates
Loch Ericht from the west, while on the eastern shores

rises *Beinn Udlaman*, 3,306 ft. To the north-west of Dalnaspidal are two prominent hills known as the *Sow of Atholl*
and the *Boar of Badenoch*, and away to the east are the
desolate 3,000-ft. high hills of the Forest of Atholl, stretching
northwards to the great Gaick Forest. See **Dalnacardoch**
and **Dalwhinnie.** *Iter. 138, 140, 143, 147, 149, 150.*

DALNESS FOREST, Argyll.   Map 18, NN 1 5.
See **Glencoe** and **Kingshouse.**

DALRY, Ayr. 4,024.   Map 8, NS 2 4.
E.C. Wed. An iron-working town in the Ayrshire
coal-field, standing on the River Garnock.   1½ m.
S.E. is *Blair House*, a fine mansion, retaining two 17th
cent. doorways and incorporating a 14th cent. keep. Through
the park flows the Dusk Water, and in the glen is a stalactite
cave. *Iter. 63, 85.*

DALRY, Kirkcudbright. 775.   Map 3, NX 6 8.
E.C. Thurs. Properly named *St. John's Town of Dalry*,
this little *Galloway* (*q.v.*) village, in the Glenkens district
of the county, is well situated for touring the Galloway
Highlands. *St. John's Stone* is the name given to an ancient
block in the village street. There are distant views of
the lofty *Rhinns of Kells* to the north-west, dominated by
Corserine, 2,668 ft., and *Carlins Cairn*, 2,650 ft. James IV
rested here in 1507, and returned in the following year.
The Water of Ken circles the Churchyard, in which a Covenanter's Stone is to be seen. Across the river valley, to the
west, is the Glenlee power station of the Galloway Power
Scheme, supplied from the *Clatteringshaws* (*q.v.*) loch.
4½ m. N.E. is *Lochinvar*, with slight remains of an island
castle, the home of the "Young Lochinvar" of the famous
ballad.   **2 m.** N.N.E., on the road to Carsphairn, which
proceeds along the west bank of the Water of Ken, is Earlston
Linn, where the Ken is joined by the Polharrow Burn.
To the east stands *Earlston Tower*, dating from 1655, now
replaced by the later *Earlston Lodge* in the near vicinity.
Iter. 75, 76.

DALRYMPLE, Ayr.   Map 8, NS 3 1.
Iter. 68.

DALTULICH BRIDGE, Moray; Nairn.   Map 25, NH 9 4.
See **Ferness** and **Logie.**

DALVEEN PASS, Dumfries; Lanark.
                            Map 4, NS 8 0 and 9 0.
See **Carronbridge** and **Elvanfoot.** *Iter. 25, 26.*

DALVOURN, Inverness.   Map 25, NH 6 3.
Lies in Strath Nairn, with *Culloden* (*q.v.*), or Drummossie
Muir rising to the north-east, and crossed by a road leading
northwards towards Inverness.   **3 m.** S.W. of Dalvourn,
off a by-road, is *Dunlichity* Church, built in 1758 to replace
an earlier structure, of which some walls remain. On two
stones there are cuts remaining, said to have been made by
clansman sharpening their weapons before Culloden fight,
in 1746. A watchtower, near the entrance to the Church,
was used as a means of preventing the theft of corpses by
body-snatchers in the 19th cent. *Iter. 212.*

DALWHINNIE, Inverness. 180.   Map 19, NN 6 8.
E.C. Wed. Situated on the River Truim, on the great
trunk road linking Perth with Inverness, and convenient
for winter sports in the *Grampian* (*q.v.*) hills of the Drumochter Forest area, lying away to the south-east. Westwards, on the fringe of *Badenoch* (*q.v.*), stretches the lonely
Loch Ericht, 15 miles in length, the waters of which are
used in connection with a big hydro-electric scheme. At
the far western extremity rises the remote peak of *Ben
Alder*, 3,757 ft., and facing it across the loch is *Beinn Udlaman*, 3,306 ft. Wade's road to Inverness and his road to
Fort Augustus over the *Corrieyairack Pass* (*q.v.*) fork just
north of the village, which stands at a height of 1,200 ft.,
and here Sir John Hope failed to intercept Prince Charles
Edward in 1745. A year later the Prince was a fugitive in
this same district, one of his hiding-places being the so-
called "Cluny's Cage," below the southern slopes of Ben
Alder, and described by R. L. Stevenson in "Kidnapped."
To the north of the village, the Inverness road descends
gradually through Glen Truim, past the Falls of Truim.

into less desolate country. Away to the east stretches the extensive and wild Gaick Forest. See **Drumgask, Drumochter Pass** and **Wade Roads.** *Iter. 138, 140, 143, 147, 149, 150.*

DAMNAGLAUR, Wigtown.   Map 2, NX 1 3.
Iter. 82.

DARNAWAY CASTLE, Moray.   Map 25, NH 9 5.
See **Forres.**

DARNICK, Roxburgh.   Map 10, NT 5 3.
The fine old *Darnick Tower,* commenced in 1569, on the site of an earlier structure, retains its iron entrance yett, and was much coveted by Sir Walter Scott. It stands in a picturesque setting near the River Tweed, a little to the west of *Melrose* (*q.v.*). Between the tower and the river is *Skirmish Hill,* where a Border battle took place in 1526, described in Scott's "The Monastery." To the south-east rise the triple-peaked *Eildon* hills, and southwards lies the attractively wooded "Rhymer's Glen," with Cauldshiels Loch to the west. In the glen is *Chiefswood,* once the home of J. G. Lockhart, the biographer of Scott. Some **2 m.** N.W. of Darnick, off the Galashiels road, is the entrance to the lonely valley of the Allan Water, in which are situated in close proximity, among the hills to the north, the three Border peel towers of *Glendearg Colmslie* and *Langshaw,* the first-named associated with Scott's "The Monastery." See **Earlston.** *Iter. 13, 43.*

DARVEL, Ayr. 3,309. SB.   Map 8, NS 5 3.
E.C. Wed. A lace-making town, and the birthplace in 1881 of Sir Alexander Fleming, the discoverer of penicillin. The prehistoric *Dragon Stone* stands in Burn Road. *Iter. 20, 69.*

DAVA, Moray.   Map 26, NJ 0 3.
The lofty Dava Moor lies between the valleys of the Spey and the Findhorn, giving wide views in the direction of the Moray Firth to the north, and southwards towards the distant *Cairngorm* (*q.v.*) range. A little to the north is the hill known as the *Knock of Braemoray,* 1,493 ft., and to the east is a lonely area of hill and moor culminating in *Cairn Kitty,* 1,711 ft. See **Dulsie Bridge** and **Lochindorb.** *Iter. 172, 176, 177.*

DAVIOT, Inverness.   Map 25, NH 7 3.
The village is situated in a dip of Strath Nairn, which lies between the high ground of the Glen of Moy to the south-east and Drummossie Moor to the north-west. The Church, with its unusual steeple, is a landmark. Wade's old military road follows a course parallel to the main Daviot to Inverness road, but keeps about a mile to the west, along the west side of the wooded *Dunmore Hill.* To the north-east of Daviot, there are roads on both sides of the River Nairn leading towards *Cawdor* (*q.v.*), that on the north bank going by way of *Culloden* (*q.v.*). *Iter. 140, 150, 195, 212.*

DAWYCK WOODS, Peebles.   Map 9, NT 1 3.
See **Stobo.**

DECHMONT, West Lothian.   Map 9, NT 0 7.
Iter. 16.

DEERNESS, Orkney.   Map 33, HY 5 0.
See **Orkney Islands** (Mainland). *Iter. 265.*

DEESIDE, Aberdeen; Kincardine.
          Map 20, NO 1 9 etc. and 21, NO 6 9 etc.
The long and picturesque wooded valley of the River Dee, famous for its salmon, extends westwards from Aberdeen across the Mar division of the county, with a brief intrusion into Kincardineshire in the vicinity of the pleasant resort of *Banchory* (*q.v.*) and *Crathes Castle* (*q.v.*). From here its finest and most typical reaches may be said to commence. The valley, to which has been given the proud title of "Royal Deeside," now becomes increasingly lovely, with rich woodlands near the river banks. Nearing *Aboyne* (*q.v.*), views are opened up of lofty hills to the south-west in the extensive Forest of Birse, dominated by the *Hill of Cat,* 2,433 ft., and *Mount Battock,* 2,555 ft. The most famous stretch of Deeside is that lying between the well-known Highland resorts of *Ballater* (*q.v.*) and *Braemar* (*q.v.*). Here

are situated the Royal Castle of *Balmoral* (*q.v.*) and the little Church of *Crathie* (*q.v.*), where the Royal Family worship when in residence at the Castle. Queen Victoria did much to introduce this district to the public, and in the course of her numerous visits with the Prince Consort made many excursions into the surrounding mountains, including the ascent by pony of the great peak of *Lochnagar* (*q.v.*). This famous peak dominates the country across the Royal Forest of Ballochbuie from its position at the northern extremity of the extensive, elevated plateau of the *White Mounth* (*q.v.*). Many of the heather-clad moors on Deeside are shot over for grouse during the season. Along the whole stretch of the Dee between Aboyne and Balmoral there are good motoring roads on both sides of the river, from each of which there are attractive views to be obtained of this beautiful part of the Scottish Highlands, much of which is given over to deer.

Braemar, a summer and winter resort, famed for its annual September Gathering, presents Deeside in its most characteristic vein, the surrounding hill country being rich in forest and heather. Fine views may be obtained from many points towards the lofty ridges of the great *Cairngorm* (*q.v.*) range, which rises away to the north-west, and includes a larger area of ground over the 4,000-ft. level than any other part of Scotland, the highest point reached being *Ben Macdhui,* which attains 4,296 ft. The Dee becomes much wilder and swift-flowing to the west of Braemar, and beyond *Inverey* (*q.v.*) is the well-known Linn of Dee, a rocky cleft, in which Byron once nearly lost his life. Beyond the *Devil's Point,* 3,303 ft. and *Cairn Toul,* 4,241 ft., far up Glen Dee, in the fastnesses of the Cairngorms, are the Pools of Dee, situated in the wild and lonely pass of the *Lairig Ghru* (*q.v.*). The actual source of the Dee, known as the Wells of Dee, is located high up near the summit of the 4,248-ft. high peak of *Braeriach.* Deeside is linked to the upper valley of the Don, to the north, in the vicinity of *Cock Bridge* (*q.v.*), by narrow roads leading into the hills from points near Braemar and Ballater respectively. These roads converge at *Gairnshiel Lodge* (*q.v.*), and continue over the narrow and steep Glas Choille section, which is liable to be snowbound in winter. *Iter. 141, 152, 160, 167, 168, 174, 179.*

DELGATIE CASTLE, Aberdeen.   Map 27, NJ 7 4.
See **Turriff.**

DENHOLM, Roxburgh. 365.   Map 10, NT 5 1.
On the River Teviot, with a pleasant green. This village was the birthplace of John Leyden, the 18th cent. poet and friend of Scott, and also of Sir James Murray, associated with the Oxford English Dictionary. An obelisk was set up in Leyden's memory in 1861, and a tablet on a thatched cottage records his birth in 1776. *Westgate Hall* is 17th cent. **2 m.** N.E., beyond the river, on the summit of the steep *Minto Crags,* is the ruined *Fatlips Castle,* dating from the 16th cent. Westwards lies *Minto House,* now a hospital. To the south of Denholm rises "dark" *Ruberslaw,* 1,392 ft., of old a Covenanters' retreat, and to the east flows the Rule Water. Alexander Peden preached formerly from a rock known as "Peden's Pulpit" near the summit of Ruberslaw. See **Sorn.** *Iter. 30, 36.*

DENNY, Stirling. 7,390. SB.   Map 16, NS 8 8.
E.C. Wed. A small paper manufacturing town, together with *Dunipace,* to the north, on the River Carron, and situated to the east of the *Kilsyth* hills. A narrow and hilly moorland road leads westwards from Denny to follow the Carron and later the Endrick Water between the *Campsie Falls* and *Fintry* hills towards *Fintry* (*q.v.*). See **St. Ninian's.** *Iter. 50, 87, 99, 114, 144.*

DENNYLOANHEAD, Stirling. 3,136.   Map 16, NS 8 8.
A small mining town. *Iter. 17, 50, 87, 97, 98, 99, 113, 115.*

DERE STREET (Roman Road), Roxburgh
          Map 5, NT 7 0 etc.
See **Carter Bar** and **Oxnam.**

DERVAIG, Isle of Mull, Argyll.   Map 12, NM 4 5.
At the head of the narrow Loch Cuan, in Glen Bellart, in a picturesque setting. To the south-east, the inland road

Darnick, Roxburgh. Darnick
Tower, which Sir Walter Scott
greatly desired to purchase. It
was erected in 1425, and after
being burnt by the English under
Hertford, was re-built in 1569 by
Andrew Heiton

Daviot, Inverness. The Church, as seen from A9. From points
in the vicinity there are distant views of Ben Wyvis, in Easter Ross

Deeside, Aberdeen. The Bridge
of Feugh, dated 1799, though
probably of earlier date. It spans
the river near its junction with
the Dee, on the outskirts of the
resort of Banchory

Darvel, Ayr. The prehistoric
Dragon Stone, in Burn Road,
around which New Year's Day
processions were once held

Denholm, Roxburgh. The
'Text House,' embellished
with exhortations, erected by
a local eccentric, Dr. Haddon

PLATE 44 (facing page 134)

Devil's Elbow, Perth. The double bends known as the 'Devil's Elbow,' at a height of 1,950 feet, on the Blairgowrie to Braemar road (A93), in the Grampian mountains

Deskford, Banff. The richly-carved Sacrament House in the ruined Church, donated by Alexander Ogilvy of Deskford, in 1551. There are inscriptions in English and Latin

Dingwall, Ross and Cromarty. The shaft of the old Mercat Cross, neighboured by the iron 'yett,' or gate from the former town gaol

Devil's Beef Tub, Dumfries. A view of the deep Annandale hollow off the Moffat to Edinburgh road (A70). It was used by Annandale raiders to secrete stolen cattle. See Crook Inn (Plate 39)

Dirleton, East Lothian. The 13th century de Vaux Castle, captured by the Bishop of Durham for Edward I. Later it resisted Cromwell's troops, before falling to General Monk, who dismantled it in 1650. In the foreground is an old dovecote

Dollar, Clackmannan. The portico of Dollar Academy, erected in 1818, the work of W. H. Playfair

PLATE 45 (facing page 135) [For DEVIL'S BEEF TUB see also Plate 173

to *Salen* (*q.v.*) goes within a short distance of Loch Frisa on the way to Glen Aros. The road leading eastwards towards *Tobermory* (*q.v.*) is narrow, with hairpin bends, in the vicinity of the Mishnish Lochs. See **Calgary**. *Iter. 248, 250.*

DESKFORD, Banff. 541.   Map 26, **NJ 5** 6.
Kirktown of Deskford is the full name of this village, which lies on the Burn of Deskford. The Church (A.M.) not now in use, is noted for its Sacrament House, dating from 1551, with an inscription in English as well as in the usual Latin, and is one of the best examples of this Church fitting, which is peculiar to certain parts of Scotland. Away to the north-west of the village rises the *Bin of Cullen*, 1,050 ft. See **Fordyce**. *Iter. 169.*

DEVIL'S BEEF TUB, Dumfries.   Map 9, **NT 0** 1.
See **Moffat**. *Iter. 10, 24.*

DEVIL'S ELBOW, Perth.   Map 20, **NO 1** 7.
See **Glenshee**. *Iter. 141, 152, 160, 167, 168.*

DINGWALL, Ross and Cromarty. 3,576. SB.
   Map 25, **NH 5** 5.
E.C. Thurs. M.D. Wed. A busy little Easter Ross town, with a long main street, created a Royal Burgh in 1226, and situated on Cromarty Firth. Slight remains of the former castle are preserved near the present mansion. The harbour was constructed by Telford. The Tolbooth dates from 1730 and shows the Town Arms, a starfish. The shaft of the former Cross stands near the iron yett of the old town gaol. Near the church is a statue (1714) to the 1st Earl of Cromarty.

1. Tolbooth, with cross-shaft and iron yett from gaol. 2. Cromarty statue.

On a hill south of the town is a tower commemorating the birth of General Sir Hector Macdonald. *Tulloch Castle*, to the north of the town, has been since 1760 a seat of the Davidsons. Far away to the north-west is *Ben Wyvis*, 3,426 ft., a landmark for many miles around. See **Conon Bridge**, **Evanton** and **Strathpeffer**. *Iter. 200, 201, 202, 203, 206, 213.*

DINNET, Aberdeen. 93.   Map 21, **NO 4** 9.
The road leading northwards towards Huntly crosses Dinnet Moor, on which prehistoric remains are to be found. To the south, beyond Dinnet Bridge across the Dee, lie Glen Tanner and the wilds of Glen Tanner Forest. See **Aboyne**, **Bridge of Ess** and **Cambus o'May**. *Iter. 152, 168, 174, 191.*

DIPPIN, Isle of Arran, Bute.   Map 7, **NS 0** 2.
Iter. 242.

DIRK HATTERAICK'S CAVE, Kirkcudbright.
See **Creetown**.   Map 2, **NX 5** 5.

DIRLETON, East Lothian. 400.   Map 10, **NT 5** 8.
The attractive village of *Dirleton* lies almost exactly half-way between the famous golfing resorts of *Gullane* (*q.v.*) and *North Berwick* (*q.v.*), and has a Church dating from the early 17th cent., the interior having been modernized. The massive remains of *Dirleton Castle* (A.M.), situated on its rock, date largely from the 13th cent., the structure having been partly dismantled by General Monk in 1650. There is a three-storey Renaissance portion still standing. By the garden is a bowling green of the 17th cent. In 1298, the stronghold was invested by Edward I, and was a home of the de Vaux family. To the west is

Archerfield House, which took the place of the Castle as a residence, and a 16th cent. circular dovecote has survived nearby. The surroundings of the house are associated with R. L. Stevenson's "Pavilion on the Links." To the north, beyond the expanse of the North links, is the tiny island of *Fidra*, with a lighthouse. *Iter. 2, 36, 37.*

DOLLAR, Clackmannan. 1,612. SB.   Map 16, **NS 9** 9.
E.C. Thurs. GOLF. This residential town near the River Devon stands at the foot of the *Ochil* hills, and is noted for its Academy, the buildings of which date from 1818. About a mile to the north, between the Burn of Sorrow and the Burn of Care, the former flowing through the narrow and steep Windy Pass, stands the ruined *Castle Campbell*, in the wooded Dollar Glen (A.M. and N.T. Scot.). Its setting is one of the most romantic in Scotland, being protected by deep ravines, with a view extending southwards over the windings of the Devon towards the Firth of Forth and the distant *Pentland* hills. The structure, which was once known as *Castle Gloume*, or *Gloom*, has a fine 14th cent. square tower joined to a 16th cent. wing, and is open weekdays, 10 to 4 or 7; Sun., 2 to 4 or 7 (see note page 90). In 1645 it was sacked by Montrose, and was at one time associated with John Knox and also Mary, Queen of Scots. To the north-west of the Castle, in the Ochils, is *King's Seat*, 2,111 ft., behind which rises *Ben Cleuch*, 2,363 ft., the highest point in the range, forming a splendid viewpoint. **2 m. N.E.** of Dollar, off the Milnathort road, is *Cowden House*, noted for its Japanese garden. *Iter. 136.*

DOLPHINTON, Lanark; Peebles. 184.   Map 9, **NT 1** 4.
Outside the door of the small and ancient church is the grave of a Covenanter. On *Kippit Hill*, to the north-east, a sandstone cist, perhaps 2,000 years old, was uncovered in 1920.

DONIBRISTLE (near Cowdenbeath), Fife.
   Map 17, **NT 1** 8.
Iter. 97, 133.

DONIBRISTLE (near Inverkeithing), Fife.
   Map 17, **NT 1** 8.
See **Aberdour**.

DOONFOOT, Ayr.   Map 8, **NS 3** 1.
Iter. 49, 80.

DORES, Inverness.   Map 25, **NH 5** 3.
A *Loch Ness* (*q.v.*) village, at the south-western extremity of Strath Dores. A little to the east is Loch Ashie, and beyond it, to the south, is the larger Loch Duntelchaig, both at a height of over 700 ft. **2 m. N.**, where Loch Ness begins to narrow, is the 18th cent. *Aldourie Castle*. To the south of Dores there is a choice of routes to Fort Augustus, the more westerly road following the shores of Loch Ness, and the easterly road climbing steeply on to moorland by way of *Errogie* (*q.v.*). *Iter. 211.*

DORNIE, Ross and Cromarty.   Map 24, **NG 8** 2.
E.C. Wed. Here, in a beautiful North-West Highland setting of mountain and loch, where *Loch Duich* (*q.v.*) meets Loch Long, is a road bridge, spanning the last-named loch, and replacing the former ferry which linked the small crofting village with *Ardelve* (*q.v.*), on *Loch Alsh* (*q.v.*). A little to the north-east of Dornie, on Loch Long, is the clachan of *Bundalloch*, where byres of several old crofters' cottages, once known as "black houses," are still to be found. Facing Loch Duich, with a view towards Totaig, on the opposite side of the loch, is the picturesque *Eilean Donan Castle*, an ancient structure, once surrounded by water, but now completely restored and linked to the mainland by a causeway. The Castle incorporates a War Memorial to the Clan Macrae, and is open to view on weekdays, 10 to 12.30 and 2 to 6. Closed in Oct. (See note page 90). In 1719, during an abortive Jacobite rising, a British frigate bombarded the structure. **2 m. S.E.** of Dornie, on the road to *Shiel Bridge* (*q.v.*), the road climbs above Loch Duich to a height of more than 500 ft. at Carr Brae, or Keppoch, a splendid viewpoint, looking towards the *Five Sisters of Kintail*, dominated by *Scour Ouran*, 3,505 ft., which form part of the *Kintail* (*q.v.*) estate. See **Inverinate**. *Iter. 207, 220.*

DORNOCH, Sutherland. 856. SB.　　　　Map 31, **NH 7 8.**
E.C. Thurs. GOLF. A small golfing resort and Royal
Burgh, with a good bathing beach and sands, looking

1. Cathedral.　　　　2. Bishop's Castle.
3. Witch's Stone.

over the Dornoch
Firth, into which
a narrow spit of
land projects ter-
minating at Dor-
noch Point. Only
the lofty tower is
still standing
from the Bishop's
Castle, destroyed
in 1570. The
Cathedral dates
from 1224, the
choir having been
probably com-
pleted c. 1539.
After severe
damage in 1570,
and later much
neglect, consider-
able restorations
took place, first
in 1835 to 1837, and latterly in 1924. No fewer than 16
Earls of Sutherland are said to be buried in the Cathedral,
and there is a statue by Chantrey of the first Duke.
Dornoch was the scene, in 1722, of the last judicial execution
for witchcraft to take place in Scotland, the Witch's Stone
on the golf course recalling the event. **2 m. N.** is the late
18th cent. mansion of *Embo House. Iter. 231.*

DORNOCK, Dumfries.　　　　Map 4, **NY 2 6.**
In the vicinity are remains of a stone circle and also two
ancient towers. *Iter. 26, 27, 28, 42, 67.*

DOUGLAS, Lanark. 2,263.　　　　Map 9, **NS 8 3.**
GOLF. This little town, in the valley of the Douglas Water,
lies in a coal-mining district, and colliery operations were
responsible for the demolition of *Douglas Castle,* which
had been rebuilt by Adam in 1759. Only the Chapel and
porch remain, and nearby is a fragment of Scott's " Castle
Dangerous." The restored chancel of *St. Bride's* Church
(A.M.) stands in the churchyard and contains the tomb of
the Earl of Angus, known as " Bell-the-Cat," who died in
1514. There is also a notable range of Douglas tombs,
and some 13th and 15th cent. French stained glass. Near
the building stands a tower, built in 1618, in which is a clock
dated 1565, said to be the gift of Mary, Queen of Scots.
Facing the tower is a monument to commemorate the raising
of the Cameronian Regiment in 1689. The " *Sun* " and
" *Cross Keys* " are old inns, the former dating from 1621.
A house in Main Street has an inscribed panel of 1695
recalling an atrocity perpetrated on James Gavin, a Covenanter. See **Lauder.** *Iter. 21, 35.*

DOUGLAS HALL, Kirkcudbright.　　　　Map 3, **NX 8 5.**
A small resort on Sandyhills Bay, overlooking the waters of
the Solway Firth, with *Criffell,* 1,866 ft., rising away to the
north-east. In the vicinity are two natural rock archways on
a delightful stretch of coast, with Sandyhills Bay facing
Craigneuk Point and the Mersehead Sands to the east.
See **Rockcliffe.** *Iter. 73.*

DOUNBY, Orkney.　　　　Map 33, **HY 2 2.**
See **Orkney Islands** (Mainland). *Iter. 264.*

DOUNE, Perth. 866. SB.　　　　Map 16, **NN 7 0.**
E.C. Wed. The River Teith is crossed here by a picturesque
bridge, built originally in 1535. The builder was James Spittal,
the wealthy tailor to James IV, who, when arriving at the
former ferry without any money, was refused a passage by the
ferryman, and built the bridge out of spite in order to deprive
the ferryman of a living. In the small town, once noted for
the manufacture of pistols, stands a fine Mercat Cross.
Doune Castle, situated between the Teith and the smaller
Ardoch, and open daily, 9 to 6 or dusk (see note page 90), is a
splendid, though mixed example of its period, and overlooks the swift-flowing rivers. The building dates from the

early 15th cent., the work of the Regent Albany. Subsequent to his execution in 1424 it passed to the Crown.
The castle has two fine towers, between which is the hall,
and has been well restored. In 1745, the castle was held for
Prince Charles Edward, and the hero of Scott's " Waverley "
was confined within, while at one period, Home, the author
of " Douglas," escaped from the castle, using a rope of
bedclothes. See **Callander** and **Dunblane.** *Iter. 141, 142,
144, 146.*

DOUNREAY, Caithness.　　　　Map 30, **NC 9 6.**
Situated on the far northern coast of Scotland. Here stands
Scotland's first nuclear power station, commenced in 1954.

DOWNAN, Banff.　　　　Map 26, **NJ 1 3.**
A road junction in the vicinity of the famous *Glenlivet (q.v.)*
distillery. At Downan, the River Avon is joined by the
Livet Water, and there is a choice of alternative routes to
Tomintoul (q.v.), the more westerly road traversing Strath
Avon, backed by the *Cromdale* hills, and the easterly road
going by way of the Braes of Glenlivet. *Iter. 192.*

DREGHORN, Ayr. 1,849.　　　　Map 8, **NS 3 3.**
E.C. Wed. The town stands on the Annick Water, which,
to the west, is joined by the River Irvine, on its way to
Irvine Bay. *Iter. 66, 69, 85.*

DREM, East Lothian.　　　　Map 10, **NT 5 7.**
At *East Fortune,* some 2½ m. E., is a monument commemorating the start of the first two-way crossing of the Atlantic in
1919 by the airship R34.

DRIMNIN, Argyll.　　　　Map 12, **NM 5 5.**
Situated on the Sound of Mull, with a small pier. The
village lies on a narrow, hilly road in the *Morven (q.v.)*
district north-west of *Lochaline (q.v.),* giving views across
the Sound to the island of Mull. Beyond the hills, to the
north-east, is Loch Teacuis, an inlet of Loch Sunart, with
the islands of Carna and Oronsay off-shore. *Iter. 218.*

DRONGAN, Ayr. 1,125.　　　　Map 8, **NS 4 1.**
A new town is being developed here, on the edge of the
Ayrshire coalfield. *Iter. 85.*

DRUMBEG, Sutherland.　　　　Map 28, **NC 1 3.**
Lies on the exceptionally picturesque, but narrow and steep
coast road linking *Lochinver (q.v.)* with *Kylesku (q.v.).* The
district is one of crofting and fishing, and in the vicinity are
numerous small lochs, among which are Loch Drumbeg,
and, farther to the south-west, the larger Loch Poll. To
the east is Loch Nedd, an inlet of the island-studded
Eddrachillis Bay, which provides seascapes of considerable
beauty, while inland the view ranges over the bizarre,
isolated Torridon sandstone peaks of Sutherland, from
Quinag, 2,653 ft., to *Suilven,* 2,399 ft., with its twin-peaked
mile and a half long summit ridge. Away to the north-west
of Drumbeg, off the coast, lies the island of Oldany. See
Stoer. *Iter. 227.*

DRUMCLOG, Lanark.　　　　Map 8, **NS 6 3.**
See **Loudounhill.** *Iter. 20, 69.*

DRUMELZIER, Peebles. 149.　　　　Map 9, **NT 1 3.**
The Drumelzier Burn comes down from its wooded dell to
join the Tweed near the reputed burial place of Merlin, the
wizard of Arthurian legend. Of the 16th cent. Castle, only
fragments remain, situated near the Tweed, about a mile to
the south-west. The Church preserves the ancient burial
vault of the Tweedies, and away to the east, is the ruined
Tinnis or *Thanes Castle,* with *Pykestone Hill,* 2,414 ft., rising
in the background. *Iter. 24.*

DRUMGASK, Inverness.　　　　Map 19, **NN 6 9.**
Here, in the lonely valley of the Upper Spey, roads from
Dalwhinnie (q.v.) and *Newtonmore (q.v.),* meet on their way
through Strath Mashie to *Loch Laggan (q.v.).* ½ m. W.,
the old Wade road to Fort Augustus over the *Corrieyairack
Pass (q.v.)* diverges to the north, and **6 m. W.,** along the
track, beyond Loch Crunachan, is Wade's *Garva,* or *St.
George's* Bridge, dating from 1732, over the Upper Spey.
Beyond this point the river leaves the track and its source
is farther to the west near the small Loch Spey. **2 m. N.E.,**
beyond *Laggan* Church and bridge, is *Cluny Castle,* the

Dornoch, Sutherland. The Witch's Stone, on the golf course, where, in 1722, the last judicial execution for witchcraft took place in Scotland. This witch was said to have changed her daughter into a pony, which was then shod by the Devil

Douglas, Lanark. A house in Main Street, its inscription recalling the atrocity perpetrated in 1695 on James Gavin, a Covenanter

Doune, Perth. The original bridge of 1535 was built by the wealthy tailor to James IV. He was refused a passage by the ferryman, as he had no money with him, and built the bridge out of spite in order to ruin him

Douglas, Lanark. The Monument which commemorates the raising of the Cameronian Regiment in 1689

Drem, East Lothian. The Monument marking the start of the first Atlantic double crossing by air, by the British airship R34, in July 1919. It stands 2½ miles east, at East Fortune, on B1377

Drumgask, Inverness. A stone, near Mains of Glentruim, on a by-road on the south bank of the River Spey. It is said to mark the geographical centre of Scotland

PLATE 46 (facing page 136)

[For DOUNE see also Plate 174

Drumlanrig Castle, Dumfries. The Castle of the Dukes of Buccleuch, erected 1676–89 for the 1st Duke of Queensberry, who spent only a single night there

Drumochter Pass, Inverness; Perth. A sign at the summit of the Pass which carries A9 through the Grampian mountains

Dryburgh Abbey, Berwick. Founded in 1150 by monks from Alnwick, in Northumberland, but many times destroyed and rebuilt, the Abbey is now the burial-place of Field-Marshal Earl Haig and Sir Walter Scott

Drummore, Wigtown. A churchyard gravestone in the form of a lighthouse

Drynoch Bridge, Isle of Skye, Inverness. This bridge across a mountain burn issuing into Loch Harport is said to be the highest masonry road bridge in Scotland

Duddingston, Midlothian. The jougs, or iron collar for malefactors, hanging outside the 12th and 17th century Church, partially renewed

[For DUFFTOWN see following plate

PLATE 47 (facing page 137)

ancient home of Cluny Macpherson, with whom Prince Charles Edward hid in a cave after Culloden, in 1746. In the background, to the north, rise the lonely *Monadhliath* mountains, with *Carn Dearg* attaining 3,093 ft. On a by-road on the south side of the Spey, near the Glen Truim estate, a little to the south-east of Cluny Castle, is a stone with some arrow markings, situated by the road, at an altitude of some 950 ft., which is said to mark the geographical centre of Scotland. See **Wade Roads.** *Iter. 143, 208.*

DRUMLANRIG CASTLE, Dumfries. Map 3, NX 8 9.
This magnificent house, containing much fine woodwork, and belonging to the Duke of Buccleuch, stands in a lovely wooded setting in Nithsdale, a little to the west of the river. Its construction dates from 1676 to 1689, the designer being Sir William Bruce, and it was occupied in 1745 by Prince Charles Edward. The first Duke of Queensberry, for whom the house was built, lived in it for one day only. In the park, to the south-east, is the ruined *Tibber's Castle*, destroyed by Bruce in 1311.

DRUMLEMBLE, Argyll. Map 6, NR 6 1.
Iter. 123.

DRUMLITHIE, Kincardine. Map 21, NO 7 8.
Lies a little to the north-east of the fertile Howe of the Mearns, and just off the Brechin to Stonehaven road. *Glenbervie House*, to the west, is an old mansion, with fine gardens. 3½ m. E., off the Stonehaven road, to the south, is the charming little *Fiddes Castle.*

DRUMMOND CASTLE, Perth. Map 16, NN 8 1.
See **Crieff.**

DRUMMORE, Wigtown. 352. Map 2, NX 1 3.
The small fishing port of *Drummore*, in the Rhinns of Galloway, facing Luce Bay, stands in the parish of *Kirkmaiden* (q.v.), the most southerly in Scotland. The Church dates from 1639, the old Church having been situated some **3 m. S.,** near Mull Farm. A gravestone in the churchyard is in the form of a lighthouse. Beyond here, at the foot of the cliffs, are fragments of *St. Medan's* Chapel, the oldest in *Galloway* (q.v.). See **Mull of Galloway, Port Logan** and **Port William.** *Iter. 82.*

DRUMMOSSIE MUIR, Inverness. Map 25, NH 7 4.
See **Culloden.**

DRUMMUIR, Banff. Map 26, NJ 3 4.
Prettily situated in a wooded part of Strath Isla, with the small Loch Park, its banks thickly clothed with trees, lying a little to the south-west, on the road to Dufftown. Nearer the village, in a park, stands *Drummuir Castle*, while in the background rise *Knockan*, 1,219 ft., to the north, and *Carran Hill*, 1,366 ft., to the south. *Iter. 169.*

DRUMNADROCHIT, Inverness. Map 25, NH 5 3.
E.C. Wed. The green and fertile Glen Urquhart, in which lies the little Loch Meiklie, extends between bare moorlands, with the extensive Balmacaan Forest to the south, while the eastern extremity of the glen opens out to the shores of Urquhart Bay, on *Loch Ness* (q.v.). Here stands the village of *Drumnadrochit*, on the River Enrick, which traverses the glen before flowing into the loch. The road through Glen Urquhart was constructed by Telford, and gives access to the grand scenery of Glens Affric and Cannich, described under *Cannich.* A little to the south of Drumnadrochit is the clachan of *Lewiston* (q.v.), beyond which a footpath leads to the picturesque Divach Falls. On the south side of Urquhart Bay is Strone Point, and here is situated the picturesque, ruined 13th to 16th cent. *Urquhart Castle* (A.M.), which was blown up in 1692 to prevent it being occupied by the Jacobites. It is accessible weekdays, 10 to 4 or 7; Sun., 2 to 4 or 7 (see note page 90). **1 m. W.** of Drumnadrochit, a road leaves Glen Urquhart in a northerly direction to ascend steeply over moorland, with good views, and descend later into Glen Convinth in the direction of *Lovat Bridge* (q.v.). *Iter. 206, 207, 210, 213.*

DRUMOAK, Aberdeen. Map 21, NO 7 9.
To the north-east is *Drum Castle*, a mansion of the 17th cent., joined to a much older tower, which has walls 12 to 15 ft. in thickness. *Iter. 152.*

DRUMOCHTER PASS, Inverness; Perth.
Map 19, NN 6 7.
The main Inverness road, accompanied by the railway, on its way from Blair Atholl to Speyside, traverses this lofty and desolate pass in the *Grampians* (q.v.), an altitude of 1,506 ft. being reached near the point where the counties of Perth and Inverness meet. The *Sow of Atholl* and the *Boar of Badenoch* are strangely-named hills rising to the west, while eastwards are the 3,000-ft. summits of the vast Forest of Atholl, with the Gaick Forest farther south. In Drumochter Forest, which lies on both sides of the northern end of the pass, *Beinn Udlaman*, 3,306 ft., rises to the west, and *Chaoruinn*, 3,004 ft., to the east, winter sports being sometimes possible in this area. Wade built the original road through the pass in 1729, and it was traversed in 1745 by Prince Charles Edward. In 1829, Telford redesigned the road, which now follows a slightly different course, though the original Wade road, with its derelict bridges, may still be seen in places on the hillsides. See **Dalnaspidal, Dalwhinnie, Drumgask** and **Wade Roads.** *Iter. 138, 140, 143, 147, 149, 150.*

DRYBURGH ABBEY, Berwick. Map 10, NT 5 3.
The situation of this Abbey (A.M.), standing in a loop of the River Tweed, is one of great beauty. It has become a place of pilgrimage for many thousands who come to visit the *St. Mary's Aisle*, burial-place of Sir Walter Scott and members of his family, together with J. G. Lockhart, his biographer, and also of Field-Marshal Earl Haig. The Abbey was founded in 1150, but in 1322, 1385, and finally in 1544, it was badly damaged by English forces. In 1918, the remains were presented to the nation by Lord Glenconner. The West front, with its 13th cent. portal, and parts of the nave, transepts, and Chapter House, are still standing, showing 12th to 15th cent. work. Much of the cloistral buildings can also be seen, notably the refectory, with its rose window, and the calefactory, retaining a large fireplace. To the north of the Abbey, on the slopes of *Bemersyde Hill*, is the lofty *Wallace* statue. See **Bemersyde** and **Smailholm.** *Iter. 13, 43.*

DRYMEN, Stirling. 304. Map 15, NS 4 8.
E.C. Wed. GOLF. The " *Buchanan Arms* " Inn has fine gardens, from which *Loch Lomond* (q.v.) is well seen. Drymen Bridge, spanning the Endrick Water, was built in 1765 and widened in 1929. In extensive grounds, bordered by the Endrick Water, to the west of the village, stood formerly the 19th cent. *Buchanan Castle*, a seat of the Duke of Montrose, the head of Clan Graham. See **Balmaha.** *Iter. 104, 106, 109, 112, 115, 137.*

DRYNOCH BRIDGE, Isle of Skye, Inverness.
Map 23, NG 4 3.
A bridge spanning a burn here is said to be the highest in Scotland. *Iter. 255.*

DUART CASTLE, Isle of Mull, Argyll. Map 13, NM 7 3.
See **Craignure.**

DUDDINGSTON (Edinburgh), Midlothian.
Map 10, NT 2 7.
Picturesquely situated below the Queen's Drive and *Arthur's Seat*, 822 ft., a magnificent viewpoint with an indicator, overlooking Edinburgh and the Firth of Forth. Duddingston Loch is now a bird sanctuary. The Church, much altered in the 17th cent., preserves a Norman chancel arch and south door, and also the medieval jougs. The " *Sheep's Heid* " Inn is an ancient hostelry. There are several interesting houses in the neighbourhood, among which is *Duddingston House*, built by Sir William Chambers, in 1768, a good example of its period. The delightful *Peffermill House* dates from 1636, and *Prestonfield House* was designed in 1687 by Sir William Bruce. This latter house was visited by Dr. Johnson and Boswell in 1773 as guests of the Dick family.

DUFFTOWN, Banff. 1,458. SB. Map 26, NJ 3 3.
Outside the town, in the vicinity of which are situated several well-known distilleries, the River Fiddich is joined by the Dullan Water, which flows along the attractive Glen Rinnes, to the south-west, under the slopes of *Ben Rinnes*, 2,755 ft.

To the north, near the station, stands the picturesque, ruined *Balvenie Castle* (A.M.), an ancient Atholl stronghold, perhaps of 15th cent. date, and preserving a good example of a yett. It was visited by Edward I in 1304 and by Queen Mary in 1562. The Castle is open weekdays, 10 to 7 in summer and 10 to 4 in winter; Sun., 2 to 4 or 7 (see note page 90). The fine road leading south-eastwards from Dufftown towards Alford and Rhynie ascends over the Glacks of Balloch Pass, 1,197 ft. The pass leads from the Fiddich, issuing from the lonely glen of that name, and backed by *Cooks Cairn*, 2,478 ft., to the more important Deveron, which flows north-eastwards into the Strathbogie district of Aberdeenshire. Almost adjoining Dufftown, to the south, is the modernised 12th cent. Church of *Mortlach*, attractively situated near the Dullan Water. The Churchyard preserves a "Battle Stone" recalling a victory over the Danes in 1010. The road to *Keith* (q.v.) leaves Dufftown in a north-easterly direction to traverse the pleasantly wooded Strath Isla, with the tiny Loch Park, beyond which lies *Drummuir* (q.v.). See **Auchindown, Craigellachie** and **Glenlivet.** *Iter 169, 177, 190, 195, 197.*

DUFFUS, Moray. 860.   Map 26, **NJ 1** 6.
St. Peter's Kirk has a curious porch, and faces the shaft of the old Parish Cross (A.M.), dating probably from the 14th cent. The Church was founded by a member of the Freskyn family, ancestors of several notable Scottish families, among which are the Murrays. 1½ m. S.E. is a mound on which stand the remains of *Duffus Castle* (A.M.), with walls of great thickness, and also considerable outer defences. A little to the north-east of Duffus is *Gordonstoun School*, founded in 1934, and occupying a 17th cent. mansion. The Duke of Edinburgh was a pupil here. The Moray coast, with the fishing villages of *Hopeman* (q.v.) and *Burghead* (q.v.), on its sandy bay, lies a little to the north-west. *Iter. 199.*

DULL, Perth.   Map 19, **NN 8** 4.
A Strath Appin hamlet, with an old Cross. Prehistoric cairns, standing stones and remains of stone circles are in the vicinity. Adamnan, or Eonan, the biographer of St. Columba, is said to have been buried near Dull, and a

college was founded here in his memory. The ruined *Comrie Castle* stands a little to the west.

DULNAIN BRIDGE, Moray.   Map 25, **NH 9** 2.
Roads from *Aviemore* (q.v.) and *Carrbridge* (q.v.) converge here, near the point where the River Dulnain flows into the Spey. **1 m. W.** is the old tower of *Muckerach*, dating from 1598. *Iter. 172, 195.*

DULSIE BRIDGE, Nairn.   Map 25, **NH 9** 4.
The River Findhorn, after having traversed the lonely Streens valley of Strath Dearn, overlooked by hills rising to more than 2,000 ft., flows here through a narrow and rocky gorge, spanned by a single-arched 18th cent. bridge, in a richly wooded setting, one of the most picturesque spots in the country. The great Moray floods of 1892 came near to damaging the bridge, the river rising to 40 ft. above normal. To the north, in the grounds of *Glenferness House*, is the "Princess Stone," a sculptured tablet, situated near a cairn supposed to mark the grave of a Celtic princess. Dulsie Bridge is approached from the Carrbridge to Forres road by a short link traversing a ford, while to the north-west, one of the old military roads leads in the direction of *Cawdor* (q.v.) and the Moray Firth. See **Ferness.** *Iter. 173, 177.*

DUMBARTON, Dunbarton. 26,175. LB.   Map 8, **NS 3** 7.
E.C. Wed. GOLF. An important shipbuilding town and Royal Burgh, standing at the point where the River Leven, flowing southwards from *Loch Lomond* (q.v.), joins the Clyde. Dumbarton was, in medieval times, the capital of the ancient kingdom of Strathclyde, which extended from the Clyde as far as Lancashire. St. Patrick is said to have been born here, and was later taken by raiders to Ireland. The *College Bow*, an arch from *St. Mary's* Collegiate Church, founded 1453, has been re-erected in Church St. The Castle (A.M.) stands in a commanding situation on the summit of a 240-ft. high rock, and consists mainly of modern barracks, while a 12th cent. gateway, and a sundial, the gift of Mary, Queen of Scots, have been preserved. The view from the Castle is very notable. In 1548, the ill-fated Queen, at the age of 6,

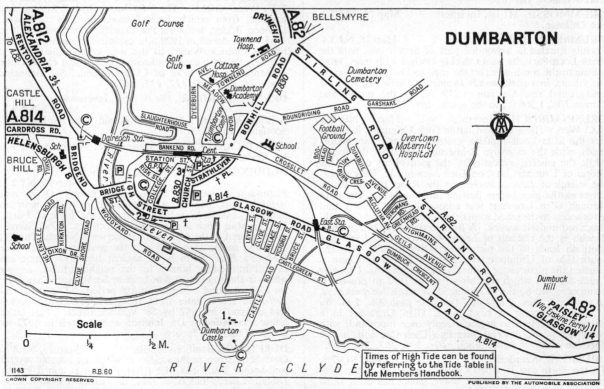

Times of High Tide can be found by referring to the Tide Table in the Members Handbook.

CROWN COPYRIGHT RESERVED   1143   R.B. 60   PUBLISHED BY THE AUTOMOBILE ASSOCIATION

1. Castle.   2. Glencairn House, dating from 1623.   3. College Bow; arch from former St. Mary's Collegiate Church.

Dufftown, Banff. The 'Battle Stone,' reputed to commemorate the defeat of the Danes in 1010. It stands in the churchyard of the modernized 12th century Mortlach Church, south of the town

Dull, Perth. The old Church, near which one of the three former Crosses of the Abbey still stands, in a mutilated condition

Dulnain Bridge, Moray. The bridge spanning the River Dulnain at the junction of A95 and A938

Dulsie Bridge, Nairn. The 18th century bridge, which spans the River Findhorn in what is considered its most picturesque reach

Duffus, Moray. The shaft of the ancient Parish Cross facing the ruined Church

Dumbarton, Dunbarton. An ancient arch from St. Mary's Collegiate Church, which is known as the College Bow

PLATE 48 (facing page 138)

Dumfries, Dumfries. The 15th century Old Bridge across the River Nith, which is now used only as a footbridge

Dumfries, Dumfries. A panel on the Mid Steeple giving distances to Scottish and English towns, including Huntingdon. The Earldom of Huntingdon was held by three early Kings of Scotland

Dumfries, Dumfries. A tablet on the house adjacent to that in which Robert Burns died in 1796

Dunbar, East Lothian. The carved Victorian 'barometer' monument of 1856, set up in honour of the fishermen of Dunbar

Dunadd, Argyll. A rock outcrop, carrying the remains of a fort, and carved with symbols. It is associated with the early kingdom of Argyll, or Dalriada, and lies 1½ miles north-west of Kilmichael, off A816

Dunbar, East Lothian. The great monument in the Parish Church to the 1st Earl of Dunbar, who died in 1610

PLATE 49 (facing page 139)

[For DUNBAR see also Plate 51

DUMFRIES

Scale ¼ MI.

Academy	1.
Burns' House, where he died.	9.
Burns' Mausoleum, in St. Michael's Churchyard, key at Burns' house	11.
Burns' Statue	4.
County Buildings, Information Bureau	13.
Court House	5.
Greyfriars Church	2.
'Globe' Inn (Burns' 'Howff')	8.
'Hole in the Wa' (Burns' Inn)	12.
Mid Steeple (Old Town Hall)	6.
Old Bridge (Footbridge)	7.
St. Michael's Church	10.
Town Hall	3.

1½ m. N. Lincluden Abbey. 7 m. S.W. New Abbey (Sweetheart Abbey).

CROWN COPYRIGHT RESERVED   DRAWN AND PUBLISHED BY THE AUTOMOBILE ASSOCIATION

was sent from here to France, and in 1571, under cover of night, the Castle was captured from her followers. Dumbarton Castle is open summer 10 to 6, winter 10 to 4; Sun., 2 to 4 or 6 (see note page 90). *Glencairn House* (A.M.) dates from 1623. *Castlehill* (N.T. Scot.) consists of two wooded mounds, and nearby is the Cunninghame-Graham Memorial (N.T. Scot.). The Royal Scots, the oldest British regiment, has for its regimental march 'Dumbarton's Drums.' See **Cardross, Old Kilpatrick** and **Port of Menteith.** *Iter. 102, 111.*

DUMFRIES, Dumfries. 27,430. LB.   Map 4, NX 9 7.
E.C. Thurs. M.D. Wed. GOLF. The important town of *Dumfries* stands about 7 miles inland from the Solway Firth and Nith estuary. The river divides Dumfries from Maxwelltown, in the county of Kirkcudbright, but the two towns were almalgamated in 1929. In the 12th cent. Dumfries became a Royal Burgh, but it suffered many vicissitudes, and was badly treated by Prince Charles Edward in 1745. Robert Burns came to the town in 1791, and did much of his work there. Among the buildings with which he is associated are the *Burns House*, in which he died in 1796, now preserving personal relics, and *St. Michael's* Church (see below). In the Churchyard is the mausoleum in which Burns, his wife and several of his children lie buried. The "*Hole in the Wa'*" and "*Globe*" taverns, or "howffs," contain Burns relics, and in front of the modern *Greyfriars* church is the poet's statue. *St. Michael's* Church dates from 1744–54, later restored, and has, on the south wall of the interior, a tablet recording the gratitude of Norwegians who took refuge in Scotland during the Second World War. A tablet marks the pew formerly used by Robert Burns. In the former Greyfriars Monastery Church, in 1306, Robert Bruce stabbed the "Red Comyn," an action which is said to have altered the course of Scottish history. A plaque on a building in Castle Street marks the supposed place of the murder. The picturesque *Mid Steeple*, or old Town Hall, dates from 1707. It shows distances to important Scottish towns, and in addition to Huntingdon, in England, the earldom of which was held by three successive early Kings of Scotland. On the south face is sculptured

the old Scots "ell" measure of 37 inches. Sir James Barrie was a pupil at the Academy. The Guid Nychburris Festival is held generally in the early summer. Four bridges link the town with Maxwelltown, of which the Old Bridge, for foot passengers only, dates back to the 15th cent., and was built by Devorgilla, who endowed Balliol College, Oxford. The Town Museum in Maxwelltown contains Burns relics, and there is also a camera obscura. **2 m. N.W.** is the mansion of *Terregles*, rebuilt in 1789, and said to have been Mary, Queen of Scots' last resting-place before her final journey to England, though this was more likely *Dundrennan* (*q.v.*). The 18th cent. *Terregles* Church preserves a restored choir, dating from 1583, containing several interesting tombs and stalls, and also a notable medieval painting on wood. For *Dumfries House*, see under *Cumnock*. See **Amisfield, Auldgirth, Brow, Caerlaverock, Irongray, Lincluden Abbey, Lochfoot, New Abbey, New Bridge, Ruthwell** and **Shawhead.** *Iter. 24, 26, 27, 28, 45, 46, 47, 48, 56, 67, 70, 71, 72, 73, 74, 75, 76.*

DUNADD, Argyll.   Map 14, NR 8 9.
See **Kilmichael.**

DUNAN, Isle of Skye, Inverness.
                    Map 23, NG 5 2.
Faces Loch na Cairidh, which separates Skye from the small island of Scalpay, beyond which lie Longay and the three Crowlin Islands. To the north-west of Dunan, the *Sligachan* (*q.v.*) road makes a circuit of Loch Ainort, backed by the Red *Coolins* (*q.v.*), or Red Hills, in Lord Macdonald's Forest, and giving views of *Blaven*, 3,042 ft., the great Black Coolin peak rising to the south-west of the roadless Strath Mor. *Iter. 251, 252, 253.*

DUNBAR, East Lothian. 4,159. SB.   Map 10, NT 6 7.
E.C. Wed. GOLF. An old fishing port, Royal Burgh and resort, with a beach of sand and pebbles. It is situated on the edge of rich farming country, notable for its reddish soil, in which the famous "Dunbar Red" potatoes flourish. The town is bordered to the south by the *Lammermuir* hills, and looks north-westwards out to sea to the lonely *Bass Rock* near *North Berwick* (*q.v.*), and south-

DUNBAR

Scale ¼ M.

Times of High Tide can be found by referring to the Tide Table in the Members' Handbook.

CROWN COPYRIGHT RESERVED   R.B. 60   DRAWN AND PUBLISHED BY THE AUTOMOBILE ASSOCIATION

1. Church, with Home monument (1611).   3. Castle.
2. Old Town House and Market Cross.

139

DUNDEE

Times of High Tide can be found by referring to the Tide Table in the Members Handbook

Scale of Miles

PUBLISHED BY THE AUTOMOBILE ASSOCIATION

CROWN COPYRIGHT RESERVED

A.A. SUB-OFFICE: 12 Victoria Chambers, Victoria Road.   Tel.: Dundee 2088.   Tel. Add. Dunfanum, Dundee.

Albert Institute	2.	
Caird Hall	4.	
	1	
Dundee Law and War Memorial	7.	Mains of Fintry Castle
Information Bureau, Town		Mills Observatory
Clerk's Office, City Square	11.	Royal Arch, 1844
	9.	St. Mary's Tower, City
	6.	Churches (Old Steeple)
	10.	
University College	5.	
Wishart Arch	8.	

DUNDEE, Angus.

The 15th century Old Steeple of the City Churches, whose defenders surrendered to General Monck (or Monk) in 1651, after being threatened with burning

The Royal Arch, commemorating Queen Victoria's visit to the docks in 1844

The plaque on the wall of St. Paul's Episcopal Cathedral, in the High Street, recording the site of the vanished castle

The tablet on an old house, now a shop, the birthplace in 1651 of Anna (or Anne) Scott, wife of the Duke of Monmouth, who was executed in 1685. They were created Duke and Duchess of Buccleuch in 1663. Sir Walter Scott's 'Lay of the Last Minstrel' is associated with the Duchess

The ruined Mains of Fintry Castle, dating from 1582, a former home of the Grahams

[For DUNDEE see also following plate

PLATE 50 (facing page 140)

Dundonald, Ayr. The ruined Castle, in which Robert II died in 1309. Dr. Johnson came here during his tour of 1773

Dundee, Angus. The East Port, where George Wishart is said to have preached in 1544 during an outbreak of plague

Dundrennan, Kirkcudbright. A 13th century monument to a former Abbot at the ruined Abbey. He may have been murdered by the man on whose effigy he stands

Dunblane, Perth. The 13th century and later Cathedral, the west front of which John Ruskin considered a masterpiece

Dundonnell, Ross and Cromarty. The so-called Destitution Road (A832), leading to Braemore Lodge. It was built during the potato famine of 1851

Dunbar, East Lothian. The old Town House, dating from 1620

[For DUNBAR see also Plate 49
[For DUNDEE see also preceding plate

PLATE 51 (facing page 141)

eastwards along a long stretch of coastline towards the distant St. Abb's Head. There is a quaint old Town House, with a six-sided tower, dating from c. 1620. Close to it is the old Market Cross. The Parish Church has a 108-ft. high tower, visible out to sea, and a notable sight is the great *Home* monument, dated 1611. The ruined Castle stands on a rock above the harbour, and has a long history, including a notable siege in 1339, and was associated with Mary, Queen of Scots in 1556 and 1567, after which it was destroyed. The battle of Dunbar, fought in 1650, in which Cromwell defeated the Covenanters under General Leslie, took place a little to the south-east of the town off the Great North Road, close to *Broxburn* (*q.v.*), where a stone was erected, in 1950, to commemorate the fight. See **East Linton, St. Monance, Spott, Stenton** (for *Biel House*) and **Whittinghame.** *Iter. 2, 39, 40.*

DUNBEATH, Caithness. 575.   Map 30, **ND 1** 2.
E.C. Thurs. A fishing village, situated on the Dunbeath River, where it flows into the narrow bay. The name is said to have been taken from the broch of *Dun Beath*, which stands in the angle formed by the river and the Burn of Houstry, to the north-west of the village. The Castle, captured by Montrose in 1650, is situated **1 m. S.**, on a lofty promontory off the *Berriedale* (*q.v.*) road, preserving a 15th cent. keep, and having been enlarged in the 19th cent. West of the village, on the moors inland, in the vicinity of *Braemore*, near the Berriedale Water, is a granite cross marking the place where the Duke of Kent was killed in a flying accident in 1942. The coast road leading south-westwards from Dunbeath gives an excellent picture of the lofty Caithness plateau, which has been carved out in a number of places by its rivers. *Iter. 200, 236.*

DUNBLANE, Perth. 2,789. SB.   Map 16, **NN 7** 0.
E.C. Wed. GOLF. Situated on the Allan Water, at the south-western extremity of Strath Allan, and forming a good touring centre for the *Ochil* hills to the east, and the Perthshire Highlands to the west and north. This old-world city, with its narrow streets containing a few good 17th cent. houses, is best known for the Cathedral (A.M.), which is a building dating chiefly from the 13th cent., but retaining a Norman tower, probably of the 11th cent. The West front, with its central doorway and tall lancet windows, was greatly praised by Ruskin, and is one of the finest compositions in Scottish church architecture. The nave roof collapsed in the 16th cent., but a restoration took place in 1893, and the choir was restored in 1914. In the south aisle of the nave are the six very finely carved 15th cent. Ochiltree stalls. The north aisle contains a stone with curious carvings and a Celtic Cross. Three blue slabs in the pavement of the choir are in memory of the three Drummond sisters, associated with James IV, and all poisoned in 1501. There are scanty remains of the Bishop's Palace; in the 18th cent. Dean's House is a small museum; and the Leighton Library is housed in a building dated 1687, near the churchyard gate. **2½ m. E.**, on the moors, is the site of the indecisive battle of *Sheriffmuir*, fought in 1715, between the Pretender's forces under the Earl of Mar and the Royal troops under the Duke of Argyll. The "Gathering Stone" of the clans commemorates the fight. See **Bridge of Allan** and **Doune.** *Iter. 135, 138, 140, 141, 146.*

DUNDEE, Angus. 179,225.   Map 17, **NO 3** 3
E.C. Wed. M.D. Tues., Fri. GOLF. The fourth largest city in Scotland, situated on the Firth of Tay, to the north-east of the fertile *Carse of Gowrie* (*q.v.*), and overlooking the coast of Fife, to which it is linked by car ferry to *Newport* (*q.v.*), and also by the famous two-mile long Tay Bridge. This bridge, built 1883–1888, carries the main railway line from Edinburgh to Aberdeen, and is the successor to the ill-fated earlier structure, which was blown down in a gale in 1879 while a train was making the crossing, with heavy loss of life. *Dundee* is essentially a modern city, its best known industry being jute, but engineering, ship-building and preserve manufacturing are all of considerable importance, and the docks cover more than 35 acres. In 1190, Dundee became a Royal Burgh, and later it suffered severely in wars with the English. Montrose stormed the

city in 1645, and General Monk captured it in 1651, while there are also associations with both the Old and the Young Pretenders, in 1715 and 1745 respectively.

The most notable building is the splendid Old Steeple, or Tower of *St. Mary*, belonging to the *City Churches*, which formerly comprised four separate Churches. The Churches were almost destroyed by fire in 1841, but were later restored. This Old Steeple, 156 ft. high, is of 15th cent. date, and considered the largest and finest of its kind in Scotland. It surrendered to General Monk, in 1651, only after burning straw had been piled at its base. The University has been combined with that of *St. Andrews* (*q.v.*) since 1897. A house in the High Street was the birth-place, in 1651, of Anne Scott, Duchess of Buccleuch (See **Dalkeith** and **Hawick**), and in the same building General Monk stayed. Among the many fine modern buildings the *Caird Hall* is outstanding. From the *East Port*, or *Wishart Arch*, George Wishart is said to have preached during the plague of 1544. The ornate *Royal Arch* leading to the docks commemorates Queen Victoria's visit in 1844. The Museum and Art Gallery in the *Albert* Institute are of much interest, and in the old cemetery, known as the *Howff*, are many quaint gravestones. William Wallace was educated at the Grammar School, and Hector Boece, the historian, was born in the city, c. 1465 (See **Grampians**). *Dundee Law*, 571 ft., a good viewpoint, is surmounted by a War Memorial. *Dudhope Castle*, 15th cent., restored, is used as a technical school, and *Mains o₁ Fintry Castle*, a ruin, dating from 1582, stands in *Caird* Park. The *Mills* Observatory is situated in *Balgay* Park. To the north-west of the city is *Camperdown House*, built by the son of Lord Duncan, victor of the battle of Camperdown in 1797, and farther away to the north rise the *Sidlaw* hills, with the high point of *Craigowl Hill*, 1,493 ft. **5 m. N.** of the city, to the west of the Forfar road, is *Kirkton of Tealing* (*q.v.*). **3 m. N.**, off the Forfar road, is the ruined *Pourie Castle*. See **Broughty Ferry, Fowlis Easter, Glamis, Longforgan** and **Newtyle.** For "Through Routes" see page 43. *Iter. 94, 126, 127, 154, 155, 156, 157, 158, 159, 160, 161.*

DUNDONALD, Ayr. 465.   Map 8, **NS 3** 3.
The Church was built in 1803. On a height, a little to the west, is the ruined *Dundonald Castle*, where Robert II died, in 1390. This castle was visited by Dr. Johnson in 1773, who also went to the 17th cent. *Auchans House*, situated to the north-west of the castle, where he was received by the Countess of Eglinton. *Iter. 85.*

DUNDONNELL, Ross and Cromarty.   Map 29, **NH 1** 8.
This remote *Wester Ross* village stands at the head of Little Loch Broom, in the green valley of Strath Beg. At *Ardessie*, **2½ m. W.N.W.**, and also near *Corryhallie*, **3 m. S.E.**, in a picturesque gorge along the road to *Braemore Lodge* (*q.v.*), there are fine waterfalls. The road to Braemore Lodge climbs to a height of over 1,100 ft. at Fain Hill along the so-called "Destitution Road," which was built during the potato famine of 1851. There are magnificent views of the grand red Torridon sandstone peaks of *An Teallach*, nearly 3,500 ft. high, some of the wildest mountains on the Scottish mainland, situated to the north-west, above Dundonnell Forest and the remote valley of Strath na Sheallag. In the heart of the *Teallach* range, at a height of about 2,000 ft., is the tiny loch of *Toll an Lochain*, in a spectacular rocky setting, overlooked by an extraordinary ridge of white quartzite slabs facing the great cliffs at the base of *Sgurr Fiona*, 3,474 ft. This loch, which is one of the most remarkable sights in the Scottish Highlands, can be reached by a rough climb on foot from a point on the Braemore Lodge road about **2 m. S.E.** of Dundonnell. East of the village, in Strath Beg, is Dundonnell Lodge, and from here a track goes northwards over the hills to *Aultnaharrie* (*q.v.*), on Loch Broom, facing *Ullapool* (*q.v.*), to which it is linked by a passenger ferry. Beyond the track, and overlooking Little Loch Broom, rises *Ben Goleach*, 2,052 ft. See **Gruinard Bay.** *Iter. 206, 222.*

DUNDRENNAN, Kirkcudbright. 89.   Map 3, **NX 7** 4.
This village, in an attractive setting on the Abbey Burn, which flows into the Solway Firth near Abbey Head to the south, is built partly of stones from its Abbey. On the coast,

DUNFERMLINE

Scale 0 ½ M.

1. Abbey, with Norman nave and brass plate in choir marking burial-place of Robert Bruce.
2. Pittencrieff Glen, with museum in 17th cent. mansion.
3. Carnegie's Birthplace and Memorial.
4. Carnegie Library.
5. Abbot's House.
6. Information Bureau.

near the outflow of the river, is *Abbey Burnfoot*, sheltered by Abbey Head, and to the east is *Port Mary*, where stands the rock from which Mary, Queen of Scots stepped on to the boat which took her, after her last night in Scotland, probably at the Abbey, to Workington in England. *Dundrennan Abbey* (A.M.), Cistercian, dates from 1142, and was annexed to the Chapel Royal at *Stirling* (q.v.), in 1621. Much of the building is irretrievably ruined, but the 13th cent. Chapter House remains are of interest, and parts of the 13th cent. transepts of the Church can be seen. There are some incised slabs; the Cellarer's Monument, dated 1480; and a fine 13th cent. monument to an abbot, who may have been murdered by the man on whose effigy his figure stands. See **Clarkston** and **Dumfries**. *Iter. 73.*

DUNECHT, Aberdeen. Map 27, NJ 7 0.
Off the *Echt* (q.v.) road, to the south, stands *Dunecht House*, in its park, once well known for its observatory, and possessing fine gardens. 2½ m. N.W. is *Castle Fraser*, described under Kemnay. For *Iter.* see *Waterton-Dunecht*.

DUNFERMLINE, Fife. 46,270. LB. Map 17, NT 0 8.
E.C. Wed. M.D. Tues. GOLF. A Royal Burgh and modern linen-manufacturing town, noted for its magnificent Abbey Church, in which Robert Bruce is buried. The town has had an historic past, and was the birthplace of James I in 1394 and also of Charles I in 1600 and his sister Elizabeth. Andrew Carnegie was born in a small cottage, in 1835, and the Carnegie Trusts have benefited the town to a very great extent. The first of the numerous Carnegie libraries was founded here in 1881 and contains many treasures. A memorial building adjoins his birthplace. The attractive Pittencrieff Glen, with its splendid flower gardens, was presented to the town by Carnegie in 1903, and in the 17th cent. mansion is a museum. There are slight remains of the Royal Palace, which was built out of the former monastery, notably a 200-ft. long buttressed wall, and also a mound with the remains of *Malcolm's Tower*. The Pends archway links the Palace with the Abbey. The Abbey Church (A.M.), founded soon after 1070, and associated with Queen Mar-

garet, contains a magnificent Norman nave, reminiscent of Durham Cathedral, and dating from 1150, the finest of its period in Scotland. The original steeple and south-western tower fell in 1753 and 1807 respectively. The choir was rebuilt in 1817–1822. The West front, with its fine door and twin towers, has been much rebuilt, and of special note are the massive 16th cent. buttresses against the north and south sides of the nave. A brass plate marks the burial-place of Robert Bruce in 1329 in the choir. The battlemented 100-ft. high square tower has the words; " King Robert the Bruce " cut out in stone around the four sides. The Abbot's House dates from the 16th cent., and an inscription on its door lintel was made use of by Scott in his " Fair Maid of Perth." To the north-east of the town is the tiny Town Loch, and still farther in the same direction lies the larger Loch Fitty. 2½ m. S.W. is *Pitfirraine Castle*, which retains a 15th cent. tower. See **Charlestown, Culross** and **Melrose**. *Iter. 89, 92, 97, 133.*

DUNGLASS, East Lothian.
Map 11, NT 7 7.
In the grounds of the modern *Dunglass House* is a fine, partially restored cruciform 14th cent. Collegiate Church, preserving notable sedilia. (A.M.)

DUNINO, Fife. Map 17, NO 5 1.
Near the Church is a very ancient carved stone, topped by a sundial of 1698. In the vicinity is a picturesque small glen.

DUNKELD, Perth. 841. Map 16, NO 0 4.
E.C. Thurs. GOLF. This ancient little Cathedral city is beautifully situated in the richly wooded valley of the Tay, where it is crossed by a bridge erected in 1809 by Telford. A house in The Square has on it the delineation of a Scottish " ell " (37 inches), dated 1706. An Abbey for Celtic monks from Iona was founded here in 315. The ancient Cathedral (A.M.) dates from the 12th to the 15th cents., but was desecrated in 1560, and although the 14th cent. choir, now used as the Parish Church, was restored in 1815 and 1908, much of the structure is still roofless. Some of the damage was caused in 1689, in the Battle of Dunkeld, when the Highlanders were defeated. The nave, with its fine window tracery, was begun in 1406, and the massive tower is late 15th cent. work, and contains some wall paintings. In the choir is a tomb, believed to be that of the Wolf of Badenoch, the destroyer of *Elgin Cathedral* (q.v.) The 15th cent. Chapter House is now the Atholl tomb-chapel. Cathedral Street and The Cross have been the scene of an ambitious group-restoration project, where the " little houses " have been given new life by The National Trust for Scotland. In the grounds of *Dunkeld House*, to the west, are the remains of a prehistoric fort. Fine Japanese larches grow on the estate. Across the Tay is *Little Dunkeld*, where, in the Churchyard, is the grave of Niel Gow, the famous fiddler, born **1 m.** W. at

DUNKELD

1. Cathedral.
2. Little Dunkeld Church.
3. Inver Village.
4. Ossians Hall.
5. Hermitage.

Dunfermline, Fife. The inscription over the door of the 16th century Abbot's House, which Sir Walter Scott used in his '*Fair Maid of Perth*'

Dunfermline, Fife. The Abbey Church, with its massive buttresses. A brass plate in the choir marks the resting place of Robert Bruce

Dunkeld, Perth. The Scottish 'ell' (37 inches), portrayed on a house in The Square, dating from 1706

Dunino, Fife. An ancient carved stone, topped by a sundial of 1698. It stands near the south wall of the church

Dunkeld, Perth. The tomb of Niel Gow, the famous fiddler, who died in 1807. It stands in the church-yard of Little Dunkeld, across the River Tay

Dunkeld, Perth. The gateway to Dunkeld House, in the grounds of which are the remains of a prehistoric fort

PLATE 52 (facing page 142)

Dunnottar Castle, Kincardine. The ruined 14th to 16th century Castle, in which the Scottish regalia were kept for safety for a period during the Commonwealth Wars in the 17th century. See Kinneff (Plate 100)

Dunrobin, Sutherland. The Castle, built originally in the 13th century, but greatly altered during the Victorian period

Dunnet, Caithness. The saddleback tower of the Church, which may be of 14th century date

Dunning, Perth. The Memorial recording the burning here in 1657 of Maggie Wall as a witch. It stands a mile to the west, on B9062

Dunoon, Argyll. The statue to Robert Burns's 'Mary,' who was born at Auchnamore Farm near the town. It was unveiled by Lady Kelvin in 1896

Dunlichity, Inverness. The watch-tower of the 18th century Church, used in the 19th century for preventing the theft of corpses. It stands 3 miles south-west of Dalvourn, in Strath Nairn, on an unclassified road off B851

PLATE 53 (facing page 143)   [For DUNS see under MERSE (Plate 121)

Inver. Nearby is *Ossians Hall* (N.T. Scot.), a restored 18th cent. "folly," open at times in the summer (see note page 90). To the south is the *Hermitage Bridge* (N.T. Scot.) in Strath Bran, below the Falls of Bran. Beyond the falls is *Rumbling Bridge,* where the river enters a picturesque chasm. North-west of Inver, above the Tay, is the hill of *Craig Vinean,* from the vicinity of which Dunkeld and its Cathedral are well seen. The wooded hill of *Craigiebarns,* 1,106 ft., above the river north-west of the town, is also an excellent viewpoint. See **Aberdour, Amulree, Birnam** and **Butterstone.** *Iter.* 139, 140, 141, 148, 150, 157, 166.

DUNLICHITY CHURCH, Inverness. Map 25, NH 6 3. See **Dalvourn.**

DUNLOP, Ayr. 553. Map 8, NS 4 4.
E.C. Wed. The district is noted for "Dunlop" cheeses. The Laigh Kirk of 1835 contains the *Dunlop* aisle of 1641 and has also much stained glass. The adjacent mausoleum and church hall were erected by Viscount Clandeboyes. *Iter.* 62.

DUNNET, Caithness. 200. Map 30, ND 2 7.
E.C. Thurs. M.D. Tues. Overlooks Dunnet Bay, with a sandy beach. To the north is St. John's Loch, and **3 m.** N.N.W. of the loch is Dunnet Head, a bold promontory, with a lighthouse, on the most northerly point of the mainland, forming a magnificent viewpoint. Across the waters of the stormy Pentland Firth can be seen the detached *Old Man of Hoy.* (See **Orkney.**) The little early Presbyterian Church of Dunnet, with a saddleback tower, may be of 14th cent. date. Timothy Pont, an early cartographer, was minister here from 1601 to 1608, and his revised surveys were incorporated in Blaeu's atlas, published in 1654, at Amsterdam. See **John o' Groats.** *Iter.* 240.

DUNNICHEN, Angus. Map 21, NO 5 4. See **Forfar.**

DUNNING, Perth. Map 16, NO 0 1.
Situated to the north of the *Ochil* hills, overlooking Strath Earn. The rebuilt Church, dedicated to St. Serf, retains its fine 13th cent. tower. See **Forteviot.** *Iter.* 86.

DUNNOTTAR CASTLE, Kincardine. Map 21, NO 8 8·
The ruins of this great Castle stand in a picturesque setting on a rocky headland overlooking the North Sea. The oldest parts are the tower and chapel, dating from c. 1392, and the fine gate-house dates from c. 1575. Montrose besieged the castle in 1645, and during the Commonwealth Wars the Scottish regalia was kept here, being removed in 1652 and hidden in the pulpit of the Church at *Kinneff* (q.v.). In 1685, no less than 167 Covenanters were confined in the dungeon, and when Scott visited the old churchyard, **2 m.** inland, near the Carron Water, he met "Old Mortality" cleaning the headstones of the graves. To the south of the castle, the coast is rocky, with magnificent cliff scenery. See **Caerlaverock.** *Iter.* 155.

DUNOON, Argyll. 8,957. SB. Map 14, NS 1 7.
E.C. Wed. GOLF. The largest and best known of the *Cowal* (q.v.) resorts. It is situated on the Firth of Clyde. facing Cloch Point in Renfrewshire, and forming a splendid centre for yachting and excursions by steamer in the neighbouring waters. The Cowal Highland Gathering takes place here at the end of August, and the Clyde Yachting Fortnight in July is also associated with the town. The modern castle dates from 1822, but traces of an ancient castle can be seen on a rock above the pier, and at the foot is a statue of Burns's "Highland Mary," who was born at a farm near the town. A coast road goes southwards for Toward Point, giving fine views, and inland to the west of Dunoon are lofty moorlands rising to *Bishop's Seat,* 1,651 ft., looking westwards across Loch Striven to the *Kyles of Bute* (q.v.). See **Benmore Estate, Hunter's Quay, Innellan** and **Kirn.** *Iter.* 102, 137.

DUNPHAIL, Moray. Map 25, NJ 0 4.
Iter. 172.

DUNRAGIT, Wigtown. Map 2, NX 1 5.
Iter. 25, 26, 80.

DUNROBIN, Sutherland. Map 31, NC 8 0.
The magnificent *Dunrobin Castle,* belonging to the Duke of Sutherland, stands in a great park overlooking the sea. The original structure dates back to c. 1275, but some extensive additions were made in 1856. An old yett is preserved, and in the grounds is a museum. A private railway was formerly situated on the estate. See **Golspie** (for *Dunrobin Glen*). *Iter.* 200, 231.

DUNROSSNESS, Shetland. Map 33, HU 3 1.
See **Shetland Islands** (Mainland). *Iter.* 269.

DUNS, Berwick. 1,958. SB. Map 11, NT 7 5.
E.C. Wed. M.D. 2nd Mon. GOLF. A pleasant little

DUNOON

Scale
0 ¼ M.

CROWN COPYRIGHT RESERVED 1557/RB.60 DRAWN AND PUBLISHED BY THE AUTOMOBILE ASSOCIATION

1. Castle House.
2. Old Castle ruins.
3. Statue of "Highland Mary".

DUNS

Scale
0 ¼ M.

CROWN COPYRIGHT RESERVED 1562 R.B.60

1. Parish Church (1790).
2. Mercat Cross.
3. Castle.

market town, lying at the foot of *Duns Law*, 713 ft., on which the town was at one time situated, before being destroyed by the English in 1545. On the summit of the hill is a "Covenanters' stone," recalling the presence of General Leslie's army in 1639. The Parish Church dates from 1880, and the Mercat Cross stands in a public park. There is a 19th cent. Town Hall. The modern *Duns Castle*, to the north-west, retains an ancient tower. In the grounds is a fine lime avenue, and nearby is a tiny loch, known as the *Hen Poo*. To the north-west of Duns rise the foothills of the *Lammermuirs*, through which penetrate two narrow roads, the westerly of which gives access to *Longformacus* (*q.v.*), and the easterly of which goes by the valley of the Whiteadder Water to *Cranshaws* (*q.v.*). **2 m. S.** of Duns is *Nisbet House*, dating from the 17th and 18th cents., and notable for its wealth of gun loops, unusual at so late a period. **2 m. E.** of the town is *Manderston House*, with its fine gardens. See **Abbey St. Bathans**, **Chirnside** and **Preston**. *Iter. 3, 9, 33, 38, 39, 41.*

DUNSCORE, Dumfries. Map 3, NX 8 8.
Lies in the fertile valley of the Cairn Water. **6 m. W.**, under *Bar Hill*, on the Kirkcudbright border, is *Craigenputtock* farm, where Carlyle wrote "Sartor Resartus." **1½ m. N.E.** is the ruined tower of *Lag*, associated with Sir Robert Grierson, a noted persecutor of the Covenanters in the 17th cent. See **Auldgirth** and **Ringford**. *Iter. 74.*

DUNSKEATH, Ross and Cromarty. Map 31, NH 7 7.
On the north shore of the Cromarty Firth narrows, with a passenger ferry to *Cromarty* (*q.v.*). To the east is the cave-riddled North Sutor, facing its southern namesake across the water.

DUNSTAFFNAGE CASTLE, Argyll. Map 14, NM 8 3.
This isolated Campbell stronghold stands on a promontory guarding Dunstaffnage Bay, where the waters of Loch Etive join those of the Firth of Lorne, and is easily reached from the Oban to Connel road. The four-sided structure has three round towers, and dates probably from the 15th cent., some of the walls being 10 ft. thick. In 1746, Flora Macdonald was imprisoned here, and Scott introduced the Castle into his "Legend of Montrose" and "Lord of the Isles." A brass gun from a Spanish galleon, wrecked in Tobermory Bay, is preserved on the battlements. The site is said to have been the seat of early Scottish government in the time of the original kingdom of Dalriada, before the union with the Picts. The famous Coronation Stone, formerly held here, was later removed to *Scone* (*q.v.*). The Chapel near the Castle is now the burial-place of the Campbells of Dunstaffnage, and is perhaps of 13th cent. date. See **Forteviot**. *Iter. 110, 117, 124, 125, 144, 145.*

DUNSYRE, Lanark. Map 9, NT 0 4.
The mansion of *Newholm* has Covenanting associations. Dunsyre Church retains the old jougs and in the churchyard are interesting gravestones. To the south rises *Black Mount*, 1,689 ft.

DUNTOCHER, Dunbarton. 2,960. Map 8, NS 4 7.
An ancient bridge is situated here. Northwards rise the *Kilpatrick* hills, with their numerous small lochs, or reservoirs. *Iter. 100, 101, 102, 113.*

DUNTULM, Isle of Skye, Inverness. Map 22, NG 4 7.
The ruins of *Duntulm Castle* are situated near the extremity of the Trotternish peninsula, in the far north of the island, and overlook Duntulm Island, in the bay of that name. The Castle was formerly a stronghold of the Macdonalds of the Isles, and was the successor to *Dunscaith Castle*, near *Isle Ornsay* (*q.v.*). Away to the north-west, beyond the waters of the Minch, rise the hills of Harris, in the Outer Hebrides. To the north of Duntulm, beyond the shores of Score Bay, is the promontory of Rudha Hunish, at the northern extremity of Skye. *Iter. 254.*

DUNURE, Ayr. Map 8, NS 2 1.
A small fishing village and resort with sandy shores, situated to the south-west of the Heads of Ayr, and lying slightly to the west of the Ayr to Girvan road. There are fragmentary remains of the former Castle on the cliffs, and an old dove-cote is preserved. In the background, inland, is *Brown Carrick Hill*, 940 ft., a good viewpoint. **2 m. S.**, on the Girvan road, is *Croy Brae*, better known as the "Electric Brae," where a curious optical illusion is created that the road descends, whereas, in effect, it is ascending, this being due to certain factors in the configuration of the land on either side of the road. A car which is stopped on this stretch of road will start to roll backwards, although appearing to be facing a descent. Away to the south-west are *Croy* sands, at the northern extremity of *Culzean* (*q.v.*) Bay. *Iter. 49.*

DUNURE MAINS, Ayr. Map 8, NS 2 1.
See **Dunure**. *Iter. 49, 80.*

DUNVEGAN, Isle of Skye, Inverness. Map 22, NG 2 4.
The famous Castle of *Dunvegan* stands at the head of the island-studded Loch Dunvegan, between the Vaternish and Duirinish peninsulas. Near it, to the south, is the pleasant village, to the south-east of which lies the ruined Church of *Duirinish*. The Castle, which is shown Mon. to Fri., 2 to 5, May to mid-Oct. (see note page 90), is entered by a bridge spanning the former moat, and dates from the 15th to 19th cents., much of it having been restored. It has long been the seat of the Macleod of Macleod. In the 15th cent. tower is the dungeon, while the south tower, of early 16th cent. date, contains the Fairy Room, the towers having been linked in the 17th cent. by the 12th Chief, known as Rory More. Among the Castle's treasures are Rory More's drinking horn; a richly carved Irish Communion Cup; relics of Prince Charles Edward; letters from Dr. Johnson and Scott; and, most priceless of all, the "Fairy Flag" of Dunvegan.

A memorial Cairn to the MacCrimmons, the hereditary pipers to the Macleods, stands **8 m. N.W.**, at *Boreraig*, where a piping College once stood. This clachan lies on a by-road traversing the western shores of Loch Dunvegan, beyond which is Dunvegan Head, with black cliffs 100 ft. in height. To the south-west of the head are lonely cliffs reaching a height of nearly 1,000 ft. Another by-road diverges to the west, about half-way along the loch, and leads to the head of Loch Pooltiel and Glen Dale, continuing thence towards Waterstein Head, 966 ft., in Moonen Bay, with some of the finest cliff scenery in Skye, accessible only on foot. Beyond the Head is Neist Point, the most westerly in Skye, with its lonely lighthouse in a splendid setting of cliffs overlooking the Little Minch. South-west of Dunvegan are the twin flat-topped hills known as *Macleod's Tables*, both around 1,600 ft. high, which form notable landmarks in the Duirinish peninsula, and overlook Loch Bracadale, to the east. Beyond these two hills the peninsula narrows to terminate in Idrigill Point, near which, off the coast, are the trio of isolated stacks of basalt rock known as *Macleod's Maidens*. See **Trumpan**. *Iter. 255.*

DURISDEER, Dumfries. Map 3, NS 8 0.
This tiny hamlet lies to the east of Nithsdale, under a lofty ridge of green Lowland hills, and a little to the east of the Thornhill to Crawford road. An ancient path, known as the Well Path, possibly part of a Roman Road, leads north-eastwards through the hills towards the Dalveen Pass. The striking little Church dates from 1699, and is noted for its elaborate *Queensberry* monuments, including some work by John Nost. In the churchyard is the "factor's stone," where the children of John Lukup, a Queensberry master of works in 1685, were buried. There is also a Martyr's Stone to a Covenanter shot in 1685. See **Enterkinfoot**. *Iter. 25, 26.*

DURNESS, Sutherland. 413. Map 28, NE 4 6.
E.C. Wed. One of the most northerly localities in Scotland, the village of *Durness*, the nearest place to *Cape Wrath* (*q.v.*), is situated on Sango Bay. To the north extends a narrow and level peninsula terminating in Fair Aird, or Far Out Head, reached on foot, and providing notable coast views. A little to the north-west of Durness, overlooking the sandy shores of Balnakeil Bay, stands the roofless old *Balnakeil* Church, dating from 1619, and preserving an old font and the quaintly-carved monument of Donald Makmurchou. Also buried here is Robert Donn, the illiterate "Burns of the North." A nearby 18th cent. house, now a farm, was once a residence of the Bishops of Caithness. In the vicinity of

Dunstaffnage Castle, Argyll. Remains of the mainly 15th century Castle, where Flora Macdonald was imprisoned for a period of 10 days during 1746 before she was taken to London

Duntocher, Dunbarton. The old twin-arched bridge, in its wooded setting

Dunure, Ayr. The ancient dovecote by the ruined Castle. The Commendator of Crossraguel Abbey was twice nearly roasted to death in the castle by the fourth Earl of Cassillis, in 1570, before surrendering his lands

Dunvegan, Isle of Skye, Inverness. The restored 15th to 19th century Castle of the Macleods, in which is kept the famous 'Fairy Flag' of Dunvegan. Dr. Johnson and Boswell came here during their tour of 1773

Durisdeer, Dumfries. The notable Queensberry monument in the Church. It was designed by John Nost, early in the 18th century

Dunvegan, Isle of Skye, Inverness. Fairy Bridge, which in the old days had an evil reputation. It was said that no horse would cross the bridge without shying. The bridge is situated 4 miles north-east, on A850

[For DUNTOCHER see also under ROMAN WALL
(Plate 142)
[For DUNTULM see under SKYE (Plate 151)

PLATE 54 (facing page 144)

Dyce, Aberdeen. The ruined Church, in the churchyard of which is a watch-house erected to prevent body-snatchers rifling the graves. It lies 1½ miles north-west, on an unclassified road between the River Don and the railway

Dykehead, Angus. The fountain in memory of the Antarctic explorers, Captain Scott and Dr. Wilson, who reached the South Pole in 1912. It stands in Glen Prosen, on an unclassified road to the north-west

Eaglesham, Renfrew. The Church, which was built in 1790, and has an eagle for a weather-cock

East Kilbride, Lanark. An old mounting stone by the churchyard

Dysart, Fife. The doorway of a house, dated 1583, inscribed: 'My hoip is in the Lord'

[For EAST LINTON see following plate

PLATE 55 (facing page 145)

Durness are several small lochs noted for fishing. South-west of the village, the road to *Rhiconich* (*q.v.*) reaches the shores of the Kyle of Durness, and from the "*Cape Wrath*" Hotel, just off the road, a passenger ferry crosses the narrow Kyle to the Cape Wrath side, but the hire car belonging to the hotel, at times kept on the far side, is at present not available. There is an 11-mile stretch of moorland, known as The Parph, which must be traversed to reach the lonely Cape Wrath lighthouse, where the striking reddish cliffs exhibit rugged scenery. See **Smoo Cave**. *Iter. 225, 229*.

DUROR, Argyll.   Map 18, **NM 9** 5.
A small *Appin* (*q.v.*) clachan, in the vicinity of which the famous Appin murder was committed, in 1752, for which James Stewart, whose home was at the nearby farm of Acharn, was tried at *Inveraray* (*q.v.*), and unjustly hanged at *Ballachulish* (*q.v.*). **2 m. S.W.**, on the shores of *Loch Linnhe* (*q.v.*), is the ruined kirk of *Keil*, where James Stewart lies, and is commemorated by a tablet. *Iter. 124*.

DURRIS, Kincardine.   Map 21, **NO 7** 9.
Iter. 168, 174.

DUTHIL, Inverness.   Map 25, **NH 9** 2.
Iter. 195.

DYCE, Aberdeen. 809.   Map 27, **NH 8** 1.
The airport for Aberdeen is situated here. The village lies west of the River Don, and farther away to the west is *Tyrebagger Hill*, 823 ft., a good viewpoint, with indicators. There are prehistoric remains on the slopes of the hill. **1½ m. N.W.**, on the west bank of the river, is the ruined Church, in the churchyard of which are preserved two sculptured stones (A.M.). A watchhouse, erected a century ago, was used to prevent body-snatchers entering the precincts. *Iter. 180*.

DYKEHEAD, Angus.   Map 20, **NO 3** 6.
Situated where two roads fork, each of which proceeds northwards up one of the long and picturesque Angus glens. The right fork follows the South Esk River, and later divides into two branches, one on each side of the river, to reach *Clova Church* (*q.v.*) in Glen Clova. The left fork proceeds into the well-wooded Glen Prosen, and about a mile up the glen is a fountain, commemorating Captain Scott and Dr. Wilson, the Antarctic explorers, which is overlooked by *Tulloch Hill*, 1,230 ft., on which stands the prominent Airlie monument. The road continues up the beautiful glen, shortly afterwards accompanied by the Prosen Water, for about seven miles, before terminating near Glen Prosen Lodge, beyond which a path leads into the lonely eastern Grampian hills in the Braes of Angus, dominated by *Mayar*, 3,043 ft. See **Cortachy** and **Kirriemuir**. *Iter. 161*.

DYKEND, Angus.   Map 20, **NO 2** 5.
Here, roads from Alyth and Kirriemuir converge at the entrance to the delightful Glen Isla, with the River Isla flowing a little to the west. *Creigh Hill*, 1,630 ft., rises to the north-east, and **2⅓ m. S.E.**, on the Kirriemuir road, is Loch Lintrathen, a reservoir for Dundee's water supply. See **Bridge of Craig**. *Iter. 160, 162*.

DYSART, Fife.   Map 17, **NT 2** 9.
E.C. Wed. This picturesque little Royal Burgh, with its old houses, is now united with *Kirkcaldy* (*q.v.*). The Tolbooth dates from 1576, and was damaged by Cromwell's soldiers. The ruined Church of *St. Serf* carries the date 1570, and has

a fortress-like tower. In the vicinity of the church stands an old house, with a courtyard, carrying an inscription and the date 1583. See **Kirkcaldy** (for Town Plan) and **Pathhead** (Fife). *Iter. 128*.

EAGLESHAM, Renfrew. 1,906.   Map 8, **NS 5** 5.
GOLF. An 18th cent. village, the creation of the 12th Earl of Eglinton, with a number of houses dating from late in the period. The Parish Church of 1790 has an eagle on the spire. In the churchyard is a Covenanter's monument. *Eaglesham* achieved fame during the Second World War, when Rudolf Hess, the deputy German Fuehrer, made his sensational 1941 landing from the air in the vicinity. To the south-west, traversed by the Kilmarnock road, is Eaglesham Moor, over 900 ft. high, providing wide views. Beyond the Lochgoin reservoir, across the Ayrshire border, is a Covenanter's monument to John Howie, erected in 1896. The nearby farmhouse contains interesting Covenanting relics. *Iter. 19*.

EARLISH, Isle of Skye, Inverness.   Map 22, **NG 3** 6.
Iter. 254.

EARLSFERRY, Fife. 924. SB. with Elie.   Map 17, **NO 4** 0.
See **Elie**.

EARLSHALL, Fife.   Map 17, **NO 4** 2.
See **Leuchars**.

EARLSTON, Berwick. 1,200.   Map 10, **NT 5** 3.
E.C. Wed. Lies in the pleasant Lauderdale valley, threaded by the Leader Water, and was once named *Ercildoune*. To the south of the town stands part of the ancient *Rhymer's Tower*, associated with the almost legendary "Thomas the Rhymer," a 13th cent. poet and prophet. In Earlston Church is a stone inscribed "Auld Rymer's Tace lies in this place." **1 m. S.** of the town, near the Leader Water, is the 16th cent. and later house of *Cowdenknowes*, associated with the Border family of Home in old ballads. *Iter. 4, 7, 13, 33, 36, 41, 43*.

EAS-COUL-AULIN, Sutherland.   Map 28, **NC 2** 2.
See **Kylesku**.

EASDALE, ISLE OF, Argyll.   Map 13, **NM 7** 1.
See **Clachan Bridge**.

EASSIE, Angus.   Map 17, **NO 3** 4.
In the churchyard is a fine example of a sculptured stone, inscribed with a cross and some Pictish symbols (A.M.). *Iter. 151, 153*.

EAST CALDER, Midlothian. 1,374.   Map 9, **NT 0** 6.
Iter. 18, 19, 20, 22.

EASTER ROSS, Ross and Cromarty.
                    Map 25, **NH 5** 6 etc.
                    and 31, **NH 7** 8 etc.
The name given to the rather flat, eastern part of the county, between the Dornoch and Cromarty Firths and once known as Cromarty. It forms a striking contrast to the wilder and more picturesque *Wester Ross* (*q.v.*) district. See **Cromarty, Dingwall** and **Dornoch**.

EAST KILBRIDE, Lanark. 17,000.   Map 8, **NS 6** 5.
E.C. Wed. GOLF. Has been chosen as one of the new towns, incorporating extensive research laboratories, and is noted also for dairy-farming. In the vicinity were born the brothers Hunter, 18th cent. anatomists, now commemorated by a monument. The first Scottish Society of Friends meeting took place here, in 1653. The Church has a 19th cent. "crown" tower and the date 1774 is carved above the tower entrance. Near the churchyard is an old mounting-stone. There is an 18th cent. *Stuart* mausoleum. At *Mount Cameron* farm lived Jean Cameron, associated with Prince Charles Edward and the '45. **1 m. N.** is the ruined *Mains Castle*, probably of early 16th cent. date. *Iter. 18, 19, 29, 56*.

EAST LINTON, East Lothian. 950. SB.   Map 10, **NT 5** 7.
E.C. Wed. An old-world village on the River Tyne, which flows here through a miniature gorge, and is crossed by a 16th cent. bridge. John Rennie, the famous engineer and bridge builder, was born in 1761 in the mansion of *Phantassie*,

to the east. The Rennie memorial is situated beside the East Linton by-pass road. To the north of the village is the little Church of *Prestonkirk*, erected in 1770, but retaining the interesting 13th cent. square-ended chancel from its predecessor, and now used as a mortuary Chapel. There is also a 17th cent. tower. **2 m. S.W.**, near the Tyne, is the ruined 13th to 15th cent. *Hailes Castle* (A.M.), preserving its original water-gate and dungeons, and associated with Mary, Queen of Scots. It was dismantled by Cromwell in 1650. Open summer 10 to 7, winter 10 to 4; Sun., from 2. (See note page 90). To the south of the Castle rises *Traprain Law*, 724 ft., where excavations, in 1919, revealed a hoard of Roman silver, now in the National Museum of Antiquities, Edinburgh. *Preston Mill* (N.T. Scot.), on the river bank near East Linton, dates from the 17th cent., and can be inspected. See **Athelstaneford, Whitekirk** and **Whittinghame**. *Iter.* 1, 40.

EAST MEY, Caithness. Map 30, ND 3 7.
Near Mey Bay, to the north-west, is *Castle of Mey*, formerly Barrogill Castle, dated 1606, and now the property of Her Majesty, Queen Elizabeth, the Queen Mother. To the north of East Mey is St. John's Point and the dangerous reef known as the " Merry Men of Mey," overlooking the Pentland Firth, with Stroma Island lying off-shore beyond the Inner Sound. See **Canisbay**. *Iter.* 240.

EAST NEUK, Fife. Map 17, NO 6 1.
The name given to the extreme eastern corner of the county, around Fife Ness. It includes several of the picturesque, small coastal Royal Burghs and villages of Fife. See **Crail, Pittenweem** and **St. Monance**.

EASTRIGGS, Dumfries. Map 4, NY 2 6.
Iter. 26, 27, 28, 42, 67.

EAST SALTON, East Lothian. 141. Map 10, NT 4 6.
At *Salton Hall*, to the north-west, was born, in 1653, Andrew Fletcher of Saltoun, the well-known Scottish patriot. The Hall is mainly modern, but retains a 17th cent. nucleus. The village was the first place in Britain to weave fine hollands, and the first in Scotland to produce pot barley. Salton Mill, near the station, is of late 17th cent. date. See **Pencaitland**. *Iter.* 3.

EAST WEMYSS, Fife. 3,528. Map 17, NT 3 9.
GOLF. A small coal-port on a rocky stretch of coast, with caves, or " weems," including the Glass Cave, situated to the south-west in the direction of *West Wemyss* (*q.v.*). Just beyond East Wemyss, to the north-east, is the massive ruin of *Macduff's Castle*, with an old dovecote nearby. *Iter.* 128.

ECCLEFECHAN, Dumfries. 611. Map 4, NY 1 7.
E.C. Thurs. The birthplace, in 1795, of Thomas Carlyle, who described the village in his " Sartor Resartus " under the name of " Entepfuhl." The house (N.T. Scot.) in which he was born, known as the " Arched House," is built over a pend, and contains personal relics. Open weekdays, 10 to 8 or sunset. (See page 90). A Carlyle statue stands in the village, and in the churchyard are the graves of the author and his parents. Archibald Arnott, who was doctor to Napoleon at St. Helena, is also buried in the churchyard. See **Dunscore, Hoddom Bridge, Kirtlebridge** and **Lockerbie**. *Iter.* 10, 13, 29, 50, 51.

ECCLES, Berwick. Map 11, NT 7 4.
There are slight remains of a Cistercian convent, burnt in 1545. A tall Cross stands by the road to the south-west of Crosshall Farm. *Iter.* 39, 46.

ECHT, Aberdeen. Map 21, NJ 7 0.
To the north-west is the Barmekin of Echt, an isolated hill, crowned by prehistoric fortifications. **1½ m. W.**, near *Sunhoney* farm, is the stone circle of *Cullerlie* (A.M.), dating probably from the late Bronze Age. See **Dunecht** and **Midmar Castle**. *Iter.* 179, 197.

ECKFORD CHURCH, Roxburgh. Map 11, NT 7 2.
Stands on the east bank of the River Teviot. The Church still preserves the jougs of 1718, and also the old watch-house in the churchyard. The Kale Water joins the Teviot at this point. See **Morebattle** and **Oxnam**. *Iter.* 30, 47.

EDDERTON, Ross and Cromarty. 432. Map 31, NH 7 8.
To the north-east are Edderton Sands, an inlet of the Dornoch Firth. The little Church dates from 1793. See **Fearn**. *Iter.* 201.

EDDLESTON, Peebles. 484. Map 10, NT 2 4.
E.C. Thurs. A hamlet in the valley of the Eddleston Water, overlooked to the east by the *Moorfoot* hills, with *Blackhope Scar* rising to 2,136 ft., and to the west by the lower *Cloich* hills. *Darnhall*, a 17th cent. house, and formerly a seat of the Murrays, is now the " *Black Barony* " Hotel. In the vicinity are the pre-historic Milkieston Rings. On the Peebles road, to the south, a tablet commemorates George Kemp (1795–1844) who designed the well known Scott Monument at Edinburgh. **2½ m. N.N.E.**, in the hills, is Portmore Loch, at a height of 1,000 ft. A narrow road leads south-westwards from Eddleston, and climbs between the twin *Meldon* hills to descend into Tweeddale. See **Walkerburn**. *Iter.* 24, 40.

EDDRACHILLIS CHURCH, Sutherland.
Map 28, NC 1 4.
Overlooks Badcall Bay, an inlet of the larger island-studded Eddrachillis Bay. Inland, across a landscape of many tiny lochans, rises the sharp gneiss cone of *Ben Stack*, 2,364 ft. The rough and hilly road leading south-eastwards towards the ferry at *Kylesku* (*q.v.*) passes near the shores of the little Calva Bay, with its two islands off-shore, and then turns inland by Loch Allt nan Airbhe. See **Scourie**. *Iter.* 225.

EDINBAIN, Isle of Skye, Inverness. Map 22, NG 3 5.
By the head of Loch Greshornish, at the southern extremity of the Vaternish peninsula, with a background of lonely moors. **4 m. N.E.**, on the Portree road, are the shores of Loch Snizort Beag. *Iter.* 255.

EDINBURGH, Midlothian. 465,671. Map 10, NT 2 7.
E.C. Tues./Wed./Sat. MD. Tues./Wed. GOLF.
The capital of Scotland, and the second largest in population, a city whose beauty, interest and historic associations are alike famous, the Royal Burgh of *Edinburgh* owes not a little to its superb natural setting, overlooked by the dominating mass of Arthur's Seat, a mountain in miniature, with the prominent Salisbury Crags on its lower flanks. To the south of the city's outskirts, and well seen from Arthur's Seat, is the long range of the Pentland Hills, approaching 2,000 ft. in height, and providing a splendid playground for the citizens of Edinburgh. The waters of the Firth of Forth wash the outer boundaries of the city, and here is situated the important port of *Leith*, incorporated since 1920 within the administration of the parent city. Edinburgh itself has been not inaptly described as the modern Athens, while the name " Auld Reekie," by which it is sometimes affectionately known, is a reference to the smoke curling upwards from its chimneys. The city is a great centre of education, noted for the University, and a number of well-known schools, among which are the Royal High School, the Academy, Fettes, Loretto, Heriot's and Donaldson's Hospitals, and George Watson's, Stewart's and Merchiston Colleges. Its varied industries include both printing and brewing, but it is essentially as a showplace that the fame of Edinburgh has resounded throughout the world. The outline of the historic Castle, on its rocky site 445 ft. high above the former Nor' Loch, now drained and occupied by pleasant gardens, through which runs the railway to the great Waverley Station, may be said to divide the historic Old Town from the New Town, the latter of which dates mainly from the 18th cent.

The Old Town descends eastwards along the ridge from the Castle, its most noteworthy feature being the historic " Royal Mile," commencing with Castle Hill and the Lawnmarket. This is succeeded by the longer High Street and Canongate, with its picturesque multi-storeyed houses and quaint Closes, or Wynds. At the foot are the portals of the Palace of Holyroodhouse, backed by the Salisbury Crags below Arthur's Seat.

The late 18th cent. New Town is dignified by broad and stately streets and squares, among which George Street and Charlotte Square are perhaps the finest, and some of the most characteristic buildings of the great Georgian architect

East Linton, East Lothian. The memorial to the engineer and architect, John Rennie. He was born at the mansion of Phantassie near here in 1761

East Neuk, Fife. The Sauchope Stone, an inscribed standing stone. It stands in the Victoria Gardens at Crail, a Royal Burgh at the extremity of the Fife coast, which is known as the East Neuk

East Salton, East Lothian. The 17th century mill, commenced by Fletcher of Saltoun, the Scottish patriot

Ecclefechan, Dumfries. The birthplace (N.T. Scot. in 1785 of Thomas Carlyle

Eccles, Berwick. An ancient wheel-headed Cross near Crosshall Farm

Eddleston, Peebles. The memorial on A703, to the south, in memory of George Kemp, who served as an apprentice here. He later designed the Scott Monument (1840–44) in Edinburgh *(see following plate)*

[For EDINBURGH see Plates 57 to 61 and also 174
[For EAST LINTON see also under LOTHIANS (Plate 17)
[For EDDRACHILLIS see under HIGHLANDS (Plate 84)

PLATE 56 (facing page 146)

The Monument to Sir Walter Scott, the work of George Kemp between 1840 and 1844. It stands in Princes Street Gardens See Eddleston (Plate 56)

Easter Coates, one of the 17th century houses engulfed by the expanding city. It is now used as a choir school by St. Mary's Cathedral

The tower (1495) of St. Giles' Church, with its 'crown' steeple, the finest of the three examples to be found in Scotland

A tablet on the 'Old Tolbooth' of the former Water of Leith village. The inscription reads: 'God Bless the Baxters of Edinbrugh uho built this hous 1675'

A boy's head and scroll at the entrance to Paisley Close, High Street. The boy was the sole survivor when the original house fell in 1861. The scroll reads: 'Heave awa chaps, I'm no dead yet'

The fountain in memory of Greyfriars Bobby, a terrier who watched over his master's grave from 1858 to 1872. It stands in Candlemaker Row, near the Greyfriars Church

PLATE 57 (facing page 147)

[For EDINBURGH see also Plates 58 to 61 and 174

Robert Adam grace the district. In George Street are the Assembly Rooms of 1787 and Music Hall of 1843, in which Paderewski and Pachmann gave piano recitals; Dickens and Thackeray lectured; and Gladstone addressed political meetings. Most famous of all is the splendid avenue of *Princes Street*, with its array of shops, clubs and hotels on the north side. Its south side is noted for the unique vista over the beautifully-tended Princes Street Gardens, with the prominent *Scott Monument*, the Scottish-American War Memorial, and the well-known *Floral Clock*, with the guardian bastion of the Castle rising in the background. Away beyond the eastern end of Princes Street lies Calton Hill, with its notable group of buildings, dominated by the unfinished *National Monument*.

Among the city's parks, that of Blackford, the oldest, lies on the 300-ft. high Blackford Hill, where the Royal Observatory is situated. The view from here was described by Scott in his "Marmion." The Royal Botanic Garden and Arboretum, which contains an attractive Rock Garden, lies on the way to Granton, and to the west of the Arboretum is Inverleith Park. Farther to the south-west, in the Corstorphine direction, are the *Murrayfield* Rugby Football Ground and the Zoological Park, the latter on the slopes of Corstorphine Hill.

Although Holyrood Abbey was already founded in 1128, the early history of Edinburgh is bound up mainly with that of its ancient Castle, which is described separately below. The city superseded Perth as Scotland's capital in 1437, and was ravaged both in 1544 and 1547 by Henry VIII. In the 17th cent., it played a part in the religious and civil struggles of the period, among the events which took place in Edinburgh being the occupation of the city in 1650 by Cromwell, and the executions, in 1650 and 1661, of the Marquis of Montrose and the Marquis of Argyll. The Scottish Parliament ceased to function after the amalgamation of Scotland with England in 1707, and the unfortunate Porteous Riots of 1736 reflected this loss of privilege. Prince Charles Edward held a gay, but brief, court at Holyroodhouse in 1745, while later in the century, and during the commencement of the one following, the limelight became focused principally on Edinburgh's literary activities. Many famous names are associated with the city, both Sir Walter Scott and Robert Louis Stevenson having been born within its boundaries. Of Scott's several Edinburgh homes, perhaps the best known is 39 Castle Street, where many of the Waverley novels were written. A modern development, which has added increased lustre to the city's world-wide renown, is the establishment, since 1947, of the Edinburgh International Festival of Art, Drama and Music, which takes place annually in the late summer, the concerts being held in the Usher Hall and the Freemasons' Hall. Opera, ballet, plays and a military tattoo are other features of the Festival. The city airport lies some 7 m. W., at *Turnhouse*, off the road to Glasgow. In order to appreciate fully the many places of interest in Edinburgh, outstanding among which are the Castle, the Palace of Holyroodhouse, the Church of St. Giles and the picturesque Royal Mile in the Old Town, the purchase of a detailed guide-book, of which many are available, is strongly advised. The majority of the principal buildings are described briefly below, together with times of admission where available (see note page 90). The racecourse is situated 6 m. E., at *Musselburgh* (q.v.).

The most notable nearby physical feature of Edinburgh is the 822-ft. high *Arthur's Seat*, together with the Salisbury Crags on its lower slopes, which rises almost directly above Holyroodhouse, and is easily climbed from various points. The view from the summit is superb, and includes the city itself, the *Pentland* hills, and also the distant coast of Fife. On the lower slopes of the hill are St. Margaret's Well, the remains of St. Anthony's Chapel, and also the tiny St. Margaret's and Dunsappie Lochs. The hill is encircled by Holyrood Park, around the perimeter of which extends the beautiful Queen's Drive, which, itself, provides beautiful views across *Duddingston* loch and village, and also towards *Craigmillar Castle*. The Water of Leith flows along the western side

of the city and is spanned by the Dean Bridge, built by Telford. Farther upstream is the picturesque village of *Dean*. Downstream, near *Stockbridge*, is a curious Doric temple covering *St. Bernard's Well*, which was erected in 1789. Some of the more interesting of the outer districts of the city have been described separately in the gazetteer, these being: *Barnton, Colinton, Corstorphine, Craigmillar Castle, Duddingston, Fairmilehead, Granton, Hillend, Leith, Liberton, Newhaven* and *Portobello*. The famous *Forth Bridge*, situated 8 m. W.N.W. of the city centre, is described under *Queensferry, South*.

CATHEDRALS AND CHURCHES

CHURCH OF ST. GILES. The finest of the city's Churches, erected largely in the 14th and 15th cents., the tower dating from c. 1495 and being surmounted by the famous "Crown" steeple, the finest of the three surviving examples in Scotland. The others are the Tolbooth at *Glasgow* (q.v.) and King's College Chapel, *Aberdeen* (q.v.). Many of the Church's altars and precious relics were destroyed in 1556, and in 1559 John Knox became minister of St. Giles, the building being later subdivided at one period into as many as four Churches. Under Charles I, in 1663, St. Giles obtained for a short period Cathedral status, and in 1637 occurred the notorious incident of a stool being thrown at the Dean for reading the service from Laud's book. Again under Charles II St. Giles became a Cathedral, but lost the rank finally in 1688. Considerable and damaging restorations took place in the 19th cent. The latest addition is Sir Robert Lorimer's fine, ornate Thistle Chapel, which dates from 1911. In the Chepman aisle lie the remains of the great Marquis of Montrose, and both the Moray and Albany aisles are of considerable interest. The colours of the Scottish regiments hang in the nave, and by the wall of the Preston aisle is the Royal pew. A side chapel beyond the south transept contains a monument to R. L. Stevenson, who is buried in Samoa, and in St. Elio's Chapel is a monument to the Covenanter Marquis of Argyll.

ST. MARY'S CATHEDRAL. This imposing, three-towered structure, carrying a 276-ft. high spire, was designed by Sir Gilbert Scott and commenced in 1874, though not finally completed until 1917. Nearby stands the attractive small mansion of *Easter Coates*, built in c. 1615 by John Byres, and probably the oldest house in the New Town. It is now used as the choir school.

GREYFRIARS CHURCH. This Church was built originally in 1612, and was altered a century later, being for long divided into two parts. In 1936, the building was restored and made into a single Church. Copies of Covenanters' flags hang above the pillars. The Greyfriars Churchyard has historic associations, the National Covenant having been signed here in 1638, while, in 1679, some 1,200 Covenanter prisoners were confined here after the battle of *Bothwell Brig* (q.v.), and are commemorated by the Martyrs' Memorial. Many eminent personages are buried in the graveyard, including Captain Porteous, Regent Morton and Allan Ramsay. Nearby, in Candlemaker Row, is a fountain in memory of "Greyfriars Bobby," a faithful Edinburgh terrier of 1858, who lingered near his master's grave for 14 years.

TRON CHURCH. Dates from 1637 to 1663, and owes its name to a public "tron," or weighing beam, situated nearby. The stone steeple, erected in 1824, replaced the former wooden one which was burnt. Hogmanay, or New Year, is celebrated annually outside the Church.

ST. GEORGE'S CHURCH. An imposing structure in the Georgian Charlotte Square (see page 150), of which the north side is one of Robert Adam's best works. The church was built in 1811 by Robert Reid in the Graeco-Roman style and incorporates a dome.

MAGDALEN CHAPEL. Founded in 1547, under the patronage of the guild of Hammermen, and preserving the founder's tomb. Outstanding in the Chapel is the notable pre-Reformation stained glass, while the little

CENTRAL EDINBURGH

A.A. OFFICE, FANUM HOUSE, 20/22 Melville Street.   Telephone: CALedonian 6591.   Telegrams: "FANUM EDINBURGH"

Assembly Rooms
1. Camera Obscura
2. Castle and Scottish National War Memorial
3. City Chambers
4. Edinburgh Festival Office
5. Floral Clock
6.

7. Freemasons' Hall
8. Greyfriars Church and Greyfriars Bobby Fountain
9. Holyroodhouse, with ruined Abbey
10. Huntly House

11. John Knox's House
12. National Gallery
13. National Monument and Nelson Monument
14. National Portrait Gallery and Museum of Antiquities

15. Scottish Tourist Board
16. (Government Offices)
17. New University
18. Old University
19. Parliament House
20. Register House

21. Royal Scottish Museum
22. St. Andrew's House
23. St. Giles' Church and Mercat Cross
24. St. Mary's Episcopal Cathedral

25. St. Mary's R.C. Cathedral
26. Scott Monument
27. Tolbooth (Canongate)
28. Usher Hall
29. White Horse Close, with 17th cent. "White Horse" Inn

Scale

Heriot's Hospital School (1628–93), founded by
George Heriot, the 'Jingling Geordie' of Sir Walter
Scott's *Fortunes of Nigel*

Originally this figure on a roof in Ramsay Gardens was a
representation of 'Auld Nick' complete with wings and
horns, but erosion has eaten these away to give now the
appearance of a cat

The Canongate Tolbooth, in the 'Royal Mile,'
dating from 1591 and once used as a prison.
It is an interesting survival of contemporary
municipal architecture.

Metal plates, marking
where the Flodden
Wall once stood, let
into the roadway at
the crossing of High
Street, Jeffrey's Street
and St. Mary's Street

The so-called John Knox's House, 16th century, built
reputedly by the goldsmith to Mary, Queen of Scots

The tablet on a 17th century house in Bible Land (187–197
Canongate), facing Moray House

PLATE 58 (facing page 148)   [For EDINBURGH see also Plates 57, 59 to 61 and 174

The site of the Old Tolbooth, the 'Heart of Midlothian,' which was stormed in the 1736 Porteous Riots, and demolished in 1817. It is situated near the Mercat Cross in the High Street of the Old Town (see below)

No. 11 Picardy Place, where Sir Arthur Conan Doyle, the creator of 'Sherlock Holmes,' was born in 1859. The name Picardy recalls a settlement here of French weavers employed by the British Linen Company in the 18th century

The cannon ball embedded in a side gable of the 17th century Cannon Ball House, on Castle Hill, near the Castle. It is sometimes said to have been fired in the 1745 Jacobite Rising

THIS TREE WAS PLANTED BY MARY QUEEN OF SCOTS ABOUT 1561

The remains of a tree planted by Mary, Queen of Scots, about 1561, at Little France, where her French attendants lived. It stands on the Old Dalkeith road (A68), about 3 miles from the city centre

The modern Mercat Cross, from which Royal Proclamations are read. Part of the ancient shaft was restored in 1885 by Mr. Gladstone

The Stevenson Memorial House, in Howard Place, where Robert Louis Stevenson was born in 1850. It contains relics and books associated with the writer

[For EDINBURGH see also Plates 57, 58, 60, 61 and 174

PLATE 59 (facing page 149)

ENVIRONS OF EDINBURGH

NORTH BERWICK   BERWICK UPON TWEED   To A.1   LAUDER

Scale
0 ¼ ½ 1 2 3 Mls.

REFERENCE

Route avoiding City Centre
A.A. Recommended Routes
Other Roads
A.A. Telephone Boxes

*The area within the dotted line indicates
area of large scale plan.*

CROWN COPYRIGHT RESERVED   DRAWN AND PUBLISHED BY THE AUTOMOBILE ASSOCIATION   8/59   1074

S. QUEENSFERRY   LINLITHGOW   MID CALDER   CARNWATH
GLASGOW

steeple dates from 1618 to 1628. The building was at one period used as a mortuary, and in 1685 the body of the Earl of Argyll was taken here after he had been executed. The Chapel is now situated within the premises of the Edinburgh Medical Missionary Society, and ranks as one of the oldest surviving structures in the city. Open daily.

FAMOUS BUILDINGS

EDINBURGH CASTLE (A.M.), the most notable landmark in the city, overlooks Princes Street and the picturesque streets of the Old Town. The history of the Castle goes back to legendary times, and the building has changed hands on a number of occasions, being taken by Edward I in 1296, re-fortified later by Edward III, and captured by the Scots in 1341. In 1573, much damage was caused when Mary, Queen of Scots lost the fortress to the Regent Morton, and Cromwell took the castle in 1650. Prince Charles Edward, though occupying the city, failed to capture this key-point in 1745. In Argyll's Tower is the dungeon where the Marquis of Argyll was confined before his execution in 1661. The view from the King's Bastion is exceedingly fine, and from the Half-moon Battery, built in 1573, royal salutes are fired, and a time gun is fired daily at 1 p.m. The restored Chapel of *St. Margaret*, commemorating the Saintly Queen Margaret, who died in 1093, is one of Scotland's oldest ecclesiastical buildings, being mainly of Norman date, and has an enriched chancel arch. Facing the Chapel is *Mons Meg*, an ancient cannon, said to have been made in 1486, at Mons in Belgium. On the north side of Palace Yard is the very impressive *Scottish National War Memorial* designed by Sir Thomas Lorimer, and opened in 1927, considered one of the finest of modern inspirations. The Old Palace, 15th to 17th cent., contains the Crown Room in which the Regalia of Scotland are kept. (See **Dunnottar Castle** and **Kinneff**.) Queen Mary's Apartments contain relics, and the Old Parliament, or Banqueting Hall, is historically famous, and is now an interesting armoury. The adjacent barracks contains the Scottish Naval, Military and Air Force Museum, illustrating changes in military uniforms, and including Highland weapons, models of old Scottish warships, and a collection of tartans. King David's Tower, built in 1367, and of great strength, is also of historic interest. The Castle is shown weekdays, 9.30 or 10 to 4, 5 or 6; Sun., 11 to 4, 5 or 6. At the corner of Castle Hill is the Outlook Tower, with a camera obscura, which is viewable weekdays 10 to 6.30; Sun., 12.30 to 6. On Castle Hill stands *Cannon Ball House*, dating from 1630, which has a cannon ball embedded in one of its gables. It was, by tradition, fired during the '45 Rising, but this is hardly likely to have been the case. The ancient *Flodden Wall* descended originally from the castle, and parts of it, including a tower, are still to be seen in the Vennel, which ascends southwards in steps beyond the Grassmarket towards *Heriot's Hospital School* (See page 151).

PALACE OF HOLYROODHOUSE (A.M.). Scotland's premier Royal Palace, and a structure of poignant memories, was commenced c. 1500 by James IV, the work being continued by James V. In 1544 and 1547 serious damage was caused and from 1561 to 1567, Mary, Queen of Scots was in residence for 6 years, which ended in tragedy. Sir William Bruce made extensive alterations to the fabric from 1670 to 1679, and Prince Charles Edward held his brief court here in 1745. The historical apartments associated with Mary, Queen of Scots and Darnley are of paramount interest, in the former having taken place the Queen's famous interview with John Knox, and at a later date the stabbing of her favourite, David Rizzio. The Picture Gallery contains portraits of more than 100 Scottish Kings, painted by Jacob de Wet, 1684-86. Mary, Queen of Scots was married to Bothwell at Holyrood in 1567, and Prince Charles Edward gave a ball here in 1745, which Scott has described in his "Waverley." The State Apartments, used by the present Queen, contain notable tapestries and paintings. The Palace is shown, in the absence of the Royal Family, or Lord High Commissioner, weekdays, 9.30 or 10 to 4, 5 or 6; Sun., 11, 1 or 2 to 4, 5 or 6, the State Apart-

ments being however closed Sundays. The remains of the adjacent Abbey, the Chapel Royal, consist solely of the nave, the fine west front and the north-west tower. The Abbey was founded in 1128, but suffered severe damage, together with the Palace, in 1544 and 1547. In the Revolution of 1688, the Church was sacked, and the collapse of a roof in 1768 completed the damage. Among famous personages buried in the Chapel are David II, James II, James V, Darnley and Rizzio. In the grounds of the Palace stands *Queen Mary's Bath House*, a small, ancient tower, in which, during repairs of 1852, a richly-decorated dagger was discovered. The murderers of Rizzio are said to have escaped through this tower.

PARLIAMENT HOUSE. This building dates from 1640, but the façade was replaced in 1829. Before the union of 1707, the Scottish Parliament met here. The Courts of Justice are now held in a part of the structure behind the Parliament Hall, with its fine roof. An inscription in the pavement of Parliament Square marks the grave of John Knox, who died in 1572. Parliament House is open Mon. to Fri., 10 to 5; Sat., 10 to 1.

NATIONAL LIBRARY OF SCOTLAND, George IV Bridge. The new buildings of the library, completed in 1956, contain many rare treasures, which were formerly kept in *Parliament House*. The exhibition is open weekdays, 9.30 to 5 (Sat., 9.30 to 1); Sun., 2 to 5.

NATIONAL MONUMENT, CALTON HILL. This is situated on the 350-ft. high Calton Hill, a splendid viewpoint, and was built to commemorate the Scottish fallen in the Napoleonic campaigns. It was commenced in 1822, but owing to lack of funds was left in an incomplete state. In the vicinity stands the 102-ft. high Nelson Monument, carrying a time-ball, which is lowered daily at 1 p.m. for the benefit of mariners. The monument is open daily, 8 to dusk. The City Observatory and the Playfair Monument are other notable structures on Calton Hill, on the lower slopes of which stand the fine Royal High School buildings, the Burns Monument and *St. Andrew's House*, the administrative centre for Scotland, erected in 1937.

THE UNIVERSITY. The old buildings were designed in 1789 by Robert Adam, and completed by Playfair in 1827, while the dome dates from 1883. The library is of particular interest, and in more recent years modern extensions to the University, including the McEwan Hall, have been built. On the site of the old buildings once stood a house belonging to the Kirk o'Field, and in this house, in 1567, Darnley and his page were blown up by gunpowder. The University was actually founded in 1582, and was at one time known as the College of King James. In the vicinity, to the south, off Meadow Walk, is George Square (1766), with fine classic-style houses. No. 25 was Sir Walter Scott's home during his earlier years.

CHARLOTTE SQUARE. "Robert Adam, Architect to the Square, 1791" is the signature on the original drawings now preserved in the City Chambers. The square is pre-eminent among the architectural ensembles of Britain, and indeed Europe. It was the fitting culmination of the New Town development and to Adam's work as Scotland's greatest architect. No. 5, on the superb north side, is now the office of The National Trust for Scotland.

REGISTER HOUSE. An imposing design of 1772 by Robert Adam, the building housing the archives of Scotland and other interesting papers and relics, including the Articles of Union of 1706, with the relevant signatures. Open Mon. to Fri., 10 to 4 (Sat., 10 to 1). Nearby is East Register Street, ascending steeply to the 18th cent. St. James's Square. Robert Burns lived here in 1787.

GLADSTONE'S LAND. A fine old six-storeyed house, in the Lawnmarket, the work of Thomas Gladstone, an Edinburgh burgess, in 1620, and now N.T. Scot. It preserves Edinburgh's last arcaded ground floor and also several notable painted ceilings. Open Mon. to Fri., 10 to 5. The house is now the home of the Saltire Society. Nearby are the picturesque Riddle's Close and Macmorran's Close, the latter containing the old house of Bailie Macmorran, who was shot during a school riot in 1595.

The historic Castle, which was captured by Edward I in 1296 and re-taken by the Scots in 1341. The original name was 'Duneadain', meaning 'Fort on a slope.' It overlooks Princes Street and the Old Town

A small building, known as the Queen's Bath House, outside the Palace of Holyroodhouse. It was originally a lodge, or pavilion, and a richly decorated dagger was found here during restoration work in 1852

Remains of the Chapel Royal of Holyrood Abbey, which was sacked in 1688

The unfinished National Monument on Calton Hill, commenced in 1822 in honour of the Scottish dead in the Napoleonic campaigns

Gladstone's Land, a 16th and 17th century house in the Lawnmarket, which has been preserved by the National Trust for Scotland. It is the only building in Edinburgh to preserve its arcaded front.

The archway made from the jawbones of a whale, which stands on The Meadows, to the south of the Old Town

[For EDINBURGH see also Plates 57 to 59, 61 and 174

PLATE 60 (facing page 150)

Edinburgh, Midlothian. The inscription at the entrance to World's End Close, off the High Street, near John Knox's House. It was probably so named owing to its distance from the centre of the town when originally built

Edinburgh, Midlothian. White Horse Close, a courtyard in the 'Royal Mile,' in which is situated the restored 17th century 'White Horse Inn,' associated with Sir Walter Scott's *Waverley*

Edinburgh, Midlothian. The tablet on Huntly House, the former residence of the Marquis of Huntly, which dates from 1570 and is now a museum, including old panelling and manuscripts of Robert Burns and Sir Walter Scott

Ednam, Roxburgh. The obelisk to James Thomson, at Ferniehill, to the south, off A699. He was born at Ednam, in 1700, and wrote the words of '*Rule Britannia*'

Edzell, Angus. A memorial arch (1887) on B966, erected in memory of the 13th Earl of Dalhousie

Edrom, Berwick. The Norman entrance doorway to a burial vault at the church

[For EDINBURGH see also plates 57 to 60 and 174

PLATE 61 (facing page 151)

MERCAT CROSS. This famous Cross, facing the City Chambers in the Royal Mile, is modern, but preserves part of the ancient shaft, having been restored in 1885 by Gladstone. Royal Proclamations are read from here. The former Cross, which saw many historic events in the city, was demolished in 1756. Nearby is the site of the old Tolbooth, Scott's " Heart of Midlothian," now marked by setts and a heart-shaped design in the causeway. The old building, built originally in 1466, became later a prison, and was stormed in the Porteous Riots of 1736, being finally demolished in 1817. The well-known Advocate's Close is situated in the neighbourhood. See *Heriot's Hospital School*, below.

JOHN KNOX'S HOUSE. A picturesque 16th cent. building, thought to have been lived in by John Knox, and shown daily, 10 to 5. The house preserves old wooden galleries, and was built by the goldsmith to Mary, Queen of Scots. Nearby stood the former Netherbow, one of the old city gates, associated with the '45 Rising, and removed in 1764.

CANONGATE TOLBOOTH. One of the most fascinating old landmarks of the Royal Mile, dating from 1591, and showing a curious projecting clock, the building having been used formerly as a prison and courthouse. It is open weekdays, 10 to 5. The restored *Canongate* Church, built in 1688, and with a stag's antlers supporting a cross on the gable, stands nearby, and in the churchyard is buried Adam Smith, the famous 18th cent. economist.

MORAY HOUSE and ACHESON HOUSE. Two interesting old houses in the Royal Mile, the former, which dates from 1628, and has historic associations, preserving fine ceilings, and being used as a school, while the latter, built in 1633, possesses a quaint courtyard, and has been well restored. Facing Moray House are *Bible Land* and *Morocco Land*, both of 17th cent. date, showing interesting carvings. Adjacent is the old-world Bakehouse Close, and nearby is the site of *Panmure House*, once the home of Adam Smith (see above).

WHITE HORSE CLOSE. Perhaps the most picturesque of the various courtyards, or closes in the Royal Mile, and in which is situated the restored " White Horse " Inn, an early 17th cent. posting house, associated with Scott's " Waverley."

HERIOT'S HOSPITAL SCHOOL. This splendid structure, commenced in 1628 by William Wallace, was not completed until 1693, and was at first used as a military hospital. It was founded by George Heriot, a wealthy jeweller, and the " Jingling Geordie " of Scott's " Fortunes of Nigel." The building, which possesses a fine quadrangle, is now a well-known school. Open Mon. to Fri., 9 to 5; Sat., 9 to 1. Between Heriot's Hospital and the Castle is the *Grassmarket*, the scene of execution of many Covenanters in the 17th cent., the site of the gallows being marked by a cross in the pavement. The Porteous Riots of 1736 ended here with the hanging of Captain Porteous by a furious mob.

ART GALLERIES AND MUSEUMS

NATIONAL GALLERY. A modern building, containing a large collection of paintings of various important schools. Open weekdays, 10 to 4 or 5; Sun., 2 to 5.

ROYAL SCOTTISH ACADEMY. Founded in 1823, and originally known as the Royal Institution. An exhibition is held annually from April to August, and other collections are on view weekdays only, 10 to 9 in summer; 10 to 5 in winter, when exhibitions are held.

ROYAL SCOTTISH MUSEUM. Opened in 1866, and containing important collections of botany, zoology, geology and other subjects. Open weekdays, 10 to 5; Sun., 2 to 5. There are reliefs from the Scottish Survey, and models of famous old ships.

NATIONAL PORTRAIT GALLERY. The exterior is embellished by statues of eminent Scotsmen by native artists. There are collections of historical portraits, and also statuary. (See below. Open weekdays, 10 to 4 or 5; Sun., 2 to 5.

NATIONAL MUSEUM OF ANTIQUITIES. Housed in the same building as the National Portrait Gallery, described above. The exhibits consist of prehistoric and historic collections, illustrating the development of human life in Scotland. Among many interesting objects are relics associated with Mary, Queen of Scots, Prince Charles Edward, Sir Walter Scott, and Robert Burns. There is also a remarkable collection of antiquities excavated at Traprain Law near *East Linton* (q.v.), as well as a fine oak door from the tower of *Amisfield* (q.v.). Open weekdays, 10 to 4 or 5; Sun., after 2. The annexe at 18 Shandwick Place, known as the *Museum Gallery*, is open weekdays only, 10 to 5.

HUNTLY HOUSE: CITY MUSEUM. This fine old house, once the town residence of the Marquis of Huntly, dates from 1570, and preserves a unique timbered front. There are collections of special interest to lovers of Edinburgh, including some relics of both Burns and Scott. Open weekdays, 10 to 5; on Wed., from June to Sept., open 6 to 9.

LADY STAIR'S HOUSE. A severely restored old house, dating from 1622, and situated in Lady Stair's Close. It is now a branch of the City Museum, and contains relics of Burns, Scott and Stevenson. Open weekdays, 10 to 4; Sat., 10 to 1. During Festival period, 10 to 5.

STEVENSON MEMORIAL HOUSE. The birthplace, in 1850, of Robert Louis Stevenson, containing an interesting collection of relics, books and photographs. Open Mon. to Fri., 10 to 4; Sat., 10 to 1.

MUSEUM OF CHILDHOOD. Situated in Hyndford's Close, in the Royal Mile, and containing an exhibition of children's toys, clothes and books, made for and also by children. Open weekdays, 10 to 1 and 2.15 to 5 (except Sat. afternoon).

See also **Cramond Bridge, Currie, Dalkeith, Lasswade, Musselburgh, Pinkie House, Queensferry (South), Roslin** and **Swanston.** For " Through Routes " see page 41. *Iter. 1, 2, 3, 4, 5, 6, 7, 8, 9, 10, 11, 12, 13, 14, 15, 16, 17, 18, 19, 20, 21, 22, 23, 24, 25, 89, 90, 91, 92, 93, 94, 95, 96.*

EDNAM, Roxburgh. 412. Map 11, NT 7 3. The birthplace, in 1700, of James Thomson, who wrote the words of " Rule Britannia," and to whom an obelisk has been erected at *Ferniehill*, to the south. The village stands on the Eden Water, here spanned by a bridge, on which, in 1952, a plaque was affixed, to commemorate Henry Francis Lyte, the hymnologist, and author of " Abide with me," who was born in a nearby house. **2 m. W.** of Ednam, across the Eden Water, is the mansion of *Newton Don*, partly 17th cent. *Iter. 39, 46.*

EDROM CHURCH, Berwick. Map 11, NT 8 5. In this Church (A.M.), the *Blackadder* aisle has a tomb dated 1553. A Norman outside doorway is the entrance to a burial vault.

EDZELL, Angus. 943. Map 21, NO 6 6. E.C. Thurs. GOLF. This little inland resort lies between Strathmore and the Howe of the Mearns, and is situated just to the west of the North Esk River, which forms here the Kincardine boundary. The river flows through the attractive Glen Esk, to the north-west, which is threaded by a road penetrating as far as lonely *Lochlee* (q.v.) in the eastern Grampian, or Benchinnan mountains, with *Mount Keen*, 3,077 ft., rising in the background to the north. A little to the west of Edzell, near the West Water, a tributary of the North Esk, stands the ruined *Edzell Castle* (A.M.) of the Lindsays, preserving the fine Stirling tower, and the bower used by Mary, Queen of Scots. The most remarkable feature of the lay-out is the walled garden, dating from 1604, with its curious square recesses in the walls, perhaps unique. A turreted garden-house has also survived, and at the adjoining farm is a fine dovecote. Open 10 to 7, summer; 10 to 4, winter; Sun., from 2. (See note page 90). See **Fettercairn, Gannochy Bridge** and **Tarfside.** *Iter. 156, 163, 164.*

EGILSAY, ISLE OF, Orkney. Map 33, HY 4 2 and 4 3.
See Orkney Islands (Egilsay).

EIGG, ISLE OF, Inverness. Map 12, NM 4 8.
See Rum.

EILDON HILLS, Roxburgh. Map 10, NT 5 3.
The triple-peaked *Eildons*, attaining 1,385, 1,327 and 1,216 ft. respectively, with an indicator on the highest point, form a prominent feature in the landscape of the *Scott Country* (*q.v.*). The views from the summit are far-reaching and include a long stretch of the River Tweed. To Sir Walter Scott these hills were especially dear. See **Melrose** and **Scott's View.**

EILEAN DONAN CASTLE, Ross and Cromarty.
See **Dornie.** *Iter. 207, 220.* Map 24, NG 8 2.

ELDERSLIE, Renfrew. 3,113. Map 8, NS 4 6.
GOLF. The town is the traditional birthplace of William Wallace. A modern memorial has been erected near an old house, perhaps on the site of the patriot's former home. *Iter. 58, 63.*

ELECTRIC BRAE, Ayr. Map 8, NS 2 1.
See **Dunure.** *Iter. 49, 80.*

ELGIN, Moray. 11,423. SB. Map 26, NJ 2 6.
E.C. Wed. M.D. Fri. GOLF. The windings of the River Lossie, in the fertile Laigh of Moray, almost encircle the Royal Burgh of *Elgin*, known best for its ruined Cathedral (A.M.), one of the finest ecclesiastical monuments in Scotland. Part of the town was burned in 1390 by the notorious Wolf of Badenoch, whose castle was *Lochindorb* (*q.v.*), and who treated the Cathedral likewise, while in 1452 Elgin again suffered severely. The town was visited by Prince

Bishop's Palace	5.
Cathedral, 13th–15th cent.	1.
Grant Lodge Library	3.
Greyfriars Chapel	6.

Information Bureau, City Chambers	7.
Little Cross, restored, 17th cent.	2.
Panns Port	4.

Charles Edward before Culloden, and in 1773 Dr. Johnson and Boswell stayed there. Near *St. Giles'* Church, modern, is the rebuilt Muckle Cross, and in the High St. is the restored 17th cent. Little Cross. The 15th cent. *Greyfriars* Chapel has been restored. The Georgian *Grant Lodge* houses the Museum and Library, and the house of Duff of Braco, with its arches, dates from 1694. On Lady Hill, where stood the former castle, is the Gordon Monument. The Cathedral, once known as the " Lantern of the North," had already suffered from a serious fire before the visitation of the Wolf of Badenoch, and in the 16th and 17th cents. more disasters befell it, culminating in the fall of the central tower in 1711, after which the building became a quarry until 1807. Of the surviving portions, much work of the 13th cent. can still be

admired, notably the choir, in which is situated the founder's grave, while the nave and chapter house date from the 15th cent., the latter in a tolerably good state of preservation. A cross-slab, possibly of 6th cent. date, with strange Pictish symbols, can be seen in the choir. In the south choir aisle are several noteworthy tombs, and in the burial ground, south of the Cathedral, are numerous tombstones with quaint inscriptions. The Panns Port, or East Gate, is the sole surviving gate from the precincts, and a wing of the Bishop's Palace, dated 1406, is still standing. **5 m.** N.E. is *Innes House*, a fine mansion, built between 1640 and 1653, perhaps by the designer of *Heriot's Hospital School* at *Edinburgh* (*q.v.*). **6 m.** N. is the well-known resort of *Lossiemouth* (*q.v.*), with its harbour of *Branderburgh*. See **Birnie, Duffus, Lhanbryde, Pluscarden** and **Spynie.** *Iter. 175, 189, 190, 192, 198, 199.*

ELGOL, Isle of Skye, Inverness. Map 23, NG 5 1.
The terminal point of the narrow and hilly road which crosses the low Strathaird peninsula on its way from *Broadford* (*q.v.*). The situation of *Elgol*, on the outer shore of *Loch Scavaig* (*q.v.*), is very fine, and from the 1,128-ft. high hill behind the village known as *Ben Meabost*, the view of the *Coolins* (*q.v.*), grouped above Loch Scavaig, has been described as one of the finest in the world. A path goes northwards along the lochside from Elgol to *Camasunary*, from which Loch na Creitheach, under the fine peak of *Blaven*, 3,042 ft., can be reached. The path then turns westwards towards the rocky slopes of *Sgurr na Stri*, 1,623 ft., and fords a stream before reaching the notorious " Bad Step," which requires some care. Access is thus gained to the magnificent scenery of *Loch Coruisk* (*q.v.*), separated by a narrow ridge from Loch Scavaig. The usual approach to Loch Coruisk from Elgol is by motor boat. The island of Soay lies in Outer Loch Scavaig, and away to the south-west is the lofty mountain outline of the island of Rum. To the south of Elgol is Strathaird Point, and north-east of here is the curious Spar Cave, with its stalagmites, generally visited by boat. Curious eroded cliffs, showing deep fissures, overlook the scene. *Iter. 252.*

ELIE, Fife. 924. SB. with Earlsferry. Map 17, NO 4 0.
E.C. Wed. GOLF. The twin resorts of *Elie* and *Earlsferry* stand on either side of a bay between Chapel Ness, to the west, and Elie Ness, to the east. Good sands and bathing are available, and garnets have been found on the beach near Elie. *Gillespie House*, in South Street, Elie, has a fine carved door, dated 1682. The Parish Church is 17th cent. East of the town, near the sea, stands the *Lady's Tower*, built originally for Lady Janet Anstruther, whom Thomas Carlyle has described. The remains of *Ardross Castle* are not far distant. At Earlsferry is *Kincraig House*, dating from 1680. Westwards from Earlsferry is Kincraig Point, near which is Macduff's Cave. See **Kilconquhar** and **St. Monance.** *Iter. 94, 98, 132.*

ELLISLAND, Dumfries. Map 3, NX 9 8.
See **Auldgirth.**

ELLON, Aberdeen. 1,477. SB. Map 27, NJ 9 3.
E.C. Wed. M.D. Mon. GOLF. On the River Ythan, in the agricultural Formartine district. The Earl's Mount is an ancient mote-hill. Below the old Castle is a fine terrace and a notable sundial stands in the gardens. See **Collieston, Methlick** and **Tarves.** *Iter. 181, 183, 185, 187.*

ELPHIN, Sutherland. Map 29, NC 2 1.
Lies almost on the Ross-shire border, on the fringe of the wild *Assynt* country, and in a lonely setting of mountain and loch. To the south rise the *Cromalt* hills, forming the boundary with Ross and Cromarty, and eastwards lies Loch Urigill. Westwards, in Drumrunie Forest, is *Cul Mor*, 2,786 ft., overlooking Loch Veyatie and the Cam Loch, a little to the north of Elphin. Beyond rises the spectacular double-topped peak of *Suilven*, 2,399 ft., the sharp eastern cone of which is well seen from Elphin. See **Inchnadamph.** *Iter. 224, 225.*

ELSRICKLE, Lanark. Map 9, NT 0 4.
Iter. 37, 52.

Eilean Donan Castle, Ross and Cromarty. The restored Macrae stronghold, bombarded by the British frigate 'Worcester' in 1719, in order to dislodge a party of Spaniards supporting an abortive Jacobite Rising. It stands near the meeting point of Lochs Duich, Alsh and Long, south of Dornie Bridge, and is linked by a causeway to A87

Elderslie, Renfrew. The Memorial to William Wallace, who is said to have been born near here

Electric Brae, Ayr. This hill, known also as Croy Brae, is on the Girvan road (A719), 2 miles south of Dunure. Owing to certain configurations of the land, a car appears to be descending the hill when it is in fact ascending

Elgin, Moray. The ruined Cathedral, which has suffered many vicissitudes, including its sack by the Wolf of Badenoch in 1390

Elie, Fife. The carved doorway of Gillespie House, in the High Street, which is dated 1682

Elgin, Moray. The inscription on a gravestone of 1687 in the Cathedral churchyard

16 IK 87
HEIR IS TE BURIALPIAC
APOINED FOR IOHN
GEDDES GLOVER BUR
GES IN ELGIN
AND ISSOBELL
McKEAN HIS SPOUS
& TER RELATON
THIS WORLD IS ACITE
FULL OF STREETS &
DEATH IS TE MERCAT
THAT ALL MEN MEETS
IF LYFE WERE A THING
HAT MONIE COULD
BUY TE POOR COULD
NOT LIVE & TE RICH
WOULD NOT DIE

[For ELGIN see also under LAIGH OF MORAY (Plate 104)]

PLATE 62 (facing page 152)

Elvanfoot, Lanark. Plaque in the burial ground near the bridge over the River Clyde. It records the death from cholera, in 1847, of 37 men working on the Caledonian Railway who were afterwards buried on the spot

Erskine Ferry, Renfrew. The tall Monument in memory of the 11th Lord Blantyre, who was killed in the Brussels riots of 1830. It stands off B815, some 2 miles to the west

Ewes, Dumfries. The 300-year old church bell, which hangs in the fork of a tree

Ettrick, Selkirk. The grave of James Hogg, the poet, known as the ' Ettrick Shepherd,' who died in 1835. Nearby is the grave of Tibbie Shiel, who was hostess of the famous inn by St. Mary's Loch which bears her name

Eyemouth, Berwick. The early 17th century Linthill House, where, in 1751, the wealthy Mrs Patrick Hume is said to have been murdered by her butler. It stands 1½ miles to the south-west, on an unclassified road

Ettrick Bridge End, Selkirk. Kirkhope Tower, c. 1600, once a home of the Scotts of Harden. It stands on an unclassified road to the north-west

Eyemouth, Berwick. Gunsgreen House, a centre for smugglers' activities during the 18th century. The nearby tower is believed to have been erected by Cromwell in 1650

PLATE 63 (facing page 153)   [For ETTRICK BRIDGE END see also Plate 173

ELVANFOOT, Lanar .   Map 9, NS 9 1.
Here, in a setting of Lowland hills, the Elvan Water unites with the Clyde in the upper part of Clydesdale. The Telford bridge over the Clyde on A74 has been replaced by a new bridge. South of the village, the tiny Clydes Burn is joined by the combined streams of the Daer Water and the Potrail Water, Elvanfoot being the first place on the true Clyde river. To the north-west is *Harryburn Brae*, 1,629 ft., and to the east rise *Harleburn Head*, 1,776 ft., and *Clyde Law*, 1,789 ft., the latter forming the border with Peeblesshire. A road leading south-westwards towards the Nith Valley traverses the picturesque, winding Dalveen Pass, which attains a height of 1,140 ft. across the Dumfries border, and above which, to the north, rises *Comb Head*, 1,998 ft., an outlier of the *Lowther* hills. Another road leads south-westwards, by way of *Leadhills* (*q.v.*), and reaches Nithsdale through the fine Mennock Pass. See **Beattock, Enterkinfoot** and **Mennock**. *Iter. 25, 49, 56.*

EMBO, Sutherland.   Map 31, NH 8 9.
A coastal village on the Outer Dornoch Firth.

ENOCHDHU, Perth.   Map 20, NO 0 6.
Iter. 159, 162, 167, 168.

ENTERKINFOOT, Dumfries.   Map 3, NS 8 0.
A hamlet in Upper Nithsdale, from which an old track climbs through the hills to emerge near the northern extremity of the Mennock Pass, over 1,400 ft. in height, on the outskirts of *Leadhills* (*q.v.*). This track goes by way of the narrow and deep Enterkin Pass, overshadowed by *Green Lowther*, 2,403 ft., and where a party of dragoons was once trapped by the Covenanters, as described by Defoe. To the south-east of Enterkinfoot, a short link connects with the fine road traversing the Dalveen Pass, with *Comb Head*, 1,998 ft., an outlier of the *Lowthers*, rising to the west. This pass reaches a height of 1,140 ft. before descending to *Elvanfoot* (*q.v.*) in the valley of the Clyde. See **Carronbridge** and **Mennock**. *Iter. 27, 48, 67.*

ERIBOLL, Sutherland.   Map 28, NC 4 5.
Situated on the road traversing the eastern shores of the wild and beautiful Loch Eriboll, a safe anchorage, which penetrates deep into the Sutherland mountains, with *Grann Stacach*, 2,630 ft., and *Beinn Spionnaidh*, 2,537 ft., to the west at its head. Away to the south-east, beyond Loch Hope, is *Ben Hope*, 3,040 ft., the most northerly peak of over 3,000 ft. in Scotland. South-westwards, beyond Strath Beag, rises *Foinaven*, 2,980 ft., with the lonely Loch Dionard at its foot. See **Heilim** and **Hope Lodge**. *Iter. 225.*

ERISKAY, ISLE OF, Inverness.   Map 32, NF 7 0.
See **Hebrides, Outer** (South Uist).

ERROGIE, Inverness.   Map 25, NH 5 2.
A hamlet on the west shores of Loch Mhor, situated at an altitude of over 600 ft., a few miles east of *Loch Ness* (*q.v.*). Near the east shores of Loch Mhor is the estate of *Easter Aberchalder*, noted for its fine rock gardens. Loch Mhor is now a reservoir, uniting the water of Lochs Garth and Farraline, and feeding the Foyers river for use in the aluminium works near *Foyers* (*q.v.*). Beyond Loch Mhor, to the east, stretch lonely moorlands culminating in *Carn Odhar*, 2,618 ft. and other summits. See **Inverfarigaig**. *Iter. 211, 212.*

ERROL, Perth. 2,012.   Map 17, NO 2 2.
E.C. Thurs. A village in the fertile *Carse of Gowrie* (*q.v.*), near the Firth of Tay, facing the Fife coast. The Earls of Errol take their title from the name. **2 m. N.** is *Megginch Castle*, dating partly from 1575. *Iter. 154.*

ERSKINE FERRY, Renfrew.   Map 8, NS 4 7.
This car ferry across the Clyde is of great use to motorists from the South wishing to by-pass Glasgow, and connects with *Old Kilpatrick* (*q.v.*), in Dunbartonshire. The 19th cent. *Erskine House*, now a hospital, was built for Lord Blantyre, to whom a tall obelisk stands in the vicinity. The Parish Church of Erskine was built in 1813. See **Bishopton**. *Iter. 88, 109, 110, 111, 112, 113.*

ESHA NESS, Shetland.   Map 33, HU 2 7.
See **Shetland Islands** (Mainland). *Iter. 267.*

ESKBANK, Midlothian.   Map 10, NJ 3 6.
See **Newbattle**. *Iter. 9, 11, 12, 37.*

ESKDALEMUIR CHURCH, Dumfries. 378.
    Map 4, NY 2 9.
Roads from Lockerbie and Langholm converge here, at the northern end of picturesque Eskdale. The continuation northwards through lonely hill country, with *Ettrick Pen*, 2,269 ft., to the west, leads towards the valley of the Ettrick Water, reaching a height of nearly 1,100 ft., near the Selkirk border. To the north of the Church is the Roman Camp of *Raeburnfoot*. **3 m. N.** of the road junction is the well-known *Eskdalemuir* observatory, erected in 1908, and situated at a height of nearly 700 ft. Prehistoric remains are to be found in the district in various places, and **4 m. S.** of Eskdalemuir Church, in the angle formed by the White Esk and Black Esk Rivers before their junction, is the notable hill-fort of *Castleoer*, on a lofty ridge. *Iter. 12, 42.*

ETTRICK, Selkirk. 299.   Map 10, NT 2 1.
The little Church of *Ettrick* stands about a mile to the west of the Selkirk to Eskdalemuir road, on the Ettrick Water, which emerges from a valley hemmed in by lofty hills, dominated by the remote and lonely *Ettrick Pen*, 2,269 ft. In the churchyard lies James Hogg, the " Ettrick Shepherd," who died in 1835, and also the well-known Tibbie Shiel (See **Tibbie Shiel's Inn**), who died in 1878 at the age of 96. A little to the east of the Church stands the Hogg monument, on the site of the former cottage where he was born in 1770. The Eskdalemuir road follows the valley of the Tima Water southwards, climbing to a height of more than 1,000 ft. nearing the Dumfries border. See **Ettrick Bridge End, St. Mary's Loch** and **Tushielaw Inn**. *Iter. 12, 42.*

ETTRICK BRIDGE END, Selkirk.   Map 10, NT 3 2.
On the Ettrick Water, and in the extensive Ettrick Forest, formerly a Royal hunting-ground, and which once gave its name to the county. The old river bridge was washed away in 1777, but a stone from it, bearing the Harden coat of arms, and associated with Sir Walter Scott, has been built into the present structure. A by-road leads north-westwards over the hills to *Yarrow* (*q.v.*), passing near the 16th cent. tower of *Kirkhope*, once a home of the Scotts. **2 m. N.E.**, near the river, in a picturesque setting, is *Oakwood Tower*, the home of Scott's grandfather, having been built by Robert Scott in 1602. In the vicinity are remains of the Roman fort of *Oakwood*. **5 m. S.W.**, off the road to *Tushielaw* (*q.v.*), is *Deloraine*, the home of William of Deloraine, in Scott's " Lay of the Last Minstrel." See **Broadmeadows, Ettrick** and **Selkirk**. *Iter. 42.*

EVANTON, Ross and Cromarty. 372.   Map 25, NH 6 6.
E.C. Thurs. Stands just inland from the waters of Cromarty Firth, where the Allt Grand river flows into the Firth. The river, known farther west as the Glass, emerges from Loch Glass, **5m. N.W.**, in the foothills of *Ben Wyvis*, 3,429 ft. To the north of Loch Glass is the smaller Loch Morie, below *Meall Mor*, 2,419 ft. A little to the west of Evanton, a path leads near the stream to the remarkable ravine known as the Black Rock of Novar. **2½ m. S.W.** of Evanton is the Clan Munro seat of *Foulis Castle*, the original structure having been burnt in the mid-18th cent. *Iter. 200, 201.*

EVELIX, Sutherland.   Map 31, NH 7 9.
Iter. 200, 231.

EVIE, Orkney.   Map 33, HY 3 2.
See **Orkney Islands** (Mainland). *Iter. 263.*

EWES CHURCH, Dumfries.   Map 4, NY 3 9.
The Church bell, 300 years old, hangs outside, high up in the fork of a lime tree. On Sorbie Bridge, in the vicinity, a tablet commemorates the Rev. Henry Scott Riddell, the author of " Scotland Yet."

EYE CHURCH, Isle of Lewis, Ross and Cromarty.
    Map 32, NB 5 3.
See **Hebrides, Outer** (Lewis). *Iter. 259.*

EYEMOUTH, Berwick. 2,159. SB.   Map 11, NT 9 6.
E.C. Thurs. GOLF. A busy little fishing town and resort, on the Eye Water, where it flows into the sea between Hare

Point and Nestends. The beach is partly sandy with bathing. In 1881 a gale destroyed much of the fishing fleet, with heavy loss of life. The coast scenery, both to the north and to the south, is rocky and picturesque, with caves and caverns once used for smuggling, and at Hare Point are remains of a fort. *Netherbyres* was at one time the home of Sir Samuel Brown, who, in 1820, built the Union Suspension Bridge across the Tweed near *Paxton* (*q.v.*). **1½ m. S.W.** is *Linthill House*, early 17th cent., with crow-stepped gables. The house, once a seat of the Humes, is said to have been the scene of a gruesome tragedy in the 18th cent. See **Burnmouth** and **Coldingham**. *Iter. 2, 41.*

FAILFORD, Ayr.   **Map 8, NS 4 2.**
Here, the Water of Fail flows into the River Ayr. A monument commemorates the parting of Robert Burns from his " Highland Mary," an Argyllshire dairymaid by the name of Mary Campbell. *Iter. 35.*

FAIR ISLE, Shetland.   **Map 33, HZ 2 7.**
See **Shetland Islands (Fair Isle)**.

FAIRLIE, Ayr. 975.   **Map 8, NS 2 5.**
E.C. Wed. A small Firth of Clyde resort, with a sandy beach and a pier. In *St. Margaret's* Church is the ancient Fairlie Stone. The resort is situated opposite the island of *Great Cumbrae*, on which stands *Millport* (*q.v.*). South of the island is *Little Cumbrae*, which is separated by a narrow channel from the much larger island of *Bute* (*q.v.*). Away to the south-west rise the mountains of Arran. In a glen to the east is the ruined *Fairlie Castle*, dated 1521, and to the north of the town is *Kelburne Castle*, a late 16th cent. tower, joined to a house dating from 1700. **3 m. S.S.W.** of Fairlie is *Hunterston Castle*, an old tower, with modern additions. *Iter. 66, 88.*

FAIRMILEHEAD (Edinburgh), Midlothian.
     Map 9, NT 2 6.
A little to the west, on the road to *Colinton* (*q.v.*), is the cottage known as the *Hunter's Tryst*, associated with R. L. Stevenson's " St. Ives." Nearby is the *Caiy Stone* (N.T. Scot.), a prehistoric monolith, the history of which is not known. See **Swanston**. *Iter. 14, 25.*

FAIRNILEE, Selkirk.   **Map 10, NT 4 3.**
On the River Tweed, with the mansion of *Yair House*, built in 1788, situated west of Yair Bridge over the river, and having as a background the hill known as *Three Brethren*, 1,523 ft. *Fairnilee House*, and its ruined tower, stand high above the Tweed, among trees, and in the tower Alison Cockburn wrote in the 18th cent., her version of the " Flowers of the Forest." *Iter. 14.*

FALKIRK, Stirling. 37,072. LB.
     Map 16, NS 8 7.
E.C. Wed. GOLF. A town of importance for its coal-mining and the great Carron iron works, but once noted as a collecting-place, or tryst for cattle, brought to *Stenhousemuir*, about three miles to the north-west, along the numerous drove roads radiating from all parts of the Highlands. Two battles were fought near Falkirk, in 1298 and 1746, in the former of which Wallace was defeated, while in the latter Prince Charles Edward was victorious. The Prince spent the night in a bootmaker's shop opposite the new Falkirk Steeple. In the High Street is the " *Cross Keys* " Inn, visited by Burns. In the private grounds of the fine mansion of *Callendar House*, east of the town, are some well-preserved portions of the Antonine, or *Roman Wall* (*q.v.*). Mary, Queen of Scots visited the house on several occasions between 1562 and 1567, and Prince Charles Edward was also here. Other sections of the wall (N.T. Scot.) lie to the west of Falkirk, towards Bonnybridge, including the fort known as

" Rough Castle." See **Glenelg, Grangemouth, Polmont** and **Westerglen**. *Iter. 17, 95, 113, 114, 115.*

FALKLAND, Fife. 1,066. SB.   **Map 17, NO 2 0.**
E.C. Thurs. This picturesque little Royal Burgh, with its cobbled streets and old houses, is best known for the very interesting *Falkland Palace* (N.T. Scot.), a favourite seat of the Scottish Court from the time of James V, who died here, after having done much to improve its amenities. His daughter, the future Mary, Queen of Scots, used to hunt from the Palace. Both Charles I and Charles II visited Falkland, and Rob Roy occupied it in 1715, after the battle of Sheriffmuir. The Royal Tennis court of 1539 still exists. The buildings are in the Renaissance style, dating from 1530–1540, with a fine façade to the south wing, and containing a banqueting-hall, now a Chapel, showing a good screen and 17th cent. tapestries. In 1654, the east wing was burnt when occupied by Cromwell's troops. Scott, in his " Fair Maid of Perth," has introduced the story of the Duke of Rothesay, who is said to have been starved to death in one of the dungeons. The Palace is open weekdays, 11 to 5; Sun., 2 to 5, April to Oct. (See note page 90). The Town House, with its spire, dates from 1805. A house in the square carries an inscribed panel to Richard Cameron, a Covenanter martyr, born in 1648, who is associated with the raising of the Cameronian regiment. On Green Hill stands a monument to O. Tyndall-Bruce, an Englishman, who, in 1849, restored the Palace and built the Church. To the south rise the *Lomond* hills, with *East Lomond*, 1,471 ft., in the immediate background, and *West Lomond*, 1,713 ft., the highest point in the range, farther to the west, overlooking *Loch Leven* (*q.v.*). See **Linlithgow**. *Iter. 130.*

FALLIN, Stirling.   **Map 16, NS 8 9.**
Iter. 96.

FALLS OF BRUAR, Perth.   **Map 19, NN 8 6.**
See **Struan**.

FALLS OF CLYDE, Lanark.   **Map 9, NS 8 4.**
See **Lanark**.

FALLS OF CRUACHAN, Argyll.   **Map 14, NN 0 2.**
These falls are situated at the eastern end of the dark and gloomy Pass of Brander, overlooking the waters of Loch

1. Bootmaker's shop where Prince Charles Edward spent a night in 1746.

Failford, Ayr. The Monument which commemorates Robert Burns's parting from his 'Highland Mary,' on May 14th, 1786

Fairlie, Ayr. The entrance to the 16th century and later Kelburne Castle, a seat of the Earl of Glasgow

Fairmilehead, Midlothian. The Caiy Stone (N.T. Scot.), a prehistoric monolith

Falkirk, Stirling. The bootmaker's shop on the site of a house in which Prince Charles Edward spent a night during the '45 Rising

Falkland, Fife. The entrance to the 16th century Palace, from which Mary, Queen of Scots, used to hunt. It is now the property of the National Trust for Scotland

Falkland, Fife. A house in the Square, with an inscribed panel to Richard Cameron, a local schoolmaster and Covenanter-martyr, born in 1648. He is associated with the raising of the Cameronian Regiment in 1689

PLATE 64 (facing page 154)

Farr, Sutherland. An ancient sculptured stone in the churchyard

Fearn, Ross and Cromarty. The restored Abbey Church, which was moved here in 1338 from its original site at Edderton, near the Dornoch Firth

Fettercairn, Kincardine. The shaft of the old Kincardine Town Cross of 1670, which is notched to show the measurement of the Scottish 'ell' (37 inches)

Fenwick, Ayr. One of a number of Covenanter monuments in the churchyard

Ferryden, Angus. The lighthouse at Scurdy Ness

Ferniehirst Castle, Roxburgh. The late 16th century Castle, which is now used as a Youth Hostel. It was a seat of the old Border family of Ker

PLATE 65 (facing page 155)

Awe. In 1308, Robert Bruce routed the MacDougalls of Lorne in the pass. In the background is *Ben Cruachan*, 3,689 ft., with its twin summits, which can be climbed from a point west of the falls, and which forms a magnificent viewpoint, the prospect embracing the picturesque *Lorne* (*q.v.*) country, including Loch Etive and *Loch Linnhe* (*q.v.*). See **Kilchurn Castle** and **Loch Awe**. *Iter. 110, 117, 125, 144, 145.*

FALLS OF GLOMACH, Ross and Cromarty.
Map 24, NH 0 2.
These lofty falls, with a drop of over 350 ft., are situated in an estate of more than 2,000 acres (N.T. Scot.), and are some of the highest in Britain, but are somewhat difficult of access. They can be approached from *Ardelve* (*q.v.*) by means of a road along Loch Long, which continues through Glen Elchaig. The falls themselves can be reached only on foot, from the western end of Loch na Leitreach in Glen Elchaig, and by means of a rough and arduous climb of more than a mile along the west bank of the stream descending from the hills. Another method of approach is from the head of *Loch Duich* (*q.v.*), at *Croe Bridge* (*q.v.*), a long-distance walkers' path leading for about 7 miles through the hills to the falls by way of Dorusduain and the rough and steep 2,000-ft. high Bealach na Sroine. South-east of the falls rises the remote and massive peak of *Sgurr nan Ceathreamhnan*, 3,771 ft. See **Kintail** and **Kylesku**.

FALLS OF LENY, Perth. Map 15, NN 5 0.
See **Callander**. *Iter. 107, 111, 139, 141, 142, 144.*

FALLS OF MEASACH, Ross and Cromarty.
Map 29, NH 2 7.
See **Braemore Lodge**. *Iter. 204, 206, 222.*

FALLS OF ROGIE, Ross and Cromarty. Map 25, NH 4 5.
These picturesque falls, on the River Blackwater, have an attractive wooded background, and can be reached from the road near *Achilty Inn* (*q.v.*). *Iter. 204, 205, 206, 221.*

FALLS OF SHIN, Sutherland. Map 29, NH 5 9.
See **Inveran Bridge**.

FALLS OF TUMMEL, Perth. Map 20, NN 9 5.
See **Bridge of Garry** and **Pitlochry**.

FARR, Inverness. Map 25, NH 6 3.
Iter. 212.

FARR, Sutherland. Map 30, NC 7 6.
A little to the south of the village, which lies just off the Bettyhill to Thurso road, is the delightful little Farr Bay, and northwards is Farr Point, overlooking the stormy waters of the Pentland Firth. The little 18th cent. Church, south of Farr Bay, preserves a very fine sculptured stone in the churchyard. See **Bettyhill**. *Iter. 232, 234, 240.*

FASKALLY, Perth. Map 20, NN 9 5.
See **Pitlochry**.

FASLANE, Dunbarton. Map 14, NS 2 8.
Near the head of the Gare Loch. In a local graveyard are buried men from the submarine K.13, which sank in the loch in 1917. Large vessels are broken up here for scrap, these having included the battleships "Malaya" and "Renown," and also the famous Cunard liner "Aquitania." *Iter. 102, 111, 116.*

FEARN, Ross and Cromarty. Map 31, NH 8 7.
Lies in the fertile stretch of country between the Cromarty and Dornoch Firths. The restored Abbey Church was originally situated at *Edderton* (*q.v.*), but was moved to its present site in 1338. In 1742, the Chapel roof collapsed, killing a number of people. An interesting tomb may be seen in the South Chapel, near the Shandwick burial-place. 2½ m. N.E., near the shores of Loch Eye, is the ruined *Lochslin Castle*. 4½ m. N.E. is *Geanies House*, with fine gardens and views of the Moray Firth. See **Balintore**.

FEARNAN, Perth. Map 16, NN 7 4.
A small *Loch Tay* (*q.v.*) resort, to the west of the wooded *Drummond Hill*. It is convenient for visiting the beautiful Glen Lyon, which can be reached by way of *Fortingall* (*q.v.*), along a short piece of road crossing the River Lyon a mile to the north of Fearnan. See **Kenmore**. *Iter. 120, 138.*

FENWICK, Ayr. Map 8, NS 4 4.
Situated on the Fenwick Water, with a moorland area to the east. The restored Church, built originally in 1643, contains a post-Reformation pulpit and the jougs are preserved. There are Covenanter monuments in the churchyard, and one inscription recalls Scott's "Old Mortality." 2 m. S. stands the seat of *Crawfurdland Castle*, given to the Hewison-Crawfurds by James V as a reward for his rescue from footpads at *Cramond Bridge* (*q.v.*). *Iter. 19, 55, 61.*

FEOLIN FERRY, Isle of Jura, Argyll. Map 6, NR 4 6.
See **Jura**.

FERNESS, Nairn. Map 25, NH 9 4.
On the River Findhorn, which, to the south, enters upon one of its loveliest reaches, in a setting of woods and high rocky banks, culminating in what is perhaps the finest scenery of its entire length at *Dulsie Bridge* (*q.v.*). 4 m. N.E. of Ferness, near *Daltulich Bridge*, off the *Forres* (*q.v.*) road, is the Morayshire beauty spot known as "Randolph's Leap," reached on foot, and situated in the Findhorn Glen at a point near the confluence of the Findhorn and the Divie, another most picturesque scene. Nearby are the fine grounds of *Relugas House*. A stone, near the meeting of the two rivers, commemorates the record height of the waters reached during the great floods of 1829. See **Ardclach Church** and **Logie**. *Iter. 173, 176.*

FERNIEHIRST CASTLE, Roxburgh. Map 10, NT 6 1.
This fine late 16th cent. Castle, now a Youth Hostel, stands a little to the east of the Jed Water, in a lovely wooded setting, and replaced an earlier structure, destroyed in 1571. It played its part in the many fierce Border fights throughout the years, and was many times besieged and frequently changed hands. The castle is L-shaped, and carries the Ker arms on several panels, while the great hall is of note and contains a huge fireplace. See **Jedburgh**. *Iter. 4, 43, 52.*

FERRYDEN, Angus. Map 21, NO 7 5.
On the estuary of the South Esk River, facing *Montrose* (*q.v.*). *Craig House* dates from 1637 and later. East of the village is Sandy Ness, with its lighthouse.

FESHIE BRIDGE, Inverness. Map 25, NH 8 0.
The bridge crosses the fine gorge of the River Feshie, to the east of the little village, which stands at the mouth of the picturesque, wooded Glen Feshie, extending deep into the *Cairngorms* (*q.v.*), rising north of Glen Feshie Forest. (See **Kincraig**.) Wade planned to build a road through the glen, in order to link Speyside with Deeside, reaching the latter near the *Linn of Dee* by *Inverie* (*q.v.*), but the road was never constructed. Apart from the walkers' track through the wild *Lairig Ghru Pass* (*q.v.*), the only means of proceeding from the Spey valley to that of the Dee is by making the long road detour by way of *Tomintoul* (*q.v.*). See **Insh** and **Rothiemurchus**. *Iter. 138, 149.*

FETLAR, ISLE OF, Shetland. Map 33, HU 6 9.
See **Shetland Islands** (Yell).

FETTERCAIRN, Kincardine. 232. Map 21, NO 6 7.
E.C. Thurs. An attractive village, on the edge of the fertile Howe of the Mearns, with the heights of the eastern Grampians in the background. In the square is the shaft of the old Kincardine Town Cross, dating from 1670, and notched to show the measurements of the Scottish "ell." An arch commemorates the visit of Queen Victoria and the Prince Consort in 1861. At *Fettercairn House*, interesting letters and papers relating to the Boswell family were discovered in 1931. 2 m. N.E., off the Stonehaven road, are the ruins of *Kincardine Castle*, on the site of the former county town of Kincardine, and once a Royal residence. This Castle is associated with Macbeth, whose head was brought here to the waiting Malcolm, after the defeat of the former at *Lumphanan* (*q.v.*). 1 m. S.W. is *Balbegno Castle*, which dates partly from the 16th cent. See **Cairn o' Mounth** and **Clattering Bridge**. *Iter. 156, 163, 165.*

FEUGHSIDE INN, Kincardine. Map 21, NO 6 9.
Situated near the Water of Feugh, almost on the Aberdeen border, and on the road linking the *Cairn o' Mounth* (*q.v.*) with Deeside in the vicinity of *Kincardine o' Neil* (*q.v.*). An

alternative road to the main Deeside road, linking Aboyne with Banchory, also passes by the Feughside Inn. Away to the west extends the great Forest of Birse. *Iter. 165, 174.*

FIFE KEITH, Banff.   Map 26, NJ 4 5.
See **Keith.** *Iter. 169, 170, 175, 178, 187, 189.*

FINCASTLE, Perth.   Map 19, NN 8 6.
To the north-west is *Old Fincastle*, a 17th cent. house, with a small loch. *Iter. 138, 148.*

FINDHORN, Moray. 480.   Map 26, NJ 0 6.
E.C. Thurs. A little resort and fishing village, situated on the east side of the sandy Findhorn Bay, facing the Moray Firth. The two previous villages have both vanished, the first being engulfed by the *Culbin Sands* (q.v.), and the second by the floods of 1701. Findhorn was once one of the chief exporting towns of Moray. To the south, across the bay, into which flows the River Findhorn, can be seen the distant town of *Forres* (q.v.). See **Kinloss.** *Iter. 199.*

FINDOCHTY, Banff. 1,528. SB.   Map 26, NJ 4 6.
A quaint little fishing village, situated between Craig Head and Long Head, on a rocky part of the coast, with Spey Bay to the west. See **Portessie** and **Portknockie.** *Iter. 199.*

FINDON, Kincardine.   Map 21, NO 9 9.
A fishing village, known also as *Finnan*, a name which has become associated with smoked haddocks.

FINGAL'S CAVE, Isle of Staffa, Argyll. Map 13, NM 3 3.
See **Staffa.**

FINHAVEN, Angus.   Map 21 NO 4 5.
On the River South Esk, and known alternatively as *Finavon*. The ruined *Finhaven Castle*, to the south of the river, was a former Crawford stronghold. Beyond the Castle rises the *Hill of Finhaven*, a viewpoint with a vitrified fort on the eastern summit. *Iter. 151, 156, 166.*

FINNART, Dunbarton.   Map 14, NS 2 9.
An oil-port on the eastern bank of *Loch Long* (q.v.), to the north of the Gare Loch. *Iter. 102, 111.*

FINSTOWN, Orkney.   Map 33, HY 3 1.
See **Orkney Islands (Mainland).** *Iter. 263, 264.*

FINTRY, Stirling. 356.   Map 15, NS 6 8.
The village is set in a hollow, threaded by the Endrick Water, between the *Fintry* hills to the north, and the more extensive and slightly higher *Campsie Fells* to the south, in the heart of what is known as the *Lennox* country. *Culcreuch Tower*, an ancient structure, with 17th cent. additions, lies a little to the north. The Crow Road, leading south-eastwards to *Lennoxtown* (q.v.), crosses the *Campsies*, and reaches a height of 1,154 ft., with fine views over the Clyde valley. **3 m.** E. of Fintry, near the Walton reservoir, is the Loup of Fintry, a waterfall on the Endrick Water, the fall being over a 100-ft. high ledge of rock. The narrow and hilly moorland road continues eastwards from here, passing near the site of the former *Sir John de Graham's Castle*, and keeping to the north of the *Kilsyth* hills to reach the flat, industrial area of the county at *Denny* (q.v.). *Iter. 107, 114.*

FINZEAN, Aberdeen.   Map 21, NO 5 9.
Iter. 174.

FIONPHORT, Isle of Mull, Argyll.   Map 13, NM 3 2.
See **Bunessan.** *Iter. 249.*

FIRTH OF CLYDE, Argyll; Ayr; Bute; Renfrew.
      Map 7, NS 1 5 etc.
The name given to the stretch of water separating the Ayrshire and Renfrewshire coasts from the islands of Arran and Bute and the Cowal shores of the Argyll mainland. The Firth is noted particularly for yachting, and regattas are held both here and in the more confined waters of the Kyles of Bute, which lie farther to the north-west. Among the well-known resorts on the Firth are Ardrossan, Largs, Wemyss Bay and Dunoon, all of which are described individually. *Rothesay* (q.v.), in the island of Bute, is associated particularly with the Clyde Yachting fortnight.

FLODIGARRY, Isle of Skye, Inverness. Map 22, NG 4 7.
Famous as the early home of Flora Macdonald, who married Allan Macdonald of Kingsburgh, in 1750. The old house is now neighboured by an hotel. In 1746, Flora Macdonald escorted Prince Charles Edward, who was disguised as her maid, from *Benbecula*, in the *Outer Hebrides* (q.v.) to *Portree* (q.v.) in Skye. Dr. Johnson and Boswell were entertained here in 1773, and later her family emigrated to North Carolina, but they returned, and in 1790 Flora Macdonald was buried at *Kilmuir* (q.v.). Off-shore, opposite Flodigarry, is the little Eilean Flodigarry, while a little inland are the rocks and pinnacles of *Leac na Fionn*, rising above Loch Langaid, and neighboured by the fantastic *Quiraing* (q.v.). *Iter. 254.*

FLOORS CASTLE, Roxburgh.   Map 10, NT 7 3.
This magnificent house, in its great park, bordered by the River Tweed, stands immediately to the north-west of *Kelso* (q.v.). It was originally designed, in 1718, by Vanbrugh, but was altered later by Playfair, and shows Tudor-style work. The palatial entrance gates giving access to Roxburgh St. in Kelso were set up in 1929. A holly-tree in the grounds is said to mark the spot, where in 1460, James II, while laying siege to the castle of *Roxburgh* (q.v.), met his end through the bursting of a cannon. The grounds and gardens are shown Wed., 10 to 4, in summer (see note page 90). *Iter. 32, 46.*

FOCHABERS, Moray. 800.   Map 26, NJ 3 5.
E.C. Wed. Lies to the east of the River Spey, on the edge of extensive woodlands, and with the great park of *Gordon Castle* to the north. The Castle, with the exception of one tower, was demolished in 1955. The village stood formerly nearer the Castle, but was removed in the 18th cent., only the Market Cross and jougs remaining. The 19th cent. Church has a pillared portico. Across the Spey, to the west of Fochabers, is *Mosstodloch* (q.v.), the bridge over the river being the successor to that destroyed in the floods of 1829. See **Methlick** and **Spey Bay.** *Iter. 175, 187, 198.*

FOGO, Berwick.   Map 11, NT 7 4.
The Church has two laird's lofts, dated 1671 and 1677 respectively, one having an outside staircase.

FOGORIG, Berwick.   Map 11, NT 7 4.
Iter. 8.

FORD, Argyll.   Map 14, NM 8 0.
A small anglers' resort, with a steamer pier, between the south-western extremity of *Loch Awe* (q.v.), and the little Loch Ederline. The road along Loch Awe follows the south shores, and passes, after two miles, the ruined *Fincharn Castle*, which is faced across the loch by Inverliver Woods. Another road parallels the north shores of the loch and leads to Dalavich and *Kilchrenan* (q.v.). See **Kilmartin** and **Portinnisherrich.** *Iter. 119.*

FORDOUN, Kincardine.   Map 21, NO 7 7.
GOLF. The tiny village lies **3 m.** N.N.W. of Fordoun station, which is situated on the Brechin to Stonehaven road. There is a small Church, in the churchyard of which, on a steep bank above the River Luther, is a fragment of the ancient Chapel of *St. Palladius*, an Irish Bishop. Almost adjacent to Fordoun is the village of *Auchinblae*. A road goes north-westwards from here, circling round *Finella Hill*, 1,358 ft., and passing *Drumtochty Castle*, now a school, before reaching *Clattering Bridge* (q.v.). **1½ m.** N.E. of Auchinblae stands *Monboddo House*, once the home of the 18th cent. judge, Lord Monboddo. *Iter. 151.*

FOREST MILL, Clackmannan.   Map 16, NS 9 9.
Iter. 86, 91, 98.

FORDYCE, Banff.   Map 26, NJ 5 6.
Delightfully situated a little to the south of the Portsoy to Cullen road. In the centre of the village stands the small late 16th cent. *Fordyce Castle*, with some fine corbelling, dormer windows, and an angle tower overlooking the street. **1½ m.** N.W. is the mansion of *Birkenbog*, with a fine walled garden. Here, in 1645, Thomas Nicholson, the first Vicar-Apostolic of Scotland, was born. See **Deskford.** *Iter. 198.*

FORFAR, Angus. 10,022. SB.   Map 21, NO 4 5.
E.C. Thurs. M.D. Mon./Fri. GOLF. The Royal Burgh of *Forfar* stands in flat country between the two little lochs of Forfar and Fithie, lying respectively to the west and east,

Findon, Kincardine. A scene at the village, which has given its name to smoked haddocks, known as 'Finnan haddies.' They were at one time cured here in the local peat-reek

Fintry, Stirling. The Loup of Fintry waterfall, which lies 3 miles to the east, off B818

Floors Castle, Roxburgh. The 18th century and later Castle, designed originally by Vanbrugh. It stands just outside Kelso, to the north-west, off A6089. In Roxburgh Street, Kelso, are the so-called 'golden gates' leading to the castle drive, which were erected in 1929, and display ornate wrought-iron work overlaid with gold-leaf

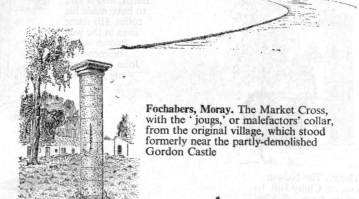

Fochabers, Moray. The Market Cross, with the 'jougs,' or malefactors' collar, from the original village, which stood formerly near the partly-demolished Gordon Castle

Fogo, Berwick. The Church, which has an outside staircase giving access to the private laird's loft of the Trotters of Charterhall, dating from 1671

Fordyce, Banff. The small 16th century Castle, which is still lived in, and overlooks the village street

[For FORFAR see following plate

PLATE 66 (facing page 156)

Forfar, Angus. The Town Hall, in which is kept the Forfar ' bridle ' or gag, used for witches

Forfar, Angus. The ruined 12th to 15th century Restenneth Priory, situated 2 miles north-east, off B9113. It was once the Parish Church of Forfar

Forres, Moray. The Nelson Monument, on Cluny Hill, to the east of the town, off A96

Fort Augustus, Inverness. The grave of John Anderson, a carpenter, who died here in 1832. He was an old friend of Robert Burns, and is said to have made his coffin. His name lives in the well known verses commencing: ' John Anderson, my jo John '

Forres, Moray. The 23-foot high carved Sueno's Stone, of unknown origin. It may, however, commemorate the defeat of Malcolm II by Sweyn in 1008

Fort Augustus, Inverness. The Benedictine Monastery of 1876, on the site of the former castle, which was built after the Jacobite Rising of 1715, and taken by the Highlanders during the 1745 Rising

[For FORTEVIOT see following plate

PLATE 67 (facing page 157)

and at the north-eastern extremity of the fertile Vale of *Strathmore* (*q.v.*), here known as the Howe of Angus. Near the Forfar Loch was once fought a battle between the Scots and the Picts. In the Town Hall is preserved the Forfar " bridle," or gag. The site of the Castle is marked by an octagonal turret, once the Town Cross. A track, known as the " King's Codger's Road," formerly led to the coast at *Usan* (*q.v.*), along which fresh fish was brought to the former

1. Castle Turret.   2. Town Hall.

Royal Castle. To the north-east, between the two roads leading towards Brechin, is the *Hill of Finhaven*, a fine viewpoint, crowned by a vitrified fort. (See Finhaven.) **2 m.** N.E. of Forfar, near Loch Fithie, is the ruined *Restenneth Priory* (A.M.), with a very early tower, the remainder of the work being mainly of the 12th cent. though the broach spire dates probably from the 15th cent. **4 m. S.E.** of the town, and a little to the east of the Carnoustie road, is *Dunnichen*, once known as *Nectan's Mere*, near which was the scene, in 685, of a great battle, when Ecgfrith, King of the Angles, was defeated and slain. As a result of this battle Scotland's future as an independent country was at the time assured. **See Glamis and Kirriemuir.** *Iter.* 151, 153, 156, 162.

FORGUE, Aberdeen.   Map 27, NJ 6 4.
Lies on the Burn of Forgue, a tributary of the Deveron, which flows a few miles to the north of the village. *Iter.* 184.

FORRES, Moray. 5,014. SB.   Map 26, NJ 0 5.
E.C. Wed. M.D. Tues. GOLF. The town, which is of great antiquity, stands a little to the right of the widening River Findhorn, near the point where it enters Findhorn Bay. Shakespeare, in " Macbeth," has mentioned it under the name of " Fores." A little to the east, where the roads to *Findhorn* (*q.v.*) and *Elgin* (*q.v.*) diverge, stands the well-known *Sueno's Stone* (A.M.), a remarkable carved pillar, of unknown origin. In the near vicinity is the " Witches' Stone," where local witches were once burnt. On *Cluny Hill*, to the east of the town, is the Nelson Monument, a good viewpoint. **6 m. S.W.**, to the south of the road to *Auldearn* (*q.v.*), and on the west bank of the Findhorn, is Darnaway Forest, in which stands the modern *Darnaway Castle*, retaining the 15th cent. hall of an earlier structure, and belonging to the Earls of Moray. Mary, Queen of

1. Witches' Stone.   2. Nelson Monument.

Scots stayed here in 1562. The scenery in the valley to the south, where the river flows between the forest and the woods of *Altyre*, is of exceptional beauty. **See Brodie, Culbin Sands, Ferness, Findhorn, Kinloss, Lochindorb and Logie.** *Iter.* 172, 173, 175, 198, 199.

FORSINARD, Sutherland.   Map 30, NC 8 4.
An anglers' resort, lying between Strath Halladale and Achintoul Forest, with *Ben Griam Beg*, 1,803 ft., and *Ben Griam Mhor*, 1,936 ft., to the west. **4 m. S.** is Loch an Ruathair, off the Helmsdale road. *Iter.* 234.

FORT AUGUSTUS, Inverness. 600.   Map 24, NH 3 0.
E.C. Wed. The village of *Fort Augustus*, once known as *Kilcummin*, or *Killichiumen*, stands on the fine modern highway, partly on the line of General Wade's road of 1725–26, linking Fort William with Inverness by way of *Glen More* (*q.v.*). Fort Augustus is well known to anglers, and is situated in a setting of hills and woods, at the south-western extremity of *Loch Ness* (*q.v.*), near the point where it is entered by the *Caledonian Canal* (*q.v.*), with its six locks. The former fort, which took its name from Augustus, Duke of Cumberland, was built after the 1715 rising, and Wade enlarged it in 1730. In 1745, the Highlanders took it, but the government regained it after the battle of Culloden, and in 1876 a Benedictine Abbey was built on the remains of the fort. Wade linked Fort Augustus with Speyside by means of his famous road over the lofty *Corrieyairack Pass* (*q.v.*), but the crossing is no longer possible, except for hardy long-distance walkers. Neil Munro, in his " New Road," has described the making of the road. From Fort Augustus, a military road went formerly north-westwards over the hills to reach Glen Moriston, and was used in 1773 by Dr. Johnson and Boswell, who stayed at Fort Augustus, the former declaring that he spent there his best night for 20 years. The old Wade road to Inverness climbs steeply eastwards from Fort Augustus, crossing the wooded Glen Doe, and passing Loch Tarff, before ascending to 1,275 ft., with good views, on the way to *Whitebridge* (*q.v.*). There are Forestry Commission developments on the western shores of Loch Ness, including the newly-founded village of *Inchnacardoch*. **See Invergarry and Wade Roads.** *Iter.* 210, 211, 212, 213.

FORTEVIOT, Perth. 458.   Map 16, NO 0 1.
A pleasant Strath Earn village, once a Pictish capital, as was also *Dunstaffnage* (*q.v.*). The river is a little to the north, where it is joined by the Water of May, flowing through the village from the heights of the *Ochil* hills. To

the south-west is *Broomhill* farm, at which recent excavations have revealed the outlines of a large Roman camp. 1½ m. S.E. is *Invermay House*, associated with Scott's "Redgauntlet." **2 m. N.** is Dupplin Loch, and eastwards, in a fine wooded park is the modern *Dupplin Castle*. A battle was fought near here in 1332. A carved Early Christian Cross stands near the River Earn. *Iter. 86.*

FORT GEORGE, Inverness.   Map 25, NH 7 5.
Situated on a narrow spit of land, where the waters of Inner and Outer Loch Moray unite to face Chanonry Point in the *Black Isle* (*q.v.*). The fort dates from the 18th cent., and was visited in 1773 by Dr. Johnson and Boswell. It is now the depot of the Seaforth Highlanders. **See Ardersier and Fortrose.** *Iter. 199.*

FORTH, Lanark.   Map 9, NS 9 5.
Iter. 22, 86.

FORTH BRIDGE, Fife; West Lothian.   Map 17, NT 1 7.
See Queensferry, South. *Iter. 17, 89, 90, 94, 96.*

FORTINGALL, Perth. 350.   Map 19, NN 7 4.
E.C. Wed. This very attractive village lies on the River Lyon, a little to the north of *Loch Tay* (*q.v.*), from which it is separated by the wooded *Drummond Hill*. Fortingall is often said to have been the birthplace of Pontius Pilate. A yew-tree in the churchyard is of outstanding size, and is one of the oldest extant, Pennant, in 1772, having assessed its girth as 56 ft. *Glen Lyon House* was once a Campbell home. To the south-west of the village are earthworks, perhaps once a Roman outpost, and to the east, for some five miles, flows the River Lyon, prior to its confluence with the more important Tay, which has issued from the loch of that name near *Kenmore* (*q.v.*). Westwards from Fortingall stretches Glen Lyon, in the *Breadalbane* (*q.v.*) country, one of the longest and loveliest of Scottish glens, approached by the richly wooded Pass of Lyon, in which is situated the romantic " Macgregor's Leap." **2 m. W.** in the glen, and to the south of the road, are the Allt do Ghob Falls, after which the road continues westwards, between the peaks of *Cairn Mairg*, 3,419 ft., to the north, and *Ben Lawers*, 3,984 ft., and its satellites, to the south. **See Bridge of Balgie** and **Fearnan.** *Iter. 107, 138.*

FORTROSE, Ross and Cromarty. 846. SB.
      Map 25, NH 7 5.
GOLF. A quiet *Black Isle* (*q.v.*) resort and Royal Burgh, facing the Inner Moray, or Inverness Firth, and separated by a narrow neck of land, terminating in Chanonry Point, from the Outer Moray Firth. On the opposite shore, facing the Point, is *Fort George* (*q.v.*). The ruined Cathedral (A.M.) is in the styles of the 14th and 15th cents., and the most interesting portion is the vaulted South aisle, in which are several monuments and an old font. The detached Chapter House is now used as a Court House. Cromwell is thought to have used some of the stones of the already derelict building to raise his fortress at *Inverness* (*q.v.*). Inland, to the north-west, is the elevated, wooded ridge known as *Millbuie*, the lordship of which Mary, Queen of Scots bestowed on Darnley. **See Rosemarkie.** *Iter. 203.*

FORT WILLIAM, Inverness. 2,812. SB.   Map 18, NN 1 7.
E.C. Wed. GOLF. An important touring centre for *Lochaber* (*q.v.*) and the Western Highlands, situated near the western extremity of the Great Glen, or *Glen More* (*q.v.*), at the head of *Loch Linnhe* (*q.v.*), and at the foot of *Ben Nevis* (*q.v.*), 4,406 ft., the highest mountain in the British Isles. For the ascent the town makes a very convenient base. The Ben itself is not visible from the streets of Fort William, but is a landmark for many miles around, and can be well seen from the summit of *Cow Hill*, 942 ft., which rises behind the town. The view includes, in addition, the lower reaches of the beautiful Glen Nevis (See **Ben Nevis**), backed by *Sgurr a' Mhaim*, 3,601 ft., in the *Mamores* (*q.v.*), with its white quartzite peak. The entrance to Glen Nevis is near Bridge of Nevis, at the north-east end of the town. The east side of the glen is traversed for the commencement of the long ascent of Ben Nevis. The original Fort was built in 1655, by General Monk, and was rebuilt under William III, when, for a short time, the town was

called Maryborough. Both in 1715, and again in 1745, the Jacobites failed to capture the fort. It had been strengthened by General Wade after the first siege. A garrison occupied the fort until 1855, soon after which it was dismantled. The very interesting West Highland Museum is noted for the Prince Charles Edward room, containing relics, which include the well-known " secret portrait," and preserves the 17th cent. panelling which was formerly in the house of the governor of the Fort. The gateway from the Fort was re-erected in 1896 at *The Craigs*, the old cemetery. From The Rock, west of the gateway, cannons fired on the fort in 1746. The Lochaber Gathering at Fort William takes place usually during the latter half of August.

To the north-east of the town is a large aluminium factory and power house, fed by the waters of the Lochaber Power Scheme, which are brought here by means of a 15-mile long tunnel through Ben Nevis. Fort William was one of the first towns in Great Britain to be lit by electricity, this having been inaugurated in 1896. Still farther north-east, by the shores of the River Lochy, is the ruined *Inverlochy Castle*, probably dating from the 15th cent. Comyn's Tower, the largest of its circular towers, had walls 10 feet thick and

1. West Highland Museum.
2. Town Hall.
3. The Craigs Burial Ground with gateway from the old fort.
4. Scottish Art and Crafts Exhibition (Summer months).

rooms 20 feet across. In 1431, the Earls of Mar and Caithness were defeated here in a battle. Another battle was fought near the Castle in 1645, in which the great Marquis of Montrose, of Clan Graham, after some remarkable forced marches through the Lochaber mountains, defeated the Covenanters. The fight has been described in Scott's " Legend of Montrose," and also in Neil Munro's " John Splendid." The modern *Inverlochy Castle* stands about **2 m. N.E.,** in a loop of the little River Lundy, being known also as *Torlundy Castle*, and in the vicinity of which the rearing of cattle is now being carried on in a large way. The main road leading north-eastwards past the Castle towards the Great Glen, on the line of General Wade's original road, gives access beyond *Loch Lochy* (*q.v.*) to *Invergarry* (*q.v.*). From here commences the fine road to *Cluanie* (*q.v.*), Glen Shiel and *Kyle of Lochalsh* (*q.v.*), the terminal point of one of the " Roads to the Isles."

South-westwards from Fort William, the road to *Kinlochleven* (*q.v.*) follows the shores of Loch Linnhe and Loch Leven, but the old road went inland over the lonely hills past Loch Lundavra. Westwards from the town stretch the waters of *Loch Linnhe* (*q.v.*), and to the north-west is Loch Eil, paralleled by the romantic Road to the Isles, " By Ailort and by Morar to the Sea," leading to *Mallaig* (*q.v.*), in a land poignant with memories of Prince Charles Edward and the '45. This road was originally constructed, as far as Arisaig, by Thomas Telford, in 1800–04. The waters of Loch Eil mingle with those of Loch Linnhe beyond the narrows near *Corpach* (*q.v.*), where the *Caledonian Canal* (*q.v.*) has its western terminus. By rounding the head of Loch Eil, and utilizing a narrow and winding road, access

Forteviot, Perth. A splendidly carved Early Christian Cross, situated near Bankhead Farm, off B9112, on a hill near the River Earn

Forth Bridge, Fife; West Lothian. The famous late 19th century railway bridge, 2,765⅓ yards in length, supported by Inchgarvie Island in the Firth of Forth. A road bridge across the Firth is now under construction to the west

Fortrose, Ross and Cromarty. The ruined 14th and 15th century Cathedral. Cromwell is said to have used some of its stones to erect his fort at Inverness

Fortingall, Perth. The large churchyard yew, which is perhaps the oldest in Great Britain

Fort William, Inverness. The secret portrait mirror of 'Bonnie Prince Charlie,' which is kept in the West Highland Museum

Fort William, Inverness. Lochy Bridge, north-west of the town, leading to the picturesque 'Road to the Isles,' which terminates at Mallaig, facing the island of Skye

[For FORTINGALL see also under BREADALBANE (Plate 22)

PLATE 68 (facing page 158)

Foulden, Berwick. The two-storeyed tithe barn

Fowlis Easter, Angus. The richly carved Sacrament House inside the 15th century Church

Fowlis Wester, Perth. The lych-gate of the Church, the inscription above which carries the date 1644

Foyers, Inverness. A stone on B852, near Loch Ness, some 5 miles north-east. It records the site of a 'Change House' (for horses), visited by Dr. Johnson and Boswell during their Highland tour of 1773

Fraserburgh, Aberdeen. The Mercat Cross of 1736 in the fishing port which Sir Alexander Fraser founded in the mid-16th century

Freswick, Caithness. The ruined 15th century Bucholly Castle of the Mowats. It stands near Ness Head

PLATE 69 (facing page 159)

is gained to the beautiful *Ardgour* (*q.v.*) district, but this journey can be shortened by some 25 miles by following the shores of Loch Linnhe from Fort William, and then utilizing the ferry at *Corran* (*q.v.*). The proposed new name for the communities of Fort William, Inverlochy, Banavie, Corpach and Caol is *Nevisburgh*. See **Ballachulish, Glenfinnan, Kinlocheil, North Ballachulish, Roy Bridge** and **Spean Bridge.** *Iter. 100, 124, 125, 126, 142, 143, 208, 209, 210, 211, 212, 213, 214, 215, 220.*

FOULA, ISLE OF, Shetland.   **Map 33, HT 9 3.**
See **Shetland Islands** (Mainland).

FOULDEN, Berwick.   **Map 11, NT 9 5.**
Here is an unusual two-storeyed and crow-stepped tithe barn (A.M.). An inscribed churchyard gravestone is dated 1592. *Iter. 3, 9, 33.*

FOWLIS EASTER, Angus.   **Map 17, NO 3 3.**
The restored Church, dedicated to *St. Marnan*, dates from 1453, and is of much interest. There is a bell dated 1508, a well-carved font and also a series of notable painted panels. The Sacrament House is one of the finest in Scotland, and is elaborately carved. Beside the south door still hang the jougs.

FOWLIS WESTER, Perth.   **Map 16, NN 9 2.**
A quaint little village, lying a short distance to the north of the Crieff to Perth road, with a restored 15th cent. Church, and a Celtic cross, having the jougs attached. There is a lych-gate dated 1644, and a 10-ft. high cross-slab preserves Pictish symbols and Celtic sculpture (A.M.). A little to the north-west, on the moors, are some prehistoric standing stones.

FOYERS, Inverness. 250.   **Map 25, NH 4 2.**
E.C. Wed. Overlooking *Loch Ness* (*q.v.*), and best known for its Falls, in a lovely, wooded setting, the upper one being 30 ft. high and the lower 90 ft. high. The volume of water has been much reduced, owing to the demands of the nearby aluminium works, which are fed from the *Loch Mhor* reservoir, on the banks of which stands the little hamlet of *Errogie* (*q.v.*). This hydro-electric scheme, the first in Britain, was completed in 1896. Across Loch Ness rises *Mealfuarvonie*, 2,284 ft., the highest point in the extensive Balmacaan Forest. Foyers is on the line of Wade's road linking Fort Augustus with Inverness, and here the General built for himself a shelter, called the General's hut, the exact location of which is not known today. See **Inverfarigaig** and **Wade Roads.** *Iter. 211.*

FRASERBURGH, Aberdeen. 10,411. SB.   **Map 27, NJ 9 6.**
E.C. Wed. M.D. Tues. GOLF. An important *Buchan*

FRASERBURGH
Scale
0   ¼ M.
Kinnairds Head
B.9031
ROSEHEARTY 4½
WATERMILL 22¼
TURRIFF 22¼
BANFF 25¼
A.98
COLLEGE BOUNDS
DENMARK ST.
BARRASGATE RD.
NORTH ST.
CASTLE ST.
DUKE ST.
HIGH ST.
FINLAYSON ST.
ALBERT ST.
CHARLOTTE STREET
GALLOWHILL ROAD
MID STREET
CROSS ST.
SEAFORTH ST.
BROAD ST.
COMMERCE ST.
Thomas Walker Hospital
Balaclava
Harbour
Outer Harbour
Faithlie
Herbr.
DENNYDUFF RD.
VICTORIA ST.
THE HEXAGON
KING EDWARD ST.
QUEEN ST.
SALTOUN PL.
ABERDEEN 42¾
PETERHEAD 18
A.981
INVERURIE 36
STRICHEN ROAD
MACCONACHIEH
A.92
Terminus
Times of High Tide can be found by referring to the Tide Table in the Members Handbook.   R.8.60
CROWN COPYRIGHT RESERVED THE AUTOMOBILE ASSOCIATION

1. Mercat Cross (1736).   3. Old Town House.
2. Old Parish Church,   Information Bureau.
    rebuilt 1899.   4. Wine Tower.

(*q.v.*) herring port and resort, situated on Fraserburgh Bay, with fine sands, and sheltered to the west by Kinnaird's Head, which was mentioned originally by Ptolemy. The town was founded in the 16th cent. under the original name of *Farthlie*. The Mercat Cross dates from 1736. The Parish Church was rebuilt in 1899. The lighthouse on Kinnaird's Head, overlooking the North Sea, stands on the remains of a tower built in 1574. Nearby is the *Wine Tower*, probably dating from the 15th cent., built above a 100-ft. long cave called the Scalch's Hole. 3 m. S.E., near the Water of Philorth, is the restored *Cairnbulg Castle*. See **Inverallochy, Rosehearty** and **Sandhaven.** *Iter. 181, 182, 185, 186, 196, 197.*

FRESWICK, Caithness.   **Map 30, ND 3 6.**
Situated a little inland from Freswick Bay, which is sheltered to the north by Skirsa Head, and to the south by Ness Head. Beyond the latter are remains of the 15th cent. *Bucholly Castle*. There are various prehistoric sites in the neighbourhood. 2 m. N., on the *John o' Groats* (*q.v.*) road, is the low Warth Hill, from which the distant Orkneys can be glimpsed. *Iter. 200.*

FRIOCKHEIM, Angus. 585.   **Map 21, NO 5 4.**
This curious name is said to be derived from Freke, a one-time bailie of Forfar, and "heim," meaning home, the suffix having been added in 1830 by one John Andson, who had been domiciled in Germany. See **Guthrie.** *Iter. 153, 163.*

FURNACE, Argyll.   **Map 14, NS 0 9.**
A *Loch Fyne* (*q.v.*) village, known for its large granite quarry. Smelting-works were formerly situated here. *Iter. 118, 121.*

FUSHIEBRIDGE, Midlothian.   **Map 10, NT 3 6.**
See **Carrington, Crichton** and **Temple.** *Iter. 9, 11, 12.*

FYVIE, Aberdeen.   **Map 27, NJ 7 3.**
The magnificent *Fyvie Castle*, one of the most imposing in Scotland, stands in a finely wooded park, threaded by the River Ythan. The rich south front, dating from the 15th and 16th cents., was added to in the 17th cent., and the four old turreted towers are named after their builders, Gordon, Meldrum, Preston and Seton. In 1644, Montrose evaded capture here by Argyll. Inside the Castle is an exceptionally fine spiral stone staircase. Lord Dunfermline, who completed the 17th cent. alterations, later worked at *Pinkie House* (*q.v.*) in Midlothian. *Iter. 180.*

GAILES, Ayr.   **Map 8, NS 3 3.**
GOLF. See **Troon.**

GAIRLOCH, Ross and Cromarty. 300.   **Map 22, NG 8 7.**
E.C. Wed. Overlooks the beautiful Gair Loch of *Wester Ross*, in which lie the islands of Eilean Horrisdale and Longa. The small resort of *Gairloch* boasts one of the loveliest settings in the Scottish Highlands, and has sandy shores providing good bathing and fishing. Away to the south-west, across the Inner Sound, there are distant views of the *Coolin* hills in the southern part of the island of Skye. Southwards, the view ranges over the Flowerdale Forest peaks, in which *Baeshven*, 2,869 ft., is the highest, while still farther south rises *Beinn Alligin*, 3,232 ft., one of the splendid, wild Torridon peaks overlooking lonely *Torridon* (*q.v.*). The road leading southeastwards to *Loch Maree* (*q.v.*) passes through the beautifully wooded Kerrysdale, in which a hydro-electric scheme is in operation. A branch off this road gives access to the coast between Opinan and Red Point. Another road leads north-westwards from Gairloch along the coast as far as *Melvaig*, beyond which lies the lonely Rudha Reidh, with its lighthouse. See **Gruinard Bay** and **Poolewe.** *Iter. 205, 206, 222.*

GAIRLOCHY, Inverness.   **Map 18, NN 1 8.**
Here, the *Caledonian Canal* (*q.v.*) is raised to the level of *Loch Lochy* (*q.v.*) by means of two locks. The River Lochy formerly flowed into the loch at this point, but its waters have been diverted over the picturesque Mucomer Falls into those of the River Spean, which itself joins the loch a little farther east. 2½ m. S.W., to the north of the road to *Corpach* (*q.v.*), along which magnificent views of *Ben Nevis* (*q.v.*), 4,406 ft., and its lofty neighbours can be obtained, is

the entrance to the roadless Glen Loy, down which Prince Charles Edward marched in 1745. In the glen are slight remains of the old Caledonian Forest. See **Loch Arkaig**. *Iter. 214*.

GAIRNEYBRIDGE, Fife.　　　　Map 17, **NT 1** 9.
Lies to the south of *Loch Leven* (*q.v.*), with *Benarty Hill*, 1,167 ft., rising to the east. A monument here commemorates the foundation, in 1733, of the first Secession Presbytery. See **Blairadam**. *Iter. 90, 92*.

GAIRNSHIEL LODGE, Aberdeen.　　Map 20, **NJ 2** 0.
Situated amid lofty hills and moors, in Glen Gairn, at the junction of roads coming from Braemar and Ballater in the Dee valley. To the north-east, beyond Glen Finzie, rises *Morven*, 2,862 ft. The continuation northwards leads over the hills along the narrow and steep Glas Choille section, rising to over 1,800 ft., and liable to be blocked by snow in winter, before descending towards the fertile valley of the Don in the vicinity of *Cock Bridge* (*q.v.*). *Iter. 160, 174*.

GALASHIELS, Selkirk. 12,205. SB.　　Map 10, **NT 4** 3.
E.C. Wed. GOLF. A busy Border manufacturing town, noted especially for tweeds and woollen hosiery. There is a well-known Woollen Technical College, and the Mercat Cross dates from 1695. The War Memorial includes a

GALASHIELS

Scale

0　¼　½ M.

1. Town Hall. Information Bureau.
2. Old Gala House.
3. Scottish Woollen Technical College.
4. Catrail.
5. Mercat Cross.
6. Municipal Buildings, with town crest.

CROWN COPYRIGHT RESERVED　　　　DRAWN AND PUBLISHED BY THE AUTOMOBILE ASSOCIATION

Clock Tower by Sir Robert Lorimer, in front of which is a representation of a Border "Reiver," or moss-trooper. *Old Gala House* dates from the 16th and 17th cents., with modern alterations, and is now an art centre. The granting of a charter in 1599 is celebrated in early summer by the "Braw Lads" Gathering. The town crest, with its motto "Soure Plums," as depicted on the Municipal Buildings, recalls the deaths of some English soldiers in a Border foray of 1337, after gathering plums. An old track, known as the "Catrail," or Pict's Ditch, passes westwards of the town, on high ground, and is thought to have extended for more than 50 miles in a southerly direction, another stretch being visible near *Shankend* (*q.v.*), on the Hawick to Newcastleton road. On the slopes of *Buckholm Hill*, to the north of Galashiels, stands the well-preserved *Old Buckholm Tower*. About 1½ m. S.E. of the town, on the Melrose road, near *Langlee*, is an inscribed tablet recording Sir Walter Scott's last journey to *Abbotsford* (*q.v.*) on his return from Italy in 1832 shortly before his death. See **Bowland, Darnick** and **Melrose**. *Iter. 11, 32, 33, 52*.

GALLATOWN, Fife.　　　　Map 17, **NT 2** 9.
Iter. 93, 94, 126, 127, 129, 130.

GALLOWAY, Kirkcudbright; Wigtown. Map 2, **NX 1** 5 etc. and 3, **NX 5** 7 etc.
Within this area, which consists of the counties of Kirkcudbright and Wigtown, is included some of the wildest, but least known scenery in Scotland, particularly in the so-called "Galloway Highlands." The mountains here, dominated by the 2,764-ft. high peak of the *Merrick*, and the fine *Rhinns of Kells* range, are bare and lonely, sheltering remote little lochs containing pike. Perhaps the loveliest parts are in the neighbourhood of *Loch Trool* (*q.v.*), where an extensive National Forest Park is situated. Galloway was administered in the 14th and 15th cents. by the Douglas family, and afterwards by hereditary stewards under the Crown until 1747. The district was later to a large extent bound up with the Covenanters. At one time Galloway also included *Carrick* (*q.v.*), which is however now part of the county of Ayr. An extensive power scheme has been developed in Galloway, harnessing the local water resources, and the large *Clatteringshaws Dam* (*q.v.*) was constructed in connection with the project, while there are also a number of power-houses. (See **Carsphairn** and **Tongland**.) The dark Galloway cattle are well known, and the breed of horses known as "Galloways" is thought to have originated partly from animals which swam ashore from wrecked Spanish Armada galleys. S. R. Crockett's "Raiders" introduces the country of the Merrick, in wildest Galloway, and the lofty hill of *Cairnsmore of Fleet*, near *Creetown* (*q.v.*), is associated with John Buchan's "The Thirty-Nine Steps." See **Mull of Galloway** and **Stewartry**.

GALSTON, Ayr. 4,547. SB.　　　Map 8, **NS 4** 3.
E.C. Wed. GOLF. The town stands in a pleasant wooded setting in the valley of the River Irvine. *Barr Castle* is an old tower. To the north is the great pile of *Loudoun Castle*, dating largely from 1811, but retaining a 15th cent. tower, and damaged by fire in 1941. 1½ m. S.E., near the Burn Anne, is *Cessnock Castle*, mainly modern, but preserving an old tower. *Iter. 20, 69*.

GANNOCHY BRIDGE, Angus; Kincardine.
Map 21, **NO 5** 7.
The North Esk, flowing here through a picturesque, rocky and wooded defile, forms the boundary between Angus and Kincardine. North-westwards stretches the beautiful valley of the river, traversed by a road leading to *Tarfside* (*q.v.*) and *Lochlee* (*q.v.*). The hills to the north-west include the *Hill of Wirren*, 2,220 ft., and *Bulg*, 1,986 ft. *Iter. 156, 163, 164*.

GARDENSTOWN, Banff.　　　　Map 27, **NJ 8** 6.
Under lofty red cliffs in Gamrie Bay lies this picturesque fishing village, with a small harbour, and houses rising in tiers to the heights above. It takes its name from a certain Alexander Garden. More Head lies to the west, and Crovie Head, sheltering the fishing village of *Crovie* (*q.v.*), to the east. Near More Head is the hill of *Gamrie Mhor*, 536 ft., overlooking the ruins of the Old Church of *St. John*, founded in 1004, to commemorate a Scottish victory over the Danes. *Iter. 182*.

GARELOCHHEAD, Dunbarton. 550.　　Map 14, **NS 2** 9.
E.C. Wed. This well-known resort stands at the head of the fine Gare Loch, with its background of hills, prominent among which is the long ridge overlooking Loch Long and known as *Argyll's Bowling Green*. Yachts anchor in the loch during the season, and large ships are often laid up in its waters, while at *Faslane* (*q.v.*), a little to the south, on the *Shandon* (*q.v.*) road, is a ship-breaking yard. To the east of Garelochhead rises a range of lonely hills overlooking the head of Glen Fruin (See **Helensburgh**), in which *Beinn Chaorach* attains 2,338 ft. There are roads on both sides of the Gare Loch, that on the west side giving access to the *Rosneath* (*q.v.*) peninsula. See **Whistlefield**. *Iter. 102, 111, 116*.

GARGUNNOCK, Stirling. 613.　　　Map 16, **NS 7** 9.
A small village is the flat country traversed by the serpentine course of the River Forth. To the south rise the *Gargunnock*

Gairneybridge, Fife. The Monument commemorating the founding of the first Secession Presbytery, on the 6th December, 1733. It was erected in 1883

Galashiels, Selkirk. The Town Crest, on the Municipal Buildings, with its motto: 'Sour Plums,' commemorating a Border foray of 1337, when some English soldiers were caught picking plums and afterwards slain

Galston, Ayr. Loudoun Castle, mainly 19th century, but retaining a 15th century tower. The structure was partially burnt in 1941. It stands to the north of Galston, off A719

Galloway, Kirkcudbright; Wigtown. The Monument to the 18th century Professor Alexander Murray, a celebrated linguist, who began as a shepherd boy in the hills of Galloway. It stands 4½ miles south-west of the Clatteringshaws Dam, on the Newton Stewart to New Galloway road (A712)

Gannochy Bridge, Angus; Kincardine. The bridge over the North Esk River, forming the boundary between Angus and Kincardine. It was erected in 1732 by James Black, a local farmer, who is said to have built the parapet with his own hands

Gardenstown, Banff. The cliff-bound fishing village, which was founded by Alexander Garden of Troup

[For GALASHIELS see also under SCOTT COUNTRY (Plate 148)

PLATE 70 (facing page 160)

Garmouth, Moray. Charles II landed near this village in 1650, and signed the Solemn League and Covenant in the cottage which carries this plaque

Garvald, East Lothian. The jougs, or iron collar for wrongdoers, on the west gable of the Church

Gatehouse of Fleet, Kirkcudbright. The ruined 15th century Cardoness Castle, overlooking Fleet Bay. It was once the home of the McCullochs and later of the Gordons of Lochinvar

Gatehouse of Fleet, Kirkcudbright. The 'Murray Arms' Inn, where Robert Burns is said to have written down the words of '*Scots wha ha'e*'

Gifford, East Lothian. The early 18th century Church. Its predecessor stood formerly near Yester House

PLATE 71 (facing page 161)

hills, with their high-lying reservoirs, beyond which are the *Fintry* hills, both ranges attaining a height of about 1,500 feet. Eastwards from Gargunnock lie the lower *Touch* hills, threaded by the Touch Burn. *Gargunnock House* is a 16th to 18th cent. mansion, situated to the east of the village. *Iter. 108, 112, 137.*

GARLIESTON, Wigtown.   Map 2, NX 4 4.
A small port on Garlieston Bay, with Eggerness Point to the north-east, near which are slight remains of *Eggerness Castle*. To the south of Garlieston, on the coast near Rigg, or Cruggleton Bay, stands *Galloway House* (1740), once the seat of the Earls of Galloway, and noted for its wealth of trees and shrubs. It is now a school. See **Cruggleton.** *Iter. 82.*

GARLOGIE, Aberdeen.   Map 21, NJ 7 0.
Iter. 179.

GARMOUTH, Moray.   Map 26, NJ 3 6.
Now a quaint little village, but once a port, near which Charles II landed in 1650. See **Kingston** and **Mosstodloch.** *Iter. 199.*

GARRABOST, Isle of Lewis, Ross and Cromarty.
Iter. 259.   Map 32, NB 5 3.

GARTOCHARN, Dunbarton. 773.   Map 15, NS 4 8.
E.C. Wed. A small resort near the the south-eastern shores of *Loch Lomond* (*q.v.*) and its numerous wooded islands. To the north-west, by the lochside, stands the mansion of *Ross Priory*, with its lovely grounds, notably the yew avenue. It was once visited by Sir Walter Scott. *Iter. 109, 112, 114, 137.*

GARVALD, East Lothian.   Map 10, NT 5 7.
A tiny village on the northern slopes of the *Lammermuir* hills, with *Clints Dod*, 1,307 ft., a good viewpoint, rising to the south-east. The Church dates partly from the 12th cent., and retains a sundial dated 1633, and also the ancient jougs, attached to the west gable. To the south-east is the mansion of *Nunraw*, mainly 19th cent., but preserving a late 16th cent. tower. It is now occupied by Trappist monks. Eastwards of Garvald lies a wooded glen in which stands the ruined tower of *Stoneypath*. A narrow and hilly road threads its way south-eastwards from Garvald into the hills below *Spartleton Edge*, and later crosses the " Hungry Snout," before descending to the Berwickshire valley of the Whiteadder Water near *Cranshaws* (*q.v.*).

GARVE, Ross and Cromarty. 149.   Map 24, NH 3 6.
E.C. Tues. Situated between Loch Garve, a little to the south-east, and the entrance to Strath Garve, which is traversed by the lonely road leading towards Ullapool. The main road westwards continues along Strath Bran, passing Loch Luichart, to the south, and giving views of the distant *Fannich* peaks away to the north-west, beyond Kinlochluichart Forest. A large hydro-electric scheme now operates in the Fannich district. Beyond Loch Luichart, and to the south of the road, are the smaller Lochs a'Chuilinn and Achanalt, with *Sgurr Vuillin*, 2,845 ft., rising in the background. To the north-east of Garve is *Little Wyvis* 2,497 ft., backed by the larger mass of *Ben Wyvis*, 3,429 ft. *Iter. 204, 205, 206, 221.*

GARVELLACH ISLANDS, Argyll.   Map 13, NM 6 1.
See **Clachan Bridge.**

GARYNAHINE, Isle of Lewis, Ross and Cromarty.
                    Map 32, NB 2 3.
See **Hebrides, Outer** (Lewis). *Iter. 257, 260.*

GATEHOUSE OF FLEET, Kirkcudbright. 876.
                    Map 3, NX 6 5.
E.C. Thurs. M.D. Sat. GOLF. A pleasant little *Galloway* (*q.v.*) town, the " Kippletringan " of Scott's " Guy Mannering," situated on the Water of Fleet, which flows southwards into Fleet Bay, an inlet of Wigtown Bay. On the moors in the vicinity Burns composed " Scots wha ha'e," and the room in the " *Murray Arms* " Hotel in which he wrote it down is still pointed out. To the south of the town, which is well known to anglers, is *Cally House*, designed by Robert Mylne in 1763, in its fine grounds. **1 m. S.W.,** on a rocky height overlooking Fleet Bay, are the remains of the late

15th cent. *Cardoness Castle* (A.M.), a former home of the McCullochs of Galloway, and retaining its original stairway. **3 m. N.W.,** in the beautiful valley of the Fleet Water, is the ruined, but imposing *Rusco Castle*, dating from c. 1500, once the home of an old Galloway family, the Gordons of Lochinvar. Farther east rises *Bengray*, 1,203 ft., below which lies Loch Whinyeon. Beyond Fleet Bay, to the south-west, are the *Murray Isles* (N.T. Scot.), in Wigtown Bay. The old road to *Creetown* (*q.v.*) went inland, where the lonely Gatehouse of Fleet station now stands, some **6 m. N.W.** of the town. The present road follows the curve of Wigtown Bay, and is one of the loveliest coast roads in southern Scotland, passing *Dirk Hatteraick's Cave* beyond Ravenshall Point, and also the ruined castles of *Barholm* and *Carsluith*. The hills in the background include *Cairnharrow*, 1,497 ft. See **Anwoth Church** and **Kirkcudbright.** *Iter. 26, 72, 73.*

GATESIDE, Fife.   Map 17, NO 1 0.
Iter. 130, 136.

GATTONSIDE, Roxburgh.   Map 10, NT 5 3.
Iter. 33.

GELSTON, Kirkcudbright.   Map 3, NX 7 5.
Iter. 72.

GEORGEMAS, Caithness.   Map 30, ND 1 5.
See **Halkirk.** *Iter. 236.*

GIFFNOCK, Renfrew. 9,144.   Map 8, NS 5 5.
E.C. Tues. GOLF. Situated on the south-western fringes of Glasgow. Away to the east, over the Lanark border, is the attractive, wooded public park of Cathkin Braes. See **Clarkston.** *Iter. 18, 29, 55, 61.*

GIFFORD, East Lothian. 338.   Map 10, NT 5 6.
E.C. Wed. GOLF. This delightful 18th cent. village, retaining its Mercat Cross, is situated on the Gifford Water, with views to the south of the *Lammermuir* hills. These are given over largely to sheep, and to the south, near the Berwick border, rises *Lammer Law*, 1,733 ft., a fine viewpoint. The Church at Gifford dates from 1708. Its predecessor stood near *Yester House*. In it is preserved a late medieval bell, and also a 17th cent. pulpit. South-east of the village, in a woodland setting, threaded by the Hopes Water, is *Yester House*, a fine Adam mansion, dating from 1745. Beyond it lie the remains of *Yester Castle*, best known for the remarkable underground chamber known as the " Goblin Ha'," which dates perhaps from 1267. Scott has introduced the scene in his " Marmion." A beech tree in the park is 142 ft. in height. Near the mansion is the little, restored 15th cent. Collegiate *Bothan's* Church, the burial-place of the Tweeddales since 1710, with a number of old monuments. A narrow, hilly and winding road climbs south-eastwards from Gifford into the *Lammermuirs*, attaining some 1,400 ft., and passing later over the " Hungry Snout " to descend to the Berwickshire valley of the Whiteadder Water near *Cranshaws* (*q.v.*), on the way to *Duns* (*q.v.*). See **Garvald** and **Whittinghame.** *Iter. 3.*

GIGHA, ISLE OF, Argyll.   Map 6, NR 6 4.
This small island lies a little way off the west coast of Kintyre, from which it is separated by the Sound of Gigha. It is only about 6 miles in length, and is flat, with rocky shores. The ruined Church of *Kilchattan* is of 13th cent. date. The gardens of *Achamore* are notable, and are shown at times in the summer (see note page 90). The well-known " Songs of the Hebrides " include verses written by Dr. Kenneth MacLeod, the Gaelic scholar, of Gigha parish. To the south is the tiny island of *Cara*. Access to Gigha is by steamer from West Loch Tarbert (see **Tarbert;** Argyll), or by passenger ferry from *Tayinloan* (*q.v.*) in Kintyre (*q.v.*).

GILLOCK, Caithness.   Map 30, ND 2 5.
Iter. 239.

GILMERTON, Midlothian.   Map 10, NT 2 6.
A little to the east is the fine mid-18th cent. mansion known as *The Drum*, built by William Adam, the father of the even more famous Robert Adam. **2 m. N.N.E.,** near the little village of *Edmonston*, is *Woolmet House* (N.T. Scot.), dating from 1686, and altered in the 18th cent. *Iter. 4, 5, 9, 11, 12, 13.*

GILMERTON, Perth.   Map 16, NN 8 2.
A by-road proceeding north-westwards, and later leading to *Crieff* (*q.v.*), circles the fine park of *Monzie Castle*, threaded by the Shaggie Burn. To the south-east, and south of the Perth road, are the mansions of *Cultoquhey*, *Abercairney* and *Inchbrackie*. **4 m. N.** of Gilmerton is the very beautiful *Sma' Glen* (*q.v.*). **5½ m. E.,** off the Perth road, are slight remains of the 13th cent. *Inchaffray Abbey*. See **Fowlis Wester.** *Iter.* 89, 140, 141, 145.

GIRVAN, Ayr. 5,931. SB.   Map 2, NX 1 9.
E.C. Wed. GOLF. A well-known resort in the *Carrick* (*q.v.*) division of the county, with a sandy beach and bathing.

1. Town House.

The Town House, moved from its original site in 1828, was at one time used as a gaol. About ten miles out to sea is the lonely, rocky *Ailsa Craig*, 1,114 ft. high, and two miles in circumference, a breeding-place for birds, and noted for its granite quarries, which supply material for the manufacture of curling-stones. A lighthouse and an ancient ruined Castle are also situated on Ailsa Craig, which is known as " Paddy's Milestone," owing to its position about half-way between Glasgow and Belfast. **3 m. N.E.,** in the valley of the Water of Girvan, is the picturesque *Killochan Castle*, dating from c. 1586. It is shown daily, 2 to 6, except Sat., mid-May to mid-Sept. (See note page 90). **4 m. S.S.W.** is *Kennedy's Pass*, perhaps the finest piece of scenery on the lovely coastal road to *Ballantrae* (*q.v.*). **2 m. S.** is *Ardmillan House*, 16th cent. and restored, where Mary, Queen of Scots once stayed. Hugh Rodger, once Burns's schoolmaster, is said to have been married in the hall of this house. See **Barr, Culzean Castle, Dailly, Kirkoswald** and **Turnberry.** *Iter.* 55, 68, 71, 74, 78, 80, 85.

GLADSMUIR, East Lothian.   Map 10, NT 4 7.
Iter. 1.

GLAMIS, Angus. 876.   Map 20, NO 3 4.
Famous for *Glamis Castle*, one of the most notable of its period in Scotland, and standing in fine grounds, bordered by the Dean Water. Shakespeare's " Macbeth " was Thane of Glamis, but the events the poet has described lack historical foundation. In 1715, the Old Pretender lodged for a

short period in the Castle, which is the ancestral home of the Earl of Strathmore, father of H.M. Queen Elizabeth, the Queen Mother, and was the birthplace, in 1930, of Her Royal Highness Princess Margaret. The greater part of the structure dates from 1675–1687, but an older tower, with 15-ft. thick walls, has survived, and there have also been early 19th cent. alterations. The drawing-room and the panelled Chapel are notable, and in the Castle is preserved the " lion-cup " of Glamis, associated with Scott's " Waverley." The Castle is reputedly ghost-haunted. It is open from 2 to 5.30, Wed. and Thurs. in May and June; Wed., Thurs. and Sun. in July, Aug. and Sept. (See note page 90.) From the battlements there are splendid views of the Vale of *Strathmore* (*q.v.*) leading to the Howe of Angus, and of the *Sidlaw* hills and the distant eastern *Grampians*. The great sundial in the grounds is over 21 ft. in height and has 84 dials. In the village, the old jougs hang near the churchyard gate. *Kirk Wynd* cottages (N.T. Scot.) contain the Angus folk museum, open daily, 1 to 6, Easter to Sept. (See note page 90). **2½ m. N.E.,** beyond the station, near *Cossans* farm, is the richly-carved *St. Orland's Stone* (A.M.), of the Early Christian period. *Iter.* 151, 153, 161.

GLASGOW, Lanark. 1,079,364.   Map 8, NS 5 6.
E.C. Tues. MD. Wed. GOLF. The largest city and sea-port of Scotland, and the third largest in population of the British Isles, *Glasgow* has grown with enormous rapidity within the last 150 years, due largely to the enterprise of Glaswegians in developing the River Clyde and establishing large docks and shipbuilding yards. Among other important industries established on Clydeside are chemicals, textiles, and both engineering and iron-works, these being made possible by the proximity of the important Lanarkshire coalfield. The patron saint of the city is St. Kentigern, or St. Mungo, who began his missionary work here in the 6th cent. The first Cathedral was finished in 1136, on the site of the early Church of *St. Kentigern*. The University was founded in 1450, and 4 years later Glasgow became a Royal Burgh. In 1650, and also in the following year, Cromwell was in the city, and Prince Charles Edward, on his retreat from England in 1745, levied toll on Glasgow. He had been proclaimed Regent at the 17th cent. Glasgow Cross. This was later demolished and replaced by the present Cross, erected in 1929. On Glasgow Green, where the Prince reviewed his troops after the retreat, stands the prominent Nelson obelisk. In the vicinity is the *People's Palace*, containing the Old Glasgow Museum. A great Empire Exhibition was held at Bellahouston Park in 1938.

Among the various parks, the best known are perhaps Glasgow Green, Kelvingrove Park and Queen's Park, the last-named having a memorial to mark the site of the battle of Langside, in 1568, after which Mary, Queen of Scots commenced her flight from Scotland. (See **Clarkston.**) South-east of Queen's Park is the famous *Hampden Park* football ground. Rouken Glen Park contains a waterfall and lake, and to the south-east of the city, near Calderpark, is the Zoological Park. In Victoria Park, Whiteinch, is a notable fossil grove. The old-established Glasgow Fair holidays take place in the 2nd or 3rd week of July. Many Clyde pleasure steamers start from the *Broomielaw*, on the north bank, adjacent to the George V bridge. The airport is situated near *Renfrew* (*q.v.*). The most important structure in the city is the very fine 13th cent. Cathedral, and prominent among the places of interest are the University, the splendid Art Gallery and Museum, and Provand's Lordship and Provan Hall, two interesting old houses. All these are described in detail below, together with other buildings, and times of admission are given where available (see page 90). In George Square stands an 80-ft. high column crowned by a statue to Sir Walter Scott, and the nearby Cenotaph is by Sir John Burnet. The mid-18th cent. *St. Andrew's* Church, in St. Andrew's Square, has a notable interior of the period. The imposing *St. Vincent Street* Church, and also the stone-built terraces in Great Western Road, are the work of the Glasgow architect Alexander Thomson (1817–1875), who was known as ' Greek' Thomson. Although situated on the fringe of a great industrial and shipbuilding area, Glasgow is exceptionally fortunate in the

Girvan, Ayr. The 16th century Killochan Castle, an ancient stronghold of the Cathcarts of Carleton. It stands some 3 miles north-east, off B741

Glamis, Angus. The great sundial, with its 84 dials, which stands in the grounds of the 17th century Castle, situated in large policies to the north of the village

Glasgow, Lanark. The statue of Sir Walter Scott, which dominates George Square

Glamis, Angus. The Kirk Wynd cottages, restored by the National Trust for Scotland, and now housing the Angus Folk Museum.

ON THIS SPOT
ALEXANDER ROSS
SPECIAL CONSTABLE
WAS SHOT DEAD
WHILE IN EXECUTION OF HIS DUTY
12TH JULY 1831

Girvan, Ayr. A stone in memory of Alexander Ross, a special constable, who was shot here in 1831. It stands at the junction of A77 and B734, to the north-east

PLATE 72 (facing page 162)   [For GLASGOW see also Plates 73 and 74

The Cathedral, partly the work of Bishop Bondington in the 13th century. It is noted for the crypt, or 'Laigh Kirk,' consecrated by Bishop Jocelin in 1197

Provand's Lordship, of 15th century date, probably the oldest house in the city. It was once part of the Hospital of St. Nicholas, and was built by Bishop Muirhead

The 'crown' steeple of the former 17th century Tolbooth, which Sir Walter Scott has portrayed in his '*Rob Roy*'

The 17th century Merchants' Hall steeple, the work of Sir William Bruce

The Memorial in Queen's Park commemorating the battle of Langside, in 1568, which was fatal to the cause of Mary, Queen of Scots

The Nelson obelisk on Glasgow Green. In the vicinity Prince Charles Edward reviewed his forces after the retreat from England in 1745

PLATE 73 (facing page 163)

[For **GLASGOW** see also Plates 72 and 74

CENTRAL GLASGOW

Street Car Parking...........
One Way Streets..............
No Waiting...................

Unilateral waiting is allowed on certain streets in the Central Area of Glasgow

Scale

440 Yds.   ½ Mile
220

A.A. OFFICE, FANUM HOUSE, BLYTHSWOOD SQUARE. Telephone: Glasgow CENtral 9191. Telegrams: Fanum, Glasgow

1. Cathedral, 12th to 15th cent.
2. City Chambers
3. Information Bureau
4. Mercat Cross, 1929
5. Merchants' Hall Steeple, late 17th cent. in Fish Market
6. Mitchell Library
7. People's Palace, with Old Glasgow Museum
8. Provand's Lordship, old house, 1471
9. St. Vincent Street Church, 1857–59
10. Tolbooth Steeple, early 17th cent.

DOCKS

Queen's Dock Area, follow YELLOW arrows.

A. Broomielaw.
B. Anderson Quay.
C. Lancefield Quay.

Prince's Dock Area, follow RED arrows.

D. Kingston Dock.
E. Bridge Wharf. (River steamers only).
F. Springfield Quay.

Art Gallery and Museum
Kelvin Hall, rebuilt 1926

1.
2.

Langside Memorial, at Queen's
Park (Battle of 1568)
University

3.
4.

GLASGOW

DOCKS

Queen's Dock Area, follow
YELLOW arrows.

A1. Stobcross Quay.
B1. Queen's Dock.
C1. Yorkhill Quay.
D1. Meadowside Quay.
E1. Merklands Wharf

Prince's Dock Area, follow RED
arrows.

F1. Mavisbank Quay.
G1. Plantation Quay.
H1. Prince's Dock.

For King George V Dock,
off Renfrew Road (A8). on west
of plan, follow BLUE arrows.

country by which it is surrounded, more particularly to the west and north. Within easy reach are such world-famous districts as the *Kyles of Bute* (*q.v.*), *Loch Lomond* (*q.v.*) and the *Trossachs* (*q.v.*), while almost on the city's doorstep, to the north are the *Kilpatrick*, *Campsie* and *Kilsyth* hills. To the south-east, beyond *Hamilton* (*q.v.*), the Clyde flows through increasingly attractive orchard country, with a series of notable waterfalls in the immediate vicinity of *Lanark* (*q.v.*).

FAMOUS BUILDINGS

GLASGOW CATHEDRAL (A.M.). The first Cathedral, built in 1123-1136 over the grave of St. Kentigern (or St. Mungo), was burned in 1192. Its successor was commenced soon afterwards, and part of the original crypt of 1197 has survived. The choir and tower are of beautiful 13th cent. workmanship, but the spire dates from 200 years later. The nave was not completed until 1480, and at a later date the building was divided into three congregations, the nave, choir and crypt. Glasgow Cathedral is the most complete in Scotland, and has never been roofless, but the Western towers were removed during the 19th cent. The crypt, or " Laigh Kirk " is the finest feature, and is notable for the pillars and vaulting, while, in the centre, is the site of St. Mungo's tomb. The Chapter House, of the same date, though not completed until later, has a richly carved entrance doorway and preserves a gravestone of nine martyred Covenanters. The 13th cent. choir contains a splendid 15th cent. stone screen. Below is Blackader's aisle, or aisle of St. Fergus, an interesting vaulted crypt. Behind the Cathedral is the Necropolis, with a statue to the Reformers and John Knox.

TOLBOOTH STEEPLE. This is the surviving portion of the Tolbooth of c. 1628, which is associated with the prison described in Sir Walter Scott's " Rob Roy," and has been reconditioned. The " crown," at the summit of the 113-ft. high steeple, is one of three similar examples in Scotland, the others being *St. Giles'* at *Edinburgh* (*q.v.*) and King's College Chapel in *Aberdeen* (*q.v.*).

MERCHANTS' HALL STEEPLE. Built by Sir William Bruce in the late 17th cent., and now surrounded by the buildings of the modern fish market. The tower is noted for its effect of diminishing storeys.

TRON STEEPLE. Formerly attached to the Church of *St. Mary*, which was destroyed by fire in 1793. The steeple, which is 126 ft. high, dates from 1637. Nearby stands the *Tron* Church.

PROVAND'S LORDSHIP. Probably Glasgow's oldest house, having been built in 1471 as part of the old Hospital of *St. Nicholas*. It is said that James II, James IV and Mary, Queen of Scots all lived in the house at different times, the last-named in 1566. The rooms in the house now contain much 17th cent. furniture, old stained glass, portraits and tapestries. Open daily, except Sun. and Thurs., summer, 10 to 1 and 2 to 5; winter, 11 to 1 and 2 to 4. See **Provan Hall**, below.

PROVAN HALL. Known also as the *Old Hall, Mailing*, and now Scottish National Trust property, this 15th cent. house, very well restored, is one of the finest buildings of its period in Scotland. It was formerly the country residence of the Prebendary of *Provand's Lordship*. (See above.) There are two buildings, facing each other across a court-yard, the original structure showing a corbie-stepped gable, and the 17th and 18th cent. wing being now the caretaker's residence. The house is situated near the forsaken Monk-land Canal, to the east of the city, and a little to the north of the Coatbridge road. It is open Mon., Tues., Thurs. and Sat., 10 to 4 or 8; Sun., 2 to 4 or 8. Also on Bank Hols.

ART GALLERY AND MUSEUM. Situated in Kelvingrove Park, and opened in 1901, this building, which received war damage in 1941, houses a magnificent collection of works of art and objects of scientific interest, including the famous Burrell collection. The paintings form one of the most comprehensive collections in Great Britain, and are representative of the Dutch, French and Scottish schools. Open weekdays, 10 to 5; Sun., 2 to 5.

THE UNIVERSITY. Founded in 1450, the University is no longer housed in its old building, but occupies a commanding site on Gilmorehill, the structure having been designed in 1868-1870 by Sir Gilbert Scott, and incorporating a tower and spire 300 ft. high. The imposing Bute Hall was added in 1882. The Old Lodge, which stands near the entrance, is built of stones from the Old College. In the *Hunterian* Museum and Library, open weekdays, 10 to 5, (Sat., 10 to 12), are valuable collections bequeathed by Dr. William Hunter, who died in 1783. The University library contains many rare volumes, and is open weekdays, 10 to 5 (Sat., 10 to 12). See **Lesmahagow.**

KELVIN HALL. Rebuilt in 1926, the hall is the largest of its kind in Great Britain, and is used for exhibitions.

CITY CHAMBERS. This fine, modern building has a tower 240 ft. in height, and the interior of the edifice is on a rich and lavish scale, with a notable banqueting hall. Open weekdays, except alt. Thurs. afternoons, 10.30 to 12 and 2 to 4; Sat., 10.30 to 12.

MITCHELL LIBRARY. A modern building, in which are numerous rare books, including an important Burns collection. The free library is the largest in Scotland. Open weekdays, 9.30 to 9; Sun., from Oct. to March, 2 to 8.

BOTANIC GARDENS. These are situated off the Great Western road, and contain rare plants and trees. In the *Kibble Palace*, re-erected here in 1872, and once used for meetings, the Earl of Beaconsfield and Mr. Gladstone delivered their rectorial addresses. Rare tree-ferns are now housed in the building.

See **Bearsden, Bothwell, Clarkston, Clydebank, Govan, Mount Vernon, Paisley, Pollokshaws, Renfrew** and **Rutherglen.** For Through Routes see page 42. *Iter. 15, 16, 17, 51, 52, 53, 54, 55, 56, 57, 58, 59, 97, 98, 99, 100, 101, 102, 103, 104, 105, 106, 107, 108.*

GLASSERTON, Wigtown. Map 2, **NX 4 3.**
On the coast, **2 m. S.**, reached by means of a by-road, and later a path, is *St. Ninian's* Cave, on Port Castle Bay, possibly an oratory used by the Saint, and in which carved stones are preserved. Burrow Head lies a little to the south-east. See **Isle of Whithorn** and **Whithorn.** *Iter. 82.*

GLEN AFFRIC, Inverness. Map 24, **NH 1 2 and 2 2.**
See **Cannich.** *Iter. 206, 210.*

GLEN ALMOND, Perth. Map 16, **NN 7 3 and 8 3.**
See **Methven** (for Trinity College; Glenalmond), **Newton Bridge** and **Sma' Glen.** *Iter. 147.*

GLENBARR, Argyll. Map 6, **NR 6 3.**
On the western shores of the narrow *Kintyre* (*q.v.*) peninsula, at the mouth of the Barr Glen, which leads into lonely hills rising in the background to more than 1,400 ft. Beyond the modernised *Glenbarr Abbey*, the Barr Water flows into the sea, with Glenacardoch Point to the north. *Iter. 121.*

GLENBARRY, Banff. Map 26, **NJ 5 5.**
Iter. 170, 193.

GLENBORRODALE CASTLE, Argyll. Map 12, **NM 6 6.**
Iter. 216.

GLENBRITTLE, Isle of Skye, Inverness. Map 23, **NG 4 2.**
Remotely situated on Loch Brittle, in the Minginish district, overlooked by the 150-ft. high Eas Mor waterfall. The western flanks of the *Coolins* (*q.v.*) rise steeply from the green valley of the River Brittle, showing from this side Coire Lagan and Coir' a Ghrunnda, two of their finest corries, the first-named being dominated by the great precipices of *Sron na Ciche*. *Sgurr Alasdair*, 3,251 ft., the highest point in the range, with its well-known " Stone Shoot," is usually climbed from here, Glenbrittle being best known as a climbers' rendezvous. A very narrow and rough road leads northwards through the upper part of the glen, now partly afforested by the Forestry Commission, and continues over high ground to reach the shores of Loch Harport. Turning eastwards, access is gained to the better road through Glen Drynoch to *Sligachan* (*q.v.*), near the northern extremity of the main Coolin ridge. A path leads southwards from Glenbrittle, along the shores of the loch, towards the picturesque headland of Rudh'an Dunain,

Glasgow, Lanark. Provan Hall, a 15th century house, cared for by the National Trust for Scotland. It stands near the Monkland Canal, off B806, to the east of the city

Glasgow, Lanark. The lofty Tron Steeple (1637), once attached to St. Mary's Church, which was burnt in 1793 by drunken members of the so-called 'Hell-Fire' club

Glasgow, Lanark. The Old Lodge, which forms part of Glasgow University. It is built of stones from the old college, founded originally in 1450

Glasgow, Lanark. The spacious Kelvin Hall (1926), used for exhibition purposes

Glen Affric, Inverness. The westerly view from Loch Benevean. Hydro-electric developments have taken place in the vicinity. The loch lies on an unclassified road south-west of Cannich

Glasgow, Lanark. The 19th century University Buildings, seen from Kelvingrove Park

[For GLASGOW see also Plates 72 and 73
[For GLEN AFFRIC see also under AFFRIC (Plate 5)

PLATE 74 (facing page 166)

Glencaple, Dumfries. A village associated with Sir Walter Scott's '*Guy Mannering*,' under the name of 'Portanferry'

Glencoe, Argyll. The site of the 1692 massacre of Glencoe, when Government troops treacherously slew more than 40 Macdonalds, whose Chieftain had been a few days late tending allegiance to William III. The order for the savage massacre is sometimes said to have been written on a playing card, the Nine of Diamonds, a card known since as the 'Curse of Scotland'

Glencoe, Argyll. The monument to the Macdonald Chief, who was slain in the massacre of 1692, and is buried on an island in Loch Leven

Glenelg, Inverness. The remains of the early 18th century Bernera Barracks, which fell into disuse after 1790. They lie to the north-west, facing Skye across the narrow and fast-flowing strait of Kyle Rhea

Glencorse, Midlothian. The entrance to the barracks of the Royal Scots, Britain's oldest regiment, whose regimental march is '*Dumbarton's Drums*.' The Earl of Dumbarton was appointed their Colonel by Charles II

Glenelg, Inverness. One of the two well preserved brochs which stand in Glen Beag, on an unclassified road to the south

PLATE 75 (facing page 167)

from which the views out to sea, and also towards the Coolins, are extremely fine. *Iter. 252.*

GLENBUCHAT CASTLE, Aberdeen.   Map 26, NJ 3 1.
See **Glenkindie**.

GLEN CANNICH, Inverness.   Map 24, NH 1 3.
See **Cannich**. *Iter. 206, 210.*   and **2** 3.

GLENCAIRN CHURCH, Dumfries.   Map 3, NX 8 9.
See **Moniaive**.

GLENCAPLE, Dumfries.   Map 4, NX 9 6.
A small bathing place on the estuary of the River Nith, associated with Scott's " Guy Mannering." It is known locally as *The Auld Quay.* Robert Burns, when working as an exciseman, once composed a poem here. See **Caerlaverock**. *Iter. 28.*

GLENCARSE, Perth.   Map 17, NO 1 2.
Pitfour Castle is a late 18th cent. mansion, and *Inchyra House* is of the same period. *Iter. 154.*

GLEN CLOVA, Angus.   Map 20, NO 3 7 and 3 6.
See **Braedownie and Clova Church**. *Iter. 161.*

GLENCOE, Argyll.   Map 18, NN 1 5.
The famous pass through Glen Coe, in Gaelic the " glen of weeping," is perhaps the best known in all Scotland, due as much to its grim historical associations as to the magnificent and wild mountain setting of north-east *Lorne* (*q.v.*) in which it lies. Some 13,000 acres in the neighbourhood are now the property of the Scottish National Trust, including the site of the main part of the Glencoe massacre, and also the lofty peak of *Bidean nam Bian*, 3,766 ft., Argyll's highest mountain. Contiguous with this property are the mountains of *Dalness* Forest, facing Glen Etive, and including the twin *Buchaille Etive* peaks, separated by the lonely Lairig Gartain pass, this district having been acquired by the Trust in 1937. The new road, dating from 1935, leading through Glen Coe from the east, which attains just over 1,000 ft. in height, has been constructed at a lower level than the old one. In the heart of the defile, above the road, is a rock platform known as the " Studdie," or " Study," which provides perhaps the finest view of the savage, bare mountains which overhang the pass.

On the south side are the *Three Sisters of Glencoe*, known as *Beinn Fhada, Gearr Aonach* and *Aonach Dubh*, all around 2,500 to 3,000 ft. high, and being outliers of the peaks of *Stob Coire nan Lochan* (3,657 ft.) and *Bidean nam Bian*. High up on *Aonach Dubh*, overlooking Loch Triochatan, is Ossian's Cave, a deep cleft. On the north side of the glen extends the pinnacled ridge of *Aonach Eagach*, with a number of 3,000-ft. summits, overlooking Loch Leven and the *Mamore Forest* (*q.v.*) mountains of *Lochaber* (*q.v.*) beyond its shores. At the western end of this ridge is the conical *Pap of Glencoe*, 2,430 ft., which is a conspicuous feature in the view from the neighbourhood of Loch Leven and *Ballachulish* (*q.v.*). Lower down the glen, beyond Loch Triochatan, the old and new roads part company, the latter keeping to the south of the river and looking across its waters to the little " Clachaig " Inn. From the Signal Rock, in the vicinity, came, on a mid-winter's dawn in 1692, the signal for the hideous massacre of the Macdonalds of Glencoe by Campbell of Glen Lyon, more than 40 being slain, while others fled into the hills to die of want and exposure. All the hamlets in the glen were burnt down by the soldiers. A monument has been set up to the memory of the murdered chief, who is buried on the island of *Eilean Munde*, in Loch Leven, near the entrance to the glen. R. L. Stevenson, in his novel " Kidnapped," has described the scenery of Glencoe. See **Bridge of Orchy**, **Carnach** and **Kingshouse** (for *Buchaille Etives*). *Iter. 100, 125, 142.*

GLENCORSE, Midlothian.   Map 10, NT 2 6.
GOLF. Here are the barracks of the Royal Scots, the oldest regiment to be found in Britain, the nucleus having been the companies formed by Louis XIII in 1633, with which were incorporated the famous Scots brigade from the Swedish army. The old Kirk, to the north of Milton Bridge, was described by R. L. Stevenson in his " Weir of Hermiston." Farther north, in the foothills of the Pentlands, is Glencorse

reservoir, at a height of 740 ft., with *Black Hill*, 1,628 ft., in the background. In the vicinity is *Rullion Green*, where the Covenanters were defeated by General Tom Dalyell in 1666. An inscribed stone, set up in 1738, recalls the fight. A service is held annually in a field at *Flotterstane*, to the northeast, in commemoration. Farther to the north rises *Castle Law*, 1,595 ft., preserving a small Iron Age hill fort (A.M.). See **Swanston** and **West Linton**. *Iter. 10, 24.*

GLEN CROE, Argyll.   Map 14, NN 2 0.
See **Rest and be Thankful**. *Iter. 88, 101, 102, 103, 137.*

GLENDARUEL, Argyll.   Map 14, NR 9 8.
A pleasant glen, stretching from the head of Loch Riddon, an inlet of the *Kyles of Bute* (*q.v.*), and extending to the hills bordering *Loch Fyne* (*q.v.*). In *Kilmodan* Church is a memorial to Colin Maclaurin, the mathematician, who organised Edinburgh's defences during the '45. A little to the south of Glendaruel, a narrow, winding and hilly (1 in 4) road, attaining 1,026 ft., leads to *Otter Ferry* (*q.v.*) on Loch Fyne. See **Colintraive**. *Iter. 102, 103.*

GLENDEVON, Perth. 139.   Map 16, NN 9 0.
In the heart of the picturesque, winding Glen Devon, which penetrates the *Ochil* hills, and merges to the north into Glen Eagles. The highest point of the road in Glen Devon attains nearly 900 ft., giving a fine northerly view over Strath Earn towards the distant Perthshire mountains. To the southeast rises *Innerdownie*, 2,004 ft., with several large reservoirs in the vicinity. See **Crook of Devon, Gleneagles Hotel** and **Rumbling Bridge**. *Iter. 89.*

GLENEAGLES HOTEL, Perth.   Map 16, NN 9 1.
E.C. Wed. GOLF. This famous golfing resort, one of the best known in Scotland, is situated on the moors between Strath Earn and Strath Allan, and a little beyond the northern extremity of Glen Eagles, with views of the *Ochil* hills away to the south. 2 m. S., off the road through the glen, stands *Gleneagles House*, dating from 1624, and in the near vicinity are remains of the former castle. *Iter. 89, 135, 146.*

GLENEGEDALE AIRPORT, Isle of Islay, Argyll.
See **Port Ellen**. *Iter. 243.*   Map 6, NR 3 5.

GLENELG, Inverness.   Map 23, NG 8 1.
This little village on Glenelg Bay lies in a picturesque, remote situation on the shores of the narrow Sound of Sleat, noted for its exceptionally strong currents, and which separates the mainland from the island of Skye. Steamers call off-shore, and the village is accessible by one road only, this crossing a high ridge of hills to the west of *Loch Duich* (*q.v.*) by means of the well-known pass of *Mam Rattachan* (*q.v.*). Dr. Johnson and Boswell reached Glenelg over the pass on their Highland tour, in 1773. A curious point, not often realized, is that the name of Glenelg is a palindrome, reading the same both backwards and forwards. On the north side of Glenelg Bay are the remains of Bernera Barracks, erected c. 1722, soldiers having been quartered there continuously until after 1790. A carved stone in the churchyard, dated 1730, is in memory of one of the garrison officers. Opposite the barracks are the narrows of Kyle Rhea, facing *Kylerhea* (*q.v.*), in Skye, which is overlooked by *Beinn na Caillich*, 2,396 ft., and *Sgurr na Coinnich*, 2,401 ft. Cattle were formerly ferried from Skye across these narrow waters, being driven over the Mam Rattachan Pass and thence down through the Highlands to the great cattle trysts near *Falkirk* (*q.v.*). A car ferry, operated during the summer, connects with Kylerhea in Skye. 1 m. S. of Glenelg is the entrance to the lovely Glen Beag, in which are situated two notable Pictish brochs, *Dun Telve* and *Dun Troddan* (A.M.), perhaps the finest existing on the mainland; farther east is another example, *Dun Grugaig*, near which is a waterfall. To the south rises *Ben Sgriol*, 3,196 ft., a splendid viewpoint. The narrow, rough and hilly coast road from Glenelg around Outer *Loch Hourn* (*q.v.*) to *Arnisdale* (*q.v.*) is one of the loveliest in Scotland, providing exquisite views from the high ground above the Sound of Sleat towards the islands of Skye and Rum. Across the mouth of Loch Hourn rises *Ladhar Bheinn*, 3,343 ft., one of the highest of the remote *Knoydart* (*q.v.*) peaks. *Iter. 207.*

GLENFARG, Perth. 295.   Map 17, **NO 1 1**.
E.C. Thurs. Situated at the southern end of the delightful and narrow defile of Glen Farg. which winds through the outliers of the main *Ochil* range towards the flat country near the estuary of the River Earn, where it flows into the inner Firth of Tay. *Iter. 90, 91, 92.*

GLENFINNAN, Inverness.   Map 18, **NM 8 8**.
One of the most beautiful and romantic places in the Western Highlands, where the well-known " Road to the Isles " passes the head of *Loch Shiel* (*q.v.*) on its way to *Morar* (*q.v.*) and *Mallaig* (*q.v.*), on the picturesque north-west coast. At the head of the loch, in its superb mountain setting, near the point where the little River Finnan flows down from Glen Finnan into the loch, stands the prominent *Prince Charles Edward* monument (N.T. Scot.), set up in 1815, to commemorate the Highlanders who followed the Prince in the '45, the Royal Standard having been raised here on August 19th, 1745. In the R.C. Church, standing in the grounds of *Glenfinnan House*, a little to the west, a tablet recalls the Prince. The Church bell carries the delineation of an Irish wolfhound and is placed at ground level. Westwards from Glenfinnan, the road follows a valley between lofty hills, notable for their steep rock-strewn flanks, with *Beinn Odhar Mhor*, 2,853 ft., to the south, and *Fraoch Bheinn*, 2,489 ft., to the north. In about three miles this road begins to descend, and on the right, by climbing a small bluff on foot, a magnificent view is opened up, extending over Loch Eilt to the Sound of Arisaig and the islands of Eigg and Rum. There is a steamer service along the whole 18-mile length of Loch Shiel, terminating at *Acharacle* (*q.v.*). To the north of Glenfinnan, beyond the railway viaduct, is the lonely Glen Finnan, at the head of which rise the bare and stony peaks of *Sgurr Thuilm*, 3,164 ft., and the twin *Streaps*, 2,988 ft. and 2,916 ft. See **Kinlocheil, Lochailort** and **Spean Bridge**. *Iter. 209.*

GLEN ISLA, Angus.   Map 20, **NO 1 6** and **2 5**.
See **Kirkton of Glenisla** and **Lair**.

GLENKINDIE, Aberdeen.   Map 26, **NJ 4 1**.
Situated in the upper Don valley. Near *Glenkindie House* is a remarkable weem, or Pict's House. **1 m. S.S.W.**, across the river, is *Towie* Church, with an ancient sculptured Cross in the churchyard, while nearby are the remains of *Towie Castle*. **3 m. W.N.W.**, beyond the Bridge of Buchat, is the ruined *Glenbuchat Castle* (A.M.), dating from c. 1590. John Gordon, the last laird, fought in the 1715 and 1745 Risings and escaped after the battle of Culloden, in 1746. See **Kildrummy**. *Iter. 167, 176.*

GLENLIVET, Banff.   Map 26, **NJ 2 2**.
Lies a little to the west of the Tomintoul to Dalnashaugh Inn road by way of Tomnavoulin, and is best known for the famous distillery, which was founded in 1824. Glen Livet extends south-eastwards from here towards the *Ladder Hills*, and James VI fought a battle in the glen in 1594. There are scanty remains of *Blairfindy Castle* (A.M.), while at *Bridgend*, a little to the north, near the Livet Water, is a picturesque, ruined bridge. Farther west, near the River Avon, which is here joined by the Livet Water, stands the ancient *Drumin Tower*, situated on an alternative road to Tomintoul by way of Strath Avon and the *Cromdale* hills. Away to the north-east of Glenlivet, overlooking the Duff-town road traversing Glen Rinnes, rises *Ben Rinnes*, 2,755 ft. *Iter. 169, 177, 192.*

GLENLUCE, Wigtown. 750.   Map 2, **NX 1 5**.
E.C. Wed. GOLF. A short way inland from the sandy shores of Luce Bay stands this *Galloway* (*q.v.*) village, to the west of which flows the Water of Luce on its way to the bay. The remains of *Luce Abbey* (A.M.), founded in 1191, are near the river, to the north of the village on the road to *New Luce* (*q.v.*), but are inconsiderable, though the chapter-house shows some good 15th cent. work. Part of the adjoining land is N.T. Scot. **1 m. S.W.** is the *Castle of Park* (A.M.), a fine castellated house, dating from 1590, as shown by the inscription above the main entrance. **2 m. N.E.**, off the Newton Stewart road, is the ruined 17th cent. *Carscreuch Castle*, built by the first Lord Stair, and associated

with Scott's " Bride of Lammermoor." See **Castle Kennedy** and **Kirkcowan**. *Iter. 25, 26, 78, 80, 81, 82.*

GLEN LYON, Perth.   Map 15, **NN 5 4** and **6 4**.
See **Bridge of Balgie** and **Fortingall**. *Iter. 107.*

GLEN MORE, Inverness.   Map 18, **NN 2 9** etc. and **2 4**, **NH 3 0** etc.
Known also as the " Great Glen of Alban," or simply the " Great Glen," this well-known trough extends diagonally in a straight line across north-west Scotland, from *Inverness* (*q.v.*) in the north-east, to *Fort William* (*q.v.*) in the south-west. It forms a remarkable physical feature, dividing the mainland into two unequal portions. A chain of lochs, the largest of which is *Loch Ness* (*q.v.*), is situated in the glen, and these are linked together by the famous *Caledonian Canal* (*q.v.*), by means of which small vessels coming from the North Sea can reach the Atlantic without having to navigate the stormy waters of the north coast of Scotland. For much of the distance lofty hills look down upon the glen, these increasing in height towards the west, and culminating in *Ben Nevis*, 4,406 ft. (*q.v.*), the highest mountain in the British Isles. The Glen More National Forest Park will be found in a different Glen More, situated in the same county, but to the east of *Aviemore* (*q.v.*), in the foot-hills of the *Cairngorms* (*q.v.*). General Wade's road through the Great Glen, linking Inverness with Fort William, traverses the glen almost from end to end, the line of the present magnificent road being, however, only partly on the line of the Wade road. See **Fort Augustus, Loch Lochy, Loch Oich** and **Wade Roads**. *Iter. 207, 210, 213, 214.*

GLEN MORE NATIONAL FOREST PARK, Inverness.
See **Aviemore** and **Loch Morlich**.   Map 25, **NH 9 1**.

GLEN NEVIS, Inverness.   Map 18, **NN 1 6** and **1 7**.
See **Ben Nevis**.

GLEN PROSEN, Angus.   Map 20, **NO 2 6** and **3 6**.
See **Dykehead**.

GLENRINNES, Banff.   Map 26, **NJ 2 3**.
In the heart of the pleasant valley of Glen Rinnes, with *Ben Rinnes*, 2,755 ft., rising to the north-west, and *Corryhabbie*, 2,563 ft., to the south. *Iter. 169, 177.*

GLENROTHES, Fife. 8,100.   Map 17, **NO 2 0**.
A new town, in course of development, situated on the Fife coalfield. *Iter. 93, 126, 130.*

GLENSHEE, SPITTAL OF, Perth.   Map 20, **NO 1 6**.
Lies in the heart of the *Grampians* (*q.v.*), at a height of 1,125 ft., in Glen Shee, on the fine road through the hills linking Blairgowrie and the south with Braemar on Royal Deeside. In former days a travellers' hospice stood at this point. Climbing and ski-ing can be enjoyed in the neighbourhood, and a ski-lift is situated on *Ben Gulabin*, 2,641 ft., which lies a little to the north, and west of the Braemar road. A little to the east of the Spittal is a stone circle, and also a tumulus, known as the Tomb of Diarmid, associated with the ancestors of the Clan Campbell. **5 m. S.E.** stands the modern *Dalnaglar Castle*, beyond the Shee Water. **5 m. N.N.E.**, on the Braemar road, beyond Gleann Beag, is the *Devil's Elbow*, 1,950 ft., notorious in the early days of motoring, with a gradient reaching 1 in 5, and having double bends. The road attains a height of 2,199 ft. at the nearby *Cairnwell Pass* (*q.v.*) summit, on the Aberdeenshire border, the highest main road in Great Britain, and liable to be blocked by snow in winter. To the west is the *Cairnwell* itself, 3,059 ft., and to the east rises *Glas Maol*, 3,502 ft., the highest of an extensive group of 3,000-ft. peaks, culminating far to the north-east in *Lochnagar* (*q.v.*). The long descent northwards leads along Glen Clunie, with the lofty mass of the *White Mounth* (*q.v.*) rising to the east, and a range of lesser hills guarding Glen Ey forest away to the west. *Iter. 141, 152, 160, 167, 168.*

GLEN SHIEL, Ross and Cromarty.   Map 24, **NG 9 1**.
One of the loveliest of Scottish glens, traversed by one of the two well known " Roads to the Isles," and considered by many good authorities to exceed even *Glencoe* (*q.v.*) in scenic grandeur. It extends for nearly 10 miles from Glen Cluanie to the head of *Loch Duich* (*q.v.*) at *Shiel Bridge*

Glenfinnan, Inverness. The Monument (N.T. Scot.) to the Highlanders who followed Prince Charles Edward in the '45. It was erected in 1815 by Macdonald of Glenaladale, a grandson of one of the Prince's original supporters

Glenfinnan, Inverness. The bell of the Church, with its delineation of a wolf. It lies at ground level

Glenlivet, Banff. The well-known distillery, which was founded in 1824

Glenrothes, Fife. Part of the shopping centre in one of Scotland's New Towns, now in course of development

Glenluce, Wigtown. The remains of Luce Abbey, which was founded by the Lord of Galloway in 1191, and was lived in during the 13th century by Michael Scott, the 'Wizard'

PLATE 76 (facing page 168)

Gordon, Berwick. Greenknowe Tower (1581), once the home of the Covenanter, William Pringle. It stands a little to the north, off A6105

Gorebridge, Midlothian. The ornate gateposts at the entrance to the Palladian mansion of Arniston. The house stands to the south-west, off B6372

Glen Torridon, Ross and Cromarty. The peak of Liathach, 3,456 feet. It rises above B858, dominating Upper Loch Torridon, to the south-west of Kinlochewe

Golspie, Sutherland. The inscribed memorial to the Clan Sutherland on a bridge in the village

Gourock, Renfrew. Granny Kempock's Stone, on Tower Hill, probably of prehistoric origin. In 1622, Mary Lamont was burnt as a witch on a charge of intending to throw the stone into the sea to cause shipwrecks

Gosford House, East Lothian. The entrance gateway to the 18th century Gosford House, a seat of the Earls of Wemyss. The house is partly the work of Robert Adam and stands in a park off A198

PLATE 77 (facing page 169)

(*q.v.*). High mountains overhang the glen on both sides, and in the lower reaches Bonnie Prince Charlie lay in hiding after the '45. On the east side, overlooking Loch Duich, are the famous *Five Sisters of Kintail*, with *Scour Ouran*, 3,505 ft., rising direct from the road-side. To the west is a line of hills culminating in the serrated ridge of *The Saddle*, 3,317 ft., with its sharp-pointed outlier of *Faochag*, 3,010 ft. In the heart of the glen, at Bridge of Shiel, spanning the River Shiel, is the site of a skirmish with Spanish troops who landed from frigates in Loch Duich during a Jacobite rising of 1719. *Sgurr nan Spainteach*, 3,129 ft., one of the Five Sisters, thus obtained its name. Dr. Johnson and Boswell traversed the glen on horseback in 1773 during their Highland tour, and the scenery in Glen Shiel determined the Doctor to write his classic " Journey to the Western Isles." A boulder in the glen, known as " Clach Johnson," is still pointed out as one under which he rested. The glen is partly on the line of one of the former military roads. See **Kintail** and **Mam Rattachan Pass**. *Iter. 207, 220.*

GLEN STRATHFARRAR, Inverness.   Map 24, **NH 2** 4.
See **Struy Bridge**.

GLEN TORRIDON, Ross and Cromarty. Map 24, **NG 9** 5.
See **Kinlochewe** and **Torridon**. *Iter. 223.*

GLEN TROOL NATIONAL FOREST PARK,
Ayr; Kirkcudbright.   Map 2, **NX 4** 6 etc.
See **Loch Trool** (for main portion) **Barr, Clatteringshaws Dam** and **Newton Stewart**.

GLENUIG, Inverness.   Map 12, **NM 6** 7.
See **Kinlochmoidart** and **Lochailort**.

GLENWHILLY, Wigtown.   Map 2, **NX 1** 7.
On the narrow, hilly and gated road traversing the moors between New Luce and Barrhill, the Cross Water of Luce flowing beside the road for some distance in the vicinity. *Iter. 78.*

GLIMPS HOLM, Orkney.   Map 33, **ND 4** 9.
Iter. 266.

GLOMACH, Ross and Cromarty.   Map 24, **NH 0** 2.
See **Falls of Glomach**.

GOGAR, Midlothian.   Map 9, **NT 1** 7.
GOLF. A little to the north-west stands the picturesque old *Gogar House*, which dates from 1625, and has angle turrets and a balustraded roof. Away to the north lies the Edinburgh airport at *Turnhouse*. *Iter. 15, 16.*

GOLSPIE, Sutherland. 1,328.   Map 31, **NH 8** 9.
E.C. Wed. GOLF. A resort and fishing village, with a sandy beach, in an arable stretch of the county having a background of lofty moors culminating in *Beinn Lundie*, 1,464 ft. On a bridge in the village is an inscribed Sutherland clan memorial. Nearer to the village is *Beinn a' Bhragie*, 1,256 ft., on which stands a statue by Chantrey to the first Duke of Sutherland. To the north-west of Golspie is the pretty Dunrobin Glen, with its burn, overlooked to the north by *Ben Horn*, 1,706 ft. A bridge spanning the burn carries a rare Gaelic, or Ogham inscription. See **Dunrobin**. *Iter. 200, 231, 233.*

GONFIRTH, Shetland.   Map 33, **HU 3** 6.
Iter. 270.

GORDON, Berwick. 673.   Map 10, **NT 6** 4.
The village is associated with the " Gay Gordons," who moved to Aberdeenshire in the 14th cent.   (See **Huntly**.) A circular clock tower stands in the main street. To the north of the village is *Greenknowe Castle* (A.M.), dating from 1581, and retaining its yett, above which is inscribed the date, between two carved shields. The castle was the 16th cent. home of the Covenanter, William Pringle. See **Mellerstain**. *Iter. 6, 33, 41.*

GORDON ARMS INN, Selkirk.   Map 10, **NT 3** 2.
A fishing inn and junction of roads, situated on Yarrow Water, in the heart of Ettrick Forest, within easy reach of the charming *St. Mary's Loch* (*q.v.*). Here, in 1830, Sir Walter Scott and James Hogg, the " Ettrick Shepherd," parted for the last time. A little to the north is the farm of *Mount-benger*, once tenanted by Hogg, and to the south is *Eldinhope*,

formerly *Altrive Lake* farm, where he died in 1835. The road leading northwards through the hills into Peeblesshire towards *Traquair* (*q.v.*) is known as the " Paddy Slacks." 3 m. N.W., in the valley of the Douglas Burn, leading off the road to St. Mary's Loch, is the ruined *Blackhouse Tower*, associated with both Scott and Hogg, and the birthplace, in 1780, of Willie Laidlaw, the friend and amanuensis of Scott. *Iter. 12, 13, 34, 46.*

GORDONSTOUN, Moray.   Map 26, **NJ 1** 6.
See **Duffus**.

GOREBRIDGE, Midlothian.   Map 10, **NT 3** 6.
E.C. Wed. A short distance to the south-west is the fine Palladian mansion of *Arniston*, the seat of the Dundas family. The entrance to the house has gateposts showing a lion and an elephant, and there are lovely walled gardens. See **Borthwick Castle**. *Iter. 40.*

GORTHLECK, Inverness.   Map 25, **NH 5** 2.
Iter. 211, 212.

GOSFORD HOUSE, East Lothian.   Map 10, **NT 4** 7.
This magnificent 18th cent. house, partly by Robert Adam, and one of the best examples of his work, stands in a park overlooking Gosford Bay in the Firth of Forth. *Iter. 2, 37.*

GOURDON, Kincardine.   Map 21, **NO 8** 7.
A coastal village sheltered by Doolie Ness.

GOUROCK, Renfrew. 9,131. SB.   Map 8, **NS 2** 7.
E.C. Wed. GOLF. One of the best known of the Firth of Clyde resorts, with a pier and a pebble beach. Its situation,

1. Granny Kempock's Stone.

on a bay facing *Kilcreggan* (*q.v.*) in the Rosneath peninsula, and looking north-westwards towards Loch Long and the Holy Loch, backed by the hills of *Cowal* (*q.v.*), is one of great natural beauty. Gourock is a good centre for yachting and for steamer trips in the waters of the Firth, and also in the *Kyles of Bute* (*q.v.*). The ancient *Granny Kempock's* Stone is probably prehistoric. 2½ m. S.W., on the coast, beyond the suburb of Ashton, is the ruined *Levan Castle*, in a wooded setting, near which stands the white *Cloch* (*q.v.*) lighthouse, a notable landmark. See **Inverkip**. *Iter. 59, 65, 66, 85, 88, 112, 113.*

GOVAN (Glasgow), Lanark. 35,969.   Map 8, **NS 5** 6.
E.C. Tues. Now part of Glasgow, in the industrial Clydeside district, but, until 1856, a village composed largely of hand-loom weavers. The modern Church, on the site of an ancient monastery, stands among early Christian monuments, and in the chancel is a sarcophagus, which may have been raised over the tomb of St. Constantine, the founder, who under-took missionary work at the request of St. Mungo, the patron saint of Glasgow. *Haggs Castle*, to the south-east, an old home of the Maxwells, although altered and restored, carries the date 1585 on a door enriched by ornamental

panels. A car ferry across the Clyde connects with Partick. *Iter. 59.*

GOWANBANK, Angus. Map 21, NO 6 4.
Iter. 163.

GRAMISDALE, Isle of Benbecula, Inverness.
Map 32, NF 0 5.
See **Hebrides, Outer** (Benbecula). *Iter. 262.*

GRAMPIANS. Map 18, NN 1 4, etc.
The name *Grampians* is essentially a literary one, having been first used, in 1520, by Hector Boece, the historian (See **Dundee**), who found, and misread, the name "Mons Graupius," which Tacitus gave as the scene of Agricola's victory over the Picts, c. A.D. 84. Modern research places the scene of this battle at some distance to the north of the River Tay. The grass and heather-covered mountains which stretch across the *Highlands* (*q.v.*), from Argyllshire, in the west, across Perthshire to Aberdeenshire, in the north-east, are generally termed the Grampians. The range was known earlier as the Mounth, a name still preserved in the well-known pass of the *Cairn o' Mounth* (*q.v.*) in Kincardineshire, and in the great plateau of the *White Mounth* (*q.v.*), south of the Dee valley, of which the highest point is the famous granite peak of *Lochnagar* (*q.v.*). Across the valley is the even higher mass of the *Cairngorms* (*q.v.*), with their lonely lochs and corries, and a large area of flat tops exceeding 4,000 ft., a height surpassed in Scotland only by *Ben Nevis* (*q.v.*) and several of its neighbours. A considerable number of the Grampian summits exceed 3,000 ft. in height, and are known generally as "Munros," the name given to all the tops in Scotland of 3,000 ft. and over, numbering in all 543, of which 276 are separate mountains. The title Munro recalls Sir Hugh Munro, who was mainly responsible for their classification.
The passes across the Grampian barrier were used by the invading armies of the Romans and the English, just as they are now used by travellers in the 20th century. Of these, the best known are the Pass of Leny, near *Callander* (*q.v.*); the *Cairnwell Pass* (*q.v.*), with the highest main road summit in Britain; the bare and lonely *Drumochter Pass* (*q.v.*), traversed by Wade's great highway linking Dunkeld with Inverness; the famous Lecht road, linking *Cock Bridge* (*q.v.*) in the Don valley, with *Tomintoul* (*q.v.*), the loftiest village in the Highlands; and the Cairn o' Mounth, already mentioned. Around the lonely head of Glen Isla, in the picturesque Braes of Angus district, the eastern Grampians are sometimes given the name of *Benchinnan* mountains. Here, the by-road from *Kirkton of Glenisla* (*q.v.*) terminates, and a long-distance walkers' track climbs *Monega Hill*, eventually reaching a height of 3,318 ft., the highest right-of-way in Scotland. West of Drumochter Pass and *Dalwhinnie* (*q.v.*), beyond Loch Ericht and the remote *Ben Alder*, the Grampians intersect the ridge known as Drum Alban, the backbone of the country, and situated near the main watershed. This ridge extends northwards from *Ben Lomond*, above *Loch Lomond* (*q.v.*), and finally reaches *Ben Hope*, the most northerly 3,000-ft. peak in the country, situated beyond *Altnaharra* (*q.v.*), in Sutherland. Many of the high moors in the Grampians are shot over for grouse during the season, and deer-stalking takes place in the hills, which carry snow in the winter months and provide opportunities for ski-ing in places. See **Glenshee, Spittal of.**

GRANDTULLY, Perth. 500. Map 20, NN 9 5.
E.C. Wed. GOLF. A small village in Strath Tay, where a bridge over the river links the roads traversing the north and south shores. **2 m. S.W.,** off the Aberfeldy road, is *Grandtully Castle,* dating from 1560, with enlargements of 1626 and 1893. It is one of those castles which Scott may have had in mind when describing "Tullyveolan" in "Waverley." A little to the south is the old Church of *St. Mary* (A.M.), which is notable for its 17th cent. painted ceiling. In the background, beyond the river to the north, rises *Farragon Hill,* 2,559 ft., below which is Loch Derculich, from which flows the Derculich Burn to join the Tay. *Iter. 120, 139, 149, 157, 158.*

GRANGEMOUTH, Stirling. 16,661. SB.
Map 16, NS 9 8.
E.C. Wed. A Forth estuary port and oil-refining town, with important docks, situated at the point of convergence of the River Carron and the Forth and Clyde Canal. The latter, which is 38 miles long, was the work of Smeaton, in 1790, and crosses the narrow waist of Scotland to enter the Clyde at *Bowling* (*q.v.*). *Iter. 17.*

GRANTON (Edinburgh), Midlothian. Map 17, NT 2 7.
The harbour dates from 1835, and faces *Burntisland* (*q.v.*), some five miles across the Firth of Forth. On the southern outskirts of Granton is the beautiful old mansion of *Caroline Park,* commenced in 1685, the picturesque south front, with its ogee-shaped tower roofs, dating from 1696. There is some notable ironwork in the house. Farther to the west lies *Drylaw,* another house from about the same period, also with good ironwork.

GRANTOWN-ON-SPEY, Moray. 1,551. SB.
Map 26, NJ 0 2.
E.C. Thurs. M.D. Sat. GOLF. A well-known Highland summer and winter resort, at a height of nearly 700 ft., beautifully situated in Strath Spey, and having been founded in 1776. It is built almost entirely of granite, and makes an excellent touring centre for Strath Spey and the fine mountain country in the district. There are good distant views of the lofty *Cairngorms* (*q.v.*) away to the south, while eastwards rise the nearer *Cromdale* hills, over 2,000 ft. high in places. The bridge over the Spey, on the Craigellachie road, has a concrete arch of 240 ft., and a little farther east is the older three-span bridge, dating from 1754. This rapid-flowing river is the second longest in Scotland, and is famous for its salmon. The road leading south-eastwards from the Spey into the hills towards *Tomintoul* (*q.v.*) climbs to more than 1,400 ft., with fine views, on the way to *Bridge of Brown* (*q.v.*), 2½ m. N. of Grantown is the fine old mansion of *Castle Grant,* 16th to 18th cent. See **Dulnain Bridge** and **Lochindorb.** *Iter. 141, 149, 160, 171, 172, 176, 177, 195.*

GRANT'S HOUSE, Berwick. Map 11, NT 8 6.
Situated on the Eye Water. **3 m. S.E.,** off the Great North Road, is the old mansion of *Houndwood,* with its fine gardens. *Iter. 1, 38, 39.*

GREAT GLEN, Inverness. Map 18, NN 2 9 etc.
and 24, NH 3 0 etc.
See **Glen More.** *Iter. 207, 210, 213, 214.*

GREENLAW, Berwick. 831. Map 10, NT 7 4.
E.C. Wed. This little town, on the Blackadder Water, in the foothills of the *Lammermuirs,* takes its name from a low "green law," or isolated hill, a little to the south-east, where the village was formerly situated. Greenlaw was between 1696 and 1853 the county town of Berwickshire until replaced by Duns. The Market Cross dates from 1696, but is not on the original site. The tower of the Church dates from 1712, though built in the style of the late 15th cent. **3 m. S.** is the ruined *Hume Castle,* at a height of some 600 ft., having been captured by Cromwell in 1651, and to a certain extent restored in 1794. The Castle makes a fine viewpoint, and was at one period a seat of the Earls of Home. **3 m. S.E.** is the mansion of *Rowchester,* with its attractive gardens. **4 m. E.N.E.,** off the Berwick road, is the motor-racing track of *Charterhall.* See **Gordon** and **Polwarth.** *Iter. 5, 8, 33, 41.*

Grampians, Argyll; Perth. An old bridge, at a height of 1,125 feet, at the Spittal of Glenshee, on the Blairgowrie to Braemar road (A93), in the Grampian mountains. Near this point a hospice once stood

Grampians, Argyll; Perth. The point north of Dalwhinnie, on A9, in the Grampian mountains, where General Wade's road to Inverness diverges from his famous road over the Corrieyairack Pass, leading to Fort Augustus, now derelict

Granton, Midlothian. The south front of Caroline Park, a house built in 1685–96 by George Mackenzie, first Viscount Tarbat

Greenlaw, Berwick. The Market Cross of 1696, which has been moved from its original site

Greenlaw, Berwick. The restored Hume Castle, the predecessor of which was captured by Cromwell in 1651. In 1804, as the result of a false alarm, a beacon was lit here to give warning of an impending Napoleonic invasion. It stands 3 miles south, off B6364

Grantown-on-Spey, Moray. The Old Spey Bridge (1754), now closed to traffic

PLATE 78 (facing page 170)

Gretna, Dumfries. Gretna Hall, built in 1710. Between 1825 and 1855, some 1,134 runaway marriages were performed in Gretna according to records preserved at the Hall

Greenock, Renfrew. The Cross on Lyle Hill, in memory of Free French sailors who gave their lives during the Second World War battle of the Atlantic

Gruinard Bay, Ross and Cromarty. The view towards the great Teallach peaks. On the west side of the bay, in the Rudha Mor peninsula, is the little Loch na Beiste, where a monster is said to have been destroyed by the throwing-in of 14 barrels of lime

Guardbridge, Fife. The old (1419) and new (1938) bridges spanning the River Eden in close proximity. On the old bridge are the arms of the builder, Bishop Wardlaw

Guildtown, Perth. An inscription of 1835 on the wall of a cottage, probably commemorating a local marriage, and depicting a mason's tools

Gullane, East Lothian. The remains of the 12th century Church. James VI dismissed the last vicar for smoking tobacco, and the building was destroyed in 1631

[For GRETNA see also under SOLWAY FIRTH (Plate 152)

PLATE 79 (facing page 171)

GREENLOANING, Perth. Map 16, NN 8 0.
In Strath Allan, and a junction of roads leading from Dunblane to Crieff and Perth. The Allan Water is joined here by the Knaik Water, the latter flowing down from *Braco* (*q.v.*), noted for its great Roman earthworks. See **Blackford**. *Iter.* 135, 138, 140, 146.

GREENOCK, Renfrew. 77,778. LB. Map 8, NS 2 7.
E.C. Wed. M.D. Tues. GOLF. An important industrial and shipbuilding town on the Clyde estuary, damaged by bombs in the Second World War. The well-known road-stead in the river immediately off Greenock is known as the "Tail of the Bank." The town was the birthplace, in 1736, of James Watt, and a statue of him by Chantrey is in the Watt

1. Birthplace of James Watt. 2. Watt Library and Institution.
3. Cemetery. The Watt Cairn.

Library and Institution. In the cemetery is the Watt Cairn, and nearby is the tombstone of Burns's "Highland Mary," which has been removed to the old North Kirk. A Cross on the viewpoint of Lyle Hill is a monument to Free French sailors who lost their lives in the Battle of the Atlantic during the Second World War. Behind the town are moors, on which the waterworks are situated, commanding good views of the Clyde estuary and its mountain background. See **Gourock** and **Tarbolton**. *Iter.* 59, 64, 65, 85, 88, 112, 113.

GRETNA, Dumfries. 2,057. Map 4, NY 3 6.
E.C. Wed. Famous as the place where runaway couples from England formerly came to be married, the ceremony being performed in accordance with 18th cent. Scots law by means of a declaration before witnesses. These took place at the Sark Toll Bar (See **Sark Bridge**); in local inns; at *Gretna Hall*; and at the well-known smithy at *Gretna Green*, interesting records having been kept at the two latter places. In 1856, an Act was passed necessitating three weeks residence north of the Border before a marriage could take place. The bridge over the River Sark is the actual Border, and a little to the south-west the river flows into the Solway Firth, noted for its dangerous tides, which occasionally form a "bore" nearly 4 ft. in height. About **3 m. N.E.** is the site of the battle of Solway Moss, in 1542, where the Scots were defeated. **1 m. S.**, near the Solway Firth shore, is the *Lochmaben Stone*, 7 ft. high and weighing 10 tons, probably having formed part of a stone circle. The stone has been on various occasions a meeting place for con-ferences, and in 1398 details of a truce between Scotland and England were discussed here. See **Canonbie, Lamber-ton, Sark Bridge and Springfield**. *Iter.* 10, 13, 20, 27, 28, 29, 42, 50, 51.

GRETNA GREEN, Dumfries. Map 4, NY 3 6.
See **Gretna**. *Iter.* 10, 13, 29, 50, 51, 67.

GREY MARE'S TAIL, Dumfries. Map 4, NT 1 1.
See **Birkhill** and **Moffat**. *Iter.* 13, 46.

GRIBUN, Isle of Mull, Argyll. Map 13, NM 4 3.
Situated on Loch na Keal, with a remarkable range of lofty cliffs, below which lies the road from *Salen* (*q.v.*) to Loch Scridain. Off-shore is the island of *Inch Kenneth*, where Dr. Johnson and Boswell were once entertained. Farther out are the islands of Ulva, Gometra, Little Colonsay and *Staffa* (*q.v.*). In the background, to the east, rises *Ben More*, 3,169 ft., the monarch of the island, and a splendid viewpoint. To the west of the Gribun cliffs is the almost roadless Ardmeanach peninsula, showing notable cliff scenery, and with the experimental farm of *Burg* (N.T. Scot.) facing Loch Scridain (See **Kilfinichen Church**). The road linking Gribun with the south-west corner of Mull goes east of the hilly Ardmeanach country by way of Glen Seilisdeir, and then rounds the head of Loch Scridain. *Iter.* 249.

GROGPORT, Argyll. Map 7, NR 8 4.
Lies in a small bay of the Kilbrennan Sound, looking across its waters to *Beinn Bharrain*, 2,345 ft., one of the Arran peaks. *Iter.* 122.

GRUDIE BRIDGE, Ross and Cromarty.
See **Loch Maree**. Map 24, NG 9 6.

GRUIDS MILL, Sutherland.
Iter. 232. Map 29, NC 5 0.

GRUINARD BAY, Ross and Cromarty.
Map 29, NG 9 9.
One of the loveliest bays of *Wester Ross* in the North-West Highlands, having fine sands and picturesque outcrops of grey rock in a background of low, rugged hills. The bay is approached from the west by de-scending the once-notorious Gruinard Hill (1 in 6), from the summit of which the view is remarkably fine, taking in the great *Teallach* range, and also the *Coigach* hills away to the north-east. A little to the west of the summit are the curiously-named clachans of *Second Coast* and *First Coast*. Two rivers, the Little Gruinard and the Gruinard, flow into the bay, in which is situated Gruinard Island. *Gruinard House*, behind which the Gruinard River flows through a gorge, is situated on the shores of the bay. The course of the river is south-eastwards towards the lonely Loch na Sheallag, above which rise the Torridon sandstone peaks of *An Teallach*, nearly 3,500 ft. high, best visited from *Dundonnell* (*q.v.*). To the south of Gruinard Bay lies the lonely Fisherfield Forest, dominated by *Beinn Dearg Mhor*, 2,974 ft. *Iter.* 206, 222.

GRULINE, Isle of Mull, Argyll. Map 12, NM 5 3.
Iter. 248, 249.

GUARDBRIDGE, Fife. 977. Map 17, NO 4 1.
The old bridge over the River Eden dates from c. 1420, and carries on one of the keystones a shield of arms and a pastoral staff recalling its building by Bishop Wardlaw, an early Bishop of St. Andrews. A new bridge, situated alongside, now carries the traffic. To the north is a large paper mill. The Eden flows into St. Andrews Bay, on the north shore of which is the lonely and extensive Tents Moor, with its forestry plantations. See **Tayport**. *Iter*, 93, 94, 131, 136.

GUILDTOWN, Perth. Map 17, NO 1 3.
See **Stobhall**. *Iter.* 152.

GULLANE, East Lothian. 1,482. Map 10, NT 4 8.
E.C. Wed. GOLF. A well-known resort and golfing centre on the Firth of Forth, with excellent sands and bathing. The championship course at *Muirfield*, the headquarters of the Hon. Company of Edinburgh Golfers, situated a little to the north-east, is world-famous. The roofless Old Church at Gullane retains a little Norman work. *Saltcoats Castle*, to the south, is of 16th cent. date, and preserves its old

dovecote. R. L. Stevenson's novel " Catriona " contains local colour. There are fine views over the Firth towards the Fife coast, backed by the distant *Lomond* and *Ochil* hills. See **Aberlady** and **Dirleton**. *Iter. 2, 36, 37.*

GUTHRIE, Angus.   Map 21, NO 5 5.
The square *Guthrie Tower* dates largely from 1468, and the gardens are picturesque. To the west, off the Forfar road, are the small Balgavies Loch and the larger Rescobie Loch. *Iter. 153.*

HADDINGTON, East Lothian. 4,683. SB.
     Map 10, NT 5 7.
E.C. Thurs. M.D. Mon. GOLF. A Royal Burgh, noted for its grain market, situated on the River Tyne, with the *Lammermuir* hills as a background away to the south. It is now by-passed by the Great North Road. The town was burnt on several occasions by the English in the middle ages, and its name was at one time given to the county as a whole. Alexander II was born here in 1198, and John Knox is thought to have been born in the town in 1505. The Town House, with its curfew bell, is the work of William Adam, the tower having been added in 1831 by Gillespie Graham. The Mercat Cross is topped by a goat. The town library includes the valuable 17th cent. collection amassed by John Gray, born in the town in 1646. *Bothwell Castle* is a ruined 16th or 17th cent. town house. Both *Haddington House* and *Moat House*, Eastgate, date from the 17th cent. The fine, restored Church (A.M.), known as the " Lamp of Lothian," dating mainly from the 15th cent., is a cruciform structure, but the choir and transepts are ruined. The splendid central tower was once surmounted by a crown, as at *St. Giles* in *Edinburgh (q.v.).* The West front of the nave is impressive, with a good double doorway, and in the choir is the tomb of Jane Welsh, the wife of Thomas Carlyle. The ruined Church of *St. Martin*, nearby, is of 12th cent. date. Two fine old bridges span the Tyne, the *Nungate Bridge*, 16th cent., from which criminals were hanged, and the *Abbey Bridge*, about a mile to the east of the town, a structure of the early 16th cent. **2 m.** N., near the *Garleton* hills, are remains of the 16th cent. *Barnes Castle.* A monument to the 4th Earl of Hopetoun is situated on the hills. **2 m.** N.E. of the town is the restored 16th and 18th cent. *Stevenson House*, near the River Tyne. **3 m.** E. of Haddington, situated off a by-road, stands the lonely little Church of *Morham*, dating from 1685 and 1724, and preserving a bell dated 1681, which was probably cast in Holland. See **Aberlady, Bolton** (for *Lennoxlove*), **Garvald** and **Gifford**. *Iter. 1, 36, 40.*

HALBEATH, Fife.   Map 17, NT 1 8.
Iter. 97, 133.

HALKIRK, Caithness. 363.   Map 30, ND 1 5.
E.C. Wed. A village laid out in symmetrical fashion, and situated on the River Thurso, noted for its fishing. The main Wick to Thurso road passes a little to the east of Halkirk. Across the river, to the north, is the ancient *Brawl Castle*, with walls 8 to 10 feet thick, perhaps 14th cent. work. A modern house adjoins the old tower. **4 m.** W. is Loch Calder, with numerous prehistoric remains in the vicinity, and to the east are Loch Scarmelett (4 m.) and the larger Loch Watten (6½ m.), the latter noted for trout fishing. *Iter. 239.*

HALKIRK ROADSIDE, Caithness.   Map 30, ND 1 6.
See **Halkirk**. *Iter. 236, 237, 239.*

HAMILTON, Lanark. 41,022. LB.   Map 8, NS 7 5.
E.C. Wed. M.D. Fri. GOLF. The centre of a mining

district, with some of the pleasantest wooded stretches of the River Avon lying to the south-east. To the east of the town, the Avon has its junction with the more important Clyde. Beyond the meeting of the waters, away to the south-east, the Clyde flows through attractive orchard country in the direction of *Crossford (q.v.).* Mary, Queen of Scots rested at Hamilton after escaping from *Loch Leven Castle (q.v.),* and in 1651 Cromwell made his headquarters in the town. The octagonal Parish Church was designed in 1732 by William Adam. Facing it is the Celtic *Netherton* Cross. A Covenanters' monument, with four heads in relief, is in the churchyard. The palatial *Hamilton Palace*, now demolished, owing to subsidences caused by mining, stood formerly in the *Low Parks*, to the north-east. In the parks are the racecourse, and the Hamilton Mausoleum, which

1. Town Hall. Information Bureau.	2. Parish Church (1732) and Netherton Cross.
3. Hamilton Mausoleum.	4. Barncluith House, 16th cent.

3 m. N.W. by exit A724, Livingstone Memorial at Blantyre.

cost some £150,000 to build around 1850 and was designed by David Bryce. South of Hamilton are the *High Parks*, in which stands the ruined *Cadzow Castle*, visited by Mary, Queen of Scots, in 1568. The wild, white cattle of Cadzow Park are probably unique in Scotland. *Chatelherault Lodge* is an 18th cent. design by William Adam. Above the Avon stands the 16th cent. house of *Barncluith*, with its fine gardens, both house and gardens being constructed in a series of terraces. See **Blantyre** (for *Livingstone Memorial*) and **Bothwell**. *Iter. 19, 51, 53, 87.*

HAMPDEN PARK (Glasgow), Lanark.   Map 8, NS 5 6.
See **Glasgow**.

HANDA, ISLE OF, Sutherland.   Map 28, NC 1 4.
This tiny island lies a little to the north-west of *Scourie (q.v.)* Bay, and is separated from the mainland by the narrow Sound of Handa. On the island, which is reached by boat from Scourie, there are red Torridon sandstone cliffs 400 ft. high, which command a fine view of the mainland mountains in the lonely Forest of Reay. Handa is preserved as a sanctuary for sea-fowl.

HARDGATE, Dunbarton. 1,463.   Map 8, NS 5 7.
Iter. 113.

HARLAW, Aberdeen.   Map 27, NJ 7 2.
See **Inveramsay**.

HARRABOL, Isle of Skye, Inverness.   Map 23, NG 6 2.
Iter. 251, 253.

Haddington, East Lothian. The Mercat Cross, which is surmounted by the figure of a goat

Haddington, East Lothian. The Town House, designed originally in 1748 by William Adam

Halkirk, Caithness. Massive walls of the 14th century Brawl Castle, which stands on the farther side of the River Thurso

Harlaw, Aberdeen. The Monument, erected in 1911, to commemorate the battle of Harlaw (1411), ending in the defeat of the Highlanders under Donald, Lord of the Isles. It stands north of the River Urie, off B9001

Hamilton, Lanark. The octagonal Parish Church, the work of William Adam in 1732. In front of it stands the Celtic Netherton Cross

PLATE 80 (facing page 172)

HAWICK, Roxburgh.

The Monument in Wilton Lodge Park to the well known racing motor-cyclist, Jimmie Guthrie, who was killed in Germany in 1937

Hawick Mote, the mound of a Norman Castle, which was probably 12th century work by one of the Lovels who then held Hawick

The Horse Monument, which recalls the defeat of English marauders at Hornshole Bridge in 1514, by the local ' callants,' or youths, the grown men having been practically wiped out at Flodden a year earlier

A pillar near Hornshole Bridge, over the River Teviot (off A698), some 2 miles north-east, commemorating the victory of the Hawick youths in 1514 (see above)

Branxholm Tower (1571), an old home of the Scott family. It stands some 3 miles south-west, in Teviotdale, off A7

PLATE 81 (facing page 173)   [For HEBRIDES, OUTER, see two following plates

HARRIS, Inverness.   Map 32, NG 0 9 etc.
(Part of Isle of Lewis, Ross and Cromarty.)
See **Hebrides, Outer** (Harris and Lewis). *Iter.* 256.

HARTHILL, Lanark. 4,840.   Map 9, NS 9 6.
E.C. Wed. A small mining town, on the edge of moorland
country. *Iter. 15, 18.*

HASSENDEAN, Roxburgh.   Map 10, NT 5 1.
A village associated with the song " Jock o' Hazeldean."
The old Church was demolished in 1690.

HATTON, Aberdeen.   Map 27, NK 0 3.
Iter. 181, 187.

HAWICK, Roxburgh. 16,631. SB.   Map 10, NT 5 1.
E.C. Tues. **M.D.** Thurs. GOLF. One of the most
important of the Border towns, situated in the heart of
Teviotdale, at the confluence of the River Teviot and the
Slitrig Water, and noted especially for woollens, yarn and
hosiery. In 1570, the town was almost completely burnt
down, one of the few earlier buildings still remaining being
part of what is now the " *Tower* " Hotel. Anne, the widow
of the executed Duke of Monmouth, and with whom Scott's
" Lay of the last Minstrel " is associated, lived here once,
while the building was visited also by Wordsworth and Scott.

HAZELBANK, Lanark.   Map 9, NS 8 4.
Iter. 53.

HEBRIDES, INNER, Argyll; Inverness.
(Western Isles.)   Maps 6, 12, 13, 22 and 23.
The islands of this group lie off the much-indented west
coast. They extend from Skye, the most northerly, which is
separated from the *Outer Hebrides* (*q.v.*) by the waters of
the Little Minch, to Islay, in the south, which lies off the
narrow Kintyre peninsula, and is at one point only some
25 miles distant from the coast of Northern Ireland. The
largest and most picturesque island is Skye, famous for
the precipitous Coolin mountains, while Iona and Staffa,
two of the smallest, are both of unique interest, the former
for its Cathedral and associations with St. Columba, and
the latter for its strange basaltic rocks and the well-known
Fingal's Cave. The principal islands are fully described
individually, and, in addition, all places of interest on
Skye, Mull and Islay have their own separate entries. See
Colonsay, Iona, Islay, Jura, Mull, Rum (also for **Eigg**),
Skye, Staffa and **Tiree.** *Iter.* 243 to 255.

HEBRIDES, OUTER, Inverness; Ross and Cromarty.
(Western Isles.)   Map 32.
The chain of islands 130 miles in length, known as the *Outer
Hebrides,* or *Long Island,* is separated from
the Scottish mainland by the Minch, and
from the nearer island of Skye, in the Inner
Hebrides, by the Little Minch. The much-
indented and sandy western Hebridean seaboard, with its many small islands off-shore,
receives the full force of the great Atlantic
breakers. In the extreme north is the Butt
of Lewis, and the most southerly point is
the small island of Berneray, where a lighthouse is situated on Barra Head. The
largest of the group is *Lewis,* which belongs
to Ross and Cromarty, but its southern
quarter, *Harris,* forms part of Inverness-
shire, as do all the smaller islands to the
south, chief among which are North and
South Uist, Benbecula, and Barra. Except
in Harris, where there are bare and lonely
mountains over 2,500 ft. high, the surface
of the islands is almost universally flat, with
lonely moors and a multiplicity of small
lochans. The soil is mainly of poor quality
and lacking in trees. Some of the primitive, thatched " black " houses in which
the Gaelic-speaking inhabitants live are still
to be seen, though in rapidly diminishing
numbers. Roads on the large island of
Lewis are fair, but many are narrow and
winding, more particularly in the district of
South Harris. There are altogether about
170 miles of good motoring roads in Lewis and Harris.
On the smaller islands the road mileage is very limited, but a
viaduct links Benbecula with South Uist. A new causeway now connects Benbecula and North Uist. Excellent
fishing and shooting are available in the islands, and manufacture of the famous handwoven Harris Tweed is of great
importance.

In the 11th cent. the Norsemen settled in the islands,
but after their defeat at *Largs* (*q.v.*) in Ayrshire, in 1263,
the Scottish supremacy was established. In the 14th cent.,
John of Islay, a supporter of Robert Bruce, became the first
Lord of the Isles. Prehistoric remains, such as cairns,
brochs and forts, notably the famous standing stones of
Callanish, as well as numerous small ruined churches, are a
feature of the Outer Hebrides, which are described individually below. A number of ports in the islands, from
Stornoway, in Lewis, to *Castlebay,* in Barra, are linked by
steamer to various mainland ports, for which see details in
the steamship communications section at the end of the
book. A map of the **Western Isles** appears on Pages 34
and 35 of the atlas. There are air services to Stornoway,
Barra and Benbecula from Glasgow (Renfrew airport) and
also an additional service to Stornoway from Inverness.

HAWICK

1. Horse Monument.
2. St. Mary's Church (1763).
3. Wilton Lodge Park (Museum and War Memorial).
4. Town Hall. Information Bureau.

The tower of *St. Mary's* Church dates from 1764. The
extensive Mote Hill, 30 ft. high and 300 ft. round, nearby,
is the mound of a Norman Castle. Hawick is well
known for the picturesque ceremony known as the " Common
Riding " which takes place annually early in June, and commemorates a victory over the English in 1514. The Horse
Monument in the town recalls the event, and a pillar, dated
1514, stands **2 m. N.E.,** near a bridge over the Teviot at
Hornshole. *Wilton Lodge* is now a museum of much interest,
open regularly. (See note page 90.) **2 m. S.W.,** in Teviotdale, is the ancient tower of *Goldielands,* owned formerly by
a branch of the Scott family. A mile farther is *Branxholm
Tower,* an old home of the Scotts, dated 1571 and later, the
original tower having been blown up in 1570. It is associated
with Sir Walter Scott's " Lay of the last Minstrel." **4½ m. W.,**
beyond the valley of the Borthwick Water, is the much-
restored *Harden House,* 16th or 17th cent., associated with
Scott's ancestors. See **Bonchester Bridge** (for **Border
National Forest Park**), **Dalkeith, Denholm, Dundee, Hassendean, Hermitage Castle, Roberton** and **St. Mary's Loch.**
Iter. 11, 30, 31, 34, 36, 44, 45.

HAWTHORNDEN, Midlothian.   Map 10, NT 2 6.
See **Lasswade.**

173

LEWIS.

Known also as *The Lews*, this island, together with its southern extension of Harris (see below), is some 60 miles long and 18 to 28 miles wide. It was for a time, after 1918, a possession of Lord Leverhulme, whose efforts to modernise the islands' trade failed owing to the indifference of the inhabitants. The largest town in the Outer Isles is the important herring fishing port and tweed-spinning town of **Stornoway** (5,245. SB), situated on the east coast, with a fine natural harbour, an airport, and linked by a narrow neck of land to the **Eye** peninsula. There is a GOLF course. In *St. Peter's* church is an ancient font, and Livingstone's Prayer Book is preserved. The modern *Stornoway*, or *Lewis Castle*, in its fine, wooded grounds, donated by Lord Leverhulme, is now a technical college. South of the town, on Arnish Moor, beyond the Creed estate, a cairn and a loch commemorate the night spent by Prince Charles Edward in a local farm after the battle of Culloden, in 1746. At the north-east extremity of the Eye peninsula, looking over the sandy Broad Bay to Vatisker Point and Tolsta Head on the main part of the island, is *Tiumpan Head*, with rock scenery and a lighthouse, giving views extending across the Minch towards the distant cliffs of Cape Wrath. The ruined 14th cent. or earlier *Eye* Church of *St. Columba* contains monuments of interest, including the Macleod tombs, one of which may be of Roderick Macleod VIII of Lewis. The building stands in the south-western corner of the peninsula, near the Stornoway road.

On the secondary road leading north-eastwards on the main part of the island from Stornoway, following the sandy bays of the coast, is *Gress*, where the ruined church of *St. Olaf* is said to be the only one in the island group dedicated to a Norse saint. There are some notable caves, including the Seal Cave, accessible by boat. Farther to the north-east, beyond *Tolsta*, is Tolsta Head, with impressive, rocky cliffs, a lighthouse, and fine silver sands. The bay of *Geiraha* is one of the most picturesque in Lewis. Another road from Stornoway proceeds at first north-westwards by way of moorland, dotted with tiny lochans, passing near the *Barvas* hills, nearly 1,000 ft. in height, and then follows the west coast to **Port of Ness** and the Butt of Lewis, at the northern extremity of Lewis, with a lighthouse, some wild rock scenery and extensive views. The restored 12th cent. Teampull of *St. Molua* stands nearby. Some 15 miles distant from Stornoway along this road, and about a mile from the Atlantic coast in the district known as Barvas, a left turn leads to the very notable 18-ft. high monolith at **Shader** known as the *Clach an Trushal*. In the vicinity is the ruined *Steinacleit* chambered cairn and stone circle (A.M.) of the Neolithic period, situated at the southern extremity of Loch an Duin.

Some **16 m.** W. of Stornoway, in a landscape of innumerable tiny lochans, and beyond the fishing centre of **Garynahine**, is the famous group of Standing Stones at **Callanish** (A.M.), situated just off the main road, and forming the most remarkable antiquity in the Western Isles, being exceeded in importance only by Stonehenge. There is a well-marked megalithic avenue, comprising 19 monoliths, ending in a circle of 13 stones, with rows of other stones fanning out, and forming probably remains of additional circles. A great cairn, 40 ft. in diameter, stands within the circle. Nearby stood formerly a typical crofter's "black house". Opposite Callanish is the island of *Great Bernera*, now accessible by means of a road bridge, with Loch Roag to the west and East Loch Roag to the east. About **7 m.** N.W. of Garynahine, on Loch Carloway, an inlet of the larger East Loch Roag, is the well-known and exceptionally well-preserved **Carloway** broch (A.M.). A road leads north-eastwards from here, along a coastline dotted with crofting communities, notably *Shawbost* and *Bragor*, the last-named still having thatched roof "black" houses. It links up with the direct Stornoway to Port of Ness road. Another road can be followed from Garynahine in a south-westerly direction, through remote country with many lochans, beyond which lies the large expanse of Loch Langabhat. This road traverses some of the farthest west parts of Lewis by way of Little Loch Roag,

and goes through the picturesque trough of Glen Valtos to reach Uig, near which are large stretches of silver sands and fine cliff scenery, with Gallen Head overlooking the island-studded Loch Roag, to the north. On Loch Bharabhat is an example of a defensive dun on a small island, linked to the shore by a narrow causeway. Far out to sea, to the north-west, are the lonely *Flannan* islands, known also as the " Seven Hunters." Some **4 m.** S.W. of Uig are *Ardroil Sands*, backed to the south by a range of remote and rocky hills, in which rises *Mealasbhal*, 1,885 ft. Beyond its eastern flanks and the hill of *Tarain* extends the long and narrow Loch Suainaval, over 200 ft. deep in places, the greatest depth reached in the Lews. South of the hills, in a roadless district, is the headland of Gearraidh na h-Airde Moire, with its collection of beehive houses near the mouth of Loch Resort, opposite which rises the precipitous, rocky hill of *Tarran Mor*, in Harris.

South-westwards from Stornoway, the road to Harris passes near many small lochs, and also the heads of Lochs Luirbost and Erisort, to reach the very picturesque Loch Seaforth and the county boundary at **Aline**, facing Seaforth Island. This south-eastern corner of Lewis is known as *Park*, with a high point of 1,874 ft. at *Beinn Mhor*, and off its shores, beyond the inlet of Loch Shell, lie the tiny *Shiant* islands.

HARRIS.

The lower reaches of Loch Seaforth mark the change of scenery from Lewis to Harris, the country becoming hilly, with lofty, bare hills of gneiss to the west, dominated by *Clisham*, 2,622 ft., the highest mountain in the Outer Isles, and its neighbour *Mulla fo dheas*, 2,439 ft. Along its eastern spurs climbs the road from Stornoway, before descending to Ardhasig Bridge, with views of West Loch Tarbert and the lonely hills away to the north-west. Farther west still are other rocky hills, in the remote Forest of Harris, including *Uisgnaval*, 2,392 ft., *Oreval*, 2,165 ft., *Ullaval*, 2,153 ft., and *Tirga More*, 2,227 ft., the last-named being the most westerly. These extend from Loch Resort to West Loch Tarbert, and outstanding among them is the great rock-face of *Strone Ulladale*, 1,398 ft., to the north of Ullaval, overlooking Glen Ulladale and Loch Resort. Of the several passes through the hills, perhaps the finest traverses Glen Meavaig, between *Uisgnaval* and *Oreval*, passing the craggy hill of *Strone Scourst*, just over 1,600 ft. in height, rising above Loch Scourst. The track ends **4 m.** N. of West Loch Tarbert at Loch Voshimid, which is associated with the " island that likes to be visited " in Sir James Barrie's " Mary Rose " (see below). To the east rises *Stulaval*, 1,887 ft., on the Lewis border, overshadowing Loch Langabhat, a long and narrow sheet of water. Outer Loch Seaforth displays fine, fjord-like scenery, and has given its name to the famous Seaforth Highlanders, the regiment having been raised by the Mackenzie who hunted in the *Park* district, to the east of the loch. **Tarbert**, the principal village of Harris, is situated on the narrow isthmus dividing West and East Loch Tarbert, and has a steamer pier on the latter. Away to the west rises *Ben Luskentyre*, over 1,600 ft. high, overlooking the island of Taransay.

About **10 m.** N.W. of Tarbert, on an attractive, narrow road along West Loch Tarbert, beyond Ardhasig Bridge, is *Amhuinnsuidhe Castle*, where Barrie wrote much of " Mary Rose." Still farther west is *Husinish Bay*, with fine scenery, and to the north-west lies the small island of Scarpa. South of Tarbert, and looking across East Loch Tarbert towards *Scalpay*, a calling-place for steamers, a road leads through the delightful district of South Harris, turning westwards by way of Glen Laxdale, noted for its funeral cairns, to reach Luskentyre Bay, with its silver sands. Beyond lies the Sound of Taransay with Taransay Island. The road continues past sandy bays, with views of the Toe Head peninsula, on which is situated Cape Difficulty, one of the only three " capes " in Great Britain. It then traverses Glen Coishletter, near the shores of the Sound of Harris, to reach the most southerly part of Harris at **Leverburgh**, or *Obbe*, where Lord Leverhulme tried unsuccessfully to create a fishing station. **3 m.** S.E., on Rodel Bay, is **Rodel**, where the well-known, restored cruciform Church of *St. Clement* (A.M.)

The remarkable collection of Standing Stones, amounting to nearly 50 in all, which are to be found at Callanish, on A858, some 16 miles west of Stornoway

Rodel Church, dating from 1500, which contains some notable Macleod tombs. It stands on A859, in the extreme south of Harris, near Obbe

A primitive, thatched crofter's 'black house,' near Daliburgh, on the island of South Uist

Stornoway, or Lewis Castle, built in the 19th century, and now a technical college. Lord Leverhulme presented it to the town

The Memorial cairn on the site of the former birthplace (1722) of Flora Macdonald, which stands at Milton, on the island of South Uist

The new bridge across an 'arm of the Atlantic,' which links the islands of South Uist and Benbecula

[For **HEBRIDES, OUTER** see also following plate

Hebrides, Outer, Inverness; Ross and Cromarty. The remains of
Kishmul, or Kiessimul Castle, 15th century and later, an ancient
MacNeil stronghold, on an island facing Castlebay, in the island
of Barra. At one period a retainer is said to have announced
daily from the castle walls: " MacNeil has dined, the Kings,
Princes and others of the earth may now dine "

**Helensburgh,
Dunbarton.** The
obelisk to Henry Bell,
who, in 1812, designed
the ' Comet,' Europe's
first steam-driven craft

Helensburgh, Dunbarton. The
flywheel of the ' Comet,' the
first steam-driven craft in
Europe, and also the anvil
used by Henry Bell, its
designer, which are both
preserved in Hermitage Park

Helensburgh, Dunbarton.
The Cross set up by Sir
James Colquhoun, to
celebrate the centenary
of the Burgh (1802–
1902)

Helmsdale, Sutherland. The remains of the Castle (1488) of the Sutherlands. A
double murder took place here in 1567, when the 11th Earl and his Countess
were slain by Isobel Sinclair

PLATE 83 (facing page 175)

[For HEBRIDES, OUTER, see also preceding plate

dates from 1500, and has some curious sculptures on the tower. The church was built by the eighth Macleod chief of Dunvegan Castle in Skye. Of particular note is the fine, recessed *Macleod* tomb, dated 1528, and in the churchyard is the tomb of a Macleod of Berneray who once fought for Prince Charles Edward. There are also some good examples of Highland grave slabs. Overlooking the village is *Roneval*, 1,506 ft., rising away to the north, and forming a fine view-point. **4 m. N.E.** of Rodel is the small port of *Finsbay*, on the loch of that name, and reached by a very narrow and winding road, with blind corners and acute bends. This road continues along the east coast, passing the head of Loch Stockinish, with a steamer calling-place at *Stockinish*, and linking up with the main road leading back to Tarbert.

NORTH UIST.

This island, in which many standing-stones, stone circles and chambered cairns are to be found, is separated from Lewis and Harris by the Sound of Harris, in which lie the fair-sized islands of Berneray and Pabbay, together with many smaller ones. North Uist consists almost of more water than land, and a road encircles the northern portion of the island, giving a picture, more especially in the east and south, of myriads of tiny lochans and inlets of the sea. Loch Scadavay is the largest inland loch, and its innumerable indentations give it a length of shore out of all proportion to its actual size. The western side of the island includes the *Paible* district, and farther to the north-west is Hoglan Bay, on the exposed Atlantic coast. Far out to sea lie the remote *Haskeir* islands. The most important centre is **Lochmaddy**, having a pier on Loch Maddy, with its numerous islets. *South Lee*, 920 ft., to the south of Lochmaddy, gives a comprehensive panorama of the loch-studded landscape to the west. Farther south still rises *Eaval*, 1,138 ft., the highest point on the island, overlooking Loch Obisary and Loch Eport, with its narrow entrance, to the north, and also the tidal island of Grimsay, to the south. The road to the west coast of the island goes south-west from Lochmaddy, to pass, after 5 miles, the notable chambered cairn of *Langass Barp*. Some 3 miles farther, a branch road to the south gives access to *Carinish*, from which the *North Ford* is crossed by a new causeway connecting with *Grimsay* island and the larger island of *Benbecula* (see below). The ruined *Teampull na Trionaid*, or *Temple of Carinish*, stands on a small eminence, and is of massive 14th or 16th cent. construction. Away to the west lies *Baleshare* island, and farther west still are the *Monach* isles, separated from North Uist by the Sound of Monach.

BENBECULA.

This small island, the surface of which is literally a maze of small lochs, lies between North and South Uist, and is linked to the former by means of a new causeway from **Gramisdale.** The island of South Uist is reached by a viaduct commencing at **Creagorry.** A road links both these points, but apart from this there are only a few very narrow roads on the island. Benbecula is perhaps best known for its associations with Prince Charles Edward, who sailed from here, in 1746, with Flora Macdonald, to Port Kilbride near *Uig* (*q.v.*), in Skye. **2 m. N.W.** of Creagorry stands the ruined *Borve Castle*, a former stronghold of the chiefs of Benbecula. **2 m. W.** of Gramisdale is the airport of *Balivanich*.

SOUTH UIST.

A road traverses the entire length of this large island, commencing at **Carnan**, in the extreme north, at the end of the viaduct which links the island with Benbecula. It then crosses the expanse of Loch Bee by means of a narrow, raised causeway. This road, from points on which *St. Kilda* (*q.v.*), 60 miles out in the Atlantic, can be seen at times, is a little over 20 miles in length and terminates at **Pollachar** near Kilbride, in the extreme south, on the Sound of Eriskay. From here there are views looking south-eastwards to the island of *Eriskay*, where Prince Charles Edward first set foot on Scottish soil, in 1745, and which is noted for its charming folksongs. The ship " *Politicia*," carrying a large export cargo of whisky, went aground off

Eriskay in 1941. On the east coast of South Uist is an area of high ground, dominated by the peaks of *Beinn Mhor*, 2,034 ft., and *Hecla*, 1,988 ft., the latter overlooking outer Loch Skiport, to the north. Between these hills the Prince sheltered in a forester's hut for three weeks, in 1746. Farther south, beyond Loch Eynort, rises *Stulaval*, 1,227 ft., with Loch Snigisclett below its northern slopes. **5 m. N.** of Pollachar, at **Daliburgh** Church, a short branch from the north to south road leads eastwards to **Lochboisdale** (GOLF), the chief centre of the island, noted for fishing, and with a pier on Loch Boisdale. **4 m. N.** of Daliburgh Church, and to the west of the main road from Benbecula, are the remains of Flora Macdonald's early home at *Milton*, near the shores of Loch Kildonan. **2½ m.** farther north, a by-road leads north-westwards to the ruined castle of *Ormaclett*, dating from c. 1701 and burnt in 1715.

BARRA.

This is the most southerly island of importance in the chain of the Outer Islands. Barra, separated from South Uist by the Sound of Barra and the island of Eriskay, is mainly sterile, and has a busy herring fishing station and pier at **Castlebay**, in the south, situated on Castle Bay. On an island in the bay stands the picturesque, ruined *Kishmul Castle*, dating from c. 1427, the largest in the Outer Hebrides, and the ancient home of the MacNeils of Barra. The island of Barra is noted for its pure Gaelic, and also for the native Hebridean folk-songs and lore. In the southern half rises *Heaval*, 1,260 ft., a fine viewpoint. A road about 12 miles in length encircles Barra, giving access to the sandy *Traigh Mor*, or Great Cockle Shore, in the north, where aircraft landings are made. At the north point rises *Ben Eoligarry*, 338 ft., a good viewpoint. The ruined *Cille-bharra*, where several carved slabs are still to be seen, was once the church of St. Barr. Beyond is a narrow peninsula, extending past the old burial-ground of Kilbar and the former MacNeil dwelling of *Eoligarry House* to Scurrival Point, washed by the waters of the Sound of Fuday. To the south of Barra are the islands of Vatersay, Sandray, Pabbay and *Mingulay*, the last-named with some very remarkable heights on the west side known as the *Biulacraig* cliffs. Finally, *Berneray* terminates the long chain, and has a lighthouse on the 580-ft. high Barra Head, the southernmost point in the Outer Hebrides. See **St. Kilda.**

HEILIM, Sutherland.   Map 28, **NC 4 5.**
Lies on the north-east shore of Loch Eriboll, a sheltered anchorage from storms, in a rugged setting, with a fine mountain background. A little to the south of Heilim is a ruined broch by the loch-side. To the north-west, on the road to *Tongue* (*q.v.*), is the head of Loch Hope, at the southern end of which rises *Ben Hope*, 3,040 ft., the most northerly of the 3,000-ft. peaks of Scotland. See **Eriboll** and **Hope Lodge.** *Iter.* 225.

HELENSBURGH, Dunbarton. 8,583. SB.
                         Map 15, **NS 2 8.**
E.C. Wed. GOLF. A well-known watering place and centre for steamer trips and yachting, situated at the point where the beautiful Gare Loch merges into the broadening estuary of the Clyde. The main steamer pier is at *Craigendoran* (*q.v.*). An obelisk in the town commemorates Henry Bell, designer of the " Comet," one of the earliest steamboats. J. Logie Baird, the inventor of television, was a native of the town. A road leading north-eastwards gives access to the shores of *Loch Lomond* (*q.v.*), and a left fork, a mile and a half from Helensburgh, leads into Glen Fruin, with *Beinn Chaorach*, 2,338 ft., rising to the north. In this glen was fought, in 1603, a savage clan battle between the Macgregors and Colquhouns, which gave the glen its name meaning " glen of sorrow." See **Bowling, Rhu** and **Torphichen.** *Iter.* 102, 111, 114, 116.

HELL'S GLEN, Argyll.   Map 14, **NN 1 0.**
See **Lochgoilhead** and **Rest and be Thankful.** *Iter.* 102.

HELMSDALE, Sutherland. 732.   Map 31, **ND 0 1.**
E.C. Wed. Where the green valley of Strath Ullie, traversed by the Helmsdale River and noted for its fishing, reaches the

sea between ridges of elevated moorland, stands the little fishing port of *Helmsdale*, with its safe anchorage. There is also bathing from a sandy beach. The ruined Castle dates from 1488, and was the scene of a double murder, in 1567, when the Earl of Sutherland and his wife were poisoned. To the north, the road to *Berriedale* (*q.v.*) winds through the picturesque Navidale ravines to enter Caithness near the rocky Ord of Caithness, at a height of more than 700 ft., with fine views towards the bare hills in the background to the north-west. See **Kildonan** (Sutherland) and **Portgower**. *Iter. 200, 231, 233, 234, 235, 236.*

1. Castle.

HERIOT, Midlothian.   Map 10, NT 4 5.
Lies in a pleasant and lofty setting on the main Carlisle to Edinburgh road, with the *Moorfoot* hills to the west. The Church stands **2 m. S.W.**, on the delightful road following the Heriot Water and the Dewar Burn through the hills, and reaching a height of about 1,200 ft. where the counties of Midlothian and Peebles meet. The descent later follows the valley of the Leithen Water towards Tweeddale, with *Windlestraw Law*, 2,161 ft., rising to the east. See **Crichton**. *Iter. 9, 11.*

HERMISTON, Midlothian.   Map 9, NT 1 7.
GOLF. The estates of *Riccarton* and *Dalmahoy*, to the south of the road leading to Mid-Calder, are both noted for their trees. A little to the north stands the restored Church of *Ratho*, of 12th cent. dedication, where the last Earl of Lauderdale, who lived at *Hatton House*, now demolished after a fire, is buried. *Iter. 18, 19, 20, 22.*

HERMITAGE CASTLE, Roxburgh.   Map 5, NY 4 9.
This famous, restored 13th cent. Liddesdale Castle (A.M.), a stronghold of the Douglases, stands on a height surrounded by moorlands overlooking the Hermitage Water, a little to the west of the Newcastleton to Hawick road, and is a structure of immense strength, dating from the 14th cent. Its history is long and particularly cruel, and the castle was visited in 1566 by Mary, Queen of Scots, who nearly died there from a fever, after riding to and from *Jedburgh* (*q.v.*), about 40 miles, in a single day. Swinburne has described the castle in one of his poems. The building consists of four towers and connecting walls, outwardly almost perfect, and the interior contains remains of the original tower. Open summer, 10 to 7, winter, 10 to 4; Sun., 2 to 7 or 4. (See note page 90). To the east, beyond the Whitterhope Burn, is *Ninestane Rig*, 943 ft., on which is a stone circle. *Iter. 31.*

HIGH BLANTYRE, Lanark.   Map 8, NS 6 5.
See **Blantyre**.

HIGHLANDS, THE
Scotland is traditionally divided into two distinct areas, known as the *Highlands* and the *Lowlands* (*q.v.*) respectively, but no definite line of demarcation exists between the two, and the junction is essentially an artificial one, created by the geological structure of the land itself. It is often said that the Highlands can be taken to consist of the entire district of hills, glens, lochs and islands lying to the north and west of, and including the grassy and heather-clad *Grampian* (*q.v.*) mountains. The rather scanty population is largely of Celtic extraction, and to some extent still employs the Gaelic speech. The Northern Highlands were at one time mainly Pictish territory, while Argyllshire, in the Southern High-

lands, formed the ancient kingdom of Dalriada. The rock formation of the Highland mountains, with their 543 tops of more than 3,000 ft., tends to make them rugged and precipitous in many places. Their most notable features are the granite of Arran and the plateau of the Cairngorms, the latter range including an extensive National Nature Reserve; the wild hills around Glencoe, including also Ben Nevis and the Mamores; the black gabbro of the serrated Coolins of Skye, the finest rock peaks in Britain, and forming a paradise for the mountaineer and hill walker; the Archaean gneiss rock of the remote Assynt district; and finally the grand Torridon red sandstone of Wester Ross and Sutherland. All these form a striking contrast compared with the more softly rounded contours of the green Lowland hills.

The *Highland Line*, or geological boundary between the two areas, may be said to commence in the Firth of Clyde, thence skirting the Cowal coast of Argyllshire to cross the mouth of the Gare Loch, and pass later over the lower reaches of Loch Lomond. It then follows, approximately, a line linking Aberfoyle with Callander and Comrie, where, at the last-named place, occasional earth tremors occur as the result of the so-called Highland "fault" being situated in the vicinity. Continuing past the entrance to the Sma' Glen, the line reaches the Tay to the south of Dunkeld, and then stretches north-eastwards through central Angus towards the Dee valley at Dinnet. From here it traverses Banff and Moray in a north-westerly direction to reach the shores of the Moray Firth at *Nairn* (*q.v.*). Across the Firth, to the north, lies the remote county of Caithness, which exhibits however characteristics entitling it to be regarded more as a Lowland than as a Highland county. A remarkable topographical feature of the Highlands is the deep rift, known as the Great Glen, or *Glen More* (*q.v.*), stretching across the country to link Fort William with Inverness, and in which lies a chain of lochs, the largest being *Loch Ness* (*q.v.*), threaded by the *Caledonian Canal* (*q.v.*). It is overlooked near its western extremity by the great bulk of *Ben Nevis* (*q.v.*), the highest mountain in the whole of Great Britain, together with its lesser satellites.

That part of the Highlands lying to the west of the rift is known generally as the North-West Highlands, and includes what is considered to be the finest and most memorable of the wild mountain and loch scenery for which Scotland is renowned. The picturesque Hebridean island of *Skye* (*q.v.*) is outstanding, and along the much-indented shores of the mainland, several of the great sea lochs, notably those of *Hourn* and *Nevis* (both *q.v.*), can be compared with the Norwegian fjords. Among the inland lochs, those of *Shiel*, *Morar*, *Duich*, *Quoich* and *Maree* (all *q.v.*) are perhaps the most memorable. The mountains of the North-West Highlands include the great hills on both sides of picturesque *Glen Shiel* (*q.v.*), extending as far as *Loch Duich*; the little-known peaks dominating Glens Affric and Cannich (See **Cannich**); Suilven and the other strange, isolated summits of the lonely Assynt district; the great cirque of the Teallachs, near *Dundonnell* (*q.v.*) in Wester Ross; and the grand Torridon peaks of Liathach and Ben Eighe near *Kinlochewe* (*q.v.*), where the Ben Eighe Nature Reserve, the first of its kind to be created in the British Isles, is to be found. Much of the mountain area in the Highlands is given over to deer-forest, and grouse-shooting takes place on some of the moors. Fishing can be enjoyed in many of the lochs and rivers, and pony-trekking is a newly-introduced sport (See **Kingussie** and **Newtonmore**). Ski-ing takes place in the Glencoe, Grampian and Cairngorm mountains, a notable centre for the last-named range being *Aviemore* (*q.v.*), which is convenient for visiting the *Glen More National Forest Park*, at the foot of the peak of Cairn Gorm.

A recent and much-debated feature of the Highlands is the advent of hydro-electric schemes to certain areas. (See **Cannich, Inveruglas, Pitlochry** and **Tomdoun**.) As a result, the villages and lonely crofts now enjoy the benefit of electric power, but the effect on the scenery is questionable, and though the construction of new roads is often of considerable help to the tourist, the primeval beauty of the scenery must inevitably suffer to some degree by the introduction of immense dams and other ancillary works, how-

Hermitage Castle, Roxburgh. The restored
14th century Douglas stronghold. Mary, Queen of
Scots, nearly died here from a fever in 1566
after riding from Jedburgh to visit Bothwell

Highlands. A view of Loch Katrine, in Perthshire, which
has associations with Sir Walter Scott's '*Lady of the Lake.*'
This loch forms part of the richly wooded Trossachs district

Highlands. The Sutherlandshire peaks of
Stack Polly and Cul Beag, in the lonely Assynt
country, seen from a point on A835, between
Ullapool and Inchnadamph

Highlands. Ben
Lomond, the highest
mountain in Stirlingshire,
rising above the northern
reaches of Loch Lomond,
and prominent in the
view from Tarbet, on its
western shores

Highlands. A view of the
islands in the lonely bay
of Eddrachillis, on the north-west
Sutherland coast, as seen from A894
between Kylesku Ferry and Scourie

Highlands. The ruined 16th
century Carnasserie
Castle, erected by a Bishop of the
Isles, who is said to have published
the first book in Gaelic. It was
burnt in 1685, and stands 1½ miles
north of Kilmartin, in Argyllshire,
on an unclassified road off A816

PLATE 84 (facing page 176)

Hoddom Bridge, Dumfries. The 16th century Trailtrow, or ' Repentance ' Tower. The name recalls John Maxwell, who repented of his decision to use his forces against his compatriots in the 16th century, and later defeated the English

Houston, Renfrew. The Mercat Cross, which was restored in 1713

Hopetoun House, West Lothian. A magnificent Scottish country house, commenced in 1696 by Sir William Bruce and completed by William Adam. It stands on an unclassified road off A904, near the Firth of Forth

Howwood, Renfrew. The ancient Clochodrich Stone, its name taken perhaps from an early ruler of Strathclyde. It stands on the Lochwinnoch road (unclassified), to the north-west

Humbie, East Lothian. A village associated with the Edinburgh Children's Holiday Fund. During the Second World War, the first German bomber to crash on British soil fell near Humbie

[For HUNTLY see following plate
[For HUNTER'S QUAY see under COWAL (Plate 36)
[For HUNTINGTOWER see under STRATHMORE (Plate 157)
[For HUNA see Plate 172

PLATE 85 (facing page 177)

ever carefully these may be planned. See **Arran, Ben Nevis, Cairngorms, Kintail, Knoydart, Lochaber, Mamore Forest, Moidart, Morven, Mull, Rum, Skye** and **Tomintoul.**

HILLEND (Edinburgh), Midlothian.　　Map 10, NT 2 6.
Situated on the outskirts of the *Pentland* hills, looking westwards towards the *Caerketton Crags* and the summit of *Allermuir Hill*, 1,617 ft. **2 m. S.S.W.** is *Woodhouselee House*, visited frequently by Sir Walter Scott. *Iter. 14, 25.*

HILLEND, Fife.　　Map 17, NT 1 8.
Iter. 93, 94, 134.

HILLFOOT, Dunbarton.　　Map 8, NS 5 7.
Iter. 105, 108, 113.

HILLSIDE, Kincardine.　　Map 21, NO 9 9.
Iter. 151, 155, 156.

HILLSWICK, Shetland.　　Map 33, HU 2 7.
See **Shetland Islands** (Mainland). *Iter. 267.*

HODDOM BRIDGE, Dumfries.　　Map 4, NY 1 7.
The bridge spans the River Annan, and a little to the west, on the south side of the Annan, stood *Hoddom Castle*, demolished in 1953. On a hill above stands the 16th cent. *Trailtrow*, or *Repentance Tower*, taking its name from the word "Repentance" which appears in raised lettering on the door lintel. *Hoddom Church*, on the Ecclefechan road, was once the See of St. Mungo. *Iter. 42.*

HOLY LOCH, Argyll.　　Map 14, NS 1 8.
A small inlet of the Clyde estuary, near the entrance to Loch Long. At *Sandbank* (*q.v.*) was launched, in 1958, the yacht "Sceptre," Britain's losing challenger for the America's Cup. See **Hunter's Quay, Kilmun** and **Kirn.** *Iter. 102, 137.*

HOLYROODHOUSE, Midlothian.　　Map 10, NT 2 7.
See **Edinburgh.**

HOLYTOWN, Lanark. 3,300.　　Map 9, NS 7 5·
Lies to the east of the Clyde valley, in a mining area. See **Carfin.** *Iter. 18.*

HOLYWOOD, Dumfries.　　Map 4, NX 9 8.
Iter. 27, 48, 56, 67.

HOPE LODGE, Sutherland.　　Map 28, NC 4 6.
Finely situated at the northern extremity of the long and narrow Loch Hope, with *Ben Hope*, the most northerly 3,000-ft. peak in Scotland, rising beyond the head of the loch. Westwards lies Loch Eriboll, and to the east is the Kyle of Tongue, at the far end of the lonely moors of A'Mhoine. To the north, and not accessible by road, is the cave-ridden Whiten Head, with very fine cliff scenery. See **Melness.** *Iter. 225.*

HOPEMAN, Moray. 1,161.　　Map 26, NJ 1 6.
GOLF. A fishing village and small resort, with a harbour and lighthouse. See **Duffus.** *Iter. 199.*

HOPETOUN HOUSE, West Lothian.　　Map 16, NT 0 7.
This splendid mansion, rich in treasures, including a museum, is one of the finest of its period in Scotland, and stands in a park overlooking the estuary of the Forth. It was commenced in 1696 by Sir William Bruce, but left unfinished, and the completion of the house was by the hands of William Adam, and his more famous son Robert. The house is shown daily, exc. Thurs. and Fri., 2 to 6, May to end of Sept. (See note page 90.) *Iter. 96.*

HOSPITALFIELD, Angus.　　Map 17, NO 6 4.
See **Arbroath.**

HOUNAM, Roxburgh.　　Map 11, NT 7 1.
On the Kale Water. *Heatherhope Loch*, noted for its heather-clad surroundings, lies to the south-east, and is now a reservoir for Kelso. The main *Cheviot* range rises beyond here, and farther east is The Cheviot, 2,676 ft., in Northumberland. The *Auchopecairn*, 2,382 ft., on its western slopes, is a fine viewpoint, and lies actually on the Scottish border.

HOUSTON, Renfrew.　　Map 8, NS 4 6.
The Mercat Cross was restored in 1713. North of the town is *St. Peter's Well*, and on a hill farther north stands the 11-ft. high Celtic *Barochan Cross* (A.M.), moved from its original site. *Houston House* is mainly 19th cent.

HOWE OF FIFE, Fife.　　Map 17, NO 2 1.
The fertile area to the north-east of the *Lomond Hills*.

HOWGATE, Midlothian.　　Map 9, NT 2 5.
Known for its associations with Dr. John Brown's "Rab and his Friends." 4 m. S.E., on the slopes of the *Moorfoot* hills, is the large *Gladhouse* reservoir. See **Carrington, Penicuik** and **Temple.** *Iter. 14, 37.*

HOWWOOD, Renfrew.　　Map 8, NS 3 6.
Away to the west is Castle Semple Loch, near which stands *Castle Semple* Church (*q.v.*). To the north-west, on the Lochwinnoch road, is the ancient *Clochodrich* Stone. *Iter. 58, 63.*

HOY, ISLE OF, Orkney.　　Map 33, ND 2 9.
See **Orkney Islands** (Hoy).

HUMBIE, East Lothian. 490.　　Map 10, NT 4 6.
At the foot of the *Lammermuir* hills and noted as a "Children's Village," being associated with the Edinburgh Children's Holiday Fund early in this century. To the south is *Johnstounburn House*, with its beautiful gardens. *Iter. 36.*

HUME CASTLE, Berwick.　　Map 10, NT 7 4.
See **Greenlaw.**

HUNA, Caithness.　　Map 30, ND 3 7.
Situated about halfway between St. John's Point and Duncansby Head, on the Inner Sound of the Pentland Firth, facing the island of Stroma. Farms in the vicinity display the characteristic Caithness flagstones, used in place of fences. See **Canisbay** and **John o' Groats.** *Iter. 240.*

HUNTER'S QUAY, Argyll.　　Map 14, NS 1 7.
This little Firth of Clyde resort is the headquarters of the Clyde Yachting Club, and the annual Clyde Yachting Fortnight, held in July, is based on Hunter's Quay, which takes its name from the Hunters of *Hafton House*, a little to the north-west. Across the mouth of the Holy Loch, to the north, is Strone Point and the small resort of *Strone* (*q.v.*). See **Kirn** and **Sandbank.** *Iter. 102.*

HUNTERSTON, Ayr.　　Map 7, NS 1 5.
Construction of a nuclear power station in the vicinity is now proceeding.

HUNTINGTOWER, Perth.　　Map 16, NO 0 2.
Huntingtower Castle (A.M.), formerly called *Ruthven Castle*, has associations with James VI and the so-called "Ruthven Raid," in 1582, as a result of which, two years later, the Earl of Gowrie was executed. The restored 15th cent. buildings include two towers joined by lower buildings, the space between the towers being traditionally known as the "Maiden's Leap." Open summer, 10 to 7, winter, 10 to 4; Sun., after 2. (See note page 90). See **Pitcairngreen.** *Iter. 145, 147.*

HUNTLY, Aberdeen. 3,966. SB.　　Map 26, NJ 5 3.
E.C. Thurs. M.D. Wed. GOLF. Immediately to the north of this important market town, which is situated in Strathbogie, the River Bogie is joined by the better-known Deveron, which has come from the higher ground to the west, overlooked by *Clashmach Hill*, 1,229 ft. The town makes a pleasant summer resort, and is noted for its good fishing facilities. The imposing, ruined Castle (A.M.), noted for the elaboration of the topmost storey, was once the home of the Gordon Marquesses of Huntly, the Gay "Gordons," one of whom bore the title of the "Cock o' the North." It was formerly known as the *Palace of Strathbogie*, and dates from 1602, the medieval structure having been burnt 8 years previously. In the 18th cent., the structure gradually became derelict, and some of the stones were used in the construction of *Huntly Lodge*, now an hotel, which stands to the north of the town. The castle is open weekdays, 10 to 7 in summer; 10 to 4 in winter. Sun., 2 to 7 or 4. (See note page 90.) See **Gordon** and **Rhynie.** *Iter. 165, 167, 175, 178, 187, 193, 194, 195, 196.*
(See page 178 for Town Plan of **HUNTLY**).

HURLFORD, Ayr. 4,147.　　Map 8, NS 4 3.
A small town having iron and fireclay works. The house of *Carnell* has a 15th cent. pele tower. *Iter. 67, 69.*

HUNTLY

Scale

A.96 ELGIN 27½
DEVERON RD
A.97 BRAEMAR 57½
BANFF 20¾ ABERDEEN 38¾
A.96

1. Castle.

and near the St. Lawrence River in Canada. Small lochs abound in the sterile country around Inchnadamph, and in one loch is found the very rare gilaroo trout. Picturesque *Loch Assynt* (*q.v.*) stretches north-westwards for some 7 miles, and on its northern shore stands the ruin of the late 16th cent. *Ardvreck Castle*, where, in 1650, the great Marquis of Montrose, of the Clan Graham, was betrayed by the laird after his last battle, fought at *Carbisdale* near *Invershin* (*q.v.*). In the vicinity stands the ruined 17th cent. *Calda House*, once a home of the Mackenzies. Near Inchnadamph is a National Nature Reserve of 3,200 acres, which includes an area of limestone country containing caves and underground streams. The Allt nan Uamh bone caves show traces of occupation by early man. **4 m. S.E.** of the village stands *Ben More Assynt*, 3,273 ft., the highest mountain in the county, and composed mainly of gneiss, being linked to the subsidiary height of *Conaveall*, 3,234 ft., on the slopes of which rises the Traligill, a partly subterranean stream. To the south-west of Inchnadamph are *Canisp*, 2,779 ft., and the sharp cone of *Suilven*, 2,399 ft., two remarkable Torridon sandstone hills, separated by the lonely Loch Gainimh. Northwards from Loch Assynt, the road to *Kylesku* (*q.v.*) climbs under the slopes of *Glasven*, 2,541 ft., to the east, and the strangely-shaped ridge of *Quinag*, 2,653 ft., to the west. See **Altnacealgach** and **Lochinver** (for *Suilven*). *Iter.* 225, 227, 228.

INCHTURE, Perth.   Map 17, NO 2 2.
In the heart of the fertile district known as the *Carse of Gowrie* (*q.v.*), between the *Sidlaw* hills and the Firth of Tay, and noted for the cultivation of strawberries. To the north is *Rossie Priory*, in its fine grounds, situated below *Rossie Hill*, 567 ft. See **Kinnaird** and **Longforgan.** *Iter.* 154.

INNELLAN, Argyll. 1,500.   Map 7, NS 1 7.
E.C. Wed. GOLF. A Firth of Clyde and *Cowal* (*q.v.*) resort, with a steamer pier, facing Wemyss Bay on the Renfrew coast. **2½ m. S.S.W.** is Toward Point, with a lighthouse, and a modern Castle to the west. A road continues westwards, passing the ruined *Castle Toward*, and proceeding thence along the east shore of Loch *Striven*, with views up the *Kyles of Bute* (*q.v.*), and across to the bay of *Rothesay* (*q.v.*) in the island of Bute. The road comes to an end shortly beyond *Inverchaolin* (*q.v.*) Church, with its background of lonely hills, dominated by *Bishop's Seat*, 1,651 ft. *Iter.* 102.

INNER HEBRIDES, Argyll; Inverness.
     Maps 6, 12, 13, 22 and 23.
See **Hebrides, Inner.**

INNERLEITHEN, Peebles. 2,389. SB.   Map 10, NT 3 3.
E.C. Tues. GOLF. A woollen town, with mineral springs, situated on the Leithen Water, near its confluence with the Tweed a little to the south-east. The summer Cleikum Ceremony is associated with the 7th cent. St. Ronan, and the town may be the original of Sir Walter Scott's " St. Ronan's Well." There are numerous hill-forts in the vicinity. Northwards lie the Leithen Water and Glentress Water valleys, in a delightful setting of hills, and with *Windlestraw Law* rising to 2,161 ft. near the point where the counties of Peebles, Selkirk and Midlothian meet. To the south of Innerleithen, across the Tweed, is situated the famous old mansion of *Traquair* (*q.v.*). **2 m. N.W.,** across the Tweed, is the ancient tower of *Cardrona.* See **Walkerburn.** *Iter.* 12, 14, 32, 33, 34, 52.

INNERMESSAN, Wigtown.   Map 2, NX 0 6.
The Roman site of " Rericonium " is thought to have been a little to the north, where stands the isolated *Craigcaffie Castle*, overlooking Loch Ryan, and dating from c. 1570, a good example of its period. *Iter.* 55, 80, 84.

INNERPEFFRAY, Perth.   Map 16, NN 9 1.
See **Crieff.**

INNERWICK, East Lothian.   Map 11, NT 7 7.
The ruined Castle was destroyed in the English invasion of 1547. There are also some remains of *Thornton Castle.* The Church dates from 1784. A school of 100 whales came ashore here in 1950. To the south is *Monynut Edge*, with *Heart Law*, near the Berwick border, attaining 1,283 ft.

HUTTON, Berwick.   Map 11, NT 9 5.
On the Whiteadder Water stands *Hutton Castle*, a modern structure incorporating an ancient pele tower. Sir William Burrell, its former owner, donated the famous Burrell Art Collection to Glasgow in 1944.

HYNDFORD BRIDGE, Lanark.   Map 9, NS 9 4.
The bridge spans the River Clyde, and is overlooked by *Cairngryfe Hill*, 1,131 ft., to the east. To the north-west of Hyndford Bridge, on Lanark Moor, is the *Lanark* (*q.v.*) racecourse. *Iter.* 21, 35, 48, 50, 53.

IMACHAR, Isle of Arran, Bute.   Map 7, NR 8 4.
Iter. 242.

INCHBARE, Angus.   Map 21, NO 6 6.
Iter. 156, 163, 164.

INCHCOLM ISLAND, Fife.   Map 17, NT 1 8.
This little island lies a mile and a half out to sea, to the south of *Aberdour* (*q.v.*). On it stands the very interesting ruined Abbey of *St. Columba* (A.M.), founded in 1123, and comprising some of the most complete monastic remains in Scotland. Much of the existing structure dates from the 13th and 15th cents., the tower on the octagonal Chapter House being of note, while remains of frescoes have been discovered in the choir. The island is mentioned in Shakespeare's " Macbeth."

INCHINNAN CHURCH, Renfrew.   Map 8, NS 5 6.
See **Renfrew.**

INCHKEITH ISLAND, Fife.   Map 17, NT 2 8.
The fortified island of *Inchkeith*, with its powerful lighthouse, stands three miles out to sea off the Fife coast, to the south-east of *Kinghorn* (*q.v.*). Between 1549 and 1567 it was held by the French. In 1773 it was visited by Dr. Johnson and Boswell, and in 1817 by Carlyle.

INCHMAHOME PRIORY, Perth.   Map 15, NN 5 0.
See **Port of Menteith.**

INCHNADAMPH, Sutherland.   Map 29, NC 2 2.
This small fishing resort is situated in the remote *Assynt* district of the North-West Highlands, in the heart of some of the strangest and most notable mountain scenery in Great Britain. Geologically, this part of Sutherland is of the greatest interest, many of the surrounding peaks being composed of Torridon sandstone. topped in places by gleaming white quartzite, the mountains tending to form isolated summits instead of being part of a range. Much of the land to the north-west is composed of Archaean gneiss rock, some of the oldest formations known to exist in the world, found elsewhere only in the Outer Hebrides,

Huntly, Aberdeen. The ruined Castle, known formerly as the Palace of Strathbogie, and once the home of the Gordon Marquesses of Huntly, the 'Gay Gordons,' one of whom was nicknamed the 'Cock o' the North'

Inchnadamph, Sutherland. The 16th century Ardvreck Castle, by Loch Assynt, off A837, to the north-west. In 1650, the great Marquis of Montrose was brought here as a prisoner and later betrayed by the laird, it is said for £20,000. See Invershin (Plate 89)

Innerpeffray, Perth. The oldest library in Scotland, founded in 1691. It stands 4 miles east of Crieff, on a by-road off B8062, near the River Earn

Innerpeffray, Perth. The Faichney Stone (1707), carved by a mason during his life-time, with the dates of birth of his 10 children. It is situated on a by-road off B8062, near the River Earn, 4 miles east of Crieff

Innermessan, Wigtown. The late 16th century Craigcaffie Castle, to the north, off A77. Its foundations are said to have been strengthened with bags of wool to counteract the danger of sinking in the marshy sub-soil

Insh, Inverness. The Church by Loch Insh, which is reputed to stand on an Early Christian site

Inverallochy, Aberdeen. The ancient stronghold of the Comyns, situated some 2 miles south, off B9033

Inveraray, Argyll. A Celtic Cross brought from Iona

Inveraray, Argyll. The 18th century Castle of the Duke of Argyll, the head of the Clan Campbell. In 1773, Dr. Johnson was entertained here by the 5th Duke during his tour of the Highlands

Inverbervie, Kincardine. The white-harled and richly-corbelled early 17th century Allardyce Castle, near the Bervie Water, to the north-west, off B967

Inveresk, Midlothian. The loftily situated Parish Church, erected in 1805. A mound in the churchyard is said to have served Cromwell as a battery site

[For INVEREY see following plate
[For INVERARAY see also under
Loch Fyne (Plate 112)

PLATE 87 (facing page 179)

INNERWICK CHURCH, Perth. Map 15, NN 5 4.
This lonely little church, in its setting of green hills in Glen Lyon, preserves an ancient bell. *Iter. 107.*

INSCH, Aberdeen. 1,421. Map 27, NJ 6 2.
E.C. Thurs. **M.D.** Mon. A large village, to the west of which is the conical hill of *Dunnideer,* crowned by a vitrified fort, on which stands a ruined 16th cent. Castle. The hill of *Christ's Kirk,* 1,021 ft., faces it across the Shevock Burn. To the north-west rise the *Foudland* hills, attaining over 1,500 ft. On their southern side, at *Mireton,* some 2½ miles from Insch, is the inscribed Pictish *Picardy Stone* (A.M.). See **Leslie** (Aberdeen) and **Oyne.** *Iter. 178.*

INSH, Inverness. Map 19, NH 8 0.
On the shores of the tiny Loch Insh, in the upper Spey valley. The Church, which stands on a hillock close to the bridge over the River Spey, is said to be the sole example of a Scottish Church on a site used continuously since the 6th cent. An ancient Celtic hand-bell has been preserved. See **Feshie Bridge.** *Iter. 138, 149.*

INVERALLOCHY, Aberdeen. Map 27, NK 0 6.
A coastal village, situated to the east of Fraserburgh Bay, with its fine sands. The Castle, which lies inland, some **2 m. S.,** was built by the Comyns, as was also the restored *Cairnbulg Castle,* standing **2 m. S.W.** of Inverallochy, on the Water of Philorth. See **St. Combs.**

INVERAMSAY, Aberdeen. Map 27, NJ 7 2.
Lies on the River Urie. Beyond the river, to the south-east, is *Harlaw House,* and the tall monument commemorating the battle of Harlaw, fought in 1411, with great loss of life, and which is associated with Scott's " The Antiquary." As a result of this important battle, the southward progress of the Highlanders under Donald, the Lord of the Isles, was checked, and the predominance of the Lowlanders made certain. *Iter. 175, 178.*

INVERAN BRIDGE, Sutherland. Map 29, NH 5 9.
Noted for fishing on the turbulent River Shin, here spanned by a three-arched bridge. The Falls of Shin lie about a mile to the north. To the south, the Shin meets the waters of the Kyle of Sutherland near *Invershin* (q.v.). *Iter. 228, 232.*

INVERARAY, Argyll. 521. SB. Map 14, NN 0 0.
E.C. Wed. This pleasant little Royal Burgh stands in a richly wooded setting on *Loch Fyne* (q.v.) facing Strone Point, at the eastern extremity of the small inlet known as Loch Shira. The well-known *Inveraray Castle* is the seat of the Duke of Argyll, the head of Clan Campbell, and known in Gaelic as " MacCailean Mor." (See **Glenshee.**) The Campbells have a long history, in which the Earls and Dukes of Argyll had their full share. The eighth Earl and his son were executed in Edinburgh, in 1661 and 1685 respectively, and Scott has introduced the former into his " Legend of Montroe," while in the " Heart of Midlothian " is portrayed the second Duke. The town, which stood formerly near the ancient castle, was moved to its new site in the mid-18th cent. The present Castle is shown weekdays, 10 to 12.30 and 2 to 6 (exc. Fri.); Sun., 2 to 6, April to end of June; daily, July 1 to end of Sept. (see page 90). It was designed by Roger Morris and Robert Mylne, and dates from c. 1780, with a large park, through which flows

Map legend:
DALMALLY, OBAN
A.819
ARROCHAR, TARBET
A.83
FRONT STREET
Archway
MAIN STREET
INVERARAY
(One way streets »»)
G.P.O.
A.83
LOCHGILPHEAD, CAMPBELTOWN R860

1. Castle. 3. Cross.
2. Church. 4. Old Court House.

the River Aray. A silver fir in the park is thought to be the bulkiest tree in Great Britain. A cannon, taken from the wreck of the sunken galleon Florida, of the Armada fleet, has been brought here from *Tobermory* (q.v.) in Mull. The hill of *Duniquoich,* 850 ft., surmounted by a tower, rises near the park, and was described in the " Legend of Montrose." In the town stands the Church, built in 1794, in which services in English and Gaelic are held in separate divisions. A Celtic Cross from Iona stands at the junction of Front Street and Main Street. R. L. Stevenson's novel " Catriona " contains much local colour towards the end. The famous Appin murder trial was held at Inveraray, in the old Courthouse, in 1752. Dr. Johnson visited the Castle in 1773, and tasted whisky for the first time at an inn. At the head of Loch Shira, the little River Shira, which has descended through Glen Shira, overlooked by *Beinn Bhuidhe,* 3,106 ft., is spanned by a fine 18th cent. ornamental bridge. Below the Ben, to the north-west, hydro-electric works are situated. North of the town, the road traversing Glen Aray, with its falls, is richly wooded, before climbing on to the open moors. In the glen, on an eminence, is a memorial to Neil Munro, the author, who was a native of Inveraray. **4 m. N.E.,** on the road to Glen Croe, and overlooking Loch Fyne, is the well-restored *Dundarave Castle,* dating from 1598, and described under the name of " *Doom Castle* " in Neil Munro's " John Splendid." See **Ballachulish, Cladich, Duror, Kilchrenan** and **Oban.** *Iter. 88, 101, 102, 117, 118, 119, 120, 121.*

INVERASDALE, Ross and Cromarty. Map 22, NG 8 8.
See **Poolewe.**

INVERBERVIE, Kincardine. 940. SB. Map 21, NO 8 7.
E.C. Wed. A little flax-spinning Royal Burgh, known also as *Bervie,* and situated on Bervie Bay, where the Bervie Water has its outlet into the sea. To the south of the town is a picturesque stretch of rocky coastline, with caves and gullies. ½ m. S. stands *Hallgreen Castle.* **1 m. N.W.,** standing in a bend of the Bervie Water, is the delightful little *Allardyce Castle,* dating from c. 1600, with its fine corbelling and white-harled walls. See **Arbuthnott** and **Kinneff.** *Iter. 155.*

INVERCANNICH, Inverness. Map 24, NH 3 3.
See **Cannich.**

INVERCHAOLIN, Argyll. Map 7, NS 0 7.
Shortly beyond the Church, the road following the eastern shores of Loch Striven comes to an end. *Bishop's Seat,* 1,651 ft., rises in the background, and farther to the north-west are higher hills overlooking Glen Lean. *Iter. 102.*

INVERDRUIE, Inverness. Map 25, NH 9 1.
Iter. 138, 149, 171.

INVERESK, Midlothian. Map 10, NT 3 7.
Pleasantly situated on the River Esk, and almost adjoining *Musselburgh* (q.v.). It was once a Roman station, numerous remains having been excavated, and is now best known for its paper mills. The Parish Church is set on a height, from which the view ranges over a large extent of country. It replaced an older church in 1805, and has a tall spire and an exceptionally lovely churchyard. There are some Georgian houses, including *Halkerston* and the Manor House. Roman remains have been excavated at *Inveresk House.* See **Carberry Hill** and **Pinkie House.**

INVEREWE, Ross and Cromarty. Map 22, NG 8 8.
See **Poolewe.**

INVEREY, Aberdeen. Map 20, NO 0 8.
A *Deeside* (q.v.) hamlet, where the main stream is joined by the Ey Water, in a beautiful, wooded setting on the road leading westwards from *Braemar* (q.v.) towards the *Cairngorm* (q.v.) foothills. A memorial tablet recalls John Lamont (1805-79), who became Johann von Lamont, Astronomer Royal of Bavaria. Eastwards, off the Braemar road, is the Linn of Corriemulzie, a picturesquely situated waterfall. Away to the south, up the rugged valley of the Ey Water, is a deep chasm, known as the " Colonel's Bed," thought to have been the hiding place of Colonel John Farquharson,

who fought in 1689 at *Killiecrankie* (*q.v.*). North-west-wards of Inverey, beyond the Dee, a path leads through Glen Lui and Glen Derry into the Cairngorms, under the slopes of *Derry Cairngorm*, 3,788 ft. and farther north below *Beinn Mheadoin*, 3,883 ft., which overlooks the remote Loch Avon. This path is known as the Lairig an Laoigh, and gives access for long-distance walkers to *Nethybridge* (*q.v.*), on the edge of the Forest of Abernethy. Another pass leads westwards from Glen Lui through Glen Lui Beg, giving access to Glen Dee and the *Lairig Ghru* (see below). **2 m. W.** of Inverey by road is the well-known *Linn of Dee*, a wild and rocky cleft through which the river cascades, situated on the edge of the extensive Mar Forest. It was here that Byron was once nearly drowned.

Farther to the west, along the valley of the Upper Dee, in surroundings which become progressively wilder, the path leading towards the southern Cairngorms, accompanied by the river, turns northwards into Glen Dee. From here onwards it is known as the *Lairig Ghru* (*q.v.*), the most famous of the walkers' passes in the Cairngorms, dominated to the west by *Beinn Bhrotain*, 3,797 ft., and later by the *Devil's Point*, 3,303 ft. Where the path diverges into Glen Dee, the river is spanned by the White Bridge, and a short distance to the east of the bridge is the rock cataract and pool known as the Chest of Dee, a notable scene.

At the Linn of Dee, a road crosses the river and doubles back to the east, crossing the Lui Water, and passing by the modern *Mar Lodge*, which replaces an older mansion, burnt down. The road terminates near the Linn of Quoich, a deep, wooded ravine, where the Quoich Water flows down from Glen Quoich, backed by *Bheinn a'Bhuird*, 3,924 ft. and 3,860 ft., one of the loftiest Cairngorms peaks. *Iter. 179.*

INVERFARIGAIG, Inverness.   Map 25, NH 5 2.
Lies in a richly-wooded setting on *Loch Ness* (*q.v.*), with a pier. The narrow and wooded Pass of Inverfarigaig is picturesque, and leads in an easterly direction towards *Errogie* (*q.v.*) on Loch Mhor. The Black Rock section of the original 18th cent. Wade road, at the foot of the pass, near Loch Ness, had to be blasted by miners. To the north of the bridge over the Farigaig River is a narrow, winding track, rising steeply on to the moors to the north-east. See **Foyers** and **Wade Roads.** *Iter. 211.*

INVERGARRY, Inverness.   Map 18, NH 3 0.
E.C. Thurs. Here, on the west side of *Loch Oich* (*q.v.*), is the commencement of a magnificent road through the West Highland glens and mountains, by way of *Cluanie* (*q.v.*) and *Glen Shiel* (*q.v.*). It forms one of the famous " Roads to the Isles," and terminates at *Kyle of Lochalsh* (*q.v.*), on the *Wester Ross* coast facing the island of Skye. The River Garry flows into the loch to the north of the ruined *Invergarry Castle* where Prince Charles Edward slept before and after Culloden, and which was afterwards burnt by the Duke of Cumberland. The Castle belonged to the Macdonells of Glengarry, many of whose descendants emigrated in 1803 to Canada and founded a new Glengarry. The Kyle of Lochalsh road climbs westwards through the richly wooded Glen Garry on the first stage of its journey, traversing after a few miles the lovely tree-lined shores of Loch Garry, beyond the opposite shores of which rises *Ben Tee*, 2,956 ft. A hydro-electric scheme now operates in this district. See **Loch Lochy** and **Tomdoun.** *Iter. 210, 214, 220.*

1. Castle.

INVERGORDON, Ross and Cromarty. 1,555. SB.
          Map 25, NH 7 6.
E.C. Wed. **GOLF.** A former naval base, with a fine harbour, on the Inner Cromarty Firth, facing Udale Bay and Cromarty Bay in the *Black Isle* (*q.v.*). The view east-wards is over the Bay of Nigg, and across to *Cromarty* (*q.v.*), guarded by the twin Sutors of Cromarty. See **Logie Easter** and **Saltburn.** *Iter. 201.*

INVERGOWRIE, Angus.   Map 17, NO 3 3.
Iter. 154.

INVERIE, Inverness.   Map 23, NG 7 0.
This remote little place is situated in the *Knoydart* (*q.v.*) district, on Inverie Bay, an inlet of Outer *Loch Nevis* (*q.v.*), in a beautiful setting of mountain and loch. It is not approachable by road, access being gained by motor-launch from *Mallaig* (*q.v.*). A bridle path leads north-eastwards from Inverie through Glen Dulochan, over-shadowed by *Sgurr Coire na Coinnich*, 2,612 ft., and the fine peak of *Ladhar Bheinn*, 3,343 ft., the most westerly 3,000-ft. summit on the mainland. This path climbs to nearly 1,100 ft., before descending into Glen Barrisdale, which debouches into Barrisdale Bay, on the picturesque shores of *Loch Hourn* (*q.v.*).

INVERINATE, Ross and Cromarty.   Map 24, NG 9 2.
On the lovely shores of *Loch Duich* (*q.v.*), in the North-West Highlands. 1½ m. S.E., on the lochside, is the little Church and manse of *Kintail* (*q.v.*). **2 m. N.W.**, on the road to *Dornie* (*q.v.*), is Carr Brae, or Keppoch Hill, situated at a height of over 500 ft. It gives magnificent views over Loch Duich and towards the *Mam Rattachan Pass* (*q.v.*), as well as south-eastwards to the splendid group of mountains known as the *Five Sisters of Kintail*, with *Scour Ouran*, 3,505 ft., as their highest point. These mountains form part of the *Kintail* estate (N.T. Scot.). See **Croe Bridge** and **Shiel Bridge.** *Iter. 207, 220.*

INVERKEILOR, Angus. 1,190.   Map 21, NO 6 4.
To the east is Lunan Bay, with some " singing " sands, stretching between Boddin Point and Lang Craig, while to the south of the latter, is the fine promontory of Red Head, associated with Scott's " The Antiquary." At Lunan Bay is the ruined *Red Castle*, destroyed in 1579. Farther north, at Boddin Point, is the curious Rock of St. Skeagh. See **Usan.** *Iter. 155.*

INVERKEITHING, Fife. 4,052. SB.   Map 17, NT 1 8.
E.C. Wed. A Royal Burgh, on the Firth of Forth, retaining a 16th cent. Mercat Cross, with carved armorial bearings, surmounted by a unicorn, added in 1688. The Old Town House, dated 1770, and also the 15th cent. Greyfriars Hospital, now a public library, are of interest. The Church has an old font, but only the tower remains from the original 15th cent. structure. In 1651, a battle was fought to the north, in which the forces of Cromwell were vic-torious, defeating a Royalist army led by a Maclean of Duart. The town is now best-known as a centre for ship-building and shipbreaking. **2 m. N.** is the 16th cent. *Fordell Castle*, on the estate of which a private railway formerly transported coal to the coast. See **Rosyth.** *Iter. 90, 93, 94, 134.*

INVERKIP, Renfrew. 413.   Map 8, NS 2 7.
Situated a little inland from the sandy coast of the Firth of Clyde, with moors to the south-east. *Ardgowan House*, built in 1798, and the 15th cent. *Inverkip Castle*, stand in a park facing Lunderston Bay. On high ground, to the east, are large reservoirs holding Greenock's water supply. 2½ m. N., at Cloch Point, on the fine coast road to *Gourock* (*q.v.*), is the white *Cloch* (*q.v.*) lighthouse. *Iter. 59, 64, 65, 66, 68.*

INVERKIRKAIG, Sutherland.   Map 29, NC 0 1.
The River Kirkaig, forming the border between Ross and Cromarty and Sutherland, and on which are situated some falls, flows here into Loch Kirkaig. The stream has its source in the Fionn Loch, lying to the south-east, and dominated by *Suilven*, 2,399 ft., one of the strange, isolated Torridon sandstone peaks of Sutherland. The picturesque,

Invergarry, Inverness. The ruined Castle, burnt by the Duke of Cumberland after Prince Charles Edward had slept there both before and after the battle of Culloden, in 1746

Inverey, Aberdeen. The memorial to John Lamont (1805–79), born at Corriemulzie, who became Johann von Lamont, Astronomer Royal of Bavaria

Inverkeithing, Fife. The 16th century Mercat Cross, topped by a unicorn placed there in 1688

Inverkeilor, Angus. The remains of Red Castle, burnt and sacked in 1579 by a son of Lord Gray, who for this action was declared an outlaw. It stands in Lunan Bay, to the north-east, on an unclassified road off A92

Inverkeithing, Fife. The Old Town House of 1770, which has an outside staircase

Inverkirkaig, Sutherland. The isolated Sutherland peaks of Suilven, Cul Mor, Cul Beag and Ben More Coigach, seen from a point just south of Inverkirkaig, on an unclassified road

PLATE 88 (facing page 180)

Inverlochy Castle, Inverness. The ruined 15th century Castle, near which the Marquis of Montrose defeated the Covenanters in 1645. It stands off A82, to the north-east of Fort William

Invermoriston, Inverness. The inscribed cairn in memory of Roderick Mackenzie, who was killed during the '45 Rising, after he had feigned to be the fleeing Prince Charles Edward. It stands 13 miles to the west, on the south side of A887, near the meeting of the Rivers Moriston and Doe in Glen Moriston

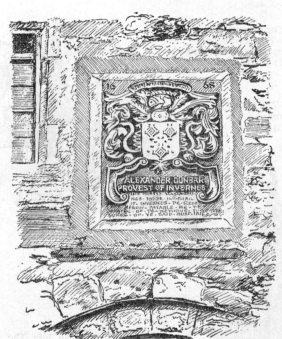

Inverness, Inverness The inscription over the doorway of Dunbar's Hospital, dated 1668

Inverness, Inverness. The Mercat Cross, incorporating the ' Stone of the Tubs,' on which women drawing water from the river used to rest their tubs

Invershin, Sutherland. The modern Carbisdale Castle, on a height to the south, near which Montrose's last battle was fought in 1650

Inveruglas, Dunbarton. The power station of the Loch Sloy hydro-electric scheme, which was inaugurated in 1950

PLATE 89 (facing page 181)

[For INVERNESS see also following plate

narrow and hilly road leading southwards from *Lochinver* (*q.v.*) into Ross-shire by way of Inverkirkaig has been called the " mad little road of Sutherland." It pursues a tortuous and hilly course, first along the steep, island-studded shores of Enard Bay, and later inland towards Loch Sionascaig, passing numerous little rocky lochans, and giving magnificent views, but demanding great care in driving. See **Achiltibuie** and **Baddagyle.** *Iter. 226.*

INVERLOCHY CASTLE, Inverness.   Map 18, NN 1 7.
See **Fort William.**

INVERMORISTON, Inverness. 160.   Map 24, NH 4 1.
E.C. Tues. Lies at the eastern end of the long Glen Moriston, bordered to the north by the heights of Invermoriston Forest, and faces *Loch Ness* (*q.v.*), near the point where the River Moriston enters the Loch. The road through

Glen Moriston is part of the through route from Loch Ness to the north-west coast, joining the road from Invergarry and the south near *Cluanie* (*q.v.*). From Invermoriston, the first part of the glen is well wooded, the road later emerging on to bare moors, and being joined by the track of an old military road from *Fort Augustus* (*q.v.*), over the mountains through Inchnacardoch Forest. By means of this route, Dr. Johnson and Boswell travelled on their Highland tour in 1773, staying the night at Invermoriston, where the Doctor presented the landlord's daughter with a text-book on arithmetic. At a point **13 m. W.** of Invermoriston, the river is joined by the Doe, flowing from the north-west, and a few miles up its glen is *Corriedoe* cave, a hiding-place used by Prince Charles Edward in the '45, when he was guarded by the " Eight Men of Glenmoriston." A cairn, situated near the meeting of the rivers, commemorates Roderick Mackenzie, who feigned to be the Prince, and was killed by the soldiers searching for him. Developments in connection with a hydro-electric scheme have taken place in Glen Moriston. **5 m. N.E.**, above loch Ness, rises the prominent hill of *Mealfuarvonie*, 2,284 ft., a local landmark. *Iter. 207, 210, 213.*

INVERNESS, Inverness. 28,225. LB.   Map 25, NH 6 4.
E.C. Wed. M.D. Tues./Fri. GOLF. Known as the " Capital of the Highlands," and finely situated on the Ness at the north-eastern extremity of *Glen More* (*q.v.*) and the *Caledonian Canal* (*q.v.*). Here, the waters of the Beauly Firth and the Inner Moray, or Inverness Firth unite at the narrows which are overlooked to the north by Craigton Point. In 1652-57, Cromwell erected a fort, known as " The Sconce," on the right bank of the Ness, but of this only slight traces now remain, though the clock tower still stands on the site. *Inverness* was the terminal point of the two great military roads built in the 18th cent. by General Wade, commencing at Dunkeld and Fort William respectively. Wade's barracks, on the site of the old Castle, which surrendered to Mary, Queen of Scots in 1562, were named by him *Fort George*, and after their destruction by Prince Charles Edward, in 1746, a new *Fort George* (*q.v.*) was built away to the north-east. In the town are the late 13th and 18th cent. *High* Church; *Dunbar's* Hospital, dating from 1668; the Mercat Cross, enclosing the so-called " Clach-na-Cudainn " or " Stone of the tubs "; the Museum, housing Jacobite relics; the modern Castle; the Episcopal Cathedral of 1866-71; the Tolbooth Steeple of 1791; and Queen Mary's former lodgings of 1562 in Bridge St. The 16th cent. *Abertarff*

House retains an ancient turnpike stair. The view from Castle Hill extends over a large expanse of Highland country, and far away to the north-west rises *Ben Wyvis*, 3,429 ft. To the west of the town is *Tomnahurich Hill*, another good viewpoint, and a little to the north is *Craig Phadraig*, 550 ft., crowned by a vitrified fort. The town is associated with Shakespeare's " Macbeth." The Northern Piping Competition, which takes place annually in September, is an important event. **6 m. N.E.**, on the road to Fort George, near *Dalcross* airport, is *Castle Stewart*, dating from 1625, and restored, a good example of the Scottish baronial style. See **Cawdor, Clachnaharry, Croy, Culloden, Loch Ness, South Kessock** and **Wade Roads.** *Iter. 140, 150, 175, 176, 177, 195, 198, 199, 200, 201, 202, 203, 204, 205, 206, 207, 210, 211, 221.*
(See page 182 for Town Plan of **INVERNESS**).

INVERORAN, Argyll.   Map 14, NN 2 4.
At the western end of Loch Tulla, on the line of the old Glencoe road, and at the foot of the *Black Mount*, looking to *Stob Ghabhar*, 3,565 ft. Near Inveroran was born, in 1724, Duncan Ban MacIntyre, the famous bard, whose monument stands at *Dalmally* (*q.v.*).

INVERSANDA, Argyll.   Map 18, NM 9 5.
Faces Inversanda Bay, on *Loch Linnhe* (*q.v.*), on the picturesque road through the *Ardgour* (*q.v.*) country, and near the eastern end of Glen Tarbert, which leads towards *Loch Sunart* (*q.v.*). **1 m. W.** up this glen is the wild Coire an Iubhair, leading off to the north, and giving access on foot to the splendid rock scenery of *Garbh Bheinn*, 2,903 ft., the finest peak of Ardgour, well-known to cragsmen. To the south of the glen rises *Creach Bheinn*, 2,800 ft., a notable viewpoint. The road through Glen Tarbert leads south-westwards round the head and southern side of Loch Sunart to *Lochaline* (*q.v.*), on the Sound of Mull, and an alternative route to Lochaline can also be followed from Inversanda along the shores of Loch Linnhe by way of *Camasnacroise* (*q.v.*). See **Strontian.** *Iter. 216, 217, 218.*

INVERSHIEL, Ross and Cromarty.   Map 24, NN 9 1.
See **Shiel Bridge.**

INVERSHIN, Sutherland. 90.   Map 29, NH 5 9.
E.C. Wed. Here, the River Shin meets the Kyle of Sutherland, and nearby, on an eminence beyond the combined streams, is the modern *Carbisdale Castle*. It is situated actually in Ross and Cromarty, and is famous for its proximity to the scene of Montrose's last battle, fought in 1650, after which he fled, before being betrayed by the laird at *Ardvreck Castle* near *Inchnadamph* (*q.v.*). Farther to the south-east, the widening Kyle is known at this point as the Maikle Pool. *Iter. 228, 229, 230, 232.*

INVERSNAID, Stirling.   Map 15, NN 3 0.
Finely situated on the eastern shores of *Loch Lomond* (*q.v.*), facing a splendid group of mountains on the opposite shore of the loch, including *Ben Ime*, 3,318 ft., *Ben Vane*, 3,004 ft., and *Ben Vorlich*, 3,092 ft. A fort to repress the Macgregors was constructed here in 1713 and was at one time under the command of General Wolfe, of Quebec fame. The road from *Aberfoyle* (*q.v.*) terminates at this point, and the loch steamers call here. Nearby are the Arklet Falls, on the Arklet Water flowing from Loch Arklet, a little to the east, at the far end of which is *Stronachlachar* (*q.v.*), on the beautiful Loch Katrine. The Falls are associated with Wordsworth's " Highland Girl," and a path going north-wards by Loch Lomond leads to Rob Roy's Cave, described by Dorothy Wordsworth. Robert Bruce is believed to have sheltered here in 1306. South-east of the falls rises *Cruachan*, 1,762 ft., a good viewpoint. On the western shore of Loch Lomond is the power house at *Inveruglas* (*q.v.*), which forms part of the Loch Sloy hydro-electric scheme. *Iter. 105.*

INVERUGLAS, Dunbarton.   Map 15, NN 3 0.
Here, on the western shores of *Loch Lomond* (*q.v.*), is the power station of the Loch Sloy hydro-electric scheme, opened by Her Majesty Queen Elizabeth, the Queen Mother, in October, 1950. Loch Sloy itself lies away to the north-west, beyond Glen Sloy, and is overlooked by *Ben Vane*,

INVERNESS

Scale

Abertarff House, 16th cent.	**5.**	
Castle, incorporating the Sheriff's Court House	**10.**	
Clock Tower and remains of Cromwell's Fort	**9.**	
Dunbar's Hospital, 1668	**6.**	
Museum, Public Library	**2.**	
Old High Church, 13th cent.	**7.**	
Queen Mary's House	**4.**	
St. Andrew's Cathedral	**11.**	
Tolbooth Steeple, 1791	**3.**	
Tourist Board Information Bureau	**8.**	
Town Hall. In front are the Mercat Cross, and the Clach-na-Cudainn Stone	**1.**	

3,004 ft., from the south, and by *Ben Vorlich*, 3,092 ft., from the north. The surrounding country was MacFarlane property, their ancient rallying cry being "Loch Sloy." *Iter. 100, 110, 111.*

INVERURIE, Aberdeen. 5,027. SB.   Map 27, **NJ 7** 2.
E.C. Wed. **M.D.** Thurs. **GOLF.** Immediately to the south of the town, which is situated in the Garioch district, is the confluence of the Rivers Urie and Don, and in the vicinity is situated a 50-ft. high natural mound known as the "Bass," the site of an ancient stronghold, and visited by Mary, Queen of Scots, in 1562. In the nearby churchyard is an inscribed Pictish Stone. Another ancient stone, carrying an Ogham inscription, and known as the *Brandsbutt Stone* (A.M.), stands ½ m. N.W. of the town. The town has long been a Royal Burgh, and contains railway workshops. *Keith Hall*, to the east, stands on the farther bank of the River Urie. Away to the west rises the *Mither Tap of Bennachie*, 1,698 ft., a notable local landmark. **2 m. S.,** near the Don, is the ruined *Kinkell* Church (A.M.), rebuilt in 1528, and preserving one of the rare Sacrament Houses. See **Chapel of Garioch, Inveramsay, Kintore** and **Old Meldrum.** *Iter. 175, 178, 184, 197.*

INVERVAR, Perth.   Map 15, **NN 6** 4.
Iter. 107.

IONA, ISLE OF, Argyll.   Map 13, **NM 2** 2.
This famous Inner Hebridean island, only 3 miles long by 1½ miles broad, is separated by the narrow Sound of Iona from *Fionphort*, near *Bunessan* (q.v.), in the south-western tip of *Mull* (q.v.), to which it is connected by passenger ferry. *Iona*, which has no motoring roads, is generally visited from *Oban* (q.v.) by steamer. Its associations stretch back through the centuries to the coming of *St. Columba* from Ireland in 563. The Saint founded a small monastery here, and for 34 years carried on his great work of introducing Christianity to the Scottish mainland and islands until his death, in 597. Although buried in Iona, his remains were later removed to Ireland. The island became for many years a resort of pilgrims, and also the burial place of early Scottish Kings and Chieftains. The Norsemen ravaged Iona time and again, the monastery suffering severely, and having to be constantly rebuilt. In 1203, the Benedictines founded a new monastery, but the buildings were destroyed in 1561. Near the landing place are remains of a nunnery, founded in 1203, and in the Chapel adjoining the nave is the tomb of the last Prioress, who died in 1543. *McLean's Cross*, richly-carved and possibly of 15th cent. date, stands on the road which parallels the ancient "Road of the Dead," leading to *St. Oran's* Cemetery. This is the oldest Christian burial ground in

Inverurie, Aberdeen. The ancient Brandsbutt Stone, which bears Pictish symbols and an Ogham inscription. It stands just to the north-west of the town

Inverness, Inverness. The Clock Tower, on the site of The Sconce, the fort erected by Cromwell in 1652–57

Inverness, Inverness. The Tolbooth, or Town Steeple, dating from 1791

Inverness, Inverness. Queen Mary's House, much-restored, where Mary, Queen of Scots, is said to have stayed in 1562, when denied entrance to the Castle

Inverness, Inverness. The Monument to Flora Macdonald, which stands on the terrace south of the modern Castle. The old Castle was blown up by Bonnie Prince Charlie in 1745

Inverness, Inverness. Castle Stewart, built by the 3rd Earl of Moray, in 1625. It stands 6 miles north-east of the town, off B9039, near the Inner Moray Firth

[For INVERNESS see also preceding plate
[For IONA see following plate

PLATE 90 (facing page 182)

Iona, Argyll. The restored Cathedral, mainly of 15th or 16th century date, which is faced by the ancient St. Martin's Cross, nearly 17 feet in height. Adjoining the Cathedral are the newly-restored monastic buildings, including the chapter house, refectory, undercroft and cloister

Irvine, Ayr. The 14th century remains of Seagate Castle. In 1297, the Treaty of Irvine was signed here, and Mary, Queen of Scots, came to the castle in 1563

Irongray, Kirkcudbright. A Covenanter's tomb of 1685, situated on a mound to the west. Near Irongray is Skeogh Hill, where, in 1678, a great gathering of Covenanters took place. An obelisk, set up on the moors in 1870, marks the spot

Irvine, Ayr. The 120-foot high Town House. Between 1781 and 1783, Robert Burns worked in the town as a flax-dresser

Isle of Whithorn, Wigtown. The ruined 13th century Chapel. The site is traditionally associated with St. Ninian (4th century), the first Christian missionary in Scotland

PLATE 91 (facing page 183)

Scotland, and contains the graves of many Kings, among them 48 Scottish, the last being Duncan, said to have been murdered by Macbeth in 1040. Among many carved Celtic slabs are those of former Clan Chiefs, bearing the designs of their galleys. In 1932, the ashes of Margaret Kennedy-Fraser, the transcriber of Gaelic songs, were buried here.

The restored, Romanesque *St. Oran's* Chapel, thought to have been built originally in 1080 by Queen Margaret, is the oldest of the island's surviving buildings, and is entered by a carved Norman doorway. In the chapel is the tomb of Scott's "Lord of the Isles." The granite *Great Cross of Iona*, or *St. Martin's* Cross, 16ft. 8 in. high, boldly carved with Runic ornament, and possibly dating from the 9th or 10th cent., stands facing the Cathedral. This was founded in the 13th cent., but is mainly the work of two or more centuries later, and has been much added to and restored. The present cruciform structure of granite has a low square tower, and inside the Church are pier capitals carved with a variety of birds, animals and flowers. There are a number of tombs of interest, and below the east window is preserved the so-called *St. Columba's* pillow. Fragments of the monastery, which adjoins the Cathedral, are in process of restoration. The 9th cent. Celtic *St. John's* Cross has been blown down by a gale and awaits re-erection. At the southern extremity of *Iona* is *Port na Curaich*, where St. Columba is thought to have landed. On the west coast is a "spouting" cave, and in the northern part of the island is *Dun I*, 332 ft., a good viewpoint, overlooking beautiful sands. The colouring of the scenery and the profusion of wild flowers and sea-shells give added interest to Iona. At the time of Dr. Johnson's visit, in 1773, the island was known as *Icolmkill*, and the Doctor referred to it as "that luminary of the Caledonian regions." See **Staffa**. *Iter. 249.*

IRONGRAY, Kirkcudbright.   Map 4, **NX 9** 7.
Lies in the pleasant valley of the Cluden Water. In the churchyard is a tombstone erected by Scott in memory of Helen Walker, said to be the original of Jeannie Deans in the "Heart of Midlothian," which was first published in 1818. ¼ m. W., on a knoll, is a Covenanter's inscribed tomb, dating from 1685. A little to the north, across the Cluden Water, is *Fourmerkland Tower*, dated 1590. **4 m. W.,** beyond the Cairn Water, is *Skeogh Hill*, 1,286 ft., reached by way of Routin Bridge. An obelisk, on the south-eastern slopes of the hill, marks the Communion Stones, where John Welsh, the local minister in 1678, and a great-grandson of John Knox, gave the Sacrament to a body of 3,000 Covenanters. *Iter. 74.*

1. Town House (Information Bureau) with Mercat Cross.
2. Seagate Castle.
3. Burns Club.
4. Relief Church.

IRVINE, Ayr. 15,832. SB.   Map 8, **NS 3** 3.
E.C. Wed. GOLF. A Royal Burgh, manufacturing town and port, on the Ayrshire coast, where the waters of the River Irvine and the Annick Water flow into the sea by the estuary of the Garnock. Burns lived in the town between 1781 and 1783, and a plaque on a cottage in Glasgow Vennel records his sojourn as a flax-dresser. Irvine is noted for its Burns Club and on the Town Moor is a statue of the poet. John Galt, the novelist, was born here in 1779. The Academy was founded in 1572 from the revenues of a former monastery. The ruined 14th cent. *Seagate Castle* was visited by Mary, Queen of Scots, in 1563. Facing the exotic 120-ft. high Town House is the old Mercat Cross. The Buchan-ite Sect originated in the *Relief* Church, in 1783. Marymass Week, an annual summer event, includes some of the oldest racing extant. To the north-west is *Bogside* racecourse. See **Crocketford** and **Kilwinning**. *Iter. 60, 66, 69, 85, 88.*

ISBISTER, Shetland.   Map 33, **HU 3** 9.
See **Shetland Islands** (Mainland). *Iter. 267*

ISLAY, ISLE OF, Argyll.   Map 6, **NR 2** 6, etc.
Lying off the west coast of *Kintyre* (q.v.), and separated by the narrow Sound of Islay from its smaller, but hillier Inner Hebridean neighbour *Jura* (q.v.), the island of *Islay* is the most southerly of the Hebrides, and has for industries, agriculture, fishing and distilleries. In size, 25 miles long and some 20 miles broad, and enjoying a mild climate, it is gaining in popularity, being reached by steamer, calling at Port Ellen or Port Askaig, from West Loch Tarbert (See **Tarbert**; Argyll). There are also regular air services to Glenegedale airport, near Port Ellen, from Glasgow (Renfrew airport). On the west side of the island, Lochs Indaal and Gruinart are separated by only a narrow neck of land, the fine coastal district to the south-west being known as the Rhinns of Islay. Away to the south-east, beyond Laggan Bay, is the Mull of Oa peninsula, with lofty cliffs, accessible by road from Port Ellen, to the north-east of which are hills rising to more than 1,500 ft. There are a number of sculptured stones, Celtic Crosses and caves on the island. No road encircles Islay, but there are some well-surfaced, classified roads linking the coastal villages, the others being mostly poor and very narrow. Some 75 miles of road can be traversed by car. See **Bowmore, Bridgend, Bruich-laddich, Claggain Bay, Kilchoman, Kildalton, Mull of Oa, Port Askaig, Port Charlotte, Port Ellen, Portnahaven** and **Sanaigmore**. *Iter. 243 to 247.*

ISLE OF WHITHORN, Wigtown.   Map 2, **NX 4** 3.
This tiny mainland port is situated on rocky shores, sheltered by Isle Head, while away to the south-west is Burrow Head. The ruined Chapel (A.M.), possibly of 13th cent. date, is traditionally associated with St. Ninian, the first Christian missionary in Scotland, who worked in the 4th cent. *St. Ninian's* Shrine at Whithorn became an important place of pilgrimage, and was visited regularly by James IV. *Isle Tower* is a 17th cent. building. Away to the west, on the shores of Luce Bay, and reached by a track off the Port William road nearing *Glasserton* (q.v.), is *St. Ninian's Cave* (A.M.) in Port Castle Bay. This is perhaps an oratory used by the Saint, and in it are preserved some sculptured stones and Crosses. In the vicinity, to the east, is the 17th cent. house of *Tonderghie*. See **Whithorn**. *Iter. 82.*

ISLE ORNSAY, Isle of Skye, Inverness. Map 23, **NG 6** 1.
A small coastal and fishing resort in the fertile peninsula of Sleat, facing an island in the Sound of Sleat, on which are situated a lighthouse and the remains of a small nunnery. **2 m. S.W.,** off the *Armadale* (q.v.) road, a rough and hilly by-road goes north-westwards to *Ord*, on Loch Eishort, which is associated with Alexander Smith, author of "A Summer in Skye." The views of the *Coolins* (q.v.) across Loch Eishort from here are superb. South-west of Ord, on the coast, is the ruined *Dunscaith Castle*, on an isolated rock, and once the home of the Macdonalds of Sleat, before they removed to *Duntulm* (q.v.). See **Teangue**. *Iter. 253.*

JAMESTOWN, Dunbarton.   Map 15, **NS 3** 8.
Iter. 109, 112.

JARLSHOF, Shetland. Map 33, HU 4 0.
See **Shetland Islands** (Mainland).

JEANTOWN, Ross and Cromarty. Map 24, NG 9 3.
See **Lochcarron.**

JEDBURGH, Roxburgh. 4,056. SB. Map 10, NT 6 2.
E.C. Thurs. M.D. Fri. GOLF. One of the most famous of the border Abbeys is situated here, in the delightful valley of the Jed Water, which flows northwards to join the Teviot beyond Bonjedward. The former Castle, once a residence of Scottish Kings, has vanished, but the modern castle, built as a gaol in 1823, stands at the top of Castlegate. In the town is preserved *Queen Mary's House,* where she may have lain ill in 1566 after her ride to *Hermitage Castle* (*q.v.*). This house, restored after its partial destruction in 1523, is now a museum, with relics of the period. *Blackfriars* Church, built in 1746, was reconstructed in 1818, and has an ornate iron lantern set in the portico.

JEDBURGH
Scale
0   ¼ Mile

1. Abbey.
2. Blackfriars Church.
3. New Gate.
4. Queen Mary's House (Museum).

The *New Gate,* surmounted by a tall steeple, carries the dates 1720, 1755 and 1761. Sir Walter Scott was an advocate here in 1793 and his associations with the town are recalled by a bronze tablet on the County Buildings. A quaint old custom perpetuated is the Candlemas Ba'. on February 2nd, when the " Uppies " play the " Doonies," while the Callants' Festival, in early summer, dates from 1947. The very interesting and imposing remains of the Abbey (A.M.), founded in c. 1118, and sacked on numerous occasions in medieval times, are built of red sandstone, and are noted for the splendid nave, dating from the Transitional period, with beautiful detail-work. The West front has a fine rose window, known as *St. Catherine's Wheel,* and there is a richly-carved Norman doorway. The central tower has been many times restored, and the choir is much rebuilt, but the fine North transept of the 14th cent. is in good condition, and contains interesting monuments. The three-arched 16th cent. bridge off Canongate is of interest. The town has many

houses displaying characteristic crow-stepped gables and is one of the most attractive in the Lowlands. Burns once lodged in a house in Canongate; Prince Charles Edward stayed in Blackhills Close; and Wordsworth and his sister visited a house in Abbey Close. A tablet marks the house where Sir David Brewster, founder of the British Association, was born. **1 m. S.,** near the river, and to the right of A.68, is the " Capon Tree," a lone survivor of the former Forest of Jethart. To the south-west of Jedburgh rise *Dunian Hill,* 1,095 ft., and *Black Law,* 1,110 ft., overlooking a wide stretch of country. 1½ m. N.W. of the town, on Lanton Moor, are the ancient earthworks and ruined 17th cent. tower of *Timpendean.* See **Ancrum Bridge, Denholm** and **Ferniehirst Castle.** *Iter. 4, 43, 47, 52.*

JERICHO, Angus. Map 20, NO 4 4.
A strangely-named, tiny village, lying just to the south of the main Glamis to Forfar road.

JOHN O' GROATS, Caithness. 140. Map 30, ND 3 7.
E.C. Wed. M.D. Thurs. This well-known place is situated near the extreme north-eastern tip of the Scottish mainland. It is 873 miles distant by road from Land's End in Cornwall, and 280 miles from Kirkmaiden, Scotland's most southerly parish, associated with Burns's " Frae Maidenkirk to Johnny Groats'." John O' Groats over-looks the stormy

JOHN O' GROATS

1. Site of John O' Groat's House.

waters of the Pentland Firth, with Stroma Island lying off-shore beyond the Inner Sound. On the beach are found small shells called " Groatie Buckies." Farther to the east is the imposing headland of Duncansby Head, the ' Vervedrum ' of Ptolemy, with its lighthouse, a notable view-point. To the south of the head rise the three curious detached stacks of Duncansby, together with a fine range of sandstone cliffs extending towards the distant Skirsa Head. The cliffs are pierced in places by deep gashes known as " goes." At John O' Groats, the curious eight-sided house erected in memory of the Dutchman John de Groot, c. 1509, has vanished, the site being marked by a mound and flagstaff. The views from here to the north, beyond Stroma, extend to South Ronaldsay and the cliffs of Hoy, in the *Orkneys* (*q.v.*), and between which, to the north lies the famous naval anchorage of Scapa Flow, screened by numerous islets. Nearer to Duncansby Head, and lying to the north-east, are the islands known as the Pentland Skerries. See **Canisbay Church, Freswick, Huna** and **Kirkmaiden.** *Iter. 200, 240.*

JOHNSHAVEN, Kincardine. Map 21, NO 7 6.
A fishing village, just off the Montrose to Stonehaven road, situated on a rocky and picturesque stretch of coast. See **St. Cyrus.** *Iter. 155.*

JOHNSTONE, Renfrew. 16,413. SB. Map 8, NS 4 6.
E.C. Tues. GOLF. A spinning town, situated on the Black Cart Water. *Iter. 64.*

JOHNSTONE BRIDGE, Dumfries. 627. Map 4, NY 1 9.
The picturesque bridge here spans the River Annan, which flows in a southerly direction through the delightful Annandale valley, with its memories of Border warfare. See **Lockerbie.** *Iter. 10, 13, 29, 50, 51.*

JOPPA, Midlothian. Map 10, NT 3 7.
See **Portobello.**

Jedburgh, Roxburgh. 'Queen Mary's House,' a late 16th century bastel-house. Mary, Queen of Scots, is said to have lain ill at Jedburgh in 1566, after riding to visit Bothwell at Hermitage Castle

Jedburgh, Roxburgh. The New Gate, which dates from the 18th century, and carries a lofty steeple. It gives access to the Abbey precincts

Jedburgh, Roxburgh. The ruined Abbey, founded early in the 12th century, and colonised by monks from Beauvais in France. Alexander III was married here in 1285

John O'Groats, Caithness. The mound and flagstaff on the site of the former house lived in by the Dutchman John de Groot, in the 16th century. This house was octagonal with eight entrances, and each of his eight descendants entered by his own door and sat at the ' head ' of an octagonal table, to assert his claim to the estate

Jericho, Angus. The sign pointing to the village, which lies off A94, between Glamis and Forfar

[For JEDBURGH see also under BORDER COUNTRY (Plate 20)]

PLATE 92 (facing page 184)

Kelso, Roxburgh. John Rennie's bridge across the River Tweed, erected in 1803. This is virtually a model of old Waterloo Bridge, in London, which he built in 1811, and the demolition of which was begun in 1934

Keills, Argyll. The carved Celtic Cross at the Chapel

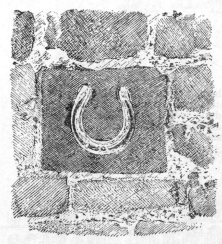

Kelso, Roxburgh. The mark in Roxburgh Street where Prince Charles Edward's horse is reputed to have cast a shoe at the time of the '45 Rising

Keiss, Caithness. The remains of the old Castle, facing the sea near the modern building

Keith, Banff. A bridge across the River Isla, built in 1609, linking Keith with Fife-Keith

Kelso, Roxburgh. Remains of the 12th century Abbey, founded by David I, which suffered one of its worst blows in 1545, when it was destroyed by the Earl of Hertford

PLATE 93 (facing page 185)

JUNIPER GREEN, Midlothian.   Map 9, **NT 1** 6.
See Colinton. *Iter. 21, 23.*

JURA, ISLE OF, Argyll.   Map 6, **NR 5** 7 and 13, **NR 5** 8.
This picturesque Inner Hebridean island is separated
from *Knapdale* (*q.v.*), on the mainland coast, by the Sound
of Jura, and from the neighbouring island of *Islay* (*q.v.*),
by the Sound of Islay. It is perhaps best known for the
three *Paps of Jura*, all about 2,500 ft. in height, forming
notable viewpoints, and being prominent objects in the
view from many points on the mainland. The island is
some 28 miles long and 8 miles broad, but it is comparatively little visited, due mainly to lack of accommodation.
Jura is linked by passenger ferry from *Feolin Ferry*, on the
Sound of Islay, to *Port Askaig* (*q.v.*), in Islay, and there is
a pier at *Craighouse* for the steamers serving *Tarbert* (*q.v.*).
A fair, waterbound road extends from Feolin Ferry along
the eastern shores of the island for 24 miles as far as *Ardlussa*, where it terminates. The sea loch of Tarbert divides
Jura almost into half, and in the southern sector rise the
well-known *Paps*. Off the north coast is the Strait of Corryvreckan, noted as a whirlpool, and audible from afar. This
strait separates Jura from the small island of Scarba.
See **Colonsay**.

JUSTINHAUGH BRIDGE, Angus.   Map 21, **NO 4** 5.
Iter. 166.

KAMES, Argyll. 297.   Map 7, **NR 9** 7.
E.C. Wed. M.D. Wed. A small *Cowal* (*q.v.*) resort on the
Kyles of Bute (*q.v.*), with a pier. A little to the west, near
the large powder-mills, a by-road branches southwards and
continues almost as far as Ardlamont Point, with views
towards the island of Bute and also to the northern tip of
Arran across the Sound of Bute. 1½ m. S.W. of Kames is
the little village of *Millhouse*, from which a road leads north-
westwards to *Kilfinan* (*q.v.*), while a branch road goes south-
westwards to the shores of *Loch Fyne* (*q.v.*), from which
the wooded Glenan Bay can be reached on foot. See **Tighnabruaich**. *Iter. 103.*

KEIG, Aberdeen.   Map 27, **NJ 6** 1.
A little to the east, near a winding stretch of the River Don,
is the modern *Forbes Castle*, with *Cairn William*, 1,469 ft.,
rising away to the south-east.

KEILLS, Argyll.   Map 13, **NR 6** 8.
Situated between the Sound of Jura and the southern reaches
of Loch Sween. A ruined chapel here has a notable Celtic
Cross. Loch na Cille lies to the south.

KEIR, Dumfries.   Map 3, **NX 8** 9.
See **Penpont** (for *Courthill*).

KEISS, Caithness.   Map 30, **ND 3** 6.
This little fishing village lies on Sinclair's Bay. A little to
the north, on the coast, is the ruined *Keiss Castle*, near the
modern castle. Beyond, to the left of the road, is a Baptist
chapel in memory of Sir William Sinclair, founder of the
country's first Baptist church in the mid-18th cent. The
main road leading southwards towards Wick crosses the
wide Keiss Links, with the Loch of Wester to the west.
See **Reiss**. *Iter. 200.*

KEITH, Banff. 4,357. SB.   Map 26, **NJ 4** 5.
E.C. Wed. M.D. Sat. An agricultural centre in Strath
Isla, on the river of that name, and once famous for its fair.
The town consists of the regularly-planned Keith, and also
Fife-Keith, to the west of the river, which is linked to the
former by two bridges, one of which dates from 1609.
Milton Tower, in ruins, was formerly a castle of the Oliphants.
To the south-east of the town is a hill known as the *Balloch*,
1,199 ft., a good viewpoint. See **Deskford** and **Drummuir**.
Iter. 169, 175, 178, 187, 189.

KELLIE CASTLE, Fife.   Map 17, **NO 5** 0.
See **Pittenweem**. *Iter. 94, 98.*

KELLS CHURCH, Kirkcudbright.   Map 3, **NX 6** 7.
See **New Galloway**.

KELSO, Roxburgh. 4,206. SB.   Map 11, **NT 7** 3.
E.C. Wed. M.D. Fri. GOLF. A most attractive Border
town on the River Tweed, with a wide market-place, or

1. Abbey.   2. Floors Castle.

square, in which stands the Court House, where a nightly
curfew is sounded. Just outside the town, best known for
its ruined Abbey, the Tweed is joined by the Teviot. *Kelso*
has many historical associations, including visits from Mary,
Queen of Scots, and Prince Charles Edward, while Scott
lived here for 6 months, in 1783, as a school-fellow at the
former grammar school, staying at *Garden Cottage*, now
Waverley Lodge. At a later date, the first edition of Scott's
" Minstrelsy of the Scottish Border " was printed in Kelso.
The Abbey (A.M.) was founded in 1128, but only a small
portion is still to be seen of what was perhaps the greatest
of the Border Abbeys. In 1545, the building was almost
totally destroyed, after having been besieged, while in earlier
years it had already suffered severely. All that now remains
are the West façade and transepts, part of the tower and
two of the nave bays, showing some fine Norman and early
Gothic detail, notably in the North transept. From the
fine 5-arched bridge over the river, built by Rennie in 1803,
there is a fine view of *Floors Castle* (*q.v.*). On the bridge
are two lamp-posts from Rennie's demolished Old Waterloo
Bridge in London. To the south-west is the Teviot bridge,
which appears to be modelled on Rennie's structure at
Kelso. *Springwood Park*, dated 1756, and *Wooden House*,
early 19th cent., are both fine houses. *Ednam House*, above
Kelso Bridge, dates from 1761. **6 m. N.W.** is *Mellerstain
House* (*q.v.*), a notable old Berwickshire mansion, by
William and Robert Adam, open daily, except Sat., 2 to 5.30,
June to end of Sept. (See note page 90). See **Ednam**, **Rox-
burgh** and **Yetholm**. *Iter. 6, 7, 30, 32, 39, 46.*

KELTY, Fife. 7,750.   Map 17, **NT 1** 9.
Situated on the edge of the Fife coal-field. *Iter. 92.*

KEMNAY, Aberdeen.   Map 27, **NJ 7** 1.
The wooded curves of the Don lie to the west of the village,
and beyond its banks stands *Fetternear House*, once the
country seat of the Bishops of Aberdeen. *Kemnay* is best
known for its granite quarries, some of the material having
been used in the construction of the Forth Bridge, and also
the Thames Embankment, in London. 3 m. S.S.W., off
the *Monymusk* (*q.v.*) road, is *Castle Fraser*, a very fine

example of the Scottish baronial style, dating from 1454 to 1618, and notable for its turrets. *Iter. 177.*

KEN BRIDGE, Kirkcudbright. Map 3, NX 6 8.
Iter. 25, 71, 75, 76.

KENMORE, Perth. 150. Map 16, NN 7 4.
E.C. Thurs. GOLF. A pleasant little resort at the eastern end of *Loch Tay* (*q.v.*) in a rich setting of hills, where the River Tay issues from the loch, *Drummond Hill,* well-wooded, rises to the north, and behind it the River Lyon flows through the long and beautiful Glen Lyon, prior to its junction with the Tay. Burns admired the view from the bridge over the Tay, and set it to verse, which is recorded in the parlour of a local inn. William and Dorothy Wordsworth also visited the village. In the loch nearby is a small island, with the ruins of a Priory, dating from 1122. *Taymouth Castle,* the modern replacement of an older structure, once the home of the Earls of Breadalbane, was visited in 1842 by Queen Victoria and the Prince Consort. There are fine views down the loch, which is dominated by *Ben Lawers,* 3,984 ft., Perthshire's highest mountain. (**See Lawers.**) A very steep road (1 in 4), with a poor surface and sharp bends, leads southwards over the hills, ascending to a height of 1,672 ft., and later passing Loch Freuchie, in Glen Quaich, on its way to *Amulree* (*q.v.*). **1½ m. S.W.** of Kenmore, on the southern shore of Loch Tay, are the falls of *Acharn.* **2 m. E.** is the stone circle of *Croftmoraig.* See **Aberfeldy** and **Fortingall.** *Iter. 120.*

KENNEDY'S PASS, Ayr. Map 2, NX 1 9
See **Ballantrae, Girvan** and **Lendalfoot.** *Iter. 55.*

KENNETHMONT, Aberdeen. Map 26, NJ 5 2.
The full name is *Kirkhill of Kennethmont.* A little to the north is *Leith Hall* (N.T. Scot.) largely 17th cent., with a noted rock garden. The house can be seen Thurs. and Sat., 10 to 6, during the summer. (See note page 90). *Iter. 178.*

KENNOWAY, Fife. Map 17, NO 3 0.
Iter. 127, 129.

KENTALLEN, Argyll. Map 18, NN 0 5.
On Kentallen Bay, an inlet of *Loch Linnhe* (*q.v.*), with the great horseshoe curve of *Ben Vair,* 3,362 ft., rising in the background. From the summit of this fine peak, the Glencoe mountains provide a wonderful spectacle, with *Bidean nam Bian,* 3,766 ft., Argyll's highest mountain, dominating the scene. To the south of Kentallen is the wooded, but roadless Glen Duror. There are fine views from the Ballachulish road over Loch Linnhe towards the Ardgour mountains, the best known of which is *Garbh Bheinn,* 2,903 ft. *Iter. 124.*

KERRERA, ISLE OF, Argyll. Map 14, NM 8 2.
See **Oban.**

KERRYCROY, Bute. Map 7, NS 1 6.
See **Kilchattan Bay.**

KESSOCK, Inverness; Ross and Cromarty.
Map 25, NH 6 4.
See **North Kessock** and **South Kessock.** *Iter. 202, 203.*

KETTLEBRIDGE, Fife. Map 17, NO 3 0.
Iter. 93.

KILBARCHAN, Renfrew. 2,905. Map 8, NS 4 6.
E.C. Wed. A town noted for tartan-weaving. On the Church steeple, which is now used for secular purposes, is the statue of a well-known local piper of the 17th cent. An 18th cent. Weaver's Cottage is preserved (N.T. Scot.), and is open regularly (See note page 90). A fountain has been erected in memory of Robert Allan, a local weaver-poet.

KILBIRNIE, Ayr. 6,535. Map 8, NS 3 5.
E.C. Wed. GOLF. On the River Garnock, with Kilbirnie Loch to the east. The Church dates from 1654, and contains a carved pulpit and the grandiose *Garnock* gallery of the Crawford family. *Kilbirnie Place,* an ancient mansion situated to the west, was damaged by fire in the 18th cent. *Ladyland* and *Glengarnock Castle* are two other ruined structures in the vicinity. *Iter. 58, 85.*

KILCHATTAN BAY, Bute. Map 7, NS 1 5.
A quiet resort, with a steamer pier and a sandy bay, facing the twin Cumbraes across the Firth of Clyde. **3 m. S.W.,**

on a narrow road, and reached by way of Kingarth, beyond which are the Standing Stones of Lubas, is the ruined Chapel of *St. Blane.* Near it, to the west, on the sandy Dunagoil Bay, is a vitrified fort. Southwards lies Garroch Head, looking towards the island of Arran. To the north of Kilchattan, some four miles distant, on the coast, is the palatial modern mansion of *Mount Stuart,* a seat of the Marquis of Bute, beyond which lies the model village of *Kerrycroy.* Another road leads north-westwards from the resort, and gives access to the sandy bays of Scalpsie and St. Ninian's, the latter facing the island of Inch Marnock, in the Sound of Bute. *Iter. 241.*

KILCHOAN, Argyll. Map 12, NM 4 6.
This remote village is situated on the picturesque, rocky Ardnamurchan coast, and has a pier, known as *Mingary* from which there is a service to *Tobermory* (*q.v.*) in Mull. The pier lies on a by-road about **1 m. S.E.,** looking eastwards across the water to the impressive, but ruined *Mingary Castle,* where James IV held his court in 1495, and which was taken for Montrose in 1644. The castle, described in Scott's "Lord of the Isles," was the ancient home of the MacIains, a sept, or branch of the Clan Macdonald. Beyond the castle rises *Ben Hiant,* 1,729 ft., a very fine viewpoint, looking eastwards towards *Loch Sunart* (*q.v.*). To the north-west of Kilchoan and its bay, a rough, gated road gives access to the most westerly point of the Scottish mainland at *Ardnamurchan Point* (*q.v.*), with its lonely lighthouse. To the west of this road, some 2 miles from Kilchoan, is the low hill of *Beinn na Seilg,* 1,123 ft. From its rocky summit the panorama is wide and beautiful, and on the eastern slopes is a stone circle. **6 m. N.E.** of Kilchoan, off the Salen road, and reached partly by means of a by-road and partly on foot, are the silver sands of Kilmory Bay, with Ockle Point lying to the east. *Iter. 216.*

KILCHOMAN, Isle of Islay, Argyll. Map 6, NR 2 6.
The Church, situated a little to the south of the road, contains a notable example of a sculptured Celtic cross. To the north-east is Loch Gorm, with the remains of an ancient castle of the Macdonalds. There are good sands at Machir Bay, in the Rhinns of Islay, to the west, and also at Saligo Bay, to the north, the latter reached by a narrow road. Near the former are the graves of some of those drowned in the sinking of the "Otranto," in 1918, and there are also several standing stones in the vicinity. See **Port Ellen** and **Sanaigmore.** *Iter. 246.*

KILCHRENAN, Argyll. 349. Map 14, NN 0 2.
E.C. Wed. Situated a little to the north of *Loch Awe* (*q.v.*), and linked to *Portsonachan* (*q.v.*) by a passenger ferry from Taychreggan pier. In the Churchyard is a block of granite commemorating Mac Cailean Mor, killed in 1294, the founder of the Argyll fortunes. Near the shores of the loch, away to the south-west, are Forestry Commission developments, including the newly-founded village of *Dalavich,* the road continuing by the loch to reach *Ford* (*q.v.*). Through the wooded Glen Nant, to the north of Kilchrenan, goes the road to *Taynuilt* (*q.v.*). *Iter. 117.*

KILCHURN CASTLE, Argyll. Map 14, NN 1 2.
This romantic, ruined Castle (A.M.), the keep of which was built by Sir Colin Campbell, the founder of the Breadalbane family, dates originally from 1440, and was garrisoned by Hanoverian troops in 1746. It stands most picturesquely in upper Loch Awe, on a site which was once an island. The south and north sides of the building are of 16th and 17th cent. date respectively, and in 1879, the great gale which at the same time wrecked the Tay Bridge, blew down one of the castle's tower tops. The Rivers Orchy and Strae enter the loch at this point, and behind Loch Awe, to the north-west, rises *Ben Cruachan,* 3,689 ft., the monarch of the surrounding country. The Dalmally to Taynuilt road now passes quite near the castle, a new bridge over an inner reach of Loch Awe having been constructed. *Iter. 110, 117, 125, 144, 145.*

KILCONQUHAR, Fife. Map 17, NO 4 0.
An attractive village, on the north shore of Kilconquhar Loch. *Kilconquhar House* has an old tower. See **Colinsburgh.** *Iter. 132.*

Kenmore, Perth. The tablet on the bridge over the River Tay, which dates from 1774

Kenmore, Perth. The entrance to the modern Taymouth Castle, seen from A827, to the north-east. The former 16th century structure was the work of Colin Campbell of Glenorchy and became later a home of the Breadalbanes

Kilbarchan, Renfrew. The inscription above the door of an 18th century Weaver's Cottage, now under the guardianship of the National Trust for Scotland

Kilbarchan, Renfrew. The statue of Habbie Simpson, a local piper of the 17th century, which stands on the Church steeple

Kilchrenan, Argyll. A granite block, showing what is said to be a carving of a claymore, set up in 1866, and commemorating MacCailean Mor, the ancestor of the Clan Argyll, killed in 1294

Kilchurn Castle, Argyll. The 15th to 17th century Castle, built by the Breadalbanes, whose ancestor, Sir Colin Campbell, Knight of Rhodes, erected the keep. The gale which destroyed the Tay Bridge in 1879 blew down one of the tower tops

PLATE 94 (facing page 186)

Kildonan, Sutherland. Parallel rows of ancient stones near Leirable Hill, to the north-west, off A897

Kilcreggan, Dunbarton. Knockderry Castle, the 'Knock Dunder' of Sir Walter Scott's '*Heart of Midlothian.*' It stands some 3 miles to the north, on the Coulport road (B833)

Kildrummy, Aberdeen. The ruined Castle of the Earls of Mar, rebuilt in 1303 by a Bishop of Caithness. It was besieged in 1404 by the son of the Wolf of Badenoch, and dismantled after the 1715 Jacobite Rising

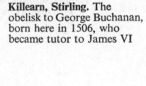

Killearn, Stirling. The obelisk to George Buchanan, born here in 1506, who became tutor to James VI

Killin, Perth. The entrance tower of the former Breadalbane stronghold of Finlarig Castle, which contains what is reputed to be the sole surviving example of a 'beheading pit'

Killiecrankie, Perth. Scenery in the gorge of Killiecrankie (part N.T. Scot.), famous for the battle which was won by the Highlanders in 1689

[For KILMACOLM see following plate]

PLATE 95 (facing page 187)

KILCREGGAN, Dunbarton. 815. SB. with Cove.
Map 14, NS 2 8.
At the southern extremity of the Rosneath peninsula, with a pier, overlooking the mouth of Loch Long and across to the Holy Loch. The resort faces *Gourock* (*q.v.*), on the opposite shores of the Firth of Clyde. Beyond Baron's Point, west of Kilcreggan, is *Cove*, also with a pier. A little farther to the north, on the road to *Coulport* (*q.v.*), is the Castle of *Knockderry*, standing on the dungeons of an old tower, and associated with Scott's "Heart of Midlothian" under the name of "Knock Dunder." See **Rosneath**. *Iter.* 116.

KILDALTON, Isle of Islay, Argyll. Map 6, NR 4 4.
In the churchyard are two finely sculptured Celtic crosses. Inland, to the north-west, rises *Beinn Sholum*, 1,136 ft., the most southerly in a long line of hills extending towards the Sound of Islay. The Kildalton estate extends towards the shores of Loch a' Chnoic, with numerous small islands offshore. *Iter.* 245.

KILDONAN, Isle of Arran, Bute. Map 7, NS 0 2.
GOLF. Here, situated on a loop off the main road, are remains of *Kildonan Castle*, on a rocky stretch of coast looking seawards towards the tiny island of Pladda, with its lighthouse. To the north-east is Dippin Head, near Dippin rocks, from which magnificent marine views may be obtained. *Iter.* 242.

KILDONAN, Sutherland. Map 31, NC 9 2.
The tiny village lies in Strath Ullie, which is threaded by the Helmsdale River, noted for its fishing. Gold was discovered in the Kildonan Burn in 1868. There are numerous prehistoric remains in the neighbourhood, notably on *Leirable Hill*, to the north-west, and some examples of parallel rows of ancient stones are to be found. In the vicinity stands *Suisgill Lodge*, with its fine gardens. To the north and south of the Strath rise moorlands and bare hills. See **Lybster**. *Iter.* 234, 235.

KILDROCHET, Wigtown. Map 2, NX 0 5.
Iter. 81, 82.

KILDRUMMY, Aberdeen. Map 26, NJ 4 1.
The imposing ruins of the great Castle of *Kildrummy* (A.M.), accessible always (see note page 90), lie a little to the south-west, at a height of nearly 800 ft., in a picturesque setting, guarded on two sides by a ravine, and overlooking the valley of the Upper Don. The castle was rebuilt in 1303, and added to at various times later, having the usual stormy history common to so many Scottish castles. Several of the towers are still in a fair state of preservation, one of its two round towers, the *Snow* Tower, being almost equal in size to the outstanding example at *Bothwell* (*q.v.*). There are also remains of the Chapel, with a triple lancet window. **1 m. N.E.** of the castle, and a little to the east of the main road, near the modern Kildrummy Church, are remains of the older Kirk, retaining a Norman wall, and also a vault containing monuments, known as the Elphinstone aisle, dating from 1605 and restored in 1862. Farther to the north, and to the left of the Huntly road, is Drumnahive Wood, in which lies *Lulach's Stone*, traditionally associated with the slaying of Lady Macbeth's son. *Iter.* 167, 176.

KILFINAN, Argyll. Map 14, NR 9 7.
Lies a little to the east of Kilfinan Bay, on *Loch Fyne* (*q.v.*), with the heights of Knapdale beyond the farther shore of the loch. The road leading southwards from here, passing Loch Melldalloch, continues as far as *Tighnabruaich* (*q.v.*), on the *Kyles of Bute* (*q.v.*). See **Kames**. *Iter.* 103.

KILFINICHEN CHURCH, Isle of Mull, Argyll.
Map 13, NM 4 2.
Situated on the northern shores of Loch Scridain. A by-road leads westwards along the shores of the loch and gives access to the 2,000-acre Scottish National Trust farm property known as *Burg*, with lofty cliffs rising farther west, at the extremity of the lonely and hilly Ardmeanach peninsula. On the shore is preserved *McCulloch's Tree*, a noted geological specimen. The road which leaves Kilfinichen in a northerly direction proceeds through Glen Seilisden towards the remarkable *Gribun* (*q.v.*) cliffs. To the north-east of

Kilfinichen rises *Ben More*, 3,169 ft., the highest point in the island, and a splendid viewpoint, the Outer Hebrides being visible at times. *Iter.* 249.

KILKENZIE, Argyll. Map 6, NR 6 2.
Iter. 121.

KILLEAN, Argyll. Map 6, NR 6 4.
Near the modern Church are remains of an earlier structure, which retains a good double window. *Iter.* 121.

KILLEARN, Stirling. 1,054. Map 15, NS 5 8.
E.C. Wed. A pleasant village, situated to the north-west of the *Campsie Fells*, among which *Earl's Seat*, 1,896 ft., is the principal summit, and *Dumgoyne*, 1,401 ft., is prominent with its conical top. In the village stands an obelisk in memory of George Buchanan, the historian, scholar and tutor to James VI, who was born at Killearn, in 1506. To the west and north are the windings of the River Forth. **2 m. N.W.**, near the small village of *Gartness*, is the *Pot of Gartness*, a cascade and ravine on the Endrick Water. *Iter.* 108, 114.

KILLEYAN, Isle of Islay, Argyll. Map 6, NR 2 4.
Iter. 244.

KILLICHONAN, Perth. Map 19, NN 5 5.
Iter. 147, 148.

KILLIECRANKIE, Perth. Map 20, NN 9 6.
E.C. Thurs. This famous wooded defile, through which pass the road, the railway and the River Garry, is best known for the battle, fought in 1689, about **1 m. N.** of the head of the pass. In the fight, won for James VII and II by the Highlanders, Graham of Claverhouse, Viscount Dundee, defeated General Mackay, but was himself slain in the moment of victory, a stone now marking the spot where he fell. Both Scott in his "Bonnie Dundee," and Macaulay, have graphically portrayed the battle. In the heart of the pass is the Soldier's Leap (N.T. Scot.), where two rocks almost bridge the gorge. At the south end is *Bridge of Garry* (*q.v.*), where the roads leading to Loch Tummel and Pitlochry diverge. Much of the pass was given to the Scottish National Trust in 1947, and adjoins the Trust's Falls of Tummel property, which can be reached on foot from Bridge of Garry, or by road from *Pitlochry* (*q.v.*). See **Blair Atholl** and **Queen's View**. *Iter.* 138, 140, 143, 150.

KILLIN, Perth. 423. Map 15, NN 5 3.
E.C. Wed. GOLF. A delightful little summer and winter sports resort, overlooking *Loch Tay* (*q.v.*), and situated at the eastern extremity of the mountain-encircled Glen Dochart and Glen Lochay. Through the former flows the River Dochart, with its picturesque falls, and the river is joined by the Lochay, flowing through Glen Lochay, also graced by beautiful falls, before the combined streams enter the loch. Near the Dochart bridge, built in 1760 and repaired in 1830, are two small islands, on one of which, *Inch Buie*, was the burial place of the Clan MacNab. At the head of the loch is the ruined *Finlarig Castle*, preserving sculptured stones and an ancient beheading pit and thought to be the only surviving example. The castle is described in Scott's "Fair Maid of Perth." At *Kinnell House*, to the south of the Dochart, is a famous vine, one of the largest in Europe. The views across Loch Tay towards *Ben Lawers*, 3,984 ft., Perthshire's highest mountain, are very fine. Nearer to Killin rise the peaks of the *Tarmachan* group, attaining 3,421 ft. West of the village is *Stronachlachan*, 1,708 ft. and 1,977 ft., a good viewpoint. **2½ m. S.W.**, in Glen Dochart, is the entrance to the gloomy defile of Glen Ogle, between steep slopes, the road attaining a height of nearly 1,000 ft. on the way to *Lochearnhead* (*q.v.*). See **Lawers**. *Iter.* 107, 120, 138.

KILMACOLM, Renfrew. 2,652. Map 8, NS 3 6.
E.C. Wed. GOLF. A pleasant resort in Strath Gryfe, with good views from some of the low hills in the neighbourhood. Adjoining the modern Church is the aisle from an older structure. In the church are buried the Earls of Glencairn. **2 m. S.E.**, on a by-road leading towards Houston, is the ruined Church of *St. Fillan*, with a doorway

dated 1635. **2 m. S.W.** are scanty remains of *Duchall Castle*, which has ghostly associations. See **Bridge of Weir.** *Iter. 64, 85.*

KILMAHOG, Perth.   Map 15, **NN 6 0.**
Iter. 106, 107, 111, 139, 141, 142, 144.

KILMALUAG, Isle of Skye, Inverness.   Map 22, **NG 4 7.**
Away to the north-west is Rudha Hunish, a narrow promontory, at the tip of the Trotternish peninsula, forming the northern extremity of Skye, and looking across to Eilean Trodday, a tiny island. The Kilmaluag River flows northwards through the village to the bay of that name. See **Flodigarry.** *Iter. 254.*

KILMANY, Fife.   Map 17, **NO 3 2.**
The Church, built in 1768, is associated with Dr. Thomas Chalmers, a famous 19th cent. preacher. *Goales Den* is pretty. *Mountquhanie* is a ruined 16th cent. castle. *Iter. 126.*

KILMARNOCK, Ayr. 44,307. LB.
                                                      Map 8, **NS 4 3.**
E.C. Wed. M.D. Fri. GOLF. An important manufacturing town in the Cunningham division of the county, noted for whisky, Kilmarnock "bonnets," carpets and boots. There are numerous Burns associations, including the " *Angel* " Hotel, the former Laigh Kirk, and an epitaph by the poet on " Tam Samson " in the churchyard, in which are also several Covenanters' monuments. The steeple of the old Kirk, dating from 1410, survived the fire of 1668. The present Laigh Kirk dates from 1802. In Kay Park is an interesting Burns museum, contained within a monument. In 1786, the first edition of Burns's poems was published from the town. The Dick Institute contains an interesting museum of rural life. Johnnie Walker, a grocer in King Street founded, in 1820, what has become the largest whisky bottling concern in the world. **1 m. N.**, near the Fenwick Water, is *Dean Castle*, early and late 15th cent., preserving two towers. *Craigie Hill*, 500 ft., to the south of the town, is a notable viewpoint, with an indicator, erected originally in 1915 by the Glenfield Ramblers. See **Fenwick** (for *Crawfurdland Castle*), **Kilmaurs** and **Symington** (Ayr). *Iter. 19, 55, 61, 62, 66, 67, 69.*

KILMARTIN, Argyll. 460.
                                                      Map 14, **NR 8 9.**
Situated in an attractive glen, and famous for its various groups of Bronze Age cup and ring marked rocks, in particular those at *Balvachraig* (A.M.). Of even greater note are the chambered cairns, notably those of *Nether Largie* (A.M.), which are attributed to the Bronze Age. In Kilmartin Churchyard are several richly-sculptured slabs, while inside the War Memorial gateway is the well-known *Kilmartin* Cross, and nearby is a notable, though mutilated Crucifixion (all A.M.). A ruined Castle is situated near the village. **1½ m. N.**, on an eminence, are the remains of the 16th cent. *Carnasserie Castle* (A.M.) overlooking the Kilmartin valley. This stronghold was built by a Bishop of the Isles, who published the first book in the Gaelic language, in 1567. **4 m. S.W.** of Kilmartin, on the shores of the Crinan Loch, stands the modernized *Duntroon Castle*. *Iter. 118, 119, 122.*

KILMAURS, Ayr. 2,176.   Map 8, **NS 4 4.**
E.C. Wed. This old burgh, once well known for its cutlery, retains its Tolbooth, on which the jougs are still hanging. **2 m. N.E.** is *Rowallan Castle* (A.M.), an interesting old structure, parts of which date back to 1560 and earlier.

There are two impressive circular towers, and a Renaissance door leads into the forecourt. The grounds are always open and the castle is viewable on application to the head gardener (see note page 90). *Iter. 62.*

KILMELFORD, Argyll. 279.   Map 14, **NM 8 1.**
E.C. Wed. A small angling resort, situated at the head of Loch Melfort, which is sheltered from the open sea by numerous islands, large and small, including those of *Luing* and *Shuna*, which are separated by the Sound of Luing from the more mountainous island of *Scarba*. Eastwards from Kilmelford, a very rough and narrow road climbs towards Loch Avich, giving a fine distant view of *Ben Cruachan*, 3,689 ft. Northwards, on the *Kilninver* (*q.v.*) road, is the picturesque, wooded Pass of Melfort, above the valley of the River Oude. The road through part of the pass has been reconstructed. **4 m. S.W.**, on the shores of Loch Melfort, and off the Ardrishaig road, is *Arduaine*

CROWN COPYRIGHT RESERVED   PUBLISHED BY THE AUTOMOBILE ASSOCIATION

1. Burns's Monument and Museum in   2. Laigh Kirk (1802) with Tower and
   Kay Park.   Graveyard of former church.
3. Town Hall. Information Bureau.

When approaching Kilmarnock from the north and making for Irvine and the coast, the town can be avoided by turning right along Western Road and joining A7, the Irvine road, 1 m. west of the town centre.

House, the notable gardens of which are sometimes shown in the summer. (See note page 90.) *Iter. 118, 119, 122.*

KILMICHAEL, Argyll.   Map 14, **NR 8 9.**
Known also as *Kilmichael Glassary*, this small village, situated on the edge of the Moine Mhor, or Great Moss of Crinan, was once known for its cattle fairs. Prehistoric standing stones are to be seen in the vicinity. **1½ m. N.W.**

Kilmacolm, Renfrew. The Holy Well of St. Fillan, where children were formerly brought to be cured of rickets. It is situated on an unclassified road some 2 miles to the south-east

Kilmacolm, Renfrew. The rock on which St. Fillan sat when baptising children. It is situated on an unclassified road some 2 miles to the south-east

Kilmany, Fife. The remains of the 16th century Mount-quhanie Castle, whose 17th century owner, Robert Lumsden, refused to give up Dundee to General Monk, and was later executed

Kilmartin, Argyll. The ancient carved Cross of Kilmartin

Kilmarnock, Ayr. The Burns Museum in Kay Park. In it is preserved the announcement of the poet's death on July 21st, 1796, as printed in the '*Kilmarnock Standard*'

Kilmaurs, Ayr. The partly 16th century Rowallan Castle, off B751, to the north-east. It bears the arms of the Mures of Rowallan, and is the home of Lord Rowallan, the former Chief Scout

PLATE 96 (facing page 188)   [For KILMARNOCK see also Plate 174
[For KILMARTIN see also under Highlands (Plate 84)

Kilmory Knap, Argyll. Castle Sween, a 13th century stronghold, facing Loch Sween, on an unclassified road some 2½ miles north-north-east. It was largely destroyed by Colkitto Macdonald in 1645

Kilmuir, Isle of Skye, Inverness. The Celtic Cross, inscribed with lines by Dr. Johnson in memory of Flora Macdonald, who died in 1790

IN·MEMORY·OF
ARCHIBALD·CLARK
WHO DIED AT AROTARIC 2º SEP 1854
AGED·20·YEARS.
·DEEPLY·REGRETTED·
BY·HIS·SORROWING·RELATIONS.

Kilmun, Argyll. A carved tombstone in the churchyard to a shepherd boy, who was found frozen to death on a hillside more than 100 years ago

Kilsyth, Stirling. The rebuilt Colzium House, which adjoins the site of Montrose's defeat of the Covenanters in 1645. It is now partly a museum

Kilwinning, Ayr. A rare example of a wooden Cross, surmounting the Mercat Cross

Kincardine-on-Forth, Fife. The Parish Church, which dates from the early 19th century. During the Second World War, the Polish General Sikorski lived at the modern Tulliallan Castle, on the outskirts of the town

[For **KINCARDINE-ON-FORTH** see also Plate 174

PLATE 97 (facing page 189)

is *Dunadd*, where a fort-crowned rock (A.M.), carved with symbols of sovereignty, is associated with the first dynasty of the Kings of Scotland, the ancient kingdom of Argyll, known originally as Dalriada, and early capitals of which were *Dunstaffnage* and *Forteviot* (both *q.v.*). *Iter. 118, 119, 122.*

KILMICHAEL, Bute.   Map 7, NR 9 7.
See **Port Bannatyne.**

KILMORACK, Inverness.   Map 25, NH 4 4.
Lies on the Beauly River, in the district known as The Aird, and is visited for the well-known Falls of Kilmorack, in a richly-wooded setting. To the south-east, beyond the river, is the impressive *Beaufort Castle*, damaged by fire in 1937, and situated in fine grounds. The Castle is the seat of Lord Lovat, the Chief of Clan Fraser. **See Crask of Aigas.** *Iter. 206, 210.*

KILMORY KNAP, Argyll.   Map 6, NR 7 7.
Situated in *Knapdale* (*q.v.*), on a narrow neck of land separating the attractively wooded Loch Sween from Loch Killisport, and known for the carved Celtic slabs and the *MacMillan Cross* (A.M.), which are preserved in the churchyard. There are fine views over the Sound of Jura towards the conical Paps of Jura. 2½ m. N.N.E. is *Castle Sween* (A.M.), incorporating *MacMillan's Tower*, and being one of the earliest stone castles in Scotland, dating from the 13th cent. Much of the structure was destroyed by Colkitto Macdonald in 1645. **See Tayvallich.** *Iter. 122.*

KILMUIR, Isle of Skye, Inverness.   Map 22, NG 3 7.
Lies on Score Bay, and on the road leading round the northern tip of the island linking *Uig* (*q.v.*) with *Flodigarry* (*q.v.*), and is famous as the burial-place of Flora Macdonald, who died in 1790. A tall Celtic cross marks her grave, on which is inscribed Dr. Johnson's tribute. The graveyard lies a little to the north-east of the road. 2 m. S. of Kilmuir, and off the Uig road, facing the sea, is Loch Chaluim Cille, now drained, and on an island of which stood a Celtic monastery, the remains of which are still distinct and show the original plan. *Iter. 254.*

KILMUN, Argyll.   Map 14, NS 1 8.
On the north shore of the Holy Loch, in the *Cowal* (*q.v.*) peninsula, and retaining the tower of the Collegiate Church, founded in 1442. The Marquis of Argyll, executed in 1661, is buried in the vault. In the churchyard are interesting carved tombstones. Artistic sea stones, set in stucco, are a feature of garden gates in the village. There are fine woods and rhododendrons in the vicinity. To the south-east is Strone Point, overlooking the Firth of Clyde. 2 m. N.W. of Kilmun is the delightful little *Puck's Glen*, incorporating a fine viewpoint, and beyond it, to the north-west, stretches Glen Masson, ringed by high hills. **See Ardentinny, Benmore Estate** and **Sandbank.** *Iter. 102.*

KILNINIAN, Isle of Mull, Argyll.   Map 12, NM 4 4.
In the Churchyard are some stones with carved Celtic inscriptions. The road to the north-west climbs over moors, with hairpin bends, to reach *Calgary* (*q.v.*). 4½ m. S.E., of Kilninian are the Laggan Falls, facing Loch Tuath and the island of *Ulva*, described under *Ulva Ferry*. *Iter. 248.*

KILNINVER, Argyll.   Map 14, NM 8 2.
Stands on Loch Feochan, an inlet of the Firth of Lorne, with views of the mountainous island of *Mull* (*q.v.*) to the west. The road leading south-eastwards to *Kilmelford* (*q.v.*) goes through the wooded Glen Callon on the way to the picturesque Pass of Melfort. 4 m. S.E., beyond Glen Euchar, is the attractive, hill-encircled *Loch Scamadale*. See **Clachan Bridge.** *Iter. 118, 119, 122.*

KILRENNY, Fife. 3,302. SB. with Anstruther.
     Map 17, NO 5 0.
See **Anstruther.** *Iter. 94, 98.*

KILSYTH, Stirling. 10,329. SB.   Map 15, NS 7 7.
E.C. Wed. GOLF. A mining town at the foot of the *Kilsyth* hills, the highest point of which, *Meikle Bin*, 1,870 ft., rises away to the north-west. Montrose defeated the Covenanters here, in 1645, a victory which gained him for a time command of all Scotland. Relics of the fight are preserved in the mansion of *Colzium*, which has become partly a museum, open daily, except Thurs., 9 to 6 (see note page 90). *Iter. 98, 113, 115.*

KILWINNING, Ayr. 7,134. SB.   Map 8, NS 2 4.
E.C. Wed. An iron-working town, known formerly as *Segdoune*, on the River Garnock. It claims to be the earliest home of Freemasonry in Scotland. There are very scanty remains of the former Priory, and the present Church is 18th cent. and later. The Mercat Cross is a shaft topped by a rare wooden Cross. Kilwinning has for many years been associated with archery contests. 1½ m. S.E. is *Eglinton Castle*, dating from 1798, and now roofless. The Eglinton Tournament was held here in 1839. See **Abington.** *Iter. 57, 63, 66, 69, 85, 88.*

KINBRACE, Sutherland   Map 30, NC 8 3.
A lonely crofting village, with a number of chambered cairns in the vicinity, especially near the Kinbrace Burn, to the south. Land reclamation schemes were attempted here by the 3rd Duke of Sutherland. *Iter. 234, 235.*

KINCARDINE BRIDGE, Fife; Stirling.   Map 16, NS 9 8.
This bridge, which dates from 1936, spans the Forth some 10 miles south-east of Stirling. It is the last bridge before the estuary widens, and by using it traffic proceeding from Glasgow and the south to Fife and the adjacent counties can avoid passing through Stirling. See **Kincardine-on-Forth.** *Iter. 86, 91, 97, 98.*

KINCARDINE CHURCH, Perth.   Map 16, NS 7 9.
This early 19th cent. Church contains Drummond monuments and also a rare example of a Scottish brass, of 17th cent. date.

KINCARDINE O'NEIL, Aberdeen.   Map 21, NO 5 9.
Formerly of importance as the Dee bridgehead of the road leading over the *Cairn o'Mounth Pass* (*q.v.*), the erstwhile bridge, and at a later date a ferry, being utilized. The modern bridge over the river stands 2 m. S.E. at *Potarch*, the road towards the pass proceeding thence by way of *Feughside Inn* (*q.v.*). At Kincardine o'Neil there are remains of the Auld Kirk, and a fair was at one time held in the village. 1½ m. W., the Dee is joined by the Dess Burn, on which is the picturesque Slug of Dess Waterfall, near a road leading northwards to the small Loch of Auchlossan and *Lumphanan* (*q.v.*). See **Deeside** and **Midmar Castle.** *Iter. 152, 191.*

KINCARDINE-ON-FORTH, Fife.   Map 16, NS 9 8.
E.C. Tues. GOLF. A small port, on the estuary of the River Forth, which is spanned here by the fine Kincardine Bridge (see above). The town has a notable 17th cent. Mercat Cross displaying the arms of the Earl of Kincardine. The ruined Church dates from 1675. Sir John Dewar, inventor of the vacuum flask, was born here in 1842. Many houses in the little town carry date inscriptions. Behind the Church is the ruined late 15th cent. *Tulliallan Castle*, of considerable architectural interest, notably the ground floor vaulting. In the background lies Tulliallan Forest, now in the hands of the Forestry Commission. See **Culross.** *Iter. 86, 91, 97, 98, 134.*

KINCRAIG, Inverness. 400.   Map 25, NH 8 0.
E.C. Wed. On the north side of Loch Insh, through which flows the River Spey. It is joined, after leaving the loch, by the Feshie, emerging from the long glen of that name, finely wooded in its deeper recesses beneath the western outliers of the lofty *Cairngorms* (*q.v.*). In the Glen Feshie Forest, the Feshie is joined by the Eidart, which has come down from the Great Moss on the lofty Cairngorm plateau. See **Feshie Bridge, Insh** and **Rothiemurchus.** *Iter. 140, 147, 150, 208.*

KINGARTH, Bute.   Map 7, NS 0 5.
Iter. 241.

KING EDWARD, Aberdeen.   Map 27, NJ 7 5.
The name King Edward is a corruption through Kinedart of the Gaelic Ceann-eador. The ruined *Kinedart Castle* lies 1 m. S., on the road leading to *Turriff* (*q.v.*). 2 m. N.W., near the River Deveron, are the ruins of *Eden Castle*. The modern mansion, in its fine grounds, stands in the vicinity. *Iter. 180.*

KINGHORN, Fife. 2,335. SB.   Map 17, **NT 2** 8.
E.C. Thurs. GOLF. A Royal Burgh and resort on the Firth of Forth, with good sands, associated with King Alexander III, who died in 1286 as a result of a fall, and is commemorated by a monument erected on the King's Crag on the *Pettycur* promontory. There are fine views obtainable from this promontory, notably towards *Inchkeith Island* (*q.v.*). Pettycur was at one time the terminal point of a ferry across the Firth, which explains the various milestones in the district which carry its name. 1½ m. N.E., on the coast, is the old tower of *Seafield*. *Iter. 134.*

KINGLASSIE, Fife.   Map 17, **NO 2** 9.
A village once known by the name of *Goatmilk*, a corruption of Gaytmylkshire. On *Redwells Hill*, 605 ft., stands the unfinished 52-ft. high tower known as " Blythe's Folly," erected in 1820.

KINGSBARNS, Fife.   Map 17, **NO 5** 1.
Stands a little inland from a stretch of coast between Babbet Ness and Cambo Ness. 2 m. S.E., off the Crail road, is the 17th cent. *Randerston House*, now a farm. *Iter. 94.*

KINGSBURGH HOUSE, Isle of Skye, Inverness.
                    Map 22, **NG 3** 5.
See Uig (Isle of Skye).

KINGSHOUSE, Argyll.   Map 18, **NN 2** 5.
This well-known climbing centre lies a little to the east of the new Glencoe road, and stands actually on a section of the former road through the glen. At the inn here, the soldiers under Captain Campbell are said to have gathered before the massacre of *Glencoe* (*q.v.*). The setting is magnificent, with the great rock peak of *Buchaille Etive Mor*, 3,345 ft., the " Shepherd of Etive," towering to the west. To the south rise the peaks of the *Black Mount*, outstanding among which are *Sron na Creise*, 2,952 ft., *Meall Bhuiridh*, 3,636 ft., noted for ski-ing, *Clachlet*, 3,602 ft., and still farther south, *Stob Ghabhar*, 3,565 ft. Buchaille Etive is famous among rock climbers, and its sensational Crowberry Ridge is one of the best known in Scotland. The wild Lairig Gartain pass separates the peak from *Buchaille Etive Bheag*, 3,129 ft., to the west. Kinghouse is described in Neil Munro's " John Splendid." Glen Etive stretches away to the south-west, and the mountains dividing it from Glencoe are part of *Dalness* Forest, acquired by the National Trust for Scotland in 1937. The narrow road diverging from the main Glencoe road and traversing Glen Etive comes to an end at the picturesque head of *Loch Etive* (*q.v.*), where there is a steamer pier. *Ben Starav*, 3,541 ft. high, dominates the loch at this point.
On the Glencoe road, 3 m. N.W. of Kingshouse, is *Altnafeadh*, from which point commenced the former military road to *Kinlochleven* (*q.v.*) over the so-called " Devil's Staircase," rising to 1,754 ft. The old road from Kingshouse to the south, over the exposed *Black Mount*, which climbed to about 1,450 ft., and is now disused, was built by soldiers under General Caulfeild, in 1757, using Kingshouse as a rest-house. The present road, re-aligned farther to the east, crosses part of the vast and desolate *Rannoch Moor*, passing by the shores of Loch Ba, and is easily graded all the way. This region has been graphically described in R. L. Stevenson's " Kidnapped," On the watershed, at a height of 1,143 ft., a cairn marks the division of waters flowing eastwards to the North Sea and westwards to the Atlantic. Beyond Rannoch Moor, away to the east, is *Rannoch* (*q.v.*) station, but there is no road link across the ten desolate miles of moorland. See **Bridge of Orchy, Glencoe** and **Kinloch Rannoch.** *Iter. 100, 125, 142.*

KINGSMUIR, Angus.   Map 21, **NO 4** 4.
Iter. 162.

KINGSTON, Moray.   Map 26, **NJ 3** 6.
Near the Spey estuary. Charles II landed at *Garmouth* (*q.v.*) near here in 1650. The name Kingston is derived from Kingston-upon-Hull, and was given to the village in 1784 by two Yorkshiremen, who came here to purchase timber.

KINGUSSIE, Inverness. 1,029. SB.   Map 19, **NH 7** 0.
E.C. Wed. GOLF. A well-known *Badenoch* (*q.v.*) resort, in the wooded *Strath Spey* (*q.v.*), with fine views of the lofty *Cairngorm* (*q.v.*) range away to the east. *Craig Beg*, 1,593 ft., is a good viewpoint, and overlooks the attractive golf course. Kingussie was the birthplace of James Macpherson, the 18th cent. translator of the Ossianic poems. The Highland Folk Museum, known as *Am Fasgadh*, was originally founded in Iona in 1935, and contains exhibits of much interest. Pony-trekking is a recently-introduced sport to this district.

|1. Highland Folk Museum.

Westwards lie the *Monadhliath* mountains, with several tops over 3,000 ft. high, including *Carn Dearg*, 3,093 ft. and *Carn Mairg*, 3,087 ft., but they are comparatively little visited, and have not the fascination of the better-known Cairngorms. The former fortress of the Wolf of Badenoch stood on a site across the Spey, on a minor road leading north-eastwards towards *Rothiemurchus* (*q.v.*) Forest, and where are now the ruins of Wade's *Ruthven Barracks*, a grim reminder of the '45. These barracks were built in 1716, and added to by Wade in 1734, but were destroyed by the Highlanders in 1746, after the failure of the '45. General Wade's military road from the south reached the barracks over the hills from Glen Truim. To the south-east of Kingussie, across the Spey, and east of the barracks, is *Tromie Bridge* (*q.v.*), leading to the long valley of Glen Tromie, which penetrates into the great Gaick Forest, where Loch an't Seileich lies amid lofty hills. The wild Minigaig Pass, for long-distance walkers only, leads out of the glen to the south-east, and crosses the hills at a high altitude, before descending into Glen Bruar, north of *Struan* (*q.v.*). 3 m. N.E. of Kingussie, off the Aviemore road, is the mansion of *Balavil*, built by James Macpherson, who is commemorated by an obelisk at the point where the Raitts Burn passes under the road on its way to join the lower Spey. See **Corrieyairack Pass, Drumgask, Feshie Bridge, Kincraig, Newtonmore** and **Wade Roads.** *Iter. 140, 147, 150, 208.*

KINKELL CHURCH, Aberdeen.   Map 27, **NJ 7** 1.
See **Inverurie.**

KINLOCHBERVIE, Sutherland.   Map 28, **NC 2** 5.
Beautifully situated on Loch Inchard, on a narrow and winding road leading north-westwards from *Rhiconich* (*q.v.*), with splendid views towards the lonely mountains of the Reay Forest, dominated by *Foinaven*, 2,980 ft. The fisheries at Kinlochbervie are of increasing importance. The road continues for some four miles towards the open sea, giving fine views, and terminating beyond Balchrick at the little fishing village of *Sheigra*. From here it is possible to follow the coast on foot to the remote *Sandwood Bay*, which has been described as almost the loveliest in all Scotland, and where, in the present century, a mermaid is said to have been seen. Lofty cliffs, with detached stacks of red Torridon sandstone, overlook the reddish sands of this little-visited bay. Far away to the north, at the extremity of a cliff-bound stretch of coast, is the lonely lighthouse at *Cape Wrath* (*q.v.*). *Iter. 229.*

KINLOCHEIL, Inverness.   Map 18, **NM 9** 7.
Near the western extremity of Loch Eil, which forms the boundary between Inverness and Argyll. Here, the road to *Ardgour* (*q.v.*) and Ardnamurchan leaves the " Road to the Isles " and continues along the south shore of the loch in the opposite direction. There are associations with Prince Charles Edward, who halted at Kinlocheil a few days after

Kingussie, Inverness. The Highland Folk Museum of Am Fasgadh, which was founded in 1935 in the island of Iona

Kinghorn, Fife. The Monument (1886) on the Pettycur promontory to Alexander III, who died here from a fall in 1286

Kinglassie, Fife. ' Blythe's Folly,' an unfinished 52-foot high tower, erected in 1820 on Redwells Hill

Kinlochbervie, Sutherland. The view up Loch Inchard, a lonely sea loch penetrating some 3 miles inland towards Rhiconich, with the mountains of the Reay Forest in the background

Kingshouse, Argyll. The ' Kingshouse ' Inn, situated just off the new road through Glencoe. Soldiers, commanded by Captain Campbell, are said to have met here in 1692 prior to the massacre of Glencoe. The great rock peak of Buchaille Etive Mor rises a short distance to the west

[For KINLOCHEIL see following plate
[For KINGUSSIE see also under BADENOCH (Plate 13

Kinlocheil, Inverness. Fassifern House, which gave shelter to Prince Charles Edward for a night in 1745 at the commencement of the Jacobite Rising. It stands 3 miles to the east, on A830

Kinlochewe, Ross and Cromarty. Sgurr Ban, at the south-eastern extremity of the Ben Eighe ridge. On its slopes lies the first National Nature Reserve to be formed in Great Britain

Kinlochleven, Argyll; Inverness. The westerly view down Loch Leven towards the conical Pap of Glencoe

Kinlochmoidart, Inverness. The row of beech trees commemorating the ' Seven Men of Moidart,' who defended Prince Charles Edward faithfully during the '45 Rising

Kinloch Rannoch, Perth. The mansion of The Barracks, erected originally for soldiers after the '45 Rising. It stands west of Loch Rannoch, on an unclassified road south of B846

PLATE 99 (facing page 191)

the raising of his Standard at *Glenfinnan* (*q.v.*), in 1745. *Ben Nevis*, 4,406 ft. is seen in the distance, and to the west rise the lofty hills guarding *Loch Shiel* (*q.v.*). **3 m. E.**, on the Fort William road, is *Fassifern House*, encircled by trees, where, in 1745, the Prince spent a night as the guest of John Cameron. See **Corpach**. *Iter. 209, 215.*

KINLOCHEWE, Ross and Cromarty. 140.
                                                           Map 24, **NH 0** 6.
E.C. Thurs. A centre in *Wester Ross* for some of the very finest mountain scenery on the mainland of Scotland. Here, the road having descended Glen Docherty divides, the south-western branch entering Glen Torridon, and the north-western branch continuing towards the nearby head of beautiful *Loch Maree* (*q.v.*), dominated by *Slioch*, 3,260 ft., rising steeply above its eastern shores. Beneath its south-eastern flanks access is gained on foot through Glen Bannis-dail to the solitary *Lochan Fada*, to the north-west of which lie the great cliffs of Glen Tulacha, part of *Ben Lair*, 2,817 ft., with *A'Mhaigdhean*, 3,060 ft., a splendid rocky peak, rising to the east and overlooking the lonely *Dubh* and *Fionn Lochs*. This is one of the most spectacular, but remote and least-known mountain districts in Scotland, due mainly to lack of roads and paths. South-west of Kinlochewe, the *Torridon* (*q.v.*) road skirts the base of *Ben Eighe*, with its array of 3,000-ft. high white quartzite peaks, and passes Loch Clair, where the beautiful private road to *Achnashellach* (*q.v.*) by way of Loch Coulin is joined. The scenery in Glen Torridon is wild and rocky, and to the north, overhanging the road, rises *Liathach*, 3,456 ft., one of the finest peaks in Scotland, built up of ledge upon ledge of red Torridon sandstone and most difficult to climb. Behind the peak are wild corries, notably Coire na Caime. Between *Liathach* and *Ben Eighe* lies a deep cleft, which gives access to the stupendous cliffs of *Coire Mhic Fhearchair*, rising above a tiny lochan, and reached only by means of a long and arduous walk. A little to the north of Kinlochewe, on the west bank of Loch Maree, are the woodlands of Coille na Glas-Leitire, which, with the lofty slopes of Kinlochewe Forest and Ben Eighe in the background, now form the *Ben Eighe National Nature Reserve*, the first of its kind to be formed in Great Britain. Scots pine and birch flourish in the woods, while the wild life in the area, which is more than 10,000 acres in extent, includes deer, wild cats and eagles. *Iter. 205, 222, 223.*

KINLOCH HOURN, Inverness. Map 18, **NG 9** 0.
Situated in a green hollow, sheltering a grove of eucalyptus trees, at the head of *Loch Hourn* (*q.v.*), perhaps the finest of the great sea lochs of the Western Highlands. Access is by means of a road from *Tomdoun* (*q.v.*), first along the shores of *Loch Quoich* (*q.v.*) where a hydro-electric scheme now operates. The narrow and very rough road later descends steeply (1 in 6) on the final 600 ft. to the loch, amid a wilder-ness of glaciated, grey rocks on the rugged slopes of *Sgurr nan Eugallt*, 2,933 ft., to the west, and *Sgurr a'Mhoraire*, 3,365 ft., to the east. The view from the summit of the last-named peak is one of the loveliest in the Highlands, taking in the whole length of Loch Hourn, and extending towards the *Coolins* (*q.v.*) of Skye. A path leads for a short distance along the south shore of the Inner Loch, giving good views of the wooded northern shores under the slopes of *Druim Fada*, 2,327 ft. Prince Charles Edward wandered in these lonely mountains after his defeat at *Culloden* (*q.v.*), in 1746, and narrowly missed the sentries posted on the slopes of *Sgurr a'Mhoraire*. The superb mountain scenery at the head of Inner Loch Hourn is reminiscent of the Norwegian fjords, and is probably the finest of its kind in Great Britain, its only rival being the freshwater *Loch Coruisk* (*q.v.*) in Skye. *Iter. 214.*

KINLOCHLEVEN, Argyll; Inverness. 1,742.
                                                           Map 18, **NN 1** 6.
E.C. Wed. A busy industrial centre, at the head of the beautiful *Loch Leven*, in a fine mountain setting. The power for the aluminium works is supplied by means of the water stored in the great Blackwater Reservoir, away to the east of the town. Loch Leven is traversed by picturesque roads on both shores, giving splendid views of mountain and water. To the north rises the grand *Mamore Forest* (*q.v.*) group, with

Binnein Mor attaining 3,700 ft., and to the south are the ridges of *Aonach Eagach*, 3,168 ft., overlooking *Glencoe* (*q.v.*) on their far side. The old military road over the " Devil's Staircase " from *Kingshouse* (*q.v.*), which rises to 1,745 ft., reached Kinlochleven from the south-east, and continued inland over the hills in a north-westerly direction past Loch Lundavra towards *Fort William* (*q.v.*), but the modern road goes by way of Loch Leven and the shores of Loch Linnhe. See **Ballachulish, Carnach** and **North Ballachulish**. *Iter. 100, 124, 125.*

KINLOCHMOIDART, Inverness. Map 12, **NM 7** 7.
Lies at the head of *Loch Moidart*, in the historic *Moidart* (*q.v.*) district, with fine woodlands on the shores of the loch. The River Moidart, issuing from the lonely glen of that name, flows here into the loch. Prince Charles Edward was given hospitality here, in 1745, by the Macdonalds, before the raising of his Standard at *Glenfinnan* (*q.v.*). A line of beeches in a meadow commemorates the " Seven Men of Moidart," who were among the most faithful of the Prince's companions. To the north of Glen Moidart rise lofty hills, culminating in *Fros Bheinn*, 2,876 ft., a splendid viewpoint, overlooking Rum and Skye beyond the Sound of Arisaig. A path leads westwards from Kinlochmoidart along the northern shores of the loch, and reaches the coast by way of Glen Uig, at the little village of *Glenuig*, on the Sound of Arisaig, and associated with the Prince. The path continues eastwards towards Loch Ailort, eventually reaching *Loch-ailort* (*q.v.*), on the " Road to the Isles," the seaward views all the way being magnificent. See **Acharacle** (for *Castle Tioram*) and **Dalilea**. *Iter. 217.*

KINLOCH RANNOCH, Perth. 300. Map 19, **NN 6** 5.
E.C. Wed. This little fishing resort lies on the River Tummel, at the eastern end of *Loch Rannoch* (*q.v.*), in the *Breadalbane* (*q.v.*) country. The river flows eastwards through a reservoir, which is part of the extensive Tummel-Garry hydro-electric scheme, while power-houses are situated at the far western end of the loch, and also at *Tummel Bridge* (*q.v.*). To the south-east of Kinloch Rannoch, is *Dalchoisnie*, where English invaders are said to have

fought Robert Bruce in 1306, and farther south extends Glen Sassunn, beyond which rise the various 3,000-ft. peaks of the extensive *Carn Mairg* group. Loch Rannoch has well-wooded roads on both north and south shores, these roads converg-ing some five miles east of the remote *Rannoch* (*q.v.*) station, which lies almost on the Argyll border. Near the point where the roads meet, a mansion, known as *The Barracks*, was erected for the troops after the '45. The desolate expanse of *Rannoch Moor* stretches westwards from the railhead, and contains Loch Laidon and Loch Ba, while beyond the ridge of the Black Corries are the large Blackwater Reservoir and the small Lochan a Chlaidheimh, the latter associated with a sword thrown into its waters by a 15th cent. Earl of Atholl in connection with a land claim against the Camerons. From the Moor, views of the lofty *Black Mount*, the *Glencoe* (*q.v.*) and the *Grampian* (*q.v.*) mountains may be obtained. This country has been graphically described in R. L. Steven-son's " Kidnapped." Northwards from Loch Rannoch, and linked by a tunnel aqueduct, lies the lonely Loch Ericht, overlooked by the fine peak of *Ben Alder*, 3,757 ft., but not accessible by road except at the far north-east extremity near *Dalwhinnie* (*q.v.*). To the south-east of Kinloch Rannoch rises the sharp quartzite cone of *Schiehallion*, 3,547 ft., one of the best known landmarks and viewpoints in the Central Highlands, and the focal point in the panorama from the famous *Queen's View* (*q.v.*) near Loch Tummel, away to the east. Beyond Schiehallion, to the west, is *Geal Charn*, 2,593 ft., which rises at the head of Gleann Mor. From the south shores of Loch Rannoch, on the edge of the picturesque Black Wood of Rannoch, where the native Caledonian pine is still to be seen growing, a path leads over the hills giving access to Glen Lyon. Beyond the reservoir, to the east of the village, a road diverges northwards, climbing to over 1,000 ft., and later descending through Glen Erochy to reach *Struan* (*q.v.*) in Glen Garry. Another road climbs steeply on to the moors to the south-east of Kinloch Rannoch, and after passing the ruined *St. Blane's* Chapel at *Lassentulich*, goes close to the lower slopes of Schiehallion on the way to the little Loch Kinardochy near *White Bridge* (*q.v.*). See **Trinafour**. *Iter. 89, 147, 148.*

KINLOSS, Moray.   Map 26, NJ 0 6.
The once-famous *Kinloss Abbey* was founded in 1150, but little is now left, the scanty remains including the foundations and two fine round-headed arches. 2½ m. N.E. is *Milton Brodie*, with an old Abbey garden and retaining a hexagonal tower. *Iter. 199.*

KINNAIRD, Perth.   Map 17, NO 2 2.
Situated on the slopes of the *Sidlaw* hills, overlooking the fertile *Carse of Gowrie* (*q.v.*), beyond which lies the Firth of Tay. The 12th to 15th cent. *Kinnaird Castle*, built of red stone, has been well restored. *Iter. 154.*

KINNEFF, Kincardine.   Map 21, NO 8 7.
The legend is that to the little Church of Kinneff the Scottish regalia was brought, in 1652, from *Dunnottar Castle* (*q.v.*). The jewels were hidden behind the pulpit, until the Restoration, by a Mrs. Grainger, to whom a monument has been erected.

KINNESSWOOD, Kinross.   Map 17, NO 1 0.
GOLF. Lies in an attractive setting to the east of *Loch Leven* (*q.v.*), and at the foot of *Bishop Hill* and *White Craigs* 1,492 ft. in the *Lomonds*. It is noted as the birthplace, in 1746, of Michael Bruce, the poet, whose cottage has been preserved (See **Portmoak**), and also of Alexander Buchan, of weather-lore fame, whose theory of cycles of recurring cold and warm periods is well-known. *Iter. 98.*

KINROSS, Kinross. 2,544. SB.   Map 17, NO 1 0.
E.C. Thurs. GOLF. Situated to the west of *Loch Leven* (*q.v.*), with its famous island-castle, and well-known as an angling resort, while skating and curling can be enjoyed in winter. The 17th cent. Tolbooth was repaired by the Crown in 1771 and decorated by Robert Adam. On the carved Town Cross are the old jougs. The steeple of the former Town Kirk is 18th cent. *Kinross House*, dating from 1685 to 1692, a notable example of its period, in a splendid setting, was designed by Sir William Bruce, famous for his work at *Holyroodhouse* at *Edinburgh* (*q.v.*). There are beautiful gardens. To the south of Loch Leven rises *Benarty Hill*, 1,167 ft., on the Fife border. See **Cleish**. *Iter. 90, 91, 92, 98.*

KINTAIL, Ross and Cromarty.   Map 24, NG 9 1.
The *Kintail* district of Wester Ross lies around the head of *Loch Duich* (*q.v.*), and includes some of the grandest mountain scenery in Scotland. About 15,000 acres are now the property of the Scottish National Trust, and among the mountains on the estate are the well-known *Five Sisters of Kintail*, of which *Scour Ouran*, 3,505 ft., is the highest, and shows on its western flanks what is said to be the longest continuous grass slope in the Highlands, dropping steeply from the summit almost to the roadside in picturesque *Glen Shiel* (*q.v.*). A smaller, contiguous estate belonging to the Trust contains the famous, but very remote *Falls of Glomach* (*q.v.*). The little Church and manse of Kintail stand on the eastern shore of Loch Duich, near *Inverinate* (*q.v.*). One of the finest views of the loch is that obtained from the summit of the lofty *Mam Rattachan* (*q.v.*) Pass, on the road to

Glenelg, which gives a wonderful picture of the Kintail peaks in the background beyond Loch Duich. See **Shiel Bridge**.

KINTORE, Aberdeen. 854. SB.   Map 27, NJ 7 1.
E.C. Wed. GOLF. A tiny Royal Burgh, with a Tolbooth dating from 1740. The Church retains one of the rare Sacrament Houses, a feature peculiar to churches in some parts of Eastern Scotland. In the vicinity there are prehistoric remains, such as hill forts and stone circles. *Balbithan House* is 17th cent. 1½ m. S.W. is *Hallforest*, a ruined tower, entirely without staircases, inhabited until 1639, and said to have been visited by Mary, Queen of Scots, in 1562. See **Inverurie**. *Iter. 175, 178, 184, 197.*

KINTRAW, Argyll.   Map 14, NM 8 0.
Lies at the head of Loch Craignish. Just north of the village, a by-road to the south-west diverges for *Craignish* Church, on the shores of the loch. Beyond, lie *Craignish Castle* and Craignish Point, looking towards the turbulent channel known as the Dorus Mor, or Great Door, near which lie several tiny islands. The road leading south-eastwards from Kintraw climbs high over moorland, with sharp curves, before descending towards *Kilmartin* (*q.v.*). *Iter. 118, 119, 122.*

KINTYRE, Argyll.   Map 6, NR 6 1 etc.
The long and narrow Kintyre peninsula, an appendage of the Argyllshire Highlands, stretches southwards towards the Atlantic and the Northern Irish coast, from which it is some 12 miles distant, and has an average width of not much over 5 miles. It is traversed for most of its length by roads on both west and east sides, the former providing fine views towards Islay, Jura, and the distant Irish shores, and the latter looking across Kilbrennan Sound to the mountainous outline of the island of Arran. Only a few miles from the western shores of Kintyre is the small island of Gigha, which is reached from *Tayinloan* (*q.v.*). The northern boundary of Kintyre is formed by West Loch Tarbert, with steamer services from *Tarbert* (*q.v.*) to the large island of Islay. Beyond here lies the district of *Knapdale* (*q.v.*). The most southerly point of the peninsula is the *Mull of Kintyre* (*q.v.*), where a lighthouse is situated. A ridge of hills extends down the peninsula for most of its length, in which *Beinn an Tuirc*, near *Saddell* (*q.v.*), attains 1,491 ft. See **Campbeltown**, **Gigha** and **Machrihanish**. *Iter. 121, 122, 123.*

KIPPEN, Stirling. 426.   Map 15, NS 6 9.
An attractive village, lying to the south of the winding River Forth, and with the *Gargunnock* and *Fintry* hills forming a lofty background. To the north of the river, across the Perthshire border, is the treacherous Flanders Moss, perhaps the remains of a former forest. A vine in Kippen is claimed to be the largest in existence. There is a fine old dovecote (N.T. Scot.). The modern Church, built in 1825, is considered to be one of the finest of its kind in Scotland, and its 20th cent. renovation is associated with Sir David Cameron, the Scottish artist. *Iter. 107, 108, 112, 137.*

KIPPFORD, Kirkcudbright.   Map 3, NX 8 5.
A small yachting resort, off the main road, and pleasantly situated on Rough Firth, the estuary of the Urr Water, forming an inlet of the Solway Firth. The beach is rocky and stony, and care should be exercised when bathing. See **Rockcliffe**. *Iter. 73.*

KIRK, Caithness.   Map 30, ND 2 5.
Iter. 238.

KIRKANDREWS, Kirkcudbright.   Map 3, NX 5 4.
The Church, farm and laundry together form a group of curious, modern castellated structures, the work of James Brown, a business man from Manchester. In Wigtown Bay lie the small Islands of Fleet.

KIRKBEAN, Kirkcudbright.   Map 3, NX 9 5.
Lies a little inland from the waters of the Solway Firth, and is dominated by *Boreland Hill*, 1,632 ft., and the bulky *Criffell*, 1,866 ft., a fine viewpoint. The font in the Church was presented in 1945 by the American Navy to commemorate Paul Jones (see below), who died in Paris in 1792. Off the Dalbeattie road is the ancient *Preston* Cross. 1½ m. S.E. of Kirkbean is the estate of *Arbigland*, where Paul Jones, the

Kinneff, Kincardine. In this Church, the regalia of Scotland were temporarily hidden in 1652. A Monument has been erected to Mrs. Grainger, who secreted them behind the pulpit, where they remained until the Restoration. See Dunnottar Castle (Plate 53)

Kinross, Kinross. The old jougs, or iron collar for wrongdoers, on the Town Cross, which was restored in 1886

Kippen, Stirling. The ancient dovecote, the property of the National Trust for Scotland

Kintail, Ross and Cromarty. The Five Sisters of Kintail peaks (N.T. Scot.), at the head of Loch Duich, seen from Auchtertyre Hill, on A890, between Kyle of Lochalsh and Strome Ferry

Kintore, Aberdeen. The Tolbooth of 1740, which has a dual outside staircase

Kirkandrews, Kirkcudbright. Castellated farm and laundry buildings, built by James Brown, a Manchester business man, early in this century.

PLATE 100 (facing page 192)

[For KIRKBEAN see following plate
[For KINNAIRD see Plate 172

Kirkbean, Kirkcudbright. The ancient Preston Cross, situated off the road to Dalbeattie (A710)

Kirkcaldy, Fife. Restored 17th century and earlier houses known as the 'Sailors' Walk' (N.T. Scot.)

KIRKCALDY BURGH SCHOOL
ERECTED BY THE TOWN COUNCIL 1725
HERE ADAM SMITH, L.L.D. AUTHOR OF THE
"WEALTH OF NATIONS" WAS A PUPIL
1729 - 1737
ROBERT ADAM. BORN IN GLADNEY HOUSE,
LINKS. 1728. EMINENT ARCHITECT AND
DESIGNER. COURT ARCHITECT TO KING
GEORGE III. ATTENDED THIS SCHOOL 1734-1739
BURIED IN WESTMINSTER ABBEY 1792
THOMAS CARLYLE. WAS SCHOOLMASTER
1816 - 1818
SCHOOL CLOSED 1843

Kirkcaldy, Fife. A tablet on the former Burgh school, where both Adam Smith and Robert Adam were pupils, and Thomas Carlyle once taught

Kirkconnell Church, Dumfries. The graves of 'Fair Helen of Kirkconnell Lee and her lover' in the churchyard of the ruined church. It lies 2½ miles north-east of Kirtlebridge, on an unclassified road off B722

Kirkcudbright, Kirkcudbright. The 16th to 17th century Tolbooth, with the Mercat Cross of 1610. Witches were tried and imprisoned here, the last one to be put to death in the town being Elspeth McEwen, in 1698. Paul Jones, the 'founder' of the American navy, to whom the Tolbooth is now a memorial, was also once held prisoner here

[For KIRKCALDY see also Plate 175
[For KIRKCUDBRIGHT see also under STEWARTRY (Plate 154)

Kirkcowan, Wigtown. The external stairway of the Church, giving access to the gallery

PLATE 101 (facing page 193)

KIRKCALDY

Scale
0   ¼   ½ M.

Times of High Tide can be found by referring to the Tide Table in the Members' Handbook.

CROWN COPYRIGHT RESERVED 1575   10/59   PUBLISHED BY THE AUTOMOBILE ASSOCIATION

Beveridge Park	1.	Ravenscraig Castle, 15th cent. ruin,	St. Serf's Church ruins; Dysart	7.
Dysart Tolbooth	2.	Pathhead	5.	Site of house where Adam Smith
Museum and Library	3.	Sailors' Walk (N.T. Scot.)	6.	was born	8.
Parish Church	4.		

privateer, sometimes described as the "father" of the American navy, was born in 1747. Here also was born Dr. Craik, Washington's personal medical assistant. The nearby *House on the Shore* has lovely gardens, and there are views across the rocky shores of the firth towards the Lake District mountains. See **Carsethorn** and **Southerness**. *Iter. 72, 73.*

KIRKCALDY, Fife. 51,825. LB.   Map 17, NT 2 9.
E.C. Wed. GOLF. An industrial town and coal port, well-known for the manufacture of linoleum. The town has been a Royal Burgh since 1450. Its boundaries now include *Dysart (q.v.)*, lying beyond Pathhead, to the north-east, while the long main street, which extends for nearly 4 miles in this direction, has caused Kirkcaldy to become known as the "Lang Toun." In the predecessor of a house in the High St., marked by a tablet, was born, in 1723, Adam Smith, author of the "Wealth of Nations." Opposite stands the 17th cent. *Old Dunnikier House*, now used as shops. The Parish Church retains its 13th cent. tower. Thomas Carlyle and his friend Edward Irving were masters at the burgh school, the former having lived in Kirk Wynd, where a tablet has been set up. There are old cottages in this steep lane. Robert Adam, the famous architect, was born at Kirkcaldy, in 1728. Near the harbour are several fine 17th cent. houses, now restored, known as the *Sailors' Walk* (N.T. Scot.). The Links Market fair, held in the spring, is well-known as the largest in Scotland. Behind the town is *Beveridge Park*, noted for motor cycle and small car racing, and giving access into the large park surrounding *Raith House.* **2 m. W.** of Kirkcaldy is *Balwearie Tower*, in ruins, with 7-ft. thick walls. See **Kinghorn** and **Pathhead** (Fife). *Iter. 93, 94, 97, 126, 127, 128, 129, 130, 133, 134.*

KIRKCOLM, Wigtown.   Map 2, NX 0 6.
On the west side of Loch Ryan, in the Rhinns of Galloway peninsula, with the little Loch Connel to the west. Beyond the loch, to the west, is situated *Balsarroch House*, the birthplace, in 1777, of Sir John Ross, the Arctic explorer. **4 m. N.W.** of Kirkcolm is Corsewall Point, with a lighthouse, and in the vicinity stands the ruined *Corsewall Castle*. See **Stranraer**. *Iter. 83.*

KIRKCONNEL, Dumfries. 4,066.   Map 9, NS 7 1.
E.C. Thurs., Sat. A mining town, on the edge of the Ayrshire coalfield, and situated on the River Nith. To the south are slight remains of the ancient Devil's Dyke, the origin of which is not clear. (For *Kirkconnell* Church, see **Kirtlebridge**.) *Iter. 27, 49, 67.*

KIRKCONNELL CHURCH, Dumfries.   Map 4, NY 2 7.
See **Kirtlebridge**.

KIRKCOWAN, Wigtown. 977.   Map 2, NX 3 6.
E.C. Wed. The Tarf Water and the River Bladnoch unite to the south-east of the village. The Church has an external stair to the gallery. There are some remains of the old Church. **5 m. S.S.W.**, beyond the Tarf Water, is the fine, restored *Old Place of Mochrum*, or *Drumwalt Castle*, incorporating much 15th and 16th cent. work. The oldest part consists of two towers of picturesque appearance. Beyond the house is Mochrum Loch and to the west of it lies the Castle Loch. **6 m. N.W.** of Kirkcowan, in the district known as *The Moors*, lies Loch Ronald. See **Glenluce**. *Iter. 81.*

KIRKCUDBRIGHT, Kirkcudbright. 2,526. SB.
Map 3, NX 6 5.
E.C. Thurs. M.D. Fri. GOLF. A market town, Royal Burgh, and the most important town in the *Stewartry (q.v.)*, situated on the River Dee, with a small harbour at the head of Kirkcudbright Bay. The ruined *Maclellan's Castle* (A.M.) is a prominent feature in the town and dates from 1582. It was built by Sir Thomas Maclellan of Bombie, Provost of Kirkcudbright, whose Renaissance tomb is in the Old Greyfriars Kirk. Open summer, 10 to 7: winter, 10 to 4; Sun., after 2. (See note page 90). Two previous castles have both vanished. There is a fine 16th to 17th cent. Tolbooth preserving two old bells; the building is now a memorial to Paul Jones, founder of the American navy, who was at one time imprisoned here. (See **Kirkbean**). The Mercat Cross dates from 1610 and stands on the outside stair of the Tolbooth, which has on its north-west wall the old jougs. There are a number of good 18th cent. houses in the town. *Auchengool House* and *Broughton House* date from the 17th

193

1. Tolbooth and Mercat Cross.   2. MacLellan's Castle.
3. Town Hall.   Information Bureau.

and 18th cents. respectively, and there is also a Museum of interest. At the "*Selkirk Arms*" Hotel, Burns wrote the well-known "Selkirk Grace." In the churchyard of *St. Cuthbert* are the graves of three Covenanters, executed in 1684–85, and also of William Marshall, a noted Galloway tinker, who died at the age of 120. Part of the former "yett", or town entrance has been incorporated in the entrance. In Kirkcudbright Bay is *St. Mary's Isle*, a peninsula, on which is a heronry, situated in private grounds. Farther south, near the open sea, is *Little Ross Island*, on which stands a lighthouse, built by the father of R. L. Stevenson. See **Dundrennan** and **Tongland.** *Iter. 70, 72, 73, 77.*

KIRKFIELDBANK, Lanark.   Map 9, **NS 8** 4.
Situated on the River Clyde, a little to the west of *Lanark* (*q.v.*), the pretty village of *Kirkfieldbank* has old (17th cent.) and new bridges spanning the river in close proximity. The district is noted for its orchard setting, the fruit-growing district extending north-westwards along the river valley, and showing a wealth of blossom in the spring. *Iter. 53, 69.*

KIRKGUNZEON, Kirkcudbright. 467.   Map 3, **NX 8** 6.
Lies on a stream known as the Kirkgunzeon Lane. In the churchyard are numerous tall monuments. Two old towers, *Drumcoltran* (A.M.), 1½ m. N.E., and *Corra*, 1 m. S., stand in the vicinity, the former being a characteristic 16th cent. example. Away to the south-east rises *Criffell*, 1,866 ft., a landmark for many miles around. *Iter. 76.*

KIRKINNER, Wigtown.   Map 2, **NX 4** 5.
There is a Celtic Cross in the churchyard. About a mile and a half to the north, near the Bladnoch Water, are the remains of *Baldoon Castle*, described under *Bladnoch*. *Iter. 82.*

KIRKINTILLOCH, Dunbarton. 15,867. SB. Map 8, **NS 6** 7.
E.C. Wed. GOLF. An ancient town, adjacent to which, on the south side, is *Lenzie*. Both lie in a detached portion of the county, and are on the Forth and Clyde canal, which traverses the flat country to the south of the *Campsies* and the *Kilsyth* hills. The old name of the town was "Caerpentulach," recalling one of the forts on the *Roman Wall* (*q.v.*), which can still be traced in the neighbourhood. A corbiestepped house in the town dates from 1644. *Iter. 98, 113.*

KIRKLAND, Dumfries.   Map 3, **NX 8** 9.
See **Moniaive.** *Iter. 25, 74.*

KIRKLISTON, West Lothian.   Map 9, **NT 1** 7.
On the River Almond, and visited for its Church, of which

parts date back to the 12th cent., notably the west tower, with its saddle-back roof, 17th cent. bell-cote, and also two carved doorways. The tomb of the first Countess of Stair is associated with Scott's "Bride of Lammermoor." To the east, across the Almond, and in Midlothian, lies *Turnhouse*, where the airport for Edinburgh is situated. **2 m. W.** is the ruined *Niddry Castle*, also known as *Niddrie-Seton*, 15th and 17th cent., where Mary, Queen of Scots, accompanied by Lord Seton, passed her first night after escaping from *Loch Leven Castle* (*q.v.*), in 1568, as described in Scott's "The Abbot." **2 m. S.W.** is the mansion of *Newliston*, by Robert Adam. See **Abercorn, Dalmeny** and **Hopetoun House.** *Iter. 91, 95.*

KIRKMADRINE CHURCH, Wigtown.   Map 2, **NX 0** 4.
See **Sandhead.**

KIRKMAIDEN, Wigtown.   Map 2, **NX 1** 3.
The most southerly parish in Scotland, associated with Burns's "Frae Maidenkirk to Johnny Groats." The distance to John o' Groats is some 280 miles. In the churchyard of the ruined Church are some sculptured stones. *Iter. 82.*

KIRKMICHAEL, Ayr.   Map 8, **NS 3** 0.
Iter. 79, 85.

KIRKMICHAEL, Perth. 819.   Map 20, **NO 0** 6.
Lies in a setting of Perthshire hills, on the River Ardle, in Strath Ardle. The road leading northwards, and later westwards, towards Pitlochry, climbs steadily through Glen Brerachan, attaining a height of 1,260 ft., with views of *Ben Vrackie*, 2,757 ft., before descending to the valley of the Tummel. Off Glen Brerachan extends Glen Fernalt, through which one of the former drove-roads led towards north-east Scotland. *Iter. 159, 162, 167, 168.*

KIRK OF MOCHRUM, Wigtown.   Map 2, **NX 3** 4.
The Church contains a fine pulpit of carved oak.

KIRK O'SHOTTS, Lanark.   Map 9, **NS 8** 6.
The Scottish Television Transmitter is situated here. To the south-east lies the Lanark coalfield. *Iter. 15, 18.*

KIRKOSWALD, Ayr. 203.   Map 8, **NS 2** 0.
A pleasant village, famous for its Burns associations. In the churchyard are the graves of "Tam o'Shanter" and "Souter Johnnie," two of Burns's best known characters. The new Church was designed by Robert Adam in 1777. An 18th cent. thatched cottage (N.T. Scot.), the home of Souter Johnnie, contains Burns relics, and in the garden are stone figures of the Burns characters. Open daily, 2 to dusk. (See note page 90). To the south of the village are the farms of *Shanter* and *Jameston*, associated with "Tam" and "Johnnie." See **Alloway** and **Culzean Castle.** *Iter. 55, 68.*

KIRKPATRICK DURHAM, Kirkcudbright.
    Map 3, **NX 7** 7.
In the churchyard is a Covenanter's stone in memory of John Neilson, Laird of Corsock, martyred at Edinburgh in 1666.

KIRKPATRICK FLEMING, Dumfries. 1,067.
    Map 4, **NY 2** 7.
To the west, beyond the Kirtle Water, on the *Cove* estate, is a cave said to have once sheltered Robert Bruce. See **Kirtlebridge.** *Iter. 10, 13, 29, 47, 50, 51.*

KIRKTON, Fife.   Map 17, **NT 2** 8.
Iter. 134.

KIRKTON, Roxburgh.   Map 10, **NT 5** 1.
Iter. 44.

KIRKTON OF GLENISLA, Angus.   Map 20, **NO 2** 6.
Lies on the River Isla, in the heart of Glen Isla, one of the long and picturesque glens of Angus, which thread their way into the remote fastnesses of the eastern Grampians, in the Braes of Angus district. The road up the glen continues northwards, and after four miles a fork to the right rejoins the River Isla, passing the ruins of *Forter Castle*, burnt in 1640. With a deteriorating surface, this road reaches, after five miles, the lodge of *Tulchan*, beyond which a track goes still farther northwards, climbing to the picturesque Canlochan Glen, on the left, under the slopes of *Monega Hill*,

Kirkfieldbank, Lanark. The 17th century bridge over the River Clyde, which has now been superseded by a modern bridge close by

Kirkgunzeon, Kirkcudbright. A tomb with a spire, one of several tall monuments in the churchyard

Kirkoswald, Ayr. Souter Johnnie's House (N.T. Scot.), dating from 1786, a thatched cottage associated with a famous poem by Robert Burns. In the garden are life-size figures of the Souter and his friend Tam o'Shanter (see below)

Kirkliston, West Lothian. Niddry Castle, where Mary, Queen of Scots, spent a night in 1658, after her escape from Loch Leven Castle. It lies 2 miles west, off an unclassified road

Kirkoswald, Ayr. The grave of 'Tam o'Shanter', made famous by Robert Burns, in the churchyard. Nearby is the grave of Tam's friend 'Souter Johnnie' (see above)

Kirkton of Glenisla, Angus. The remains of Forter Castle, perhaps the 'Bonnie Hoose o'Airlie' associated with the lines:

" Lady Ogilvie looks o'er her bower window,
  And O, but she looks weary,
  And there she spied the great Argyle,
  Come to plunder the castle o' Airlie."

The castle was burnt by Argyle in 1640, and stands on B951, some 4 miles to the north-west

Kirktown of Tealing, Angus. The late 16th century dovecote

Kirriemuir, Angus. The birthplace (N.T. Scot.), in 1860, of Sir James Barrie

Kirtlebridge, Dumfries. The 15th century Merkland Cross, said to mark the spot where a Master of Maxwell was murdered in 1484. It stands to the south-east, on an unclassified road off A74

Knockando, Moray. The Church, which has an internal gallery. The Grant brothers, made famous by Charles Dickens as the 'Cheeryble brothers' in 'Nicholas Nickleby' lived in this parish

Knapdale, Argyll. Locks on the Crinan Canal, near the meeting of A816 and B841 at Cairnbaan, on the northern fringe of the district of Knapdale

Kyleakin, Isle of Skye, Inverness. The remains of Castle Moil. It is said to have been built by the daughter of a Norwegian king, who installed a chain across the strait to extract a toll from passing ships, and became known as 'Saucy Mary'

[For KYLE OF LOCHALSH see following plate

PLATE 103 (facing page 195)

2,917 ft., and *Glas Maol*, 3,502 ft. The *Monega Pass*, for long-distance walkers, formerly a drove road for cattle, attains a height of 3,318 ft., and is said to be the highest right-of-way in Scotland. By means of this path, the *Cairnwell Pass* (*q.v.*), on the Aberdeen-Perth border, can be reached. See **Lair**. *Iter. 160, 162.*

KIRKTON OF KINGOLDRUM, Angus. Map 20, NO 3 5.
Iter. 162.

KIRKTOWN OF ALVAH, Banff. Map 27, NJ 6 5.
To the north is Bridge of Alvah, in a very beautiful wooded reach of the River Deveron. **2 m. N.W.** is *Inchdrewer Castle*, where in 1713, the third Lord Banff was burnt to death.

KIRKTOWN OF AUCHTERLESS, Aberdeen.
Map 27, NJ 7 4.
In the Howe of Auchterless, with some stone circles and earth-houses in the vicinity.

KIRKTOWN OF TEALING, Angus. Map 17, NO 4 3.
A late 16th cent. dove-cote and an earth-house of Iron Age date, both (A.M.), are of interest.

KIRKWALL, Orkney. 4,305. SB. Map 33, HY 4 1.
See **Orkney Islands** (Mainland). *Iter. 263, 264, 265, 266.*

KIRK YETHOLM, Roxburgh. Map 11, NT 8 2.
See **Yetholm**.

KIRN, Argyll. Map 14, NS 1 7.
A Firth of Clyde resort, situated to the north-east of *Dunoon* (*q.v.*) to which it is contiguous. See **Hunter's Quay**. *Iter. 102.*

KIRRIEMUIR, Angus. 3,526. SB. Map 20, NO 3 5.
E.C. Thurs. M.D. Fri. GOLF. Famous as the birthplace, in 1860, of Sir James Barrie, and the "Thrums" of his novels. His birthplace, containing relics, together with the washhouse behind, which Barrie used as a theatre, is now (N.T. Scot.) and can be visited. Opposite stands the "Auld Licht Manse," and in the weavers' suburb of Southmuir is the cottage known as "A Window in Thrums." The gable of the "Auld Licht Kirk" is preserved in the new Church, and in the pavilion behind the cemetery, where, in 1937, Barrie was buried, is a camera obscura, open Wed., Sat. and Sun., 2 to 6, June 1 to Sept. 30. (See note page 90). Kirriemuir, which lies at the north-eastern extremity of the fertile valley of *Strathmore* (*q.v.*), or Howe of Angus, has picturesque narrow streets, and is to-day noted for jute-manufacturing. The town makes a good centre for explorations of the beautiful Braes of Angus, which include Glen Glova, Glen Prosen and Glen Isla, all penetrating deep into the lonely eastern Grampian mountains. **1½ m. S.** is *Logie*, a mainly 17th cent. house, with fine gardens. **4 m. N.E.**, near the South Esk river, is *Inverquharity Castle*, a well-preserved four-storeyed tower, dating from c. 1450. See **Clova Church, Dykehead, Edzell, Glamis** and **Kirkton of Glenisla**. *Iter. 161, 162, 166.*

1. Birthplace of Sir   2. "A Window in Thrums."
   James Barrie.   3. Camera obscura.

KIRTLEBRIDGE, Dumfries. Map 4, NY 2 7.
Near the Kirtle Water, a little to the south-east, stand the old towers of *Robgill* and *Bonshaw*. The former, dating from the 16th cent., is now incorporated in a modern mansion, and the latter dates from the same period. **2½ m. N.E.**, by the Kirtle Water, is the ruined Church (A.M.) of *Kirkconnell*,

which is visited for the graves of "Fair Helen of Kirkconnell Lee" and her lover. **1 m. S.E.**, off the Gretna road, and on a by-road, stands the notable 15th cent. *Merkland Cross* (A.M.). *Iter. 10, 13, 29, 50, 51.*

KISHORN, Ross and Cromarty. Map 23, NG 8 4.
Known also as *Courthill*, and situated near the head of Loch Kishorn, an inlet of the larger Loch Carron. The view westwards, over the Inner Sound towards Skye, is very fine, and above the loch rise *Sgurr a'Charaochain*, 2,539 ft., and its rugged outlier *The Cioch*, in the *Applecross* hills of red Torridon sandstone. Near the head of the loch is *Rassall Ashwood*, now a Nature Reserve and forming the most northerly habitat of this tree in Great Britain. Through this tiny village passes the road leading to *Applecross* (*q.v.*), which makes the climb over the wild and lofty Pass of the Cattle, described under *Tornapress*. The miniature Pass of Kishorn is traversed by the road leading eastwards from Kishorn to *Lochcarron* (*q.v.*). See **Shieldaig**. *Iter. 219, 223.*

KNAPDALE, Argyll. Map 7, NR 7 6 etc.
A small district, consisting mainly of low hills, lying between the Sound of Jura and *Loch Fyne* (*q.v.*), and separated from the *Kintyre* (*q.v.*) peninsula, to the south, by West Loch Tarbert. Knapdale is almost encircled by roads around its perimeter, but only one road penetrates into the interior, that leading from Ardrishaig to the inner reach of Loch Killisport, on the west coast. The *Crinan* (*q.v.*) Canal, linking Loch Gilp and Loch Fyne with the Sound of Jura, lies on the northern fringe of Knapdale. See **Ardrishaig, Kilmory Knap** and **Tayvallich**. *Iter. 122.*

KNOCKANDHU, Banff. Map, 26 NJ 2 2.
Iter. 169, 177, 192.

KNOCKANDO CHURCH, Moray. Map 26, NJ 1 4.
The galleried Parish Church preserves carved slabs in the churchyard. The village lies a little to the south, near the winding course of the Spey in one of its most delightfully wooded reaches, with *Ben Rinnes*, 2,755 ft., rising away to the south-east beyond the river valley. *Iter. 171.*

KNOYDART, Inverness. Map 23, NG 7 0 etc.
This very picturesque and mountainous tract of the Western Highlands, dominated by *Sgurr na Ciche*, 3,410 ft., and *Ladhar Bheinn*, 3,343 ft., lies between *Loch Hourn* (*q.v.*) and *Loch Nevis* (*q.v.*). and is sometimes referred to under the name of the "Rough Bounds," possibly due to its comparative inaccessibility, though the fringe of the area is traversed by the narrow and rough road leading from *Tomdoun* (*q.v.*) to *Kinloch Hourn* (*q.v.*). Cattle ranching on an extensive scale is being introduced into the district. Some of the finest mountain and loch scenery in Scotland is to be found in Knoydart, and has been somewhat affected as a result of a new hydro-electric scheme now being operated in the district around *Loch Quoich* (*q.v.*).

KYLEAKIN, Isle of Skye, Inverness. Map 23, 18 7 2.
The arrival point for the car ferry from *Kyle of Lochalsh* (*q.v.*), Kyleakin overlooks the narrow strait of Kyle Akin, the name being derived from an early King of Norway, who sailed through the narrows, in 1263, on his way to *Largs* (*q.v.*). The ruined *Castle Moil* stands on the shore to the east, with a fine view up the waters of Loch Alsh, which extend inland towards the mountains of *Kintail* (*q.v.*). In the background rises *Beinn na Cailleach*, 2,396 ft., a notable viewpoint, beyond which are the narrows of Kyle Rhea. *Iter. 251.*

KYLE OF LOCHALSH, Ross and Cromarty. 350.
Map 23, NG 7 2.
E.C. Thurs. Finely situated at the western extremity of Loch Alsh, where the narrow strait of Kyle Akin, crossed by a car ferry, separates the mainland from *Kyleakin* (*q.v.*) in Skye. Kyle of Lochalsh, the *Wester Ross* railhead of the line from Inverness, is sometimes known as the "Gateway to Skye," and is the terminal point of one branch of the "Road to the Isles." As well as being a fishing port, there are regular steamer services to Mallaig, Skye, and both the Inner and Outer Hebrides. Motor boats provide a service to Loch Toscaig for *Applecross* (*q.v.*). From numerous points in the

STROME FERRY, DORNIE PLOCKTON
A.87

KYLE OF LOCHALSH

Hotel.

Sta.
Pier

BROADFORD, PORTREE

A.850

Pier

Kyleakin

S K Y E

N

Kyle

Ferry

Akin

Loch
Alsh

CROWN COPYRIGHT RESERVED   R.B.60

vicinity magnificent views towards the Coolins of Skye, and over *Loch Alsh* (*q.v.*), Loch Carron and the Inner Sound, with the Crowlin Islands, can be obtained. Beyond the Crowlins rise the lofty *Applecross* hills and westwards lies the narrow island of Raasay. Kyle of Lochalsh is situated partly within the extensive N.T. Scot. estate of *Balmacara* (*q.v.*). See **Plockton**. *Iter. 207, 220, 221, 222, 251.*

KYLERHEA, Isle of Skye, Inverness. Map 23, **NG 7** 2.
On the narrow strait of Kyle Rhea, facing Glenelg in Inverness-shire. From here, a narrow road, with good views, climbs very steeply (1 in 5) to over 900 ft. through Glen Arroch, before descending to the coast road linking *Kyleakin* (*q.v.*) with *Broadford* (*q.v.*). *Beinn na Cailleach*, 2,396 ft., rises to the north-west of Kylerhea and commands a fine prospect. A car ferry, operated in the summer, connects with *Glenelg* (*q.v.*), on the mainland.

KYLESKU, Sutherland. Map 28, **NC 2** 3.
One of the most beautiful and remote places in the Northern Highlands, where the narrows of Loch Cairnbawn, an inlet of the picturesque Eddrachillis Bay, are guarded by several small islands. The waters are crossed by a car ferry to Kylestrome, opposite which is the small island of Garbh. To the east, the waters of Loch Glendhu and Loch Glencoul penetrate deep into the wild and roadless hills in the manner of Norwegian fjords. The distant peak of *Ben Leoid*, 2,597 ft., overlooks the latter, and at its head is the little-known 600-ft. high waterfall of *Eas-coul-Aulin*, descending to a valley beyond Loch Beag, and approachable only on foot or by boat. It is considered to be about thrice the height of Niagara when in full spate. South of Kylesku, the road to *Inchnadamph* (*q.v.*) follows the pass between *Quinag*, 2,653 ft. and *Glasven*, 2,541 ft. Westwards goes the picturesque, but rough, hilly and narrow road along Loch Cairnbawn's southern shores leading towards *Drumbeg* (*q.v.*) and *Lochinver* (*q.v.*), providing magnificent views, both inland towards the mountains and out to sea for the whole of the distance. See **Scourie**. *Iter. 225, 227.*

SCOURIE, DURNESS

Kylestrome

A.894

Garbh
Island

Kylesku
Ferry

Loch
Cairnbawn

Inn

Unapool

KYLESKU

Loch Glendhu

Loch Glencoul

N

A.894

R.B.60
CROWN COPYRIGHT RESERVED

LOCHINVER, ULLAPOOL

KYLES OF BUTE, Argyll; Bute. Map 7, **NR 9** 7 etc.
The name given to the picturesque, curved, strait traversed by the Clyde steamers, which encircles the northern extremity of the island of *Bute* (*q.v.*), washing the shores of the *Cowal* (*q.v.*) peninsula of Argyll, on the mainland. The Kyles of Bute, and the wider expanse of the Firth of Clyde, to the east, are a favourite venue of yachtsmen and regattas are held in the summer. About halfway along the coast of Cowal, the inlet of Loch Riddon bites into the land, and farther east is Loch Striven, which penetrates even deeper, to the north,

with a background of pleasant green hills. At the mouth of Loch Striven is Strone Point, a little to the west of which lies *South Hall*, where the woods have been so planted as to show the positions of the opposing armies at the battle of Waterloo. Between the two inlets stands *Colintraive* (*q.v.*), with a steamer pier, and also a ferry service to *Rhubodach* (*q.v.*), in Bute. The small *Burnt* Islands almost block the channel to the west, facing the northern tip of Bute, where two standing stones, known as the " Maids of Bute," form prominent landmarks. See **Rothesay** and **Tighnabruaich**. *Iter. 102, 103, 241.*

KYLESTROME, Sutherland. Map 28, **NC 2** 3.
The wild and lonely road to the north-west passes several small lochans before reaching the sea at Calva Bay, an inlet of the larger, island-studded Eddrachillis Bay. See **Kylesku**. *Iter. 225.*

LADYBANK, Fife. 1,177. SB. Map 17, **NO 3** 0.
GOLF. Lies in the fertile Howe of Fife, to the north-east of the *Lomond* hills. **3 m.** N. is the notable *Melville House*, now a school, described under *Monimail*.

LADYKIRK, Berwick. Map 11, **NT 8** 4.
On the River Tweed. The picturesque cruciform Church dates from 1500, but the tower was probably completed by William Adam in 1743. The building, built entirely of stone, in order to obviate the risk of damage by fire, is said to have been erected by James IV as a thank-offering for his escape from drowning in the river nearby. On the Northumberland side of the river is the ruined Norham Castle. *Iter. 46.*

LAGAVULIN, Isle of Islay, Argyll. Map 6, **NR 4** 4.
See **Port Ellen**. *Iter. 245.*

LAGG, Isle of Arran, Bute. Map 7, **NR 9** 2.
Stands near the south shores of the island, in a setting of woods and tropical plants, with the village of *Kilmory*, on the Water of Kilmory, situated a little to the north-east. Still farther east on the coast is Bennan Head, the most southerly point of Arran, on a rocky stretch of coast. North-west of Lagg, within a mile, diverges the inland road through Glen Scorrodale leading to *Lamlash* (*q.v.*). The coast road continues to Tor Chaistel, a barrow with two stone circles, on the way to *Blackwaterfoot* (*q.v.*). *Iter. 242.*

LAGGAN BRIDGE, Inverness. Map 19, **NN 6** 9.
See **Drumgask** and **Loch Laggan**. *Iter. 208.*

LAGGAN LOCKS, Inverness. Map 18, **NN 2** 9.
These locks lie on the *Caledonian Canal* (*q.v.*) at the north-west extremity of *Loch Lochy* (*q.v.*). The main mountain ridge of Scotland, known as Drum Alban, cuts across the Great Glen, or *Glen More* (*q.v.*), at this point, forming an important watershed at a height of 115 ft., rivers to the west flowing into the Atlantic, and those to the east entering the North Sea. **1 m.** S.W., on the north bank of Loch Lochy, is *Kilfinnan*, where the mausoleum is the burial ground of the Glengarry chiefs. *Iter. 210, 214, 220.*

LAG TOWER, Dumfries. Map 3, **NX 8** 8.
See **Dunscore**.

LAIDE, Ross and Cromarty. Map 22, **NG 8** 9.
Iter. 206, 222.

LAIGH OF MORAY, Moray. Map 26, **NJ 2** 6 etc.
The name given to the fertile, flat countryside, watered by the River Lossie, and bordering the shores of the Outer Moray Firth. In the centre of the district stands the town of *Elgin* (*q.v.*).

LAIR, Perth. Map 20, **NO 1** 5.
Situated in Glen Shee, surrounded by hills, with *Mount Blair*, 2,441 ft., to the east. A road leads eastwards from here across the River Shee to enter Angus and reach, within a few miles, the beautiful valley of Glen Isla, which is traversed by a picturesque road for the greater part of its length. See **Kirkton of Glenisla**. *Iter. 141, 152, 160, 162, 167, 168.*

LAIRG, Sutherland. 305. Map 29, **NC 5** 0.
E.C. Wed. A network of roads stretches westwards and northwards across the country from *Lairg*, leading to the wild and beautiful scenery of the far North-West Highlands. The featureless Loch Shin, where hydro-electric develop-

Kylesku, Sutherland. The meeting of Lochs Cairnbawn, Glencoul and Glendhu. The narrows here are crossed by a car ferry

Kyle of Lochalsh, Ross and Cromarty. The car ferry across Loch Alsh to Kyleakin, in the island of Skye

Lag Tower, Dumfries. This ruined 16th century Nithsdale tower was once the seat of Sir Robert Grierson (1650–1736), a persecutor of the Covenanters. It stands on an unclassified road, 1½ miles north-east of Dunscore

Ladykirk, Berwick. The Church, which James IV had built c. 1500 as a thanks-offering for his escape from drowning in the River Tweed. It was built entirely of stone to avoid the risk of fire

Laigh of Moray, Moray. The rebuilt Muckle Cross (1888) at Elgin, in the flat country near the Outer Moray Firth. It is associated with the raising, in 1778, of the Macleod Highlanders, later the Highland Light Infantry

Kyles of Bute, Argyll; Bute. A view of the small resort of Tighnabruaich, facing the island of Bute. Its Gaelic name means ' House on the Brae,' and refers to the solitary house which once stood there

PLATE 104 (facing page 196)

Lamlash, Isle of Arran, Bute. Holy Island, in Lamlash Bay, which is associated with the naval battle of Largs against the Norwegians in 1263

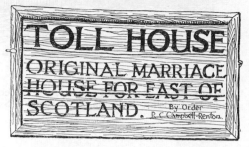

Lamberton, Berwick. The notice board on the former toll house at Lamberton Bar, where runaway marriages used to be performed

Lamington, Lanark. The Norman doorway of the old Church

Lake of Menteith, Perth. A view of the 13th century Inchmahome Priory, on an island in one of the only two 'lakes' in Scotland. Mary, Queen of Scots, was sent here at the age of 5, attended by her servants, the Four Marys

Lammermuir Hills, Berwick; East Lothian. The former Douglas stronghold of Cranshaws Tower, in Berwickshire, which is still inhabited. It stands on B6355, the road which crosses the hills to link Gifford with Duns

Lammermuir Hills, Berwick; East Lothian. The old watch-house of the Church at Spott, erected as a protection against body snatchers. The village stands at the northern extremity of the hills, near Dunbar, in East Lothian

[For LANARK see following plate

PLATE 105 (facing page 197)

ments have taken place, extends in a north-westerly direction away from the village, and in the distance rises *Ben More Assynt*, 3,273 ft., Sutherland's highest mountain. Lairg is known to anglers, and is a busy centre for local bus routes. Important lamb sales take place here. Southwards from Loch Shin flows the turbulent River Shin, in a wooded setting. There are numerous remains of archaeological interest, especially hut circles and tumuli, in the neighbourhood, notably to the north of Lairg, where the Scourie and Tongue roads fork, the latter continuing northwards thro ugh Strath Tirry towards the low *Crask* (*q.v.*) Pass. See **Inveran Bridge, Overscaig** and **Rosehall**. *Iter.* 224, 229, 230, 232, 233.

LAIRIG GHRU PASS, Aberdeen; Inverness.

Map 20, **NH 9 0**.

This famous pass, essentially for hardy long-distance walkers only, links Speyside with Deeside by cutting through the heart of the great *Cairngorm* (*q.v.*) range, the distance from *Aviemore* (*q.v.*) to *Braemar* (*q.v.*) being about 28 miles. The northern extremity of the pass is overshadowed to the east by the great cliffs of *Cairn Lochan*, 3,983 ft., and also by the *Lurcher's Crag*, 3,448 ft., the path descending from this point into the woodlands of the great forest of *Rothiemurchus* (*q.v.*). The track reaches a height of more than 2,700 ft. between the shoulders of *Ben Macdhui*, 4,296 ft., and *Braeriach*, 4,248 ft., amid a wilderness of huge boulders, near which are situated the Pools of Dee. These are not, however, the source of the river, which rises high up in the remote fastnesses of Braeriach, at a height of more than 4,000 ft. On the descent towards Glen Dee and the extensive Mar Forest, to the south of the great peaks, rises the *Devil's Point*, 3,303 ft., to the west. Below it is situated the ruined Corrour bothy, well known as a shelter to walkers. The path then keeps near the Dee and follows the river to *Inverey* (*q.v.*). Another branch diverges south-eastwards from the bothy and goes through Glen Lui Beg and Glen Lui to reach Inverey. See **Coylumbridge**.

LAKE OF MENTEITH, Perth. Map 15, **NN 5 0** and **NS 5 9**. See **Port of Menteith**. *Iter.* 109, 111, 139.

LAMANCHA, Peebles. Map 9, **NT 2 5**. Situated a little to the west is *Lamancha House*, dating from 1663. *Iter.* 10, 14, 37.

LAMBERTON, Berwick. Map 11, **NT 9 5**. On the Great North Road, and at the Border between Scotland and England, situated a little to the north of *Berwick-upon-Tweed* (*q.v.*). At the former *Lamberton Bar*, the toll-keeper once performed runaway marriages similar to those which took place at *Gretna* (*q.v.*). The coastline in the vicinity is characterized by lofty cliffs. *Iter.* 1, 2.

LAMB HOLM, Orkney. Map 33, **HY 4 0**. *Iter.* 266.

LAMINGTON, Lanark. Map 9, **NS 9 3**. A small Clydesdale village, looking towards *Tinto Hill*, 2,335 ft., a noted viewpoint to the west, and also to *Culter Fell*, 2,454 ft., situated among a network of lesser heights away to the east. The Church, once visited by Robert Burns, has a good Norman doorway, and retains the jougs. *Lamington Tower*, in ruins, to the north, carries the date 1589. *Iter.* 25.

LAMLASH, Isle of Arran, Bute. 1,000. Map 7, **NS 0 3**. GOLF. The largest village in Arran, attractively situated on Lamlash Bay, with bathing, sheltered by Kingscross Point to the south and Clauchlands Point to the north. From the former, Bruce is said to have embarked for the mainland in 1307. In the bay, associated with the naval battle of *Largs* (*q.v.*) in 1263, when Haco of Norway rallied his defeated fleet, lies *Holy Island*, on which *Mullach Mor* attains 1,030 ft. Below the hill, facing the bay, is the cave of *St. Molus*, with Runic inscriptions. Inland from Lamlash, a road ascends through the Monamore Glen to nearly 1,000 ft., a steep, twisting climb, with a gradient of 1 in 6, prior to descending through Glen Scorrodale towards the south-west coast, which is reached near *Lagg* (*q.v.*). The road to *Brodick* (*q.v.*) keeps inland, but a path goes round by the coast, affording fine views, and traversing the fringe of the low *Clauchland* hills to the west. See **Whiting Bay**. *Iter.* 242.

LAMMERMUIR HILLS, Berwick; East Lothian. Map 10, **NT 5 5** etc. See **Cranshaws, Duns, Garvald, Gifford, Longformacus** and **Soutra Hill**. *Iter.* 3.

LANARK, Lanark. 8,201. SB. Map 9, **NS 8 4**. E.C. Thurs. M.D. Mon. GOLF. This Clydesdale town, which is of considerable antiquity, though visible relics of its past are lacking, stands high above the banks of the winding River Clyde, which flows through what are perhaps its most picturesque reaches within a short distance of Lanark. The Parish Church dates from 1777, and has a large statue of Wallace, who is said to have lived in the town. There are slight remains of the 12th cent. *St. Kentigern's* Church. Pageants are held to celebrate Lanimer Day, or " Beating the Bounds," which is held on the Thursday following June 6. " Whuppity Scoorie," another local festival, possibly associated with ancient pagan rites, and including a children's race round the Parish Church, takes place annually on March 1. To the west of Lanark, the Mouse Water, spanned by an ancient bridge, possibly Roman, flows into the Clyde, and nearby are the lofty Cartland

1. R.C. Church.
2. St. Kentigern's Church, ruins.
3. Parish Church, with Wallace Statue.
4. Information Bureau.

Crags, overlooking a deep chasm. The racecourse is situated on Lanark Moor, where there is a small loch. **1 m. S.** of the town is *New Lanark*, founded in 1784, with its textile mills, beyond which are the picturesque Falls of Clyde, including Cora Linn, the finest, and also the Bonnington Falls. Above Cora Linn is situated the ruined *Cora Castle*, associated with one of Wordsworth's poems. The Stonebyres Linn Fall lies **2 m. W.** of Lanark, and nearby is *Blackhill* (N.T. Scot.), a fine viewpoint. The mansion of *Stonebyres* is 15th to 16th cent., with large later additions. All the various Falls have been affected by developments in hydro-electric schemes. *Braxfield House*, on the way to New Lanark, is associated with R. L. Stevenson's " Weir of Hermiston." A little to the west of Lanark, on the south bank of the Clyde, is the pretty village of *Kirkfieldbank* (*q.v.*), in a district of orchards, which extend along the river valley in a north-westerly direction. See **Crossford** and **Douglas**. *Iter. 22, 23, 37, 48, 50, 53, 54, 69, 86.*

LANGBANK, Renfrew.   Map 8, **NS 3 7.**
E.C. Wed. *Iter. 59, 65, 88, 112, 113.*

LANGHOLM, Dumfries. 2,365. SB.   Map 4, **NY 3 8.**
E.C. Wed. An Eskdale town, noted for woollens, and also an angling resort, situated on the wooded River Esk, where it is joined by the Wauchope Water from the south-west, and also by the picturesque Ewes Water from the north. A picturesque Border Riding ceremony is held annually, having been inaugurated in 1816, and the town is associated with the 16th cent. Border reiver, Johnny Armstrong. (See **Canonbie** and **Teviothead**). The poet Hugh MacDiarmid was born in the town. *Whita Hill*, 1,162 ft., to the east, a splendid viewpoint, is crowned by a monument to General Sir John Malcolm, who is buried in Westminster Abbey. There are very scanty remains of *Langholm Castle*, on the Castle Holm. **2½ m. N.N.W.,** near a bend of the Esk, is the mote of the former *Barntalloch Castle*. *Iter. 11, 12, 30, 45.*

LAPHROAIG, Isle of Islay, Argyll.   Map 6, **NR 3 4.**
Iter. 245.

LARACHBEG, Argyll.   Map 12, **NM 6 4.**
A tiny *Morven* (*q.v.*) clachan, situated in a valley between Loch Aline and Loch Arienas, where smallholdings were given to many of the inhabitants of the island of *St. Kilda* (*q.v.*) following its evacuation in 1930. At the head of Loch Aline is the 15th cent. *Kinlochaline Castle*, a square, turreted structure. The road leading north-eastwards towards *Loch Linnhe* (*q.v.*) climbs through the hills by way of Gleann Geal, and later divides into two branches, the main one traversing the south-east shores of *Loch Sunart* (*q.v.*). See **Lochaline**. *Iter. 218.*

LARBERT, Stirling. 3,416.   Map 16, **NS 8 8.**
E.C. Wed. GOLF. Known for the large Carron ironworks, at which guns used in the battle of Waterloo were cast. For plan, see **Falkirk**. *Iter. 95, 97, 98.*

LARGO, Fife.   Map 17, **NO 4 0.**
E.C. Wed. Situated on Largo Bay, and consisting of Lower Largo, on the coast, and Upper, or Kirkton of Largo, a little inland, dominated by the cone of *Largo Law*, 948 ft., a good viewpoint. The Parish Church, at Upper Largo, has a 16th cent. chancel, tower and spire, the last-named added in 1623. There is also a Celtic cross-slab near the church-yard gate. Sir Andrew Wood, of naval fame, was buried here, in 1515, and of his once-great Castle, only a tower, with its conical cap, still remains. To the west of the Church, beyond Largo House, is Kiels Den, a charming glen. In Lower Largo was born, in 1676, Alexander Selkirk, the prototype of Defoe's " Robinson Crusoe," and a statue to him stands near the harbour. In the 15th cent., a naval victory over the English was gained by Sir Andrew Wood, among his ships being the " Great Michael," launched in 1507 at *Newhaven* (*q.v.*). **1 m. N.W.** of Upper Largo stands the old *Pitcruvie Castle*. See **Lundin Links**. For *Iter.* see *Upper Largo*.

LARGOWARD, Fife.   Map 17, **NO 4 0.**
Iter. 128, 132.

LARGS, Ayr. 7,739 SB.   Map 8, **NS 2 5.**
E.C. Wed. GOLF. A popular Clyde coast yachting resort on the Gogo Water and Largs Bay, facing the island of *Great Cumbrae* (See **Millport**), in the Firth of Clyde. The beach is pebble. The splendid mausoleum of the former Parish Church of *St. Columba* dates from 1636, and is known as the *Skelmorlie* Aisle (A.M.). There is a painted wooden roof, and the tombs of Sir Robert Montgomery, the founder, and also of his wife, are in the aisle. This remarkable monument dates from 1636. Another fine monument is to the Boyles of Kelburne. A round tower, situated at

1. St. Columba's Parish Church, with   2. Information Bureau.
   Mausoleum or Skelmorlie Aisle.   3. Municipal Chambers.

Bowen Craig to the south of the town, commemorates a battle in which the Norsemen failed to effect a permanent landing in 1263. As a result of this battle, Haco, the King of Norway, lost the Hebrides and the Isle of Man. The Colm's Day Festival in honour of St. Columba is held generally in the early summer. To the north-east stood formerly *Brisbane House*, birthplace of Sir Thomas Brisbane, governor of New South Wales, who gave his name to the Australian city of Brisbane. In the background lies a large moorland area, in which the highest point is the *Hill of Stake*, 1,711 ft. The town makes a good centre for excursions by steamer, notably to the *Kyles of Bute* (*q.v.*). See **Fairlie**. *Iter. 58, 66, 88.*

LARKHALL, Lanark. 14,309.   Map 9, **NS 7 5.**
E.C. Wed. A mining town, on the Avon Water. *Iter. 51.*

LASSWADE, Midlothian. 5,874. SB. with Bonnyrigg.
          Map 10, **NT 3 6.**
Situated in the deep valley of the North Esk River. Here, Scott lived in a cottage for six years, between 1798 and 1804, being visited during the period by Wordsworth. *Lasswade* is thought to be the " Gandercleugh " of his " Tales of my Landlord." In the churchyard of the ruined Norman

Lanark, Lanark. Remains of the 12th century St. Kentigern's Church, where William Wallace may have been married

Largo, Fife. The 'Robinson Crusoe' statue. Alexander Selkirk, the prototype of Daniel Defoe's hero, was born at Lower Largo, in 1676

Largo, Fife. The tower of the former castle of Sir Andrew Wood, the 15th century naval commander of the 'Yellow Carvel'

Lanark, Lanark. The 18th century Parish Church, with its statue of William Wallace. The church is connected with the local 'Whuppity Scoorie' festival, held annually in March

Largs, Ayr. The Skelmorlie Aisle of the old Parish Church, which contains the tomb of the founder, Sir Robert Montgomery, who died in 1639

Lasswade, Midlothian. Mavisbush, now De Quincey cottage, where Thomas de Quincey, the writer, lived between 1840 and 1859. It stands at Polton, 2 miles south-west of Lasswade, on an unclassified road

PLATE 106 (facing page 198)

Latheron, Caithness. A whalebone archway near Latheronwheel, on the south-east side of A9. It was taken from a whale washed ashore in 1869

Lauder, Berwick. The entrance gates on A697, south-east of the town, to the 16th to 19th century Thirlestane Castle, which stands in large policies

Laurieston, Kirkcudbright. The monument to S. R. Crockett, the author, who died in 1914 at Tarascon, in France. He is buried in Balmaghie churchyard, near the shores of Loch Ken, to the east

Laxford Bridge, Sutherland. A view of the conical peak of Ben Stack, which rises to 2,364 feet beyond the western shores of Loch Stack

Leadhills, Lanark. A churchyard gravestone in memory of John Taylor, who lived to the age of 137

Leith (Edinburgh), Midlothian. The so-called Signal Tower, at the corner of Tower St. and The Shore, which Robert Mylne erected originally as a windmill in 1686

[For LEITH see also following plate
[For LATHERON see also Plate 175

PLATE 107 (facing page 199)

Church are the graves of William Drummond, the poet, and Henry Dundas, 1st Viscount Melville, a famous late 18th cent. benevolent despot, and virtual ruler of the country, whose home was the nearby 19th cent. *Melville Castle*, now an hotel. **2 m. S.W.**, near the river, is *Mavisbush*, now De Quincey Cottage, where De Quincey lived between 1840 and 1859. **2½ m. S.W.**, also near the river, is *Hawthornden House*, rebuilt in 1638, by Drummond (see above), and beautifully situated on a height overlooking the North Esk, in a setting of lovely gardens. An ancient bell tower is incorporated in the house, and below are artificial caves of great age. In the grounds stands Ben Jonson's tree, recalling the poet's visit in 1618-19.

LATHERON, Caithness.   Map 30, **ND 1** 3.
On a hill above the Church stands a detached tower, in which the church bells were formerly hung. Near the Post Office is a large Standing Stone of great antiquity. The moorland road which links Latheron with Thurso, on the Pentland Firth, was built in the late 18th cent. There are numerous hut circles and Pictish remains in the neighbourhood. **1 m. S.S.W.** is *Latheronwheel*, or *Janetstown*, with a quaint little harbour. **2½ m. N.E.**, on the rock-bound coast, is the ruined *Forse Castle*, and farther inland are some recently excavated stone structures of very early date, known as *The Wag* (A.M.). *Iter. 200, 236.*

LATHONES, Fife.   Map 17, **NO 4** 0.
Iter. 128.

LAUDER, Berwick. 580. SB.   Map 10, **NT 5** 4.
E.C. Thurs. A small Royal Burgh, the only example in the county, situated in Lauderdale, on the Leader Water, which flows southwards from the *Lammermuirs*, on the East Lothian border. It forms a good angling centre, and a Border Riding ceremony is still held annually. There is a curious little Tolbooth, approached by a flight of steps. The cruciform Church, dating from 1573 and later, may be partly the work of Sir William Bruce. In 1482, several favourites of James III were hanged from the former Lauder Bridge by the Earl of Angus, who earned for himself the soubriquet of " Bell-the-Cat." James Guthrie, minister at Lauder from 1642 to 1649, was the first Covenanter martyr to be recorded on the Greyfriars churchyard monument in Edinburgh. He was executed in 1661. Outside Lauder is the park of *Thirlestane Castle*, an imposing structure, dating from 1595, 1675 and 1841, with a fine west front by Sir William Bruce. The castle is associated with the ancient tower of *Thirlestane*, situated **2½ m. E.** of Lauder, off the Greenlaw road. A fine moorland road leads westwards from Lauder, reaching a height of over 1,100 ft., and later descending to the Gala Water at *Stow* (*q.v.*). See **Douglas** and **Gordon**. *Iter. 4, 9, 13, 36.*

LAURENCEKIRK, Kincardine. 1,419. SB.
      Map 21, **NO 7** 7.
E.C. Wed. **M.D.** Mon. A small town, founded in 1779, once noted for the manufacture of snuff-boxes, and situated in the fertile Howe of the Mearns. To the south-east rises *Garvock Hill*, 915 ft., topped by the Johnstone Tower. See **Drumlithie**. *Iter. 151.*

LAURIESTON, Kirkcudbright. 122.   Map 3, **NX 6** 6.
A *Galloway* (*q.v.*) village, to the north of which lies the little Woodhall Loch. Its name prior to the 18th cent. was *Clachanpluck*. There is a monument to S. T. Crockett, the author, whose novels introduced much local colour, and who lies buried in the churchyard at *Balmaghie*, situated **3 m. E.**, near the shores of Loch Ken. In the churchyard are also Covenanters' gravestones. *Iter. 77, 95.*

LAURISTON CASTLE, Midlothian.   Map 9, **NT 2** 7.
See **Barnton**.

LAWERS, Perth.   Map 15, **NN 6** 3.
Situated on *Loch Tay* (*q.v.*), at the foot of *Ben Lawers*, 3,984 ft. (N.T. Scot.), the highest mountain in the county, and noted especially for its botanical interest. The mountain can be easily ascended from Lawers, while the view from the summit is very rewarding, including the whole of the *Breadalbane* (*q.v.*) country and much of the *Grampians* (*q.v.*).

From the summit, a descent can be made westwards to the tiny Lochan na Lairige, on the steep, narrow and rough mountain road linking Loch Tay with *Bridge of Balgie* (*q.v.*), in Glen Lyon. The slopes of Ben Lawers and its satellites provide good ski-ing in suitable conditions, and Coire Odhar, on *Beinn Ghlas*, 3,657 ft., is used by the Scottish Ski Club. To the west of Lochan na Lairige rise the peaks of the *Tarmachan* group, reaching a height of 3,421 ft. *Iter. 120, 138.*

LAXAY, Isle of Lewis, Ross and Cromarty.
Iter. 256.   Map 32, **NB 3** 2.

LAXDALE, Isle of Lewis, Ross and Cromarty.
Iter. 258, 260.   Map 32, **NB 4** 3.

LAXFORD BRIDGE, Sutherland.   Map 28, **NC 2** 4.
This remote place in the Northern Highlands is situated on the Laxford River, a famous salmon stream, which flows through Laxford Bay into the island-studded Loch Laxford, a little to the north-west. To the south-east rises the gneiss cone of *Ben Stack*, 2,364 ft., below which is Loch Stack, drained by the Laxford River, and along the south shore of which goes the picturesque road leading south-eastwards to *Lairg* (*q.v.*). North of the loch is *Arcuil*, 2,580 ft., with its rough quartzite scree slopes, and farther east rises *Meall Horn*, 2,548 ft., both in the great Reay Forest. The whole district is noted especially for a multiplicity of tiny lochans, forming a fisherman's paradise. From the summits of the mountains in the vicinity the view shows almost more water than land, the latter consisting largely of bare outcrops of Archaean grey gneiss, some of the oldest rocks in the world. See **Rhiconich**. *Iter. 225, 229.*

LAXO, Shetland.   Map 33, **HU 4** 6.
See **Shetland Islands** (Mainland). *Iter. 270.*

LEADBURN, Midlothian.   Map 9, **NT 2** 5.
Lies in a moorland district. **2 m. S.W.**, over the Peebleshire border, is *Whim*, a fine 18th cent. Adam mansion. See **Lamancha**. *Iter. 10, 14, 24, 37.*

LEADERFOOT BRIDGE, Roxburgh.   Map 10, **NT 5** 3.
Iter. 4, 33, 36, 41, 43.

LEADHILLS, Lanark. 670.   Map 9, **NS 8** 1.
E.C. Thurs. **GOLF.** This pleasant village was once noted especially for its lead, though gold and silver have also been extensively mined as long ago as the 12th cent. It is situated at a height of 1,350 ft., and is exceeded in height only by its near neighbour to the south-west, *Wanlockhead* (*q.v.*), the road linking the two villages attaining a height of 1,531 ft. on the Lanark-Dumfries boundary. A stone in the churchyard is in memory of John Taylor, who died at the age of 137 years. To the south-east rise the rounded *Lowther* hills, of which *Green Lowther*, 2,403 ft., and *Lowther Hill*, 2,377 ft., are the principal summits, commanding wide views over the Lowlands and into Cumberland. In the late 17th cent. these hills were a refuge for the persecuted Covenanters. The golf course, at an altitude of 1,500 ft., is said to be the highest in Britain. William Symington, a pioneer of steam navigation, was born at Leadhills in 1763, and is commemorated by a monument below the churchyard. Here also was born, in 1686, Allan Ramsay, author of the " Gentle Shepherd," and founder of an early Edinburgh theatre. See **Bowling** and **Mennock**. *Iter. 48, 49.*

LECHT ROAD, Aberdeen; Banff.   Map 26, **NJ 2** 1.
See **Cock Bridge**. *Iter. 141, 160, 174, 176, 191.*

LEDAIG, Argyll.   Map 14, **NM 9** 3.
Iter. 124.

LEGERWOOD, Berwick.   Map 10, **NT 5** 4.
The Church has a Norman chancel arch and there is a 17th-century Ker monument. *Corsbie Tower* is a ruined 16th-century stronghold.

LEITH (Edinburgh), Midlothian. 62,472. Map 17, **NT 2** 7.
E.C. Wed. Known officially as the *Port of Leith*, the town has been, since 1920, incorporated within the Edinburgh boundaries. It suffered many attacks from the English, and was devastated in 1544 and 1547. Through the town

flows the Water of Leith, dividing it into North and South Leith. The important harbour has well-equipped docks and shipyards. The shore was the old landing-place, and the visit of George IV, in 1822, is recorded on a stone by the quay wall. Among the town's manufacturing interests are sawmills, biscuits and chemical works. In Kirkgate is the restored 15th cent. *St. Mary's* Church, and nearby is *Trinity House*, in which are some notable paintings. The fine 16th cent. and later Merchant's House in Water Close, known as *Lamb's House* (N.T. Scot.), where Mary, Queen of Scots spent her first day after landing in 1561, is being restored as an Old Folks' Centre. Only scanty remains of the Citadel of 1650 now exist, and in the vicinity is *Leith Fort*, built in 1779. The *Signal Tower*, built originally in 1686 as a windmill, still stands near the shore. On Leith Links, now a park, Charles I played golf in 1641.

LEITHOLM, Berwick.　　　　　　　Map 11, **NT 7** 4.
Iter. 39, 46.

LENDALFOOT, Ayr.　　　　　　　Map 2, **NX 1** 9·
Situated on a fine stretch of coast, with Bennane Head to the south-west. There is a memorial recalling the drowning of some Arran men in 1711. The Lendal Water flows into the sea at Lendalfoot, and a little inland is the ruined *Carleton Castle*, associated with the legend of a baron, who pushed his first seven wives over the cliffs, but was himself thus disposed of by the eighth. On the way to Bennane Head is some fine rock scenery at *Gamesloup*, and beyond the Head is Bennane Cove, associated with Crockett's "Grey Man." To the north of Lendalfoot, on the coast road, one of the most picturesque in the country, is the delightful *Kennedy's Pass*. See **Ballantrae.** *Iter. 55, 80.*

LENNEL, Berwick.　　　　　　　Map 11, **NT 8** 4.
Iter. 38.

LENNOXLOVE, East Lothian.　　　Map 10, **NT 5** 7.
See **Bolton.**

LENNOXTOWN, Stirling. 4,966.　　Map 15, **NS 6** 7.
E.C. Wed. GOLF. This town stands below the *Campsie Fells*, at the foot of the road leading over the hills to *Fintry* (*q.v.*) by way of the head of *Campsie Glen* (*q.v.*), at a height of 1,154 ft., and is noted for its nail-works. The name *Lennox* was formerly applied to the county of Dunbarton, and included also parts of the adjacent counties, but is now only used to describe the various hill ranges in north-west Stirlingshire, which are known generally as the *Lennox* hills. *Iter. 107, 115.*

LENY FALLS, Perth.　　　　　　Map 15, **NN 5** 0.
See **Callander.** *Iter. 107, 111, 139, 141, 142, 144.*

LENZIE, Dunbarton.　　　　　　Map 8, **NS 6** 7.
See **Kirkintilloch.**

LERWICK, Shetland. 5,623. SB.　　Map 33, **HU 4** 4.
See **Shetland Islands** (Mainland). *Iter. 267, 268, 269, 270.*

LESLIE, Aberdeen.　　　　　　　Map 27, **NJ 5** 2.
On the Gady Burn, looking towards the long ridge of *Bennachie*, to the south-east. The Castle dates from 1661. 2½ m. E., beyond *Auchleven*, is the restored mansion of *Lickleyhead*, built in 1629.

LESLIE, Fife. 2,838. SB.　　　　Map 17, **NO 2** 0.
E.C. Wed. GOLF. A small industrial town, with old houses and a green, which claims to be the scene of the 15th-cent. poem "Christ's Kirk on the Green." The 'bull stone' on the green was formerly used to tether bulls when bull-baiting was in progress. *Leslie House*, two wings of which were destroyed in the 18th cent., dates partly from 1670, and stands to the east of the town. **2 m. W.** is the restored *Strathendry Castle*, with a view over *Loch Leven* (*q.v.*). See **Markinch.** *Iter. 98.*

LESMAHAGOW, Lanark. 3,084.　　Map 9, **NS 8** 4.
E.C. Thurs. GOLF. Known also as *Abbey Green*, and situated on the edge of an extensive moorland area lying to the south-west. The River Nethan flows northwards through the town on its way to join the Clyde at *Crossford* (*q.v.*). The former Priory was famous for its orchards, and the monks may have pioneered the important fruit-

growing industry of Clydesdale. In the Hunterian Museum at the University of *Glasgow* (*q.v.*) is preserved the bronze Lesmahagow Flagon, found here in 1810. *Iter. 29, 51, 56.*

LESWALT, Wigtown.　　　　　　Map 2, **NX 0** 6.
Iter. 83.

LEUCHARS, Fife. 656.　　　　　Map 17, **NO 4** 2.
E.C. Wed. GOLF. Famous for its Norman Church, one of the finest of its period in the country. noted especially for the chancel and apse, both interior and exterior being richly carved. A 17th cent. bell turret has been added to the structure above the apse. The two carved *Earlshall* stones are of interest. To the east, on the borders of the lonely Tents Moor, with its forestry plantations, is the picturesque old mansion of *Earlshall*, dating from 1546 to 1607, with beautiful gardens, the house having been well restored by Sir Robert Lorimer. See **Guardbridge** and **Tayport.** *Iter. 94.*

LEVEN, Fife. 8,899. SB.　　　　Map 17, **NO 3** 0.
E.C. Thurs. GOLF. A Firth of Forth resort and coal port on Largo Bay, with fine sands. The River Leven flows here into the Firth. A re-erected Cross marks the jubilee of King George V. On the promenade is a curious "shell" house. See **Lundin Links.** *Iter. 128.*

LEVENHALL, Midlothian.　　　　Map 10, **NT 3** 7.
Iter. 1, 2, 3.

LEVENWICK, Shetland.　　　　　Map 33, **HU 4** 2.
Iter. 269.

LEVERBURGH (Isle of Lewis), Harris, Inverness.
　　　　　　　　　　　　　　　Map 32, **NG 0** 8.
See **Hebrides, Outer** (Harris). *Iter. 256.*

LEWIS, ISLE OF, Ross and Cromarty
　(includes **Harris,** Inverness).　Map 32, **NB 0** 2, etc.
See **Hebrides, Outer** (Lewis and Harris). *Iter. 256 to 260.*

LEWISTON, Inverness.　　　　　Map 25, **NH 5** 2.
A hamlet lying a little to the south of *Drumnadrochit* (*q.v.*), at the foot of Glen Urquhart. *Balmacaan House* is now the headquarters of the College of Celtic Art. To the south-west, and reached on foot, are the picturesque Divach Falls, on a tributary of the River Coiltie. *Iter. 207, 210, 213.*

LEYLODGE, Aberdeen.　　　　　Map 27, **NJ 7** 1.
Iter. 197.

LHANBRYDE, Moray.　　　　　　Map 26, **NJ 2** 6.
Lies in a wooded setting, with the little Loch na Bo to the south-east. **1 m. S.W.** is the well-preserved and white-harled *Coxton Tower*, with its characteristic iron yett, the building dating from 1641, a particularly fine example of its kind. *Iter. 175, 187, 198, 199.*

LIATHACH, Ross and Cromarty.　Map 24, **NG 9** 5.
See **Torridon.**

LIBERTON (Edinburgh), Midlothian.　Map 10, **NT 2** 6.
To the west rise the *Braid* hills, 698 ft., a public park. *Liberton House* is of early 17th-cent. date, a sundial bearing the date 1683. The house is the successor to the ruined 15th-cent. *Liberton Tower*, situated on a slight ridge, and forming a conspicuous landmark. A little to the south of Liberton is *Stenhouse Mansion* (N.T. Scot.), dated 1623, and restored, containing fine plaster ceilings. **1 m. N.N.E.** is *The Inch*, an early 17th-cent. house, with modern additions. *Iter. 10, 24.*

LIDDESDALE, or LIDDISDALE, Roxburgh.
　　　　　　　　　　　　　　　Map 5, **NY 4** 8, etc.
See **Canonbie, Hermitage Castle, Newcastleton** and **Riccarton.** *Iter. 31, 47.*

LILLIESLEAF, Roxburgh.　　　　Map 10, **NT 5** 2.
The Church of 1771 has been enlarged. **2 m. S.W.** is the *Riddell* motte, crowned by a tower of 1885. The old house of *Riddell* was burnt down in 1942.

LIMEKILNS, Fife.　　　　　　　Map 16, **NT 0** 8.
See **Charlestown.**

LINCLUDEN ABBEY, Kirkcudbright.　Map 3, **NX 9** 7.
The red sandstone remains of this Abbey, or College (A.M.),

Leith (Edinburgh), Midlothian. A stone in the quay wall recording the visit of George IV in 1822

Lendalfoot, Ayr. The Memorial recording the drowning of a number of men from the island of Arran in 1711

Leuchars, Fife. The richly carved Norman Church, perhaps the finest of its period in Scotland

Leven, Fife. The curious 'shell' car on the promenade. A 'shell' house stands adjacent to it

Leslie, Fife. The Bull Stone on the green, which was once used to tether bulls during bull-baiting

Liberton, Midlothian. The ruined 15th century Liberton Tower of the Dalmahoys

[For LEITH see also preceding plate
[For LENDALFOOT see also under LOWLANDS
(Plate 118)

PLATE 108 (facing page 200)

Linlithgow, West Lothian. The gateway of Linlithgow Palace, which was burnt down accidentally in 1746 by General Hawley's soldiers

Linlithgow, West Lothian. The Cross Well, a reconstruction of 1807. An earlier well was destroyed in 1659 by Cromwell's troops

Lix Toll, Perth. An old toll house, the 59th, which stands at the junction of A85 and A827, in Glen Dochart

Linn of Dee, Aberdeen. A view below the bridge. The poet Byron, as a boy, narrowly escaped drowning in this reach of the river

Linlithgow, West Lothian. The plaque facing the County Buildings, which records the shooting in the street of the Earl of Moray, in 1570

PLATE 109 (facing page 201)   [For LOCHABER see following plate lie in a lovely setting, near the meeting of the River Nith and the Cluden Water, a little to the north-west of Dumfries, off the Thornhill road. A Benedictine Convent was founded here in the 12th cent., and in the 14th and 15th cents. it was rebuilt as a Collegiate Church, and still retains portions of the medieval domestic buildings. Of the Church, the richly decorated choir preserves the sedilia and piscina, the stone rood-screen, a fine sacristy door, and a tomb of very great beauty to Princess Margaret, who died c. 1430. The arms of the Douglas family appear in various places. **See Irongray.** *Iter. 27, 48, 56, 67, 74.*

LINDORES, Fife. Map 17, NO 2 1.
Situated near the small and reed-surrounded Lindores Loch. About 2½ m. N.W., and to the east of *Newburgh* (q.v.), lie the scanty remains of *Lindores Abbey*, founded in 1178. The groined entrance arch, and a portion of the West tower are the sole substantial survivals of the former structure. In the vicinity is the ruined 16th-cent. *Denmylne Castle. Iter. 131, 132.*

LINLITHGOW, West Lothian. 4,223. SB. Map 16, NS 9 7.
E.C. Wed. **M.D.** Mon. **GOLF.** This ancient Royal Burgh, famous for its Palace and Church stands on the south shore of Linlithgow Loch, noted for skating. Its name was at one time given to the county as a whole. In the town are some late 16th-cent. houses (several N.T. Scot.), and the fountain of *St. Michael*, dated 1720, inscribed " Saint Michael is kind to strangers." The curious Cross Well, erected in 1807, with its thirteen water jets, is a reproduction of an earlier example. The Earl of Moray, Regent of Scotland, was shot in the street outside the present County Buildings, in 1510, and a plaque set up in 1875 recalls the fact. The last Scottish National Parliament met in the Palace in 1646, and Cromwell garrisoned the town between 1651 and 1659.

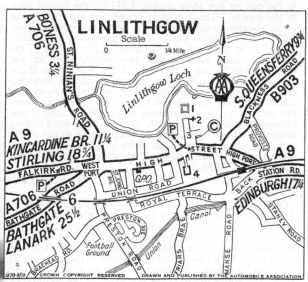

1. Palace.
2. St. Michael's Church (1424).
3. Cross Well.
4. County Buildings

A fine gateway, erected by James V, leads to the precincts, in which the Palace and Church are situated. *St. Michael's* Church, one of the finest in Scotland, exhibits strong French characteristics, and was rebuilt after a fire in 1424, though the apse was not finished until 1531. The nave and choir are a fine composition, and in place of transepts there are two chapels, in the southerly of which James IV had the vision of his coming end at Flodden. The window tracery, notably in the Katherine's aisle, is partly in the flamboyant style, and is outstanding for its beauty. The splendid, ruined Palace (A.M.) overlooks the loch, and is the successor to an older building, burnt in 1424. The chapel and magnificent Great Hall are late 15th-cent. work and

there is also notable work from the early 16th cent. A fine quadrangle inside the building contains a richly-carved 16th-cent. fountain. The Royal apartments are on the west side of the quadrangle, and on the 1st floor is the room, where, in 1542, Mary, Queen of Scots, was born, while her father, James V, lay dying at *Falkland Palace* (q.v.). Queen Margaret's Bower is the little room in a turret where the Queen kept vigil while James IV fought at Flodden. Prince Charles Edward stayed in the Palace in 1745, but in 1746 it was burnt, probably by accident, by troops of General Hawley. In 1914, King George V held a court in the Lyon Chamber. The Palace is open weekdays, summer, 10 to 7, winter, 10 to 4; Sun., 2 to 4 or 8. (See note page 90). **2** m. N., beyond Linlithgow Loch, on a hill 559 ft. high, is a monument to General Hope, a hero of the Indian Mutiny. **See Abercorn, Blackness, Hopetoun House** and **Torphichen.** *Iter. 86, 91, 95, 96.*

LINN OF DEE, Aberdeen. Map 20, NO 0
See **Inverey.** *Iter. 179.*

LINTMILL, Banff. Map 26, NJ 5 6.
Iter. 169.

LINTON CHURCH, Roxburgh. Map 11, NT 7 2.
See **Morebattle.**

LINWOOD, Renfrew. Map 8, NS 4 6.
Iter. 64.

LISMORE, ISLE OF, Argyll. Map 14, NM 8 3 and 8 4.
This flat, green and treeless island lies in Outer *Loch Linnhe* (q.v.), where its waters mingle with those of the Firth of Lorne and the Sound of Mull. Between Lismore and the nearest point on the mainland is the Lynn of Lorne, threaded by the steamers, whose calling-place is *Achnacroish* pier, on the east side of the island. Lismore was formerly the seat of the Argyll diocese, and the tiny Cathedral, now modernized, is used as the Parish Church. There are associations with St. Moluag, an early saint, who was contemporary with St. Columba. The ruined *Castle Coeffin* is situated on the west coast, in a picturesque setting, not far from the little village of *Clachan*. There are splendid views obtainable from many points on the island, looking northwards to the hills of *Morven* (q.v.), and westwards towards the rugged island of *Mull* (q.v.). A steamer service serves *Oban* (q.v.), and a passenger ferry connects with *Port Appin* (q.v.), on the mainland coast.

LIVINGSTON, West Lothian. Map 9, NT 0 6.
Iter. 18.

LIX TOLL, Perth. Map 15, NN 5 3.
Iter. 107, 111, 120, 138, 139, 142, 144, 145.

LOANHEAD, Aberdeen. Map 27, NJ 7 2.
See **Old Meldrum.**

LOANHEAD, Midlothian. 5,209. SB. Map 10, NT 2 6.
Situated a little to the north of the North Esk River, with the *Pentland* hills rising away to the west.

LOANS, Ayr. Map 8, NS 3 3.
See **Troon.** *Iter. 9, 60, 66.*

LOCHABER, Inverness. Map 18, NN 1 6, etc.
The district of *Lochaber*, one of the loveliest in the Highlands, is inseparably bound up with the fortunes and wanderings of Prince Charles Edward. It stretches roughly east of the Great Glen, or *Glen More* (q.v.), from Loch Leven and Loch Linnhe to *Loch Lochy* (q.v.) and Glen Spean, where it touches the borders of the almost equally lovely *Badenoch* (q.v.) country. The boundaries of Lochaber have varied at different times in the course of history, and at one time the district extended from the Atlantic as far as the country of *Strath Spey* (q.v.). The name Lochaber is probably derived from a loch of that name, which has long since dried up. The district is divided into the Cameron country of Nether Lochaber, south of *Ben Nevis* (q.v.), including the *Mamores* (q.v.), and Brae, or Upper Lochaber, the original land of the MacDonnells of Keppoch, famous for their Gaelic bards, and which lies beyond the Ben. The head of Clan Cameron is Cameron of Lochiel, whose ancestral home of *Achnacarry House* stands near the

richly wooded shores of *Loch Arkaig* (*q.v.*). *Fort William* (*q.v.*) is the scene of the annual Lochaber gathering. The Lochaber Power Scheme is described under *Ben Nevis*, *Fort William* and *Loch Laggan*. See **Corran Ferry, Gairlochy, Roy Bridge** and **Spean Bridge**.

LOCH ACHRAY, Perth.   Map 15, NN 5 0.
See **Trossachs**. *Iter. 106, 111, 139*.

LOCHAILORT, Inverness. 58.   Map 12, NM 7 8.
Beautifully situated at the head of the sea loch of Loch Ailort, backed by a range of high hills, among which *Fros Bheinn*, 2,876 ft., a fine viewpoint, is the most prominent feature. At the seaward end of the loch is the tiny island of Eileen nan Gobhar, where the French ship bringing Prince Charles Edward anchored in July, 1745, at the start of the great, but hopeless adventure, which ended one year later where it had begun. The little River Ailort flows into the loch at Lochailort, having issued, **2 m. E.**, from the exceptionally beautiful *Loch Eilt*, with its picturesque tree-crowned islets, backed by steep rock-strewn hills. The well-known Road to the Isles, "By Ailort and by Morar to the sea," traverses the shores of Loch Eilt from end to end. From the western extremity of this loch, a path climbs northwards through the hills, reaching a height of over 1,000 ft. This path gives a superb view down the narrow and little-known *Loch Beoraid* in the South Morar country. This loch stretches away to the east, hemmed in by lonely mountains, some of which show outcrops of grey, glaciated rocks. In the vicinity is a cave in which the Prince hid during his wanderings. The path descends by the Meoble River to the lonely clachan of Meoble, and eventually reaches the remote shores of Loch Morar (See **Morar**). From Lochailort, another path leads south-westwards into the picturesque *Moidart* (*q.v.*), first along the shores of Loch Ailort, and later reaching the Sound of Arisaig. Here lies the tiny village of *Glenuig*, at which the Prince landed on his way from *Borrodale House*, near the head of *Loch nan Uamh* (*q.v.*), on his way to *Kinlochmoidart* (*q.v.*). The seaward views along the entire length of this path are splendid. See **Arisaig**. *Iter. 209*.

LOCHALINE, Argyll.   Map 12, NM 6 4.
Lying at the seaward end of Loch Aline, with a pier, overlooking the Isle of Mull beyond the Sound of Mull, and with a background of low hills, *Lochaline* is a small, but pleasant *Morven* (*q.v.*) village. Across the narrow mouth of Loch Aline is a flat, wooded stretch, terminating in Ardtornish Point, on which stand the ruins of the 14th-cent. *Ardtornish Castle*, associated with Scott's "Lord of the Isles." Near the Church of Lochaline, at *Keil*, which has carved slabs of interest, one depicting what is perhaps the earliest portrayal of the wearing of the kilt, is an old Cross, which was formerly on the island of *Iona* (*q.v.*). There are important deposits of silica sand along the west shore of Loch Aline. See **Drimnin** and **Larachbeg** (for *Kinlochaline Castle*). *Iter. 218*.

LOCH ALSH, Ross and Cromarty.   Map 23, NG 7 2.
                                                               and 8 2.
One of the finest of the sea lochs of *Wester Ross*, extending inland from the narrow strait of Kyle Akin, which separates Skye from the mainland, to the point where it joins Loch Duich and Loch Long at the *Dornie* (*q.v.*) bridge. The road from Dornie leading westwards towards *Kyle of Lochalsh* (*q.v.*) gives views of the loch and of *Beinn na Cailleach*, 2,396 ft., one of the Skye hills rising above the narrows of *Kyle Rhea*. See **Ardelve, Balmacara** and **Kyleakin**. *Iter. 207, 220, 221, 222*.

LOCHANS, Wigtown.   Map 2, NX 0 5.
A small Rhinns of Galloway village, a little to the south-east of which are the remains of *Garthland Tower*. *Iter. 81, 83*.

LOCHARBRIGGS, Dumfries.   Map 4, NX 9 8.
E.C. Thurs. *Iter. 24, 46*.

LOCH ARD, Perth.   Map 15, NN 4 0.
See **Aberfoyle**.

LOCH ARKAIG, Inverness.   Map 18, NN 0 9.
This beautiful loch is separated from *Loch Lochy* (*q.v.*), in the Great Glen, by the short length of the River Arkaig. Near the point where the river enters Loch Arkaig is *Achnacarry House*, among its woods, looking westwards to Glen Mallie. This is the ancestral home of Cameron of Lochiel, Chief of Clan Cameron, one of whose ancestors, known as the " gentle Lochiel," was associated with Prince Charles Edward in the '45. The estates were later forfeited by the family, and the original castle burnt in 1746, but in 1784 they were handed back. There are several magnificent tree-lined avenues, the best-known of which is the so-called " Dark Mile," traversed by the road leading from *Gairlochy* (*q.v.*) to Loch Arkaig, with the picturesque Cia-aig Falls on the right. A rough and narrow road, degenerating later into a path, leads west along the whole length of the loch, at first in a richly-wooded setting, and later in surroundings becoming gradually wilder, with the bare peaks of *Gulvain*, 3,224 ft., and the *Streaps*, 2,988 ft. and 2,916 ft., rising to the west. At the far end of the loch, paths continue through Glen Dessary and the rocky Glen Pean to the remote shores of *Loch Nevis* (*q.v.*) and Loch Morar respectively. In Glen Dessary lived Jenny Cameron, who was present when the standard of Prince Charles Edward was raised at *Glenfinnan* (*q.v.*), in 1745. A path leading from this glen to Loch Nevis traverses the very picturesque and rugged pass known as the Mam na Cloiche Airde. This wild country in the neighbourhood of Loch Arkaig is associated with the wanderings of Prince Charles Edward after the failure of the '45. *Iter. 214*.

LOCH ARKLET, Stirling.   Map 15, NN 3 0.
See **Inversnaid**. *Iter. 105*.

LOCH ASSYNT, Sutherland.   Map 29, NC 1 2 and 2 2.
A lonely and delightful loch, situated in the heart of the wild, rocky Sutherland mountains, which are dominated to the east by *Ben More Assynt*, 3,273 ft., the highest peak in the county. The district is known for rare plants and ferns. Nearer to the loch, on the north side, rises *Quinag*, 2,653 ft., its original Gaelic name signifying a " Waterstoup." On the south side is *Canisp*, 2,779 ft., one of the strange, isolated Torridon sandstone peaks, which are the most notable feature of this part of the North-West Highlands. At the south-eastern extremity of the loch lies *Inchnadamph* (*q.v.*), a fishing resort, to the north-west of which is the shell of *Ardvreck Castle*, late 15th cent., where the great Marquis of Montrose, of the Clan Graham, was betrayed and captured, in 1650. A picturesque road leading towards *Lochinver* (*q.v.*) traverses the northern shores of the loch, and gives fine mountain views in a bare and austere setting of Archaean, grey gneiss rocks. See **Invershin**. *Iter. 225, 227, 228*.

LOCH AVON, Banff.   Map 20, NJ 0 0.
See **Cairngorms**.

LOCH AWE, Argyll.   Map 14, NM 9 0 etc.
This narrow and delightful loch, noted for its fishing, is some 23 miles in length, and has a uniform width of about a mile, except at the north-eastern end. The loch is one of the best-known in the West Highlands, and there are roads along both its east and west banks, The name, in its old form " Lochow," is associated with the Clan Campbell. Loch Awe forms the southern boundary of the picturesque land of *Lorne* (*q.v.*). The finest reach lies under the shadow of the twin-peaked *Ben Cruachan*, 3,689 ft., where the loch is drained by the River Awe, flowing through the wild Pass of Brander towards *Taynuilt* (*q.v.*), near the shores of Loch Etive. (See *Kilchurn Castle*). In the vicinity is the wooded island of Fraoch Eilean, with a romantic ruined castle, half-hidden by trees, and dating from 1596, having been erected by the McNaughtons. On the nearby island of Inishail stands an ancient burial-ground. To the south-west of Loch Awe station stands the beautiful modern Church of *St. Conan*, dedicated in its present form in 1930. See **Falls of Cruachan, Ford, Portinnisherrich** and **Portsonachan**. *Iter. 110, 117, 119, 125, 144, 145*.

LOCH BEORAID, Inverness.   Map 12, NM 8 8.
See **Lochailort**.

Lochaber, Inverness. The view across the head of Loch Leven towards the Mamore Forest mountains from A82, near Kinlochleven, in the district of Nether Lochaber

Lochaline, Argyll. A gravestone in Keil churchyard, which depicts what is considered to be perhaps the earliest portrayal of a kilt

Loch Arkaig, Inverness. The Cia-aig Falls, in the tree-lined avenue known as the 'Dark Mile' (B8005), situated near the eastern end of Loch Arkaig, which is said to contain treasure hidden by the Jacobites

Loch Assynt, Sutherland. The remains of Calda House, a one-time home of the Mackenzies, situated off A837, near the south-eastern extremity of the loch. Ardvreck Castle, seen in the distance, is illustrated under Inchnadamph (Plate 86)

Loch Awe, Argyll. The notable modern Church of St. Conan (1881–1930), which stands near the station, on A85, at the northern end of the loch

PLATE 110 (facing page 202)

Loch Doon, Ayr; Kirkcudbright. The ruined 14th century Loch Doon Castle, also known as Balliol's Castle. It stood formerly on an island in the loch and was re-erected on its banks

Loch Duich, Ross and Cromarty. A heather-thatched cattle byre, built in the shape of one of the former 'black houses,' several of which used to stand in the clachan of Bundalloch, by Dornie, where Loch Alsh, Loch Duich and Loch Long meet

Lochearnhead, Perth. The scanty remains of St. Blane's Chapel, at the south-western extremity of Loch Earn

Lochearnhead, Perth. The tombstone to a band of seven Glencoe men, killed when attempting to raid Ardvorlich House, in 1620. It is situated 4 miles east, off the unclassified road on the south shore of the loch, near the entrance to Glen Vorlich

Loch Eilt, Inverness. Windswept trees on a small island, almost the last to have survived the gales which blow up this valley. The 'Road to the Isles' (A830), which links Fort William with Mallaig, traverses the shores of the loch

PLATE 111 (facing page 203)

LOCHBOISDALE, South Uist, Inverness. Map 32, NF 7 1. See **Hebrides, Outer** (South Uist). *Iter. 262.*

LOCH BROOM, Ross and Cromarty.   Map 29, NH 0 9. This fine *Wester Ross* sea loch stretches south-eastwards from the *Coigach* district into the hills separating the Dundonnell and Inverlael Forests. Near its mouth stands the small fishing town and resort of *Ullapool* (*q.v.*). *Beinn Dearg*, 3,547 ft., dominates the Strath More valley at the head of the loch. To the west of Ullapool, across the loch, rises *Ben Goleach*, 2,082 ft., and beyond it lies Little Loch Broom, along the shores of which goes the road linking Ullapool with *Dundonnell* (*q.v.*), with the great *An Teallach* range dominating the landscape to the south.

LOCHBUIE, Isle of Mull, Argyll.   Map 13, NM 6 2. On the south side of the island, on the shores of picturesque Loch Buie, overlooked by *Ben Buie*, 2,354 ft., to the north. The ruined *Moy Castle* was a former Maclaine stronghold, and was once visited by Dr. Johnson. To the east is the little Loch Uisg, near which stands a stone circle, and beyond lies the almost land-locked Loch Spelve, traversed by the road leading towards *Craignure* (*q.v.*). Above the road rises *Creach Bheinn*, 2,289 ft., and the cliff scenery in the neighbourhood is remarkable. At the entrance to Loch Buie, on the south-eastern shore, looking towards the Firth of Lorne, is Lovat's Cave, 300 ft., long and 150 ft. high, accessible only by boat. See **Carsaig Bay**. *Iter. 250.*

LOCHCARRON, Ross and Cromarty.   Map 24, NG 9 3. Known also as *Jeantown*, this attractive village lies on the shores of Inner Loch Carron, at the point of divergence of the road leading to the famous Pass of the Cattle, which gives access from *Tornapress* (*q.v.*) to *Applecross* (*q.v.*). There is a little fishing harbour at Slumbay, to the south-west of the village. On the Tornapress road, to the west, is the miniature Pass of Kishorn, which leads towards the shores of Loch Kishorn and the tiny village of *Kishorn* (*q.v.*). This loch leads into Outer Loch Carron, the widening waters of which merge into the Inner Sound facing Skye. Perhaps the most picturesque spot on Loch Carron is the village of *Plockton* (*q.v.*). See **Shieldaig** and **Strome**. *Iter. 221, 222, 223.*

LOCH CORUISK, Isle of Skye, Inverness.
                                                    Map 23, NG 4 2.
This wild and picturesque loch lies in what is considered to be the grandest mountain amphitheatre in Great Britain, and is separated from the sea loch of *Loch Scavaig* (*q.v.*) by a narrow neck of land. Access is generally gained by boat from *Elgol* (*q.v.*), but long-distance paths are also available, from Elgol by way of Camasunary and the notorious " Bad Step," and also from *Sligachan* (*q.v.*) by means of the low Drumhain ridge. By far the most impressive view of the loch is gained by climbing the steep and rocky little peak of *Sgurr na Stri*, 1,623 ft., which rises at the south-eastern extremity of Loch Coruisk. This hill faces directly towards the great cirque of the *Coolins* (*q.v.*) massed to the west, with a view, beyond the corrie of Coire-uisg, of the almost unapproachable " Inaccessible Pinnacle " perched near the rocky summit of *Sgurr Dearg*, 3,206 ft. Sir Walter Scott, in his " Lord of the Isles," has described the loch, and John Buchan's " Mr. Standfast " contains local colour, while Turner and countless others have essayed to portray the savage beauty of the scene in its deep-set mountain-girdled hollow. The grandeur of the mountain scenery of Loch Coruisk is rivalled only by *Loch Hourn* (*q.v.*), the finest of the great sea lochs of the Western Highlands. *Iter. 252.*

LOCHDONHEAD, Isle of Mull, Argyll. Map 13, NM 7 3. See **Craignure**. *Iter. 249, 250.*

LOCH DOON, Ayr; Kirkcudbright.   Map 2, NX 4 9. A long, narrow loch, surrounded by hills. At its northern extremity lies the picturesque Ness Glen. A road traverses the western shores, passing the 14th-cent. island-castle of *Loch Doon* (A.M.), now carefully re-erected by the roadside. The waters of the loch form part of the extensive Galloway Power Scheme. West of the loch is the Carrick Forest area, part of the Glen Trool National Forest Park. The lonely Lochs Recar and Macaterick are situated here,

with the waters of the Eglin Lane and the Gala Lane to the east. The hills rising to the south of Loch Doon include *Shalloch on Minnoch*, 2,520 ft., *Kirriereoch Hill*, 2,562 ft., *Corserine*, 2,668 ft. and *Carlin's Cairn*, 2,650 ft., some of the best known of the *Galloway* heights. See **Dalmellington**. *Iter. 74, 75, 76, 77.*

LOCH DUICH, Ross and Cromarty.   Map 24, NG 8 2. A very beautiful North-West Highland sea loch, extending from *Shiel Bridge* (*q.v.*), at the northern extremity of the magnificent mountain-encircled defile of *Glen Shiel* (*q.v.*), to *Dornie* (*q.v.*). There it is joined by Loch Long, the combined waters then uniting to join Loch Alsh, which stretches as far as the shores of Skye. Beyond Shiel Bridge, there are roads on both sides of Loch Duich, that on the eastern shore proceeding towards Dornie and *Kyle of Lochalsh* (*q.v.*), forming part of one of the " Roads to the Isles," and considered one of the loveliest roads in Scotland. That on the western shore terminates at *Totaig*, which is linked by a passenger ferry to the *Ardelve* (*q.v.*) side of Dornie Bridge. A branch to the left off the road leading towards Totaig climbs over the steep and narrow *Mam Rattachan Pass* (*q.v.*) to *Glenelg* (*q.v.*). The outstanding feature of the views from Loch Duich is the fine ridge known as the *Five Sisters of Kintail*, dominated by *Scour Ouran*, 3,505 ft., which towers over Glen Shiel, away to the south-east of the loch, and forms part of the *Kintail* (*q.v.*) estate (N.T. Scot.). See **Croe Bridge, Dornie** (for *Eilean Donan Castle*) and **Inverinate**. *Iter. 207, 220.*

LOCHEARNHEAD, Perth. 300.   Map 15, NN 5 2. E.C. Wed. A small touring centre, situated at the western extremity of the charmingly wooded Loch Earn, which stretches eastwards for some six miles, with the delightful resort of *St. Fillan's* (*q.v.*) at the far end. Near the south shore of the loch is the ruined *St. Blane's* Chapel, and a little farther east is the entrance to Glen Ample, with a waterfall, facing the old, castellated mansion of *Edinample*. The glen is associated with Scott's " Legend of Montrose," as is also *Ardvorlich House*, **2 m. E.**, by the lochside. In this house is preserved the Clach Dearg, a famous talisman of rock-crystal. By the road-side near the house is a stone recalling the slaying of seven Macdonalds of Glencoe, who were trying to raid Ardvorlich. North of the loch rise the hills of the *Breadalbane* (*q.v.*) country, and to the south are the lofty summits of *Ben Vorlich*, 3,224 ft., and *Stuc a'Chroin* 3,189 ft. Roads traverse the shores of the loch on both sides, the main road on the north bank giving the best mountain views, while that to the south is narrow and hilly. To the north of Lochearnhead is the gloomy defile of Glen Ogle, leading towards Glen Dochart and *Killin* (*q.v.*), the road through the pass attaining a height of 948 ft. See **Balquhidder**. *Iter. 107, 111, 138, 139, 141, 142, 144, 145.*

LOCH ECK, Argyll.   Map 14, NS 1 8 and 1 9. This lonely and charming hill-encircled loch lies in the *Cowal* (*q.v.*) peninsula, which divides *Loch Fyne* (*q.v.*) from Loch Long and the Clyde estuary. To the south-west of the loch rises *Beinn Mhor*, 2,433 ft., one of the highest points in this district. The slopes of some of the hills overlooking Loch Eck are now clothed with a forest of variegated spruces, making an unusual and attractive picture. A delightful road traverses the eastern shores of the loch, linking *Strachur* (*q.v.*) with the inner waters of the Holy Loch and the well-known resort of *Dunoon* (*q.v.*). See **Kilmun**. *Iter. 102, 137.*

LOCH EILT, Inverness.   Map 12, NM 8 8. See **Lochailort**. *Iter. 209.*

LOCH ERICHT, Inverness; Perth.   Map 19, NN 5 6 etc. See **Dalwhinnie** and **Kinloch Rannoch**.

LOCH ETIVE, Argyll.   Map 14, NM 9 3 and NN 0 3. This narrow sea loch extends from the Firth of Lorne to the foot of Glen Etive, where there is a steamer pier, and a narrow road, bordered by the *Dalness* Forest (N.T. Scot.) mountains, leads towards *Kingshouse* (*q.v.*), *Ben Starav*, 3,541 ft. and *Stob Coir'an Albannaich*, 3,425 ft., dominate the head of the loch, to the east. Farther to the south, beyond Glen Kinglass and Glen Noe, rises the twin-peaked

Ben Cruachan, 3,689 ft., and here the loch turns westwards to reach the narrows at *Connel* (*q.v.*), where the Falls of Lora are situated.

LOCH ERIBOLL, Sutherland.　　Map 28, NC 4 5 and 4 6. See **Eriboll, Heilim** and **Rispond.** *Iter. 225.*

LOCHFOOT, Kirkcudbright.　　　　　　Map 3, NX 8 7. A tiny village on the northern shores of the small Loch-rutton Loch.　1½ m. S.E. is the restored *Hills Castle*, mid-16th cent., joined to an early 18th-cent. house, and preserving a rare gatehouse of the early 17th cent.

LOCH FYNE, Argyll.　Map 7, NR 8 7 and 14 NR 9 9 etc. One of the best-known of the Scottish sea lochs, famous for its herrings, and stretching for about 40 miles from a little beyond *Inveraray* (*q.v.*), in the north, to the Sound of Bute, which separates the Island of Bute from the shores of the *Kintyre* (*q.v.*) peninsula. As with most of the sea lochs, the finest scenery is around the head, near *Cairndow* (*q.v.*), where the peaks of *Beinn Bhuidhe*, 3,106 ft., *Binnein an Fhidleir*, 2,658 ft., and *Beinn an Lochain*, 3,021 ft., overlook its waters. From here, a picturesque road climbs through Glen Kinglas, and descends past *Rest and be Thankful* (*q.v.*) to Glen Croe and the head of Loch Long at *Arrochar* (*q.v.*). Beyond *Otter Ferry* (*q.v.*), in the hilly *Cowal* (*q.v.*) country, the loch widens, with the heights of *Knapdale* (*q.v.*) forming a background to the western shores. See **Ardrishaig** and **Tarbert** (Argyll). *Iter. 88, 101, 102, 103, 118, 121, 122, 137.*

LOGHGAIR, Argyll.　　　　　　　　Map 14, NR 9 9. Situated on Loch Gair, a tiny inlet of *Loch Fyne* (*q.v.*). To the north-west is the little Loch Glashan. *Iter. 118, 121.*

LOCHGELLY, Fife. 9,388. SB.　　　　Map 17, NT 1 9. A town situated on the Fife coalfield. The little Loch Gelly lies just to the south-east.

LOCHGILPHEAD, Argyll. 1,229. SB.　　Map 14, NR 8 8. **E.C.** Tues. **M.D.** Mon. This small town stands at the head of Loch Gilp, an inlet of the larger *Loch Fyne* (*q.v.*). The Crinan Canal flows to the west on its way from *Crinan* (*q.v.*) to Loch Gilp at *Ardrishaig* (*q.v.*). There are views to the south-west of the low *Knapdale* (*q.v.*) hills. A little to the north is the chambered cairn of *Auchnahoish*, a notable prehistoric monument. See **Kilmartin, Kilmichael** and **Lochgair.** *Iter. 118, 121.*

LOCHGOILHEAD, Argyll. 300.　　　　Map 14, NN 2 0. Situated in a hollow below lofty *Cowal* (*q.v.*) hills, with a pier at the head of picturesque Loch Goil, a short stretch of water diverging from the larger Loch Long to the south-east. A steep and narrow road leads northwards from Lochgoilhead, dividing after about two miles, the eastern fork leading towards the well-known *Rest and be Thankful* (*q.v.*). The western branch traverses the rocky and lonely *Hell's Glen*, before debouching on to the eastern shores of *Loch Fyne* (*q.v.*) by means of steep zig-zags. On the western shores of Loch Goil, and well seen from the loch steamers, stands the ruined *Carrick Castle*, perhaps 14th cent., which was burnt down in 1685. A narrow road leads from Lochgoilhead along the shores of the loch as far as this point. Across the loch, and extending along the western shore of Loch Long, is a range of hills attaining a little over 2,000 ft., known as *Argyll's Bowling Green*. These form part of the Ardgoil estate (Argyll National Forest Park), which has been donated to the city of Glasgow. See **Arrochar.** *Iter. 102.*

LOCH HOURN, Inverness.　　　　Map 18, NG 8 1 and 23, NG 7 1 etc. Competent judges declare this loch, which lies in the remote district of *Knoydart* (*q.v.*), to be the grandest of the great sea lochs of the Western Highlands. Its mountain setting is certainly unequalled, the scenery providing a picturesque blending of savage, rocky slopes, together with stretches of woodland, consisting partly of Scots pines from the ancient forests, and partly of trees newly-planted by the Forestry Commission. The whole picture comes perhaps nearest in Great Britain to approximate in grandeur to the Norwegian fjords, especially in the land-locked inner reach around

Kinloch Hourn (*q.v.*). Loch Hourn is divided by a narrow strait, known as Caolas Mor, into the Inner and Outer lochs, and each section has a poor and narrow road leading steeply to its shores. The magnificent Inner Loch is reached by a road commencing at *Tomdoun* (*q.v.*) in Glen Garry, and later passing *Loch Quoich* (*q.v.*) before descending steeply (1 in 6 and very rough) the 600 ft. to Kinloch Hourn, on its shores, amid a wilderness of glaciated grey rocks on the lofty mountain flanks. The Outer Loch can be reached from *Glenelg* (*q.v.*) by means of a rough road traversing the shores of the Sound of Sleat, facing across to Skye, and providing magnificent seaward views. This road bends round Outer Loch Hourn and terminates near *Arnisdale* (*q.v.*), dominated by *Ben Sgriol*, 3,196 ft. Across the loch rises *Ladhar Bheinn*, 3,343 ft., the most westerly 3,000-ft. peak on the mainland, forming a splendid viewpoint. The mountain can be climbed from *Inverie* (*q.v.*) on *Loch Nevis* (*q.v.*), which is linked to Loch Hourn by a path from Barrisdale Bay through Glen Dulochan, the track reaching a height of nearly 1,100 ft. Perhaps the finest of all views of the loch is that obtained by climbing the rock-strewn peak of *Sgurr a'Mhoraire*, 3,365 ft., which rises to the east of the Inner Loch, and can be approached from the steep road leading inland from Kinloch Hourn towards Loch Quoich. *Iter. 207, 214.*

LOCHINCH, Wigtown.　　　　　　Map 2, NX 1 6. See **Castle Kennedy.**

LOCHINDORB, Moray.　　　　　　Map 25, NH 9 3. This little loch, situated high up on the west side of the bleak *Dava Moor*, is best known for the ruins of the sinister *Lochindorb Castle*, on its island site, once occupied by Edward III, in 1303, and later becoming a stronghold of the notorious Wolf of Badenoch. In the reign of James II the structure was destroyed. A narrow road, diverging from the Grantown-on-Spey to Forres main road, climbs on to moorland to traverse the eastern shores of the loch, and then leads south-westwards towards a road which attains some 1,200 ft., linking Carrbridge with Forres. See **Badenoch** and **Kingussie.** *Iter. 173, 177.*

LOCHINVAR, Kirkcudbright　　　　Map 3, NX 6 8. See **Dalry** (Kirkcudbright).

LOCHINVER, Sutherland.　　　　　Map 29, NC 0 2. One of the most beautiful small resorts on the wild, rocky coast of the *Assynt* district in the North-West Highlands, with a pier at the head of the small Loch Inver. Into the loch flows the River Inver, at the end of its short, but pic-

turesque partly-wooded course from the western extremity of *Loch Assynt* (*q.v.*). Lochinver is well known for fishing, being surrounded by numerous tiny lochans in all directions, while to the south-east lies the Glen-canisp Forest, in which are situated the isolated Torridon sandstone peaks of *Canisp*, 2,779 ft., and *Suilven*, 2,399 ft. The latter, one of the most striking on the mainland, has been called the "Matterhorn" of Scotland. Its summit, a notable viewpoint, forms a ridge a mile and a half long, with a sharp eastern peak, well seen from the neighbourhood of *Altnacealgach* (*q.v.*). The better-known western peak resembles a gigantic sugarloaf, virtually unclimbable, and is a striking object when seen from various points on the coast around Lochinver, notably from the rocky shores of Loch Roe, which lies to the north-west, on

Lochinver, Sutherland. The 'sugar-loaf' double peak of Suilven, 2,399 feet high, seen from a point on A837, some 5 or 6 miles to the south-west. The view from the summit ranges over a barren landscape of isolated peaks interspersed with innumerable small lochs

Lochgoilhead, Argyll. The remains of the 14th century Carrick Castle, of the Earls of Argyll, burnt in 1685. It stands 5 miles south, on an unclassified road on the west shore of Loch Goil

Loch Fyne, Argyll. An archway in the town of Inveraray, on Loch Fyne. It spans A819, leading northwards towards the richly wooded Glen Aray

Loch Fyne, Argyll. The 18th century bridge carrying A83 across the River Shira, where it enters Loch Shira, an inlet of Loch Fyne, a little to the north-east of Inveraray

Lochfoot, Kirkcudbright. Hills Castle, 16th to 18th century, which has its original 'yett,' or grated iron door. It stands on an unclassified road about 1½ miles to the south-east

Lochindorb, Moray. The ruined island-castle, once occupied by Edward I, and later a stronghold of the notorious Wolf of Badenoch. It lies on the bleak Dava Moor, off an unclassified road between A939 and B9007

PLATE 112 (facing page 204)

Loch Katrine, Perth. Ellen's Isle, facing the now submerged 'Silver Strand,' associated with Sir Walter Scott's poem, *'The Lady of the Lake'*

Lochlee, Angus. The ruined Invermark Castle of the Stirlings, which stands between the church and Loch Lee, on an unclassified road

Loch Leven, Kinross. The 15th century island-castle from which Mary, Queen of Scots, made her sensational escape in 1568. The notorious Wolf of Badenoch, and Patrick Grahame, Primate of Scotland, were also imprisoned here at different times

Loch Lochy, Inverness. The former 'Letterfinlay' Inn, which General Wade's soldiers used as a road-house during the construction of the road in the early 18th century. It stands on the east shore of the loch, on A82

Loch Lomond, Dunbarton; Stirling. A plinth, with the figure of a child, placed in the loch near Luss, a Dunbartonshire village on A82. It was erected by William Kerr, who made a fortune in England and returned to visit his boyhood home some 70 years ago

Loch Linnhe, Argyll; Inverness. The view at the Corran narrows, looking towards the lighthouse on the Ardgour side. A car ferry crosses the loch at this point

[For LOCH LEVEN (Argyll) see under LOCHABER (Plate 110)
[For LOCH KATRINE see also under HIGHLANDS (Plate 84)
[For LOCH LINNHE see also under ARDGOUR (Plate 8)

PLATE 113 (facing page 205)

the road to Stoer. It is also seen from points on the very wild and beautiful road leading southwards towards *Inverkirkaig* (*q.v.*) and the lovely Enard Bay. This narrow and hilly road has been described as the " mad little road of Sutherland." North-westwards from Lochinver, a most picturesque road, narrow and steep in places, follows the coast by way of *Stoer* (*q.v.*) to *Kylesku* (*q.v.*), giving magnificent views of the remarkable Sutherland peaks, and of the distant island of Skye beyond the Minch. See **Achiltibuie, Drumbeg, Inchnadamph** and **Loch Lurgain**. *Iter. 226, 227, 228.*

LOCH KATRINE, Perth; Stirling.
Map 15, NN **40** and **4** 1.
This Perthshire loch, the north-western extremity of which extends into Stirlingshire, is one of the loveliest in the Highlands, and is ringed with hills, the most prominent of which is the bare and rocky *Ben Venue*, 2,393 ft., which rises beyond the south-east corner. There are associations with the romantic works of Sir Walter Scott, notably the " Lady of the Lake," in which Ellen's Isle and the now-vanished " Silver Strand " appear. Steamers ply on the loch from Loch Katrine pier, but no roads encircle the shores, that on the north bank being private, though available for pedestrians who can reach *Glengyle*, the birthplace of Rob Roy. The waters of the loch are used in connection with Glasgow's water supply by means of a subterranean aqueduct. The richly-wooded *Trossachs* (*q.v.*) district, with *Ben A'an*, 1,750 ft., fringes the loch, and part of the Queen Elizabeth Forest Park is in the vicinity. See **Aberfoyle** and **Stronachlachar**. *Iter. 106, 111, 139.*

LOCH LAGGAN, Inverness. Map 19, NN **4** 8 and **5** 8.
Works in connection with the Lochaber Power Scheme (See **Ben Nevis** and **Fort William**) have caused the appearance of wooded Loch Laggan to be greatly changed. A large reservoir is now situated to the south-west, at the far end of which is the great *Laggan Dam*, near the outflow to the River Spean, in *Glen Spean*. A tunnel connects with the waters of Loch Treig, away to the south. During works in connection with the scheme, several ancient dug-out canoes were taken from the loch. Lofty mountains rise above the north shore of Loch Laggan, and beyond *Aberarder* farm, about halfway along the loch, is the entrance to the wild Coire Ardair, with its remote lochan, above which rises *Creag Meaghaidh*, 3,700 ft., the highest point in a range of hills which falls but little below the 3,000-ft. level for nearly 10 miles. Beyond the dam, farther to the west, on the north side of the road, are " Parallel Roads," similar to the better known examples to be found near *Roy Bridge* (*q.v.*). At the north-east extremity of the loch, the River Pattack, on which is situated the Linn of Pattack, flows near the Kingussie road prior to entering the loch. See **Dalwhinnie, Drumgask, Newtonmore** and **Tulloch**. *Iter. 143, 208.*

LOCHLEE CHURCH, Angus. Map 21, NO **4** 8.
Beyond the Church, a little to the south-west, is situated the little Loch Lee, at the terminal point of the long and beautiful valley of Glen Esk, threaded by the North Esk River. The glen extends far into this corner of the eastern Grampian, or *Benchinnan* mountains from the neighbourhood of *Edzell* (*q.v.*). A short distance from the Church, to the east of the loch, where the Water of Mark comes down from Glen Mark, stand the remains of *Invermark Castle*. To the north rises *Mount Keen*, 3,077 ft., climbed by Queen Victoria and the Prince Consort in 1861, and away to the west is the *White Mounth* (*q.v.*) group, dominated by *Lochnagar*, 3,786 ft. (*q.v.*). On the path leading towards Mount Keen is the Queen's Well, commemorating the ascent by Queen Victoria, and along the western shoulder of the mountain goes the Mounth track, giving access for walkers through Glen Tanner to *Aboyne* (*q.v.*). See **Tarfside**. *Iter. 164*

LOCH LEVEN, Argyll; Inverness. Map 18, NN **1** 6 etc.
See **Ballachulish, Carnach, Kinlochleven** and **North Ballachulish**. *Iter. 100, 124, 125, 142.*

LOCH LEVEN, Kinross. Map 17, NT **1** 9 and NO **1** 0.
This attractive loch, situated immediately to the east of *Kinross* (*q.v.*), is famous both for its pink-trout fishing and for its historic associations. On *St. Serf's* island are the

remains of an old Priory, and on Castle Island is the ruined 15th cent. *Loch Leven Castle* (A.M.), from which Mary, Queen of Scots made her celebrated escape, in 1568, after having spent nearly a year imprisoned in the tower. The Queen escaped with the help of William Douglas, a friend of George Douglas, the gaoler's son. William Douglas, after having stolen the castle keys and locked the building, threw them into the loch after the Queen had entered a boat. Scott's novel, " The Abbot," has immortalised the well-known story. To the east of the loch rise the *Lomond* hills, with *Bishop Hill* and *West Lomond*, the latter rising to 1,713 ft., while away to the south is *Benarty Hill*, 1,167 ft. See **Carberry Hill** and **Kirkliston**. *Iter. 90, 92, 98.*

LOCH LINNHE, Argyll; Inverness.
Map 14, NM **8** 4 and **1** 8, NN **0** 6 etc.
This fine sea loch extends for a distance of some 35 miles, from its meeting with Loch Eil at the western extremity of the Great Glen, or *Glen More* (*q.v.*), to Duart Point in the island of Mull, beyond the smaller island of Lismore in the Firth of *Lorne* (*q.v.*). Loch Linnhe falls naturally into two sub-divisions, an inner and an outer loch, which are separated by the Corran narrows, crossed by the car ferry at *Corran* (*q.v.*) linking the *Lochaber* (*q.v.*) and *Ardgour* (*q.v.*) districts. The inner stretch of the loch, to the north-east of the narrows, is dominated by *Ben Nevis* (*q.v.*) and the range of *Mamore Forest* (*q.v.*). Over the water, facing *Fort William* (*q.v.*), the *Caledonian Canal* (*q.v.*) issues into Loch Linnhe and Loch Eil at *Corpach* (*q.v.*). Beyond the Corran narrows, after being joined by Loch Leven, the loch broadens out, and its waters are overlooked by the *Ben Vair* ridges of the *Appin* (*q.v.*) country, and also by the sharp peak of *Garbh Bheinn* in Ardgour, rising behind *Inversanda* (*q.v.*). There are roads on each shore of the inner loch, and also for some distance on both shores of the outer loch, but the best way to appreciate the splendid mountain scenery along its entire length is to make a journey on one of the regular steamers which link Fort William with Oban in the summer months. *Iter. 100, 124, 125, 142, 215, 216, 217, 218.*

LOCH LOCHY, Inverness. Map 18, NN **2** 8 and **2** 9.
One of the chain of lochs in the Great Glen, or *Glen More* (*q.v.*), forming part of the waterway known as the *Caledonian Canal* (*q.v.*), and at the north-western extremity of which are situated the *Laggan Locks* (*q.v.*). The shores of Loch Lochy are for the most part hilly and sometimes wooded, the highest mountains being on the north side, in Glengarry Forest, where *Sron a'Choire Ghairbh* attains 3,066 ft., and the sharp cone of *Ben Tee* is 2,956 ft. in height. The main Fort William to Inverness road traverses the eastern shores of the loch, and about half-way along its length is the former " *Letterfinlay* " Inn, a road-house for General Wade's soldiers when the original road was being built, and once visited by Wordsworth and his sister. About **4** m. S.W. of Letterfinlay is the entrance to Glen Gloy, a long, roadless valley leading into lonely hills, in which are situated some " Parallel Roads," similar to the better-known examples near *Roy Bridge* (*q.v.*). See **Gairlochy, Loch Arkaig** and **Loch Oich**. *Iter. 210, 214, 220.*

LOCH LOMOND, Dunbarton; Stirling.
Map 15, NS **3** 9 etc.
This famous and beautiful inland loch, known as the " Queen of Scottish Lakes," and noted for its fishing, is the largest in Great Britain. It is some 24 miles long and 5 miles broad at its widest point, though a long stretch in the north is less than a mile in width. Steamers, calling at various points, traverse the full length of the loch, from *Balloch* (*q.v.*) in the south, to *Ardlui* (*q.v.*) in the north. The writings of Sir Walter Scott have done much to make the loch so well known, and Smollett admired it greatly, but both Dr. Johnson and Wordsworth were less enthusiastic. In the lower part of the loch are a number of wooded islands, and roads traverse both the east and west shores, but beyond *Rowardennan* (*q.v.*), on the eastern side, there is no road. On *Inchmurrin* island, to the north of Balloch, are situated the ruins of *Lennox Castle*. *Ben Lomond*, 3,192 ft., the most prominent feature in views of Loch Lomond, rises to the east of the loch, opposite *Tarbet* (*q.v.*), and is best climbed

from Rowardennan. The view from the summit is very extensive, extending from the Arran hills to Ben Cruachan. A narrow neck of land on the west side separates Loch Lomond from the northern extremity of Loch Long at *Arrochar* (*q.v.*). Later, lofty hills close in beyond the shores, the most notable being to the west, where *Ben Ime*, 3,318 ft., *Ben Vane*, 3,004 ft., and *Ben Vorlich*, 3,092 ft., make an impressive picture. Between the two last-named mountains lies Glen Sloy, with Loch Sloy, whose waters are now harnessed to one of the new hydro-electric schemes. The power-house at *Inveruglas* (*q.v.*) was opened by Her Majesty Queen Elizabeth, the Queen Mother, in October, 1950. The head of Loch Lomond, near Ardlui, is very beautiful, and the fine road along the whole length of the wooded western shores, which is traversed annually by many thousands of tourists, continues northwards into Perthshire, through picturesque Glen Falloch, towards *Crianlarich* (*q.v.*). See **Inversnaid** and **Luss**. *Iter. 88, 100, 101, 104, 105, 110, 111, 115, 137.*

LOCH LONG, Argyll; Dunbarton.
Map 14, **NS 2** 8 etc.
A long and narrow sea loch, extending for some 16 miles from its head at Arrochar to its mouth, where the waters are joined with those of the widening Clyde estuary. Near Arrochar rises the prominent rock peak of *Ben Arthur* (*The Cobbler*), 2,891 ft., and farther south is the line of hills known as *Argyll's Bowling Green*, which overlooks Loch Goil near its junction with Loch Long. At the mouth of Loch Long is Strone Point, where the Holy Loch also meets the Clyde estuary, into which at this point extends the *Rosneath* peninsula, dividing Loch Long from the Gare Loch. On the eastern bank, north of the Gare Loch, is the new oil-port of *Finnart*. See **Ardentinny, Arrochar, Coulport, Kilcreggan** and **Whistlefield**. *Iter. 88, 101, 102, 103, 111, 116, 137.*

LOCH LONG, Ross and Cromarty.
Map 24, **NG 8** 2 and **9** 2.
See **Ardelve, Dornie** and **Falls of Glomach**. *Iter. 207, 220.*

LOCH LURGAIN, Ross and Cromarty. Map 29, **NC 1** 0.
This remote North-West Highland loch is comparatively little known, owing to its situation away from any main road, but its mountain setting is one of the finest in Scotland, and a visit to its shores is eminently worth the extra trouble involved. A narrow road, leading off the Ullapool to Inchnadamph road, traverses its northern shores, above which rise *Cul Beag*, 2,523 ft., and later *An Stac*, or *Stack Polly*, 2,009 ft., an amazing little mountain, with a summit ridge of sharp and practically unclimbable rock pinnacles overlooking Inverpolly Forest. Behind these two peaks is the still higher *Cul Mor*, 2,786 ft., one of the isolated Torridon sandstone hills of the district. Beyond the roadless south shore of the loch is *Beinn Eun*, which faces *Ben More Coigach*, 2,438 ft., a magnificent viewpoint, overlooking Outer Loch Broom, and the Coigach district. Between these two hills lies the tiny Lochan Tuath, overlooked by the great crag of *Sgurr an Fhidhleir*, 2,285 ft. At the west end of Loch Lurgain lies Loch Baddagyle, along the shores of which the road continues towards *Baddagyle* (*q.v.*) and the picturesque, rocky seaboard at *Achiltibuie* (*q.v.*) and Enard Bay. *Iter. 226.*

LOCHMABEN, Dumfries. 1,213. SB. Map 4, **NY 0** 8.
E.C. Thurs. GOLF. A small Annandale Royal Burgh, situated between the Castle Loch, to the south-east, the Kirk and Mill Lochs, to the north-west, and the Brumel Loch, to the east. In the Castle Loch, and also in two other lochs in the vicinity, is found the vendace, a rare species of fish. Lochmaben's Mercat Cross displays sundials on the faces of the top block. At the southern extremity of the Castle Loch stands the ruined *Lochmaben Castle* (A.M.), which may have been the birthplace of Robert Bruce, though *Turnberry* (*q.v.*) also claims this honour. To the north of Lochmaben, the Water of Ae is joined by the Kinnel Water, the combined streams shortly uniting with the River Annan, which flows to the east of the Castle Loch in a series of acute bends through Annandale. **2 m. N.N.W.** of Lochmaben, on the banks of the Water of Ae, stands the late 16th-cent. *Elshieshields Tower*, partly modernised and joined to an 18th-cent.

house. **3 m. S.W.** is *Skipmyre*, the birthplace, in 1658, of William Paterson, who is associated with the founding of the Bank of England. See **Lockerbie** and **Torthorwald**. *Iter. 45.*

LOCHMADDY, North Uist, Inverness. Map 32, **NF 9** 6.
See **Hebrides, Outer** (North Uist). *Iter. 261.*

LOCH MAREE, Ross and Cromarty.
Map 22, **NG 8** 7 and 24, **NG 9** 6 etc.
One of the loveliest of the North-West Highland lochs in *Wester Ross*. It is well known to fishermen, being some 12 miles in length, and separated by less than two miles of land, traversed by the short River Ewe, from the sea loch of Ewe, which may at one time have been joined to Loch Maree. The finest mountain scenery is at the south-east end of the loch, where *Slioch*, 3,260 ft., a notable landmark and a grand viewpoint, rises in steep, rocky slopes above the eastern shores. To the north-west of Slioch is *Ben Lair*, 2,817 ft., with its great cliffs, and farther away is *Beinn Airidh Charr*, 2,593 ft. The road along Loch Maree traverses the western shores, passing *Grudie Bridge*, from where a magnificent view is gained towards the grand Torridon peaks to the south, from *Beinn a Chearcaill*, 2,376 ft., to the much loftier *Ben Eighe*, 3,220 ft., and *Liathach* 3,456 ft. Beyond Grudie Bridge is situated the "*Loch Maree*" Hotel, opposite which lie a number of picturesque, wooded islands, one of which is *Isle Maree*, on which are slight remains of a chapel, the successor to an early hermitage of *St. Maelrubha*. South of the hotel rise *Beinn an Eoin*, 2,801 ft., and *Baeshven*, 2,896 ft., overlooking the remote Shieldaig and Flowerdale Forests. From the clachan of *Slattadale*, near which are the Victoria Falls, so named to commemorate a visit by Queen Victoria, the road bears away from the wooded shores of the loch on the way to *Gairloch* (*q.v.*), and passes through the narrow and beautiful Kerrysdale, in which a hydro-electric scheme is now operating. On the far side of Loch Maree, opposite the hotel, is *Letterewe*, where iron-smelting for cannons, using charcoal now exhausted, was in full swing until the mid-17th century. One of the best views of Loch Maree, seen from the north-western extremity, and looking towards Slioch, can be obtained from the southern outskirts of *Poolewe* (*q.v.*) on Loch Ewe. Another splendid view of the loch, from the south-east, can also be had from the road leading to *Kinlochewe* (*q.v.*) and Glen Docherty. Here, above the south-west shore of the loch, in Kinlochewe Forest, on the slopes of Ben Eighe, Britain's first National Nature Reserve has been established, and is described under *Kinlochewe*. *Iter. 205, 222.*

LOCH MORAR, Inverness. Map 23, **NM 7** 9.
See **Morar**.

LOCH MORLICH, Inverness. Map 25, **NH 9** 0.
This loch, with its sandy shores, lies in the heart of the Glen More National Forest Park, to the south of the peak of *Cairngorm*, 4,084 ft., which has given its name to the range as a whole. *Glenmore Lodge* is now a mountaineering training centre. There is a camping ground in the vicinity, and the district is becoming well known for ski-ing. Swedish reindeer were introduced here as an experiment in 1952 and the herd has since increased. To the north-east of the loch is the extensive Abernethy Forest, reached by means of a track over the Ryvoan Pass, with the picturesque little Green Loch. North-west of Loch Morlich, the Sluggan Pass gives access by means of another track to the Spey valley near *Boat of Garten* (*q.v.*). See **Nethybridge** and **Rothiemurchus**.

LOCHNAGAR, Aberdeen. Map 20, **NO 2** 8.
This famous granite peak, with its twin summits of 3,786 ft., and 3,768 ft., respectively, is the culminating point of the extensive, high-lying *White Mounth* (*q.v.*) plateau. It rises near the meeting-point of Aberdeen and Angus, overlooking the Royal Forest of Balmoral, and is separated from the great *Cairngorm* (*q.v.*) range by the beautifully-wooded Dee Valley. Lochnagar is a prominent feature in the view from many points on Deeside, and is also well seen from places far afield in Angus. The ascent can be made from *Braemar* (*q.v.*) up Glen Callater; from *Ballater* (*q.v.*) up Glen Muick by way of Loch Muick, above which rises *Cuidhe Crom*, 3,552 ft., a

Loch Long, Argyll; Dunbarton. Ben Arthur, 2,891 feet high, better known as ' The Cobbler,' rising to the north-west of the loch

Loch Lurgain, Ross and Cromarty. A view of the mountain of Stack Polly, 2,009 feet, its curious, pinnacled summit having the appearance of a porcupine's quills

Lochmaben, Dumfries. The Mercat Cross, which has sundials on the faces of its upper portion

Loch Maree, Ross and Cromarty. A tablet with a Gaelic inscription, recording Queen Victoria's visit in October, 1877, to the ' Loch Maree ' Hotel, on the west side of the loch, on A832

Loch Maree, Ross and Cromarty. The peak of Slioch, 3,260 feet, dominating the head of the loch, as seen from A832 on its western shores

Loch Morlich, Inverness. Cairn Gorm, 4,084 feet, from which the Cairngorm range takes its name, seen across the loch. It forms the background to the Glen More National Forest Park

[For LOCH MORLICH see also under CAIRNGORMS (Plate 26)

Loch Oich, Inverness. The Well of the Seven Heads, recording in four languages, Gaelic, English, French and Latin, the fate which overtook seven brothers who murdered the two sons of a 17th century Clan Keppoch chief

Loch Ness, Inverness. The Memorial to John Cobb, the racing motorist, who lost his life when his speedboat capsized in the loch in September, 1952. It is situated on A82, between Drumnadrochit and Invermoriston

Lochnaw Castle, Wigtown. The modernised 16th to 18th century Castle, which was the seat of the Agnews, formerly Sheriffs of Galloway

Loch Nan Uamh, Inverness. This loch saw the arrival, aboard a French ship, of Bonnie Prince Charlie at the start of the '45 Rising. A year later he fled to France by ship, departing from the same loch

Loch Nan Uamh, Inverness. The Memorial Cairn, set up in 1956 by the '45 Association, on the traditional spot from which Bonnie Prince Charlie left to set sail for France on the 20th September, 1746, after having wandered through the Highlands as a fugitive, with a price of £30,000 on his head

PLATE 115 (facing page 207)

south-eastern buttress of Lochnagar; and also from *Braedownie* (*q.v.*) in Glen Clova. Queen Victoria and the Prince Consort made the ascent from *Balmoral* (*q.v.*) on ponies, in 1848, by way of Glen Gelder. The view from the summit, where there is an indicator, is exceptionally fine, and below the peak is a deep corrie overhung by tremendous cliffs surrounding a tiny lochan. One of Byron's best-known poems has portrayed the mountain.

LOCH NAN UAMH, Inverness. Map 12, NM 6 8.
A picturesque West Highland sea loch, forming an offshoot of the Sound of Arisaig, and famous for its associations with Prince Charles Edward, who arrived on board a French frigate, on August 5th, 1745, and landed at Borrodale, where the tiny Borrodale Burn flows into the bay. *Borrodale House*, burnt after Culloden, but still preserving much of the original structure, has many associations with the Prince, and here took place the fateful interview with Lochiel, when the whole issue of the Jacobite Rising hung in the balance. The following year the Prince returned, this time as a fugitive, and was forced to hide in the nearby Glen Beasdale woods, before he was able to cross to the Outer Hebrides. Later, he returned to the mainland, and after again hiding in a cave near Borrodale, was taken on board the French frigate " *L'Heureux*," on September 20th, 1746, and left Scotland for the last time. A memorial cairn was set up on the shore in 1956 by the '45 Association. Behind the shores of the inner loch and the tiny Loch Beag is Gleann Mama, leading to Loch Mama, in the hills of South Morar. The views out to sea, towards Eigg and Rum are very noteworthy. See **Culloden, Glenfinnan, Kinlochmoidart, Lochailort** and **Morar.** *Iter. 209.*

LOCHNAW CASTLE, Wigtown. Map 2, NW 9 6.
Situated in the northern half of the peninsula known as the Rhinns of Galloway, and about half-way between Loch Ryan and the North Channel, in a setting of woods and rhododendrons. The Castle, 16th to 18th cent., and modernised, stands near a small loch, and is the ancient seat of the Agnews, once sheriffs of *Galloway* (*q.v.*). To the east of the castle lies the pretty *Aldouran Glen*, traversed by the Stranraer road. To the west is the ruined 16th-cent. *Galdenoch Castle. Iter. 83.*

LOCH NESS, Inverness. Map 25, NH 4 1 etc.
Extending for 24 miles, from a point south-west of *Inverness* (*q.v.*) to *Fort Augustus* (*q.v.*), this narrow loch is over 700 ft. deep in parts, and has not been known to freeze. In recent years it has acquired notoriety due to the appearance of the famous " Loch Ness Monster," first reported in 1932, and reputedly seen by a number of people, though its possible existence is still a matter of considerable speculation. St. Adamnan, the 7th-cent. Abbot of Iona and biographer of St. Columba (See **Dull**), refers in his writings to a much earlier Loch Ness monster, which he describes as an " aquatilis bestia." The splendid Inverness to Fort William road traverses the wooded western shores of the loch, while on the eastern side a road extends south-westwards as far as *Foyers* (*q.v.*), after which it veers inland, and only reaches the loch again near Fort Augustus. This road follows partly the course of Wade's original Fort Augustus to Inverness military road. There are no high hills in the immediate vicinity of Loch Ness, but *Mealfuarvonie*, 2,284 ft., is a conspicuous feature rising above the western shores opposite Foyers. The *Caledonian Canal* (*q.v.*) traverses its length in progressing through the Great Glen, or *Glen More* (*q.v.*). One of the most picturesque views from the loch extends into Glen Urquhart, stretching westwards from its bay, and guarded by the ruins of *Urquhart Castle* near *Drumnadrochit* (*q.v.*). In September 1952, when attempting to beat the water speed record with his jet speedboat, John Cobb, the well-known racing motorist, lost his life when his craft capsized and sank. A cairn has been erected in his memory between Invermoriston and Drumnadrochit. See **Inverfarigaig, Invermoriston** and **Loch Oich.** *Iter. 206, 207, 210, 211, 213.*

LOCH NEVIS, Inverness. Map 23, NM 7 9 and 8 9.
This magnificent sea loch, inferior in grandeur perhaps only to *Loch Hourn* (*q.v.*), is divided, like its rival, into an Inner and Outer loch, separated by the narrow strait of Kylesknoy-

dart. The mountain background is very impressive, with the rugged *Knoydart* (*q.v.*) hills to the north, and the lower hills of North Morar to the south dividing it from *Loch Morar* (See **Morar**). Finest of all are the lofty peaks at the head of Inner Loch Nevis, dominated by *Luinne Bheinn*, 3,083 ft., *Ben Aden*, 2,905 ft., and the sharp cone of *Sgurr na Ciche*, 3,410 ft. Unlike Loch Hourn, no roads give access to the shores of Loch Nevis, which is therefore almost isolated, and can only be visited by boat, or by long-distance walkers, and is reached by motor launch from *Mallaig* (*q.v.*) to *Inverie* (*q.v.*), on its north-west shores. From the head of the Inner Loch, a path traverses the wild pass of the Mam na Cloiche Airde, giving access for hardy walkers to *Loch Arkaig* (*q.v.*). Perhaps the finest view of the loch is that obtained from *Carn a'Ghobhair*, 1,794 ft., which can be climbed from Mallaig, the panorama from the summit including also the whole length of Loch Morar.

LOCH OICH, Inverness. Map 18, NN 3 9 and NH 3 0.
A short, but beautiful loch, forming one of the chain of lochs in the Great Glen, or *Glen More* (*q.v.*), through which penetrates the *Caledonian Canal* (*q.v.*), here reaching its highest point above sea-level. Along the western shores goes the fine Fort William to Inverness road, passing through *Invergarry* (*q.v.*), the gateway to some of the finest scenery in the North-West Highlands, while along the wooded eastern shores went Wade's former military road, now a minor road. At the northern end of the loch is *Aberchalder Lodge*, where Prince Charles Edward rallied his forces before crossing the *Corrieyairack Pass* (*q.v.*), in 1745, on his way to Edinburgh and England. On the west side of the loch, near its southern extremity, is the historic "Well of the Heads." This was erected to commemorate the fate which overtook seven brothers, who had killed the two sons of a 17th cent. Clan Keppoch chief, and whose gory heads were washed in the well by the avenger. The inscription on the monument is in four languages, Gaelic, English, French and Latin, the seven heads being carved around the top of the pillar, and surmounted by a hand clasping a dagger. See **Laggan Locks, Loch Lochy, Loch Ness** and **Roy Bridge.** *Iter. 210, 220.*

LOCH QUOICH, Inverness. Map 18, NG 9 0 and NH 0 0.
A most beautiful loch, penetrating westwards from Glen Garry into the rocky *Knoydart* (*q.v.*) mountains, its northern shores being traversed by the road from *Tomdoun* (*q.v.*) to *Kinloch Hourn* (*q.v.*), very rough at the end. King Edward VII visited Glen Quoich Lodge for the shooting on numerous occasions. Half-way along the road is *Quoich Bridge*, where the River Quoich flows into the loch from Glen Quoich. This roadless glen is surrounded by lofty hills, *Sgurr a'Mhoraire*, 3,365 ft., to the west, and *Gleourach*, 3,395 ft., and *Spideann Mialach*, 3,268 ft., to the east, and leads towards Glen Shiel, far to the north, having been traversed, in 1654, by General Monk and his troops. To the south of Loch Quoich rises the fine peak of *Gairich*, 3,015 ft., a notable landmark. From the south-western extremity of the loch, at Kinlochquoich, a walkers' track penetrates into the wild and lonely district known as the " Rough Bounds," dominated by *Sgurr na Ciche*, 3,410 ft., passing the very picturesque and tiny rock-girt Lochan nam Breac on the way to the distant shores of *Loch Hourn* (*q.v.*). Prince Charles Edward wandered in the district as a fugitive, in 1746, and had many narrow escapes from capture. There is much rugged scenery all around Loch Quoich, which is noted for its exceptionally high rainfall figures. A hydro-electric scheme now operates in the district. *Iter. 214.*

LOCH RANNOCH, Perth. Map 19, NN 5 5 and 6 5.
This inland sheet of water, 10 miles in length, extends westwards from *Kinloch Rannoch* to a point near Bridge of Gaur, on the road leading to the remote *Rannoch* (*q.v.*) station. High hills rise to the south of the loch, from *Schiehallion*, 3,547 ft., and *Carn Mairg*, 3,419 ft., in the south-eastern corner, to *Garbh Mheall*, 3,054 ft., lying to the south-west. The southern shores of the loch are bordered by the Black Wood of Rannoch. The waters of Loch Rannoch now form part of the Tummel-Garry hydro-electric scheme and there is a large power station. See **Kinloch Rannoch.** *Iter. 147, 148.*

LOCHRANZA, Isle of Arran, Bute.   Map 7, **NR 9 5**.
GOLF. The most northerly resort on the island, with a
steamer pier. It is situated on an attractive bay, at the foot
of Glen Chalmadale, with the Cock of Arran away to the
north-east, facing the Sound and Island of Bute, backed by
the hills of Cowal. The picturesque, ruined double-towered
Castle dates from the 14th cent., and overlooks Loch Ranza,
where Bruce is said to have landed, in 1306, from Ireland.
The fine road leading southwards towards *Pirnmill* (*q.v.*)
hugs the coast at the foot of a range of hills for the whole
of the distance, and passes, within two miles, the delightful
bay of *Catacol*, on Kilbrennan Sound. From here, Glen
Catacol extends southwards into the hills, with *Beinn
Bhreac* and *Beinn Bharrain* both exceeding 2,300 ft. in height.
They overlook the lonely Loch Tanna, which lies at an
altitude of 1,051 ft., beyond the head of the glen. To the
south of the loch extends the lengthy Glen Iorsa. Glen
Diomhan is a small National Nature Reserve to the south-
west, below *Meall nan Damh*, 1,870 ft., in Glen Catacol,
and contains rare whitebeam trees. See **Sannox**. *Iter. 242.*

LOCH SCAVAIG, Isle of Skye, Inverness.
                    Map 23, **NG 4 1** and **5 1**.
The beautiful sea loch of *Scavaig* lies immediately to the
south of the great *Coolin* (*q.v.*) range, and is crossed by the
motor boats from *Elgol* (*q.v.*) on their way to its head.
Beyond here, separated by a narrow barrier of land, lies the
wild and impressive *Loch Coruisk* (*q.v.*), with the jagged
peaks of the Coolins overhanging the far end. A little to
the west, the so-called " Mad Burn," impressive when in
spate, falls through its narrow ravine into the waters of
Scavaig. *Gars Bheinn*, 2,934 ft., the most southerly Coolin
peak, rises above the loch to the north-west, and off-shore is
the flat island of *Soay*, accessible from *Mallaig* (*q.v.*). Farther
out to sea is the mountainous island of Rum, and also Eigg,
with the curious Sgurr of Eigg. Perhaps the loveliest views
of Scavaig, with its superb mountain background, are those
which are to be obtained from the heights in the immediate
neighbourhood of Elgol. *Iter. 252.*

LOCH SHIEL, Argyll; Inverness.
                    Map 12, **NM 7 7** and **18 NM 8 7**.
A long and narrow fresh-water loch, in the romantic Clanranald country, stretching south-westwards from the Prince
Charles Edward monument (N.T. Scot.) at *Glenfinnan* (*q.v.*)
to *Acharacle* (*q.v.*). It forms the boundary between the
Ardgour (*q.v.*) district of Argyll and the *Moidart* (*q.v.*) district
of Inverness. For the whole of its 18 miles its breadth
nowhere exceeds a mile. The setting of this loch is one of
exceptional beauty, justifying its claim to be one of the very
finest in the Western Highlands, while its historical associations with the '45 give it much added interest. (See **Dalilea**
and **Kinlochmoidart**.) Lofty mountains look down on the
loch for much of its length, the finest being to the north,
where *Bheinn Odhar Bheag*, 2,895 ft., towering above the
west shore, faces *Meall nan Creag Leac*, 2,784 ft. In the
background, behind the Prince's monument, rise parallel
ranges of rock-strewn hills guarding Glen Finnan. Farther
down the loch, the mountains of Moidart recede, and
interest turns to the eastern shore, where *Ben Resipol*, 2,774
ft., tapers to a sharp, rocky peak. Near its foot, in the
narrows of Loch Shiel, is the little island of *Eileen Fhionain*,
with an ancient burial-ground, preserving a very rare example
of a Celtic bell. To the east, where the Polloch River flows
into the loch from the tiny Loch Doilate, is an opening in
the hills threaded by the lonely, wooded Glen Hurich. At
the far end of Loch Shiel, the short course of the Shiel River
connects with Outer Loch Moidart, in flat, mossy surroundings. Loch Shiel is difficult of access by road, except at the
two extremities. A steamer links Glenfinnan with Acharacle,
at its south-western extremity, and the magnificent mountain
views to be obtained from this lovely loch make the journey
by boat eminently worth undertaking. *Iter. 209, 217.*

LOCH SHIN, Sutherland.   Map 29, **NC 4 1** etc.
See **Lairg** and **Overscaig**.

LOCH SLOY, Dunbarton.   Map 15, **NN 2 1**.
See **Inveruglas** and **Loch Lomond**. *Iter. 100, 110, 111.*

LOCH SUNART, Argyll.   Map 12, **NM 6 5** etc.
A delightful sea loch, extending inland from the Ardnamurchan peninsula on the Sound of Mull for a distance of
some 20 miles. Its head lies in an amphitheatre of hills,
where the districts of *Ardgour* (*q.v.*) and *Morven* (*q.v.*) meet,
and is dominated to the north-east by the fine rock peak of
Garbh Bheinn, 2,903 ft., and to the south-east by *Creach
Bheinn*, 2,800 ft. Both of these are notable viewpoints, and
between them a road threads its way through Glen Tarbert,
giving access to Loch Linnhe. This picturesque, though
narrow and hilly road, traverses the northern shores of Loch
Sunart, providing lovely views of the wooded southern
shores, with some low hills beyond. It passes the small
resorts of *Strontian* (*q.v.*) and *Salen* (*q.v.*), behind which rises
the prominent cone of *Ben Resipol*, 2,774 ft., from the
summit of which the panorama is one of the finest in the
Western Highlands, overlooking the whole length of
picturesque *Loch Shiel* (*q.v.*) and across the sea to the islands
of Eigg and Rum. *Iter. 216, 217, 218.*

LOCH TAY, Perth.   Map 15, **NN 6 3** etc.
This large and deep Highland loch, nearly 15 miles long, is
noted for its salmon fishing, and is overlooked, to the north,
by *Ben Lawers*, 3,984 ft. (N.T. Scot.), Perthshire's highest
mountain. (See **Lawers**.) Facing Ben Lawers, to the west,
are the peaks of the *Tarmachans*, 3,421 ft., the views from
these mountains being very extensive, including almost the
whole of the *Breadalbane* (*q.v.*) country and much of the
Grampians (*q.v.*). Roads traverse both shores of Loch Tay,
the main road being on the north side, but the views from the
wooded south shore are more beautiful, though the road is
somewhat narrow and hilly. From this side paths lead into
the hills, that from Ardeonaig, with its mill and waterfall,
giving access to Glen Lednoch, and that from Ardtalnaig,
farther to the north-east, leading towards Glen Almond.
Loch Tay has been well described in Scott's " Fair Maid of
Perth." The River Tay, some 120 miles in length, and with
the largest volume of water of any river in Britain, flows
from the eastern extremity of Loch Tay towards *Aberfeldy*
(*q.v.*). See **Kenmore**, **Killin** and **Tyndrum**. *Iter. 107, 120,
138, 139.*

LOCH TORRIDON, Ross and Cromarty.
                            Map 22, **NG 7 6** etc.
See **Torridon**. *Iter. 223.*

LOCH TROOL, Kirkcudbright.   Map 2, **NX 4 7**.
This beautiful loch, in the heart of the remote *Galloway* (*q.v.*)
Highlands, and reached from *Bargrennan* (*q.v.*), on the
Girvan to Newton Stewart road, lies in a most picturesque
setting in Glen Trool. It is now becoming better known,
due mainly to the creation of the Glen Trool National Forest
Park. The Park has a total area of over 110,000 acres, and
consists in all of five forests, several of which are contiguous.
The Glen Trool Forest contains the finest scenery, and a
camping site is situated near the loch, at Caldons Farm.
(The remaining forests in the Park are described under **Barr**,
Clatteringshaws Dam and **Newton Stewart**.) To the north
of the loch rises the *Merrick*, 2,764 ft., the highest mainland
mountain south of the Highlands proper. This, together
with its lesser satellites, is included within the Park, and
below its eastern and southern slopes lie Loch Enoch and
Loch Neldricken, the latter incorporating the remote
" Murder Hole." South-east of Loch Enoch are the remote
Round and Long Lochs of the Dungeon. At the east end
of Loch Trool is the Bruce Memorial, a fine viewpoint, the
stone commemorating a victory over the English by Bruce
in 1307. At the south-western extremity of the loch, near
Caldons Farm, is an inscribed Martyrs' Stone, dominated
in the background by *Muldonach* and *Lamachan Hill*,
2,349 ft., in the hills of the Minnigaff district. Away to the
north-east rise the *Rhinns of Kells*, dominated by *Corserine*,
2,668 ft., and *Carlins Cairn*, 2,650 ft. Farther south are
Millfire, 2,350 ft. and *Meikle Millyea*, 2,446 ft., between which
lies the lonely Loch Dungeon. Much of the fine, wild
mountain country of the Merrick district is described in
S. R. Crockett's " Raiders." *Iter. 71, 79.*

LOCH TULLA, Argyll.   Map 15, **NN 2 4**.
See **Inveroran**.

Loch Shiel, Argyll; Inverness. A view from Glenfinnan of the 18-mile long loch up which Prince Charles Edward sailed with some of his followers at the start of the '45 Rising. The monument to the Prince is visible in the foreground, and is illustrated also under Glenfinnan (Plate 76)

Loch Sunart, Argyll. Ben Resipol, 2,774 feet, seen from a point near Strontian, which lies on the northern shore of the loch

Loch Trool, Kirkcudbright. The Bruce Memorial, at the eastern end of the loch, which commemorates one of his victories, in 1307

Loch Tay, Perth. Ben Lawers, 3,984 feet (N.T. Scot.), Perthshire's highest mountain, and of great botanical interest, seen from the unclassified road along the south shore

Loch Tulla, Argyll. A view of the loch, which lies on the edge of the Black Mount, to the west of the new road leading to Glencoe. In the vicinity was born, in 1724, Duncan Ban MacIntyre, who has been described as the ' Burns of the Highlands '

PLATE 116 (facing page 208)

Logierait, Perth. Examples of mortsafes in the churchyard, formerly used to prevent the the removal of corpses for sale as anatomical specimens

Longforgan, Perth. The 15th century Castle Huntly, on a rocky site to the south-west, off an unclassified road. It was erected by Lord Gray of Foulis, Master of the Household to James II, and was at one period known as Castle Lyon

Lorne, Argyll. Inverawe House, partly 16th century, which is associated with a ghost story. It stands north of the River Awe, at Bonawe, off A85, in the district of Lorne

Loth, Sutherland. The Monument commemorating the slaying by Hunter Polson, c. 1700, of the last wolf in Sutherland. It stands at the foot of Glen Loth, to the south-west, and on the north side of A9

Lothians. The remains of the 15th century Soutra Aisle, a one-time hospice and sanctuary. It stands just to the south-west of Soutra Hill, on B6368, in Midlothian

Lothians. Preston Mill, a 17th century water-mill (N.T. Scot.), perhaps the oldest in Scotland, at East Linton, an East Lothian village, situated between the Lammermuir Hills and the Firth of Forth

PLATE 117 (facing page 209)

LOCH TUMMEL, Perth.　　　　Map 19, NN 8 5.
See **Queen's View** and **Tummel Bridge.** *Iter. 138, 148.*

LOCH VENNACHAR, Perth.　　　Map 15, NN 5 0.
See **Callander** and **Trossachs.** *Iter. 106, 111, 139.*

LOCHWINNOCH, Renfrew. 1,950.　　Map 8, NS 3 5.
E.C. Wed. GOLF. A small textile and furniture manufacturing town, on Castle Semple Loch. At the south end
of the loch are the remains of *Barr Castle* and *Peel Castle*.
To the north-west lies an extensive and lofty moorland area,
which rises to 1,663 ft. at *Misty Law*, and 1,711 ft. at the
Hill of Stake, the former being a splendid viewpoint. Both
of these hills are situated on the borders of Ayrshire. See
Howwood. *Iter. 58, 85.*

LOCHY BRIDGE, Inverness.　　　Map 18, NN 1 7.
Iter. 143, 208, 209, 210, 214, 215, 220.

LOCKERBIE, Dumfries. 2,668. SB.　　Map 4, NY 1 8.
E.C. Tues. M.D. Thurs. GOLF. An Annandale market
town, noted for its August lamb fair, which dates back to
the 17th cent. The Old Tower was formerly the town gaol.
To the east flows the Water of Milk, near which stands the
mansion of *Castle Milk* with its fine gardens, situated **3 m.**
S. of Lockerbie. A Roman Camp, comprising a remarkable
group of fortifications, is situated near the flat-topped
Birrenswark Hill, to the south-east of the town. **5 m.**
N.N.W., to the west of the Moffat road and beyond the
River Annan, is *Spedlins Tower*, dated 1605, though some
portions of the structure are 15th cent. work. See **Loch-**
maben. *Iter. 10, 13, 29, 42, 45, 50, 51.*

LOGAN HOUSE, Wigtown.　　　　Map 2, NX 0 4.
See **Port Logan.**

LOGIE, Moray.　　　　　Map 26, NJ 0 5.
Situated a little to the east of the River Findhorn, which
flows here through a deep and picturesque gorge, with the
Altyre Woods and Darnaway Forest to the north. (See
Forres.) 1½ m. S.W. of Logie is the beauty spot known as
" Randolph's Leap," reached on foot, in the picturesque
Findhorn Glen, near the confluence of the river with the
Divie. The fine grounds of *Relugas House* lie nearby, and
farther to the south-west, off the road to *Ferness* (q.v.) is
Daltulich Bridge, spanning the Findhorn, on the Nairn
border. See **Dulsie Bridge.** *Iter. 172, 173.*

LOGIE COLDSTONE, Aberdeen.　　Map 26, NJ 4 0.
Iter. 141, 167, 191.

LOGIE EASTER, Ross and Cromarty. 528.
　　　　　　　　　　　　　Map 31, NH 7 7.
An agricultural village, well known for its herds of cattle.
1 m. S.W., beyond the Balnagown River, is the 13th to 16th
cent. turreted *Balnagown Castle*, once the home of the Earls
of Ross. The castle has fine gardens. **2 m.** W., near the
Balnagown River, lies *Marybank* churchyard, in which are
preserved some ancient stones. See **Milton** (Ross and Cromarty) and **Nigg.** *Iter. 201.*

LOGIERAIT, Perth.　　　　Map 20, NN 9 5.
Once famous for a Royal Castle, the seat of the Regality
Courts of Atholl. From its gaol, Rob Roy made an escape
in 1717. The village is situated in Strath Tay, and a little to
the south-east the River Tay is joined by the Tummel. In
the Church are preserved some sculptured stones, and there
are mortsafes in the churchyard. Standing stones and
remains of stone circles exist at various places on the east
bank of the Tay. *Iter. 120, 158.*

LONGFORGAN, Perth.　　　　Map 17, NO 3 2.
In the fertile *Carse of Gowrie* (q.v.), between the *Sidlaw* hills
and the Firth of Tay. **1 m.** S.W., on a rocky site, is the
impressive *Castle Huntly*, once known as *Castle Lyon*, and
dating from the 15th cent., with considerable additions from
the latter half of the 17th cent. See **Fowlis Easter** and
Kinnaird. *Iter. 154.*

LONGFORMACUS, Berwick. 320.　　Map 10, NT 6 5.
A remote little place in the foothills of the *Lammermuirs*,
situated on the Dye Water, not far from its junction with
the Whiteadder Water away to the north-east. *Longformacus
House* is Georgian. *Dirrington Great Law* 1,309 ft., rises

to the south, overlooking the Duns road. The hilly and
winding road leading north-westwards from Longformacus
into the hills gives access to the village of *Gifford* (q.v.). To
the west of this road, on the Lammermuir heights, near the
East Lothian border, are the so-called " Mutiny Stones," a
relic of the Stone Age. *Iter. 3.*

LONGHAVEN, Aberdeen.　　　　Map 27, NK 1 4.
Iter. 181, 182, 187.

LONGMANHILL, Banff.　　　　Map 27, NJ 7 6.
Iter. 181, 183, 188.

LONGNIDDRY, East Lothian.　　　Map 10, NT 4 7.
GOLF. The village stands just inland from a stretch of
flat, sandy coast, where there is a well-known golf course.
Between 1643 and 1647, John Knox was a tutor here.
1½ m. N.E., is the ruined 16th to 17th cent. mansion of
Redhouse. See **Gosford House** and **Seton.** *Iter. 2, 37.*

LONGRIDGE, West Lothian.　　　Map 9, NS 9 6.
Iter. 86.

LONGSIDE, Aberdeen.　　　　Map 27, NK 0 4.
Iter. 188, 189.

LONGTOWN, Cumberland (England).　　Map 4, NY 3 6.
E.C. Wed. M.D. Thurs. *Iter. 11, 12, 30, 31, 51, 67.*

LONMAY, Aberdeen.　　　　Map 27, NK 0 5.
A little to the east is the Loch of Strathbeg, near the shores
of Strathbeg Bay. 2½ m. N.E. is *Cairness House*, dating
from 1792. **3 m.** N.N.W., near the village of *Rathen*, is
the Bronze Age burial cairn of *Memsie* (A.M.). *Iter. 181,
182.*

LORNE, Argyll.　　　　Map 14, NM 9 2 etc.
The name given to the picturesque stretch of country lying
between the Firth of Lorne, at the seaward end of *Loch
Linnhe* (q.v.), and *Loch Awe* (q.v.), farther to the south.
The eastern boundary of the district is formed by the
mountains surrounding Loch Etive, beyond which, to the
west, lie the districts of *Benderloch* and *Appin* (both q.v.),
in reality a part of Lorne itself, which extends in a northerly
direction as far as Loch Leven and the wild *Glencoe* (q.v.)
country. *Oban* (q.v.) is the principal centre of Lorne, and
is well placed for explorations in one of the loveliest parts
of the Western Highlands of Scotland. The Duke of Argyll
takes one of his titles from the name Lorne. A magnificent
panorama of the entire Lorne country can be obtained from
the summit of *Ben Cruachan*, 3,689 ft., which may be
climbed from a point near the *Falls of Cruachan* (q.v.), on
the shores of Loch Awe, near the Pass of Brander.

LOSSIEMOUTH, Moray.　　　　Map 26, NJ 2 7.
5,161. SB. with Branderburgh.
E.C. Thurs. GOLF. A well-known resort on Spey Bay, at
the mouth of the River Lossie, with good sands and bathing;
there are extensive sandhills to the east beyond the river.
The harbour, at *Branderburgh*, at the west end of the town,
serves as the port of *Elgin* (q.v.). The Rt. Hon. Ramsay
Macdonald was born in 1866 at Lossiemouth. To the west
of the harbour, about two miles distant, is *Covesea*, with its
lighthouse, and also a number of caves showing fantastic
rock formations. At *Kinnedar*, to the south-west of Lossiemouth, the Bishops of Moray formerly had a castle, of
which there are but scanty remains still in existence. See
Duffus and **Spynie Palace.** *Iter. 187, 192, 199.*

LOTH, Sutherland.　　　　Map 31, NC 9 1.
A monument at the foot of Glen Loth, a little to the south-
west, commemorates the slaying of the last wolf in the county.
East of Lothbeg Bridge, at the foot of the glen, are remains
of an early long cairn, and in Glen Loth itself are standing
stones, while in the background rise *Beinn Dobhrain*,
2,060 ft., and *Ben Uarie*, 2,046 ft. **2 m.** S.W., on the coast,
is the ruined broch of Cinn Trolla. *Iter. 200, 231, 233.*

LOTHIANS.　　Map 9, NS 9 7 and 10, NT 6 7 etc.
The Lothian district now comprises a large expanse of
country bordered by the Firth of Forth, and extending
roughly from Dunbar, in the east, to Linlithgow, in the
west, incorporating the greater part of the *Lammermuir*,
Moorfoot and *Pentland* hills. It is divided into the counties

of East Lothian, Midlothian, which includes the city of Edinburgh, and West Lothian. In former times the Lothians extended as far south as the River Tweed, and were part of the ancient kingdom of Northumbria. The family of Kerr takes its title of Marquis from the name Lothian. An extensive panorama of much of the Lothian country can be obtained from the summit of *Soutra Hill* (*q.v.*), on the Edinburgh to Lauder road.

LOUDOUNHILL, Ayr. Map 8, NS 6 3.
Near *Loudoun Hill*, 1,043 ft., an isolated cone of rock, was fought, in 1307, a battle in which Robert Bruce defeated the English. A little to the north of the hill, in 1679, the battle of *Drumclog* was won by the Covenanters. To the east of Loudoun Hill is Wallace's Cairn, commemorating a successful skirmish by Sir William Wallace. This region is well depicted by Scott in "Old Mortality." *Loudoun Castle* is described under Galston. *Iter. 20, 69.*

LOVAT BRIDGE, Inverness. Map 25, NH 5 4.
About a mile to the south-east of this bridge over the Beauly River, a road diverges southwards from the Inverness road, and leads by way of the fertile district of *The Aird*, through Glen Convinth, in the direction of Glen Urquhart. Another branch, narrow and poor, forks south-eastwards from the glen, and climbs towards the tiny Loch Laide. *Iter. 200, 201, 203, 204, 205, 210, 213, 221.*

LOWLANDS, THE
That part of Scotland known as the *Lowlands*, as distinct from the *Highlands*, and which includes also the tumbled Border Country, separated from England by the *Cheviots* (*q.v.*), is sometimes described as being the area lying to the south and east of the *Grampian* (*q.v.*) mountains. A rather more definite geological line of demarcation is often quoted, which has been given in detail in the separate article describing the *Highlands*. Broadly speaking, the Lowlands are perhaps best known as the country situated to the south of the Clyde estuary and the Firth of Forth, or simply to the south of a line linking Glasgow, Stirling and Edinburgh. The landscape is characterised by rounded green hills, pleasant valleys and some excellent farming country. Much of this area has become famous owing to its associations with Sir Walter Scott and Robert Burns, and the romantic Border Country is especially delightful. It must, however, not be forgotten that nearly all the country lying near the east coast between the Firth of Forth and the Moray Firth, and even the distant county of Caithness, beyond the latter, is true Lowland country. This area is often better described as the *North-East Lowlands*. A remarkable feature of the Lowlands in the south-west is the less well-known district of *Galloway*, where the lonely, rugged hills, dominated by the lofty *Merrick*, 2,764 ft., exhibit many of the features of real Highland mountains. Most of Scotland's industrial area is centred in the Lowlands, notably between the Clyde and Forth estuaries. See **Border Country, Burns Country, Galloway, Highlands, Scott Country** and **Wanlockhead.**

LUCE ABBEY, Wigtown. Map 2, NX 1 5.
See **Glenluce.** *Iter. 78.*

LUGAR, Ayr. 1,148. Map 8, NS 5 2.
A cave here was the scene of early experiments in coal-gas lighting by William Murdoch, who was born at Bello Mill in the village, in 1754. The large ironworks date from 1845. See **Muirkirk** (for *Airds Moss*). *Iter. 21, 68.*

LUGTON, Ayr. Map 8, NS 4 5.
GOLF. *Iter. 57, 60, 62.*

LUING, ISLE OF, Argyll. Map 14, NM 7 0
See **Clachan Bridge.** and 7 1.

LUMPHANAN, Aberdeen. 831. Map 27, NJ 5 0.
E.C. Thurs. GOLF. Situated a little to the north of the winding River Dee, beyond the Loch of Auchlossan. To the north is Macbeth's Cairn, where he made his last stand in 1057. After he had been killed, his head was taken to Malcolm at *Kincardine Castle*, near *Fettercairn* (*q.v.*). See **Craigievar Castle** and **Torphins.** *Iter. 165, 190.*

LUMSDEN, Aberdeen. Map 26, NJ 4 2.
Lies in a valley between the *Correen* hills, to the east, and

the *Buck of Cabrach*, 2,368 ft., to the west. **2 m. N.**, off the Dufftown road, to the left, is the ruined *Auchindoir* Church, with a richly-carved 12th or 13th cent. doorway, and also a Sacrament House. Near the Church is a mote, on which stood formerly the Norman castle. To the west, on the Burn of Craig, stands the 16th cent. *Craig Castle. Iter. 165, 167, 177, 190.*

LUNCARTY, Perth. Map 16, NO 0 2.
Near the River Tay, on which is situated at this point a salmon hatchery. A battle is said to have been fought in the vicinity in 990, when the Danes were defeated, the Scots having been rallied by a peasant armed only with a plough-yoke. It is sometimes thought that the adoption of the thistle as the Scottish national emblem arose out of an incident in this battle. *Iter. 148, 149, 150.*

LUNDIE, Angus. Map 17, NO 2 3.
A *Sidlaw Hills* village, to the south of Loch Long. The Church contains Norman work.

LUNDIN LINKS, Fife. 400. Map 17, NO 4 0.
E.C. Thurs. GOLF. A golfing resort, on Largo Bay, with its good sands. Three standing stones are preserved near the station. A tall 14th cent. tower from a former mansion of the Lundins can still be seen. *Iter. 94, 98, 128.*

LUSS, Dunbarton. 495. Map 15, NS 3 9.
E.C. Wed. An exceptionally pretty village, at the mouth of Glen Luss, on the western shores of *Loch Lomond* (*q.v.*) facing a group of wooded islands, and looking northwards to *Ben Lomond*, 3,192 ft. There is a steamer pier. Coleridge, and also Wordsworth and his sister visited Luss, in 1803. **3 m. S.**, on a promontory facing Loch Lomond, is *Rossdhu House*, a seat of the Colquhouns. 3½ m. N., off the *Tarbet* (*q.v.*) road, is the entrance to Glen Douglas, set between lofty hills, and threaded by a road leading to the shores of Loch Long. At *Inverbeg*, **3 m. N.**, of Luss, Loch Lomond is crossed in summer by a passenger ferry, giving access to *Rowardennan* (*q.v.*). *Iter. 88, 100, 101, 110, 137.*

LYBSTER, Caithness. Map 30, ND 2 3.
E.C. Thurs. GOLF. On Lybster Bay, situated on a wild and rocky stretch of coast, with Clyth Ness to the east, and of some importance for its fishing industry. The Church, built of dressed local flagstones, has a West door in the ancient native tradition, and the chancel entrance is in the same form. See **Kildonan** (Sutherland) and **Mid Clyth.** *Iter. 200.*

LYNE, Peebles. Map 9, NT 1 4.
The Church, one of the smallest in Scotland, contains a pulpit and two canopied pews said to be of Dutch workmanship. Near the Church is a Roman camp. A little to the south, beyond Lyne station, and across the River Tweed near its junction with the Lyne Water, is *Barns Tower*, dating from 1488, and retaining its iron yett. It is associated with an early novel by John Buchan. In the vicinity is the whiteharled *Barns House*. To the north of Lyne are the twin *Meldon* hills, facing each other across a narrow road leading to *Eddleston* (*q.v.*). Farther north, and to the west of this road, rises *Crailzie Hill*, 1,561 ft., with the interesting Harehope Rings and the prehistoric Harehope Fort. See **Broughton** and **Romanno Bridge.** *Iter. 14, 35, 52, 53.*

LYNE OF SKENE, Aberdeen. Map 27, NJ 7 1.
Iter. 197.

LYNWILG, Inverness. Map 25, NH 8 0.
On Loch Alvie, in a pleasant wooded setting, with a Waterloo cairn, and a monument to the last Duke of Gordon standing on *Tor of Alvie Hill*, to the south-east. From the summit, the view extends eastwards over the great *Rothiemurchus* (*q.v.*) forest towards the distant *Cairngorms* (*q.v.*). In Alvie churchyard, at the western extremity of the loch, is buried Sir George Henschel. To the north-west of Lynwilg rises *Geal Charn Mor*, 2,702 ft., from the summit of which the distant view of the Cairngorms has been described as one of the finest panoramas in the country. *Iter. 140, 147, 150, 208.*

MACDUFF, Banff. 3,404. SB. Map 27, NJ 7 6.
E.C. Wed. GOLF. An important herring-fishing town,

Luss, Dunbarton. The gateway, on A82, leading to the mansion of Rhos Dhu, the seat of the Colquhouns

Lundin Links, Fife. A trio of prehistoric standing stones, which are situated off the Leven road (A915)

Lowlands. The remains of Carleton Castle, at Lendalfoot, on the Ayrshire coast. Its former baronial owner is said to have pushed his first seven wives over the cliff, but was himself thus disposed of by the eighth

Lumphanan, Aberdeen. Macbeth's Cairn, locally reputed to commemorate his last stand in 1057 before he was slain. It stands a little to the north, off A980

Lugar, Ayr. A scene on the Lugar Water. Near this spot is a cave in which William Murdoch conducted experiments in coal-gas lighting during the 18th century

Lumsden, Aberdeen. Craig Castle, which stands off B9002, some 3½ miles to the north. Patrick Gordon, slain at Flodden Field in 1513, built the original tower three years previously

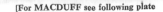

[For MACDUFF see following plate

Macduff, Banff. Rock outcrops near the Howe of Tarlair, to the east

Mallaig, Inverness. The fishing port of Mallaig, which faces the island of Skye across the Sound of Sleat

Magus Muir, Fife. The gravestone of five Covenanters, taken prisoner at the battle of Bothwell Brig, in 1679, and later executed here. It is situated 3 miles north-east of Pitscottie, on B939. In a wood nearby is a cairn marking the spot where Archbishop Sharp was murdered in the same year

Manor, Peebles. The stone which David Ritchie, the original of the 'Black Dwarf,' or 'Bowed Davie' of Sir Walter Scott's novel, 'The Black Dwarf,' is said to have carried here from the bed of the River Tweed, nearly a mile distant (see below)

Manor, Peebles. The cottage in which David Ritchie, the original of the 'Black Dwarf' of Sir Walter Scott's novel is said to have lived, showing the special 'dwarf' door

PLATE 119 (facing page 211)

situated in *Banff Bay*, with a large harbour. Across the mouth of the River Deveron, to the west, is the town of *Banff* (*q.v.*). Macduff was formerly known as *Down*, the name being changed in 1783. On the *Hill of Down*, a viewpoint, is a lofty War Memorial. A little to the east is the Howe of Tarlair, with Tarlair Well, and some fantastic rock outcrops by the shore, where there is also a bathing pool. See **Crovie**, **Gardenstown** and **King Edward**. *Iter. 180, 181, 182, 183, 188.*

MACHRIE, Isle of Arran, Bute. Map 7, NR 8 3.
GOLF. Situated on Machrie Bay, on the Kilbrennan Sound, facing the *Kintyre* (*q.v.*) peninsula. The Machrie Water flows into the bay at this point, and about 1½ m. E., on its south bank, are the Standing Stones of Tormore, with remains of some 10 circles. The coast road to the south leads inland to *Blackwaterfoot* (*q.v.*), and a path from it diverges to the coast for the King's Caves, in the largest of which Fingal and Bruce are traditionally said to have sheltered. North of Machrie, a road goes eastwards inland to link up with the String Road, leading to the east coast of the island at *Brodick* (*q.v.*). The coast road goes due north towards Dougrie Point, near which is the seaward end of the long and desolate Glen Iorsa, hemmed in by high hills at its head. *Iter. 242.*

MACHRIE, Isle of Islay. Argyll. Map 6, NR 3 4.
GOLF. See **Port Ellen**. *Iter. 243, 244.*

MACHRIHANISH, Argyll. 130. Map 6, NR 6 2.
E.C. Thurs. GOLF. A *Kintyre* (*q.v.*) resort on Machrihanish Bay, looking towards the open Atlantic, with good sands for bathing, and also extensive sand dunes to the north, on which is situated a very well-known golf course. The airport for *Campbeltown* (*q.v.*) lies between that town and Machrihanish. **4 m. S.S.W.** is *Cnoc Moy*, 1,462 ft., whose slopes overlook the sea, and are honeycombed with caves which contain stalactites. These are best reached by way of *Southend* (*q.v.*). *Iter. 123.*

MACMERRY, East Lothian. Map 10, NT 4 7.
Iter. 1.

MAESHOWE, Orkney. Map 33, HY 3 1.
See **Orkney Islands** (Mainland). *Iter. 263.*

MAGGIEKNOCKATER, Banff. Map 26, NJ 3 4.
This tiny village is situated in a finely-wooded glen between the heights of *Ben Aigan*, 1,544 ft., to the north-west, and *Knockan*, 1,219 ft., to the north-east. *Iter. 170.*

MAGUS MUIR, Fife. Map 17, NO 4 1.
See **Pitscottie**.

MAIDENS, Ayr. Map 8, NS 2 0.
A small fishing village and resort on Maidenhead Bay, with a sandy beach. See **Culzean Castle**, **Kirkoswald** and **Turnberry**. *Iter. 80.*

MAINLAND, Orkney. Map 33, HY 4 1 etc.
See **Orkney Islands** (Mainland).

MAINLAND, Shetland. Map 33, HY 4 4 etc.
See **Shetland Islands** (Mainland).

MAINSRIDDLE, Kirkcudbright. Map 3, NX 9 5.
See **Southerness**. *Iter. 72, 73.*

MALLAIG, Inverness. 600. Map 23, NM 6 9.
E.C. Wed. A fishing port and calling-place for the Inner and Outer Hebridean steamers, lying in a splendid setting on the shores of North Morar. It forms the terminal point of the romantic Road to the Isles, " By Ailort and by Morar to the sea." Steamers, carrying cars, maintain a service to *Armadale* (*q.v.*), and also *Portree* (*q.v.*) in Skye. Motorboats serve the island of *Soay* (See **Loch Scavaig**). There are connections by motor launch to *Inverie* (*q.v.*), on the hill-girt inlet of *Loch Nevis* (*q.v.*), which lies on the threshold of the rugged *Knoydart* (*q.v.*) country, in which *Ladhar Bheinn*, 3,343 ft., rises to the south of *Loch Hourn* (*q.v.*). Prince Charles Edward landed at Mallaig, as a fugitive, in 1746, and after much wandering in the lonely hills in the vicinity finally reached *Loch nan Uamh* (*q.v.*). **3 m. E.** of Mallaig rises the pathless, wild and rocky hill of *Carn a'Ghobhair*, 1,794 ft., from the summit of which

the view is one of the very finest in Scotland, taking in the whole length of both Loch Morar and Loch Nevis, with their background of picturesque, rocky peaks. The panorama extends westwards over the sea to distant Ardnamurchan Point, and across towards the mountainous outline of Rum, and also Skye, in which the jagged Coolin peaks are the dominating feature. See **Arisaig** and **Morar**. *Iter. 209.*

MAMORE FOREST, Inverness. Map 18, NN 1 6 and 2 6.
The fine group of mountains known as the *Mamore Forest*, or simply the *Mamores*, lies in the heart of *Lochaber* (*q.v.*), between Glen Nevis and Loch Leven. The highest peak is *Binnein Mor*, 3,700 ft., rising above *Kinlochleven* (*q.v.*). The next highest is *Sgurr a'Mhaim*, 3,601 ft., with its white quartzite summit, neighboured by *Stob Ban*, 3,274 ft., both of which form a prominent feature in the view up Glen Nevis at the foot of *Ben Nevis* (*q.v.*). The ridges of the Mamores extend from east to west for a distance of 8 miles, the average height being rarely less than 3,000 ft., providing some of the finest ridge-walking to be found in Scotland. In winter, under snow conditions, they present an impressive sight from many points in the vicinity. A magnificent view of the entire group of hills can be obtained from the summit of Ben Nevis, or from the lofty peaks around *Glencoe* (*q.v.*).

MAM RATTACHAN PASS, Inverness; Ross and Cromarty. Map 24, NG 9 1.
This splendid pass, which rises to 1,116 ft., the summit being on the county boundary between Inverness and Ross and Cromarty, links the shores of *Loch Duich* (*q.v.*) with the remote village of *Glenelg* (*q.v.*), on the narrow strait separating the mainland from the island of *Skye* (*q.v.*). The climb is steep (1 in 6) and winding, with hairpin bends, and the surface poor, and considerable recent afforestation has somewhat changed the magnificent views in the vicinity. From the summit, Loch Duich, the jewel of *Kintail* (*q.v.*), is seen in all its beauty, backed by the famous *Five Sisters of Kintail*, dominated by *Scour Ouran*, 3,505 ft., overlooking the defile of *Glen Shiel* (*q.v.*). The whole picture is one of the grandest in Scotland. The descent to the west, following the Glenmore River, is more gradual, while to the south-west is seen the prominent *Ben Sgriol*, 3,196 ft., one of the rugged peaks which guard *Loch Hourn* (*q.v.*). Dr. Johnson and Boswell crossed the pass on horseback during their Highland Tour in 1773 on the way to Glenelg, and the Doctor described it as " a terrible steep to climb." See **Shiel Bridge**. *Iter. 207.*

MANOR, Peebles. Map 9, NT 2 3.
The little Church of *Manor* stands at the northern extremity of the long and beautiful valley of the Manor Water, which flows into the Tweed to the west of *Peebles* (*q.v.*). In the churchyard is the tombstone of the " Black Dwarf " (see below). The setting is one of green, rounded Lowland hills, becoming loftier as the valley is ascended, and culminating in *Dollar Law*, 2,680 ft. Once a centre of population, the valley is now only sparsely occupied, and several ruined towers, among them *Castlehill* and *Posso*, recall the past. Near the latter is the isolated *Woodhill*, on which stood traditionally a building known as *Macbeth's Castle*. To the south of the Church is *Hallyards Manor*, associated in 1797, with Sir Walter Scott, when visiting David Ritchie, the original of the " Black Dwarf." The present " Black Dwarf's Cottage " is situated a little to the south, and

beyond it, to the south-east, rises *Canada Hill*, 1,713 ft. See **Lyne**.

MARCHMONT HOUSE, Berwick.　　Map 11, NT 7 5.
See **Polwarth**.

MARKINCH, Fife. 2,456. SB.　　Map 17, NO 2 0.
E.C. Wed. A paper-making town, noted for *St. Drostan's Church*, the tower of which dates from the 11th or 12th cent., with a later upper storey. General Leslie, the Covenanter, who died in 1661, is buried in the Church. North of the town is the Stob Cross, marking the limits of a former sanctuary. **2 m. N.W.**, on high ground, is *Bandon Tower*, dating from c. 1580. See **Glenrothes** and **Milton of Balgonie**. *Iter. 98.*

MARNOCH, Banff.　　Map 27, NJ 5 5.
Iter. 189.

MARWICK, Orkney.　　Map 33, HY 2 2.
See **Orkney Islands** (Mainland). *Iter. 264.*

MARYBANK, Ross and Cromarty.　　Map 25, NH 4 5.
Situated at the eastern extremity of Strath Conon. The road through this wooded glen, backed by shapely hills at its farthest extremity where Loch Beannachan is situated, leaves the Beauly to Garve road at Marybank. A little to the south, beyond the windings of the River Orrin, and stretching away to the west, in a district of lonely hills, extends the picturesque, but roadless Glen Orrin, on the Inverness border.

MARYBURGH, Ross and Cromarty.　　Map 25, NH 5 5.
Iter. 200, 202, 203, 206, 213.

MARYCULTER, Kincardine.　　Map 21, NO 8 9.
See **Culter** (Aberdeen). *Iter. 168, 174.*

MARYKIRK, Kincardine.　　Map 21, NO 6 6.
A village on the North Esk River, situated on the edge of the Vale of *Strathmore* (*q.v.*), near the point where it merges into the country of the *Mearns* (*q.v.*). **3 m. N.W.** is *Inglismaldie Castle*, c. 1700 and later, once the seat of the Earls of Kintore. *Iter. 165.*

MARYWELL, Aberdeen.　　Map 21, NO 5 9.
Iter. 174.

MARYWELL, Angus.　　Map 21, NO 6 4.
Iter. 155.

MAUCHLINE, Ayr. 2,988.　　Map 8, NS 4 2.
E.C. Wed. GOLF. A town visited principally for its associations with Robert Burns, and formerly noted for the manufacture of wooden snuff-boxes. Some of Burns's children and friends, including Gavin Hamilton, are buried in the churchyard, the scene of the poet's " Holy Fair," but the Church itself was rebuilt in 1829. The " Burns House," where he set up home with Jean Armour, is now a museum, and nearby is " Auld Nanse Tinnock's," now a hostel. In the house of Gavin Hamilton, once Burns's landlord, is the room in which the poet was married in 1788. " Poosie Nansie's " cottage, and the former " *Whitefoord Arms* " Inn both have well-known Burns associations. *Mauchline Castle*, or Abbot Hunter's Tower (A.M.) is of 15th cent. date, and contains a fine vaulted hall. An obelisk recalls five Covenanters hanged in 1685. About a mile to the north of the town is the *Burns Memorial Tower*, neighboured by some model cottages. A little farther west is *Mossgiel* farm, rented by Burns and his brother between 1784 and 1788, and where much of his first volume of poems was completed, before he visited Edinburgh, in 1786. The farm was rebuilt in 1859. To the north-west, about 2 miles distant, is *Lochlea* farm, where the Burns family lived from 1777 to 1784. **3 m. W.S.W.** of Mauchline, on the Ayr road, is *Failford* (*q.v.*). See **Auchinleck, Catrine, Sorn, Stair** and **Tarbolton**. *Iter. 35, 67.*

MAUD, Aberdeen.　　Map 27, NJ 9 4.
Iter. 189.

MAVIS, GRIND Shetland.　　Map 33, HU 3 6.
See **Shetland Islands** (Mainland). *Iter. 267.*

MAXTON, Roxburgh.　　Map 10, NT 6 2.
Near a loop of the River Tweed, and retaining an old cross

shaft. The Church, of 12th cent. foundation, has been much altered. There is a ruined tower of the Kers. See **St. Boswells Green** (for *Mertoun House*). *Iter. 32, 46.*

MAXWELLHEUGH, Roxburgh.　　Map 11, NT 7 3.
Iter. 6, 7.

MAXWELLTOWN, Kirkcudbright.　　Map 4, NX 9 7.
See **Dumfries**.

MAXWELTON HOUSE, Dumfries.　　Map 3, NX 8 8.
See **Moniaive**.

MAYBOLE, Ayr. 4,962. SB.　　Map 8, NS 3 0.
E.C. Wed. GOLF. This small town, once the capital of the *Carrick* (*q.v.*) district, now manufactures shoes and agricultural implements. The restored 17th cent. *Maybole Castle*, in the High St., formerly the town house of the Earls of Cassillis, has picturesque turrets with oriel windows. The partly ancient Tolbooth was formerly a mansion of the Kennedy family. The Collegiate Church (A.M.), founded in 1371, fell into disrepair, and became a burial chapel for the Earls of Cassillis. A little to the north, near *Cargilston* farm, is a monument to six Covenanters, drowned in a slave ship off the Orkney Islands, after having been captured in the battle of *Bothwell* (*q.v.*) Brig in 1679. **3½ m. N.E.**, near the banks of the River Doon, is *Cassillis House*, incorporating an old peel tower, and associated with Burn's " Hallowe'en." **1 m. S.** is *Kilhenzie Castle*, 16th to 17th cent., and now a farm. **4 m. S.** is the late 17th cent. *Kilkerran House*. See **Crossraguel Abbey, Culzean Castle, Dunure** (for *Electric Brae*) and **Kirkoswald**. *Iter. 49, 55, 68, 84.*

MAY, ISLE OF, Fife.　　Map 17, NT 6 9.
See **Anstruther**.

MEARNS, Renfrew.　　Map 8, NS 5 5.
See **Newton Mearns**.

MEARNS, THE, Kincardine.　　Map 21, NO 6 7 etc.
An alternative name for the county of Kincardine, one particular district of which, between the Rivers North Esk and Bervie Water, is known as the " Howe of the Mearns." This forms a north-eastern extension of the fertile valley of *Strathmore* (*q.v.*) in the counties of Perth and Angus. The " Men o' the Mearns " are supposed to be of particular strength and noted for their efficiency.

MEASACH FALLS, Ross and Cromarty.　　Map 29, NH 2 7.
See **Braemore Lodge**. *Iter. 204, 206, 222.*

MEAVIG, Isle of Lewis, Ross and Cromarty.　　Map 32, NB 0 3.
Iter. 257.

MEIGLE, Perth. 759.　　Map 17, NO 2 4.
To the north of the village, with its old houses, and situated in the *Strathmore* (*q.v.*) valley, flows the River Isla. There is a museum (A.M.) containing a very notable collection of ancient sculptured stones, and Meigle is said to be the place of burial of Queen Guinevere. In the churchyard lies Sir Henry Campbell-Bannerman, the politician, who died in 1908. *Drumkilbo*, a mansion to the east, has fine gardens. See **Alyth, Eassie** and **Newtyle**. *Iter. 151, 153, 160.*

MEIKLEOUR, Perth.　　Map 17, NO 1 3.
A little to the south, near the meeting of the Rivers Tay and Isla, is the famous beech hedge, bordering the grounds of the modern *Meikleour House*. This hedge, which was planted in 1746, is now 85 ft. high and borders the Perth to Blairgowrie road for more than 600 yards. In the village of Meikleour is a Cross, dating from 1698, and the joug stone is still standing. See **Caputh**. *Iter. 152, 157.*

MELLERSTAIN, Berwick.　　Map 10, NT 6 3.
This notable 18th cent. mansion, designed by William and Robert Adam, is associated with an old 17th cent. custom, that of giving a white rose to the reigning monarch when on a visit. There are fine walled gardens adjoining the house, which looks southwards across a lake to the distant Cheviots. Lady Grizel Baillie, a heroine of Covenanting times, is associated with the house. It is shown daily (exc. Sat.), June to end of Sept., 2 to 5.30. (See note page 90.) See **Pathhead** (Midlothian). *Iter. 6, 7.*

Meikleour, Perth. The famous beech hedge, now 85 feet high. It was first planted in 1746

Meikleour, Perth. The 'joug' stone, or place of punishment, which stands opposite the Mercat Cross, to the left of the Dunkeld road (A984)

Maxwelton House, Dumfries. The modernized 17th century home of 'Annie Laurie,' the subject of the famous song, written originally c.1700. It stands on an unclassified road off A702, near Moniaive

Maybole, Ayr. The Monument to six Covenanters, drowned in a slave ship off the Orkneys in 1679. It stands near Cargilston Farm, on an unclassified road a little to the north

Mauchline, Ayr. The Memorial to five Covenanters, executed on the Loan Green in 1685

Markinch, Fife. The Stob Cross, reputed to be an old sanctuary stone, situated at the northern entrance to the town

PLATE 120 (facing page 212)

Methven, Perth. Millhaugh Old Bridge, built in 1619, which carries an unclassified road across the River Almond, some 3 miles north-west of Methven

Melness, Sutherland. Moin House, situated off A838, on the moors to the west. It was built originally as a refuge when the road was being constructed in 1830

Merse, Berwick. The Mercat Cross at Duns, which was removed to the park at the beginning of this century. The town stands at the northern edge of the Merse plain

Melrose, Roxburgh. The ruined Cistercian Abbey, founded by monks from Rievaulx, in Yorkshire, in 1136, and showing some of the finest 14th century work in Scotland. It was presented to the nation in 1918 by the Duke of Buccleuch

Methlick, Aberdeen. The remains of the Old Church

Merse, Berwick. A tall column at Coldstream, erected in 1832 in honour of Charles Marjoribanks, a former M.P. for the county. The village stands on the River Tweed, on the southern edge of the plain of the Merse

PLATE 121 (facing page 213)

MELNESS, Sutherland.   Map 28, **NC 5** 6.
Situated at the mouth of the Kyle of Tongue, on Tongue Bay, overlooking the Rabbit Islands. A sloop, carrying French gold for Prince Charles Edward, ran aground here, in 1745. Away to the north-west, not accessible by road, is Whiten Head, on a lonely rockbound stretch of coast, noted for its numerous caves, near the mouth of Loch Eriboll. Inland rises *Beinn Thutaig*, 1,340 ft., overlooking the moors of A'Mhoine, traversed by the road leading westwards towards the shores of Loch Eriboll. **6 m. S.W.** of Melness, on the moors, is *Moin House*, built in 1830 as a refuge while the road was being built. See **Port Vasco** and **Tongue.** *Iter. 225.*

MELROSE, Roxburgh. 2,177. SB.   Map 10, **NT 5** 3.
E.C. Thurs. GOLF. Here, beautifully situated near the River Tweed, famous for its salmon, and with the triple-peaked *Eildon Hills* (*q.v.*) rising just to the south, are the picturesque remains of what is perhaps the finest and best known ruined Scottish Abbey. *Melrose* itself is the " Kennaquhair " of Scott's " Abbot " and " Monastery," while the Abbey was described by him in the " Lay of the Last Minstrel." There are some old houses in the town, and the Cross, which carries the arms of Scotland, dates from 1642. The tower of the Parish Church dates from 1810.

1. Abbey.   2. Parish Church.   3. Mercat Cross (1642).

An old custom kept up is the " Masons' Walk " from the Cross to the Abbey and back by torchlight, on St. John's Day, December 27th. The Cistercian Abbey (A.M.) was founded in 1136, but was almost wrecked by the English during several invasions, more especially in 1322 and 1385, while in 1545 it suffered further serious damage. Parts of the nave and choir date from a rebuilding of 1385, and represent the best and most elaborate work of this period in Scotland. The flying buttresses, pinnacles and rich window tracery, wrought in red sandstone, are all of much interest. The five-light window in the South transept, with its flowing flamboyant tracery, is the finest in the Abbey. A gargoyle on the roof shows a pig with a set of bagpipes. On a west buttress of the south side are carved the Royal Arms. The heart of Robert Bruce is said to have been interred under the East window of the chancel, after it had been brought back from Spain (See **Dunfermline**). In the chancel is also the supposed tomb of Michael Scott, the Wizard, associated with Deloraine in " The Lay." The ground plan of the cloisters and other parts of the monastic buildings has been revealed by recent excavations. The Abbey museum is housed in a 15th to 16th cent. building, possibly the former Abbey guest-house. There are interesting tombs in the old graveyard, including those of Scott's wood-forester, Tom Purdie, and of his coachman, Peter Matheson. The whole of the Melrose district is redolent with memories of Sir Walter Scott. See **Abbotsford, Ashiestiel, Darnick, Dryburgh, Earlston, Edinburgh,** New-

stead, **Sandyknowe, Scott Country** and **Smailholm.** *Iter. 13, 32, 41, 43, 52.*

MELVICH, Sutherland. 500.   Map 30, **NC 8** 6.
E.C. Thurs. Lies at the seaward end of the long valley of Strath Halladale, on Melvich Bay. There is fine cliff scenery in the vicinity, notably at *Bighouse*, to the east of the Halladale River, and also at *Portskerra* (*q.v.*). *Iter. 232, 234, 240.*

MEMSIE, Aberdeen.   Map 27, **NJ 9** 6.
Iter. 186, 197.

MENNOCK, Dumfries.   Map 9, **NS 8** 0.
A tiny Nithsdale village, the starting point of the fine road which winds north-eastwards through the Mennock Pass, rising to more than 1,400 ft. in height. *Lowther Hill*, 2,377 ft. and *Green Lowther*, 2,403 ft., overlook the pass on the short descent to *Wanlockhead* (*q.v.*), Scotland's highest village, after which the road climbs again to a height of 1,531 ft. before reaching *Leadhills* (*q.v.*). Wordsworth and his sister journeyed over the pass in 1803. Across the Nith, to the west of Mennock, is *Eliock House*, which has claims to be the birthplace, in 1560, of the " Admirable Crichton." See **Clunie** and **Enterkinfoot.** *Iter. 27, 48, 49, 67.*

MENSTRIE, Clackmannan. 1,325.   Map 16, **NS 8** 9.
A small weaving and furniture-making town, at the foot of *Dumyat*, 1,375 ft., on the fringe of the *Ochil* hills. The 16th. cent. Castle, where Sir William Alexander, a 17th cent. North American Colonist, was born, is being restored, with a Nova Scotia exhibition room. Menstrie was also the birthplace, in 1734, of Sir Ralph Abercromby, the victor of the battle of Alexandria in the Napoleonic wars. *Iter. 136.*

MENTEITH, Perth.   Map 15, **NN 5** 0.
See **Port of Menteith.**

MERCHISTON (Edinburgh), Midlothian.   Map 9, **NT 2** 6.
See **Colinton.**

MERKLAND LODGE, Sutherland.   Map 28, **NC 4** 2.
On Loch Merkland, one of the chain of lochs whose shores are traversed by the road leading from Lairg to the wild north-western seaboard of Scotland, near Loch Laxford. To the north rises *Ben Hee*, 2,864 ft., in the great Reay deer forest, and to the west is *Ben Leoid*, 2,597 ft. *Iter. 229.*

MERSE, THE, Berwick.   Map 11, **NT 8** 5 etc.
A name given to that part of the county of Berwickshire which lies near the valley of the Tweed, and extends in a north-easterly direction towards the Whiteadder Water. It forms the largest plain in Scotland, and contains some of the richest agricultural land. At one time, the Merse included all the flat country between the Cheviots and the Lammermuirs, and the name is still sometimes applied to the whole of Berwickshire. The main road linking Berwick-upon-Tweed with Kelso cuts right through the heart of the Merse.

MERTOUN HOUSE, Berwick.   Map 10, **NT 3** 6.
See **St. Boswells Green.**

METHIL, Fife. 21,458. SB. with Buckhaven.
                                              Map 17, **NT 3** 9.
E.C. Thurs. An important port for the Fife coalfield, and now linked with *Buckhaven* (*q.v.*), which lies to the south-west. *Iter. 128.*

METHLICK, Aberdeen. 1,399.   Map 27, **NJ 8** 3.
On the River Ythan, with a modern Church, near which, in the burial ground, are the remains of the ancient Old Church. **3½ m. N.W.,** near the river, are the remains of the ancient *Castle of Gight*, in a picturesque, wooded setting, having been besieged by Montrose in 1639. Lord Byron's mother, Catherine Gordon of Gight, was heiress to the estate, but was forced to sell it, in 1787, in order to pay her husband's debts. **2 m. S.S.E.,** in a fine park, is the 18th cent. Adam mansion of *Haddo House*. **3 m. S.E.,** is the fine old, restored *House of Schivas*. See **Fochabers, Fyvie** and **Tarves.** *Iter. 186, 197.*

METHVEN, Perth. 643.   Map 16, **NO 0** 2.
Lies at the south-western extremity of the fertile valley of *Strathmore* (*q.v.*). Only a fragment remains from the 15th cent. Church. In 1306, Robert Bruce was defeated by the

English in Methven Wood, and in 1644, near *Tibbermuir*, to the south-east, Montrose defeated the Covenanters. 1½ m. E. is *Methven Castle*, in a splendid wooded park. **3 m.** N.W. is Millhaugh Old Bridge, built in 1619, and spanning the River Almond. 4½ m. N.W., near the River Almond, is *Trinity College, Glenalmond*, a well-known public school, situated in the eastern part of Glen Almond, the finest stretches of which lie beyond the *Sma' Glen (q.v.)*. See **Huntingtower**. *Iter. 145*.

MEY, Caithness.   Map 30, **ND 2 7.**
See **East Mey.** *Iter. 240*.

MID CALDER, Midlothian. 2,793.   Map 9, **NT 0 6.**
E.C. Wed. Lies on the River Almond, in a district noted for its oil shales. The Church has an apsidal choir, which was rebuilt in 1541. There is some flamboyant 16th cent. window tracery, and also corbels carved with heraldic devices. The remainder of the building is modern. John Knox first administered the Communion under the Protestant rite, in 1556, at *Calder House*, a partly ancient mansion, and here also Chopin stayed in 1848. *Linhouse* is a 16th and 17th cent. house. 2½ m. S.W. of Mid Calder is *Alderston*, a 17th cent. house, with modern additions, and preserving an old dovecote. *Iter. 18, 19, 20, 22*.

MID CLYTH, Caithness.   Map 30, **ND 2 3.**
On the hill-slopes behind the village are 22 parallel rows of prehistoric stones, comprising 192 in all, the best examples in the county. **2 m. N.W.**, off the Wick road, is the picturesque little sandstone inlet of *Whaligoe. Iter. 200*.

MIDDLETON, Midlothian.   Map 10, **NT 3 5.**
A small village on the northern slopes of the *Moorfoot* hills. From here, a road deviates from the main Galashiels road to penetrate into the hills, attaining a height of over 1,200 ft., and later reaching Tweeddale at *Innerleithen (q.v.)*. See **Borthwick Castle.** *Iter. 9, 11, 12*.

MIDMAR CASTLE, Aberdeen.   Map 21, **NJ 7 0.**
This splendid example of a late 16th cent. or early 17th cent. Scottish castle in the baronial style is situated to the north of the *Hill of Fare*, 1,545 ft., just off the Aberdeen to Tarland road, and is notable for a characteristic display of turrets. The Castle is said to have been built originally by Sir William Wallace, and was formerly known as *Ballogie*. The old Churchyard of Midmar, in the near vicinity, contains a slab, dated 1575, to the memory of George Bell, probably the master-mason of the castle. *Iter. 179*.

MILLERSTON, Lanark.   Map 8, **NS 6 6.**
Iter. 17, 97, 99.

MILLHOUSE, Argyll.   Map 7, **NR 9 7.**
See **Kames.** *Iter. 103*.

MILLPORT, Great Cumbrae Island, Bute. 1,655. SB.
GOLF.   Map 7, **NS 1 5.**
Faces Millport Bay, on the Island of *Great Cumbrae*, in the Firth of Clyde, and is reached by steamer from *Largs (q.v.), Fairlie (q.v.)* or *Wemyss Bay (q.v.)* on the mainland. There are good sands and bathing. The modern Collegiate Church was consecrated in 1876 as the Episcopal Cathedral of Argyll and the Isles. On the eastern shores of the island, adjacent to *Keppel* pier, is a Marine Biological Station and museum. The island is only about 10 miles in circumference, and a road encircles its shores, giving good views. To the south is *Little Cumbrae* island, on which stands a lighthouse. Off its eastern shores lies the tiny Castle Island, on which are the remains of a Castle, destroyed by Cromwell, in 1653.

MILNATHORT, Kinross. 1,180.   Map 17, **NO 1 0.**
E.C. Thurs. M.D. Mon. GOLF. A small woollen-manufacturing town, standing a little to the north of *Loch Leven (q.v.)*. To the east is the ruined *Burleigh Castle*, dated 1582 (A.M.), a former stronghold of the Balfours, and with which Scott's "Old Mortality" is associated. In the vicinity, a few miles to the south-east, are the standing stones of *Orwell. Iter. 90, 91, 92, 98, 136*.

MILNGAVIE, Dunbarton. 8,206. SB.   Map 8, **NS 5 7.**
E.C. Tues. GOLF. A small town in a pleasant setting, with the Mugdock and Craigmaddie reservoirs to the north. Beyond the reservoirs, amid woodlands, stands *Mugdock*

Castle, preserving an old tower. To the south of the town are faint traces of the former Antonine, or *Roman Wall (q.v.)*. **2 m. E.** is the 16th cent. *Bardowie Castle*, facing its tiny loch. **2 m. N.E.** is *Craigmaddie Castle*, only the foundations remaining. See **Strathblane.** *Iter. 105, 108*.

MILTON, Dunbarton.   Map 8, **NS 4 7.**
Iter. 88, 100, 101, 102, 109, 110, 111, 112.

MILTON, Inverness.   Map 25, **NH 4 3.**
Iter. 206, 210, 213.

MILTON, Perth.   Map 16, **NN 9 3.**
Lies in Strath Bran, which is here joined by Glen Cochill, traversed by the road leading to *Aberfeldy (q.v.)*. To the north-west rises *Meall Dearg*, 2,258 ft. overlooking the lonely little Loch Fender. *Iter. 89, 140, 141, 147*.

MILTON, Ross and Cromarty.   Map 31, **NH 7 7.**
An old-world village, known also as *Milntown. Tarbat House* faces the Bay of Nigg.

MILTON, Stirling.   Map 15, **NS 6 7.**
Iter. 115.

MILTON BRIDGE, Midlothian.   Map 9, **NT 2 6.**
See **Roslin.** *Iter. 10, 24*.

MILTONISH, Wigtown.   Map 2, **NX 1 7.**
Iter. 78.

MILTON OF BALGONIE, Fife.   Map 17, **NO 3 0.**
David Leslie, Lord Newark, the Covenanting general, whom Cromwell defeated in 1650, at *Dunbar (q.v.)*, died in 1661 at the ruined *Balgonie Castle*, to the west. It dates probably from the 15th cent., and was besieged in 1716 by the celebrated Rob Roy. See **Markinch.** *Iter. 98*.

MINARD, Argyll.   Map 14, **NR 9 9.**
The 19th cent. *Minard Castle* looks out over Minard Bay, an inlet of *Loch Fyne (q.v.)*. *Iter. 118, 121*.

MINGARY CASTLE, Argyll.   Map 12, **NM 4 6.**
See **Kilchoan.**

MINGULAY, ISLE OF, Inverness.   Map 32, **NL 5 8.**
See **Hebrides, Outer** (Barra).

MINISHANT, Ayr.   Map 8, **NS 3 1.**
Iter. 55, 79.

MINNIGAFF, Kirkcudbright.   Map 2, **NX 4 6.**
See **Newton Stewart.**

MINTLAW, Aberdeen.   Map 27, **NJ 9 4.**
See **Old Deer.** *Iter. 185, 188, 189*.

MOFFAT, Dumfries. 2,057. SB.   Map 4, **NT 0 0.**
E.C. Wed. GOLF. This little resort stands on the River

1. St. Andrew's Parish Church.   2. Colvin Fountain.

Mid Clyth, Caithness. Rows of prehistoric stones, nearly 200 in all, on the Hill of Clyth behind the village

Midmar Castle, Aberdeen. The 16th to 17th century Castle, said to have been originally built by Sir William Wallace, and formerly known as Ballogie. It stands to the south of A974, about 14 miles west of Aberdeen

Milnathort, Kinross. The ruined Burleigh Castle, a former Balfour fortress, dated 1582. It stands to the east of the town, on A911

Milton of Balgonie, Fife. The ruined 15th century Balgonie Castle, to the west, off A911. It was besieged by Rob Roy in 1716, and became later the home of the Covenanter General Leslie

Mingary Castle, Argyll. The ruined Clan Macdonald fortress, visited by James IV in 1495, and captured for Montrose in 1644. It stands near Kilchoan, on an unclassified road off B8007

Millerston, Lanark. The Monument on the site of the house in which Sir John Menteith, the 'fause' Menteith, betrayed William Wallace and a co-patriot in 1305. It stands 2 miles north-west, on an unclassified road

[For MOFFAT see following plate

PLATE 122 (facing page 214)

Moffat, Dumfries. The Colvin fountain, with its ram, signifying the importance of the local sheep farming industry

Moniaive, Dumfries. The Monument to James Renwick, the last of the Covenanter martyrs, who was executed at Edinburgh in 1688, at the age of 26

Monikie, Angus. The Panmure Monument, on a hillside to the south. It commemorates the first Lord Panmure of Brechin, who died in 1852

Monimail, Fife. The remaining fragment of Monimail Palace (1573), now known as Cardinal Beaton's Tower

Montrose, Angus. The Town Hall, erected in 1763. Dr. Johnson, after his visit in 1773, spoke of its " good dining-room and other rooms for tea drinking "

Montrose, Angus. The Medicine Well, well known as a spa during the 18th century

PLATE 123 (facing page 215)

Annan, in a delightful setting of Lowland hills. It makes a good centre for walks in Annandale, as well as being noted for angling. The *Colvin* fountain, surmounted by a ram, stands in the town, and signifies the importance of sheep-farming in this district. A sulphur spring, situated 1½ m. N.E. of the town, was discovered in 1630, and brought some fame to Moffat as a spa, among the visitors for its waters being Boswell and Burns. From the 18th cent. *Moffat House*, now a hotel, James Macpherson published, in 1759, his " Ossianic Fragments." John Macadam, who lived at *Dumcrieff House*, on the Moffat Water to the southeast, was buried in the churchyard, in 1836. *St. Andrew's* Parish Church, the successor to an older building, dates from 1887. The Edinburgh road, leaving the town in a northerly direction, climbs into the hills, and reaches, after five miles, the well-known *Devil's Beef Tub*, a spectacular Upper Annandale hollow by the side of the road at Ericstane Brae, over-shadowed by steep, green slopes, and associated with Scott's " Redgauntlet." There is a memorial stone (1955) to John Hunter, a Covenanter, shot on a nearby hillside, in 1685. A little farther to the north-west, at a height of more than 1,300 ft., is the meeting point of the counties of Dumfries, Lanark and Peebles, near which is the watershed where the Rivers Annan, Clyde and Tweed (See **Tweedsmuir**) all have their sources. Eastwards from Moffat, the road towards *St. Mary's Loch* (q.v.) follows the Moffat Water past the *Burns Cottage*, near which is Craigieburn Wood, associated with the poet. Beyond this point, *Hart Fell*, 2,651 ft., and *White Coomb*, 2,695 ft., rise to the west, and the road later reaches the notable waterfall known as the *Grey Mare's Tail*, some 200 ft. high, where the Tail Burn joins the Moffat Water. In a setting of high hills in the background lies the lonely Loch Skene. See **Beattock** and **Birkhill**. *Iter. 10, 13, 24, 46, 49.*

MOIDART, Inverness.   Map 12, NM 7 7 etc.
The name applied to the wild and mountainous Clanranald country, lying between the western shores of *Loch Shiel* (q.v.) and the Sound of Arisaig, and associated very largely with Prince Charles Edward and the '45. Loch Ailort and *Loch nan Uamh* (q.v.) are two picturesque inlets of the Sound, the last-named having witnessed both the arrival and the departure of the Prince. At the western extremity of Moidart lies Loch Moidart, which divides the district from the remote Ardnamurchan peninsula. See **Acharacle, Dalilea, Kinlochmoidart** and **Lochailort.**

MOLLINBURN, Lanark.   Map 8, NS 7 7.
Iter. 17, 97, 99.

MONALTRIE, Aberdeen.   Map 20, NO 2 9.
South-west of the ruined *Monaltrie House* is the Farquharson Cairn-na-Cuimhne, or Cairn of Remembrance, near the River Dee, off A93.

MONDYNES. BRIDGE, Kincardine.   Map 21, NO 7 7.
See **Drumlithie** *Iter. 151, 156.*

MONIAIVE, Dumfries. 527.   Map 3, NX 7 9.
E.C. Thurs. Three streams meet in the vicinity of this pleasant village to form the Cairn Water. The village Cross dates from 1638, and there is a monument to James Renwick, the last Covenanter martyr, who died in 1688. **3 m. E.S.E.** is *Maxwelton House*, 17th cent., but altered and modernised, carrying the date 1641, and long the seat of the Laurie family, being well known as the one-time home of the heroine of " Annie Laurie." To the south-west of the house is the little village of *Kirkland*, and also *Glencairn* Church, where Annie Laurie and her husband are said to be buried. **2¼ m. W.** of Moniaive, off the Carpshairn road, is *Craigdarroch*, built by William Adam in 1729, with its lovely gardens, formerly the married home of Annie Laurie, and where she died. See **Penpoint.** *Iter. 25, 74.*

MONIFIETH, Angus. 3,386. SB.   Map 17, NO 4 3.
E.C. Wed. GOLF. A small resort, with a sandy beach, to the east of which are the Barry Links, on which is situated a large military training-ground. Farther to the south-east is Buddon Ness. See **Broughty Ferry.** *Iter. 155.*

MONIKIE, Angus.   Map 17, NO 5 3.
Beyond the reservoirs, to the west of the station, stands the

battlemented and turreted 15th cent. keep of *Affleck Castle* (A.M.), in which is a vaulted chapel and also a solar of great merit. The castle is viewable on weekdays, 10 to 4 or 7. (See note page 90). South of Monikie, in a prominent position on a hillside, is the *Panmure* monument.

MONIMAIL, Fife.   Map 17, NO 2 1.
The Church has the Melville gallery and a notable Adam ceiling. *Melville House*, to the south-west, now a school, is a fine house of 1692, with an imposing lay-out and an interesting interior attributed to Sir William Bruce. *Monimail*, or *Beaton's Tower* dates from 1578 and is the surviving portion of an ecclesiastical palace.

MONKTON, Ayr. 653.   Map 8, NS 3 2.
Stands a little inland from Ayr Bay, its Church preserving a Romanesque doorway. See **Symington** (Ayr), and **Tarbolton.** *Iter. 88.*

MONREITH, Wigtown.   Map 2, NX 3 4.
Situated on Monreith Bay, in the Machers peninsula, between Barsalloch Point and the Point of Lag. Near the latter is the ancient, restored Church of *Kirkmaiden-in-Fernis*. *Monreith House*, about **2 m. N.E.** of Barsalloch Point, is well known from the essays of Sir Thomas Maxwell, and possesses very notable woodland gardens, with magnificent rhododendrons. In the park is the White Loch of Myrton, and in the grounds of the mansion stands the carved, wheel-headed *Monreith Cross* (A.M.). In the vicinity is the ruined *Myrton Castle*. *Iter. 82.*

MONTROSE, Angus. 10,778. SB.   Map 21, NO 7 5.
E.C. Wed. M.D. Fri. GOLF. A well-known resort, fishing port, and Royal Burgh, with excellent sands and bathing, situated on the estuary of the South Esk River. This flows through Montrose Basin, a tidal lagoon, some two miles square, behind the town. Montrose has a long history, and formerly possessed a strong castle, which was occupied in 1296 by Edward I, before Wallace destroyed it during the following year. The Old Pretender sailed from the harbour at the close of the 1715 rising, and at *Old Montrose*, beyond the Basin, was born, in 1612, the famous Marquis of

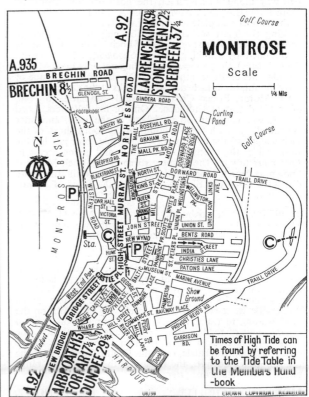

1. Church, 18th cent.   2. Town Hall.   3. Medicine Well.

Montrose. Both the Town Hall and the Church date from the late 18th cent., the spire of the latter being a 19th cent. addition by Gillespie Graham. The restored Medicine Well was much visited as a spa during the 18th cent. See **Ferryden, Inverkeilor, St. Cyrus** and **Usan**. *Iter. 153, 155, 164, 165, 166.*

MONYMUSK, Aberdeen. 114. Map 27, NJ 6 1.
A village situated just off the Alford to Inverurie road, and which was formerly the site of a Priory and later of a monastery. The remains of the Priory Church, probably of Norman date, are incorporated in the present Parish Church. The well-known Monymusk Reliquary, a casket of the Celtic period, is now in the National Museum of Antiquities in Edinburgh. *Monymusk House* is partly of 15th cent. date. To the north-west of the village rises *Cairn William,* 1,469 ft., and below its wooded eastern shoulder, known as *Pitfichie Hill,* is the ruined *Pitfichie Castle,* beyond which flows the River Don in a delightful wooded setting. 1½ m. S. of Monymusk is the modern *Cluny Castle.* See **Kemnay.** *Iter. 177.*

MOORFOOT HILLS, Midlothian. Map 10, NT 3 5.
See **Eddleston, Heriot** and **Temple.** *Iter. 12, 40.*

MORAR, Inverness. Map 23, NM 6 9.
Situated on the narrow neck of land separating Loch Morar from the outer waters of the Sound of Sleat, and through which flows the Morar River, on which are situated the Falls of Morar, now harnessed to a local hydro-electric scheme. The bay formed by the estuary is famous for its white sands, and looks across the sea to the picturesque outlines of the islands of Rum and Eigg. Loch Morar, a little to the east, has a depth of 180 fathoms, almost the deepest known hollow in Europe, and the scenery along its shores, notably at the east end, where the hills are highest, is of great beauty. On an island in the lake stood formerly an 18th cent. Catholic college, and also the residence of the Pope's Vicar Apostolic of Scotland. Loch Morar is separated by a narrow neck of land, at South Tarbet Bay, about half-way along its length on the northern side, from the more impressive *Loch Nevis* (q.v.). A feature of both lochs is the almost complete absence of roads along their shores, making the finest scenery accessible only to long-distance walkers. Perhaps the finest view of Loch Morar is that which is obtained by climbing *Carn a'Ghobhair,* 1,794 ft. from *Mallaig* (q.v.), the panorama including not only Loch Morar, but also the entire length of Loch Nevis, with the cirque of lofty mountains at its head. In the hills at the eastern end of Loch Morar, Prince Charles Edward wandered, in 1746, after his defeat at Culloden. One of his followers, Lord Lovat, was captured on an island in the loch, and later beheaded. A path from a point on the south shore of the loch leads into the hills by way of Meoble, later passing the west end of the lonely Loch Beoraid, and giving access to *Lochailort* (q.v.). The country surrounding Loch Morar is known as North Morar and South Morar, while the entire district is often described generally by the name of Morar. *Iter. 209.*

MOREBATTLE, Roxburgh. 195. Map 11, NT 7 2.
This little village is almost encircled by the windings of the Kale Water, which flows southwards from the outliers of the *Cheviot* (q.v.) hills, and then turns westwards in order to join the Teviot. The lonely valley to the south, threaded by the Kale Water, was once a refuge for the persecuted Covenanters. Across the river, to the north of the village, is *Linton Church,* an ancient structure, now restored, with a Norman font, a bell in the belfry dated 1697, and the notable carved Somerville stone set above the porch. 2½ m. S.W., on the road leading to *Oxnam* (q.v.), are the remains of *Cessford Castle,* built of reddish stone, with walls 14 ft. thick. The castle surrendered to the English in 1545. Away to the south-east of Morebattle, over the English border, rises the *Cheviot* itself, 2,676 ft., the highest of the whole long range of hills. See **Hounam.** *Iter. 47.*

MORTON LOCHS, Fife. Map 17, NO 4 2.
See **Tayport.**

MORVEN, Argyll. Map 12, NM 6 5 etc.
The district of *Morven,* or *Morvern,* is bounded to the north by *Loch Sunart* (q.v.), and to the west and east by the Sound of Mull and *Loch Linnhe* (q.v.) respectively. It is mainly a country of low hills, though *Creach Bheinn,* in the north-eastern corner, attains 2,800 ft., and forms a very fine viewpoint. Some of the best views of the Morven landscape are those obtained from the steamers linking Fort William with Oban in summer. See **Drimnin, Larachbeg** and **Lochaline.** *Iter. 218.*

MOSCOW, Ayr. Map 8, NS 4 4.
A small village on the little River Volga. From its moorland setting there are westerly views towards the Firth of Clyde.

MOSSBANK, Shetland. Map 33, HU 4 7.
See **Shetland Islands** (Mainland). *Iter. 270.*

MOSSEND, Lanark. Map 9, NS 7 6.
Iter. 18.

MOSSGIEL, Ayr. Map 8, NS 4 2.
See **Mauchline.**

MOSSTODLOCH, Moray. Map 26, NJ 5 5.
A pleasant village, situated immediately to the west of Fochabers Bridge across the Spey, the predecessor of the bridge having been destroyed in the floods of 1829. 3 m. N. of Mosstodloch, and on the left bank of the Spey before it reaches the sea, stands *Garmouth* (q.v.), once a port. See **Fochabers** and **Spey Bay.** *Iter. 171, 175, 187, 198, 199.*

MOTHERWELL, with Wishaw, Lanark. 71,384. LB. Map 9, NS 7 5.
E.C. Wed. GOLF. The centre of an important coal-mining area, forming, together with *Wishaw,* a single Burgh,

and noted for iron, steel and engineering works. The great Dalzell works were founded by David Colville in 1871. The site of the original " well " is marked by a plaque in Ladywell Road. North of the town is *Jerviston House,* an ancient tower of the Baillie family. To the south-east of *Motherwell,* near the River Clyde is *Dalzell House,* 17th cent. and later, incorporating a 15th cent. tower. *Iter. 19, 54, 87.*

MOULIN, Perth. 2,775. Map 20, NN 9 5.
E.C. Thurs. A picturesque little village, in the vicinity of which are the remains of *Castle Dhu.* To the east is *Kinnaird Cottage,* where R. L. Stevenson lived and wrote, in 1881. *Craigour,* 1,300 ft., (N.T. Scot.), to the north-west, is a good viewpoint, and to the north rises *Ben Vrackie,* 2,757 ft. The

Morar, Inverness. The White Sands of Morar, which fringe the bay. Loch Morar, to the east, is 180 fathoms in depth, one of Europe's greatest hollows

Morar, Inverness. The Falls of Morar, its waters now used by a local hydro-electric scheme. This district is said to be the setting for L. A. G. Strong's novel, '*The Brothers*'

Morebattle, Roxburgh. The ruined Cessford Castle, which surrendered to the Earl of Surrey in 1545. It stands 2½ miles to the south-west, on an unclassified road

Moulin, Perth. The inscribed panel on Kinnaird Cottage, where Robert Louis Stevenson wrote several of his shorter works, including '*Thrawn Janet*,' during 1881

Moscow, Ayr. The sign at the small village of Moscow, which actually stands on the River Volga

PLATE 124 (facing page 216)

Mound, Sutherland. Thomas Telford's embankment across Loch Fleet, built in 1815, at a cost of £9,600, in order to obviate the use of a ferry

Moy, Inverness. The obelisk to Sir Aeneas Mackintosh, who died in 1820. It stands on an island of Loch Moy, and is visible from A9

Muchalls, Kincardine. The 17th century Muchalls Castle, which was built by the Burnetts of Leys

Muir of Ord, Ross and Cromarty. The restored 17th century Kilcoy Castle of the Stewarts and later of the Mackenzies. It stands 4 miles east-north-east, off an unclassified road between A832 and B9162

Mull of Galloway, Wigtown. The lighthouse, which commands a wide view from a height of more than 200 feet

Musselburgh, Midlothian. The mid-16th-century footbridge across the River Esk, for the repair of which an Act of Parliament was passed in 1597

PLATE 125 (facing page 217)   [For MUSSELBURGH see also following plate road leading north-eastwards towards Kirkmichael climbs to 1,260 ft. before descending into Glen Brerachan. See **Pitlochry.** *Iter. 159, 162, 167, 168.*

MOUND STATION, Sutherland.　　　Map 31, **NH 7** 9.
The 1,000-yard long embankment, which here carries both the road and the railway across the waters of Loch Fleet, was constructed by Telford, in 1815, in order to reclaim some of the land and obviate the use of a ferry. *Iter. 200, 231, 233.*

MOUNT VERNON (Glasgow), Lanark. 4,721.
　　　　　　　　　　　　　　　Map 8, **NS 6** 6.
On the south-eastern outskirts of Glasgow, near the River Clyde, and adjacent to Calderpark, where the Zoological Park of *Glasgow* (*q.v.*) is situated. *Iter. 51, 54.*

MOUSA, Shetland.　　　　　　Map 33, **HU 4** 2.
See **Shetland Islands** (Mainland).

MOY, Inverness.　　　　　　　Map 25, **NH 7** 3.
To the east is Loch Moy, on an island of which are remains of a castle, and also an obelisk to the memory of Sir Aeneas Mackintosh. *Moy Hall,* at the north end of the loch, was commenced in 1955 to replace a former house, and is the seat of the chief of the Clan Mackintosh. An episode, known as the " Rout of Moy," took place in the vicinity during the '45, when a force under Lord Loudoun fled in disorder. **3 m. N.,** on the Inverness road, beyond the tiny Lochan a' Chaoruinn, a fine view is opened up over Strath Nairn, and towards the far-distant *Ben Wyvis,* 3,429 ft., to the north-west. *Iter. 140, 150, 195.*

MUCHALLS, Kincardine. 500.　　　Map 21, **NO 9** 9.
E.C. Wed./Thurs.　Situated just off the Stonehaven to Aberdeen road, on a picturesque stretch of coast, with cliffs and gullies. The Castle dates from the 17th cent. and belonged to the Burnetts of Leys. It is shown Tues. and Sun., 3 to 5.30, May to Sept., or by arrangement (see note page 90). To the north are the little fishing villages of Skateraw, Porthlethen and *Findon* (*q.v.*). *Iter. 151, 155, 156.*

MUCK, ISLE OF, Inverness.　　　Map 12, **NG 4** 7.
See **Rum.**

MUIRDRUM, Angus.　　　　　Map 17, **NO 5** 3.
Iter. 155, 162.

MUIRFIELD, East Lothian.　　　Map 10, **NT 4** 8.
GOLF. See **Gullane.** *Iter. 2, 36, 37.*

MUIRHEAD, Angus.　　　　　Map 17, **NO 3** 3.
See **Fowlis Easter.** *Iter. 157, 158, 159, 160.*

MUIRHEAD, Lanark. 3,229.　　　Map 8, **NS 6** 6.
GOLF. The small lochs of Johnston, Bishop, Woodend and Lochend lie to the south-east. *Iter. 17, 97, 99.*

MUIRKIRK, Ayr. 3,214.　　　　Map 8, **NS 6** 2.
In a district of coal-mines and ironworks, and situated on the River Ayr. The Church was built in 1650. To the south-east rise *Cairn Table,* 1,944 ft., and *Stony Hill,* 1,843 ft., on the Lanark border, the former crowned with prehistoric cairns. Still farther south is *Three Shire Hill,* where a boulder marks the meeting of three counties: Ayr, Dumfries and Lanark. **5 m. S.W.** is Airds Moss, a barren expanse of moorland, where, in 1680, a fight took place between Royalists and Covenanters, in which Richard Cameron, who gave his name to a famous regiment, was slain. A monument commemorates the action. *Iter. 21, 25, 35, 68.*

MUIR OF ORD, Ross and Cromarty.　Map 25, **NH 5** 5.
GOLF. Now the centre of a crofting district, and formerly noted for its cattle fairs. **2 m. S.E.,** near the Beauly Firth, is *Taradale House,* where Sir Roderick Murchison, the 19th cent. geologist, was born. **4 m. E.N.E.** is *Kilcoy Castle,* 17th cent., restored, a good example of the Scottish baronial style, with the Stuart arms carved on the west tower. See **Marybank.** *Iter. 200, 201, 204, 205, 206, 213, 221.*

MULBEN, Moray.　　　　　　Map 26, **NJ 3** 5.
Iter. 170, 189.

MULL, ISLE OF, Argyll.　　Map 13, **NM 5** 3 etc.
The picturesque, hilly island of *Mull,* one of the Inner Hebrides, lies in the approaches to *Loch Linnhe* (*q.v.*), and is separated from the mainland coast of *Morven* (*q.v.*) by the Sound of Mull, and from the coast of *Lorne* (*q.v.*) by the Firth of Lorne. Irregular in shape, and only about 30 miles in length, the rocky coastline, owing to its numerous sea-lochs and indentations, measures approximately 300 miles. The island is almost cut in two at one point opposite the Sound of Mull, where the inlet of Loch na Keal, on the west coast, is separated from the Sound by only 3 miles of land. Mull is accessible by steamers from Oban calling at Craignure, Salen or Tobermory. With the exception of the stretch between Salen and Tobermory, the chief centre on the island, the roads are narrow, winding and difficult for passing, while some of the surfaces are poor. About 120 miles of road are suitable for motoring. The road which goes round the north-western extremity of Mull, from Tobermory to the shores of Loch Tuath and thence to Loch na Keal, is winding and hilly (1 in 6), with hairpin bends, but is scenically of much interest. The shores of Loch na Keal, in which lies the small island of Forsa, are traversed for their entire length by a road providing fine scenery, and in the background, to the south, rises *Ben More,* 3,169 ft., the monarch of the island. The road along the south shore of the loch is overlooked by the steep Gribun cliffs, facing the islands of Inch Kenneth and Ulva, and later turns south to reach the northern shore of Loch Scridain. The south-western peninsula of the island is known as the Ross of Mull, and is traversed by the road leading to Fionphort, west of Bunessan. From Fionphort a passenger ferry plies to *Iona* (*q.v.*), to the north of which lies the island of *Staffa* (*q.v.*). In the south-east corner of Mull lie the picturesque Lochs Buie and Spelve, while near Craignure stands the well-known restored Duart Castle. The island was visited by Dr. Johnson during his Highland tour of 1773, and his comment was " O Sir! a most dolorous country ". See **Bunessan, Calgary, Carsaig Bay, Craignure** (for *Duart Castle*), **Dervaig, Gribun, Kilninian, Lochbuie, Pennyghael, Salen** (Mull), **Tobermory** and **Ulva Ferry.** *Iter. 248, 249, 250.*

MULL OF GALLOWAY, Wigtown.　　Map 2, **NX 1** 3.
The most southerly point on the mainland of Scotland, at the extremity of the Rhinns of Galloway peninsula. The lighthouse stands at a height of 210 ft., and commands an extensive view. Nearby are ancient entrenchments, thought to have been the last defences of the Picts against the Scots. There are scanty remains of *St. Medan's* Chapel, near Mull Farm, by the cliffs overlooking Luce Bay. See **Drummore.** *Iter. 82.*

MULL OF KINTYRE, Argyll.　　　Map 6, **NR 5** 0.
This wild headland, the terminal point of the long and narrow *Kintyre* (*q.v.*) peninsula, is approached by a rough and narrow road from *Southend* (*q.v.*), which descends about 1,000 ft. in a mile and a half. The last portion of the road is private. A lighthouse is situated near South Point, built originally in 1788, and having been remodelled by Robert Stevenson. The views from here are remarkable, and extend towards the open Atlantic and the coast of Northern Ireland, with Rathlin Island some 12 miles distant, the Mull being the nearest point in Scotland to the Irish coast. Behind the lighthouse rises *Beinn na Lice,* 1,405 ft. *Iter. 123.*

MULL OF OA, Isle of Islay, Argyll.　　Map 6, **NR 2** 4.
Situated in the extreme south of the island, in the Oa peninsula, with fine cliff scenery and caves. A little to the east is an American memorial to the soldiers drowned in the loss of the " Tuscania," in the First World War. (See **Port Ellen.**) The road from Port Ellen ends about a mile short of the Mull itself, which is accessible on foot only. *Iter. 244.*

MUNLOCHY, Ross and Cromarty.　　Map 25, **NH 6** 5.
Iter. 203.

MURRAYFIELD (Edinburgh), Midlothian. Map 9, **NT 2** 7.
See **Corstorphine.**

MURTHLY CASTLE, Perth.　　　Map 16, **NO 0** 3.
See **Caputh.** *Iter. 148.*

MUSSELBURGH, Midlothian. 18,173. SB.
　　　　　　　　　　　　　Map 10, **NT 3** 7.
E.C. Wed./Thurs. **GOLF.** The town stands on the estuary

of the River Esk, and looks out over the Firth of Forth to the distant coast of Fife, with the *Lomond* hills rising dimly in the background. *Musselburgh* has a number of local industries, and mussels are still gathered, a picturesque ceremony still observed being the annual autumn fishermen's " Walks of Thanksgiving," which take place in the town and in the adjoining village of *Fisherrow*, across the river. There is a Tolbooth, dating from c. 1591, in which an old clock, given by the Dutch, in 1496, is preserved. Nearby stands the Mercat Cross. A statue in the town commemorates David Moir, the " Delta " of Blackwood's Magazine. An old three-arched footbridge still spans the river upstream from Rennie's bridge of 1807. An Act of Parliament was passed in 1597 for its repair, and the structure may date from the mid-16th cent. Near the links, noted for golf, horse-racing and archery, and on which Cromwell camped after the battle of *Dunbar* (q.v.), in 1650, stands *Loretto College*, a well-known Public School. A chapel of " Our Lady of Loretto " stood formerly on the site, and the stones are said to have been used in the building of the Tolbooth at Musselburgh. See **Carberry Hill, Inveresk, Pinkie House** and **Prestonpans.** *Iter. 1, 2.*

MUTHILL, Perth. 605.   Map 16, NN 8 1.
E.C. Wed. **GOLF.** A Strath Earn village, in a wooded setting, on the outskirts of the park of *Drummond Castle.* (See *Crieff.*) The ancient Church, which was abandoned many years ago, dated mainly from the 15th cent., but the fine Romanesque tower, 12th cent. or earlier, with a later gabled roof, is still standing, and the old chancel arch is intact. *Iter. 89, 140.*

MYBSTER, Caithness.   Map 30, ND 1 5.
Iter. 236.

NAIRN, Nairn. 4,666. SB.   Map 25, NH 8 5.
E.C. Wed. **M.D.** Thurs. **GOLF.** A well-known Royal Burgh, watering-place and golfing centre on the Moray Firth, with good sands and bathing, and a particularly dry and sunny climate. The town, once known as *Invernairn*, stands on the River Nairn, and makes an excellent centre for visiting the wooded country in the vicinity, as well as the exceptionally picturesque reaches of the River Findhorn near *Dulsie Bridge* (q.v.) and *Ferness* (q.v.). Dr. Johnson and Boswell visited Nairn during the course of their Highland tour of 1773. Near the harbour, built by Telford in 1820, but badly damaged in the great 1829 floods, is the Fishertown.

1. The Old Cross.

An old Cross stands in the High St. The town is held to mark the division between the Highlands and the Lowlands; at one time it was said that Gaelic was spoken in the south-western quarter and English in the north-eastern quarter. **3 m. S.** is *Rait Castle*, 16th to 17th cent., with a round tower. See **Auldearn, Cawdor** and **Forres.** *Iter. 175, 176, 199, 212.*

NATIONAL FOREST PARKS.
Argyll, See **Arrochar** (for Ardgartan) and **Benmore Estate.**
Border, See **Bonchester Bridge** and **Newcastleton.**
Glenmore, See **Aviemore.**
Glen Trool, See **Loch Trool** and also **Barr, Clatteringshaws Dam** and **Newton Stewart.**
Queen Elizabeth, See **Aberfoyle, Rowardennan** and **Trossachs.**

NATIONAL OR LOCAL NATURE RESERVES.
These reserves, which are controlled by the Nature Conservancy (see page 31), are to be found at or near the following places which are described in the gazetteer. Those printed in black type have public access; those in italics require permits, obtainable locally. See **Aberlady,** *Anstruther* (*for Isle of May*), **Caerlaverock, Cairngorms,** *Cape Wrath,* **Clatteringshaws Dam, Inchnadamph, Kinlochewe** (for **Ben Eighe**), *Kishorn,* **Lochranza,** *Newburgh* (*Aberdeen*), *Rannock, Rum, St. Kilda, Shetland* and *Tayport.*

NEDD, Sutherland.   Map 28, NC 1 3.
Iter. 227.

NEIDPATH CASTLE, Peebles.   Map 9, NT 2 4.
See **Peebles.**

NEILSTON, Renfrew.   Map 8, NS 4 5.
At the foot of the moors, with the Balgray reservoir to the east. The Church is 18th cent., and nearby is a monument to John Robertson, who manufactured the engines for the " Comet," one of the earliest steamships, launched in 1812 at *Bowling* (q.v.). **4 m. S.W.**, above Loch Libo, stands the 15th cent. *Caldwell Tower.*

NENTHORN, Berwick.   Map 10, NT 6 3.
About **2 m. E.** stands *Newton Don*, with fine 18th cent. furnishings and lovely gardens. *Iter. 6.*

NETHER LOCHABER, Inverness.   Map 18, NN 0 6.
See **Corran Ferry** and **Lochaber.**

NETHYBRIDGE, Inverness. 387.   Map 26, NJ 0 2.
E.C. Thurs. **GOLF.** On the River Nethy, which has its junction with the more important Spey a little to the north of the village. The village has become a centre for early spring ski-ing. To the north-east is *Abernethy* Church, near which stands the ruined *Castle Roy.* South of Nethybridge lies the great Forest of Abernethy, through which wander many paths, giving access by the Ryvoan Pass, with the picturesque little Green Loch, to *Loch Morlich* (q.v.) in the Glenmore National Forest Park. (See *Aviemore.*) Other paths lead southwards towards the Lairig an Laoigh, one of the two well-known passes in the *Cairngorms* (q.v.), in this case linking Speyside with *Inverey* (q.v.) on Deeside, but suitable only for long-distance walkers. The road leading from Nethybridge to Aviemore traverses the fringe of Abernethy Forest, keeping to the east of the Spey, and passing the little Church of *Kincardine*, beyond which lies Loch Pityoulish. *Iter. 149, 169, 170, 171.*

NEVIS, Inverness.   Map 18, NN 1 7.
See **Ben Nevis** (for *Glen Nevis*) and **Fort William.**
See also **Loch Nevis.**   Map 23, NM 7 9 and 8 9.

NEW ABBEY, Kirkcudbright.   Map 3, NX 9 6.
Beautifully situated on the Pow Burn, in a wooded setting, and backed by the outlines of *Meikle Hard Hill*, 1,300 ft. and the bulky *Criffell*, 1,866 ft. The village is known chiefly for the ruined Cistercian *New Abbey*, or *Sweetheart Abbey* (A.M.), built of red sandstone, and founded, in 1273, by Devorgilla, who also endowed Balliol College at Oxford and built the 13th cent. bridge over the River Nith at *Dumfries* (q.v.). Devorgilla was buried in front of the high altar, together with the heart of her husband, the Abbey thus obtaining its name of " Dulce Cor " or Sweetheart. The picturesque, roofless remains, mainly 13th and 14th cent. work, include the 90-ft. high central tower, much of the nave

Musselburgh, Midlothian. The Tolbooth of c. 1591, built of stones from the Chapel of Our Lady of Loretto. For this act the town was excommunicated for a period of two centuries

Muthill, Perth. A dog-headed drinking fountain on A822

Nairn, Nairn. The ancient Cross shaft, which stands in the High Street

Neilston, Renfrew. The Monument to John Robertson, who made the engines for the ' Comet,' the earliest steam-driven craft in Europe, launched on the Clyde in 1812

New Abbey, Kirkcudbright. This Abbey, also known as Sweetheart Abbey, was founded by Devorgilla in 1273, and not dissolved as a monastery until 1605. The last Abbot, Gilbert Brown, was exiled to Paris

Nethybridge, Inverness. Broomhill Bridge, across the River Spey, to the north of the village. It carries an unclassified road linking A95 and B970

[For MUSSELBURGH see also preceding plate
[For NETHYBRIDGE see also under STRATH SPEY (Plate 158)

PLATE 126 (facing page 218)

New Aberdour, Aberdeen. The ruined Dundarg Castle, looking across Aberdour Bay

Newark Castle, Selkirk. The ruined, mainly 15th century Castle, associated with Sir Walter Scott's '*Lay of the Last Minstrel*.' It stands near the Yarrow Water, a mile south-east of Broadmeadows, off A708

Newbattle, Midlothian. Newbattle Abbey, now a college. The original Cistercian structure was founded in 1140, and the later house became a seat of the Marquess of Lothian

New Bridge, Kirkcudbright. Part of the 'Twelve Apostles' stone circle, consisting actually of 11 stones in two adjacent fields. They are situated off B729, a little to the north-west

Newbigging, Lanark. The Mercat Cross of 1693

New Galloway, Kirkcudbright. The carved 'Adam and Eve' stone in the churchyard of Kells, which is situated a little to the north of the town, on A762

PLATE 127 (facing page 219)

and transepts, and a short aisleless choir. A little to the north-east of the structure stands the isolated Abbot's Tower, and a short distance beyond is the estuary of the River Nith, on the Solway Firth. A circular *Waterloo* tower crowns Glen Hill, to the west. **2 m. N.E.** is *Kirkconnel Tower*, 16th to 18th cent. **1 m. N.W.** is *Shambellie Wood*, which contains what are considered to be the finest Scots pines in the country. *Iter. 72, 73.*

NEW ABERDOUR, Aberdeen. Map 27, **NJ 8** 6.
Stands a little to the south of the red sandstone cliffs of Aberdour Bay, which is overlooked by the ruined tower of *Dundarg Castle*. The little River Dour flows into the bay to the west of the castle. The cliffs in the vicinity are riddled with caverns. See **Pitsligo.** *Iter. 182.*

NEW ALYTH, Perth. Map 20, **NO 2** 4.
See **Alyth.** *Iter. 166.*

NEWARK CASTLE, Fife. Map 17, **NO 5** 0.
See **St. Monance.**

NEWARK CASTLE, Renfrew. Map 8, **NS 3** 7.
See **Port Glasgow.**

NEWARK CASTLE, Selkirk. Map 10, **NT 4** 2.
See **Broadmeadows.**

NEWARTHILL, Lanark. Map 9, **NS 7** 5.
Stands partly at an altitude of over 500 ft. *Iter. 87.*

NEWBATTLE, Midlothian. 7,455. Map 10, **NT 3** 6.
On the River South Esk, and well-known for *Newbattle Abbey*, now used as a college. Of the former Cistercian Abbey, founded in 1140, the crypt and basement chapel still survive, and are incorporated in the present buildings. The earlier structure was burnt in 1544. There are some notable portraits and interior furnishings, and in the fine park stand two fine sundials. Newbattle Church, rebuilt in 1727, preserves the pulpit and other memorials of Archbishop Leighton, minister from 1641 to 1653. The former "*Sun*" Inn was well-known in coaching days. *Iter. 9, 11, 12.*

NEWBIGGING, Lanark. Map 9, **NT 0** 4.
The old Cross carries the date 1693. *Iter. 37, 52.*

NEWBRIDGE, Midlothian. Map 9, **NT 1** 7.
Here is a crow-stepped, gabled inn, dated 1683. At *Cliftonhall*, to the south-west, lived at one time Euphame McCalzean, who was burnt as a witch in 1591 after a trial in Edinburgh. *Iter. 15, 16.*

NEW BRIDGE, Kirkcudbright. Map 3, **NX 9** 7.
The bridge spans the Cluden Water. A little to the north-west, off the Moniaive road, are the remains of a large stone circle, known as the "Twelve Apostles," and of which 11 stones are still to be seen, including five in an upright position. See **Irongray.** *Iter. 27, 48, 56, 67, 74.*

NEWBURGH, Aberdeen. Map 27, **NJ 9** 2.
GOLF. A small harbour, on the estuary of the River Ythan, in the Formartine division of the county. The river is known for its mussel-pearls and also for fishing. Across the estuary are the Sands of Forvie, now a National Nature Reserve of 1,774 acres. To the south, the coast-line is flat and sandy. *Iter. 182.*

NEWBURGH, Fife. 2,464. SB. Map 17, **NO 2** 1.
A small Royal Burgh, with a harbour, on the Firth of Tay, and noted for the manufacture of linoleum. The *Mugdrum* Cross is more than 1,000 years old. The pedestal of *Macduff's* Cross stands on a hill to the south of Newburgh. Opposite the harbour, the Firth is divided by Mugdrum Island into the North and South Deeps. A little to the east are the remains of *Lindores Abbey* (q.v.), and to the south-east lies Lindores Loch. **3 m. N.E.** of Newburgh, beyond Lindores Abbey, stands the ruined *Ballanbreich Castle*, overlooking the Firth of Tay. The Earls of Rothes once owned this 14th cent. stronghold. In the background rises *Normans Law*, 936 ft. *Iter. 131, 132.*

NEW BYTH, Aberdeen. Map 27, **NJ 8** 5.
A small village, founded in 1764, in order to promote home industries, among which hand-loom weaving was formerly practised on a considerable scale. *Iter. 183.*

NEWCASTLETON, Roxburgh. Map 5, **NY 4** 8.
Founded in 1793 as a weaving village, *Newcastleton* has hill views to east and west, and is situated in the delightful Liddesdale valley, on the Liddel Water, which forms the boundary between England and Scotland for some miles to the south-west. The valley is associated with Scott's "Guy Mannering." The Forestry Commission have planted great new forests on the hill-slopes in the vicinity, which together with Wauchope Forest (See **Bonchester Bridge**), form part of the Border National Forest Park, extending across the English border. To the north-east of Newcastleton are the *Larriston Fells*, 1,677 ft., beyond which rise the lonely *Cheviot* hills, and to the north-west of the village is *Roan Fell*, 1,862 ft., on the borders of Dumfriesshire. The English-Scottish border traverses the *Larriston Fells*, which, on their west side, were once crossed by a road linking Liddesdale with the North Tyne valley in Northumberland. The inscribed *Bloody Bush* stone, showing the various toll charges of former days, still stands on the fells some 2½ miles east of the Newcastleton-Jedburgh road. **1½ m. S.S.W.** is the former Border stronghold of *Mangerton Tower*. See **Hermitage Castle** and **Riccarton.** *Iter. 31, 47.*

NEW CUMNOCK, Ayr. 3,871. Map 8, **NS 6** 1.
E.C. Wed. GOLF. This mining parish was separated from *Cumnock* (q.v.) in 1650, and is situated on the River Nith, not very far from its source in the hills, and where it is joined by the Afton Water. The latter flows through the delightful Glen Afton, to the south, overlooked at the head of the valley by *Blackcraig Hill*, 2,298 ft. Glen Afton is associated with Sir William Wallace, and Burns wrote the well-known lines commencing: "Flow gently, sweet Afton." *Iter. 27, 67.*

NEW DAILLY, Ayr. Map 2, **NS 2** 0.
See **Dailly.** *Iter. 74, 85.*

NEW DEER, Aberdeen. Map 27, **NJ 8** 4.
See **Old Deer.** *Iter. 183, 186, 189 197.*

NEW ELGIN, Moray. 1,329. Map 26, **NJ 2** 6.
Iter. 190, 192.

NEW FOWLIS, Perth. Map 16, **NN 9** 2.
See **Fowlis Wester.** *Iter. 145.*

NEW GALLOWAY, Kirkcudbright. 293. SB.
Map 3, **NX 6** 7.
E.C. Thurs. GOLF. A tiny Royal Burgh and angling centre, on the River Ken, in the Glenkens district, with Loch Ken immediately to the south. On the west side of the loch is *Kenmure Castle*, 16th to 17th cent. and modernised, the ancient seat of the Lochinvar chiefs. Farther to the south, the shores of the loch are well-wooded. In *Kells* Churchyard, a little to the north of New Galloway, is the grave of a Covenanter, shot in 1685. There is also a curious carved Adam and Eve stone. Other stones have unusual carvings and inscriptions. Away to the north-west rise the lofty *Rhinns of Kells*, with *Corserine* reaching a height of 2,668 ft. South-westwards, on the *Newton Stewart* (q.v.) road, lies *Clatteringshaws Dam* (q.v.), with the Cairn Edward Forest, part of the Glen Trool National Forest Park, situated in the immediate vicinity. The Glenlee power station in connection with the Galloway Power Scheme lies to the north-west of the town. New Galloway railway station lies some **5 m. S.E.**, on the Kirkcudbright road, near the point where the Black Water of Dee enters Loch Ken. See **Balmaclellan** and **Dalry** (Kirkcudbright). *Iter. 25, 71, 77.*

NEWHAVEN (Edinburgh), Midlothian. Map 10, **NT 2** 7.
This little fishing port was founded by James IV, c. 1500. the original population being of Dutch, or Danish strain. Some early warships were built here, including the "Great Michael," launched in 1507, on which served Sir Andrew Wood of *Largo* (q.v.). *Newhaven* is noted for its fish dinners, and also for the curious dresses worn by the fishwives. The old fishergirl cries of "Caller ou" (fresh oysters) and "Caller herrin" (fresh herrings) were characteristic of Edinburgh in former days. The "*Peacock*" Inn has long been known for sea food.

NEWHOUSE, Lanark.   Map 9, **NS 7** 6.
Iter. 15, 18, 50, 52, 87.

NEW LEEDS, Aberdeen.   Map 27, **NJ 9** 5.
Iter. 185.

NEW LUCE, Wigtown.   Map 2, **NX 1** 6.
Lies in that part of *Galloway* (q.v.) known as The Moors, and is situated at the junction of the Main Water of Luce with the Cross Water of Luce, which together form the Water of Luce flowing southwards to *Glenluce* (q.v.) and Wigtown Bay.   The hilly and narrow road leading northwards to *Barrhill* (q.v.) in Ayrshire is gated, and goes through lonely moorlands rising to about 1,000 ft.   From 1659 to 1662, Prophet Peden was minister at New Luce. *Iter. 78.*

NEWMACHAR, Aberdeen.   Map 27, **NJ 8** 1.
Iter. 180.

NEWMAINS, Lanark. 6,396.   Map 9, **NS 8** 5.

E.C. Wed. This town is situated on the extensive Lanark coalfield, with large iron and steel works. *Murdostoun Castle*, to the north of Newmains, is partly 15th cent., and has an old dovecote. To the east, on the Midlothian border, are the *Gladsmuir* hills. *Iter. 19, 20, 50, 52.*

NEWMILL, Roxburgh.   Map 5, **NT 4** 1.
Iter. 11, 30, 45.

NEWMILLS, Fife.   Map 16, **NT 0** 8.
GOLF. See **Culross** and **Valleyfield**. *Iter. 97, 134.*

NEWMILNS, Ayr. 4,011. SB.   Map 8, **NS 5** 3.
A small town specializing in the manufacture of muslins. Several Covenanters' tombstones stand in the churchyard. The former Tolbooth dates from 1739. *Iter. 20, 69.*

NEW ORLEANS, Argyll.   Map 7, **NR 7** 1.
Situated on the east side of the Kintyre peninsula.

NEW PITSLIGO, Aberdeen. 1,438.   Map 27, **NJ 8** 5.
E.C. Wed. A large *Buchan* (q.v.) village, to the north-west of which rises the hill of *Turlundie*. See **Pitsligo**. *Iter. 188.*

NEWPORT-ON-TAY, Fife. 3,332. SB.   Map 17, **NO 4** 2.
E.C. Wed. A Firth of Tay resort, linked to *Dundee* (q.v.), on the opposite shore, by a car ferry. To the south-west, commencing at *Wormit*, is the famous two-mile long Tay Bridge, built 1883–1888, and replacing its ill-fated predecessor, which was blown down, in 1879, while a train was making the crossing, causing heavy loss of life. 2½ m. S. of Newport-on-Tay, on the Leuchars road, is the strangely named ' *Pickletillem*' Inn. See **Tayport**. *Iter. 94, 126, 127.*

NEW SCONE, Perth.   Map 17, **NO 1** 2.
See **Scone**. *Iter. 151, 153.*

NEWSTEAD, Roxburgh.   Map 10, **NT 5** 3.
An old-world village, standing on the south bank of the River Tweed, to the west of the point where it is joined by the Leader Water. On Leaderfoot Hill is a monument marking the site of the Roman Camp of *Trimontium*, where excavations, between 1905 and 1910, revealed treasures which are now in the National Museum of Antiquities in Edinburgh. To the south rise the triple-peaked *Eildon* hills. **2 m. E.**, in a bend of the Tweed, is *Old Melrose*, the site of a monastery founded in the 7th cent. *Iter. 13, 41, 43.*

NEWTON BRIDGE, Perth.   Map 16, **NN 8** 3.
Situated a little beyond the northern extremity of the delightful *Sma' Glen* (q.v.). Here, the by-road leading westwards into Glen Almond, threaded by the River Almond, diverges from the main road eading northwards on the line of General Wade's military road towards *Amulree* (q.v.). Away to the west, and dominating Glen Almond, rises *Ben Chonzie*, 3,048 ft. *Iter. 89, 140, 141, 147.*

NEWTON MEARNS, Renfrew. 4,317.   Map 8, **NS 5** 5.
A mile to the south-east is *Mearns*, on the edge of an extensive and high-lying moorland district. The Church here dates from the late 18th cent. Nearer to Newton Mearns stand the 15th cent. *Blackhouse Castle* and the restored *Pollok Castle*, with its 17th cent. garden architecture. To the south-west, on the Kilmarnock road, is a monument to Robert Pollok, an early 19th cent. poet. See **Eaglesham**. *Iter. 55, 61.*

NEWTONMORE, Inverness. 655.   Map 19, **NN 7** 9.
E.C. Wed. GOLF. A Speyside resort, with both a summer and a winter-sports season, situated beneath the foothills of the *Monadhliath* mountains to the west, and with views towards the *Cairngorms* (q.v.) to the east. Pony-trekking is a recently-introduced local sport. The Clan Museum contains numerous treasures of the Clan Macpherson. Outside the village, to the south-west, the Spey is joined by the Calder, which has come down through the wild Glen Banchor. To the north-east of the town, the Spey receives the waters of the Tromie, issuing from the long glen of that name, which extends far into the wilds of the great Gaick Forest, a wilderness of lonely hills. **3 m. S.W.**, off the road leading towards *Drumgask* (q.v.) and *Loch Laggan* (q.v.), near the meeting-point of the Spey and the Truim, is the site of a clan battle, fought in 1386. The site is overlooked to the north by *Craig Dhu*, 2,350 ft., a gathering-place of the Clan Macpherson, and giving its name to their battle cry. In a cave on the steep cliffs of this hill, Cluny Macpherson hid for some years after the '45. The wooded scenery at this point is of much beauty. See **Dalwhinnie**, **Kingussie** and **Tromie Bridge**. *Iter. 140, 147, 150, 208.*

NEWTON STEWART, Wigtown. 2,040. SB.
    Map 2, **NX 4** 6.
E.C. Wed. M.D. Fri. GOLF. This attractive little *Galloway* (q.v.) weaving town and fishing resort is situated on the River Cree, a few miles above Wigtown Bay. Houses in the town are built along the river banks, giving a delightful, almost Venetian appearance. The ornate 19th cent. *Galloway* monument is 57 feet high. The old village of *Minnigaff*, where the churchyard by the ruined Church contains carved tombstones, is linked to Newton Stewart by means of the

1. Galloway Monument.

Cree Bridge, built in 1813 to replace an earlier one washed away by the river. The scenery in the vicinity is of great charm, notably to the north, and there are distant views of the fine mountains which surround picturesque *Loch Trool* (q.v.). Beyond the Cumloden deer-park, and near the line of the Devil's Dyke, are two tall prehistoric stones known as The Thieves. To the south is the ruined 16th cent. *Garlies Castle*. Immediately to the north-east of the town, and threaded by the Penkill Burn, is Kirroughtree Forest, part of the National Forest Park of Glen Trool. **3 m. S.E.**, on the road to *Creetown* (q.v.), is the entrance to the pretty Bargaly Glen, threaded by the Palnure Burn. It is overlooked to the east by the great mass of *Cairnsmore of Fleet*, 2,331 ft., a notable landmark, which is associated with John Buchan's " The Thirty-Nine Steps." **4 m. N.W.**, on the Bargrennan road, are the *Cruives*

Newmilns, Ayr. One of a number of Covenanters' monuments in the church-yard

New Orleans, Argyll. A house situated on an unclassified road 4 miles south-east of Campbeltown, near the east coast of the Kintyre peninsula

Newport-on-Tay, Fife. The strangely named 'Pickle-tillem' Inn, which stands some 2½ miles south of the town, on A92

Newton Mearns, Renfrew. The Monument to the poet Robert Pollok, born in 1798. It stands 3 miles south-west, near A77

Newtonmore, Inverness. The notice outside the Clan Museum, which contains treasures of the Clan Macpherson

Newstead, Roxburgh. The Monument on Leader-foot Hill, above the River Tweed, marking the site of the Roman fort of Trimontium

[For **NEWTON STEWART** see following plate

PLATE 128 (facing page 220)

Newton Stewart, Wigtown. The early 19th century bridge spanning the River Cree, which replaces an older structure wrecked by floods. Earlier, the river was crossed by the Black Ford of Cree

Newton Stewart, Wigtown. The Galloway Monument, erected in 1875 to commemorate the 9th Earl of Galloway, who died in 1873

Oban, Argyll. The unfinished building, intended as a museum and art gallery, and known as ' McCaig's Folly.' It is situated on a hill at the back of the town

North Berwick, East Lothian. The archway made from the jawbones of a whale, which stands on the summit of North Berwick Law, 613 feet, off B1347

Oban, Argyll. The remains of the 12th to 13th century McDougall fortress of Dunollie, overlooking the sea between Oban and Ganavan Bay, on an unclassified road

Oban, Argyll. The Dog Stone, or Clach a'Choin, to which the legendary Fingal is said to have tied his dog Bran. It stands on an unclassified road near Dunollie Castle, between Oban and Ganavan Bay

PLATE 129 (facing page 221)

of Cree, a beautiful wooded stretch of the river, which Burns has described in verse. See **Kirkcowan**. *Iter. 25, 26, 71, 72, 73, 78, 79, 80, 81, 82.*

NEWTOWN ST. BOSWELLS, Roxburgh.
Map 10, NT **5** 3.
A railway junction, noted for livestock sales which were previously held at St. Boswells. See **St. Boswells Green.** *Iter. 4, 13, 32, 36, 52.*

NEWTYLE, Angus. Map 17, NO **2** 4.
A *Sidlaw* hills village, with the high points of *Auchterhouse Hill*, 1,399 ft., and *Craigowl Hill*, 1,493 ft., rising to the east. To the south-east of Newtyle, at the commencement of the ascent over the Glack of Newtyle in the Sidlaws, the road to Dundee passes the ruined 16th cent. *Hatton Castle.* See **Eassie.** *Iter. 160.*

NEW YORK, Argyll. Map 14, NM **9** 1.
Faces *Portinnisherrich* (q.v.) from the west bank of Loch Awe.

NIGG, Ross and Cromarty. 573. Map 31, NH **8** 7.
Overlooks the small Bay of Nigg, an inlet of the larger Cromarty Firth. The Church preserves a curious sculptured stone, perhaps 7th cent. work. To the east rises the *Hill of Nigg*, 666 ft. See **Balintore, Dunskeath, Fearn** and **Logie Easter.**

NITSHILL, Renfrew. Map 8, NS **5** 6.
Iter. 18, 29, 61.

NORTH BALLACHULISH, Inverness. 120.
Map 18, NN **0** 5.
Faces *Ballachulish* (q.v.) across the narrows of Loch Leven, which are crossed here by a busy car ferry. For motorists travelling south, this ferry can be avoided by making the long, but picturesque detour round the loch by way of *Kinlochleven* (q.v.), and rejoining the main road at *Carnach* (q.v.), near the entrance to *Glencoe* (q.v.). By the door of *St. Bride's* Church stands a copy of the High Cross of *Oronsay* Priory. See **Colonsay.** *Iter. 100, 124, 125, 142.*

NORTH BALLOCH, Ayr. Map 2, NX **3** 9.
At the head of the pleasant Stinchar valley, where the river is joined by the Balloch Burn. To the south-east is the 1,280-ft. high, lonely Nick o' the Balloch Pass, traversed by the road to *Bargrennan* (q.v.). *Iter. 84.*

NORTH BERWICK, East Lothian. 3,738. SB.
Map 10, NT **5** 8.
E.C. Thurs. GOLF. This well-known Royal Burgh, resort and fishing village on the North Sea coast is famous particularly for golf, and there is also a sandy beach for bathing. The harbour is situated between the east and west bays, and in the vicinity of the former is a fragment of the 12th cent.

1. " Auld Kirk " ruins.   2. Information Bureau.   3. Museum.

" Auld Kirk." Out to sea, to the north-east, is the famous landmark of the *Bass Rock*, 350 ft. high, with a powerful lighthouse. It was once a Covenanters' prison, and is associated also with R. L. Stevenson's " Catriona." There are traces of old fortifications, and of a chapel, while the former fort on the island was destroyed in 1694. Sea-birds now inhabit the Bass Rock in large numbers. North-west of the resort lies *Fidra* island, with its lighthouse. A little to the south of North Berwick is *North Berwick Law*, 613 ft., a fine viewpoint, crowned by a watch-tower dating from Napoleonic times, near which is an archway made from the jawbones of a whale. Farther to the south, off the road to *Haddington* (q.v.), is the 16th cent. *Fenton Tower.* **3 m.** E., on the coast, beyond Canty Bay, are considerable remains of the picturesque, moated *Tantallon Castle* (A.M.), situated on a headland, and dating probably from the 14th cent. and later. The Castle was besieged in 1528, and finally destroyed by General Monk, in 1651. Scott's " Marmion " describes this romantic Douglas stronghold. A 17th cent. " doocot," or dovecote, stands within the two inner ditches. To the south-east of the castle, in the grounds of *Seacliff House*, are slight remains of *Auldhame Priory.* See **Dirleton, Gullane, Tynninghame** and **Whitekirk.** *Iter. 2, 36, 37, 38.*

NORTH BROOMAGE, Stirling. Map 16, NS **8** 8.
Iter. 95, 97, 98.

NORTH KESSOCK, Ross and Cromarty. Map 25, NH **6** 4.
A crofting and fishing village, facing the narrows which divide the waters of the Beauly Firth from those of the Inner Moray Firth. It is known as North Kessock to distinguish it from *South Kessock* (q.v.) on the Ness estuary, in Inverness-shire, on the opposite shore of the narrows, to which it is connected by car ferry, giving access thereby to *Inverness* (q.v.). Above North Kessock, to the north-east, is *Ord Hill*, crowned by a large vitrified fort. *Iter. 202, 203.*

NORTH QUEENSFERRY, Fife. Map 17, NT **1** 8.
See **Queensferry, North.** *Iter. 89, 90, 93, 94.*

NORTH UIST, ISLE OF, Inverness. Map 32, NF **7** 7 etc.
See **Hebrides, Outer** (North Uist). *Iter. 261.*

NORTH-WEST HIGHLANDS.
See **Highlands.**

OA CHURCH, Isle of Islay, Argyll. Map 6, NR **3** 4.
See **Mull of Oa.** *Iter. 244.*

OAKLEY, Fife. 3,591. Map 16, NT **0** 8.
In the vicinity, to the west, is situated the *Comrie* coal mine, one of the most modern and up-to-date in Scotland. *Iter. 133.*

OBAN, Argyll. 6,124. SB. Map 14, NM **8** 3.
E.C. Thurs. **M.D.** Wed. GOLF. A famous West Highland resort, yachting centre, and starting point for picturesque drives in the district of *Lorne* (q.v.), notable for its magnificent seascapes and island scenery. Many of the finest excursions can be made by steamer to such well-known places as the islands of Mull, Lismore, Iona and Staffa, which are all described under their own headings. There are also regular steamer sailings to several of the Outer Hebridean islands. Yachting is a great feature of the waters in the vicinity, while during the second week of September is held the annual Argyll Gathering. The island of *Kerrera* faces Oban Bay, being linked by passenger ferry, and is separated from the mainland by the Sound of Kerrera. On the south-western shores of the island, in a very striking setting, stands the ruined *Gylen Castle*. Oban itself has a modern R.C. Cathedral of granite, built by Sir Giles Scott, and on a hill behind the town is the curious, unfinished structure known as " McCaig's Folly," and also an uncompleted hydropathic. From Pulpit Hill, to the south, the view is remarkable, an indicator being provided, and sunsets seen from here are sometimes memorable.

On the east side of Oban Bay is the Clach a'Choin, or, " Dog Stone," traditionally associated with Fingal's dog, Bran. Nearby is the ruined McDougall stronghold of *Dunollie Castle*, 12th or 13th cent., overlooking the Firth of Lorne. In the modern mansion of *Dunollie* is preserved the Brooch of Lorne, supposed to have been worn by Robert Bruce. Beyond the old Castle lies Ganavan Bay, with its fine, sandy bathing beach. To the east of the town, in Glen

1. Cathedral (R.C.)   2. McCaig's Folly.   3. Information Bureau.

Cruitten, stands *Glencruitten House*, its park noted for the "Cathedral of Trees." Dr. Johnson and Boswell visited Oban in their tour of 1773, and found a "tolerable" inn. Sir Walter Scott came here in 1814. The road leading southwards from the town towards Loch Feochan and *Kilninver* (*q.v.*) passes near the ruined *Kilbride* Church, and the restored 16th cent. *Lerags Cross*. A little to the east of the Kilninver road is the pretty Loch Nell, on the south-west shore of which is a curious 80-yard long boulder ridge, known as the "Serpent's Mound." At the far end of the loch, in Glen Lonan, is a tall granite monolith called Diarmid's Pillar, adjacent to which is the burial-place of Diarmid, the ancestor of the Clan Campbell. Another road, with gates and bad bends, leads direct from Oban into Glen Lonan, and provides an alternative route to *Taynuilt* (*q.v.*) and Loch Etive. See **Connel, Dunstaffnage Castle, Lismore** and **Tyndrum**. *Iter.* 110, 117, 118, 119, 122, 124, 125, 144, 145.

OBBE (Isle of Lewis), Harris, Inverness.   Map 32, NG 0 8.
See **Hebrides, Outer** (Harris). *Iter.* 256.

OCCUMSTER, Caithness.   Map 30, ND 2 3.
Iter. 200.

OCHIL HILLS, Clackmannan; Kinross; Perth.
Map 16, NN 8 0 etc.
See **Alva, Bridge of Allan, Dollar, Dunblane, Glendevon, Gleneagles Hotel, Glenfarg** and **Tillicoultry.** *Iter.* 86, 89, 135, 136, 146.

OCHILTREE, Ayr. 642.   Map 8, NS 5 2.
Lies at the junction of the Burnoch Water with the better-known Lugar Water, in a dairy-farming district. A tablet marks the house in which was born George Douglas Brown, whose "House with the Green Shutters" contains much local colour. The former *Ochiltree House* was the scene of the marriage, in 1684, of Claverhouse, while in an earlier house, in 1564, John Knox was married. See **Stair.** *Iter.* 21, 27, 68.

OICH BRIDGE, Inverness.   Map 18, NH 3 0.
See **Loch Oich.** *Iter.* 210.

OLD DAILLY, Ayr.   Map 2, NX 2 9.
See **Dailly.** *Iter.* 78.

OLD DEER, Aberdeen. 212.   Map 27, NJ 9 4.
An attractive *Buchan* (*q.v.*) village, visited for the scanty remains of the Cistercian Abbey (A.M.), founded in 1218,

and situated a little to the north-west, in the grounds o *Pitfour House*. Excavation has revealed the ground plan of the buildings, but there is little to see, though the riverside setting, near the South Ugie Water, is charming. A monastery was founded here in the 6th cent. by St. Columba, this being recalled by the well-known Book of Deer, incorporating the first known characters in Gaelic script, and now in the University Library at Cambridge. *Iter.* 189.

OLDHAMSTOCKS, East Lothian.   Map 11, NT 7 7.
A secluded village, once noted for the biennial fairs held on the green by the now-vanished Mercat Cross. The Church has an elaborate 16th cent. sundial.

OLD KILPATRICK, Dunbarton. 3,227.   Map 8, NS 4 7.
E.C. Wed. Situated on the north bank of the River Clyde, here crossed by

1. St. Patrick's Well.

the *Erskine* car ferry, much used by motorists from the south desiring to bypass Glasgow. The *Kilpatrick* hills look down upon the village, which was on the line of the Antonine, or *Roman Wall* (*q.v.*), of which vestiges are still traceable. St. Patrick may have been born here, and a Holy Well bears his name. The Forth and Clyde canal passes through Old Kilpatrick on its way westwards towards *Bowling* (*q.v.*), a short distance away, where it joins the Clyde. See **Dumbarton.** *Iter.* 88, 109, 110, 111, 112, 113.

OLD MELDRUM, Aberdeen. 1,095. SB.   Map 27, NJ 8 2.
E.C. Wed. The Church dates from 1684. About a mile to the south is *Barra Hill*, 634 ft., crowned by a prehistoric fort, overlooking the Formartine and Garioch districts. A battle is said to have been fought here, in 1308, by Robert Bruce. **4 m. W.**, near *Daviot*, is the very notable *Loanhead* stone circle (A.M.), situated on a low hill, and dating probably from the Neolithic-Bronze age, **2 m. S.W.**, on the Inverurie road, is the old mansion of *Barra Castle*, 17th and 18th cent. See **Fyvie** and **Tarves.** *Iter.* 180, 187, 197.

OLD RATTRAY, Aberdeen.   Map 27, NK 0 5.
Lies a little inland from the lonely Rattray Head, dividing the two bays of Rattray and Strathbeg. West of Old Rattray lies the shallow Loch of Strathbeg, at the east end of which are the remains of *Rattray Castle* and the 13th cent. Chapel of *St. Mary*. *Iter.* 182.

OLD SCONE, Perth.   Map 17, NO 1 2.
See **Scone.** *Iter.* 152.

ONICH, Inverness.   Map 18, NN 0 6.
E.C. Thurs. Finely situated on the shores of *Loch Linnhe* (*q.v.*), looking towards the *Ardgour* (*q.v.*) hills, among which *Garbh Bheinn*, 2,903 ft., is the outstanding feature in the view. There is a monument to Dr. Alexander Stewart, a noted Gaelic scholar. Near the pier is a perforated monolith, known as the Clach a' Charra. To the north, the Amhainn Righ Burn, on which are waterfalls, debouches from wooded heights into Loch Linnhe. *Iter.* 100, 124, 125, 142.

OPINAN, Ross and Cromarty.   Map 22, NG 7 7.
A clachan situated between the Gair Loch and the mouth of Loch Torridon, with views across the Inner Sound towards the distant *Cuillin* mountains of Skye.

Ochiltree, Ayr. The house in which George Douglas Brown, the author of the 'House with the Green Shutters,' was born in 1869. In this book, Ochiltree appears as 'Barbie'

Old Kilpatrick, Dunbarton. The Holy Well of St. Patrick. The Saint was by tradition born at Old Kilpatrick

Old Meldrum, Aberdeen. The Loanhead stone circle, which lies some 4 miles west of the town, near Daviot, on an unclassified road

Onich, Inverness. The perforated monolith known as the Clach a'Charra, which stands near the pier on Loch Linnhe

Old Meldrum, Aberdeen. The old mansion of Barra Castle, partly 17th century, which is situated some 2 miles south-west, on A981

PLATE 130 (facing page 222)

Orkney Islands. The 12th to 15th century Cathedral of St. Magnus at Kirkwall, the capital and largest town of Orkney

Orchardton Tower, Kirkcudbright. This circular late 15th century tower was built originally by John Cairns and became a Maxwell property. It stands a mile south of Palnackie, on an unclassified road off A711

Orkney Islands. The tower of the much reconstructed 16th century Bishop's Palace at Kirkwall

Orkney Islands. The great prehistoric chambered tomb of Maeshowe, or Maes Howe, off A965, some 3 miles west-south-west of Finstown

Orkney Islands. The prehistoric standing stones of Stenness, which are situated on B9055, between the Loch of Stenness and the Loch of Harray, some 5 miles west of Finstown

[For ORKNEY see also following plate

PLATE 131 (facing page 223)

ORCHARDTON TOWER, Kirkcudbright. Map 3, NX 8 5. See **Palnackie**.

ORKNEY ISLANDS. Map 33.

The *Orkneys* lie about 20 miles to the north of the Scottish mainland, from which they are separated by the turbulent waters of the Pentland Firth, and were known to the Romans as the Orcades. There are, in all, about 70 islands, 28 of which are inhabited, by far the largest being that of the *Mainland*, where the largest mileage of motoring roads will be found, and on which is situated **Kirkwall**, the most important centre. The Mainland is linked by the *Churchill Barriers* to several of the smaller islands to the south. Magnificent cliff scenery, notably in the island of Hoy, sometimes best viewed from a boat; wonderful seascapes; rare bird life; and some famous prehistoric antiquities, are all features of the islands. The nearest port on the mainland is *Scrabster* (*q.v.*), near Thurso, with a 2½-hour car ferry steamer service to Stromness, and there are air services to Grimsetter airport at Kirkwall. Other steamer services operate from Aberdeen and Leith, and there are also connections to the Shetlands. Owing to their geographical situation, the summer is almost nightless. The climate is mainly mild, and the soil fertile, though virtually treeless. Most of the farming is now carried on by modern mechanical methods. There is an abundance of good trout fishing to be obtained, with free loch fishing. The Picts are said to have been the first colonisers of the Orkneys, being succeeded by the Norsemen. The territory was annexed to Scotland in 1468, being pledged for 50,000 florins by King Christian I of Norway as part of the agreed dowry of 60,000 florins when his daughter Margaret married James III of Scotland. *Iter. 263 to 266*.

THE MAINLAND.

This is the largest of the Orkneys, having a deeply-indented coastline, while on it are situated *Kirkwall* and *Stromness*, the two most important ports and towns. There are nearly 200 miles of motoring roads on the island which are well-surfaced throughout. Minor roads giving access to the coast may be poor in places.

Kirkwall (4,305. SB. M.D. Mon.) was created a Royal Burgh in 1486, and is famous for *St. Magnus'* Cathedral, founded in 1137, the buildings being mainly of 12th cent. date, with additions up to 1558. After the battle of *Largs* (*q.v.*), in 1263, the body of King Haco rested here on its return to Norway. The Cathedral was later desecrated by Cromwell's soldiers, and the spire was destroyed by lightning in 1671, but restorations, some 50 years ago, have made good much of the damage. The 133-ft. high tower, built in 1525, is a good viewpoint. In the choir is a notable 15th cent. tomb, and in the North aisle of the nave is suspended a characteristic Orcadian " mort-brod," or memorial, others of which may also be seen. A tablet to the crew of the battleship " Royal Oak," torpedoed in the Second World War, with the loss of more than 800 men, was unveiled in 1948. South of the Cathedral stands the ruined Bishop's Place (A.M.), with its massive mid-16th cent. round tower. Nearby are the remains of the Earl's Palace (A.M.), dating from 1607, and associated with Scott's " The Pirate." A doorway has survived from the 16th cent. Church of *St. Ola*, and near the Cathedral is the old *Tankerness House*, dated 1574. There are picturesque, narrow alleys in the town surfaced mainly with large stone slabs, and there is a noticeable absence of footpaths. The pier lies to the north, on Kirkwall Bay. There is a GOLF course.

Kirkwall Airport (Grimsetter) lies to the south-east of the town. Beyond the bay, to the east of Wide Firth, is *Shapinsay* island, with the 19th cent. *Balfour Castle*. Eastwards of Kirkwall are the smaller bays of Meil and Berstane, each with good sands, and the latter being an inlet of the larger Inganess Bay, to the east of which lies the Tankerness peninsula. South of Kirkwall is the sandy Scapa Bay, near the western shores of which is the road overlooking *Scapa Flow*, the famous naval anchorage, used extensively in both world wars, and which saw the surrender of the German fleet, in 1918. Most of the ships were scuttled by their crews in 1919, but a number have since been salvaged. The battleship " Royal Oak " was sunk here by a U-boat in 1939. During the last war, in order to seal up the eastern approach to Scapa Flow, the *Churchill Barriers* were built, linking the Mainland with South Ronaldsay. The new road commences at **St. Mary's Holm**, 6½ m. S.S.E. of Kirkwall, on Holm Sound, and traverses the small island of Lamb Holm, where Italian prisoners, during the war, constructed an ornate little Chapel out of a Nissen hut. Glimps Holm and Burray, with its curious broch, together with the narrow waterways which separate them, are then traversed. 3 m. N.W. of Kirkwall, off the Finstown road, is *Wideford Hill*, 741 ft. (A.M.), a remarkable viewpoint. There are interesting " weems," or Picts' Houses to the west and north.

Finstown, an attractive village, with one of Orkney's few woods, stands on the Bay of Firth, in which is situated Damsay Island, with its ruined broch. To the south-east of the village, on the bay, is the notable Gallery Grave of *Rennibister* (A.M.). 3 m. W.S.W., at **Stenness**, is the very notable **Maeshowe** (A.M.), an enormous burial mound, perhaps Pictish, 36 ft. high and some 300 ft. in circumference, with many Runic inscriptions. A little farther to the west, on a narrow causeway between the Loch of Stenness and the Loch of Harray, and beyond **Stenness** Church, are the famous *Standing Stones of Stenness* (A.M.), comprising two incomplete circles, the *Circle of Stenness* and the *Ring of Brogar*, or *Brodgar* (A.M.), the latter retaining 20 stones. There are also numerous tumuli in the neighbourhood. 7 m. N.E. of Finstown, near the shores of Wide Firth and facing the island of Gairsay, is the *Hall of Rendall*, where a doocot, having flagstone landing piers for the birds, and dating perhaps from c. 1600, has survived.

Stromness (1,483. SB.), with its fine harbour, narrow paved street, quaint closes and an interesting museum, faces the hills of **Hoy** across Hoy Sound and looks south-eastwards to historic **Scapa Flow**. There is a GOLF course. It is the port for *Scrabster* (*q.v.*) and also for Hoy and other islands. Near Waith Bridge, over which the road to Kirkwall passes, is the Neolithic, or Stone Age Chambered Cairn of *Onstan* (A.M.). 9 m. S.E. of Stromness, near the shores of Scapa Flow, and close to **Orphir** Church (A.M.), is a ruined circular Church, built perhaps by Earl Haakon in the 12th cent. To the east of Orphir lies the sandy Swanbister Bay.

In the extreme north-west of the Mainland is situated **Birsay**, on the bay of that name, with the Loch of Boardhouse lying to the east. The ruined Palace of Birsay was rebuilt late in the 16th cent. Off-shore, to the north-west, is the tidal island of Brough of Birsay, with a ruined 12th cent. Church. Some **10 m.** E.S.E. of Birsay, past Costa Head, Britain's windiest spot, and by the shores of Eynhallow Sound, is **Evie**, near which stands the large broch of *Gurness* (A.M.) at Aikerness. To the south-west of Birsay Bay lies Marwick Head, reached on foot from **Marwick**, and notable for the Kitchener Memorial. The cruiser " Hampshire," which was taking the general to Russia, was sunk, in June 1916, off the coast in the vicinity. The very famous prehistoric village of **Skara Brae** (A.M.), dating from the Stone Age, and in a remarkable state of preservation, stands on the south shore of the sandy bay of Skaill, beyond **Aith,** to the west of the Birsay to Stromness road. Narrow, covered alleys give access to stone huts, while the smaller remains which have been found point to an occupation of some 250 years. Near the freshwater Loch of Skaill stands the modernised 17th cent. and later *Skaill House*. Inland, and to the east, lies the Loch of Harray, noted for fishing, to the north of which is **Dounby**, with *Klick* mill, an old watermill, in the vicinity.

In the south-east corner of the mainland, known as East Mainland, and situated on Sandside Bay, is **Deerness**, with its ruined broch. A little to the north is a chasm in the cliffs known as the Gloup of Deerness, and beyond it is the Stack of Deerness. The road leading westwards from the Deerness peninsula to Kirkwall passes the head of Deer Sound at St. Peter's Pool. On the narrow isthmus separating it from Taracliff Bay and the North

Sea, with Copinsay Island away to the south-east, is the barrow of *Dingy's Howe*. **2 m. N.N.W.** of Deerness, accessible only on foot, and overlooking Deer Sound, is a monument at *Scarva Taing* commemorating 200 Covenanters, wrecked here in 1679.

HOY.

The most spectacular and second in size among the Orkneys, *Hoy* is accessible by steamer from Stromness, and has a number of hills over 1,000 ft. in height, the loftiest being *Ward Hill*, 1,565 ft., noted for its rare plants. From *Linksness*, with its pier, in the north of the island facing Graemsay Island in Hoy Sound, access is gained on foot to the magnificent cliff scenery, riven by steep gashes called " geos." These form the great feature of the north-west coast, from St. John's Head, rising vertically to 1,140 ft., to the celebrated *Old Man of Hoy*, an impressive, isolated rock stack, 450 ft. high. This is a famous landmark, being visible from as far away as Caithness on the mainland coast across the Pentland Firth. Beyond lies Rora Head and another line of cliffs, overlooking the attractive Rackwick Valley, in which is situated the burial-chamber known as the *Dwarfie Stone* (A.M.), associated with Scott's " The Pirate," and inscribed with Hugh Miller's initials. In the south of Hoy are the coloured cliffs of Berry Head, and to the east, beyond the modern *Melsetter House*, with its fine gardens, is the South Walls peninsula, with the inlet of Long Hope. At its mouth lies the island of Flotta, looking westwards to the Scapa Flow naval base of **Lyness.** Hoy is said to be the most southerly breeding-place in Great Britain of the rare great skua.

SOUTH RONALDSAY.

This fertile island is now linked to the larger island of Mainland by the *Churchill Barriers*, which traverse the smaller islands of Burray, Glimps Holm and Lamb Holm. On the northern coast of the island is **St. Margaret's Hope,** associated with Queen Margaret, the " Maid of Norway," who died on board ship on her way to Scotland, in 1290. Hoxa Head, on the north-west side of South Ronaldsay, has a ruined broch. The southern extremity of the island, on which stands **Burwick,** linked by a road to the pretty village of St. Margaret's Hope, is separated from Duncansby Head, in Caithness, on the mainland, by the 6-mile wide turbulent stretch of the Pentland Firth.

ROUSAY AND EYNHALLOW (both uninhabited).

The island of *Rousay* is separated from Mainland by the waters of Eynhallow Sound. It has some fine rock scenery on the west coast, on which are also the notable broch and chambered cairn of *Midhope* (A.M.), in addition to other cairns. On the tiny *Eynhallow* Island is a ruined monastic Church (A.M.), and the island is also a haunt of seals and many species of rare birds, among them the skua. Fulmars and eiders also abound.

EGILSAY.

This small island, to the east of Rousay, is noted chiefly for its roofless Norman Church (A.M.), supposed to stand on the site where St. Magnus was murdered, in 1116, and famous for its curious round tower, 48 ft. high, one of the three examples to be found in Scotland. To the south-west is the little island of *Wyre*, or *Veira*, on which are slight remains of *Cobbie Row's Castle* (A.M.), which may be the earliest of all Scottish stone-built castles.

STRONSAY.

A strangely-shaped island, in the north-east sector of the group, with three large bays, Milk Bay, St. Catherine's Bay and Bay of Holland. Off the northern shores is the small island of Papa Stronsay, and farther north, across the Sanday Sound, is the large and narrow island of *Sanday*, with its Neolithic Chambered Cairn of *Quoyness* (A.M.). Beyond Sanday is *North Ronaldsay*, the most northerly of the Orkneys, noted for its indigenous breed of sheep, feeding for the most part on seaweed. A stone wall, 12 miles in circumference, has had to be built in order to keep the sheep off the cultivated land.

WESTRAY.

On this island, lying in the north-west of the group, is the ruined 16th cent. *Noltland Castle* (A.M.), destroyed in 1746, and noted for its hall, kitchen and fine, winding staircase. The Castle stands a little inland from Pierowall Bay, on the north-east coast, with its ruined Church preserving some inscribed tombstones (A.M.). There is a GOLF course. To the north-east, across Papa Sound, is the island of *Papa Westray*, with a ruined Chapel and a large chambered cairn of Neolithic date, with beehive cells and some rare megalithic engravings (A.M.). In the extreme north-west of Westray is Noup Head, with magnificent, lofty cliffs and a lighthouse. To the south is the Gentlemen's Cave, the hiding-place of several Jacobites after Culloden, in 1746. Off the south-east shores of Westray is *Eday*, preserving numerous weems and tumuli, and with Red Head overlooking the Calf Sound, beyond which rises Grey Head on the smaller island of Calf of Eday. See **Shetland Islands.**

ORMISTON, East Lothian. 1,914.   Map 10, NT 4 6.
A pleasant village, on the Tyne Water, with a 15th cent. Cross, set on modern steps. At *Ormiston House*, to the south, an old house, modernized and enlarged, George Wishart took refuge, in 1545, with Alexander Cockburn. A fragment of the old Church of Ormiston stands near the house, and preserves a notable brass to Alexander Cockburn, who died in 1563. See **Pencaitland.**

ORONSAY, ISLE OF, Argyll.   Map 13, NR 3 8.
See **Colonsay.**

ORPHIR, Orkney.   Map 33, HY 3 0.
See **Orkney Islands** (Mainland). *Iter. 264.*

ORTON, Moray.   Map 26, NJ 3 5.
Pleasantly situated in the Lower Spey valley, with wooded heights rising on each side, and *Ben Aigan*, 1,544 ft., dominating the landscape to the south. *Iter. 171, 189.*

OSE, Isle of Skye, Inverness.   Map 22, NG 3 4.
Situated on the shores of Loch Bracadale, looking towards the islands of Harlosh, Tarner and Wiay. Glen Ose extends inland to the east and on its southern slopes is the ruined broch of *Dun Arkaig*. *Iter. 255.*

OTTER FERRY, Argyll.   Map 14, NR 9 8.
Situated on *Loch Fyne* (q.v.). Across the loch rise the low hills of *Knapdale* (q.v.), and in an inlet of the loch, known as Loch Gilp, are situated the well-known resorts of *Ardrishaig* and *Lochgilphead* (both q.v.). A narrow, winding and hilly road, with gradients up to 1 in 4, and attaining a height of 1,026 ft., leads from Otter Ferry to the shores of Loch Riddon and also to *Glendaruel* (q.v.). See **Kilfinan.** *Iter. 103.*

OUTER HEBRIDES, Inverness; Ross and Cromarty.   Map 32.

See **Hebrides, Outer.**

OVERSCAIG, Sutherland. 50.   Map 29, NC 4 2.
On the northern shores of the rather featureless Loch Shin, along which proceeds the road from Lairg to Loch Laxford and *Laxford Bridge* (q.v.), on the wild north-western seaboard. Away to the west rises *Ben More Assynt*, 3,273 ft., the highest mountain in the county, while to the north, on the edge of the great Reay deer forest, is *Ben Hee*, 2,864 ft. See **Merkland Lodge.** *Iter. 229.*

OXENFOORD CASTLE, Midlothian.   Map 10, NT 3 6.
See *Pathhead* (Midlothian).

OXNAM, Roxburgh.   Map 10, NT 6 1.
Situated in a lonely valley, threaded by the Oxnam Water in a setting of low hills. A little to the north, at *Cappuck*, a Roman station has been located. The line of the Roman Dere Street, built by Agricola, can be traced to the east of Oxnam, on its way towards the *Cheviot* (q.v.) ridge, which it crosses, at a height of some 1,500 ft., near the great camp and earthworks of *Chew Green*, to the east of *Carter Bar* (q.v.). See **Morebattle.**

The remains of the 16th century Palace of Birsay, on A966, in the extreme north-west of the Mainland. It was a former residence of the Earls of Orkney, and was rebuilt by Earl Robert Stewart, in the style of Falkland Palace (Illustrated on Plate 64)

The broch of Gurness, at Aikerness, with its secondary buildings. It stands near Evie and the shores of Eynhallow Sound, facing Rousay island from an unclassified road off A966

Marwick Head, to the west of B9056, near Birsay, on which stands the Kitchener Memorial. Lord Kitchener lost his life when the cruiser 'Hampshire' was sunk off this coast during the First World War

The prehistoric village of Skara Brae, which lies on an unclassified road off B9056, on the Bay of Skaill, near Aith

The island of Hoy, seen from Black Craig, which lies on an unclassified road to the north-west of Stromness

[For ORKNEY see also preceding plate

PLATE 132 (facing page 224)

Oxton, Berwick. The Parish Church of Channelkirk, where a church dedicated to St. Cuthbert has existed since before written records. It stands a short distance to the north, on an unclassified road off A68

Oykell Bridge, Ross and Cromarty. The bridge across the turbulent River Oykell, which rises in the massif of Ben More Assynt (3273 feet), Sutherland's highest mountain

Paisley, Renfrew. The restored 17th century Place of Paisley, built originally by the Earl of Dundonald. It was the scene of the wedding, in 1684, of John Graham of Claverhouse and Lady Jean Cochrane

Paisley, Renfrew. The restored mid-15th century Abbey Church, the predecessor of which was destroyed by the English in 1307. It had been founded c. 1163 by Walter FitzAlan and monks from Wenlock Abbey, in Shropshire

Pathhead, Fife. The ruined 15th century Ravenscraig Castle, an old palace of the Sinclairs. It figures as 'Ravensheugh' in Sir Walter Scott's '*Rosabelle*'

PLATE 133 (facing page 225)

OXTON, Berwick. 125. Map 10, **NT 4** 5.
A tiny Lauderdale hamlet, situated a little to the west of the Edinburgh to Lauder road through *Carfraemill* (*q.v.*). A little to the north is the small *Channelkirk* Church, which is associated with St. Cuthbert, who spent his childhood in the district, and in whose honour it was built. A pilgrims' track formerly passed through both hamlets, leading from the *Lammermuirs* to Tweeddale, and it is probable that the Romans also came this way. **See Soutra Hill.**

OYKELL BRIDGE, Ross and Cromarty. Map 29, **NC 3** 0.
Mentioned by Ptolemy, the early geographer, and figuring also in Icelandic Sagas. To the south-east of this bridge over the River Oykell, the river is joined by the Einig, flowing from Glen Einig. A little to the west of Oykell Bridge are some picturesque falls on the Oykell, which has come down from the slopes of *Ben More Assynt*, 3,273 ft., Sutherland's highest mountain. From here it flows south-eastwards through Loch Ailsh, noted for fishing, to form the boundary between Sutherland and Ross and Cromarty for the greater part of its turbulent course. Southwards lies a wilderness of lonely hills in the extensive Freevater Forest. **5 m. N.W.** of Oykell Bridge, on the road to *Inchnadamph* (*q.v.*), near the small Loch Craggie, is a low watershed, from which the views range towards the distant, isolated Sutherland peaks of *Canisp*, 2,779 ft., and *Suilven*, 2,399 ft., with its sharp eastern peak. **See Rosehall.** *Iter.* 224, 228.

OYNE, Aberdeen. 630. Map 27, **NJ 6** 2.
This little village, on the Gady Burn, in the district of Garioch, is overlooked to the south by the mass of *Bennachie*, with *Oxen Craig* rising to 1,733 ft. To the east of the hills is the prominent *Mither Tap*, 1,698 ft., on which is situated a remarkable hill fort. *Harthill Castle*, a ruined tower, standing south-east of Oyne, dates from 1638, and was burnt by the Covenanters. **See Chapel of Garioch** and **Insch.** *Iter.* 178.

PAISLEY, Renfrew. 95,822. LB. Map 8, **NS 4** 6.
E.C. Tues. **M.D.** Mon. **GOLF.** An important Municipal Burgh and industrial town, the world's largest thread-producing centre, and at one time famous for the well-known "Paisley Shawls." In the town is the fine Cluniac Abbey Church, founded in 1163, and destroyed by the English in 1307. The present building dates largely from the mid-15th cent., but the tower, choir and North transept have been rebuilt. The West front, with a notable doorway, and the nave, which is used as the Parish Church, are the finest parts of the structure. In place of the South transept is *St. Mirren's* Chapel, built in 1499, in which is an effigy, thought to be of Marjory Bruce, the daughter of Robert Bruce. Part of the former Abbey buildings, on the south side of the Church, on the site of the refectory, are incorporated in the 17th cent. *Place of Paisley*, which has been well restored as a War Memorial. In the town museum are works by Scottish artists, and a collection of Paisley shawls. The Thomas Coats Memorial Church was built in 1894. Professor John Wilson, the "Christopher North" of Blackwood's Magazine, was born at Paisley, in 1785. At 8 Castle Street, was born, in 1774, Robert Tannahill, the weaver poet, who described the beauties of the *Braes of Gleniffer*, a fine viewpoint, to the south-west of the town. Nearby are the remains of *Staneley Castle*. On the White Cart River, **3 m. E.** of Paisley, is *Crookston Castle* (N.T. Scot.), late 14th cent., presented to the Trust in 1931, their first acquisition in Scotland. Open Mon. to Fri., 10 to 4.30 or 8; Sat. and Sun., 2 to 4.30 or 8 (see page 90). The first American troops to reach Britain during the Second World War came to Paisley in 1942. **See Clarkston, Erskine Ferry** and **Old Kilpatrick.** *Iter.* 18, 29, 58, 60, 61, 62, 63, 64, 65, 109, 110, 111.

PALNACKIE, Kirkcudbright. 177. Map 3, **NX 8** 5.
Situated on a creek of the Rough Firth, an inlet of the Solway Firth. The Urr Water flows just to the north of the village to enter the creek. **1 m. S.** is *Orchardton Tower* (A.M.), late 15th cent., and unique among *Galloway* (*q.v.*) towers in that it is circular. There are grounds for believing that Scott's "Guy Mannering" can be associated with Orchardton. To the south lies a narrow peninsula terminating in Almorness Point. **3 m. N.** are the well-known *Craignair* granite quarries, which have provided stone for the Thames embankment in London. *Iter.* 73.

PALNURE, Kirkcudbright. Map 2, **NX 4** 6.
The Palnure Burn, which has issued from the pretty Bargaly Glen, flows southwards from here to enter the winding Cree estuary. *Cairnsmoor of Fleet*, 2,331 ft., associated with John Buchan's "The Thirty-nine Steps," rises to the north-east. *Iter.* 26, 72, 73.

PANNANICH WELLS, Aberdeen. Map 20, **NO 4** 9.
Lies on Deeside, with views of *Morven*, 2,862 ft., to the north, beyond the river. To the south rises *Pannanich Hill*, 1,896 ft., a good viewpoint. The Wells of Pannanich became known in 1760, and led to the rise of the well-known resort of *Ballater* (*q.v.*), situated a little to the south-west. **2½ m. E.** is *Ballaterach* farm, associated with Byron's childhood. **See Cambus o' May.** *Iter.* 168, 174.

PARALLEL ROADS, Inverness. Map 18, **NN 2** 8.
See **Roy Bridge** and also **Loch Lochy** and **Tulloch.** *Iter.* 143, 208.

PARKGATE, Dumfries. Map 4, **NY 0** 8.
Iter. 24, 46.

PARTON, Kirkcudbright. Map 3, **NX 6** 6.
Iter. 76.

PASS OF BRANDER, Argyll. Map 14, **NN 0** 2.
See **Falls of Cruachan.**

PASS OF THE CATTLE, Ross and Cromarty. Map 23, **NG 7** 4.

See **Tornapress.** *Iter.* 219.

PATHHEAD, Fife. Map 17, **NT 2** 9.
Situated between Kirkcaldy and Dysart. The ruined 15th cent. *Ravenscraig Castle*, dismantled in 1651, is described in Scott's 'Rosabelle' and overlooks the Firth of Forth.

CROWN COPYRIGHT RESERVED

PUBLISHED BY THE AUTOMOBILE ASSOCIATION

1. Abbey, part 15th cent., and 17th cent. Place of Paisley, now War Memorial.
2. Coats Memorial Church, 1894.
3. Information Bureau.
4. Town Hall.

PATHHEAD, Midlothian. Map 10, NT 3 6.
To the north, below steep banks, flows the Tyne Water, and beyond the river is *Oxenfoord Castle*, in a fine park. A picturesque ceremonial still observed at the castle is the presentation of a red rose to the reigning monarch when on a visit. *Preston Hall* dates from c. 1794, and *Ford House*, an attractive old house, from 1680. See **Crichton, Mellerstain** and **Pencaitland.** *Iter. 4, 5, 13.*

PATNA, Ayr. 465. Map 8, NS 4 1.
E.C. Wed. Lies on the River Doon, on the edge of a coal-mining and iron-producing area. *Iter. 75, 76, 77, 85.*

PAXTON, Berwick. Map 11, NT 9 5.
Between the village and the River Tweed, to the south, stands *Paxton House*, a fine Georgian mansion, attributed to Robert Adam. Farther south, the river is spanned by the fine Union Suspension Bridge, the first of its type, erected originally by Sir Samuel Brown in 1820.

PEEBLES, Peebles. 5,662. SB. Map 9, NT 2 4.
E.C. Wed. GOLF. This well-known Royal Burgh and inland resort stands in a delightful setting of green Tweeddale hills, through which the River Tweed, famous for its salmon, flows in one of its most delightful reaches. The town is noted for its tweed mills, and is also a good angling centre. The former Castle has entirely vanished. Both Cromwell and Prince Charles Edward have occupied the town, the former in 1649 and the latter in

Chambers Institute (Queensberry
  Lodging)   1.
" Cross Keys " Inn   2.
Cross Kirk remains, 1261   3.
Parish Church (1784)   4.
St. Andrew's Church Tower 5.
Town Cross   6.

1745. An interesting ceremonial, observed yearly in June is the Border Riding, with which is combined the ceremony of crowning the " Beltane Queen." The 17th cent. " Cross Keys " Inn is said to be the " Cleikum " Inn of Scott's " St. Ronan's Well," and the " Tontine " Inn dates from 1808. At the southern end of Northgate stands the shaft of the former Town Cross, and nearby is the *Queensberry Lodging*, dated 1644, and now forming part of the *Chambers Institution*, in which is incorporated an interesting museum. The 4th Duke of Queensberry, famous as " Old Q.," was born in the Queensberry Lodging, in 1725. The Parish Church was built in 1784, but there are still some remains of the old Cross Kirk (A.M.), dating from 1261. John Buchan and his sister, Anna Buchan (O. Douglas), the novelist, lived at *Bank House*. R. L. Stevenson and Samuel Crockett also lived in Peebles at different times. The bridge

spanning the Tweed, twice widened, was built originally in 1467 and the Peebles arms appear on the present lamp-standards. Mungo Park, the famous African explorer, lived in Peebles at one period. At the western end of the town stood *St. Andrew's* Church, of which only the tower remains. The road following the river westwards reaches, within a mile, the picturesque 15th cent. *Neidpath Castle*, an early Fraser stronghold, having walls 11 feet thick, finely situated on the north bank of the Tweed, and once battered by Cromwell's artillery. The Castle passed later into the hands of the Earls of Tweeddale, and was purchased, in 1686, by the 1st Duke of Queensberry, whose successor, " Old Q.," cut down all the fine timber on the estate. South of the town lies the beautiful and comparatively little-known valley of *Glensax*, threaded by the Glensax Burn, with *Dunrig* rising to 2,433 ft. at the lonely head of the glen, on the Selkirk border. To the east of Peebles, and bordering the *Innerleithen* (q.v.) road, lies Glentress Forest. See **Lyne, Manor, Stobo** and **Traquair.** *Iter. 4, 14, 24, 32, 33, 34, 35, 40, 52, 53.*

PENCAITLAND, East Lothian. 601. Map 10, NT 4 6.
E.C. Wed. The Tyne Water divides this charming village into two. In Western Pencaitland is an old Mercat Cross, and in Eastern Pencaitland is the Church, dating from the 13th cent., preserving the original North Sacristy. There are also three old sundials, a fine 17th cent. West doorway and a laird's loft, while the tower is dated 1631. Beyond the river, to the north, is *Winton House*, dating from 1620, with later alterations. This fine structure is somewhat similar in its external details to Heriot's Hospital, at *Edinburgh* (q.v.), and is noted particularly for the tall and finely wrought chimney stacks and the enriched plaster ceilings. 1½ m. S.W. is *Penkaet*, formerly *Fountainhall*, a beautiful 17th cent. house, with much contemporary woodwork and two old dovecotes. See **Ormiston** and **East Salton.** *Iter. 3, 40.*

PENICUIK, Midlothian. 5,799. SB. Map 9, NT 2 5.
On the North Esk River, to the south of the *Pentland* hills, with *Scald Law*, the highest peak in the range, rising to 1,898 ft., in the background. To the north of the mountain, in a deep trough, lies the picturesque Loganlee reservoir. *Penicuik* is noted for paper-making, and an annual Border Riding ceremony is still observed. The Parish Church of *St. Mungo* has a Doric portico, and its belfry is the 12th cent. tower of the former church of *St. Kentigern*. In the grounds of the semi-ruined *Penicuik House*, dating from c. 1770, with its notable portico, stands an obelisk to Allan Ramsay, the poet, who was born in 1686. Part of the former stables now form a residence, and the Clerk family, owners of the estate, still live there. The " Spear " lodge, on the Carlops road, shows their arms and motto. During the Napoleonic wars, *Valleyfield Mill* was used to confine French prisoners, 300 of whom died there, and are commemorated by a monument. 2½ m. S.W., near the river, are the remains of *Brunstane Castle*. 1½ m. N.E. is *Auchendinny House*, built in 1707 by Sir William Bruce, a good example of the period. See **Carlops, Glencorse** and **Roslin.** *Iter. 10, 24.*

PENNAN, Aberdeen. Map 27, NJ 8 6.
A small fishing village, on a rocky and precipitous stretch of coast by Pennan Bay, overlooked by Pennan Head. To the west, the Tore Burn, marking the border between the counties of Aberdeen and Banff, flows into the sea, and still farther west is the bold headland of Troup Head. See **Crovie.** *Iter. 182.*

PENNYGHAEL, Isle of Mull. Argyll. Map 13, NM 5 2.
Situated on the southern shores of Loch Scridain, with *Ben More*, 3,169 ft., rising away to the north beyond the loch. A narrow road leads southwards from Pennyghael through Glen Leidle to *Carsaig Bay* (q.v.). The road which proceeds to the head of Loch Scridain winds through the lonely Glen More, in a setting of lofty hills, with *Ben Buie*, 2,354 ft., rising to the south. Later it reaches the northern shores of the almost land-locked Loch Spelve on the way to *Craignure* (q.v.). See **Kilfinichen Church.** *Iter. 249.*

Pathhead, Midlothian. The 'Lion' entrance gates to Preston Hall, a late 18th century mansion

Peebles, Peebles. The Chambers Institute, perhaps incorporating the reconstructed remains of the Queensberry Lodging of 1644. The 4th Duke of Queensberry, known as 'Old Q,' was born here in 1725

Pencaitland, East Lothian. The lodge at the entrance to Winton House, a mansion of 1620, which stands to the north of the Tyne Water, on an unclassified road

Peebles, Peebles. The White Stone, facing the 'Peebles' Hydro. At this spot the town used to give an official welcome to distinguished visitors

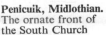

Penicuik, Midlothian. A huntsman and a hunting horn with the motto of the Clerk family, owners of the Penicuik estate. They are placed on the gable of the entrance lodge, which stands on the Carlops road (A766)

Penicuik, Midlothian. The ornate front of the South Church

PLATE 134 (facing page 226)

Perth, Perth. St. John's Church, 15th to 16th century, where John Knox delivered his famous sermon on idolatry in 1559

Perth, Perth. The 'Salutation' Hotel, which has a brass plate recording its association with Bonnie Prince Charlie and the '45 Rising

Perth, Perth. The house of Catherine Glover, the 'Fair Maid of Perth.' Her father was a noted glover, and a niche in the wall of the house once held a statue of St. Bartholomew, the patron saint of the glovers

Penpont, Dumfries. The inscription on the smithy at Keir, where Kirkpatrick Macmillan, inventor of the bicycle in 1839, was born. It stands to the south-east, on an unclassified road

Peterhead, Aberdeen. The statue of Marshal Keith, who was born near the town in 1696

1939
THE CENTENARY OF
THE BICYCLE
THE NATIONAL COMMITTEE ON CYCLING
HONOURS THE MEMORY OF
KIRKPATRICK MACMILLAN
THE INVENTOR OF THE BICYCLE
'He builded better than he knew'

[For PINKIE HOUSE see following plate
[For PETERHEAD see also under BUCHAN (Plate 25)

PLATE 135 (facing page 227)

PENPONT, Dumfries. Map 3, NX 8 9.

Lies on the Scar Water, which, within a short distance, joins the Nith. The village stands on the line of an ancient Pilgrims' track, and James IV travelled this way going from Edinburgh to *Whithorn* (q.v.), in 1507. On *Tynron Doon*, 946 ft., to the west, is a prehistoric hill-fort commanding an extensive view, and said to have sheltered Robert Bruce, in 1306. *Auchengibbert Hill*, 1,221 ft., rises away to the north. To the south of Penpont is the long ridge of the *Keir* hills. To the north-east of these hills is the hamlet of *Keir*, in the vicinity of which, at *Courthill* smithy, was born Kirkpatrick Macmillan, the inventor of the bicycle in 1839. The original machine is in the Science Museum, in London, and a plaque on the smithy commemorates the inventor. See **Drumlanrig Castle** and **Tynron**. *Iter.* 25.

PENTLAND HILLS, Midlothian. Map 9, NT 0 5 etc.
See **Carlops, Currie, Glencorse, Penicuik, Swanston** and **West Linton.**

PERTH, Perth. 40,919 LB. Map 17, NO 1 2.

E.C. Wed. M.D. Fri. GOLF. The "Fair City" of Perth, known at one time as *St. Johnstoun*, stands between the meadows of the North and South Inch at the head of the estuary of the River Tay, famous for its salmon. The city looks towards the *Sidlaw* hills to the north-east, and the *Ochil* hills to the south-west, while eastwards, on the north shores of the Firth of Tay, stretches the fertile *Carse of Gowrie* (q.v.). Near Perth are *Kinnoull Hill*, across the river, to the east, and *Moncreiffe Hill*, to the south-east, both over 700 ft. high, and providing fine views from their summits, the first-named crowned with a view indicator. Perth is an ancient Royal Burgh, once the capital of Scotland, and has a long history, having been on several occasions in the hands of the English. In 1600, the Gowrie conspiracy took place here; in 1651, the city surrendered to Cromwell; and in both Jacobite risings, in 1715 and again in 1745, it was occupied by the insurgents.

The fine, restored Church of *St. John* dates from various periods, the choir having been built in 1450, the nave c. 1490 and the central tower having a 15th cent. steeple. In 1559, John Knox delivered here his famous sermon against idolatry in the Church. Charles I, Charles II and Prince Charles Edward all attended services here, and Scott has introduced it into the scene of his "Fair Maid of Perth." In the rebuilt North transept is Sir Robert Lorimer's War Memorial Chapel. The County Buildings occupy the site of the former Gowrie House, where, in 1600, the famous conspiracy took place. There is an interesting Museum and Art Gallery. The *Fair Maid of Perth's House* is situated in Curfew Row, near the North Inch, on which took p lace the judicial Clan combat of 1396, thought to have been fought between branches of the Clan Chattan, and which Scott has so graphically described. Nearby stood the former Blackfriars Monastery, in which James I was murdered, in 1437, after Catherine Douglas, a lady of the Queen, had vainly striven to save him by placing her arm in a door in order to replace a stolen bar. The "Salutation" Hotel has associations with Prince Charles Edward and the '45. The city has today many industries, and is an important touring centre, being situated within easy reach of the *Sma' Glen* (q.v.), the Perthshire Highlands and the Vales of Strath Earn and *Strathmore* (q.v.), together with the interesting Fife coast. At Bridgend, across the Tay, John Ruskin spent part of his boyhood, and he was married in 1848 at the house of *Bowerswell*, which stands below Kinnoull Hill. 4¼ m, S.E., on the south bank of the Tay, beyond Moncreiffe Hill, is the ruined 16th cent. *Elcho Castle* (A.M.), retaining its yetts. Open summer, 10 to

7, winter, 10 to 4; Sun., after 2. (See page 90). See **Abernethy, Bridge of Earn, Huntingtower, Methven, Rumbling Bridge, Scone** and **Stobhall**. *Iter.* 86, 90, 91, 92, 130, 131, 132, 135, 145, 146, 147, 148, 149, 150, 151, 152, 153, 154.

PETERCULTER, Aberdeen. 2,309. Map 21, NJ 8 0.
E.C. Tues. GOLF. See **Culter** (Aberdeen). *Iter.* 152.

PETERHEAD, Aberdeen. 12,611. SB. Map 27, NK 1 4.

E.C. Wed. M.D. Fri. GOLF. An important *Buchan* (q.v.) herring fishing port, situated on Peterhead Bay. This is separated by Salthouse Head from Sandford Bay, beyond which is Buchan Ness, the most easterly point in Scotland. The town was founded in 1593 by the Keiths, who, for helping the Old Pretender in 1715, were exiled. On the links to the south are the remains of *St. Peter's Kirk* (1132), with a chancel arch of architectural interest. The Bell tower of 1592 contains a Dutch bell of 1647. The old Parish Church, or Muckle Kirk, dates from 1806. The Town House dates from 1788, and in front stands a statue of Marshal Keith, born in 1696, at *Inverugie Castle*, 3 m. N.W., a ruined 16th cent. structure on the River Ugie. About a mile farther up the river are the remains of the 14th cent. *Ravenscraig Castle*. Peterhead convict prison, adjacent to

CROWN COPYRIGHT RESERVED

PUBLISHED BY THE AUTOMOBILE ASSOCIATION

City Hall
County Buildings
Fair Maid's House
Information Bureau,
    King Edward Street.
    (Summer only)

3. Municipal Buildings
5. Natural History Museum
1.   and Art Gallery
9.

2. St. John's Church,
        associated with John
6. Knox's sermon of 1559 4.
    Sandeman Public Library 8.
    Sir Walter Scott's Statue 7.

Burnhaven (q.v.), lies near Salthouse Head, and the south breakwater of the harbour was built by convict labour. The well-known Peterhead granite quarries are situated beyond *Boddam* (q.v.), to the south of Buchan Ness. See **Cruden Bay, Old Deer** and **Old Rattray.** *Iter. 181, 182, 187, 188, 189.*

(See page 228 for Town Plan of **PETERHEAD**).

PINKIE HOUSE, Midlothian. Map 10, NT 3 7.

This magnificent Jacobean mansion, dating from 1613, was altered and enlarged by Lord Dunfermline, who had previously transformed *Fyvie Castle* (q.v.), in Aberdeenshire. The old tower incorporated in the house dates from 1390. Pinkie is noted particularly for the east front, the long gallery, with its splendid painted ceiling, and the well-head in the courtyard. The battle of Pinkie, in which the Scots were defeated by Lord Hertford, took place in

1. Town House.
2. Old Parish Church.
3. Bell Tower (1592) and ruins of St. Peter's Church.

PITLOCHRY

1. Power Station, Dam, and Salmon Ladder.
2. Festival Theatre.
3. Information Bureau, Council Chambers.

1547. After the battle of *Prestonpans* (*q.v.*), in 1745, Prince Charles Edward slept in the house, which now forms part of Loretto College. See **Carberry Hill** and **Musselburgh.**

PINMORE, Ayr.   Map 2, NX 2 9.
Iter. 71.

PINWHERRY, Ayr.   Map 2, NX 1 8.
Situated in the delightful valley of the River Stinchar, at the point where it is joined by the Duisk Burn. There are ivy-clad ruins of an ancient castle of the Kennedys. See **Colmonell.** *Iter. 71, 78, 84.*

PIRNMILL, Isle of Arran, Bute.   Map 7, NR 8 4.
This hamlet lies on the fine road traversing the west coast of the island, overlooking the *Kintyre* (*q.v.*) peninsula across the narrow waters of the Kilbrennan Sound. In the background rise *Beinn Bhreac* and *Beinn Bharrain*, both over 2,300 ft. high. *Iter. 242.*

PITCAIRNGREEN, Perth.   Map 16, NO 0 2.
An attractive hamlet near the River Almond. To the north-west are the Lynedoch Woods, by the river, where lie the graves of Bessie Bell and Mary Gray, who came here in 1645 to avoid an outbreak of plague in Perth.   **See Huntingtower.**

PITCAPLE, Aberdeen.   Map 27, NJ 7 2.
On the River Urie, with *Pitcaple Castle*, a 19th cent. reconstruction of an older building, which had associations with James IV, Mary, Queen of Scots, Charles II and the Marquis of Montrose. The last-named slept at the Castle as a prisoner on his last journey to Edinburgh, in 1650. See **Chapel of Garioch.** *Iter. 175, 178.*

PITCUR, Angus.   Map 17, NO 2 3.
Situated on the edge of the *Sidlaw* hills, where the Coupar Angus to Dundee road begins to cross the range by way of Tullybaccart Hill. At *Pitcur* is preserved a remarkable "weem," or Pict's House, the key of which is kept at Hallyburton House. See **Lundie.** *Iter. 157, 158, 159.*

PITLESSIE, Fife. 328.   Map 17, NO 3 0.
In the manse of *Cults*, a little to the north-east, was born, in 1785, Sir David Wilkie, the painter. One of his pictures, "Pitlessie Fair," hangs in the Scottish National Gallery at Edinburgh. The Church font emanates from the Crimea. *Crawford Priory*, to the north-east, is a large 19th cent. mansion. *Iter. 93.*

PITLOCHRY, Perth. 2,279. SB.   Map 20, NN 9 5.
E.C. Thurs. GOLF. A well-known Highland summer resort and touring centre of the *Grampians* (*q.v.*), in a wooded setting on the River Tummel, and sometimes held to be the exact centre of Scotland. The Pitlochry Festival Theatre presents plays during the summer. A little to the south-east, on a tributary of the Tummel, is the picturesque Black Spout waterfall. *Craigour*, 1,300 ft. (N.T. Scot.), reached by

path to the north-west, and situated beyond the village of *Moulin* (*q.v.*), is a fine viewpoint, the prospect extending westwards across the Tummel valley to distant *Schiehallion*, 3,547 ft. Farther to the north-east is *Ben Vrackie*, 2,757 ft., the monarch of the nearby district. There are extensive hydro-electric developments in the Pitlochry district in connection with the Tummel-Garry scheme, including the generating stations of Pitlochry and Clunie. A new loch, that of *Faskally*, has been created as a result of the construction of the Pitlochry Dam, and lies on the west side of the resort, where the Tummel flows in a wooded setting. A new salmon-pass has been made for the fish to surmount the 54-ft. high dam on their way to the higher reaches of the river, and has proved a great attraction to visitors, who can watch the fish from the Pitlochry hydro-electric station. In connection with the works, the new Aldour road bridge has been constructed at the south-eastern extremity of the resort, giving access to the west bank of the Tummel and the Falls of Tummel (N.T. Scot.). The Falls are also accessible by footpath from *Bridge of Garry* (*q.v.*). The road passing Loch Faskally continues by the side of the Tummel to reach the east end of Loch Tummel, where there is another new dam and also a salmon ladder. On the farther bank of the Tummel, nearing the loch, is the famous *Queen's View* (*q.v.*), reached from Pitlochry by way of Bridge of Garry. To the north-east of Pitlochry, a road climbs on to the moorlands leading to Glen Brerachan, and reaches a height of 1,260 ft, with views of Ben Vrackie, before descending to *Kirkmichael* (*q.v.*) in Strath Ardle. See **Blair Atholl, Killiecrankie** and **Logierait.** *Iter. 120, 139, 140, 143, 148, 150, 158, 159, 162, 167, 168.*

PITMEDDEN, Aberdeen.   Map 27, NJ 8 2.
The 600-acre *Pitmedden* estate, where the 17th cent. "Great Garden" has been re-created and is now open regularly (see note page 90), was acquired by the National Trust for Scotland in 1952. See **Udny.** *Iter. 186, 187.*

PITSCOTTIE, Fife.   Map 17, NO 4 1.
The wooded ravine of Dura Den, to the north, threaded by the Ceres Burn, is of interest to geologists for its fossils. A collection of these can be seen in the University Museum at *St. Andrews* (*q.v.*). **3 m. N.E.,** at *Magus Muir*, off the St. Andrews road, a cairn within a plantation marks the spot where Archbishop Sharp was murdered by Covenanters, in 1679. His monument is in the Town Church at St. Andrews. There is also a Martyrs' Stone within railings in memory of five Covenanters taken prisoner at the battle of *Bothwell* (*q.v.*) Brig in 1679 and executed here. The stone was set up in 1877. See **Ceres.** *Iter. 129, 132.*

PITSLIGO, Aberdeen.   Map 27, NJ 9 6.
The Church dates from 1633, and is noted for the richly-carved Forbes gallery. A little to the north is the ruined Castle, dating from 1577, and farther to the east are the remains of the 17th cent. *Pittullie Castle*. See **Rosehearty.** *Iter. 182.*

PITTENWEEM, Fife. 1,559. SB.   Map 17, NO 5 0.
E.C. Wed. One of the picturesque Royal Burghs of the county, with old houses grouped around the little harbour. An Augustinian Priory was founded here in 1141, of which slight remains are incorporated in the parsonage. The Church has a picturesque tower, dated 1592, and resembling

Pinkie House, Midlothian. In this mainly Jacobean mansion Prince Charles Edward slept after his victory at Prestonpans, in 1745. It stands off A1, on the eastern outskirts of Musselburgh

Pitcaple, Aberdeen. The rebuilt Castle, in the predecessor of which the Marquis of Montrose spent the night as a prisoner in 1650

Pitlochry, Perth. The Clunie Memorial Arch, built in the same shape as the water conduits, and marking the completion of the Tummel–Garry hydro-electric scheme in 1952

Pittenweem, Fife. The tower of the Church, which dates from 1592

Pitsligo, Aberdeen. The Church, dating from 1633, which contains the ornate Forbes gallery

Pitsligo, Aberdeen. The ruined Castle of 1577, once the home of Alexander Forbes, Lord Pitsligo, outlawed after the battle of Culloden, in 1746. It stands to the north, on an unclassified road

PLATE 136 (facing page 228)

Plockton, Ross and Cromarty. The view along Loch Carron from the east side of the village

Pluscarden Priory, Moray. The 13th century Priory, which is being rebuilt by the Benedictines. In 1390, the Wolf of Badenoch burnt down the old church

Pollokshaws (Glasgow), Lanark. Pollok House, the home of the Maxwells, which was built by William Adam in 1752. Part of the surrounding estate belongs to the National Trust for Scotland

Polmont, Stirling. The Westquarter dovecote, dating from 1647, which stands to the west, off A9. The arms of William Livingstone of Westquarter appear over the doorway

Poolewe, Ross and Cromarty. The cairn by Loch Ewe in memory of Alexander Cameron, the Tournaig bard, who died in 1933, having spent his whole life by the shores of the loch

PLATE 137 (facing page 229)

a castle more than a church tower. A robbery, which took place at Pittenweem in 1736, led to the famous Porteous Riots in Edinburgh. The cave-shrine of *St. Fillan* lies near the harbour. **2 m. N.W.** is *Balcaskie House*, dating from c.1675, from designs by Sir William Bruce. There are terraced gardens. **3 m. N.N.W.** is *Kellie Castle*, 16th cent., with numerous towers and turrets, where Sir Robert Lorimer, the eminent architect, spent his boyhood. The interior is of note and contains Italian paintings. See **Leuchars** and **St. Monance.** *Iter. 94, 98.*

PLEAN, Stirling.   Map 16, NS 8 8. *Iter. 95.*

PLOCKTON, Ross and Cromarty. 250.   Map 23, NG 8 3. A fishing and crofting village, part of the *Balmacara (q.v.)* estate (N.T. Scot.), most beautifully situated on a small inlet of Loch Carron, with views of the wild *Applecross (q.v.)* and *Torridon (q.v.)* mountains to the north. The modern *Duncraig Castle*, now a school, stands in a wooded setting to the east of the village, beneath a line of crags facing the shores of the loch. A Douglas fir, some 180 feet in height, grows on the Duncraig estate. See **Strome.** *Iter. 222.*

PLUSCARDEN PRIORY, Moray.   Map 26, NJ 1 5· Situated in a fertile valley, overlooked to the north by a well-wooded ridge, to the west of which is *Eildon Hill*, 767 ft., The well-preserved remains of *Pluscarden* have been partially restored by the Marquis of Bute, and are now being rebuilt by the Benedictines, to whom they have been presented. The original Cistercian monastery was founded in 1236, and the choir and transepts remain from the 13th cent. Church, together with the tower and part of the chapter-house. In 1390, the Church was burned by the Wolf of Badenoch, and was later restored. Large circular windows are a feature of the transepts, and alterations to the fenestration of the building took place in 1460, when the Benedictines took over the Abbey. The chapter-house is of interest, and in the calefactory, now used as a Church, is a pulpit, dating from 1680, which was originally in the old High Kirk at Elgin. The "Burgie Necklace" of jet, an ornament from the Bronze Age, is preserved in the Abbey, which is shown to visitors on request. *Iter. 198.*

POLLACHAR, South Uist, Inverness.   Map 32, NF 7 1. See **Hebrides, Outer** (South Uist).

POLLOKSHAWS (Glasgow), Lanark.   Map 8, NS 5 6. To the north of the White Cart River stands the fine mansion of *Pollok House*, built by William Adam, in 1752, and situated in extensive grounds. Part of the estate (N.T. Scot.) is now used as a recreation ground, and the house is open week-ends, Easter to May. Also daily, 2.30 to 6, except Fri., May 1st to Sept. 30 (see note page 90) *Iter. 57.*

POLMONT, Stirling. 1,106.   Map 16, NS 9 7. GOLF. To the north-east of the town, the River Avon, forming the boundary between Stirling and West Lothian, flows into the Forth estuary. The line of the Antonine, or *Roman Wall (q.v.)* is just to the north of Polmont. About **1 m. W.** of Polmont, off the Falkirk road, is the *Westquarter* dovecote, dated 1647 (A.M.). *Iter. 86, 91, 95, 96.*

POLWARTH, Berwick.   Map 11, NT 7 5. On the green, within a railing, grew once a thorn, associated with verses by Allan Ramsay. The Church, in the grounds of *Marchmount House*, to the south, was rebuilt in 1703, and in the vaults, Sir Patrick Hume, a follower of Argyll in 1685, lay hidden for a month. The mansion was built by William Adam, the father of the even more famous Robert Adam. An oak tree in the park is 128 ft. tall and nearly 15 ft. in girth. See **Carlops.** *Iter. 33, 41.*

POOLEWE, Ross and Cromarty.   Map 22, NG 8 8. Stands at the head of Loch Ewe, where the River Ewe, noted for its salmon, flows into the loch after its short course from *Loch Maree (q.v.).* On the eastern shore of the loch, about a mile from Poolewe, stands *Inverewe House* (N.T. Scot.), a Mackenzie home, well known for its woodland gardens, semi-tropical plants and palm trees. This is a remarkable fact in view of Poolewe's situation near the 58th parallel,

which cuts through Siberia and Canada's Hudson Bay territory. The gardens are shown daily, weekdays 10 to dusk; Sun. from 2 (see page 90). From the Gairloch road, southwards from Poolewe, there is a magnificent view up Loch Maree, dominated by *Slioch*, 3,260 ft., at its head. A little beyond the River Ewe, to the east, lies Loch Kernsary. Beyond it is the larger Fionn Loch, bordering the lonely Fisherfield Forest, and dominated by *A'Mhaighdean*, 3,060 ft., a notable rock peak, and also *Beinn Dearg Mhor*, 2,974 ft. **4½ m. N.W.** of Poolewe, on the shores of Loch Ewe, is *Inverasdale*, where experimental work in croft rehabilitation has recently been carried out. In both the World Wars Loch Ewe was of considerable naval importance. See **Aultbea, Gairloch** and **Gruinard Bay.** *Iter. 206, 222.*

PORT APPIN, Argyll.   Map 14, NM 9 4. This quiet little village lies between Loch Laich, an inlet of *Loch Linnhe (q.v.)*, and Airds Bay, on the Lynn of Lorne, and is a calling place for steamers. It is linked in addition by a passenger ferry to the north-eastern extremity of the island of *Lismore (q.v.)*. The mid-18th cent. *Airds House* stands a little to the south-east of the village. *Appin* Church, in the Strath of Appin, is situated **2 m. E.N.E.** of Port Appin, on the Ballachulish to Oban road. Away to the south-east of the Church, this road makes a circuit of the head of Loch Creran, with its mountain background, overlooking the lonely Glen Creran. See **Appin** and **Port-nacroish** (for *Castle Stalker*). *Iter. 124.*

PORT ASKAIG, Isle of Islay, Argyll.   Map 6, NR 4 6. Situated on the Sound of Islay, with a steamer pier, and connected by passenger ferry to *Feolin Ferry*, in the island of *Jura (q.v.)*. **3 m. S.W.**, off the *Bridgend (q.v.)* road, to the right, is Loch Finlaggan, with a ruined island-castle, belonging formerly to the Lords of the Isles. There are alternative routes leading south-westwards from Port Askaig towards *Port Ellen (q.v.)*, the inland one being known as the "glen" road, while the better way is through *Bridgend (q.v.)*, at the head of Loch Indaal. **4 m. N.** of Port Askaig, over a narrow, hilly and winding road passing the Caol Isla distillery, is Bonahaven Bay, with views across the Sound of Islay towards the conical *Paps of Jura*, and also to the more distant coast of Mull. *Iter. 243, 247.*

PORT BANNATYNE, Bute.   Map 7, NS 0 6. GOLF. A small resort on Kames Bay, facing the Firth of Clyde, looking to Toward Point on the mainland. The waters of the *Kyles of Bute (q.v.)* lie farther to the north-west near the entrance to Loch Striven. The tower of *Kames Castle*, overlooking the bay, is perhaps of 14th cent. date. Inland from Port Bannatyne, to the north-west, is the highest ground in the island, with *Windy Hill* attaining 911 ft. A road leads westwards across the narrow waist of Bute to reach the sandy Ettrick Bay, with views over the Kyles of Bute to Ardlamont Point. This road continues northwards as far as *Kilmichael*, where the ancient, ruined Chapel of *St. Michael* is still standing. Another road goes north-westwards from Kames Bay, and terminates at *Rhubodach*, which is linked to *Colintraive (q.v.)*, on the mainland, by a car ferry. See **Rothesay.** *Iter. 241.*

PORT CHARLOTTE, Isle of Islay, Argyll. Map 6, **NR 2 5.** On the western shores of Loch Indaal, at its narrowest point. In the vicinity are the graves of some American soldiers drowned in the sinking of the "Tuscania," in 1918. A road leads westwards from the village across the Rhinns of Islay peninsula to *Kilchiaran Bay*, from which a rough and narrow road follows the peninsula towards *Portnahaven (q.v.)* at its south-western extremity. See **Bruichladdich.** *Iter. 247.*

PORT ELLEN, Isle of Islay, Argyll. Map 6, **NR 3 4.** GOLF. The main port of the island, with distilleries in the vicinity, *Port Ellen* is situated on a small rocky bay, facing a prominent lighthouse on the Mull of Oa peninsula. A road goes north-eastwards along the coast past *Lagavulin*, where a ruined round tower may once have been a Macdonald stronghold, and reaches, after 7 miles, the churchyard of *Kildalton (q.v.)*. **1½ m. W.** of Port Ellen, facing the sandy Kilnaughton Bay, is a pillar commemorating the American troops drowned in the sinking of the " Tuscania " in 1918. **4 m. N.W.** of Port Ellen, to the west of the " low " road leading to *Bowmore* (*q.v.*), is *Machrie*, near Laggan Bay, noted for its sands and golf, the splendid course having been constructed on the machair, or sea-turf. A little farther to the north is *Glenegedale* Airport, with regular services to Glasgow (Renfrew airport). Machrie can also be approached from Kilnaughton Bay, to the west of Port Ellen. Another road to Bowmore, known as the " high " road, keeps well inland all the way, and a branch leading north-eastwards from it is known as the " glen " road, and leads to *Port Askaig* (*q.v.*). A better way, however to the latter is by way of *Bridgend* (*q.v.*). See **Claggain Bay, Kilchoman** and **Mull of Oa**. *Iter. 243, 244, 245, 246.*

PORT ELPHINSTONE, Aberdeen.   Map 27. **NJ 7 1.** *Iter. 175, 178, 184, 197.*

PORT ERROLL, Aberdeen.   Map 27. **NK 0 3.** See **Cruden Bay**.

PORTESSIE, Banff.   Map 26, **NJ 4 6.** This picturesque fishing village, on a sandy coast, stands on a small crescent-shaped bay, with some old cottages. To the east is Portessie Bay, sheltered by Craig Head. *Iter. 199.*

PORT GLASGOW, Renfrew. 23,155. **LB.**   Map 8, **NS 3 7. E.C.** Wed. A shipbuilding town on the River Clyde, founded in 1668, and formerly the chief custom-house port of the river before it was deepened and ships were able to proceed up the river to Glasgow. *Newark Castle* (A.M.), on the river bank, dates from the 16th and 17th cents., and is a notable example, preserving a courtyard and a hall, the latter carrying an inscription of 1597. *Iter. 59, 64, 65, 85, 88, 112, 113.*

PORTGORDON, Banff.   Map 26, **NJ 3 6.** The harbour at this little place, which is situated near the Moray border, was built by the Duke of Richmond and Gordon, in 1874. See **Tynet**. *Iter. 199.*

PORTGOWER, Sutherland.   Map 31, **ND 0 1.** A small fishing village, on a rocky stretch of coast, with moorlands rising in the background which culminate in *Beinn na Meilich*, 1,940 ft. *Iter. 200, 231, 233.*

PORTINCAPLE, Dunbarton.   Map 14, **NS 2 9.** On Loch Long, facing Loch Goil and the hills known as *Argyll's Bowling Green*.

PORTINNISHERRICH, Argyll.   Map 14, **NM 9 1.** On the east side of *Loch Awe* (*q.v.*), facing the island of Innis Shearaich. To the north is the smaller island of Innis Connel, on which are situated the remains of *Ardconnel Castle*, an ancient Campbell stronghold. The road leading northwards along the loch from the village passes, after about two miles, the outflow of the Allt Blarghour Burn, on which are some waterfalls. See **Portsonachan**. *Iter. 119.*

PORTKNOCKIE, Banff. 1,469. **SB.**   Map 26, **NJ 4 6.** A quaint little fishing village, to the west of Cullen Bay, from which it is separated by Scar Nose. See **Findochty**. *Iter. 199.*

PORT LOGAN, Wigtown. 65.   Map 2, **NX 0 4.** A small fishing village in the Rhinns of Galloway, situated on Logan Bay, on the opposite side of which can be seen a remarkable tidal fish-pond. This was commenced in 1788, taking 12 years to complete, and is notable for the extraordinary tameness of the fish, which are fed by hand. It can be seen Mon., Wed., Sat. and Sun., 12.30 to 6.30, 1st Sun. in May to 1st Sun. in Oct. (see note page 90). **2 m. N.** is the Georgian *Logan House*, famous for its grounds, shown at times, in which many rare plants and trees flourish. See **Drummore**. *Iter. 82.*

PORTMAHOMACK, Ross and Cromarty.
    Map 31, **NH 9 8.**
GOLF. A Dornoch Firth fishing village, situated on a narrow peninsula stretching into the Moray Firth, at the extremity of which is Tarbat Ness, with a lighthouse, and a wide outlook over sea and land. Near the Church, to

the south-west, are the curiously-named sandhills of *Gaza*. *Ballone Castle*, probably 16th cent., stands to the south-east.

PORT MARY, Kirkcudbright.   Map 3, **NX 7 4.** See **Dundrennan**.

PORTMOAK, Kinross.   Map 17, **NO 1 0.** Situated on the low ground to the east of Loch Leven, between the *Lomonds* and *Benarty Hill*, and including *Kinnesswood* and *Scotlandwell* (both *q.v.*) within its Parish boundary. *Portmoak* Church, the third to be built here, had, in the early 18th cent., as its minister, Ebenezer Erskine, who founded the Scottish Secession Church. In the churchyard is the grave of his wife and children, with a four-line epitaph. The cottage of Michael Bruce, a local poet of the 18th cent., is now a small museum. *Iter. 98.*

PORTNACROISH, Argyll.   Map 14, **NM 9 4.** Situated on Loch Laich, an inlet of Loch Linnhe in the *Appin* (*q.v.*) district, and looking towards the island of Shuna. *Appin House*, to the north, is 17th cent. On a tiny island off-shore is the prominent and very picturesque sea-girt *Castle Stalker*, dating from c. 1500, an ancient home of the Stewarts of Appin, and associated with James IV, the Royal Arms being carved over the entrance. The Castle is also well seen from the steamers traversing Loch Linnhe. See **Port Appin**, *Iter. 124.*

PORTNAGURAN, Isle of Lewis, Ross and Cromarty. *Iter. 259.*   Map 32, **NB 5 3.**

PORTNAHAVEN, Isle of Islay, Argyll.   Map 6, **NR 1 5.** At the south-western extremity of the Rhinns of Islay, and to the south-east of which is Rhinns Point. The island of Orsay, with its lighthouse, faces Portnahaven. A road leads north-eastwards along the rocky west side of the Rhinns peninsula to *Kilchiaran Bay*. See **Port Charlotte**. *Iter. 247.*

PORT NA LONG, Isle of Skye, Inverness.
    Map 23, **NG 3 3.**
See **Talisker**. *Iter. 252.*

PORTOBELLO (Edinburgh), Midlothian. 23,486.
    Map 10, **NT 3 7.**
A popular resort, with good sands and a bathing pool, much frequented by the citizens of Edinburgh, Linked to Portobello at its eastern extremity, is Joppa. The resort was the birthplace, in 1870, of Sir Harry Lauder. The name of Portobello is derived from a Panamanian town of that name, and was given to it by a sailor, who served there in 1739 under Admiral Vernon. A little to the west is *Restalrig* Church, an ancient building, destroyed in 1560, but later restored. The adjacent 15th cent. hexagonal Chapel (A.M.) is considered to be that of *St. Triduana*, who cured ailments of the eyes with water from the spring that bears her name. In the vicinity is *Craigentinny House*, late 16th cent., with large 19th cent. alterations and additions. W. H. Miller, an eccentric owner of the house, was buried in a strange-looking mausoleum off the Portobello Road in 1849. See **Duddingston**. *Iter. 2.*

PORT OF MENTEITH, Perth. 43.   Map 15, **NN 5 0.** A small resort on the Lake of Menteith, noted for pike, and the only " lake " in Scotland apart from the little artificial Pressmennan Lake near *Whittinghame* (*q.v.*) in East Lothian. On the largest of the lake's three islands are the remains of *Inchmahome Priory* (A.M.), founded in 1238. Parts of the nave, choir and tower arch are still to be seen, and some of the work, notably the fine West porch, is of much interest. Robert Bruce visited the Priory on three occasions. Mary, Queen of Scots, at the age of 5, was sent to the island after the battle of *Pinkie* (*q.v.*), in 1547, and her garden, known as Queen Mary's Bower, is still in existence. From here, the Queen was removed to *Dumbarton* (*q.v.*), prior to sailing for France. On Inch Tulla island is a ruined Castle, once the home of the Earls of Menteith. Overlooking the lake, to the west, rise the *Menteith* hills, attaining 1,289 ft., and in the vicinity is part of the newly-planted Loch Ard Forest. East of these hills are *Beinn Dearg*, 1,401 ft. and *Ben Gullipen*, 1,344 ft., between which lies the tiny Loch an Balloch. Off the Callander road lies Loch Rusky, which is

Port Glasgow, Renfrew. The 16th to 17th century Newark Castle, on the banks of the River Clyde. The monogram of the builder, Patrick Maxwell (1597), is above the entrance

Portknockie, Banff. The fishing harbour, which is sheltered by Scar Nose

Port Logan, Wigtown. The tidal fish-pond, in which the fish are tame and fed by hand

Portmahomack, Ross and Cromarty. The curiously named Sandhills of Gaza, which lie near the Church, to the south-west

Portobello (Edinburgh), Midlothian. The Mausoleum, noted for its decorative panels. It contains the body of W. H. Miller, the eccentric owner of Craigentinny House, who died in 1849. He was known as ' Measure Miller,' owing to his habit of measuring all the books he bought with a ruler which he carried for the purpose

PLATE 138 (facing page 230)

Portpatrick, Wigtown. The ruined early 16th century Dunskey Castle, facing the sea to the south of the resort

Prestonpans, East Lothian. The 17th century Mercat Cross, one of the finest in Scotland

Prestonpans, East Lothian. Hamilton House (1628), which has been restored by the National Trust for Scotland

Prestwick, Ayr. The ancient Mercat Cross

Prestonpans, East Lothian. The Cairn commemorating the victory of Prince Charles Edward over General Cope at the battle of Prestonpans, in 1745

PLATE 139 (facing page 231)

sometimes frozen over in the winter. The name *Menteith*, or Monteith, is applied generally to that part of the county lying to the south of Port of Menteith towards the River Forth, on the Stirling border. The flat land south of the Lake of Menteith, merging into Stirlingshire, is known as the Flanders Moss. In the vicinity of the south-western shores of the lake is the tiny Loch Macanrie, where, according to a legend, a king's son was saved from drowning by a girl while hunting. *Iter. 109, 111, 139.*

PORT OF NESS, Isle of Lewis, Ross and Cromarty.
Map 32, **NB 5** 6.
See **Hebrides, Outer** (Lewis). *Iter. 258.*

PORTPATRICK, Wigtown. 1,063.   Map 2, **NX 0** 5.
E.C. Thurs. GOLF. Now a small Rhinns of Galloway resort. It was formerly a port for steamers to Northern Ireland, but the service was transferred to *Stranraer* (*q.v.*), owing to the danger from severe south-westerly gales. The North Channel, separating Scotland from Ireland, was swum in 1947 by Thomas Blower, who crossed from Donaghadee to Portpatrick in just over 16 hours. The seaward views extend to the Irish coast, some twenty miles distant, and also towards the Isle of Man. The shores are rocky, but there are several sandy bays suitable for bathing. The remains of *Dunskey Castle*, built c. 1510, stand in a strong position on a headland to the south of Portpatrick, where the Craigoch Burn enters the sea. See **Lochnaw**. *Iter. 81, 83.*

1. Dunskey Castle ruins.

PORTREE, Isle of Skye, Inverness. 1,094.
Map 23, **NG 4** 4.
E.C. Wed. The metropolis of the island, lying at the mouth of the delightful Portree Loch, with a pleasant harbour and a pier for the steamers. Portree Bay, sheltering the fishing fleet, looks towards *Ben Tianavaig*, 1,352 ft., and also over the Sound of Raasay to Raasay Island (see below). A room in the present " *Royal* " Hotel is pointed out as that in which Prince Charles Edward said farewell to Flora Macdonald in 1746. The name Portree means " King's Haven " and commemorates a visit paid by James V. The old name of the town was *Kiltaragleann*. Off the road leading northwards towards the prominent *Storr* (*q.v.*), a landmark for many miles and the highest point in the long, elevated Trotternish ridge, lie the Storr Lochs, which have been harnessed to a hydro-electric scheme, inaugurated in 1952. A very rough hill road leads north-westwards from Portree to *Bracadale* (*q.v.*), on Loch Beag, an inlet of Loch Harport.

The island of *Raasay*, some 15 miles long, at which the Portree steamers call, is hilly for the most part, and contains *Raasay House*, now a hotel, where Dr. Johnson and Boswell were entertained in 1773. On the flat-topped *Dun Caan*, 1,456 ft., Boswell performed a solo dance. On the north-east coast of the island is the ruined Macleod Castle of *Brochel*, beyond which lies the small island of Rona, with its lighthouse. See **Coolins, Dunvegan, Sligachan, Staffin** and **Uig**. *Iter. 251, 253, 254, 255.*

PORT SETON, East Lothian. 3,335. SB. with Seton.
Map 10, **NT 4** 7.
A Firth of Forth fishing village. See **Seton**.

PORTSKERRA, Sutherland.   Map 30, **NC 8** 6.
A small fishing village on the west shores of Melvich Bay, with some cliff scenery. *Iter. 232, 234.*

PORTSONACHAN, Argyll.   Map 14, **NN 0** 2.
Lies on the south shore of *Loch Awe* (*q.v.*), with views of *Ben Cruachan*, 3,689 ft., away to the north beyond the loch. A passenger ferry connects with Taychreggan Pier for *Kilchrenan* (*q.v.*), on the opposite shore, the latter being about a mile from the loch. *Iter. 119.*

PORTSOY, Banff. 1,720. SB.   Map 27, **NJ 5** 6.
A small fishing port on a rocky stretch of coast, known for Portsoy marble, or serpentine. This marble is coloured light green and pink, and was used for two of the chimney-pieces in the Palace of Versailles. 2 m. E., overlooking the Burn of Boyne, in a wooded setting, is the ruined *Boyne Castle*, dating from 1485, an early Ogilvie fortress. 2½ m. W. is Sandend Bay, sheltered by Redhythe Point and Garron Point. See **Fordyce**. *Iter. 184, 193, 198, 199.*

PORT VASCO, Sutherland.   Map 28, **NC 5** 6.
A tiny coastal hamlet at the mouth of the Kyle of Tongue, looking eastwards towards Eilean Iosal and Roan Island out to sea. *Beinn Thutaig*, 1,340 ft., rises to the west beyond Strath Melness. *Iter. 225.*

PORT WILLIAM, Wigtown. 539.   Map 2, **NX 3** 4.
E.C. Thurs. GOLF. This little port and resort, founded by Sir William Maxwell in 1770, lies on the sandy Luce Bay, in the Machers district, from which a road climbs inland to the well-known house and park of *Monreith* (*q.v.*). There are fine views across Luce Bay towards the peninsula of the Rhinns. In the vicinity are rocks with cup and ring markings dating from the Bronze Age (A.M.). 2 m. N.E. of Port William, off the Glenluce road, is *Kirk of Mochrum* (*q.v.*). *Iter. 78, 82.*

POTARCH BRIDGE, Aberdeen.   Map 21, **NO 6** 9.
See **Kincardine o'Neil**. *Iter. 165, 168.*

POWFOOT, Dumfries.   Map 4, **NY 1** 6.
In former days only a fishing village, but now a pleasant little resort, with sandy shores, situated on the Pow Water, where it flows into the Solway Firth.

POWMILL, Kinross.   Map 16, **NT 0** 9.
Iter. 86, 89, 91, 98.

PRESSMENNAN LAKE, East Lothian.   Map 10, **NT 6** 7.
See **Whittinghame**.

PRESTON, Berwick. 417.   Map 11, **NT 7** 5.
The Whiteadder Water, flowing down from the *Lammermuir* hills, passes a little to the south of the village. The shaft of the old Cross is still standing. 2½ m. N.E., below the foothills of the Lammermuirs, is the rebuilt Church of *Bunkle*, which preserves a Norman arch said to be the earliest of its period in the country. *Iter. 38, 39.*

PRESTONKIRK CHURCH, East Lothian.
Map 10, **NT 5** 7.
See **East Linton**.

PRESTONPANS, East Lothian. 3,098. SB. Map 10, **NT 3** 7.
Once noted for salt-panning and oysters, the former industry having been established here originally in the 12th cent. by monks from *Newbattle Abbey* (*q.v.*). Sir Walter Scott stayed here as a child, and gained much local knowledge, which he utilized in his novel " Waverley." The battlefield of Prestonpans, where Prince Charles Edward defeated General Cope in 1745, is 1 m. E. Hamilton House (N.T. Scot.) dates from 1628, and has been well restored. It can be inspected by arrangement with the occupier. To the north stands the ruined 15th cent. *Preston Tower*, with a 17th cent. dovecote, while nearby is a fine 17th cent. Mercat Cross (A.M.). *Northfield House*, a fine 16th or 17th cent. dwelling, lies opposite, with a contemporary dovecote and a sundial dated 1647. In the grounds of the 17th cent. *Bankton House*, now a farm, is a monument to Colonel Gardiner, who died at *Tranent* (*q.v.*), from wounds received at the battle of Prestonpans. Scott's " Waverley " describes the incident. See **Cockenzie, Musselburgh, Pinkie House** and **Seton**. *Iter. 2, 37.*

PRESTWICK, Ayr. 11,422. SB.   Map 8, **NS 3** 2.
E.C. Wed. GOLF. Long known as a golfing resort, and now almost contiguous with *Ayr* (*q.v.*), to the south. *Prest-*

wick is now additionally famous for its great international airport, the most important in Scotland. The town has an old Mercat Cross, and the ruined Church of *St. Nicholas*, a landmark for mariners, is said to date from 1163. There is a sandy bathing beach on Ayr Bay, and also a bathing pool, while the views across the Firth of Clyde to the mountains of Arran, dominated by *Goat Fell*, 2,866 ft., are very fine. *Iter. 88.*

PRINCE CHARLES EDWARD MONUMENT,
    Inverness.   Map 18, NM 9 8.
See **Glenfinnan**. *Iter. 209.*

PROTSTONHILL, Banff.   Map 27, NJ 8 6.
Iter. 182.

PUCK'S GLEN, Argyll.   Map 14, NS 1 8.
See **Benmore Estate** and **Kilmun**.

QUARFF, Shetland.   Map 33, HU 4 3.
Iter. 269.

QUARTER, Lanark.   Map 8, NS 7 5.
In a field in the vicinity, Gordon of Earlston was slain after the battle of *Bothwell* (*q.v.*) Brig, in 1679.

QUEEN ELIZABETH FOREST PARK, Perth; Stirling.
           Map 15, NN 4 0 etc.
See **Aberfoyle, Rowardennan** and **Trossachs**.

QUEENSFERRY, West Lothian.   Map 17, NT 1 7.
See **Queensferry, North** and **South**. *Iter. 17, 96.*

QUEENSFERRY, NORTH, Fife. 1,353. Map 17, NT 1 8.
E.C. Wed. On the Ferry Hill peninsula, overlooking the Firth of Forth, and dominated by the great *Forth Bridge*, described under *Queensferry, South*, to which it is linked by car ferry. A new road bridge is to span the Firth. There are associations with Queen Margaret, who formerly journeyed this way towards Dunfermline. St. Margaret's Bay, to the north-west, is part of the naval base of *Rosyth* (*q.v.*). *Iter. 89, 90, 93, 94.*

QUEENSFERRY, SOUTH, West Lothian. 2,744. SB.
           Map 17, NT 1 7.
E.C. Wed. Situated on the south shore of the Firth of Forth, and linked by car ferry to *Queensferry, North* (*q.v.*). The ferry boats leave from the Hawes Pier, opposite which stands the " *Hawes* " Inn (1683), described in Scott's " The Antiquary " and R. L. Stevenson's " Kidnapped." The little Royal Burgh takes its name, as does also its namesake across the Firth, from Queen Margaret, who formerly journeyed this way between Edinburgh and Dunfermline. A Carmelite Chapel was founded here in 1330, and the existing structure, dating from c. 1500, and restored as a Church in 1890, has a central tower and barrel vaults. In the Burgh museum are preserved the old charters, including the original one granted by David II. There is an old Tolbooth, which was remodelled in 1720. *Plewlands House* (N.T. Scot.), dated 1643, has been restored and converted into flats. *Black Castle*, dating from 1626, shows characteristic crow-stepped gables. The picturesque Ferry Fair is held annually in the summer, and the quaint " Burry Man's " procession is another regular annual custom. Overshadowing the town is the spectacular *Forth Bridge*, built 1883–90, to carry the main railway line from Edinburgh to Aberdeen across the Firth of Forth. This great bridge, one of the finest examples of engineering in the world, has a length of 2,765¼ yards, including the approach viaducts, and crosses the firth giving a headway of 150 ft., the two main spans each having dimensions of 1,710 ft., and the top of the bridge being 361 ft. above the water. *Inchgarvie Island*, in the centre of the narrows, gives support to the structure, and had formerly a 15th cent. fort, which opposed Cromwell in 1650. The bridge was built by Sir John Fowler together with Sir Benjamin Baker, the contractor being Sir William Arrol. A road bridge has been planned to span the Firth in the vicinity, and work on the approaches has commenced. 1¼ m. S. is *Dundas Castle*, the old building dating from 1416 to 1424, and the modern building from 1818. The house was for many years the seat of the Dundas family, one of the oldest in the country. See **Dalmeny** and **Hopetoun House**. *Iter. 17, 89, 90, 93, 94, 96.*

QUEEN'S VIEW, Perth. (A.A. viewpoint.)
           Map 19, NN 8 5.
A famous outlook, visited by Queen Victoria in 1866, and situated on the north bank of the River Tummel, a little to the east of Loch Tummel. Access is by a gate to a rocky spur, from which the river, the loch and a grand array of mountains to the north and west in the *Breadalbane* (*q.v.*) country, dominated by the sharp quartzite cone of *Schiehallion*, 3,547 ft., are seen in all their magnificence. In the nearer vicinity the wooded setting forms a fitting foreground to the general picture. In 1777, Maskelyne, the Astronomer Royal, made use of Schiehallion in connection with his experiments to determine the gravity of the earth. Developments in the extensive new Tummel-Garry hydro-electric scheme have necessitated the building of a dam, and also the lengthening of Loch Tummel, which has inevitably detracted from the beauties of the view in that direction. Loch Tummel itself has roads on both north and south banks, the former being the better, and leading in a westerly direction towards *Tummel Bridge* (*q.v.*). The dam at the eastern end of Loch Tummel has a fish-ladder similar to the one at *Pitlochry* (*q.v.*). See **Kinloch Rannoch**. *Iter. 138, 148.*

QUIRAING, Isle of Skye, Inverness.   Map 22, NG 4 6.
This extraordinary collection of fantastically-shaped rock pinnacles, forming one of the most notable of the sights of Skye, lies a little inland from the road along the shores of Staffin Bay, in the Trotternish peninsula, and was used in olden times to shelter stolen cattle. The Needle Rock is 120 ft. high, and behind it lies an amphitheatre, surrounding a grass-covered rock foundation known as the " Table," while nearby is the " Prison." A little to the north are the rocks and pinnacles known as *Leac na Fionn*. The views from this wilderness of rocks, reached only on foot, are far-flung, and range over the hills of Trotternish, and eastwards to the Torridon mountains of Ross and Cromarty on the mainland. The narrow and steep mountain road linking *Staffin* (*q.v.*) with *Uig* (*q.v.*) passes directly to the south of the Quiraing. Overlooking the whole collection of rocks, and attaining a height of 1,779 ft., to the north of this road, is *Meal na Suiramach*, a hill from which the view extends over northern Skye and out to sea towards the distant Outer Hebrides in the Atlantic. See **Flodigarry**. *Iter. 254.*

QUOICH BRIDGE, Inverness.   Map 18, NH 0 0.
Hydro-electric developments on *Loch Quoich* (*q.v.*) have taken place in this neighbourhood. To the north extends the roadless Glen Quoich, which was traversed by General Monk and his soldiers in 1654. Southwards, across the loch, rises *Gairich*, 3,015 ft. See **Kinloch Hourn**. *Iter. 214.*

RAASAY, ISLE OF, Inverness.   Map 23, NG 5 3 etc.
See **Portree**.

RACHAN MILL, Peebles.   Map 9, NT 1 3.
Iter. 10, 24.

RANNOCH STATION, Perth.   Map 19, NN 4 5.
This remote West Highland railway station is situated almost on the Argyll border, and is the terminal point of the road which leads westwards from the western extremity of *Loch Rannoch* (*q.v.*). Some 10 miles of the wild and lonely moor of Rannoch lie between Rannoch and the fine new road leading from Tyndrum to Glencoe, but there is no connecting link. To the south-west of the station stretches Loch Laidon, with the *Black Corries* rising to the north, and beyond which stretches the large Blackwater Reservoir. The lonely Loch Ericht stretches away in a north-easterly direction in the *Grampian* (*q.v.*) mountains towards the north of the *Kinloch Rannoch* (*q.v.*) road. Some 3,500 acres of Rannoch Moor are now a Nature Reserve. *Iter. 148.*

RATHO CHURCH, Midlothian.   Map 9, NT 1 7.
See **Hermiston**.

RATTRAY, Perth. 5,250. SB. with Blairgowrie.
           Map 20, NO 1 4.
See **Blairgowrie**. *Iter. 141, 152, 159, 166.*

RAVENSTRUTHER, Lanark.   Map 9, NS 9 4.
Iter. 21, 23, 37.

Queensferry, South, West Lothian. The restored Carmelite Church of St. Mary, founded originally by the Laird of Dundas, in 1330. It is the only mediaeval church of this Order still functioning in Great Britain

Queensferry, South, West Lothian. The partly 17th century, but much altered 'Hawes' Inn. It is associated with Sir Walter Scott's '*The Antiquary*,' and here Robert Louis Stevenson is said to have commenced writing '*Kidnapped*,' in Room No. 13

Quarter, Lanark. The sign on A723 pointing to the village

Queen's View, Perth. The westerly view along Loch Tummel from the A.A. viewpoint on B8019

Quoich Bridge, Inverness. The bridge across a stream issuing from Glen Quoich, a glen traversed in 1654 by General Monk and his troops. Loch Quoich, now part of a large new hydro-electric scheme, lies west of Tomdoun, on the fringe of the 'Rough Bounds,' in the lonely Knoydart district

Raasay, Isle of, Inverness. A view of the southern end of Raasay (described under Portree). It is taken from A850, before turning west towards Sligachan

PLATE 140 (facing page 232)

Reiss, Caithness. The modernised Ackergill Tower, once a seat of the Earls Marischal, which stands on Sinclair's Bay, to the east

Renfrew, Renfrew. Inchinnan Church, once the property of the Knights Templars. The present building was erected by Lord Blythswood early in this century. It stands a mile to the west, off A8

Rest and Be Thankful, Argyll. The inscribed stone at the summit of the pass looking down Glen Croe. The seat which formerly stood there was described in verse by William Wordsworth

Renton, Dunbarton. The monument to the novelist, Tobias Smollett, for which Dr. Johnson wrote a Latin epitaph in 1773

Rhiconich, Sutherland. A well on A838, some 7 miles north-east, placed there in 1883 by Peter Lawson, a surveyor, as a mark of gratitude to the local people for their hospitality

Rhu, Dunbarton. The tomb of Henry Bell, who launched the pioneer Clyde steamboat 'Comet' in 1812

PLATE 141 (facing page 233)

REAY, Caithness. 719.   Map 30, NC 9 6.
Stands at the head of Sandside Bay, on the lonely Caithness coast, and gave its name to Lord Reay, Chief of Clan Mackay. Their seat was **2 m. N.E.**, near the sea, at *Dounreay Castle*, now a farm, and preserving a 16th cent. tower. *Reay* Church, built in the post-Reformation period, is typical of several in the vicinity, and in the churchyard are remains of an older Church, with a carved Celtic cross-slab. The lonely mountains and deer forest of Reay, in the county of Sutherland, lie in the vicinity of *Rhiconich* (q.v.), near the wild north-western seaboard. See **Dounreay**. *Iter. 232, 234, 240.*

REDCASTLE, Ross and Cromarty.   Map 25, NH 5 4.
On the north shore of the Beauly Firth, with the estate of *Redcastle*, an old home of the Mackenzie family. The house retains some 16th cent. work, now incorporated in a modern mansion. See **Muir of Ord**. *Iter. 203.*

REISS, Caithness.   Map 30, ND 3 5.
Lies a little inland from Sinclair's Bay, at the junction of roads leading to Thurso and John o' Groats. On the shores of the bay stands the ancient *Ackergill Tower*, now modernised. It retains a well 25 ft. deep, and also two 18th cent. dovecotes. *Iter. 200, 238.*

RENFREW, Renfrew. 17,741. SB.   Map 8, NS 5 6.
E.C. Wed. GOLF. This ancient Royal Burgh, its charter having been granted in 1396, gives the title of Baron to the Prince of Wales, and is generally considered to be the cradle of the Royal House of Stuart. The Parish Church has a sculptured tomb and a 15th cent. effigy on the tower. *Renfrew* is today best known for its important shipbuilding yards on the Clyde, which are well seen from the car ferry over the river, situated to the north of the town, and giving access to *Yoker* (q.v.), in Lanarkshire. Westwards from the

1. Parish Church.   2. Town Hall.

ferry is the park of *Blythswood House*, where, in 1685, the Earl of Argyll was captured, and later executed at Edinburgh for his share in the Monmouth rebellion. 1½ m. W. of the town, off A8, near a swing-bridge by the meeting of the Black and White Cart Waters, is the *Argyll Stone*, which was at one time thought to be stained with the Earl's blood. Off the Paisley road, south of the town, lies the important Glasgow airport, from which there are regular services to some of the outlying Scottish islands. 1 m. W. of Renfrew, across the Black Cart Water, is *Inchinnan* Church, once the property of the Knights Templar, the present modern building having been erected by Lord Blythswood. In the churchyard are preserved Celtic stones, tombs of the Templars, and also several mortsafes, recalling the days of " bodysnatching." *Iter. 59.*

RENTON, Dunbarton. 5,170.   Map 15, NS 3 7.
There is a monument to Tobias Smollett, with a Latin inscription written by Dr. Johnson in 1773. See **Alexandria**.

RESTALRIG CHURCH, Midlothian.   Map 10, NT 2 7.
See **Portobello**.

REST AND BE THANKFUL, Argyll.   Map 14, NN 2 0.
At the summit of the easily-graded, reconstructed road climbing up Glen Croe from the shores of Loch Long, and at a height of nearly 900 ft., stood formerly a rough stone seat, inscribed " Rest and be Thankful." Wordsworth, after a visit to the pass, described it in verse. The old road, with its steep gradients, is still used for motor trials. Above the summit, to the north-east, rises *Ben Ime*, 3,318 ft., a notable viewpoint, the ascent of which can be undertaken from here. *Ben Arthur*, 2,891 ft., more familiarly known as *The Cobbler*, rises to the north of the glen, while the south side is dominated by the rough, rocky slopes of *The Brack*, 2,580 ft., and farther to the west by the extensive mass of *Ben Donich*, 2,774 ft. This mountain area in *Cowal* (q.v.) is included within the Ardgoil Estate of the Argyll National Forest Park, while the summits to the north of Glen Croe form part of the Ardgartan Estate. The westerly descent from the head of the pass leads by way of lonely Loch Restil, under the slopes of *Beinn an Lochain*, 3,021 ft., to the west, and then proceeds down Glen Kinglas towards the shores of *Loch Fyne* (q.v.). A steep and narrow road gives access from the summit of Rest and be Thankful to the rocky and lonely *Hell's Glen*, and also to *Lochgoilhead* (q.v.), at the head of Loch Goil. See **Arrochar** and **Benmore Estate**. *Iter. 88, 101, 102, 103, 137.*

RESTENNETH PRIORY, Angus.   Map 21, NO 4 5.
See **Forfar**. *Iter. 153.*

RHICONICH, Sutherland.   Map 28, NC 2 5.
A little clachan, where an inn was formerly situated, finely placed at the head of Loch Inchard. It provides magnificent views of the great quartzite peaks of the Reay Forest, away to the south-east, an area given over largely to deer. *Foinaven*, 2,980 ft., dominates the range, with the rocky *Creag Dionard*, overlooking the bleak head of Strath Dionard and its lonely loch farther to the south-east. To the south rises *Arkle*, 2,580 ft., with its rough scree slopes, backed by the peak of *Meall Horn*, 2,548 ft. The whole setting around Rhiconich and the district farther south is one of innumerable lochans, lying among outcrops of Archaean grey gneiss, some of the world's oldest rocks, and has been described as being almost akin to a lunar landscape. On the road northwards to *Durness* (q.v.), the Achriesgill Water threads a picturesque little ravine just beyond Rhiconich, and to the north-east extends the lonely Strath Dionard, backed by *Grann Stacach*, 2,630 ft., and *Beinn Spionnaidh*, 2,537 ft. The Amhainn Dionard, draining Loch Dionard, flows northwards into the Kyle of Durness. See **Kinlochbervie** and **Laxford Bridge**. *Iter. 225, 224.*

RHU, Dunbarton. 1,103.   Map 14, NS 2 8.
E.C. Wed. Faces the Gare Loch and Rosneath Bay, with a pier, and is noted for yachting. Henry Bell, who launched an early steamboat, the " Comet," in 1812, is buried in the churchyard. A deep glen to the north, known as Whistler's Glen, was mentioned in Scott's " Heart of Midlothian." See **Helensburgh**. *Iter. 102, 111, 116.*

RHUBODACH, Bute.   Map 7, NS 0 7.
On the shores of the *Kyles of Bute* (*q.v.*), and also known as *Rudhabodach*, being linked to the mainland by a car ferry to *Colintraive* (*q.v.*). At one time cattle bound for Bute were made to swim across the strait. See **Port Bannatyne.** *Iter. 241.*

RHUM, ISLE OF, Inverness.   Map 23, NM 3 9.
See **Rum.**

RHYNIE, Aberdeen. 388.   Map 26, NJ 4 2.
E.C. Thurs. The *Tap o' Noth,* 1,851 ft., visible as far away as the North Sea, and crowned by a vitrified fort, dominates *Rhynie,* the full name of which is *Muir of Rhynie.* Near the Church is an inscribed stone, known as the Crow Stone. **1 m.** S.E. is *Druminnor House,* a 16th cent. former home of the Forbes family. **2½ m.** W., off the Dufftown road, is the ruined *Lesmore Castle,* once a Gordon stronghold. This road climbs to a height of nearly 1,400 ft. near the Banff county boundary, with the hill known as the *Buck of Cabrach,* 2,368 ft., rising away to the south. See **Leslie** (Aberdeen). *Iter. 165, 167, 177, 190.*

RICCARTON, Ayr.   Map 8, NS 4 3.
Iter. 55.

RICCARTON, Roxburgh.   Map 5, NY 5 9.
Situated in a remote part of Liddesdale, in a setting of hills, with the *Larriston Fells,* 1,677 ft. high, to the south. **2 m.** N.E., beyond the Liddel Water, is *Thorlieshope,* well known as the home of Dandie Dinmont in Scott's " Guy Mannering." Away to the east rises *Peel Fell,* 1,975 ft., in the *Cheviots* (*q.v.*), on the north-eastern slopes of which, near the boundary between Scotland and England, is situated the remote *Kielder Stone,* a remarkable boulder. The road leading north-eastwards towards *Jedburgh* (*q.v.*) climbs to 1,250 ft. at Note o' the Gate, in the Lowland hills. To the east of Riccarton, a lonely road penetrates the Cheviots at a comparatively low altitude, crossing the Border after about four miles, and giving access to the North Tyne valley in Northumberland. *Iter. 47.*

RICKARTON, Kincardine.   Map 21, NO 8 8.
Iter. 190, 191.

RIGG, Dumfries.   Map 4, NY 2 6.
Iter. 26, 27, 28, 42, 67.

RIGSIDE, Lanark.   Map 9, NS 8 3.
Iter. 21, 35, 48.

RINGFORD, Kirkcudbright.   Map 3, NX 6 5.
A *Galloway* (*q.v.*) hamlet, on the Tarff Water. **2 m.** N., to the left of the road leading towards *New Galloway,* is a monument recalling the killing of five Covenanters, in 1685, by Grierson of Lag, whose seat, the tower of *Lag,* is described under *Dunscore. Iter. 26, 77.*

RING OF BROGAR, Orkney.   Map 33, HY 2 1.
See **Orkney Islands** (Mainland).

RISPOND, Sutherland.   Map 28, NC 4 6.
This remote little place stands on Rispond Bay, just off the Durness to Eriboll road, with some fine cliff scenery and sandy bays at the northern extremity of picturesque Loch Eriboll. To the north is the island of Eileen Hoan, and across the mouth of the loch, to the north-east, rises Whiten Head, the most prominent feature in a line of bold, cave-ridden cliffs. See **Smoo Cave.** *Iter. 225.*

ROADS TO THE ISLES, Inverness; Ross and Cromarty.
See **Fort William, Glenfinnan, Lochailort, Morar, Mallaig,** and also **Fort William, Invergarry, Invermoriston, Cluanie, Kyle of Lochalsh.**

ROBERTON, Lanark.   Map 9, NS 9 2.
Iter. 50.

ROBERTON, Roxburgh. 283.   Map 10, NT 4 1.
The Church of this hamlet, on the Borthwick Water, dates from 1650. *Chisholme* and *Borthwickbrae* are 18th cent. houses in the vicinity. A little to the west, on the *Tushielaw* (*q.v.*) road, beyond the early 19th cent. *Greenbank* toll-house, now incorporated in a farm, is *Firestane Edge,* at an altitude of more than 1,000 ft. ,a fine viewpoint. Beyond it lies the

little Alemoor Loch, drained by the Ale Water. To the south of the ridge stretches the lonely valley of the Borthwick Water, with a range of hills forming the Dumfries border rising at its head. *Iter. 34.*

ROB ROY'S CAVE, Stirling.   Map 15, NN 3 1.
See **Inversnaid.**

ROCKCLIFFE, Kirkcudbright.   Map 3, NX 8 5.
E.C. Thurs. A quiet resort, off the main road, on Rough Firth, the estuary of the Urr Water, with small rocky and sandy bays looking towards the Solway Firth. The Mote of Mark (N.T. Scot.) is the site of a prehistoric vitrified fort. In the Firth is *Rough Island* (N.T. Scot.), a bird sanctuary. See **Kippford.** *Iter. 73.*

RODEL (Isle of Lewis), Harris, Inverness.
                             Map 32, NG 0 8.
See **Hebrides, Outer** (Harris). *Iter. 256.*

RODONO HOTEL, Selkirk.   Map 10, NT 2 2.
See **St. Mary's Loch.** *Iter. 13, 46.*

ROGART, Sutherland.   Map 31, NC 7 0.
Rovie Lodge, in Strath Fleet, into which flows the River Fleet, has beautiful gardens. *Iter. 233.*

ROGIE FALLS, Ross and Cromarty.   Map 25, NH 4 5.
See **Falls of Rogie.** *Iter. 204, 205, 206, 221.*

ROMANNO BRIDGE, Peebles. 50.   Map 9, NT 1 4.
E.C. Wed. Lies on the Lyne Water. To the south, near *Newlands* Church, are the so-called " Romanno Terraces," on the hillside, the origin of which is unexplained. **3 m.** S. of Romanno Bridge, in the valley of the Lyne Water, near its meeting with the Tarth Water, is *Drochil Castle,* left unfinished in 1581, its owner, the Regent Morton, having been executed for his complicity in the murder of Darnley. **1 m.** N.E. is the 16th cent. *Halmyre House,* an ancient Gordon residence. See **Lyne** and **West Linton.** *Iter. 10, 14, 37.*

ROMAN WALL, Dunbarton; Lanark; Stirling, West Lothian.   Map 8, NS 4 7 etc. and 16, NT 0 8 etc.
Known generally as the *Antonine Wall,* or as Graham's, or Grime's Dyke, this consisted originally of a turf rampart, together with a military road to the south and also a ditch to the north. It dates from c. 140 A.D., and was abandoned less than 50 years later. Built upon a line of forts set up by Agricola, in A.D. 78, the wall stretched from a point about a mile to the east of *Bo'ness* (*q.v.*), on the Forth estuary, and extended for 36 miles across the narrow waist of Scotland to reach the Clyde near *Bowling* (*q.v.*). There were, in all, 19 forts on the line of the wall, these having been situated at the following points, commencing near the western extremity: Old Kilpatrick, Duntocher, Castlehill, New Kilpatrick, Balmuildy, Cadder, Kirkintilloch, Auchendavy, Barhill, Croyhill, Westerwood, Castlecary, Seabegs, Rough Castle, Falkirk, Mumrills, Inveravon, Kinneil and Bridgeness. Unlike the great wall of Hadrian, in Northumberland, there are only scanty traces of the fortifications still to be seen, one of the best preserved forts being *Rough Castle* (N.T. Scot.), to the west of *Falkirk* (*q.v.*). The wall was built against incursions of tribes from the north, and Agricola's original defences were strengthened by about a dozen new forts. Perhaps the best-preserved portions of the wall are those which survive in the private grounds of *Callendar House* near Falkirk, and also in the vicinity of *Bearsden* (*q.v.*).

Roman camps and earthworks are still to be found in other parts of Scotland, the most notable being at Ardoch, near *Braco* (*q.v.*), while others are described under *Lockerbie* and *Newstead.* The most northerly penetration by the Romans is thought to have been near *Ythan Wells* (*q.v.*) in Aberdeenshire. The earliest of the Roman roads in Scotland, the Dere Street of Agricola, shown on some maps as a branch of Watling Street, crossed the Cheviots near *Carter Bar* (*q.v.*). On the Northumberland side of the Border, near this point, is the large camp of Chew Green, by the headwaters of the River Coquet. After descending the Cheviot ridge into Scotland, the line of the road crossed the Kale Water, and traces are still to be found in the vicinity of *Oxnam* (*q.v.*).

Rhynie, Aberdeen. The Crow Stone, showing Pictish symbols, which stands in a field near the church

Rispond, Sutherland. A view taken from A838, to the west, showing Whiten Head across the mouth of Loch Eriboll

Roman Wall, Dunbarton. A fragment of the Antonine Wall at Duntocher, in Dunbartonshire. The wall was erected around A.D.140, and extended from Bridgeness, east of Bo'ness, on the Forth estuary, to Old Kilpatrick, by Bowling, on the estuary of the Clyde

Roberton, Roxburgh. The former 19th century Greenbank toll house, now a farm, situated on the Tushielaw road (B711), to the west

Romanno Bridge, Peebles. The curious ' Romanno Terraces,' which lie on the hillside to the south, near Newlands Church

PLATE 142 (facing page 234)

Rosehearty, Aberdeen. A view of the pool in an attractive fishing village in the Buchan district of the county

Roslin, Midlothian. The plaque on the 17th century 'Old Rosslyn' Inn, on College Hill, which was set up in 1950, and records the names of former eminent visitors to the hostelry (see below)

Rothiemay, Banff. The old bridge spanning the River Deveron

Roslin, Midlothian. The richly carved Prentice pillar in the Church, which was founded by William Sinclair in 1446. This pillar is said to have been carved by an apprentice during his master's absence in Italy to examine the original for the proposed design. On his return, the master killed his assistant in a fit of jealousy

Rosemarkie, Ross and Cromarty. A grave-slab in the churchyard, bearing a Cross on one side and Pictish symbols on the other

[For ROTHIEMURCHUS see following plate
[For ROTHESAY see under BUTE (Plate 26)

PLATE 143 (facing page 235)

ROSEBANK, Lanark.   Map 9, NS 8 4.
Iter. 53, 69.

ROSEHALL, Sutherland.   Map 29, NC 4 0.
Situated in Strath Oykell, on the Oykell River, near the point where it is joined by the turbulent Cassley, flowing down the long and little-known valley of Glen Cassley, to the north. Near the point where the Lairg road crosses the Cassley are the remains of *Auchness Castle.* There are traces of several brochs in the vicinity, and at *Tutim,* a little to the west, on the Oykell, a fierce clan battle took place in 1408. To the east of the village the road divides, the left fork leading to *Lairg* (*q.v.*) and the right fork to *Bonar Bridge* (*q.v.*). *Iter. 224, 228.*

ROSEHEARTY, Aberdeen. 1,184. SB.   Map 27, NJ 9 6.
E.C. Thurs. GOLF. A pretty fishing village, with sands and shelving rocks to the east. To the west, beyond Braco Park, on the coast, is the cave of *Cowshaven,* where the last Lord Pitsligo, outlawed for the part he played in the '45, was hidden by his neighbours. See **Pitsligo.** *Iter. 182.*

ROSEMARKIE, Ross and Cromarty. 500.
                               Map 25, NH 7 5.
GOLF. A small, but exceptionally charming *Black Isle* (*q.v.*) resort, on Rosemarkie Bay and the Moray Firth, facing Fort George on the opposite shores of the Firth. The beach is sandy and there is some good rock scenery. In the churchyard is an interesting Celtic sculptured stone. Rosemarkie was once the seat of a bishopric, before this was transferred to *Fortrose* (*q.v.*). To the north-east are cliffs of geological interest, which have been made famous by the writings of Hugh Miller, who was born at *Cromarty* (*q.v.*). *Iter. 203.*

ROSEMOUNT, Perth.   Map 17, NO 1 4.
Iter. 158, 159.

ROSEWELL, Midlothian. 1,930.   Map 10, NT 2 6.
Iter. 37.

ROSKHILL, Isle of Skye, Inverness.   Map 23, NG 2 4.
Iter. 255.

ROSLIN, Midlothian. 1,278.   Map 10, NT 2 6.
E.C. Wed. This little mining village lies on the North Esk River, in the vicinity of which was fought a battle, in 1303, when the Scots defeated the English invaders. *Roslin* is famous both for its Chapel and its Castle, known also as *Rosslyn.* The former was founded in 1446, by William Sinclair, later Earl of Caithness, and was intended to become a Collegiate Church, but only the choir was built, this becoming the burial-place of the Sinclairs. After being damaged by rioters in 1688, the Chapel was finally restored in 1842. It is noted particularly for its profusion of rich and elaborate carving, showing continental influence, and the outstanding feature of the interior is the beautifully decorated Prentice Pillar, rich with foliage. The exterior of the Chapel has flying buttresses and finely-carved pinnacles. There is a vaulted Lady Chapel, only 15 ft. high, and also a crypt, possibly once used as a Chapel. Scott has introduced the Chapel into the "Lay of the Last Minstrel." On a wall of the one-time "Old Rosslyn" inn, on College Hill, is an inscribed plaque recording names of former visitors and set up in 1950. Dr. Johnson and Boswell (in 1773), Robert Burns, Queen Victoria (in 1856) and King Edward VII have all visited the inn. The Castle overlooks the North Esk and the picturesque Roslin Glen from the edge of a cliff. The oldest parts date from the early 14th cent., and although nearly destroyed in 1544, the buildings were later restored. The 16th and 17th cent. rooms are now shown daily, 10 to dusk (see note page 90). The Bilston Burn, which flows to the north of Roslin, is of much interest to geologists.

ROSNEATH, Dunbarton.   Map 14, NS 2 8.
E.C. Wed. A small Gare Loch resort and yachting centre, overlooking Rosneath Bay, in the south-east corner of the narrow Rosneath peninsula. At the south-eastern extremity of the bay is the old Castle, and beyond it is the modern *Rosneath House,* belonging to the Dukes of Argyll. *St. Modan's Well* (N.T. Scot.) commemorates a saint who founded the Church at Rosneath. See **Kilcreggan.** *Iter. 116.*

ROSSLYN CHAPEL, Midlothian.   Map 10, NT 2 6
See Roslin.

ROSYTH, Fife.   Map 17, NT 1 8.
A naval base on the Forth estuary, of special importance during both the World Wars. The dockyard Church contains memorials from the more recent of these wars. The former Cunard liner "Mauretania" was broken up here, in 1935. Rosyth Garden City stands on ground on which was fought, in 1651, the battle of *Inverkeithing* (*q.v.*). *Rosyth Tower* (A.M.), 15th and 16th cent., standing in the dockyard, carries the date 1561, and is mentioned in Scott's "The Abbot." *Iter. 89, 92, 134.*

ROTHES, Moray. 1,217. SB.   Map 26, NJ 2 4.
E.C. Wed. On the River Spey, which flows to the south, between *Ben Aigan,* 1,544 ft., on the east side, and *Conerock Hill,* a wooded viewpoint, on the west side. To the north of the town is the pleasant Glen of Rothes, traversed by Edward I of England in 1296, and through which goes the road to *Elgin* (*q.v.*). A ruined Castle stands in a loop of the river to the north-east of Rothes. The town was partially inundated in the great Spey floods of 1829. See **Craigellachie.** *Iter. 171, 190, 192.*

ROTHESAY, Bute. 8,934. SB.   Map 7, NS 0 6.
E.C. Wed. GOLF. A well-known resort and Royal Burgh, which gives the title of Duke of Rothesay to the Prince of Wales. The town stands on the sandy Rothesay Bay, with an open-air bathing station, overlooking the Firth of Clyde, and facing Toward Point on the mainland. There is a good harbour, which is associated with the annual Clyde Yachting Fortnight, held in July. Near the pier, where many of the Clyde steamers call, are remains of the old castle, and also of the chapel of *St. Michael,* the latter probably of 14th cent. date. The Castle (A.M.), was largely destroyed in the 17th cent., partly by Cromwell, and is considered a remarkable example of its kind. The present moated structure is 13th cent. and its strong walls enclose a circular courtyard. The original castle, captured in 1263 by King Haco of Norway, is said to have been demolished by Robert Bruce. Scott, in his "Fair Maid of Perth," has introduced the story of the Duke of Rothesay and the castle. The ruined chancel of the old Church of *St. Mary,* with its ancient tombs, stands near the Parish Church, while the *Mansion House* is of 17th cent. date. Behind the town lies the narrow Loch Fad, on the western shore of which stands *Kean's Cottage,* built by Edmund Kean, the famous actor, in 1827. A road traverses the eastern shores of the loch, and provides an alternative route to *Kilchattan Bay* (*q.v.*). The other road to the resort goes along the coast past Bogany Point to reach the model village of *Kerrycroy,* beyond which, in a wooded setting, stands *Mount Stuart,* the palatial modern seat of the Marquis of Bute. Another road leads south-westwards from Rothesay, passing the little Greenan Loch, and giving access to the sandy bays of St. Ninian's and Scalpsie, with views of the island of Inch Marnock. A branch from this road leads northwards to the sandy Ettrick Bay, looking across the waters of the *Kyles of Bute* (*q.v.*) to Ardlamont Point. See **Port Bannatyne** and **Rhubodach.** *Iter. 241.*

ROTHIEMAY, Banff.   Map 26, NJ 5 4.
Here is an old bridge over the River Deveron, which is joined a little farther to the south-west by the Isla, flowing through the strath of that name. A monument at Milltown of Rothiemay commemorates James Ferguson, an early 18th cent. astronomer. *Rothiemay Castle,* in a park beyond the Deveron, preserves some old work and has fine gardens. *Iter. 189, 193.*

ROTHIEMURCHUS, Inverness.   Map 25, NH 8 0.
This hamlet stands on a minor road linking Aviemore with Kingussie along the east bank of the River Spey, and on the fringe of the great Forest of Rothiemurchus, now partly a Nature Reserve. This once formed part of the extensive Caledonian Forest, and contains a wealth of paths and rides, dividing Speyside from the great range of the *Cairngorms* (*q.v.*). Through the forest goes the walkers' track leading to the well-known *Lairig Ghru Pass* (*q.v.*). Reindeer have in recent years been successfully introduced into the district.

To the south-east of Rothiemurchus Church, and reached on a by-road, is the beautiful *Loch an Eilean*, in richly wooded surroundings, noted for its triple echo. On an island of the loch stands the sinister ruined Castle of the Comyns, once a stronghold of the notorious Wolf of Badenoch. In the vicinity of the Church, situated in a bend of the Spey, is the mansion of *The Doune*, 16th cent. and later, with an interesting interior. South of the forest, at the head of Glen Einich, is lonely Loch Einich, one of the wildest lochs in the Highlands, situated at a height of 1,650 ft. in an amphitheatre of Cairngorm peaks, with *Braeriach*, 4,248 ft., to the east, and the great cliffs of *Sgoran Dubh*, 3,658 ft., to the south-west. Beyond *Sgoran Dubh* extends a long line of hills over 3,000 ft. in height overlooking Glen Feshie and its remote forest. Contiguous with Rothiemurchus Forest, to the north-east, is Glenmore Forest, with one of the National Forest Parks, described under *Aviemore*, the well-known *Strath Spey* (*q.v.*) resort lying some **2 m. N.** of Rothiemurchus, on the opposite bank of the Spey. In the Park is *Loch Morlich* (*q.v.*), and to the south-east rises *Cairn Gorm*, 4,084 ft., on the slopes of which there is ski-ing in Coire Cas, now easier of access due to the construction of a new road. See Coylumbridge and **Loch Morlich**. *Iter. 138, 149.*

ROTHIE NORMAN, Aberdeen.   Map 27, NJ 7 3.
The Fordoun Burn flows past the village on its way north-eastwards to join the Ythan near *Fyvie* (*q.v.*), with its great castle. *Iter. 184.*

ROUSAY, ISLE OF, Orkney.   Map 33, HY 3 3.
See **Orkney Islands** (Rousay).

ROWANTREE, Ayr.   Map 2, NX 3 8.
A little to the north is a road fork, the right-hand branch leading over the hills, attaining a height of 1,421 ft., with *Shalloch on Minnoch*, 2,520 ft., rising away to the east, and later reaching *Straiton* (*q.v.*), in the valley of the Water of Girvan. The left-hand branch crosses the lonely Nick o' the Balloch Pass, 1,280 ft. high, and descends towards *Maybole* (*q.v.*). Both these moorland roads are narrow and winding. See **Bargrennan**. *Iter. 79.*

ROWARDENNAN, Stirling. 40.   Map 15, NS 3 9.
The road along the eastern shores of *Loch Lomond* (*q.v.*) terminates here, where a steamer pier is situated. From this point there are views across to Glen Douglas, on the opposite side of the loch, with which it is connected by passenger ferry. Rowardennan is a good starting point for the ascent of *Ben Lomond*, 3,192 ft., the monarch of the whole district, and a magnificent viewpoint, notably in the direction of the richly wooded district of the *Trossachs* (*q.v.*), to the east. The lesser summit a little to the west of the Ben is known as *Ptarmigan*, and attains 2,398 ft. To the south-east lies *Rowardennan Forest* in the *Queen Elizabeth* Forest Park. See **Luss**. *Iter. 104, 115.*

ROXBURGH, Roxburgh.   Map 10, NT 6 3.
The present small village of Roxburgh stands on the west bank of the Teviot and the churchyard contains the grave of Andrew Gemmels the "Edie Ochiltree" of Scott's "The Antiquary." Of the Castle, situated some **3 m. N.E.** and **1½ m. S.W.** of *Kelso* (*q.v.*), between the Rivers Teviot and Tweed, there are only very scanty remains. The former town of Roxburgh, once adjacent, has entirely vanished, though in the 13th cent. it was one of the four Royal Burghs of Scotland. James II besieged the Castle, once a Royal residence, in 1460, and during the siege is said to have been accidentally killed by the bursting of a cannon in the park of *Floors Castle* (*q.v.*). **3½ m. S.W.** is the late 17th cent. *Fairnington House. Iter. 32, 46.*

ROY BRIDGE, Inverness.   Map 18, NN 2 8.
The bridge spans the River Roy, coming down from Glen Roy, the stream then flowing into the Spean, a short distance to the south in Glen Spean, in the *Lochaber* (*q.v.*) country. A rough and narrow road threads its way northwards through Glen Roy, which is famous for its so-called "Parallel Roads," well seen on the hillside some four miles from Roy Bridge, the uppermost "roads" being about 80 ft. apart, and the lowest situated some 200 ft. below them.

These roads portray the most striking evidence of glacial action in Scotland, and have been interpreted as marking the shores of a vanished lake. Montrose made a wonderful forced march through Glen Roy before the battle of Inverlochy, in 1645. (See **Fort William**). The 18th cent. *Keppoch House* is the successor to an older mansion of the MacDonells of Keppoch. One of the young Chiefs of Keppoch and his brother were murdered here in the 17th cent. The assassins, seven brothers, were slain seven years later, by Iain Lom, the family bard, and their gory heads washed in the "Well of the Heads," on the shores of *Loch Oich* (*q.v.*). At Roy Bridge took place the last of the clan battles, fought between the MacDonells of Keppoch and the MacIntoshes on August 4, 1688. This is said to have been the final recorded use of bows and arrows by the Highlanders. The MacDonells were victorious, but their opponent's standard-bearer jumped the River Roy and escaped. To the east, road and railway traverse the Achluachrach Gorge, on the River Spean, in which are situated the *Monessie Falls*, in their rocky setting, seen to great advantage from the railway, though their fall has been reduced since the Lochaber Power Scheme came into operation. Away to the south of Roy Bridge rise the remote peaks of the *Grey Corries*, 3,858 ft., terminating the series of lofty ridges culminating in *Ben Nevis* (*q.v.*), 4,406 ft., the monarch of the British Isles. See **Spean Bridge** and **Tulloch**. *Iter. 143, 208.*

RULLION GREEN, Midlothian.   Map 9, NT 2 6.
See **Glencorse**.

RUM, ISLE OF, Inverness.   Map 23, NM 3 9.
This mountainous Inner Hebridean island is a prominent feature in the views from various places on the West Highland mainland, notably from the Ardnamurchan peninsula, Arisaig, Morar and Mallaig. *Rum*, or *Rhum*, is now a property of the Nature Conservancy and difficult to visit. The peaks in its southern half form a splendid group, the highest being *Askival*, *Sgurr nan Gillean* and *Ashval*, all exceeding 2,500 ft., in altitude, and providing fine climbing, as well as being notable viewpoints. At the head of Loch Scresort, on the east side of the island, is the little township and Castle of *Kinloch*, and on the west side, in Glen Harris, is situated a mausoleum. The Cuillin Sound lies between Rum and the island of Skye, to the north. Separated from Rum by the Sound of Canna, to the north-west, is the small island of *Canna*, on which stands the low *Compass Hill*, the iron deposits of which sometimes affect mariners' compasses. The Sound of Rum, to the south-east of Rum, divides that island from *Eigg*, on the south side of which rises the curious *Sgurr of Eigg*, 1,289 ft., a remarkable landmark. This is well seen from *Galmisdale*, with its pier, and is prominent in views from the mainland. Scott's "Lord of the Isles" describes a tragedy in a cave on this island, when several hundred Macdonalds were deliberately suffocated by the MacLeods of Skye in the 16th cent. On the north-west side of the island is the Bay of Laig, with the clachan of Cleadale, and in the vicinity are some "singing sands." Beyond Eigg, to the south-west, across the Sound of Eigg, lies the tiny island of *Muck*, with a laird's residence at *Gallanach* and a small harbour at *Port Mor*. Steamer services link Rum, Eigg and Canna to the mainland ports of Mallaig and Kyle of Lochalsh.

RUMBLING BRIDGE, Kinross; Perth. 253.
    Map 16, NT 0 9.
E.C. Wed. This well-known beauty spot, on the River Devon, its name derived from the noise of the river when in spate, gives access to several spectacular and picturesque gorges and falls. The Devon is spanned near the hotel by two bridges, one of which, a narrow arch, dates from 1713, the other being dated 1816. The Devil's Mill and Caldron Linn are the best known falls, the former to the north-east, and the latter to the south-west of Rumbling Bridge. **3 m. S.E.** stands the restored *Aldie Castle*, overlooking the *Cleish* hills across the Pow Burn. *Iter. 86, 89.*

RUTHERGLEN, Lanark. 24,423. LB.   Map 8, NS 6 6.
E.C. Tues. Although contiguous with the city of Glasgow, *Rutherglen*, situated south of the River Clyde, has successfully retained its independence, and remains the oldest of the

Rothiemurchus, Inverness. The ancient Comyn stronghold on Loch Eilean, in which the notorious Wolf of Badenoch once lived. The loch lies off an unclassified road to the south-east, in Rothie-murchus Forest, in the foothills of the Cairngorms

Roy Bridge, Inverness. The view up the lonely Glen Roy, to the north of A86, in which lie the famous 'parallel roads,' which have been formed by glacial action

Rutherglen, Lanark. The tower of the Parish Church, which incorporates a fragment of the earlier Norman Church

Rumbling Bridge, Kinross; Perth. Two bridges spanning the River Devon, dated 1713 and 1816 respectively. A plaque showing the two bridges exists on the wall of the hotel

Rutherglen, Lanark. The Kirk Port of 1663, which retains two sentry boxes dating from the 18th century

PLATE 144 (facing page 236)

Ruthwell Church, Dumfries. The famous 18-foot high carved 8th century Cross, which is preserved in an apse built specially for it

Saddell, Argyll. An entrance arch to Saddell Castle, built in 1508. Robert Bruce was concealed in the castle after his defeat at Methven in 1306

St. Andrews, Fife. The remains of the Cathedral, founded originally in 1160. Robert Bruce attended its consecration in 1318

St. Andrews, Fife. The 14th century Gothic arches known as The Pends, which form part of a once-vaulted gate-house to the Priory precincts

St. Abb's, Berwick. A row of net houses used to store the local fishermen's gear

St. Andrews, Fife. The Club House of the Royal and Ancient Golf Club, founded in 1754, and acknowledged as the ruling authority on the game

PLATE 145 (facing page 237)   [For ST. ANDREWS see also following plate

Scottish Royal Burghs, having been thus created by David I, early in the 12th cent. The former castle has disappeared, having been burnt by the Regent Murray after the battle of Langside, in 1568, after which Mary, Queen of Scots commenced her flight from the country (See **Clarkston**). In 1679, the Covenanters affixed a declaration to the Town Cross, which led to the battles of Drumclog near *Loudounhill* (*q.v.*), and *Bothwell Brig* (*q.v.*). A gable from the former Norman Church rests against an early 16th cent. steeple containing a Dutch bell of 1635. The Kirk port dates from 1663 and has a pair of 18th cent. sentry-boxes. The present Mercat Cross is modern. Clydesdale horses were at one time tethered in the wide main street during important sales. The town is an important manufacturing centre, noted for chemicals and paper mills, and there are also collieries in the vicinity. 1½ m. S. is *Castlemilk*, incorporating a 15th or 16th cent. tower, and thought to have housed Mary, Queen of Scots before the battle of Langside. See **Cambuslang**. *Iter. 56.*

RUTHVEN, Angus.　　　　Map 20, NO 2 4. *Iter. 166.*

RUTHVEN BARRACKS, Inverness.　　Map 19, NN 7 9. See **Kingussie**. *Iter. 138, 149.*

RUTHWELL CHURCH, Dumfries.　　Map 4, NY 1 6. The Church lies a little to the north, and the village a little to the south of the Dumfries to Annan road. The very remarkable *Ruthwell Cross* (A.M.) is of the greatest interest to archaeologists, and is preserved inside the Parish Church, in an apse built specially for it. This preaching Cross, 18 ft. high, and probably of 8th cent. date, is one of Europe's most notable examples, and carries an inscription in Runic characters, depicting the earliest phrases extant of written English, in the Northumbrian dialect. The Cross was overthrown in 1642, but was restored again in 1823. At Ruthwell, in 1810, the Rev. Henry Duncan set up Scotland's first savings bank. The local pronunciation of Ruthwell is " Rivvie." See **Brow**. *Iter. 28, 47.*

SADDELL, Argyll. 932 with Skipness.　　Map 7, **NR 7** 3. Stands in a picturesque setting on Saddell Bay, at the foot of Saddell Glen, with slight remains of a Cistercian monastery, possibly of 12th cent. date. This is said to have been founded by Somerled, the first Lord of the Isles, from whom sprang the Clan Donald. In the churchyard are some stones carved with Celtic inscriptions, and one of the recumbent effigies may be that of Somerled himself. On the south side of the bay stands *Saddell Castle*, dated 1508, with a machicolated parapet, and once the residence of the Bishops of Argyll. Above the date panel over the door is carved a representation of the " Galley of Lorne." To the west of Saddell rise the highest of the *Kintyre* (*q.v.*) hills, with *Beinn an Tuirc* attaining 1,491 ft. and *Beinn Bhreac* only slightly less high at 1,398 ft. See **Carradale**. *Iter. 122.*

ST. ABB'S, Berwick.　　　　Map 11, NT 9 6. A small resort and fishing village, with sands, on a cliff-bound stretch of coast. There is a row of picturesque, tiny buildings used for the storage of the local fishermen's gear. Towards St. Abb's Head, with its lighthouse, to the north, the red cliffs rise to over 300 ft., forming an impressive headland, and are riddled with the caves of former smugglers. From the small inlet of Pettycarwick Bay the rugged coast scenery can be well glimpsed. See **Coldingham**. *Iter. 2.*

ST. ANDREWS, Fife. 9,559. SB.　　Map 17, NO 5 1. E.C. Thurs. GOLF. This fascinating old University town and well-known summer resort, situated on St. Andrews Bay looking out over the North Sea, can justly claim to be one of the most interesting in Scotland, and was once the ecclesiastical capital of the country. The town stands on a promontory, and steep cliffs guard the narrow harbour, but north-westwards lie extensive stretches of sand fringing a shallow bay. At this end lie the golf-courses for which St. Andrews is today most celebrated, the Royal and Ancient Golf Club being the foremost in the world and the ruling authority on the game, which is said to have been played at St. Andrews in the 15th century. There are four courses in all, two of which are kept up by the club and two by the Corporation, and championship meetings take place from time to time. During the annual autumn meeting, the captain for the following year plays himself into office.

St. Andrews was made a Royal Burgh in 1140, and in 1160 the Cathedral (A.M.) was founded, becoming the largest in the country, and having been completed in 1318. James V and Mary of Guise were married within its walls, and in 1559, after sermons delivered by John Knox, a certain amount of destruction of ornaments took place. By 1649 the Cathedral was reduced, mainly by neglect, to a state of ruin. Today, only parts of the west and east ends, together with a portion of the south nave wall are still standing, though the ground plan can still be traced. There are fairly extensive monastic remains, including the chapter house and refectory. Close to the Cathedral stands the small *St. Regulus'* or *St. Rule's* Church (A.M.), with its 108-ft. high tower, dating from the early 12th cent., which is ascended by a spiral staircase. The nave has vanished, but the narrow, roofless choir, with its round-headed windows, has survived.

The University is the oldest in Scotland, having been founded in 1412, and now includes *Dundee* (*q.v.*) University, incorporated in 1897. The United Colleges of *St. Salvator* and *St. Leonard*, founded in 1455 and 1512, and combined in 1747, are famous for the Church of *St. Salvator*, now the College Chapel. This 15th cent. Church has a tall tower, with an octagonal broach spire, and the interior contains the tomb of the

ST. ANDREWS

Scale

0　　¼ Mile

N

Blackfriars Monastery	5.	Madras College	6.
Castle	1.	Queen Mary's House	9.
Cathedral	2.	St. Mary's College	8.
Information Bureau		St. Regulus' Church	3.
adjacent to Town Hall	11.		

Town Church (Holy Trinity)　　4.
United Colleges (St. Salvator's Church)　7.
West Port　10.

founder, Bishop Kennedy; the oldest Sacrament House in a Scottish Church; and John Knox's pulpit, formerly in the Town Church. *St. Mary's College*, founded in 1537 by Cardinal Beaton, preserves a quadrangle between the older buildings, while a thorn tree, planted by Mary, Queen of Scots, still flourishes. The University Museum contains interesting fossils from Dura Den, near *Pitscottie* (*q.v.*). There are still slight remains of the original *St. Leonard's* College, in which John Knox resided, and nearby is the little 16th cent. *St. Leonard's* Chapel, with monuments of interest. The Town Church, *Holy Trinity*, founded in 1412, but so much altered that it is now virtually a new structure, retains its 16th cent. tower, of " Fife " type. The interior contains an elaborately-carved 17th cent. marble monument to Archbishop Sharp, murdered in 1779, at Magus Muir, near Pitscottie. John Knox preached his first public sermon in the Church, in 1547. The Playfair aisle contains monuments to the family. There are also two choir stalls of c. 1505; some notable modern windows by Douglas Strachan; and a wall tablet to the famous golfer, Tom Morris. The Session House contains interesting relics, including two " cutty," or repentance stools and the branks or scold's bridle. In the grounds of the modern *Madras* College stands the Blackfriars Chapel, dating from 1525, a fragment of the former monastery, founded originally in 1274. In the Town Hall are portraits, and among some interesting relics is the headsman's axe, as well as a stone dated 1565, which came from the old tolbooth, taken down in 1862. A house in South Street, built by Hugh Scrymgeour in 1523, and now *St. Leonard's* School library, is said to have once housed Mary, Queen of Scots. Nearby are *The Pends* two Gothic arches, perhaps 14th cent., forming the entrance to the Priory precincts, once completely encircled by a wall, the work of Prior Hepburn in the 16th cent., of which considerable portions are still in situ. A number of fine old houses may still be seen in South Street, the west end of which is spanned by the *West Port* (A.M.), built in 1589. The *Teinds Yett*, in Abbey Walk, is another old gate. A picturesque custom is the " Kate Kennedy " procession, held annually in the spring.

The ruined Castle (A.M.) is situated on a rock overlooking the sea, and was founded in 1200, being rebuilt late in the 14th cent. Cardinal Beaton was murdered here, in 1546, and in the following year John Knox was among the garrison when the Castle was taken by the French fleet, and the prisoners, among them Knox, taken to the galleys in France. In the Sea Tower is a 24-ft. deep dungeon known as the Bottle Dungeon, and to the southeast of the courtyard is an underground passage containing mine fragments from a siege of 1546. Near the Club House of the Royal and Ancient Club is the Martyrs' Monument, commemorating some of the reformers who were burnt at St. Andrews in the 15th and 16th cents. The town makes an excellent centre for visits to the various old-world Royal Burghs situated along the Fife coast, from *Crail* (*q.v.*) in the east, to *Culross* (*q.v.*) in the west beyond *Dunfermline* (*q.v.*). **2 m. S.E.** of St. Andrews is Kinkell Ness, with the strange, basalt rock pillars known as the " Rock and Spindle." **2 m. S.W.** is the park of *Mount Melville*, now the *Craigtoun* public park. The 19th-cent. novelist, G. J. Whyte-Melville, formerly lived here. See **Ceres, Dairsie, Leuchars** and **Pitscottie** (for *Magus Muir*). *Iter. 93, 94, 128, 129, 131, 136.*

ST. ANN'S, Dumfries. Map 4, NY 0 9.
Lies on the Kinnel Water, which flows through the delightful Raehills Glen, a little to the north-west. St. Ann's Bridge dates from c. 1800. *Lochwood Tower*, a ruined Johnstone stronghold, situated in a wood, was burnt in 1592 *Iter. 24, 46.*

ST. BOSWELLS GREEN, Roxburgh. Map 10, NT 5 3.
A spacious common links the village with *St. Boswells*, a little to the north-east, nearer the River Tweed, where *Lessudden House* is a fine, modernised 16th and 17th cent. house. Across the Tweed, to the north-east, stands *Mertoun House*, designed originally by Sir William Bruce in 1703. There is a dovecote dated 1576. *Old Mertoun House* dates

back to 1677. To the north-west is *Newtown St. Boswells* (*q.v.*). In the background rise the triple-peaked *Eildon Hills*. See Dryburgh Abbey. *Iter. 4, 13, 32, 36, 41, 43, 46, 52.*

ST. CATHERINE'S, Argyll. Map 14, NN 1 0.
Situated on the eastern shore of *Loch Fyne* (*q.v.*), looking across its waters to *Inveraray* (*q.v.*). To the north-east, the road continues along the lochside to circle round its head, but two branches diverge to the east, leading to Hell's Glen and Glen Kinglas respectively, and meeting again at the summit of *Rest and be Thankful* (*q.v.*), in its mountain setting. *Iter. 102, 103, 137.*

ST. COMBS, Aberdeen. Map 27, NK 0 6.
A fishing village situated under the shelter of Inzie Head, with Strathbeg Bay lying beyond it to the south-east. *Iter. 182.*

ST. CYRUS, Kincardine. 356. Map 21, NO 7 6.
E.C. Thurs. Lies on the coast, to the north of the estuary of the River North Esk, with some rock scenery north-east of the village, and also bathing from a sandy beach. About a mile in this direction is the ruined *Kaim of Mathers*, a refuge, built in 1421, near which is the promontory of Milton Ness. The former village of Mathers was destroyed by the sea, in 1795. **2 m. N.E.**, and west of the Inverbervie road, is the wooded *Den Finella*, with a waterfall. *Iter. 155.*

ST. FERGUS, Aberdeen. Map 27, NK 0 5.
Iter. 181, 182.

ST. FILLAN'S, Perth. 170. Map 15, NN 6 2.
E.C. Wed. GOLF. Charmingly situated at the eastern extremity of Loch Earn, and on the River Earn, where it commences its journey down Strath Earn. To the south rise the wooded slopes of *Dundurn*, 2,011 ft., an ancient Pictish fortified hill, and below is the smaller *Dunfillan Hill*, 600 ft., topped by a rock known as *St. Fillan's* Chair. A ruined Chapel stands in a cemetery near the village, and has long been used as the burial-place of the Stewarts of *Ardvorlich House*, near *Lochearnhead* (*q.v.*). The font from the Chapel is now in the Parish Church. In the loch, west of the village, is the wooded Neish Island. Roads traverse Loch Earn's north and south shores, the main road on the north bank giving fine mountain views, which include *Ben Vorlich*, 3,224 ft., and *Stuc a'Chroin*, 3,169 ft., rising beyond the loch to the south. *Iter 138, 141, 145.*

ST. JOHN'S TOWN OF DALRY, Kirkcudbright.
See **Dalry** (Kirkcudbright). Map 3, NX 6 8.

ST. KILDA, ISLES OF, Inverness.
Situated some 40 miles to the west of *North Uist*, in the Outer Hebrides, this small group of lonely islands, for long owned by the Macleod of Macleod, was given to the Scottish National Trust in 1957, and is leased to the Nature Conservancy. The inhabitants were removed, in 1930, mostly to *Larachbeg* (*q.v.*), in Argyllshire. There are magnificent cliffs on the largest of the islands, rising to more than 1,300 ft. Wild Mouflon sheep and sea-fowl predominate on St. Kilda, which is now a bird sanctuary, the rare Leach's fork-tailed petrel being found. The world's largest gannetry is situated on Boreray and the Stacs, and there are myriads of fulmars and puffins. In 1734, Lady Grange was sent in exile to St. Kilda for harbouring Jacobite secrets, being buried at *Trumpan* (*q.v.*), in Skye. Some 180 miles distant in the Atlantic is the minute island of *Rockall*, only 83 ft. in diameter and 70 ft. high, first discovered in 1810, when it was actually mistaken for a French privateer.

ST. MARGARET'S HOPE, Orkney. Map 33, ND 4 9.
See **Orkney Islands** (South Ronaldsay). *Iter. 266.*

ST. MARY'S HOLM, Orkney. Map 33, HY 4 0.
See **Orkney Islands** (Mainland). *Iter. 265, 266.*

ST. MARY'S LOCH, Selkirk. Map 9, NT 2 2.
In its setting of rounded, green Lowland hills in Ettrick Forest, this beautiful loch, some three miles in length, makes a charming picture, and its praises have been sung by Wordsworth in " Yarrow Visited " and by Scott in his

St. Andrews, Fife. The West Port, spanning South Street. Its building contract is dated 18th May, 1589, but it was extensively restored in 1843 and the side arches added

St. Andrews, Fife. The ruined Castle, of 14th to 17th century date, in which Cardinal Beaton was murdered in 1546. A year later John Knox was taken from here to the galleys in France

St. Fillan's, Perth. The ancient ruined Chapel in a cemetery near the village

St. Boswells Green, Roxburgh. The knocker on the entrance door to the 16th to 17th century Lessudden House. It stands at St. Boswells, to the north-east, on B6404, near the River Tweed

St. Cyrus, Kincardine. The 15th century refuge known as the Kaim of Mathers, which was built by a Barclay, in 1421, after he had slain a sheriff of the Mearns. It lies to the north-east, near Milton Ness

St. Andrews, Fife. The ruined early 12th century St. Rule's Church, which has a tower 108 feet high. It was built originally for Bishop Robert. In the nearby cemetery is buried Tom Morris (1821-1908), the famous golfer of early days

[For ST. ANDREWS see also preceding plate
[For ST. MARY'S LOCH see following plate

PLATE 146 (facing page 238)

St. Mary's Loch, Selkirk. A view of the loch, in its setting of hills in the Southern Uplands

St. Monance, Fife. An old dovecote near the ruined Newark Castle, on the cliffs to the south-west

St. Mary's Loch, Selkirk. The statue of James Hogg, the 'Ettrick Shepherd,' which stands near 'Tibbie Shiel's' Inn, between St. Mary's Loch and the Loch of the Lowes, on A708

St. Vigean's, Angus. The Drosten Stone, in the Church carrying Pictish symbols and a contemporary inscription

Saltburn, Ross and Cromarty. A Cromarty Firth village, recalling the days when salt was smuggled ashore to evade the salt tax

PLATE 147 (facing page 239)

"Marmion." At the south-western extremity, separated by a narrow spit of land carrying a road, on which stands the famous "*Tibbie Shiel's*" Inn (*q.v.*), is the little *Loch of the Lowes*. St. Mary's Loch has associations with Hogg, the 'Ettrick Shepherd,' who herded on the hills in the neighbourhood, and his statue stands near Tibbie Shiel's. The Megget Water flows into the loch on the north side, at *Coppercleuch*, while a rough track traverses the valley through which the stream flows, and gives access to the lonely Talla Reservoir. near *Tweedsmuir* (*q.v.*), overlooked by *Broad Law*, 2,754 ft., one of the loftiest of the Lowland hills. To the south of the Megget Water outflow is the picturesquely situated "*Rodono*" Hotel, taking its name from the old barony of Rodonna of which the Megget family formed a part. On the hillside, north of the loch, is the old churchyard of *St. Mary's* Kirk. Farther to the north-east is the ruined *Dryhope Tower*, said to be the birthplace of Mary Scott, the "Flower of Yarrow," who married "Auld Wat of Harden," an ancestor of Sir Walter Scott. (See **Hawick**.) North-eastwards. in the extensive Ettrick Forest, lies the beautiful Vale of *Yarrow* (*q.v.*), one of the loveliest of the Border valleys. See **Ettrick, Ettrick Bridge End, Gordon Arms Inn** and **Tushielaw Inn**. *Iter*. 13, 46.

ST. MONANCE, Fife. 1,468. SB.   Map 17, NO 5 0.
E.C. Wed. A charming little fishing port, also known as *St. Monans*, with old houses clustered near the water's edge. A beautiful little 14th cent. Church stands almost on the foreshore, having been built by David II, and consisting of an unfinished cruciform structure, topped by a curious stone steeple. A model of a three-masted ship hangs usually from one of the transept roofs. The original "Fifie" fishing boats were built in the town's shipyard, which now specialises in yachts. On the cliffs, to the south-west, are remains of the 17th cent. *Newark Castle*, with an old dovecote close by. The Castle was once the home of General Leslie, the Covenanter, who won the battle of *Philiphaugh*, near *Selkirk* (*q.v.*), but was later defeated by Cromwell in the battle of *Dunbar* (*q.v.*). *Iter*. 94, 98.

ST. NINIAN'S, Stirling. 3,932.   Map 16, NS 7 9.
This old village, known also as *St. Ringan's*, is situated to the south of *Stirling* (*q.v.*). It stands at the junction of roads leading towards Airdrie and Falkirk, with the famous battlefield of *Bannockburn* (*q.v.*) in close proximity to the south-west. 2½ m. S. of St. Ninian's, and off the road to Denny, is the 16th cent. mansion of *Auchinbowie*. In the vicinity, to the west, is the probable site of the battle of *Sauchieburn*, in 1488, when James III was defeated, wounded and afterwards murdered. *Iter*. 50, 87, 95, 99.

ST. VIGEAN'S, Angus.   Map 21, NO 6 4.
The village lies a little to the north of Arbroath, on the Brothock Water, and is known chiefly for its Church, founded in the 11th cent., but much restored. There is a remarkable collection of Celtic inscribed stones, and outstanding is the so-called *Drosten Stone*, carrying Pictish symbols. 3 m. N., near the Brothock Water, is *Colliston House*, dating from 1583.

SALEN, Argyll. 136.   Map 12, NM 6 6.
A small fishing resort on the beautifully-wooded shores of *Loch Sunart* (*a.v.*), a long and narrow sea loch, which divides Ardnamurchan from Morven, and whose waters mingle with those of the Sound of Mull away to the west. Eastwards rises *Ben Resipol*, 2,774 ft., a splendid viewpoint, and northwards goes the road to *Acharacle* (*q.v.*), at the western extremity of *Loch Shiel* (*q.v.*), with its memories of Prince Charles Edward and the '45. See **Strontian**. *Iter*. 216.

SALEN, Isle of Mull, Argyll. 119.   Map 12, NM 5 4.
A steamer port on the Sound of Mull, situated on the narrowest part of the island, and separated by only 3 miles of land from the western sea loch of Loch na Keal. This loch may be the "Loch Gyle" of Campbell's famous poem," Lord Ullin's Daughter" (See **Ulva Ferry**). Roads traverse both north and south shores of its waters, that on the north

side leading ater by the shore of Loch Tuath, in which lies the island of *Ulva*, with its caves, and eventually reaching *Calgary* (*q.v.*). The road on the south side of Loch na Keal passes near the north-western extremity of the beautiful inland Loch Ba. Later it gives views of Ulva, beyond which lies the smaller island of *Gometra*, before passing under the magnificent *Gribun* (*q.v.*) cliffs on the way to Loch Scridain. In the background, to the east, rises *Ben More*, 3,169 ft., Mull's highest peak, and a fine viewpoint. To the east of Salen, a road leads along the shores of the Sound of Mull, overlooked by a range of 2,500-ft. high hills. 2 m. N.W. of Salen, overlooking the Sound of Mull, and near the entrance to Glen Aros, on the inland road to *Dervaig* (*q.v*), is the ruined *Aros Castle*, once a stronghold of the Lords of the Isles. 2 m. E. stands the ruined *Pennygowan* Chapel, in which some carved cross-slabs are preserved. See **Craignure** and **Tobermory**. *Iter*. 248, 249, 250.

SALINE, Fife.   Map 16, NT 0 9.
GOLF. At the foot of *Saline Hill*, 1,178 ft., an outlier of the *Cleish* hills, which stretch away north-eastwards, partly in Kinross-shire, their highest point being *Dumglow*, 1,241 ft. Sir Walter Scott stayed here at times.

SALTBURN, Ross and Cromarty.   Map 25, NH 7 6.
A Cromarty Firth village, adjacent to *Invergordon* (*q.v.*), its name recalling the days of the salt tax, when this commodity used to be smuggled ashore and hidden in burns. *Iter*. 201.

SALTCOATS, Ayr. 13,740. SB.   Map 8, NS 2 4.
E.C. Wed. GOLF. A well-known resort, with a harbour, sands and bathing, facing Irvine Bay to the south-east. The resort and steamer pier of *Ardrossan* (*q.v.*) lies to the north-west across a bay. Saltworks were originally established at Saltcoats by James V, in the 16th cent. See **Stevenston**. *Iter*. 88.

SANAIGMORE, Isle of Islay, Argyll.   Map 6, NR 2 7.
Lies on Sanaigmore Bay, near which, in 1847, the emigrant ship "Exmouth" foundered with heavy loss of life. Away to the north-east, on a rocky stretch of coast, is Ardnave Point, at the mouth of Loch Gruinart. A narrow road leads southwards from Sanaigmore, keeping inland from the rocky coast, in which some notable caves are to be found. It passes near the shores of Loch Gorm, with remains of an ancient castle of the Macdonalds, on the way to the sandy Saligo Bay, in the Rhinns of Islay. See **Kilchoman**. *Iter*. 246.

SANDBANK, Argyll. 1,161.   Map 14, NS 1 8.
E.C. Wed. Situated on the south shores of the Holy Loch, which is almost encircled by the road from Dunoon to Ardentinny, providing fine marine views for the whole of the distance. A little to the north-west is the entrance to Glen Lean, threaded by the narrow and hilly road leading to the heads of Lochs Striven and Riddon, and thence to *Glendaruel* (*q.v.*) and *Loch Fyne* (*q.v.*). The yacht "Sceptre," the unsuccessful 1958 challenger for the America's Cup, was launched at Sandbank in the spring of that year. See **Ardnadam**. *Iter*. 102, 137.

SANDHAVEN, Aberdeen.   Map 27, NJ 9 6.
A coastal village, with the ruined 17th cent. *Pittullie Castle* standing a little inland to the south-west. *Iter*. 182.

SANDHEAD, Wigtown.   Map 2, NX 0 4.
On Luce Bay, with the extensive Sands of Luce, backed by the sand dunes of the Torrs Warren, to the north-east, where a battle between the Picts and the Scots once took place. 2 m. S.W., on a by-road away from the coast, is *Kirkmadrine* Church, in the porch of which are preserved several remarkable inscribed stones (A.M.), showing that a very early Christian settlement must have existed in the locality. *Iter*. 82.

SANDNESS, Shetland.   Map 33, HU 2 5.
See **Shetland Islands** (Mainland). *Iter*. 268.

SANDWICK, Isle of Lewis, Ross and Cromarty.
Iter. 259.   Map 32, NB 4 3.

SANDWICK, Shetland.   Map 33, HU 4 2.
See **Shetland Islands** (Mainland). *Iter*. 269.

SANDWOOD BAY, Sutherland.   Map 28 **NC 2** 6.
See **Kinlochbervie**. *Iter.* 229.

SANDYKNOWE, Roxburgh.   Map 10, **NT 6** 3.
At this farmhouse, situated near the picturesque *Smailholm Tower* (*q.v.*), Sir Walter Scott spent some of his childhood years, living with his grandfather.

SANNOX, Isle of Arran, Bute.   Map 7, **NS 0** 4.
Situated on Sannox Bay, at the seaward end of the picturesque and lonely Glen Sannox. This penetrates into the heart of the granite hills of Arran, the head of the valley being dominated by *Cir Mhor*, 2,618 ft., and *Caisteal Abhail*, 2,817 ft. The hills which overlook the lower half of the valley are *Suidhe Fhearghais*, 1,756 ft., to the north, and *Cioch na'h Oighe*, 2,168 ft., to the south. By traversing a ridge to the south of *Cir Mhor*, access is gained for climbers to Glen Rosa and *Brodick* (*q.v.*). From the bay, views are obtained towards the islands of Bute and the twin Cumbraes. The road leading north-westwards from Sannox to *Lochranza* (*q.v.*) traverses the fine North Glen Sannox. See **Corrie**. *Iter.* 242.

SANQUHAR, Dumfries. 2.519. SB.   Map 9, **NS 7** 0.
E.C. Thurs. GOLF. A small Nithsdale town, the River Nith being joined, to the east, by the Crawick Water, flowing down from the lonely hills on the Lanarkshire border. These are traversed by a winding and narrow road reaching Clydesdale by way of *Crawfordjohn* (*q.v.*). The site of the former Town Cross, to which the Covenanters affixed the two famous Declarations of Sanquhar, in 1680 and 1685, is commemorated by a modern granite monument. The Tolbooth dates from 1735. The Riding of the Marches festival takes place in the summer, The ruined castle above the Nith belonged once to the Crichtons and later to the Douglases. West of Sanquhar are remains of an earthwork called the "Devil's Dyke," the origin of which is obscure. In the latter half of the 17th cent., the neighbourhood of the *Lowther* hills, to the east, was long a retreat for the persecuted Covenanters, or "Men of the Moss Hags." See **Enterkinfoot** and **Mennock**. *Iter.* 27, 48, 49, 67.

SARCLET, Caithness.   Map 30, **ND 3** 4.
On a rocky piece of coast, with the Stack of Ulbster to the south, near Loch Sarclet.

SARK BRIDGE, Dumfries.   Map 4, **NY 3** 6.
This bridge over the River Sark, which flows from here into the Solway Firth, forms the border between Scotland and England, and carries the road (built in 1830 to supersede the road via Longtown) leading from Carlisle to Glasgow and Stranraer. The former Sark Toll Bar house was the scene of many runaway marriages. See **Gretna** and **Springfield**. *Iter.* 10, 13, 26, 27, 28, 29, 42, 50, 51.

SATTERNESS, Kirkcudbright.   Map 3, **NX 9** 5.
See **Southerness**.

SCALLOWAY, Shetland.   Map 33, **HU 3** 3.
See **Shetland Islands** (Mainland). *Iter.* 270.

SCAPA FLOW, Orkney.   Map 33, **HY 3** 0.
See **Orkney Islands** (Mainland).

SCARBA, ISLE OF, Argyll.   Map 13, **NM 6** 0.
See **Clachan Bridge**.

SCHIEHALLION, Perth.   Map 19, **NN 7** 5.
See **Kinloch Rannoch** and **Queen's View**. *Iter.* 89, 138, 147, 148, 149.

SCONE, Perth. 2,292.   Map 17, **NO 1** 2.
Famous for the former Abbey and Palace, which stood **2 m.** W. of *New Scone*, a little to the west of the Perth to Blairgowrie road, and between *Old Scone* and the River Tay. It was destroyed in 1559 by a mob from Perth, who had been fired by John Knox's oratory. The mote-hill of Scone was known already in the 8th cent., and the celebrated Stone of Scone, traditionally identified with Jacob's pillow at Bethel, and later the Stone of Destiny at Tara in Ireland, was brought here about a century later, to be carried away to England by Edward I in 1297. It was later placed under the seat of the Coronation Chair in Westminster Abbey,

from which it was sensationally taken in December 1950. Early in 1951, the Stone found a temporary resting place in the Abbey at *Arbroath* (*q.v.*), before being returned to England. All the early Scottish Kings were crowned at Scone until the time of James I. The last King to be crowned here was Charles II, in 1651. The Old Pretender kept court in Scone Palace, in 1716, and 29 years later Prince Charles Edward slept there. The present early 19th cent. Palace on the old site is the successor to the rebuilt 16th cent. house. In the park are preserved the old Cross of Scone and also a group of Sacred Stones. See **Dunstaffnage**. For *Iter.* see *New Scone* and *Old Scone*.

SCONSER, Isle of Skye, Inverness.   Map 23, **NG 5** 3.
In their tour of 1773, Dr. Johnson and Boswell dined at an inn here. *Iter.* 251, 252, 253.

SCOONIE, Fife.   Map 17, **NO 3** 0.
See **Leven**. *Iter.* 94, 98, 128.

SCOTLANDWELL, Kinross.   Map 17, **NO 1** 0.
Takes its name from springs which bubble up in a parapeted stone cistern west of the main street. To the north rises *White Craigs*, 1,492 ft., an outlier of the *Lomonds*, and south-westwards is situated *Benarty Hill*, 1,167 ft. *Iter.* 98.

SCOTS DYKE, Dumfries.   Map 4, **NY 3** 7.
See **Canonbie**.

SCOTT COUNTRY, THE   Map 10, **NT 53** etc.
The Scott country may be taken to comprise that part of the picturesque *Border* (*q.v.*) country in the *Lowlands* (*q.v.*) which is threaded by the River Tweed, and has for its centre the town of *Melrose*. Numerous places in the district have achieved fame for their personal links with the great novelist, or are associated, either with his ancestors, or with characters from his works. Of these places *Abbotsford House* is perhaps the best known, having been Sir Walter's last and best-loved home, while to *Dryburgh Abbey* falls the honour of being his place of burial. Although not part of the Scott Country proper, the beautiful *Trossachs* (*q.v.*) country, in Perthshire, is bound up with the novelist's " Laay of the Lake " and " Rob Roy," and is visited yearly by countless admirers of his genius. Two other places, *Riccarton* (*q.v.*) and *Gatehouse of Fleet* (*q.v.*), are particularly associated with " Guy Mannering," and *Caerlaverock* (*q.v.*) has the tomb of Robert Paterson, Scott's " Old Mortality." See **Abbotsford House, Ashiestiel, Darnick, Dryburgh Abbey, Edinburgh, Ettrick Bridge End, Galashiels, Hawick, Irongray, Kelso, Manor, Melrose, Peebles, St. Mary's Loch, Selkirk, Sandyknowe, Shetland** and **Smailholm**. *Iter.* 13, 43.

SCOTT'S VIEW, Berwick. (A.A. viewpoint.)
          Map 10, **NT 53**.
From this point a beautiful view is disclosed, much loved by Sir Walter Scott, looking across the Tweed towards the *Eildon Hills* (*q.v.*). See **Bemersyde**.

SCOURIE, Sutherland. 51.   Map 28, **NC 1** 4.
E.C. Wed. A small crofting village and fishing resort, situated on Scourie Bay, with views to the east of the sharp gneiss cone of *Ben Stack*, 2,364 ft. Palm trees growing in the vicinity of Scourie are thought to be the most northerly in the world. The landscape around this remote Sutherland village is one of innumerable tiny lochans. To the south is the small inlet of Badcall Bay, forming part of the larger island-studded bay of *Eddrachillis* (*q.v.*). To the north-west of Scourie Bay, separated from the mainland by the Sound of Handa, is the island of *Handa* (*q.v.*), now a sea-fowl sanctuary. See **Kinlochbervie** and **Rhiconich**. *Iter.* 225.

SCOUSBURGH, Shetland.   Map 33, **HU 3** 1.
See **Shetland Islands** (Mainland).

SCRABSTER, Caithness.   Map 30, **ND 0** 7.
On the sandy Thurso Bay, sheltered by Holborn Head, with its curious arched chasms. From the pier, the mail-steamer for Stromness in the *Orkneys* (*q.v.*) crosses the turbulent Pentland Firth. See **Thurso**. *Iter.* 236.

SEA MILL, Ayr.   Map 8, **NS 2** 4.
See **West Kilbride**. *Iter.* 66, 88.

Sandyknowe, Roxburgh. The farmhouse where Sir Walter Scott spent some of his childhood days

Sanquhar, Dumfries. The ruined Castle, above the River Nith, which was once owned by the Crichtons and later by the Douglases

Sark Bridge, Dumfries. The Sark Toll Bar house, on A74, the 'First House in Scotland,' where runaway marriages were performed. Above the entrance door is 'the marriage room' tablet. The former main road to Scotland followed A6071 by way of Longtown and Springfield (see Plate 153), marriages being first performed in the latter village

Schiehallion, Perth. The 3,547-foot high peak, which rises south-east of Kinloch Rannoch. West of the peak lies Glen Sassunn, near which English invaders are said to have fought Robert Bruce

Scott Country. The tablet at Langlee, on the Melrose road (A6091), about 1½ miles south-east of Galashiels, in Selkirkshire. It records Sir Walter Scott's last journey to his home at Abbotsford, on his return from Italy in 1832, shortly before his death

Scotlandwell, Kinross. A stone cistern, dated 1838, in which is contained the spring from which the village takes its name

PLATE 148 (facing page 240)

Seton, East Lothian. The unfinished 15th century Collegiate Church. It stands in the grounds of the Castle, which Robert Adam built in 1790 to replace the old Palace, where Charles I was entertained in 1633

Selkirk, Selkirk. The Flodden Monument, which was erected in 1913, on the 400th anniversary of the battle, and is inscribed, 'O Flodden Field'

SITE OF OLD FOREST INN
WHERE
BURNS
WROTE HIS EPISTLE TO WILLIE CREECH
13TH MAY 1787.

Selkirk, Selkirk. The Old Court House, facing which stands a statue of Sir Walter Scott, who was sheriff of the county from 1799 to 1832

Selkirk, Selkirk. The tablet on the West Port recalling the former 'Forest' Inn, where Robert Burns once lodged

Shandwick, Ross and Cromarty. A carved Celtic stone by the roadside

Shawhead, Kirkcudbright. One of a number of examples of modern sculpture by Henry Moore, set up on the slopes of the hills near Glenkiln, to the north-west

PLATE 149 (facing page 241)

[For SHETLAND see following plates

SEIL, ISLE OF, Argyll.   Map 14, NM 7 1.
See **Clachan Bridge**. *Iter. 122.*

SELKIRK, Selkirk. 5,757. SB.   Map 10, NT 4 2.
E.C. Thurs. GOLF. A Royal Burgh, on the edge of Ettrick
Forest, situated on the Ettrick Water, which has received the
waters of the Yarrow a little farther to the south-west. A
picturesque Border Riding ceremony is still kept up annually,
and the town is today noted especially for its tweed mills.
A nightly curfew is sounded from the Town Hall, with its
110-ft. high spire. The Mercat Cross is modern. There are
statues in the High Street to Sir Walter Scott, who was once

1. Town Museum and Library.   2. Town Hall.

Sheriff of the county, and to Mungo Park, the eminent
explorer. Another monument recalls the tragic news of
Flodden Field. In the Town Museum is kept a flag, said to
have been captured at Flodden, and there are relics of James
Hogg, the "Ettrick Shepherd," Mungo Park and Andrew
Lang, the writer. Burns lodged at the former "*Forest*" Inn,
now marked by a tablet, in the West Port. Selkirk was once
famous for its "Sutors" or shoemakers. South of the town
stands *The Haining*, (1794–1819), a Palladian house, near
which is the shell of an earlier mansion, burnt in 1944. To
the south-west of Selkirk, where the Ettrick and Yarrow
Waters meet, is *Philiphaugh*, a mansion with fine gardens,
recalling the battle, fought in 1645, when Leslie and the
Covenanters defeated Montiose. A monument now commemorates the event. (See **Traquair**.) Between the two
rivers is *Carterhaugh*, the scene of the ballad of "Tamlane".
Nearby, to the north-west, is the park of *Bowhill*, a fine
house, enlarged by Sir Charles Barry in the 19th cent., and
containing notable portraits. See **Bowden**, **Broadmeadows**
and **Ettrick Bridge End**. *Iter. 11, 13, 14, 41, 42, 43, 46.*

SETON, East Lothian.   Map 10, NT 4 7.
There stood here formerly *Seton Palace*, one of the most
magnificent of Scottish buildings, which was replaced by
Seton Castle, by Robert Adam, dating from 1790. Mary,
Queen of Scots is associated with Seton, having been here
in 1566, with Darnley, after the murder of Rizzio, and again
in 1567, with Bothwell, after Darnley had been murdered.
In the grounds of the Castle is the late 14th cent. unfinished
Collegiate Church of *Seton* (A.M.), noted for its fine vaulted
chancel and apse, with good window tracery. There are also
splendid tombs and a good example of a piscina. A little
to the north of Seton lie the twin fishing-villages of Port
Seton and *Cockenzie* (*q.v.*). *Iter. 2, 37.*

SHADER, Isle of Lewis, Ross and Cromarty.
    Map 32, NB 3 5.
See **Hebrides, Outer** (Lewis). *Iter. 258.*

SHANDON, Dunbarton.   Map 14, NS 2 8.
GOLF. Situated on the Gare Loch, looking westwards
across the loch to the hills of *Cowal* (*q.v.*). *Iter. 102, 111
116.*

SHANDWICK, Ross and Cromarty.   Map 31, NH 8 7.
Here, in a field west of the road, is a carved Celtic Stone.

SHANKEND, Roxburgh.   Map 5, NT 5 0.
On the Slitrig Water, in a setting of Lowland hills. To the
south, the line of the ancient "Catrail," or Picts' Ditch
crosses the road which leads towards Liddesdale and the
English border. The summit of this road is reached at
Limekiln Edge, **3 m. S.** of Shankend, at an altitude of about
1,200 ft., overlooked to the west by the strangely-shaped
Maiden Paps, 1,677 ft. The Catrail keeps to the north of
the Paps, and then turns northwards, another stretch being
visible in the vicinity of *Galashiels* (*q.v.*). *Iter. 31.*

SHAWBOST, Isle of Lewis, Ross and Cromarty.
Iter. 260.   Map 32, NB 2 4.

SHAWHEAD, Kirkcudbright.   Map 3, NX 8 7.
On the slopes of the hills to the north-west, at *Glenkiln*, are
placed a number of modern bronzes by Henry Moore, a
head by Rodin, and other carvings.

SHEIGRA, Sutherland.   Map 18, NC 1 6.
See **Kinlochbervie**. *Iter. 229.*

SHERIFFMUIR, Perth.   Map 16, NN 8 0.
See **Dunblane**.

SHETLAND ISLANDS.   Map 33.
Known locally as *Shetland*, these consist in all of some 100
islands, of which less than 20 are inhabited, and form the
most northerly portion of the United Kingdom. By far the
largest of these is *Mainland*, on which stands **Lerwick**, the
only important town. The islands lie about 60 miles from
Orkney and are remarkable for their prehistoric antiquities
and for their splendid cliff and sea loch scenery, the local
name for the latter being "voes." Knitting, fishing and
crofting are the principal industries, Shetland hosiery being
known the world over. The land is treeless and the summer
is short, but during June and part of July the "Simmer
dim" as it is called gives nights with little or no darkness,
and the beauty of a "Simmer dim" night has to be seen
to be realised. The sea trout fishing in the islands is particularly good and in many places the fishing is free. Shetland
wool has a world-wide reputation and Shetland ponies are
equally well known. Many of the roads on the Mainland
are excellent, but in the lesser islands they range from
middling to poor. The Picts are supposed to have been the
first colonisers of Shetland and were succeeded by the
Norsemen. In 1468 however, when Margaret, daughter of
Christian the First, King of Denmark, Sweden and Norway,
married James the Third, King of Scotland, Christian by
the marriage contract agreed to pay 60,000 florins as her
dowry. He pledged the Orkney islands for 50,000 and
agreed to pay the balance before Margaret left for Scotland,
but could only produce 2,000, and pledged Shetland for the
remaining sum due, 8,000 florins. *Iter. 267 to 270.*

MAINLAND.

This island, which is the most southerly of the Shetland
group, has on its eastern shore the capital of the islands,
Lerwick (5,623. SB. E.C. Wed.) standing on Bressay Sound.
It is the most northerly town in Britain and is a busy
fishing port. King Haco of Norway visited the harbour
when on his way to the battle of Largs in 1263. In Lerwick
there is celebrated the picturesque festival of Up Helly 'A'
every year on the last Tuesday in January. This is a Norse
Festival in which a Viking ship is escorted round the town
by torch bearers and afterwards burnt. The Festival is
supposed to celebrate the return of the sun. In Charles the
Second's time, *Fort Charlotte* (A.M.), overlooking the town,
was built, but in a subsequent Dutch war it was burnt by a
Dutch frigate together with some of the best houses in the
place. Repaired in George the Third's time, it was until
recent years used as a headquarters for the Royal Naval
Reserve who drilled there in the winter time. After being

repaired it took its name from George the Third's Queen. There is a narrow paved street running the length of the old town and narrow "closes" run up to the top of the hill. At the south end of the town a number of the houses are built into the sea, being in earlier days known as "lodberries," or loading piers, which were used extensively before the harbour works were made. Lerwick possesses a fine Town Hall in which there are some notable stained glass windows.

On the Ward of **Bressay,** which lies across Bressay Sound there is a fine viewpoint, and near Bard Head, in the extreme south, is the stalactite Cave of the Bard, noted for its echo. The Lerwick GOLF course is at Bressay. A visit to the island of **Noss,** now a Nature Reserve, should certainly be undertaken to view the myriads of birds which frequent its great cliffs.

A road to Dunrossness, the most southerly parish in Shetland, proceeds southwards from Lerwick, and a short distance from the town *Clickhimin* Loch is passed, at which there is a fine specimen of a "Pictish" broch (A.M.). The road follows the east coast and passes **Sandwick,** which is situated on Mousa Sound. Here, at Leebitton, a boat may be hired to convey tourists to the island of *Mousa,* where the best specimen of a "Pictish" broch (A.M.) extant can be examined.

Some eight miles farther to the south is **Dunrossness,** the district so frequently mentioned in Sir Walter Scott's novel "The Pirate" as the abode of Norna of Fitful Head. Here is also **Jarlshof,** the residence of Mr. Basil Mertoun. This place has now acquired considerably more fame than it originally had as a dwelling as being the site of very important archaeological discoveries from the Bronze and Iron age periods and also a Viking age house (A.M.). North of Jarlshof, between the West Voe of Sumburgh and the Pool of Virkie, is **Sumburgh** airport. The main road ends near Jarlshof, but a secondary one leads to Sumburgh lighthouse, where a view of the dangerous "Roost" or current which upsets seaborne passengers in more ways than one can be had. Returning to Dunrossness, a detour can be made by branching off at the Parish Church and continuing in a south-westerly direction to Quendale school, then continuing round the west side of Loch Spiggie to **Scousburgh,** where there are two hotels. Continuing northwards past St. Ninian's Bay and Island, this road later joins the main road at Channerwick. Those who are fond of hill-climbing on foot can have ample opportunity of doing so by tackling *Fitful Head,* 928 feet high, beyond Quendale Bay, away to the north-west, but the view from the top is ample reward for the toil involved.

Scalloway, situated some 6½ miles west of Lerwick, is the ancient capital of the islands and seat of the justiciary. It lies at the head of Clift Sound, which is sheltered by the islands of Trondra, Papa and Oxna. Farther down the Sound lie East and West Burra. In this latter isle there was an ancient Christian Church where early Christian sculptured stones have been discovered. *Scalloway Castle* (A.M.), built about 1600 by the notorious Earl Patrick Stewart, is a conspicuous landmark, and to the west of the village lies the Gallows Hill, where witches were formerly burnt. To the north of Scalloway, in the fertile valley of **Tingwall,** are the lochs of Asta and Tingwall, both good trout fishing lochs. In the loch of Tingwall there is a small hold, or islet, at one time reached by stepping-stones, where the Island Parliament met. The loch has been lowered and the stepping-stones are no longer required. Proceeding northwards and westwards, Weisdale Voe is encircled, and the road climbs in a southerly direction until the top of the hill is reached where a splendid view unfolds itself at the Scord of Sound.

At **Twatt** a road turns south to *Reawick,* with a fine sandy bay. Farther west from Twatt and just beyond the Bridge of Walls is the village of **Walls,** on Vaila Sound. This is the port for the Foula mail boat. *Foula,* with a cliff 1,220 feet high, is a home of the Great Skua, and here the film "The Edge of the World" was made in 1938. To the north-west of Walls is the district of **Sandness,** a part of the parish of Walls, and across the Sound of Papa is the island

of *Papa Stour.* The caves in the island have been described by Dr. Macculloch, a well known authority, as being the best in Britain. Out at sea from Papa Stour lie the dangerous "Vee Skerries," on which many ships have been wrecked. The islands are the haunt of large flocks of seals.

The main road leading to the North Mainland from Lerwick passes near the head of Wadbister Voe, and goes along the west side of the Loch of Girlsta, to the north-east of which lies the Nesting peninsula looking seawards to Whalsay island. At South Nesting Bay, close to Brettabister, a road turns off inland to Dury and **Laxo,** where a gated and switchback branch road goes northwards, passing near Vidlin to reach *Lunna,* with its interesting, ancient church, displaying an outside stair to the gallery. The old mansion nearby is associated with the Norwegian escape route during the Second World War. From Laxo the road proceeds westwards past the shores of Voe Loch to the small township of **Voe** at the head of Olnafirth Voe. Here, the direct road from Lerwick to Voe meets the road from Nesting. The continuation northwards overlooks Dales Voe (Delting), and later reaches **Mossbank,** where, at Toft's Voe, it connects with a passenger ferry service to *Ulsta,* in the island of Yell. Some **6 m.** north-west of Voe is **Mavis Grind,** an isthmus less than 50 yards in width, separating the parish of Northmavine from the rest of the Mainland, and so narrow that it is possible to throw a stone from the shore of the North Sea on the east side into the waters of the Atlantic on the west side.

In a northerly direction from Mavis Grind is situated **Hillswick,** on Ura Firth, an inlet of St. Magnus Bay, where there is good accommodation. This is an excellent place for trout fishing. **Eshaness,** to the west, shows some remarkable rock scenery, such as the "Holes of Scraada." There were originally two holes, but about 50 years ago the bridge connecting them fell in, leaving only one. The "Grind of the Navir" is another of these peculiar rock formations. This is a breach smashed in the face of the cliff by the force of the sea. On the north side of Ronas Voe rises *Ronas Hill,* 1,475 ft., the highest hill in Shetland and a very fine viewpoint, from whence, on a fine clear day, most of the islands can be seen. To the east and north-east lie the townships of Collafirth and Burravoe. The road which passes the heads of the inlets on which they lie terminates at **Isbister,** in North Roe. Still farther north is Fethaland, the northernmost point of the mainland.

YELL.

This island is separated from the Mainland by Yell Sound, and is almost cut in two by Whalefirth on the west side and Raefirth or Mid Yell Voe, as it is sometimes called, on the east side. In the north of Yell is Gloup Voe, almost like a miniature Norwegian fjord. Off the east coast of Yell lies the island of *Fetlar,* noted for the breeding of Shetland ponies. Passenger ferries connect *Ulsta* with Toft's Voe (*Mossbank*) in the Mainland and also *Gutcher* with the island of **Unst** at *Belmont.* The mail and passenger steamer "*Earl of Zetland*" from Lerwick calls at *Burravoe, Mid Yell,* to the west of Hascosay, and *Cullivoe,* which are all on the east side of the island.

UNST.

The most northerly of the Shetland Islands and scenically and mineralogically perhaps the most interesting. This island is separated from Yell by Blue Mull Sound, access being by passenger ferry from *Gutcher* in Yell. Here, for many years, was the home of the rare Great Skua, which was preserved from extinction by the endeavours of the Edmonstons, the principal proprietors of the island. At the south-east end of the island is *Muness Castle,* built in 1598, but now a ruin. Midway on the isle is the principal port *Baltasound,* once a very busy herring fishing port, and farther north is situated *Haroldswick,* which has the farthest north post office in Great Britain. Burrafirth, a large sea loch opening to the north, has some very fine caves, and the *Hermaness* district, on its western shores, is now a National Nature Reserve. The Great Skua breeds here, and many other species of birds breed on the sea cliffs. Out at sea is

The 45-foot high broch of Mousa, the only one that survives to approximately its original height. It stands on the island of Mousa, reached by boat from Leebitton, on the Sound of Mousa, near Sandwick

The Bronze Age excavations at Jarlshof, which lie near the airfield at Sumburgh, in the southern extremity of the Mainland. The nearby 16th cent. laird's house has associations with Sir Walter Scott's 'The Pirate'

The lighthouse at Sumburgh Head, in the extreme south of the Mainland. It was erected by Robert Stephenson in 1820. A dangerous current off-shore at this point is known as the 'Roost'

The ruined Scalloway Castle (c. 1600), built by Earl Patrick Stewart, which stands 6 miles west of Lerwick, facing Clift Sound

The 50-yard wide isthmus of Mavis Grind, from which a stone can be thrown from the waters of the Atlantic Ocean into those of the North Sea. It lies on A970, some 6 miles north-west of Voe, on Olna Firth

[For SHETLAND see also following plate

PLATE 150 (facing page 242)

Shetland Islands. The broch of Clickhimin, and its secondary buildings, on Clickhimin Loch to the south-west of Lerwick, off A970

Skelmorlie, Ayr. The entrance door of the partly 16th century Skelmorlie Castle, which stands a mile to the south, on A78

Skipness, Argyll. The ruined Castle. Its red sandstone quoins may have been brought from the island of Arran across the narrow Kilbrennan Sound

Skirling, Peebles. Examples of curious wrought-iron work incorporating painted birds and animals, which are a feature of this village

Skye, Isle of, Inverness. The 2,537-foot high Red Cuillin hill of Glamaig, seen from A850, at the head of Loch Ainort, between Broadford and Sligachan. In 1899, Haskabir Thapa, a Ghurka, visiting Skye with General Bruce, of Himalayan fame, climbed the hill in 37 minutes and made the descent in 18 minutes

Skye, Isle of, Inverness. Duntulm Castle, a 15th century stronghold of the Macdonalds of the Isles, in the extreme north of the island, off A855. It is mentioned between 1577 and 1595 under the name of Duncolmen

[For SHETLAND see also preceding plate

PLATE 151 (facing page 243)

the Mukkle Flugga lighthouse, on its lonely rock, Great Britain's most northerly inhabited place. The mail steamer "*Earl of Zetland*" calls at *Uyeasound* on the south side and at *Baltasound* on the east side of the island.

FAIR ISLE (N.T. Scot.).
This small, lonely island is situated half-way between Orkney and Shetland. There are two lighthouses on it, and a bird-watching station, which was founded in 1948. A Spanish Armada ship was wrecked here in 1588. The female inhabitants of the isle are mostly employed in making the variegated woollen hosiery famous all over the world under the name of Fair Isle hosiery.

SHETTLESTON, Lanark. Map 8, NS 6 6.
A town engaged in the coal and iron industry. *Iter. 16.*

SHIEL BRIDGE, Ross and Cromarty. Map 24, NG 9 1.
Most beautifully situated at the head of the lovely sea loch of *Loch Duich* (*q.v.*), near the clachan of *Invershiel*, and in the heart of the 15,000-acre *Kintail* (*q.v.*) estate (N.T. Scot.). This includes *Ben Attow*, 3,383 ft., and the famous *Five Sisters of Kintail*, dominated by *Scour Ouran*, 3,505 ft. The road descending from the grand defile of *Glen Shiel* (*q.v.*), between the Five Sisters, to the east, and *The Saddle*, 3,317 ft., to the west, divides here, the eastern fork continuing round Loch Duich towards *Dornie* (*q.v.*), and the western fork climbing the well-known pass of *Mam Rattachan* (*q.v.*) on its way to *Glenelg* (*q.v.*). Another road leaves the Mam Rattachan road, and continues along the western shore of Loch Duich, passing Glen Shiel Church on its way to *Totaig*, facing *Ardelve* (*q.v.*), to which it is linked by a passenger ferry. See **Croe Bridge** and **Inverinate**. *Iter. 207, 220.*

SHIELDAIG, Ross and Cromarty. Map 22, NG 8 5.
A little crofting and fishing village, picturesquely situated on Loch Shieldaig, an inlet of Loch Torridon, beyond which, to the north-east, rise the great Torridon sandstone peaks of Ben Alligin, 3,232 ft., *Beinn Dearg*, 2,995 ft. and, finest of all, *Liathach*, 3,456 ft. Although *Torridon* (*q.v.*) is only seven miles distant, at the head of the loch, there is no driving road, and the track, which passes the Falls of Balgy, is only for walkers. A new road is being made to bridge the gap. To the south of the track rises the fine peak of *Ben Damh*, 2,958 ft., and also the cone of *Meall a'Chinn Deirg*, 3,060 ft. Another walkers' track goes westwards from Shieldaig, and follows the coast to *Applecross* (*q.v.*), giving magnificent views over the Inner Sound towards the islands of Raasay and Skye. The road leading south-eastwards to *Tornapress* (*q.v.*) climbs to over 400 ft. before descending to Loch Coultrie, with views of Coir Each and Coire na Poite, two of the wild corries of *Beinn Bhan*, 2,936 ft., the highest of the Applecross hills, showing characteristic horizontal bands of red Torridon sandstone. *Iter. 219, 223.*

SHORTWOODEND, Dumfries. Map 4, NT 1 0.
Iter. 13, 46.

SHOTTS, Lanark. Map 9, NS 8 6.
GOLF. See **Kirk o'Shotts** and **Newmains**.

SILVERBURN, Midlothian. Map 9, NT 2 6.
A *Pentland* hills hamlet, at the foot of *Scald Law*, 1,898 ft., the highest point in the range, which overlooks the picturesque Loganlee reservoir, and can be climbed from here. *Iter. 25.*

SINCLAIRTOWN, Fife. Map 17, NT 2 9.
Iter. 93, 94, 126, 127, 129, 130.

SKAIG BRIDGE, Sutherland. Map 29, NC 2 2.
See **Inchnadamph**. *Iter. 225, 227, 228.*

SKARA BRAE, Orkney. Map 33, HY 2 1.
See **Orkney Islands** (Mainland). *Iter. 264.*

SKEABOST BRIDGE, Isle of Skye, Inverness.
Map 22, NG 4 4.
Spans the River Snizort, where it flows into one of the inlets of Loch Snizort Beag. There is a picturesque old church-yard. *Iter. 255.*

SKELLISTER, Shetland. Map 33, HU 4 5.
Iter. 270.

SKELMORLIE, Ayr. 1,327. Map 8, NS 1 6.
A Firth of Clyde resort, linked to *Wemyss Bay* (*q.v.*), having a fine beach, and giving views across the Firth to Toward Point and westwards to the island of Bute. In the waters of the Firth, opposite Skelmorlie, is a "Measured Mile" where smaller vessels are tested for speed. 1½ m. S., on the coast road to *Largs* (*q.v.*), is *Skelmorlie Castle*, parts of which date back to 1502. See **Corrie**. *Iter. 66, 88.*

SKENE, Aberdeen. Map 27, NJ 8 0.
E.C. Wed. North-west of the village, off the Alford road, is the little Loch of Skene. See **Dunecht**. *Iter. 176.*

SKERRAY, Sutherland. Map 28, NC 6 6.
A crofting township, with a pier and a sandy bay, looking towards the islands of Roan and Eilean Co'omb.

SKERRYVORE, Argyll. Map 13.
See **Tiree, Isle of.**

SKIBO CASTLE, Sutherland. Map 31, NH 7 8.
This impressive modern Castle, built for Andrew Carnegie, is situated just to the south of the Bonar Bridge to Dornoch road, and succeeds a former structure, which was once an episcopal residence. *Iter. 200, 231.*

SKIPNESS, Argyll. Map 7, NR 8 5.
Faces the waters of Kilbrennan Sound and the Sound of Bute, from the eastern side of the *Kintyre* (*q.v.*) peninsula, with fine views of the northern half of the island of Arran. There are remains of an ancient Chapel, and also of a large 13th cent. castle, overlooking Skipness Bay. *Iter. 122.*

SKIRLING, Peebles. Map 9, NT 0 3.
An attractive village, with a green. It is noted for some curious wrought-iron work and painted animals and birds, which are a local feature, making the village probably unique in Scotland. It was the idea of Lord Carmichael, who also designed his own house here, and died in 1926. The iron-work was carried out by Thomas Hadden of Edinburgh. The former castle was demolished in 1568. *Iter. 35, 53.*

SKYE, ISLE OF, Inverness. Maps 22 and 23.
The largest of the Inner Hebrides, known as the "Winged Isle," or "Isle of Mist," and perhaps the most picturesque of all the islands lying off the Scottish mainland. *Skye* is most famous for its range of jagged black mountains, known as the *Coolins*, or *Cuillin*, which provide the most sensational rock scenery in the British Isles. The island is 50 miles long and over 600 square miles in area, and is deeply indented by sea lochs at many points, being thus broken up into a series of individual peninsulas. All these are dominated from far or near by the serrated tops of the Coolins, while no part of the island is more than about 5 miles from the sea. The chief places of interest are linked by fairly good roads, while others are narrow, hilly and less well-surfaced, many being provided with passing-places. Some 165 miles of road fall within the Class 'A' category. The mild and misty climate gives rise often to weather effects of unique beauty. Crofting and fishing are the main local industries. The name of Prince Charles Edward is inseparably linked with the island, notably in connection with the heroic exploits of his intrepid helper Flora Macdonald, who is buried at *Kilmuir*. In 1773, Dr. Johnson and Boswell paid their memorable visit to Skye, and since that time many thousands of tourists have delighted in the splendour of mountain, loch and coast scenery, which is unsurpassed in Scotland. The seaboard of the island is largely rocky, and bathing is generally from stones or gravel. Some of the finest cliff scenery lies in the Duirinish district, west of Dunvegan, but is only accessible on foot. Among the most notable sights of Skye are the wild and beautiful *Lochs Coruisk* and *Scavaig* in the *Coolins*; the fantastic rock towers of the *Quiraing* near *Staffin*, in the Trotternish peninsula; the famous castle of *Dunvegan*; and the magnificent panoramic view of the *Coolins* rising beyond *Loch Scavaig* as seen from above *Elgol*. The island is most easily accessible for motorists by way of *Kyle of Lochalsh* (*q.v.*) and the ferry over the narrow strait of Kyle Akin to *Kyleakin*, and there are steamer piers at both Portree and Armadale, with services to the mainland. All places of interest in Skye are described under their own separate headings and the most noteworthy

243

are indexed below. See **Armadale, Broadford, Coolins, Dunvegan, Elgol, Flodigarry, Glenbrittle, Kilmuir, Kyleakin, Kylerhea, Loch Coruisk, Loch Scavaig, Portree, Quiraing, Storr** and **Uig**. *Iter. 251 to 255.*

SLAMANNAN, Stirling.   Map 9, NS 8 7.
A village on the River Avon, with the Black Loch to the south.

SLATEFORD, Midlothian.   Map 9, NT 2 7.
Iter. 21, 23.

SLIDDERY, Isle of Arran, Bute.   Map 7, NR 9 2.
Iter. 242.

SLIGACHAN, Isle of Skye, Inverness.   Map 23, NG 4 2.
Situated near the head of Loch Sligachan, on the river of that name, and at the northern extremity of the boggy Glen Sligachan, which extends southwards into the fastnesses of the black *Coolins* (*q.v.*). *Sligachan* is a resort of anglers, and is, above all, famous among mountaineers, who, from here can climb, among other notable hills, *Sgurr nan Gillean*, 3,167 ft., the great pinnacled Cuillin peak which rises majestically almost directly above the village, to the south. The path down Glen Sligachan gives access to various well-known rock peaks in the range. Farther down the glen, a long and poorly-defined path over the Drumhain ridge leads to the spectacular *Loch Coruisk* (*q.v.*) in its deep basin below the Coolins. *Bruach na Frithe*, 3,143 ft. a magnificent view-point, and comparatively easy to climb, is best approached over the Bealach a'Mhaim, south-west of Sligachan. Below the peak lies the gloomy Harta Corrie, in which the Bloody Stone commemorates the final clan battle between the Mac-donalds and Macleods, fought in 1601. To the east of Sligachan, in Lord Macdonald's Forest, are the rounded, red granite peaks of the Red Coolins, or Red Hills, among them *Glamaig*, 2,537 ft. and *Marsco*, 2,414 ft., forming a striking contrast to the precipitous Black Coolins. Two roads diverge from Sligachan away from the loch, that to the north leading through Glen Varragill to *Portree* (*q.v.*), and that to the west proceeding through Glen Drynoch towards Loch Harport. This latter road continues thence towards the Duirinish and Vaternish peninsulas of the island, between which lies the famous castle of *Dunvegan* (*q.v.*). Nearing Loch Harport, a rough and narrow road branches southwards, giving access to *Glenbrittle* (*q.v.*), a well-known climbers' rendezvous in the southern Coolins. The road leading alongside Loch Sligachan from Sligachan follows the coast, and later rounds the head of Loch Ainort, on the way to *Dunan* and *Broadford* (both *q.v.*), providing fine views, especially towards the islands of Raasay and Scalpay. See **Bracadale, Elgol** and **Talisker**. *Iter. 251, 252, 253, 255.*

SLOCHD SUMMIT, Inverness.   Map 25, NH 8 2.
The highest point on the main road linking Strath Spey with Inverness and the north, a height of 1,332 ft. being reached, where both road and railway traverse the lonely Slochd Mor gorge. *Iter. 140, 150, 195.*

SLUG ROAD, Kincardine.   Map 21, NO 7 9.
See **Banchory** and **Stonehaven**. *Iter. 190, 191.*

SMA' GLEN, Perth.   Map 16, NN 8 2 and 9 2.
This beautiful, richly-wooded and rocky glen, which lies on the road linking Crieff with Dunkeld, is threaded by the River Almond. It forms one of the loveliest sights in the Perthshire hills, which rise to more than 2,000 ft. on both sides of the glen. The road through the glen was made originally by General Wade, in 1730. Overlooking the glen, on the eastern side, is *Dun Mor*, 1,520 ft., surmounted by a partly vitrified hill-fort. Below it, between the road and the river, is *Ossian's Stone*, which was moved from its original site by Wade's soldiers, and has been celebrated in verse by Wordsworth. At the northern extremity of the Sma' Glen, at *Newton Bridge* (*q.v.*), the Almond leaves the road, and flows westwards through the delightful valley of Glen Almond, surrounded by lonely hills, dominated by *Ben Chonzie*, 3,048 ft. See **Gilmerton** (Perth) and **Methven**. *Iter. 89, 140, 141, 147.*

SMAILHOLM, Roxburgh. 207.   Map 10, NT 6 3.
Near the church is *Smailholm House*, dating from 1707. To the south-west stands *Smailholm Tower* (A.M.), probably of 16th cent. date, in a romantic and wild situation on a rocky knoll, with fine views all round, especially towards the triple-peaked *Eildon* hills. The land was acquired in the 17th cent. by the Scotts of *Harden* near *Hawick* (*q.v.*), and Sir Walter himself spent some of his childhood years here at the nearby farm of *Sandyknowe* (*q.v.*). Scott later brought Smailholm into the Introduction to the Third Canto of "Marmion," and it also forms the scene of his ballad "Eve of St. John." On *Brotherstone Hill* are the ancient "Brothers' Stones" and the "Cow Stone." *Iter. 7.*

SMOO CAVE, Sutherland.   Map 28, NC 4 6.
A well-known cave, on the wild northern coast of Sutherland, situated in a deep cove in the cliffs, and extending beneath the road. It consists of three chambers, the outermost, which is accessible, being 33 ft. high, 203 ft. long and 130 ft. broad. Sir Walter Scott visited the cave in 1814 and admired it greatly. *Iter. 225.*

SNIZORT CHURCH, Isle of Skye, Inverness.
Map 22, NG 4 5.
On Loch Snizort Beag, an inlet of the larger Loch Snizort. A little to the south-west of the Church, on the right bank of the River Snizort, is the notable chambered cairn of Cairn Liath. See **Uig** (for *Kingsburgh House*). *Iter. 254.*

SOAY, ISLE OF, Inverness.   Map 23, NG 4 1.
See **Loch Scavaig**.

SOCIETY, West Lothian.   Map 17, NT 0 7.
A quaintly named hamlet, perhaps a corruption of "Sea City," on the shores of the Firth of Forth, near Abercorn.

SOLLAS, North Uist, Inverness.   Map 32, NF 7 7.
Iter. 261.

SOLWAY FIRTH, Dumfries, Kirkcudbright.
Map 4, NY 0 5 etc.
The waters of this inlet divide England from Scotland, and the Firth is noted for its rapid tides. *Criffell*, 1,868 ft., dominates the Firth from its position overlooking the Nith estuary, and forms the finest viewpoint for a panoramic view of the Solway, including within its orbit the distant Lake District mountains of Cumberland, to the south.

SORBIE, Wigtown. 145.   Map 2, NX 4 4.
A little to the east stands the ruined *Old Place of Sorbie*, and beyond it, on Garlieston Bay, is the small port of *Garlieston* (*q.v.*). *Iter. 82.*

SORN, Ayr.   Map 8, NS 5 2.
This attractive village, on the River Ayr, has a 17th cent. Church, on the walls of which still hang the jougs; its lofts are reached by external stairs. *Sorn Castle*, dating partly from 1409 and partly from 1795 to 1805, lies a little to the north-west. Alexander Peden, the preacher, was born, in the early 17th cent., at a lonely farm on the moors to the north, and ended his days as a fugitive in a cave in this same district. See **Denholm**. *Iter. 35.*

SOUTHDEAN, Roxburgh. 402.   Map 5, NT 6 0.
A little to the south of the Parish Church, in which a window recalls James Thomson, the author of "Rule Britannia," flows the Jed Water. On the river is the ruined *Souden Kirk*, where the Scottish leaders gathered in 1388 before the battle of Otterburn. The Redeswire Raid of 1575 took place in this parish. (See **Carter Bar**.) Among relics excavated from the 13th cent. Church is a super-altar only 9¼ inches long, bearing 5 incised crosses. *Souden Law*, rising above the river, is crowned by a hill-fort, and there are numerous other prehistoric remains in the vicinity. To the south is the long line of the *Cheviots*, dominated by *Peel Fell*, 1,975 ft. and *Carter Fell*, 1,815 ft. *Iter. 44.*

SOUTHEND, Argyll. 200.   Map 6, NR 6 0.
GOLF. A small resort, with fine seaward views over the North Channel to the coast of Northern Ireland. Off-shore, and separated by the Sanda Sound, lies the small island of Sanda. It is traditionally believed that St. Columba first set foot on Scottish soil near Southend. The narrow road

Smoo Cave, Sutherland. The entrance to the famous cave, one of the three chambers of which is accessible. It is situated east of Durness, off A838

Sma' Glen, Perth. 'Ossian's Stone,' which may have marked his grave, lying between the road and the River Almond. Wordsworth has described it in verse. The stone has been moved from its original site

Smailholm, Roxburgh. The 16th century Smailholm Tower, near which Sir Walter Scott spent part of his childhood. He last came here in 1831, with the painter Turner, who made a sketch of the building

Society, West Lothian. A rare example of a VR letterbox of Queen Victoria's time. The curious name of this tiny village may be a corruption of ' Sea City '

Solway Firth, Dumfries; Kirk-cudbright. The historic 7-foot high Lochmaben Stone, which weighs 10 tons. It stands across fields to the south of Gretna, near the Dumfries-shire shores of the Firth, off an un-classified road

Southdean, Roxburgh. The tablet on the ruined Souden Kirk, near the Jed Water where the Scottish leaders gathered in 1388 before invading England

[For SOUTHEND see following plate
[For SLOCHD SUMMIT see Plate 174

PLATE 152 (facing page 244)

Southerness, Kirkcudbright. The disused lighthouse at Southerness Point. An older name for the village was Satterness

Southend, Argyll. According to local legend these are the footprints of St. Columba, who landed at this point. They are situated near Dunaverty Castle, to the west, off B842

Spinningdale, Sutherland. The remains of the 18th century mill, which is associated with Mackintosh, of water-proof fame

Spean Bridge, Inverness. The Commando Memorial, designed by Scott Sutherland in 1952. They trained in this district during the Second World War. It stands to the north-west, in the angle between A82 and B8004

Springfield, Dumfries. Runaway marriages were once performed here. This Border village, founded by weavers in 1791, stands on the former main road from Carlisle to Glasgow through Longtown. When the new road (A74) by way of Sark Bridge (see Plate 148) was built, the ' marriage trade ' was lost

Spittal of Glenshee, Perth. A memorial Cross by A83, near Glenshee post office, in memory of an American girl killed here in 1906, when the horse pulling her coach bolted. The original Cross was replaced by her brother 41 years later

[For SPYNIE PALACE see following plate
[For SPITTAL OF GLENSHEE see also under GRAMPIANS (Plate 78)

PLATE 153 (facing page 245)

leading westwards to the *Mull of Kintyre* (*q.v.*) passes, within a short distance, the slight remains of *Dunaverty Castle*, where, in 1647, the garrison, to the number of some 300, were put to death by the Covenanters under General Leslie. In 1306, Robert Bruce spent several nights here on his way to Ireland. To the north, the road to *Campbeltown* (*q.v.*) traverses the Conie Glen, and a branch road leads first westwards and then north-westwards to terminate at the head of Glen Breakerie, from which a track leads to the coast. Here, under the slopes of *Cnoc Moy*, 1,426 ft., are caves containing stalactites. See **Machrihanish**. *Iter. 123.*

SOUTHERNESS, Kirkcudbright. Map 3, NX 9 5.
GOLF. A pleasant little resort, also known as *Satterness*, situated off the main road, on a rocky piece of coast, with a no longer used lighthouse on Southerness Point, overlooking Gillfoot Bay, an inlet of the Solway Firth. There are views towards the distant Lake District mountains. *Criffell*, 1,866 ft., rises away to the north, beyond the village of *Kirkbean* (*q.v.*). *Iter. 73.*

SOUTH KESSOCK, Inverness. Map 25, NH 6 4.
Faces the narrows which divide the waters of the Beauly Firth from those of the Inner Moray Firth. A car ferry connects with *North Kessock* (*q.v.*) on the opposite shore. South Kessock stands on the estuary of the River Ness, and is less than two miles distant from the Highland town of *Inverness* (*q.v.*). *Iter. 202, 203.*

SOUTH NESTING BAY, Shetland. Map 33, HU 4 5.
Iter. 270.

SOUTH QUEENSFERRY, West Lothian. Map 17, NT 1 7.
See **Queensferry, South.** *Iter. 17.*

SOUTH RONALDSAY, ISLE OF, Orkney.
Map 33, ND 4 8.
See **Orkney Islands** (South Ronaldsay). *Iter. 266.*

SOUTH UIST, ISLE OF, Inverness. Map 32, NF 7 2 etc.
See **Hebrides, Outer** (South Uist). *Iter. 262.*

SOUTHWICK, Kirkcudbright. Map 3, NX 9 5.
Pleasantly situated off the main road, and on the Southwick Water, which flows into the Solway Firth, with the Mersehead and Barnhourie Sands situated off-shore. In the background, to the north-east, rises *Criffell*, 1,866 ft., a fine viewpoint, with its spur of *Boreland Hill*, 1,632 ft., in the foreground. *Iter. 72, 73.*

SOUTRA HILL, Berwick; East Lothian; Midlothian.
Map 10, NT 4 5.
This well-known viewpoint, at a height of 1,131 ft., on the road leading south-eastwards from Edinburgh towards Lauder, is situated near the meeting point of Berwick, East Lothian and Midlothian. The *Moorfoot* hills rise away to the south-west, while the main ridge of the *Lammermuirs*, their slopes largely given over to sheep, extends north-eastwards towards the distant coast in the neighbourhood of *Cockburnspath* (*q.v.*). There are prehistoric remains in the vicinity of Soutra Hill, and the road itself is on the line of an ancient Pilgrims' Way. This is recalled by the *Soutra Aisle*, the remains of a hospice, or chapel, possibly of 15th cent. date, which stands a little to the south-west, on a lonely moorland road giving access to the valley of the Gala Water. The Romans knew the road across Soutra Hill, and it was used at different times by Edward I, Edward III and James IV of Scotland, among others. The view is very extensive, and stretches from the *Eildon* hills, to the south, away to the *Ochils* beyond the Forth estuary, taking in also *Arthur's Seat*, overlooking the city of Edinburgh. *Iter. 4, 5, 13.*

SPEAN BRIDGE, Inverness. 135. Map 18, NN 2 8.
E.C. Thurs. The bridge, built by Telford in 1819, spans the turbulent River Spean, which flows westwards through a picturesque reach to enter *Loch Lochy* (*q.v.*) near *Gairlochy* (*q.v.*). About **2 m. W.** on this reach is *High Bridge*, 100 ft. above the gorge, the remains of one of the bridges, built in 1736, on General Wade's road, the line of which deviated from the present road through Spean Bridge. The bridge cost £1087 6s. 8d. to construct. A preliminary skirmish took place here, in 1745, three days prior to the raising of Prince Charles Edward's standard at *Glenfinnan* (*q.v.*), this being

1. Commando Memorial.

virtually the commencement of the '45. The last repairs to the bridge took place in 1893, but in 1913 part of it collapsed, and nothing has been done to it since. The road leading south-westwards from Spean Bridge towards Fort William crosses an elevated moorland ridge, giving magnificent views of the *Grey Corries*, 3,858 ft., *Aonach Mor*, 3,999 ft., and the great northern corries of distant *Ben Nevis*, 4,406 ft. (*q.v.*), which are usually streaked with snow as late as June, and sometimes right through the summer. A memorial to the Commandos in the Second World War has been erected to the north-west of Spean Bridge. Eastwards extends Glen Spean, which gives access to *Roy Bridge* (*q.v.*), for the famous "Parallel Roads." See **Wade Roads.** *Iter. 143, 208, 210, 220.*

SPEY BAY, Moray. 200. Map 26, NJ 3 6.
E.C. Wed. GOLF. A small resort, with a shingle beach, some sand at low tide, and bathing, at the mouth of the Spey, the second-longest river in Scotland, famous for its salmon. The best-known reaches are to the south-west, in the foothills of the Cairngorms, where Speyside, or Strath Spey, is at its best around *Grantown-on-Spey* (*q.v.*) and *Aviemore* (*q.v.*). See **Fochabers.** *Iter. 171, 199.*

SPEYSIDE, Inverness. Map 25, NH 8 0 and 26, NJ 1 3 etc.
See **Strath Spey.**

SPINNINGDALE, Sutherland. Map 31, NH 6 8.
On the Dornoch Firth, with the ruins of an 18th cent. mill, associated with Mackintosh, of waterproof fame. See **Creich.** *Iter. 200, 231.*

SPITTAL OF GLENSHEE, Perth. Map 20, NO 1 6.
See **Glenshee.** *Iter. 141, 152, 160, 167, 168.*

SPOTT, East Lothian. Map 10, NT 6 7.
In the modern Church is preserved a beautifully-carved early 18th cent. pulpit, with a sounding-board. The jougs still hang near the door, and near the Church gate is an old watch-house. At Spott Loan is a Witch's Stone, recalling the fact that the last witch to be burnt south of the Forth suffered her fate at Spott. In the vicinity there are various pre-historic remains, among them hut circles and cairns.

SPRINGBURN (Glasgow), Lanark. Map 8, NS 6 6.
Iter. 98, 107.

SPRINGFIELD, Dumfries. Map 4, NY 3 6.
A village founded by a band of weavers in 1791. Runaway marriages were performed here during the 18th cent. in competition with *Gretna* (*q.v.*). The main Glasgow to Carlisle road formerly went through the village and crossed the River Esk at Longtown before the present A74 road by way of *Sark Bridge* (*q.v.*) was constructed in 1830. *Iter. 51, 67.*

SPRINGHOLM, Kirkcudbright. Map 3, NX 8 6.
See **Kirkpatrick Durham.** *Iter. 26, 70.*

SPYNIE PALACE, Moray. Map 26, NJ 2 6.
This ruined palace, situated near the shores of the little Loch Spynie, slightly to the east of the Elgin to Lossiemouth road, was formerly the Castle of the Bishops of Moray. The prominent square tower, known as Davie's Tower, dates from *c.* 1470, and over the main entrance to the courtyard, with its three small towers, are the arms of the early 15th cent. Bishop John Innes. The Church of Spynie, once the

In the map image: FORT AUGUSTUS, INVERNESS, A.82; GAIRLOCHY; B. 8004; Allt Ottan; Ch.; R. Spean; Sta. G.P.O.; Golf Course; FORT WILLIAM, A.82; LOCH LAGGAN, NEWTONMORE, A.86; SPEAN BRIDGE; CROWN COPYRIGHT RESERVED; RB.60

Cathedral of Moray, stood until 1736, but only the church-yard now remains. *Iter. 192.*

STAFFA, ISLE OF, Argyll.　　　　Map 13, **NM 3** 3.
The tiny, uninhabited Inner Hebridean island of *Staffa* is usually visited by steamer from *Oban (q.v.).* It is famous for its basaltic formations and the extraordinary caves, the best known of which is *Fingal's Cave*, 227 ft. long, and 66 ft. in height above the sea at mean tide. The name is derived from the Ossianic giant Finn McCoul, who is credited with the construction of both Staffa and the well-known Giant's Causeway in Northern Ireland. Fingal's Cave can be seen on foot or by boat, and the black pillared walls and columns flanking the aperture are amazingly symmetrical. Mendelssohn's " Hebrides Overture " was inspired by the scenery of the cave. Many famous people have visited Fingal's Cave, and, in 1847, Queen Victoria and the Prince Consort were rowed into it by barge. Other curious caves on the island are the Boat Cave, Mackinnon's Cave, and the remarkable Clam Shell Cave, with its columns suggesting the ribs of an old wooden ship. The last-named is near the usual landing-place, and has in close proximity, the Great Causeway, reminiscent of the Giant's Causeway in Northern Ireland. Staffa was introduced to the world, in 1772, by the explorer Sir Joseph Banks, then on his way to Iceland, while Pennant's " Tour in Scotland," written in 1774, provides the earliest description. To the west of Staffa are the tiny Treshnish Islands, the most southerly of which is known as the " Dutchman's Cap," owing to its curious configuration. See **Iona.**

STAFFIN, Isle of Skye, Inverness.　　　Map 22, **NG 4** 6.
Faces the sandy Staffin Bay, in the Trotternish peninsula, with Staffin Island off-shore, and has notable cliffs of basalt. A little to the south-east, off the Portree road, is the well-known *Kilt Rock*, best seen from a boat, and farther south still, where the road nears the seashore, the waters of Loch Mealt pour into the sea as a waterfall. The road leading northwards from the village divides into two branches, one continuing along the coast towards *Flodigarry (q.v.),* and the other, narrow and steep, climbing to nearly 900 ft., with a hairpin bend below the fantastic rock masses of the *Quiraing (q.v.).* This road provides splendid views of Staffin Bay, on the way to *Uig (q.v.).* A hydro-electric scheme, inaugurated in 1952, operates along the road to Portree. *Iter. 254.*

STAIR, Ayr.　　　　　　　　　　Map 8, **NS 4** 2.
Stair House, a picturesque old building, situated in a bend of the River Ayr, dates from the early 17th cent., and has been modernised. *Iter. 85.*

STANLEY, Perth. 1,305.　　　　　Map 17, **NO 1** 3.
Stands on the River Tay, in the *Strathmore (q.v.)* valley. On the river, a little to the north-east, are the Campsie Linn rapids. Off a by-road, 4½ m. N.E., near the Tay, are remains of the rectangular enclosure of *Kinclaven Castle,* said to have been destroyed in 1336. *Iter. 148.*

STAXIGOE, Caithness.　　　　　　Map 30, **ND 3** 5.
A fishing village having a small harbour, situated on a rocky stretch of coast between the Tails of Elzie and Silkey Head, with the more prominent Noss Head to the north, overlooking Sinclair's Bay. The airport for *Wick (q.v.)* lies a little to the south-west of Staxigoe.

STENHOUSEMUIR, Stirling. 4,601.　　Map 16, **NS 8** 8.
See **Falkirk.**

STENNESS, Orkney.　　　　　　　Map 33, **HY 3** 1.
See **Orkney Islands** (Mainland). *Iter. 263, 264.*

STENTON, East Lothian.　　　　　Map 10, **NT 6** 7.
An attractive village, with the 14th cent. Rood well, topped by a cardinal's hat. The medieval Wool Stone, used formerly for the weighing of wool at Stenton Fair, stands on the green. *Biel*, a fine old mansion, now modernised, with 16th cent. terraced gardens, lies to the north-east.

STEPPS, Lanark. 2,897.　　　　　Map 8, **NS 6** 6.
The small Frankfield Loch lies to the south-west. *Iter. 17, 97, 99.*

STEVENSTON, Ayr. 9,812. SB.　　　Map 8, **NS 2** 4.
E.C. Wed. GOLF. A town of ancient foundation, overlooking Irvine Bay in the Firth of Clyde. There are coal-mines, chemical works, and an explosives factory in the neighbourhood. *Iter. 57, 63, 66, 69, 88.*

STEWARTON, Argyll.　　　　　　Map 6, **NR 6** 1.
Iter. 123.

STEWARTON, Ayr. 3,378. SB.　　　Map 8, **NS 4** 4.
E.C. Wed. M.D. Thurs. The town stands on the Annick Water, and is noted for its woollen manufactures. See **Kilmaurs.** *Iter. 62.*

STEWARTRY, THE, Kirkcudbright.
　　　　　　　　Map 2, **NX 4** 7 and 3, **NX 8** 7.
This name is sometimes applied to Kirkcudbright, as an alternative to the title of county. It is derived from the fact that the lordship of the Balliols, when it was taken away from them, was placed under the jurisdiction of a Royal Steward, an office which was held by the family of Maxwell. between 1526 and 1747. The Stewartry, together with the adjacent county of Wigtown, comprises the district known as *Galloway (q.v.).*

STIRLING, Stirling. 26,947. LB.　　Map 16, **NS 7** 9.
E.C. Wed. M.D. Thurs. GOLF. A famous old Royal Burgh, known as the " Gateway to the Highlands," and situated on one of the numerous loops of the River Forth. Stirling Bridge spans the river at the north end of the town, and close to it is the Old Bridge (A.M.), dating from c. 1400, and still in use for foot passengers. Remains of the original burgh gate are still to be seen at one end of the structure. This bridge was for centuries of great strategic importance as the sole exit to the north. Until the opening of the new bridge at *Kincardine-on-Forth (q.v.),* lower down the Forth, Stirling was the last place where the river could be crossed before the estuary widens. The battle of Stirling Bridge, fought in 1297, in which Wallace defeated the Earl of Surrey, is thought to have taken place near a now-vanished wooden bridge, about a mile upstream.

The history of Stirling is bound up with its great Castle (A.M.), in which several of the early Scottish Kings died. Wallace recaptured the Castle from the English in 1297, but Edward I retook it after a siege in 1304. Later, Stirling became a favourite Royal residence, and within its walls were born James II, in 1430, and James V, in 1512, while both Mary, Queen of Scots, and James VI spent some years in the Palace. General Monk took the Castle, in 1651, but Prince Charles Edward failed to capture it in 1746. Stirling Castle stands in a commanding situation, but has long been used as a barracks, though restoration work is in progress. James III built several of the older towers in the 15th cent., and the splendid Renaissance buildings of the Palace date from the following century. The Parliament Hall, 125 ft. long, abuts on the Inner Court, and on the north side of the Court is the Chapel Royal, rebuilt in 1594 by James VI, and preserving early 17th cent. wall-paintings. In the historic, restored Douglas Room are kept various interesting relics. The hereditary keeper of Stirling Castle is the Earl of Mar and Kellie. The Castle is open weekdays, 10 to 4 or 7; Sun., 1 to 4 or 7. (See note page 90). The view from the 420-ft. high Queen Victoria's look-out is famous, and extends well into the Highlands. On the Esplanade is a statue of Bruce, and the Ladies' Rock is another good view-point, overlooking the King's Knot (A.M.) and King's Garden. Queen Mary's look-out has the inscription: M.R. 1561.

In the town are several 17th cent. houses; the fine Tol-booth, dating from 1701; the old Mercat Cross, with a modern shaft; and *Darnley's House*, associated with James VI and his son. The uncompleted Renaissance structure known as *Mar's Wark* (A.M.) stands in Broad Street, and dates from 1570, retaining several curious inscriptions. *Argyll's Lodging* (A.M.), one of the most noteworthy of its period in Scotland, was built by the Earl of Stirling, in 1630, and has for many years been used as a military hospital. The 17th cent. Guildhall, or *Cowane's* Hospital retains old relics and bears a statue of John Cowane, the founder, who

Spynie Palace, Moray. The ruined 15th century Palace, once a castle of the Bishops of Moray. It stands near Loch Spynie, to the east of A941

Stenton, East Lothian. The ancient Rood Well, surmounted by a cardinal's hat, and associated with the Abbey at Melrose

Stenton, East Lothian. The Wool Stone, formerly used in the weighing of wool at Stenton Fair. In the background is an old dovecote, formerly the tower of a church

Stewartry, Kirkcudbright. Maclellan's Castle, at Kirkcudbright, dating from 1582, and built by Sir Thomas Maclellan of Bombie, a former Provost of the town. The Stewartry is a name applied to the county, recalling its former jurisdiction by a Royal Steward

Stirling, Stirling. The Castle, dating mainly from the 15th and 16th centuries, and long used as a barracks. James II and James V were born here, in 1430 and 1512 respectively

Stirling, Stirling. The old Mercat Cross, which has a modern shaft

[For STIRLING see also following plate

PLATE 134 (facing page 246)

Stirling, Stirling. The 16th or 17th century Darnley's House, perhaps the nursery of James VI and his son Prince Henry, but more probably associated with the Erskines of Gogar. It was reconstructed in 1957

Stirling, Stirling. The Old Bridge of c. 1400, for many years famous as the sole 'Gateway to the Highlands.' One of the arches was blown up in 1745 to prevent the entry of the Highlanders

Stobo, Peebles. The ancient 'jougs,' or iron collar for wrongdoers, which is preserved outside the Church

Stirling, Stirling. The entrance to Argyll's Lodging, built in the 16th and 17th centuries, and used as a military hospital since 1799

Stirling, Stirling. The Wallace Monument, which was erected in 1869 at a cost of £16,000. It stands near Causewayhead, to the north-east of the town, off A997

Stirling, Stirling. Mar's Wark, dated 1570 and never completed, the Town House of the Regent Mar. It has the Royal Arms above the main entrance

[For STOBO see also under TWEEDDALE (Plate 166

PLATE 155 (facing page 247)

died in 1634. In the *Smith* Institute are pictures and relics of interest. The fine Church of the *Holy Rude* is mainly of two dates. The nave was commenced c. 1414, and retains a notable oak roof, while the choir dates from between 1507 and 1520, and has, as its outstanding feature, a remarkable five-sided apse. The square 90-ft. high battlemented tower still shows the shot marks made by guns in the 1651 siege. In 1543, Mary, Queen of Scots was crowned in the Church at the age of 9 months, and 24 years later James VI, when a year old, was crowned in the choir, the sermon being preached by John Knox. Between 1656 and 1936 the nave and choir were used as separate Churches. In the former tilting ground, now a cemetery, between the Castle and the Church, is a marble representation, in a glass case, of the Covenanting Wigtown Martyrs (See **Wigtown**), who, in 1685, were tied to stakes and drowned by the incoming waters of the Solway Firth.

A little beyond Stirling Bridge is *Causewayhead*, overlooked by the 362-ft. high Abbey Craig, which is crowned by the well-known 220-ft. high *Wallace Monument*, erected in 1869 at a cost of £16,000, containing Wallace's sword, and providing an extensive view. About a mile to the south, near one of the bends of the Forth, in the fertile district known as the "Links of the Forth," are the rather scanty remains of *Cambuskenneth Abbey* (A.M.), founded in 1147, and retaining a fine 14th cent. detached tower, which can be ascended for the view. James III and his Queen were buried before the high altar in 1488, and Queen Victoria erected a monument to them, in 1864. A Scottish Parliament, under Bruce, was held at Cambuskenneth, in 1326. See **Bannockburn, Bridge of Allan, Dundrennan** and **St. Ninian's**. *Iter. 50, 87, 95, 96, 99, 108, 111, 112, 133, 134, 135, 136, 137, 138, 139, 140, 141, 142, 144.*

STOBHALL, Perth. Map 17, NO 1 3. Here, situated on a ridge, on the east bank of the River Tay, is a picturesque and well-preserved group of buildings overlooking a courtyard, the ancient home of the Drummonds (A.M.). The larger house consists of a chapel and tower dating from 1578, the former retaining the old Holy Water stoup, the aumbry, with its original door, and a painted ceiling, above which is a loft. Millais, the painter, lived for a time in the house. Nearby is the dower-house, dated 1761, and attached to it is the gateway, with its heraldic panel, which leads to the whole enclosure. To the south-west of Stobhall are the Campsie Linn rapids.

STOBO, Peebles. 237. Map 9, NT 1 3. The small, restored Church of *Stobo*, overlooking the River Tweed, is of Norman date, with additions in the 16th and 17th cents. The barrel-vaulted porch enshrines a 13th cent. doorway, and the jougs still hang by the porch. *Stobo Castle*, a little to the south-west, is a modern building. On the opposite bank of the river are the remarkable *Dawyck Woods*, some of the best-known in the country, and the place where the larch was introduced into Scotland, in 1725. There are also Douglas firs, a pinetum and a wealth of Chinese rhododendrons and other shrubs and trees. The lime avenue was mentioned in an early novel by John Buchan. *Iter. 24.*

STOBS CAMP, Roxburgh. Map 5, NT 5 0. *Iter. 31.*

STIRLING

Scale
0   R.B.60   ½m

CROWN COPYRIGHT RESERVED   PUBLISHED BY THE AUTOMOBILE ASSOCIATION

Argyll's Lodging		**6.**	King's Knot (A.M.) and	Queen Mary's Look-out	**2.**
Bruce's Statue	**4.**		Garden **10.**	Queen Victoria's Look-out	**3.**
Castle	**1.**		Ladies' Rock **5.**	Smith Institute	**14.**
Guildhall (Cowane's			Mar's Wark **7.**	Tolbooth and Mercat	
Hospital)	**9.**		Municipal Buildings.	Cross	**15.**
High Church or Church			Information Bureau **11.**	Wallace Monument,	
of the Holy Rude			Old Bridge **13.**	Causewayhead	**12.**
		8.			

Field of Bannockburn—to the south by exit A.80.

STOCKIEMUIR, Stirling. Map 15, NS 4 8. From this elevated stretch of moorland a wide panoramic view can be obtained, and glimpses of *Loch Lomond* (q.v.), away to the north-west, are sometimes possible. A little to the west, on the slopes of *Auchineden Hill*, 1,171 ft., is the curious chasm known as the *Whangie*. *Iter. 104, 106.*

STOER, Sutherland. Map 28, NC 0 2. A remote little North-West Highland village, on the picturesque, narrow and hilly road linking *Lochinver* (q.v.) with *Kylesku* (q.v.). There is bathing from the sandy shores of the Bay of Stoer. The neighbourhood is one of innumerable tiny lochans, many of which provide good fishing. From the low hill of *Cnoc Poll*, to the north-west, the view ranges inland towards the strange, isolated Sutherland mountains of red Torridon sandstone, from *Quinag*, 2,653 ft., to *Canisp*, 2,779 ft., and the double-peaked *Suilven*, 2,399 ft. Beyond Cnoc Poll is the Stoer peninsula, terminated by Rhu Stoer, and the Point of Stoer, between which is situated the rock pillar known as the " Old Man of Stoer." To the south-east of Stoer, off the Lochinver road, is the sandy Achmelvich Bay, near which is the rocky inlet of Loch Roe. See **Drumbeg.** *Iter. 227.*

STONEHAVEN, Kincardine. 4,461. SB.

Map 21, NO **8** 8.
E.C. Wed. M.D. Thurs. GOLF. A fishing port and resort, with a bathing beach of stone and shingle, and much fine cliff scenery, both to the north and south. The Carron Water divides the new town from the old and is joined, near its outflow, by the Cowie Water, flowing from the lonely

STONEHAVEN
Scale

1. Mercat Cross and 18th cent. Steeple.   2. Town Hall.

hills to the west through an attractive glen. On the quay is a 16th cent. Tolbooth, formerly a storehouse of the Earls Marischal, and used later until 1784 as a prison. Local Episcopal ministers were lodged here in 1745. The building is to become a Folk Museum. Near the harbour stands the Mercat Cross, and the 18th cent. Steeple, where the Old Pretender was proclaimed king in 1715. At Hogmanay, fireballs made from tallowed rope are carried through the town. The road leading north-westwards from Stonehaven over the hills to *Banchory* (*q.v.*) is known as the *Slug Road.* It rises to nearly 800 ft., at one point. To the north of this road, within 4 miles of Stonehaven, is the Roman Camp of *Raedykes.* See **Cowie, Dunnottar Castle** and **Muchalls.** *Iter. 151, 155, 156, 190, 191.*

STONEHOUSE, Lanark.   Map 9, NS **7** 4.
Iter. 20, 29, 69.

STONES OF CLAVA, Inverness.   Map 25, NH **7** 4.
See **Culloden.**

STONEYKIRK, Wigtown.   Map 2, NX **0** 5.
Iter. 82.

STORNOWAY, Isle of Lewis,   Map 32, NB **4** 3.
  Ross and Cromarty. 5,245. SB.
See **Hebrides, Outer** (Lewis). *Iter. 256 to 260.*

STORR, THE, Isle of Skye, Inverness.   Map 22, NG **4** 5.
The peninsula of Trotternish, which extends northwards from *Portree* (*q.v.*), has for its backbone a 10-mile long ridge, averaging some 2,000 ft. in height, precipitous in many places to the east, and dominated by the lofty *Storr,* 2,360 ft. high, with its wild crags. This fine viewpoint looks southwards to the great *Coolins* (*q.v.*) range; westwards over the Minch to the Outer Hebrides; and eastwards towards the Applecross mountains on the mainland. Below the Storr stands the well-known *Old Man of Storr,* a 160-ft. high detached pinnacle of rock, forming a notable landmark. The hilly road linking Portree with the northern extremity of the island passes below the Storr cliffs, and provides splendid views of the steep contours and varied forms of the whole range from many places. On the Portree road lie the Storr Lochs, which have been harnessed to a hydro-electric scheme, inaugurated in 1952. *Iter. 254.*

STOW, Midlothian. 462.   Map 10, NT **4** 4.
E.C. Thurs. A delightful village, situated on the Gala Water, with a fine pack-horse bridge, dating from 1655. The old Church is in ruins. The modern Church has a 140-ft. high spire. In the vicinity, once known as the " Stow of Wedale," the Saxons are said to have been routed by King Arthur, who founded a Church as a thanksgiving. A delightful road proceeds eastwards from Stow, crossing the moors at a height of over 1,100 ft., before descending into Lauderdale, and reaching the small town of *Lauder* (*q.v.*). To the west of Stow rise the lonely *Moorfoot* hills. *Windlestraw Law,* attaining 2,161 ft., is situated a little farther to the south, near the point where the counties of Midlothian, Peebles and Selkirk meet. *Iter. 9, 11.*

STRACHAN, Kincardine. 546.   Map 21, NO **6** 9.
E.C. Wed. On the Water of Feugh, near its junction with the Water of Dye, flowing along the long valley of Glen Dye, which is traversed by the well-known road climbing over the *Cairn o' Mounth* (*q.v.*). Away to the west is the extensive Forest of Birse, extending to the lonely hills on the borders of Aberdeen and Angus. Some 12 miles west of Strachan, on a by-road, stands the restored, partly 16th cent. Aberdeenshire Castle of *Birse,* a former home of the Gordons of Clunie. To the south-east of Strachan rises *Kerloch,* 1,747 ft. See **Feughside Inn.** *Iter. 163, 174.*

STRACHUR, Argyll. 580.   Map 14, NN **0** 0.
E.C. Wed. A small resort near *Loch Fyne* (*q.v.*), once visited by Chopin, and situated in the *Cowal* (*q.v.*) peninsula, with a pier about a mile to the north-west. The road leading inland from Strachur gives access to *Loch Eck* (*q.v.*), a long and narrow sheet of water surrounded by hills. The highest of these are *Beinn Bheula,* 2,557 ft., to the north-east, and *Beinn Mhor,* 2,433 ft., overlooking the western shores of the loch. See **Inveraray** and **St. Catherine's.** *Iter. 102, 137.*

STRACHUR PIER, Argyll.   Map 14, NN **0** 0.
See **Strachur.** *Iter. 102, 103, 137.*

STRAITON, Ayr. 1,080.   Map 8, NS **3** 0.
An attractive *Carrick* (*q.v.*) village, on the Water of Girvan, with a pre-Reformation aisle in its restored Church. To the west, near the river, is the old mansion of *Blairquhan.* A narrow and hilly road leads southwards, climbing over the moors towards *Rowantree* (*q.v.*), and attains a height of 1,421 ft., with views of *Shalloch on Minnoch,* 2,520 ft., to the south-east, beyond which lies the remote Loch Macaterick. To the east of Straiton, off the Dalmellington road, is the glen of the Lambdoughty Burn, in which are several waterfalls. One of these is called the Rossetti Linn, having been much admired by Dante Gabriel Rossetti when staying at *Penkill Castle,* near *Dailly* (*q.v.*). *Iter. 49, 74, 79.*

STRAITON, Midlothian.   Map 10, NT **2** 6.
Iter. 10, 24.

STRANRAER, Wigtown. 8,895. SB.   Map 2, NX **0** 6.
E.C. Wed. M.D. Fri. GOLF. An important port for the mail-steamers to Larne in Northern Ireland, having taken the place of *Portpatrick,* which is too much exposed to gales. Stranraer is situated in the Rhinns of Galloway at the head of Loch Ryan, the Reregonius Sinus of the Romans, and the

Stones of Clava, Inverness. Standing stones and burial cairns (N.T. Scot.), dating from the Bronze Age, 1800–1500 B.C. They stand 1 mile south-east of the battlefield of Culloden, across the River Nairn

Stow, Midlothian. The pack-horse bridge spanning the Gala Water, which was built in 1655

Strachur, Argyll. The upper reaches of Loch Fyne, which in the vicinity is said to attain its greatest depth of some 82 fathoms

Stranraer, Wigtown. The 16th to 17th century Castle, which at one period was used as the gaol

Stranraer, Wigtown. The North-West Castle, once the home of Sir John Ross, the Arctic explorer (1777–1856)

PLATE 156 (facing page 248)

Strathdon, Aberdeen. Poldullie Bridge, which spans the River Don, to the south-west

Strathaven, Lanark. Strathaven, or Avondale Castle, a 15th century ruin, last occupied by the Duchess of Hamilton in the 17th century

Strathmiglo, Fife. The Tolbooth of 1734, built from the stones of a former castle owned by Sir William Scott of Balwearie

Strathmore, Angus; Perth. The cottage at Kirriemuir, Angus, known as 'A Window in Thrums,' associated with Sir James Barrie. Strathmore lies between the Lower Grampian and the Sidlaw Hills

Strathdon, Aberdeen. The Church, with its tall spire, a landmark for many miles around

Strathmore, Angus; Perth. Huntingtower, formerly Ruthven Castle, 15th century, where the historic 'Ruthven Raid' of 1582 took place, resulting in the putting to death of the Earl of Gowrie. It stands on A85, west of Perth, at the south-west extremity of Strathmore

PLATE 157 (facing page 249)

R.B.60

A.A. PORT OFFICE, STRANRAER HARBOUR STATION. Tel. 570.
1. Castle.   2. North West Castle House.   3. Information Bureau.

sea passage from here to Larne is only 35 miles in length. *Stranraer Castle* stands in the centre of the town, and is probably of early 16th cent. date, with some 17th cent. reconstruction, having long been used as a gaol. Claverhouse is said to have lived there, in 1682, when rounding up the Covenanters. Near the pier is a house called the *North West Castle*, formerly the home of Sir John Ross, the Arctic explorer. Stranraer was the home port of the ill-fated cross-channel steamer "Princess Victoria," lost in the great storm of early January, 1953. See **Castle Kennedy** (also for airport), **Innermessan, Kirkcolm** and **Portpatrick.** *Iter.* 25, 26, 55, 82, 83, 84.

STRATHAN, Sutherland.   Map 29, **NC 0** 2.
Iter. 226.

STRATHAVEN, Lanark. 4,288.   Map 8, **NS 7** 4.
E.C. Wed. M.D. Tues.   GOLF. A weaving town, situated at a height of over 600 ft. on the edge of an extensive moorland district stretching away to the west. The Powmillon Burn, spanned here by an ancient bridge, threads its way through the town on its way to join the Avon Water, to the south-east. The remains of *Strathaven*, or *Avondale Castle*, dating from the 15th cent., overlook the burn. To the west of Strathaven, on A71, stands the house of *Lauder Ha'*, formerly the home of Sir Harry Lauder, who was born, in 1870, at *Portobello* (q.v.). *Iter.* 20, 29, 56, 68, 69, 87.

STRATHBLANE, Stirling. 1,161.   Map 15, **NS 5** 7.
GOLF. This small resort, on the Blane Water, has calico-printing works. It is situated at the foot of the *Strathblane* hills and the loftier *Campsie Fells*, in which *Earl's Seat*, 1,896 ft., is the highest point of the range. About a mile to the east, on the Ballagan Burn, are the falls known as the Spout of Ballagan. **2 m. N.W.,** off the Killearn road, stands the partly 15th cent. *Duntreath Castle*, in which the medieval stocks and dungeons are preserved. See **Campsie Glen, Milngavie** and **Stockiemuir.** *Iter.* 105, 108, 115.

STRATHCARRON STATION, Ross and Cromarty.
Map 24, **NG 9** 4.
Lies immediately to the south of the road from Inverness to *Kyle of Lochalsh* (q.v.), near the north-eastern extremity of Loch Carron, and is overlooked by the lonely hills of *Attadale Forest*, in which *Beinn Dronaig* attains 2,612 ft. See **Lochcarron.** *Iter.* 221, 222, 223.

STRATHDON, Aberdeen. 747.   Map 26, **NJ 3** 1.
Here, the River Don, noted for fishing, is joined by the Water of Nochty, flowing from the *Ladder Hills*. The spire of the Church is a local landmark, and to the south-west of the village the Don is spanned by *Poldullie Bridge*, dating from 1715. There is some attractive river and hill scenery in the neighbourhood. The Lonach Highland Gathering is usually held at Strathdon in mid-August. 1½ m. E.S.E., near the Don, are slight remains of the 16th cent., but never completed *Colquhonnie Castle*. See **Cock Bridge** and **Glenkindie.** *Iter.* 141, 176, 191.

STRATHFARRAR, Inverness.   Map 24, **NH 2** 3.
See **Struy Bridge.**   and **3** 3.

STRATH GLASS, Inverness.   Map 24, **NH 3** 3.
See **Cannich** and **Struy Bridge.** *Iter.* 206, 210.

STRATHKANAIRD, Ross and Cromarty.
Map 29, **NC 1** 0.
In the valley of Strath Kanaird, between the remote Rhidorroch Forest and the *Coigach* hills. The valley is traversed by the picturesque Ullapool to Inchnadamph road, which, to the south-west of Strathkanaird, goes by the shores of Loch Kanaird, with Isle Martin lying offshore. On the north side of the estuary of the Kanaird River, on the coast, stands *Dun Canna*, a ruined broch, with *Ben More Coigach*, 2,438 ft., rising in the background, and dominating the Coigach district. *Iter.* 224, 225, 226.

STRATHLACHLAN, Argyll.   Map 14, **NS 0** 9.
On Lachlan Bay, a small inlet of *Loch Fyne* (q.v.), stands *Castle Lachlan*, in its wooded setting. **2 m. N.E.,** a road climbs over the hills of *Cowal* (q.v.) to descend towards *Glendaruel* (q.v.), in the long and pleasant glen of that name. *Iter.* 103.

STRATHMIGLO, Fife.   Map 17, **NO 2** 1.
Here is a Tolbooth dating from 1734. To the south rise the *Lomond* hills. See **Falkland.** *Iter.* 130, 136.

STRATHMORE, Angus; Perth.   Map 20, **NO 1** 3 etc.
A pleasant, fertile valley, lying to the south of the *Grampian* (q.v.) foothills, and north of the *Sidlaw* hills. It extends from south-west to north-east across the area, at first

1. Castle ruins.

249

parallel with the River Tay, and later with its tributary, the Isla. The greater part of Strathmore is in Perthshire, commencing a little to the west of Perth, but it stretches also into Angus, in the direction of *Kirriemuir* (*q.v.*), where it is known as the Howe of Angus.

STRATH NAVER, Sutherland.　Map 30, **NC 6** 4 etc.
Situated in the long and lonely valley of Strath Naver, largely de-populated in the early 19th cent., and stretching from *Altnaharra* (*q.v.*), on Loch Naver, to the coast at *Bettyhill* (*q.v.*), where the River Naver flows into the sea. The river was known to Ptolemy, the early historian from Alexandria, and is famous for its salmon. There are many prehistoric remains in the valley. See **Syre Church.** *Iter.* 232, 235.

STRATHPEFFER, Ross and Cromarty.　Map 25, **NH 4** 5.
E.C. Thurs. GOLF. This well-known Highland spa and resort stands in a sheltered and wooded setting to the north

1. Eagle Pillar.

of Strath Conon. There are chalybeate springs here, and as a touring centre Strathpeffer is convenient for the Moray Firth district, and for explorations of the beautiful lochs and mountains of *Wester Ross* (*q.v.*). *Ben Wyvis*, 3,429 ft., the highest mountain in Easter Ross, rises to the north, and is a notable landmark for

many miles around. A Clan battle was fought at Strathpeffer in 1478. An upright stone, bearing incised Pictish symbols, stands near the old pump. To the north of the village is the turreted *Castle Leod*, dating from 1616, with later alterations. Eastwards of Strathpeffer is the ridge of *Druim Chat*, on which is situated the vitrified fort of *Knock Farril*. See **Achilty Inn, Dingwall, Garve** and **Rogie Falls.** *Iter.* 201, 206.

STRATH SPEY, Inverness.　Map 25, **NH 8** 0
and 26, **NJ 1** 3 etc.
The name Strath Spey, or Speyside, is applied to the wide lower valley of this rapid-flowing salmon river. The Upper Spey rises near the *Monadhliath* mountains, and the well-wooded lower valley extends north-eastwards between that range and the lofty *Cairngorms*. The river then flows along the Banff and Moray border to reach the sea at *Spey Bay* (*q.v.*). See **Aviemore, Boat of Garten** and **Grantown-on-Spey.**

STRATHY, Sutherland.　Map 30, **NC 8** 6.
Lies a little inland from Strathy Bay, to the west of which stretches a peninsula terminated by the headland of Strathy Point, with its multitude of caves. Strathy itself has flagstone quarries, and on the west side of the Strathy Water are prehistoric remains, including hut circles and mounds. *Iter.* 232, 234, 240.

STRATHYRE, Perth. 107.　Map 15, **NN 5** 1.
E.C. Thurs. This village, noted as a summer resort and centre for walks in the surrounding Perthshire hills, lies in the heart of the country so graphically described by Scott in his " Lady of the Lake " and " Legend of Montrose." A large new forest has been planted in the vicinity. The Balvaig Burn flows through the village, and is crossed by an old bridge. Immediately to the south, in a setting of hills, is the narrow Loch Lubnaig, noted for fishing, its wooded eastern shore traversed by the road leading southwards towards the Pass of Leny, with its falls, to near *Callander* (*q.v.*). To the south-west is *Ben Vane*, 2,685 ft., and to the east rise *Stuc a'Chroin*, 3,189 ft., and *Ben Vorlich*,

3,224 ft. At the southern end of the loch is a tiny churchyard on the site of *St. Bride's* Chapel, and across the water rises *Ben Ledi*, 2,875 ft. See **Balquhidder.** *Iter.* 107, 111, 139, 141, 142, 144.

STRICHEN, Aberdeen. 1,040.　Map 27, **NJ 9** 5.
E.C. Wed. Lies to the south-west of *Mormond Hill*, 749 ft., the sole eminence in a large expanse of the flat *Buchan* (*q.v.*) country, and forming a prominent local landmark. On the southern slopes of this hill is carved a White Horse, dating from 1700, and on the overgrown eastern slopes is a Stag, carved in 1870. *Iter.* 186, 197.

STROMA, Caithness.　Map 30, **ND 3** 7.
A small island, with a rapidly-diminishing population, situated in the turbulent Pentland Firth between the mainland and the Orkneys. To the east lies the even smaller Pentland Skerries group.

STROME, Ross and Cromarty.　Map 23, **NG 8** 3.
Situated on the narrows of Loch Carron, here crossed by a

1. Castle ruins (North Strome).

car ferry. Overlooking the loch, on the north side, are slight remains of *Strome Castle* (N.T. Scot.), the building having been destroyed after a long siege, in 1609. There are fine views from here of the distant *Coolins* (*q.v.*) in Skye. The road leading towards the ferry on the north side was constructed by Telford, he and the poet Southey being

the first to travel over the road in a wheeled carriage, in 1819. On the south side, the road first climbs steeply, before descending to Strath Ascaig, and then crossing the hills towards *Auchtertyre* (*q.v.*). See **Lochcarron** and **Plockton.** *Iter.* 219, 220, 221, 222.

STROMNESS, Orkney. 1,483. SB.　Map 33, **HY 2** 0.
See **Orkney Islands** (Mainland). *Iter.* 263.

STRONACHLACHAR, Stirling.　Map 15, **NN 4** 1.
Here is a steamer pier on *Loch Katrine* (*q.v.*), and a short length of road connects by way of Loch Arklet with *Inversnaid* (*q.v.*) on *Loch Lomond* (*q.v.*). Another road leads southwards towards the shores of Loch Chon, eventually reaching *Aberfoyle* (*q.v.*). A path leading north-westwards from Stronachlachar gives access to the lonely house of *Glengyle*, in Glen Gyle, on the Perthshire border, the birthplace, in 1671, of the famous freebooter, Rob Roy, immortalised by Scott. See **Balquhidder** and **Trossachs.** *Iter.* 105.

STRONE, Argyll.　Map 14, **NS 1** 8.
GOLF. A small holiday resort at the mouth of Loch Long, facing the Firth of Clyde, with a pier at Strone Point, at the eastern extremity of the Holy Loch, and looking across to *Hunter's Quay* (*q.v.*). Almost adjoining Strone, to the north, is the little resort of *Blairmore*, also with a pier. See **Ardentinny** and **Kilmun.** *Iter.* 102.

STRONSAY, ISLE OF, Orkney.　Map 33, **HY 6** 2.
See **Orkney Islands** (Stronsay).

STRONTIAN, Argyll.　Map 12, **NM 8** 6.
Picturesquely situated at the eastern end of *Loch Sunart* (*q.v.*), a long and beautiful sea loch, with richly wooded scenery farther towards the west, on the road to *Salen* (*q.v.*). The loch separates the districts of Sunart and Ardnamurchan, on the north side, from Morven, on the south side. The Strontian River flows through the village into the loch, and in the glen to the north are deserted lead-mines, which once

Strath Spey, Inverness. The remains of Castle Roy, an old stronghold of the Comyns, Lords of Badenoch, which stands a little to the north-east of Nethybridge, on B970

Strathpeffer, Ross and Cromarty. An upright stone, bearing incised Pictish symbols. In a clan battle here of 1478, the Munros were defeated by the Mackenzies

Strathyre, Perth. The old bridge over the Balvaig Burn

Strichen, Aberdeen. A White Horse, carved in 1700, and said to be the only one in Scotland, on the southern slopes of Mormond Hill. On the eastern slopes is a carving of a stag (1870), now much overgrown. The hill rises some 2 miles north-east of Strichen

Strome, Ross and Cromarty. The remains of the Castle (N.T. Scot.), destroyed in 1602. It overlooks the narrows of Loch Carron at North Strome

PLATE 158 (facing page 250)

Struie Hill, Ross and Cromarty. The north-westerly panorama from the A.A. viewpoint, at an altitude of about 700 feet, giving a distant glimpse of Ben More Assynt, the highest mountain in Sutherland

Struan, Perth. The picturesque Falls of Bruar, in Glen Bruar, off A9, to the east

Swanston, Midlothian. A village in which Robert Louis Stevenson spent some of the holidays of his youth between 1870 and 1880

Symington, Ayr. Round-headed Norman windows of 12th century date in the chancel of the old Church, much reconstructed

Tain, Ross and Cromarty. The 17th century Tolbooth, which has a conical spire

Tantallon Castle, East Lothian. The 14th century and later Douglas stronghold, which General Monk dismantled in 1651. It figures in Sir Walter Scott's 'Marmion,' and stands 3 miles east of North Berwick, off A198

PLATE 159 (facing page 251)

[For TARBERT see following plate

formed an important feature of the locality. Among other rare minerals found at the time was that which received the name of strontianite. The name of Scotstown, by which one of the settlements in the glen is known, recalls the miners who came here in the 18th cent. from the Lowlands. From the glen it is possible to climb the prominent peak of *Ben Resipol*, 2,774 ft., which rises to the north-west of Strontian, and provides a magnificent view from the summit, notably over the waters of *Loch Shiel* (*q.v.*), and southwards across the Morven district. *Iter. 216, 217.*

STRUAN, Perth. Map 19, NN 8 6.
Lies at the junction of Glen Garry with Glen Erochy, and is divided by the River Garry, with its noted falls and salmon leap, from *Calvine*, which stands on the main Perth to Inverness highway. A little to the east of Calvine, and situated actually in Glen Bruar, are the well-known Falls of Bruar, the upper fall being a short distance up the glen, which is dominated to the east by *Beinn Dearg*, 3,304 ft., in the Forest of Atholl hills. A path leads up this glen by means of which long-distance walkers can traverse the lonely hills of the wild Gaick Forest, and after crossing the remote Minigaig Pass eventually reach *Kingussie* (*q.v.*) in the Spey valley. The road which leads westwards from Struan through Glen Erochy, climbing to a height of over 1,000 ft., gives access to the Tummel valley and *Kinloch Rannoch* (*q.v.*). The Clan Donnachie is associated with Struan. See **Blair Atholl**. *Iter. 147, 149.*

STRUIE HILL, Ross and Cromarty. (A.A. viewpoint.)
Map 31, NH 6 8.
A lofty height overlooking the waters of Dornoch Firth.

STRUY BRIDGE, Inverness. Map 24, NH 4 4.
On the River Farrar, near its confluence with the Glass, the combined streams being thence known as the Beauly River. There are roads on both sides of the delightful Strath Glass, which extends to the south-west, these roads meeting later near *Cannich* (*q.v.*). In the 18th and 19th centuries, large numbers of people emigrated from these old Clan Chisholm lands to America and Canada. Westwards from Struy Bridge stretches the long and beautiful Glen Strathfarrar, traversed for some distance by a private road. Hydro-electric developments are taking place in the glen. Cattle-ranching has been introduced into this district. The valley continues into the fastnesses of the Ross-shire mountains, many exceeding 3,000 ft. in height, and in the heart of which lies the lonely Loch Monar, dividing Ross and Cromarty from Inverness. Beyond the loch stretches West Monar Forest, in which *Squrr a'Chaorachain* attains 3,452 ft., and looks northwards towards the lonely Glencarron Forest. Ptolemy of Alexandria, the early historian, mentions the Farrar River in his writings. Immediately to the north-east of Struy Bridge stands the modernised *Erchless Castle*, once the seat of the head of Clan Chisholm. See **Crask of Aigas** and **Kilmorack**. *Iter. 206, 210.*

SUILVEN, Sutherland. Map 29, NC 1 1.
See **Lochinver**.

SUMBURGH, Shetland. Map 33, HU 4 0.
See **Shetland Islands (Mainland)**. *Iter. 269.*

SUMMER ISLES, Ross and Cromarty. Map 29, NB 9 0.
See **Achiltibuie**. *Iter. 226.*

SWAINBOST, Isle of Lewis, Ross and Cromarty.
Iter. 258. Map 32, NB 5 6.

SWANSTON, Midlothian. Map 9, NT 2 6.
A tiny hamlet, at the north-eastern extremity of the *Pentland* hills, visited for its associations with the novels of R. L. Stevenson, notably " St. Ives." *Swanston Cottage* was the summer home of the Stevensons between 1867 and 1881, and in it are preserved relics belonging to the author. *Caerketton* and *Allermuir* hills, in the Pentlands, overlook Swanston from the south. See **Colinton**.

SWEETHEART ABBEY, Kirkcudbright. Map 3, NX 9 6.
See **New Abbey**. *Iter. 72, 73.*

SWINTON, Berwick. 571. Map 11, NT 8 4.
On the Mercat Cross, dating from 1769, there are several

sundials. The Church contains a tomb dating from c. 1200. *Iter. 38, 46.*

SYMINGTON, Ayr. Map 8, NS 3 3.
The small, restored Church shows a trio of round-headed windows, dating from the 12th cent., and also an ancient roof of open-work timber. *Craigie Castle*, an old Wallace stronghold, to the north-east, is in ruins.

SYMINGTON, Lanark. 652. Map 9, NS 9 3.
E.C. Wed. To the west rises *Tinto Hill*, 2,335 ft., a prominent landmark for many miles, with a wide view from the summit, extending as far as the English Lake District mountains and the coast of Northern Ireland. Near the eastern slopes of the hill stands the ruined *Fatlips Castle*. Away to the north of Symington, beyond the River Clyde, is *Quothquan Law*, 1,097 ft. *Iter. 35, 53.*

SYRE CHURCH, Sutherland. Map 30, NC 6 4.
Situated in the *Strath Naver* (*q.v.*) valley. To the north and south are numerous prehistoric remains, notably ruined brochs and hut circles. Westwards from Syre lies the lonely little Loch Syre, and still farther west, beyond Loch Loyal, rises the multi-peaked *Ben Loyal*, 2,504 ft. This, the finest mountain in this part of Sutherland, is seen perhaps at its best from the vicinity of *Tongue* (*q.v.*). See **Bettyhill**. *Iter. 232, 235.*

TAIL OF THE BANK, Renfrew. Map 8, NS 2 7.
See **Greenock**.

TAIN, Ross and Cromarty. 1,642. SB. Map 31, NH 7 8.
E.C. Thurs. **M.D.** Alt. Fri. GOLF. An ancient Royal Burgh of Easter Ross, on the Dornoch Firth, with a fine 17th cent. Tolbooth having a peal of bells. Nearby is the restored Market Cross. The Collegiate Church of *St. Duthac* was built in 1371, and has some good fenestration, and in the churchyard stands a ruined Chapel of *St. Duthac*. The remains of another Chapel to the same saint are on a knoll near the golf links, and to this Chapel fled, in 1306, the wife and daughter of Robert Bruce, who were later given up to Edward I. In the 15th and 16th cents., James IV made regular pilgrimages to Tain, and a road leading southwards from the town, crossing Glen Aldie in the direction of *Logie Easter* (*q.v.*), is still known as the King's Causeway, and recalls the rides of that monarch. His son, James V, also traversed the road on foot, in 1527. Eastwards of the town lies Loch Eye, with the ruined *Lochslin Castle*, and away to the north of the loch, bordering the Dornoch Firth, is a large expanse of sandy links, known as the Morrich More. See **Fearn**. *Iter. 201.*

TALISKER, Isle of Skye, Inverness. Map 23 NG 3 3.
The well-known *Talisker* distillery is situated at the village of *Carbost*, on the western shores of Loch Harport, reached along a by-road leaving the Sligachan to Bracadale road in a westerly direction near the head of Loch Harport. A narrow and rough road goes westwards over the hills from Carbost to Talisker Bay, with the imposing mass of *Preshal More* rising to the south of the road near the coast. Away to the south of the bay lies a splendid range of lofty cliffs, accessible only on foot. Another by-road leads north-westwards from Carbost, along the shores of Loch Harport towards Fiskavaig Bay. To the north of this road, near Ardtreck Point, is *Port na Long*, noted for its Harris tweed weavers. *Iter. 252.*

TANNADICE, Angus. 871. Map 21, NO 4 5.
Situated on the South Esk River, in the fertile Vale of *Strathmore* (*q.v.*), looking towards the *Hill of Finhaven* beyond the river. See **Finhaven**. *Iter. 166.*

TANTALLON CASTLE, East Lothian. Map 10, NT 5 8.
See **North Berwick**. *Iter. 2, 38.*

TARBERT, Argyll. 1,426. Map 7, NR 8 6.
E.C. Wed. GOLF. On East Loch Tarbert, an inlet of *Loch Fyne* (*q.v.*), and well known as the headquarters of the Loch Fyne herring industry. There are sands providing good bathing, and also a steamer pier. The ruined 14th cent. Castle, which overlooks the harbour, was once the home of Robert Bruce and, at a later period, of James II. To the south-west of the town, about two miles distant, is

West Loch Tarbert Pier, used by the steamers which serve Gigha and the Inner Hebridean islands of Jura, Colonsay and Islay. Magnus Barefoot of Norway is said to have been dragged in a galley across the isthmus separating the two lochs, in 1093. North-west of Tarbert rise the hills of South Knapdale, among which *Sliabh Gaoil* attains 1,840 ft. West Loch Tarbert, a narrow sheet of water, some ten miles in length divides the districts of *Knapdale* and *Kintyre* (both *q.v.*), and exhibits much pleasant, wooded scenery. Roads encircle the loch on both sides, that on the north, somewhat rough and hilly, continuing westwards, and later northwards, to overlook the waters of the Sound of Jura and Loch Killisport. The road along the south side extends along the narrow Kintyre peninsula, with views towards the island of *Gigha* (*q.v.*), and eventually reaches *Campbeltown* (*q.v.*). See **Skipness.** *Iter. 121, 122.*

TARBERT (Isle of Lewis), Harris, Inverness.
Map 32, NB 1 0.
See **Hebrides, Outer** (Harris). *Iter. 256.*

TARBET, Dunbarton. 162. Map 15, NN 3 0.
E.C. Wed. A resort on *Loch Lomond* (*q.v.*), at the eastern extremity of the narrow neck of land separating it from

Arrochar (*q.v.*) on Loch Long. Across here Magnus of Norway dragged his ships, in 1263, when laying waste the country. From Tarbet, the view across Loch Lomond includes the fine peak of *Ben Lomond*, 3,192 ft., while westwards, beyond Loch Long, rises *Ben Arthur*, or *The Cobbler*, 2,891 ft. The road leading northwards on Loch Lomond's shores reaches, after some 4 miles, the *Inveruglas* (*q.v.*) power-station of the Loch Sloy hydro-electric scheme, which was opened by Her Majesty Queen Elizabeth, the Queen Mother, in October, 1950. *Iter. 88, 100, 101, 103, 110, 111, 137.*

TARBOLTON, Ayr. 1,855. Map 8, NS 4 2.
E.C. Wed. Well known for its associations with Robert Burns. The family lived at *Lochlea* farm from 1777 to 1784 and here his father died. At Tarbolton, in 1781, the poet became a Freemason, while one year previously he had founded the Bachelors' Club, which met in the upper part of a thatched house. In 1938, this house became the property of the N.T. Scotland, and now contains various Burns relics from the Lochlea period of the poet. The Church has stone stairs leading to the loft and the spire rises to 90 feet. *Willie's Mill*, on the Water of Fail, to the north-east of Tarbolton, has Burns associations, as has also *Failford* (*q.v.*), farther to the south-east. In the vicinity stands *Montgomerie Castle*, where Mary Campbell, Burns's "Highland Mary" was in service. It was known formerly as *Coilsfield*, from the tradition that " Auld King Coil " was killed here by Fergus, King of the Scots. **2 m. N.** of Tarbolton is the prominent 19th cent. *Barnweil* Monument, associated with William Wallace and the burning of the Barns of Ayr. John Knox preached in the ruined *Barnweil* Church. *Iter. 85.*

TARFSIDE, Angus. Map 21, NO 4 7.
Lies in the picturesque valley of Glen Esk, in the foothills of the eastern Grampian, or *Benchinnan* mountains. The Water of Tarf flows into the Esk at this point. Away to the north-west rises *Mount Keen*, 3,077 ft., and to the north-east is *Mount Battock*, 2,555 ft., near which the counties of Angus, Kincardine and Aberdeen meet. A walkers' track

goes northwards from Tarfside through the hills, crossing a shoulder of the *Hill of Cat*, 2,435 ft., and is known as the Fir Mount road, giving access to Glen Tanner and *Aboyne* (*q.v.*). See **Lochlee Church.** *Iter. 164.*

TARLAND, Aberdeen. 682. Map 21, NJ 4 0.
GOLF. On the outskirts of this village, to the north-east, stands the *House of Cromar*, re-named *Alastrean House*, and donated to the Royal Air Force by the late Lady MacRobert in memory of her three sons, who gave their lives during the Second World War. **4 m. N.E.**, on the Aberdeen road, is the Slack of Tillylodge, a fine viewpoint, the prospect extending westwards towards *Morven*, 2,862 ft., and the distant Cairngorms. About a mile farther stands the ruined *Corse Castle*, dated 1581. **3 m. S.E.**, off the Aboyne road, are the remains of *Coull Castle*, on a rocky knoll near the Church, and in the vicinity is the stone circle of *Tomnaverie* (A.M.), probably dating from the Bronze Age. See **Craigievar Castle.** *Iter. 179.*

TARVES, Aberdeen. Map 27, NJ 8 3.
Here, in the 19th century, the Duthie family perfected the famous Collynie breed of shorthorn cattle. Situated on a by-road, **2 m. S.**, are the interesting remains of *Tolquhon Castle* (A.M.), dated 1584 and 1589, with an entrance between two round towers showing grated windows and a fine carved panel over the door. The courtyard has buildings on all four sides. Open summer 10 to 7, winter, 10 to 4; Sun., 2 to 4 (see note page 90). *Iter. 186.*

TAY BRIDGE, Angus; Fife. Map 17, NO 3 2.
See **Dundee, Newport** and **Wormit.** *Iter. 94, 126, 127.*

TAYINLOAN, Argyll. Map 6, NR 6 4.
Stands on the west side of the narrow *Kintyre* (*q.v.*) peninsula, looking across the Sound of Gigha towards the island of *Gigha* (*q.v.*), to which it is linked by a passenger ferry. See **Killean.** *Iter. 121.*

TAYMOUTH CASTLE, Perth. Map 16, NN 7 4.
See **Kenmore.**

TAYNUILT, Argyll. 415. Map 14, NN 0 3.
E.C. Wed. A small resort near the shores of picturesque Loch Etive, where the village of *Bonawe* (*q.v.*) stands opposite the narrows which divide the lower and the upper loch. Near *Muckairn* Church is a monument to Lord Nelson, which was erected in 1805, before his remains had been brought back to England. To the south-east, beyond the River Awe, is the entrance to the gloomy Pass of Brander, threaded by the River Awe, and in which are situated the *Falls of Cruachan* (*q.v.*). The views from Taynuilt are very extensive, taking in *Ben Cruachan*, 3,689 ft., and also the mountains overlooking Upper Loch Etive, the highest of which is *Ben Starav*, 3,541 ft., far to the north-east. Southwards from the village is the wooded Glen Nant, traversed by the road leading to *Kilchrenan* (*q.v.*). Another road, gated and with bad bends, leads westwards by way of Glen Lonan, and passes near Loch Nell on the way to *Oban* (*q.v.*). *Iter. 110, 117, 125, 144, 145.*

TAYPORT, Fife. 3,164. Map 17, NO 4 2.
GOLF. Overlooks the Firth of Tay, and was formerly known as *Ferry Port on Craig*, but the ferry service to Broughty Ferry, on the opposite shore, is no longer in operation. The Church has a 17th cent. tower and carries the date 1794. *Scotscraig*, a mansion to the south-west, below Hare Law, preserves an archway dated 1697, the crest recalling Archbishop Sharp, its one-time owner, who was murdered at Magus Muir. (See **Pitscottie**.) To the south-east of Tayport is the Tents Moor, with its forestry plantations, on the western extremity of which are the *Morton Lochs*, an important breeding ground and resting place for migrating birds, around which an area of 47 acres has been declared a National Nature Reserve for the study of wildfowl. Surrounding the reserve is Forestry Commission property, planted mainly with Corsican pine. Part of it forms the 92-acre *Tentsmuir Point* National Nature Reserve. *Iter. 94.*

TAYVALLICH, Argyll. Map 14, NR 7 8.
Lies in the *Knapdale* (*q.v.*) district, on a small inlet of Loch

Tarbert, Argyll. The remains of the 14th century Castle, once a stronghold of Robert Bruce. It overlooks the inlet of East Loch Tarbert

Tarbet, Dunbarton. A milestone on A83 between Arrochar and Tarbet

Tarbolton, Ayr. The tall 19th century Barnweil Monument, off B730, some 2 miles north. It commemorates the burning of the Barns of Ayr by William Wallace

Tarbolton, Ayr. The Bachelors' Club, which Robert Burns founded in 1780. It is now the property of the National Trust for Scotland

Tarland, Aberdeen. The ruined Corse Castle (1581), which stands 5 miles north-east, off A974. When owned by Patrick Forbes, in the early 16th century, it is said to have been visited by the Devil, who, after an argument, carried off the castle front

Tayport, Fife. The sundial and plaque on the Church, which records its re-building in 1794 by the Rev. Dr. Robert Dalgleish of Scotscraig. The 17th century tower is out of true

PLATE 160 (facing page 252)

Temple, Midlothian. Deuchar's Arch, the sole remaining fragment of a former large mansion. It is situated to the east of the village

Temple, Midlothian. A churchyard monument, which is perhaps unique, being inscribed with the details of the Will of the Rev. James Goldie, who died in 1847

Teviothead, Roxburgh. The Monument to the song writer, Henry Scott Riddell, who died here in 1870. It stands a little to the north and is accessible by a path

Thornhill, Dumfries. The tall column of 1714, surmounted by the 'winged horse' emblem of the Queensberry family

Thurso, Caithness. Pennyland House, n which Sir William Alexander Smith, the founder of the Boys' Brigade, was born in October, 1854

Thurso, Caithness. The Sinclair burial-place, known as Harold's Tower, which stands beyond the Castle, where Sir John Sinclair, the agriculturist, was born in 1754

PLATE 161 (facing page 253)

Sween, with its richly wooded shores. To the west, beyond a small neck of land, is Carsaig Bay, in the Sound of Jura. The road leading south-westwards from Tayvallich terminates at *Keills* (*q.v.*). *Iter. 122.*

TEANGUE, Isle of Skye, Inverness.   Map 23, **NG 6** 0.
In the fertile Sleat peninsula, facing Knock Bay, an inlet of the Sound of Sleat. On a crag above the bay are the remains of *Knock Castle*, from which the views towards the lofty mainland mountains are very fine. About a mile to the north-west of Teangue, a rough and hilly by-road crosses the peninsula to *Ord*, on Loch Eishort, which is described under *Isle Ornsay*. *Iter. 253.*

TEMPLE, Midlothian.   Map 10, **NT 3** 5.
This pleasant village is situated on the steep banks of the South Esk River, and is visited for its roofless 13th to 14th cent. Church, which has a 17th cent. east gable belfry. *Temple* was formerly the chief Scottish seat of the Knights Templar, the order having been suppressed in 1312, and the property passing to the Knights of St. John of Jerusalem. In the churchyard of the modern Church is a gravestone to the Rev. James Goldie, on which appears his will. East of the village stands "Deuchar's Arch," the sole remnant of a vanished mansion. **3 m.** S.W., on the lower slopes of the *Moorfoot* hills, at a height of 900 ft., is the large Gladhouse reservoir, beyond which rises the lonely hill of *Blackhope Scar*, 2,136 ft. See **Gorebridge**. *Iter. 40.*

TENTSMUIR, Fife.   Map 17, **NO 4** 2.
See **Tayport**.

TERREGLES, Dumfries.   Map 4, **NX 9** 7.
See **Dumfries**.

TEVIOTHEAD, Roxburgh. 307.   Map 5, **NT 4** 0.
In the churchyard of the lonely Church, situated among the rounded hills of Teviotdale, is a memorial to Johnny Armstrong, an early 16th cent. Border "reiver," or outlaw. He was associated with the district around *Canonbie* and *Langholm* (both *q.v.*), and was hanged near Teviothead by order of James V. On the high ground a little to the north stands a monument to Henry Scott Riddell, a writer of patriotic songs, the best known of which are perhaps "Scotland Yet" and "Oor ain Folk." Formerly a minister of the parish, he was buried in the churchyard in 1870. *Iter. 11, 30, 45.*

THIRLESTANE, Berwick.   Map 10, **NT 5** 4.
See **Lauder**.

THIRLESTANE, Selkirk.   Map 10, **NT 2** 1.
See **Tushielaw**.

THORNHILL, Dumfries. 1,262.   Map 3, **NX 8** 9.
E.C. Thurs. M.D. Sat. GOLF. A small town overlooking the fertile valley of the River Nith in one of its most pleasant stretches, with a backing of Lowland hills, dominated by *Queensberry*, 2,285 ft., rising to the east. There are tree-lined streets, and a museum with Burns and Covenanters' relics. A tall column, erected in 1714, is topped by a winged horse, the emblem of the Queensberrys. Near the bridge over the Nith, a little to the west, is the 15th cent. *Boatford Cross*, marking the old ford and ferry. **2 m.** S., off the Dumfries road, and near the river, is *Dalgarnock* churchyard, where a Cross commemorates 57 Nithsdale Covenanters, who gave their lives in various parts of the country. See **Carronbridge, Closeburn, Drumlanrig Castle, Enterkinfoot** and **Penpont**. *Iter. 27, 48, 56, 67.*

THORNHILL, Perth. 450.   Map 15, **NS 6** 9.
E.C. Wed. *Iter. 107, 111, 139.*

THORNTON, Fife. 2,342.   Map 17, **NT 2** 9.
An important mining centre on the East Fife coalfield. *Iter. 93, 126, 130.*

THREAVE CASTLE, Kirkcudbright.   Map 3, **NX 7** 6.
See **Castle Douglas**.

THRUMSTER, Caithness.   Map 30, **ND 3** 4.
A tiny Caithness village, with three small lochs in the vicinity. To the north-east is the bare Loch Hempriggs;

to the south-west is the Loch of Yarehouse; and to the south, close to the village of *Sarclet*, and almost on the rocky coast between Sarclet Head and the Stack of Ulbster, lies Loch Sarclet. *Iter. 200.*

THURSO, Caithness. 4,127. SB.   Map 30, **ND 1** 6.
E.C. Thurs. M.D. Tues. GOLF. Finely situated on the Thurso River, flowing into Thurso Bay. There are good views north-westwards towards the most northerly point on the Scottish mainland, the cliffs of Dunnet Head, and also to the distant cliffs of Hoy, in the Orkneys, across the Pentland Firth. To the north-west of the town are the riven

1. Bishop's Palace remains.   3. St. Peter's Church.
2. Castle.   4. Town Hall, with Library and Museum adjacent.

cliffs of Holborn Head. Once an important port, *Thurso* is today mainly a fishing town and resort, while the quarrying of Caithness flagstones is a local industry, most of the fields and roads in the vicinity being lined by them in place of trees or hedges. The ruined Church of *St. Peter* is a reconstruction of the 17th cent. The town has some 17th cent. houses, and in the Museum is a collection of plants and fossils and a small Runic Cross. At *Thurso Castle*, northeast of the town, and partially demolished, was born Sir John Sinclair, the 18th cent. agriculturist and statistician, to whom a statue has been erected opposite the Church. Beyond the Castle stands *Harold's Tower*, the Sinclair burial-place, erected over the grave of Harold, a former Jarl of Caithness, killed in 1196. West of the town, on the shores of the bay, are the remains of the medieval *Bishop's Palace*, and in the vicinity is *Pennyland*, where Sir William Smith, the founder of the Boys' Brigade, was born in 1854. Farther to the north-west is *Scrabster* (*q.v.*), the port for the Orkney steamer. **2½ m.** W., near the foot of Scrabster Hill, is a broch known as "Things Va." See **Bridge of Forss, Dounreay, Dunnet** and **East Mey.** *Iter. 232, 234, 236, 237, 238, 239, 240.*

TIBBIE SHIEL'S INN, Selkirk.   Map 9, **NT 2** 2.
This well-known anglers' inn stands on the narrow neck of land separating picturesque *St. Mary's Loch* (*q.v.*) from the Loch of the Lowes. Here, many famous names are recalled, among the visitors to the inn having been de Quincey, Brewster and Lockhart, while here also took place one of the "Noctes Ambrosianae" of Christopher North (Professor Wilson) and James Hogg, better known as the "Ettrick Shepherd." See **Ettrick.** *Iter. 13, 46.*

TIGHARY, North Uist, Inverness.   Map 32, **NF 7** 7.
Iter. 261.

TIGHNABRUAICH, Argyll. 1,500.   Map 7, **NR 9** 7.
E.C. Wed.   A favourite *Kyles of Bute* (*q v.*) and *Cowal* (*q.v.*) resort, with a steamer pier, facing the Island of Bute in one of the narrowest reaches of the Kyles.   The road from the eastern shores of *Loch Fyne* (*q.v.*) terminates here.   Adjacent to Tighnabruaich, to the south-west, is the smaller resort of *Auchenlochan*, also with a pier.   See **Kames.**   *Iter. 103.*

TILLICOULTRY, Clackmannan. 3,994. SB.
Map 16, **NS 9** 9.
E.C. Tues.   GOLF.   The town stands on the River Devon, at the foot of the main ridge of the *Ochil* hills, dominated by *Ben Cleuch*, 2,363 ft., the highest point in the range. Tartans and woollens are manufactured at Tillicoultry.   In the picturesque glen behind the town several burns converge. To the north-east, on the slopes of the hills, is the modern *Harviestoun Castle*, described by Robert Burns, and formerly the home of Archibald Campbell Tate, headmaster of Rugby School, and later Archbishop of Canterbury. *Iter. 136.*

TILLYFOURIE, Aberdeen.   Map 27, **NJ 6** 1.
Lies below the wooded *Tillyfourie Hill*.   **2 m. S.E.** is the ruined, ivy-clad *Tillycairn Castle*, built to an L-plan.   To the south-west rise the wooded hills of Corrennie Forest. *Iter. 176, 177.*

TINGWALL LOCH, Shetland.   Map 33, **HU 4** 4.
See **Shetland Islands** (Mainland).   *Iter. 270.*

TINWALD, Dumfries.   Map 4, **NY 0** 8.
The Church, rebuilt in 1763, has a martyr's monument in the churchyard.

TIREE, ISLE OF, Argyll.   Map 13, **NL 9** 4 etc.
This flat, crofting Inner Hebridean island, which has an airport, lies beyond the western shores of Mull, and is noted both for horses and its variegated coloured marble.   On the east side of the island, and situated between Goth and Hynish Bays, stands *Scarinish*, with its pier and lighthouse. Tiree has been called the "Granary of the Hebrides," owing to its exceptional fertility.   Some ten miles west, on an isolated rock in the Atlantic, is the lonely *Skerryvore* lighthouse, built by Alan Stevenson, and one of the best known of Scotland's lighthouses.   The tower was erected in 1843, and is 135 ft. high, its construction having been attended by immense difficulties.   To the north-east of Tiree, separated by only a few miles of water, is the flat island of *Coll*, devoted mainly to crofting, while there are some remains of early forts, and also a ruined Castle.   Dr. Johnson paid a visit to the island, in 1773, when he inspected the castle.   Both Tiree and Coll are connected to Oban, on the mainland, by steamer service, and Tiree has a direct air service from Glasgow (Renfrew airport).

TIUMPAN HEAD, Isle of Lewis, Ross and Cromarty.
Iter. 259.   Map 32, **NB 5** 3.

TOBERMORY, Isle of Mull, Argyll. 667. SB.
Map 12, **NM 5** 5.
E.C. Wed.   GOLF.   The largest and best-known resort on the island, with a steamer pier overlooking Tobermory Bay, sheltered by Calve Island in the Sound of Mull.   There are views of the Ardnamurchan and Morven coast on the mainland to the north and east.   The town stands in a pleasant wooded setting, with several waterfalls, and is noted for sea fishing.   Its name means St. Mary's Well.   Tobermory has long been associated with a Spanish Armada galleon, probably the " Florida," which was blown up and sunk in the bay in 1588.   The ship was actually destroyed as the result of the work of a Scottish hostage.   Numerous attempts, including some in recent years, have been made to retrieve the treasure which is believed to be hidden in the wreck. Various articles have at different times been salvaged from the galleon, including a cannon, now resting at *Inveraray Castle* (*q.v.*).   Dr. Johnson and Boswell visited Tobermory in 1773 and noted 12 to 14 vessels in the harbour.   From the pier a service connects with Mingary, near *Kilchoan* (*q.v.*), on the Ardnamurchan coast.   To the south-east of the town

are the fine grounds of *Aros House*.   The road leading westwards towards *Calgary* (*q.v.*) passes near the shores of the Mishnish Lochs, to the north of Loch Frisa, beyond which, after some hairpin bends, it reaches *Dervaig* (*q.v.*), on the narrow Loch Cuan.   Away to the north of Tobermory, near the coast, is the modern *Glengorm Castle*, in its fine grounds. See **Salen** (Mull).   *Iter. 248, 249, 250.*

TODHILLS, Angus.   Map 17, **NO 4** 3.
Iter. 156, 161.

TOLQUHON CASTLE, Aberdeen.   Map 27, **NJ 8** 2.
See **Tarves.**

TOMATIN, Inverness. 166.   Map 25, **NH 8** 2.
E.C. Wed.   A Strath Dearn village, in the midst of fir plantations, and situated on the River Findhorn, which has come down from a wilderness of lonely hills away to the south-west, dominated by the *Monadhliath* range.   The bridge over the river at Tomatin replaces one built originally by Telford in 1833.   From here the river flows north-eastwards through a roadless part of Strath Dearn known as *The Streens*, overlooked by hills rising to more than 2,000 ft., and leading towards *Dulsie Bridge* (*q.v.*), situated in what is the Findhorn's most picturesque reach.   See **Moy** and **Slochd Summit.**   *Iter. 140, 150, 195.*

TOMDOUN HOTEL, Inverness.   Map 18, **NH 1** 0.
An anglers' resort, beautifully situated in Glen Garry, to the west of Loch Garry.   The road climbing northwards over a 1,424-ft. high shoulder of *Creag a' Mhaim* leading to *Cluanie* (*q.v.*) will eventually no longer be usable owing to the construction of the Loch Loyne reservoir in connection with the Loch Garry hydro-electric scheme.   A new road (**4 m. E.**) now crosses low hills from the north side of Loch Garry to reach the eastern end of Loch Cluanie.   Both these lochs are now reservoirs.   The continuation of this road westwards gives access to Cluanie for *Glen Shiel* (*q.v.*) and *Kyle of Lochalsh* (*q.v.*).   Westwards from Tomdoun goes a road following the continuation of Loch Garry, formerly known here as Loch Poulary.   This road gives access to the very lovely *Loch Quoich* (*q.v.*), its contours also changed due to hydro-electric works, and terminates (very rough and narrow) at *Kinloch Hourn* (*q.v.*).   The whole of this *Knoydart* (*q.v.*) district is one of lonely mountain grandeur, with *Gairich*, 3,015 ft., prominent in the westerly view from Tomdoun itself.   Depopulation of the neighbourhood took place in the 18th and 19th centuries, many of the emigrants departing to Canada, where they founded a new Glengarry.   See **Invergarry.**   *Iter. 214, 220.*

TOMINTOUL, Banff. 457.   Map 26, **NJ 1** 1.
E.C. Wed.   The loftiest village in the Highlands, being situated at a height of 1,160 ft.   It is well known as an angling resort in summer, and also as a winter sports resort. *Tomintoul* lies on a plateau, with the main range of the *Cairngorms* (*q.v.*) rising away to the south-west beyond the valley of the River Avon, their lonely foothills and distant *Ben Avon*, 3,843 ft. being visible at various points from the road leading north-westwards towards *Grantown-on-Spey* (*q.v.*).   To the east flows the Conglass Water, which is crossed by the road climbing north-eastwards, and reaching a height of more than 1,200 ft. nearing the Braes of Glenlivet, before descending to *Tomnavoulin* (*q.v.*) and *Glenlivet* (*q.v.*). South-eastwards from Tomintoul, the famous *Lecht* road, described under *Cock Bridge*, reaches a height of 2,090 ft. near the Aberdeen and Banff border on its way to the valley of the Don, and is liable to be blocked by snow in winter. The Avon flows to the west of Tomintoul, being joined by the Conglass Water, and a road follows Strath Avon and the *Cromdale* hills in a northerly direction towards *Dalnashaugh* (*q.v.*), on the threshold of the Spey valley.   This point is also accessible by the Glenlivet road, mentioned previously.   To the south-west of Tomintoul, the Avon flows through the remote foothills of the Cairngorms.   Just outside the village, near *Delnabo*, it is joined by the Water of Ailnack.   This stream, together with the Water of Caiplach, flows along the Banff and Inverness border in a series of spectacular gorges, most difficult of access, with *Geal Charn*, 2,692 ft., rising in the background.   Tomintoul is not the highest village in Scotland, this distinction falling to

Tobermory, Isle of Mull, Argyll. A view of the bay, in which Dr. Johnson, during his visit of 1773, counted 12 to 14 ships. A Spanish Armada galleon was sunk here in 1588, and efforts have been made at various times to salvage treasure from the wreckage

Tolquhon Castle, Aberdeen. The ruined Castle, dated 1584 and 1589, which was built by William Forbes. It stands 2 miles south of Tarves, on an unclassified road off B999

Tomintoul, Banff. A fountain presented by Robert Grant M.D., in 1915, as a memento of his boyhood

Tomdoun, Inverness. A view looking towards the dam on Loch Garry, off A87, to the east. It is part of a large new hydro-electric scheme extending westwards to Loch Quoich

Tomintoul, Banff. A cattle-grid, at a height of 2,090 feet, on the Lecht road (A939), which was built in 1754 as a military road, and leads south-eastwards to Corgarff, in the Upper Don valley

[For TIGHNABRUAICH see under KYLES OF BUTE (Plate 104)

Tongland, Kirkcudbright. A power station in connection with the extensive Galloway hydro-electric scheme

Tornapress, Ross and Cromarty. A view down the famous Pass of the Cattle, or 'Bealach nam Bo' (2,054 feet), which climbs over the hills to descend to Applecross Bay, facing the islands of Raasay and Skye

Tongue, Sutherland. Ben Loyal, 2,504 feet, which rises to the south of Tongue, and is well seen from both A836 and A838

Torphichen, West Lothian. The 12th to 16th century Church, which was once the property of the Knights Hospitallers of St. John of Jerusalem, and outwardly resembles a castle more than a church

Torphichen, West Lothian. A churchyard stone bearing cup marks. It has been associated with an area of sanctuary connected with the church

Torridon, Ross and Cromarty. Part of a moraine deposit, known as the 'Corrie of a Hundred Hills,' which lies in Glen Torridon

PLATE 163 (facing page 255)

Wanlockhead (*q.v.*), a Lowland village, which is situated at an altitude of 1,380 ft. *Iter. 141, 160, 169, 174, 176, 177, 191, 192.*

TOMNAVOULIN, Banff. Map 26, **NJ 2 2.**
Situated in Glen Livet, with the famous *Glenlivet* (*q.v.*) distillery situated on a by-road to the north-west. East of Tomnavoulin is an area of lonely hills and moors, dominated by *Corryhabbie*, 2,563 ft., overlooking Glen Suidhe and Glen Fiddich. The Tomintoul road goes southwards, rising to more than 1,200 ft. beyond the Braes of Glen Livet. *Iter. 169, 177, 192.*

TONGLAND, Kirkcudbright. Map 3, **NX 6 5.**
The dam here was constructed as part of the important *Galloway* (*q.v.*) hydro-electric scheme, which utilises the fall in the level of the River Ken before joining the Dee at the foot of Loch Ken. The generating station at Tongland was built in 1935. Tongland Bridge, over the River Dee, is of early 19th cent. date. A fish pass for the salmon has been constructed, and is said to be one of the highest in the country. Of the former 12th cent. Abbey, only a mere fragment still remains in the burial-ground near the Parish Church. *Iter. 70.*

TONGUE, Sutherland. 828. Map 28, **NC 5 5.**
E.C. Mon. This pleasant resort, also known as *Kirkiboll*, lies on the Kyle of Tongue, the outer waters of which are known as Tongue Bay. There are exposed sandy shores providing good bathing, while fishing is also to be had. The ruined *Castle Varrich*, situated on the Allt an Rian, where it flows into the Kyle, is traditionally the former home of an 11th cent. Norse king. *Tongue House*, to the north of the village, is of 17th and 18th cent. date, replacing a one-time home of the Lords of Reay. Beyond it, to the north-east, is the craggy height of *Cnoc an Freiceadain*, 1,009 ft., well seen from the road to *Bettyhill* (*q.v.*). Away to the south, the road to *Altnaharra* (*q.v.*) skirts the shores of Loch Loyal, and westwards rises the multi-peaked, granite *Ben Loyal*, 2,504 ft., one of the finest mountains in Sutherland, though not of great interest to climbers. Ben Loyal is also a prominent feature in the view from the road which rounds the Kyle of Tongue, passing near the little Loch Hacoin, before it turns northwards towards the desolate moorlands of A'Mhoine. See **Melness** and **Reay**. *Iter. 225, 230, 234, 235, 240.*

1. Castle Varrich ruins.   2. Tongue House.

TORE, Ross and Cromarty. Map 25, **NH 6 5.**
Iter. 202, 203.

TORGYLE BRIDGE, Inverness. Map 24, **NH 3 1.**
In Glen Moriston, where the road through the glen crosses the Moriston River, with its fine rapids. To the east, the country is well wooded, but westwards the glen becomes bare, with high mountains rising away to the west dominated by *Sgurr nan Conbhairean*, 3,634 ft. *Iter. 207.*

TORNAPRESS, Ross and Cromarty. Map 23, **NG 8 4**
Lies at the head of Loch Kishorn, an inlet of Loch Carron. This is the starting point of the famous mountain road to *Applecross* (*q.v.*) over the Pass of the Cattle, or "Bealach nam Bo," the nearest approach to an Alpine climb in Great Britain, and liable to be blocked by snow in winter. This rough and narrow, but spectacular road ascends from sea-level to a height of 2,054 ft. within six miles, almost the highest in Scotland, having a maximum gradient of 1 in 4,

while near the summit are situated several sharp hair-pin bends. The view from the top is superb, ranging westwards towards the Coolins of Skye and the distant Outer Isles, and eastwards over Lochs Kishorn and Carron to the serried Ross-shire and Inverness-shire peaks. The descent to Applecross is less difficult, but the return journey must be made over the same road. To the south of the pass rises *Meall Gorm*, 2,325 ft., and on the north side is *Sgurr a'Chaorachain*, 2,539 ft., both composed of red Torridon sandstone. Nearer to Tornapress itself is the peak of *Beinn Bhan*, 2,936 ft., with its remarkable, lonely corries, notably Coire na Poite. See **Shieldaig**. *Iter. 219, 223.*

TORNESS, Inverness. Map 25, **NH 5 2.**
On the River Farigaig, with three lochs, those of Ruthven, Duntelchaig and Ashie, lying to the north-east. *Iter. 211.*

TORPHICHEN, West Lothian. 525. Map 9, **NS 9 7.**
This village stands high, in a situation away from main roads, and is visited for its fine Church (A.M.), once belonging to the Order of Hospitallers, or Knights of St. John of Jerusalem. A meeting of the Order, the first for 400 years, was held here in 1947. Outwardly, the structure is more in the nature of a castle than a Church, the upper storeys of the tower, with its saddle-back roof, having doubtless formed part of the original "Hospital," or domestic buildings. A 16th cent. Parish Church has been built over the former nave, and of the original Norman Church, built for the Knights Templar, the chancel arch has survived. Only the foundations of the choir remain. There are 13th cent. transepts, while the crossing, tower and upper storeys are 15th cent. work. There is a sanctuary stone in the church-yard. Torphichen Mill was the birthplace, in 1767, of Henry Bell, designer of the "Comet," one of the earliest steamboats. Near the mill, a bridge, built c. 1800 and repaired in 1930, spans the River Avon. To the south-east rise the *Bathgate* hills, the highest point being *The Knock*, 1,017 ft., a good viewpoint. **2 m. S.W.** is *Bridge Castle*, standing on a rocky eminence, and dating mainly from the 16th and 17th cents., having been formerly in the possession of the Earls of Linlithgow. About **2 m. E.** of Torphichen is *Cairnpapple Hill* (A.M.), a Neolithic sanctuary remodelled in the Bronze Age and recently excavated. See **Bowling**. *Iter. 86.*

TORPHINS, Aberdeen. 473. Map 27, **NJ 6 0.**
E.C. Thurs. M.D. Alt Mon. A pleasant small village, lying to the north of the Dee valley. It may have taken its name from Thorfinn, a Scandinavian ally of Macbeth, the latter having been killed in the neighbourhood of nearby *Lumphanan* (*q.v.*). **2 m. S.** is the ruined *Castle Maud*, which is said to date back to the time of Robert Bruce. *Iter. 165, 190.*

TORRANCE, Stirling. Map 8, **NS 6 7.**
Iter. 107, 113.

TORRIDON, Ross and Cromarty. Map 24, **NG 9 5.**
Lies at the western end of Glen Torridon, perhaps the finest and wildest of the *Wester Ross* (*q.v.*) glens. It is of great interest to geologists for the grand mountains of red Torridon sandstone, topped in places with white quartzite, lining both sides of the valley, which extends inland in the direction of *Loch Maree* (*q v.*). West of Torridon is Inner Loch Torridon, its northern shores traversed by a narrow road which continues as far as the hamlet of Diabaig, on the Outer Loch, the latter half of the road being rough and steep with hairpin bends and gradients of 1 in 3½. Above the Inner Loch, beyond Coire Mhic Nobuil, rises *Ben Alligin*, 3,232 ft., showing the "Horns of Alligin," and to the north-east is *Ben Dearg*, 2,995 ft., from which all the Torridon peaks can be very well seen. In Glen Torridon, the monarch of the hills is *Liathach*, 3,456 ft., one of Scotland's finest peaks, composed of more than 3 miles of steep terraces of red sandstone, most difficult to climb, and towering over the spectacular corrie of Coire na Caime, to the north. These hills of Torridon stone make a striking picture when lit by the rays of the evening sun. Situated in the glen is the curious so-called "Corrie of a Hundred Hills," probably an ancient moraine deposit. North-eastwards lie the quartzite

peaks of *Ben Eighe*, all over 3,000 ft. in height. (See **Kinlochewe**). A new road is being made on the south side of the Inner Loch leading to *Shiedaig* (*q.v.*), and will go near the foot of *Ben Damh*, 2,958 ft. *Iter. 223.*

TORRIN, Isle of Skye, Inverness.   Map 23, **NG 5** 2.
Faces Loch Slapin, beyond which, on the Strathaird peninsula, rises the great black *Coolin* (*q.v.*) peak of *Blaven*, 3,042 ft., with its notable rock ridge of *Clach Glas*, well known to climbers. A little to the east of Torrin, on the Broadford road, is the little Loch Cill Chriosd, in Strath Suardal, with the ruined Church of *Kilchrist*, probably of 16th or 17th cent. date. See **Elgol**. *Iter. 252.*

TORRYBURN, Fife.   Map 16, **NT 0** 8.
Lies on Torry Bay, an inlet of the Forth estuary, and is a small coal port. In 1822, Alison Cunningham, who was nurse to R. L. Stevenson, and to whom he later dedicated his " Child's Garden of Verses," was born in a house in the village. Preston Island, in Torrie Bay, once had a coalmine. 2½ m. W., on the coast, is the famous little Royal Burgh of *Culross* (*q.v.*). *Iter. 97, 134.*

TORTHORWALD, Dumfries.   Map 4, **NY 0** 7.
The old, ruined Castle keep of the Carlyles overlooks the fertile Nithsdale valley, to the west, from its 250-ft. high eminence, and is probably of late 14th cent. date. *Iter. 45.*

TOSCAIG, Ross and Cromarty.   Map 22, **NG 7** 4.
See **Applecross**.

TOTAIG, Ross and Cromarty.   Map 23, **NG 8** 2.
See **Ardelve** and **Loch Duich**.

TOWN YETHOLM, Roxburgh.   Map 11, **NT 8** 2.
See **Yetholm**.

TRABBOCH, Ayr.   Map 8, **NS 4** 2.
Iter. 85.

TRANENT, East Lothian. 6,058. SB.   Map 10, **NT 4** 7.
A mining town, situated a few miles inland from the coast of the Firth of Forth. Colonel Gardiner, who died here from wounds received at the battle of *Prestonpans* (*q.v.*), in 1745, is associated with Scott's " Waverley." The Parish Church was built in 1800, on the foundations of a much older structure, and in the churchyard are numerous interesting monuments. A nearby doocot dates from 1587. **2 m. S.S.W.** is the 15th cent. *Elphinstone Tower*, where walls 8 ft. in thickness have numerous small rooms with staircases built into them, and from which an extensive view can be obtained. **2 m. S.W.** is the ruined 15th and 16th cent. *Falside Castle*, also situated on high ground. See **Ormiston** and **Pencaitland**. *Iter. 1, 3.*

TRAPRAIN LAW, East Lothian.   Map 10, **NT 5** 7.
See **East Linton**.

TRAQUAIR, Peebles. 431.   Map 10, **NT 3** 3.
An attractive little village, lying on the Quair Water, one of the tributaries of the Tweed. *Traquair House*, perhaps the Tully-Veolan of Scott's " Waverley," is one of the finest and most picturesque of early Scottish mansions, and is shown daily, except Fri., 2 to 5.30, May to end of Sept. (See note page 90.) It is one of the oldest inhabited houses in the country, and was once the home of William the Lion, who held a court here in 1209. The main block dates from 1642, and wings were added later in the same century. Mary, Queen of Scots and Darnley stayed in the house in 1566. The main avenue gates have not been opened since 1796, when the 7th Countess of Traquair died, but tradition has it that they were closed already after 1745, not to be re-opened until a Stuart should once more ascend the throne. There are fine gardens at the house known as the *Riggs of Traquair*. South-west of the Church, which has outside gallery stairs, lies *Glen*, with its fine gardens, an early home of the 1st Countess of Oxford and Asquith. To the east of Traquair, on the Selkirk border, rises *Minchmuir*, 1,856 ft., a fine viewpoint, traversed by an old drovers' track linking Peebles with Selkirk, which was used as an escape route by Montrose, in 1645, after the battle of *Philiphaugh* near *Selkirk* (*q.v.*). Montrose is said to have halted at *Traquair House* during his flight. The road leading south-

wards towards the picturesque Vale of *Yarrow* (*q.v.*) climbs over the hills, and is known as the " Paddy Slacks." It reaches a height of over 1,100 ft. near the meeting-point of the counties of Peebles and Selkirk, on the northern fringe of Ettrick Forest. See **Blairgowrie**. *Iter. 12, 34.*

TRESTA, Shetland.   Map 33, **HU 3** 5.
Iter. 268, 270.

TRINAFOUR, Perth.   Map 19, **NN 7** 6.
Situated in the lonely moorlands of Glen Erochy, on the road linking the Tummel valley with the main Perth to Inverness highway in Glen Garry at Calvine, near *Struan* (*q.v.*). The Errochty River has been harnessed to a hydro-electric scheme, in conjunction with the Tummel-Garry undertaking, and for this purpose the Errochty reservoir and power station have been constructed. To the north of Trinafour, a rough track leading to *Dalnacardoch* (*q.v.*) is part of Wade's original military road, constructed in 1730, and climbing to a height of 1,452 ft. before descending into Glen Garry. The view of the mountains to the north in the extensive Forest of Atholl from the hairpin bend on this track, above Trinafour, is extremely fine. A better route to Glen Garry is to continue through Glen Erochy, as mentioned above. See **Kinloch Rannoch** and **Wade Roads**. *Iter. 147, 149.*

TROCHRY, Perth.   Map 16, **NN 9** 4.
Iter. 140, 141.

TROMIE BRIDGE, Inverness.   Map 19, **NN 7** 9.
To the south extends the long, partly wooded expanse of Glen Tromie, which gives access by paths to the lonely Gaick Forest. Here, Loch an't Seilich, set beneath steep hills, is linked to Loch na Cuaich, their combined waters being taken by aqueduct to Loch Ericht, an important link in the Rannoch hydro-electric scheme. Another Gaick Forest loch, that of Vrotten, is passed on the way southwards by footpath to the Inverness–Perth border, where Loch-an-Duin, a sheet of water in the Grampians at a height of some 1,700 ft., has scenery reminiscent of Wastwater in the English Lake District. From here paths continue southwards through the Forest of Atholl to reach Glen Garry near *Dalnacardoch* (*q.v.*). *Iter. 138, 149.*

TROON, Ayr. 9,951. SB.   Map 8, **NS 3** 3.
E.C. Wed. GOLF. A well-known golfing resort and coal port, with ship-building yards. It lies on a narrow spit of rocky land dividing Ayr Bay from Irvine Bay, and faces

1. Marr College.

256

Torthorwald, Dumfries. The ruined 14th century Castle of the Carlyles, situated on a hill to the east. One of its earliest owners was given the title of Lord Torthorwald by James VI

Tranent, East Lothian. The dovecote of 1587 which stands near the Church

Tranent, East Lothian. The 15th century Elphinstone Tower, some 2 miles south-south-west, off B6414. Here, in 1545, George Wishart was brought as a prisoner of Cardinal Beaton

Troon, Ayr. Marr College, erected from the proceeds of a legacy donated to the town in 1919 by Charles Kerr Marr, who was born at Troon

Traquair, Peebles. Perhaps Scotland's oldest inhabited mansion, the present Traquair House, of the 16th century and later. William the Lion hunted in Traquair Forest in 1209, and Mary, Queen of Scots, stayed here with Darnley in 1566

Traquair, Peebles. The main entrance gates to Traquair House, which have been closed since the '45 Rising, and it is said will not be re-opened until a Stuart once again ascends the throne

PLATE 164 (facing page 256)

Trossachs, Perth. The Loch Katrine steamer at the Trossachs pier

Trossachs, Perth. A milestone on A81, between Aberfoyle and Balfron, on the southern edge of the Trossachs. It gives an unusual spelling for Aberfoyle

Tullibardine, Perth. The Collegiate Church of 1446, which contains a remarkable open timber roof

Tullynessle, Aberdeen. The ruined Terpersie Castle, dated 1561. It stands in a farmyard to the north-west, off an unclassified road

Tummel Bridge, Perth. One of General Wade's bridges, dating from 1730. The modern bridge is behind it

Turnberry, Ayr. The ruined Castle, which may have been the birthplace of Robert Bruce. The Scottish Barons met here in 1286, and at the same place, 21 years later, Bruce defeated the English

PLATE 165 (facing page 257)

the waters of the Firth of Clyde, with distant views of the Arran mountains. The fourth Duke of Portland commenced the development of the harbour in the 18th cent. *Marr College* dates from 1919. The south sands provide good bathing, and beyond the north sands lie *Barassie* and *Gailes*, both known for their excellent golfing facilities. Off-shore is Lady Isle, a bird sanctuary. Louis Philippe of France stayed, in 1801, at *Fullarton House*, which lies inland to the east of the town. See **Dundonald** and **Symington** (Ayr). *Iter. 19, 88.*

TROSSACHS, THE, Perth. 250. Map 15, NN 4 0 and 5 0.
The fame of the *Trossachs* district is due not only to its extraordinary lovely combination of mountain, loch and woodland, but also to the graphically-written descriptions in Scott's " Lady of the Lake " and " Rob Roy," which have served as an introduction to many thousands of visitors. The word Trossachs means " bristly country," and the richly-wooded gorge of the Trossachs extends actually from Loch Achray to Loch Katrine, though the road through the pass does not follow quite the same course as in Scott's time. Part of the area lies within the newly-created *Queen Elizabeth Forest Park*. The rugged hills of *Ben Venue*, 2,393 ft., to the south, and rocky *Ben A'an*, 1,750 ft., to the north, both fine viewpoints, dominate the scene, and over-look the eastern end of picturesque *Loch Katrine* (*q.v.*). Here, opposite Ellen's Isle, was the former " Silver Strand," associated with the " Lady of the Lake," but now sub-merged since the level of the lake was raised in connection with the buildings of the subterranean aqueduct conveying water supplies for Glasgow. A steamer plies on the loch in summer from Loch Katrine Pier, where the public road terminates, to *Stronachachar* (*q.v.*) Pier, from which Rob Roy's birthplace at *Glengyle* can be visited on foot. The private road from Loch Katrine Pier along Strath Gartney and the northern shores of the loch, which also gives access to Glengyle, can only be used by pedestrians.

A road diverges southwards from the Trossachs by the wooded shores of Loch Achray, leading over the hills to *Aberfoyle* (*q.v.*), with fine views. To the west of this road, and traversed by paths, is the picturesque Pass of Achray, and also the Bealach nam Bo, or Pass of the Cattle, along which the MacGregors once drove their plunder. The road leading eastwards along the northern shores of Loch Achray passes the " *Trossachs* " Hotel, behind which rises the hill of *Sron Armailte*, 1,149 ft., a good viewpoint. Later it reaches the well-known *Brig o' Turk*, familiar to lovers of the " Lady of the Lake." This bridge spans the Finglas Water, or River Turk, which has descended from Glen Finglas. Beyond the bridge stretches picturesque Loch Vennachar, with *Ben Ledi*, 2,875 ft., rising to the north, the road following the north bank of the loch towards *Callander* (*q.v.*). To the south of Loch Vennachar lies the smaller Loch Drunkie, which is well seen from the picturesque " Duke's " Road linking the Trossachs with Aberfoyle. The whole of this district has associations with Scott's novels. See **Inversnaid**. *Iter. 106, 111, 139.*

TRUMPAN, Isle of Skye, Inverness. Map 22, NG 2 6.
In an isolated and lonely setting on the narrow Vaternish peninsula, washed by the waters of Loch Snizort and Loch Dunvegan. The ruined Macleod Church was burnt by the Macdonalds, and here is buried Lady Grange, who had been exiled, in 1734, to *St. Kilda* (*q.v.*). To the north of the village is Vaternish Point, and eastwards, in Loch Snizort, lie the Ascrib Islands. *Iter. 255.*

TULLIBARDINE, Perth. Map 16, NN 9 1.
The interesting Collegiate Church of *Tullibardine* (A.M.) dates from 1446, and stands in a delightful Strath Earn setting. The most notable feature is the open timber roof, and at the fortified west end of the building is a small tower. The Church, at one time the Atholl mausoleum, is now the burial-place of the Strathallan family. The Castle of *Strathallan* lies a little to the north, near the point where the Machany Water flows into the River Earn.

TULLIBODY, Clackmannan. Map 16, NS 8 9.
Situated within a large bend of the River Devon, near the

point where it flows into the Forth. The village was the birthplace, in 1811, of the geologist, Robert Dick.

TULLOCH, Inverness. Map 19, NN 3 8.
On the River Spean, in Glen Spean, with one of the curious " Parallel Roads " well seen on the hillside to the north. (See **Roy Bridge**.) To the south-east, and traversed only by the railway, are the shores of Loch Treig, surrounded by lofty hills exceeding 3,000 ft. in height. The loch is now included in the great Lochaber power scheme, its waters being carried by means of a 15-mile long tunnel through *Ben Nevis* (*q.v.*). To the south-east of Loch Treig is the lonely Loch Ossian, beyond the shores of which rise the peaks of *Beinn Eibhinn*, 3,611 ft., and *Ben Alder*, 3,757 ft. The road leading north-eastwards from Tulloch passes a reservoir, dominated by the great mass of *Creag Meaghaidh*, 3,700 ft., rising away to the north, and later reaches the shores of *Loch Laggan* (*q.v.*). *Iter. 143, 208.*

TULLOCHGORUM, Inverness. Map 25, NH 9 2.
Situated on the north bank of the River Spey, with *Creag an Fhithich*, 1,325 ft., a wooded hill, rising to the west. The name Tullochgorum is that of a well-known 18th cent. Strathspey tune, the words of which were written about 150 years ago by John Skinner, a bishop of Aberdeen.

TULLYNESSLE, Aberdeen. Map 26, NJ 5 1.
Lies on the Suie Burn, a tributary of the River Don. A little to the north-west, in the foothills of the *Correen* hills, stands the ruined three-storeyed stronghold of *Terpersie Castle*, dated 1561, and showing the Gordon crest on a window-sill. *Iter. 165.*

TUMMEL BRIDGE, Perth. Map 19, NN 7 5.
This bridge was built by General Wade, in 1730, and stands on the line of his military road from Crieff to Dalnacardoch. A power station, in connection with the Tummel-Garry hydro-electric scheme, is now situated nearby on the south bank of the River Tummel. Mendelssohn spent some time at an inn here in 1829. Eastwards lies Loch Tummel, per-haps the loveliest aspect of which is to be obtained from the celebrated *Queen's View* (*q.v.*). Roads traverse both shores of the loch, that on the north side being the finer of the two. Farther east still are the Falls of Tummel (N.T. Scot.), des-cribed under *Pitlochry*. To the south of Tummel Bridge, the Wade road climbs over the hills past *White Bridge* (*q.v.*), reaching a height of nearly 1,300 ft., with *Schiehallion*, 3,547 ft., to the west, before descending into Strath Appin. See **Kinloch Rannoch** and **Wade Roads**. *Iter. 138, 148, 149.*

TUNDERGARTH, Dumfries. Map 4, NY 1 8.
Iter. 45.

TURNBERRY, Ayr. 500. Map 8, NS 2 0.
E.C. Tues. GOLF. Situated on the sandy Turnberry Bay,

1. Castle ruins.

looking across to the mountains of the island of Arran, and well-known for its golf-course. Motor racing is a more recent addition to the attractions of the resort. There are scanty remains of *Turnberry Castle*, to the north, at Turnberry Point, and Robert Bruce is some-times thought to have been born here, though *Lochmaben* (*q.v.*) disputes this claim. Bruce is said to have landed at Turn-berry, in 1307, to commence his fight for Scotland's free-dom, which culminated 7 years later at *Bannockburn* (*q.v.*). See **Culzean Castle**, **Dunure** (for *Electric Brae*) and **Kir-koswald**. *Iter. 80.*

TURNHOUSE, Midlothian.　　　Map 9, **NT 1** 7.
In the vicinity lies the airport for Edinburgh. *Iter. 91, 95.*

TURRIFF, Aberdeen. 2,836. SB.　　Map 27, **NJ 7** 4.
E.C. Wed.　**M.D.** Tues./Thurs.　GOLF.　Stands on the
Idoch Water, which joins the more important River Deveron,
forming the Aberdeen-Banff boundary, a little to the north-
west. The Knights Templars once had a church here. The
present Church has a 16th cent. choir, a double belfry, dated
1635, and also some monuments of interest. The old Market
Cross was re-erected in 1865. A skirmish, known as the" Trot
of Turriff," was fought here, in 1639, between the Covenanters
and the Royalists. To the east, in wooded grounds, stands
the 14th to 16th cent. *Delgatie Castle*, the home of the Clan
Hay. It is shown each Wed., and the 1st Sun. in the month,
3 to 6, May to Sept. (See note page 90). 4½ m. N.E. stands
Craigston Castle, an early 17th cent. structure. **3 m. S.E.**,
off the Fyvie road, is *Hatton Castle*, with part of the ancient
Balquholly Tower. See **Auchterless** and **King Edward**. *Iter.
180, 189, 196.*

TUSHIELAW INN, Selkirk.　　　Map 10, **NT 3** 1.
Lies in a picturesque setting on the Ettrick Water, surrounded
by the characteristic green and rounded hills of the Lowlands.
In the valley, to the south-west, threaded by the river, are
the remains of *Tushielaw Castle*, where, in 1528, Adam Scott,
a well-known Border raider, is said to have been hanged in
his own stronghold by James V. **2 m. S.W.** is the ruined
Thirlestane Tower, associated with Sir John Scott, a follower
of the same king. *Thirlestane House* is of early 19th cent.
date. A fine moorland road climbs in an easterly direction
from the inn, passing, after five miles, into Roxburghshire,
on the way to Hawick. See **Buccleuch, Ettrick, St. Mary's
Loch** and **Tibbie Shiel's Inn**. *Iter. 12, 34, 42.*

TUTIM, Sutherland.　　　　　Map 29, **NC 4** 0.
See **Rosehall**.

TWATT, Orkney.　　　　　　Map 33, **HY 2** 2.
Iter. 263, 264.

TWATT, Shetland.　　　　　　Map 33, **HU 3** 5.
Iter. 268.

TWEEDDALE, Peebles.　　　Map 10, **NT 1** 3 etc.
An alternative name for Peeblesshire, through the centre of
which flows the River Tweed, famous for its salmon-fishing,
and which, during its course, is joined by numerous tributaries rising within the county. Perhaps the loveliest reaches
of Tweeddale are those which extend from *Melrose* (*q.v.*)
through *Peebles* (*q.v.*) itself to the lonely head of the river
at *Tweedsmuir* (*q.v.*), associated with the novels of John
Buchan. Beyond here, ranges of lofty hills close in near the
meeting-point of Dumfries, Lanark and Peebles. *White
Coomb*, 2,695 ft. and *Hart Fell*, 2,651 ft., both on the Dumfries border, are the highest of these hills, and to the north-
west of the latter rises the 1,766-ft. high *Crown of Scotland*.
Captain Armstrong, a local historian, failed to explain the
curious name of this hill when describing it in 1775.

TWEEDSMUIR, Peebles. 242.　　Map 9, **NT 1** 2.
Near the lonely Church, with its lofty spire, a landmark for
many miles around, is a standing stone 5 ft. high. In the
churchyard is an inscribed Covenanter's stone, dated 1685.
Lofty, rounded hills rise in all directions, while the ridge to
the east, with the flat-topped *Broad Law*, 2,754 ft., and
Dollar Law, 2,680 ft., is the highest in the Lowlands after the
Merrick in *Galloway* (*q.v.*). John Buchan spent part of his
youth in this parish at the south-western extremity of
Tweeddale (*q.v.*) and his novels include much local colour.
A track leads south-eastwards from Tweedsmuir by the side
of the *Talla* reservoir, in its hilly setting, holding water for the
city of Edinburgh. To the south-east is the Megget Stane,
near the Selkirk border. Beyond rises the Megget Water
flowing towards *St. Mary's Loch* (*q.v.*). At the south-
eastern extremity of the reservoir, the Gameshope Burn
flows down by Talla Linn foot, with its cascades, noted for
the famous Covenanters' meeting of 1682, described by
Scott in his " Heart of Midlothian." **8 m. S.W.** of Tweedsmuir, on the Moffat road, near the meeting-point of

Dumfries, Lanark and Peebles, is the watershed where the
Rivers Annan, Clyde and Tweed all rise in close proximity.
The last-named rises at Tweed's Well, situated at a height of
1,500 ft., a little to the east of the road. At this point on the
road, known as *Tweedshaws*, stands a cairn and tablet in
memory of the devoted guard and driver of the Edinburgh
mail-coach who lost their lives in a great snowstorm in 1831.
The highest point of the road lies a little farther south and
attains 1,348 ft. See **Crook Inn** and **Moffat**. *Iter. 10, 24.*

TWYNHOLM, Kirkcudbright.　　Map 3, **NX 6** 5.
Barwhinnock to the north-west, is a notable example of a
small Regency mansion, with a walled garden. *Iter. 26.*

TYNDRUM, Perth. 90.　　　Map 15, **NN 3** 3.
E.C. Wed. This well-known angling, climbing and winter
sports resort is situated at a height of about 800 ft. in Strath
Fillan, near its junction with Glen Lochy. Dominating the
latter is the fine peak of *Ben Lui*, 3,708 ft., with its great
northern corrie, on the Argyll border, and to the east of
which rises *Beinn Oss*, 3,374 ft., above Glen Coninish. On
the slopes of *Ben Lui* rises the Fillan Water, which is later
known as the Dochart, and after emerging from *Loch Tay*
(*q.v.*) becomes the Tay, a river having the largest volume of
water in Scotland. Another fine group of mountains lies
to the south-east, where Glens Falloch and Dochart meet
at *Crianlarich* (*q.v.*). About **2 m. S.E.** of Tyndrum, near the
Fillan Water, is *Dalry*, where Robert Bruce was worsted in
a skirmish, in 1306, and lost his brooch, which is now
treasured in the Macdougall mansion of *Dunollie* near *Oban*
(*q.v.*). *Beinn Chaluim*, 3,354 ft. and *Creag Mhor*, 3,305 ft., are
the principal heights rising to the north-east of Tyndrum
in the Forest of Mamlorn mountains and facing the head
of Glen Lochay in the *Breadalbane* (*q.v.*) country. See
Bridge of Orchy. *Iter. 100, 110, 120, 125, 142, 144, 145.*

TYNET BRIDGE, Banff.　　　Map 26, **NJ 4** 6.
In the vicinity stands *Tynet* Church, one of Scotland's oldest
Post-Reformation structures, still in use. *Iter. 178, 198.*

TYNNINGHAME, East Lothian.　　Map 10, **NT 6** 7.
In the richly wooded grounds of *Tynninghame House*, 18th
and 19th cent., to the north-east, near Tynninghame Sands
on the coast by the Tyne estuary, are the remains of the 12th
cent. Church, now a burial chapel of the Earls of Haddington. This Chapel must have been one of the best examples
of parochial Romanesque architecture in Scotland, as shown
by the rich carving on the surviving arch of the apse.
Beyond the park of the house stretch the links, terminating
in a narrow promontory, with a rock known as *St. Baldred's
Castle*. Nearby is a cairn dating from the Bronze Age.
Farther to the north are the Peffer Sands. See **East Linton**.
Iter. 2, 38.

TYNRON, Dumfries.　　　　Map 3, **NX 8** 9.
On the Shinnel Water. There is an inscribed martyr's stone
in the churchyard.

TYRIE, Aberdeen.　　　　　Map 27, **NJ 9** 6.
Iter. 181, 196.

UDDINGSTON, Lanark. 6,292.　　Map 8, **NS 6** 6.
E.C. Wed. GOLF. A town having large iron-foundries,
situated on the River Clyde, to the south-east of Glasgow.
Iter. 51.

UDNY, Aberdeen.　　　　　Map 27, **NJ 8** 2.
Situated in the Formartine district, which takes in much of
the country between the Rivers Don and Ythan, and also
the sandy coast to the east. The modern Castle retains an
ancient four-storeyed tower. See **Pitmedden**.

UIG, Isle of Lewis, Ross and Cromarty.　Map 32, **NB 0** 3.
See **Hebrides, Outer** (Lewis). *Iter. 257.*

UIG, Isle of Skye, Inverness.　　Map 22, **NG 3** 6.
On the picturesque Uig Bay in the Trotternish district, overlooking Loch Snizort, the Ascrib Islands, and the Vaternish
peninsula. A little to the north-west. on the coast, is the
rugged Stack Skudiburgh, in its rocky setting. Farther
north, off the *Duntulm* (*q.v.*) road, near *Port Kilbride*, stands
Monkstadt House, near which Flora Macdonald and Prince
Charles Edward, the latter disguised as " Betty Burke," her

Turriff, Aberdeen. The double belfry (1635) of the Church. The Knights Templars formerly owned a church here

Tweeddale, Peebles. The Dawyck Woods, at Stobo, to the south of the River Tweed, and south-west of Peebles. They are considered some of the finest in Scotland

Tweeddale, Peebles. The 15th century Neidpath Castle, once battered by Cromwell's guns. It stands to the west of Peebles, on the banks of the Tweed, off A72

Tweeddale, Peebles. Barns Tower, dating from 1488, which stands near Lyne, to the south of the Tweed, on an unclassified road in the vicinity of Manor Church

Tweedsmuir, Peebles. The cairn (1931) at Tweedshaws, 8 miles south west, on A701, which tells the story of the snowstorm of 1831, when the driver and guard of the mail coach lost their lives

Uig, Isle of Skye, Inverness. A house in the form of a round tower overlooking Uig Bay

Urquhart Castle, Inverness. The ruined Castle, blown up in 1692 to prevent its occupation by the Jacobites. It stands on Loch Ness, off A82, to the south-east of Drumnadrochit

Ullapool, Ross and Cromarty. A memorial clock to Sir Arthur Fowler of Braemore, who died in 1899

Usan, Angus. The curious rock of St. Skeagh, said from certain angles to resemble an elephant. It is situated near Boddin Point, on an unclassified road to the south-west

Wade Roads. A by-passed Wade bridge near A9, at Dallnamine, 2 miles south-east of Dalnacardoch, in the Grampian mountains of Perthshire

Wade Roads. General Wade's Sluggan Bridge of 1728 across the River Dulnain. It stands 2 miles west of Carrbridge, Inverness-shire, on the original line of his road from Kingussie to Inverness

PLATE 167 (facing page 259)

maid, landed on June 29, 1746, from the remote island of *Benbecula* in the Outer Hebrides. Some six miles off the road leading south from Uig towards Loch Snizort Beag stands the successor to the former *Kingsburgh House*, where the Prince sheltered and Flora Macdonald stayed, and where, in later years, Dr. Johnson and Boswell were entertained. A well nearby, to the north, where the Prince quenched his thirst, is still known as Prince Charles's Well. The road leading westwards and then northwards from Uig makes an abrupt double bend before ascending Idrigil Hill, and then divides into two branches, the westerly of which continues round the head of the Trotternish peninsula towards *Kilmaluag* (*q.v.*). The easterly branch, narrow and steep, accompanied by the little River Rha, leads into the remote hills looking towards the wild *Quiraing* (*q.v.*). Later it descends steeply, with a hairpin bend, towards *Staffin* (*q.v.*) and the shores of Staffin Bay, with fine views, both of the Quiraing and out to sea beyond Staffin Island. See **Flodigarry, Kilmuir** and **Hebrides, Outer** (Benbecula). *Iter. 254.*

UIST, NORTH AND SOUTH, Inverness.
Map 32, NF 7 7 etc. and NF 7 2 etc.
See **Hebrides, Outer** (North Uist and South Uist).

ULLAPOOL, Ross and Cromarty. 538. Map 29, **NH 1** 9.
E.C. Tues. An attractive *Wester Ross* (*q.v.*) fishing town and resort, founded by the Fisheries Association, in 1788, to further the herring industry. It forms a convenient base from which explorations of some of the finest mountain scenery of the North-West Highlands can be made. There is a safe anchorage for boats, and both bathing and angling are available. *Ullapool* is very beautifully situated on *Loch Broom* (*q.v.*), with grand views towards the head of the loch, and faces *Aultnaharrie* (*q.v.*), dominated by *Ben Goleach*, 2,052 ft., on the opposite shore, to which it is linked by passenger ferry. Beyond Loch Broom, away to the south-east, is the fertile, wooded valley of Strath More, above which rise the lofty peaks of the *Ben Dearg* group. North-west of Ullapool, a rugged and picturesque stretch of road traverses the shores of Loch Kanaird, on the edge of the rugged *Coigach* district, with the low-lying Isle Martin off-shore, before turning inland through Strath Kanaird, with *Ben More Coigach*, 2,438 ft., prominent to the north-west. Farther out to sea are the delightful Summer Islands in Baden Bay, looking towards *Achiltibuie* on the mainland coast. There are several ruined brochs in the neighbourhood of Ullapool, including Dun Canna (See **Strathkanaird**), and also two examples on the farther shore of Loch Broom, south-east of Aultnaharrie. The Ullapool River flows into Loch Broom at Ullapool, having emerged from Loch Achall, to the east, at the farther extremity of which lies Glen Achall, in a setting of lonely hills, with Rhidorroch Forest to the north. See **Achiltibuie, Baddagyle, Braemore Lodge, Dundonnell** and **Loch Lurgain.** *Iter. 204, 222, 224, 225, 226, 235.*

ULVA FERRY, Isle of Mull, Argyll. Map 12, **NM 4** 3.
Situated a little to the west of the road which skirts the shores of Loch Tuath and Loch na Keal, in the north-west sector of the island. A narrow piece of water, crossed by a passenger ferry, separates Mull from the smaller island of *Ulva* at this point, while beyond the island, to the south-west, are Little Colonsay and the well-known island of *Staffa* (*q.v.*). Ulva has caves, and cliffs of basalt, and was visited in 1773 by Dr. Johnson and Boswell, while later visitors include Sir Walter

Scott and David Livingstone. Campbell's famous poem about Lord Ullin's daughter is associated with the island, but it is thought that the "Loch Gyle" in the poem may refer to Loch Goil in the *Cowal* (*q.v.*) district. A little to the west of Ulva is the island of *Gometra*, which shows basaltic columns, and looks out towards the tiny islands of Lunga and Fladda in the Treshnish group. The road leading eastwards from Ulva Ferry winds high above the shores of Loch na Keal, with fine views of *Ben More*, 3,169 ft., to the south, before descending to the lochside. **2 m. N. of Ulva Ferry,** near the shores of Loch Tuath, are the Laggan waterfalls, off the road to *Kilninian* (*q.v.*). *Iter. 248.*

UNAPOOL, Sutherland. Map 28, **NC 2** 3.
On Loch Glencoul, near its junction with Loch Glendhu, and on the road leading northwards to the ferry at *Kylesku* (*q.v.*). This enables cars to cross the narrows which link the two lochs with Loch Cairnbawn, an inlet of the bay of *Eddrachillis* (*q.v.*). The mountain which dominates the remote head of Loch Glencoul is *Ben Leoid*, 2,597 ft. The road leading in a southerly direction towards *Inchnadamph* (*q.v.*) is dominated by the long ridge of *Quinag*, 2,653 ft., with its outlying peak of *Sail Gorm*, 2,551 ft. *Iter. 225, 227.*

UNST, ISLE OF, Shetland. Map 33, **HP 5** 0 etc.
See **Shetland Islands** (Unst).

UPHALL, West Lothian. Map 9, **NT 0** 7.
GOLF. The Church, partly of Norman date, has a burial-vault of the 17th cent., and contains some tombs of interest. The manse was once a 17th cent. dower-house of the Dowager Lady Cardross. *Houston*, a 16th cent. mansion, standing to the south of the village, was the birthplace, in 1819, of Principal Shairp, the writer, who is buried in the Church. *Iter. 16.*

UPLAWMOOR, Renfrew. Map 8, **NS 4** 5.
A small village, its name being derived from *Ouplaymuir*. To the south-west, across the Ayrshire border, stands the Adam mansion of *Caldwell*, built in 1772.

UPPER LARGO, Fife. Map 17, **NO 4** 0.
See **Largo.** *Iter. 94, 98, 128.*

URAFIRTH, Shetland. Map 33, **HU 3** 7.
Iter. 267.

URQUHART CASTLE, Inverness. Map 25, **NH 5** 2.
See **Drumnadrochit.** *Iter. 207, 210, 213.*

USAN, Angus. Map 21, **NO 7** 5.
Once a thriving fishing village of some importance, known as *Fishtown of Usan*, its port and mill being mentioned in 1608. It is now a quiet village and coastguard station, with a rocky foreshore, situated between Scurdy Ness and Boddin Point. Near the latter is the curious rock of *St. Skeagh*, and beyond lies the wide expanse of Lunan Bay, sheltered by Lang Craig and Red Head to the south. A track, known as the "King's Codger's Road," once led westwards inland to *Forfar* (*q.v.*) along which fresh fish was conveyed to the former Royal Palace at that town. To the north of Usan is *Ferryden* (*q.v.*), overlooking *Montrose* (*q.v.*) across the estuary of the River South Esk.

VALLEYFIELD, Fife. Map 16, **NT 0** 8.
A garden village on Torry Bay, with the small coal port of *Torryburn* (*q.v.*) situated a little to the south-east. See **Culross.**

VOE, Sutherland. Map 53, **HU 4** 6.
See **Shetland Islands** (Mainland). *Iter. 267, 270.*

WADE ROADS. Map 19, **NN 6** 8 etc., 20, **NO 0** 4 etc.
and 25, **NH 6** 4 etc.
A number of great military roads were constructed by General George Wade in the Highlands between 1726 and approximately 1740. Modern research considers, however, that by no means all the roads built for military purposes in this part of Scotland were actually the work of Wade. The road mileage definitely attributed to the General is 234½, and between approximately 1728 and 1737 a total sum of £23,316.0.6 was paid out to him. The most notable road constructed by Wade was that linking Dunkeld with Inverness, involving the crossing of the *Grampians* (*q.v.*), a road

which is very largely followed by the course of the present splendid modern highway. A link road, which commenced at Crieff, followed a northerly course through the Sma' Glen to Aberfeldy, where, what is perhaps Wade's finest bridge, still spans the Tay. The continuation led over the Perthshire hills by way of Tummel Bridge, also Wade's work, to reach the main highway at Dalnacardoch, where, in the vicinity, the Wade Stone is still standing. Part of this link road is incorporated in modern roads, and part is still in existence as a rough track. Beyond Dalnacardoch, the road climbed northwards through Drumochter Pass to descend towards Dalwhinnie, where another famous Wade road diverged to the left into the Upper Spey valley (see below). From here a short spur was constructed to rejoin the more important road nearing Kingussie, at which point Wade reconstructed the well-known Ruthven Barracks, still to be seen, although in a ruinous state. The main highway from Kingussie continued to Fort George, now known as Inverness, a new Fort George having been constructed away to the north-east of the town at a later date.

The road from the Upper Spey led north-westwards to climb the famous Corrieyairack Pass in steep zigzags, reaching a height of more than 2,500 ft., amid a lonely wilderness of hills, before the descent through Glen Tarff commenced. This great road, traversed in 1745 by Prince Charles Edward, gradually fell into disuse, and is today little more than a track, which, in places, is barely discernible, and can only be crossed on foot, involving a long and arduous journey. From Glen Tarff, the road led to Fort Augustus, in the Great Glen, or *Glen More* (*q.v.*), where Wade rebuilt and enlarged the former barracks, and on the remains of which, in 1876, the present Benedictine Monastery was built. Fort Augustus lies on the road which Wade built from Fort William to Inverness through the Great Glen, and along parts of which the line of the present magnificent road now goes. Between Fort Augustus and Inverness, the Wade road kept to the east, and the modern road keeps to the west of Loch Ness. Inverness thus became the meeting-point of what are perhaps Wade's two best-known roads, both of which are to some extent incorporated in the present modern highways.

In 1740, Wade was relieved of his command in Scotland, and four years later he fought in a campaign in Flanders. He played a part in the '45 Rising, but retired when Cumberland took over the supreme command of the English army. After living at Highgate, in London, for some years. Wade died at Bath in 1748, at the age of 75, and was buried in Westminster Abbey, a monument being erected by Roubiliac in his memory.

Perhaps the best known of General Wade's successors was General Caulfeild, who was the reputed author of the well-known lines:

" If you'd seen these roads before they were made,

You'd lift up your hands, and bless General Wade."
Caulfeild was responsible for a large number of the military roads which were constructed in later years, and spent on them some £167,000 in all. Among these were the roads linking Dumbarton with Inveraray (1746-1750); Coupar Angus to Braemar and over the Lecht road to Tomintoul, Grantown-on-Spey and the present Fort George (1748 onwards); Stirling to Tyndrum, Kinlochleven and Fort William by way of the now disused Devil's Staircase near Kingshouse (1748–1751); and Fort Augustus to Bernera Barracks at Glenelg (1750–1784), this road later being abandoned. A map of the military roads was first produced in 1755, and a list of these roads in Scotland towards the end of the 18th cent. gives their total mileage as 1,103. By the year 1800, only some 600 miles of these roads were kept in a state of repair, and in 1814 they were taken over by the Commissioners of the Road and Bridge Act of 1812.

See **Aberfeldy, Corrieyairack Pass, Dalnacardoch, Dalwhinnie, Drumgask, Fort Augustus, Foyers, Inverfarigaig, Inverness, Kingussie, Sma' Glen, Spean Bridge, Tummel Bridge** and **Weem.**

WALKERBURN, Peebles. Map 10, NT 3 3.
A textile-manufacturing village, on the River Tweed. A Border Riding ceremony is held here annually. On *Purvis*

Hill, to the north, high above the Tweed, are some remarkable earthen terraces. 2¼ m. E., on the south bank of the river, is the ruined *Elibank Tower,* dating perhaps from 1595, and built, or enlarged, by one of the Murrays of *Darnhall* near *Eddleston* (*q.v.*). The daughter of this Murray, known as " Muckle Mouthed Meg," married a Scott of *Harden* near *Hawick* (*q.v.*), and has been commemorated in ballads by both Hogg and Browning. *Iter. 14, 32, 33, 52.*

WALLS, Shetland. Map 33, **HU 2 4.**
See **Shetland Islands** (Mainland). *Iter. 268.*

WALLYFORD, Midlothian. Map 10, NT 3 7.
Iter. 37.

WANLOCKHEAD, Dumfries. Map 9, NS 8 1.
The loftiest village in Scotland, standing 1,380 ft. above sea level in a setting of rounded *Lowther* hills, with *Green Lowther* 2,403 ft., and *Lowther Hill,* 2,377 ft., as the principal summits, both being fine viewpoints. Many of the persecuted Covenanters hid in these hills during the late 17th cent. Lead mines in the neighbourhood of the village were opened originally in 1680, while other metals, including gold and silver, have also been mined, both here and at the nearby almost equally loftily-situated village of *Leadhills* (*q.v.*). The road linking these two villages attains a height of 1,531 ft. on the Dumfries-Lanark border. Leading south-westwards towards the Nith valley, a road traverses the fine *Mennock* (*q.v.*) pass, and attains a height of more than 1,400 ft. just beyond Wanlockhead. *Tomintoul* (*q.v.*), the highest village in the Highlands, stands only 1,160 ft. in altitude, more than 200 ft. lower than Wanlockhead, which lies in the heart of the Lowlands. *Iter. 48, 49.*

WATERLOO, Lanark. Map 9, NS 8 5.
Iter. 20, 54.

WATERTON-DUNECHT, Aberdeen. Map 21, NJ 7 0.
See **Dunecht.** *Iter. 176, 197.*

WATTEN, Caithness. Map 30, ND 2 5.
Situated a little to the south of Loch Watten, well known for its trout-fishing. At the south-eastern extremity of the loch is the ancient Mill of Watten. *Iter. 237.*

WEEM, Perth. 25. Map 19, NN 8 4.
E.C. Wed. M.D. Thurs. Lies on the north bank of the River Tay, at the east end of Strath Appin, overlooked by the 800-ft. high *Rock of Weem,* a good viewpoint. A local inn has hanging outside a portrait of General George Wade, inscribed " Soldier and Engineer." The Renaissance Church contains monuments to the Menzies, and their seat, *Menzies Castle,* a fine structure dating partly from 1571, stands west of the village in beautifully-wooded grounds. See **Aberfeldy, Dull** and **Wade Roads.** *Iter. 89, 107, 147, 149.*

WEISDALE, Shetland. Map 33, HU 3 5.
Iter. 268, 270.

WEMYSS, Fife. Map 17, NT 3 9.
GOLF. See **East Wemyss** and **West Wemyss.** *Iter. 128.*

WEMYSS BAY, Renfrew. 376. Map 8, NS 1 6.
E.C. Wed. GOLF. A popular Clyde coast resort, with a rock and pebble beach and a busy steamer pier. There are good views across the firth to the hills of Bute and Cowal. The Kelly Burn separates Wemyss Bay from the neighbouring Ayrshire resort of *Skelmorlie* (*q.v.*). To the east of Wemyss Bay is the burnt-out *Kelly House,* and to the north, near Wemyss

1. Castle.

Walkerburn, Peebles. The late 16th century Elibank Tower, 2½ miles east, on an unclassified road south of the River Tweed. Here is said to have taken place the wedding of Scott of Harden and 'Muckle Mou'd Meg'

Wanlockhead, Dumfries. What is said to be the highest petrol pump in Scotland, at an altitude of some 1,500 feet

Watten, Caithness. The old Mill of Watten, which lies at the south-eastern extremity of Loch Watten, on B870

Weem, Perth. Menzies Castle, which dates partly from 1571, and stands on the west side of the village, off B846

Weem, Perth. The sign of the Inn, where General Wade, 'Soldier and Engineer,' stayed in 1733

Wemyss, Fife. The remains of Macduff's Castle, near which stands an ancient dovecote. It is situated at East Wemyss, overlooking the Firth of Forth, off A955

PLATE 168 (facing page 260)

Wester Ross, Ross and Cromarty. The view from the Wester Ross railhead of Kyle of Lochalsh towards the Skye hill of Beinn na Caillich, across the narrows of Loch Alsh

Westerkirk, Dumfries. The Memorial to the engineer and architect, Thomas Telford, born near here in 1757

Westruther, Berwick. One of a pair of gate-houses incorporating milestones and coaching clocks, leading to the former Spottiswoode House. They stand some 3 miles south-west, on the Lauder road (A697). The inscription on the milestone is shown in the small illustration to the right

West Linton, Peebles. Lady Gifford's Well, on which is a figure carved locally in 1666

West Wemyss, Fife. The old Tolbooth, with its outside staircase

Whitekirk, East Lothian. The two-storeyed tithe barn, incorporating part of a 16th century castle, which stands beyond the churchyard

PLATE 169 (facing page 261)

Point, is the 19th cent. *Castle Wemyss*. See **Millport**. *Iter. 59, 64, 65, 66, 88.*

WEST BARNS, East Lothian. Map 10, NT 6 7. *Iter. 2, 40.*

WEST CALDER, Midlothian. 2,687. Map 9, NT 0 6. E.C. Wed. GOLF. Shale oil mining is carried on in the neighbourhood. See **Mid Calder**. *Iter. 19, 20, 22.*

WESTERGLEN, Stirling. Map 16, NS 8 8. Here is a B.B.C. radio transmitter.

WESTERKIRK, Dumfries. 372. Map 4, NY 3 9. A lonely Eskdale village, surrounded by green Lowland hills. A memorial Cross stands to the memory of Thomas Telford, the famous engineer, who was born in the vicinity, in 1757, and was buried in Westminster Abbey. Among his many achievements in Scotland was the construction of the *Caledonian Canal* (*q.v.*). *Iter. 12.*

WESTERN ISLES. Maps 6, 7, 12, 13, 22, 23 and 32. The name given collectively to the island groups off the West Coast of Scotland, consisting chiefly of the Inner and Outer Hebrides. All these, in addition to Arran, Bute and the Cumbraes, which lie farther south in the Firth of Clyde, are shown, together with their mainland communications, in the special map on pages 34 and 35 of the atlas. See **Arran, Bute, Colonsay, Hebrides (Outer), Iona, Islay, Jura, Millport** (for *Cumbraes*), **Mull, Rum, Skye, Staffa** and **Tiree**.

WESTER ROSS, Ross and Cromarty. Map 22, NG 7 2 etc., 24, NG 9 6 etc. and 29, NC 0 0 etc. This is the name applied to the picturesque and hilly western half of the county of Ross and Cromarty, as distinct from *Easter Ross* (*q.v.*), which comprises the more level country facing the North Sea. The coast of Wester Ross is indented by numerous fine sea lochs, and includes the railhead of *Kyle of Lochalsh* (*q.v.*) facing the island of Skye, and also the beautiful little resort of *Gairloch* (*q.v.*), to the east of which lies the delightful *Loch Maree* (*q.v.*), in a notable setting of North-West Highland hills. See **Dundonnell, Gruinard Bay, Loch Broom, Torridon** and **Ullapool**.

WEST GORDON, Berwick. Map 10, NT 6 4. See **Gordon**.

WEST KILBRIDE, Ayr. 4,241. Map 8, NS 2 4. E.C. Wed. GOLF. The old village lies off the main road, a little inland from the modern resort of *Sea Mill*, with its good sands, on the Firth of Clyde. To the north-west is Farland Head, with the ruined *Portencross Castle*, overlooking the twin Cumbraes. Off the headland a Spanish Armada galleon is thought to have foundered. *Kilbride Tower*, or *Law Castle*, stands on high ground off the road to Dalry. See **Fairlie**. *Iter 66, 88.*

WEST LINTON, Peebles. 1,624. Map 9, NT 1 5. E.C. Thurs. GOLF. This village lies at the foot of the *Pentland* hills, at a height of nearly 800 ft. It was formerly well known for its stonemasons, who worked largely on tombstones, and whose craftsmanship, dating from 1666, is displayed on the figure, re-erected in 1861, surmounting " Lady Gifford's Well." The dates 1660 and 1678 occur on a house opposite, the carvings being probably by the same hand. To the north-west, the Lyne Water flows down from the *Windy Gowl*, below the main Pentland ridge. A road, following the stream, climbs into the hills and then becomes a track, which was formerly one of the best known of the old drove roads, and is called the *Cauld Stane Slap*. This track crosses the Pentlands at a height of 1,430 ft., under the slopes of *East Cairn Hill*, 1,839 ft., and cattle were formerly driven over this drove road making for Stenhousemuir near *Falkirk* (*q.v.*). Opposite the track, to the southwest, rises the even higher *West Cairn Hill*, 1,844 ft. **9 m.** S.W. of West Linton, above the hamlet of *Dunsyre* (*q.v.*), rises *Black Law*, 1,460 ft., on which is situated the grave of a nameless Covenanter, slain at Rullion Green, in 1666. See **Glencorse** and **Romanno Bridge**. *Iter. 25.*

WEST LOCH TARBERT PIER, Argyll. Map 7, NR 8 6. See **Tarbert** (Argyll). *Iter. 121, 122.*

WESTRAY, ISLE OF, Orkney. Map 33, HY 4 4. See **Orkney Islands** (Westray).

WESTRUTHER, Berwick. Map 10, NT 6 4. Situated on the southern hill slopes of the *Lammermuirs*, with *Dirrington Great Law*, 1,309 ft., rising away to the north-east. Near the modern Church are remains of the former structure. Two lodges, with clocks over their gables, and milestones, remain from the former *Spottiswoode House*, and stand some **3 m.** S.W., off the Lauder road (A697). 1½ m. N.E. is *Wedderlie House*, partly 17th cent. *Iter. 9.*

WEST WEMYSS, Fife. Map 17, NT 3 9. GOLF. Lies a little to the south-east of the Kirkcaldy to Leven road, and is a small coal-port on the Firth of Forth. There is a curious old Tolbooth. The coast to the northeast is rocky, with caves, or " weems," notable for their Bronze and Iron Age and Early Christian carvings, though some of the caves have collapsed. *Wemyss Castle*, dating from 1421, 1670 and 1880, is of historic interest for the first meeting between Mary, Queen of Scots and Darnley, in 1565. See **East Wemyss**. *Iter. 128.*

WHALSAY, ISLE OF, Shetland. Map 33, HU 5 6. See **Shetland Islands** (Mainland).

WHANGIE, THE, Stirling. Map 15, NS 4 8. See **Stockiemuir**.

WHAUP HILL, Wigtown. Map 2, NX 4 4. *Iter. 78.*

WHISTLEFIELD, Dunbarton. Map 14, NS 2 9. On the watershed between the Gare Loch and *Loch Long* (*q.v.*), looking towards the hills of *Argyll's Bowling Green*. See **Portincaple**. *Iter. 102, 111.*

WHITBURN, West Lothian. 5,835. SB. Map 9, NS 9 6. A police training college is situated in this district of coal mines and iron foundries. *Iter. 18, 86.*

WHITEBRIDGE, Inverness. Map 25, NH 4 1. Here, the River Foyers is joined by the Fechlin, which has emerged from Loch Killin, in the hills to the south-east. *Whitebridge* is on the line of General Wade's military road from Fort Augustus to Inverness, constructed in 1732, and the former military rest-house at this point became at one time an inn. The Fort Augustus road first follows the Foyers, and then climbs to a height of 1,275 ft., with good views, on to moorlands, on which is situated Loch Tarf, before descending steeply to the wooded Glen Doe. There is a choice of routes leading northwards from Whitebridge, one road being hilly and descending to *Foyers* (*q.v.*) on *Loch Ness* (*q.v.*), and an alternative going by way of *Errogie* (*q.v.*), both routes converging at *Dores* (*q.v.*). See **Fort Augustus**. *Iter. 211, 212.*

WHITE BRIDGE, Perth. Map 19, NN 7 5. At a height of over 1,000 ft. in the Perthshire hills, on the line of one of the Wade roads, and near a road fork of two routes leading northwards to the Tummel valley. Between these roads lies the little Loch Kinardochy, and the westerly of the two roads passes near the loch-side to climb over the moorlands below *Schiehallion*, 3,547 ft., with fine views, before descending later to *Kinloch Rannoch* (*q.v.*). The more easterly of the roads reaches a height of 1,263 ft. shortly after leaving White Bridge. *Iter. 89, 138, 147, 149.*

WHITECAIRNS, Aberdeen. Map 27, NJ 9 1. *Iter. 186.*

WHITEHILLS, Banff. Map 27, NJ 6 6. This small fishing village lies in a sandy and rocky bay between Stake Ness and Knock Head. The coast to the west is rocky, with a succession of lonely headlands nearing *Portsoy* (*q.v.*). See **Boyndie Bay**. *Iter. 199.*

WHITEHOPE, Peebles. Map 10, NT 3 4. *Iter. 12.*

WHITEHOUSE, Argyll. Map 7, NR 8 6. *Iter. 121.*

WHITEKIRK, East Lothian. Map 10, NT 5 8. The interesting 15th cent. cruciform Church has a barrel-vaulted chancel and porch, and a massive tower, surmounted by a wooden spire. The structure was damaged by suffragettes in 1914, and has since been repaired. The carved wooden front of the north gallery is of 17th cent. date. A Holy Well was formerly situated in the near vicinity, and was visited, among others, by Aeneas Silvius, later Pope Pius II, the Church owing its origin to this Well, which was discovered in 1294. Near the Church is a two-storeyed tithe barn, incorporating part of a 16th cent. castle, and once used for the storage of grain by monks from Holyrood. **2 m. S.W.** stands the mansion of *Newbyth*, with fine walled gardens. See **Tynninghame.** *Iter. 2, 38.*

WHITE MOUNTH, Aberdeen. Map 20, **NO 2** 8.
The great mountain plateau of the *White Mounth* lies on the Angus border and faces Deeside and Balmoral Forest to the north, which separates it from the more important *Cairngorm* range. *Lochnagar* is the most famous White Mounth peak, its twin summits attaining 3,786 and 3,768 ft. respectively. *Broad Cairn*, 3,268 ft., *Cairn Bannoch*, 3,314 ft., *Fafernie*, 3,274 ft., and *Cairn Taggart*, 3,430 ft. are the other principal heights. Glen Callater, with its loch, to the west, and Glen Muick, also with its loch, to the east, lie on either side of the mountains, and provide means of access from Braemar and Ballater. The only access from the Angus side is by mountain paths from *Braedownie* (q.v.).

WHITERASHES, Aberdeen. Map 27, **NJ 8** 2.
Iter. 180.

WHITHORN, Wigtown. 1,026. SB. Map 2, **NX 4** 4.
An ancient Royal Burgh, in the bleak Machers peninsula, with the remains of a 12th and 15th cent. Priory Church, preserving a good late 12th cent. carved doorway. This Church may have been built on the site of *St. Ninian's* "White House," or "Candida Casa," though *Isle of Whithorn* (q.v.) claims the distinction that *St. Ninian's* Christian Chapel, built in 397, perhaps the earliest in Scotland, stood near the ruined Chapel at that place. *St. Ninian's Shrine* at Whithorn became an important place of pilgrimage, and was visited regularly by James IV. Whithorn Priory Church (A.M.) is approached by a 17th cent. archway known as "The Pend," which has a panel carved with the Royal Arms of Scotland before the Union; here has been set up a museum in which some carved stones are preserved. These include the 7th cent. *St. Peter's* Stone and the 5th cent. *Latinus* Stone, the latter possibly the oldest in Scotland. There are a number of small 18th cent. houses in George Street. **2 m. N.W.** is *Castle Wigg*, partly 16th and 18th cent. See **Cruggleton** and **Monreith.** *Iter. 82.*

WHITING BAY, Isle of Arran, Bute. Map 7, **NS 0** 2.
GOLF. This attractive small resort, with bathing, lies on Whiting Bay, facing the Firth of Clyde. There is a steamer pier. Inland extends the pretty Glen Ashdale, with its falls. Away to the north-east, beyond Kingscross Point, is Holy Island, described under *Lamlash*. See **Kildonan.** *Iter. 242.*

WHITLETTS, Ayr. Map 8, **NS 3** 2.
Iter. 20, 35.

WHITTINGHAME, East Lothian. 463. Map 10, **NT 6** 7.
E.C. Wed. *Whittinghame House*, built in 1817, was the birthplace, in 1848, of the Earl of Balfour, and in the grounds is his tomb. An old yew tree is said to mark the spot where Darnley's murder was plotted. The old *Whittinghame Tower* stands in the neighbourhood of the house, and dates from the 15th cent. **2 m. S.E.** is the little artificial *Pressmennan Lake*, the only "lake" in Scotland, apart from the much better known Lake of Menteith, described under *Port of Menteith*. **1½ m. E.** is the modernised 17th cent. house of *Ruchlaw*, which preserves two old sundials and a dovecote. See **Stenton.**

WICK, Caithness. 7,770. SB. Map 30, **ND 3** 5.
E.C. Wed. M.D. Thurs. GOLF. Situated on Wick Bay, where the Wick Water flows into the sea, the important herring fishing town and ancient Royal Burgh of *Wick* has a harbour which was designed by Telford. It was later improved by Thomas Stevenson, but is accessible to large steamers at high water only. The suburb of *Pulteneytown* was founded by the British Fishery Society early in the 19th

1. Parish Church. 2. Town Hall.

cent. In the Parish Church is the old Sinclair Aisle, in which the Earls of Caithness are buried. The quaint Town Hall is surmounted by a cupola. The airport lies about **2 m.** to the north-east. There is much fine cliff and rock scenery, both to the north and to the south of the town. **3 m. N.E.** is Noss Head, with its lighthouse, overlooking the sandy Sinclair's Bay, on the shores of which stand, in close proximity, the ruined Castles of *Sinclair* and *Girnigoe*, both demolished during Clan battles in the 17th cent. The latter was defended by a complicated system of moats, portcullis and guardrooms. **1½ m. S.E.** is the Castle of *Old Wick*, or *Castle Oliphant*, dating from the 14th cent., and known to mariners as the "Old Man of Wick." Nearby are curious rock stacks called the "Brig o' Tram" and the "Brough." See **East Mey, Reiss** and **Staxigoe.** *Iter. 200, 237, 238, 239.*

WIGTOWN, Wigtown. 1,345. SB. Map 2, **NX 4** 5.
E.C. Wed. This old town became a Royal Burgh in 1457, and stands on Wigtown Bay, near the estuary of the River Bladnoch, where there is a derelict quay. The old Cross, dating from 1748, retains its sundial, and is neighboured by a modern example. In the broad main street is an enclosure, once used to pen cattle. The churchyard contains an inscribed stone in memory of the "Wigtown Martyrs," a woman and a young girl, named Margaret McLauchlan and Margaret Wilson respectively, who are said to have been tied to stakes and drowned at the mouth of the Bladnoch in 1685. because of their Covenanting beliefs. A stone on the shore marks the spot. Another Covenanters' memorial stands on high ground behind the town, from which an extensive view can be obtained. **3 m. N.W.**, off the road to *Kirkcowan* (q.v.), are the standing stones of *Torhousekie* (A.M.), dating probably from the Bronze Age. They consist of 19 stones and form a complete circle. See **Bladnoch** and **Stirling.** *Iter. 81, 82.*

WILSONTOWN, Lanark. Map 9, **NS 9** 5.
A mining village, standing at an altitude of more than 900 ft., in a district of lonely moors and fells. *Iter. 22, 86.*

WINCHBURGH, West Lothian. 2,206. Map 9, **NT 1** 7.
A centre of the oil-shale industry, which is of considerable importance locally, but has left its mark in places to the detriment of the countryside. *Iter. 91, 95.*

WINDYGATES, Fife. 1,446. Map 17, **NO 3** 0.
The village stands a little way inland from the Fife coast, on the River Ore. *Iter. 94, 98, 127, 129.*

Whithorn, Wigtown. Remains of the 12th to 15th century Priory Church, later adapted for parish use. Fragments of St. Ninian's original 'White House,' or Candida Casa, survive on the site

Whithorn, Wigtown. The 17th century Pend archway, carved with the Royal Arms of Scotland before the Union

Wick, Caithness. The old Town Hall, which is surmounted by a cupola

Wick, Caithness. The 14th century Castle of Old Wick, or 'Old Man of Wick.' It stands 1½ miles to the south-east, off A9

Wigtown, Wigtown. The Covenanters' Memorial, which stands on a hill behind the town. It was erected in 1858

Wigtown, Wigtown. The stone on the shore commemorating the Wigtown Martyrs of 1685, a woman and a young girl, who were tied to stakes and drowned in the Bladnoch estuary

PLATE 170 (facing page 262)

Wormit, Fife. The 2-mile long railway bridge across the Firth of Tay, built 1883–88 to replace its ill-fated predecessor, blown down in 1879. The supports of the old bridge are still visible nearby

Yarrow, Selkirk. The rebuilt Church, which takes the place of two previous structures, both burnt down. Sir Walter Scott's great-grandfather was once minister of the church

Yarrow, Selkirk. The Yarrow, or Liberalis Stone, a memorial to two British Christian chieftains of the 6th century, Nudus and Dumnogenus, sons of Liberalis. It stands on A708, at Whitefield, to the south-west, and was excavated by a plough in the 19th century

Yetholm, Roxburgh. An old house in Kirk Yetholm, which was formerly the ' Palace ' of the Scottish gipsies

PLATE 171 (facing page 263)

WINTON HOUSE, East Lothian. Map 10, NT 4 6.
See **Pencaitland.** *Iter. 3.*

WISHAW, Lanark. 71,384. LB with Motherwell.
Map 9, NS 7 5.
E.C. Wed. GOLF. *Wishaw House,* to the north, and
Cambusnethan Priory, to the south-west, are Victorian
mansions by Gillespie Graham. J. G. Lockhart, Scott's bio-
grapher, was born at Cambusnethan manse in 1794. See
Motherwell. *Iter. 19, 54.*

WISTON, Lanark. Map 9, NS 9 3.
The old Church in this village was replaced in the 19th
cent. *Tinto Hill,* 2,335 ft., a fine viewpoint, rises to the north.

WORMIT, Fife. Map 17, NO 3 2.
The first stone of the ill-fated original Tay Bridge carrying
the railway into Fife was laid here in 1871. The present
bridge was built 1883–88. See **Newport.** *Iter. 126.*

YARROW CHURCH, Selkirk. 402. Map 10, NT 3 2.
The beautiful Vale of Yarrow, threaded by the Yarrow
Water, and well wooded in places, lies in the heart of the
green, rounded hills of Ettrick Forest, in the Lowlands, and
has been praised in verse and song by many well-known
writers and composers. "The Braes of Yarrow" by
Hamilton of Bangour; "The Dowie Dens of Yarrow" by
Scott; and Wordsworth's three famous poems, all vividly
recall Yarrow Vale. Scott's great-grandfather was once
minister of Yarrow Kirk, which has twice been burnt, and
which now contains relics associated with Wordsworth and
Hogg, the "Ettrick Shepherd." A little to the north-east of
the Kirk is the picturesque, derelict *Deuchar Bridge,* dating
from 1653. To the south, a by-road leads over the hills to
Ettrick Bridge End (*q.v.*). About ⅓ m. W. of the Kirk, off
the Moffat road, is the *Yarrow,* or *Liberalis* Stone, at Whitefield, excavated by chance by a plough during the 19th cent.
It commemorates the battle of Yarrow, in 592, when two
sons of Liberalis died. Some of the loveliest scenery in the
Vale is in the vicinity of *Broadmeadows* (*q.v.*), lying to the
north-east, in a richly-wooded setting. *Iter. 13, 46.*

YELL, ISLE OF, Shetland. Map 33, **HP 4** 8 etc.
See **Shetland Islands** (Yell).

YESTER HOUSE, East Lothian. Map 10, NT 5 6.
See **Gifford.**

YETHOLM, Roxburgh. 295. Map 11, NT 8 2.
E.C. Wed. Situated at the foot of the *Cheviot* (*q.v.*) hills,
with the *Cheviot,* 2,676 ft., away to the south-east, across
the Northumberland border. Nearer hills, traversed partly
by the Border line, are *The Curr,* 1,849 ft. and *The Schel,*
1,985 ft., below which lies the lonely valley of the College
Burn. The village is divided by the Bowmont Water into
Kirk Yetholm and *Town Yetholm,* and is overlooked by the
Cheviot foothill of *Staerough,* 1,086 ft. The former was
once the headquarters of the Scottish gipsies, and the last
" Queen," Esther Faa Blythe, was buried here, in 1883. Her
so-called " palace " in the village is still pointed out, and
her son, who became " King " in 1898, died four years later.
The character of " Meg Merrilees," in Scott's " Guy
Mannering," is supposed to have been suggested by one of
the earlier gipsy " Queens." *Iter. 7, 47.*

YETTS OF MUCKHART, Perth. Map 16, NO 0 0.
GOLF. A meeting-place of roads in the hills around *Glendevon* (*q.v.*), with the River Devon flowing to the south-east
below *Lendrick Hill,* 1,496 ft. See **Crook of Devon** and
Rumbling Bridge. *Iter. 86, 89, 136.*

YOKER (Glasgow), Lanark. Map 8, NS 5 6.
Here is a car ferry across the River Clyde, giving access to
Renfrew (*q.v.*).

YTHAN WELLS, Aberdeen. Map 27, NJ 6 3.
Lies in the Strathbogie district of the county. The River
Ythan rises in the vicinity and flows eastwards to enter the
North Sea near *Newburgh* (*q.v.*). 1½ m. W., at *Glenmailen,*
are traces of Roman occupation, considered to be the most
northerly in Britain. 3 m. N. stands the ancient house of
Frendraught, with which a tragedy of 1630 is associated,
when the tower was set on fire, causing the deaths of Lord
Aboyne and Gordon of Rothiemay.

Explanatory Glossary including Gaelic (G) and Norse (N) Words

In **Gaelic** the stress accent falls on the first syllable, except in compound names, where the chief stress falls on the qualifying word. The aspirated digraphs "bh" and "mh" are represented by "v" in English; "fh" is silent; "ch" is equivalent to the guttural sound heard in the German word Nacht.

In the respelt word the vowels have the following phonetic values: "a" as in "father," "ā" as in "shake," "â" as in "all," "e" as in "pen," "ē" as in "feet," "ê" as in "where," "i" as in "tin," "ī" as in "time," "o" as in "cot," "ō" as in "mote," "oo" as in "foot," "ow" as in "cow," "u" as in "tub," and "ū" as in "tube." Of the consonants, "g" is always hard as in "gate."

The definite article varies according to gender, number, case and the initial letter of the noun to which it is prefixed; its forms are am, an, an t-, a', na, na h-, nam, nan.

A, Ay, a (*N*).—Island, *e.g.*, Soa, sheep isle, Pabby, priest's isle.

Aber, Abar, Obar (*G*).—Mouth or confluence of a river.

Abhainn, Amhuinn (*pron.* av'-uin) (*G*).—River. Usually **Avon.**

Ager, Acker (*N*).—Arable or cultivated land.

Ailean (*pron.* al'-yen) (*G*).—A green place; plain.

Airt.—Direction.

Aisle.—In Scotland, sometimes applied to a small building attached to a church, such as an apse or mausoleum. See **Arbuthnott** and **Largs.**

Allt (*pron.* âlt) (*G*).—Brook, burn, stream. Conventional forms: **Ald, Alt, Auld, Ault.**

Ambry or Aumbry.—Small cupboard for holding altar vessels, etc.

Archæan.—Of the earliest geological period (See **Hebrides, Outer (Harris)** and **Inchnadamph**).

Ard, Aird (*G*).—A high point, promontory.

Àth (*pron.* ah) (*G*).—A ford; also a kiln.

Avon (*G*).—Conventional form of **Abhainn** (*q.v.*).

Bad (*pron.* bât) (*G*).—A thicket, tuft.

Bagh (*pron.* bàh) (*G*).—A bay.

Baile (*pron.* bal'-y) (*G*).—Town. Usually **Bal, Bali.**

Bailey.—Enclosure (See **Mote**).

Bailie or Baillie.—Magistrate, cf. alderman.

Bàn (*G*).—White, fair.

Barbican.—Outer defence, especially double tower over gate or bridge.

Bard (*N*).—Extremity, point, headland.

Bàrd (*G*).—A poet; a dyke, enclosure.

Barp (*G*).—Conical heap of stones, a chambered cairn. See **Hebrides, Outer** (North Uist).

Barr (*G*).—A point, top, extremity.

Bartizan.—Battlemented parapet, or turret at top of tower.

Bastel House.—House capable of being defended.

Bastion.—Projecting part of fortification.

Bayeux Tapestry.—(See **Mote**.)

Beag (*pron.* bāk) (*G*).—Little, small. Conventional form, **Beg.**

Bealach (*pron.* byall'-ach) (*G*).—Breach, pass, gap. See **Tornapress.**

Beck (*N*).—A brook.

Beinn (*pron.* byān) (*G*).—A mountain. Conventional form, **Ben.**

Beith (*pron.* bā) (*G*).—A birch tree.

Beltane.—May-day Festival when great fires are lit and traditional ceremonies observed. See **Peebles.**

Bing.—Slag-heap.

Binnean or Binnein (*pron.* bin'-en) (*G*).—A pinnacle, little mountain.

Birlinn.—Barge.

Black House.—Highland cottage of unmortared stones with fire in middle of floor, and interior blackened by smoke. See **Dornie.**

Blindstorey.—Triforium below clearstorey of church, admits no light.

Bo, plural **Ba** (*G*).—Cow, cows.

Bodach (*pron.* bott'-ach) (*G*).—An old man, hobgoblin, spectre.

Both, Bothan (*pron.* bo, bo'-han) (*G*).—A hut, both or bothy (*q.v.*).

Bothy.—Farm servants' hut.

Braigh (*pron.* brai'-h) (*G*).—Top, summit. Usually **Brae, Bread.**

Breac (*pron.* brechk) (*G*).—Spotted, pie-bald, speckled, trout.

Brig.—Bridge.

Broch or "**Pictish Tower**" (*N*).—Massive cylindrical drystone tower peculiar to Scotland. Skilfully constructed with intra-mural chambers, stair and galleries. All openings, except entrance tunnel, look on roofless inner court about 40–50 feet in diameter. Period unknown, but relics prove occupation by civilized community engaged in farming, weaving, etc., during early Iron Age. Chiefly found north of Inverness. See **Altnaharra, Glenelg, Orkney** and **Shetland.**

Bronze Age.—From approximately 1800 B.C. to 400 B.C. tools, weapons and ornaments were made of bronze, well-designed and serviceable.

Bruaich (*pron.* broo'-ach) (*G*).—A bank, brae, brim, steep place.

Buachaille (*pron.* buo'-ach-ilyu) (*G*).—A herdsman. See **Kingshouse.**

Buidhe (*pron.* boo'-i) (*G*).—Yellow, golden coloured.

Burgh.—cf., borough, a chartered town. (1) Royal Burgh had charter from the Crown. (See **Culross**, etc.) (2) Burgh of Barony was created by the baron. (See **Aberdeen**.) (3) Police Burgh, managed by commissioners.

Burn (*G*).—A stream: Anglo-Saxon, Burne.

By (*N*).—Village, town.

Cailleach (*pron.* kyl'-ach) (*G*).—A nun, old woman.

Cairn.—Pyramidal heap of undressed stones erected as sepulchre, monument or landmark.

Cairn, Chambered.—Enclosing one or more burial chambers or cists. Were round, oval, rectangular, elongated or horned (with horn-like projection, found only in Scotland). See **Kilmartin** and **Orkney** (Maeshowe).

Camas (*pron.* k'-mas) (*G*).—Bay, bend, channel.

Caol (*pron.* kaol) (*G*).—Strait, firth, narrow. Other form **Kyle.** Alternative Gaelic form: **Caolas.**

Carn (*G*).—A heap of stones, cairn.

Carse (*N*).—Alluvial fertile land alongside a river. See **Carse of Gowrie.**

Ceann (*pron.* kyenn) (*G*).—Head, headland. Usually **Ken, Kin.**

Ceilidh (*pron.* kaylee) (*G*).—Smaller, indoor Gaelic gathering. See **Mod.**

Chapter House.—Special building in which members of monastic or knightly order met to hear chapters of the rule read and transact business.

Chief.—See article on Highland Clans and Lowland Families.

Choir.—See Quire

Cill (*pron.* Kil) (*G*).—A cell, church. Usually Kil.

Cinerary Urn.—Urn holding ashes after cremation.

Cioch (*pron.* kioch) (*G*).—A pap, woman's breast.

Cist.—Prehistoric stone coffin, found in a cairn or underground, sometimes containing a cinerary urn (*q.v.*).

Clach (*pron.* klach) (*G*).—A stone. **Clachan,** stones, hamlet.

Cladach (*pron.* klad'-ach) (*G*).—Shore, beach.

Cladh (*pron.* klugh) (*G*).—A churchyard, burying-ground.

Clan.—See article on Highland Clans and Lowland Families.

Clearstorey or Clerestory.—Section over aisle roofs lighting upper part of church. See **Blindstorey.**

Cleuch or Cleugh.—Ravine.

Huna, Caithness. A farmhouse with fences made from the local flagstones, in a far northern hamlet

Ballater, Aberdeen. The bridge over the River Dee which links A93 and A973

Crail, Fife. An old dovecote standing near the shore of one of the earliest Royal Burghs in the county

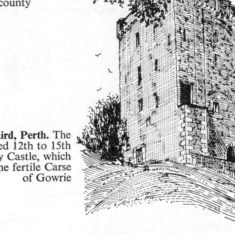

Kinnaird, Perth. The restored 12th to 15th century Castle, which overlooks the fertile Carse of Gowrie

Sorn, Ayr. The ancient Church, with its outside staircase, and the 'jougs,' or collar for wrongdoers, hanging on the wall below

Crossraguel Abbey, Ayr. The ruined Kennedy stronghold of Baltersan Tower, which stands to the north-east of the ruined Abbey

PLATE 172 (facing page 264)

Crichton, Midlothian. The tower of the 15th century Collegiate Church, built by Sir William Crichton, Chancellor of Scotland

Ettrick Bridge End, Selkirk. Oakwood Tower (1602), showing characteristic crow-stepped gables. It was once the home of Sir Walter Scott's grandfather, and stands 2 miles north-east, on B7009

Devil's Beef Tub, Dumfries. The Memorial Stone (1935) to John Hunter, a Covenanter martyr, who was shot near here in 1685

Culloden, Inverness. The Well of the Dead, where the Chief of the MacGillivrays fell in the battle which terminated the '45 Rising

Dunsyre, Lanark. The 'jougs,' or iron collar for wrongdoers, hanging on a wall of the Church

Culross, Fife. The 17th century house known as The Study. This tiny Royal Burgh, now partly in the hands of the National Trust for Scotland, was once famous for its girdles, or baking-plates

PLATE 173 (facing page 265)

Close.—Common entry leading to a "land" (q.v.).

Cluain (G).—A field, pasture, green plain, meadow.

Cnap (pron. krap) (G).—A knob, hillock.

Cnóc (pron. knochk, krochk) (G).—A knoll. Usually **Knock.**

Coill, or **Coille** (pron. kolyi) (G).—A wood, forest.

Coire (pron. kor'-e) (G).—A cauldron, kettle, circular hollow. Other form: **Corrie.**

Col.—Depression in mountain chain.

Collegiate Church.—Church served by a staff of clergy (XIV and XV centuries). See **Crichton, Seton,** etc.

Commendator.—Person appointed to collect the fruits of a benefice during a vacancy.

Corbel.—Projection of stone or timber which supports part of building.

Corbie-steps.—Crow steps (where the gable has stepped instead of sloping sides).

Covenanter.—Upholder of the Covenants which played an important part in Scottish history. (1) The National Covenant, 1638, repelled Episcopacy and the Scottish Prayer Book (sometimes called "Laud's Liturgy"). (2) The Solemn League and Covenant, 1643, a league with England for the suppression of Episcopacy. The Covenants were declared illegal after the Restoration and the Covenanters took up arms in 1665. In 1685, adherence to the Covenants was declared treasonable and mercilessly repressed. The name "Covenanter" is specifically applied to the persecuted—"the men of the moss hags," hunted down during the "Killing Time," 1685–9. See **Sanquhar,** etc.

Crannog.—Lake-dwelling. See **Cambus o' May.**

Creag (pron. krāg) (G).—A rock, cliff, English form: **Craig.**

Croft.—Small-holding.

Cromlech.—Prehistoric monument consisting of flat stone laid across upright ones.

Crow-steps.—See Corbie-steps.

Cruach (pron. kroo'-ach) (G).—Stack, heap, haunch.

Cul (pron. kool) (G).—The back, a nook.

Culdee (Keledei).—Member of Celtic religious order occupied in maintaining the round of divine service.

Cup-Mark, Cup-and-Ring Mark.—Cup-shaped hollow, sometimes surrounded by concentric rings, found in groups on earth-fast boulders and covers of cists. Purpose unknown. See **Kilmartin.**

Curtain.—Wall connecting towers and surrounding castle enclosure.

Damh (pron. dav) (G).—A bullock, heifer.

Dearg (G).—Red.

Doire (G).—Grove, hollow.

Dolmen.—See Cromlech.

Donjon, Dungeon. — Originally the mound or mote: then the tower on the mound; later the strongest tower of a castle; lastly its prison cell.

Doocot.—Dovecote.

Druim (G).—The back, ridge. Usually **Drem, Drom, Drum.**

Dubh (pron. doo) (G).—Black, dark. Other form: **Dhu.**

Dún (pron. doon) (G).—A fort, castle.

Eaglais (pron. āklash) (G).—A church, temple.

Earth House.—Low, curved, subterranean gallery. Also called Pict's House, Fairy House, or Weem (Cave). See **Pitcur.**

Eas (pron. es) (G).—A waterfall. Other form; **Easach** (pron. es'-ach).

Easg (pron. āsk) (G).—Bog, fen, natural ditch.

Eilean (pron. ēl'an) (G).—An island.

Entresol.—Intervening floor between vaulted basement and hall of tower.

Ey (N).—An island. See **Ay.**

Fad (G).—Long, e.g. **Beinn Fhada,** long mountain. See **Croe Bridge.**

Fair, Far (Norwegian, **Faar**) (N).—Sheep.

Fearn (pron. fern) (G).—An alder tree.

Fell, Field (Norwegian, **Fjeld**) (N).—Mountain.

Feu.—To let.

Fifteen. The, or **The '15.**—Jacobite Rising of 1715, attempted to restore the House of Stewart in the person of James Francis Edward Stewart, Chevalier de St. George, sometimes referred to as "the Old Pretender." His standard was raised at **Braemar** (q.v.), 6th September, 1715.

Firth, Frith (Lat. **Fretum**) (N).—Strait, estuary of a river.

First Pointed.—See **Gothic.**

Flamboyant. — "Flame-like" tracery used in late French Gothic, and in Scotland in preference to English Perpendicular. (See **Melrose.**)

Forest.—District reserved for hunting (originally woodland).

Forty-five, The, or **The '45.**—Attempt renewed by Jacobites in 1745 when Prince Charles Edward Stewart (or Stuart) ("Bonnie Prince Charlie," sometimes called the "Young Chevalier" or "Young Pretender"), raised his standard at **Glenfinnan** (q.v.).

Fuar (pron. foo'-ar) (G).—Cold.

Gabbro. — Black rock, excellent for climbing, found chiefly in the **Coolins** (q.v.) of Skye.

Gabhar, or **Gobhar** (pron. go'ur) (G).—A goat.

Gait, Gate.—Way, road.

Garbh (pron. garv) (G).—Rough. Other spelling: **Garve.**

Garth (Norwegian, **Gaard**) (N).—An enclosure, yard, farm.

Geal (pron. gel) (G).—White, clear.

Geo.—See **Gio.**

Ghillie.—A sportsman's attendant.

Gill (N).—A ravine.

Girth.—Sanctuary Enclosure.

Gio, Geo (N).—A chasm, rift. See **Orkneys** (Hoy).

Girdle, or **Griddle.**—Round iron baking-plate.

Glac (G).—A hollow, dell, defile.

Glas (G).—Grey, pale, wan; green.

Glais.—A stream.

Gleann (pron. glyan') (G). — Narrow valley, dale, dell. Usually **Glen.**

Gneiss. — Archaean (q.v.) grey rock found near **Inchnadamph** (q.v.) and in **Harris.** (See **Hebrides, Outer.**)

Gorm (G).—Blue, azure, green.

Gothic.—Style of architecture that developed the use of the pointed arch. Prevalent from XII to XVI centuries. Periods of development styled Early, Middle and Late Pointed, corresponding to Early English, Decorated and Perpendicular in England. "Scottish Baronial" (q.v.). Gothic was attempted revival of Gothic forms in mansions of XIX century, characterised by excessive use of pepper-pot turrets, battlements, etc.

Grind (N).—A gate. See **Shetland** (Mainland).

Haar.—Drizzling rain; mist.

Harl.—Rough-cast.

Haugh, Hauch.—Water-meadow.

Hogmanay.—New Year's Eve.

Holm (N).—An island in river, or sea, near the shore.

Hope (N).—An inner bay.

How (Haugr) (N).—A burial mound.

Howe.—(1) A hollow or sheltered place. (2) A (sepulchral) mound.

Howff.—Resort, or meeting place. See **Dumfries.**

Hut Circle.—Stone foundation of prehistoric round dwelling.

I (pron. ē) (G).—An island.

Inbhir (pron. in'-ver) (G).—Confluence, place at the meeting of river and sea. Other form: **Inver,** cf. **Aber.**

Innis (pron. in'-ish) (G). — Island, meadow. Usually **Inch.**

Inver (G).—See **Inbhir.**

Iron Age.—Period from about 400 B.C. to introduction of Christianity, about A.D. 400 at **Whithorn** (q.v.).

Jacobite.—Adherent of House of Stewart after deposition of James VII and II in 1689. (See the Fifteen and Forty-five.)

Jougs.—An iron collar, with a lock, which was fastened round a wrong-doer's neck and attached by a chain to a tolbooth or churchyard wall for a period of punishment. See **Duddingston** and **Fowlis Easter,** etc.

Kale, Kail.—Greens, or Broth made of greens.

Kelpie.—Water-sprite.

Ken or Kin.—See **Ceann.**

Kil.—See **Cil.**

Knock.—See **Cnoc** (G).

Kyle.—See **Caol** (G).

L-Plan.—Plan of tower with wing projecting at right angles. See **Craigievar Castle,** etc.

Lag (*pron.* lak) (G).—A hollow in a hill. Usually **Logan, Logie.**

Laigh.—Low.

Laird.—Landed proprietor.

Lairig (G).—The sloping face of a hill, a pass. See **Lairig Ghru.**

Land.—Tenement. See Close.

Lane.—(In Galloway.) A slow-moving river. See **Kirkgunzeon.**

Law (N).—A conical hill.

Lax (N).—A salmon.

Leathad (*pron.* le'ud) (G).—A slope, declivity.

Leathan (*pron.* lya-un) (G).—Broad.

Liath (*pron.* lēa).—Grey.

Links.—Sandy ground, Golf Course.

Linne (*pron.* lyēn'a) (G). — A pool, sound, channel.

Loch (G).—A lake, arm of the sea. **Lochan.**—Small loch.

Machair (*pron.* mach'-ar) (G).—A plain or extensive beach.

Machicolation.—Projecting parapet with spaces left between supports to permit of missiles being dropped on assailants. See **Borthwick Castle.**

Màm (G).—A round or gently rising hill.

Manse.—Minister's house. (In Aberdeen, Professor's house.)

Maol (*pron.* mull) (G).—Headland, bald top, cape.

Meadhon (*pron.* me'-un) (G).—Middle, central.

Meall (*pron.* myal) (G).—Knob, lump, rounded hill.

Megalith.—Large stone.

Meikle.—Great, much.

Mercat Cross.—At one time a proclamation centre, or where criminals were punished. See **Aberdeen, Inverkeithing, Prestonpans,** etc.

Mon.—Gaelic Musical Festival. See Ceilidh.

Mòd (G).—A court of justice, meeting, small knoll.

Moine or **Mointeach** (*pron.* mò'-entyach) (G).—Moss-land, mossy. See **Cairngorms** and **Kilmichael.**

Mol (N).—Shingly beach. **(Möl.)**

Monadh (*pron.* mon'-a) (G). — Moor, heath, hill, mountain. See **Newtonmore.**

Monolith.—Single block of stone.

Mòr (G).—Great, large, tall. English form : **More.**

Mote, Motte. — Steep-sided earthen mound on which Norman castle stood. A Mote-and-bailey Castle stood on a mote, with bailey or forecourt enclosed by a palisade and ditch, as illustrated in the Bayeux Tapestry (early XII century).

Mounth.—An expanse of mountain. Came to be applied to the passes of the Grampians. See **Cairn o' Mounth.**

Muc (*pron.* moocht) (G).—A sow, pig. Usually **Muck, Muic.**

Muileann (*pron.* mool'ān) (G).—Mill.

Muir (*pron.* mur) (G).—The sea.

Nab (Norwegian, **Knabb**) (N).—A rock projection.

Neolithic.—See Stone Age.

Ness (N).—A point, headland.

Norman.—See Romanesque.

Noup (N).—A lofty headland. See **Shetland** (Mainland).

Òb (G).—A bay, creek, haven. Other form : **Tob.**

Odhar (*pron.* ò'-ur) (G).—Dapple, drab, dun-coloured, sallow.

Ogee.—A curve produced by the merging of a convex and a concave line.

Ogham, Ogam.—Celtic form of writing on stone. The essential feature is a central line with strokes at right angles to it, and groups of dots representing vowels. See **Golspie.**

Ord (G).—A round, steep, or conical hill.

Papa (N).—Spiritual father, a prefix to several of the smaller Orkney and Shetland Islands.

Parish Church.—Has been Presbyterian in Scotland since 1688, when Episcopacy was disestablished, and penalized for adherence to House of Stewart. Catholicism fell in Scotland in 1560.

Peel or **Pele.**—A tower. Has come to have special reference to Border towers. See **Cranshaws.**

Pend.—Vaulted passage through buildings, usually ending in court, or yard.

Picts.—A mysterious people whose race has never been authoritatively determined. The Romans called them Picti, which may mean " painted." Chiefly in the north-east, they left sculptured stones bearing symbols of unknown significance. (See **Elgin, Ballater,** etc.) Finally dominated by the Scots, losing their language and individuality. Pictish towers — see Brochs. Pict's House — see Earth House.

Pinetum.—Plantation of various kinds of pines grown for botanical or ornamental purposes. See **Stobo.**

Piscina.—Stone basin with drain for rinsing altar vessels.

Policies.—Park or grounds.

Poll (*pron.* poul) (G).—A pool, pond, pit.

Porphyry. — Volcanic rock containing crystals.

Provost.—(1) cf. mayor; (2) cf. dean.

Pulpitum.—The most important screen in a mediæval church, with platform on top from which Epistle and Gospel were read. Position varied with position of the quire.

Quire, Choir.—The Eastern part of a monastic, cathedral or collegiate church.

Rathad (*pron.* ra'-ud) (G).—A road, way.

Reek, Reekie.—Smoke, smoky. " Auld Reekie "—name applied to **Edinburgh.**

Reiver.—Outlaw.

Riabhach (*pron.* rē'-ach) (G).—Drab, greyish, brindled, grizzled. Other form : **Riach.**

Righ (*pron.* rè) (G).—A King. Other form : **Ree.**

Romanesque or **Norman.**—Architectural style, XI–XII centuries, characterised by the round arch (but see also Transitional).

Ros (G).—A point, promontory. Other form : **Ross.**

Ruadh (*pron.* roo'-a) (G).—Red, reddish.

Rudha (*pron.* roo'-a) (G).—Promontory. Usually **Ru, Rhu, Row.**

Runes.—(1) Letters of earliest Teutonic alphabet (*e.g.* **Ruthwell**). (2) Marks of hidden meaning. (3) Secret counsel.

Sacrament House.—Interior niche often elaborately carved, for the reservation of the Elements. See **Cullen, Deskford** and **Fowlis Easter.**

Scaur, Scar.—Precipitous slope.

Scottish Baronial.—Name given to style of building of many late XVI and early XVII century castles, as at **Craigievar** and **Midmar,** etc. (*q.v.*). See also under Gothic.

Sean (*pron.* shen) (G). — Old, aged, ancient.

Sedilia.—Recessed seats south of altar.

Sept.—Branch of clan.

Sett.—Pattern of tartan.

Sgeir (*pron.* skeir) (G).—A reef, sea-surrounded rock.

Sgorr or **Sgurr** (*pron.* skor, skoor) (G).— A peak, conical sharp rock. Sometimes **Scaur, Scour.**

Shieling, Sheiling.—Summer pasture, or Herdsman's hut at summer pasture.

Sith (*pron.* she) (G).—A fairy. **Sithean** (*pron.* shee'-an).—A fairy hillock or knoll.

Skerries (N).—Isolated rocks, or islets. See **Shetland** (Mainland).

Slack, Slug.—Opening between hills.

Slochd (G).—A deep hollow. See **Slochd Summit.**

Slogan.—Battle-cry .

Sneachd (*pron.* snyachg) (G).—Snow.

Souter or **Sutor.** — Shoemaker. See **Cromarty** and **Selkirk.**

Kilmarnock, Ayr. The surviving steeple of the former Laigh Kirk, which was burnt in 1668 and replaced by the present building in 1802

Mid Calder, Midlothian. The Parish Church, which has an apsidal choir, re-built in 1541

Kincardine-on-Forth, Fife. The 17th century Mercat Cross

Edinburgh, Midlothian. The Canongate Church, built in 1688, with a stag's antlers on the gable Cross. The Old Town of Edinburgh has been described as 'Auld Reekie,' referring to the smoke formerly emitted by the closely packed tall houses

Doune, Perth. The old Mercat Cross of a small town formerly well known for the manufacture of pistols

Slochd Summit, Inverness. The highest point (1,332 feet) on A9, where it traverses the gorge of Slochd Mor between Carrbridge and the valley of the River Findhorn on the way to Inverness

PLATE 174 (facing page 266)

Benderloch, Argyll. Part of the hill known as Beregonium, or Dun Mac Sniochan. On the summit is a prehistoric fort showing traces of vitrifaction, or burning

Closeburn, Dumfries. The 14th century Closeburn Tower, which still preserves the iron 'yett,' or grille, to its first-floor entrance doorway

Latheron, Caithness. A prehistoric standing stone, which is situated near the station

Crail, Fife. The 16th century Tolbooth, into which prisoners were formerly taken through the blocked-up doorway under the window at the side

Auchtermuchty, Fife. The Tolbooth of 1728, which displays characteristic crow-stepped gables

Kirkcaldy, Fife. A cottage in the Kirk Wynd, in which Thomas Carlyle lodged between 1816 and 1818

PLATE 175 (facing page 267)

Srath (*pron.* stra) (*G*).—A valley, plain beside a river, strath.

Sròn (*G*). — Nose, peak, promontory. Other form: **Strome**.

Sruth (*pron.* stru) (*G*). — A stream, current. Usually **Struan**.

Stac (*pron.* stak) (*G*).—A steep rock, conical hill.

Stack (*N*). A columnar rock.

Standing Stone.—Monolith of unhewn stone.

Stewartry.—Lands governed through a Steward. Usually refers to the county of **Kirkcudbright**.

Stob (*pron.* stop) (*G*).—A point.

Stone Age.—Stage of civilisation at which tools and weapons were of stone. Distinction made between the Palæolithic, Older Stone Age, and the Neolithic—New Stone Age, when polished stone and flint implements used, and great sepulchral cairns built; approximately between 2500 and 1800 B.C.

Stor, Stour (*N*).—Big, large, great.

Strath.—Wide valley. See **Srath**.

Stuc (*pron.* stook) (*G*).—A pinnacle, peak, conical steep rock.

Suidhe (*pron.* sooi'-ye) (*G*). — Sitting, resting place.

Sutor.—See Souter.

Tacksman.—Tenant (generally a kinsman of the Chief).

Taigh or **Tigh** (*pron.* ty) (*G*).—A house. Usually **Tay, Ty**.

Tairbeart (*pron.* tar'-pyart) (*G*).—An isthmus. Other forms: **Tarbet, Tarbert**.

Teampull (*G*).—A church. See **Hebrides, Outer** (North Uist).

Thing, Ting (*N*).—A provincial parliament. See **Shetland** (Mainland).

Tir (*pron.* tyĕr) (*G*).—Country, region, land.

Tir-nan-Og (*G*).—The land of the ever young.

Tobar (*G*).—A well, spring, fountain. Usually **Tober**.

Tolbooth.—Once the booth for collecting tolls or taxes. Later, came to refer to the Town Hall. See **Culross, Edinburgh, Tain**, etc.

Tom (*pron.* tōm) (*G*).—A hillock, mound.

Torc (*pron.* tork) (*G*).—A boar.

Torr (*G*).—A mound, heap, hill.

Traigh (*pron.* try) (*G*).—Sea-shore, beach, strand, sands.

Transitional.—In architecture, refers to the transition from Romanesque to Gothic, i.e. to the period in which the round and the pointed arch were used simultaneously, late XII to early XIII centuries. (Note, however, that round-headed doorways were common in Scotland in Gothic times.)

Tulach (*pron.* too'-ach) (*G*).—Knoll, hillock, eminence. Anglicised forms: **Tilly, Tully, Tulloch**.

Uachdar (*pron.* ooach'-ur) (*G*).—Upperland. Usually **Auchter, Ochter**.

Uaine (*pron.* ooin'e) (*G*).—Green.

Uamh (*pron.* oo'-av) (*G*).—A cave, a grave.

Uig (*pron.* ooēg) (*G*).—A nook, bay.

Uisge (*G*).—Water, rain.

Undercroft.—Basement under church.

Vennel.—Alley.

Vik, Wik (*N*).—A creek.

Vitrified Fort.—Hill-fort with walls fused by fire. See **Finhaven**, etc.

Voe (*N*).—A little bay, inlet. See **Shetland** (Mainland).

Weem.—Cave. See Earth House.

Whal (Norwegian, **Hval**) (*N*).—A whale.

Whaup.—Curlew.

Wynd.—Alley.

Yett.—Gate, particularly massive iron-barred grille defending entrance to tower. See **Cawdor**, etc.

Z.—Represents an obsolete symbol for a sound resembling initial " y " (*e.g.* **Drumelzier** (*q.v.*) pronounced Drummell-yer); or, after " n," the " g " in " swing " (*e.g.* Menzies pronounced Ming-ies).

HIGHLAND CLANS AND LOWLAND FAMILIES

THE CLAN MAP on page 36 of the Atlas gives a general idea of the districts occupied by the principal Highland clans, and indicates also the Lowland areas in which certain families were dominant.

HIGHLANDS: It will be understood that the districts outlined were not clan reserves, nor were they clearly delimited by hard-and-fast boundaries like a modern county. Clansmen always moved about freely. Moreover, whereas some clans, notably the Campbells, continually enlarged their holdings, others, as for example the MacGregors, gradually lost every rood of land. Then again, in certain districts there was a mixture of clans from the earliest recorded times; for instance, in Glen Lyon there were Robertsons, MacGregors, members of Clan Menzies and others. Other districts were debatable lands, such as Lochaber, where Camerons, Mackintoshes, Macdonalds and Macleans had conflicting claims. As a general rule, however, a particular clan was in the majority, as the map suggests.

The word clan means " children " or " descendants," and Mac means " son." Thus MacDonald means the son of Donald the " world-ruler " from whom all MacDonalds claim descent. The Chief of a clan is the representative of this common ancestor, and is known to his own people by a

patronymic which proclaims this relationship. Hence the Duke of Argyll, head of Clan Campbell is MacCailein Mor, Son of the Great Colin. The tie of blood was always insisted upon, and a remarkable and enduring feature of Highland life was the love the clansmen gave their Chief. Travellers like Dr. Johnson were invariably impressed by it. General Wade reported to the Government that the chiefs " have an Inherent Attractive Virtue, which makes their people follow as Iron Claps to the Loadstone." The Chief was the clan's leader in war, and at home he was responsible for its welfare and conduct, and was the holder of the land it occupied. Legally he had the right of administering justice, which included the power of life and death. This hereditary jurisdiction was taken away after the Jacobite Rising of 1745. At the same time the clans were disarmed and forbidden to wear their national dress. The results of this measure were far-reaching, for it broke up the military organisation which was the basis of clan life, and in so doing, it struck a blow at the whole social system of the Highlands. The Chief, who had been the leader and father of his people, became their landlord. The clansman ceased to be a warrior and became a peasant.

HIGHLAND DRESS: The embargo on Highland dress, mentioned above, may seem trivial, but the tartan set the Highlander apart from the Lowlander, and also distinguished clan from clan. There is nothing fortuitous about the sett or pattern of tartan. It was possible to tell where a man lived by looking at his plaid. Writing about 1695, Martin Martin noted that " the women are at great pains first to give an exact pattern of the plaid upon a piece of wood, having the number of every thread of the stripe on it." The belted-plaid was from four to six yards in length and two yards broad. It was plaited from the belt to the knee, thrown round the shoulders and fastened on the breast with a bodkin. It was kilt, plaid and coat in one. The division of this garment into three seems to have come about in the XVIII cent., giving rise to the philabeg (or small kilt) as now worn. The arms forbidden by the Disarming Act of 1746 were broadsword, targe, dirk, pistol, or gun. The use of the distinguished and expressive Gaelic language, once universal in the Highlands, was steadily discouraged by religious and educational agencies. The 1951 provisional Census figures show a decline in the number of Gaelic and English speakers from 230,806 in 1901 to 91,630 in 1951, while the number of persons who speak Gaelic alone has dropped from 28,106 to 2,178.

LOWLANDS: On the Border, social conditions in the Middle Ages approximated to conditions in the Highlands. In both cases the people needed land to live on, and a leader who would defend them. Where the Highlander looked to his Chief for protection and leadership in war, the Borderer looked to a Douglas, a Ker, or a Home. An old rhyme tells of the dominance of Lord Cassillis, head of the Kennedy family:

> Frae Wigtown to the town of Ayr,
> Port Patrick to the Cruives of Cree,
> Nae man need think for to bide there
> Unless he court a Kennedy.

Both in the Highlands and on the Border, as surnames became usual, the dependants of a great house—even although they were not kinsmen—adopted the family name, so that it became the commonest name in a district. In the Lowlands, as in the Highlands, the people showed devotion to the head of the family, a " clannishness " that appears to be part of the common Celtic heritage of the race. The sense of mutual obligation, and the way it worked out in practice on the Border, appears in ballads—" Jamie Telfer of the Fair Dodhead," or " Kinmont Willie."

HIGHLAND CLANS: Brief notes follow on some of the clans mentioned in the Gazetteer.

CLAN CAMERON: Famous Chiefs were Sir Ewen Cameron ("Evandhu") who fought at **Killiecrankie** (q.v.), and his grandson the " gentle Lochiel " whose influence was decisive in rallying the clans to Prince Charles Edward's banner in 1745. The clan badge is the cranberry or the oak. The slogan is interpreted—" Sons of the hounds come hither and get flesh!" (See **Lochaber** and **Loch Arkaig**.)

CLAN CAMPBELL: The name means "wry-mouthed." The Chief is the Duke of Argyll, known to his people as MacCailein Mor, Son of the Great Colin, who founded the family of Campbell of **Loch Awe** (q.v.), a race of statesmen, with high literary gifts. In 1715 and 1745 they supported the Government. The mythical progenitor of the family was Diarmid (See **Oban** and **Glenshee**). Their badge is the wild myrtle or fir club moss, and their slogan " Cruachan!" (See **Loch Awe** and **Inveraray**.)

CLAN CHATTAN: See Mackintosh.

CLAN CHISHOLM: The clan territory is Strath Glass and its lovely tributary glens. (See **Struy Bridge**.)

CLAN DONALD: Donald means "world-ruler." The clan claims descent from Donald, grandson of the great Somerled who broke the power of the Scandinavians and prepared the way for the Celtic Lordship of the Isles. (See **Inveramsay** and **Saddell**.) The clan supported Prince Charles Edward from the outset of his ill-fated adventure (See **Loch nan Uamh, Kinlochmoidart**, etc.). This widespread and once-powerful clan includes the families of Sleat in Skye (the House of the Isles, See **Duntulm**); Glengarry (See **Invergarry**); and Clanranald (See **Acharacle** and **Dalilea**), whose Chiefs decide precedence by lot, if more than one is present at a gathering of Clansmen. Other branches noted in the Gazetteer are Clanranald of Lochaber (MacDonells of Keppoch, See **Roy Bridge**), Clan Iain Abrach (MacDonalds of **Glencoe**, q.v.) and Clan Iain of Ardnamurchan (See **Kilchoan**). The badge is the common heath. " Fraoch Eilean! "—" Heather Isle " is one of the clan slogans and the various branches have much distinctive pipe music, including the fine Lament, " The Massacre of Glencoe."

CLAN DONNACHIE: The Robertsons of **Struan** (q.v.) are believed to be the descendants of the ancient Celtic Earls of Atholl. The badge is the fine-leaved heath, and the slogan means " Fierce when roused! "

THE FARQUHARSONS' lands lie in Aberdeenshire, and the royal estate of **Balmoral** (q.v.) was bought from them. Their slogan is " Carn na cuimhne!"—" Cairn of Remembrance!" See **Monaltrie**.

THE FRASERS are a family of Norman origin, who first settled in Tweeddale (See **Peebles**) and in the XIII cent. were granted the forfeited estates of the Bissets in Inverness-shire (See **Kilmorack**).

GORDON is a " place " name (See **Huntly**). The clan became so powerful in the Highlands that the Chief was known as " Cock o' the North." (See **Fochabers, Aboyne** and **Methlick**.)

GRAHAM is an ancient name, traditionally derived from the hero who overthrew the Roman Wall, locally known as Grim's, or Graeme's Dyke. The family was distinguished by its loyalty to the House of Stewart and produced the two most distinguished soldiers of the Civil Wars, the great Marquis of Montrose, and Graham of Claverhouse, the "Bonnie Dundee" of Scott's ballad (See **Fort William** and **Killiecrankie**). The Chief of Clan Graham is the Duke of Montrose.

CLAN GRANT is a branch of Clan Alpin. The present Chief is Lady Seafield. The clan has many distinguished branches. The badge is the pine or the cranberry, and their slogan "Stand fast, Craigellachie!" (See **Cullen** and **Aviemore**.)

CLAN GREGOR: "'S Rioghail mo Dhream"—"Royal is my Race"—is the motto of this ancient and unfortunate clan which (with Macaulays, Mackinnons and others) claims descent from Griogar, son of King Alpin (c. A.D. 787). The name Macgregor was proscribed from 1603 to 1774. The famous Rob Roy was a Macgregor of Glengyle, but frequently used the name of Campbell. (See **Balquhidder**.)

THE MACDOUGALLS: Like Clan Donald, Clan Dougall is descended from the mighty Somerled, and once had wide domains. These Lords of Lorne were on the losing side in the contest for the throne between Bruce and Balliol, and many of their lands passed to the Campbells, but Dunollie still remains the seat of the Chief. (See **Oban** and **Tyndrum**.) The badge is bell heather and the slogan means "Victory or Death!"

CLAN MACKAY: The Highland designation of the Chief, Lord Reay, is Mac Aoidh—"Son of Hugh." The badge is reed grass or broom, and the slogan means "the White Banner of Mackay!" (See **Reay**.)

THE MACKENZIES: The "z" here represents an obsolete letter formerly rendered by "g" or "y," and an old form is the name of MacKengie. The clan rose to great power after the forfeiture of the MacDonalds, Lords of the Isles. The Chief of the Mackenzies of Kintail was the Earl of Seaforth. Their badge is variegated holly, and the slogan "Tulach Ard!"—(A hill in Kintail.) See **Gairloch**.

CLAN MACKINTOSH or Macintosh and **CLAN MACPHERSON**: These are the leading clans of the Clan Chattan Confederacy, and are believed by some authorities to have formed the "Clan Quhele" which took part in the Clan combat at **Perth** (q v) The badge of both is boxwood or whortleberry, and their slogans are "Loch May!" and "Creag Dhubh!" (See **Drumgask, Moy** and **Newtonmore**.)

THE MACLEANS or **CLAN GILLEAN** belong to the Western Isles and claim descent from Gillean of the Battle-axe, who fought at the battle of Largs. The Chief is Maclean of Duart and the 26th Chief acquired and restored the historic Castle Duart in Mull (See **Craignure**). Ardgour is almost the only clan territory to have been held by Macleans in continuity. Crowberry, holly and blaeberry are the badges of various families, and the clan slogans mean "Death or Life!" and "Another for Hector!" (See **Inverkeithing**.)

THE MACLEODS are an Island family, and the names of the early chiefs suggest that they were of Norse, or mixed Norse and Celtic descent. The historic seat of the Chief is **Dunvegan** (q.v.) in Skye. The badge of the Macleods of Harris is juniper, and a famous pipe tune is "The Lament for Rory Mor."

THE MACNABS are a branch of the ancient Clan Alpin, and claim descent from the lay Abbot of Glendochart (Clann-an-Aba, Sons of the Abbot). Their badge is the heath (See **Killin**).

THE MACPHERSONS: See Clan Mackintosh.

THE MACRAES of Kintail mustered strong in the Seaforth Highlanders when the regiment was first raised in 1778. The Chief held from 1520 the post of Hereditary Constable of Eilean Donan Castle (See **Dornie**).

CLAN MENZIES fought for Bruce at Bannockburn. The slogan means "Up with the Red and the White!" (See **Weem**.)

CLAN MUNRO'S Chief is Munro of Foulis and the slogan is "Casteal Folais na theine!"—"Foulis Castle on Fire!" Many noted soldiers came of this clan. (See **Evanton**.)

CLAN STEWART: There are many septs of this royal clan. The Stewarts of Appin played a gallant part in the '45, led by Stewart of Ardshiel (See **Portnacroish**). The badge is the oak and the slogan is "Creag-an-Sgairbh!"—"The Cormorant's Rock."

THE MURRAYS: This powerful family claims descent from Hugh Freskyn (See **Duffus**), a Fleming, whose son assumed the title "de Moravia" because of his wide domain in Moray. The Duke of Atholl is Chief of Clan Murray of Atholl (See **Blair Atholl**). An old saying ran:

> Duke of Atholl, King in Man
> And the greatest man in a' Scotlan'.

OGILVIE: The Chief is the Earl of Airlie, who claims descent from the Celtic Earls of Angus. His seat is Cortachy Castle (See **Dykehead**). The family suffered heavily in the Stewart cause.

FERRY
LOCATION
MAP
SCALE
0   10   20   30   40 MILES

Ferries indicated thus ◯ operate daily.
   "   "   "   ▢ do not operate
                        on Sundays.
(The numbers refer to the list of
  ferries on the following pages.)

JOHN O'GROATS

Outer Hebrides

KYLESKU 58

LAIRG

Skye

57 STROME
56 KYLE OF LOCHALSH
KYLEAKIN
KYLERHEA GLENELG
55 Summer only

ARMADALE
54 MALLAIG
Advance reservation required

SPEAN BRIDGE
FORT WILLIAM
53 CORRAN
ARDGOUR
52 BALLACHULISH
CONNEL BRIDGE
50 OBAN 51 BONAWE
Mull
CUAN
49

Jura

Islay

Kintyre

Arran

KESSOCK
59 INVERNESS

ELGIN   BANFF   FRASERBURGH
                      PETERHEAD
INVERMORISTON   HUNTLY
FORT AUGUSTUS
INVERGARRY   KINGUSSIE
                        ABERDEEN
BRAEMAR
BLAIR ATHOLL   STONEHAVEN
PITLOCHRY
FORFAR
DUNDEE 60 NEWPORT
PERTH

STIRLING
NORTH QUEENSFERRY
SOUTH QUEENSFERRY 61 EDINBURGH
GLASGOW
DUNOON
ROTHESAY
SEE INSET

AYR

N

SEE
INSET

CROWN COPYRIGHT RESERVED   Ⓒ THE AUTOMOBILE ASSOCIATION

COLINTRAIVE DUNOON 43
48 RHUBODACH   GOUROCK   OLD KILPATRICK YOKER
BUTE   PARTICK
ROTHESAY 42 WEMYSS BAY 44 ERSKINE RENFREW GOVAN GLASGOW
                                    PAISLEY
MILLPORT 45 FAIRLIE   47
41 ARDROSSAN
ARRAN 41 SUMMER ONLY   KILMARNOCK
BRODICK Scale
         0   5   10 MLS
Nov. 1950

270

FERRIES IN SCOTLAND

The following abridged information is correct at the time of going to press. Owing to frequent changes, the service times and charges should be verified direct with the ferry operators or any A.A. Office. Every possible care is taken to ensure the accuracy of the following information but the Automobile Association cannot be held responsible for errors or omissions or their consequences.

Tide and weather conditions may sometimes cause delay to **services,** and at certain ferries on popular routes congestion occurs during the touring season.

Some ferry services *do not operate on Sundays.*

Advance bookings are not accepted and are not required, unless otherwise stated.

Petrol tanks need not be emptied.

The **charges** shown are for single journeys unless otherwise stated and are at owner's risk. Members staying in the vicinity of a ferry should enquire whether period tickets at reduced rates are available.

Commercial vehicle rates may be obtained direct from the ferry operators.

Where passengers are allowed to remain in their vehicles on ferries, care should be taken to leave sufficient room between vehicles so that doors can be opened to allow passengers to escape in an emergency.

INDEX TO FERRIES

The second column gives the National Grid Reference to the Atlas at the end of the book.

The third column gives the paragraph number on the succeeding pages where particulars of the ferries are listed in clockwise order from the Firth of Clyde to the Firth of Forth.

271

41. FAIRLIE–BRODICK (all year) **and ARDROSSAN–BRODICK** (Summer only) (across the Firth of Clyde to the Isle of Arran). (Map 7 NS 2 4 & 2 5.)

Vehicles should be available for shipment 15 minutes before the advertised time of departure. It is advisable to reserve space prior to the date of travel, particularly for weekends. Bookings should be sent direct to: The General Manager, Caledonian Steam Packet Co. Ltd., Gourock, Renfrewshire. *Telephone:* Gourock 31261.

Service.—Weekdays only. NO SUNDAY SERVICE. October to May, two morning services from Fairlie only (also 4.10 p.m., 5.40 after 31st March, Saturdays). June to September, two services from Fairlie and two from Ardrossan from 6.40 a.m. to 6.5 p.m. (5.30 p.m. Saturday). For times see Scottish Region railway timetable.

Capacity.—45 cars. **Time in Transit.**—60 minutes.

Charges (return, including driver).—Car, according to length £3 to £6; Trailer-caravan, small £4 15s., large £6 15s.; Motor cycle, solo 13s. 6d.; with sidecar £1 2s. 6d. Passengers 9s. 1d. return. Pier Dues. At Ardrossan, Cars 2s. 6d.; Motor cycle, solo or with sidecar 1s. At Brodick, each way, Car 6s.; Motor cyle, solo 1s.; with sidecar 1s. 6d.

42. WEMYSS BAY–ROTHESAY and MILLPORT (across the Firth of Clyde to the Isles of Bute and Cumbrae). (Map 7, NS 1 5 & 1 6.)

Vehicles should be available for shipment 15 minutes before the advertised time of departure. It is advisable to reserve space prior to date of travel, particularly for weekends and for services to Millport. Bookings should be sent direct to: The General Manager, Caledonian Steam Packet Co. Ltd., Gourock, Renfrewshire. *Telephone:* Gourock 31261.

Service.—Several crossings daily to and from Rothesay weekdays between 7.45 a.m. and 6.20 p.m. (7.45 p.m. Saturdays); Sundays, April to September from 9.45 a.m.; during the period October to March the Sunday service operates in conjunction with service 43 from Gourock instead of Wemyss Bay. Service to Millport on Mondays, Wednesdays and Fridays only. For times of all services, see Scottish Region railway timetable.

Capacity.—34 cars. **Time in Transit.**—30 minutes to Rothesay; 50-80 minutes to Millport.

Charges (return including driver).—Car, according to length £1 10s. to £2 10s.; Trailer-caravan, small £2 6s. 3d., large £3 9s. 3d.; Motor cycle, solo 8s. 9d.; with sidecar 17s. 6d. Passengers 5s. 11d. to Rothesay or Millport. A circle ticket for cars (£1 4s. to £2) and passengers (5s. 8d.) is available from Wemyss Bay to Rothesay and Dunoon to Gourock or vice versa. Motorists make their own way between Dunoon and Rothesay using **Ferry No. 48.** Pier Dues. At Rothesay, Car 1s.; Motor cyle, solo 6d.; with sidecar 9d. At Millport, Car 5s.; Motor cyle, solo or with sidecar 3s.

43. GOUROCK–DUNOON (across the Firth of Clyde). (Map 7, NS 1 7 & 2 7.)

Vehicles should be available for shipment 15 minutes before the advertised time of departure. It is advisable to reserve space prior to the date of travel, particularly for weekends. Bookings should be sent direct to: The General Manager, Caledonian Steam Packet Co. Ltd., Gourock, Renfrewshire. *Telephone:* Gourock 31261.

Service.—Several crossings daily, weekdays from 6.45 a.m. to 6.10 p.m. (8 p.m. Saturdays); Sundays, October to March from 10.45 a.m. to 6 p.m. April to September from 9.20 a.m. to 7.50 p.m. For times see Scottish Region railway timetable.

Capacity.—34 cars. **Time in Transit.**—20 minutes.

Charges (including driver).—Car, according to length, single 14s. to 25s., return £1 1s. to £1 17s. 6d.; Tri-car single 16s. 6d., return £1 4s. 9d.; Motor cycle, solo single 5s. 6d., return 8s. 3d.; with sidecar, single 11s., return 16s. 6d.; Trailer-caravan, small single £1 3s., return £1 14s. 9d.; large single £1 14s. 9d., return £2 6s. 3d. Passengers single 2s. 4d. A circle ticket for cars (£1 4s. to £2) and pas-

sengers (5s. 8d.) is available from Gourock to Dunoon and Rothesay to Wemyss Bay or vice versa. Motorists make their own way between Dunoon and Rothesay using **Ferry No. 48.** Pier Dues. At Dunoon, Car 1s.; Motor cycle, solo 6d.; with sidecar 9d.

44. ERSKINE–OLD KILPATRICK (across the River Clyde). *Telephone:* Glasgow CENtral 2695. (Map 8, NS 4 7.)

Service.—Weekdays, April to September 6 a.m. to 11 p.m (October to March 10 p.m. weekdays, 11 p.m. Saturdays); Sundays, April to September 8 a.m. to 11 p.m. (October to March 10 p.m.).

Capacity.—12–15 cars. **Time in Transit.**—3 minutes (subject to congestion).

Charges (including driver).—Car 1s. 6d.; Tri-car 1s. 6d.; Motor cycle, solo 6d., with sidecar 9d.; Trailer-caravan 1s. Passengers 2d.

45. RENFREW–YOKER (across the River Clyde). *Telephone:* Glasgow CENtral 2695. (Map 8, NS 5 6.)

Service.—Continuous day and night.

Capacity.—15–18 cars. **Time in Transit.**—2 minutes (subject to congestion).

Charges (including driver; double rates, midnight to 5 a.m.).—Car 1s.; Tri-car 1s.; Motor cycle, solo 4d., with sidecar 6d.; Trailer-caravan 9d. Passengers 1d.

46. WHITEINCH–LINTHOUSE

This ferry has ceased to operate and will be replaced by a road tunnel which is being constructed under the Clyde between Whiteinch and Linthouse and is due for completion in 1963.

47. GOVAN–PARTICK (across the River Clyde). *Telephone:* Glasgow CENtral 2695. (Map 8, NS 5 6.)

Service.—Weekdays continuous 6 a.m. to 10 p.m. NO SUNDAY SERVICE

Capacity.—15 cars. **Time in Transit.**—4 minutes.

Charges.—Free.

48. COLINTRAIVE–RHUBODACH (across the Kyles of Bute to the Isle of Bute). *Telephone:* Rothesay 304. (Map 7, NS 0 7.)

Service.—Daily from 8 a.m. (Sunday 9 a.m.) to dusk.

Capacity.—4 cars. **Time in Transit.**—4 minutes.

Charges (including driver).—Car 7s. 6d. and 9s. 6d.; Motor cycle, solo 2s. 6d., with sidecar 5s.; Trailer-caravan 15s. Passengers 1s.

49. CUAN (across Cuan Sound to the Island of Luing). (Map 14, NM 7 1.)

Service.—This ferry is dependent on the tides and does not operate during certain periods of low water. A timetable is displayed on a notice board near Kilninver Post Office. For Tide Table see *Members Handbook.* March to September 8 a.m. to 6 p.m., October to February 9 a.m. to 4 p.m. NO SUNDAY SERVICE for cars. When the car ferry is not operating a passenger launch service is available.

Capacity.—2 cars. **Time in Transit.**—15 minutes.

Charges.—Free.

50. CONNEL BRIDGE. A railway bridge with a track for vehicles across Loch Etive. *Telephone:* Connel 281. (Map 14, NM 9 3.)

Service.—Open continuously 24 hours, weekdays and Sundays.

Charges.—Car (excluding driver and passengers) according to horsepower 4s. to 6s.: Tri-car 4s.; Motor cycle, solo 1s. 3d., with sidecar 2s. 6d.; Trailer-caravan 6s. Passengers 2d. Weekly, fortnightly and monthly tickets available.

51. BONAWE (across Loch Etive). *Telephone:* Bonawe 210. (Map 14, NN 0 3.) This ferry is not advised if towing a caravan.

Service.—Weekdays 8 a.m. to 5 p.m. (or dusk if earlier—noon on Saturdays). NO SUNDAY SERVICE.

Capacity.—2–4 cars. **Time in Transit.**—5 minutes.

Charges.—Car 5s.; Tri-cars 4s.; Motor cycle, solo 2s. 6d., with sidecar 3s. 6d. Passengers 3d.

52. BALLACHULISH (across Loch Leven). *Telephone:* Ballachulish 215; Fort William 149. (Map 18, NN 0 5.)

If towing a caravan or trailer it is advisable to use the road round Loch Leven.

Service.—Daily from 8 a.m. (Sundays 9 a.m.) to 8 p.m. or dusk if earlier. From May to August inclusive the service is extended to 9.30 p.m. or dusk if earlier.

Capacity.—6 cars. **Time in Transit.**—5 minutes (subject to congestion).

Charges (including driver and passengers).—Car, according to length 4s. to 7s. 6d.; Tri-car 3s.; Motor cycle 2s., with sidecar 3s.

53. CORRAN–ARDGOUR (across Loch Linnhe). *Telephone:* Onich 235. (Map 18, NN 0 6.)

Service.—Weekdays 8.15 a.m. to 7.45 p.m. (summer 8.45 p.m.) Sundays from 10.30 a.m. to 7.45 p.m. (Summer 8.45 p.m.) or dusk if earlier.

Capacity.—4–5 cars. **Time in Transit.**—6 minutes.

Charges (including driver and one passenger).—Car 6s.; Tri-car 4s. 6d.; Motor cycle, solo 2s., with sidecar 3s. 6d.; Trailer-caravan (including car and passengers) 10s. Passengers 4d.

54. MALLAIG–ARMADALE (across the Sound of Sleat to the Isle of Skye).

There is no car ferry service in operation but a limited number of vehicles are carried by the combined passenger and cargo boats operated by David MacBrayne Ltd. Previous arrangements MUST be made with David MacBrayne Ltd., 44 Robertson Street, Glasgow, C.2. *Telephone:* Glasgow CENtral 9231.)

Service.—Weekdays, Mallaig departure 9.40 a.m.; Armadale departure 11.0 a.m. NO SUNDAY SERVICE.

Time in Transit.—40 minutes.

Charges.—Cars £2 8s. 1d. per ton (minimum £1 16s. 6d.); Motor cycle, solo 5s. 6d., with sidecar 11s. Passengers, 1st class, single 3s., return 4s. Reduced rates for return within three months. Pier dues. At Mallaig, Car 3s. 9d. Motor cycle, solo 1s. 3d.; with sidecar 1s. 10d. At Armadale, Car 5s. to 7. 6d. Motor cycle, solo or with sidecar 3s. 6d.

Passengers and solo motor cycles will be carried on the above service without previous booking. They will also be carried on MacLennan service which operates on weekdays only from June to September, three or four times a day. No bookings necessary.

55. GLENELG–KYLERHEA (across Kyle Rhea to the Isle of Skye). (Map 23, NG 8 1.)

This ferry is not advised if towing a caravan, and special care is necessary along the approach roads.

Service.—May to September inclusive, weekdays from 8.30 a.m. to 9.0 p.m. (or dusk if earlier). NO SUNDAY SERVICE.

Capacity.—2 cars. **Time in Transit.**—4 minutes.

Charges (including driver and passengers).—Car 10s.; Motor cycle, solo 2s. 6d., with sidecar 5s.

56. KYLE OF LOCHALSH–KYLEAKIN (across Kyle Akin to the Isle of Skye). *Telephone:* Kyleakin 202. (Map 23, NG 7 2.)

Service.—Weekdays only. May to September 7.0 a.m. to 9.45 p.m.; October to April 8 a.m. to 8.45 p.m. NO SUNDAY SERVICE.

Capacity.—4–6 cars. **Time in Transit.**—10 minutes (subject to congestion).

Charges (including driver).—Car, single 9s., & 12s. 6d. return 16s. & 20s.; Tri-car, single 9s., return 16s.; Motor cycle solo, single 3s. 2d., return 5s.; with sidecar, single 6s. 3d., return 10s.; Trailer-caravan single 9s., return 16s. Passengers 6d.

57. STROME (across Loch Carron). *Telephone:* Lochcarron 219. (Map 23, NG 8 3.)

Service.—Weekdays, June to August 8 a.m. to 9 p.m. (or dusk if earlier). September to May 9 a.m. to dusk. NO SUNDAY SERVICE.

Capacity.—2–6 cars. **Time in Transit.**—8 minutes (subject to congestion).

Charges (including driver and passengers).—Car 10s.; Tri-car 10s.; Motor cycle, solo 2s., with sidecar 3s.; Trailer-caravan £1 (10s. if conveyed at same time as car); Luggage-trailer 5s.

Alternative service by rail. Facilities for the conveyance of cars by specified passenger trains are available on week-days only (3 trains a day) between Kyle of Lochalsh or Strome and Strathcarron Stations. Two days' notice must be given to the Stationmaster. The petrol tank must be emptied. *Telephone:* Kyle 205, or Lochcarron 204. Charges vary from about £1 7s. to £2.

58. KYLESKU (across Loch Cairnbawn). *Telephone:* Kylestrome 202. (Telephone available on north side of ferry). (Map 28, NC 2 3.)

If towing a caravan it is advisable to proceed via Lairg as special care is necessary along the approach roads to this ferry.

Service.—Daily, mid-April to mid-September 9 a.m. to 9 p.m. Mid-September to mid-April 9 a.m. to dusk.

Capacity.—4 cars. **Time in Transit.**—5 minutes (subject to congestion).

Charges.—Free.

59. KESSOCK (across Beauly Firth). *Telephone:* Inverness 270. (Map 25, NH 6 4.)

Service.—From South Kessock. Weekdays half-hourly 7.15 a.m. to 10.45 p.m. Sundays half-hourly 9.45 a.m. to 5.45 p.m.

From North Kessock. Weekdays half-hourly 7.30 a.m. to 10.30 p.m. Sundays half-hourly 10 a.m. to 6 p.m.

Additional services from June to mid-September every 15 minutes from each side. Weekdays 10.15 a.m. to 6.30 p.m. Sundays 2 p.m. to 5.15 p.m. then half-hourly until 9.45 p.m.

Capacity.—8–10 cars. **Time in Transit.**—7 minutes.

Charges (including driver).—Car 3s.; Tri-car 2s.; Motor cycle, solo 1s. 3d., with sidecar 2s.; Trailer-caravan 3s.; Luggage-trailer 1s. 6d. Passengers 6d.

60. DUNDEE–NEWPORT (across the Firth of Tay). *Telephone:* Dundee 25364, Newport (Fife) 3252. (Map 17, NO 4 2.)

Service.—From Dundee. Weekdays half-hourly from 7 a.m. to 10 p.m. (October to April hourly between 7 p.m. and 10 p.m.) Sundays hourly from 10 a.m. to 8 p.m. then 9.15 p.m. (October to April to 7 p.m. then 8.15 p.m. only.) Services from Newport half-hour later than Dundee.

Capacity.—16–40 cars. **Time in Transit.**—15–20 minutes.

Charges (including driver).—Car, according to horsepower or engine capacity, from single 5s. 9d. to 9s. 6d., return 8s. 8d. to 14s. 3d.; Tri-car single 4s. 11d., return 7s. 5d.; Motor cycle solo, single 1s. 4d., return 2s.; with sidecar, single 2s. 7d.; return 3s. 11d.; Trailer, per foot length, single 1s. 4d., return 2s. Passengers, single 10d., return 1s. 3d. Return tickets are available for one month. Motorists and motor-cyclists using this and **Ferry No. 61** successively should, when obtaining a ticket, ask for a voucher entitling them to a reduction of 20 per cent. This allowance is made when the second crossing is booked and applies to both fares. The outward journey must be completed within seven days and return journey by both ferries within one month from date of issue of the vouchers.

61. QUEENSFERRY (across the Firth of Forth). *Telephone:* South Queensferry 253. (Map 17, NT 1 7.)

The Forth road bridge is under construction and is due for completion in 1963.

Service.—From 6.45 a.m. to 11.10 p.m. daily, including Sundays and Public Holidays. 3 or 4 sailings per hour from each side, but this may be reduced to half-hourly service in the evenings and on Sundays, particularly from October to March inclusive.

Capacity.—24–28 cars. Time in Transit.—12 minutes.

Charges (including driver).—Car, according to horsepower or engine capacity, 4s. 6d. to 8s. 3d.; Tri-car 4s.; Motor cycle solo, 1s. 9d. or 2s. 3d., with sidecar 4s.; Trailer, per foot length, 1s. 9d. Passengers 7d. For reduced rates when using this ferry and that across the Tay, see **Ferry No. 60**.

The information given is CORRECT AT THE TIME OF GOING TO PRESS. Conditions at the ferries are continually changing and SERVICE TIMES AND CHARGES should be verified.

SHIPPING SERVICES TO THE ISLANDS

Regular shipping services for passengers are maintained throughout the year to most of the larger islands and also, less frequently, to many others. Particulars of the more important services are given on the following pages. These services also convey passengers to a number of remote mainland piers. The shipping companies (see page 276) publish timetables giving full particulars of services, including also details of numerous summer season excursions and tours.

The information is correct at the time of going to press, but the service times and charges should be verified direct with the shipping companies concerned.

There is no **air ferry service** for the transport of vehicles between the mainland and the islands off the coast of Scotland, but British European Airways operate passenger services from the mainland towns of Glasgow, Edinburgh, Aberdeen, Inverness, Wick and Campbeltown serving the islands of Islay, Tiree, the Outer Hebrides, Orkney and Shetland. Timetables showing the routes served can be obtained from any office of British European Airways and from most travel agencies.

TAKING A VEHICLE TO THE ISLANDS

The distances from the mainland to the islands vary between the half-mile ferry crossing to Bute and Skye and the 270 miles from Edinburgh to Shetland, so that the decision whether or not to take a motor vehicle to any of the islands is a matter of personal preference and is influenced by the cost of shipping the vehicle and the extent of motoring road available. If it is considered not worthwhile to ship a vehicle to one of the islands, arrangements can usually be made for it to be garaged on the mainland, but it is advisable to reserve accommodation in advance.

As a rule it is essential to give previous notice to reserve space on the vessels. The A.A cannot undertake to make reservations and bookings should be made direct with the shipping company. Solo motor cycles are usually accepted without previous notice, except to the very small islands. On all the larger islands there are piers at which vehicles can be landed.

All vehicles are conveyed at owner's risk and it is advisable to make sure that the vehicle insurance policy covers the journey. The shipping charges are quoted as a guide only and the exact charges should be confirmed direct with the company concerned. In addition to the shipping charges, pier dues are levied at most piers on arrival and departure. Further details and addresses will be found on the following pages under the heading "The Shipping Companies."

INDEX TO ISLANDS SERVED

The following index shows the mainland ports of departure, the names of the piers on the islands and the shipping company operating each service. It also shows the service number given on the following pages where all essential particulars of each shipping service are given. These numbers also appear on the maps on pages 33, 34 and 35 of the Atlas at the end of the book.

Island			Atlas Page	Service No.	Shipping Company	Vehicles & Passengers	*Island Piers* Passengers* Only	Mainland Port
Arran	...	...	7	1, 2 & 3	CSP	Brodick	Whiting Bay	Fairlie
							Lochranza	Ardrossan
Barra	...	...	32	11	MAC	Castlebay		Oban
Benbecula	...	32	11 & 12	MAC	via South Uist			Oban, Mallaig or Kyle of Lochalsh
Bute	...	...	7	2, 3, 5 & 6 (see also ferry 48)	MAC	Rothesay		Wemyss Bay (*Weekdays*) Gourock (*Sundays*)
Canna	...	...	23	12	MAC		Canna	Mallaig or Kyle of Lochalsh
Coll	...	...	12	11	MAC		Coll	Oban
Colonsay	...	13	7	MAC	Colonsay			Tarbert West
Cumbrae	...	7	4	CSP	Millport			Wemyss Bay
Eigg	...	...	12	12	MAC		Eigg	Mallaig or Kyle of Lochalsh
Eriskay	...	32	11	MAC		via South Uist		Oban
Gigha	...	...	6	7	MAC	Gigha		Tarbert West
Harris	...	...	32	12	MAC	Tarbert	Rodel	Kyle of Lochalsh or Mallaig
Iona	...	...	13	8	MAC		Iona	Oban
Islay	...	...	6	7	MAC	Port Askaig		Tarbert West
						Port Ellen		Tarbert West
Jura	...	...	6	7	MAC	Craighouse		Tarbert West
Lewis	...	...	32	16	MAC	Stornoway		Kyle of Lochalsh or Mallaig
Lismore	...	...	14	10	MAC	Lismore		Oban
Mull	...	...	12 & 13	10	MAC	Salen	Craignure	Oban
						Tobermory		
North Uist	...	32	12	MAC	Lochmaddy			Mallaig or Kyle of Lochalsh
Orkney	...	...	33	17 & 18	NS	Stromness		Thurso (Scrabster)
						Kirkwall		Aberdeen
						Kirkwall		Edinburgh (Leith)
Raasay	...	...	23	15	MAC		Raasay	Kyle of Lochalsh
Rum	...	...	23	12	MAC		Rum	Mallaig or Kyle of Lochalsh
Shetland	...	....	33	19	NS	Lerwick		Aberdeen
						Lerwick		Edinburgh (Leith)
Skye	...	...	22 & 23	13, 14 & 15 (see also ferries 55 & 56)	MAC	Armadale	Portree	Mallaig or Kyle of Lochalsh
South Uist	...	32	11 & 12	MAC	Lochboisdale			Oban, Mallaig or Kyle of Lochalsh
Staffa	...	...	13	8	MAC		Staffa	Oban
Tiree	...	...	13	11	MAC	Tiree		Oban

*Solo motor cycles are usually accepted without previous notice except to the very small islands.

CSP = Caledonian Steam Packet Co. Ltd. . . . . Services 1 to 5
MAC = David MacBrayne Ltd. . . . . Services 6 to 16
NS   = North of Scotland and Orkney and Shetland Shipping Co. Ltd. . . . . Services 17 to 19
The conditions of carriage and methods of charging vary. For essential details applicable to each company refer to the following paragraphs.

THE SHIPPING COMPANIES
FIRTH OF CLYDE
(Services 1 to 5, operated by the Caledonian Steam Packet Co. Ltd.)

Specially constructed car-carrying vessels, which can be loaded by ramp at any state of the tide, are employed on these services. Vehicles should be available for shipment 15 minutes before the advertised departure time. A timetable is available from the address below. Shipping charges vary according to the length of the vehicle. All vehicles must be accompanied and must be driven on and off the vessel under their own power. The petrol tank need not be emptied. Where passengers are allowed to remain in their vehicles, care should be taken to leave sufficient room between vehicles so that doors can be opened to allow passengers to escape in an emergency. If it is intended to take a vehicle (other than a solo motor cycle) on any of these services, it is advisable to make advance arrangements, especially for weekends during the summer season. Applications for reservation of shipping space should be sent direct to:

The Manager, The Caledonian Steam Packet Co. Ltd., Gourock, Renfrewshire.
Telephone: Gourock 31261.

The application should give the following particulars:
1. Date of crossing.
2. Registration number.
3. Make, type and overall length of vehicle.

WESTERN ISLES
(Services 6 to 16, operated by David MacBrayne Ltd.)

Advance arrangements must be made with the shipping company if it is intended to take a vehicle (other than a solo motor cycle) to any of the islands served by David MacBrayne Limited. A map of the services is included in a free timetable available from the company at the address below. It also contains full details of the services, including departure times, ports of call, passenger fares and vehicle shipping charges.

The shipping charges for cars and caravans vary according to weight and distance and those quoted are for vehicles weighing between 10 and 20 hundredweights. Reduced rates are available (except for motor cycles) when a return journey by the same route is made within three months.

For a car or caravan a weight certificate, obtainable at any public weighbridge, must be produced at the time of shipment. There are no petrol restrictions. Vehicles are usually loaded by net slings.

Application for the reservation of shipping space on all the MacBrayne's services (except those from Oban) should be sent direct to:

David MacBrayne Ltd., 44 Robertson Street, Glasgow C.2.
Telephone: Glasgow CENtral 9231.

For departures from Oban application should be sent to:

David MacBrayne Ltd., North Pier, Oban, Argyllshire.
Telephone: Oban 2285.

The application should give the following particulars:
1. Date of crossing.
2. Registration number.
3. Make and type of vehicle.
4. Weight of vehicle.

ORKNEY AND SHETLAND
(Services 17 to 19, operated by the North of Scotland, and Orkney and Shetland Shipping Co. Ltd.)

Advance arrangements must be made direct with the shipping company if it is intended to take a vehicle to Orkney or Shetland, except on the daily service between Thurso (Scrabster) and Stromness (Orkney) on which previous booking is not required or accepted. A map of the services is included in a free timetable available from the company at the address below. It also contains full details of the services, including departure times, ports of call, passenger fares and vehicle shipping charges.

The shipping charges for vehicles vary according to weight and those quoted are for vehicles weighing between 10 and 40 hundredweights. Special return rates for accompanied vehicles are available for three months.

Motorists visiting Shetland from Leith or Aberdeen may arrange for the vehicle to be discharged and reloaded at Orkney for an extra handling charge of £1 plus pier dues. For a car or caravan, a weight certificate, obtainable at any public weighbridge, must be produced at the time of shipment. Petrol must be kept to the minimum. Vehicles are loaded by net slings.

Applications for the reservation of shipping space on these services should be sent direct to:

North of Scotland, and Orkney and Shetland Shipping Co. Ltd., Matthews Quay, Aberdeen.
Telephone: Aberdeen 29111.

The application should give the following particulars:
1. Date of crossing.
2. Registration number.
3. Make and type of vehicle.
4. Weight of vehicle.

SERVICES

The service numbers are those shown on the maps on pages 33, 34 and 35 of the Atlas at the end of the book and also in the index on page 275.

Services 1 to 5 are operated by the Caledonian Steam Packet Co. Ltd.; 6 to 16 by David MacBrayne Ltd.; and 17 to 19 by the North of Scotland, and Orkney and Shetland Shipping Co. Ltd. It is essential to reserve space for the conveyance of motor vehicles, except solo motor cycles. Bookings should be made direct with the company concerned. The conditions of carriage and methods of charging vary according to the company operating the service. In some cases a weight certificate must be produced at the time of shipment. Essential details are given below and on the previous pages. Further information can be obtained direct from the shipping company concerned.

1. ARRAN.

Fairlie to Brodick (also from and to Ardrossan in summer). Service: Weekdays only. Return freight charges (including driver): Car £3 10s. to £6; Motor cycle, solo 13s. 6d., with sidecar £1 2s. 6d. Passengers 8s. 8d. return.

2. ARRAN, BUTE and CUMBRAE (passenger service only).

A tourist service from Gourock via Dunoon—Rothesay (Bute)—Largs—Fairlie—Millport, Cumbrae (Saturdays excepted)—Lochranza (Arran) to Campbeltown. Passenger fares 7s. to 15s.

3. ARRAN and BUTE (passenger service only).

A circular tour from Gourock or Wemyss Bay calling at Rothesay (Bute)—Kyles of Bute—Brodick (Arran)—Whiting Bay (Arran). Service: Mondays and Wednesdays only from June to September. Fares, from Gourock 12s. 6d.; from Wemyss Bay 11s. 6d.

4. CUMBRAE.

Wemyss Bay to Millport. Service: For vehicles Mondays, Wednesdays and Fridays. Passengers only other weekdays and Sundays. Return freight charges (including driver): Car £1 16s. 3d. to £2 10s.; Motor cycle, solo 8s. 9d., with sidecar 17s. 6d. Passengers 3s. 11d.

5. BUTE.

Wemyss Bay to Rothesay. Service: Daily. (From October to March the Sunday service operates from Gourock instead of Wemyss Bay.) Return freight charges (including driver): Car £1 16s. 3d. to £2 10s.; Motor cycle, solo 8s. 9d., with sidecar 17s. 6d. Passengers 5s. 8d. return. A circle ticket for cars (£1 7s. 6d. to £2), is available from Wemyss Bay to Rothesay and from Dunoon to Gourock (or vice versa). Motorists make their own way between Rothesay and Dunoon using the ferry between Rhubodach and Colintraive. For further details, including the charges on the ferry, see page 272—Ferries No. 43 and 48.

6. BUTE (passenger service only).

Ardrishaig Mail Service. Service: Weekdays at 9.30 a.m. from Gourock to Dunoon, Rothesay and Tarbert East (also to Ardrishaig from May to September). There is a coach connection between Tarbert East and West for the Islay Mail Service. Fares to Rothesay 4s. 7d.; to Tarbert 11s. 10d.

7. ISLAY, JURA, GIGHA and COLONSAY.

Islay Mail Service. Service: From Tarbert West at 1.30 p.m. on Mondays, Wednesdays and Fridays to Port Askaig (Islay), Craighouse (Jura) and on Tuesdays, Thursdays and Saturdays to Port Ellen (Islay) and Gigha. On Mondays only (Fridays also during the summer) there is a service to Colonsay. Freight charges, single: to Islay, Car £3 10s. to £6 19s. 11d.; Motor cycle, solo 12s. 6d., with sidecar £1 5s. To Jura and Gigha, car £3 7s. 7d. to £6 15s. 1d.; Motor cycle, solo 8s., with sidecar 16s. To Colonsay, Car £3 18s. 10d. to £7 17s. 8d.; Motor cycle, solo 15s. 10d., with sidecar £1 11s. 8d. Passengers, 1st class return: To Islay and Jura £1 13s. 8d.; to Gigha 18s. 8d.; to Colonsay £2 5s. 9d. As an alternative vehicles may be left at Gourock whence there is a passenger ship service to Tarbert, **Service No. 6.** There is a passenger ferry between Port Askaig (Islay) and Feolin (Jura).

8. IONA and STAFFA (passenger service only).

A circular tour from Oban every weekday from June to mid-September. The tour takes a whole day. Fare £1 17s. 6d. There is also a passenger ferry between Fionphort (Mull) and Iona.

9. OBAN and FORT WILLIAM (passenger service only).

A tourist service on weekdays from June to September. Fare, 13s. 9d.

10. MULL and LISMORE.

Tobermory Mail Service. Service: Weekdays only from Oban to Craignure (Mull), Lochaline (mainland), Salen (Mull), Drimnin (mainland) and Tobermory. There is a passenger ferry between Tobermory and Mingary (mainland). Vehicles for Mull can be disembarked at Salen or Tobermory. Freight charges, single: Car £2 17s. 2d. to £5 14s. 5d.; Motor cycle, solo 12s. 6d., with sidecar £1 5s. Passengers, 1st class return: Salen 14s. 4d.; Tobermory 19s. 9d. There is a weekday service between Oban and Lismore—for charges and fares apply to shipping company.

11. COLL, TIREE, BARRA and SOUTH UIST.

Inner Islands Mail Service. Service: From Oban at 6.30 a.m. Mondays, Wednesdays and Fridays. For an alternative service to South Uist see 12 below. Freight charges single: to Tiree, Car £4 0s. 4d. to £8 0s. 7d.; Motor cycle, solo 15s. 10d., with sidecar £1 11s. 8d. To Barra and South Uist, Car £4 16s. 11d. to £8 13s. 10d.; Motor cycle, solo £1 3s., with sidecar £2 6s. Passengers, 1st class return: to Coll £1 11s. 2d.; to Tiree £1 19s. 2d.; to Barra £3 4s. 5d.; to South Uist £4 1s. 7d. A bus service connects South Uist with Benbecula and a passenger ferry connects South Uist and the islands of Eriskay and Barra.

12. HARRIS, NORTH UIST, SOUTH UIST, CANNA, RUM and EIGG.

Outer Islands Mail Service. Service: Departures from the mainland three times a week following a circular route from Kyle of Lochalsh to Tarbert (Harris), Lochmaddy (North

Uist), Lochboisdale (South Uist) then back to the mainland at Mallaig and Kyle of Lochalsh. Calls are made at the piers of the smaller islands of Canna, Eigg and Rum. The first service each week operates in the reverse direction and for this reason it is important to ascertain which mainland port will be most convenient at the proposed time of crossing. Lochboisdale (South Uist) can also be reached by the Inner Islands Service from Oban. See **Service No. 11.** There are passenger ferries between Rodel or Leverburgh (Harris) and Newton Ferry (North Uist). Freight charges, single: Cars to Harris, North and South Uist £4 6s. 11d. to £8 13s. 10d. The charges for Motor cycles are by the shortest route. Motor cycle, solo to Harris 15s. 10d., with side-car £1 11s. 8d.; to North and South Uist, solo 18s. 4d., with sidecar £1 16s. 8d. Passengers, 1st class single, by the shortest route (apply to shipping company for fares by other routes). From Mallaig to Eigg 5s. 6d.; Rum 10s. 1d.; Canna 14s. 9d.; Lochboisdale £1 7s. 1d. From Kyle to Tarbert £1 1s. 9d.; Lochmaddy £1 12s. 1d.

13. SKYE (passenger service only).

A tourist service from Mallaig to Loch Scavaig on Thurs-days between mid-May and mid-September. Fare £1. For other weekday services see **Service Nos. 14** and **15** and also page 273—**Ferries Nos. 55** and **56.**

14. SKYE.

Mallaig to Armadale. Service: Weekdays only from Mallaig at 9.40 a.m. and from Armadale at 11 a.m. For details see **Ferry No. 54,** page 273. For alternative ferry services see page 273—**Ferries Nos. 55** and **56.**

15. RAASAY and SKYE (passenger service only).

Kyle of Lochalsh—Raasay—Portree. Service: Weekdays only at 2.40 p.m. Fares: 1st class return, Raasay 13s. 4d.; Portree 15s. 6d. There is also a passenger ferry from Kyle to Toscaig (for Applecross). For alternative services to Skye see above and also page 273—**Ferries Nos. 55** and **56.**

16. LEWIS.

Mallaig and Kyle of Lochalsh to Stornoway. Service: Weekdays only from Mallaig at 12.30 p.m. and from Kyle at 2.30 p.m. Freight charges, single: Cars £4 6s. 10d. to £8 13s. 10d.; Motor cycle, solo from Kyle 15s. 10d., from Mallaig £1 3s.; with sidecar, from Kyle £1 11s. 8d., from Mallaig £2 6s. Passengers, 1st class return from Mallaig £3 13s. 4d.; from Kyle £2 11s. 4d.

17. ORKNEY.

Thurso (Scrabster) to Stromness. Service: Weekdays only Thurso (Scrabster), 1.30 p.m. Stromness 9.15 a.m. Sunday service during July and August only. Vehicles must be alongside one hour before departure time. Bookings are not required or accepted. Freight charges, return: accompanied, Car £4 7s. 6d. to £6 10s.; Motor cycle, solo £1; with sidecar £2. Passengers, return £1 10s. (See below for alternative service from Edinburgh and Aberdeen on which booking is required.)

18. ORKNEY.

Edinburgh (Leith) and Aberdeen to Kirkwall. Service: From Edinburgh (Leith) three times a week; from Aberdeen twice a week. Apply to shipping company for further details. Freight charges, return: accompanied, Car £8 12s. 6d. to £13; Motor cycle, solo £1 15s.; with sidecar £3. Passengers, 1st class return, from Edinburgh £5 15s.; from Aberdeen £5.

19. SHETLAND.

Edinburgh (Leith) and Aberdeen to Lerwick. Service: from Edinburgh (Leith) twice a week; from Aberdeen twice a week via Kirkwall (Orkney) and twice a week direct. Apply to shipping company for further details. Freight charges, return: accompanied, Car £8 12s. 6d. to £13; Motor cycle, solo £1 15s.; with sidecar £3. Motorists visiting both Orkney and Shetland may arrange for discharge and reloading at the intermediate port for an extra charge plus pier dues. Passengers, 1st class return, from Edinburgh £7; from Aberdeen £6; from Kirkwall to Lerwick £3 5s.

BARTHOLOMEW'S
ROAD ATLAS OF SCOTLAND

Showing Ministry of Transport Road Numbers, A.A. and R.A.C. Telephone Boxes, Mileages and National Grid

SCALE: FIFTH-INCH TO MILE

THE COUNTIES OF
SCOTLAND

County Towns •
Scale

0 10 20 30 40 50 MILES

SHETLAND ISLANDS

Foula   Lerwick

Fair Isle

ORKNEY ISLANDS

Kirkwall

Wick

CAITHNESS

SUTHERLAND

Lewis

Harris

Dornoch

ROSS AND CROMARTY

N. Uist

Skye

Dingwall   Nairn   Elgin   Banff

Inverness   NAIRN   MORAY

S. Uist

BANFF

ABERDEEN   Aberdeen

Canna

INVERNESS

Barra

Rum   Eigg

KINCARDINE   Stonehaven

Muck

ANGUS

Coll

PERTH   Forfar

Tiree   Mull

Iona

Perth   Cupar

Inveraray

KINROSS   FIFE

Scarba   CLACKMAN   Kinross

Colonsay   Jura

Stirling   Alloa

DUNBARTON   STIRLING   Linlithgow   Haddington

Dumbarton   W. LOTHIAN   EAST LOTHIAN

Islay   Rothesay   Renfrew   Edinburgh

Gigha   Bute   RENFREW   MIDLOTHIAN   Duns

LANARK   Peebles   BERWICK

Arran   Lanark   PEEBLES   Selkirk   Jedburgh

Ayr   SELKIRK   ROXBURGH

AYR   DUMFRIES

Dumfries   ENGLAND

KIRKCUDBRIGHT

WIGTOWN   Kirkcudbright

Wigtown

CROWN COPYRIGHT RESERVED   R.B.35   1118

PUBLISHED BY THE AUTOMOBILE ASSOCIATION

CONTENTS

THE NATIONAL GRID AND THE A.A. ROAD BOOK

GENERAL

The Atlas on the following pages has had the network of the National Grid superimposed upon it and the map references in the gazetteer portion of the Road Book give the page number of the Atlas, followed by the National Grid reference. In conformity with the present Ordnance Survey practice, National Grid references in the text of the book are given in the new form of letters and figures instead of in the original form of figures only.

The advantage of the National Grid is that it provides one system of reference for the whole country, which is correct for any scale of map, the degree of accuracy of the reference depending on the scale of the map and the number of 'co-ordinates' or figures given in it. The co-ordinates are the figures given in the margin of the Atlas, and it will be noted that the figures at the top and bottom of the page are heavier than those at the sides. The heavy figures are the 'eastings' and are invariably given first in the reference after the Major Square letters. The lighter figures, or 'northings', are always given second.

HOW TO USE THE GRID

On page iv will be found an index map showing the Major Squares into which the country is divided, each square with its own letters shown in a circle. These letters are repeated in the pages of the Atlas, the thick lines indicating the borders of the Major Squares. The Major Square number formerly used (preceded by a letter in the case of Orkney and Shetland) is shown in brackets below the letters to assist in reference to maps published before the adoption of the letter designation. Each Major Square contains 100 smaller Squares, Square **0** 0 being in the bottom left hand corner and Square **9** 9 being in the top right hand corner.

On page iii will be found a reproduction of Major Square **NT**. Along the top and bottom of the square are the figures **0-9** in heavy type. These are the 'eastings' and at the sides of the square are the 'northings' in lighter type. These figures are the 'co-ordinates' (mentioned above) which give the map reference within the Major Square, and are shown in the margin of the pages throughout the Atlas. 'Eastings' are denoted throughout the text by heavy type figures. 'Northings' are shown in light type. Major Square letters are also shown in heavy type in the text.

In the National Grid system of map reference the letters of the Major Square are always given first, and in the gazetteer section of this book, these letters follow the map page, e.g. Glasgow Map 8, **NS 5** 6 will be found on page 8, in Major Square **NS**, smaller square **5** 6. To avoid confusion, the smaller squares into which the Major Squares are sub-divided by the east and north co-ordinates, are spoken of by giving the figures separately, e.g. **1** 4 as 'one four', **2** 5 as 'two five', etc.

EXAMPLES

By reference to the map on page iii, the Grid reference for Edinburgh will be found to be **NT 2** 7, indicating that Edinburgh lies within Major Square **NT**, two lines east and seven lines north. Peebles is in the left centre of the square to the right of the vertical line **2** and just above horizontal line **4**; therefore its Grid reference is **NT 2** 4 (NT, two, four). Hawick is just to the right of vertical line **5** and above horizontal line 1, and its Grid reference is **NT 5** 1 (NT, five, one). Moffat is an example of a town in the smaller square **0** 0 and its reference **NT 0** 0 (NT, nought, nought).

An alphabetical list of the map references for some of the towns which lie in Major Square **NT** is given above the map.

BIGGAR	- -	- **NT 0** 3	EDINBURGH	-	- **NT 2** 7	KIRKCALDY	-	- **NT 2** 9

BIGGAR - - - **NT 0** 3 EDINBURGH - - **NT 2** 7 KIRKCALDY - **NT 2** 9

BONNYRIGG - - **NT 3** 6 GALASHIELS - - **NT 4** 3 LEADBURN - - **NT 2** 5

CARTER BAR - - **NT 6** 0 HADDINGTON - - **NT 5** 7 MID CALDER - **NT 0** 6

COLDSTREAM - - **NT 8** 3 HAWICK - - - **NT 5** 1 MOFFAT - - **NT 0** 0

DUNBAR - - - **NT 6** 7 JEDBURGH - - **NT 6** 2 NORTH BERWICK - **NT 5** 8

DUNFERMLINE - - **NT 0** 8 KELSO - - - **NT 7** 3 PEEBLES - - **NT 2** 4

DUNS - - - **NT 7** 5 SELKIRK - - **NT 4** 2

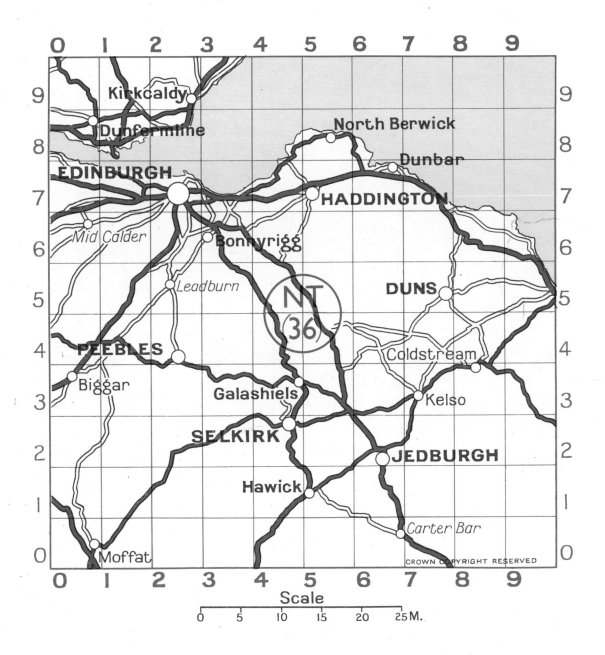

Scale

0   5   10   15   20   25 M.

Each Major Square is 62½ miles across and each smaller square 6¼ miles.

INDEX TO MAJOR SQUARE NUMBERS

OF THE NATIONAL GRID

The National Grid is superimposed by permission of the Controller of
H.M. Stationery Office and the Director General of Ordnance Survey

SCALE OF MAP PAGES 2-31
FIFTH-INCH TO MILE

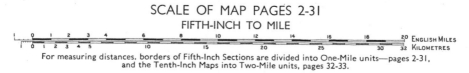

For measuring distances, borders of Fifth-Inch Sections are divided into One-Mile units—pages 2-31,
and the Tenth-Inch Maps into Two-Mile units, pages 32-33.

Printed by JOHN BARTHOLOMEW & SON LTD EDINBURGH   Published by THE AUTOMOBILE ASSOCIATION

INDEX TO MAP PAGES

A.A. Offices .... ●
A.A. Sub Offices .... □

Scale of Index.

0 10 20 30 40 50 MILES

ORKNEY ISLANDS

Kirkwall

33

SHETLAND ISLANDS

Lerwick

Stornoway

HEBRIDES OR WESTERN ISLES

32

John o'Groats

Thurso

Tongue

Wick

Scourie

28

30

29

Ullapool

31

Dornoch

Portree

22

Kinlochewe

Cromarty

Elgin

Banff

Fraserburgh

Dingwall

Nairn

24

25

Inverness

Grantown-on-Spey

26

27

ABERDEEN

Dornie

23

Fort Augustus

Kingussie

Ballater

Stonehaven

Arisaig

18

Fort William

19

Blair Athol

20

21

Brechin

12

Forfar

Montrose

Salen

Tyndrum

Perth

DUNDEE

14

Oban

Inveraray

15

Cupar

13

Callander

16

Kinross

17

Stirling

Kirkcaldy

Bowmore

Dumbarton

Greenock

Linlithgow

EDINBURGH

Haddington

Rothesay

Paisley

GLASGOW

Duns

Berwick upon Tweed

6

7

8

Lanark

9

Peebles

10

11

Brodick

Ayr

Selkirk

Wooler

Campbeltown

Cumnock

Hawick

Jedburgh

Alnwick

Moffat

Girvan

Langholm

4

5

New Galloway

Dumfries

Hexham

NEWCASTLE-UPON-TYNE

Stranraer

Wigtown

2

3

Hawick

Kirkcudbright

CARLISLE

Durham

Penrith

Middlesbrough

Keswick

Appleby

CONTOUR COLOURING OF MAP PAGES

	Feet
	3000
	2000
	1000
	500
	100
	Sea Level

CROWN COPYRIGHT RESERVED

PUBLISHED BY THE AUTOMOBILE ASSOCIATION

REFERENCE TO MAP PAGES, 2-33

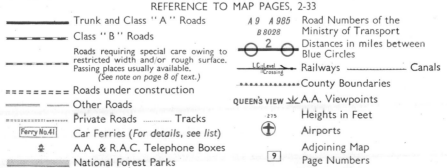

Trunk and Class "A" Roads

Class "B" Roads

Roads requiring special care owing to restricted width and/or rough surface. Passing places usually available. *(See note on page 8 of text.)*

Roads under construction

Other Roads

Private Roads .... Tracks

Ferry No.41 Car Ferries *(For details, see list)*

A.A. & R.A.C. Telephone Boxes

National Forest Parks

A 9 A 985   Road Numbers of the
B 8028   Ministry of Transport

2   Distances in miles between Blue Circles

L.C. Level Crossing   Railways .... Canals

County Boundaries

QUEEN'S VIEW A.A. Viewpoints

275   Heights in Feet

Airports

9   Adjoining Map Page Numbers

Closed Roads ××××

Roads requiring special care owing to restricted width
and/or rough surface. Passing places usually available - - - -

Closed Roads xxxx

OUTER HEBRIDES

Scale: Tenth Inch to the Mile

Copyright–John Bartholomew & Son.

SHETLAND

HP (N42)

HT (N31)

HZ (N40)

HU (N41)

ORKNEY

Scale : Tenth-inch to the Mile

See "Shipping Services to the Islands"

HY (N30)

ND (39)

THE WESTERN ISLES
SHIPPING SERVICES TO THE ISLANDS

KEY TO ROUTES

The Service Numbers shown thus **12** *refer to the Shipping Services to the Islands article on the preceding pages.*

All the year round – WITH CARS	————
All the year round – NO CARS	————
Summer only – WITH CARS	– – – –
Summer only – NO CARS	– – – –
Cars may be disembarked at places shown	●
No disembarkation facilities for cars	- - - -
(Solo Motorcycles can usually be handled)	
Car Ferries	●━━━● Ferry No 50
Passenger Ferries	●━━━● P

STORNOWAY

Lewis

OUTER HEBRIDES

Harris

TARBERT

SCALPAY

RODEL

Leverburgh

Newton Ferry

North Uist

LOCHMADDY

Benbecula

South Uist

LOCHBOISDALE

Ludaig

Eoligarry

Eriskay

Barra

CASTLEBAY

THE MINCH

LITTLE MINCH

RAASAY

PORTREE

Skye

TOSCAIG

KYLE OF LOCHALSH

Ferry No.55
(Summer Only)

Glenelg

Ferry No.56

Kyleakin

Kylerhea

LOCH SCAVAIG

ARMADALE

MALLAIG

EIGG

CANNA

RUM

Muck

12 15 16 14 13 11

The services to Orkney and Shetland are shown on page 33 of the Atlas

© THE AUTOMOBILE ASSOCIATION

Drawn & Published by The Automobile Association

CROWN—COPYRIGHT RESERVED

This map has been adjusted to portray the Island connections more plainly—therefore the sea distances are not correct

Crown Copyright Reserved

GLASGOW
Old Kilpatrick
Ferry No.44
Erskine
Ferry No.43
GOUROCK
WEMYSS BAY
FAIRLIE
ARDROSSAN
RIVER CLYDE
FIRTH OF CLYDE
Ferry No.48
DUNOON
MILLPORT
ROTHESAY
WHITING BAY
Rhubodach
BRODICK
LOCH-RANZA
Arran
COINTRAIVE
TIGHNA-BRUAICH
Rhubodach
ARDRISHAIG
TARBERT (East)
Kintyre
TARBERT (West)
CAMPBELTOWN
CRAIGHOUSE
GIGHA
Feolin P.
PORT ASKAIG
Islay
PORT ELLEN
COLONSAY
Jura
Scarba
Seil
Luing
Ferry No.49
OBAN
Connel Br.No.50
Connel
Ballachulish
Ferry No.52
N. Ballachulish
Corran
Ferry No.53
Ardgour
CRAIGNURE
Mull
STAFFA
Fionphort
IONA
SALEN
LISMORE
LOCHALINE
DRIMNIN
MINGARY
TOBERMORY
COLL
TIREE
FORT WILLIAM

Ferry No.53
Ferry No.52
Connel Br.No.50
Ferry No.49

Nov 1959

N

HIGHLAND CLANS
AND FAMILIES

Scale of English Miles

Mileage chart between Scottish towns: ABERDEEN, ARDROSSAN, ARROCHAR, AYR, BANFF, BERWICK-UPON-TWEED, BRAEMAR, CALLANDER, CAMPBELTOWN, CARLISLE, CRIANLARICH, DINGWALL, DORNOCH, DUMFRIES, DUNDEE, DUNFERMLINE, DUNOON, DURNESS, EDINBURGH, ELGIN, FORT AUGUSTUS, FORT WILLIAM, FRASERBURGH, GAIRLOCH, GALASHIELS, GIRVAN, GLASGOW, GRANTOWN-ON-SPEY, HAWICK, HU...